THE
INTERNATIONAL SERIES
OF
MONOGRAPHS ON CHEMISTRY

GENERAL EDITORS

J.S. ROWLINSON

J.E. BALDWIN

DISORDER
IN CRYSTALS

BY

N. G. PARSONAGE

Lecturer in Physical Chemistry at the
Imperial College of Science and Technology,
University of London

AND

L. A. K. STAVELEY

Fellow of New College, Oxford
and University Reader in
Inorganic Chemistry

CLARENDON PRESS · OXFORD
1978

Oxford University Press, Walton Street, Oxford OX2 6DP

OXFORD LONDON GLASGOW
NEW YORK TORONTO MELBOURNE WELLINGTON
IBADAN NAIROBI DAR ES SALAAM LUSAKA CAPE TOWN
KUALA LUMPUR SINGAPORE JAKARTA HONG KONG TOKYO
DELHI BOMBAY CALCUTTA MADRAS KARACHI

© Oxford University Press 1978

British Library Cataloguing in Publication Data

Parsonage, Neville George
    Disorder in crystals. - (The international series
    of monographs on chemistry).
    1. Crystals - Defects
    I. Title II. Staveley, Lionel Alfred Kilby
    III. Series
    548'.81   QD931   77-30456

    ISBN 0-19-855604-7

Printed in Great Britain
by Thomson Litho Ltd,
East Kilbride

TO CLARISSA AND JOYCE

PREFACE

The object of this book is to survey present knowledge of all aspects of disorder in crystals - the thermodynamic background, the statistical mechanics involved in order-disorder transitions, the experimental methods used in investigating disorder, and the information now available on particular crystals.

While we have attempted to cover in a representative way all kinds of crystal (alloys, salts, molecular solids and so on), we have given special attention to the detailed studies which have been carried out on structurally simple solids, as being the most suitable for tests of various models and theories. We have concentrated our attention on stoichiometric solids, and we do not specifically discuss crystal defects.

We write as two chemists engaged in research work in this field, and the book is primarily for chemists and crystallographers; but we hope that it will be of interest to solid state physicists, who have made so many valuable contributions to the subject. We include a chapter on magnetic disorder, even though this is a subject on which there are already accounts written by physicists, partly because of its intrinsic interest, but also because many theories and concepts originally developed for magnetic systems have since been applied to other types of disorder.

We are indebted to a number of colleagues who have read sections of the book. Their expert comments and criticisms have been of great value to us. We would particularly mention Dr. A.H.Cooke, Sir Rex Richards, and Dr. L.E.Sutton. We are grateful to Dr. A.S.Bailey for advice on the formulation and nomenclature of organic compounds, to Dr. C.K.Prout for help with crystallographic points, and to Joyce Staveley for assistance with the references. We have also benefited from the interest taken by the editor of this series, Professor J.S.Rowlinson, who has corrected a number of flaws, both scientific and

literary. The responsibility for residual errors of all
kinds remains, of course, ours alone.

    Finally, it is a pleasure to acknowledge the invaluable
help we have received from the Clarendon Press.

N.G.P.   L.A.K.S.
London   Oxford.

ACKNOWLEDGEMENTS

Acknowledgement is made to the editors, authors, and publishers of the
following works and journals for permission to use figures and tables.

To the American Institute of Physics:
for the *Journal of Chemical Physics*, Vols. 55, 60, 55, 49, 28, 39, 36, 18,
43, 31, 41, 44, 40, 51, 57, 55, 58, 57, 39, 44, 58, 44, 23, 9, 61, 62, 48,
55, 40, 37, 41, 47, 59, 44, 5, 58, 56, 54, 51, 59, 41, 61, for Figs. 3.18,
3.19, 4.1. 4.8, 4.10, 4.12, 4.13, 4.14, 4.16, 4.19, 4.22, 4.23, 4.24,
5.4, 7.1, 7.2, 7.4, 7.5, 7.25, 7.31, 7.34, 7.35, 7.41, 7.50, 7.54, 8.6,
8.7, 8.9, 8.10, 9.3, 9.8, 9.9, 9.10, 9.14, 9.16, 9.17, 9.18, 9.22, 9.23,
9.24, 10.1, 10.2, 10.13, 10.23, 11.4, 11.20, 11.21, 12.49;
for *Reviews of Modern Physics*, Vol.10, for Figs. 5.1, 5.2, 5.8;
for the *Physical Review*, Vols. 183, B12, 162, 38, B9, B8, B5, 133A, B9, B7,
133, B6, B1, 116, 90, 110, B2, 188, 165, 176, B5, 135, 140, for Figs.
3.11, 3.13, 4.2, 7.6, 7.28, 7.29, 7.37, 7.51, 8.20, 9.2, 9.4, 9.6, 9.7,
12.5, 12.17, 12.27, 12.30, 12.41a, 12.42, 12.43, 12.44, 12.45, 12.47,
12.50;
for *Physical Review Letters*, Vols. 24, 19, 27, 15, 26, 7, for Figs.
2.6, 7.24, 7.53, 12.25, 12.40 and Table 12.2;
for *Journal of Applied Physics*, Vols. 22, 32, 39, for Figs. 5.13, 12.11,
12.23.
To Macmillan Journals Ltd:
for *Nature*, Vols. 215, 217, 224, for Figs. 4.4, 9.13, 9.15.
To the North-Holland Publishing Company:
for *Physica*, Vols. 5, 59, 76, 31, 51, 61, 31, 58, 69, for Figs. 2.3a,
4.26, 7.22, 7.47, 7.48, 7.49, 12.19, 12.20, 12.38, 12.48;
for *Chemical Physics Letters*, Vols. 1, 19, for Figs. 4.17, 7.27.
for *Progress in Low-temperature Physics*, Vol. 4, for Fig.12.10a, and
Tables 3.3, 3.5.
To the Chemical Society:
for the *Transactions of the Faraday Society*, Vols. 65, 56, 63, 61 for
Figs. 7.38, 10.17, 11.17, 11.13, 11.18, 11.15, 11.6 and Tables 11.9,
11.7;
for the *Discussions of the Faraday Society*, Nos. 23, 48, for Figs. 4.31,
9.12;

for the *Journal of the Chemical Society* (1947) for Fig.11.1.

To the American Chemical Society:

for the *Journal of the American Chemical Society*, Vols. 56, 75, for Figs. 4.28, 7.26;

for *Analytical Chemistry*, Vol.25, for Fig.6.9;

for the *Journal of Physical Chemistry*, Vols. 69, 68, 74, 60, 69, 74, for Figs. 4.11, 4.25, 7.16, 8.4, 10.18, 10.25;

for *Chemical Reviews*, Vol.66, for Table 3.20.

To the Royal Society of Canada:

for the *Symposium 'Physics and Chemistry of Ice, 1973'*, for Figs.8.11, 8.13.

To Pergamon Press Ltd:

for the *Journal of the Physics and Chemistry of Solids*, Vols. 18, 28, 26, 29, 13, 37, 18, for Figs. 3.10, 4.18, 7.17, 7.19, 7.46, 10.5, 10.28;

for *Solid State Communications*, Vols. 10, 2, 15, 13, 9, for Figs. 2.3b, 4.21, 7.39, 7.40, 8.18, 12.18, 12.37.

To Gordon and Breach:

for *Molecular Crystals and Liquid Crystals*, Vols. 6, 1, 9, 28, 17, for Figs. 4.2, 4.33, 10.11, 10.12, 10.26, 10.27.

To the Japan Academy:

for the *Proceedings of the Japan Academy*, Vol.48, for Fig.8.5.

To the Commonwealth Scientific and Industrial Research Organization, Australia:

for the *Australian Journal of Chemistry*, Vol.20, for Fig.7.15.

To the Gmelin-Institut:

for the *Gmelin Handbuch 'Quecksilber' Teil B1, System-Nr.34*, for Fig.6.10.

To the Chemical Society of Japan:

for the *Bulletin of the Chemical Society of Japan*, Vols. 36, 38, 46, 41, 44, 43, for Figs. 7.3, 7.23, 8.18, 10.3, 10.4, 10.16(b), 10.24.

To the Physical Society of Japan:

for the *Journal of the Physical Society of Japan*, Vols. 36, 13, 17, 15, 28, 12, 7, 20, 22, 27, 37, 24, 28, 18, 25, 17, 30, for Figs. 5.9, 5.16, 5.17, 5.18, 5.19, 5.20, 6.1, 6.6, 7.7, 7.8, 7.14, 7.18, 7.20, 7.33, 7.52, 7.55, 7.56, 8.17, 11.8, 12.21, 12.51.

To the Royal Society:

for the *Philosophical Transactions of the Royal Society*, Vol.264, for Figs. 4.5, 4.6;

for the *Proceedings of the Royal Society*, Vols. A225, A243, A206, for

Figs. 11.6a, 11.6b, 12.10b.

To Akademische Verlagsgesellschaft Geest und Portig, K.G.:

for *Zeitschrift für physikalische Chemie* Vol.B38, for Fig.4.3.

To Akademie-Verlag Berlin:

for *Physica Status Solidi*, Vol.45b, 50b, for Fig.4.7, 12.32.

To the National Research Council of Canada:

for the *Canadian Journal of Chemistry*, Vols. 50, 52, 46, 49, for Figs. 4.15, 6.11, 11.11 and Table 11.5;

for the *Canadian Journal of Physics*, Vol.40, for Fig.9.1.

To the International Atomic Energy Agency:

for *Proceedings of the Symposium on the Inelastic Scattering of Neutrons, 1964*, for Fig.4.20.

To Geschäftsstelle der deutschen Bunsen-Gesellschaft für physikalische Chemie:

for *Berichte der Bunsengesellschaft Phys.Chem.* Vols. 75, 68, for Figs. 6.3, 6.4, 6.7;

for *Zeitschrift für Elektrochemie*, Vol.62, for Fig.10.14.

To Akademie der Wissenschaften in Göttingen:

for *Nachr.Wiss.Göttingen Math.Phys.Kl.2*, Vol.4, for Fig.6.5.

To Johann Ambrosius Barth:

for *Zeit.Anorg.Allg.Chemie*, Vol.279, for Fig.6.8.

To John Wiley and Sons, Inc.:

for *Progress in Inorganic Chemistry*, Vol.1, for Fig.6.12,

for *The Physical Principles of Magnetism* for Figs. 2.11, 12.8, 12.16;

for *Advances in Chemical Physics*, Vol.2 for Table 11.3;

for *Introduction to Solid State Physics*, 2nd edition, for Fig.12.24;

for *Advanced Inorganic Chemistry*, for Fig.12.14a.

To the American Association for the Advancement of Science:

for *Science*, Vol.115, for Figs. 8.2, 8.3.

To the Plenum Publishing Corporation:

for the *Journal of Low-Temperature Physics*, Vol.3, for Fig.9.21;

for *Low-temperature Physics* LT9, for Fig.9.20;

for Proceedings of the *International Symposium on the Physics of Ice, 1969*, for Figs. 8.8, 8.12;

for *Treatise on Solid State Chemistry*, Vol.5 for Fig.3.17a,b.

To Academic Press, Inc.:

for the *Journal of Magnetic Resonance*, Vol.1, for Figs. 4.27, 8.16;

for the *Journal of Solid State Chemistry*, Vol.5, for Fig.7.11;

for *Phase Transitions and Critical Phenomena*, Vols. 1, 3 for Figs.3.17c,d,

Table 3.2;

for *Journal of Chemical Thermodynamics*, Vol.14, for Fig.11.24, Table 11.11.

To the Institute of Physics:

for the *Proceedings of the Physical Society*, Vol.89, for Fig.9.11;

for the *Journal of Physics*,Vols.9C, 4C, 5C for Figs. 10.6, 12.14b, 12.35;

for the *Reports on Progress in Physics*, Vol.38 for Fig.12.33.

To the *Japanese Journal of Applied Physics*, Vol.6, for Fig.7.9.

To Pion Ltd.:

for *High-temperature, High-pressure*,Vols.4, 1, for Figs. 7.10, 7.44.

To Springer-Verlag Komm.Ges.:

for *Monatshefte für Chemie*, Vol.93, for Fig.7.45.

To *Acta Chemica Scandinavica*, Vol.28A for Figs. 7.42, 7.43.

To Taylor and Francis, Ltd.,:

for *Molecular Physics*,Vols.25, 4, 7, 3, 13, 1 for Figs. 7.36, 11.2,
11.5, 11.7, 11.12 and Table 11.4;

for *Advances in Physics*, Vols.23, 20, for Figs. 3.15, 12.2, 12.39 and
Tables 3.4, 3.7, 3.8.

To *Journal de Chimie physique*, Vol.68, for Fig.10.15.

To Akademische Verlagsgesellschaft Wiesbaden:

for *Zeitschrift für physikalische Chemie N.F.*, Vol.43, for Fig.7.32.

To *Compte rendus Acad.Sci.Paris*,Vols.268C, 267B, for Figs.10.7, 12.22.

To the Cambridge University Press:

for *The Elements of Classical Thermodynamics*, for Figs.2.4, 2.5.

To the McGraw-Hill Book Company:

for *Statistical Mechanics*, for Figs.3.5 and 3.7.

To the National Bureau of Standards (U.S.A.):

for *Miscellaneous Publication No.273*, for Figs.3.9, 3.14.

To Pergamon Press (Inc).,:

for *Acta Metallurgica*, Vol.22, for Fig.5.14.

To the American Society for Metals, Metals Park, Ohio,:

for *Metallurgical Transactions*, Vol.4, for Fig.5.15.

To the International Union of Crystallography:

for *Acta Crystallographica*, Vols. 5, 7, 8 for Figs. 11.14, 11.22, 11.23,
12.46.

To Oxford University Press:

for *Structural Inorganic Chemistry*, for Figs.11.9 and 11.10.

To Masson (éditeur):

for *Annales de Chimie et de Physique*, for Fig.12.28.

To the Institute of Electrical and Electronic Engineers (U.S.A.):

for the *Proceedings of the Institute of Radio Engineers*, Vol.43 for Fig.12.7.

To *Journal de Physique Paris*, Vol.34 for Figs.12.29, 12.31.

To Springer-Verlag, Heidelberg,:

for *Zeitschrift für angewandte Physik*, Vol.32 for Fig.12.34.

To Bell Laboratories (U.S.A.):

for *Bell Systems Technical Journal*, Vol.43 for Fig.12.26.

CONTENTS

CONTENTS

LIST OF SYMBOLS

a major semi-axis of ellipsoid of revolution

a range of repulsive forces (equation 3.16)

a_τ, $a_{\mathcal{H}}$ scaling parameters characteristic of the system
(equation 3.35)

A Helmholtz free energy

A' $U - HM - TS$, magnetic free energy

A activity (in radiotracer studies)

A per cent (infrared) absorption

A pre-exponential factor in Arrhenius equation

A quadrupole coupling constant

b minor semi-axis of ellipsoid of revolution

b range of attractive forces (equation 3.16)

B NMR line-width above line-width transition region

B parameter in Debye-Waller factor

$\mathcal{B}$ number of cells or spins in Ising or lattice gas model

c per cent of ortho-hydrogen molecules

c_g capacitance of gas-phase

c interlayer spacing

c_{11}, c_{12}, c_{66} elastic constants

C Curie constant

C NMR line-width below line-width transition region

C_i Flinn operator (p.194)

C heat capacity. C^m, magnetic contribution to -; $C_{\mathcal{H}}$, - at
constant field; C_M, - at constant magnetization; $C_{M'}$,
at constant sub-lattice magnetization; C_p, - at constant
pressure; C_V, - at constant volume; C_{int}, contribution of
internal modes to -; C_{rot}, rotational contribution to -;
C_{vib}, contribution of vibration of whole molecules
against environment to -

$\tilde{C}$ stiffness matrix

d dimensionality

$\tilde{D}$ compliance matrix

D demagnetization factor

D molecular diameter

D self-diffusion coefficient

e electronic charge

eq maximum component of electric field gradient

eQ molecular quadrupole moment

E e.m.f.

E electric field

E, E_a activation energy. E_c, - for creep process; E_D, - for diffusion; E_R, - for reorientation

E energy. E, - of a particular configuration; E_c, - of a system at the critical point; E_0, ground-state -; E_{JT}, Jahn-Teller -

f atomic scattering factor

f recoil-free fraction (Mössbauer)

f frequency ($= \omega/2\pi$). f_{max} = - of maximum in dielectric absorption

$f(h)$ NMR line-shape derivative

$f(T,p)$ order parameter (NQR)

F structure factor

g magnetic g-factor

$g(\ )$ degeneracy of configuration specified in the brackets

g, $g(h)$ shape-factor for NMR absorption line

g_K Kirkwood's orientational correlation factor

G Gibbs free energy

h $\mathcal{H} - \mathcal{H}_0$ (NMR)

h Planck's constant

h_m amplitude of field modulation (NMR)

hnn   horizontal nearest neighbour

H enthalpy. ΔH_s, - of sublimation; ΔH_t, - of transition; $\Delta H^{0\ddagger}$, - of activation

H'' $m\mathcal{H}/kT$ (equation 3.23) magnetic field. $\mathcal{H}'$, staggered -; $\mathcal{H}^*$, - at the tricritical point; $\mathcal{H}_0$ - at NMR line centre; $\mathcal{H}_{int}$, internal -; $\mathcal{H}_a$, applied -; $\mathcal{H}_{sf}$ = spin-flop -; δH = NMR line-width within line-width transition region; $\mathcal{H}^c$, $\mathcal{H}^a$, - required to rotate spins from easy axis to c and a, respectively

$\hat{\mathcal{H}}$ Hamiltonian operator

i, I electric current

I moment of inertia

I nuclear spin quantum number

I_3 octupole moment (p.582)

J rotational quantum number

J, J' Ising or Heisenberg constants. J_{aa}, - for spins on sub-lattice a

k Boltzmann's constant

k rate constant

$\underline{k}$ wave-vector. k, modulus of -; k_x, x-component of -

K crystalline anisotropy energy

K J/kT (equation 3.23)

L Avogadro constant

L latent heat of transition

m (linear dimension of domain)/(interatomic spacing)

m magnetic moment

M magnetization. M^*, - at tricritical point; M', sub-lattice M_0, spontaneous -; $M_0(T)$, spontaneous - at temperature T; M_s, saturation -; M_{dis}, - of disordered phase in two-phase region; M_{ord}, - of ordered phase in two-phase region

M number of cells per domain

M component of rotational quantum number J

M_2 second moment (NMR)

n number of particles per nucleus

n (thickness of domain wall)/(interatomic spacing)

nn nearest neighbour. nnn = next -

n_α number of α-sites

n number of carbon atoms in a carbon chain

n number of spins in chain

n refractive index

N_0 Avogadro constant

N_{AB}, N_{BB} molecular field constant at B-site due to A and B spins, respectively

$N_{\alpha\beta}$ number of nn α - β pairs of molecules

N_1, N_2 number of possible molecular orientations in high- and low-phases, respectively

p fraction of 'bonds' or 'atoms' open (Percolation Problem) p_c^a, p_c^b, critical values of - for 'atom' and 'bond' problems, respectively

p pressure. p^*, tricritical -; p_I, contribution to - from magnetic interaction; p_0, contribution to - from ordinary interactions

$\underline{p}$ electric dipole moment. p , magnitude of -

p short-range order parameter

p specific polarization

P polarization. P_s, spontaneous -.

P probability. $P_\alpha(i)$, (p. 192). $P(B_j|A_i)$, (p. 193). $P_\infty^a(p)$, (p. 83). $P_\infty^b(p)$, (p. 82)

q electric charge

$\underline{q}$ wave-vector. q modulus of -

q,q' coordination number

q_c classical partition function for a one-dimensional oscillator

q_{qmo} quantum mechanical partition function for a one-dimensional oscillator

Q partition function. Q, isothermal-isochoric -;

Q' isothermal-isochamp -; $Q^{hr}(Q_c^{hr})$, (classical approximation to) - for a two-dimensional hindered rotor

Q initial total activity (radiotracer diffusion study)

Q_{JT} Jahn-Teller distortion

$\underline{r}$ interparticle vector r, length of -

r_α fraction of α-sites with 'right' occupation. $r_{\alpha p}$, see p. 221

R the gas constant

R nearest neighbour separation

$\mathcal{R}$ a long-range order parameter (Pople-Karasz model)

$\underline{s}$ spin operator

s,S magnetic spin number

s_i^z z-component of the spin-vector at site i

S entropy. S_c, - at the critical point; S(cal), calorimetric ('third law') -; S(spec), - calculated from spectroscopic data; S(stat), - calculated taking account of the consequences of nuclear spin; S(eq), - evaluated from equilibrium study; S(res), residual -; S_∞, - at $T=\infty$; ΔS_m, - of fusion; ΔS_t, - of transition; ΔS_τ, excess - of transition (p. 693); $\Delta S^{\ddagger}$, - of activation

$\mathcal{S}$ a long-range order parameter

t time

T temperature. T^*, tricritical -; T_c, critical or Curie -, (see also p. 230); T_{c+}, T_{c-}, critical - approached from above and below, respectively; T_{comp}, compensation - (ferrimagnet); T_g, glass-transition -; T_m, melting -;

T_{min}, - at which minimum in T_1 occurs; T_n, - at which NMR line begins to narrow; T_r, - of reorientation transition; T_t, transition -; T_D, Jahn-Teller transition -; T_N, Néel -; T_{SK}, Stanley-Kaplan -; T_λ - of maximum in heat capacity in gradual or partly gradual transition (see p.230); T_χ, - of maximum in X

T_0 Curie-Weiss constant

T_1 spin-lattice relaxation time (NMR). T_1^*, T_{1D}, - in local nuclear dipole field; T_{1D}, - for diffusion; T_{1R}, - for reorientation; $T_{1\rho}$, - in rotating frame

T_2 spin-spin (transverse) relaxation time (NMR)

$\bar{u}$ mean square displacement

U internal energy

U_{SF} stacking-fault energy

vnn   vertical nearest neighbour

V voltage

V volume. V_m, molar -; $V^\ddagger$, - of activation; V_s; molar - of solid at melting-point

V potential energy. V, (- difference between minima)/2; V_0, height of - barrier

w_α fraction of α-sites wrongly occupied. $w_{\alpha p}$, see p.221

W number of complexions (microstates)

W, W' energy contributions in Pople-Karasz model

W_0 degeneracy of lowest energy state

W_i potential barrier for process i

x mole-fraction

x occupancy factor of sites or positions

x non-ordering parameter. x^*, tricritical value of -

x displacement

y, y_1, y_2 occupancy factor of sites or positions

Y partition function for constant T and $\mu_a - \mu_b$

z_i activity of species i

Z configurational part of canonical partition function; Z_g, - for gas; $Z_{cl,1}$, $Z_{cl,2}$, - for clathrate cavities, types 1 and 2, respectively

α $(dV/dT)_p / V$

α, α' critical indices for $>T_c$ and $<T_c$, respectively

α_{ij} order parameter (equation (5.2)). α_{ij}^{∞}, limit of - in fully ordered state

α polarizability. α_0, static -; α_{∞}, electronic -

α_t, α_t', α_u, α_u' tricritical indices

β critical index

β_t, β_u, β_-, β_+ tricritical indices

γ gyromagnetic ratio

γ, γ' critical indices

$\gamma(\mathcal{R}, \mathcal{S})$ number of configurations having $\mathcal{R}$ and $\mathcal{S}$ with values given

γ_t, γ_t', γ_u, γ_u' tricritical indices

γ_λ $(dp/dT)_\lambda = dp/dT$ along λ-line

Γ quadrupole coupling constant. Γ_{eff}, effective - in actual lattice; Γ_0, - for rigid lattice

Γ tunnelling integral

$\Gamma(T; \underline{r})$ pair correlation function (equation 3.11)

δ critical index

δ (dielectric) loss angle

δ Jahn-Teller splitting

δ_t, δ_u tricritical indices

Δ critical index (p.218)

Δ crystal field splitting

Δ Curie-Weiss constant

Δ energy difference (Schottky anomaly)

Δ non-ordering parameter (p.26)

Δ tunnelling splitting constant

ϵ $(T-T_c)/T_c$

ϵ (crystal field splitting)/2

ϵ permittivity of free space

ϵ, ϵ_i energy associated with a vertex (section 3.7)

ϵ_{ij} energy of interaction of particles of types i and j

ϵ_0 energy gap

$\dot{\epsilon}$ creep rate

ϵ, ϵ_r relative permittivity. ϵ_0 = - (static); ϵ_{∞} = - at $\nu = \infty$; ϵ', real part of -; ϵ'', imaginary part of -, (loss factor)

ϵ^* total permittivity

ϵ^* Lennard-Jones energy parameter

ζ ordering 'field' parameter (Ch.2)

ζ $= \Gamma_{eff}/\Gamma_0$

η critical index

η, η_i order parameters

θ $4qs(s+1)J/3k$ = Weiss constant

θ angular displacement

θ canting angle

θ scattering angle (in diffraction)

θ_{jk} angle between vector and applied field

θ_D Debye temperature

κ specific conductivity (electrolytic)

κ, κ_T $= -(dV/dT)_p/V$ = isothermal compressibility

κ_s $= -(dV/dT)_s/V$ = adiabatic compressibility

κ^{-1} correlation range

λ fraction of B-atoms in tetrahedral sites in a spinel (p.258)

λ wave-length

λ, λ' mean-field coupling coefficients (Jahn-Teller) (p.862)

μ chemical potential

μ_B Bohr magneton

μ_{eff} effective spin magnetic moment

μ_i s_i^z/s

ν frequency. $\bar{\nu}$, - expressed in wave-numbers; ν_D = Debye -; ν_R = jump - of reorientation; ν_{TO}, - of transverse optic mode; ν_{LO} = - of longitudinal optic mode

ν $q'W'/qW$ (p.67)

ν, ν' critical indices

ν_1, ν_2 stoichiometric coefficients

ξ $= I_3^2/R^7$ (p.584)

ρ density

ρ electrical resistivity

ρ length parameter in repulsion energy expression, $\exp(-r/\rho)$

ρ mole-fraction of diluent

σ area

σ interfacial surface free energy per unit area

σ neutron scattering cross-section. σ_s = total -

σ relative second harmonic intensity

σ stress

$\sigma, \bar{\sigma}$ Lennard-Jones length parameters

σ^x, σ^z Pauli operators

τ Jahn-Teller operator (p.862)

τ mean molecular jump time

τ relaxation time. τ_I, Ising contribution to -; τ_D, diffusional contribution to -

τ_c correlation time (NMR)

χ magnetic susceptibility. χ, χ_T, isothermal -; χ_s, adiabatic -; χ', χ_T' staggered -; $\chi_|$, $\chi_\perp$, components of - for anisotropic systems

ψ_j spin-wave eigenfunction

ω angular frequency. ω_{LO}, - of longitudinal optic mode; ω_{TO}, - of transverse optic mode

ω octupole moment (p.582)

Ω electrical resistance

Ω number of conformations of an aliphatic chain

Ω octupole moment (p.582)

Ω volume per atom

1

INTRODUCTION

The acceleration in activity in this field has been quite remarkable. If one leaves out of consideration magnetic ordering, and this may be justified on the grounds that it is only in recent years that the analogy between this and other forms or ordering has been clearly drawn, then the study of ordering can be said to have started with the work of Tammann. His paper of 1919 summarized his work published in the previous five years on the resistance to chemical attack of a variety of alloys. His method of investigation has not proved to be of general importance, but his discussion, in which he called upon the then recently determined structures of pure metals, generated a great deal of interest in the possible effects of order and disorder. In subsequent years, the main lines of experimental investigation were X-ray diffraction and calorimetry. Approximate theoretical methods for treating these systems followed, notably those by Bragg and Williams in 1934-5 (section 3.1.2) and Bethe in 1935 (section 3.1.3). It is, however, since the mid-1940s that the main growth has taken place. On the theoretical side, one would undoubtedly pick out Onsager's famous paper of 1944 (section 3.1.4) on the Ising model, and this has been followed by a great deal of splendid work involving both analytic and computer methods. Experimentally, a great variety of new techniques has become available, of which the principal are neutron diffraction and scattering and nuclear magnetic resonance. Dielectric measurements, which were in their infancy in 1939, have been developed, and refinements in X-ray diffraction and calorimetry have been made. The application of infrared and Raman spectroscopy to crystals started about 1950, when the use of group theory made analysis of the spectra feasible. One difficulty faced by us, as authors, has been to make the best selection from the vast amount of work which has been carried out.

The title given to this book, *Disorder in crystals*,

needs some qualification, since it may suggest different
things to different people. Before elaborating on the
sense in which we have interpreted the word 'disorder',
we must point out that a number of factors have imposed limitations on our treatment of the subject, such as our own
interests, the desire to keep the book within reasonable
bounds, and the fact that there already exist thorough
treatments of the disorder associated with lattice defects
and with non-stoichiometry. For this last reason, we may
state at the outset that we do not specifically consider
defects - though admittedly some of the aspects of the sub-
jects we do treat cannot be adequately discussed if all
mention of defects is omitted - and we do not deal with
non-stoichiometric crystals. It is true that we have a
chapter on clathrates, which will have a non-stoichiometric
'formula' when not all the cavities are filled, but at least
there is usually in such systems a definite ratio between
the number of cavities and the number of units composing
the host lattice. We have included a chapter on magnetic
disorder, in spite of the periodic reviews of high quality
which are carried out. This is because we believe that
this field has in recent years been the mainspring for the
development of the whole subject of disordering and no
book on disorder would be complete without an account of it.

We shall deal with three main kinds of disorder: disorder
of position, orientational disorder, and magnetic disorder.
By disorder of position we mean, for instance, that the
lattice is one in which there are more sites to accommodate
a particular kind of particle than there are particles of
that kind available and that there is at least some randomness in the way in which the particles are distributed among
the sites in question. Another possibility for positional
disorder arises when there are, for example, N A-atoms and
N B-atoms which together occupy $2N$ sites, again in a partially
or wholly random way. Orientational disorder can arise when
diatomic or polyatomic molecules or ions have access to two
or more orientations in the crystal lattice which are distinguishable. Magnetic disordering is a disordering of the
orientations of magnetic spins and is encountered in the

common paramagnetic state. However, a clear-cut distinction
cannot always be made between positional and orientational
disorder. Thus the famous case of the disorder in the
ordinary form of ice can be considered either as a problem in
the number of different ways in which protons can be placed
in the hydrogen bonds between oxygen ions in a tetrahedral
network of these ions, subject to certain conditions, of which
one is that of the four protons surrounding any one oxygen
two are close and two remote, or alternatively it can be
regarded as a problem in orientational disorder, with the
limitation that a molecule cannot adopt any of the six possible orientations independently of those of neighbouring
water molecules.

With regard to the significance we have given to the
word 'disorder', the literature will be found to contain
the terms 'dynamic' and 'static' disorder. We have made
relatively little use of these adjectives, since they have
been given different meanings by different authors. References to dynamic disorder often simply imply a rather large
degree of thermal movement, as for example a molecule or ion
undergoing torsional oscillations[†] through a somewhat large
angle. Some authors, however, have made the distinction
between static and dynamic disorder on the basis of a comparison of the time-scale of the relevant molecular or
ionic movement with the time-scale of some observation.
Suppose, for example, that we have a crystal in which each
molecule or ion has two possible distinguishable orientations
available to it. If the potential barrier which must be
surmounted to pass from one orientation to the other is so
high that the rate of passage is negligible on the time-
scale of the observation, then if the molecules or ions are
found to be distributed between the two orientations the
situation can certainly be described as one of static disorder. But if the transit happens many times during the
period of the observation, this is sometimes referred to as

[†]Motion of this kind is often described as libration, a word originally
used for an apparent oscillation of the moon by virtue of which the
surface near the edge of the disc is alternately visible and invisible.

dynamic disorder. From this standpoint, whether the disorder qualifies for description as static or dynamic depends
inter alia on the potential barrier height, temperature, and
time-scale of the observation, and the difference becomes
one of degree and not of kind. Even if the term dynamic
disorder is simply used to mean a relatively large amount
of thermal motion, the distinction between this and static
disorder can become rather blurred. For example, ammonium
salts are known in which as the ammonium ion is rotated it
passes through more than one potential energy minimum, some
of which at least correspond to distinguishable orientations, but in which the barrier separating such minima is
relatively low, say 4 kJ mol^{-1}. At temperatures within
the range of thermal stability of some salts of this kind,
a not negligible fraction of the ions in the crystal can
reach energy levels above the barrier top, and an instan-
taneous photograph on a molecular scale would show some of
the ions in the act of librating anharmonically and with a
rather large amplitude, and others undergoing a somewhat
non-uniform rotation.

        If we take a crystal disordered in one or more ways
- and examples will be found in this book of solids simultaneously disordered in two or even three ways - and cool
it down, in principle one of two things can happen. Either
the disorder remains (becomes frozen-in) so that there
would still be disorder at 0 K. Or else, and this is the
commoner occurrence, the crystal undergoes some kind of
transition and becomes ordered. (We leave out of consideration here various artificial models such as the one-
dimensional Ising model and models in which the entities
behave completely independently, for which the entropy becomes
zero at 0 K but which display no transition.) Sometimes the
crystal may have to pass through more than one transition
to reach a completely ordered state. These order-disorder
transitions vary greatly in detail and we shall not elaborate
on this at this stage; but it will be clear that discussion
of disorder in crystals is inseparable from discussion of
transitions in solids. In distinguishing between different
phases of a solid, or perhaps we should provisionally

deliberately use the less precise word 'forms', we have
adopted the widely used system of numbering them with Roman
numerals, I being the form stable at the highest temperatures,
which on cooling transforms to II, which on further cooling
gives III, and so on. However, there are certain classes of
polymorphic solid, for example, long-chain organic compounds
and simple molecular solids such as nitrogen and oxygen, where
the alternative system of lettering the forms α, β, γ, etc., is
rather thoroughly entrenched. Since the latter system can
have advantages, as for example in considering long-chain
compounds, where similar forms share a common Greek letter,
we have, at the risk of being thought inconsistent, occasionally employed it.

   The thorough study of disorder in a particular crystal
involves a number of experimental techniques, and we have
thought it worth while to give an account of the more widely
used of these, not to provide a *vade mecum* for anyone wishing
to carry out experimental work in this field, but rather to
illustrate the kind of information which a specific technique may be expected to supply. The experimentalist will
not only be concerned with discovering whether a given crystal
is disordered or not, and, if it is, in establishing the
character of the disorder. He will also wish to determine
the characteristics of any order-disorder transitions involved. Moreover, the dynamics of any relevant motion in
the lattice must be investigated. For example, numerous
ammonium salts can exist in forms in which the ammonium ions
are orientationally disordered, and quantitative information
on the rate at which such an ion can change its orientation
contributes to a fuller understanding of the disordering
process. Since comparative information on the rate parameters involved which covers a range of different ammonium
salts is of obvious value, we have not hesitated to quote
results for salts which do not themselves exhibit any order-
disorder transitions.

   With regard to the reviews we present of the experimental information at present available on disorder in various
types of solid, we hope that the material surveyed is representative, but we have not aimed at including every known case

of disorder. Rather, we have sought to give fairly detailed accounts of studies on solids in which the molecules or ions are either small or at least highly symmetrical, since such solids offer the best hope of solving
the theoretical problems involved. As for the theoretical
background of the subject, disorder in a crystal usually
has clear thermodynamic consequences, in that if frozen-
in on cooling it will lead to a crystal still possessing
entropy at the absolute zero, or if not it will probably be
associated with one or more transitions. Then there arises
the question of whether a model can be applied to the solid
in question which, with the aid of statistical mechanics, can
be shown to reproduce the main features associated with the
disorder. Our subject has in fact supplied theoreticians
in the past three or four decades with some celebrated and
difficult statistical mechanical problems. Those un-
familiar with the subject may be surprised to learn how complicated apparently straightforward problems in this field
can prove to be. The theoretical handling will generally
be easy for systems in which the molecules or ions behave
independently of each other. Unfortunately, these systems
are usually the ones of least interest. If, by contrast,
the tendency of a particle to switch to another state is
determined by the current state of the other particles then
we have the far more interesting situation of cooperative
behaviour. In such systems the disordering process becomes
'easier' the further it proceeds and leads to what is sometimes termed a 'catastrophe' at a particular temperature.

In contemplating the fascinating duel - as it appears
to us - between the forces in a crystal which favour an
ordered structure with the thermal agitation tending to produce disorder, the nature of the force or forces involved
in any particular case naturally excites curiosity. Here
too there is considerable variety. Possible factors which
favour an ordered arrangement of molecules or ions in a
lattice can include the anisotropy of dispersion forces and
of short-range repulsion forces, the interaction between
electric dipoles, the interaction between electric quadrupoles (as in crystalline nitrogen or hydrogen), octupoles

(as in methane, or between ammonium ions), or even higher
multipoles (for example, hexadecapoles in sulphur hexafluoride) and hydrogen bonding. Magnetic ordering often
proves to be far stronger than would be expected simply on
the basis of magnetic interactions through space, and often
involves the participation of intermediate atoms, ions, or
ligands ('superexchange').

   We are therefore concerned in this book with phenomena
which occur in a very large number of crystals of widely
diverse chemical types. These phenomena have been investigated by a variety of experimental techniques, and a tremen-
dous amount of factual information is now available. In
seeking an understanding of this information, recourse at
some stage or other to thermodynamics, statistical mechanics,
and quantum mechanics is inevitable.

Tammann, G. (1919). *Z.anorg.allg.Chem.* 107, 1.

2

THERMODYNAMICS

2.1. INTRODUCTION

On cooling a substance we might expect disorder to disappear until, at least by 0 K, the substance was fully
ordered. However, there are certain systems for which experiment indicates that this does not happen. The true
equilibrium state at 0 K may be presumed to be fully ordered,
so that the disorder which is found in the real system
must be a consequence of the failure of the kinetic process
by which the degree of disorder is brought into correspondence with the temperature of the other degrees of
freedom. Such a system is said to have 'frozen-in' disorder.
It is most likely to be found if the sample is cooled very
rapidly from a temperature at which the equilibrium state is
disordered to a temperature low enough for the rate of
ordering to be virtually zero. Generally speaking, therefore,
the more complicated the molecules or ions, or rather the
ordering process, then the greater is the chance of
'freezing-in' disorder. Nevertheless, it is possible that
some very simple solids can be 'caught' in the disordered
state. For example CO is generally considered to be
disordered with respect to the head-tail arrangements of the
molecules (Clayton and Giauque 1932). The reason for this is,
in part, that the two ends of the molecule are so similar.
The other consideration is that the structure adopted, which
is determined by the relatively large quadrupoles, is such
as to reduce the importance of differences between the two
ends of the molecules. Thus the difference in energy between
the ordered and disordered states which arises from the dipolar interactions has been calculated to be $18 \cdot 9$ J mol^{-1}
(Melhuish and Scott 1964), which only becomes comparable
with RT at $\sim$ 2 K. At such a temperature the chance that a
molecule would possess the activation energy necessary
to perform a head-tail interchange is exceedingly small, so
that, for all intents and purposes, the process does not
take place at all. Recent experimental work has suggested

that the behaviour may be more complicated than has been indicated here (section 9.3). Other substances showing this type
of behaviour are NO (section 9.3), N_2O (section 9.5.1) and
ClO_3F (p.571).

Another type of disorder in solids can be illustrated by
a consideration of the cooling of glycerol. In the absence
of nuclei the liquid is readily supercooled below the melting-
point (291 K), and because of its considerable stability with
respect to crystallization the supercooled liquid can be
easily studied. It is found that over a small range near
183 K the supercooled liquid changes its character, the new
state being known as a 'glass'. Fig.2.1 shows the heat

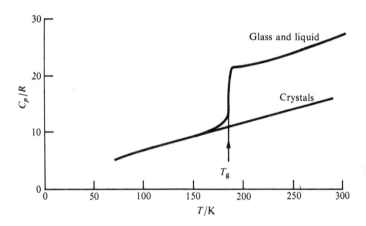

Fig.2.1. C_p against T for glycerol in the liquid, glassy and crystalline
forms (from Gibson and Giauque 1923).

capacity curves for the glass and supercooled liquid and
also for the crystalline solid (Gibson and Giauque 1923,
Simon and Lange 1926, Oblad and Newton 1937) and the equilibrium liquid. The transformation from the supercooled
liquid to the glass (the 'glass transition') corresponds to
the loss of some degrees of freedom and the freezing-in of
the corresponding parameters at the values which they had
in the supercooled liquid at the transition temperature.
The glass transition is not a true thermodynamic transition,
and the position and nature of it depend somewhat on the

thermal history (but particularly on the cooling rate) of
the sample. The observed glass transition temperature (T_g)
is the temperature at which the time required for relaxation of the degree(s) of freedom concerned becomes comparable with that allowed by the experiment. The lower the
cooling rate, the lower the glass transition temperature
since the degree(s) of freedom involved will then be able
to remain in equilibrium until a lower temperature is
reached. Thus by allowing a longer time for equilibration,
Oblad and Newton (1937) were able to extend the heat capacity
curve for the supercooled liquid below the glass transition
temperature found by normal calorimetric means (Gibson and
Giauque 1923), thereby reducing the value for the zero-
point entropy of the glass below the value of $20 \cdot 9$ J K^{-1}
mol^{-1} found by the earlier workers. The effect of cooling
rate on T_g is not very marked, however, because of the high
rate of change of relaxation rate with temperature. Thus
in the transition to the 'glassy crystal' in c-$C_6H_{11}OH$
(see below) at $T_g \approx 150$ K, the time constant of the ordering
process was found to change from $11 \cdot 9$ h at 144 K to 125 h at
133 K. Nevertheless, this dependence of T_g on the time-
scale of the experiment has led Kauzmann (1948) to define
T_g as the temperature where C_p or α shows a more or less
sudden change due to relaxation effects when 10 min to 1 h
is allowed for equilibration.

     According to Cohen and Turnbull (1959-70) it should be
possible to obtain even the simplest substances in a glassy
form. For a system of hard spheres this form would be the
dense random structure (density $\approx 0 \cdot 85 \times$ that of the close-
packed crystal) considered by Bernal in his studies of the
liquid state. Experimental studies of the glass-forming
properties of some fairly simple substances have been carried
out by **Staveley** *et al*. (Thomas and Staveley 1952, de Nordwall
and **Staveley** 1954, 1956). Their observations were of the
'devitrification temperature', at which, on heating the vitreous material, heat is evolved and the substance becomes
crystalline, rather than of T_g. They found such devitrification processes for $C_2H_5OH, C_6H_5CH_3, p\text{-}C_6H_4(CH_3)_2$,
$C_5H_5N, NH_3, CH_3NH_2, CH_3Cl$, and $Sn(CH_3)_4$, and suggested

that these samples must have been, at least partly, vitreous. Substances with more symmetric molecules (C_6H_6, CS_2, $c\text{-}C_5H_{10}$, and CH_2Cl_2) showed no such behaviour, and it was assumed that these substances were not in the glassy state. These experiments do not, in fact, distinguish between the glass and the supercooled liquid, but rather between these two and the crystalline form.

To distinguish the supercooled liquid from the glass it is necessary to observe the glass transition. Seki *et al.* (Sugisaki, Suga, and Seki 1967, 1968) have employed conventional adiabatic calorimetry on samples made by cooling from the vapour, and have shown that CH_3OH, H_2O, and iso-C_5H_{12} can be made in glassy forms with $T_g \approx 130$ K, ≈ 135 K, and ≈ 65 K, respectively. They also found that on supercooling the f.c.c. I-form of $c\text{-}C_6H_{11}OH$ below the temperature at which it would normally be transformed into the II-form there was a glass transition to give what they termed a 'glassy crystal' (Fig.10.3). In all the cases studied by Seki's group, crystallization occurred a few degrees above T_g, thereby supporting the relevance of the experiments of Staveley *et al.* to the location of glass transitions. A similar calorimetric study of diethyl phthalate and *o*-terphenyl has shown that each of these substances undergoes a supercooled liquid-glass transformation, the residual entropy at 0 K being 20-23 and 15 J K^{-1} mol^{-1}, respectively (Chang, Harman, and Bestul 1967, Chang and Bestul 1972).

Another group of glass-forming substances are the chalcogens (Chaudhari, Beardmore, and Bever 1966, Gattow and Buss 1969) and the chalcogenides of elements such as As and Ge (Kolomiets 1970, Taylor, Bishop, and Mitchell 1971, Ward 1972). These are of interest because many of them are semiconductors. Here the process which can become frozen is the equilibrium between chains and rings of atoms.

Many polymers also show glass transitions: on cooling, the elastic, supercooled form goes over to the brittle, glassy form over a fairly narrow range of temperature (often ~ 20°). Such glass transitions are normally associated with the loss of the degrees of freedom which arise from internal rotation about the bonds of the carbon skeleton of the polymer

(Tobolsky 1960).

A good discussion of glass transitions from the thermodynamic point of view has been given by Prigogine and Defay
(1954). A more recent paper of general interest is that
by Moynihan and Macedo (1971). From the assumption that the
relaxation process goes by a first-order kinetic law, they
have shown quantitatively how the heat capacity versus temperature curve depends upon the calorimetric heating rate
and have reproduced the frequently observed minimum and
maximum in the curve at the beginning and end of the transition region. A useful collection of data on glass transitions known up to 1960 is to be found in a paper by Wunderlich (1960). We will not, however, consider these transitions further here.

2.2. CLASSIFICATION OF TRANSITIONS (EHRENFEST)

For the moment, we shall restrict our attention to those
cases where all the degrees of freedom remain in equilibrium
at all temperatures. This still leaves a very large number
of systems of interest, and considerable effort has been put
into the task of dividing their transitions into a small
number of classes. The most famous attempt in this direction
was made by P.Ehrenfest (1933). He defined the 'order' of
a transition as being the order of the lowest derivative of
the Gibbs free energy which showed a discontinuity at the
transition point. Thus, a simple isothermal transition involving a latent heat and a volume change, e.g. melting, has
no discontinuity in G at the transition point, but it does
show abrupt changes in the first derivatives of G with respect to T and p, i.e. S and V. It is, therefore, said to
be a first-order transition (Fig.2.2a). On this basis, a
second-order transition is one for which there is a dis-
continuity in the second derivatives of G, i.e. C_p, $(\partial V/\partial p)_T$
and $(\partial V/\partial T)_p$, but only a change of slope for S and V, at the
transition point (Fig.2.2b).

Ehrenfest obtained a relationship for dT_t/dp, the rate of
change of the transition temperature with pressure, for a
second-order transition. This is analogous to the well-known
Clapeyron equation for a first-order transition. Since the

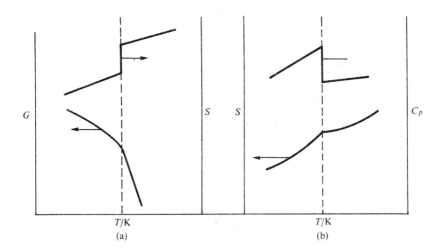

Fig.2.2. Transitions in Ehrenfest's classification; (a) first-order,
(b) second-order.

entropies of the low- and high-temperature forms are equal,
$S_1 = S_2$, then changes in T and p such that the forms remain
in equilibrium must lead to $dS_1 = dS_2$. That is:

$$(\partial S_1/\partial T)_p dT + (\partial S_1/\partial p)_T dp = (\partial S_2/\partial T)_p dT + (\partial S_2/\partial p)_T dp . \quad (2.1)$$

Therefore

$$\frac{dp}{dT} = \frac{C_{p2}/T - C_{p1}/T}{V(\alpha_2 - \alpha_1)} , \quad \text{where } \alpha = (\partial V/\partial T)_p/V . \quad (2.2)$$

Likewise, consideration of the continuity of V yields

$$\frac{dp}{dT} = \frac{\alpha_2 - \alpha_1}{\kappa_{T2} - \kappa_{T1}} , \quad \text{where } \kappa_T = -(\partial V/\partial p)_T/V . \quad (2.3)$$

Third-order transitions can be treated in a similar way.
Using the continuity of C_p, α and κ_T, the set of relationships

$$\frac{dp}{dT} = \frac{(\partial C_{p2}/\partial T)_p - (\partial C_{p1}/\partial T)_p}{TV\{(\partial \alpha_2/\partial T)_p - (\partial \alpha_1/\partial T)_p\}} = \frac{(\partial \alpha_2/\partial T)_p - (\partial \alpha_1/\partial T)_p}{(\partial \kappa_{T2}/\partial T)_p - (\partial \kappa_{T1}/\partial T)_p} = \frac{(\partial \alpha_2/\partial p)_T - (\partial \alpha_1/\partial p)_T}{(\partial \kappa_{T2}/\partial p)_T - (\partial \kappa_{T1}/\partial p)_T}$$

$$(2.4)$$

is derived.

However, very few systems show the finite discontinuity
in C_p and α which the second-order class should have. A

transition which fairly certainly corresponds to Ehrenfest's
second-order type is the superconducting-normal transition
in, for example, tin (Fig.2.3a). Those in $TmVO_4$ (Fig.2.3b)

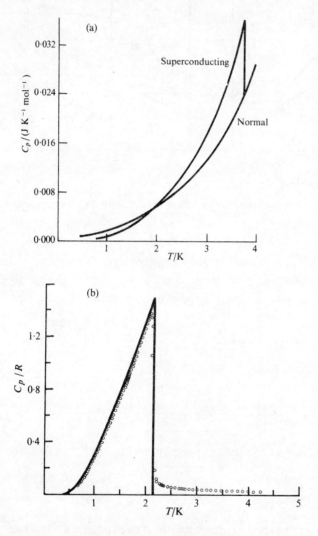

Fig.2.3.(a) C_p against T for tin in the normal and superconducting
forms (from Keesom and Van Laer 1938); (b) C_p against T for $TmVO_4$
(from Cooke, Swithenby, and Wells 1972).

and some related zircons may also be of this type (section
12.13.1).

  A further weakness in Ehrenfest's treatment which was
almost immediately realized is exposed by considering the

way in which the graphs of G against T for the two forms
meet at the transition temperature.   Since there is no discontinuity in slope the two curves must touch at T_t (Fig.2.4).

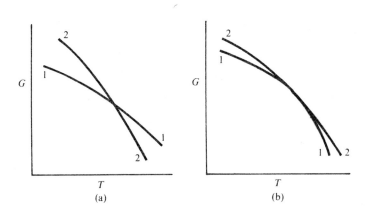

Fig.2.4. G against T for the low (1) - and high (2) - temperature forms
in Ehrenfest's treatment; (a) first-order transition, (b) second-order
transition (after Pippard 1964).

It is therefore clear that the same form must be stable both
above and below the transition temperature! The same ob-
jection does not apply to third-order transitions as different forms would then be stable above and below T_t (Justi
and von Laue 1934). The source of the trouble with regard
to second-order transitions is the assumption that there are
two phases each of which could be imagined to be present both
above and below T_t. Thus the λ-lines are being compared with
the corresponding lines of heterogeneous equilibrium rather
than, as turns out to be more appropriate, with a set of
critical points. The state of the system is, as we shall see,
better described by means of an order parameter (η) which
below T_t decreases with increase in temperature and finally
becomes zero at T_t and remains so for all higher temperatures.
Thus a continuation of the low-temperature phase into the
region above T_t would have no meaning, for one could not
suggest that η is there becoming increasingly negative (Mayer
and Streeter 1939). Indeed, the two modifications become increasingly alike until at T_t they become identical. Below T_t
the possibility of two phases can be discussed, and indeed

some of the examples given above of frozen-in disorder
correspond to the system with $\eta = 0$.

2.3. CLASSIFICATION OF TRANSITIONS (PIPPARD)

A.B.Pippard (1964a) has made a classification which is considerably more elaborate than that of Ehrenfest. Instead of
the second- and third-order transitions of Ehrenfest, he
suggests four subdivisions of each. These are best described in terms of the C_p versus T curves (Fig.2.5). Types 2

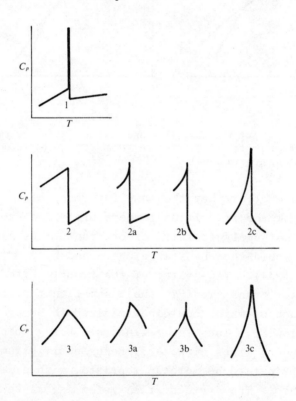

Fig.2.5. C_p against T curves for various types of transition in Pippard's
classification (from Pippard 1964).

and 3 are the straightforward transitions as envisaged by
Ehrenfest; 2a and 3a each have infinite dc_p/dT but finite c_p
on one side of the transition; 2b and 3b each have infinite
dc_p/dT but finite c_p on both sides of the transition; 2c and
3c both have infinite c_p at the transition. The discontinuity

in C_p, whether finite or infinite, is present in all the
types of second-order transition whereas, of course, the third-
order transitions only show the discontinuities in dC_p/dT.
It should be remarked that there is no reason why C_p should
not become infinite at a transition point, provided that the
integral under the curve of C_p against T remains finite. It
is, therefore, acceptable for C_p to go to infinity as
$\ln|T-T_t|$ or as $|T-T_t|^{-1/2}$, but not as sharply as $|T-T_t|^{-1}$.
There is also no reason why C_V should not remain finite
even though C_p becomes infinite. Similar considerations to
those for C_p apply to α, which can also become infinite at
transition points.

For further information on the superconducting-normal
transition in zero magnetic field (in non-zero field it is
first-order) the reader is referred to the account by Pippard.
The Bragg-Williams and similar approximations also lead to
this type of heat capacity behaviour, as will be seen later
(section 3.1.2). Types 2c and 3c, both of which are known as
λ-transitions, are of frequent occurrence, being found, for
example, for β-brass, many NH_4^+ salts, solid H_2, liquid ^4He
and in many magnetic transitions.

An important part of Pippard's work has been to derive
equations for the λ-line equivalent to those obtained by
Ehrenfest for finite discontinuities. Starting from the
relationships:

$$\gamma_\lambda = (dp/dT)_\lambda = -(\partial^2 s/\partial T^2)/(\partial^2 s/\partial T \partial p) = -(\partial^2 s/\partial T \partial p)/(\partial^2 s/\partial p^2)$$
$$(2.5)$$

he then makes an assumption about the form of $S(T,p)$. For
this purpose, he employs the so-called 'cylindrical approximation', namely that close to the λ-line $S(T,p)$ can be represented as $S = S_\lambda(p)+f(p-\gamma_\lambda T)$. The curvature of $S_\lambda(p)$ is
assumed to be negligible compared with that of $f(p-\gamma_\lambda T)$, and
hence

$$(\partial^2 s/\partial T^2)_p = \gamma_\lambda^2 f'' , \quad (\partial^2 s/\partial T \partial p) = -\gamma_\lambda f'' \text{ and } \partial^2 s/\partial p^2 = f''. (2.6)$$

This leads to the relationship:

$$C_p = \gamma_\lambda V T_\lambda \alpha + \text{const, where } \alpha = (\partial V / \partial T)_p / V. \qquad (2.7)$$

A similar discussion of the surface for $V(T,p)$ yields

$$\alpha = \gamma_\lambda \kappa_T + \text{const'}. \qquad (2.8)$$

In the case of a type 2c transition the curvature must be evaluated on the side of the transition remote from the discontinuity; for a type 3c transition no such stipulation need be made.

Experimental tests near the λ-line are limited to a small number of substances: NH_4Cl (Garland and Jones 1963 Renard and Garland 1966; see also section 7.5.1.), ^4He (Buckingham and Fairbank 1961), β-brass (Garland and Jones 1963), sulphur (Klement 1966), $NaNO_3$ (Klement 1970; Fig. 7.16), and quartz (Hughes and Lawson 1962). In the latter work, equations similar to (2.7) and (2.8) gave values for γ_λ which deviated from the directly determined value by ~35% and ~2%, respectively. However, the α-β quartz transition is not truly second order, there being a small first-order component. Fig.7.25 shows the results for NH_4Cl as a plot of C_p/T against $V\alpha$. Corresponding equations may be derived for magnetic and ferroelectric transitions, e.g. $C_{\mathcal{H}=0}/T$ should vary linearly with $(\partial \chi_T / \partial T)_{\mathcal{H}=0}$. Wright (1972) has found that this relationship is not well obeyed for $CoCl_2.6H_2O$ just above the Curie point. He noted, however, that the equivalent relationship for ferroelectric systems was in good agreement with experiment for KH_2PO_4 at temperatures just above the transition point. Janovec (1966) has also made a very careful analysis of ferroelectric data by means of the corresponding Pippard equations. From measurements of the heat capacity, elastic compliances, and pyroelectric and piezoelectric coefficients of the aniso-tropic dielectric triglycine sulphate, he was able to evaluate the slope of the transition line $(dT/dp)_\lambda$ in several ways. The results obtained ranged over about one order of magnitude. This was attributed to differences in the domain configurations between the various experiments.

2.4. THE TISZA APPROACH

Tisza (1961) has considered in detail the thermodynamics of
transitions from the point of view of an enlarged Gibbsian
space. For one-component systems he enlarged the Gibbsian
space, $U(S,V)$, by adding one or more symmetry parameters
(η_i) in those cases where a phase can exist in two or more
forms which are not superimposable either by rotation or
translation. On raising the temperature the η_i decrease and
become zero at the corresponding critical points. For such
a more generalized system the temperature of the λ-point(s)
is a function of the external parameter p (conjugate to V)
and so forms a λ-line, in contrast to the situation in pure
fluids where the critical behaviour occurs at an isolated
point. The extra degree of freedom to account for this
difference arises from the parameter η_i. If there is a single
η and its conjugate field is zero, then η will be a function
of S and V such that U is minimized.

        Since in this book we are not concerned with fluids,
it is more instructive to consider the case of a single component magnetic system. The complete treatment would require consideration of S, V, and M as the independent variables, where M, the magnetization, is the order parameter. The
problem may be simplified by assuming that the variable V is,
for our purposes, unimportant. The stable state is now one
which minimizes U for the particular values of the independent
variables (S,M). The stability of a phase with respect to
small changes in S and M requires that the surface $U(S,M)$ be
convex to the S and M axes. In other words, the quantity
$\delta^2 U$, defined by the equation:

$$\delta^2 U = (\partial^2 U/\partial S^2)(\delta S)^2 + 2(\partial^2 U/\partial S \partial M)\delta S \delta M + (\partial^2 U/\partial M^2)(\delta M)^2 \quad (2.9)$$

should be positive definite, that is >0 for all values of
δS and δM. In the unstable region $\delta^2 U$ will be indefinite
($\lessgtr 0$). On the boundary between these regions, where the
system is said to be in a critical state, $\delta^2 U$ should be
positive semi-definite. That is, $\delta^2 U \geq 0$ according to the
choice of δS and δM, which determines the direction of the

virtual displacement. The necessary and sufficient condition for $\partial^2 U$ to be positive semi-definite is that the deter-
minant of the stiffness matrix:

$$\tilde{D} = \begin{pmatrix} \partial^2 U/\partial S^2 & \partial^2 U/\partial S\,\partial M \\[2mm] \partial^2 U/\partial M\,\partial S & \partial^2 U/\partial M^2 \end{pmatrix} = \begin{pmatrix} T/C_M & T(\partial\mathcal{H}/\partial T)_M/C_M \\[2mm] T(\partial\mathcal{H}/\partial T)_M/C_M & 1/\chi_S \end{pmatrix}$$

$$(2.10)$$

where $C_M = (\partial U/\partial T)_M$ and $\chi_S = (\partial M/\partial\mathcal{H})_S$, should be zero. This
does not enable any simple statements to be made about the
individual elements of the matrix. However, it can be said
that the elements of the compliance matrix, which is the
inverse of $\tilde{D}$, must each be infinite in the critical state.
Since, for this system,

$$\tilde{C} = \tilde{D}^{-1} = \begin{pmatrix} C_{\mathcal{H}}/T & (\partial M/\partial T)_{\mathcal{H}} \\[2mm] (\partial M/\partial T)_{\mathcal{H}} & \chi_T \end{pmatrix}$$

$$(2.11)$$

then $(\partial M/\partial T)_{\mathcal{H}}, C_{\mathcal{H}}$ and χ_T must each become infinite at the
critical condition.

For more general systems in which U is a function of
several variables $x_1, x_2, x_3 \ldots x_r$ the requirement for critical
behaviour is:

$$\det \tilde{D} = \begin{vmatrix} \partial^2 U/\partial x_1^2 & \partial^2 U/\partial x_1 \partial x_2 & \cdots & \partial^2 U/\partial x_1 \partial x_r \\ \partial^2 U/\partial x_2 \partial x_1 & & & \\ \vdots & & & \\ \vdots & & & \\ \vdots & & & \\ \partial^2 U/\partial x_r \partial x_1 & & & \partial^2 U/\partial x_r^2 \end{vmatrix} = 0$$

$$(2.12)$$

The way in which the order parameter should be chosen
has been ignored so far. As an example of the procedure
we consider the $U(S,V,..)$ surface, as the $U(S,M...)$ surface

turns out to be over-simple. If a plane is simultaneously
tangent to the surface at two points, then these two points
represent two states which are in equilibrium with each
other and the line joining them is known as a generator.
As the tangent plane rolls over the $U(S,V..)$ surface a continuous series of generators is formed. As we proceed towards a critical state these generators become shorter and
the two states corresponding to their ends become more
alike. The order parameter is defined by the direction of
the generator in the limit as the critical state is reached.
As an example, for a generator of a pure fluid we have that
$\Delta S:\Delta U:\Delta V = \mathrm{d}p/\mathrm{d}T:T(\mathrm{d}p/\mathrm{d}T):1$, where p is the vapour pressure.
The correct order parameter is given by the corresponding
direction at the critical point. In ferromagnetic ordering
the generators are always parallel to the magnetization axis,
so that the correct order parameter is simply the magnetization.

2.5. LANDAU'S THEORY OF PHASE TRANSITIONS

L.D. Landau (1937) proposed a theory of gradual transitions
which assumed that the free energy remained analytic at a
critical point. This assumption is now known to be incorrect and the theory consequently fails in the immediate
neighbourhood of critical points. Nevertheless, it is
worthy of consideration for three reasons. Firstly, it has
exerted a considerable influence on the study of transitions
over a long period of time. Secondly, its predictions, which
usually attract the adjective 'classical', are often used
as standards with which experimental results and those from
more exact theories are compared. Finally, the theory
usually gives results which are at least qualitatively
correct.

As elsewhere in this book, we will consider the special
case of a ferromagnetic transition because we believe that
this will assist in the understanding of the treatment.
Other kinds of disordering transition may be discussed in
the same way, with similar results, and indeed Landau's
original work is written in more general terms.

The Helmholtz free energy $A(T,M) \equiv U-TS$ is expanded in ascending powers of the magnetization (M):

$$A(T,M) = a_0(T) + a_2(T)M^2 + a_4(T)M^4 + a_6(T)M^6 + \ldots$$
$$(2.13)$$

Terms in odd powers of M are omitted in order that A should be symmetric with respect to the $M = 0$ axis. It follows that:

$$\mathcal{H} = (\partial A/\partial M)_T = 2a_2(T)M + 4a_4(T)M^3 + 6a_6(T)M^5 + \ldots \qquad (2.14)$$

We shall want to know how various thermodynamic quantities behave as the critical point is approached.

Consider the approach to the critical point along the critical isotherm ($T=T_c$). Since $a_2(T_c) = 0$, (2.14) reduces to:

$$\mathcal{H} = 4a_4(T)M^3 + 6a_6(T)M^5 + \ldots \qquad (2.15)$$

or $\mathcal{H} \sim M^3$ as the critical point is approached.

Now consider the situation at $\mathcal{H}=0$ and at a temperature slightly below T_c, and let us expand the coefficient a_2 in terms of (T_c-T) in equation (2.14):

$$0 = 2\{a_{21}(T_c-T)+a_{22}(T_c-T)^2+..\}M + 4a_4(T)M^3+6a_6(T)M^5+.. \qquad (2.16)$$

This leads to the solution for M as $T \rightarrow T_c$:

$$4a_4(T)M^2 \sim 2a_{21}(T_c-T) . \qquad (2.17)$$

Likewise the heat capacity $C_M = -T(\partial^2 A/\partial T^2)_M$ in zero field can be written as:

$$C_M = -T(d^2a_0/dT^2) \qquad \text{for } T > T_c \qquad (2.18)$$

For $T < T_c$ it is necessary to substitute for M^2 from (2.17) into (2.13). Retaining the first two terms

$$A(T,M) = a_0(T)+\{a_{21}(T_c-T)+a_{22}(T_c-T)^2...\}\{a_{21}(T_c-T)/2a_4+..\}$$
$$(2.19)$$

from which as $T \rightarrow T_c$

$$C_M = -T(d^2 a_0)/dT^2) + T a_{21}^2/a_4 + 0(T_c - T) . \qquad (2.20)$$

Thus at T_c there is a discontinuity in C_M of magnitude $T_c a_{21}^2/a_4$.

Differentiation of (2.14) with respect to M yields an expression for the isothermal susceptibility:

$$1/\chi_T = (\partial \mathcal{H}/\partial M)_T = 2\{a_{21}(T_c-T)+a_{22}(T_c-T)^2+..\ \}+ 12a_4(T)M^2 + 30a_6(T)M^4+...$$
$$(2.21)$$

As $T \rightarrow T_c$ from above and with $\mathcal{H}=M=0$:

$$1/\chi_T \sim 2a_{21}(T_c-T) . \qquad (2.22)$$

It must be emphasized that Landau's theory is of general application and M is to be considered as the appropriate order parameter and $\mathcal{H}$ the conjugate 'field'. For example, when applying the theory to an antiferromagnet the appropriate ordering parameter is the sublattice magnetization (M') and the the 'field' conjugate to it is the 'staggered' field $(\mathcal{H}')$, which is oppositely directed on the two sublattices. Although $\mathcal{H}'$ is inaccessible, equations (2.13) to (2.22) are correct provided that $\mathcal{H}$, M, and χ_T are replaced by $\mathcal{H}'$, M', and χ_T', where the latter is known as the 'staggered' susceptibility. In the presence of an applied (direct) field the magnetizations of the two sublattices will not be equal and the mean of their magnitudes should be taken for M' (see below).

Landau also considered the case where a_2 and a_4 became zero at the same temperature (T^*), which is now called the tricritical temperature for reasons which are discussed in the next section. The most common real situation in which this occurs is that of a metamagnet (a type of antiferromagnet) in a magnetic field, and for that reason theoretical predictions are here expressed in terms appropriate to an antiferromagnetic system. From (2.15) it is at once clear that $\mathcal{H}' \sim M'^5$ at $T = T^*$ instead of $\sim M'^3$. The corresponding modification of (2.16) leads to the result

$$3a_6(T)M'^4 \sim a_{21}(T^*-T) . \qquad (2.23)$$

Above T^*, C_M, is given by (2.18). However, below T^* when (2.19) is modified to take account of a_4 being zero, (2.20) becomes

$$C_{M'} = -T d^2 a_0 / dT^2 - T\{3 a_{21}^{3/2} (T^*-T)^{-1/2} / 4(3 a_6)^{1/2}\}. \qquad (2.24)$$

The staggered susceptibility near T^* and at $\mathcal{K}'=M'=0$ is correctly given by (2.22).

A quantity which is frequently measured is M, the magnetization of the antiferromagnetic system, as a function of temperature along the transition line below T^*. The corresponding Landau equation is not (2.23), which refers to the ordering parameter M', but rather equations which have been derived by Bidaux, Carrara, and Vivet (1967):

$$M_{dis}/M_s = M^*/M_s + (T^*-T)M_s/2T^*M^*$$
$$\qquad\qquad\qquad\qquad\qquad\qquad\qquad\qquad (2.25)$$
$$M_{ord}/M_s = M^*/M_s - (T^*-T)M_s/2T^*M^*$$

where M_{dis} and M_{ord} refer to the disordered ($M'=0$) and ordered ($M'\neq0$) phases which coexist at temperature T, M^* is the magnetization at the tricritical point, and M_s is the saturation magnetization.

2.6. FURTHER CONSIDERATIONS ON λ-LINES AND TRICRITICAL POINTS
A number of workers have examined the possibility of there being restrictions on the type of behaviour which can occur along lines of λ-points. O.K.Rice (1954) concluded that, on producing a λ-line by coupling the ordering process with the compressibility of the lattice, an infinity in C_V would give way to a first-order transition, rather than permit there to be a line along which C_V was infinite. Domb (1956), who considered only the Ising model, reached a similar conclusion. Both of the above treatments involve approximations which could well have an important influence on the properties near the transition. A similar treatment by Renard and Garland (1966) is presented in section 3.1.8. Fisher (1968) criticized the above theories on the grounds that they did not allow for fluctuations in density from place to

place in the sample. Fisher's argument, which is concerned
with the effect on a transition of 'hidden' variables (the
volume, in this example) led him to predict a renormalization
of the critical exponents (section 3.3) rather than conversion
to a first-order transition. It has subsequently been demonstrated that Fisher's treatment is correct only for certain
types of constraint (Baker and Essam 1971, Imry, Entin-Wohl
man, and Bergman 1973); other types can, indeed, lead to
first-order transitions. Sak (1974) has shown that for the
compressible Ising lattices the normal behaviour is to show
a first-order transition, although in certain cases it may
be very close to being second-order. The Heisenberg model,
on the other hand, does not alter the character of its
transition on allowing the lattice to be compressible.
Achiam and Imry (1975) found that critical behaviour may
remain Ising-like, become renormalized, become first-order,
or even become tricritical (see below) when the ordering
process is coupled to another, non-ordering parameter. Likewise, Friedman and Gunther (1975) have concluded that whether
a first- or renormalized second-order transition is obtained
depends, for a compressible system, on the magnitude of the
applied pressure: for $p < p^*$ and $p > p^*$, where p^* is the
tricritical pressure, the transition would be first- and
second-order, respectively. Although this area is still
somewhat uncertain, it has been shown rigorously, without
appeal to a model, that it is not compatible with thermodynamic stability for there to be a line along which
$C_V = \infty$ (Wheeler and Griffiths 1968).

Attention has also been directed by Griffiths (1970)
to the λ-lines which are generated when a non-ordering field,
that is one which is not conjugate to the relevant ordering
parameter, is varied. From a consideration of the phase
diagram of ^{3}He+^{4}He mixtures, and in particular their super-
fluid-normal transition, he concluded that the phenomena
observed were representative of a more widespread class,
including especially metamagnets (section 12.6.1). He
observed that the situation is simplified if the phase diagram is plotted in terms of 'fields', these being the quantities which must have the same values in phases which are

in equilibrium. If the 'fields' concerned are the temperature and those conjugate to the ordering parameter (ζ) and
to a non-ordering parameter (Δ), then the characteristic
phase diagram is probably as in Fig.2.6. The surfaces A, B,
and B' are first-order in the sense that movement across

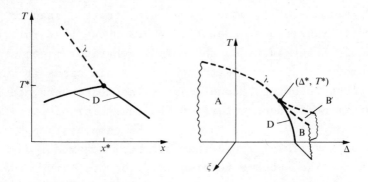

Fig.2.6. Phase diagrams showing a tricritical point $(T^*,x^*,\Delta^*,\zeta^*=0)$.
(a) T against the non-ordering parameter x. The two arms of the coexistence curve are labelled D; the λ-line is indicated by the dashed
line. (b) T against the 'field' variables Δ (non-ordering) and
ζ (ordering). The λ-line is indicated by the dashed curve (after
Griffiths 1970).

them leads to a first-order transition. Each of these planes
is terminated in one direction by a λ- or critical line.
The point of intersection of the three critical lines is the
tricritical point, at which three phases (the two mirror-
image antiferromagnetic phases and a disordered phase)
become indistinguishable. The term 'disordered' for the
third phase, though often used (as in section 2.5), is
somewhat misleading: it is based on the fact that both
sublattices have the same magnetization, with respect to sign
as well as magnitude, and so the long-range antiferromagnetic order has been lost. In this phase, with the high
values of the direct field which are necessary to sustain
it, the sublattice magnetization may be quite large. It is
possible to argue that this phase is ordered - by the applied
direct field (Δ), as Griffiths has done. It frequently
happens that one of the fields is inaccessible, and for that

reason only a section of the phase diagram of Fig.2.6(b)
is observed. If it is not possible to alter ζ from the
value zero, as in metamagnetism, then what is observed is
that on increasing the non-ordering field (Δ) the critical
temperature at first decreases, whilst remaining a critical
point; at the tricritical point the transition goes over to
being first-order and remains so with further increase in
Δ.

Such phenomena had indeed been predicted by Landau
(1937) on the basis of the assumed analytic behaviour of the
free energy at the critical point (section 2.5). However,
many of the details of the behaviour of real systems are not
well represented by his theory. Thus, it predicts that,
plotted in the manner of Fig.2.6(a), the λ-line should
intersect with the right-hand branch of the coexistence
curve at the tricritical point without change in slope.
Experimental work on the ^{3}He+^{4}He mixtures, discussed by
Griffiths, and on metamagnets indicates that there is a
change of slope. Experiment also casts doubt on the existence of a discontinuity in C_M which follows from the
classical theory (Note: bearing in mind that this system is
an antiferromagnet (2.24) refers to $C_{M'}$, not to C_M). Experiments on the isotopic helium mixture also suggests a
divergence in the analogue of $(\partial M/\partial \mathcal{H})_T$ which is not predicted by Landau's theory.

Tricritical behaviour will be encountered in the section on NH_4Cl (Section 7.5.1) as well as that on magnetism
(Chapter 12). Experimentally, the tricritical point is important because as it is approached it becomes increasingly
difficult to evaluate the true asymptotic values for the
critical indices (section 3.3). Even though the experimental region examined does not include the tricritical
point, nevertheless a knowledge of its proximity may be
important in understanding the results observed. The cross-
over from λ-line to tricritical behaviour has recently been
examined using the renormalization group method of Wilson
(Nelson and Rudnick 1975).

2.7. FERROELECTRICS AND ANTIFERROELECTRICS

A sample which has a non-zero electric polarization (electric dipole moment per unit volume) even when there is no applied field is said to be pyroelectric. If, as in the large majority of instances, this spontaneous polarization can be re-versed by application of a small field then the substance is described as being ferroelectric. Since, in practice, crystals usually carry electric charges on the exposed surfaces which counterbalance the bulk polarization, ferro-electrics are not normally recognized by their spontaneous polarization. Rather, they are identified by the hysteresis loop which is found when the electric field is cyclically varied. For the discussion of the fundamentals of ferro-electricity, however, the spontaneous polarization (P_s) is a valuable quantity. It is obtained by extrapolation to $E=0$ of the linear (saturation) part of the P versus E loop as shown in Fig.2.7. For a single-domain system the loop is very 'rectangular', and the value of P_s so found differs only slightly from the value of P at $E=0$ on that part of the loop; for a multi-domain crystal the discrepancy can be larger.

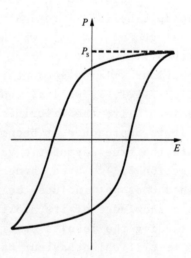

Fig.2.7. Polarization (P) against electric field (E) for a ferroelectric, showing the linear extrapolation used to evaluate the spontaneous polari-zation (P_s).

P_s falls to zero at the transition temperature, and remains zero, of course, in the upper, paraelectric phase.
The manner in which P_s goes to zero, and hence the order of
the ferroelectric- paraelectric process, may be discontinuous
(for a first-order transition) or gradual (for a higher-order
transition) (Fig.2.8).   In many real systems there is a

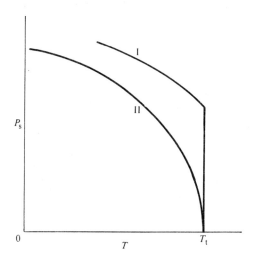

Fig.2.8. Spontaneous polarization (P_s) against T for a first-order (I)
and a second-order (II) ferroelectric-paraelectric transition.

gradual fall in P_s with increase in T, but the final disappearance of the polarization is achieved discontinuously.
A few substances melt before losing their ferroelectric
order.   Above the transition temperature the permittivity
of almost all ferroelectrics obeys the Curie-Weiss law:
$\varepsilon = C/(T-T_0)$, so that the onset of ferroelectricity is often
heralded by a peak in ε (Fig.2.9).   However, T_0 is generally
not equal to T_t, in which case ε may not be infinite at T_t.
    Since in the ferroelectric state the centre of positive
charge must not coincide with the centre of negative charge
there are restrictions on the types of crystal structure
which can show ferroelectric behaviour.   Only the ten polar
crystal classes can show spontaneous polarization (Jona
and Shirane 1962).   Although a structure having a centro-
symmetric point group cannot have $P_s \neq 0$, the absence of a

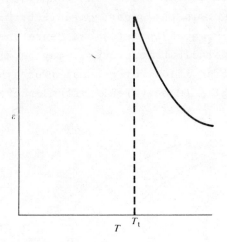

Fig.2.9. Permittivity (ε) against T for a paraelectric in the neighbour-hood of the ferroelectric transition (T_t).

centre of symmetry is not itself sufficient to ensure a polar class.

As mentioned above, all ferroelectrics are also pyro-electric, that is on changing the temperature a current will pass in an external circuit connected to the faces of the crystal. This current is equal to the rate of change of P_s and is, therefore, proportional to the temperature coeffi-cient of P_s:

$$I \propto (dP_s/dt) = (dP_s/dT)(dT/dt) \qquad (2.26)$$

All ferroelectrics are also piezoelectric, although the reverse is not true, e.g. quartz is piezoelectric without being ferroelectric. KH_2PO_4 and Rochelle salt, two of the most well-studied ferroelectric substances, remain piezo-electric above the transition temperature at which they lose their piezoelectric and ferroelectric characters simul-taneously.

Ferroelectric anomalies are often associated with anomalies in the elastic coefficients, piezoelectric be-haviour (as in $BaTiO_3$ and triglycine sulphate above), and

also in expansivities and the heat capacity. Because, therefore, the strain is coupled to the ferroelectric and other
properties, different behaviour of these quantities is observed according to whether the crystal is clamped or not.

Antiferroelectrics are substances in which two (or more)
sublattices each have spontaneous polarizations, but these
cancel so as to give $P_s=0$ overall. The experimental recognition of antiferroelectrics is more difficult than of ferroelectrics. The most important information comes from crystal
structure and heat capacity determinations; permittivity
measurements, which frequently yield a peak at the transition
temperature, are also useful.

Chemically, there is often very little difference between substances which favour ferroelectric and antiferroelectric phases. For example, KH_2PO_4 (known in theoretical
work as KDP) shows ferroelectric behaviour whilst $NH_4H_2PO_4$,
with the same basic crystal structure, has only antiferro-
and paraelectric phases. Again, many of the titanates, zircon-
ates, and niobates related to the ferroelectric $BaTiO_3$ are
antiferroelectric. Indeed, the same substance sometimes
forms both ferro- and antiferroelectric phases, and it can be
said that whether a substance adopts a ferro- or antiferroelectric structure is often rather a delicately balanced
decision. It should also be added that in ferroelectrics
the phase sequence may be more complicated than the simple
one discussed above, namely ferroelectric below a transition
temperature and paraelectric above. For example, Rochelle
salt is only ferroelectric within a fairly narrow range of
temperature (253 to 297 K), and is paraelectric at both
higher and lower temperatures.

A related effect, known as ferroelasticity, can occur
in crystals which have two or more stable orientational states
in zero electric field and in the absence of mechanical stress.
It may then be possible for the crystal to transform from
one state to the other if a mechanical stress is applied
(Aizu 1969). The distortions involved are generally very
small (a few parts in 10^3) and the atomic displacements are
of the order of 0·01 nm. On removal of the stress these displacements do not become zero as would happen in a normal

phase. Pure ferroelastic phases are rare, this distortion usually being coupled to other cooperative processes. A good review of the early work on these phases has been given by Abrahams (1971).

For detailed accounts of ferroelectricity and topics related to it the reader is referred to the books by Fatuzzo and Merz (1967), Burfoot (1967), and Jona and Shirane (1962).

2.8. MAGNETIC AND ELECTRIC HYSTERESIS

It is frequently found that the results of what are apparently equilibrium measurements depend upon the direction from which the final state is approached. Such phenomena are of considerable importance in studies of ferromagnetic and ferroelectric materials, on which most of the studies of hysteresis have been concentrated.

Hysteresis in particles of magnetic materials which are not too small (usually $\nmid$ 0·1 µm diameter) is explained in terms of the formation of magnetic domains or regions in which the magnetization is uniformly in one direction. A single crystal may then be comprised of many domains, such that on passing from one to another the direction of magnetization changes. The boundaries between domains are called domain walls, and it is the motion of these that largely determines the magnetic hysteresis of the sample.

Before considering the kinetics of domain wall motion we should answer the question, why are domains formed at all? Would not the system be more stable if each crystal were a single domain, for this would eliminate the inter-domain surface energy arising from the presence of neighbouring magnetic spins which are not parallel to each other, and therefore not in the situation of lowest energy? The answer is that whereas the short-range forces may favour parallel alignment, the long-range forces may oppose this. The short-range forces referred to are of the exchange type; the long-range forces, on the other hand, are the normal dipolar forces of classical magnetic theory. Thus in Fig.2.10 the magnetization of region B favours an opposite magnetization for region A, which is illustrated by sketching in the lines of force. This effect is measured by the demagnetization factor of the

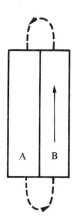

Fig.2.10. The demagnetizing effect of magnetization in region B on the material in region A.

specimen. From the diagram it will be appreciated that there would be no tendency for the formation of a domain wall in the horizontal direction. As a consequence of this, if the specimen is a thin needle with its large dimension parallel to the 'easy' direction of magnetization the specimen would suffer very little from demagnetization and so would remain as a single-domain crystal. On the other hand, if the crystal is large in directions perpendicular to the 'easy' axis then we may expect to find a number of domains, for by breaking into oppositely magnetized regions the magnetic field, and hence the demagnetization term, are greatly reduced. We may summarize by saying that in the equilibrium situation the subdivision into domains occurs until the energy of an additional boundary, separating domains magnetized in different directions, would be greater than the consequent reduction in magnetostatic energy (Carey and Isaac 1966a), where the energy referred to is to be taken as the free energy. The existence of magnetic domains can be directly demonstrated by removing the strained outer layers by electropolishing and covering the surface with a colloidal suspension of magnetic particles, when the strong fields at the domain edges attract the particles. Other methods are, however, available for their observation (Carey and Isaac

1966b). The Barkhausen noise, which can be heard when a
ferromagnetic specimen is magnetized, is attributed to the
reorientation of the domains, and a similar effect is observed in ferroelectrics (Brophy 1965).

Now consider the process of changing the magnetization
of a specimen by alteration of the applied field. We could
envisage the individual spins reorientating themselves in
accordance with the dictates of the new value of the applied
field without regard to the states of the neighbouring spins.
However, a process requiring a smaller activation energy
would be one in which those domains in which the magnetization was correctly orientated grew at the expense of those
in which it was not. This would involve the movement of the
domain walls, and any process which impeded this movement
would tend to prevent the response of the sample to the
change of applied field and might cause hysteresis. Important contributors to the impedance of wall motion, are,
frequently, the inhomogeneous strains brought about, for
example, by magnetostriction. Another important factor can
be the 'pinning' of the walls by included impurities. When
the wall passes through a non-magnetic inclusion the wall
energy is generally less, and this will correspondingly increase the activation energy required to move the wall
(Carey and Isaac 1966c).

So far we have discussed hysteresis entirely in terms
of each crystal having a domain structure. However, if the
particles are sufficiently small the advantage gained by
domain formation in destroying the demagnetization term is
more than overcome by the increase in exchange energy along
the domain interface. There is, indeed, a critical size for
any particular substance below which the crystal will remain
as a single domain. For example, the critical size for iron
at its saturation magnetization has been variously estimated
and typical values are a diameter of 15 nm for spheres and
a minor diameter of 60 nm for a prolate ellipsoid having
a/b = 10. If the particles are below this critical size, so
that they consist of a single domain, the magnetic hysteresis
becomes largely determined by 'shape anisotropy'. Stoner
and Wohlfarth (1948) calculated M versus $\mathcal{H}$ curves for pro-

late and oblate ellipsoids of various axial ratios and
showed that the prolate, though not the oblate, particles
showed hysteresis (Fig.2.11). It will be noted that for the

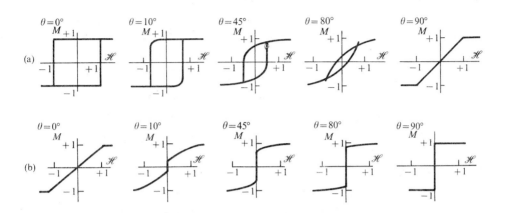

Fig.2.11. M against $\mathcal{H}$ curves for ellipsoids; (a) prolate, (b) oblate.
Resolved part of the magnetization in the direction of the field, reduced
by the total magnetization, against the applied field, reduced by the difference of the demagnetizing fields for the minor and major axes. [θ = angle
between the field and the polar axis of the ellipsoid.] (After Morrish 1965.)

prolate ellipsoids there is no hysteresis if $\mathcal{H}$ is perpendicular to the major axis ($\theta = 90°$), but at all other angles
hysteresis results. Indeed, the coercive force, a measure
of the hysteresis, is proportional to the difference of
the demagnetization coefficients for the principal directions.
These calculations have also been used, with appropriate reinterpretation of the parameters, to deal with hysteresis
arising from crystalline or strain anisotropy. Subsequently,
it has been shown that the behaviour of single-domain particles of other shapes can be related to those of suitably
chosen ellipsoids (Brown and Morrish 1957).

     For still smaller single-domain particles it has been
shown that the chance of a switch of all the spins in the
particle as a result of thermal fluctuations may be sufficiently great that it would remain effectively in equilibrium
with an applied field. No hysteresis would then be expected.
As the size of the particle increases the rate of approach
to equilibrium falls off sharply, and if one sets a maximum
time for which one is prepared to wait for equilibrium, the

time-scale of the experiment, say 10^2s, then another critical
particle size can be defined. This critical size is, of
course, dependent upon the temperature as well as upon the
material, the field, and the chosen time interval. Since particles smaller than the critical size behave like large paramagnetic molecules, the term 'superparamagnetic' has been
coined to describe them. For iron at 300 K the critical diameter is found to be about 10 nm (Brown 1965).

There are similarities, but also differences, between
the domain behaviour of ferroelectrics and ferromagnetics.
For example, the thickness of the domain walls is much less
in ferroelectrics (a few lattice constants) than it is in
most ferromagnets (several hundred lattice constants).
Again, within the domain walls in ferromagnetics the intensity of magnetization remains constant but its direction
changes gradually across the wall; by contrast, in ferroelectrics the orientation of the electric polarization stays
the same but the magnitude gradually changes (Burfoot 1967a).
A good discussion of techniques for observing ferroelectric
domains is given by Fatuzzo and Merz (1967). In ferroelectrics,
both nucleation of new domains and movement of domain walls
are important in the switching process. With regard to the
latter, both the nature and thickness of the walls are significant, in that these largely determine the available intermediate states when the wall is being moved. According to
Burfoot (1967b), for a given wall energy the wall is less
likely to move if it is very thin. In view of what has been
said about the importance of wall motion in determining hysteresis properties, it is not surprising that repolarization
of the ferroelectric forms of triglycine sulphate and barium
titanate is helped by applying ultrasonic vibration to the
sample (Rudyak and Baranov 1965), or that hysteresis can be
induced by radiation damage (Glower and Hester 1965, Glower,
Hester, and Warnke 1965, Gesi and Takagi 1964, Rewaj 1964).

2.9. THERMAL HYSTERESIS
So far we have considered hysteresis which occurs when the
external field acting on a ferromagnet or ferroelectric is
changed. Now let us examine hysteresis in processes in which

the variable changed is temperature (or pressure).

In these processes the change will, in general, involve a volume change as one form disappears and the other replaces it. Thomas and Staveley (1951) have, indeed, concluded that for this type of hysteresis to occur at all it is necessary for there to be a discontinuous change of volume, that is, the transition must be, at least to some extent, first-order (isothermal); they noted that transitions which on the evidence then available appeared to be entirely gradual seemed to be hysteresis-free. $PrAlO_3$ shows both types of behaviour, the gradual transition at 151 K and the first-order transformation at 205 K being without and with hysteresis, respectively (Cohen, Riseberg, Nordland, Burbank, Sherwood, and van Uitert 1969).

The mechanism of this type of hysteresis can be pictured as follows. Consider a crystal of the pure stable α-form, and let us suppose that we alter the temperature so that the stable form is now the β-form. The free energy change which would arise from the formation of a nucleus of the β-phase containing n particles could then be written as:

$$\Delta G_n = An^{2/3} + Bn + Cn \tag{2.27}$$

where the terms represent, respectively, the interfacial free energy, the difference in the bulk free energies of the two forms, and the strain free energy. The nucleus will, because of the volume change attendant upon its formation, be in a state of compression or tension, the stress being such as to tend to prevent the formation of the nucleus. For this reason C will be positive. A will also be positive, but B will be negative. Close to the transition temperature $C > |B|$ and so ΔG should increase monotonically with n. In real systems, C will fall as n increases, leading to a maximum in ΔG at a particular value of n. Nuclei larger than this critical size should be able to grow spontaneously, and it is the rate of production of such nuclei, rather than their rate of subsequent growth which is considered to be the rate-determining factor in the hysteresis. This rate is taken to be proportional to

$\exp(-\Delta G^*/kT)$, where ΔG^* is the free energy of formation
of a nucleus of the critical size. Thomas and Staveley pro-
ceeded by adapting a treatment of Turnbull and Fisher (1949)
for liquids which did not include the strain term. This led
to the expression:

$$\Delta G = 16\pi\sigma^3/3\{-\Delta S_t \Delta T + (\Delta V_t)^2/2\kappa_T\}^2 \tag{2.28}$$

where σ = the interfacial surface free energy per unit
               area,
      ΔT = the deviation of the temperature from the true
               transition temperature,
ΔS_t and ΔV_t = the discontinuous part of the entropy and
               volume change, respectively,
and κ_t = the isothermal compressibility of either
               phase.

In the absence of the strain term ($\Delta V_t = 0$) and taking reasonable values for σ and ΔS_t, the rate of nucleation was found
to be extremely sensitive to ΔT. Inclusion of the strain term
would increase this sensitivity still further.

      This theory assumes that the various nuclei behave in-
dependently of each other. As the process goes towards completion this would be expected to become a poor approximation. It is also based on the supposition that homogeneous nucleation is the governing step. The presence of
defects, impurities, or other factors leading to heterogeneous nucleation would cause the rate of nucleation to be
increased and hence the hysteresis, as measured by ΔT_h, to be
reduced. Criticism of Fisher and Turnbull's theory of homogeneous nucleation, on which the above treatment of hysteresis is based, has arisen as a result of experiments on
liquid-liquid nucleation in methylcyclohexane-perfluoro-
methylcyclohexane mixtures having immiscibility gaps. It
is found that the degree of undercooling (the amount by
which the sample can be cooled below the true transition
temperature before the second phase appears) exceeds that
predicted by the theory by factors varying from 8·5 at
$\Delta T=10°$ to 340 at $\Delta T=0·3°$ (Sundquist and Oriani 1962).

This discrepancy, in the opposite direction to effects which could be attributed to heterogeneous nucleation, has been confirmed by other workers (Heady and Cahn 1973, Huang, Vernon, and Wong 1974). It appears that the nucleation theory fails increasingly as the critical solution temperature is approached. Huang *et al*. (1974) found that their results covering the range $(T_c-T)/T_c = 2 \cdot 10^{-2}$ to $2 \cdot 10^{-5}$ were in agreement with a theory of Sarkies and Frankel (1971) and Sarkies, Richmond, and Ninham (1972) in which the treatment of the thermodynamic properties of the fluid phases utilizes a non-classical approach, that is one not conforming to the theory of Landau. In view of this work, one must question the Thomas and Staveley approach to hysteresis wherever the change occurs near to a critical point.

A theory similar in spirit to the Lindemann theory of melting has been put forward by E.B.Smith (1959) to relate the temperature and pressure ranges of a hysteresis (ΔT_h and Δp_h). It is postulated that there is a maximum amount of strain-free energy which the crystal can withstand (before breakdown). When the transition actually occurs at a temperature differing from the equilibrium transition temperature by ΔT_h the free energy difference between the forms is $\{(\partial G_\alpha/\partial T)_p - (\partial G_\beta/\partial T)_p\}\Delta T_h = \Delta S_t \cdot \Delta T_h$. Similarly, when the change is brought about by changing the pressure at constant temperature the free energy difference is $\Delta p_h \cdot \Delta V_t$. According to the above postulate, therefore, $\Delta S_t \Delta T_h = \Delta p_h \Delta V_t$. It has not been possible to test this equation since suitable Δp_h values are not available.

A number of theories of hysteresis based upon the sigmoid shape of many theoretical isotherms have also been advanced. A particularly clear example of this type of treatment is a theory that has been proposed by Bean and Rodbell (1962), involving a modification of the Ising model so as to couple volume change with the order-disorder process. A theory of this type is dealt with in section 3.1.8 (together with the criticism of it). Flandrois (1974) has reviewed the various theories for the kinetics of phase changes.

2.10. FLUCTUATIONS

A characteristic of a substance at a λ-point is that it displays singularities in the compliance coefficients, e.g. α, κ_T, as well as C_p (see section 2.4). A consequence of this is that there can be wide (infinite) fluctuations in the values of some of the thermodynamic properties about their mean values.

For a fluid system at a constant pressure and temperature, the relative fluctuation in the enthalpy can be represented by the equation (Hill 1956):

$$\frac{\langle H^2 \rangle - \langle H \rangle^2}{\langle H \rangle^2} = \frac{kT^2 C_p}{\langle H \rangle^2} . \tag{2.29}$$

For normal systems the right-hand side vanishes for large systems as $\langle N \rangle^{-1}$. However, if $C_p / \langle N \rangle$ becomes infinite, as at a critical point, the right-hand side will go to zero more gradually than $\langle N \rangle^{-1}$. There will also be fluctuations in volume, and these will be given by a very similar formula:

$$\frac{\langle V^2 \rangle - \langle V \rangle^2}{\langle V \rangle^2} = \frac{kT\kappa_T}{\langle V \rangle} . \tag{2.30}$$

These fluctuations in volume can be considered alternatively as fluctuations in density. Since fluctuations in density lead to corresponding fluctuations in refractive index and thence to the scattering of radiation we have a very powerful method of observing them. The most familiar manifestation of this effect is the so-called critical opalescence of fluid systems near the gas-liquid critical point, at which $\kappa_T \to \infty$. Whereas, remote from the critical point, the fluctuations in different spatial regions can be considered to be independent of each other, near the critical point this is no longer true. Long-range correlations between the fluctuations in different regions develop rapidly as the critical point is approached. These correlations lead to interference between the radiation scattered from different places and consequently to a strong dependence of the scattered intensity on the angle of scattering.

It was for some time thought that corresponding fluc-

tuations in solid-phase order-disorder systems did not occur
or, at least, would not be observable (Münster 1965). However, this turns out not to be so, and in recent years a
variety of studies of fluctuation phenomena in solids have
been made. The fluctuations in magnetization (M) at constant
T and $\mathcal{H}(=0)$ given by $\langle M^2 \rangle = 3kT\chi_T$, where χ_T is the isothermal
magnetic susceptibility, lead to effects in the magnetic
scattering of neutrons analogous to critical opalescence.
Examples of this type of work are: iron (Palevsky and Hughes
1953), Fe_3O_4 (McReynolds and Riste 1954), and dysprosium
aluminium garnet (Norvell, Wolf, Corliss, Hastings, and
Nathans 1969).

Since the scattering of phonons by magnetic fluctuations should affect the thermal conductivity, measurements
of this quantity in the transition region provide information on fluctuations. Furthermore, application of a magnetic
field removes the critical singularities and hence suppresses
the critical fluctuations. This has been used to separate
out that part of the thermal resistivity (the reciprocal of
the thermal conductivity) of $K_2CuCl_4 \cdot 2H_2O$ which arises
from critical fluctuations (Dixon and Walton 1969).

Critical fluctuations in the order parameter of alloys
have been similarly observed using X-ray scattering. The
λ-transition in β-brass was studied by Walker and Keating
(1963); subsequently, Guttman and Schnyders (1969) examined
the order-disorder transition in Fe_3Al at temperatures such
that $2\cdot5 \times 10^{-2} > (T-T_c)/T_c > 2 \times 10^{-4}$.

In the case of ferroelectrics, critical fluctuations
of the *total* polarization can be inferred from measurements
of the noise current in an external circuit (Brophy 1965b) .
It is only the very few ferroelectrics which have critical
or near-critical transitions, e.g. triglycine sulphate,
which would be expected to show substantial effects; the
majority of substances, having first-order transitions,
would not be suitable objects of study. So far, no experimental method has been found for observing fluctuations
of the *local* polarization, which should be relatively much
larger. These would be equivalent to the local density
fluctuations in fluids.

To the experimentalist concerned with measurements near
critical points there is one very irritating feature associated with the phenomena discussed above. This is that the
times required for systems to reach equilibrium can become
very long indeed. This may be appreciated by considering
energy equilibrium. A small inequality in temperature between one spatial region and another requires a large heat
flow to redress it because of the large value of the heat
capacity. Since the thermal conductivity does not take
similarly large values the time required for thermal equilibrium will be long.

REFERENCES

Abrahams, S.C. (1971). *Mater.Res.Bull.* 6, 881.

Achiam, Y. and Imry, Y. (1975). *Phys.Rev.* B12, 2768.

Aizu, K. (1969). *J.phys.Soc.Japan* 27, 387.

Baker, G.A. and Essam, J.W. (1971). *J.Phys.(Paris).* Suppl.1.
     Pt. 2, C1, 1015.

Bean, C.P. and Rodbell, D.S. (1962). *Phys.Rev.* 126, 104.

Bidaux, R., Carrara, P., and Vivet, B. (1967). *(J).Phys.Chem.*
     Solids, 28, 2453.

Brophy, J.J. (1965). In *Fluctuation phenomena in solids* (ed.
     R.E.Burgess), (a) p.25; (b) p.12. Academic Press, New
     York and London.

Brown, W.F. (1965). *Fluctuation phenomena in solids* (ed.
     R.E. Burgess), p.43. Academic Press, New York and
     London.

————   and Morrish, A.H. (1957). *Phys.Rev.* 105, 1198.

Buckingham, M.J. and Fairbank, W.M. (1961). *Prog.Low Temp.*
     Phys. 3, 80.

Burfoot, J.C. (1967). *Ferroelectrics,* (a) p.208; (b) p.210.
     Van Nostrand, Princeton and Toronto.

Carey, R. and Isaac, E.D. (1966). *Magnetic domains,* (a) p.13;
     (b) p.62; (c) pp.33-38. English University Press,
     London.

Chang, S.S. and Bestul, A.B. (1972). *J.chem.Phys.* 56, 503.

————   , Harman, J.A., and Bestul, A.B. (1967). *J.Res.*
     Natn.Bur.Stand. A71, 293.

Chaudhari, P., Beardmore, P., and Bever, M.B. (1966). *Phys. Chem.Glasses*, 7, 157.

Clayton, J.O. and Giauque, W.F. (1932). *J.Am.chem.Soc.* 54, 2610.

Cohen, E., Riseberg, L.A., Nordland, W.A., Burbank, R.D., Sherwood, R.C., and Van Uitert, L.G. (1969). *Phys.Rev.* 186, 476.

Cohen, M.H. and Turnbull, D. (1959). *J.chem.Phys.* 31, 1164.
———   ———   (1960). *J.chem.Phys.* 34, 120.
———   ———   (1964). *Nature*, Lond. 203, 964.
———   ———   (1970). *J.chem.Phys.* 52, 3038.

Cooke, A.H., Swithenby, S.J., and Wells, M.R. (1972). *Solid St.Communs.* 10, 265.

Dixon, G.S. and Walton, D. (1969). *Phys.Rev.* 185, 735.

Domb, C. (1956). *J.chem.Phys.* 25, 783.

Ehrenfest, P. (1933). *Commun.Kamerlingh Onnes Lab., Leiden Suppl.* 75b.

Fatuzzo, E. and Merz, W.J. (1967). *Ferroelectricity*. Vol.7 of *Selected topics in solid state physics* (ed. E.P.Wohlfarth). North-Holland, Amsterdam.

Fisher, M.E. (1968). *Phys.Rev.* 176, 257.

Flandrois, S. (1974). *J.Chim.phys.* 71, 979.

Friedman, Z. and Gunther, L. (1975). *Phys.Rev.* B12, 5123.

Garland, C.W. and Jones, J.S. (1963). *J.chem.Phys.* 39, 2874.

Gattow, G. and Buss, B. (1969). *Naturwiss.* 56, 35.

Gesi, K. and Takagi, Y. (1964). *J.phys.Soc.Japan* 19, 632.

Gibson, G.E. and Giauque, W.F. (1923). *J.Am.chem.Soc.* 45, 93.

Glower, D.D. and Hester, D.L. (1965). *J.appl.Phys.* 36, 2175.
———   Hester, D.L., and Warnke, D.F. (1965). *J.Am. ceram.Soc.* 48, 417.

Griffiths, R.B. (1970). *Phys.Rev.Lett.* 24, 715.

Guttman, L. and Schnyders, H.C. (1969). *Phys.Rev.Lett.* 22, 520.

Heady, R.B. and Cahn, J.W. (1973). *J.chem.Phys.* 58, 896.

Hill, T.L. (1956). *Statistical Mechanics*, p.102. McGraw-Hill, New York, Toronto and London.

Huang, J.S., Vernon, S., and Wong, N.C. (1974). *Phys.Rev. Lett.* 33, 140.

Hughes, A.J. and Lawson, A.W. (1962). *J.chem.Phys.* 36, 2098.

Imry, Y., Entin-Wohlman, O., and Bergman, D. (1973). *J.Phys.* C6, 2846.

Janovec, V. (1966). *J.chem.Phys.* 45, 1874.

Jona, F. and Shirane, G. (1962). *Ferroelectric Crystals*. Pergamon, New York.

Justi, E. and Von Laue, M. (1934). *Z.tech.Phys.* 15, 521.

Kauzmann, W. (1948). *Chem.Rev.* 43, 219.

Keesom, W.H. and Van Laer, P.H. (1938). *Physica* 5, 193.

Klement, W. (1966). *J.chem.Phys.* 45, 1421.

———   (1970). *J.phys.Chem.* 74, 2753.

Kolomiets, B. (1970). *Soviet Sci.Rev.(GB)*, 1, 22.

Landau, L.D. (1937). *Phys.Z.Sowjetunion*, 11, 26. In *Collected Papers of L.D.Landau* (1965) (ed. D.ter Haar), p.193. Pergamon, Oxford.

McReynolds, A.W. and Riste, T. (1954). *Phys.Rev.* 95, 1161.

Mayer, J.E. and Streeter, S.F. (1939). *J.chem.Phys.* 7, 1019.

Melhuish, M.W. and Scott, R.L. (1964). *J.phys.Chem.* 68, 2301.

Morrish, A.H. (1965). *The Physical Principles of Magnetism*. Wiley, New York, London and Sydney.

Moynihan, C.T. and Macedo, P.B. (1971). *J.phys.Chem.* 75, 3379.

Münster, A. (1965). In *Fluctuation Phenomena in Solids* (ed. R.E. Burgess), p.180. Academic Press, New York and London.

Nelson, D.R. and Rudnick, J. (1975). *Phys.Rev.Lett.* 35, 178.

De Nordwall, H.J. and Staveley, L.A.K. (1954). *J.chem.Soc.* 224.

———   ———   (1956). *Trans.Faraday Soc.* 52, 1061, 1207.

Norvell, J.C., Wolf, W.P., Corliss, L.M., Hastings, J.M., and Nathans, R. (1969). *Phys.Rev.* 186, 567.

Oblad, A.G. and Newton, R.F. (1937). *J.Am.chem.Soc.* 59, 2495.

Palevsky, H. and Hughes, D.J. (1953). *Phys.Rev.* 92, 202.

Pippard, A.B. (1964). *The Elements of Classical Thermodynamics* (a) Chap.9; (b) p.129. Cambridge University Press.

Prigogine, I. and Defay, R. (1954). *Chemical Thermodynamics*. Translated by D.H.Everett. Longmans Green, London, New York and Toronto.

Renard, R. and Garland, C.W. (1966). *J.chem.Phys.* 45, 763.

Rewaj, T. (1964). *Phys.St.Solidi*, 6, 163.

Rice, O.K. (1954). *J.chem.Phys.* 22, 1535.

Rudyak, V.M. and Baranov, A.I. (1965). *Izv.Akad.Nauk SSSR*, *Ser.Fiz.* 29, 951.

Sak, J. (1974). *Phys.Rev.* B10, 3957.

Sarkies, K.W. and Frankel, N.E. (1971). *J.chem.Phys.* 54, 433.

—————— , Richmond, P., and Ninham, B.W. (1972). *Aust. J.Phys.* 25, 367.

Simon, F.E. and Lange, F. (1926). *Z.Phys.* 38, 227.

Smith, E.B. (1959). *(J).Phys.Chem.Solids.* 9, 182.

Stoner, E.C. and Wohlfarth, E.P. (1948). *Phil.Trans.R.Soc.* A240, 599.

Sugisaki, M., Suga, H., and Seki, S. (1967). *Bull.chem.Soc. Japan* 40, 2984.

——————   ——————   —————— (1968). *Bull.chem.Soc. Japan* 41, 2586, 2591.

Sundquist, B.E. and Oriani, R.A. (1962). *J.chem.Phys.* 36, 2604.

Taylor, P.C., Bishop, S.G., and Mitchell, D.L. (1971). *Phys.Rev.Lett.* 27, 414.

Thomas, D.G. and Staveley, L.A.K. (1951). *J.chem.Soc.* 2572.

——————   —————— (1952). *J.chem.Soc.* 4569.

Tisza, L. (1961). *Ann.Phys.* 13, 1.

Tobolsky, A.V. (1960). *Properties and Structure of Polymers*. Wiley, New York and London.

Turnbull, D. and Fisher, J.C. (1949). *J.chem.Phys.* 17, 71, 429.

Walker, C.B. and Keating, D.T. (1963). *Phys.Rev.* 130, 1726.

Ward, A.T. (1972). *Advances in Chemistry Series*, No.110, 163.

Wheeler, J.C. and Griffiths, R.B. (1968). *Phys.Rev.* 170, 249.

Wohlfarth, E.P. (1959). *Adv.Phys.* 8, 87.

Wright, P.G. (1972). *J.Phys.* A5, 1206.

Wunderlich, B. (1960). *J.phys.Chem.* 64, 1052.

3

STATISTICAL MECHANICS

3.1. THE ISING MODEL

Many order-disorder systems can be profitably considered
in terms of the model originally employed by Lenz and Ising
in 1925 for ferromagnets. In recent years, there have been
great advances in the solution of problems of this type, and
whereas the results have been most frequently applied to
ferromagnets they have equal significance for any other
system which can be formulated in the same way. It is for
this reason that we shall devote so much attention to them.

In its simplest form the Ising model involves the supposition that the system can be divided into $\mathscr{B}$ cells, and
that each one may be occupied in either of two ways, $s^z = \pm 1/2$.
These two states correspond to two possible orientations for
the atomic magnetic moments in a ferromagnet, but they could
just as well be two possible orientations for a molecule or
the two possible ways in which a lattice site could be
occupied in a binary solid solution. The restriction to only
two possible states for each cell is mathematically very
convenient and the overwhelming majority of calculations have
been of this type, but a few results have also been obtained
for systems in which each cell could be occupied in a larger
number of ways ($s^z = -s, -s+1, \ldots +s$, where s may be integral or half-integral). The next assumption is that only
interactions between nearest-neighbour(nn) cells are non-
zero. Again there have been a few calculations in which
the effects of interactions between more remote neighbours
have been taken into account. Finally, the energy of interaction for an array of cells is assumed to take the form:

$$E = -\frac{J}{s^2} \sum_{\substack{i>j \\ nn}} s_i^z s_j^z - \frac{m\mathcal{H}}{s} \sum_i s_i^z \qquad (3.1)$$

where the first term represents the intercell interaction
and the second gives the contribution which arises when the
system is in a magnetic field ($\mathcal{H}$). J and m are constants

which are characteristic of the system. For ferromagnets, for example, m is the maximum value of the component of the magnetic moment in the direction of the field. The constant-field partition function is then given by

$$Q'(\mathcal{B},T,\mathcal{H}) = \sum_{s_i^z} \exp(-E/kT) \tag{3.2}$$

where the summation is taken over all possible values for $s_1^z, s_2^z, \ldots s_{\mathcal{B}}^z$.

$Q'(\mathcal{B},T,\mathcal{H})$ is related to a magnetic free energy (A') by

$$U-HM-TS = A' = -kT \ln Q' \tag{3.3}$$

where U is the internal energy and M the magnetization. The fundamental thermodynamic equation for A' is

$$dA' = -SdT - Md\mathcal{H} + \mu d\mathcal{B} \tag{3.4}$$

where μ is here the chemical potential per spin.

From (3.4), expressions for S,M and μ in terms of the partition function Q' are readily obtained.

For the simple, two-state Ising model the partition function may be written as

$$Q'(\mathcal{B},T,\mathcal{H}) = \exp(m\mathcal{H}\mathcal{B}/kT)\exp(q\mathcal{B}J/2kT) \sum_{N_-} \exp(-2m\mathcal{H}N_-/kT)$$

$$\sum_{N_{+-}} g(N_-,N_{+-},\mathcal{B})\exp(-2JN_{+-}/kT) \tag{3.5}$$

where q is the coordination number and $g(N_-,N_{+-},\mathcal{B})$ is the number of configurations in which there are N_- cells having $s^z = -1/2$ and N_{+-} pairs of dissimilar nn pairs. The summations are taken first over all values of N_{+-} for a fixed value of N_-, and then over all values of N_-. Equation (3.5) is very convenient as a starting point for the discussion of the equivalence of the magnetic with other types of Ising problem.

As another example, and also because of its general interest to us, we shall consider the application of the Ising model to a binary solid solution (Hill 1956a). For such a system the canonical partition function is given by

$$Q(N_a, N_b, T) = \exp\{-(N_a \varepsilon_{aa} + N_b \varepsilon_{bb})q/2kT\} \sum_{N_{ab}} g(N_a, N_{ab}, \mathscr{B}) \exp(-2JN_{ab}/kT) \quad (3.6)$$

where N_a, N_b are the numbers of A and B particles, respectively, $\mathscr{B} = N_a + N_b$, q is the coordination number, $2J = \varepsilon_{ab} - (\varepsilon_{aa} + \varepsilon_{bb})/2$, and $\varepsilon_{aa}, \varepsilon_{bb}$ and ε_{ab} are the energies of interaction for one nn pair of AA, BB, and AB particles, respectively.

Equation (3.6) can be rearranged to give

$$Q(N_a, \mathscr{B}, T) = \exp(-q\mathscr{B}\varepsilon_{bb}/2kT)\exp\{(\varepsilon_{bb} - \varepsilon_{aa})N_a q/2kT\} \sum_{N_{ab}} g(N_a, N_{ab}, \mathscr{B}) \exp(-2JN_{ab}/kT)$$
$$(3.7)$$

A function similar in mathematical form to $Q'(\mathscr{B}, T, \mathscr{H})$ (equation 3.5) may be obtained by multiplication of equation (3.7) by $\exp\{N_a(\mu_a - \mu_b)/kT\}$, followed by summation over all values of N_a:

$$Y(\mathscr{B}, T, \mu_a - \mu_b) = \exp(-q\mathscr{B}\varepsilon_{bb}/2kT) \sum_{N_a} \exp[\{q(\varepsilon_{bb} - \varepsilon_{aa})/2 + (\mu_a - \mu_b)\}N_a/kT]$$
$$\sum_{N_{ab}} g(N_a, N_{ab}, \mathscr{B}) \exp(-2JN_{ab}/kT) \quad (3.8)$$

This function is related to the thermodynamic properties of the system by the equations

$$kT \ln Y = -\mathscr{B}\mu_b \quad (3.9)$$

and
$$N_a = kT(\partial \ln Y / \partial(\mu_a - \mu_b))_{T, \mathscr{B}} \quad (3.10)$$

A comparison of equations (3.8), (3.9), and (3.10) with (3.4) and (3.5) enables a table of equivalents to be drawn up (Table 3.1).

If, in a relationship which has been deduced for a ferromagnet by use of the simple Ising model, every quantity is replaced by its binary solid equivalent then the resultant equation will be valid for the Ising model of the binary system. The table can, of course, be greatly extended by considering the derivative quantities. For ferromagnet-

TABLE 3.1

*Equivalent quantities in the Ising models of ferromagnets
and binary solid systems*

Ferromagnet	Binary Solid Solution
$\mathcal{B}$	$N_a + N_b$
N_-	N_a
$(1 - M/M_{max})/2\ ^{\dagger}$	$x_a = N_a/(N_a + N_b)$
$-2m\mathcal{H}$	$q(\varepsilon_{bb} - \varepsilon_{aa})/2 + (\mu_a - \mu_b)$
$A' + m\mathcal{H}\mathcal{B}$	$\mathcal{B}\mu_b - q\mathcal{B}\varepsilon_{bb}/2$

$\dagger\ M/M_{max} = (\mathcal{B} - 2N_-)/\mathcal{B}$

lattice gas correspondence, see Fisher (1966).

A non-magnetic order-disorder system in which a molecule can adopt only two orientations, and for which the
crystal lattice causes one orientation to have a higher
energy than the other can be simulated by treating it as
the ferromagnet case but with the magnetic field term replaced by a term which gives the intrinsic difference in
energy of the two orientations.

In order to describe the order in a system it is useful
to define an infinite set of pair correlation functions.
For spins with inter-spin vector $\underline{r}$, and in zero field, we
define

$$\Gamma(T;\underline{r}) = \langle s_0^z s_{\underline{r}}^z \rangle / s^2 \tag{3.11}$$

where $\langle\ \rangle$ denotes the ensemble average. As $|\underline{r}| \to \infty$, (3.11)
becomes

$$\Gamma(T;\infty) = \mathscr{S}^2 \tag{3.12}$$

where $\mathscr{S}$ is the long-range order parameter. $\mathscr{S}$ may also be identified with $\langle s_i^z \rangle / s$ provided that $\langle \rangle$ is here taken to be the magnitude of the average over the whole system, rather than the ensemble average. In zero field, of course, the latter will be zero since it will sample equally both positive and negative regions.

Whereas $\Gamma(T;\infty)$ and $\mathscr{S}$ go to zero at the critical point, the other correlation functions have an inflexion point at T_c, but only go to zero asymptotically as $T \to \infty$ (Fig.3.1).

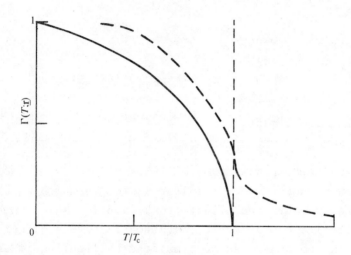

Fig.3.1. The decay of the pair correlation in zero field with increase of temperature. $\Gamma(T,\underline{r})$ is the pair correlation function for interspin vector $\underline{r}$. Full line: long (infinite) range $[\Gamma(T;\infty)]$. Broken line: a typical shorter-range function (after De Jongh and Miedema 1974).

3.1.1. Availability of solutions

Having expressed order-disorder in terms of the Ising model the question now arises, to what extent can the nearest neighbour Ising problems be solved?

We may summarize the situation in the following way. In one dimension the problems can readily be solved both in the presence and in the absence of a magnetic field. However, no transitions are predicted and the results are not in any way exciting. The two-dimensional problem of a simple quadratic lattice in zero field was solved exactly by Onsager

(1944) in what is recognized as one of the outstanding pieces of statistical mechanics. This work showed that there was a critical point marked by a logarithmic divergence of the heat capacity. The corresponding problem in a magnetic field has not been solved. Subsequently, solutions have been found for several other important two-dimensional lattices in zero field (Green and Hurst 1964). No problem in three dimensions, even in the absence of a field, has been solved exactly. Fortunately, we have a large amount of approximate data of high quality from the very careful work of Domb, Essam, Fisher, Sykes and their associates. These data, most of which have been obtained by series expansion methods, will be considered in greater detail in later sections.

Prior to all the above work, except that for one dimension, several approximate treatments were proposed, which can be expressed in terms of the Ising model. These have the advantage that they enable the partition function and hence the thermodynamic functions, to be evaluated in closed form. The most important of these are the Bragg and Williams approximation and the Bethe-Guggenheim or quasichemical approximation, and we shall first look at these before considering the exact solutions and numerical methods.

Except where explicitly stated otherwise we shall restrict our attention to the $s = 1/2$ Ising model.

Authoritative accounts of the present achievements in the solutions of Ising and other lattice problems are given in the series edited by Domb and Green (1972-).

3.1.2. Bragg and Williams theory (1934-5)

This approximation is an example of a class of widely used approximate treatments known as 'molecular field' or 'mean field' theories. Two other well-known members of this class are Weiss's theory of ferromagnets and van der Waals' treatment of the attractive interactions in fluids. In its behaviour in the immediate vicinity of the transition point it also resembles Landau's theory of transitions (section 2.5).

The main assumption made was that an adequate description could be given in terms of the long-range order parameter ($\mathscr{S}$) alone, no account being taken of shorter-range correlations.

The lattice of a 1:1 binary mixture (AB) is divided into two sublattices (α and β), each consisting of alternate sites. Where there is an A atom on an α-site or a B atom on a β-site we put $s^z = +1/2$, and otherwise we put $s^z = -1/2$. For the energy of interaction of the ith particle with each of its nns (on the other sublattice) we put $-4Js_i^z\langle s^z \rangle$, where $\langle s^z \rangle$ is the mean value of s^z taken over the sublattice which includes the nns.

The partition function may then be written as

$$Q = \sum_{s_i^z} \exp(\sum_i 2Jqs_i^z\langle s^z \rangle/kT) = \prod_i 2\cosh(2Jq\langle s^z \rangle/kT) \qquad (3.13)$$

where q is the coordination number; and in the exponent we have divided by 2 in order to avoid counting each inter- action twice. The summation over configurations should strictly be taken in two stages: first, over all s_i^z values for a given $\langle s^z \rangle$, and secondly over all $\langle s^z \rangle$ values. However, since the summand is sharply peaked, it is permissible to use only the one value of $\langle s^z \rangle$ in the summation.

Now

$$\partial \ln Q/\partial(Jq\langle s^z \rangle/kT) = \sum_{s_i^z} 2s_i^z \exp(\sum_i Jq\langle s^z \rangle s_i^z/kT)/Q$$
$$= 2\mathscr{B}\langle s^z \rangle = \mathscr{B}\mathscr{S}$$

Therefore

$$\mathscr{B}\mathscr{S} = \sum_i \tanh(Jq\langle s^z \rangle/kT) = \mathscr{B} \tanh(Jq\mathscr{S}/2kT) \qquad (3.14)$$

$\mathscr{S}=0$ is always a solution of this equation, but for

$$T < T_c = Jq/2k \qquad (3.15)$$

there is an additional solution with $\mathscr{S} > 0$. Where two solu- tions exist it can be shown that the one with $\mathscr{S} > 0$ is the stable one. The C $vs.T$ curve is of Ehrenfest second-order type (Fig.3.2).

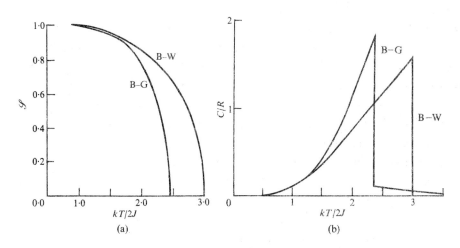

Fig.3.2. (a) Long-range order($\mathscr{S}$) and (b) heat capacity (C) against temperature for the simple cubic lattice. B-W: Bragg-Williams; B-G: Bethe-Guggenheim.

There are various ways of considering the Bragg and Williams approximation. The first comes from the realization that that form of equation would be valid if the forces between the particles were of infinitely long range and infinitely weak, the latter requirement being necessary to prevent the total interaction energy of the system from becoming infinite (Kac, Uhlenbeck, and Hemmer 1963). It would then follow that any one particle would be equally influenced by all the other particles in the system, and geometrical proximity would not be of any significance. It is clear that the long-range order parameter would be the only one necessary to describe the interaction energy of the system and hence its thermodynamic properties. When put in this way the approximation is not very acceptable as a model for real systems. However, it may usefully be visualized as being, in a sense, the opposite of the simple Ising model: in the latter it is said that only nn cells interact, whereas in the former we say that all interact equally. The true picture is somewhere in between, the interactions of non-nearest neighbours being non-zero but usually of less importance than the nn interactions and decreasing in importance as the distance apart of the cells

increases. Since coulombic and dipolar forces are of longer
range than magnetic exchange, dispersion and repulsion forces
it might be expected that substances in which the former are
important, such as the ferroelectrics, would show large
deviations from the behaviour of the simple Ising model and
exhibit some of the character of the Bragg-Williams model
(Ginzburg 1961, Gonzalo 1970). However, Friedman and
Felsteiner (1974) have shown that although the mean-field
approximation is exact for infinite-range direction-indepen-
dent interactions, it is a poor approximation if the interactions are strongly angle-dependent. Their theoretical
work is supported by the observation that for $Dy(C_2H_5SO_4)_3$.
$9H_2O$ and $Ce_2Mg_3(NO_3)_{12}.24H_2O$, in which the magnetic interactions are almost purely dipolar, the observed transition
temperature is about one-half of the value expected from
mean-field theory.

One further point about the range of applicability of
the Bragg and Williams approximation may be made. Since it
does not take proper account of fluctuations, it would be
expected to be particularly poor where the fluctuations
are known to be large, namely in the vicinity of the critical point. Indeed, Fisher (1967) has proposed that the
limits of validity may be expressed in the form:

$$|T - T_c|/T_c \simeq c(a/\lambda b)^d \qquad (3.16)$$

where a and b are the ranges of the repulsive and attractive
forces, respectively, c and λ are parameters of order unity,
and d is the dimensionality of the system. Since the factor
$(a/\lambda b)$ is less than unity, it would follow that the Bragg
and Williams approximation could be taken closer to T_c, the
higher the dimensionality of the system.

*3.1.3. Bethe-Guggenheim (quasichemical) approximation
(Fowler and Guggenheim 1956).*
The basis of the quasichemical approach, due to Guggenheim,
is that the relative numbers of (++), (--), and (+-) nn
spins are the same as would be found if the pairs behaved
independently. Thus, considering the hypothetical chemical

reaction:

$$(++) + (--) = 2 (+-)   \Delta E = 4J \tag{3.17}$$

we would expect the equilibrium relationship:

$$\frac{N_{+-}^2}{4N_{--}N_{++}} = \exp(-4J/kT) . \tag{3.18}$$

Bethe's First Approximation starts from an apparently quite different point but, nevertheless, turns out to be equivalent to the quasichemical approach. In it, inter-actions of a particle with nns are treated exactly, whilst the effects of more remote particles are allowed for by a mean-field treatment. Thus, when considering spin 0 (Fig. 3.3) the correlations between spins 1 and 2 via the outer

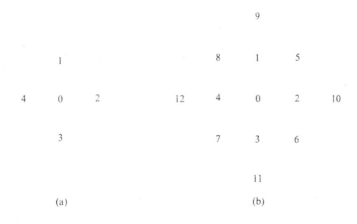

Fig.3.3. Cores for (a) First Approximation and (b) Second Approximation of Bethe.

parts of the system are treated by an approximation which is equivalent to that of Bragg and Williams. In his Second Approximation, Bethe included the next shell of particles (5 to 12) in the core of the system within which inter-actions were treated exactly. Thus correlations of 1 and 2 via the path 1-5-2 would now be considered exactly, al-though longer correlation paths would still only be

represented by the mean-field approximation. We shall not
pursue the Second Approximation here as the improvement over
the First is not sufficiently great and, as a consequence, it
has not been widely used.

To evaluate $Q'(\mathscr{B},T,\mathcal{H})$ from equation (3.5) an approximation for the statistical factor $g(N_-,N_{+-},\mathscr{B})$ is needed.
Now the numbers of nn pairs of each type may be written as:

$$\underset{--}{(qN_--N_{+-})/2} \qquad \underset{++}{\{q(\mathscr{B}-N_-)-N_{+-}\}/2} \qquad \underset{-+}{N_{+-}/2} \qquad \underset{+-}{N_{+-}/2}$$

The approximation is then made by setting

$$g(N_-,N_{+-},\mathscr{B}) = \text{const.}\frac{(q\mathscr{B}/2)!}{\{(qN_--N_{+-})/2\}![\{q(\mathscr{B}-N_-)-N_{+-}\}/2]!\{(N_{+-}/2)!\}^2} \tag{3.19}$$

the constant being chosen so as to satisfy the equation

$$\sum_{N_{+-}} g(N_-,N_{+-},\mathscr{B}) = \mathscr{B}!/\{N_-!(\mathscr{B}-N_-)!\} \tag{3.20}$$

This leads to the equations

$$\left(\frac{N_-}{\mathscr{B}-N_-}\right)^{q-1}\left(\frac{q\mathscr{B}-qN_--N_{+-}}{qN_--N_{+-}}\right)^{q/2} = \exp(-2m\mathcal{H}/kT) \tag{3.21}$$

and

$$\frac{N_{+-}^2}{(qN_--N_{+-})(q\mathscr{B}-qN_--N_{+-})} = \exp(-4J/kT) \ . \tag{3.22}$$

Simultaneous solution of (3.21) and (3.22) gives the values
of N_- and N_{+-} which maximize the typical term of the partition function. These values are now put back into equation (3.5) to yield the maximum term, which is equated with
the partition function in the usual way. Equation (3.22)
is equivalent to (3.18).

The C versus T curve (Fig.3.2b) differs from that for
the corresponding Bragg-Williams treatment in having a high-
temperature 'tail' and also in having its peak at a lower
temperature.

3.1.4. *Results for Ising models with $s = \frac{1}{2}$*

One dimension. The partition function per spin is the larger root of the quadratic equation in λ:

$$\{\exp(K+H'') - \lambda\}\{\exp(K-H'') - \lambda\} - \exp(-2K) = 0 \qquad (3.23)$$

where $K = J/kT$ and $H'' = m\mathcal{H}/kT$.

In zero field the long-range order is zero at all temperatures above 0 K. The physical reason for this is easy to appreciate. Imagine a one-dimensional array of spins in an ordered arrangement at 0 K (Fig.3.4a). At any higher

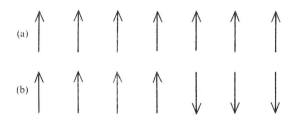

(a)

(b)

Fig.3.4. One dimensional array of Ising ($s=1/2$) spins. (a) Fully ordered; (b) containing a single pair of antiparallel neighbours.

temperature there will, of course, be the occasional pair of nn spins which are antiparallel (Fig.3.4b). As a consequence of this we would expect no correlation between the orientations of the first and last spins as the number of particles between becomes infinite, since there is only one path of communication between the terminal spins however large the system.

The more general problem in which the interaction is not restricted to nns, but instead falls off gradually with distance has been examined by Thouless (1969). Writing the energy of a configuration as

$$E = -4 \sum_{m=2}^{N} \sum_{n=1}^{m-1} J(m-n) s_m^z s_n^z \qquad (3.24)$$

where the interaction parameter $J(m-n)$ depends upon the difference between m and n as

$$J(m-n) \propto (m-n)^{-r} \qquad (3.25)$$

he showed that provided $r > 2$ there is no long-range order at non-zero temperatures.

There is also a more general theorem, due to van Hove, not restricted to the Ising lattice, according to which a one-dimensional system of particles interacting by forces of finite range cannot have any singularities in its thermo-dynamic properties (Münster 1969).

In zero field C is the same as for a Schottky anomaly involving two non-degenerate states with energy separation $2J$. The graph of C *versus* T shows a smooth maximum at $T = 0 \cdot 833 J/k$ (Fig.3.5).

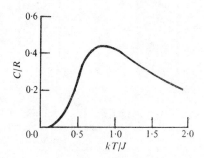

Fig.3.5. Heat capacity (C) against temperature for a one-dimensional array of Ising ($s=1/2$) spins in zero field (from Hill 1956).

Two dimensions, zero field. For the simple quadratic lattice (Fig.3.6) Onsager (1944) found the partition function per spin to be given by the equation:

$$\ln Q - \frac{1}{2} \ln(2 \sinh K) = \frac{1}{2\pi} \int_0^{\pi} \gamma(\omega) \, d\omega \qquad (3.26)$$

where $\cosh \gamma = \coth 2K \cosh 2K' - \mathrm{cosech}\, 2K \sinh 2K' \cos \omega$ and $K = J/kT$ and $K' = J'/kT$. J and J', the Ising parameters for nn spins whose inter-spin vectors lie along the two axes of the lattice, need not be equal.

The long-range order does not fall to zero as soon as T becomes non-zero. Instead, there is a gradual loss of long-

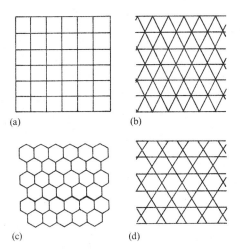

(a)   (b)

(c)   (d)

Fig.3.6. Common two-dimensional lattices. (a) Quadratic (square); (b) triangular; (c) hexagonal (honeycomb); (d) Kagomé.

range order up to a critical point, at which it becomes zero. Fig.3.7 shows C *versus* T. One feature to note is that the energy and entropy gained below T_c is very similar in

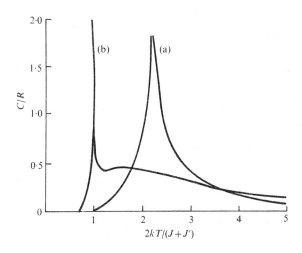

Fig.3.7. Heat capacity (C) of quadratic Ising ($s=1/2$) system in zero field. (a) $J' = J$; (b) $J' = 0 \cdot 01 J$ (from Hill 1956).

magnitude to that gained above T_c (Table 3.2). This contrasts with the result for the Bragg and Williams treatment.
Another interesting feature is that if $J{\ne}J'$ then there is

TABLE 3.2

The entropy and energy gained below the critical point
(S_c and E_c - E_0) and above the critical point (S_∞-S_c and
$-E_c$) for several types of array of s = 1/2 Ising ferro-
magnets; q is the lattice coordination number and
θ = 4qs(s+1)J/3k = qJ/k; all nn parameters are assumed to be
equal to J (after Domb 1974).

Lattice	q	T_c/θ	S_c/R	$(S_\infty-S_c)/R$	$(E_c-E_0)/R$	$-E_c/RT_c$
Hexagonal	3	0·50621	0·26471	0·42844	0·22737	0·76035
Quadratic	4	0·56730	0·30647	0·38668	0·25814	0·62323
Triangular	6	0·60683	0·33028	0·36287	0·27465	0·54931
Diamond	4	0·6761	0·510	0·183	0·417	0·323
Simple cubic	6	0·75180	0·5579	0·1352	0·4451	0·2200
Body-centred cubic	8	0·79416	0·5820	0·1111	0·4576	0·1720
Face-centred cubic	12	0·81627	0·5902	0·1029	0·4609	0·1516

a reduction of the fraction of the energy gained under the
logarithmic peak and more becomes absorbed into the smooth
hump. In the extreme case, where $J'=0$, the system becomes
a number of one-dimensional arrays, the graph loses its
peak, and becomes a smooth Schottky-like hump.

Apart from the quadratic lattice, exact solutions have
been found for a number of other two-dimensional lattices,
among them the triangular (Fig.3.6b) and the hexagonal or
honeycomb (Fig.3.6c) lattices. Good accounts of these and
of other two-dimensional lattices are given by Domb (1960)
and Green and Hurst (1964). The behaviour shown by these
lattices is qualitatively similar to that of the quadratic
lattice provided that the interactions are ferromagnetic

(all $J > 0$) (Table 3.2). If the interactions are antiferromagnetic (all $J < 0$) the behaviour may even be *qualitatively* dependent upon the lattice involved. For example,
in zero field there is no difference at all between the
thermodynamic properties of arrays of Ising ferromagnets and
antiferromagnets on a quadratic lattice (either can be
accommodated in the same theory by referring to the number
of 'correctly' or 'incorrectly' oriented nn pairs rather
than by stipulating that they are parallel or antiparallel).
On the triangular lattice, by contrast, antiferromagnets
having equal interaction parameters for the three directions
are unable to find an unique configuration of lowest energy.
In fact, the ground state comprises a large number of configurations (W_0) of equal energy, such that $\ln W_0$ is $O(\mathscr{B})$,
where $\mathscr{B}$ is the number of antiferromagnets in the system.
Wannier (1950) has shown that the zero-point entropy of this
system is $0\cdot3383R$, a value which has been subsequently
corrected to $0\cdot32306R$ (Domb 1960). For ferromagnets on the
same lattice there are two ground configurations of equal
energy. Thus $W_0 = 2$ and $\ln W_0$ is $O(1)$. Since in thermodynamics we are only concerned with the limit as $\mathscr{B} \to \infty$ we
can consider the ground state of the system of ferromagnets
as being unique. If the interaction parameters of the antiferromagnet along the three directions are not equal then
the system can become ordered as a consequence of there now
being a unique configuration of lowest energy.

Two dimensions, non-zero field.   There is a limited class
of so-called 'decorated' lattices for which exact solutions
in non-zero field have been found (Fisher 1960, Green and
Hurst 1964a). In the two examples given in the references
a quadratic lattice is 'decorated' with spins on every
bond, each 'decorated' spin ($\times$) interacting only with the
two adjacent ordinary spins ($\cdot$) (Fig.3.8a,b). In Fisher's
model all horizontal interactions have parameter $+J$ and all
vertical interactions are characterized by $-J$. Green and
Hurst's model assumes that the interaction parameters for
each 'decorated' spin with its two nns are equal in magnitude but opposite in sign. An important feature of both of

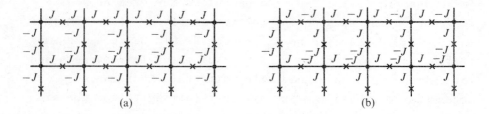

Fig.3.8. Decorated Ising lattices; (×) decorated spin, (·) ordinary spin.
(a) Fisher's model; (b) Green and Hurst's model.

these models is that only the 'decorated' spins interact with
a magnetic field. For these rather artificial conditions
transformations can be found which relate the properties
to those of the quadratic lattice in zero field, which Onsager
had solved. The only extensive application of these results
to real systems seems to have been in the discussion of 2-
and 3-component liquid systems (Widom 1967, Neece 1967, Clark
1968, Clark and Neece 1968).

Three dimensions, zero field.   Although none of these systems
can be solved exactly, Griffiths (1967) has shown that if
we compare a three-dimensional ferromagnetic system with the
two-dimensional system generated by letting the interactions
in one direction become zero, then T_c for the former cannot
be lower than for the latter.
     Domb and associates have examined a number of these
systems using high- and low-temperature expansions of the
susceptibility and the heat capacity. The coefficients of
as many as possible of the leading terms are evaluated by
careful numerical work, and subsequent terms are estimated
by extrapolation of the coefficients or by other continuation methods. Having obtained, in effect, the complete
series, the properties in the vicinity of the critical point
can be calculated. Fig.3.9, showing a typical graph from
which a critical temperature was estimated, illustrates
the nature of the extrapolation involved. Since nearly all
the present knowledge of three-dimensional arrays comes

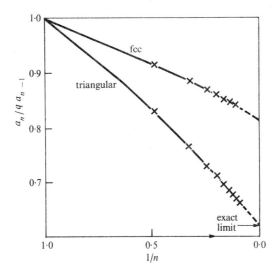

Fig.3.9. Convergence of the ratio of successive coefficients a_n and a_{n-1} in high-temperature susceptibility expansions with increase in ordinal number (n) of the term; q = coordination number of the lattice (from Domb 1966).

from this approach, it should be said that the justification for the method is that there seems to be no physical reason why the regularity among the coefficients which is observed among the early members should be lost among the later ones.

One of the general results from this work is that the approximate symmetry about T_c of the curve of C *versus* T evident in two dimensions, is lost in three: the energy and entropy gained below T_c is much greater than that gained above (Table 3.2). This is one of a number of observations which seems to be determined more by the dimensionality of the system than by the actual lattice involved. It is very satisfying that the theory for three dimensions leads to this asymmetry because λ-points in real systems usually deviate from symmetry in the same sense.

At temperatures appreciably above T_c the heat capacity is found to be proportional to T^{-2}. This result is in agreement with the behaviour of real magnetic systems, and is frequently used as a basis for the separation of the ferromagnetic from other contributions to the heat capacity (Domb

1960, Hill 1956b).

Three dimensions, non-zero field.   Fosdick (1963) has reported some Monte Carlo results for these systems, but unfortunately that method suffers from severe convergence
problems near the critical point and it is that region in
which one is usually interested.

A fairly successful Monte Carlo simulation of a metamagnetic system has been carried out by D.P. Landau (1972)
(see section 12.6.1).   For a comprehensive review of recent
Monte Carlo studies see the article by Binder in Domb and
Green (1972-), Volume 5b.

3.1.5. *Results for Ising models with s > 1/2.*

Domb has studied several of these on the face-centred cubic
lattice in zero field.   Although the precision is not as
high as for the $s=1/2$ systems, the results show clearly
that as s increases the asymmetry of the *C versus T* curve
also increases.   Table 3.3 illustrates this point with
reference to the amount of energy and entropy gained above
and below T_c.   The Table also shows the much less dramatic
change (decrease) of T_c itself for a fixed value of the
energy difference between the most- and least-favoured
states.   Thus, even when the number of allowed states goes
to infinity T_c is still more than one-third of its value
for the two-state ($s=1/2$) system.

TABLE 3.3

*Properties of the face-centred cubic Ising lattice for various
values of s (after Domb and Miedema 1964).*

s	kT_c/qJ	S_c/R	$(S_\infty - S_c)/R$	$(E_c - E_0)/RT_c$	$-E_c/RT_c$
1/2	0·816	0·591	0·102	0·463	0·150
1	0·567	0·983	0·116	0·721	0·160
2	0·432	1·486	0·123	0·990	0·167
∞	0·291	∞	0·131	1·541	0·175

3.1.6. Antiferromagnetic systems

In zero-field, long-range order disappears at a critical
point known as the Néel point. From what has been said
already, it is clear that the Ising model on an ordering
lattice predicts a *C versus T* graph identical with that
for the corresponding ferromagnet. In a non-zero field,
however, the equivalence between the ferro- and the antiferromagnetic Ising systems disappears. One experimentally
observed property of antiferromagnets which is reproduced
by the Ising model is the non-coincidence of the Néel
point (T_N) and the temperature of the maximum in the magnetic susceptibility (T_χ). For two-dimensional lattices
T_N and T_χ can differ greatly, e.g. T_χ/T_N is predicted to be
$1 \cdot 537$ and $1 \cdot 688$ for the quadratic and the hexagonal lattices,
respectively. For three-dimensional arrays, on the other
hand, this ratio is much nearer to unity, e.g. $1 \cdot 098$ and
$1 \cdot 065$ for the simple cubic and the body-centred cubic
lattices, respectively.

3.1.7. Systems with more than one type of disorder

The most common category of real systems which are of this
type is that of the 'plastic' crystals. These are solids
in which there is the possibility of both orientational
and positional disorder. Where these two disordering processes occur within a small temperature range it does not
seem reasonable to treat them as being independent. The
considerations involved, and the consequences, are made
especially clear in the theory put forward by Pople and
Karasz (1961) for 'plastic' crystals.

First, they represent the positional disordering process, in the manner of the Lennard-Jones and Devonshire
theory of melting, by supposing that there are two interpenetrating and equivalent sublattices on which any molecule
may sit, one being the 'right' lattice (α) and the other
the 'wrong' lattice (β). Two coordination numbers are introduced: q for the number of β-sites surrounding each α-site,
and q' for the number of α-sites closest to each α-site
(these are the next nearest neighbours). Secondly, the
authors assume that each molecule has a 'rotational'

coordinate which can take on either of two values (1 and 2).
Each pair of molecules occupying a nn α-β pair of sites makes
a repulsive contribution to the energy of W. A pair of molecules on neighbouring sites on the same sublattice (α or β)
but with opposite rotational states makes a repulsive contribution of W' to the energy.[†] The interaction between
the two disordering processes is represented by the fact
that in the above scheme for two nns, one on an α- and the
other on a β-site, there is no additional contribution if
the rotational coordinates are also different. By use of a
form of the Bragg and Williams approximation they were able
to obtain solutions for this model.

Their treatment proceeds as follows. Long-range order
parameters are introduced for position, $\mathcal{R}$ = fraction of particles on α-sites, and for orientation, $\mathcal{S}$ = fraction of particles having the rotational coordinate = 1. A Bragg and
Williams-like approximation is now made by assuming that the
chance of a molecule having the positional coordinate α or
the rotational coordinate 1 are simply $\mathcal{R}$ and $\mathcal{S}$, respectively,
whatever the coordinates of the neighbouring molecules. The
number of nn α-β pairs of molecules ($N_{\alpha\beta}$) is then $N\mathcal{R}.q(1-\mathcal{R})$,
the number of neighbouring α_1-α_2 pairs ($N_{\alpha_1\alpha_2}$) is $N\mathcal{R}\mathcal{S}.$
$q'\mathcal{R}(1-\mathcal{S})$, and the number of neighbouring β_1-β_2 pairs ($N_{\beta_1\beta_2}$)
is $N(1-\mathcal{R})\mathcal{S}.q'(1-\mathcal{R})(1-\mathcal{S})$.

The total energy of a configuration then becomes:

$$N_{\alpha\beta}W + N_{\alpha_1\alpha_2}W' + N_{\beta_1\beta_2}W' = qNW\mathcal{R}(1-\mathcal{R}) + q'NW'\mathcal{S}(1-\mathcal{S})(1-2\mathcal{R}+2\mathcal{R}^2)$$

$$(3.27)$$

We now require $\gamma(\mathcal{R},\mathcal{S})$, the number of configurations
which have a particular value of $\mathcal{R}$ and $\mathcal{S}$. This is

$$\gamma(\mathcal{R},\mathcal{S}) = \left[\frac{N!}{(N\mathcal{R})!\{N(1-\mathcal{R})\}!}\right]^2 \frac{(N\mathcal{R})!}{(N\mathcal{R}\mathcal{S})!\{N\mathcal{R}(1-\mathcal{S})\}!} \frac{N(1-\mathcal{R})!}{\{N(1-\mathcal{R})\mathcal{S}\}!\{N(1-\mathcal{R})(1-\mathcal{S})\}!}$$

$$(3.28)$$

[†]W' is not the potential barrier opposing rotation. Rather it is the
difference in potential energy between two minima.

The canonical partition function is then readily obtained from the expression:

$$Q = \sum_{\mathfrak{R},\mathscr{S}} \gamma(\mathfrak{R},\mathscr{S}) \exp\{-(N_{\alpha\beta}W + N_{\alpha_1\alpha_2}W' + N_{\beta_1\beta_2}W')/kT\} \qquad (3.29)$$

where the summation is taken over all values of $\mathfrak{R}$ and $\mathscr{S}$.

The well-known device of replacing the sum by its maximum term is then used. The values of $\mathfrak{R}$ and $\mathscr{S}$ for the maximum term are given by the equations:

$$\ln\{\mathfrak{R}/(1-\mathfrak{R})\} = \{qW/2kT - q'W'\mathscr{S}(1-\mathscr{S})/kT\}(2\mathfrak{R}-1) \qquad (3.30)$$

$$\ln\{\mathscr{S}/(1-\mathscr{S})\} = q'W'(1-2\mathfrak{R}+2\mathfrak{R}^2)(2\mathscr{S}-1)/kT . \qquad (3.31)$$

$\mathfrak{R}=\mathscr{S}=1/2$ is always a solution of these equations, but at sufficiently low temperatures there is an additional solution which in fact corresponds to the largest term in the summation.

If $\nu = q'W'/qW$ is small, then as the temperature is raised orientational disorder occurs first and subsequently, and essentially separately, positional disorder (melting) is achieved. If ν is larger, there can be a large, discontinuous loss of both types of order at the same temperature. Finally, if ν is larger still, loss of all residual positional order, together with some orientational order, occurs discontinuously at a single temperature. The last situation corresponds to the behaviour of liquid crystals. Pople and Karasz went on to examine the equation of state of the system, for which it was necessary to make assumptions about the variation of W and W' with volume and about the partition function factor relating to the movement of each molecule about its mean lattice position. For the latter they used the cell model of Lennard-Jones and Devonshire. Their results for the entropy and volume of transition as a function of ν are shown in Fig.3.10, and are in general accord with experimental observations.

Huberman and Streifer (1975) have employed a mean-field treatment to examine a system in which magnetic order is coupled to a lattice order parameter (equivalent to $\mathfrak{R}$ in

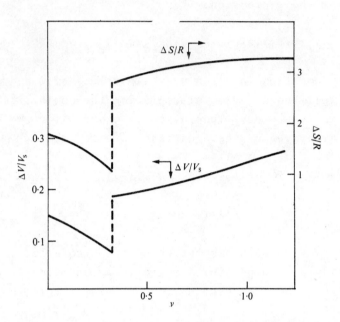

Fig.3.10. Relative volume change ($\Delta V/V_s$) and entropy change (ΔS) on melting as a function of $\nu = q'W'/qW$ in the theory of Pople and Karasz. V_s is the molar volume of the solid at the melting-point (from Pople and Karasz 1961).

the work of Pople and Karasz). They found that, depending upon the relative values of the parameters, three types of effect on the critical behaviour could occur. In the first, described as a zone of weak renormalization, the decay of magnetic order is slightly modified and the dis-ordering of the lattice occurs virtually entirely at some higher temperature. In the second, the curve of magnetic order against temperature becomes more rectangular but remains continuous, and there is a simultaneous smooth de-crease in lattice order. In the final case, disordering terminates in a first-order change involving both order parameters.

Another type of system in which two kinds of randomness can occur is that of the ferromagnetic alloys. Here we must first consider order-disorder with respect to the positions of the spins, that is, whether the magnetic and diluent atoms are randomly dispersed on the lattice or are

in an ordered arrangement. Secondly, we must consider order-
disorder of the orientations of the spins. An exact solution of a one-dimensional model of such an alloy has been
given by Kawatra and Kijewski (1969). In their treatment
diluent atoms act in the same way as holes in lattice gas
theory in that there is no interaction between neighbouring cells when either or both are occupied by the diluent.
The main feature of the heat capacity curve is that at some
diluent concentrations the curve has two separate maxima,
these arising from the 'condensation' of the magnetic atoms
and the orientational ordering of the spins. At other concentrations both processes occur simultaneously (Fig.3.11).

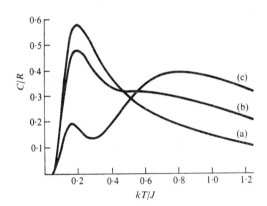

Fig.3.11. Heat capacity (C) against temperature for the one-dimensional
ferromagnetic alloy systems of Kawatra and Kijewski for various mole
fractions (ρ) of diluent. (a) $\rho = 0.75$, (b) $\rho = 0.25$, (c) $\rho = 0.05$ (from
Kawatra and Kijewski 1969).

   It should be stressed that in the treatments considered
in this section so far it is assumed that equilibrium with
respect to both kinds of disorder is maintained throughout.
In many real systems, however, it is nearer to the truth to
adopt the opposite viewpoint, namely that with respect to
one of the processes the system is frozen into the completely disordered state. McCoy and Wu (1968, 1969) have
studied a quadratic Ising array in which the horizontal
interaction parameters all have the value J, but the vertical

parameters, whilst having the same value within any row,
vary randomly from row to row (Fig.3.12). When the probability distribution of the vertical parameters is narrow

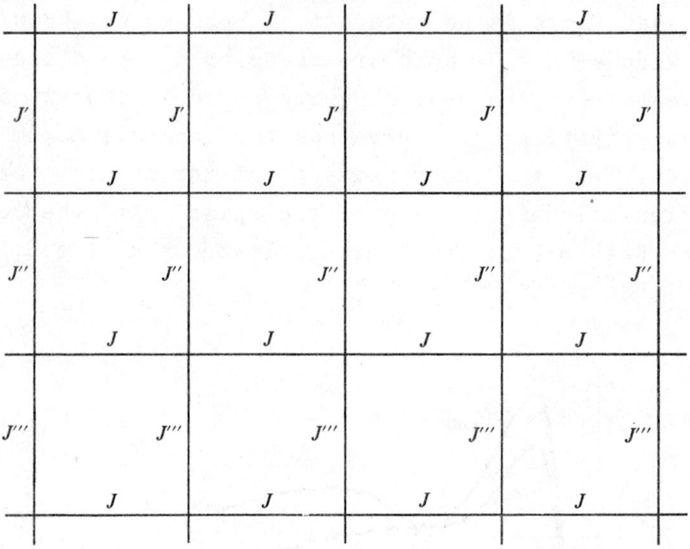

Fig.3.12. The Ising quadratic array with random vertical coupling parameters.

the heat capacity curve was found to have a smooth maximum,
instead of the logarithmic divergence of Onsager's problem.
Little success has been achieved for the Ising problem
with a broader probability distribution.

The ordering properties of pseudo-linear chain systems,
i.e. those in which the interactions are strong in one
direction but weak in the other two, might be expected to
be especially sensitive to the introduction of substitutional impurities, and this is indeed found to be so. Hone,
Montano, Tonegawa, and Imry (1975) assumed the impurity atoms
to be fixed in a random manner and applied a mean-field
approximation in the directions of weak interaction. Fig.
3.13(a) refers to the system containing no impurity atoms
and shows how T_c increases as the weak interactions (J')
are increased for a fixed value of the strong interaction

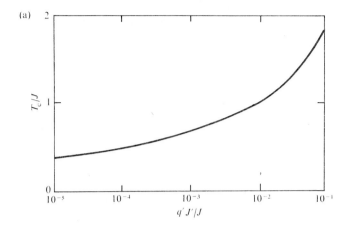

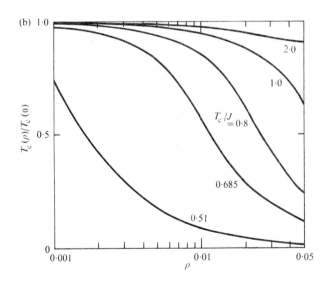

Fig.3.13. The effect of substitutional impurities on the three-dimensional transition temperature of a pseudo one-dimensional Ising $s=1/2$ system. (a) Transition temperature as a function of interchain coupling parameter (J') in the absence of impurities. q' is the number of nearest neighbours other than those in the same chain. (b) Transition temperature $T_c(\rho)$ as a function of the mole fraction of impurities (ρ) for various values of T_c/J for the pure substance (from Hone *et al.*, 1975).

(J); Fig.3.13(b) shows that the presence of even 1% of impurity atoms can bring about a drastic lowering of T_c, particularly if J'/J is small (T_c/J small).

Of considerable importance for this type of problem is
the work on the Percolation Problem (section 3.4).

3.1.8. *Effects of volume change on transitions*

All the Ising treatments which we have described have ignored the possibility of volume change, although a great
many order-disorder transitions are, in fact, accompanied
by volume changes when they occur at constant pressure.
One way in which these volume changes can be included in the
theory has been exploited by Bean and Rodbell (1962) and
Garland and Renard (1966). They consider a simple quadratic
Ising model in which the parameter J is 'volume'-dependent
(or rather area-dependent for this two-dimensional array).
Provided that the lattice has a finite compressibility and
the heat capacity at constant area is infinite at T_c the
transition can become first order and, they suggest, show
hysteresis. Their results are illustrated in Fig.3.14, which
shows how for seven temperatures $(T_1 \ldots T_7)$ the two components

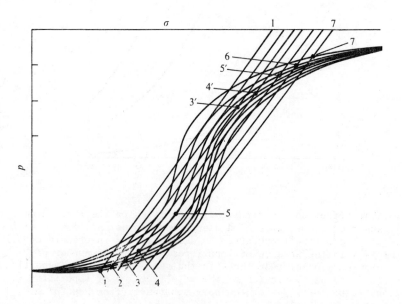

Fig.3.14. Two-dimensional pressure (p) against area (σ) at seven temperatures for compressible Ising $s=1/2$ lattice. Straight-line isotherms
are for $-T$, sigmoid isotherms are for p_I (after Garland and Renard
1966).

of the pressure, that arising from the Ising spin system
(p_I) and that which is associated with the normal attractive
and repulsive forces between the particles (p_0), vary as the
area of the system is changed. The p_0 values are based on
experimental compressibilities of three-dimensional solids;
the p_I were obtained by differentiation with respect to area
of Onsager's expression for the free energy with $dJ/d\sigma \neq 0$,
where σ is the area.

We are concerned with the condition $p = p_I + p_0 = 0$, and
we further require that $(\partial p/\partial \sigma)_T < 0$ in order to achieve
mechanical stability. For the latter condition to be satis-
fied the slope of the $-p_0$ line must be greater than that of
the p_I line. Thus at each temperature for which three inter-
sections are found the central one always represents an unstable situation. Therefore, at each such temperature there
are two values of the area which satisfy our conditions and
a change from one to the other involves a discontinuous
change in volume as at a first-order transition. At temperatures such that the curves cut at only one point there is
only one possible area for the system.

In this model, hysteresis can be pictured by considering
the heating of the system from T_1 to T_7. Initially, the
area increases smoothly through the points 1 to 5. It must
then jump to 5', after which it again increases smoothly
to 7. On cooling from T_7 the area can decrease smoothly as
far as 3', after which it jumps to 3 and then decreases
smoothly again to 1. The patterns of area *versus* temperature
on heating and cooling are, evidently, not the same. Fisher
(1966b) has expressed doubts about the validity of this kind
of treatment of the change in the nature of the transition.
His criticism is based on the fact that it ignores local
fluctuations in the density of the system.

3.2. THE HEISENBERG MODEL
The Hamiltonian is here written as

$$- \frac{J}{s^2} \sum_{i,j} \underline{s}_i \cdot \underline{s}_j - \frac{m\mathcal{H}}{s} \sum_i s_i^z \qquad (3.32)$$

Since all components of the spin are taken to be equally

important in determining the inter-spin contribution, this model can be considered as being completely isotropic; in the same sense, the Ising model, in which only one component is employed, represents the extreme of anisotropy.

Many fewer calculations have been carried out on Heisenberg than on Ising systems. However, it is now established that no long-range order can occur at non-zero temperature in one- or two-dimensional systems; it is only when we reach three dimensions that this can arise. Work by Stanley and Kaplan (1966) (see section 12.13.2) does, nevertheless, suggest that a singularity in χ_T can occur in two-dimensional systems above 0 K, even though no long-range order exists.

The absence of long-range order in the two-dimensional model can be visualized in the following, rather crude, way. Consider an ordered domain. At the domain wall the change to the new orientation may occur gradually, that is, the wall thickness may be many times the interparticle spacing. The strain arising from a pair of particles being out of alignment by $\Delta\theta$ should be proportional to $1-\cos(\Delta\theta) \simeq (\Delta\theta)^2/2$. If the linear dimension of the domain and the thickness of the domain wall are, respectively, m and n times the interparticle spacing, then the number of particles in the wall will be roughly $(m+n)^2-m^2$, and the total wall energy will be proportional to $\{(m+n)^2-m^2\}(\Delta\theta)^2$ and, therefore, to $\{(m+n)^2-m^2\}/n^2 = 1+2m/n$. The wall energy will therefore be less, the greater the wall thickness. Hence we would expect the majority of any specimen to be made up of domain walls rather than the domains themselves.

In three dimensions, on the other hand, the wall energy passes through a minimum as n increases. The domains can then occupy most of the volume and the system behaves as a ferromagnet.

Critical temperatures in Heisenberg systems are lower and the high-temperature heat capacity 'tails' are larger (Table 3.4) than for the corresponding Ising model (Table 3.2).

As with the Ising systems (Table 3.3), the effect of increase in spin number is primarily to increase the amount

TABLE 3.4

Results for s = ½ *Heisenberg systems.*   θ = 4qs(s+1)J/3k = qJ/k
(after de Jongh and Miedema 1974).

	q	T_c/θ	S_c/R	$(S_\infty - S_c)/R$	$(E_c - E_0)/RT_c$	$-E_c/RT_c$
Simple cubic	6	0·56	0·43	0·26	0·30	0˙60
Body-centred cubic	8	0·63	0·45	0·24	0·33	0·46
Face-centred cubic	12	0·67	0·46	0˙23	0˙31	0·43

TABLE 3.5

*Properties of the face-centred cubic Heisenberg lattice for
various values of* s. *(after Domb and Miedema 1964).*

s	kT_c/qJ	S_c/R	$(S_\infty - S_c)/R$	$(E_c - E_0)/RT_c$	$-E_c/RT_c$
1/2	0·679	0·479	0·220	0·31	0·44
1	0·498	0·810	0˙289	0·57	0·45
2	0˙387	1·305	0·304	0·86	0·46
∞	0·266	∞	0˙322	1·42	0·47

of entropy and energy gained below T_c. Domb's results
for the face-centred cubic lattice are given in Table 3.5.

3.3. CRITICAL INDICES AND SCALING
A great deal of attention has been given to examination
of the manner in which a number of quantities either diverge
to infinity or converge to zero as the critical point is
approached. For the quantitative discussion of this topic
a number of critical indices have been defined. A simple
example of these is β, which for a magnetic system describes
the way in which the spontaneous magnetization (M_0) goes to
zero as $T \to T_c$. The asymptotic relationship would be written
as

$$M_0 \sim (T_c - T)^\beta \qquad\qquad (3.33)$$

or, alternatively, as

$$\beta = \lim_{T \to T_c} \frac{\ln M_0}{\ln (T_c - T)} \qquad\qquad (3.34)$$

The path of the approach to T_c has been defined in this example because the discussion refers to the spontaneous magnetization, i.e. $\mathcal{H}=0$. Also, it is clear that T must approach T_c from below, since M_0 is zero above T_c. For other quantities, however, it is necessary to state clearly the approach path, on which the index may be very dependent.

It should also be noted that if the quantity goes to infinity logarithmically then the index is zero. For the same reason, if the asymptotic dependence has a logarithmic factor, e.g. $x^n \log x$, then that factor makes a contribution of zero to the index, which is then determined by the remaining factor (x^n in the example). When the index is zero as a result of a logarithmic divergence it is usual to write this as 0(log) to distinguish it from 0(finite). The latter symbol indicates that the quantity does not go to infinity at all, and would, for example, encompass the situations in which there is a cusp at the critical point. The presence of a jump discontinuity at the critical point does not affect the index.

The definitions of the most important of the critical indices are set out in Table 3.6 for the magnetic system. There are equivalent definitions in terms of gas-liquid critical behaviour and for other order-disorder systems. For comparison of the magnetic indices with analogous indices for other systems it would perhaps be better to stipulate the approach path for α and α' as being $M=0$. Justification for the above definition, apart from the fact that it corresponds more directly to actual experimental conditions, is that above T_c, $\mathcal{H}=0$ implies $M=0$, and below T_c, $M=0$ demands an equal mixture of the two magnetic phases coexisting at $\mathcal{H}=0$ (Fisher 1967). Similar arguments apply to the use of the path $\mathcal{H}=0$ for the definitions of γ, ν and η.

From rigorous thermodynamic arguments a variety of

TABLE 3.6

Definitions of some critical indices [a]

Index	Asymptotic relationship	Path
α	$C_{\mathcal{H}} \sim (T-T_c)^{-\alpha}$	$\mathcal{H}=0, T \to T_{c+}$
α'	$C_{\mathcal{H}} \sim (T_c-T)^{-\alpha'}$	$\mathcal{H}=0, T \to T_{c-}$
β	$M_0 \sim (T_c-T)^{\beta}$	$\mathcal{H}=0, T \to T_{c-}$
γ	$\chi_T \sim (T-T_c)^{-\gamma}$	$\mathcal{H}=0, T \to T_{c+}$
γ'	$\chi_T \sim (T_c-T)^{-\gamma'}$	$\mathcal{H}=0, T \to T_{c-}$
δ	$\|\mathcal{H}\| \sim \|M\|^{\delta}$	$T=T_c, \mathcal{H} \to 0$
ν	$\kappa^{-1} \sim (T-T_c)^{-\nu}$	$\mathcal{H}=0, T \to T_{c+}$
ν'	$\kappa^{-1} \sim (T_c-T)^{-\nu'}$	$\mathcal{H}=0, T \to T_{c-}$
η	$\Gamma(T_c;r) \sim r^{-d+2-\eta}$	$\mathcal{H}=0, T \to T_c, r \to \infty$

[a] $C_{\mathcal{H}}, M_0, \chi_T$, and $\Gamma(T;r)$ are, respectively, the heat capacity at constant field, the spontaneous magnetization, the isothermal susceptibility, and the spin correlation function (equation 3.11). κ describes the decay of the correlation function with distance for systems not at the critical temperature [$\Gamma(T;r) \sim \exp(-\kappa r)$]. For a discussion of the correlation range κ^{-1} and alternative correlation lengths see Fisher and Burford (1967) and Fisher (1969). In the latter a second moment distance is defined, $\xi^2 = \sum_r |r|^2 \mathcal{G}(r) / \sum_r \mathcal{G}(r)$, where $\mathcal{G}(r) = \langle s_0^z s_r^z \rangle - \langle s_0^z \rangle \langle s_r^z \rangle$, and κ^{-1} is then equated with ξ.

inequalities relating these exponents have been derived (Griffiths 1972). In these derivations no model is assumed for the system. Thus, from the requirements imposed on the curvature of the free energy in order to ensure stability, Rushbrooke showed that $\alpha'+2\beta+\gamma' \geq 2$. Likewise, Griffiths showed that $\alpha'+\beta(1+\delta) \geq 2$. Subsequently a number of other inequalities have been found. Their value lies in their use in providing consistency checks on both experimental and approximate theoretical results.

A further group of relationships, in this case equalities, can be obtained if the assumption of a 'scaling law' is made for properties in the neighbourhood of the critical point. For this region each property is divided into a regular and a singular part, and it is the latter which is then discussed. For a magnetic system the 'scaling law' assumption can be expressed in the following form: Near the critical point the singular part of the magnetic Gibbs free energy is asymptotically a generalized homogeneous function of $\tau = T - T_c$ and $\mathcal{H}$, i.e.

$$A'(\lambda^{a_\tau} \tau, \lambda^{a_{\mathcal{H}}} \mathcal{H}) = \lambda A'(\tau, \mathcal{H}) \qquad (3.35)$$

where λ is any positive number (Hankey and Stanley 1972). The constants a_τ and $a_{\mathcal{H}}$ are characteristic of the system. Corresponding homogeneity relationships can be derived for other thermodynamic quantities, enabling the critical indices to be expressed in terms of a_τ and $a_{\mathcal{H}}$. It follows that only two of the indices which refer to thermodynamic properties ($\alpha, \alpha', \beta, \gamma, \gamma', \delta$) can be independent. In particular, it is found that the relationships of Rushbrooke and Griffiths given above become equalities. 'Scaling' can also be applied to static and dynamic correlation functions, and these yield equations involving ν, ν' and η. A collection of 'scaling' relationships is contained in the paper of Hankey and Stanley (1972).

Table 3.7 shows the values of the indices predicted by some theoretical models. The indices are sensitive to the dimensionality of the system and also to the type of model e.g. mean-field, Ising or Heisenberg, but not to the actual crystal lattice or the spin number s (Ritchie and Fisher 1972) (see, however, section 3.7). For this reason discussion of real systems which are believed to be effectively one- or two-dimensional in character are frequently carried on in terms of the critical indices. Uncertainties in this approach can arise when the concentration of impurities or defects is such that their distance apart is less than or comparable with the correlation length (which goes to infinity as $T \to T_c$). Another difficulty lies in the uncertainty in

TABLE 3.7

Values of critical indices for various theoretical models
(after de Jongh and Miedema 1974).

	α	α'	β	γ	γ'	δ	η	ν	ν'
Mean-field	discont.		1/2	1	1	3	0	1/2	1/2
Ising $d=2$	$O(\ln)$	$O(\ln)$	1/8	1·75	1·75	15	0·25	1	1
Ising $d=3$	$\approx 0 \cdot 125$	$\text{to}^{0 \cdot 063}_{0 \cdot 125}$	0·312	1·25	$\text{to}^{1 \cdot 25}_{1 \cdot 31}$	≈ 5	$\text{to}^{0 \cdot 03}_{0 \cdot 05}$	$\approx 0 \cdot 63$	-
Heisenberg $d=3$	$\approx 0 \cdot 1$	-	$\approx 0 \cdot 36$	$\approx 1 \cdot 40$	-	≈ 5	$\text{to}^{0 \cdot 03}_{0 \cdot 04}$	$\approx 0 \cdot 71$	-

the location of the critical point itself. Although this
uncertainty may be small by ordinary experimental standards,
it can become important when deviations from the critical
values of, say, 1 part in 10^4 are the subject of examination.
For this reason, it is common to treat the critical parameter concerned as being adjustable and to choose both it
and the critical index so as to give the best fit to the data.
This procedure has, however, been strongly criticized by
Nagle (1975).

A more fundamental difficulty in the use of the indices
arises from the so-called Universality Hypothesis (Griffiths
1970). According to this, a real pseudo-two-dimensional
system, because it is in fact three-dimensional with very
weak interactions in the third dimension, will exhibit the
critical index values for a three-dimensional system when the
observations are carried sufficiently close to the critical
point. The more nearly two-dimensional the system is, the
closer to the critical point the observations must be taken for
the three-dimensional index values to be found. When interactions in the third dimension become zero there will be a
sudden change of the index to the value appropriate for a two-
dimensional system, but as this limit is approached the
range over which the three-dimensional values are found will
itself gradually disappear. Systems with a large amount of

mean-field character by virtue of the presence of long-
range interactions will likewise only yield the normal critical indices when the measurements are taken very close to
the critical point. The more long-range the forces, the
more restricted is the range within which the correct
asymptotic indices can be obtained (section 3.1.2). The
eight-vertex model studied by Baxter does not obey the
Universality Hypothesis, the values of the indices being
dependent upon the values of the interaction parameters,
instead of depending only upon the dimensionality and the
nature of the interactions (section 3.7).

As mentioned previously (section 2.5) Fisher (1968),
from a combination of intuition and theory, concluded that
in many real situations the indices actually observed would
not correspond to those for rigid systems, which have been
discussed in this chapter, but instead would be subject to
a renormalization process. The effect of this process
would be to convert the indices $\alpha, \alpha', \beta, \gamma,$ and γ' to
$-\alpha/(1-\alpha), -\alpha'/(1-\alpha'), \beta/(1-\alpha'), \gamma/(1-\alpha),$ and $\gamma'/(1-\alpha')$. Thus
the divergence of the heat capacity at the critical point
in the simple model is converted to a cusp (with a finite
discontinuity) on renormalization. The presence of impurities leads to similar effects.

For a substance exhibiting a tricritical point (section
2.6) in a non-ordering field, the indices should ultimately
go to the normal values, as given in Table 3.7, provided that
the non-ordering field is less than the tricritical value;
if this field has its tricritical value then the indices will
take up special values, the so-called tricritical exponents,
e.g. α_t, δ_t. For δ_t the defining path is to be taken as $T=T^*$,
$\mathcal{H} \rightarrow \mathcal{H}^*$. In terms of the ordering and non-ordering parameters (M'
and M) and the ordering and non-ordering fields ($\mathcal{H}'$ and $\mathcal{H}$) and
for $T < T^*$, the exponents may be defined by the relation-
ships $M' \sim (T^*-T)^{\beta_t}$, $(\partial M'/\partial \mathcal{H}')_{T,\mathcal{H}} \sim |T-T^*|^{-\gamma'_t}$, and
$C_M \sim |T-T^*|^{-\alpha'_t}$, where the path taken is $\mathcal{H}=\mathcal{H}^*$ (Griffiths
1973). Alternatively, a fixed-temperature path ($T=T^*$)
may be chosen, when the corresponding defining relation-
ships are $M' \sim |\mathcal{H}-\mathcal{H}^*|^{\beta_t}$, $(\partial M'/\partial \mathcal{H}')_{T,\mathcal{H}} \sim |\mathcal{H}-\mathcal{H}^*|^{-\gamma'_t}$, and
$(\partial M/\partial \mathcal{H})_{T,\mathcal{H}'} \sim |\mathcal{H}-\mathcal{H}^*|^{-\alpha'_t}$. For $T > T^*$, there are corresponding

definitions for α_t and γ_t. δ_t is defined as $(\partial M'/\partial \mathcal{H}')_{T,\mathcal{H}}$
taken along $T=T^*$. A set of subsidiary exponents (denoted
by the subscript u), which arise when considering the tricritical point as the limit of the first-order transition
line, has also been frequently used. For $T < T^*$, these are
defined from the equations $\Delta M \sim (T^*-T)^{\beta_u}$, where ΔM is the
difference in M of the two phases which are in equilibrium
$(\partial M/\partial \mathcal{H})_{T,\mathcal{H}'} \sim |T-T^*|^{-\gamma'_u}$, and $C_M \sim |T-T^*|^{-\alpha_u}$, all being taken
along the first-order line; α_u and γ_u are defined by equa-
tions similar to those for α'_u and γ'_u, but with the path
being that of constant magnetization, $M=M^*$. δ_u is defined
by $|\mathcal{H}-\mathcal{H}^*| \sim |M-M^*|^{\delta_u}$. If, however, the validity of scaling
is admitted, then the parameters of one type (say u) may be
expressed in terms of those of the other type (t) together
with a single additional parameter (Griffiths 1973).

In mean-field theory the main tricritical exponents
are known to be $\alpha_t=0$ (finite), $\alpha'_t=1/2$, $\beta_t=1/4$, $\gamma_t=\gamma'_t = 1$,
and $\delta_t=5$ (section 2.5). As the non-ordering field approaches
the tricritical value it becomes necessary to pursue measurements closer and closer to the critical point, e.g.
$|T-T_c|/T_c$ must be made smaller in the determination of β
(Nagle 1975).

3.4. THE PERCOLATION PROBLEM
In many real systems the entities which are capable of
being ordered are diluted by inert bodies, which occupy
some of the sites which could otherwise be filled by the
ordering particles. Alloys composed of ferromagnetic and
non-magnetic metals immediately come to mind as examples
of this kind of system. Another example, which will be
discussed in section 11.2.4, is that of a clathrate of a
polar molecule in which some of the cavities are vacant.
For these systems it is required to know how the dilution
affects the cooperative ordering processes, and, indeed,
whether the kind of catastrophic ordering behaviour associated with critical points will still occur at all.
Hammersley seems to have been the first to realize that
the problems presented by dilute ordering systems are
representatives of a larger class which have been given the

name 'Percolation Processes', because the archetype concerns the percolation of water through a system of pores,
as described below (Broadbent and Hammersley 1957).

Hammersley first considered what is now generally known
as the *bond* percolation problem. In this, 'atoms' are supposed to be arranged on the sites of a regular lattice.
'Bonds' are taken to be present between all nn pairs of
'atoms', some of these being designated as being 'blocked'
and some 'open'. This designation is carried out randomly.
The question is then asked, to what extent would the 'atoms'
be 'wetted' if the crystal were immersed in water and the
water could only pass along the 'open' bonds? The likeli-
hood that an infinite number of 'atoms' will be 'wetted'
turns out to be of particular importance. Hammersley was
able to show that the answer to the last question would be
the same as that to an equivalent percolation problem in
which one randomly chosen 'atom' near the centre of the
crystal was 'wetted' and water flowed from it along the
'open' bonds. Needless to say, the chance that an infinite
number of 'atoms' would be 'wetted' is dependent upon the
fraction of the total number of 'bonds' which have been
declared 'open'. As with the Ising model, this problem
has been solved exactly for a number of two-dimensional
lattices, but for no three-dimensional array. Numerical
solutions for some of the latter have, however, been obtained by Monte Carlo and series expansion methods. Fig.
3.15 shows the graphs of $P_\infty^b(p)$, the probability that an
infinite number of 'atoms' will be 'wetted', against p, the
fraction of the total number of 'bonds' which are 'open',
for several two- and three-dimensional lattices. It is
immediately seen that over a fairly small range of
$p, P_\infty^b(p)$ changes dramatically and, indeed, that there is a
critical value of $p (=p_c^b)$ below which $P_\infty^b(p)$ is zero.

The second problem which Hammersley recognized, the
atom percolation problem, is of more direct concern
to us. This differs from the bond problem in that here it
is the 'atoms', rather than the 'bonds', which are designated as being 'blocked' or 'open'. Fluid cannot 'wet'
or pass through a 'blocked atom'. In a ferromagnetic alloy,

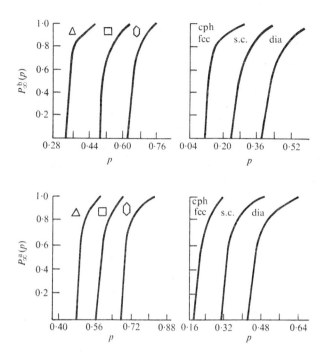

Fig.3.15. Percolation graphs for seven different lattices. The probability that an infinite number of 'atoms' will be 'wetted' in the
bond $[P^b_\infty(p)]$ and atom $[P^a_\infty(p)]$ problems against p, the fraction of the
total number of bonds or atoms which are 'open'. $\triangle$: triangular, $\square$
: square, $\lozenge$: hexagonal, s.c.: simple cubic, fcc: face-centred cubic,
dia: diamond cph: close-packed hexagonal (from Shante and Kirkpatrick
1971).

a 'blocked' site would be one occupied by a non-magnetic
atom, those occupied by ferromagnetic atoms being considered as 'open'. Once again we ask, What is the probability, $P^a_\infty(p)$, that fluid from a single, randomly chosen,
source 'atom' will 'wet' an infinite number of other atoms
if the probability of an 'atom' being 'open' is p? The
graph of $P^a_\infty(p)$ versus p is found to be similar in shape
to that for $P^b_\infty(p)$ (Fig.3.15). It can be shown that for
all lattices $P^a_\infty(p) \leq P^b_\infty(p)$ and $p^a_c \geq p^b_c$, the equality signs
only holding for $p=0$ or 1, or if the lattice is of a type
which is not of interest to us. Since for the ferromagnetic
netic alloy p is equal to the mole-fraction of ferromagnetic atoms, p^a_c is the mole-fraction of ferromagnetic atoms

below which there can be no infinite clusters of ferromagnetic atoms. In other words, for $p < p_c^a$ there can be no
long-range ferromagnetic order and no ferromagnetism.

Fisher (1961a) has shown that a bond problem on any
lattice can be transformed to an atom problem; it is not
generally possible to transform any atom problem into a
corresponding bond problem. When, however, a bond and
an atom problem are related by such a transformation the
solution of one leads immediately to the solution of the
other, and, in particular, the critical probabilities for
the two problems are equal. Table 3.8 shows the values of

TABLE 3.8

*The critical percolation probabilities of the bond (p_c^b) and
atom (p_c^a) problems for several lattices; q = lattice coordination number (after Shante and Kirkpatrick 1971).*

Lattice	q	p_c^b	p_c^a
Hexagonal	3	0·6527	0·700
Kagome (Fig.3.6d)	4	-	0·653
Quadratic	4	0·5	0·590
Triangular	6	0·3473	0·5
Diamond	4	0·388	0·425
Simple cubic	6	0·247	0·307
Body-centred cubic	8	0·178	0·243
Face-centred cubic	12	0·119	0·195
Hexagonal close-packed	12	0·124	0·204

the critical probabilities for several two- and three-
dimensional lattices, together with the lattice coordination number (q). As a rough guide to memory or prediction
it can be seen that for two- and three-dimensional lattices
$p_c^b \simeq 2/q$ and $\simeq 1·5/q$, respectively.

In all the work reported so far it has been assumed
that the distribution of 'blocks' is completely random.

If, however, there is some short-range positional order of
the 'blocks' then the results would be modified. Studies
have also been made on more complicated bond problems in
which a bond may permit passage of water in one direction
but not in the other. No further mention of these will,
however, be made in this book.

3.5. EFFECTS OF THE FINITE SIZE OF THE SYSTEM

For finite systems the partition function is the sum of a
finite number of analytic terms and must, therefore, itself
be analytic. Only for an infinite system can the partition
function and the thermodynamic functions be singular. However, it is to be expected that maxima in the heat capacity
and magnetic susceptibility will be found near to the point
at which the singularity develops as the size of the system
is increased to infinity.

Two kinds of calculation on finite systems must be distinguished: those with periodic boundary conditions and
those with free boundaries. The former are far more common,
but it is not completely clear what they correspond to; the
latter, on the other hand, clearly correspond to real systems, and this section will be mainly devoted to them.

Unfortunately, even in two dimensions there is no
general expression which gives the exact solution for finite
Ising systems of varying size. Numerical studies on very
small square lattices (2×2, 3×3, 4×4) (Ferdinand and Fisher
1969) suggest that the temperature of the heat capacity
maximum $[T_c(n)]$ was below that for the infinite system by
an amount of order n^{-1}, where n is the number of spin sites
in each direction, their actual expression being
$1-T_c(n)/T_c \simeq 1\cdot35/n$. For a quadratic Ising system of size
$n\times\infty$, Onsager (1944) found that the magnitude of the molar
heat capacity maximum was related to n by the equation:
$C/R=0\cdot48\ln n+0\cdot21$. Numerical studies have also been made
on simple cubic Ising arrays which are of finite extent in
one dimension but infinite in the other two. Using the
high-temperature series expansion method to locate the
critical temperature, Allan and Fisher (briefly reported
in Watson 1972a) concluded that the deviation of $T_c(n)$ from

$T_c(\infty)$ was as $0(n^{-1/\nu})$ where n is the number of sites in the finite dimension and ν is the index describing the way in which the correlation range goes to infinity at the critical point.   One way of interpreting this conclusion is to assume that the effect of finite size will become important when the finite linear dimension (n) is comparable with the cor- relation range for pairs of spins (κ^{-1}).   Since $\kappa^{-1} \sim |T-T_c|^{-\nu}$ near $T_c(\infty)$, the size effect should be important in a tem- perature region centred on $T_c(\infty)$ and of size $\propto n^{-1/\nu}$.   For the same system the magnetic susceptibility for the finite lattice at the critical temperature of the infinite lattice goes to infinity as $n^{\gamma/\nu}$ as $n \to \infty$, and the heat capacity is thought to diverge in a similar fashion as $n^{\alpha/\nu}$.

   Monte Carlo computations for simple quadratic Ising lattices with up to 110×110 spins have been carried out in zero and non-zero field (Stoll and Schneider 1972).   As with other Monte Carlo studies near critical points the con- vergence was not always good, even though 10^4 steps per Ising spin were allowed.   It was found that even with this large number of spins the relative magnetization (M/M_{sat}, where M_{sat} is the saturation magnetization) increased with the number of spins for fixed values of T and $\mathcal{H}$.   In zero field it was also found that application of the usual perio- dic boundary conditions caused M_0 and χ_T to increase.   The Monte Carlo estimate of the critical temperature in zero field was also affected by the boundary conditions: for the free surface (no boundary conditions) and ordinary periodic boundary conditions T_c was found to be, respective- ly, lower and higher than the rigorous value for the $\infty \times \infty$ lattice.   The latter observation can be understood as a stabilization of the ordered structure by the imposition of the boundary conditions.

   An extensive discussion of finite systems, including results obtained with periodic boundary conditions and for some non-Ising systems, has been given by Watson (1972b). In general, however, it is comforting to know that for normal samples containing $\sim 10^7$ interacting 'spins' in each direction it is only when the temperature is within about 1 part in 10^7 of the critical temperature of the infinite system that the size effects become important (Domb 1967).

3.6. EFFECTS OF LATTICE VIBRATIONS

So far in this chapter the possibility of coupling between
the order-disorder process and the vibrations of the lattice
has been neglected.

Attempts to deal with this problem have been made which
employ the Einstein model (Booth and Rowlinson 1955) and
the Born-von Karman model (Wojtowicz and Kirkwood 1960) for
the vibrational modes. The latter paper, which considers
the disordering of a 1:1 alloy, treats the order-disorder
problem by means of a method, devised by Kirkwood, which
is related to the Bethe-Guggenheim approximation (section
3.1.3). Other approximations arise from the use of a perturbation treatment, the unperturbed state being a lattice
in which all particles have the mean mass and all force
constants also have the average value. In order to be
able to neglect terms beyond the second order, it was
necessary that the masses of the atoms and the force constants should deviate little from the mean. Other approximations, whose validity is less clear, are also made. For
β-brass, to which the theory is applied, T_c is reduced to
about one-half of the value obtained if lattice vibrations
are ignored; likewise, the discontinuity in C_V is increased
from $1\cdot7R$ to $6\cdot1R$. These striking changes are in qualitative accord with those found when the Einstein model
was employed (Booth and Rowlinson 1955).

A related problem, the calculation of the frequency
distribution for disordered lattices has been successfully
attacked by Dean and coworkers (Dean 1972). The method
and results may be exemplified by the paper of Dean and
Bacon (1965), in which they examined the completely disordered solid solutions on quadratic and hexagonal lattices.
Having placed ~1000 particles (of types A and B) on the
sites randomly, the dynamics of the system was examined
numerically. By performing the same kind of computation
for various initial placements, chosen randomly, they were
able to construct a histogram showing the number of lattice
modes in each frequency range. One feature of their results

is that if one starts with pure solid A and introduces a
small amount of B (the lighter species) some impurity peaks
appear in the frequency distribution curve which correspond
to the presence of isolated B atoms. These are very
localized modes. As the concentration of B is increased
other peaks associated with clusters of B atoms of various
size grow. Above a critical mole-fraction of $0 \cdot 5 - 0 \cdot 7$ for
the quadratic and ~$0 \cdot 5$ for the hexagonal lattice the individual cluster peaks become smeared into a general, smooth
curve. These critical values may be compared with the P_c^a
values for the equivalent Percolation Problems (section 3.4).
It is obvious that such modifications of the frequency distribution curve will affect the thermodynamics of the order-
disorder transition, but, so far, these consequences have
not been evaluated. To do this it would be necessary to study
systems with intermediate degrees of order, whereas Dean's
work has been confined to the completely disordered and, of
course, the completely ordered situations. Other studies of
the frequency spectra of disordered alloys have been made,
particularly by Elliott and coworkers (Elliott and Taylor
1967, Aiyer, Elliott, Krumhansl, and Leath 1969, Leath and
Goodman 1969).

3.7. MODELS FOR HYDROGEN-BONDED SYSTEMS

In recent years considerable effort has been devoted to
models of hydrogen-bonded substances, some of them ferroelectrics and antiferroelectrics, which present similar
difficulties to those encountered, and to some extent overcome, with Ising problems (Lieb and Wu 1972). The basis
of all these treatments is the model used by Pauling in 1935
for ordinary ice. In this structure each O atom was known
to be surrounded tetrahedrally by four other O atoms, but
the disposition of the H atoms was more doubtful. In the
model used by Pauling the H atom on any O--H--O bond could
be in either of two potential minima, symmetrically placed
with respect to the centre of the bond. He further made
the important restriction that of the four H atoms which
were neighbours to each O atom, two should be in the nearer
and two in the more remote wells. These requirements are

known as the 'ice laws'. The permitted environments of any
O atom are represented diagramatically in Fig.3.16 (a), (b),
(c), (d), (e), and (f), where an arrow pointing towards the

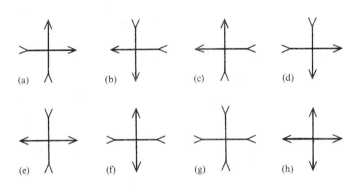

Fig.3.16. 'Ice' vertices. Arrow pointing inward (outward) indicates
that the proton is in the near (far) potential well of the hydrogen bond.

vertex indicates that the H atom on that bond is in the
well which is nearer to the O atom, and *vice versa*. Configurations such as (g) and (h) would not be allowed since
in them all four H atoms are in the near and remote wells,
respectively. Pauling put forward an approximate solution
to this problem (section 8.1), but no exact solution has
been found. However, Lieb (1967a) has solved a problem
which is a two-dimensional projection of the true problem.
He placed the O atoms at the vertices of a simple quadratic
lattice and evaluated the number of configurations of the
whole lattice in which the 'ice laws' were obeyed. He thus
assigned equal energies to the six allowed vertex environments.

A similar model for the ferroelectric KH_2PO_4 (KDP), in
which the PO_4 ions replace the O atoms of the ice model,
had been proposed by Slater (1941). The same six vertex
arrangements were permitted, but (a) and (b) were regarded
as being of lower energy than the remainder (Table 3.9).

TABLE 3.9

*Energy schemes for various proposed vertex models. ε is to
be taken as positive*

	(a)	(b)	(c)	(d)	(e)	(f)	(g)	(h)
Ice	0	0	0	0	0	0	∞	∞
Slater KDP	0	0	ε	ε	ε	ε	∞	∞
Rys F	ε	ε	ε	ε	0	0	∞	∞
Wu	ε	ε	ε	ε	0	0	2ε	2ε
Baxter 8-vertex	ε_1	ε_1	ε_2	ε_2	ε_3	ε_3	ε_4	ε_4

Since (a) and (b) both have their polarization along the
$x=y$ axis, whereas (c) and (d) have theirs along the $x=-y$
axis and (e) and (f) show no polarization at all, this energy
scheme simulates the preference of the substance for polarization along a particular axis.

For antiferroelectrics Rys (1963) put forward a model
with the same six allowed vertices, but with the energy
scheme chosen so as to favour the unpolarized arrangements
(e) and (f) (Table 3.9).

The Slater KDP and Rys F models have been solved exactly
in finite as well as in zero field (Lieb 1967b,c), and in
this respect greater progress has been made than with the
Ising model. The E-T phase diagrams for both models are
shown in Fig.3.17. For $E=0$ both models display transitions
at ε/kT_c = ln 2, though for KDP it is partly isothermal
(with a latent heat of $\varepsilon/2$ per vertex), whereas for the F
model it is of infinite order, with all the free-energy
derivatives being continuous through the transition. For
KDP in a non-zero field the latent heat disappears and T_c
increases. Both with and without the applied field
$C \sim (T-T_c)^{-1/2}$ for $T \rightarrow T_{c+}$, but $C=0$ at all temperatures below
T_c (Fig.3.18). The transition in the F model also changes
its character on applying a field and C diverges as
$(T-T_c)^{-1/2}$ for $T \rightarrow T_{c+}$. Below T_c, C is unaffected by the

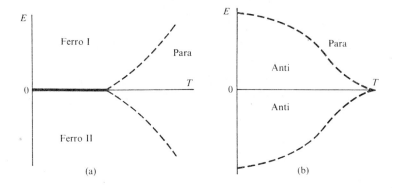

Fig.3.17. E-T phase diagram for (a) the Slater KDP model, (b) the Rys F model. Bold line: first-order transition line; broken line: second-order transition line. Ferro, Antiferro, and Para indicate regions of ferroelectric, antiferroelectric and paraelectric phases, respectively. Two mirror-image ferroelectric phases are shown for the KDP model. E is taken to be vertical (from Nagle 1975).

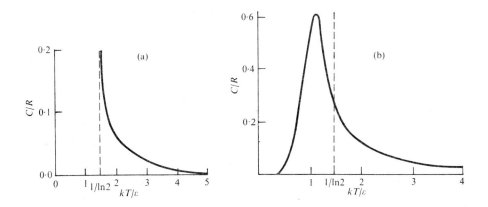

Fig.3.18. Heat capacity (C) against temperature for (a) the KDP model and (b) the Rys F model in zero field. Broken line: transition temperature (after Lieb and Wu 1972).

application of the field and has a shape reminiscent of a
Schottky anomaly (Fig.3.18). A related model for KDP, employing the mean-field approximation, is discussed in section
7.7 (see also Fig.7.51).

An alternative model of an antiferroelectric, which
turns out to be much easier to solve, has been treated by
F.Y. Wu (1969a,b). His model differs from that of Rys in
allowing the 'ionized' vertices (g) and (h), to which he
assigns the energy 2ε (Table 3.9). This problem can be
transformed into the quadratic Ising model, and as a consequence C shows a logarithmic singularity at the transition
point in zero field.

An important advance was made by Baxter (1972), who
solved rigorously for zero field a two-dimensional problem
of considerable generality (Table 3.9). All the other
models discussed in this section can be seen to be special
cases of this model. The most interesting feature of the
results obtained is that the critical exponents vary
smoothly as the values of the four parameters are varied,
thus exposing a breakdown of the Universality Hypothesis
(section 3.3). The general formulae for the heat capacity
exponents are:

$$2-\alpha = 2-\alpha' = \pi/\bar{\mu} \qquad\qquad (3.36)$$

where $\bar{\mu} = \cos^{-1}[(ab-cd)/(ab+cd)]$, $a = \exp(-\varepsilon_1/kT)$,
$b = \exp(-\varepsilon_2/kT)$ $c = \exp(-\varepsilon_3/kT)$, and $d = \exp(-\varepsilon_4/kT)$. For
certain special cases, and notably when $\varepsilon_4=0(d=0)$, equation
(3.36) is not applicable and separate consideration of the
critical exponents is necessary. In addition to the above,
rigorously obtained, results, formulae have been suggested
for other exponents. Barber and Baxter (1973) argued
forcibly that all the critical exponents should be linear in
$\pi/\bar{\mu}$, and in particular that $\beta = \pi/(16\bar{\mu})$. When they also
assumed the validity of scaling laws they obtained the
further values $\gamma=7\pi/(8\bar{\mu}) = 1/4$ and $\delta=15$. It is important to
realize that Baxter's solution does not apply to non-zero
field, and as a consequence not all of Lieb's (1967) results can be obtained from it. F.Y. Wu (1969a), who

had first proposed the model, had already shown that it could be transformed to a complicated type of Ising problem on a quadratic lattice which contained 'crossed bonds' and 'four-spin' interactions, the energy of a configuration being given by:

$$E = -\frac{J}{s^2} \underset{\underset{\text{hnn}}{i>j}}{\sum} s_i^z s_j^z - \frac{J'}{s^2} \underset{\underset{\text{vnn}}{i>k}}{\sum} s_i^z s_k^z - \frac{J''}{s^2} \underset{\underset{\text{NEnnn}}{i>l}}{\sum} s_i^z s_l^z - \frac{J'''}{s^2} \underset{\underset{\text{NWnnn}}{i>m}}{\sum} s_i^z s_m^z -$$

$$-\frac{J_4}{s^4} \underset{[ijkl]}{\sum} s_i^z s_j^z s_k^z s_l^z \qquad\qquad (3.37)$$

The first two terms are concerned with horizontal (hnn) and vertical (vnn) nearest neighbours; the third and fourth terms relate to next nearest neighbour interactions in the two possible diagonal directions indicated by N(orth) E(ast) and N(orth) W(est); the final term, which is concerned with a special interaction (over and above that given by the previous terms) of four spins situated at the corners of the smallest square on the lattice, does not appear to corres- pond to any realistic physical interaction. If the diagonal and 'four-spin' terms are omitted, correspondence between the Ising and the eight-vertex model is achieved if $\varepsilon_1 = -J-J'$, $\varepsilon_2 = J+J'$, $\varepsilon_3 = J'-J$ and $\varepsilon_4 = J-J'$. Many dimer models (section 3.8) can also be transformed into the eight-vertex model.

Salinas and Nagle (1974) have proposed and solved exactly a two-dimensional model for the hydrogen-bonded solid $SnCl_2 \cdot 2H_2O$. The solution, which was achieved by means of a transformation to an equivalent Dimer Problem, will be discussed in section 8.4. Nevertheless, it is worthy of note that they found $\alpha = \alpha' = 0(\log)$, as for a simple two-dimensional Ising model and in contrast to most other common hydrogen-bond models, except that of Wu. The solutions of two similar problems representing hydrogen- bonded solids, $NaH_3(SeO_3)_2$ and $Cu(HCOO)_2 \cdot 4H_2O$, are des- cribed in the next section.

3.8. DIMER PROBLEMS
This is another class of problem which shows relationships

to the Ising problem. The relevance to real systems is
shown in its simplest form by considering $Hg(NH_3)_2Cl_2$
(section 6.2), in which the NH_3-Hg-NH_3 units are distributed
virtually randomly on a simple cubic lattice with each unit
occupying two neighbouring lattice sites. To calculate
the zero-point entropy, therefore, it is necessary to know
the number of ways in which 'dimers' can be put onto the
cubic lattice so as just to fill all the lattice positions.
Once again, the three-dimensional problem has resisted solution but the corresponding two-dimensional problem has been
exactly solved (Fisher and Temperley 1960, Fisher 1961b,
Kasteleyn 1961). Fisher considered the situation where the
internal partition functions of the horizontal and vertical dimers are different, z_1 and z_2 being their respective activities [if the dimers lack internal degrees of
freedom, then if ε_1 and ε_2 are the energies associated with
the two dimer orientations, $z_1 = \exp(-\varepsilon_1/kT)$ and
$z_2 = \exp(-\varepsilon_2/kT)$]. His result for the partition function of
a $m \times n$ lattice was:

$$\lim_{m,n \to \infty} (mn)^{-1} \ln Q(z_1, z_2) = 1/2 \ln z_2 + 1/\pi \int_0^{z_1/z_2} \tan^{-1} v/v . dv$$

$$(3.38)$$

It follows that the free energy is a smooth function of z_1/z_2,
so that no separation of the system into phases of predominantly horizontal and vertical dimers would be expected.
The more general question of the number of ways of distri-
buting M dimers on N sites where $N > 2M$ (the monomer-dimer
problem) has not been solved even for this lattice, though
it is known that no transition is possible (Heilmann and
Lieb 1972). Kasteleyn has likened this last problem to
the Ising problem in non-zero field.

On the hexagonal or honeycomb lattice a transition
occurs when the activities of dimers with the three possible
orientations (z_1, z_2, z_3) are related by the equation
$z_1 = z_2 + z_3$. Below the temperature defined by this equation
the energy is constant and $\alpha' = 0$ (finite); above the transition temperature $\alpha = 1/2$ (Kasteleyn 1963).

Dimer problems also arise from the transformation of vertex models which have been proposed to simulate the layer-like hydrogen-bonded substances $NaH_3(SeO_3)_2$ (Nagle and Allen 1971), $Cu(HCOO)_2.4H_2O$ (Allen 1974) and $SnCl_2.2H_2O$ (Salinas and Nagle 1974).

In $NaH_3(SeO_3)_2$ each SeO_3 ion is joined to three similar ions by hydrogen bonds (Fig.3.19). In the theoretical model

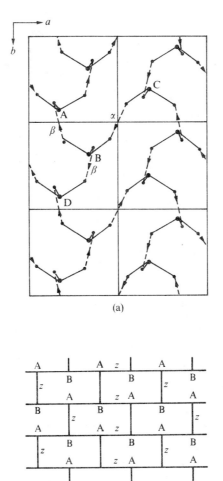

(a)

(b)

Fig.3.19. $NaH_3(SeO_3)_2$. (a) The assumed hydrogen-bond system showing SeO_3 ions belonging to the two sublattices (A and B). (b) The equivalent hexagonal lattice on which dimers must be placed. For significance of z see text (from Nagle and Allen 1971).

it is assumed that each such ion has either one or two
protons in positions close to it. If it is also assumed
that each nn SeO_3 adjacent to an ion having a single close
proton must itself have two close protons, and *vice versa* ,
then the SeO_3 arrangement breaks up into two equal sublattices
(A and B) which are together topologically equivalent to a
honeycomb lattice (Fig.3.19). Attention is now focussed
on those bonds in which the proton is near to an ion which
has no other near proton. Since each SeO_3 ion may participate in only one such bond the problem is reduced to the
Dimer Problem on the honeycomb lattice. Modifications in
which certain bonds are given higher activity (or lower
energy ε, where $\varepsilon < 0$) than others have also been solved.
Thus if all the vertical bonds of the honeycomb lattice are
given weight $v = \exp(-\varepsilon/kT)$ then a transition occurs when
$v=2$ at which $\alpha=1/2$ and $\alpha'=0$(finite). Again, if the bonds
designated z in Fig.3.19 are given weight z, then a transition at a temperature determined by the equation $v^2=2$ occurs
with the critical indices being again $\alpha=1/2$ and $\alpha'=0$(finite).
These variations, achieved by altering the weight given to
various kinds of bond, alter the ground-state arrangement
of the system but do not affect the entropy at infinite
temperature.

In $Cu(HCOO)_2.4H_2O$ the protonic ordering occurs between
the H_2O molecules which lie in layers between other layers
made up from Cu and HCOO ions (Fig.3.20). Two kinds of
oxygen atoms can be distinguished, types I and II having,
respectively, two and one near protons within the layer.
The arrangement of these oxygen atoms is shown in Fig.3.20.
By considering adjacent I-I and II-II pairs as A and B
units, respectively, the problem can be reduced to that of
placing oriented dimers on a square lattice (Fig.3.20).
Transitions, in which $\alpha'=0$ (finite) and $\alpha=1/2$, can be obtained from such a model. A modification in which parallel
nn dimer pairs are penalized leads, by means of a transformation, to an eight-vertex model for which Baxter's
solution is in good accord with experiment.

The actual properties of $NaH_3(SeO_3)_2$ and $Cu(HCOO)_2.4H_2O$
are discussed in detail in section 7.7 and section 8.4,

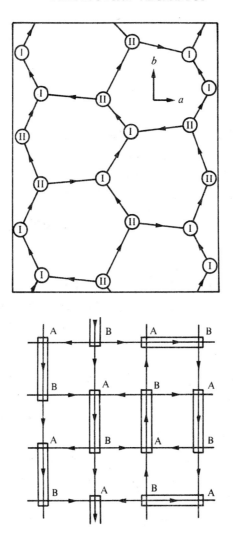

Fig.3.20. Cu(HCOO)$_2$.4H$_2$O. (a) The assumed hydrogen-bond system for the H$_2$O layers showing the two kinds of oxygen atoms (I and II) which have, respectively, two and one protons in near positions as indicated by the arrows. (b) The equivalent Dimer Problem. Each A unit corresponds to a I-I pair and has three incoming and one outgoing arrows; each B unit corresponds to a II-II pair and has one incoming and three outgoing arrows (from Allen 1974).

respectively. A further example of this type of problem, concerned with SnCl$_2$.2H$_2$O, is treated in section 8.4. In all of these Dimer Problems there is difficulty in defining an appropriate ordering parameter, and for this reason the exponents β, γ, γ', and δ have not been determined (Nagle 1975).

3.9. LATTICE MODE THEORIES OF TRANSITIONS

As opposed to the order-disorder models of transitions which have occupied all of this chapter so far, increasing recognition has been given in recent years to the validity, at least for some systems, of quite a different type of approach. For many years ferroelectrics had been divided into order-disorder-type and displacive-type, examples of the two kinds being KH_2PO_4 and $BaTiO_3$, respectively. It was considered that in KH_2PO_4 the order-disorder model of Slater was essentially correct, although it was difficult to reconcile this model with the vary large change in T_t which occurs on deuteration; in $BaTiO_3$ the mechanism was clearly connected with very small displacements of the constituent atoms. The ΔS_t values generally differed greatly, being much smaller for the displacive transitions, e.g. KH_2PO_4 ($3 \cdot 3$ J $K^{-1}mol^{-1}$) but $BaTiO_3$ ($0 \cdot 52$ J $K^{-1}mol^{-1}$). Initially, it was to treat the onset of ferroelectricity at displacive transitions that the present theory was developed by Anderson and by Cochran (1960), independently. The basic idea was that as the paraelectric phase was cooled towards the transition temperature one of the transverse optic modes with $\underline{k}=0$ became 'soft', i.e. its frequency became very small. At T_t a permanent displacement of one Bravais lattice with respect to another occurred, resulting in spontaneous polarization (since $\underline{k}=0$). (It was believed that the mode involved would have $\underline{k}=0$ because otherwise the individual sublattices would become distorted.) The explanation advanced for this shift of ν towards zero was that the contribution to the restoring force from the short-range interatomic interactions with the immediate neighbours was becoming counterbalanced by the contribution from the long-range coulombic interaction with polarizations in other parts of crystal. The temperature variation of the net restoring force was believed to arise from the anharmonicity of the short-range forces. Using a shell model for each ion, in which it was represented as a positively-charged core surrounded by a negatively-charged shell, Cochran was able to reproduce many of the properties of $BaTiO_3$ and similar displacive ferroelectrics. One result

which is considered to be characteristic of his theory is
that $\nu^2 \propto (T-T_t)$ for the 'soft' mode. A modification is
introduced by 'retardation' of the coulombic interactions,
the main effect being that the 'soft' mode is then one for
which $\underline{k}$ is not quite zero. An important feature of this
theory is that only the 'soft' or 'ferroelectric' mode is
appreciably changed in the vicinity of the transition. This
assumption has been borne out by subsequent neutron scattering experiments.

The Lyddane-Sachs-Teller equation for a cubic crystal
with two atoms per unit cell is $\nu_{LO}^2/\nu_{TO}^2 = \varepsilon_0/\varepsilon_\infty$, where ν_{LO}
and ν_{TO} are the frequencies of the longitudinal and trans-
verse optic modes at $k=0$ and ε_0 and ε_∞ are the total static
and electronic permittivities, respectively. It follows
that as ν_{TO} becomes small, ε_0 becomes large.

The theory also leads to the conclusion that the condition for the crystal to be unstable against the transverse
optic mode is;

$$\frac{4\pi}{9V_m} (\varepsilon_\infty + 2)(\alpha_0 - \alpha_\infty) = 1$$

where α_0 and α_∞ are the total static and the electronic
polarizability, respectively, and V_m is the molar volume.
Taken with the Clausius-Mosotti equation for the electronic
polarization this gives $4\pi\alpha_0/3V_m = 1$, which is the condition
for the so-called 'polarizability catastrophe'.

As considered so far, the transition would be second
order. If, however, more than one mode were involved the
transition would become first order and it would not be
necessary for any of the mode frequencies to approach closely
to zero.

The model has been described above in terms appropriate
to a cubic crystal. If the crystal is not cubic then it
is not possible to pick out optic modes which are truly
transverse. The essential features of the argument remain,
nevertheless, the same.

It now appears that this model, originally proposed
for displacive ferroelectrics, is much more widely applicable. It may be a mode other than a transverse optic one

which becomes 'soft', and $\underline{k}$ need not be at or near zero (the
zone centre). Antiferroelectric-paraelectric transitions,
for example, can be explained in terms of an equivalent model
with the 'soft' mode occurring at the Brillouin zone edge,
rather than the centre. It is clear that zero overall polarization will result when such a mode is 'frozen in'.

It is also thought that the 'soft' mode theory provides
an essentially correct description of many structural
transitions. In such transitions strains are usually strongly
coupled to the order parameter, thereby rendering them, at
least partly, first order. The quartz transition has also
been discussed in terms of this theory, a 'soft' $\underline{k}=0$ optical
mode being coupled to a pair of oppositely directed zone-
edge acoustic modes (Scott 1968).

Even KH_2PO_4 has been discussed in terms of the lattice
dynamical theory. The model used (Cochran 1969, Tokunaga
and Matsubara 1966) is one in which motion of the H atoms
between the alternative wells, which is considered to be
the primary process, is treated as cooperative tunnelling.
This ordering process then 'triggers' a lattice dynamical
transition involving modes which affect the coordinates of
the other particles (Fig.7.52). In this way it is possible
to explain both the large isotope effect and the fact that
P_s can be almost fully accounted for by the displacements
of the ions other than H. The H-bonds do, in any case, lie
in planes perpendicular to P_s and so cannot contribute
directly to it.

A 'triggering' mechanism has also been put forward to
account for the 'ferroelastic' effects of substances such as
$\beta\text{-}Gd_2(MoO_4)_3$. In this substance application of a stress
along the [010]-direction interchanges the a and b axes and
also reverses the polar direction. Since the dielectric
response is normal if the crystal is clamped it is assumed
that the spontaneous strain 'drives' P_s, but is itself
'driven' by the primary instability in a zone-boundary
lattice mode. Thus, the 'soft' mode proper is antiferroelectric, although, as a result of coupling, a non-zero value
of P_s is finally observed for the unclamped crystal (Axe,
Dorner, and Shirane 1971).

The transition in ND_4Br, which at first sight would seem
to be a case of simple order-disorder, is now thought to
involve coupling of the ND_4^+ orientation process with small
displacements of the Br^- ions (Shirane 1974) (Fig.7.28).
Coupling does not seem to be important in ND_4Cl. It might
be added that in some cases of coupling between processes
the decision as to which is primary and which secondary
appears to be rather arbitrary.

Samara, Sakudo, and Yoshimitsu (1975) have observed
that there are no known exceptions to the rule that for
displacive transitions T_t falls as p is increased for transitions involving zone-centre optical phonons, but rises as p
is increased if zone-boundary phonons are concerned. For the
former, the result may be explained in terms of the greater
sensitivity of the short-range (over the long-range) forces
to changes in pressure, the relative increase in the short-
range forces with increase in pressure tending to stabilize
the undistorted form. The explanation of the behaviour of
substances showing softening of zone-boundary phonons is
unclear.

In this book we are not concerned with displacive transitions to a great extent. Our interest in the lattice dynamical theory arises largely from its possible intrusion
into the field of order-disorder transitions, which is our
main concern. For more information on this theory and on
related experimental studies of ν-$\underline{k}$ dispersion the reader
is referred to the articles by Cochran (1960) and Shirane
(1974).

3.10. ENTROPIES OF TRANSITION

The choice of the model to be used to represent a particular
real order-disorder process is often decided, at least
in part, by an analysis of the entropy change associated with
the process[†]. A complication which may arise is that the
process is accompanied by an alteration in crystal structure

[†]The entropy change concerned may be entirely gradual, entirely isothermal, or part gradual and part isothermal. We shall discuss here
the complete entropy change arising from the disordering process, in
whatever manner this entropy is gained.

STATISTICAL MECHANICS

and a volume change, in consequence of which the lattice
vibrational frequency spectrum is altered, leading to an
associated entropy change which is incorporated into ΔS_t
(section 3.6). Where it is possible either to take this
into account (Oriani 1951, Hofmann and Decker 1953) or to
neglect it, it is often found that the entropy gain attributable to the disordering process itself is representable
with fair accuracy as $R \ln n$, where n is an integer or
simple fraction. This is illustrated in Fig.3.21, which

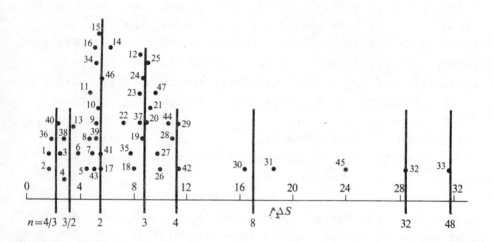

Fig.3.21. Values of ΔS_t in J $mol^{-1}K^{-1}$ for transitions in salts; n is the
simple fraction or integer for the values of ΔS_t given by the vertical
lines, where $\Delta S_t = R \ln n$. The height of the points above the baseline has
no significance. (1) NH_4NO_3,V→IV; (2) $RbNO_3$, II→I; (3) $TlNO_3$, III→II;
(4) KBH_4; (5) K_2SnCl_6; (6) n-amylammonium chloride, III→II; (7) $NaBH_4$;
(8) NaCN, III→II; (9) KCN, III→II; (10) NH_4Cl and ND_4Cl, III→II; (11)
NH_4I, III→II; (12) $NaNO_3$; (13) KNO_3, III→II; (14) $RbNO_3$, III→II; (15)
NH_4NO_3, IV→III; (16) n-amylammonium chloride (λ-transition in metastable
form of the salt); (17) $(NH_4)_2SiF_6$ (hexag.); (18) KCN, II→I; (19) NH_4Br,
II→I; (20) NH_4PF_6, II→I; (21) n-amylammonium chloride, II→I; (22) KNO_3,
III→I; (23) $RbNO_3$, IV→III; (24) $TlNO_3$, II→I; (25) $CsNO_3$, II→I; (26) NH_4PF_6,
III→II; (27) $RbPF_6$; (28) $(NH_4)_2SO_4.Al_2(SO_4)_3.24H_2O$; (29) $(NH_4)_2SO_4.Cr_2(SO_4)_3.$
$24H_2O$; (30) $(NH_4)_2SO_4$; (31) $(NH_4)_2SnBr_6$; (32) KPF_6; (33) $Ni(NO_3)_2.6NH_3$;
(34) KCNS; (35) $(NH_4)_2CuCl_4.2H_2O$; (36) NH_4CNS, II→I; (37) NH_4CNS, III→II;
(38) NH_4Br, III→II; (39) $SrCa_2(C_2H_5COO)_6$, III→II; (40) $SrCa_2(C_2H_5COO)_6$,
II→I; (41) RbCN; (42) NaCN, II→I; (43) $NaNO_2$; (44) CsCN; (45) $PbCa_2(C_2H_5COO)_6$
(46) $AgNO_3$; (47) NH_4Cl, II→I (from Newns and Staveley 1966).

shows the distribution of the measured entropy changes for
a number of transitions in salts (Newns and Staveley 1966).

The grouping around $R \ln 2$, $R \ln 3$ and $R \ln 4$ is evident.
This kind of behaviour is frequently found if in the disordered crystal some of the ions have a number of distinguishable orientations available to them of equal or approximately equal energy. If the crystal passes from a form in
which a molecule or ion has a number n_1 of distinguishable
orientations to one in which it has n_2 such orientations
then the entropy gain *on this account* is $R \ln (n_2/n_1)$. This
discussion assumes that the potential wells associated with
the various possible orientations are similar in shape. If,
on the other hand, the wells whose occupancy is increased
on going to the disordered form are narrower than those
occupied in the ordered form then the entropy change of
the transition would be correspondingly reduced. This particular complication, concerning as it does the vibration of
particles about their site positions, may be considered as
being part of the more general problem which arises from
changes in the lattice vibrational spectrum brought about
by disordering, and discussed earlier (section 3.6). In
one-component molecular solids any one molecule will have
identical molecules as its nearest neighbours and it may be
effectively prevented at any particular instant from adopting
some of the orientations which are in principle available to
it because of the orientations possessed at that moment by
its neighbours. For example, if the interaction energy
between nearest neighbours could take three values (0, J and
∞), according to the orientations of the two molecules, then
we would, in general, expect a transition at a temperature
proportional to J, but the evaluation of the entropy change
(and other properties) would be exceedingly difficult because of the effective elimination of some configurations by
the infinite potential term. The 'ice problem' (section
3.7), which may be considered to be similar to the above
example but with only two values for the potential energy
of interaction (0 and ∞), and which leads to no transitions,
illustrates the difficulties which can arise in calculating
the entropy of such a disordered structure. Further examples
of this are represented by the Dimer Problem (section 3.8)
and, in real systems, by the disordered phases of the hydrogen

halides (section 9.4). In inorganic salts and in clathrates
it often happens that the orientable entity is surrounded not
by similar particles but by other ions or molecules. These
passive nearest neighbours will, of course, be most important
in deciding which orientations are permissible, but they
can also be regarded as simplifying the problem by protecting
the central ion from the type of major interference discussed
immediately above, namely that which effectively eliminates
from consideration some of the possible arrangements. Thus,
at a temperature which is high but non-infinite the various
orientations will be approximately equally likely and the
entropy would be readily calculable. On the other hand, at
a corresponding temperature the solid without the passive
'diluent' would be in a disordered state for which the entropy could only be calculated with great difficulty.

REFERENCES

Aiyer, R.N., Elliott, R.J., Krumhansl, J.A., and Leath, P.L.
     (1969). *Phys.Rev.* 181, 1006.
Allen, G.R. (1974). *J.chem.Phys.* 60, 3299.
Axe, J.D., Dorner, B., and Shirane, G. (1971). *Phys.Rev.Lett.*
     26, 519.
Barber, M.N. and Baxter, R.J. (1973). *J.Phys.* C6, 2913.
Baxter, R.J. (1972). *Ann.Phys.* 70, 193.
Bean, C.P. and Rodbell, D.S. (1962). *Phys.Rev.* 126, 104.
Booth, C. and Rowlinson, J.S. (1955). *Trans.Faraday Soc.* 51,
     463.
Bragg, W.L. and Williams, E.J. (1934-5). *Proc.R.Soc.* A145,
     699; A151, 540; A152, 231.
Broadbent, S.R. and Hammersley, J.M. (1957). *Proc.Camb.phil.
     Soc.* 53, 629.
Clark, R.K. (1968). *J.chem.Phys.* 48, 741.
——   and Neece, G.A. (1968). *J.chem.Phys.* 48, 2575.
Cochran, W. (1960). *Adv.Phys.* 9, 387.
——   (1969). *Adv.Phys.* 18, 157.
Dean, P. (1972). *Rev.mod.Phys.* 44, 127.
——   and Bacon, M.D. (1965). *Proc.R.Soc.* A283, 64.
De Jongh, L.J. and Miedema, A.R. (1974). *Adv.Phys.* 23, 1.

Domb, C. (1960). *Adv. Phys.* $\underline{9}$, 149, 245.

────── (1966). In *Critical phenomena, Proceedings of a Conference, Washington, D.C., 1965*. U.S. Dept. Commerce and N.B.S. Misc. Pubns. No. 273, p.29.

────── (1967). *Proc. Low Temperature Calorimetry Conf., Helsinki, 1966; Ann.Acad.Sci.Fenn.*, Ser. A6, $\underline{210}$, 167.

and Green, M.S. (1972-) (eds.) *Phase transitions and critical phenomena*. Vol.1 (1972); Vol.2 (1972); Vol.3 (1974); Vol.5a (1976); Vol. 5b (1976). Academic Press, London and New York.

────── and Miedema, A.R. (1964). *Prog.Low.Temp.Phys.* $\underline{4}$, 296.

Elliott, R.J. and Taylor, D.W. (1967). *Proc.R.Soc.* A296, 161.

Ferdinand, A.E. and Fisher, M.E. (1969). *Phys.Rev.* $\underline{185}$, 832.

Fisher, M.E. (1960). *Proc.R.Soc.* $\underline{A254}$, 66.

────── (1961a). *Phys. Rev.* $\underline{124}$, 1664.

────── (1961b). *J.Math.Phys.* $\underline{2}$, 620.

────── (1966). In *Critical phenomena, Proceedings of a Conference, Washington D.C., 1965*. U.S. Dept. Commerce and N.B.S. Misc. Pubns. No.273, (a) p.21; (b) p.210.

────── (1967). *Rep.Prog.Phys.* $\underline{30}$, 615.

────── (1968). *Phys.Rev.* $\underline{176}$, 257.

────── (1969). *Phys.Rev.* $\underline{180}$, 594.

────── and Burford, R.J. (1967). *Phys.Rev.* $\underline{156}$, 583.

────── and Temperley, H.N.V. (1960). *Rev.mod.Phys.* $\underline{32}$,1029.

Fosdick, L.D. (1963). In *Methods in computational physics* (eds. B.Alder, S.Fernbach, and M.Rotenberg), Vol.1. Academic Press, New York and London.

Fowler, R.H. and Guggenheim, E.A. (1956). *Statistical thermodynamics*, p.576, Cambridge University Press.

Friedman, Z. and Felsteiner, J. (1974). *Phys.Rev.* $\underline{B9}$, 337.

Garland, C.W. and Renard, R. (1966). In *Critical Phenomena, Proceedings of a Conference, Washington, D.C., 1965*. U.S. Dept. Commerce and N.B.S. Misc. Pubns. No.273, p.202.

Ginzburg, V.L. (1961). *Sov.Phys.Solid State*, $\underline{2}$, 1824.

Gonzalo, J.A. (1970). *Phys.Rev.* $\underline{B1}$, 3125.

Green, H.S. and Hurst, C.A. (1964). *Order-disorder phenomena* Interscience, London, New York and Sydney.

Griffiths, R.B. (1967). *J.Math.Phys.* $\underline{8}$, 478.

────── (1970). *Phys.Rev.Lett* $\underline{24}$, 1479.

Griffiths, R.B. (1972). In *Phase transitions and critical phenomena* (eds. C. Domb, and M.S.Green) Vol.1., p.7. Academic Press, London and New York.

———   (1973). *Phys.Rev.* B7, 545.

Hankey, A. and Stanley, H.E. (1972). *Phys.Rev.* B6, 3515.

Heilmann, O.J. and Lieb, E.H. (1972). *Commun.Math.Phys.* 25, 190.

Hill, T.L. (1956). *Statistical mechanics.* (a) p.293; (b) p.343. McGraw-Hill, New York, Toronto and London.

Hofmann, J.D. and Decker, B.F. (1953). *J.phys.Chem.* 57, 520.

Hone, D., Montano, P.A., Tonegawa, T., and Imry, Y. (1975). *Phys.Rev.* B12, 5141.

Huberman, B.A. and Streifer, W. (1975). *Phys.Rev.* B12, 2741.

Kac, M., Uhlenbeck, G.E., and Hemmer, P.C. (1963). *J.Math. Phys.* 4, 216.

Kasteleyn, P.W. (1961). *Physica,* 27, 1209.

———   (1963). *J.Math.Phys.* 4, 287.

Kawatra, M.P. and Kijewski, L.J. (1969). *Phys.Rev.* 183, 291.

Landau, D.P. (1972). *Phys.Rev.Lett.* 28, 449.

Leath, P.L. and Goodman, B. (1969). *Phys.Rev.* 181, 1062.

Lieb, E.H. (1967a). *Phys.Rev.* 162, 162.

———   (1967b). *Phys.Rev.Lett.* 18, 1046.

———   (1967c). *Phys.Rev.Lett.* 19, 108.

———   and Wu, F.Y. (1972). In *Phase transitions and critical phenomena.* (eds. C.Domb, and M.S.Green) Vol.1, p.331. Academic Press, London and New York.

McCoy, B.M. and Wu, T.T. (1968). *Phys.Rev.* 176, 631.

———   ———   (1969). *Phys.Rev.,* 188, 982.

Münster, A. (1969). *Statistical thermodynamics,* p.298. 1st English Edition. Springer-Verlag, Berlin, Heidelberg, and New York.

Nagle, J.F. (1975). In *Treatise on solid state chemistry,* (ed. N.B.Hannay). Vol.5, p.20. Plenum, New York and London.

———   and Allen, G.R.(1971). *J.chem.Phys.* 55, 2708.

Neece, G. (1967). *J.chem.Phys.* 47, 4112.

Newns, D.M. and Staveley, L.A.K. (1966). *Chem.Rev.* 66, 267.

Onsager, L. (1944). *Phys.Rev.* 65, 117.

Oriani, R.A. (1951). *J.chem.Phys.* 19, 93.

Pauling, L. (1935). *J.Am.chem.Soc.* 57, 2680.

Pople, J.A. and Karasz, F.E. (1961). *(J.)Phys.Chem.Solids*, 18, 28.

Ritchie, D.S. and Fisher, M.E. (1972). *Phys.Rev.* B5, 2668.

Rys, F. (1963). *Helv.phys.Acta*, 36, 537.

Salinas, S.R. and Nagle, J.F. (1974). *Phys.Rev.* B9, 4920.

Samara, G.A., Sakudo, T., and Yoshimitsu, K. (1975). *Phys. Rev.Lett.* 35, 1767.

Scott, J.F. (1968). *Phys.Rev.Lett.* 21, 907.

Shante, V.K.S. and Kirkpatrick, S. (1971). *Adv.Phys.* 20, 325.

Shirane, G. (1974). *Rev.mod.Phys.* 46, 437.

Slater, J.C. (1941). *J.chem.Phys.* 9, 16.

Stanley, H.E. and Kaplan, T.A. (1966). *Phys.Rev.Lett.* 17, 913.

Stoll, E. and Schneider, T. (1972). *Phys.Rev.* A6, 429.

Thouless, D. (1969). *Phys.Rev.* 187, 732.

Tokunaga, M. and Matsubara, T. (1966). *Prog.Theor.Phys.* 35, 581.

Wannier, G.H. (1950). *Phys.Rev.* 79, 357.

Watson, P.G. (1972). In *Phase transitions and critical phenomena*, (eds. C.Domb, and M.S.Green). Vol.2 (a) p.155; (b) p.101. Academic Press, London and New York.

Widom, B. (1967). *J.chem.Phys.* 46, 3324.

Wojtowicz, P.J. and Kirkwood, J.G. (1960). *J.chem.Phys.* 33, 1299.

Wood, D.W. (1975). *Chem.Soc.Specialist Periodical Report, Statistical Mechanics*, Vol.2., p.55. Chemical Society, London.

Wu, F.Y. (1969a). *Phys.Rev.* 183, 604.

———   (1969b). *Phys.Rev.Lett.* 22, 1174.

4

EXPERIMENTAL METHODS

4.1. INTRODUCTION

In this chapter we shall review the more important experimental methods for investigating various aspects of order-disorder problems. We shall confine ourselves to approaches which have some generality. References to other kinds of investigation of more limited applicability will be found in later chapters. We shall not attempt to give a detailed exposition of either the theoretical basis of each method or of the relevant experimental technique, although the references cited will often provide further information on both of these matters. Our concern will rather be to illustrate the kind of information which each approach is capable of yielding. It will be appreciated that the various methods dealt with are frequently interdependent, in that an approach of one kind can often only be applied to the best advantage - or even usefully applied at all - when it draws on information provided by another.

4.2. THERMODYNAMIC STUDIES

Paramount among these is the calorimetric measurement of heat capacities, usually carried out by adiabatic calorimetry. On cooling a disordered substance, it may undergo a transition into an ordered phase, possibly followed at lower temperatures by one or more further transitions into still more ordered phases. A transition may be sharp (first order), wholly gradual, or partly gradual and partly isothermal. Many, probably most, transitions of this kind have been discovered calorimetrically, usually with low-temperature calorimeters operating roughly between 10 K and 300 K. It is possible, though less common, for the disorder to be 'frozen-in' on cooling, in which case the crystal at 0 K has residual entropy. The chief contribution which low-temperature calorimetry can make to the study of disorder in crystals, apart from the discovery of transitions to which other techniques can then be applied, arises from the possibility of interpreting the measured entropies of transition, residual entropies, and the heat capacities themselves.

If a transition is first order, there is usually no difficulty in making a precise determination of ΔS_t, the entropy of transition, since this is given by the ratio of the measured enthalpy of transition to the measured transition temperature. If the transition is partly or wholly gradual, ΔS_t is then given by $\int (C'_p/T)\,\mathrm{d}T$, where C'_p is the 'extra' or 'abnormal' contribution to the measured heat capacity, and the integral is taken over the temperature range in which the heat capacity appears to be 'abnormal'. There is often difficulty in deciding what the normal heat capacity is over the transition region. If this region is not too extensive, it is frequently possible to draw a reasonably reliable freehand heat capacity curve joining the experimental curve below the transition with that above. But sometimes the transition is very protracted, or alternatively is accompanied by a change in the 'normal' heat capacity, and then the evaluation of the 'extra' heat capacity is much more arbitrary. So it must be stressed that there is often an uncertainty associated with the values of ΔS_t for gradual transitions which is difficult to estimate but which is certainly not insignificant. (In some of the earlier literature especially, it is not always clear whether the quoted entropies and enthalpies of transition refer to the 'abnormal' contribution due to the transition, or to the *total* change in entropy and enthalpy over the most prominent part of the transition.) Sometimes, however, there are ways and means by which the reliability of estimates of ΔS_t in gradual transitions can be improved. One is to use as a reference the heat capacity curve of a substance which itself has no transition but which is isomorphous with the solid which does. At sufficiently high temperatures, say $T > \theta_D$, the Debye temperature, when the contribution to the overall heat capacity from the lattice vibrations is approaching the classical value, a plot of the difference in the heat capacities of the two substances can then make it easier to assess the 'abnormal' part due to the transition. At lower temperatures, it can no longer be assumed that the lattice (or background) heat capacity of the crystal under examination and that of the structurally similar reference substance will be approximately the same, but with some modification the device can still sometimes be used to good purpose. For example, Stout and his colleagues have analysed the heat capacity of anhydrous halides of transition metals in the region of their magnetic transitions by assuming that the lattice contributions to the entropy and heat capacity of a group of isomorphous solids obey the principle of corresponding states, in that these contributions are supposed to be a common function of an appropriately reduced temperature (Stout and Catalano 1955, Stout and Chisholm 1962). A suitable member of the group is chosen as a reference substance, which for the transition metal dichlorides may be either a diamagnetic salt such as $ZnCl_2$, or alternatively $MnCl_2$, which has its own magnetic transition at a much lower temperature than that in the other salts. Appropriate allowance can be made for the small residual magnetic heat capacity of the $MnCl_2$ in the region of higher temperatures in which the comparison with the other dichlorides is carried out. The lattice heat capacity and entropy of the salt under examination are then estimated by comparison with the reference substance by introducing a temperature reducing parameter, which in the simpler version of the treatment is regarded as temperature-independent, but which if necessary may itself be allowed to vary with temperature. By subtraction from the total heat capacity, the development with rising temperature of the magnetic heat capacity and entropy can then be revealed. As an illustration of this, we may cite the case of copper (II) chloride, $CuCl_2$. This substance shows a peak in its heat capacity curve at 24 K which marks the transition from an ordered antiferromagnetic state to the disordered paramagnetic condition. Since the Cu^{2+} ion has only one unpaired electron, the expected overall magnetic entropy gain for this transition is $R \ln 2$. Fig.4.1 shows the temperature dependence of the magnetic heat capacity and entropy. It will be seen that the heat capacity is 'abnormal' for a considerable range of tempera-

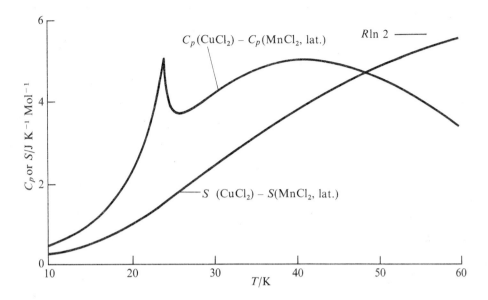

Fig.4.1. Temperature dependence of the magnetic heat capacity and entropy of $CuCl_2$, estimated using $MnCl_2$ to allow for the lattice heat capacity (Stout and Chisholm 1962).

ture above that of the peak in the heat capacity curve.   In fact, only about one-third of the magnetic entropy has been acquired by the time this peak is reached.   This is because the crystal of copper (II) chloride is essentially composed of parallel chains of the type

The peak marks the breakdown of the order due to the relative-ly weak magnetic interaction between the chains, but one-dimensional order still persists within the chains due to the stronger interaction between the copper atoms of one and the same chain, and this is only gradually dispelled.

        Another way of dealing in principle with the problem of the lattice or background heat capacity through the region of a gradual transition is to estimate it with the help of

theories of the heat capacity of crystals, but often the substances concerned are too complex for this to be possible.
The situation should improve as information on phonon spectra accumulates from the application of techniques such as
far infrared spectroscopy and slow inelastic neutron
scattering. However, many gradual magnetic order-disorder
transitions occur at such low temperatures (below 20 K or
so) that the lattice heat capacity is in any case small,
and may be represented with sufficient accuracy by such a
simple expression as aT^3 (the Debye T^3 expression), and
accordingly the ΔS_t values for such transitions have often
been estimated with relatively little uncertainty. It is
also possible to measure a magnetic heat capacity, independently of the lattice contribution, by purely magnetic measurements. The method was originally suggested by
Casimir and du Pré (1938). An account of the technique,
with examples of its potentialities, has been given by
Skjeltorp and Wolf (1973).

An indirect method of assessing ΔS_t for a first-order
phase transition is by studying the effect of pressure on
the transition temperature, and applying the Clapeyron
equation $dp/dT = \Delta S/\Delta V$. Even if one or both of the phases
only exists under pressure there is usually no difficulty
in measuring ΔV, the volume change at the transition, so
ΔS_t follows from the experimental values of ΔV and dp/dT.
This approach has been used to estimate the entropy change
on the interconversion of the high-pressure forms of ice.
The results obtained throw an interesting light on the
problem of which of the forms are ordered and which disordered (section 8.3).

To determine whether or not a crystal retains entropy
at 0 K, it is necessary to have two independent values
for the molar entropy of the compound at some stated
pressure p and temperature T, (e.g. at 1 atmosphere and
298·15 K). One of these values must be S(cal), where
S(cal) is the difference between the entropy S in the
defined state and the actual entropy of the crystal S_0 at
0 K, and is given by the equation

$$S(\text{cal}) = S - S_0 = \int_0^T (C_p/T)\,dT + \Sigma(\Delta H/T)$$

where the summation refers to phase changes. If the substance is a molecular compound, $S(\text{cal})$ should refer to the
ideal gas at a definite pressure at the temperature T.
There is usually no difficulty in determining the heat of
vaporization of a liquid by direct calorimetry, but the
determination of the heat of sublimation of a solid of only
moderate volatility is rather less easy, and is perhaps best
effected indirectly by vapour pressure measurements, though
to carry these out with sufficient precision may require a
sophisticated experimental technique. For such a substance,
the second independent figure for the molar entropy is
usually best obtained by a statistical mechanical calculation, using molecular parameters (moments of inertia and
intramolecular vibration frequencies) derived from spectroscopic data. This value of the entropy can be called
$S(\text{spec})$. It should be noted that the calculations leading
to $S(\text{spec})$ have usually taken no account of any consequences
of nuclear spin, and it should therefore be distinguished
from $S(\text{stat})$, in which these consequences are taken into
consideration. An example of a group of substances for which
it is important to distinguish between $S(\text{spec})$ and $S(\text{stat})$
are the deuterated methanes (section 9.7).

     For an ionic substance such as a salt hydrate there
is of course no possibility of calculating the entropy at
the reference temperature on a statistical basis. Instead,
it is necessary to resort to a study of a suitable equilibrium to obtain a value for the entropy, $S(\text{eq})$, for comparison with $S(\text{cal})$. In sections 6.2 and 8.4 examples will
be found of methods used to obtain $S(\text{eq})$, which include
experimental investigation of dissociation pressures (for
example, of a salt hydrate into the anhydrous salt and
water vapour), of appropriate solution thermodynamics, and
of the e.m.f. of a cell in which the reaction involves the
substance in question. If $S(\text{eq})$ or $S(\text{spec})$ exceeds $S(\text{cal})$
by more than the experimental uncertainty, then the crystal
retains entropy, $S(\text{res})$, at 0 K, given by

$S(\text{res}) = S(\text{eq}) - S(\text{cal})$, or $S(\text{spec}) - S(\text{cal})$. Here, how-ever, we must enter a caveat concerning the extrapolation of the measured heat capacities to 0 K in evaluating the in-tegral $\int_0^T (C_p/T)\,\mathrm{d}T$. Very often the C_p measurements are made to about 10 K and extrapolated to 0 K on the basis of the Debye T^3 law, with no risk of any serious mistake being made. On the other hand, there may be transitions below 10 K. For example, Worswick, Cowell, and Staveley (1974) made estimates of $S(\text{eq})$ for hexaammine nickel iodide, $\text{Ni(NH}_3)_6\text{I}_2$, and diammine nickel iodide, $\text{Ni(NH}_3)_2\text{I}_2$, by studying the two equilibria

$$\text{Ni(NH}_3)_6\text{I}_2(\text{s}) = \text{Ni(NH}_3)_2\text{I}_2(\text{s}) + 4\text{NH}_3(\text{g}); \qquad (4.1)$$

$$\text{Ni(NH}_3)_2\text{I}_2(\text{s}) = \text{NiI}_2(\text{s}) + 2\text{NH}_3(\text{g}) . \qquad (4.2)$$

All three nickel salts have magnetic transitions, from anti-ferromagnetic to paramagnetic forms, with $T \sim 58\cdot9$ K for NiI_2, $10\cdot8$ K for the diammine and $0\cdot3$ K for the hexaammine. Heat capacity measurements made to 5 K in each case would include the magnetic transition for the first two salts, but not for the hexaammine. In this case, therefore, a magnetic entropy term of $R\ln 3$ should be added to $S(\text{cal})$ for the hexaammine for comparison with the diammine and the anhydrous iodide. On the other hand, also at about $0\cdot3$ K, there is another transition in the hexaamminenickel iodide which is discussed in more detail in section 7.6. This has its origin in the partial removal on cooling of the de-generacy associated with each ammonia molecule as it rocks in its potential well, and it involves a very large molar entropy loss of $6R\ln 2$. In estimating $S(\text{cal})$ for the hexa-ammine using experimental values of ΔS^0 for reactions (4.1) and (4.2), this last transition should be disregarded if, in assessing $S(\text{eq})$, the 'ordinary' standard molar entropy of gaseous ammonia, at, say, one atmosphere and 25°C is used, since this last quantity is $S(\text{cal})$ or $S(\text{spec})$, and not an entropy which has allowed for a similar effect in crystalline ammonia at very low temperatures.

    The next task is the interpretation of ΔS_t or $S(\text{res})$

on a statistical basis. This may be very simple for some
solids, but for others it can present mathematical problems
of great complexity which have so far resisted exact solution. Some aspects of the analysis of ΔS_t values are discussed in section 3.10. It would appear that with transitions concerned with a gain in orientational disorder, the
chances of a simple statistical interpretation of ΔS_t are
best when the transition is such that ΔS_t can be estimated
reasonably accurately from the calorimetric measurements,
when the transition involves only a slight change in crystal
structure and a small volume change, and when it occurs at
lower rather than higher temperatures. In favourable circumstances, even a relatively small entropy change may be
significant, as for example in the transition of rubidium
nitrate from the rhombohedral form II to the face-centred
cubic form I at 564 K with $\Delta S_t = 0 \cdot 21R$. The crystal structure change here is so slight that a single crystal can
survive the transition without breaking up, and the ΔS_t value
may primarily reflect the increase in the number of available
orientations available to the nitrate ion from 6 in form II
to 8 in form I ($R \ln (8/6) = 0 \cdot 29R$).

When disorder persists to 0 K, it would seem that $S(\text{res})$
should be in some respects an easier quantity to interpret
than an entropy of transition, being free from some of the
complicating factors affecting ΔS_t. At the same time, the
difficulties due to the mutual interference of the ions or
molecules in the lattice still remain, and can make the
exact calculation of $S(\text{res})$ for some crystals impossibly
difficult. Perhaps the most famous example of this is
provided by the residual entropy of ice (section 8.1). A
further handicap is that the experimental values of $S(\text{res})$
sometimes carry a rather large uncertainty, as they are
obtained as a relatively small difference between the two
entropy values $S(\text{cal})$ and $S(\text{eq})$, or $S(\text{spec})$. Thus, sodium
sulphate decahydrate, $Na_2SO_4 \cdot 10H_2O$, retains entropy at 0 K
of approximately $R \ln 2$, but this is only about one per
cent of the molar entropy at 25°C.

In principle, the actual values of the heat capacity
of a crystal should throw light on the molecular or ionic

movement, but here it must be remembered that the heat
capacity which lends itself to theoretical analysis is that
at constant volume, C_V, rather than the measured C_p.[†] C_V can
be estimated using the thermodynamic relation

$$C_p - C_V = T\alpha^2 V/\kappa$$

if values of the coefficient of expansion α and of the isothermal compressibility κ are known. It is usually information on this last quantity which is lacking, and which is
laborious to obtain, so that relatively little use has been
made of this approach. Some of the experimental evidence
which disposed of the possibility that in particular cases
ions or molecules can freely rotate in the lattice took the
form of an examination of the C_V values, examples being
that of the ammonium ion in ammonium chloride (Lawson 1940),
and the molecules in the high-temperature, 'plastic' phase
of carbon tetrabromide (Marshall, Staveley, and Hart 1956).
For the latter substance, C_V was found to change very little
at the transition, retaining in the high-temperature phase
a value only slightly less than $6R$ (after deduction of the
contribution from the intramolecular vibrations), consistent with classical contributions from the lattice vibrations
and from torsional oscillations of the molecules, but not
with free rotation, where a value of $(9/2)R$ would have been
expected. Methane is another example of a crystal to which
an analysis of C_V has been applied (Smith, 1971). Clathrates
(Chapter 11) provide a rather special case in which consideration of the relation **between** heat capacity and temperature has been fruitful, since here it is possible to estimate
the heat capacity of the empty host lattice and so, by subtraction, obtain that of the guest molecules, which are
present in cavities of effectively constant volume.

[†]This statement may not be true in the immediate neighbourhood of a singularity. Fisher (1968) has argued that in this situation C_p is the
more fundamental quantity. According to his discussion, because of
the renormalization arising from the constant-volume constraint
(section 3.3), C_V would not be expected to diverge to infinity, and
in this respect would differ from the behaviour of the heat capacity
as predicted by most theories.

Sometimes the problems presented by the fact that the heat capacity measurements are made at constant pressure and not at constant volume can be circumvented by the use of a reference substance, as in the case of ammonium hexachloro-stannate (IV) [ammonium stannichloride, $(NH_4)_2SnCl_6$], where comparison of its heat capacity with that of the corresponding rubidium salt was used to show that the ammonium ions behave like restricted rotators, with a comparatively low barrier between one energy minimum and the next (Morfee, Staveley, Walters, and Wigley 1960). It may also be noted that the difference between C_p and C_V matters less as the temperature falls, becoming insignificant when dealing, for example, with a magnetic transition at low temperatures. C_p and C_V approach zero asymptotically as $T \to 0$ K, but more slowly than (C_p-C_V), which at low temperatures is proportional to T^7 (Wilson 1966).

The dependence of heat capacity on temperature in a gradual transition is in itself an interesting and important matter, since predictions of this dependence can be made on the basis of various statistical models. A relevant question which can sometimes be very difficult, if not impossible, to answer, is whether in such a transition the heat capacity reaches infinity or remains finite, and whether there is a discontinuity. Apart from the influence of incidental factors like traces of impurities, surface and particle size effects, the state of strain of the crystals and so on, a calorimetric value of a heat capacity is an average figure resulting from heating the sample over a temperature interval. Sometimes special efforts have been made to make this interval as small as possible. We show, in Fig.4.2, the heat capacity of potassium dihydrogen phosphate, KH_2PO_4, throughout the much-studied ferroelectric-paraelectric transition, carried out with a single crystal with temperature increments as small as 0·014 K (Reese and May 1967). The temperature of the heat capacity peak can be fixed to ~0·01 K, and the results can be used to examine quantitatively the temperature dependence of the excess heat capacity on either side of the peak. Nevertheless, even results obtained with such small temperature intervals do

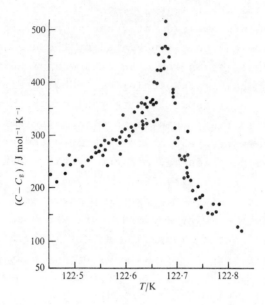

Fig.4.2. Heat capacity of KH_2PO_4 in the neighbourhood of the peak of the transition. The quantity plotted against temperature is the molar heat capacity C less the estimated lattice heat capacity C_g. The measurements were made with temperature intervals of between 0·014 K and 0·05 K (Reese and May 1967).

not enable an unambiguous decision to be made as to whether the transition is second-order or whether it is completed in a first-order transition of small latent heat. Another interesting study of this kind which probably represents the limit of what can be achieved by standard low-temperature calorimetry in its present state is that carried out on the salt hydrate $SnCl_2 . 2H_2O$ by Matsuo, Tatsumi, Suga, and Seki (1973). This showed that the transition in this compound appears in the heat capacity-temperature curve as a very symmetrical peak (Fig.8.18).

An unconventional technique which also makes it possible to measure heat capacities over very small temperature intervals ($\sim 0·01$ K) has been described by Handler, Mapother, and Rayl (1967). The method is well suited to the examination of the heat capacity in the immediate neighbourhood of the critical temperature of a λ-type transition, especially as the measurements can be made as the transition is approached

from above as well as from below. The specimen in the form
of a foil or thin crystal is periodically heated by radiation, for example by chopped light from a tungsten lamp
of constant intensity. The temperature changes of the sample
are converted by means of thermocouples into an a.c. voltage
which is amplified and measured. Schwartz (1971) has given
a detailed account of this technique, which he applied to
a study of the temperature dependence of the heat capacity
of ammonium chloride through the λ-transition at 242 K.

Much calorimetry concerned with disorder in crystals
has been limited to the region between ~10 K and room temperature, but in recent years a considerable amount of work
has been carried out from ~1 K to ~20 K, a region accessible
without magnetic cooling, and accurate adiabatic calorimetry
has also been extended above room temperature, notably by
Westrum. Some use has already been made of differential
scanning calorimetry (DSC), and this is likely to increase,
though at present the technique is inferior in accuracy to
conventional calorimetry, and less well suited to studying
the finer details of thermal anomalies. DSC and the related
technique of DTA (differential thermal analysis) have, however, obvious value in studies at higher temperatures and in
discovering transitions which may prove to be worth examining
by other methods. They also lend themselves to the investigation of the effect of pressure on the thermal characteristics of transitions. Thus, Trappeniers (1966) used DTA
to investigate the effect of pressure on the entropy change
at the λ-transition in ammonium chloride, with the surprising
discovery that the entropy of transition decreases with
rising pressure, having at 10^3 bar only about one quarter of
its value at atmospheric pressure. Pistorius and Rapoport
and their coworkers have employed DTA in their studies of
the phase diagrams of salts under pressure, references to
which will be found in Chapter 7. Würflinger (1975) has
described a DTA apparatus capable of operating from 70 K to
420 K and at pressures up to 3 kbar, with which he studied
transitions in hydrocarbons.

Occasionally, calorimetry can be applied to obtain
kinetic information. For example, on cooling ordinary ice

(ice-Ih) to ~100K, there is a slight tendency towards a
more ordered arrangement of the protons which gives rise
to a small but measurable heat evolution. By determining
the rate of this at more than one temperature, Haida, Matsuo,
Suga, and Seki (1972) obtained a value for the activation
energy for the relaxation process involved.

    In the study of magnetic ordering in paramagnetic salts,
an increasingly important part is being played by measurements of the heat capacity (and of the magnetization) in
magnetic fields. Much of the pioneering work in this field
of magneto-thermodynamics has been carried out by Giauque
and his collaborators. The heat capacity measurements are
usually made in the range ~0·01 K to ~4 K in fields which
may reach ~10^5G. To get sufficient precision, rather large
specimens of the substance under investigation have to be
used, which should be cut from single crystals and appropriately mounted with respect to the magnetic field, since
the properties under examination are anisotropic (Chapter 12).

    As already indicated, heat capacity measurements are
not particularly suitable for deciding whether a transition
is wholly gradual, or partly gradual and partly isothermal,
or for studying the thermal hysteresis sometimes associated
with transitions, (since heat capacity determinations are
much more easily made on warming than on cooling). These
aspects of a transition are better investigated by measuring
a property such as volume or permittivity (dielectric constant). Thus Fig.4.3 shows the dependence of volume on
temperature through the transitions in NH_4Cl and ND_4Cl
(Smits and MacGillavry 1933, Smits, Muller, and Kröger
1937), from which it would appear that the transition in
NH_4Cl is partly isothermal and displays hysteresis, while
that in ND_4Cl is wholly gradual and hysteresis-free (see,
however, p.328). In these investigations the volume changes
were measured dilatometrically, but there are other ways in
which the expansion or contraction can be followed; for
example, by X-ray diffraction, or by measuring the change in
length of a single crystal interferometrically. Another
possible technique, used by Fredericks (1971) on ammonium
chloride, is to make a single crystal of the salt determine

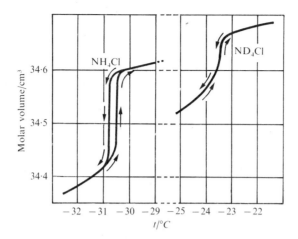

Fig.4.3. The temperature dependence of the molar volume of NH_4Cl and ND_4Cl in the final stages of the III-II transition (Smits *et al.* 1933, 1937).

the plate spacing of a capacitor, so that changes in crystal length are converted into changes in capacitance, which can be measured with great accuracy.

As might be expected, the effect of pressure on the thermal properties of disordered crystals and on the characteristics of transitions has been investigated in relatively few laboratories. Probably the most thoroughly studied system is ice, which illustrates the point that a crystal can remain disordered under extremely high pressures. Of the nine known forms of ice, three (all of them stable under pressure) have the hydrogen atoms in an essentially ordered arrangement, whereas in the other six forms these atoms are disordered, to a considerable extent at least, among the possible positions available to them. One of these forms, ice-VII, has been taken to ~200 kbar but still remains disordered. Undoubtedly, many interesting facts about the behaviour of other crystals when under pressure remain to be revealed. To give just one example, at ordinary pressures camphor can form a highly disordered crystal which has been quite thoroughly investigated (section 10.3); but at least eight high-pressure forms of camphor exist which still await examination.

If a transition has a discontinuous (first-order) stage, the magnitude of the volume change associated with this can be determined by studying the effect of pressure on the transition temperature providing the corresponding entropy change is known. Clusius and Weigand (1938) measured the small volume change at the III-II transition in H_2S and D_2S in this way. The observed effect of pressure on the temperature of the transition in solid hydrogen (section 9.2) was used by Ahlers and Orttung (1964) to show that the principal force operating to produce a preferred mutual orientation of the molecules is that between the molecular quadrupoles.

We shall end this review of experimental thermodynamic investigations of disorder by mentioning studies of the phase diagrams of two-component systems, namely temperature-composition diagrams at constant pressure. Sometimes these are carried out to examine the effect on a disordered crystal of replacing some of the molecules or ions by simpler ones incapable of the same kind of disorder. The way in which an order-disorder transition is affected by such dilution should be interpreted with the help of the results of studies of the Percolation Problem (section 3.4), provided that the assumption of random mixing of the components is acceptable for the system concerned. The system krypton-methane provides a case in point, since the krypton atoms cannot of course themselves have the orientational disorder which is possible for the methane molecules. Their presence in the mixed crystal, however, weakens the orientational forces between the methane molecules. Alternatively, binary systems have been studied where the two components separately show a rather similar behaviour. An example is the carbon tetramethyl - carbon tetrachloride system, and this and similar systems are discussed in section 10.6. Finally, a comparison of two phase diagrams may provide some information about the extent to which two pure crystalline substances resemble each other. Thus, from a comparison of the phase diagrams of the systems $Ar-N_2$ and $Ar-CO$, it appears that while the high-temperature, disordered phases of nitrogen and carbon monoxide are similar, they are not identical. (Barrett and

Meyer 1965 a,b).

4.3. DIFFRACTION METHODS

At some stage in a thorough investigation of a disordered crystal it is essential to examine its structure by a diffraction technique. Indeed, there are many examples of crystals in which the disorder was first revealed by a diffraction study. When, as so often happens, an ordered form of the substance also exists, it is valuable to determine its structure as well, for comparison with that of the disordered phase or phases. The technique most widely employed is, of course, that of X-ray diffraction, but considerable use has been made of neutron diffraction. Electron diffraction has been rather less frequently applied, but has sometimes provided useful information.

Positional disorder can arise either because there are more sites available to particles than there are particles to fill them, or because more than one kind of particle has access to a given set of lattice sites. The classic example of the latter situation, discussed in detail in Chapter 5, is found in alloys. Here, n_A atoms A and n_B atoms B have to occupy $(n_A + n_B)$ sites. Because of the difference in diffracting powers of the two atoms, lines appear in the diffraction pattern of the ordered crystal ('superlattice lines') which are absent from that of the ordered crystal. With regard to the positional disorder of the first kind, examples will be found in the so-called super ionic conductors discussed in Chapter 6; other instances of this type of disorder which have been discovered by diffraction work are provided by the mercury atoms in the compounds $Hg(NH_3)_2Cl_2$ and $Hg(NH_3)_2Br_2$ (Fig.6.9) and by the lithium ions in the monohydrates of lithium bromide and iodide (Fig.8.16).

Orientational disorder is disclosed in a diffraction study when it is found that the site symmetry of a particular molecule or ion is higher than the point-group symmetry of the molecule or ion itself. Numerous examples will be found in Chapters 9 and 10 on molecular crystals, where molecules of comparatively low symmetry can nevertheless crystallize

in a cubic phase. This can give rise to some remarkable
structural resemblances. Thus, the disordered high-temperature forms of cyclononanone, $(CH_2)_8CO$, and of fluorine have
cubic crystals with the same space group.

One of the early diffraction studies on a solidified
gas was that made by Simon and von Simson (1924) on hydrogen
chloride, which showed that the high-temperature form is
face-centred cubic, each molecule having twelve nearest
neighbours. This result prompted the suggestion that the
molecules of hydrogen chloride actually rotate in the lattice,
thereby acquiring effectively spherical symmetry. It is now
known that in such disordered crystals, with very few exceptions, the molecules do not rotate freely, but instead switch
from one orientation to another. In HCl-I, each molecule has
twelve orientations available to it. In principle, sufficiently precise diffraction studies should enable a decision
to be made between free rotation on the one hand, and jumps
between a limited number of possible orientations on the
other. Generally, the necessary precision in the intensity
measurements cannot be attained, but occasionally free
rotation can be ruled out in this way. Thus, in one of the
earliest neutron diffraction studies of its kind, Levy and
Peterson (1952) showed that the ammonium ions in ammonium
chloride above the λ-transition do not rotate, but that
the diffraction results are compatible with disorder of those
ions between two orientations. More recently, Sándor and
Farrow (1967) carried out a similar study of the high-temper-
ture phase of deuterium chloride, which supported the twelvefold disordered model, but not free rotation. This can be
seen from Fig.4.4, where the diffraction intensities calculated for free rotation and for twelvefold disorder are compared with those observed. An elegant example of the insight
which can be obtained into orientational disorder is provided by the work of Jordan, Streib, and Lipscomb (1964) on
the high-temperature form of fluorine (Fig.9.9) from which
they concluded that one-quarter of the molecules are disordered in three dimensions (spherically disordered), while
the remaining three-quarters are disordered in a plane
(cylindrically disordered). For CD_4-II, Press (1972) decided

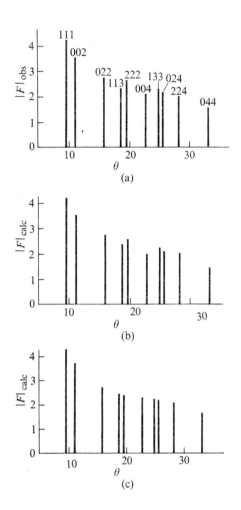

Fig.4.4. Observed and calculated structure factors F for the high-temperature face-centred cubic disordered form of DC1. (a) $|F|_{obs}$ from neutron powder diffraction experiments. (b) and (c) $|F|_{calc}$ for the twelvefold disordered model and the random-orientation model respectively (Sándor and Farrow 1967).

from his neutron diffraction study that here too the molecules fall into two groups, but now three-quarters of the molecules are ordered, while the remainder are orientationally disordered (and perhaps even rotating).

Orientational disorder can sometimes be strikingly displayed by Fourier maps. Fig.4.5 is the Fourier projection

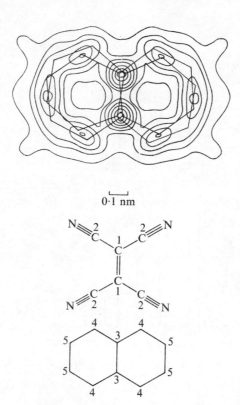

Fig.4.5. Electron density in the plane of the naphthalene molecule in the naphthalene-tetracyanoethylene complex at room temperature. The contours of electron density are at intervals of $10^3 e/nm^3$, and start at zero electron density. Results of Williams and Wallwork (1967), as presented by Herbstein and Snyman (1969).

for the 1:1 complex formed between naphthalene and tetra-cyanoethylene, an example of the charge-transfer type of complex discussed in section 10.6. Tbe naphthalene mole-cules have two possible orientations available to them in their molecular planes, in consequence of which the peaks for the pairs of carbon atoms furthest from the mole-cular centre, i.e. those numbered 5, merge to give a single peak for each pair in a mean position (Herbstein and Snyman 1969). Such disorder may also be made apparent by un-usually large Debye-Waller factors. The vibration of an atom in a lattice gives rise to a more rapid decrease in the atom scattering factor f with the scattering angle θ than would be the case if the atom were at rest. This can be allowed for by writing f as

$$f = f_0 \exp(-B \sin^2 \theta / \lambda^2)$$

where the exponential term is the Debye-Waller factor. The temperature-dependent parameter B is related to the mean square displacement $\bar{u}$ of the atom from its mean position by the equation $B = 8\pi^2 \bar{u}^2$. Typical values of B lie in the range $(2 \text{ to } 4) \times 10^{-2}$ nm^2, but it will be seen from Fig.4.6 - which like Fig.4.5, refers to the 1:1 naphthalene - tetracyanoethylene complex - that for the carbon atoms 4 and 5 of the

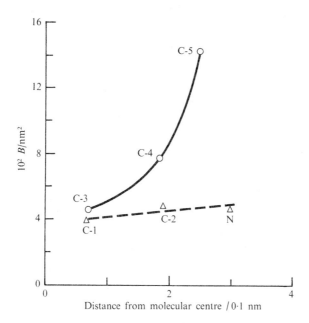

Fig.4.6. Values of the parameter B of the isotropic Debye-Waller factors of the atoms in the naphthalene molecule (upper curve) and the tetra-cyanoethylene molecule (lower curve) in the 1:1 complex at room temperature. Source as for Fig.4.5.

naphthalene molecules B is much larger.

The relation between the structures of ordered and disordered phases of a given substance can sometimes be very close. For example, on passing from phase II to phase I in thallium and caesium nitrates, there is a considerable entropy gain of $R \ln 3$, but the structures are so similar that a single crystal of phase I can be cooled to become

II without disintegrating. When the structures only differ
slightly, it is permissible to speak of the appearance of
superlattice lines on cooling, even though the disorder is
orientational rather than positional. On the other hand,
very different diffraction patterns are often obtained from
the ordered and disordered (plastic) phases of the molecular
crystals discussed in Chapters 9 and 10, and in this connection two practical problems should be mentioned. The molecules in such plastic crystals are not only disordered
among several possible orientations, but in addition they
can often diffuse in the lattice with comparative ease. As
a result, they give poor X-ray diffraction patterns. The
lines in a powder photograph can be limited to a few low-
angle lines, which are in any case rather broad, so that
it is difficult to estimate the lattice parameters with
precision. In some of the earlier work, the inherently
poor quality of the photographs was a considerable handicap.
Thus, the powder photograph of cyclobutane obtained by
Carter and Templeton (1953) had only two usable lines, the
minimum necessary to identify the unit cell as body-centred
cubic. A new method of analysing the diffraction data for
crystals of this kind has been suggested by Press and
Hüller (1973). (The same kind of experimental difficulty
can arise with highly disordered inorganic solids such as
silver iodide, as can be seen from Fig.6.1, which shows the
lines of a powder photograph for this compound in phase I
rapidly decreasing in intensity with increasing Bragg angle,
superimposed on a very considerable diffuse background
scattering.) The second practical problem relates to the
examination of low-temperature ordered phases of molecular
crystals. These often only exist well below room temperature, and generally a single crystal of the high-temperature
disordered form fragments on transforming to the ordered
phase, so that only powder photographs can be carried out on
the latter. However, Rudman and Post (1968), studying the
three members of the series $(CH_3)_n CCl_{4-n}$ with $n = 0,1$ and
3, managed to obtain single crystals of the ordered phase
II from the shattered sample formed on cooling phase I to
just below the transition temperature by annealing for

periods of up to five days. Also, occasionally advantage can
be taken of a piece of good fortune. Thus, Jordan, Smith,
Streib, and Lipscomb (1964) were able to carry out a single-
crystal study of the ordered low-temperature form II of
solid nitrogen (α-N_2) because on just one occasion out of
more than twenty a single crystal of form I (β-N_2) failed
to break up on cooling through the transition.

Although electron diffraction has not been very widely
used in order-disorder studies, its superiority over X-ray
diffraction in locating hydrogen atoms has sometimes been
put to good effect. Thus, the technique has been applied
to ice (section 8.1), and to crystalline hydrogen and deuterium sulphides (section 9.5.2). The disorder of the hydrogen atoms in ammonium hexafluorosilicate $(NH_4)_2SiF_6$,
was first disclosed by electron diffraction (Vainshtein and
Stasova 1956). The contributions from neutron diffraction
work have been extremely important, for three reasons.
(1) It is the best of all diffraction techniques for determining the position of hydrogen atoms. (2) Since neutrons are
scattered not only by atomic nuclei but also by electrons
with unpaired spins, it is invaluable in investigating magnetic ordering, since the spin configuration of the ordered
system and its relation to the crystallographic axes can be
determined. (3) It is sometimes useful in distinguishing between atoms of elements close to each other in the Periodic
Table. With regard to (1), it should be pointed out that
hydrogen atoms are often found to be involved in disorder in
crystals. In molecular solids, some of the most thoroughly
investigated transitions are those in simple hydrides (and
in hydrogen and deuterium themselves), while in ionic solids
transitions in ammonium salts have received particular attention. Neutron diffraction studies aimed at locating the
hydrogen atoms have usually been carried out on the deuterated form of the compound because the coherent scattering
amplitude of the deuteron for neutrons is larger than
that of the proton by a factor of three and has a positive
sign. The potentialities of the technique are well
illustrated by the pioneer work of Levy and Peterson on
ammonium halides (1952, 1953) (section 7.5.1) and by that

of Sándor and his colleagues on the deuterium halides (section 9.4) and of Press (1972) on tetradeuterated methane
(section 9.7). The method has also been used to investigate
positional disorder, such as that occurring in transition-
metal hydrides (Somenkov 1972). Experimental details will be
found in the book by Bacon (1975), together with some comparative observations on X-ray and neutron diffraction (see
also Hamilton and Ibers 1968). The application of neutron
diffraction to magnetic ordering concerns transition-metal
and rare-earth compounds particularly, but it has occasionally been applied to molecular solids. Thus Collins (1966)
used it to find how the magnetic moments of the oxygen
molecules are ordered in the form of the element stable at
the lowest temperatures (O_2-III, or α-O_2). Examples of the
different types of magnetic ordering in metallic compounds,
as revealed by neutron diffraction studies, have been
listed by Goodenough (1963). Finally, with regard to the
use of the technique to differentiate between atoms which
are difficult to distinguish by X-ray diffraction, examples
of this are its application to alloys such as β-brass (CuZn)
(section 5.4), and to the examination of solid dinitrogen
oxide, N_2O, for orientational disorder. The coherent scattering amplitudes of the nitrogen and oxygen atoms for
neutrons differ considerably, and Hamilton and Petrie (1961)
were able to confirm that the molecules in the lattice
are in fact disordered in an end-to-end way.

Most diffraction experiments have, naturally enough,
been carried out at or near atmospheric pressure, but there
are interesting order-disorder problems which concern phases
only stable under pressure, and some crystallographers have
mastered the technical difficulties which must be overcome
before studying these. Examples relating to the high-
pressure forms of ice will be found in section 8.3.

In order-disorder transitions, diffraction studies
can be used to observe the progressive formation of one form
and the disappearance of the other as the transition is traversed. This involves taking a sequence of photographs
at relatively small temperature intervals, and hence requires better control of the temperature of the specimen

than is usually needed in diffraction work. An early example
of this kind of investigation was that which Dinichert
(1942) carried out through the λ-transition in ammonium
chloride, which showed that the high- and low-temperature
modifications could coexist over a range of about 3 K. Such
studies can be used to estimate an order parameter, as was
done in the neutron diffraction investigation carried out
by Sándor and Johnson (1968) on the III-II transition in
deuterium bromide (section 9.4). Another example of the
analysis of neutron diffraction results in terms of an
orientational order parameter is the work of Press and
Hüller (1973) on tetradeuteromethane in which experiments
were carried out on the gradual III-II transition between
23 K and 28 K with temperature control to 0·01 K; (see also
in relation to alloys, section 5.3 and Fig.5.13).

X-ray studies have also been used to give precise information on the change in lattice parameters as a transition proceeds. Such a study can throw light on whether
the transition is first-order or not, and on any attendant
hysteresis. Although this information may be obtainable
from a dilatometric measurement of the overall volume
change, the X-ray approach gives a more detailed picture,
and it can moreover be carried out with quite a small
sample. Thus, Fig.4.7 reproduces the results obtained
by Kobayashi, Uesu, and Enomoto (1971) on the transition in
potassium dihydrogen phosphate, KH_2PO_4, at which the low-
temperature ferroelectric orthorhombic phase passes into the
high-temperature paraelectric tetragonal phase. Fig.4.7
shows the change in the a and b parameters as the transition
is approached and the appearance of the single equivalent
parameter for the tetragonal phase, both in the absence of an
electric field and in the presence of an increasing bias
field applied between the c-faces. It will be seen that the
transition normally has a first-order stage, but that this
becomes less pronounced and eventually disappears as the
bias field is increased.

Diffraction experiments can sometimes be usefully
supplemented by the examination of other properties of the
crystal, such as whether or not it is birefringent or

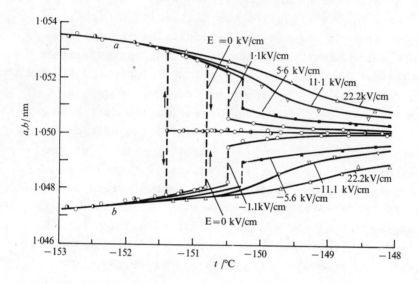

Fig.4.7. Temperature dependence of the lattice parameters a and b of KH_2PO_4 under biasing electric fields E. For $E=0$, open circles are for increasing temperature, and half-shaded circles for decreasing temperature (Kobayashi, Uesu, and Enomoto 1971).

piezoelectric. In the earlier years of the investigation of order-disorder transitions in simple molecular solids (solidified gases), Clusius and his colleagues examined numerous phases for double refraction, and in this way established that whereas disordered phases are usually cubic, the lower-temperature forms are not; (see Kruis and Clusius 1937, Clusius and Faber 1942). However, the value of the technique now lies more in the light it can throw on slight departures from highly symmetrical structures. Thus, Rudman and Post (1966) confirmed that the stable disordered phase I of carbon tetrachloride is rhombohedral and not cubic by showing that it is weakly birefringent. Ballik, Gannon, and Morrison (1973) have developed a sensitive method of studying birefringence quantitatively, that is, by measuring the refractive index difference in two directions at right angles in the plane normal to the incident light beam. With this technique, they have confirmed the conclusion reached from X-ray and neutron diffraction studies that phase III of tetradeuteromethane, CD_4,

is tetragonal, while with ordinary methane, CH_4, they observed below 18 K a time- and temperature- dependent birefringence, consistent with the view based on other experiments that spontaneous conversion between different spin
species takes place. An example of birefringence measurements in a study of a gradual order-disorder transition
in a salt will be found on page 375.

For a crystal to be piezoelectric, the unit cell must
lack a centre of symmetry. In the much-studied λ-transition in ammonium chloride, the structure remains like that
of caesium chloride throughout, but Hettich (1934) found
the crystals to be piezoelectric below the transition,
though not above. The appearance of a centre of symmetry
with the transformation into the high-temperature form is
consistent with the now accepted view that in the ordered
state the ammonium ions are all parallel to each other,
each having just one orientation, while above the λ-transition they are disordered between two possible orientations.
At one time, a structure was proposed for the ordinary low-
pressure form of ice which would have required it to be
piezoelectric. A good deal of experimental effort has been
needed to establish that it is actually neither piezoelectric
nor pyroelectric (see section 8.1).

4.4. NUCLEAR MAGNETIC RESONANCE (NMR)

Disorder in a crystal is intimately linked with the motion
of the constituent ions or molecules, and we come now to
the first and most widely used technique for obtaining information on the nature and kinetics of this motion. Powles
(1976) has contributed a valuable comparative review of the
more important methods available for investigating motion
in molecular crystals, and Richards (1968, 1969) has discussed the principles involved in the analysis of NMR data.
Earlier NMR work relevant to disordered crystals has been
reviewed by Andrew (1961) and by Powles (1961), while more
recent developments have been surveyed by Andrew and
Allen (1966) and by Slichter (1969). The nuclei most frequently involved in these experiments are protons and to a
somewhat lesser extent deuterons, but we shall later give

examples of other nuclei which have been employed in NMR
studies of disorder. Even with the restriction to the study
of H and D resonances, there is still a very large number of
molecular crystals which can be profitably investigated, as
well as inorganic systems such as ammonium salts, salt hydrates, and metal hydrides.

We shall first illustrate the use which has been made
of line-width and second-moment measurements. The resonance
line from a solid is often broadened, the two main causes
of this being either magnetic dipole-dipole interaction between nuclei, or (if the resonating nucleus, like the deuteron,
has an electric quadrupole moment) by quadrupolar coupling
between this moment and electric field gradients within the
crystal. The onset of sufficiently rapid motion of the molecules or ions in the lattice can result in these interactions
partially or completely averaging to zero, with a consequential change in line shape and width. The time-scale on
which such motion must operate to be effective is of the
order of the strength of the coupling, which for protons is
usually ~ 10 kHz. The change in the resonance line is
often expressed in terms of the second moment M_2, the mean
square width of the line about its centre. If the magnetic
field strength $\mathcal{H}$ is taken as the variable, M_2 can be defined by the equation

$$M_2 = \int_{-\infty}^{\infty} h^2 g(h)\,\mathrm{d}h \Big/ \int_{-\infty}^{\infty} g(h)\,\mathrm{d}h \ ,$$

where $g(h)$ is the shape function for the absorption line,
$h = \mathcal{H} - \mathcal{H}_0$, and $\mathcal{H}_0$ is the value of the field at the line
centre. Alternatively, M_2 can be expressed as

$$M_2 = \int_{-\infty}^{\infty} h^3 f(h)\,\mathrm{d}h \Big/ 3 \int_{-\infty}^{\infty} h f(h)\,\mathrm{d}h \ ,$$

where $f(h)$ is the line-shape derivative. The experimental
values of M_2 obtained from these equations should be ad-
justed by the amount $-h_m^2/4$ to give the true second moment,
where h_m is the amplitude of the field modulation (Andrew
1953).

Many solids are known for which, on warming the

crystals from low temperatures, the line width and second
moment show one or more marked decreases. A solid exhibiting
this behaviour need not necessarily undergo a transition in
the thermodynamic sense, a well-known instance of this
being provided by benzene (Andrew 1950, Andrew and Eades
1953). Although this substance only exists in one crystalline form, there is a considerable drop in second moment
between 90 K and 120 K (Fig.4.8). However, similar line-

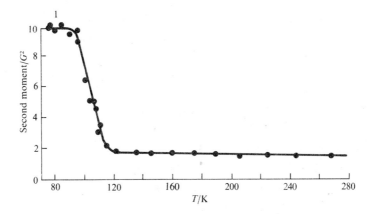

Fig.4.8. Temperature dependence of the second moment of benzene (Andrew
1950, Andrew and Eades 1953).

width and second-moment changes are frequently encountered
in solids which undergo one or more order-disorder transitions, although these changes need not coincide with thermodynamic transitions. The two main types of movement involved are sufficiently rapid reorientation of the molecules
or ions (sometimes about one axis only, sometimes of a
more general kind), which is often spoken of as rotation, and
diffusion of the molecules or ions in the lattice. A further possibility for ions or molecules containing, say, methyl
groups is intramolecular 'rotation' of these groups, a type
of motion which may operate by quantum-mechanical tunnelling
and which in consequence can persist to very low temperatures, as for example in hexamethylbenzene, in which the
methyl groups effectively undergo reorientation even at 1 K.

The second moment drop in crystalline benzene shown in
Fig.4.8 is due to the onset of molecular reorientation in
the plane of the ring, i.e. about the sixfold axis. Since
the six positions made available to each molecule by this
motion are indistinguishable, and since the time spent by
a molecule actually in transit is relatively very small,
there is no reason why this gain in molecular freedom
should be accompanied by any marked thermodynamic effects.

In principle, the type of motion responsible for a
decrease in second moment M_2 can be deduced by comparing
the experimental values of M_2 at different temperatures
with those calculated first for the rigid lattice and then
for a situation in which a particular kind of motion is
assumed to be occurring. These calculations are based on
the formula due to Van Vleck, which we can write as

$$M_2 = C \sum_k \frac{(1-3\cos^2\theta_{jk})}{r_{jk}^6} .$$

C is a parameter which depends, *inter alia*, on the gyromagnetic ratio and the nuclear spin quantum number, and
on the number of nuclei involved which are in equivalent
positions, r_{jk} is the length of the vector joining the
resonating nucleus j with the nucleus k, and θ_{jk} the angle
between this vector and the applied magnetic field. The
summation to give M_2 can be carried out if the coordinates
of all the magnetic dipoles in the lattice are known. Both
the intramolecular and the intermolecular contribution to
M_2 must be evaluated. The experiments are often performed
on polycrystalline material with randomly oriented crystallites, and $(1-3\cos^2\theta_{jk})$ is then replaced by 4/5, its
value averaged over all directions. Benzene provides
a simple example of the analysis of second moment data in
this way. The experimental value of M_2 of $9 \cdot 72 \pm 0 \cdot 06$ G^2
below 90 K agrees with the estimate of $9 \cdot 62$ G^2 calculated
for such a lattice with stationary molecules (the rigid
lattice value). The experimental value of M_2 above 120 K
is $1 \cdot 6$ G^2, while the theoretical estimate for the same
lattice but with the molecules rotating in the plane of
the ring is $1 \cdot 7 \pm 0 \cdot 5$ G^2. The case of triethylenediamine

(Smith 1965) can be taken as a second, more complicated example. This substance has a single first-order transition at 351 K, above which the crystals are highly disordered and typical of so-called plastic crystals. The molecule is approximately spherical (Fig.4.9). The course

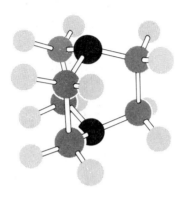

Fig.4.9. The molecule of triethylenediamine (1,4-diazabicyclo-[2,2,2]-octane). The dark circles represent the carbon atoms.

taken by the second moment with increasing temperature is shown in Fig.4.10. Up to about 140 K, M_2 is constant at $24 \cdot 7 \pm 0 \cdot 9$ G^2. The calculated rigid lattice value (assuming a C-H bond length of $0 \cdot 109 \pm 0 \cdot 002$ nm) is $24 \cdot 7 \pm 0 \cdot 9$ G^2. From 140 K upwards M_2 falls, reaching a value of $5 \cdot 52 \pm 0 \cdot 26$ G^2 between 286 K and 330 K. This drop is primarily due to reorientation about the N-N axis, but this alone would cause M_2 to fall only to about 8 G^2. That M_2 drops to a rather lower value is attributed to a wobbling of the molecule about the N-N axis, superimposed on the reorientation. An 'angle of wobble' of 10° to 15° would suffice to reduce M_2 to $5 \cdot 5$ G^2. At or very near the phase transition, M_2 drops abruptly to $1 \cdot 1 \pm 0 \cdot 26$ G^2. This value is consistent with general reorientation of the molecule, for which the calculated M_2 is between $1 \cdot 15$ and $1 \cdot 4$ G^2. Finally, as the temperature approaches the melting point, M_2 falls almost to zero due to diffusion.[†]

† see page 138.

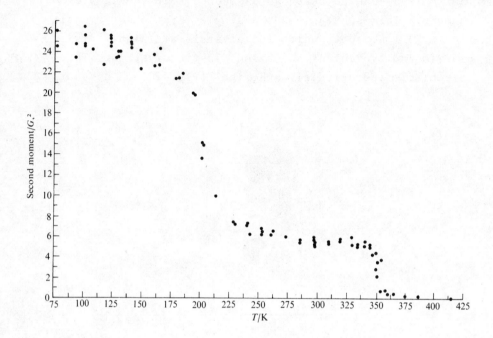

Fig.4.10. Temperature dependence of the second moment of triethylenediamine. (Smith 1965).

An illustration of the distinction which an NMR study
may make it possible to draw between intramolecular rotation
of particular groups and overall molecular rotation is provided by the work of Anderson and Slichter (1965) on the
n-alkanes. Fig.4.11 shows the resonance spectrum, presented
as the derivative curve, for n-C_7H_{16} at 150 K. It consists
of two components, a broad one associated with the effectively motionless methylene groups, and a narrow one due
to the terminal methyl groups, which at 150 K are reorienting
with a frequency greater than the line-width expressed in
frequency units (~10kHz). With falling temperature the

Footnote to page 137

[†]It should perhaps be pointed out that although we have spoken, as is
commonly done, of the decrease in the second moment, this refers to the
observable part. The *total* second moment remains constant, and strictly
speaking is not affected by a change of motion (Abragam 1961, p.453).

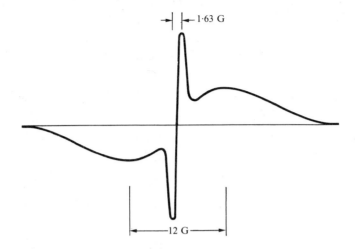

Fig.4.11. Derivative curve for n-C$_7$H$_{16}$ at 150 K (Anderson and Slichter 1965).

narrow component merges into the broad one. At 77 K it has vanished, so that at this temperature the 'rotation' of the methyl groups has ceased.

It is possible to use line-narrowing data to estimate the reorientational jump frequency and its temperature dependence and hence the activation energy for the reorientation process. From the theory of Bloembergen, Purcell, and Pound (1948), as modified by Gutowsky and Pake (1950), the connection between the jump frequency ν_R and the line width δH is given by the following approximate relation

$$2\pi\nu_R = \alpha\gamma\delta H \left(\tan\left\{ \frac{\pi}{2}[(\delta H^2 - B^2)/(C^2 - B^2)] \right\} \right)^{-1} ,$$

where B, δH, and C are respectively the line width above, within, and below the transition region, γ is the gyromagnetic ratio, and α a numerical constant. The activation energy E_R is then obtained by assuming an Arrhenius relation between ν_R and E.[†] Waugh and Fedin (1962) suggested a

[†] see page 140.

simple approximate method for deriving potential barriers to reorientation from the temperature dependence of a line-width. They assumed that the activation energy for reorientation can be identified with the barrier height V_0, that the reorientation frequency is proportional to $\exp(-V_0/RT)$, and that the potential energy V of the molecule or ion as it rotates is given by the equation $V = V_0(1 - \cos n\phi)/2$. They showed that if T_n is the temperature at which the NMR line begins to narrow and if Δ is the 'excess' line-width at low temperatures, then

$$\Delta \approx n \; \overline{\sqrt{(V_0/2I}} \; \exp(-V_0/RT_n) \; ,$$

I being the moment of inertia of the molecule. V_0 can be estimated from the experimental values of Δ and T_n. Waugh and Fedin point out that V_0 in kJ mol^{-1} proves to be approximately equal to $0\cdot155 T_n$.

In some disordered crystals, increasing freedom of translational movement is superimposed on orientational disorder, and as the melting point is approached the second moment can then fall to very small values, comparable with that for the liquid where the static dipole-dipole coupling is zero. Moreover, the line shape for such solids can become Lorentzian (which is characteristic of liquids) rather than Gaussian (which is more typical of a crystal).[‡]

Footnote to page 139.

[†]Since we shall frequently refer to activation energies obtained by plotting the logarithm of some form of rate constant against the reciprocal of the absolute temperature, it should be stressed that these are by definition Arrhenius activation energies E. For the systems which concern us, for which the pressure can be regarded as constant, the relation between E and the enthalpy of activation $\Delta H^{\circ\ddagger}$ which appears in the equation for the rate constant given by transition state theory is $E = \Delta H^{\circ\ddagger} + RT$ (Amdur and Hammes 1966). When E is small, (as it can be, for example, for the reorientation of highly symmetrical molecules or ions) the relative difference between E and $\Delta H^{\circ\ddagger}$ is considerable.

Where it is necessary to avoid confusion between activation energies for reorientation and diffusion we represent them as E_R and E_D respectively.

[‡] see page 141

Cyclohexanol undergoes a transition at 265·5 K to give a highly disordered phase, and Suga and Seki (1962) found that even only 1 K above the transition temperature the narrow resonance line already shows, under high resolution, the essential features of the chemical shift pattern displayed by the liquid.

While in the earlier NMR work on disorder in crystals the emphasis was on the investigation of line-widths and second moments, as time has passed increasing use has been made of relaxation time measurements, which are undoubtedly a superior source of quantitative information on the kinetics of reorientation and diffusion processes (Richards 1968, 1969). When a nuclear spin system is subjected to radiation at the NMR frequency, a distribution between the states available to the nuclei is established such that the spin system and the lattice are no longer in thermodynamic equilibrium. When the radiation is switched off, there is an exponential return to a condition of thermal equilibrium. The rate of restoration of the spin-lattice equilibrium is controlled by the spin-lattice relaxation time T_1. The rate at which internal equilibrium within the spin system itself is established is characterized by the spin-spin (transverse) relaxation time T_2. An important technique for extending the study of spin-lattice relaxation to measure much longer correlation times is that of relaxation in the rotating frame (Hartmann and Hahn 1962, Slichter and Ailion 1964). In this method, the

Footnote to page 140

[‡] If the line shape is Lorentzian, the dependence of the shape function g on the angular frequency ω is given by the equation

$$g = \frac{A^2}{B^2 + (\omega - \omega_0)^2}$$

where ω_0 is the frequency at which g is a maximum. For a Gaussian line shape, the corresponding relation is

$$g = D[\exp(-\tfrac{1}{2}C(\omega - \omega_0)^2]$$

A Lorentzian curve decreases much more slowly in the outer wings than a Gaussian.

alignment of the nuclear magnetization, initially along $\mathcal{H}_0$, is transferred to the rotating field $\mathcal{H}_1$. The time constant for the decay of the magnetization, usually designated $T_{1\rho}$, is the spin-lattice relaxation time of the nuclei in the relatively low field $\mathcal{H}_1$. Use is also sometimes made of the relaxation time in the local nuclear dipole field, T_1^*. The development of methods for determining greater correlation times has made it possible to get information on relatively long jump times for diffusion, as was demonstrated by the beautiful study carried out on metallic lithium by Ailion and Slichter (1965). In an informative paper, Resing (1969) reported the results of measurements of T_1, T_2, and T_1^* on the hydrocarbon adamantane (which has an interesting disordered phase considered in section 10.3), and discussed the nature of the processes which determine these relaxation times. In this particular case, the range of jump times covered was almost 10^{12} (Fig.10.12).

The establishment of thermal equilibrium between the spin system and the lattice is a consequence of the fluctuating magnetic fields set up by the movement of the magnetic nuclei in the ions or molecules (or in groups within molecules). The interaction is at its most efficient, and T_1 is therefore a minimum, when the molecular movement is characterized by a frequency about the same as the resonance frequency, which for the magnetic fields commonly used is generally in the range 10-100 MHz. The minimum in T_1 will appear in a plot of T_1 (or $\ln T_1$) against temperature T, (or $1/T$), and more than one minimum may be encountered if the temperature range covered is sufficiently wide. Thus, Fig.4.12 shows the dependence on temperature of the proton T_1 in crystalline t-butyl chloride, $(CH_3)_3CCl$. Of the three minima, that at the lowest temperature is believed to be due to intramolecular reorientation of the methyl groups, the central minimum to reorientation of the molecule as a whole ('molecular tumbling'), while the third, less prominent minimum just below the melting-point is attributed to translational movement of the molecules (Stejskal, Woessner, Farrar, and Gutowsky 1959).

It is often found that the experimental spin-lattice

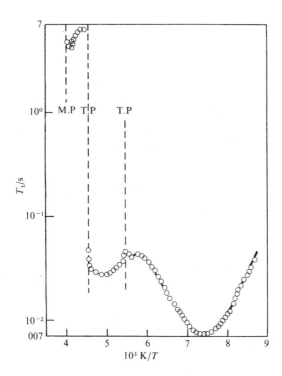

Fig.4.12. Temperature dependence of the proton spin-lattice relaxation time T_1 in solid $(CH_3)_3CCl$. The dotted lines indicate the melting-point (248 K) and the upper (220 K) and lower (183 K) transitions (Stejskal *et al*. 1959).

relaxation time for rotational movement can be successfully linked with a single correlation time (or jump time) τ_c for the molecular rotation in question. The connection between T_1 and τ_c is made on the basis of the theory of Bloembergen, Purcell, and Pound (1948), and may be expressed as

$$\frac{1}{T_1} = KI(I+1)\gamma^4\left(\frac{h}{2\pi}\right)^2 \sum_j r_j^{-6} \left[\frac{\tau_c}{1+(\omega\tau_c)^2} + \frac{4\tau_c}{1+4(\omega\tau_c)^2}\right] , \quad (4.3)$$

where γ is the gyromagnetic ratio, r_j the distance from the jth nucleus to the reference nucleus, I the nuclear spin, and K a constant which depends on the geometry associated with the motion. Thus, K will differ according to whether the movement is about one axis, or three. It is supposed that the temperature dependence of τ_c is given by the

Arrhenius-type equation

$$\tau_c = \tau_c^\circ \exp(E/RT) \qquad\qquad (4.4)$$

where E is the activation energy of the relaxation process.
It follows from equations (4.3) and (4.4) that in a plot of
T_1 against $1/T$ the minimum in T_1 should occur at $\omega\tau_c = 0\cdot6158$.
The validity of equation (4.3) (embodying the assumption of
a single correlation time) and of equation (4.4) can be
checked by comparing the experimental plot of T_1 (or $\ln T_1$)
against $1/T$ with that calculated from these equations.

If the spin-lattice relaxation process is governed by
a range of correlation times rather than just one, the
minimum in the T_1 $vs.$ $1/T$ curve tends to be broader, as
illustrated in Fig.4.13 for a solid solution of 62·5 mole
per cent of d-camphor and 37·5 mole per cent of l-camphor.

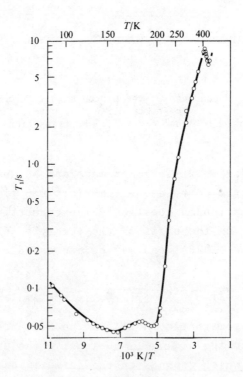

Fig.4.13. Temperature dependence of the spin-lattice relaxation time T_1
in a solid solution of 62·5 mole per cent of d-camphor and 37·5 mole per
cent l-camphor, measured at 30 MHz (Anderson and Slichter 1964).

The motion involved here is the intramolecular reorientation
of the methyl groups, and the distribution of the relaxation
times reflects the variability in environment from molecule
to molecule. (The small minimum at ~420 K is due to self-
diffusion.)

For a crystal at higher temperatures in which both molecular tumbling and diffusion contribute to the spin-lattice
relaxation time T_1, the latter can be divided into a time
for reorientation (tumbling) T_{1R} and a time for diffusion
T_{1D}, according to the equation

$$\frac{1}{T_1} = \frac{1}{T_{1R}} + \frac{1}{T_{1D}} \; .$$

The contribution made to T_1 by T_{1R} can be assessed by extrapolation of the experimental data for T_1 obtained at lower
temperatures, and the values of T_{1D} so separated can then
be used to evaluate the Arrhenius parameters for self-
diffusion.

Activation energies for reorientation and diffusion obtained from NMR measurements can sometimes be compared with
those found by other techniques - for example, for the
reorientation of polar molecules by dielectric loss studies
(section 4.8), and for diffusion by radiotracer techniques
or by using the phenomenon of plastic flow or 'creep'
(section 4.9). Occasionally there is disagreement between
the activation energies obtained from NMR measurements and
estimates made in other ways, especially where translational
movement is concerned. This is discussed in section 10.7,
but we may note here that in studying diffusion, NMR measurements are concerned with movement over very much shorter
distances than those involved, for example, in a radiotracer
investigation, and while the results from both techniques
may be affected by the degree of crystallinity of the sample
and by its purity they need not necessarily be influenced in
the same way or to the same extent (Hood and Sherwood 1966a).
In general, diffusion along grain boundaries (where impurities tend to concentrate) will proceed more rapidly and
with a lower activation energy than diffusion through the
crystal lattice, and Resing (1962) has argued that enhanced

molecular mobility at these boundaries will have much more
influence on the results of a radiotracer study than on
NMR measurements, which should scarcely by affected by grain
boundary effects. Impurities can also alter the vacancy concentration in the lattice, and thereby change the diffusion
rate. Of course, the ideal is that all experiments should
be carried out with pure single crystals. Recorded instances
of the effect of the physical condition of the sample on
the kinetic parameters for reorientation are less common,
but Fratiello and Douglass (1964) found that for a packed
sample of perfluorocyclohexane, C_6F_{12}, the **activation energy**
for reorientation in the **disordered phase** was 5 kJ mol^{-1},
whereas for the presumably superior crystals **formed** by slow
crystallization **from** the **melt** the activation energy was only
3·3 kJ mol^{-1}.

The experimentally determined temperature-independent
parameter τ_c° of equation (4.4) can be used to estimate the
entropy of activation $\Delta S^{\ddagger}$ for the process involved from the
relation

$$\tau_c^{\circ} = \nu_D^{-1} \exp(-\Delta S^{\ddagger}/R) .$$

For translational movement, ν_D can be taken to be the Debye
frequency. For reorientation, it can be assumed to be the
molecular librational frequency given by the approximate
relation

$$\nu_D \approx (n/2\pi)(E_R/2I)^{\frac{1}{2}}$$

where n is the number of nearest neighbour minima for a
revolution of 2π about the appropriate axis, I is the moment
of inertia, and E_R the activation **energy** for reorientation.

NMR spectra are very **vulnerable to** the disturbing influence of even quite small quantities of paramagnetic impurities in the substance under investigation. Thus, some
of the earlier work on crystalline methane was vitiated by
the presence of oxygen in concentrations of the order of
a few parts per million.

A few studies have been made of the effect of pressure

on relaxation times, from which it is possible to deduce the volume of activation (Benedek 1963, Jonas 1975). Such experiments are technically rather difficult, but this is undoubtedly a field in which further profitable work will be carried out. The kind of effect which an increase in pressure can produce is illustrated in Fig.4.14 for hexamethylbenzene, from which it will be seen that a pressure

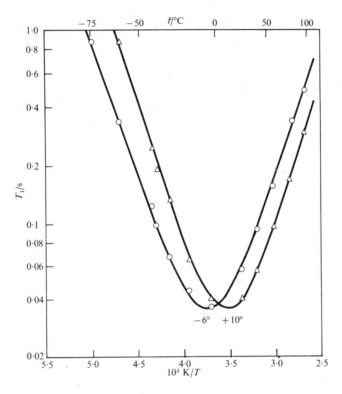

Fig.4.14. Temperature dependence of the spin-lattice relaxation time T_1 in solid hexamethylbenzene at pressures of 1 atm (circles) and 680 atm (triangles) (Anderson and Slichter 1966).

increase from one to 680 atm produces an upward shift of about 16 K in the temperature for minimum T_1 (Anderson and Slichter 1966). From experimental results for the effect of pressure on T_1 at constant temperature, the volume of activation $V^{\ddagger}$ can be evaluated from the relation

$$V^{\ddagger} = RT(\partial \ln T_1/\partial p)_T .$$

The deuteron with a spin of $I = 1$ has an electric quadrupole moment, and whereas spin-lattice relaxation with
protons is a matter of dipolar interaction, in the corresponding deuterium compounds it is primarily brought about
by quadrupolar coupling. Moreover, it appears for a deuterated species such as ND_4^+, for example, that the deuteron
quadrupole coupling constant is determined much more by
intraionic interaction than by the crystalline field, and
the coupling constant is therefore responsive in a rather
direct way to changes in the motion of the ion. Examples
of NMR studies of deuterated ammonium salts will be found
in section 7.5.1. The motion of the water molecules in salt
hydrates has also been investigated by experiments on the
deuterated forms. Thus, Ketudat and Pound (1957) concluded
from deuteron resonance experiments on single crystals of
$Li_2SO_4.D_2O$ that whereas at 148 K the water molecules are
stationary, at room temperature they switch through 180°
about the line bisecting the DOD angle. Tsang and O'Reilly
(1965) investigated the more complex hydrate $K_4Fe(CN)_6.3D_2O$,
and combined their results with an NMR study of the protonated form to draw conclusions about the movement of the water
molecules above and below the ferroelectric-paraelectric
transition (O'Reilly and Tsang 1967).

In a compound such as NH_4PF_6 spin exchange between
the protons and ^{19}F nuclei can play a part in the spin-
lattice relaxation. This cross-relaxation can be reduced
by replacing the protons by deuterons, and Albert and
Gutowsky (1973) used ND_4PF_6 to obtain from fluorine T_1
measurements the parameters governing the rate of reorientation of the anions. Another use of deuterium substitution is to separate the movement of two different hydrogen-
containing groups. Thus, in their NMR study of methylammonium chloride Albert and Ripmeester (1973) carried out
experiments on the salts $(CH_3.ND_3)Cl$ and $(CD_3.NH_3)Cl$ to
characterize separately the motion of the CH_3 and NH_3^+
groups about the C-N axis of the cation (p. 370).

Finally, some examples of resonance work involving other

nuclei may be cited. ^{19}F resonance ($I = \frac{1}{2}$) has been used
in studying the movement of ions such as BF_4^- and PF_6^- (section
7.5.4 and 7.6), and of molecules such as tetrafluoromethane
(section 10.1) and perfluorocyclohexane (section 10.2).
Yen and Norberg (1963) used the ^{129}Xe isotope ($I = \frac{1}{2}$) to
investigate diffusion in solid xenon by T_2 measurements,
while Resing (1962) studied diffusion in the high-temperature phase of white phosphorus by T_2 measurements, and reorientation of the tetrahedral P_4 molecules in the low-
temperature form by determining T_1. From ^{23}Na resonance
experiments ($I = 3/2$) on sodium nitrate, Andrew, Eades,
Hennel, and Hughes (1962) drew conclusions about the connection between the λ-transition in this salt (which is
primarily associated with orientational disorder of the
nitrate ions) and the translational movement of the sodium
ions. ^{14}N ($I = 1$), ^{35}Cl ($I = 3/2$), and ^{81}Br ($I = 3/2$)
resonances have been employed in investigations of the
ammonium halides (section 7.5.1), and the diffusion of
copper ions in CuI and CuBr has been studied with ^{63}Cu
(p.243).

4.5. INFRARED AND RAMAN SPECTROSCOPY

As in studies of molecular structure, so also in investigations of crystals, infrared and Raman spectroscopy com-
plement each other, and in general both should be investigated in a complete spectroscopic examination of a particular crystal. Useful information has been obtained from
all frequency regions, namely those associated with the
phonon spectrum and the torsional oscillations of the molecule or ion in the lattice, and with the intramolecular or
intraionic vibrations. The development of far-infrared
spectroscopy has made it possible to get direct information on low-frequency modes of motion, which in the infrared can usually only be discerned in combination bands or
as overtones.

Useful reviews of the application of infrared and
Raman spectra to obtain structural information about
crystals have been written by Vedder and Hornig (1961),
by Dows (1963), and (with particular reference to disordered

molecular crystals) by Cabana (1975). The article by Scott
(1974), although primarily concerned with the application
of various spectroscopic techniques to soft-mode transitions,
reviews some of the Raman work carried out on crystals discussed in this book, such as ammonium halides and hydrogen-
bonded ferroelectrics.

Ideally, spectroscopic studies should be carried out
on single crystals, since it is then possible to use oriented
specimens and polarized light. It is perhaps more often possible with salts, as opposed to molecular crystals, to obtain single crystals of ordered as well as of disordered
phases. The ordered phases of molecular crystals are often
only stable at relatively low temperatures, and although
the disordered forms of such substances can frequently be
obtained as single crystals by slow crystallization from the
liquid, such crystals generally break up when cooled to give
the ordered phase. Solid specimens of substances liquid or
gaseous at ordinary temperatures are often produced by the
'spray-on' technique, that is by directing the gas onto a
cooled surface. The difficulties involved in producing
specimens of such substances for low-temperature work, and
the methods of resolving these difficulties, have been described by Cabana (*loc.cit*). It should be noted that for i.r.
work the crystal should be large but very thin (e.g. between
1 and 10^3 microns thick), whereas for Raman studies specimen
size is less important. Use is also made of the mull technique in investigating i.r. spectra.

In assigning observed frequencies to translational or
torsional oscillational ('rotational') vibrations, an
assignment can often be checked by comparing these frequencies
for two isotopic forms of the substance. Thus, assuming
the torsional oscillations of ammonium ions in a lattice to
be harmonic, the corresponding frequency should be proportional to $I^{-\frac{1}{2}}$, where I is the moment of inertia of the ion,
so that the ratio $\nu(ND_4^+)/\nu(NH_4^+)$ should be approximately
$1/\sqrt{2}$, or $0\cdot707$. The frequencies assigned to this mode of
motion in phase III of ND_4Cl and NH_4Cl by Wagner and Hornig
(1950) are 281 cm^{-1} and 391 cm^{-1} respectively. Their ratio
of $0\cdot718$ is reasonably close to the theoretical value. For

translational lattice vibrations, the frequency ratio will
depend inversely on the square root of the relative molecular
masses. Bertie and Whalley (1967b) assigned a frequency of
$229 \cdot 2$ cm^{-1} in the far i.r. spectrum of ice-Ih (the ordinary,
hexagonal form of ice) to such a mode of motion (actually,
a transverse optic vibration), the corresponding frequency
for heavy ice (D_2O) being $221 \cdot 7$ cm^{-1}. The ratio of these
frequencies is $1 \cdot 034$. This is fairly close to, but not
in complete agreement with the value of $\sqrt{(20/18)}$, $= 1 \cdot 054$,
which would be expected if the vibrations are harmonic and
if the force constants in the two lattices are the same.
The discrepancy implies that one or both of these assumptions - perhaps more particularly that about the force
constants - is not quite correct. It should be noted that
rotational and translational frequencies can couple with each
other, unless such coupling is forbidden by symmetry restrictions (which in a disordered form of a substance are
usually completely lifted), and isotopic comparison is helpful in picking out such mixed vibrations. An example of
this will be found in the work of Bertie and Sunder (1973)
on the far i.r. spectra of the H and D forms of t-butyl
bromide.

It may be helpful to the reader who wishes to consult
the original literature in this field to distinguish between the groups used by spectroscopists in dealing with
crystals. A space group is an infinite array of symmetry
operations which include the translations which generate
the lattice as well as the operations familiar in point
groups. The space group can be regarded as the product of
the translation group and another finite group called the
factor group. The factor group, which can also be called
the unit cell group, is in general *not* a point group,
although the possible factor groups are isomorphous with
the 32 point groups of crystallography. The site group
denotes the local symmetry as it appears from the site in
question. It is, in other words, a point group of symmetry
operations which leaves the site invariant. A site group
must be a subgroup of the factor group, and also of the
molecular point group (see, e.g. Hornig 1948, Dows 1963).

Thus, for a tetrahedral molecule AB_4 belonging to the point group T_d, the subgroups from which a possible site symmetry must be selected are T_d, T, T_{2d}, C_{3v}, S_4, D_2, C_{2v}, C_3, C_2, C_s, and C_1.

If one considers a particular molecule or ion at a lattice site of known symmetry in a crystal lattice, group theory can be applied to determine which vibrations should be active in the i.r. spectrum, and which in the Raman. Conversely, by analysis of the observed i.r. and Raman spectra, inferences may be drawn about the site symmetry of the molecule or ion which may be a very useful supplement to knowledge of the crystal structure obtained in other ways. Spectroscopic studies of this kind have been, and will no doubt continue to be, especially valuable when applied to the low-temperature, ordered phases of molecular crystals (even when in the polycrystalline form produced by the 'spray-on' technique), since the difficulty in obtaining single crystals of such phases prevents full advantage being taken of diffraction techniques.

In using spectra associated with intramolecular vibrations to obtain information about site symmetries, a frequently used device, introduced by Hiebert and Hornig (1952), is to study the spectra of an isotopic form of the molecule present in relatively small concentration as the guest in a host lattice composed of another isotopic species. If the vibrational frequencies of the guest and host molecules are sufficiently different, as far as the guest molecules are concerned the coupling with the vibrations of neighbouring molecules is largely broken down, and the spectrum obtained from the guest molecules is essentially determined by the site symmetry. Thus, in a study of crystalline CH_4 one might examine the spectrum produced by CD_4 molecules at low concentration in CH_4. From any splitting of the degenerate vibrational modes of the guest molecules site symmetries can be deduced, and it may then be possible to eliminate some of these by using as the guest other isotopic species of different symmetry, for example CH_3D and CH_2D_2 in the case in point. To illustrate this kind of application of i.r. and Raman spectroscopy we consider phase II (the low-temperature ordered form) of silane, SiH_4. Fournier, Savoie, Nguyen Dinh The, Belzile, and Cabana (1972) examined the spectra of SiD_4 present to the extent of about one per cent in SiH_4. An isolated SiD_4 molecule has four fundamental modes of vibration, ν_1 (non-degenerate, Raman-active), ν_2 (doubly degenerate, Raman active), ν_3 and ν_4 (both triply degenerate and both infrared- and Raman-active). The i.r. and Raman spectra of SiD_4 in dilute solution in SiH_4 are shown in Fig.4.15. Since ν_1 only appears as one component

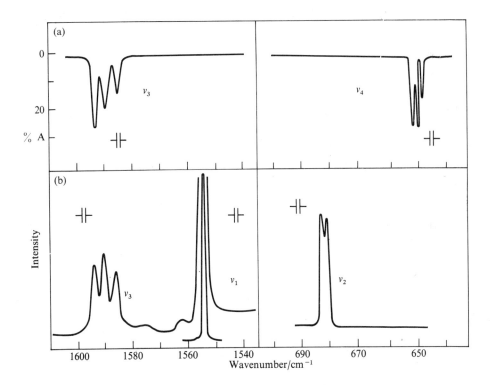

Fig.4.15. (a) Infrared spectrum of SiD_4 in 1 per cent solution in SiH_4-II at 10 K (%A = per cent absorption); (b) corresponding Raman spectrum of a 1·8 per cent solution at 40 K (Fournier et al. 1972).

(at 1554 cm^{-1}), all sites occupied by the SiD_4 molecules are identical. It will be seen that the degeneracies of ν_2, ν_3, and ν_4 are completely removed, an observation only consistent with the following site symmetries: D_2, C_{2v}, C_2, C_s, and C_1.

Of these, D_2 and C_{2v} can be eliminated by the number of
components observed in the spectra of the pure crystals,
thus leaving three possibilities. In connection with attempts of this kind to determine a site symmetry, or at
least limit the number of possibilities, it should be borne
in mind that if the molecules under examination are subjected to only very small lattice distortions, the consequential splittings may not be resolvable. In this event,
the spectroscopist may infer that the lattice is more symmetrical than it actually is, but he should never reach
the reverse conclusion.

    With regard to the differences in the spectra produced
by the ordered and disordered forms of a substance, the
spectra of the ordered crystal show more detail or fine
structure than those of the disordered form, since whereas
the environment of a molecule or ion at a particular site
in the unit cell in the ordered crystal should be uniform,
variability in this environment from molecule to molecule
is to be expected in the disordered crystal. As an illustration of this difference in an i.r. spectrum, we show in
Fig.4.16 the spectrum of the HOD molecule in solution in H_2O
in the region of the ν_{OD} band in the ordered high-pressure
form of ice-II, as compared with the spectra of the high-
pressure form V and the ordinary disordered low-pressure
form Ih. Raman and far i.r. spectra of ordered and disordered phases show similar differences. The far i.r.
spectrum of solid deuterium bromide in phases I, II, and
III is shown in Fig.4.17. (Phase III is ordered; in phase
II the molecules are disordered between two orientations,
and in I between twelve orientations). The spectrum of
III reveals both lattice translational frequencies (the
two peaks at the lowest frequencies), and torsional oscillational frequencies (the central peaks). In the intermediate form II, the spectrum has less structure, but the
translational frequencies are still apparent, whereas the
still more disordered form I has a much more diffuse spectrum, very much like that of the liquid. In general, the
spectrum of a disordered phase is no longer rigorously controlled by selection rules, but at the same time it must be

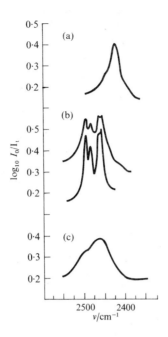

Fig.4.16. Infrared spectrum of the HOD molecule in the region of the ν_{OD} band in different phases of ice in mulls in isopentane at 100 K. (a) Ice-Ih, 95% H_2O, 5% D_2O; (b) Ice-II, upper, 95% H_2O, 5% D_2O; lower, 99% H_2O, 1% D_2O; (c) Ice-V, 95% H_2O, 5% D_2O (Bertie and Whalley 1964).

remembered that local order can persist in a disordered phase, and we shall see that spectroscopy sometimes provides a method of demonstrating the occurrence of local order and of investigating how it changes with temperature.

We may illustrate the application of spectroscopy to studies of order-disorder phenomena in salts by examples taken from the very comprehensive investigations of the i.r. and Raman spectra of the ammonium halides. In ammonium chloride the ordered phase III changes into the disordered phase II at a λ-transition with T_λ = 242·5 K. Each ammonium ion has two possible orientations in the cubic unit cell (Fig.7.21). In the ordered crystal all these ions have the same orientation, that is, they are parallel. In the disordered crystal, the ions are disordered among the two possible orientations available to each. Hornig, one of the pioneers in the application of spectroscopy to crystals, studied the i.r. spectra of NH_4Cl and ND_4Cl, and found

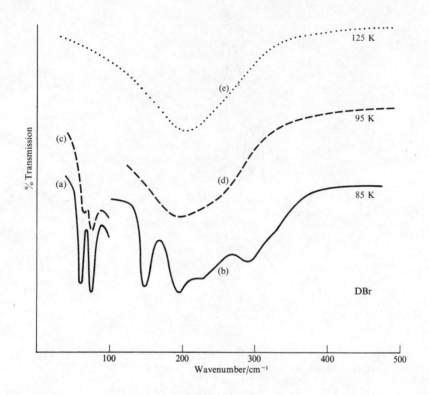

Fig.4.17. Far infrared spectrum of solid DBr; (a) and (b) phase III at
85 K; (c) and (d) phase II at 95 K; (e) phase I at 125 K (Arnold and
Heastie 1967).

that the frequency of the torsional oscillations of the
ammonium ions (ν_6) appeared in combination bands with the
frequencies of two of the internal modes of vibration of
the ion (ν_2 and ν_4)   (Wagner and Hornig 1950). In phase
III, ν_6 is 391 cm^{-1}, and it appears in the same combination
band for phase II with a not greatly altered frequency
(359 cm^{-1}). This therefore rules out the possibility that
in the disordered form II ammonium ions rotate in the lattice
- a conclusion supported by the absence of any signs of
rotational fine structure in the i.r. bands. Later, Garland
and Schumaker (1967) observed ν_6 as its binary overtone
in the i.r. spectrum of phase III, at 749 cm^{-1} at 90 K.
(It may be noted that 749 is considerably less than twice
391, a reflection of the anharmonic character of the

torsional oscillations.) From the observed values of torsional oscillational frequencies and a knowledge of the
relevant crystal structure, it is possible by assuming a
suitable potential function to estimate the height of the
barrier opposing reorientation (see for example, section
7.5.1, on the ammonium halides).

Garland and Schumaker also studied the i.r. band of the
triply degenerate bending vibration ν_4 in NH_4Cl. As the
λ-point is approached from below, a component of this band
appears at 1444 cm^{-1}, which is a consequence of the disappearance of the translational symmetry as the ammonium
ions become orientationally disordered. By applying a
theory due to Lifshitz (1942), they were able to correlate
the temperature dependence of the intensity of the 1444 cm^{-1}
component with the temperature dependence of the quantity
$p(1-p)$ (Fig.4.18); (p is a short-range order parameter,

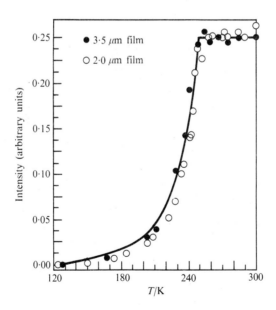

Fig.4.18. Temperature dependence of the intensity of the 1444 cm^{-1} component of the ν_4 band in ammonium chloride. The intensity scale for both
sets of points has been arbitrarily normalized to 0·25 at 300 K. The
solid line shows the variation of the quantity $p(1-p)$, where p is a
short-range parameter for the orientational order of the ammonium ions
derived from heat capacity data; T_c = 242·5 K (Garland and Schumaker
1967).

namely the probability that two nearest neighbour ammonium
ions have parallel orientations, which was estimated from
heat capacity data).   Raman spectra are likewise sensitive
to local order, and this spectrum of phase II of ammonium
chloride was used by Wang and Wright (1973) to demonstrate
that even in this phase selection rules are still operating
owing to the persistence of short-range order.   Another
example of the use of an internal mode of vibration
as a sensitive indicator of small changes in site symmetry
is provided by Wright and Wang's study (1973) of the changes
in the Raman spectrum associated with the ν_4 vibration of
the ammonium ion in NH_4Br through the III-II transition.

The connection between the phonon spectrum and the
extent and nature of the disorder prevailing in a crystal
is a matter to which spectroscopists have more recently
turned their attention, and which is likely to play an increasingly important role, since detailed studies of frequencies and life-times of phonon modes should give valuable information about the lattice dynamics, and hence
about the mechanism of order-disorder changes.   Bertie
and Whalley (1967a) have presented a theory of the effect
of orientational disorder in a crystal on the optical spectrum arising from the translational lattice vibrations.
As an example of the changes which may be observed to occur
in the region of frequencies of translational and librational modes, we show in Fig.4.19 the results of far i.r.
and Raman studies of NH_4Br in phases II, III, and IV (Durig
and Antion 1969, Perry and Lowndes 1969).   (NH_4Br-II is
like NH_4Cl-II, with the ammonium ions disordered between
two possible orientations. NH_4Br-IV has the same structure
as II but with all the ammonium ions parallel, while
NH_4Br-III is a tetragonal structure, with the ammonium ions
ordered parallel to each other along the *c*-axis, but antiparallel in the *ab*-plane.   The III-IV transition shows
pronounced thermal hysteresis.)   From a detailed study
of the temperature dependence of the Raman spectrum of
NH_4Br in the region of 56 cm^{-1}, Wang *et al*. showed that
such an investigation is yet another source of information
about the temperature dependence of order parameters in

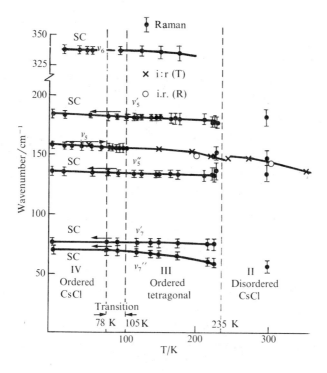

Fig.4.19. Frequency variation of the infrared and Raman modes of NH$_4$Br in phases II, III, and IV. The IV-III transition has a wide hysteresis loop. SC = single crystal, T = thin film transmission, R = reflectance spectrum (Perry and Lowndes 1969).

the neighbourhood of a transition (Wang and Fleury 1968, Wang 1971, Wang and Wright 1972). A mode at 56 cm^{-1} appeared with increasing intensity as the III→II transition was approached from below. This was attributed to a phonon of large wave vector at the zone boundary which becomes Raman-active by virtue of the development of disorder in the ordered phase III. The intensity of this 56 cm^{-1} mode correlated closely with the 'abnormal' contribution to the heat capacity of the crystal.

Illustrations of the value of Raman studies in investigating disorder in crystals where the lattice dynamic instability known as a soft mode may be involved are provided by the thiocyanates discussed in section 7.3.1 and by the hydrogen-bonded ferroelectrics considered in section

7.7.

Some work has been carried out on the Raman spectra of solids under pressure. By virtue of the observable changes in the spectrum at transitions, this kind of spectroscopy can be used to map phase diagrams. An example of this is the investigation of the phase diagram of ammonium iodide to ~6 kbar by Hochheimer, Spanner, and Strauch (1976).

Finally, the shapes of infrared and Raman bands can be analysed to yield information on the dynamics of the rotational movement of ions and molecules in crystals. It is likely that increasing use will be made of this approach, an example of which relating to the hydrocarbon $C(CH_3)_4$ will be found in section 10.1.

4.6. NEUTRON SCATTERING SPECTROSCOPY

4.6.1. *Inelastic scattering*

These experiments are carried out with neutrons with energies in the range 10^{-3} eV to 1 eV, which correspond respectively to neutron wavelengths of 0·9 nm to 0·03 nm, and to velocities of 500 ms^{-1} to 14 000 ms^{-1}. The neutron beam can exchange energy with the lattice phonons and with torsional oscillations of the molecules or ions, and the energy changes therefore give information on the phonon dispersion curve of the solid and on torsional oscillation frequencies.[†] There is accordingly some similarity between inelastic neutron scattering and the Raman effect, and the information obtained from the scattering experiments complements that from other sources, such as the analysis of heat capacity data and infrared and Raman spectroscopy. However, neutron scattering is not subject to the selection rules which operate in electromagnetic spectroscopy, and transitions forbidden in the latter are allowed in neutron scattering. A further difference between inelastic neutron scattering and the Raman effect is that, compared with a light quantum, a

[†]A phonon dispersion curve shows the dependence of the phonon frequencies on the wave vector $\underline{k}$, where $|\underline{k}| = 2\pi/\lambda$, for a particular direction in the crystal.

neutron has considerable momentum and can impart momentum to
the crystal lattice. In consequence, the intensity of a
peak or band in the neutron spectrum can depend on the
scattering angle, and this angular dependence can be used
to determine the amplitude of motion of particles in the
lattice. Useful reviews of both theoretical and experimental aspects of the subject will be found in the book
Thermal neutron scattering (ed. Egelstaff 1965).

White (1974) has reviewed the application of neutron
scattering spectroscopy to the study of disordered crystals,
while Shirane (1974) has surveyed neutron scattering investigations of transitions with a soft mode mechanism.

An inelastic scattering experiment can be carried out
in more than one way. Neutrons brought into thermal equilibrium with a moderator at a particular temperature have
a Maxwellian distribution of velocities. By using choppers,
pulses of neutrons well-defined in both energy and time
can be produced, which then interact with the specimen on
their way to the detector. The energy distribution in the
beam is determined by 'time-of-flight' measurements. Another possibility is to use a neutron crystal spectrometer,
which can be applied to measure neutron wavelengths as well
as to select a monochromatic beam. The detectors employed
depend on the secondary particles formed by absorption of
the neutrons by suitable nuclei, such as the ^{10}B nuclei in
boron trifluoride. The spectrum of the scattered neutrons
can be presented as a plot of intensity versus 'time-of-
flight', or neutron energy change, or spectrometer angle.

Fig.4.20 shows the spectrum for hydrogen chloride
(Boutin and Safford 1964). In the ordered phase HCl-II,
the molecules are associated in infinite zig-zag chains
with each molecule having a unique orientation, and it is
this phase which gives the spectrum with the most prominent
peaks. It will be seen, however, that clear indications
of some of these peaks persist in phase I, namely those at
0·026, 0·009, and 0·006 eV, so that although the molecules in
this phase are orientationally disordered among twelve possible orientations, there is still a tendency for groups
of molecules to form the zig-zag chains, and the spectrum

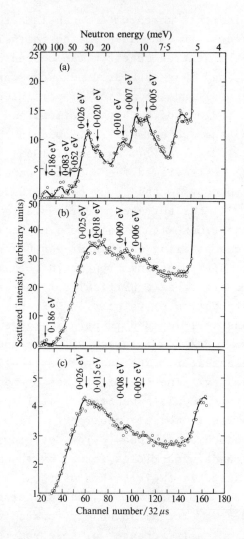

Fig.4.20. Inelastic neutron scattering spectrum of hydrogen chloride.
(a) HCl-II (ordered phase) at 85 K; (b) HCl-I (disordered phase) at
143 K; (c) liquid HCl at 183 K (Boutin and Safford 1964).

for the liquid implies that this tendency even persists in
this state as well. Fig.4.21 is part of the scattered
neutron spectrum obtained from ammonium chloride by Venkataraman, Usha Deniz, Iyengar, Vijayaraghavan, and Roy (1964)
at three temperatures, two below the λ-transition and one
above. In this experiment, energy was transferred from the
neutrons to the lattice. The main peak, at 359 cm^{-1} at 300 K,
is ascribed to the excitation of the torsional oscillation of

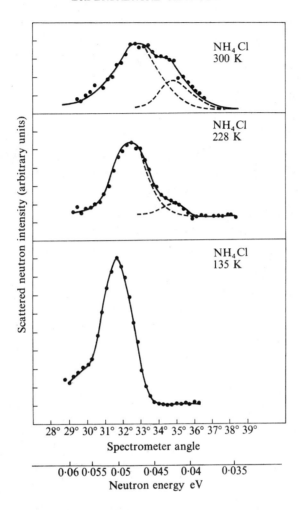

Fig.4.21. Inelastic neutron scattering spectrum of ammonium chloride (T_λ = 242·5 K) (Venkataraman *et al*. 1964).

the ammonium ion from the ground state to the first excited state, whereas the satellite peak at 315 cm^{-1} which is prominent at 300 K, less marked at 228 K, and absent at 135 K, is attributed to the transition from the first to the second excited state. At sufficiently low temperatures, of course, virtually all the ammonium ions in the specimen will be in the torsional oscillational ground state. The difference in the frequencies of the two peaks of ~44 cm^{-1} reflects the anharmonicity of the librational motion (*cf*. p.156).

Neutron scattering has been applied to some of the

numerous disordered solids which contain hydrogen atoms
by studying the dependence of the scattering cross-section
σ on the neutron wavelength. σ, defined as the ratio of
the number of neutrons scattered by a nucleus per second
to the incident neutron flux, is very large for the proton
(a consequence of the near-equality of the neutron and
proton masses), and is sensitively dependent on the movement of the protons. The theory of this dependence is
complicated (see, for example, Janik and Kowalska, Chapter 9,
Egelstaff 1965); but for sufficiently slow neutrons which
gain energy in the scattering process, the inelastic scattering cross-section is proportional to the neutron wavelength while the elastic scattering cross-section is almost
constant. The total scattering cross-section σ_s can thus
be expressed as $\sigma_s = a + b\lambda$. Fig.4.22 shows typical plots

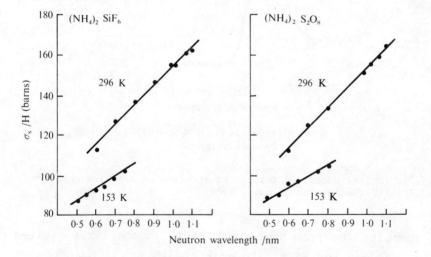

Fig.4.22. Linear dependence of the total neutron scattering cross-section
σ_s on neutron wavelength for the two ammonium salts $(NH_4)_2SiF_6$ and
$(NH_4)_2S_2O_8$ (Leung, Rush, and Taylor 1972).

of σ_s against λ for two ammonium salts, which for $\lambda > 0.5$ nm
are almost linear (see also Rush, Taylor, and Havens 1960). The
values of b, the slope of such plots, vary considerably from
salt to salt. This is because b depends on the motion of

the groups, ions, or molecules containing the protons, and
Rush, Taylor, and Havens (1962) showed that for the ammonium
ion in various salts b can be empirically correlated with
the height of the energy barrier opposing rotation of the
ion. These barrier heights can be estimated, for example,
from the torsional oscillational frequencies of the ammonium
ion obtained spectroscopically or by the analysis of heat
capacity data. In Fig.4.23, b is plotted against barrier
height for several ammonium salts, the value for zero barrier
height being that for the gaseous ammonia molecule. Given

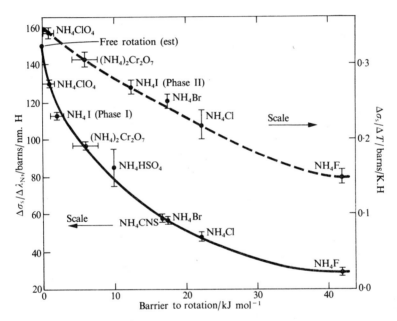

Fig.4.23. Correlation between the barrier opposing the rotation of the
ammonium ion in various ammonium salts and the temperature coefficient
of the total neutron scattering cross-section (upper curve) and the
quantity b, $= \Delta\sigma_S/\Delta\lambda_N$ (lower curve) (Leung, Rush, and Taylor 1972).

a measured b value, the curve in Fig.4.23 can be used as
a calibrated curve to estimate the barrier to rotation.
Thus, the values of b for the salts NH_4ClO_4 and NH_4PF_6 are
130 and 127 barns/nm respectively, only slightly smaller
than the value for the free ammonia molecule (155 barns/nm),
which suggests that in these two salts the barrier heights
are less than 1 kJ mol^{-1}, so that at ordinary temperatures

the ammonium ions are approaching something genuinely like free rotation. Since in the inelastic scattering under consideration the neutrons are picking up energy from molecules or ions in excited states, the number of which falls rapidly with decreasing temperature, the cross-section also falls as the temperature is reduced (for a fixed wavelength), as does the slope b. The temperature dependence of σ_s for the two ammonium salts $(NH_4)_2SiF_6$ and $(NH_4)_2S_2O_8$ is illustrated in Fig.4.24. Values of $\Delta\sigma_s/\Delta T$ from results of this kind can also be correlated with the energy barriers opposing rotation of the ammonium ion (Fig.4.23). Fig.4.25

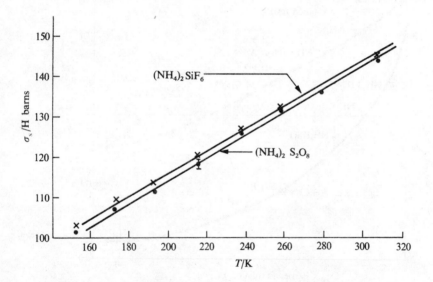

Fig.4.24. The temperature dependence of the total neutron scattering cross-section σ_s for the salts $(NH_4)_2SiF_6$ and $(NH_4)_2S_2O_8$, for a neutron wavelength of $0\cdot85$ nm (Leung, Rush, and Taylor, 1972).

shows the change in σ_s with temperature (for $\lambda \approx 1$ nm) for hexamethylbenzene (Rush and Taylor 1964). This substance undergoes a λ-transition at $\sim116\cdot5$ K, and at about this temperature there is a small but definite change in σ_s. Rush and Taylor attributed this to a fall in the barrier to rotation of the methyl groups as the crystals are heated through the λ-transition, a conclusion later confirmed by an examination of the inelastic scattering spectrum (Rush

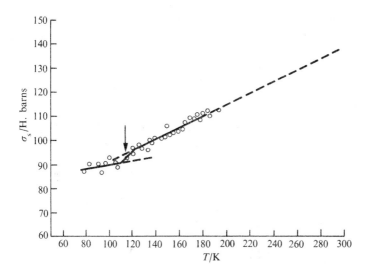

Fig.4.25. Temperature dependence of the neutron scattering cross-section σ_s per hydrogen atom for hexamethylbenzene; $\lambda_N \approx 1$ nm (Rush and Taylor 1964).

and Taylor 1966, see p. 636).

4.6.2. *Quasielastic scattering*

If inelastic neutron scattering is regarded as analogous to the Raman effect, quasielastic scattering may be compared with the Rayleigh scattering of light. The experiments are carried out with monochromatic neutrons, and owing to the movement of the ions or molecules responsible for the scattering a Döppler effect operates to broaden the elastic peak - hence the adjective quasielastic - and accordingly this broadening is a source of information about the motion in the lattice of the particles with which the neutrons interact. Roughly speaking, the more freedom of movement possessed by these particles, the broader the elastic peak. In particular, quasielastic scattering has been used to help elucidate the mechanism by which ionic or molecular reorientation occurs. Fig.4.26 shows the peak for neopentane, $C(CH_3)_4$, above and below the λ-transition at 140 K (Dahlborg, Gräslund, and Larsson 1972). Above the transition, solid neopentane is orientationally dis-

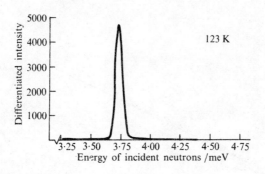

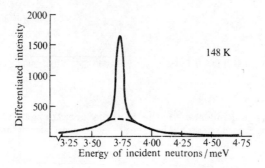

Fig.4.26. Quasielastic neutron spectrum of neopentane, $C(CH_3)_4$, above and below the transition at 140 K (Dahlborg, Gräslund, and Larsson 1972).

ordered, and behaves as a typical plastic crystal. When the ordered form is converted into the plastic phase, the intensity of the peak is reduced. With regard to the broadening, the change in the peak is not a matter of the width of the main peak itself being increased, but of the appearance beneath it of a broader component. Lechner, Rowe, Sköld, and Rush (1969) considered the interpretation of the quasi-elastic scattering on the basis of two models, (1) the rotational jump model in which reorientation was assumed to occur by relatively infrequent jumps through 120° about the threefold molecular axis, the jumps themselves occupying very little time, (2) a model in which reorientation was supposed to take place by a Brownian-like process of rotational diffusion, that is by a process involving frequent small stages. Neither model alone appeared to fit the experimental results, but de Graaf and Ściensiński (1970)

suggested that both reorientation mechanisms operate simultaneously. Dahlborg *et al.* (1972) also advanced an interpretation of their results based on a dual nature for the
type of motion in question, but concluded that in the plastic
phase the molecules spend more time actually undergoing reorientation than in executing librational motion.

The work of Rush and his colleagues on the alkaline
hydrogensulphides (p. 276) supplies an excellent example
of what can be learnt about the nature of orientational
order-disorder transitions and about the dynamics of the
motion involved by carrying out both inelastic and quasielastic scattering studies on one and the same solid.

4.7. OTHER SPECTROSCOPIC TECHNIQUES

4.7.1. Nuclear quadrupole resonance (NQR)

If a nucleus has a spin I which is ≥ 1, the charge on it has
a non-spherical distribution and the nucleus possesses a
quadrupole moment. In an *inhomogeneous* electric field the
quadrupole will be restricted to a limited number of orientations which in general correspond to different energy
levels. The pure quadrupole resonance spectrum, which lies
in the radiofrequency region, is due to transitions between these levels. The transition frequency is determined
by the quadrupole coupling constant A, where

$$A = e^2 q Q [4I(2I-1)h]^{-1} \, ,$$

eQ being the quadrupole moment and eq the maximum component
of the electric field gradient; eq is the second differential coefficient of the electrostatic potential with respect
to a suitable coordinate.

The condition that $I \geq 1$ naturally restricts the use
of this type of spectroscopy, but its potential when applied
to problems of disorder in solids is illustrated by the
work of Scott and his colleagues on crystals containing the
nitrogen molecule. For the ^{14}N nucleus $I = 1$, and Scott
has applied NQR to nitrogen itself and to the nitrogen β-
quinol clathrate. At ordinary pressures, nitrogen has a

low-temperature ordered form II (the α-form) which at 35·6 K
transforms into an orientationally disordered form I (the
β-form). α-Nitrogen gives a single pure nuclear quadrupole
resonance line of frequency ν, where ν ≈ 3·5 MHz at 4·2 K.
As the α-form is heated, ν decreases as shown in Fig.4.27,

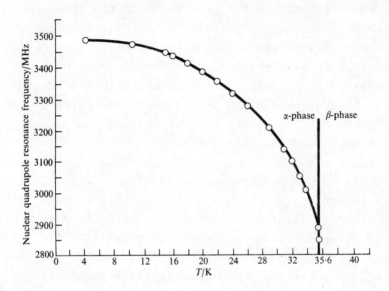

Fig.4.27. Temperature dependence of the pure quadrupole resonance frequency
of ^{14}N in α-N$_2$ (= N$_2$-II) (DeReggi, Canepa, and Scott 1969).

and at the transition drops discontinuously by a factor of
more than 10^3 (DeReggi, Canepa, and Scott 1969). In solid
nitrogen the electric field gradient acting on a nucleus
is predominantly intramolecular. It derives from the p
electrons, and is a maximum along the molecular axis. The
decrease in ν on heating reflects the increasing excitation of the librational motion of the molecules, with its
consequent disruptive effect on orientational order, and
the course taken by ν with rising temperature shows that
the transition begins gradually but is completed isothermally. The NQR frequency can be expressed as

$$\nu(T,p) = \nu_s \, f(T,p) \ ,$$

where ν_s is the resonance frequency for a static molecule
and $f(T,p)$ is an order parameter representing the averaging effect on the field gradient of the librational movement
of the molecules. The dramatic fall in ν at the transition
can be explained if in the disordered hexagonal β-phase the
molecules precess about the c axis at an angle close to
$54°44'$, since for this angle the electric field gradient
averages to zero. This interpretation has been confirmed by
X-ray diffraction studies. Brookeman and Scott (1973) used
this abrupt fall in ν at the transition to determine with
some precision the α-β phase boundary line up to $3 \cdot 3$ kbar,
at which pressure the transition temperature has increased to
$44 \cdot 5$ K. Brookeman, McEnnan, and Scott (1971) had previously
shown that the order parameter $f(T,p)$ was connected with
the mean square angular amplitude $\langle \theta^2 \rangle$ of the librations by
the equation

$$f(T,p) = 1 - 3\langle \theta^2 \rangle + \frac{9}{2}\langle \theta^2 \rangle^2 - 5\langle \theta^2 \rangle^3.$$

Applying this equation to their results for the values of
ν for the α-phase at the transition, Brookeman and Scott
found that the r.m.s. amplitude $\langle \theta^2 \rangle^{\frac{1}{2}}$ is approximately
constant at ~18-19°, implying that instability of this phase
is attained when the amplitude of the librational movement
reaches a critical figure which is little affected by
pressure or temperature. In this critical condition the
amplitude of the motion is quite large and no doubt appreciably anharmonic.

The application of NQR spectroscopy to the nitrogen
β-quinol clathrate is described in section 11.2.4.

4.7.2. Electron spin resonance (ESR)
Cyclohexane has two solid phases, a low-temperature ordered
form II and an orientationally disordered form I. If crystals of II are irradiated well below the transition temperature of 186 K with γ-rays from cobalt-60, some of the
molecules in the lattice lose a hydrogen atom to give trapped
cyclohexyl radicals whose presence can be readily detected
by the ESR technique. When the crystals of II are heated,

combination of the radicals begins a few degrees below the
transition, and with the conversion to the high-temperature
form the ESR signal disappears, implying that as the transition is taking place the radicals become free to move and
to combine with each other (Szwarc 1962).   Studies of this
kind, in which the probe is a radical formed by irradiation of the solid under investigation, can therefore throw
light on the mobility which the particles in the lattice
acquire during the actual phase changes.   Such experiments
were pioneered by Russian workers, and examples of some of
these earlier investigations have been given by Semenov
(1961).   The question arises as to how far the movement of
the radicals can be regarded as representing that of the
molecules.   Marx (1966) has reviewed this aspect of the subject, and considers that where the molecules in the lattice
are fairly large and the radical formation only involves
the removal from them of a hydrogen atom (as in the example quoted), then movement of the radicals and of the molecules is probably very similar (at least as regards diffusion).   It should be noted that the sensitivity of ESR
spectroscopy is such that only a very small concentration
of radicals need be produced in the lattice, and it is
unlikely that their presence affects the general behaviour
of the molecules.

ESR spectroscopy can therefore provide yet another
means of detecting phase transitions.   For many solids this
may often be done by simpler and more convenient techniques,
especially when the transition is one between two stable
phases, but the ESR method can be helpful when metastable
phases of the solid may be involved, depending on the thermal treatment to which the solid is subjected.   Cyclohexanol,
which has a complicated polymorphism involving metastable
forms (p. 621) provides an example. Szwarc (1966) studied
the effect of heating on the number of radicals trapped in
samples of cyclohexanol which had been irradiated after
differing thermal treatments, and found that the behaviour
varied considerably according to the thermal history.   Some
irradiated specimens showed on warming more than one region
of temperature in which there was a fall in the radical

concentration.

Examples of ESR investigations of order-disorder phenomena in which the probe itself is a normal component of the
lattice are at present relatively few. Foner, Meyer, and
Kleiner (1961) examined the ESR spectrum of the oxygen
molecules trapped in the β-quinol clathrate to obtain information about the barrier height hindering molecular rotation and about the interaction of molecules in neighbouring cavities (section 11.2.4). However, it is probable
that many as yet undiscovered cases of disorder exist in coordination and organometallic compounds, and frequently such
solids will contain transition metal ions with unpaired
electrons. It is likely, therefore, that ESR spectroscopy
will be applied to these to throw light on structural and
environmental changes associated with the development of
disorder. As an illustration we may cite the case of copper
(II) trisethylenediamine sulphate $Cu(En)_3SO_4$, crystals of
which at ordinary temperatures contain orientationally disordered sulphate ions and apparently regular octahedral
cations, in contrast to the usual Jahn-Teller deformed environment of a Cu^{2+} ion. On cooling this salt there is a
transition at 180 K at which it appears from the entropy
loss that the sulphate ions become orientationally ordered.
Simultaneously, there is an abrupt change in the ESR spectrum. From being almost isotropic above the transition, it
suddenly becomes very anisotropic, implying that in the
disordered form the copper complexes are subject to a dynamic Jahn-Teller effect (section 12.12), but that this
reverts to the more usual static distortion in the low-
temperature form (Bertini, Gatteschi, and Scozzafava 1974).

ESR spectroscopy can also be carried out on crystals
doped with a suitable probe. An example of a transition
which was discovered in this way is that in sodium azide
(Fig.7.5). The probe was the Mn^{2+} ion present to the
extent of 5 p.p.m. In such doped crystals, the environment
of the probe is not of course the same as that of the ions
or molecules of the host lattice. Nevertheless, the environmental changes reflected in the ESR signal from the probe
may be a reasonably reliable guide to those taking place else-

where in the lattice. Kuroda and Kawamori (1971) studied
the ESR spectrum of Cu^{2+} in crystals of ammonium chloride
from 150 K to 300 K, which covers the III-II λ-transition.
They considered that the Cu^{2+} probe was present as the linear
complex ion $Cu(NH_3)_2^{2+}$, and interpreted their observations
on the basis of the behaviour of the ammonia molecules in
this ion. They derived an order parameter for these molecules which in its dependence on temperature closely paral-
leled that for the ammonium ions given by an analysis of the
heat capacity of the salt.

As with molecular solids, a probe can also be introduced into a salt by irradiation. This technique has been
used, for example, by McDowell and his coworkers in investigating potassium and ammonium dihydrogenarsenates.
Thus, Dalal, McDowell, and Srinivasan (1974) carried out an
ESR study on the salt $NH_4H_2AsO_4$ in which the paramagnetic
probe was the AsO_4^{4-} ion formed from an AsO_4^{3-} ion by electron
capture on irradiation of the crystal with X-rays.

4.8. DIELECTRIC PROPERTIES

Valuable information about disorder in certain polar solids
has resulted from measurements of the relative permittivity
(the dielectric constant) and from studies of dielectric
loss. (The relative permittivity is given the symbol ε_r,
but the subscript r is often omitted when it is necessary
or desirable to introduce another subscript, such as the 0
or ∞ inserted to indicate the conditions to which the value
of the relative permittivity refers.) When a polar liquid
crystallizes, ε_r usually falls sharply to a low value characteristic of a non-polar compound. This happens, for example,
with chlorobenzene. However, for some substances there is
almost no change in ε_r on freezing. Indeed, it may actually
increase, as is shown in Fig.4.28 for hydrogen sulphide. It
was soon established that this latter behaviour was frequently displayed by substances composed of small non-polar
molecules and by organic compounds with larger molecules
which, while polar, were roughly spherical or highly symmetrical, such as the molecules of t-butyl chloride and
camphor. Such solid phases of high permittivity are in

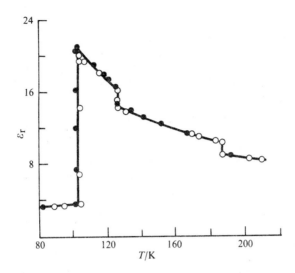

Fig.4.28. Temperature dependence of the relative permittivity ε_r of hydrogen sulphide at 5 kHz. Open circles indicate rising temperature and full circles falling temperature (Smyth and Hitchcock 1934).

fact usually plastic crystals, discussed in detail in Chapters 9 and 10. They have been described as 'rotator phases', or by some similar term, but it is now generally agreed that while the molecules in such phases undoubtedly possess remarkable molecular freedom, comparable with that in the liquid form of the substance, they do not rotate freely, but rather switch rapidly between orientations of minimum potential energy. On further cooling, a rotator phase may be expected to undergo a transition at which the permittivity drops, as illustrated in Fig.4.28. This transition may be isothermal, or partly or wholly gradual. Numerous examples of dielectric studies of such transitions will be found in Smyth's authoritative book *Dielectric behavior and structure* (1955).

In Chapters 9 and 10, reference will be made to the Onsager equation, which connects the static (limiting low-frequency) relative permittivity ε_0 of a pure polar liquid with the dipole moment p of the molecules. One form of this equation is

$$\frac{(\varepsilon_0 - \varepsilon_\infty)(2\varepsilon_0 + \varepsilon_\infty)}{\varepsilon_0(\varepsilon_\infty + 2)^2} = \frac{4\pi N_1 p^2}{9kT\varepsilon}$$

where ε_∞, the high-frequency limit of the relative permittivity, can in principle be replaced by the square of the refractive index in the far infrared. N_1 is the number of molecules per unit volume, and ε is the permittivity of free space. It has been found that the dependence of permittivity on temperature for a rotator phase often conforms quite closely to the Onsager equation, showing that, with respect to the particular aspect of molecular dynamics involved, such solids are more like liquids than conventional crystals. For hydroxylic substances in the *liquid* state, owing to the formation of hydrogen-bonded aggregates, the permittivity can be considerably higher than that expected from the Onsager equation and the same can be true of crystalline hydroxylic substances in rotator phases. Thus, cyclopentanol forms two such phases, I and II, with 'abnormally' high permittivities. On the basis of a modified Onsager equation, Green, Dalich, and Griffith (1972) derived a value for the number of molecules in an aggregate or chain in phase II, and also estimated the fraction of such chains orientated in a particular direction in the crystals. They concluded that there are about three molecules in each chain, the number being approximately independent of temperature, but that the preference of the chains for a particular orientation decreases as the II→I transition is approached.

So far in this discussion we have confined our attention to the real part of ε_r, and the effect of changing the frequency has only been used to separate out the contribution from the orientational modes. However, dielectric dispersion studies can give useful information on the kinetics of molecular reorientation. So long as the frequency of the applied alternating field is sufficiently low (which usually means $< 10^6$ Hz) the reorientation of the molecules can keep pace with the reversals of the field. The so-called displacement current is 90° out of phase with the applied e.m.f., and so has no component in phase with the voltage (Fig.4.29a,b). Consequently there is no dissipation of electrical energy as

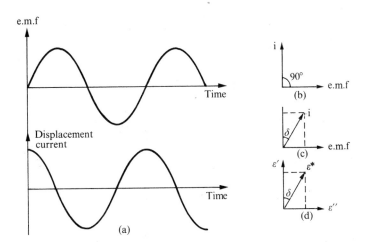

Fig.4.29. Dielectric loss

Joule heat. As the frequency is increased, the rotation or reorientation of the molecules will start to lag behind the field. This happens in the frequency range between 10^6 and 10^{12} Hz. The permittivity begins to fall, and since the displacement current now has a component of i sin δ in phase with the e.m.f. (see Fig.4.29 (c)), energy is lost as Joule heat. This is the region of dielectric loss in which the polar substance acts both as a dielectric and as a conductor, due to the component of the current in phase with the voltage. In this region, it is customary to represent the total permittivity ε^* by the complex function

$$\varepsilon^* = \varepsilon' - i\varepsilon''$$

where ε' is the real permittivity, ε'' the unreal permittivity or loss factor, and $\varepsilon''/\varepsilon' = \tan \delta$ (Fig.4.29(d)).

If the polar material is subjected to a static field, which is switched off at time $t = 0$, the polarization decreases with time. If the specific polarization has fallen to P after time t from its initial value of P_0 at $t = 0$, then it appears that the decay often follows the simple exponential equation

$$P = P_0 \exp(-t/\tau)$$

where τ is a relaxation time. It can then be shown that for a single relaxation time

$$\varepsilon^* = \varepsilon'_\infty + (\varepsilon'_0 - \varepsilon'_\infty)/(1 + i\omega\tau) \qquad (4.5)$$

and that the dependence of ε' and ε'' on the frequency ω (in radians s^{-1}) is given by the following equations (usually called the Debye equations):

$$\varepsilon' = \varepsilon'_\infty + (\varepsilon'_0 - \varepsilon'_\infty)/(1 + \omega^2\tau^2) , \qquad (4.6)$$

$$\varepsilon'' = (\varepsilon'_0 - \varepsilon'_\infty)\omega\tau/(1 + \omega^2\tau^2) , \qquad (4.7)$$

where ε'_0 and ε'_∞ are the values of the permittivity at frequencies below and above the dispersion region (Fig.4.30). The maximum value of ε'', which occurs at a frequency $f_{max} = \omega_{max}/2\pi$, is given by

$$\varepsilon''_{max} = \tfrac{1}{2}(\varepsilon'_0 - \varepsilon'_\infty) .$$

The relaxation time τ is a **macroscopic** property of the medium, but as a rule it does not differ much from the

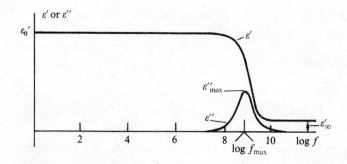

Fig.4.30. Dielectric dispersion.

microscopic or molecular relaxation time for the reorientation of the individual molecules. Elimination of $\omega\tau$ from equations (4.6) and (4.7) leads to the relation

$$\varepsilon''^2 + [\varepsilon' - (\varepsilon_0' + \varepsilon_\infty')/2]^2 = (\varepsilon_0' - \varepsilon_\infty')^2/4 , \qquad (4.8)$$

which is of the form $x^2 + y^2 = r^2$, and represents a semi-circle (since only positive values of ε'' are physically possible). Equation (4.8) is the basis of the Cole-Cole arc plots of ε'' against ε'. If the assumption of a single re-laxation time is valid, the plot is a semicircle with its centre on the ε' axis. If the system has more than one relaxation time, equation (4.5) has to be modified, and the Cole-Cole plot becomes a smaller arc, with a centre lying below the ε' axis, the more so the more extended the range of relaxation times.[†] Two examples of Cole-Cole plots are shown in Fig.4.31.

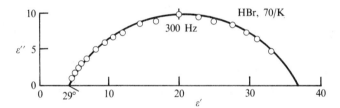

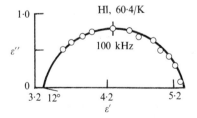

Fig.4.31. Cole-Cole plots for the ordered phases III of hydrogen bromide and hydrogen iodide (Cole and Havriliak 1957).

[†] The plot is symmetrical if the distribution of relaxation times is sym-metrical, but becomes skewed if relaxation mechanisms operating on the high-frequency side of the main dispersion are less effective.

As already indicated, the 'rotation' of the polar molecules is really a matter of an activated jump from one potential energy minimum to another. The simplest model for this is one in which a dipole has two possible positions which are equal in energy but opposite in direction, and which are separated by an energy barrier E. The dipoles oscillate in the potential wells with frequency f_0, and occasionally surmount the barrier between the two orientations. The dependence of the frequency of maximum absorption f_{max} on temperature is then given by the Arrhenius-type equation

$$f_{max} = A \exp(-E/RT)$$

where the frequency factor A can be written as $(f_0/\pi)[\exp(\Delta S^{\ddagger}/R)]$ ($\Delta S^{\ddagger}$ being the entropy of activation), or alternatively, by the application of absolute reaction rate theory, as $(kT/h)[\exp(\Delta S^{\ddagger}/R)]$. Accordingly, from experimental measurements of f_{max} at different temperatures, estimates can be obtained of the parameters E and $\Delta S^{\ddagger}$ which govern the rate of reorientation. A disordered crystal on which dielectric absorption studies have been carried out in several laboratories is the high-temperature (plastic) phase of cyclohexanol. Fig.4.32 is a plot of $\log f_{max}$ against

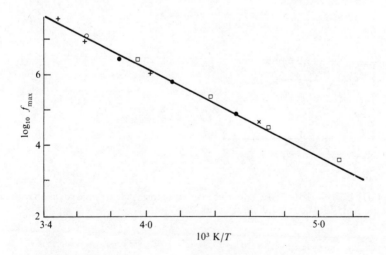

Fig.4.32. Plot of $\log_{10} f_{max}$ against $1/T$ for cyclohexanol, incorporating five different sets of results (Green and Griffith 1969).

$1/T$ for this phase, which shows the agreement between the different sets of measurements, and which leads to a value of 15 kJ mol^{-1} for the activation energy of the reorientation process.

It is possible, of course, that as the dipole rotates through 2π it passes through more than one energy minimum, and that these minima are not all equal. This situation is encountered, for example, in crystals of long-chain polar molecules, on which a considerable amount of interesting dielectric work has been carried out which is discussed in section 10.5.

Useful elementary accounts of dielectric dispersion have been presented by Davies (1965) and by Meakins (1961), and a more detailed treatment will be found in the book by Hill, Vaughan, Price, and Davies (1969). These sources describe the experimental methods available for measuring ε' and ε''. One experimental problem, especially in dealing with plastic crystals formed from the melt, is that the sample is prone to contain cavities or voids, and the presence of these may have reduced the quantitative value of some of the earlier work in this field.

With respect to salts, permittivity studies are of course of cardinal importance in investigating ferroelectric and antiferroelectric crystals (section 2.7), but even when ferroelectricity is not involved permittivity measurements on ionic solids can still be useful. The dielectric properties of such solids are chiefly determined by the ability of the ions in the lattice to move, and so are dependent on crystal imperfections and defects. The latter may be altered in an order-disorder transition, and accordingly the permittivity may change. Thus, sodium nitrate has a single gradual transition extending from ~420 K to 548 K which is associated with increasing orientational disorder of the nitrate ions, accompanied by increased freedom of the sodium ions to diffuse in the lattice. Fermor and Kjekshus (1968, 1972), using zone-refined single crystals, found that the permittivity of this salt increases by about two orders of magnitude as it is heated through the transition. Finally, since permittivity measurements are made isothermally and can be carried out with some precision with falling as well

as with rising temperature, they have frequently been used
to establish whether or not a transition has a discontinuous
stage accompanied by hysteresis.

4.9. RADIOTRACER AND CREEP STUDIES OF DIFFUSION

In some disordered solids, especially in the soft solids
known as plastic crystals (Chapters 9 and 10), the molecules
can diffuse in the lattice with comparative ease. This
self-diffusion takes place *via* the point defects in the
crystal, and can be studied quantitatively by a radiotracer
method. In this technique, which has been developed by Sherwood and his coworkers, a suitably labelled sample of the
substance is deposited on the surface of a single crystal.
In investigating self-diffusion in cyclohexane, for example,
the labelled form contained one ^{14}C atom per molecule. The
rate of diffusion of the labelled molecules into the crystal
is then measured. This can be done in more than one way,
but the best method appears to be to cut sections of the
crystal parallel to the surface on which the radioactive form
is deposited, and then to determine the activities of these
sections. In this way the activity A is determined as a
function of distance x from the surface and of the diffusion
time t. For diffusion from a very thin surface layer, of
initial total activity Q, into an effectively infinite
crystal, the following relation holds:

$$A = (Q/(\pi D t)^{\frac{1}{2}})\exp(-x^2/4Dt) \ .$$

From this equation the self-diffusion coefficient D can be
evaluated. The dependence of D on temperature T is governed
by an Arrhenius-type equation

$$D = D_0 \exp(-E_D/RT) \ ,$$

where D_0 is a constant and E_D is the activation energy for
the self-diffusion process. Accordingly, by carrying out
experiments over a range of temperature, E_D can be determined, and it is also possible to make estimates of the
entropy of activation from the value of D_0. Experimental

details will be found in the papers of Hood and Sherwood
(1966a,b). Considerable attention must be paid to the
purity and preparation of the specimen used, but there is
no doubt that, properly handled, this method gives valuable
information on intrinsic self-diffusion through the lattice
(as opposed to diffusion along dislocations and sub-boundaries
in the crystal). Fig.4.33, for cyclohexane, illustrates the

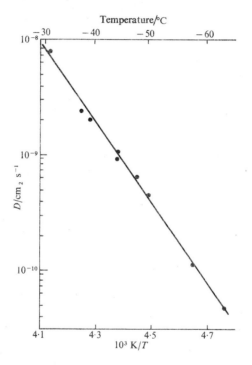

Fig.4.33. Temperature dependence of the self-diffusion coefficient D for
cyclohexane (Hood and Sherwood 1966b).

precision of which the technique is capable.

Examples will be found in section 6.2. of the use of
the radiotracer technique to study self-diffusion in the so-
called super-ionic conductors such as silver iodide and the
compound $RbAg_4I_5$. If a suitable radioactive isotope is not
available, its place can be taken by a stable isotope, the
progress of which through the crystal is followed with a
mass-spectrometer. In this way, using [6]Li, Kvist and Trolle
(1967) investigated the self-diffusion of the lithium ions
in the high-temperature disordered phase of lithium sulphate.

Quantitative information about the translational movement of the molecules in organic crystals can also be obtained by studying the phenomenon of creep. This is the
plastic flow or deformation which occurs under an applied
stress, a process previously investigated in metals at high
temperatures. The application of this method to plastic
crystals has again been due to Sherwood and his collaborators.
Essentially, a stress σ is applied to a cylindrical crystal
and its height h measured as a function of time t. The creep
rate $\dot{\varepsilon}$ (= $dh/h_0)/dt$, where h_0 is the height of the crystal at
$t = 0$) is given by the equation

$$\dot{\varepsilon} = \frac{A}{T} \sigma^n \exp(-E_c/RT) ,$$

where E_c is the activation energy for the creep process, and
A and n are constants. Quite small values of σ are adequate
in studying plastic crystals. For example, in experiments
on cyclohexane and pivalic acid, Hawthorne and Sherwood (1970)
used stresses of the order 10 kN m^{-2}. There are two possible
mechanisms by which creep can take place. The first is by
the migration of lattice vacancies across grains in the
crystal, when $n = 1$. The second is by the climbing of dislocations via point defects in the lattice, in which case
the theoretical value of n is 4·5. For both possibilities,
the creep rate is controlled by the diffusion of vacancies
in the crystal, and accordingly the activation energy for
creep (E_c) should be about the same as that for self-diffusion
(E_D). The results so far obtained by Sherwood and his coworkers do in fact show that E_c and E_D are approximately
equal, and that creep occurs by the dislocation climb mechanism, since the experimental values of n lie between ~4·4
and 6 (Sherwood 1969).

REFERENCES

Abragam, A. (1961). *The principles of nuclear magnetism*,
    Oxford University Press.

Ahlers, G. and Orttung, W.H. (1964). *Phys.Rev.* A133, 1642.

Ailion, D.C. and Slichter, C.P. (1965). *Phys.Rev.* A137, 235.

Albert, S. and Gutowsky, H.S. (1973). *J.chem.Phys.* 59, 3585.

———   and Ripmeester, J.A. (1973). *J.chem.Phys.* 58, 541.

Amdur, I. and Hammes, G.G. (1966). *Chemical kinetics*, McGraw-Hill, New York.

Anderson, J.E. and Slichter, W.P. (1964). *J.chem.Phys.* 41, 1922.

———   ———   (1965). *J.phys.Chem.* 69, 3099.

———   ———   (1966). *J.chem.Phys.* 44, 1797.

Andrew, E.R. (1950). *J.chem.Phys.* 18, 607.

——— (1953). *Phys Rev.* 91, 425.

——— (1961). *(J).Phys Chem.Solids* 18, 9.

——— and Allen, P.S. (1966). *J.Chim.phys.* 63, 85.

——— and Eades, R.G. (1953). *Proc.R.Soc.* 218A, 537.

———   ———   Hennel, J.W. and Hughes, D.G. (1962). *Proc.phys.Soc.* 79, 954.

Arnold, G.M. and Heastie, R. (1967). *Chem.Phys.Lett.* 1, 51.

Bacon, G.E. (1975). *Neutron diffraction*, 3rd ed. Oxford University Press.

Ballik, E.A., Gannon, D.J. and Morrison, J.A. (1973). *J.chem.Phys.* 58, 5639.

Barrett, C.S. and Meyer, L. (1965). (a) *J.chem.Phys.* 42, 107; (b) 43, 3502.

Benedek, G.B. (1963). *Magnetic resonance at high pressure*. Interscience Tracts on Physics and Astronomy No.24. Interscience, New York.

Bertie, J.E. and Sunder, S. (1973). *J.chem.Phys.* 59, 498.

——— and Whalley, E. (1964). *J.chem.Phys.* 40, 1646.

———   ———   (1967). (a) *J.chem.Phys.* 46, 1264; (b) 46, 1271.

Bertini, I., Gatteschi. D., and Scozzafava, A. (1974). *Inorg.Chim.Acta.* 11, L17.

Bloembergen, N., Purcell, E.M., and Pound, R.V. (1948). *Phys.Rev.* 73, 679.

Boutin, H. and Safford, G.J. (1964). *Proc.symposium on inelastic scattering of neutrons, Bombay,* II, 393.

Brookeman, J.R., McEnnan, M.M., and Scott, T.A. (1971). *Phys.Rev.* B4, 3661.

——   and Scott, T.A. (1973). *J.low Temp.Phys.* 12, 491.

Cabana, A. (1975). *Vibrational spectra and structure* (ed. J.R.Durig), Vol.4, Chap.2 , Elsevier, Amsterdam.

Carter, G.F. and Templeton, D.H. (1953). *Acta crystallog.* 6, 805.

Casimir, H.B.G. and Du Pré, F.K. (1938). *Physica* 5, 507.

Clusius,K. and Faber, G. (1942). *Z.phys.Chem.* B51, 352.

——   and Weigand, K. (1938). *Z.Elektrochem.* 44, 674.

Cole, R.H. and Havriliak, S. (1957). *Disc.Faraday Soc.*, No.23, 31.

Collins, M.F. (1966). *Proc.phys.Soc.* 89, 415.

Dahlborg, U., Gräslund, C., and Larsson, K.E. (1972). *Physica*, 59, 672.

Dalal, N.S., McDowell, C.A., and Srinivasan, R. (1974). *J.chem.Phys.* 60, 3787.

Davies, M. (1965). *Some electrical and optical aspects of molecular behaviour*, Pergamon Press, Oxford.

DeReggi, A.S., Canepa, P.C., and Scott, T.A. (1969). *J.mag. Res.* 1, 144.

Dinichert, P. (1942). *Helv.phys.Acta.* 15, 462.

Dows, D.A. (1963). *Physics and chemistry of the organic solid state*, (ed. D.Fox, M.Labes, and A.Weissberger), Vol.I., Chap.11, p.657, Interscience, New York.

Durig, J.R. and Antion, D.J. (1969). *J.chem.Phys.* 51, 3639.

Egelstaff, P.A. (Ed.) 1965. *Thermal neutron scattering*, Academic Press, London and New York.

Fermor, J.H. and Kjekshus, A. (1968). *Acta chem.scand.* 22, 1628.

——   ——   (1972). *Acta chem.scand.* 26, 3235.

Fisher, M.E. (1968). *Phys.Rev.* 176, 257.

Foner, S., Meyer, H. and Kleiner, W.H. (1961). *(J). Phys. Chem.Solids* 18, 273.

Fournier, R.P., Savoie, R., Nguyen Dinh The, Belzile, R. and Cabana, A. (1972). *Can.J.Chem.* 50, 35.

Fratiello, A. and Douglass, D.C. (1964). *J.chem.Phys.* 41, 974.

Fredericks, G.E. (1971). *Phys.Rev.* B4, 911.

Garland, C.W. and Schumaker, N.E. (1967). *(J.).Phys.Chem.Solids*
28, 799.

de Graaf, L.A. and Ściesiński, J. (1970). *Physica* 48, 79.

Green, J.R. and Griffith, W.T. (1969). *Molecular Crystals
and Liquid Crystals* 6, 23.

——————   Dalich, S.J. and Griffith, W.T. (1972). *Molecular
Crystals and Liquid Crystals* 17, 251.

Goodenough, J.B. (1963). *Magnetism and the chemical bond*,
Interscience, New York.

Gutowsky, H.S. and Pake, G.E. (1950). *J.chem.Phys.* 18, 162.

Haida, O., Matsuo, T., Suga, H., and Seki, S. (1972). *Proc.
Japan Acad.* 48, 489.

Hamilton, W.C. and Ibers, J.A. (1968). *Hydrogen bonding in
solids*, W.A. Benjamin Inc., New York.

——————   and Petrie, M. (1961). *J.phys.Chem.* 65, 1453.

Handler, P., Mapother, D.E., and Rayl, M. (1967). *Phys.Rev.
Lett.* 19, 356.

Hartmann, S.R. and Hahn, E.L. (1962). *Phys.Rev.* 128, 2042.

Hawthorne, H.M. and Sherwood, J.N. (1970). *Trans.Faraday.Soc.*
66, 1783.

Herbstein, F.H. and Snyman, J.A. (1969). *Phil.Trans.R.Soc.
London*, 264A, 635.

Hettich, A. (1934). *Z.phys.Chem.* A168, 353.

Hiebert, G.L. and Hornig, D.F. (1952). *J.chem.Phys.* 20, 918.

Hill, N.E., Vaughan, W.E., Price, A.H., and Davies, M. (1969).
Dielectric properties and molecular behaviour, Van
Nostrand Reinhold Company, London.

Hochheimer, H.D., Spanner, E., and Strauch, D. (1976). *J.
chem.Phys.* 64, 1583.

Hood, G.M. and Sherwood, J.N. (1966). (a) *J.Chim.phys.* 63,
121; (b) *Molecular crystals* 1, 97.

Hornig, D.F. (1948). *J.chem.Phys.* 16, 1063.

Jonas, J. (1975). *Ann.Rev.Phys.Chem.* 26, 167.

Jordan, T.H., Smith, H.W., Streib, W.E., and Lipscomb, W.N.
(1964). *J.chem.Phys.* 41, 756.

——————   Streib, W.E., and Lipscomb, W.N. (1964). *J.
chem.Phys.* 41, 760.

Ketudat, S. and Pound, R.V. (1957). *J.chem.Phys.* 26, 708.

Kobayashi, J., Uesu, Y., and Enomoto, Y. (1971). *Phys.St.*
    Solidi, 45B, 293.

Kruis, A. and Clusius, K. (1937). *Phys.Zeit.* 38, 510.

Kuroda, N. and Kawamori, A. (1971). *(J.).Phys.Chem.Solids* 32,
    1233.

Kvist, A. and Trolle, U. (1967). *Z.Naturforsch.*22a, 213.

Lawson, A.W. (1940). *Phys.Rev.* 57, 417.

Lechner, R.E., Rowe, J.M., Sköld, K., and Rush, J.J. (1969).
    Chem.Phys.Lett. 4, 444.

Leung, P.S., Rush, J.J., and Taylor, T.I. (1972). *J.chem.*
    Phys. 57, 175.

Levy, H.A. and Peterson, S.W. (1952). *Phys.Rev.* 86, 766.
  ———   ———   (1953). *J.Am.chem.Soc.* 75, 1536;
    J.chem.Phys. 21, 366.

Lifschitz, I.M. (1942). *Zh.eksp.teor.Fiz.* 12, 117, 137.

Marshall, J.G., Staveley, L.A.K., and Hart, K.R. (1956).
    Trans.Faraday Soc. 52, 19.

Marx, R. (1966). *J.Chim. phys.* 63, 128.

Matsuo, T., Tatsumi, M., Suga, H., and Seki, S. (1973).
    Solid St.Communs. 13, 1829.

Meakins, R.J. (1961). *Progress in Dielectrics*, 3, 151.

Morfee, R.G.S., Staveley, L.A.K., Walters, S.T., and Wigley,
    D.L. (1960). *(J).Phys.Chem.Solids* 13, 132.

O'Reilly, D.E. and Tsang, T. (1967). *J.chem.Phys.* 47, 4072.

Perry, C.H. and Lowndes, R.P. (1969). *J.chem.Phys.* 51, 3648.

Powles, J.G. (1961). *(J).Phys.Chem.Solids* 18, 17.
  ———   (1976). *Ber. Bunsenges. phys. Chem.*80, 259.

Press, W. (1972).*(J.)chem.Phys.* 56, 2597.
  ———   and Hüller, A. (1973). *Acta crystallog.* A29, 252.

Reese, R. and May, L.F. (1967). *Phys.Rev.* 162, 510.

Resing, H.A. (1962). *J.chem.Phys.* 37, 2575.
  ———   (1969). *Molecular Crystals and Liquid Crystals*
    9, 101.

Richards, R.E. (1968). *Mol.Spectrosc.Proc.Conf.4th*, 375.
  ———   (1969). *Nat.Bur.Stand.(U.S.) Spec.Publ.1967*
    (Pubd.1969). No.301, 157.

Rudman, R. and Post, B. (1966). *Science* 154, 1009.
  ———   ———   (1968). *Molecular Crystals* 5, 95.

Rush, J.J. and Taylor, T.I. (1964). *J.phys.Chem.* 68, 2534.

Rush, J.J. and Taylor, T.I. (1966). *J.phys.Chem.* <u>44</u>, 2749.

———   ———   and Havens, W.W. (1960). *Phys.*
    Rev.Lett. <u>5</u>, 507.

———   ———   ———   (1962). *J.chem.*
    Phys. <u>37</u>, 234.

Sándor, E. and Farrow, R.F.C. (1967).*Nature, Lond.* <u>215</u>, 1265.

———   and Johnson M.W. (1968). *Nature, Lond.* <u>217</u>, 541.

Schwartz, P. (1971). *Phys.Rev.* <u>B4</u>, 920.

Scott, J.F. (1974). *Rev.mod.Phys.* <u>46</u>, 83.

Semenov, N.N. (1961). *XVIIIth Intern. Congress of Pure and*
    Appl.Chem., Montreal, p.353. Butterworths, London.

Sherwood, J.N. (1969). *Molecular Crystals and Liquid Crystals*,
    <u>9</u>, 37.

Shirane, G. (1974). *Rev.mod.Phys.* <u>46</u>, 437.

Simon, F. and von Simson, C. (1924). *Z.Phys.* <u>21</u>, 168.

Skjeltorp, A.J. and Wolf, W.P. (1973). *Phys.Rev.* <u>B8</u>, 215.

Slichter, C.P. and Ailion, D. (1964). *Phys.Rev.* <u>135A</u>, 1099.

Slichter, W.P. (1969). *Molecular Crystals and Liquid Crystals*
    <u>9</u>, 81.

Smith, D. (1971). *Chem.Phys.Lett.* <u>10</u>, 174.

Smith, G.W. (1965). *J.chem.Phys.* <u>43</u>, 4325.

Smits, A. and MacGillavry, C.H. (1933). *Z.phys.Chem.* <u>A166</u>,
    97.

———   , Muller, G.H. and Kröger, F.A. (1937). *Z.phys.*
    Chem. <u>B38</u>, 177.

Smyth, C.P. (1955). *Dielectric behavior and structure,*
    McGraw-Hill, New York.

———   and Hitchcock, C.S. (1934). *J.Am.chem.Soc.* <u>56</u>,
    1084.

Somenkov, V.A. (1972). *Ber.Bunsenges.physik.Chem.* <u>76</u>, 733.

Stejskal, E.O., Woessner, D.E., Farrar, T.C., and Gutowsky,
    H.S. (1959). *J.chem.Phys.* <u>31</u>, 55.

Stout, J.W. and Catalano, E. (1955). *J.chem.Phys.* <u>23</u>, 2013.

———   and Chisholm, R.C. (1962). *J.chem.Phys.* <u>36</u>, 979.

Suga, H. and Seki, S. (1962). *Bull.chem.Soc.Japan*, <u>35</u>, 1905.

Szwarc, H. (1962). *J.Chim.phys.* <u>59</u>, 1067.

———   (1966). *J.Chim.phys.* <u>63</u>, 137.

Trappeniers, N.J. (1966). *Ber.Bunsenges.phys.Chem.* <u>70</u>, 1080.

Tsang, T. and O'Reilly, D.E. (1965). *J.chem.Phys.* <u>43</u>, 4234.

Vainshtein, B.K. and Stasova, M.M. (1956). *Kristallografiya* 1, 311. *(Soviet Phys.Crystallog. 1956,* 1, 241).

Vedder, W. and Hornig, D.F. (1961). *Adv.Spectrosc.* 2, 189.

Venkataraman, G., Usha Deniz, K., Iyengar, P.K., Vijayaraghavan, P.R., and Roy, A.P. (1964). *Solid St.Communs.* 2, 17.

Wagner, E.L. and Hornig, D.F. (1950). *J.chem.Phys.* 18, 296.

Wang, C.H. (1971). *Phys.Rev.Lett.* 26, 1226.

———   and Fleury, P.A. (1968). *Light scattering spectra of solids* (ed. G.B. Wright) Springer-Verlag, New York, p.651

———   and Wright, R.B. (1972). *J.chem.Phys.* 57, 4401.

———   ———   (1973). *J.chem.Phys.* 58, 1411.

Waugh, J.S. and Fedin, E.I. (1962). *Fizika Tver.Tela* 4, 2233 *(Soviet Phys.Solid St.,* 1963, 4, 1633).

White, J.W. (1974). *Spectrochim.Acta* 30A, 1665.

Williams, R.M. and Wallwork, S.C. (1967). *Acta crystallog.* 22, 899.

Wilson, A.H. (1966). *Thermodynamics and statistical mechanics,* p.160. Cambridge University Press.

Worswick, R.D., Cowell, J.C., and Staveley, L.A.K. (1974). *J.chem.Soc.,Faraday Trans.* I, 70, 1590.

Wright, R.B. and Wang, C.H. (1973). *(J.) Phys.Chem.Solids,* 34, 787.

Würflinger, A. (1975). *Ber.Bunsenges.phys.Chem.* 79, 1195.

Yen, W.M. and Norberg, R.E. (1963). *Phys.Rev.* 131, 269.

5
ALLOYS

5.1. INTRODUCTION

In some respects the order-disorder processes in alloys are simpler than those found in either ionic or molecular solids. It is primarily for this reason that we shall consider systems of this type first. Historically, it was the Fe-Al system which attracted the attention of W.L. Bragg and Williams to the problem of order-disorder transitions, and the first quantitative tests of their theory were made using heat capacity data for β-brass, and Cu_3Au. The comparative simplicity of alloy systems comes largely from the possibility of treating the individual units, in this case the atoms, as being spherically symmetric. This is in contrast to, for example, molecular crystals, where the units are the molecules and these may have very complicated shapes indeed.

Because alloys may often be considered simply as arrays of close-packed or near close-packed spheres it is not surprising that many of them have **very simple** crystal structures, frequently based on face-centred or body-centred cubic arrangements. In the fully ordered state each site is assigned to a particular kind of atom, A or B in the case of a binary alloy $A_x B_y$. In the disordered alloy, on the other hand, at least some of the sites are occupied in irregular fashion by either A or B atoms. It follows from this that even when the ordered and disordered forms are based on the same crystal system, the unit cell may be larger for the former than the latter. An example of such behaviour is Fe_3Al, which is discussed below. In other cases, the disordering does not affect the size of the unit cell.

It was mentioned in Chapter 3 that the order-disorder processes in binary alloys could be discussed in terms of the Ising model. Ordering alloys are then equivalent to magnetic systems having antiferromagnetic interactions between the spins, since the atoms of these alloys tend to

arrange themselves so as to minimize the number of like
nearest-neighbour pairs. Those alloys in which like nearest-
neighbour pairs are preferred tend to separate into two
phases on cooling. Several attempts have been made to simulate the ordering of alloys on a computer. These attempts
were essentially Ising model studies using Monte Carlo
methods and as such they suffered from convergence failures
in the vicinity of the critical temperatures (Fosdick 1959,
Guttman 1961, Flinn and McManus 1961).

5.2. ORDER PARAMETERS

The definitions of the order parameters which were given in
section 3.1 are suitable only for the 1:1 binary alloy discussed there. It is not possible to define a system of
order parameters which will be suitable for all order-disorder processes in alloys. Even when attention is restricted to long-range order, the situation is too complex
to admit of a simple, general solution, and, indeed, in
many it is necessary to employ several long-range order
parameters in order to describe the system adequately.

Frequently, a first step in selecting an appropriate
set of long-range parameters is to divide the lattice into
the minimum number of sublattices such that in the fully
ordered state each sublattice is entirely occupied by atoms
of one kind. This is generally possible for stoichiometric
alloys, though not for non-stoichiometric ones. The state
of an alloy may then be described by the set of values for
the probabilities that a site on a particular sublattice is
occupied by a particular kind of atom. For example, if
there are four sublattices $(\alpha,\beta,\gamma,\delta)$ and three kinds of
atom $(1,2,3)$, there would be twelve probability values of
the form $P_{\alpha}(2)$, this being the probability that a site of
the α sublattice is occupied by an atom of type 2. However,
there are relationships between these P values which must
always be satisfied, e.g. $P_{\alpha}(1)+P_{\alpha}(2)+P_{\alpha}(3) = 1$ and
$n_{\alpha}P_{\alpha}(1)+n_{\beta}P_{\beta}(1)+n_{\gamma}P_{\gamma}(1)+n_{\delta}P_{\delta}(1) = N_1$ where $n_{\alpha},n_{\beta},n_{\gamma}$, and
n_{δ} are the total numbers of sites on the α,β,γ and δ sub-
lattices, respectively, and N_1 is the total number of atoms
of type 1 in the system. It is clear that in the fully

ordered state each P value is either unity or zero. In the
fully disordered state, in which all the sites are occupied
randomly, each P value becomes equal to the mole fraction of
the type of atom concerned. These P values for the disordered state will, of course, be modified if not all of the
sublattices are involved in the randomization (see Fe_3Al).
It is often considered desirable that long-range parameters
should be defined so that they take the values 0 and 1 for
the extreme situations of disorder and order, respectively.
Such a long-range parameter could, for example, be defined
as:

$$\mathscr{S}\alpha = \frac{P_\alpha(1) - P_\alpha(1)_{dis}}{P_\alpha(1)_{ord} - P_\alpha(1)_{dis}} \tag{5.1}$$

where $P_\alpha(1)$, $P_\alpha(1)_{dis}$, and $P_\alpha(1)_{ord}$ refer, respectively, to
the state of interest and the disordered and order states,
and the α sublattice is occupied by type 1 atoms in the
ordered state. The number of independent $\mathscr{S}$ and P values
must, of course, be the same.

    An alternative method for binary alloys which has been
used by Cowley (1950, 1960, 1965) is firstly to introduce
order parameters describing the occupancy correlation of two
sites i and j by the relation:

$$\alpha_{ij} = 1 - P(B_j|A_i)/x_B \tag{5.2}$$

where $P(B_j|A_i)$ is the conditional probability that site j
will be occupied by a B atom given that there is an A atom
at site i, and x_B is the mole fraction of B atoms. Irres-
pective of the degree of order in the lattice $\alpha_{ii} = 1$.   It
is also clear that for a fully disordered lattice $\alpha_{ij} = 0$,
provided $i \neq j$. The number of independent α_{ij} values is, of
course, greatly reduced by the symmetry of the lattice, since
the correlation involved is determined by the relative rather
than the absolute positions of the sites. If the intersite
vector ($\underline{r}_{ij}$) is increased by an amount representable as
$l\underline{a} + m\underline{b} + n\underline{c}$, where $\underline{a}, \underline{b}$ and $\underline{c}$ are the unit cell vectors and l, m,
and n are integers, then α_{ij} will decrease. Above the
critical ordering temperature this fall proceeds asymptotically to zero; however below the critical temperature each

α_{ij} tends asymptotically to a finite, non-zero value (α_{ij}^{∞}), which is a measure of the long-range order. In general for a proper description of the long-range order it is necessary to know the limiting values of all of the α_{ij}, the number of which corresponds to the number of maxima in the Patterson X-ray pattern. Cowley (1965) has shown that provided the composition of the alloy can be assumed to remain uniform at all times then relationships between these long-range order parameters may be derived, thereby reducing the number which need to be specified. For example, for the alloy Cu_3Au, the structure of which is based on the face-centred cube, the long-range correlation between corner and face-centre sites (α_{cf}^{∞}) is related to that between corner sites (α_{cc}^{∞}) by the equation $3\alpha_{cf}^{\infty}+\alpha_{cc}^{\infty} = 0$. It should be emphasized that the α_{ij}^{∞} do not in general become unity for the fully ordered state, as is indeed evident from the prevous equation. Thus for the completely ordered state of Cu_3Au $\alpha_{cc}^{\infty} = 1$ but $\alpha_{cf}^{\infty} = -1/3$.

The brief discussion of order parameters for the Ising model in section 3.1 was limited to the case of zero applied field for the magnetic system and correspondingly to the equiatomic composition for the binary alloy system. To extend the treatment to problems equivalent to those of binary alloys of general composition it is necessary to modify equation (3.11) so as to render it applicable when a non-zero field is applied. We then have:

$$\alpha_{ij} = (\langle s_i^z s_j^z \rangle - \langle s_i^z \rangle^2)/(s^2 - \langle s_i^z \rangle^2) \qquad (5.3)$$

where $s=1/2$ and s_i^z and s_j^z can each take the values $\pm 1/2$ according to whether the sites i and j are occupied by atoms of type A or B. The mole fractions of A and B atoms in the alloy are $(\langle s_i^z \rangle/s +1)/2$ and $(1-\langle s_i^z \rangle/s)/2$, respectively.

Flinn (1956) introduced a scheme of operators for the discussion of order in alloys which is analogous in all respects to the Ising system outlined above. He defined an operator C_i which is related to the Ising spin operators by the equation: $C_i = x_B+(s_i^z-s)$. Occupation of the ith site by an A(B) atom corresponds to $s_i^z = +1/2(-1/2)$ and in turn to $C_i = x_B(-x_A)$. The α functions may then be related to the

Flinn operators by the equation:

$$\langle c_i c_j \rangle = x_A x_B \alpha_{ij} \quad .$$

(5.4)

In discussing long-range order parameters it has been said that the limit as the distance is increased to infinity should be taken. We must here enter a caveat. Suppose, for example, that the substance behaves as a two-dimensionally ordered crystal. In this case, the limit to which the order parameter, i.e. α_{ij} or its equivalents, tends as $\underline{r}_{ij}$ increases will depend upon the way in which $\underline{r}_{ij}$ and the increments in it are disposed with respect to the crystal axes. Thus if $\underline{r}_{ij}$ is directed along the third crystal direction and increments with the same direction are added to it, then the limit will be zero. However, if $\underline{r}_{ij}$ and its increments lie along a direction in the plane defined by the two 'important' dimensions, then the limit will be non-zero. A further difficulty arises for the so-called long-period structures (section 5.5). These may be considered as a completely regular alternating system of domains. Consider now the evaluation of a long-range order parameter in the direction of the periodicity; α_{ij}, for example, will vary periodically with $\underline{r}_{ij}$ with a repeat distance equal to that of the domain structure. If the increments in $\underline{r}_{ij}$ are multiples of the 'long period' then α_{ij} will behave normally, decreasing monotonically to a limit which defines the 'long-period order parameter'. There is no simple, general way to define a long-range parameter describing other types of order in these systems: such definitions are beset by difficulties arising from the 'domain' structure.

5.3. SPECIAL EXPERIMENTAL METHODS

As with most of the other order-disorder systems, a great deal of important information is derived from X-ray and neutron diffraction studies. These methods have been discussed in Chapter 4. However, a particular feature of alloy systems is that frequently the atoms concerned are difficult to distinguish by X-ray diffraction. This arises when, as is often the case, the elements lie close together in the

Periodic Table and therefore have similar numbers of electrons and similar scattering factors for X-rays. In the
classic case of β-brass it was not possible to show up the
ordering unless the frequency of the X-rays was very carefully chosen. Only by selecting a frequency which was close
to that of an absorption line was the ratio of the scattering
factors (f) of the Cu and Zn atoms made sufficiently different
from unity for the superlattice to be observed (Fig.5.1). A

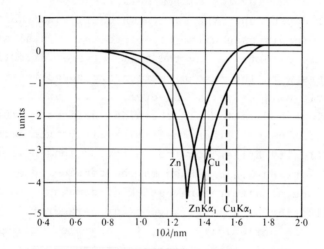

Fig.5.1. The variation with wavelength of the X-ray structure factors
for Zn and Cu atoms (full lines). Positions of nearby absorptions are
indicated by broken lines (from Nix and Shockley 1938).

similar device has been resorted to in order to distinguish
Cu and Mn atoms in Heusler alloys and Ni and Fe atoms in
Ni_3Fe. In the more recently developed technique of neutron
diffraction the scattering factors vary in an irregular
manner with atomic number, with the consequence that atoms
of adjacent elements in the Periodic Table may often be
distinguished by this means.

        Another useful method of investigation, which is almost
entirely restricted to metallic systems, is that using
electrical resistivity measurements. For alloys this is
a simple and sensitive method of detecting order-disorder
transitions, although the quantitative relationship between

resistivity and order has not been deduced in detail. The
principle of the method is, however, straightforward: the
current-carrying electrons in the alloy will be frequently
scattered in the disordered lattice, thereby increasing the
resistivity. A typical graph of resistivity against temperature is given in Fig.5.2 (Sykes and Evans 1936). The critical ordering temperature is marked by a sharp change of

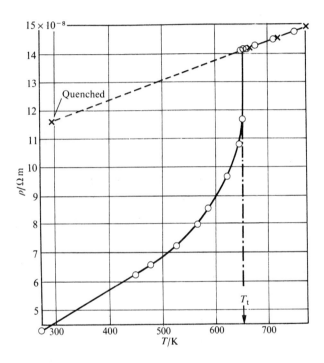

Fig.5.2. Electrical resistivity (ρ) against temperature for Cu$_3$Au;
———o——— equilibrium values, -----x----- values for sample quenched
from a high temperature to the temperature shown (from Sykes and Evans
1936).

slope. By quenching from high temperatures it is possible
to obtain results which fall on the extrapolation to lower
temperatures of the high-temperature branch of the equilibrium curve. Two kinds of complication arise. Firstly,
if the ordered form has a domain structure the scattering
of the electrons at the domain walls may cause the resistivity to be unduly large. Secondly, what has been said
about the effect of order on resistivity is valid for long-

range order, but the situation for short-range order is more
obscure. Indeed, an increase of short-range order may lead
either to an increase or a decrease in resistivity (Damask
1956; Gibson 1956). The quantity discussed in these papers
is the residual resistivity, the value obtained by quenching
the alloy from the temperature of interest and then measuring its resistivity at liquid helium temperatures. In this
way effects due to atomic vibrations are avoided. Damask
examined Cu_3Au above T_t and also α-brass ($Cu_{0.7}Zn_{0.3}$). He
found that as the temperature from which the alloy was quenched
was increased, thereby decreasing the short-range order,
Cu_3Au showed a decrease in resistivity, whilst α-brass showed
an increase.

Magnetic properties can also often be used to detect
order-disorder changes. In these experiments two types of
process can occur: magnetic ordering of the spins and positional ordering of the atoms. Incomplete positional ordering often leads to an alloy being magnetically 'hard', that
is, having a high coercivity. This is because the walls of
the magnetic domains find it difficult to move through the
disordered solid. Positional disorder will also often
affect the saturation magnetization, although it cannot
generally be said that the induced change will be in one
particular direction.

Reductions in the degree of order have often been
achieved by the deliberate introduction of strains or dislocations by means of 'cold working'. Starting from an ordered alloy, each passage of a dislocation along a slip plane
increases the antiphase boundary between domains and hence
the disorder. The most commonly employed method is to stretch
the metal, when the percentage reduction in the cross-section
is a measure of the degree of 'cold working'. An excellent
account of the effects of 'cold working' on alloys has been
given by Cohen and Bever (1960), who were primarily concerned
with Cu_3Au.

Most of the early studies of ordering alloys at high
temperatures were actually carried out with samples quenched
from the temperature concerned. It was assumed that no
changes occurred in the sample during or after the rapid

cooling to room temperature. In more recent work it is usual, wherever possible, to perform the experiments with the sample held at the temperature of interest. As a test of the above assumption, X-ray determinations of the long-range and short-range order have been made on quenched samples and on samples held at the high temperature in question. Walker (1952) found no significant difference for Cu_3Au, but Keating and Warren (1951) showed that samples of the same alloy held just below the transition temperature had appreciably less order than those quenched from the same temperature.

Values of long-range order parameters have been obtained from measurements of changes in some of the lattice constants, that is from the amount of lattice distortion associated with the change from the fully ordered or disordered forms. In these methods, unfortunately, it is necessary to assume the form of the dependence of the distortion on the order parameter. Thus for AuCu, which undergoes a tetragonal distortion on ordering, different workers have assumed that the c/a ratio is proportional to $\mathcal{S}$ and $\mathcal{S}^2$, where $\mathcal{S}$ is the Bragg-Williams long-range order parameter. In Cu_3Au, also, different dependences of c/a on $\mathcal{S}$ have been adopted. From what has been said, it seems clear that this method of determining $\mathcal{S}$ is not soundly based.

5.4. SPECIFIC SYSTEMS

Out of the large number of alloy systems which have been studied we shall, in the main, restrict ourselves to the stoichiometrically and structurally simple AB and A_3B types. We shall generally omit reference to the many interesting non-stoichiometric systems, except where the discussion of these is helpful to the understanding of the stoichiometric alloys. Another vigorous field of study which will largely be omitted is that of the superconducting and ferromagnetic properties of alloys.

5.4.1. FeAl

This ordered structure is body-centred cubic, with the Fe atoms at the cell corners and the Al atoms at the cell centres. It can, therefore, be considered as being made up

of two interpenetrating simple cubic lattices, each occupied
by one kind of atom. The unit cell of this ordered structure
is the cube shown in Fig.5.3, just as it would be if the Fe

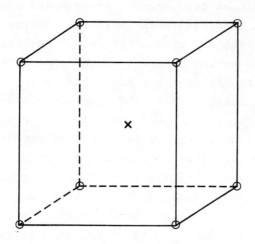

Fig.5.3. The ordered structure of FeAl; o = Fe, × = Al.

and Al atoms were distributed randomly over the sites. On
heating to ~1530 K the solid begins to melt in a manner
typical of two-component systems yielding a liquid richer
in Al and a solid depleted in Al. There does not appear
to be a disordered phase of this composition (Taylor and
Jones 1958).

5.4.2. β-CuZn (β-brass)
The ordered structure is the same as for FeAl. There is,
however, also a disordered form which is stable above ~741 K
and in which the Cu and Zn atoms are distributed over all the
lattice sites in such a way that there is no long-range
order. The β-phase is, in fact, only stable over the range
of compositions from 45·8 to 48·9 at.%Zn. However, at one
limit the composition is sufficiently close to that of CuZn
that for most discussions it is possible to ignore the discrepancy. For many years there was much discussion as to
whether below T_t, the transition temperature, there was only
a single phase present or whether there were two phases in

equilibrium. This question was answered by the careful X-ray work of Keating and Warren (1951). Since the disordered form has a slightly larger cell dimension, reflections from the two forms are correspondingly slightly displaced. The presence of both forms together would then lead to a broadening of the X-ray peaks or even to double peaks. Experiments on single crystals held at various temperatures below T_t showed only narrow single peaks.

β-brass is a particularly convenient subject for study because of its short relaxation time near the ordering temperature. This is in line with the general observation that atomic diffusivities are higher in the more open b.c.c. matrix than in, for example, a f.c.c. system (Wayman 1971). Indeed, it seems to be impossible with this alloy to 'freeze in' disorder by cooling rapidly from above T_t. Sykes and Wilkinson (1937) were able, therefore, to obtain measurements of C_p which were independent of the previous treatment of the sample. Ashman and Handler (1969) have used an a.c. calorimetric technique (section 4.2) to examine the immediate vicinity of T_t $(10^{-6}<|(T_t-T)/T_t|<10^{-1})$. Their experiments yielded relative, rather than absolute, C_p data and this was then normalized by reference to the data of Moser (1936) for 810 K (Fig.5.4). The necessity for normalization does not, of course, affect the validity of the critical indices which they obtained from their data. The discussion by Ashman and Handler was concerned with C_V, but Salamon and Lederman (1974) have pointed out that on account of renormalization (section 2.5) it is better to compare C_p, rather than C_V, with the heat capacity of the rigid Ising system. When this is done the indices are found to be $\alpha = \alpha' = 0\cdot11 \pm 0\cdot02$, in fair agreement with the theoretical values (Table 3.7) and also with the best values for the gas-liquid critical point.

Neutron diffraction studies by Als-Nielsen and Dietrich (1967) have shown that below T_t the Bragg-Williams long-range order parameter ($\mathscr{S}$) decreases as $(T_t-T)^\beta$ with $\beta = 0\cdot305 \pm 0\cdot005$. This is in fair accord with estimates of this quantity for the three-dimensional Ising model (Table 3.7). They also showed that above T_t the variation

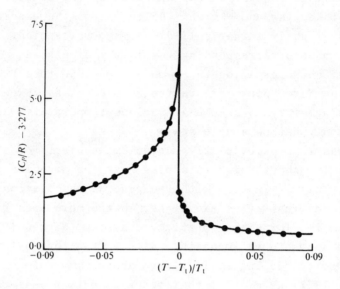

Fig.5.4. Heat capacity against temperature for β-brass: the results of Ashman and Handler (after Baker and Essam 1971).

of the short-range order with temperature followed that to be expected for the Ising model. Thus, from the critical scattering of neutrons in the range 2 - 25° above T_t they found values of the critical indices γ and ν of 1·25 and 0·65, respectively, as compared with 1.25 and 0·63 for the Ising model and 1 and 0·5 for the Bragg-Williams (mean-field) model. Münster (1973) has expressed surprise that agreement with the predictions of the Ising model is so good, since he considers that some of the assumptions involved in that model (in particular, the use of equation 3.1 for the energy of a configuration) are unreasonable for β-brass. He has also pointed out that for $T/T_t < 0·97$ the values of the long-range order parameter from X-ray determinations (Chipman and Walker 1971) are significantly higher than those predicted by the Ising model even when account is taken of the compressibility of the lattice. The values of this parameter obtained from neutron diffraction by Norvell and Als-Nielsen (1970), as corrected by Rathmann and Als-Nielsen (1974), agree with those of Chipman and Walker and also yield the value β = 0·293, which is significantly lower than

the accepted value for the three-dimensional Ising model.
The critical index γ' has also been determined by Als-Nielsen
(1969) from the critical neutron scattering from a sample
which had been enriched in ^{65}Cu to improve the cross-section
for critical scattering in comparison with that for Bragg
scattering. The scaling law result $\gamma = \gamma'$ (section 3.3)
was found to hold to within 3%.

The pressure dependence of the transition temperature
up to 10 kbar has been examined by Yoon and Bienenstock
(1968) using DTA to detect the transition. To obtain the
volume dependence of the transition temperature it was necessary to choose a value for the isothermal compressibility
(κ_T). This was done by extrapolation from lower temperatures,
ignoring Garland's suggestion (1964) that κ_S, at least,
should show a small peak at T_t. It was found that
$d \ln T_t / d \ln a$, where a is the lattice parameter, changed by
9% for a 3% change in the composition of the alloy, thereby
contradicting the nearest-neighbour Ising model, according
to which $d \ln T_t / d \ln a$ should be insensitive to composition.
This result may be explained if interactions between more
remote neighbours are included as well as those between
nearest neighbours. Theoretical results (Domb and Dalton
1966, Fan and Wu 1969) show that such a finite extension of
the range of interaction should not appreciably alter the
predicted values of the critical exponents, and so the
good agreement between experiment and the nearest-neighbour
Ising model for the indices should not be lost. A similar
study was made by Yoon and Jeffery (1970) on the ordering
transition at 995 K in α-CoFe, which is similar to that
in β-brass. The curve of T_t against composition, which
should be symmetric about the equiatomic composition according to the Ising model, was found to be markedly skew
whether or not corrections were applied to the experimental
results so as to relate them to constant volume. Thus, the
assumption of nearest-neighbour interactions only seems
again to be incorrect. Heat capacity measurements by
Orehotsky and Schroder (1974) over the range 700 - 1300 K,
because of the non-uniform temperature of the sample, were
not sufficiently precise to test the predictions of the Ising

model.

5.4.3. *CuAu*

The disordered form, stable above 683 K, is face-centred
cubic with both kinds of atom dispersed over all the sites
with no long-range order. There are two ordered forms. In
CuAu-I,[†] the structure stable at room temperature, the Cu
and Au atoms fill alternate (100) planes (Fig.5.5). As a

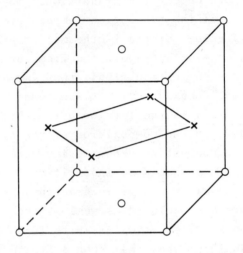

Fig.5.5. CuAu-I; o = Cu, × = Au.

consequence, the symmetry of the lattice is reduced to tetragonal and there are small changes in the lattice parameters,
with the base edges being somewhat longer than the vertical
edge. Observation of these cell lengths provides a convenient method of following the course of the ordering process,
although, as discussed above, it is dangerous to assume a
relationship between the extent of the distortion and the
long-range order parameter. In CuAu-I each Cu atom has as
nearest neighbours eight Au atoms and four Cu atoms, as

[†]The I-II nomenclature used here is that universally adopted for this
substance. It is the reverse, however, of that employed elsewhere in
this book.

compared with six Au and six Cu atoms in the disordered structure. It is possible, therefore, to attribute the stability
of this ordered structure to the tendency of each kind of
atom to surround itself with atoms of the opposite kind.
However, there is probably also a contribution from the
change in the energy of the conduction electrons. This
effect is discussed with reference to CuPt below, where it
is not masked by the nearest-neighbour affinities.

    Apart from the two forms already described, there is a
further ordered form (CuAu-II), which is stable between 653
and 683 K. It differs from CuAu-I only in that at intervals
of five lattice constants in the c direction there is a
shift by $0 \cdot 5 \times$ lattice constant in the a and b directions
(Fig.5.6). The 'antiphase domain' size seems to vary only

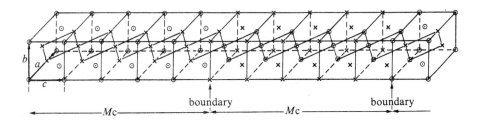

Fig.5.6. CuAu-II; $\circ$ = Cu, $\times$ = Au.

slightly from 5 over the, admittedly limited, temperature
range of the phase (Tachiki and Teramoto 1966). Since at
the 'antiphase' boundary each atom still has eight unlike
and four like nearest neighbours, the associated surface
energy would be expected to be small. This clearly facilitates the formation of the II form. However, to understand
why the II form might be more stable than the I form it is
necessary to consider the energy of the conduction electrons.
The extra periodicity associated with the 'antiphase' domains
leads to extra energy gaps in the conduction band. Considerable stabilization can result from this energy splitting if
the gaps appear in contact with the Fermi surface. This
effect is similar in character to that for CuPt discussed
below.

As presented so far it would appear that the 'anti-
phase' structure should be the stable form at low temperatures, which is not the case. Jones (1969) has shown that
this difficulty can be overcome if the 'antiphase' boundaries
are considered to be irregular, rather than planar. Thus
each element of a boundary can adopt any of a small number
of positions centred about the average position (Fig.5.7).

Fig.5.7. Jogs in an antiphase boundary of CuAu-II according to the Jones-
Inglesfield model.

The variety of possible positions of the boundaries gives an
extra entropy term to the II form, and it is this which
causes it to be preferred to the I form at the higher temperatures. Developing this explanation in greater detail,
Inglesfield (1972) represented each boundary by a square
Ising system, the fully ordered configuration of the latter
corresponding to a completely smooth boundary plane, and increasing disorder in the Ising system being equivalent to an
increasingly rough interface. If the free energy of such
a system is $G_{Ising}(T)$ then the difference in free energy
of the two forms is

$$G_{II} - G_I = \frac{\Omega}{Ma} \{U_{SF} + 2G_{Ising}(T)\} + \Delta U(M) \qquad (5.5)$$

where M is the average number of cells in each domain, a is
the length of the side of the cubic cell, Ω is the volume
per atom, U_{SF} is the stacking fault energy per unit area
of the fault, and $\Delta U(M)$ is the change in the electron
energy, which is zero if $M \geq 5$, but is large and positive
if $M < 5$. The factor '2' is arbitrarily introduced to allow
for the fact that deviations of the domain wall from the
average position may occur in two directions. It is stressed
that U_{SF} and $G_{Ising}(T)$ arise from interactions across and
within the boundary, respectively. Structure II becomes more
stable than I when $U_{SF} + 2G_{Ising}(T)$ becomes negative, provided that ΔU remains zero. When this is so, it would appear that a decrease in M would provide a further free energy
advantage. However, at this point the term ΔU enters and
prevents M from falling below 5. In evaluating the transition temperature Inglesfield used the values of $G_{Ising}(T)$
given by Onsager (1944). On this model, the upper transition
temperature (II → disordered) may be related to the critical
temperature of the Ising lattice, since this corresponds
to the temperature at which the domain walls break up, or
become completely disordered. In this way, Inglesfield was
able to show that the two transition temperatures in CuAu
should lie close together, as is found to be so.

Both transitions in CuAu are probably, at least in
part, first order. From measurements of the heat of solution
in liquid tin of the alloy and the pure metals, Orr, Luciat-
Labry, and Hultgren (1960) concluded that the latent heat
for the I→II transition was certainly not greater than
$0 \cdot 42$ kJ mol^{-1}, and was, indeed, probably zero, whilst that
for the II → disordered transition was ~$1 \cdot 6$ kJ mol^{-1}. A
study by Oriani and Murphy (1958) using liquid tin differential solution calorimetry yielded values of $0 \cdot 89 \pm 0 \cdot 15$ and
$1 \cdot 59 \pm 0 \cdot 08$ kJ mol^{-1} for the lower and the upper transitions,
respectively. However, they admit that, when proper account
is taken of the anomalous rises in C_p which usually precede
transitions, both of these values would be reduced. The

zero-point entropy of AuCu quenched from above the upper
transition temperature has been found by Hawkins and Hultgren
(1971) to be $5 \cdot 0$ J $K^{-1}mol^{-1}$, instead of the predicted value
of $R \ln 2 = 5 \cdot 76$ J $K^{-1}mol^{-1}$. The discrepancy is attributed
by these workers to gain in order during the quenching process, in support of which it is known that disordered AuCu
slowly becomes ordered even at room temperature. It is
likely, however, that a considerable part of the deviation
arises from experimental error, since they had to use some
previously obtained high-temperature data of uncertain
accuracy.

The graph of electrical resistivity against composition
(Fig.5.8) for the equilibrium Cu-Au system shows fairly sharp

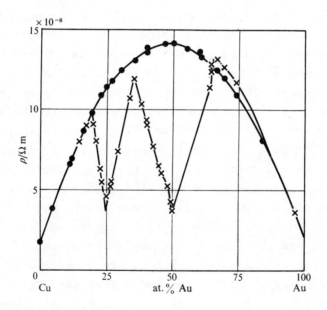

Fig.5.8. Electrical resistivity (ρ) against composition for the Cu-Au
system; ● = alloys quenched from ~925 K, × = alloys annealed at ~475 K
(after Nix and Shockley 1938).

minima at the compositions corresponding to CuAu and Cu_3Au.
On the other hand, alloys which have been quenched from temperatures above the disordering temperature show a smooth,
almost parabolic curve with no sign of minima.

The effect of pressures up to 70 kbar on the equilibrium
between the three forms was examined by Iwasaki, Yoshida,
and Ogawa (1974). They found that increase of pressure
favoured the ordered forms over the disordered, but also
favoured I over II. Form II was in fact 'squeezed-out' at
~50 kbar (Fig.5.9). They also observed that in form II M
increased from 5·1 to 5·5 as the pressure was increased to
50 kbar.

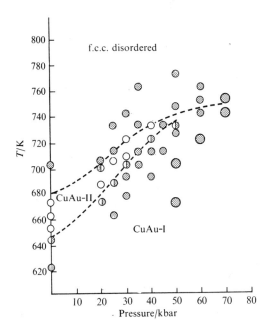

Fig.5.9. T-p diagram for CuAu. Large and small circles indicate use of different experimental methods (from Iwasaki *et al.* 1974).

An additional complication which has been found in
the structure of the II form is 'lattice modulation'. This
involves very small, regular shifts of atoms from what would
be considered to be their normal positions. The shifts
found varied from 0·0079 to 0·0028 nm for Cu atoms and from
0·0048 to 0·0004 nm for Au atoms (Okamura, Iwasaki, and
Ogawa 1968).

5.4.4. *CuPt*

Above 1083 K the structure is face-centred cubic with the
Cu and Pt distributed in disordered fashion over all the
sites. On cooling below 1083 K an ordered state in which
alternate (111) planes are occupied by Cu and Pt atoms is
formed (Fig.5.10) (Schneider and Esch 1944). This low-

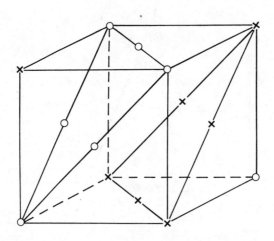

Fig.5.10. Ordered structure of CuPt; o = Cu, × = Pt.

temperature phase differs, therefore, from CuAu-I, in which
the layers of similar atoms are in the (100) planes. An
interesting feature of CuPt is that in the ordered state each
atom has the same number of unlike nearest neighbours as
it has, on average, in the disordered form. Since the ordering process does not affect the total number of unlike
nearest-neighbour pairs it is necessary to look elsewhere
for the reason for the relative stability of the ordered
structure at lower temperatures. Slater (1951) proposed
that the stabilization arises from the changes in energy of
the conduction electrons. He observed that formation of the
layered structure splits the Brillouin zone, some electron
levels moving up and some down. If the available electrons
were sufficient only to half-fill the original zone, then
in the ordered structure they would occupy the lower part of
the split zone. The lowering in energy achieved in this
way would be proportional to $\mathscr{S}^2$, where $\mathscr{S}$ is the Bragg-Williams

long-range order parameter.

5.4.5. Fe₃Al

Like FeAl this structure is based on the body-centred cube
with Fe atoms at the corners of each cell. However, in the
ordered form of Fe$_3$Al the centres of the cells are occupied
alternately by Fe and Al atoms (Fig.5.11). There is a

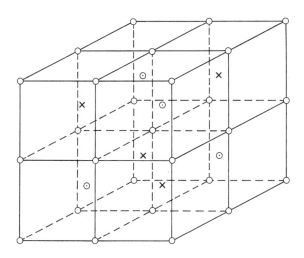

Fig.5.11. Fully ordered structure of Fe$_3$Al; o = Fe, × = Al.

non-isothermal transition at 831 K to a disordered form in
which only the body-centre positions tend to become randomly
occupied; the corner sites remain occupied entirely by Fe
atoms. The figure shows a complete unit cell of the ordered
form, and it can readily be seen that it is eight times as
large as the unit cell of the disordered form. Because the
corner atoms do not participate in the disordering process it
is reasonable to ignore them when setting up theoretical
models, thereby greatly simplifying the ensuing theory. At
~1050 K there is a further transition leading to the completely disordered phase (Selisskii 1960, Taylor and Jones
1958). The latter transition, which is sometimes referred
to as being due to a FeAl-type disordering process, has
not been very thoroughly studied. Lawley and Cahn (1961)

have reported that for alloys having <25 at.%Al the two
processes occur simultaneously, all the sublattices disordering together.

There appear to be no isothermal discontinuities at
the lower transition and it seems to be quite reversible.
Thus Guttman, Schnyders, and Arai (1969) found that the
difference between T_t values found from heating and cooling
curves was only ~0·14 ± 0·02 K. From 1-10 K below this
transition temperature they found that the long-range order
parameter, as determined from X-ray diffraction intensities,
varied as $(T_t-T)^\beta$ with $\beta = 0·307$. This value of the critical index agrees well with the Ising model prediction of
0·312. The indices describing the correlations above and
at T_t were found to be $\nu = 0·649$ and $\eta = 0·080$. These values
are in good and fair agreement, respectively, with those
expected for the Ising model (Guttman and Schnyders 1969).

There is a considerable amount of contradictory evidence on the magnetic properties of this alloy. The early
work of Sykes and Evans (1935) seemed to show that on
cooling the disordered phase it reached its Curie point and
became ferromagnetic, but that this ferromagnetism was lost
when on further cooling the Fe_3Al ordering transition was
reached. A further magnetic transition would then be expected at still lower temperatures as the positionally
ordered form became ferromagnetic. The true situation appears to be that the saturation magnetization of the ordered
form is less than that of the disordered, and this can give
the impression of a reversion to paramagnetism at the ordering transition (Lawley and Cahn 1961). Selisskii (1960)
found the following sequence of states on cooling an alloy
having 25·1 at.%Al:

disordered   ~1050K   FeAl-ordered~880K   FeAl-ordered   ~830K   Fe₃Al-ordered
paramagnetic ――――――> paramagnetic ――――――> ferromagnetic ――――――> ferromagnetic

Swann and Fisher (1966) suggested that since the energies
of positional ordering and magnetization are comparable one
must consider the effect of the magnetic ordering on the
positional ordering as well as the converse. This led them

to the conclusion that the spontaneous magnetization causes
the main disordering transition to be first-order rather
than gradual. Other evidence would appear to show that any
first-order character must be fairly small.

5.4.6. Fe_3Si

This has a gradual transition which is similar to the lower
one in Fe_3Al. The location of the transition temperature
was done by measurements of electrical and thermal conductivity (Glaser and Ivanick 1956). As it occurs at a very
high temperature (~1400 K), only ~80 K below the solidus,
it has been little studied. No structural work to elucidate
fully the nature of the transition has been carried out.
The relatively greater stability of the ordered Fe_3Si lattice,
as compared with that in Fe_3Al, is thought to arise from the
greater size difference of the component atoms which tends
to discriminate against the disordered structure.

5.4.7. Cu_3Au

Above 667 K the alloy exists as a disordered form which has
a simple face-centred cubic structure in which the Cu and Au
atoms are spread over all the sites without long-range order.
Below the transition, which is partly first-order, the Cu
atoms occupy the face-centres and the Au atoms are at the
corner positions (Fig.5.12). The unit cells of the two forms
comprise the same number of atoms, but there is a small
change in the lattice constant on ordering. As in the case of
β-brass, Keating and Warren (1951) were able to utilise
this small change to demonstrate that over a wide range of
temperature below T_t there is only one phase present. They
also determined the Bragg-Williams long-range order parameter
($\mathscr{S}$) over the range 423 to 654 K. Their results on quenched
samples and on samples held at the temperature of interest
are shown in Fig.5.13. The short-range order above T_t has
been investigated by Moss (1964), who was able to express
his results in the form of occupation numbers for sites out
to the tenth nearest neighbours. It has been pointed out
by Kikuchi and Sato (1974) that a one-dimensional degeneracy
exists in the ordered state. Without any loss in the number

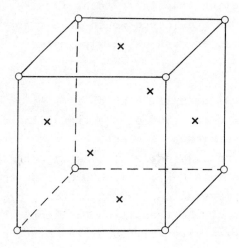

Fig.5.12. Ordered structure of Cu_3Au; × = Cu, o = Au.

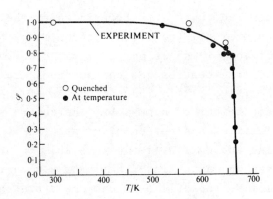

Fig.5.13. Cu_3Au. Long-range order parameter ($\mathscr{S}$) against temperature.
(after Keating and Warren 1951).

of favourable nearest-neighbour interactions a switch of the
positions of the Au atoms could occur as in Fig.5.14 (the
other two possible displacements, parallel to the other two
cubic axes, would each result in a positive interface energy).
Such a one-dimensional modification leads to thermodynamic

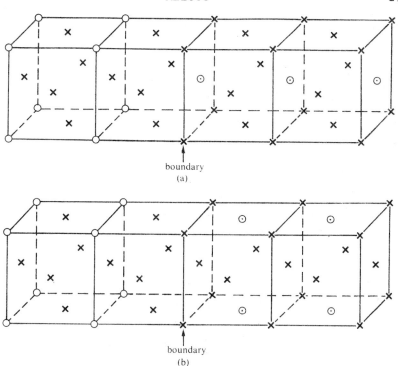

Fig.5.14. Cu$_3$Au. The one-dimensional degeneracy. o = Au, × = Cu (from Kikuchi and Sato 1974).

effects which are only $0(N^{1/3})$ in the number of atoms and so vanish in the thermodynamic limit.

Associated with the ordering transition there is both a latent heat and a sharp maximum in C_p. The heat (L_t) absorbed isothermally at T_t was found by Sykes and Jones (1936) to be 2·04 kJ mol^{-1}, but subsequent measurements have suggested that a better value may be 1·22 kJ mol^{-1} (Hultgren, Orr, Anderson, and Kelley 1963). A Bragg-Williams calculation, in which account was taken of the fact that two kinds of site were present, predicted that the transition would be part gradual, part isothermal, and gave a value of 0·392 for L_t/RT_t (Fowler and Guggenheim 1939). This is in fortuitous agreement with the experimental value of 0·372 ± 0·036. Indeed, a Bethe treatment in which the unit is taken to be a pair of sites, which may be regarded as the first improvement on the Bragg-Williams treatment, predicts no transition at all, and it is necessary to go to a

tetrahedral unit in order to recover the predicted transition (Kikuchi and Sato 1974).

A number of interesting facts on the rates of the ordering processes were shown up by examination of samples quenched from high temperatures. Sykes and Jones (1936) found that
release of 'frozen-in' energy could be observed at temperatures as low as 60°C. It was also found that more than 40%
of the ordering energy was released before long-range order
could be detected by X-ray or resistivity experiments. Since
the ordering energy evolved is directly related to the degree
of short-range order present, this result is readily understood in terms of the Bethe model or, indeed, any model which
leads to a high-temperature 'tail' in the heat capacity
curve.

The fact that well-defined phonons, as distinct from
local modes, are predominant in the disordered alloy has
been shown by Hallman (1974). This finding from his neutron
scattering study of a quenched disordered sample is in
accord with other observations on disordered non-dilute
alloys. It is to be contrasted with that found for dilute
alloys (section 3.6).

5.4.8. CuAu$_3$
This alloy has a high-temperature disordered phase and a
low-temperature ordered phase corresponding in structure
to the phases of Cu_3Au. Most simple theories of alloys
lead to the result that the order-disorder properties of
this alloy mirror those of Cu_3Au, since their compositions
are symmetrically disposed with respect to the equimolar
composition. In the Ising model, for example, Cu_3Au and
$CuAu_3$ are each equivalent to a magnetic spin system in a
field, the fields in the two cases being equal in magnitude
but opposite in direction. It is surprising, therefore, that
there is a considerable difference in their transition temperatures. Stoichiometric $CuAu_3$ has been reported as having
T_t = 472 K (Batterman 1957), but Hirabayashi (1952) found
the much higher value T_t = 516 K for an alloy which contained 74 at.% Au. Other work in this area tends to support the lower value (Orr 1960). It is also difficult to

accept that such a small difference in composition could
lead to such a large change in transition temperature.
Nevertheless, it is clear that, whichever value is taken,
there is a marked difference from T_t for Cu_3Au, which is
667 K. The difference in the ordering temperatures of Cu_3Au
and $CuAu_3$ was predicted approximately quantitatively by
Cowley (1950) in terms of their different molar volumes,
which in turn arise from the different sizes of the constituent atoms. The observed ~5% linear expansion on going
to $CuAu_3$ is sufficient to bring about an ~30% lowering of
T_t, which is to be compared with drops of 23 and 29% obtained
using the extreme experimental values for the transition temperature of $CuAu_3$. One consequence of the low ordering
temperature of $CuAu_3$ is that samples at room temperature are
always appreciably disordered, the Bragg-Williams order parameter $\mathscr{S}$ being never higher than 0·87.

5.4.9. Cu_2MnAl

This is one of the most common of the so-called Heusler
alloys. It is the β-phase which is of interest here. This
is stable at high temperatures, but on slow cooling it breaks
down eutectoidally to give the α and γ phases. However, with
ordinarily rapid cooling the β-phase can be frozen-in and
the metastable form becomes ordered on further cooling.
The structure of the ordered β-phase is similar to that of
Fe_3Al, with the Cu atoms at the cell corners and the Mn and
Al atoms occupying alternate body-centre sites. DTA shows
a peak at 898-903 K which is associated with disordering
of the atoms at the body-centre positions. However, in
contrast to Fe_3Al, some disordering of the cell corner
sites occurs simultaneously with that of the body-centre
positions (Johnston and Hall 1968). The β-phase has a
Curie point at 630 K, below which it is ferromagnetic in
spite of containing no Fe, Co, or Ni; neutron scattering
experiments have shown that the magnetic moments are centred
almost completely on the Mn atoms, each Cu atom carrying a
moment of less than $0·1\mu_B$.

5.4.10. Ni_2Al_3

This may be looked upon as being related to the FeAl ordered

structure by having three Fe atoms replaced by two Ni atoms
plus one vacancy. The symmetry is thereby changed to hexagonal.

5.4.11. Ni_3Mn.

Neutron diffraction has been used to show up the ordering
process, since this is one of the instances where X-ray diffraction suffers as a result of the similar scattering factors of the constituent atoms. The ordered form has the
face-centred cubic structure with the Ni atoms occupying
the face centres. There is a disordering transition at 753 K,
above which the long-range order of all the sites is lost.
In contrast with Cu_3Au the transition has been reported to
have no isothermal part (Marcinkowski and Brown 1961). However, a later X-ray diffraction study revealed a two-phase
region involving ordered and disordered forms, indicating
that the transition is, at least in part, first order. In
the same work the transition temperature was found to have
the much higher value of 818 K (Beers and Guttman 1974).

The dynamics of the order-disorder transition have been
investigated by neutron scattering (Collins and Teh 1973).
Critical slowing down was observed and the relaxation time
(τ) was broken down into the product of an Ising and a diffusional relaxation time (τ_I and τ_D, respectively). Setting
$\tau_I = B(T_c-T)^{-\Delta}$ the critical index Δ was found to be
$1\cdot04 \pm 0\cdot09$, in marked disagreement with a theoretical
value of $1\cdot4$ obtained by Yahata (1971) from a dynamic version of the three-dimensional Ising model, but in better
agreement with values of $1\cdot18$ and $0\cdot81$ deduced from experimental data on Cu_3Au. It should be stressed that Yahata's
model involves assumptions additional to those involved in
the ordinary, static Ising model. The later observation that
the transition is partly first-order has been reconciled with
these observations of critical slowing down, which suggest
the approach of a higher-order transition, by the suggestion
that there exists a higher-order transition at a virtual
transition temperature slightly above the actual transition
temperature and it is the approach to this virtual transition that is heralded by the slowing down (Beers and Guttman

1974).

5.4.12. U_2Mo
Below 700 K this substance has the γ'-structure shown in
Fig.5.15. It can be looked upon as a body-centred cubic

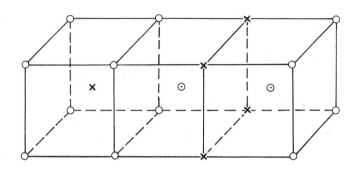

Fig.5.15. Ordered structure of U_2Mo; × = U, o = Mo (from Richman and
Davies 1973.)

structure in which every third layer perpendicular to the
[100] direction is occupied by Mo atoms (Richman and Davies
1973). Above the transition all long-range order is lost
and the phase is body-centred cubic (γ-phase) (Ivanov and
Virgiliev 1962).

5.5. LONG-PERIOD ORDER ('ANTIPHASE DOMAIN' STRUCTURES)
Some of the most interesting developments in the study of
order in alloys have been those concerning 'antiphase domain'
or long-period structures,[†] of which the best known is
CuAu-II (section 5.4.3). The latter is indeed unusual in
that on cooling it gives way to a form (I) without long-
period order: apart from non-stoichiometric Cu_3Au, almost
all other long-period forms remain stable down to 0 K. A

[†]Sato and Toth (1962) have objected to the use of the name 'antiphase
domain' structures for the systems described here. In their view that
name implies a lack of regularity in the sizes and natures of the
domains. Here we follow the normal practice of treating the two names
as being synonymous.

number of systems of this type have been carefully examined
during the past twenty years, particularly in the laboratories
of Schubert and Ogawa.

The 'antiphase' character of the lattice is often described by M, the number of unit cells between successive
'antiphase' domain walls. On the other hand, some workers
have used the term 'antiphase period', which is equal to $2M$.

Sato (1975) has discussed the relative stability of
these structures and the corresponding simple structures in
terms similar to those used by Jones for CuAu-II. He has
observed that long-period structures with very large M are
never found and also that non-stoichiometry tends to lead to
larger values of M, and he has put forward qualitative ex-
planations of these effects.

5.5.1. Cu_3Au-II.

Following on from the discovery of CuAu-II it was perhaps
natural to look for a similar form of Cu_3Au. It now appears
that gold-rich samples can adopt a long-period structure
over a limited temperature range, but that the stoichiometric
alloy cannot. Scott (1960) was successful with alloys having
31·6 and 29·2 at.% Au in the range 593 to 623 K, for which
he found $M=9$. These results were confirmed by electron diffraction and electron microscopy studies on evaporated films
of thickness 45-50 nm (Yamaguchi, Watanabe, and Ogawa 1962):
a long-period structure was found for systems with 33 and 31
at.% Au, but not for 27, 24, 21, or 19 at.% Au. They reported the value $M=10$ and a smaller range of stability
(613-623 K for 33 at.% Au, 618-633 K for 31 at.% Au) than
that which Scott had found. Yakel (1962) also found a 32·2
at.% Au alloy to have an 'antiphase domain' structure with
$M=8$-9, which was stable from 586 to 601 K. Direct observations of the regular array of 'antiphase domains' in a foil
of the alloy using electron microscopy have also been made
by Fisher and Marcinkowski (1961).

5.5.2. Ag_3Mg

Single crystal X-ray and thin-film electron diffraction
studies (Fujiwara, Hirabayashi, Watanabe, and Ogawa 1958)

showed the stable form to be as in Fig.5.16. It is an
'anti-phase' derivative of the ordered Cu_3Au structure, in
which after every progression of M unit cells in the direction

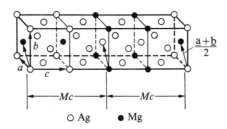

○ Ag   ● Mg

Fig.5.16. Ag_3Mg. Ordered structure, showing anti-phase domains (from
Fujiwara *et al*. 1958).

of the 'anti-phase' axis ($\underline{c}$) there is a displacement of
($\underline{a}+\underline{b}$)/2. The actual value of M varies with composition and
is ~1·8 for the stoichiometric alloy. On heating, Ag_3Mg
transforms to the disordered face-centred cubic structure.
This process is part gradual, part isothermal with a total
enthalpy of ordering of 1·4 kJ mol^{-1}. The isothermal part
of the transition occurs at 665 K (Gangulee and Bever 1968).

Gangulee and Moss (1968) defined two Bragg-Williams-
type long-range order parameters for this substance. Considering planes perpendicular to the long-period axis, those
which in the ordered state contained only Ag atoms were
denoted by 'O' and those which contained equal numbers of
Ag and Mg atoms were denoted by 'p'. Further, sites proper
to Ag and Mg atoms were represented by α and β, respectively.
Thus αO, αp, and βp represented, respectively, sites in the
pure Ag plane and sites proper to Ag and Mg atoms in the
Ag-Mg plane. The parameter corresponding to the ordering
process in Cu_3Au is $\mathscr{S} = r_\alpha - w_\beta = r_\beta - w_\alpha$, where r and w denote
right and wrong occupancy, respectively, of the sites indi-
cated by the subscript. Likewise, the 'anti-phase' order
parameter is defined as $\mathscr{S}_p = r_{\alpha p} - w_{\beta p} = r_{\beta p} - w_{\alpha p}$. From a comparison of the intensities of superlattice and satellite
reflections both $\mathscr{S}$ and $\mathscr{S}_p$ were determined. It might have

been expected that $\mathscr{S}_p$ would fall more rapidly than $\mathscr{S}$ with
rise in temperature. However, it was found that the two
parameters were very similar at all temperatures. The
largest discrepancy was at T_t, at which the 'anti-phase' parameter was the lower by only 2%. It is clear, therefore,
that the 'anti-phase' order is, for all intents and purposes,
retained up to the highest temperature at which long-range
ordering exists.

5.5.3. Au_3Cd

The room temperature form (α_1) has essentially the same long-
period superlattice as Ag_3Mg (Fig.5.16) (Schubert, Kiefer,

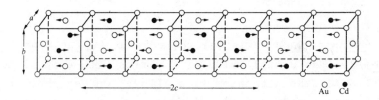

Fig.5.17. Au_3Cd. Long-period structure and lattice modulation
(from Iwasaki 1962).

Wilkens, and Haufler 1955, Hirabayashi and Ogawa 1961).
Subsequent work (Iwasaki, Hirabayashi, and Ogawa 1965) has
shown that there are also small, regular displacements from
the lattice sites ('lattice modulation') of the Cd atoms
(by $0\cdot0028 \pm 0\cdot0005$ nm) and those Au atoms which occupy cube
faces (by $0\cdot0015 \pm 0\cdot0005$ nm) (Fig.5.17).

5.5.4. Au_3Zn

(Iwasaki, Hirabayashi, Fujiwara, Watanabe, and Ogawa 1960,
Iwasaki 1962.)

On cooling Au_3Zn it passes from the disordered face-
centred cubic state to an ordered form (H) at 696 K, and on
further cooling to ~530 K it goes over to one of two more
complicated structures, (R_1) and (R_2). Which of the latter
is formed is influenced by any deviations from stoichiometry

and by the details of the cooling process.   Au$_3$Zn(H) has
the same structure as Ag$_3$Mg (Fig.5.16) and shows no lattice
modulation. (R$_1$) and (R$_2$) differ from (H) only in displaying
lattice modulation, it being different for the two (R) forms.
Figs.5.18(a) and (b) show the (R$_1$) and (R$_2$) structures.   In

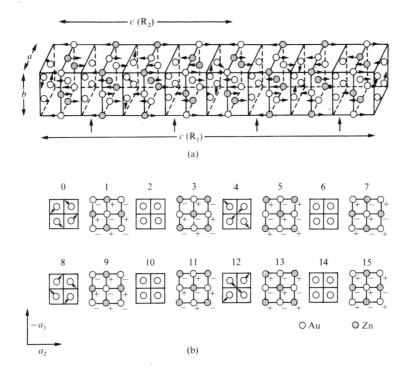

Fig.5.18. Au$_3$Zn(R$_1$). Arrows show the direction of atom shifts.   (a) The
positions of anti-phase boundaries in the Au$_3$Zn(H) structure are indicated
by vertical arrows.   The c axis of the (R$_2$) structure is also shown. (b)
The modulations in 16 successive planes of the (R$_1$) structure.   Plus and
minus indicate elevation of the atoms above and below the plane of the
drawing, respectively.   The α_1 and α_2 axes of the tetragonal (R$_1$) structure
become the a- and b-axes of the orthorhombic (R$_2$) form (from Iwasaki 1962).

those planes perpendicular to the 'anti-phase' axis which
contain only Au atoms the displacements are in the plane and
of magnitude 0·047 nm; in the remaining such planes the
displacements are perpendicular to the plane and of magnitude 0·015 and 0·018 nm for Au and Zn atoms, respectively.
     Heat capacity measurements on two near-stoichiometric
samples each showed two regions of anomalously high heat
absorption (Fig.5.19).   The low-temperature peaks were considerably the smaller, and for them the temperature of the
C_p maximum varied with the composition.   On the other hand,

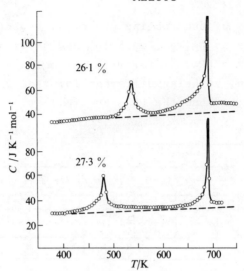

Fig.5.19. Heat capacity against temperature for Au-Zn alloys containing 26·1 and 27·3 at.% Zn.(from Iwasaki *et al.* 1960).

the temperature of the second maximum was the same for both samples. The lower anomalies are attributed to the (R) → (H) transition, whilst the upper are believed to arise from the

(H) → disordered process. The total energy absorbed in the upper transition is ~2·9 kJ mol^{-1}, of which ~0·6 kJ mol^{-1} is taken in isothermally. The corresponding value for the lower transition, which has no latent heat, is ~0·8 kJ mol^{-1}.

5.5.5. Cu_3Pd

(Schubert, Kiefer, and Wilkens 1954, Watanabe and Ogawa 1956, Hirabayashi and Ogawa 1957.)

Two 'anti-phase' structures occur in the vicinity of this composition. X-ray studies show that over the range 20·8-25·8 at.% Pd the solid has a simple, one-dimensional long-period system, with the step-shifts occurring regularly along the tetragonal axis, the structure being thus the same as for Ag_3Mg (Fig.5.20). The 'anti-phase' period was found to vary quite strongly with composition, M being 7·0 at 20·8 at.% Pd but 4·2 at 25·8 at.%Pd. On heating to 738 K the 'anti-phase' structure of the stoichiometric alloy gives way immediately to a disordered structure involving all the atoms. The total energy of this transition was found to be ~2·1 kJ mol^{-1} (Iwasaki *et al.* 1960). 'Lattice modulation' has

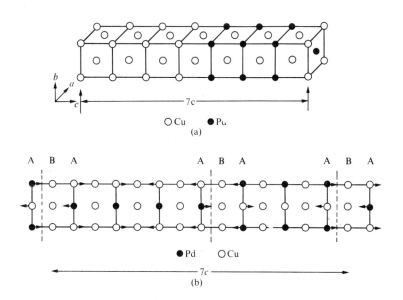

Fig.5.20. Cu₃Pd. (a) The one-dimensional anti-phase structure. (b) The lattice modulation. A projection onto the (010) plane. Arrows show direction of atom displacements. Broken lines are anti-phase boundaries (after Okamura 1970.)

been found in the 'anti-phase' structure (Okamura 1970).

Alloys slightly richer in Pd(27·3 and 28·5 at .% Pd) have a two-dimensional long-period system, there being regular step-shifts along both the a and b axes.

Other alloys showing long-period order include Cu₃Pt, Au₃Mg (Burkhardt and Schubert 1965), Pd₃Mn (Watanabe 1962), and Au₃Mn (Watanabe 1960).

REFERENCES

Als-Nielsen, J. (1969). *Phys.Rev.* <u>185</u>, 664.
——— and Dietrich, O.W. (1967). *Phys.Rev.* <u>153</u>, 717.
Ashman, J. and Handler, P. (1969). *Phys.Rev.Lett.* <u>23</u>, 642.
Baker, G.A., jr. and Essam, J.W. (1971). *J.chem.Phys.* <u>55</u>, 861.
Batterman, B.W. (1957). *J.appl.Phys.* <u>28</u>, 556.
Beers, J.C. and Guttman, L. (1974). *Phys.Rev.* <u>B9</u>, 3941.
Burkhardt, K. and Schubert, K. (1965). *Z.Metallk.* <u>56</u>, 844.
Chipman, D.R. and Walker, C.B. (1971). *Phys.Rev.Lett.* <u>26</u>, 233.

Cohen, J.B. and Bever, M.B. (1960). *Trans.Met.Soc.AIME* <u>218</u>,
    155.

Collins, M.R. and Teh, H.C. (1973). *Phys.Rev.Lett.* <u>30</u>, 781.

Cowley, J.M. (1950). *Phys.Rev.* <u>77</u>, 669.

——————   (1960). *Phys.Rev.* <u>120</u>, 1648.

——————   (1965). *Phys.Rev.* <u>138</u>, A1384.

Damask, A.C. (1956). *(J.)Phys.Chem.Solids* <u>1</u>, 23.

Domb, C. and Dalton, N.W. (1966). *Proc.phys.Soc.* <u>89</u>, 859.

Fan, C. and Wu, F.Y. (1969). *Phys.Rev.* <u>179</u>, 560.

Fisher, R.M. and Marcinkowski, M.J. (1961). *Phil.Mag.* <u>6</u>, 1385.

Flinn, P.A. (1956). *Phys.Rev.* <u>104</u>, 350.

——————   and McManus, G.M. (1961). *Phys.Rev.* <u>124</u>, 54.

Fosdick, L.D. (1959). *Phys.Rev.* <u>116</u>, 565.

Fowler, R.H. and Guggenheim, E.A. (1939). *Statistical thermo-*
    dynamics, p.600. Cambridge University Press.

Fujiwara, K., Hirabayashi, M., Watanabe, D. , and Ogawa, S.
    (1958). *J.phys.Soc.Japan* <u>13</u>, 167.

Gangulee, A. and Bever, M.B. (1968). *Trans.Met.Soc.AIME* 242,
    278.

Gangulee, A. and Moss, S.C. (1968). *J.appl.Crystallog.* <u>1</u>, 61.

Garland, C.W. (1964). *Phys.Rev.* <u>135</u>, A 1696.

Gibson, J.B. (1956). *(J.)Phys.Chem.Solids* <u>1</u>, 27.

Glaser, F.W. and Ivanick, W. (1956). *J.Metals,N.Y.* <u>8</u>, 1290.

Guttman, L. (1961). *J.chem.Phys.* <u>34</u>, 1024.

——————   and Schnyders, H.C. (1969). *Phys.Rev.Lett.* <u>22</u>,
    520.

——————   ——————   and Arai, G.J. (1969). *Phys.*
    Rev.Lett. <u>22</u>, 517.

Hallman, E.D. (1974). *Can.J.Phys.* <u>52</u>, 2235.

Hawkins, D.T. and Hultgren, R. (1971). *J.Chem.Thermodynamics*
    <u>3</u>, 175.

Hirabayashi, M. (1952). *J.Jap.Inst.Metals* <u>16</u>, 67.

——————   and Ogawa, S. (1957). *J.phys.Soc.Japan* <u>12</u>, 259.

——————   ——————   (1961). *Acta Mettall.* <u>9</u>, 264.

Hultgren, R., Orr, R.L., Anderson, P.D., and Kelley, K.K.
    (1963). *Selected values of thermodynamic properties of*
    metals and alloys. Wiley, New York and London.

Inglesfield, J.E. (1972). *J.Phys.* <u>F2</u>, 68.

Ivanov, O.S. and Virgiliev, Yu.S. (1962). *J.Nucl.Mater.* <u>6</u>, 199.

Iwasaki, H. (1962). *J.phys.Soc.Japan* 17, 1620.

———— , Hirabayashi, M. , and Ogawa, S. (1965). *J.phys. Soc.Japan* 20, 89.

———— ———— , Fujiwara, K., Watanabe, D., and Ogawa, S. (1960). *J.phys.Soc.Japan* 15, 1771.

———— , Yoshida, H., and Ogawa, S. (1974). *J.phys.Soc. Japan* 36, 1037.

Johnston, G.B. and Hall, E.O. (1968). *(J.) Phys.Chem.Solids* 29, 193.

Jones, H. (1969). *J.Phys.* C2, 760.

Keating, D.T. and Warren, B.E. (1951). *J.appl.Phys.* 22, 286.

Kikuchi, R. and Sato, H. (1974). *Acta Metall.* 22, 1099.

Lawley, A. and Cahn, R.W. (1961). *(J.)Phys.Chem.Solids* 20, 204.

Marcinkowski, M.J. and Brown, N. (1961). *J.appl.Phys.* 32, 375.

Moser, H. (1936). *Phys.Z.* 37, 737.

Moss, S. (1964). *J.appl.Phys.* 35, 3547.

Münster, A. (1973). *Z.phys.Chem.(Frankfurt)* 86, 230.

Nix, F.C. and Shockley, W. (1938). *Rev.mod.Phys.* 10, 1.

Norvell, J.C. and Als-Nielsen, J. (1970). *Phys.Rev.* B2, 277.

Okamura, K. (1970). *J.phys.Soc.Japan* 28, 1005.

———— , Iwasaki, H., and Ogawa, S. (1968). *J.phys.Soc. Japan* 24, 569.

Onsager, L. (1944). *Phys.Rev.* 65, 117.

Orehotsky, J. and Schroder, K. (1974). *J.Phys.* F4, 196.

Oriani, R.A. and Murphy, W.K. (1958). *(J.) Phys.Chem.Solids* 6, 277.

Orr, R.L. (1960). *Acta Metall.* 8, 489.

———— , Luciat-Labry, J., and Hultgren, R. (1960). *Acta Metall.* 8, 431.

Rathmann, O. and Als-Nielsen, J. (1974). *Phys.Rev.* B9, 3921.

Richman, R.H. and Davies, R.G. (1973). *Metall.Trans.* 4, 2731.

Salamon, M.B. and Lederman, F.L. (1974). *Phys.Rev.* B10, 4492.

Sato, H.(1975). *J.phys.Soc.Japan* 38, 739.

———— and Toth, R.S. (1962). *Phys.Rev.* 127, 469.

Schneider, A. and Esch, U. (1944). *Z.Elektrochem.* 50, 290.

Schubert, K., Kiefer, B., and Wilkens, M. (1954). *Z.Natur-forsch.* 9a, 987.

———— ———— ———— and Haufler, R. (1955).*Z.Metallk.* 46, 692.

Scott, R.E. (1960). *J.appl.Phys.* 31, 2112.

Selisskii, Ya.P. (1960). *Z.neorg.Khim.* $\underline{5}$, 2435. *(Russ.J.inorg. Chem.* $\underline{5}$, 1179).

Slater, J.C. (1951). *Phys.Rev.* $\underline{84}$, 179.

Swann, P.R. and Fisher, R.M. (1966). *Appl.Phys.Lett.* $\underline{9}$, 279.

Sykes, C. and Evans, H. (1935). *J.Iron Steel Inst.(London)* $\underline{131}$, 225.

———   ———   (1936). *J.Inst.Metals* $\underline{58}$, 255.

———   and Jones, F.W. (1936). *Proc.R.Soc.* $\underline{A157}$, 213.

———   and Wilkinson, H. (1937). *J.Inst.Metals* $\underline{61}$, 223.

Tachiki, M. and Teramoto, K. (1966). *(J.)Phys.Chem.Solids* $\underline{27}$, 335.

Taylor, A. and Jones, R.M. (1958). *(J.)Phys.Chem.Solids* $\underline{6}$, 16.

Walker, C.B. (1952). *J.appl.Phys.* $\underline{23}$, 118.

Watanabe, D. (1960). *J.phys.Soc.Japan* $\underline{15}$, 1030.

———   (1962). *Trans.Jap.Inst.Metals* $\underline{3}$, 234.

———   and Ogawa, S. (1956). *J.phys.Soc.Japan* $\underline{11}$, 226.

Wayman, C.M. (1971). *Ann.Rev.Mater.Sci.* $\underline{1}$, 185.

Yahata, H. (1971). *J.phys.Soc.Japan* $\underline{30}$, 657.

Yakel, H.L. (1962). *J.appl.Phys.* $\underline{33}$, 2439.

Yamaguchi, S., Watanabe, D., and Ogawa, S. (1962). *J.phys. Soc.Japan* $\underline{17}$, 1902.

Yoon, D.N. and Bienenstock, A. (1968). *Phys.Rev.* $\underline{170}$, 631.

———   and Jeffery, R.N. (1970). *(J.)Phys.Chem.Solids* $\underline{31}$, 2635.

6

POSITIONAL DISORDER IN INORGANIC COMPOUNDS

6.1. INTRODUCTION

The disorder considered in this chapter can be of two kinds, which for convenience of reference we shall arbitrarily designate as Type 1 and Type 2. Type 1 arises because the lattice offers more sites to a set of particles than there are particles available to fill them. These sites need not all be positions of the same energy, and indeed generally they are not. Consequently, in the disordered condition of the crystal the distribution of the particles in question among the sites to which they have access is not necessarily completely random. The ordered state of such a substance may have essentially the same structure but with an ordered arrangement of occupied and unoccupied sites. Alternatively, it may have a different structure in which the number of sites now equals the number of particles. The second kind of positional disorder, Type 2, is similar to that frequently encountered in alloys (section 5.4) in which two kinds of particle can be randomly distributed over a set of sites equal in number to the total number of the two sorts of particle. (In sufficiently complex crystals, more than two species of particle may be involved.) As contrasted with some alloys, however, we are dealing here with compounds in which some of the atoms occupy quite definite positions, with the disorder confined to the positions of some or all of the remaining atoms. In other words, the randomness involves one or more sublattices rather than all the lattice sites. Thus, Type 2 disorder can occur in spinels of formula AB_2O_4 in which the oxygen atoms occupy fixed positions and any disorder concerns the whereabouts of the A and B atoms.

Although we shall consider the two types of positional disorder separately, it is possible for a crystal to be simultaneously disordered in both ways, an instance of this being the high-temperature phase of the compound Ag_3SI (p. 245). Moreover, a crystal can have positional disorder and at the same time orientational disorder of a polyatomic ion or

molecule. Examples of this are provided by lithium iodide
monohydrate (p.494) and the high-temperature form of lithium
sulphate (p.252).

　　We pointed out in Chapter 1 that sometimes the distinction between positional disorder and orientational disorder
is arbitrary, citing as an example the well-known case of
ordinary ice. In this chapter we shall not discuss crystals
in which the disorder depends on the position of protons and
can alternatively be regarded as orientational disorder of
water molecules or of acid anions. Such solids are dealt
with in Chapter 8 on ice and hydrates, and in section 7.7
where various acid salts are considered.

6.2. TYPE 1 DISORDER

We shall first discuss some of the more striking cases of
Type 1 disorder which are associated with exceptional freedom of movement of cations in the lattice. Table 6.1[†] gives
some thermodynamic and structural information on various

[†]In this and similar tables in this book, the symbols λ and F are often
assigned to a transition to give a *rough* idea of its nature. In this
context, λ signifies that the transition certainly extends over a range
of temperature, while F implies that a substantial part of the transition is isothermal. The choice between the two letters is not infrequently rather arbitrary, since on the one hand a largely gradual transition often ends abruptly (a case in point being the transition in
ammonium chloride, which many would cite as the prototype of a λ-transi-
tion), while on the other hand many transitions in which most of the
change in enthalpy, entropy, and volume happens isothermally can nevertheless have a gradual beginning. Sometimes a definite view on the order
of a transition has not been expressed in the literature, but if the
available evidence (e.g. a heat capacity curve) suggests that the transition is probably largely first-order, or alternatively predominantly
gradual, this has been indicated by (?F) or (?λ) respectively. When
there is information bearing on whether a particular transition is
wholly gradual or not, this is usually mentioned in the text.

　　For a gradual or partly gradual transition, T_t in this and similar
tables in this book is the temperature at which the heat capacity reaches
a maximum, or the temperature of the abrupt part of the transition at
which the heat capacity effectively becomes infinite. In the text we
often refer to these temperatures as T_λ. In discussions of such transitions in the literature the symbol T_c also frequently appears, especially in the fitting of equations such as those involving critical indices
(section 3.3). T_c is used by some authors for the temperature of the
maximum in the heat capacity.

　　With regard to the references, those in the column headed Cal. generally relate to measurements of heat capacities and enthalpies of

[†]continued......

transitions made by conventional calorimetry, but they may include references to other types of investigation, e.g. differential scanning
calorimetry (DSC), and to freezing-point depression studies leading to
estimates of enthalpies of fusion. References in the column headed
Cryst. are usually to diffraction studies, which may be assumed to be
X-ray diffraction investigations unless stated to be electron or
neutron diffraction. Roman numerals indicate the phase or phases
examined. This column may occasionally include references to work using
other techniques (e.g. spectroscopy) which bears on the crystal structure. In the numerous later tables with a third column headed NMR, the
nature of the study is briefly indicated. LW and SM = line-width and
second moment respectively. T_1 and T_2 are respectively the spin-lattice
and spin-spin (transverse) relaxation times, $T_{1\rho}$ is the spin-lattice
relaxation time in the rotating frame, and $T_{1}^{\dagger}$ (or T_{1D}) that in the local
dipole field. The NMR column may include references to nuclear quad-
rupole resonance studies.

inorganic solids with the common feature of possessing at
least one high-temperature phase with exceptionally high ionic
conductivity. Thus, the conductivity of AgI-I just above the
II→I transition is $1 \cdot 3$ $(\Omega \text{ cm})^{-1}$, while that of the compound
$RbAg_4I_5$ at 25°C is $0 \cdot 27$ $(\Omega \text{ cm})^{-1}$. [The conductivity of a
saturated solution of sodium chloride at 25°C is $0 \cdot 25$
$(\Omega \text{ cm})^{-1}$.] The disordered phases of such solids are frequently referred to as super ionic conductors. Some of the
substances in Table 6.1, notably the halides and chalcogenides
of silver and copper, can exist with non-stoichiometric compositions, and indeed the preparation of stoichiometric
samples is sometimes rather difficult. We shall, however,
confine ourselves essentially to observations and properties
which have been recorded for stoichiometric specimens. All
of the compounds in Table 6.1 occur in at least two phases,
and frequently these have been distinguished by Greek letters,
the usual convention being to label the form stable at the
highest temperature α. Unfortunately, this convention has
not been uniformly adopted. Thus, in Gmelin's Handbuch
(1973), of the three phases of silver sulphide that stable
at the lowest temperature is designated the α̃ form, and the
high-temperature phase the γ form, and other examples of
this inverse lettering can be found in the literature[‡]. We
shall distinguish between the various phases of a solid by

[‡] see page 234.

TABLE 6.1

Thermal and structural information on some inorganic compounds with one or more positionally disordered phases. T_t and T_m are respectively the temperatures of transition and melting, and ΔS_t and ΔS_m the corresponding entropy increases; R = gas constant. For significance of F and λ see footnote on page 230. The Greek letters are those often (but not necessarily universally) applied to the phases in question.

Compound	III ←	T_t/K, ΔS_t/R → II →		T_t/K, ΔS_t/R → I ←		T_m/K, ΔS_m/R → Liquid	Cal.	Cryst.
AgI			(β) Hexagonal (B4), $P6_3mc$	421 (F), 1·75	(α) Cubic b.c. (B23), $Im3m$	831, ~1·4	1,2	1,3
CuI	Cubic (B3)	646 (F), 1·33	Hexagonal (B4)	684 (?F), 0·57	Cubic f.c. (B3), $F\bar{4}3m$	871	4,5	6,7
CuBr	Cubic (B3)	659 (?F), 1·05	Hexagonal (B4)	742 (F), 0·45	Cubic (B23)	760	5	7
Ag₂S	(β) Monoclinic, $P2_1/n$	450 (F), 1·04	(α) Cubic (B23)	~860, 0·07	Cubic f.c.	1103, 0·85	8,9	10,11
Cu₂S	(γ) Orthorhombic, $Ab2m$	376 (F)	(β) Hexagonal, $H6mcm$	717 (F), 0·28	(α) Cubic f.c.	1402, 1·97	8,12	10,13
Ag₂Se	Orthorhombic, $P2_12_12_1$	406 (F), 2·1	Cubic (B23)			1163	8,14	10,15

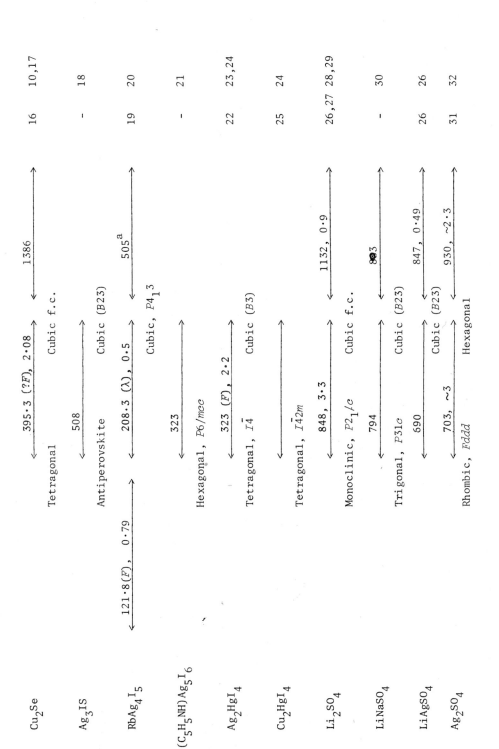

Compound	Transition sequence	Ref.	Ref.
Cu_2Se	← 121·8(F), 0·79 → Tetragonal ← 395·3 (?F), 2·08 → Cubic f.c. ← 1386 →	16	10,17
Ag_3IS	← 508 → Antiperovskite ← Cubic ($B23$) →	–	18
$RbAg_4I_5$	← 208·3 (λ), 0·5 → Cubic, $P4_13$ ← 505^a →	19	20
$(C_5H_5NH)Ag_5I_6$	← 323 → Hexagonal, $P6/mcc$	–	21
Ag_2HgI_4	← 323 (F), 2·2 → Tetragonal, $I\bar{4}$ ← Cubic ($B3$) →	22	23,24
Cu_2HgI_4	Tetragonal, $I\bar{4}2m$	25	24
Li_2SO_4	← 848, 3·3 → Monoclinic, $P2_1/c$ ← Cubic f.c. → ← 1132, 0·9 →	26,27	28,29
$LiNaSO_4$	← 794 → 8?3	–	30
$LiAgSO_4$	← 590 → Trigonal, $P31c$ ← Cubic ($B23$) → ← 847, 0·49 →	26	26
Ag_2SO_4	Rhombic, $Fddd$ ← 703, ~3 → Cubic ($B23$) ← 930, ~2·3 → Hexagonal	31	32

Footnotes to Table 6.1.

a. Incongruent melting point.

References

1.   Hoshino (1957).

2.   Nölting (1963); Perrott and Fletcher (1968a, 1969b); Nölting and Rein (1969).

3.   Strock (1934, 1935)(I); Helmholtz (1935)(II); Burley (1963, 1964)(II); Lawn (1964)(II).

4.   Nölting (1964).

5.   Nölting, Rein, and Troe (1969).

6.   Miyake, Hoshino, and Takenaka (1952)(I,II,III).

7.   Krug and Sieg (1952)(I,II).

8.   Jost and Kubaschewski (1968).

9.   Perrott and Fletcher (1969a); Thompson and Flengas (1971).

10.   Rahlfs (1936)(Ag_2S-II, Ag_2Se-I, Cu_2Se-I, $Cu_{1.8}S$-II).

11.   Ramsdell (1943); Frueh (1958, 1961); Djurle (1958).

12.   Wehefritz (1960).

13.   Buerger and Buerger (1944)(II,III)

14.   Baer, Busch, Fröhlich, and Steigmeier (1962).

15.   Wiegers (1971)(II); Asadov and Yabrailova (1972)(I,II).

16.   Kubaschewski and Nölting (1973).

17.   Borchert (1944)(II).

18.   Reuter and Hardel (1960, 1965, 1966)(I,II).

19.   Johnston, Wiedersich, and Lindberg (1969).

20.   Bradley and Greene (1967b)(I); Geller (1967)(I).

21.   Geller (1972)(II); Geller and Owens (1972).

22.   Ketelaar (1935).

23.   Ketelaar (1934b)(I); Hoshino (1955)(I,II); Browall, Kasper, and Wiedemeier (1974) (II); Kasper and Browall (1975)(I); Hibma, Beyeler, and Zeller (1976)(I).

24.   Ketelaar (1931)(II); Hahn, Frank, and Klingler (1955)(II).

25.   Chivian, Claytor, Eden, and Hemphill (1972).

26.   Øye (1963).

27.   Nolte and Kordes (1969).

Footnote from page 231.

[‡]The letters α, β, γ have also often been used to label the various phases of crystals composed of diatomic molecules (section 9.3). Here also the form stable at the lowest temperatures is called the α form.

Footnotes to Table 6.1 continued......

28.   Førland and Krogh-Moe (1957)(I).

29.   Nord (1973)(II); Alcock, Evans, and Jenkins (1973)(II).

20.   Førland and Krogh-Moe (1958)(II); Morosin and Smith (1967)(II).

31.   Kelley (1936); Hedvall, Lindler, and Hartler (1950); Ingraham
      and Marier (1965).

32.   Hermann and Ilge (1931)(II); Fischmeister (1956)(I).

means of Roman numerals, I being the form stable at the
highest temperatures, even though this system can admittedly
conceal structural similarities between the phases of different compounds, but we also give in Table 6.1 the Greek
letters most usually applied to a particular phase.

We shall first discuss disorder in silver iodide, the
most thoroughly investigated of all the super ionic conductors. [In the relevant volume of Gmelin's Handbuch (1972)
the account of the physical properties of this salt extends
to more than eighty pages.] The crystal structure of the disordered phase was elucidated by powder photography by Strock
(1934, 1935) and Hoshino (1957). A single crystal study
has apparently not yet been made. The highly disordered nature
of the crystal is revealed by the marked temperature dependence of the intensities of the Debye lines and by the strong
diffuse background (Fig.6.1). The structure of this phase
proposed by Strock and confirmed by Hoshino, which is designated B23 in the Strukturbericht classification, is shown in
Fig.6.2. The iodide ions form a body-centred cubic lattice,
while the two silver ions in each unit cell have available
to them no less than 42 different sites. These are not all
equivalent, but form three sets usually labelled (b), (d),
and (h), there being per unit cell 6 (d), 12 (d), and 24
(h) sites. The stable form of the ordered crystal AgI-II
(β-AgI) has an hexagonal, wurtzite lattice ($\underline{B}4$). There is,
however, another ordered form AgI-II' (γ-AgI) with a cubic
structure like that of zinc blende (B3). [At pressures
above 3 kbar a form III is produced with a rocksalt lattice,
and there are at least two other high-pressure forms (Jacobs
1938, Davis and Adams 1964, Moore and Kasper 1968).] It was
at one time believed that II undergoes a transition into

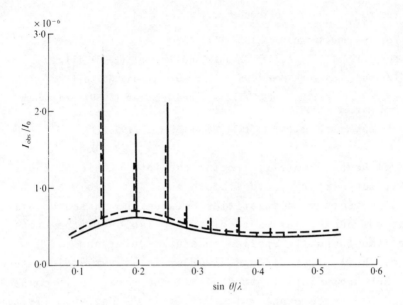

Fig.6.1. Intensities of lines in the powder photograph of AgI-I at 250°C (full lines) and 400°C (dotted lines) (Hoshino 1957).

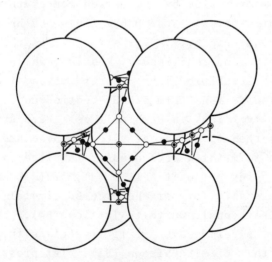

Fig.6.2. The B23 structure proposed by Strock (1934) for AgI-I. The large circles are iodide ions; ⊙, the 6 (*b*) sites per unit cell for the silver ions, o, the 12 (*d*) sites, and •, the 24 (*h*) sites.

II' at about 410 K, but doubt has been cast on this (Natarajan and Rao 1970). II and II' are certainly very similar in density and lattice energy, and they both transform to I at the same temperature. When the ordered phase is formed, it tends to be a mixture of II and II'. There is an interesting memory effect associated with the transformation (II+II')→I, in that if phase I formed by this conversion is not heated above ~445 K and is then cooled below the transition temperature of 421 K, the ordered form is produced with the same proportions of II and II' as the starting materials (Block and Möller 1931, Burley 1967). The transition of II or II' into I is accompanied by a volume decrease of 6·7 per cent, and appears from the heat capacity determinations to be largely first-order, though in some of its properties AgI-II shows signs of the beginnings of disorder well below the transition temperature. Even at room temperature the Debye-Waller factors for AgI-II are quite large (Burley 1964, Bührer and Brüesch 1975), and the phase is unusual in having a negative coefficient of expansion, which may perhaps be attributable to the migration of silver ions into the octahedral holes in the close-packed hexagonal lattice of iodide ions. For transitions such as that in AgI which lead to a high-temperature super ionic form, Rice, Strässler, and Toombs (1974) have propounded a theory in which a leading role is played by the stress field set up in the crystal by the volume change which occurs as the transition is approached.

There is a curious discrepancy between the results obtained from the two most recent heat capacity studies on AgI-I. Perrott and Fletcher (1968a) reported that for a stoichiometric sample the heat capacity between 420 K and 870 K is anomalously high, being larger by a factor of 1·5-2 than the normal values expected for such a solid. They further stated that this abnormality in the heat capacity completely vanishes for samples non-stoichiometric to the extent of as little as one mole per cent. They later claimed to have observed an order-disorder transition in AgI-I which reaches completion at 703 K (Perrott and Fletcher 1969b). Nölting and Rein (1969), however, failed to find any evidence for abnormally high heat capacities, or

for any marked dependence of the heat capacity on the degree
of non-stoichiometry, nor did they detect any transition
between the II-I phase change and the melting-point. W.
Jost (1971) and Fletcher (1971) have commented on these conflicting observations.

●The chief evidence for extreme freedom of movement of
the silver ions in AgI-I comes from electrical conductivity
measurements. The conductivity rises by about two orders of
magnitude at the II→I transition, and then increases from
$1 \cdot 3$ $(\Omega \ cm)^{-1}$ at 420 K to $2 \cdot 6$ $(\Omega \ cm)^{-1}$ at the melting-point
(828 K), which corresponds to a relatively low activation
energy of ~5 kJ mol^{-1} (Tubandt and Lorentz 1914, Kvist and
Josefson 1968). The classical transport number determinations of Tubandt (1932) proved that the conductivity is wholly
due to cation movement. ✿ (By contrast, the conductivity of
some of the substances in Table 6.1, such as Ag_2S-I, Ag_2Se-I
and Cu_2Se-I, is electronic as well as ionic.) Silver iodide
appears to be unique in that when it melts the conductivity
actually falls, by about ten per cent. The application of
pressure to phase I decreases its conductivity, whereas that
of phase II is increased (Hara, Mori, and Ishiguro, 1973;
cf. the effect of pressure on the conductivity of $RbAg_4I_5$,
p. 247 , and of Ag_2HgI_4, p. 250). Diffusion studies show that
the silver ions move as easily in AgI-I as in aqueous solution (Tubandt, Reinhold, and W.Jost 1929). It is not surprising therefore that this singular crystal has often been
described as consisting of fluid silver ions in a solid
lattice of iodide ions, and even as a 'missing link' between
the solid and liquid states. The crystals are soft and
plastic, like many of the disordered molecular solids discussed in Chapters 9 and 10.

Two other physical properties of AgI-I should be mentioned, which appear to be characteristic of such super ionic
conductors. One is that the conductivity is frequency-
dependent, decreasing with increasing frequency in the
microwave region (Fig.6.3). The other is that there is
a very broad absorption band in the far infrared (Fig.6.4),
symptomatic of very slow lattice vibrations (Funke and A.
Jost 1971).

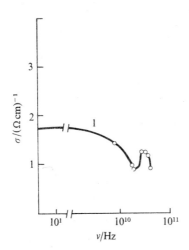

Fig.6.3. Frequency dependence of the conductivity of AgI-I at 535 K in the microwave region (Funke and Jost 1971).

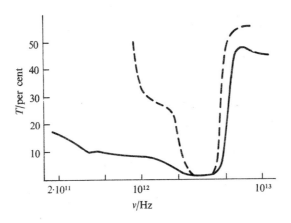

Fig.6.4. Transmittance T in the far infrared of AgI-I at 250°C (full curve), and AgI-II at 25°C (broken curve) (Funke and Jost 1971).

We have already referred to the Strock model of AgI-I, which gives the two silver ions in a unit cell a choice of 42 sites. Apart from the fact that these sites fall into

three different groups, the energy of a silver ion in any
one site must depend on what neighbouring sites happen to
be occupied. Adjacent sites can be as close as $0 \cdot 09$ nm,
and the energy barrier opposing the movement of an ion from
one site to the next cannot be large. The picture which
emerges is one in which the silver ion moves rapidly between
a large number of shallow potential wells. While trapped
within any one of these, its motion must be markedly anharmonic. Since the wells are shallow it is not impossible
for a silver ion to gain sufficient energy to pass over a
number of sites, or in other words to experience periods
of effectively translational movement. This has been incorporated in a theory of ionic movement in super ionic conductors proposed by Rice and Roth (1972). They suppose that
if the potentially mobile ions acquire an energy ε_0 they can
cross an energy gap separating localized ionic states from
a free-ion state in which they have a finite life-time. ε_0
is then the activation energy in the Arrhenius-like relation
between conductivity and temperature. This model is consistent with the frequency dependence of the conductivity,
since the efficiency of a silver ion as a conductor is naturally impaired when the time required for a unit stage of
translational movement becomes greater than half the period
of the electrical field. Studies of the conductivity dispersion can therefore give information on this time.

For a number of reasons, the interparticle energetics
in the lattice of the disordered phase must be very complicated. In the first place, although we have spoken of
the movement and position of *ions* in the lattice, there can
be little doubt that in solid silver iodide (and indeed in
some of the other compounds in Table 6.1) the interaction
between the metallic and non-metallic particles is to some
extent covalent. Further, it is probably an oversimplification to consider the iodide ions as fixed in the lattice.
It is true that they diffuse altogether more slowly than
the silver ions - by a factor of 10^4 to 10^6, according to
radiotracer studies with ^{131}I (Jost and Nölting 1956) - so
that the possibility of their migration in the lattice can
be disregarded. Nevertheless, Hoshino (1957) noted that

in AgI-I the iodide ions have a large Debye-Waller factor, and it seems likely that their displacement is correlated with the movement of the silver ions from site to site (Perrott and Fletcher 1968b). Such displacements must affect the potential of the silver ions on neighbouring sites. Considerations of this kind support W.Jost's view (1971) that perhaps the Strock model with its 42 sites per unit cell should not be taken too literally.

Although silver bromide has no phase comparable with AgI-I, the latter takes up to 10 per cent of the bromide into solid solution (Natarajan and Rao 1970). Both copper (I) iodide and bromide, however, form high-temperature dis-ordered phases in which the copper ions have freedom of move-ment comparable with that of the silver ions in AgI-I, since the very high electrical conductivity of these phases has been shown to be entirely cationic (Tubandt, Rindtorff, and W.Jost 1927, Tubandt, Eggert, and Schibbe 1921). CuBr-I only exists over a range of 18 K. Fig.6.5 reproduces

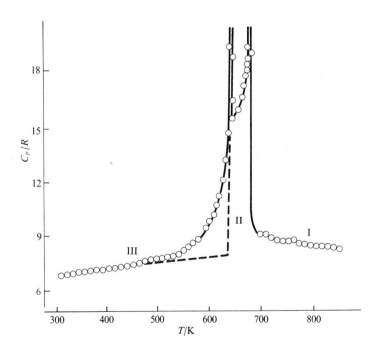

Fig.6.5. Heat capacity of copper (I) iodide, CuI (Nölting, Rein, and Troe 1969).

the heat capacity of CuI as determined by Nölting, Rein, and
Troe (1969); the measured C_p for phase I illustrates
a property frequently shown by solid phases in which particles are positionally disordered and move unusually easily,
namely that the heat capacity decreases with rising temperature. The effect seems to be too protracted to be ascribed
to the disappearance of short-range order, and it may rather
be an indication that the movement of the cations as the
temperature rises is changing from vibration to translation.

The crystal structure of CuI-I does not appear to be the
same as that of AgI-I, but it may well be essentially that
of its own low-temperature phase III (Miyake, Hoshino, and
Takenaka 1952), in which the iodide ions form a face-centred
cubic lattice and not the body-centred cubic lattice of
AgI-I. Miyake *et al*. suggested that in the disordered high-
temperature phase each copper ion has access to five sites
(Fig.6.6), a central site and four others tetrahedrally disposed about it at a distance of ~0·09 nm from the central
site. They found that this model agrees quite well with the
observed X-ray diffraction intensities, and they also pointed

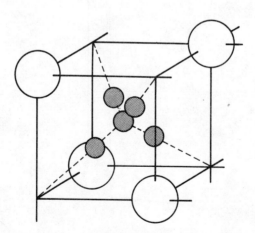

Fig.6.6. Structure of CuI-I proposed by Miyake, Hoshino, and Takenaka
(1952), showing an octant of the unit cell. Open circles are iodide
ions, shaded circles are possible positions for copper ions.

out that the combined entropy of the two transitions of
$1 \cdot 9R$ is not far from $R \ln 5$ (= $1 \cdot 61R$). CuI-I, like AgI-I,
has a frequency-dependent conductivity in the microwave
region which indicates that the duration of a cation jump
is ~10^{-10}s (Funke and Hackenburg 1972). NMR investigations
of CuI and CuBr have been carried out, using ^{63}Cu and involving both line-width and T_1 measurements (Herzog and
Richtering 1967, Guenther and Hultsch 1969, Becker, Herzog,
Kanne, Richtering, and Stadler, 1970). These show that
diffusion of copper ions has already begun in phase III at
temperatures as low as 370 K, with activation energies of
14 and $17 \cdot 5$ kJ mol^{-1} for CuBr and CuI respectively. The
phase diagram of the system AgI-CuI has been studied by
Nölting (1964) and others, and proves to be rather complicated (Fig.6.7). The high-temperature phases of the two
salts are not miscible in all proportions, though the mis-
cibility gap does not exceed ~10 mole per cent. Different
authors disagree about the position of the lowest phase-
boundary lines on the diagram, partly perhaps because of the
slow approach to equilibrium in this region and partly because of the gradual nature of the transitions involved.
It will be noted that the phase AgI-II (β-AgI) does not
appear. It seems that even small quantities of CuI stabilize the cubic zinc blende form AgI-II' (γ-AgI), and that
this and CuI-III are probably miscible in all proportions.
CuBr-I can dissolve up to 50 mole per cent of AgBr and
still retain the B23 structure (Frenzel 1963, Bremer and
Nölting 1973).

  The chalcogenides of silver and copper, which are more
prone to non-stoichiometry than the halides, all possess
highly disordered phases, some of them stable over a wide
range of temperature. These phases have high cationic conductivity, though there can also be considerable electronic conductivity, exceeding that due to the cations.
Ag_2S-II and Ag_2Se-I have structures similar to that of
AgI-I, with the anions forming a body-centred cubic lattice,
though the nominal 42 cation positions now have to accommodate four silver ions and not just two as in the iodide.
(Llabres and Messien (1968) have suggested that in these

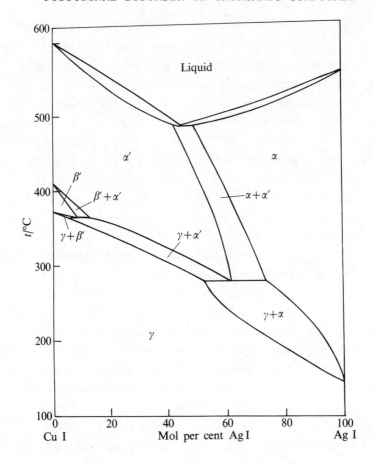

Fig.6.7. Phase diagram of the system AgI-CuI. α' = CuI-I, β' = CuI-II, α = AgI-I, γ = CuI-I or AgI-II' (γ - AgI) (after Nölting 1964).

crystals the 42 Strock sites may be reduced to 6.) A further
difference between the chalcogenides and silver iodide is
that whereas in AgI-I the iodide ions are in contact, with
the sulphide and selenide ions this is not the case. There
is disagreement, similar to that already mentioned for silver
iodide, between the thermodynamic properties of silver sulphide as reported by Perrott and Fletcher (1969a) and as
determined by others. Perrott and Fletcher state that a
stoichiometric sample has an abnormally high heat capacity
in phase II and undergoes an order-disorder transition
reaching completion at 623 K and having an entropy change
of ~0·5R. Both the abnormality in the heat capacity and

the transition are reported to have disappeared from samples
deviating from stoichiometry by only one mole per cent. The
heat capacity results of W.Jost and Kubaschewski (1968) for
Ag_2S-II, however, give no indication of the Perrott and
Fletcher transition, and in fact show C_p decreasing with
rising temperature, as it also does for Cu_2S-II. We have
already remarked on this behaviour in CuI-I. Ag_2S-II transforms with a small entropy increase into Ag_2S-I, the first
powder photograph of which showed only a single line against
a very strong diffuse background (Djurle 1958). Later,
Frueh (1961) obtained a photograph with three lines. The
structures of the ordered phases of silver sulphide (III)
and selenide (II), while not identical, are similar, and
in both the anions are already essentially in a body-centred
relationship. The disordered phases Ag_2S-II, Ag_2Se-I and
Cu_2Se-I all persist to at least 40 kbar (Clark and Rapoport
1970).

Copper (I) telluride, Cu_2Te, exists at ordinary pressures in no less than six forms. Cu_2Te-I has the anions
arranged on a face-centred cubic lattice, and the cations
are no doubt positionally disordered as in Cu_2Se-I and
Cu_2S-I. Phase II is probably also disordered as its heat
capacity decreases with rising temperature, and the combined
entropy increases at the preceding transitions amount to
$1 \cdot 15R$ (Kubaschewski and Nölting 1973).

The salts Ag_3SI and Ag_3SBr have been investigated by
Reuter and Hardel (1960, 1965, 1966). Ag_3SI has a high-
temperature phase I with the B23 structure, which is intermediate between AgI-I and Ag_2S-II in that three silver ions
are now disposed among the 42 Strock positions. Moreover,
the sulphide and iodide ions are statistically distributed
among the anion sites of the body-centred cubic lattice,
so that the crystal has positional disorder of Types 1 and 2
simultaneously. Ag_3SI-II has the same approximately antiperovskite structure as the single known form of Ag_3SBr.
Here, the halide and sulphide ions have an ordered arrange-
ment on the 0,0,0 and $\frac{1}{2},\frac{1}{2},\frac{1}{2}$ sites, so that the unit cell
is primitive. However, the structure departs slightly from
the ideal antiperovskite lattice to give each silver ion
four possible positions, and N silver ions are statis-

tically distributed among $4N$ sites. Both Ag_3SBr and Ag_3SI-II
are cation conductors, the conductivity of the latter rising
by a factor of ~10 at the II→I transition. Reuter and Hardel
(1966) have pointed out that there is an interesting correlation between the activation energy for conductivity in
the salts AgI-I, Ag_2S-II, Ag_3SI-II, Ag_3SBr, and the compound
Ag_2HgI_4 (which we shall discuss in due course), and the
degree of Type 1 disorder as given by the ratio of the number
of metal ions to the number of available sites (Table 6.2).

TABLE 6.2

E = *activation energy in kJ* mol^{-1} *for cationic conductivity
in the solids indicated. Atoms/sites = number of metal atoms
per unit cell/number of available sites per unit cell.*

	AgI-I	Ag_2S-II	Ag_3SI-II	Ag_3SBr	Ag_2HgI_4-I
E	4·9	5·8	17	23	36
Atoms/sites	2/42	4/42	3/12	3/12	(2Ag+1Hg)/4

Still more remarkable than the super ionic conductors so
far discussed are those of the formula MAg_4I_5 (M = K, Rb,
or NH_4^+), discovered independently by Bradley and Greene
(1966, 1967a, b), and by Owens and Argue (1967). These substances are thermodynamically unstable at room temperature,
but the rubidium compound can be kept indefinitely in the
absence of moisture at room temperature and below, and is
the most thoroughly studied member of the group. Its conductivity at 25°C of 0·27 $(\Omega\ cm)^{-1}$ is higher than that of
any other solid ionic conductor at the same temperature;
but even more notable is the persistence of a relatively
high ionic conductivity to quite low temperatures (Owens
and Argue 1967, 1970). Form I is cubic with four formula
units per unit cell. The iodide ions have the same arrangement as the manganese atoms in β-manganese, which form two
sets with different environments, though in both sets each
atom has twelve neighbours. A rubidium ion is surrounded
by a distorted octahedron of iodide ions, while the silver
ions are positionally disordered, with 56 sites available

to the 16 Ag^+ in the unit cell. These 56 sites, which all
lie within iodide ion tetrahedra, fall into three crystallographically non-equivalent sets, one of 8 and two of 24 each.
Due to site energy differences and the mutual repulsion of
silver ions on adjacent sites, the distribution of the
silver ions is not a random one. There are channels in the
lattice through which these ions can diffuse. The structures of the low-temperature forms II and III are not yet
known. While both of these phases are birefringent and so
cannot be cubic, there are indications that they only differ
in a minor way from I. There is no change in conductivity
at the I→II transition, but it drops by about two orders
of magnitude at the II→III transition (Owens and Argue 1970).
In phase I, from ~430 K down to the I→II transition, the
activation energy for cation conductivity is 7 kJ mol^{-1},
not very different from the activation energy for self-diffusion of the silver ions of 8·2 kJ mol^{-1} obtained from a
tracer study with ^{110}Ag (Bentle 1968). An activation energy
of between 6 and 12 kJ mol^{-1} for ionic movement has been
derived from ultrasonic attenuation experiments (Nagao and
Kaneda 1975). In phase II, the activation energy for conductivity
rises to 17 kj mol^{-1}. Studies of the effect of pressure on the
conductivity of $RbAg_4I_5$-1 showed that it falls with increasing
pressure (the activation energy increasing), the conductivity
at 60 kbar being less by a factor of ~10^3 than the initial
value (Bundy, Kasper, and Moore 1971). $RbAg_4I_5$-I, like
AgI-I, has a broad absorption band in the far infrared, no
doubt because the silver ions oscillate with very low frequencies and large amplitudes (Eckold and Funke 1973). The
Raman spectrum of $RbAg_4I_5$-I, like that of AgI-I, is also very
broad. More detail appears in these spectra on conversion
into the low-temperature modifications, but the changes in
the phonon spectrum of $RbAg_4I_5$ at the two transitions are much
less marked than those which occur at the I→II transition in
AgI at 421 K (Burns, Dacol, and Shafer, 1976, Delaney and
Ushioda 1976).

The investigation of the thermodynamic properties of
$RbAg_4I_5$ carried out by Johnston, Wiedersich, and Lindberg

(1969) proved to be very rewarding. Besides elucidating the
nature of the two transitions, the following facts were established: (1) The crystals appear to be still disordered
at 0 K, retaining entropy of $9 \cdot 4$ J K mol^{-1}, though the uncertainty of $6 \cdot 7$ J K^{-1} mol^{-1} placed on this figure is relatively rather large. (2) From ~50 K upwards, the heat
capacity is much higher than the values which would be expected in the absence of configurational effects. (3) The
configurational entropy of phase I at 300 K is $45 \cdot 2$ J K^{-1}
mol^{-1}. In estimating this, the contribution to the molar
heat capacity from the rubidium and iodide ions, $C(Rb,I)$, was
treated as a Debye function in 18 degrees of freedom, and
that from the silver ions, $C(Ag)$, as an Einstein function in
12 degrees of freedom. It seemed that there might be a
Schottky anomaly at low temperatures, with the tail of this
making a small contribution to C_p in the region of the
lowest measurements. The configurational heat capacity from
which the configurational entropy was estimated was taken
to be $C_p - (C_p - C_V) - C(Rb,I) - C(Ag) - C(Schottky)$. By
increasing the entropy of formation of the compound, the
configurational entropy makes an important contribution to
its stabilization. (4) Once again, the heat capacity of the
most disordered form I falls with rising temperature.

Most of the transitions in super ionic conductors, although often clearly partly gradual, have a first-order stage.
This does not appear to be true of the II-I transition in
$RbAg_4I_5$, which seems to lack the discontinuous stage. Pardee
and Mahan (1974) used the heat capacity results of Johnston
et al. to show that for $T < T_c$ (where $T_c = 208 \cdot 3$ K is the
temperature at which C_p is a maximum), the heat capacity con-
forms closely to the equation $C_p = $ constant $\times (-\varepsilon)^{\alpha'}$, where
$\varepsilon = (T - T_c)/T_c$ and $\alpha' = 1/16$. They point out that the value
of α' is very similar to that predicted on the Ising model.
Above the transition, C_p does not follow an equation $C_p = A\varepsilon^{\alpha}$
with $\alpha = \alpha'$, so there is no evidence of scaling symmetry in
this case (section 3.3). They conclude that the II-I transition may be a manifestation of the disappearance of order
within microdomains, that is within a group of several unit
cells in which the silver ions are ordered with respect to

their distribution on the three sets of non-equivalent sites
[*cf.* the views of Roth (1972) on domain structures in β-
alumina]. Lederman, Salamon, and Peisl (1976) measured
the heat capacity of $RbAg_4I_5$ by the a.c. technique and also
the optical birefringence. They confirmed that the II-I
transition is hysteresis-free and gradual. They too concluded that this transition is Ising-like, since the values
they derived for the critical indices, namely α (from the
heat capacity) and β (from the birefringence) of $0 \cdot 14 \pm 0 \cdot 02$
and $0 \cdot 31 \pm 0 \cdot 03$ respectively, are in fair accord with those
required by the Ising model.

Wiedersich and Johnston (1969) have advanced a theory
of disorder in $RbAg_4I_5$ which is based on the quasi-chemical
approximation (section 3.1.3) and which takes into account
both the site energy differences and the energy of repulsion
of silver ions on adjacent sites. With $3 \cdot 4$ kJ mol^{-1} for
this energy of repulsion and values of $2 \cdot 6$ and $4 \cdot 1$ kJ mol^{-1}
for the site energy differences, they were able to account
satisfactorily for the observed configurational entropy
and the 'abnormal' heat capacity of phase I, the latter
being the result of the change with temperature of the distribution on the different sites and of the concentration of
pairs of adjacent silver ions.

The formation of compounds of the type MAg_4I_5 appears
to be limited to a rather narrow range of radius of the
cation M^+. Caesium does not form this compound, though Cs^+
can replace M^+ (= K^+, Rb^+, or NH_4^+) to a limited extent in
the MAg_4I_5 phase. Bradley and Greene (1967a) report that
the corresponding copper compound KCu_4I_5 is stable between
530 K and 605 K. With larger cations M^+, similar compounds
but of different stoichiometry can be obtained. Thus, the
compound $[N(CH_3)_4]_2 Ag_{13}I_{15}$, which is rhombohedral (space
group *R*32) has its silver ions distributed over eight non-
equivalent sets of tetrahedral sites (Geller and Lind 1970).
These ions move in channels in the lattice, though the conductivity is not as high as that of $RbAg_4I_5$. Silver ions also
move in channels formed by face-sharing tetrahedra in the
compound $Ag_{31}I_{39}(C_8H_{22}N_2)_4$, in which the organic cation is
$(CH_3)_3N^+-CH_2CH_2-N^+(CH_3)_3$. This substance has a triclinic

structure ($P\bar{1}$), and the 31 silver atoms in the unit cell
are distributed among 66 tetrahedral sites (Coetzer, Kruger,
and Thackeray 1976). The pyridinium salt $(C_5H_5NH)Ag_5I_6$ (Table
6.1) does not undergo any obvious structural change on passing into its high-temperature form, but the disorder increases at the transition, perhaps because all of the silver
ions, instead of only some of them, become mobile. In this
compound, the silver ions lie at the centre of iodide octahedra, not tetrahedra (Geller 1972).

    Type 1 disorder in the compounds Ag_2HgI_4 and Cu_2HgI_4
was discovered by Ketelaar, who investigated the thermodynamic and structural properties of these substances as
well as their electrical conductivity. He also applied a
Bragg-Williams treatment to the transition from the ordered
phases II to the disordered phases I (see Ketelaar 1938, for
a summary of this work.) The transitions, which are accompanied by reversible colour changes (yellow to red in the
case of the silver compound, and red to brownish-purple for
the copper compound) begin gradually, as shown by the rise
in heat capacity and conductivity, but are completed isothermally; though for the silver salt (the more thoroughly
studied of the two) only about one-fifth of the total
enthalpy gained at the transition is assimilated in the
isothermal stage, which is accompanied by hysteresis. A
single crystal of Ag_2HgI_4-II can be heated through the
transition and remain a single crystal, the volume change
being very small. The conductivity rises by about an order
of magnitude in the final stage of the transition to a
value of $\sim 10^{-3}$ $(\Omega\ cm)^{-1}$, considerably less than the conductivity of AgI-I just above the II$\rightarrow$I transition (Suchow and
Pond 1953, Neubert and Nichols 1958). In phase I the conductivity is mainly due to the silver ions, the mercury ions
with their larger charge only contributing about 6 per cent
(Ketelaar 1934a). In phase II, there is a considerable
electronic contribution. The behaviour of the conductivity
when pressure is applied is curious. In both phases it
first increases, reaches a maximum at 4 kbar and then decreases. A new phase is formed above ~ 6 kbar which is
essentially an electronic conductor (Weil and Lawson 1964).

Ag$_2$HgI$_4$-I has a zinc blende structure in which the three cations, 2 Ag + 1 Hg, are distributed among four tetrahedral sites. It appears from the diffraction intensities observed by Kasper and Browall (1975) in their single crystal study that the ionic vibrations are rather strongly anharmonic, and some local order of the cations appears to persist in this phase (Hibma, Beyeler, and Zeller 1976). The structure of phase II is shown in Fig.6.8, though there is probably

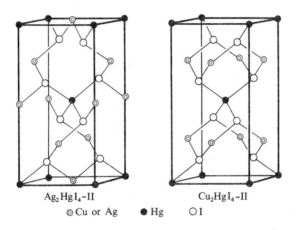

Ag$_2$HgI$_4$-II   Cu$_2$HgI$_4$-II
◎ Cu or Ag   ● Hg   ○ I

Fig.6.8. Structure of the ordered phase II of Ag$_2$HgI$_4$ and Cu$_2$HgI$_4$ (Hahn, Frank, and Klingler 1955).

considerable distortion of the actual arrangement of the iodide ions from cubic close-packing (Browall, Kasper, and Wiedemeier 1974). The ordered form of the copper compound has a different structure in which the copper atoms are arranged in layers (Fig.6.8). While the high-temperature form of Cu$_2$HgI$_4$ appears to be cubic it does not form a continuous series of solid solutions with Ag$_2$HgI$_4$-I (Suchow and Keck 1953).

Certain metallic sulphates have high-temperature phases in which the cations are positionally disordered (Table 6.1).

These sulphates undoubtedly approach more closely to purely ionic solids than the halides and chalcogenides of silver and copper. Some of their disordered phases have the B23 structure in which the sulphur atoms form the body-centred cubic lattices. In Li_2SO_4-I, however, these atoms are arranged on a face-centred cubic lattice as in CuI-I. Disorder in these high-temperature phases is reflected in their low entropies of fusion and in the large entropies of transition from the ordered phases, and it is likely that some of the disorder takes the form of orientational disorder of the anions (p.390). The cations, however, have the same kind of freedom of movement as in the solids we have already discussed, as is shown by conductivity measurements (Kvist and Lundén 1965, Kvist 1966, 1967) and by self-diffusion studies (Kvist and Trolle 1967). Thus, for Li_2SO_4, the conductivity is $\sim 3(\Omega \text{ cm})^{-1}$ at the melting point, and it only increases by ~ 30 per cent on fusion. The activation energy for the movement of the Li^+ ions in Li_2SO_4-I obtained from the temperature dependence of the conductivity is 33 kJ per mole of Li^+, as compared with the value of 43 kJ given by self-diffusion experiments using ^6Li and a mass spectrometer. (These two activation energies need not agree, as the mechanisms of conductivity and diffusion are not necessarily the same.) An interesting deduction from the diffusion experiments was that the motion of the Li^+ ions in the lattice is a cooperative process in which roughly two ions appear to move in phase. The double sulphates, which contain, besides lithium ions, either sodium or silver ions, give phases with the B23 structure which are stable over a considerable range of composition on either side of the 1:1 ratio (Schroeder and Kvist 1968). In view of the different environments of the three kinds of cation site in this structure, the possibility arises of some partial segregation of the two kinds of cation, even in the disordered phase. Krogh-Moe (1966) has pointed out that the larger Na^+ or Ag^+ ions should preferentially occupy the more spacious 12 (d) sites (Fig.6.2), the smaller Li^+ ions being more suitable for the more confined 6 (b) and 24 (h) positions. Such preferences will lead to non-random mixing, and Øye (1963) found evidence of this in

the $LiAgSO_4$ B23 phase by measurements of the entropy of
mixing of the component sulphates. Nevertheless, both kinds
of ion appear to have much the same freedom of movement.
Thus, the diffusion coefficients of the Li^+ and Ag^+ ions
in the disordered form of $LiAgSO_4$ are virtually the same
(Bengtzelius, Kvist, and Trolle 1968), and a conductivity
study of $LiNaSO_4$-I by Polishchuk and Shurzhal (1973) gave
no indication that the movement of the Na^+ ions is hindered
compared with that of the Li^+ ions.

It should be noted that an order-disorder transition
Another striking example of cation disorder is supplied
by the solid usually known as β-alumina (Roth 1972). Once
thought to be a polymorphic form of Al_2O_3, the ideal composition of the solid is $NaAl_{11}O_{17}$. The sodium can be replaced by K, Rb, or Ag, and the Al by Fe or Ga, and the
actual compositions are variable. The crystals are hexagonal (space group $P6_3/mmc$) and the monovalent ions lie in
parallel planes which are perpendicular to the hexagonal
axis and separated by spinel-like blocks (Beevers and Ross
1937, Peters, Bettman, Moore, and Glick 1971). The disorder of the monovalent ions is very much like that of the
cations in some of the super ionic conductors already discussed, except that in the β-alumina structure only two
dimensions are involved. These ions are distributed among
two kinds of site which are crystallographically different
and are therefore not randomly occupied. The ions execute
large-amplitude oscillations on these sites, from which
they are easily displaced, and they spend an appreciable
fraction of time in actually moving from one site to another. The two-dimensional conductivity is very high - that
of sodium-β-alumina is $1 \cdot 4 \times 10^{-2}$ $(\Omega \text{ cm})^{-1}$ at 298 K - and
is virtually wholly due to the monovalent cations. The acti-
vation energy for the movement of the sodium ions is only
~16 kJ mol^{-1} (Whittingham and Huggins 1971a,b).

It should be noted that an order-disorder transition
is not essential for the development in a lattice of exceptional freedom of movement of ions as the temperature
rises. Thus, sodium sulphide, Na_2S, which has an antifluorite structure, does not appear to undergo any transition, yet its conductivity, which is wholly cationic, is

~1 $(\Omega \text{ cm})^{-1}$ at 800°C, which is still far below the melting
point (1169°C) (Möbius, Witzmann, and Hartung, 1964). Also,
instances can be found of Type 1 disorder where the disordered crystals have not been reported as exhibiting unusually high cationic conductivity. Gallium (III) sulphide,
Ga_2S_3, is a case in point. It exists in two disordered
forms, a high-temperature wurtzite B4 form (β) and a low-
temperature zinc blende B3 structure (γ), the transition
temperature being ~850 K. In both of these, the gallium
atoms randomly occupy two-thirds of the sites which in wurtzite or zinc blende are filled by the zinc atoms (Hahn and
Klingler 1949). There is also a third modification of
Ga_2S_3, (α), which still contains vacant cation sites, but
these now form an ordered array, in consequence of which the
crystal is somewhat distorted as compared with the other
two structures and is in fact monoclinic (Goodyear and
Steigmann 1963). The double sulphide Al_2ZnS_4 has a high-
temperature form which was at one time thought to have a
wurtzite structure with the metal atoms disordered on the
tetrahedral sites in essentially the same way as in Ag_2HgI_4-I
(Hahn and Frank 1952). It is now known that this modification has a complex layered orthorhombic lattice in which,
however, there is some Type I disorder of the zinc atoms
on tetrahedral sites (Steigmann 1967).

In the mercury compounds $Hg(NH_3)_2Cl_2$ and $Hg(NH_3)_2Br_2$,
the mercury atoms are disordered in such a way that the
crystals present an example of the disorder of dimers on a
simple cubic lattice (section 3.8). The two substances have
cubic unit cells in which the mercury atoms occupy the face-
centred positions, the chance of finding such an atom on
any one of these sites being one-sixth (Fig.6.9). A mole
of the salt contains N linear cations NH_3-Hg^{2+}-NH_3, and
the nitrogen atoms occupy $2N$ fixed points forming a primitive
cubic lattice, so that if the cation is regarded as the
dimer the affinity with the disorder of dimers on a cubic
lattice is obvious. (The randomness can therefore alternatively be regarded as a form of orientational disorder of
the complex cations.) Crystals of mercury diamminochloride
show no transition on cooling, suggesting that the disorder

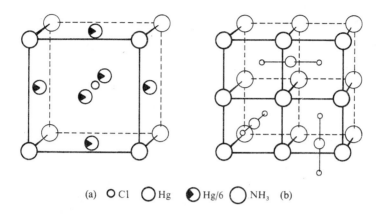

(a) ⊙ Cl ◯ Hg ◑ Hg/6 ◯ NH₃ (b)

Fig.6.9. (a) The unit cell of $Hg(NH_3)_2Cl_2$; (b) the same structure shown as a three-dimensional disordered dimer system (Lipscomb 1953).

persists to 0 K (Cooke, Linford, Worswick, and Staveley, unpublished results). This recalls the theoretical prediction
of Green and Hurst (1964) - though admittedly this was made
for a two-dimensional lattice - that a disordered dimer
system should not undergo a transition to an ordered state
on cooling (section 3.8). The persistence of disorder in
the crystal at 0 K was confirmed by comparison of the apparent calorimetric entropy $S(cal)$ with the value $S(eq)$ obtained from e.m.f. measurements on a cell based on the
reaction

$$2AgCl(s) + 2NH_3(aq) + Hg(1) = Hg(NH_3)_2Cl_2(s) + 2Ag(s) .$$

The value of the residual entropy, $S(res) = S(eq) - S(cal)$,
was $11 \cdot 1 \pm 3 \cdot 0$ J K^{-1} mol^{-1}.
    The mercury compound mercury (II) amidobromide,
$HgNH_2Br$, exists in a stable, ordered, orthorhombic form,
and an unstable cubic modification (Fig.6.10). The infinite
cations consist of alternate linear N-Hg-N units and angled
Hg-N-Hg units, so that the cation in the disordered lattice
follows the path of a random walk on a cubic lattice in
which each step is at right angles to the preceding step.
A comparison of $S(cal)$ (= $131 \cdot 0$ J K^{-1} mol^{-1}) and $S(eq)$

($= 130 \cdot 2$ J K^{-1} mol^{-1}) for the cubic form gave the rather
surprising result that the two are equal within experimental error, so that although there is no reason to doubt
the diffraction evidence for disorder in this modification
at room temperature, little if any disorder remains at 0 K.
Using a Monte Carlo method, it was estimated that the
configurational entropy which would be associated with random

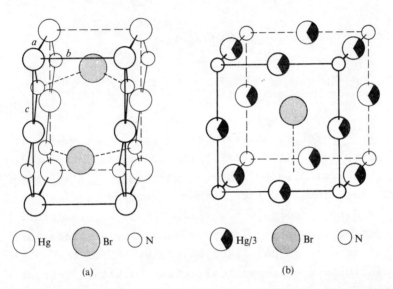

(a)   (b)

Fig.6.10. (a) Ordered, orthorhombic form of HgNH$_2$Br (Nijssen and Lipscomb
1952). (b) The disordered cubic form (Brodersen and Rüdorff 1954).
(Reproduced by permission from Gmelin's Handbuch.)

walk disorder of this kind would be approximately $6 \cdot 7$ J K^{-1}
mol^{-1} (Worswick, Mayers, and Staveley 1972).

Another mercury compound exhibiting positional disorder - though strictly neither of Type 1 nor Type 2 - is
the substance formulated as Hg$_{2 \cdot 86}$AsF$_6$, in which the mercury atoms are formally between a zerovalent and monovalent
state, the average charge per atom being +0·35. This curious
compound exists as golden, tetragonal crystals in which the
mercury atoms form linear chains in non-interacting channels
in two directions at right angles (Fig.6.11) (Brown, Cutforth,
Davies, Gillespie, Ireland, and Vekris 1974). The mercury
atoms in any one chain are disordered with respect to those

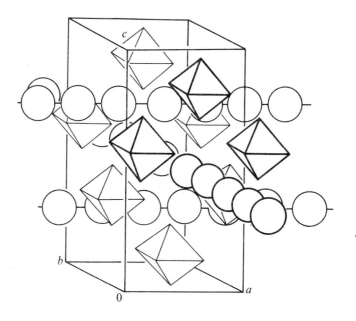

Fig.6.11. Structure of the compound $Hg_{2.86}AsF_6$. The AsF_6^- ions are shown as octahedra, the Hg atoms as circles (Brown *et al*. 1974).

in adjacent chains, so the disorder resembles that found in the hydrates $CsCl$, $1/3(H_2O, 2HCl)$ and HCl, H_2O, (p. 311) and in the urea-hydrocarbon adducts discussed in section 11.4. In such a case, the number of possible configurations for a crystal depends on its surface area rather than its volume, or alternatively, for N ordering entities on $N^{2/3}$ rather than on N, and for macroscopic crystals the corresponding configurational entropy is virtually zero.

6.3. TYPE 2 DISORDER

A simple example of Type 2 disorder is found in the compound $LiFeO_2$, formed by heating stoichiometric amounts of Fe_2O_3 and Li_2O at 700°C. The crystals obtained on quenching have a face-centred cubic lattice with the lithium and iron atoms randomly arranged on the cation sites (Collongues and Chaudran 1950). On prolonged annealing at 600°C, this form changes to the ordered zinc blende structure of chalcopyrite, $CuFeS_2$ (Collongues 1957). The compounds $ZnSnAs_2$

and $AgInS_2$ also have the chalcopyrite structure at ordinary
temperatures, but at 908 K the former transforms into a zinc
blende modification in which the Zn and Sn atoms are randomly
disordered on the cation sites (Pfister 1963), while at
~920 K $AgInS_2$ is converted into a wurtzite-like form in which
the cations are similarly disordered (Hahn, Frank, Klingler,
Meyer, and Störger, 1953). More remarkably, at 50°C and at
pressures >20kbar, the room-temperature modification of
$AgInS_2$ changes to a sodium chloride-like crystal in which the
Ag^+ and In^{3+} ions are randomly distributed on the octahedral sites. This modification is almost certainly thermodynamically unstable, owing its existence to the inability
of the cations at such a low temperature to diffuse in the
lattice and thus generate an ordered structure (Range,
Lindenberg, Keubler, Leeb, and Weiss, 1969).

Numerous examples of Type 2 disorder are to be found
among the spinels. These are solids of the general formula
AB_2X_4, where $X = O^{2-}$ or S^{2-}, or less commonly Se^{2-} or Te^{2-}.
Useful general reviews of this class of inorganic solid have
been written by Ward (1959), Greenwood (1968) and Wells
(1975). The unit cell of a spinel AB_2O_4 consists of 8 A
atoms, 16 B atoms, and 32 O atoms. The sites available to
the metal atoms A and B are (1) eight equivalent positions
in which the metal atom is tetrahedrally surrounded by four
oxygen atoms, (2) 16 sites in which the metal is at the
centre of an octahedron of six oxygen atoms (Fig.6.12). In
a normal spinel, the A and B atoms occupy tetrahedral and
octahedral sites respectively, so that its formula may be
represented as $[A]_t[B_2]_oO_4$, but in an inverse spinel the
tetrahedral sites are occupied by half the B atoms while
the remaining B atoms and the A atoms are randomly disposed
on the octahedral sites. An inverse spinel can therefore
be formulated as $[B]_t[AB]_oO_4$. A spinel in which the tetrahedral sites are not exclusively occupied by A or B atoms
can be characterized by a parameter λ, the fraction of B
atoms in these sites, so that $\lambda = 0$ for a normal spinel, $\frac{1}{2}$ for
an inverse spinel, and 1/3 for spinels with random distribution
of the A and B atoms on both kinds of site. The most common
type of AB_2O_4 and AB_2S_4 spinel is the 2:3 version, in which

the charges on A and B are +2 and +3 respectively. Most of these are either strictly normal or inverse, but which of these structures is adopted depends in a rather complicated way on a number of factors, and the energy difference between the two can be quite small (see, e.g. Blasse 1964, Greenwood 1968). Intermediate conditions, for which λ falls between 0 and $\frac{1}{2}$, are therefore not infrequently encountered. Thus, for $MgGa_2O_4$, $\lambda = 0 \cdot 42$, so it is not a pure inverse spinel $[Ga]_t[MgGa]_oO_4$, but one in which about 16 per cent of the magnesium ions are on the tetrahedral sites (Weidenborner, Stemple, and Okaya 1966). Sometimes the degree to which the occupation of sites is random depends on the thermal history of the sample, as revealed by a variable λ. For $NiMn_2O_4$, for example, λ varies between $0 \cdot 37$ and $0 \cdot 47$ (Boucher, Buhl, and Perrin 1969). Most 4:2 spinels (with charges of +4 and +2 on A and B respectively) form inverse spinels, but here too the tetrahedral sites are not always completely filled by B ions. Forster and Hall (1965) found from neutron and X-ray diffraction studies that, for Fe_2TiO_4, $\lambda = 0 \cdot 46$; therefore the tetrahedral sites are not exclusively occupied by Fe^{2+} ions.

Magnetite, Fe_3O_4, exists below ~120 K as an inverse spinel, with 8 Fe^{3+} in the tetrahedral A sites and (8 Fe^{2+} + 8 Fe^{3+}) on the octahedral sites. Verwey, Haayman, and Romeijn (1947) proposed that the two kinds of ion on the octahedral sites are ordered, and this was confirmed by a neutron diffraction study by Hamilton (1958). On heating form II it is converted between 100 K and 120 K into an orthorhombic form I. (The transition temperatures quoted in the literature vary somewhat, depending on the property studied and on the preparation or origin of the sample - which can moreover qualitatively affect the form taken by the transition. Thus, the heat capacity measurements which Voronel, Garber, and Mamnitskiĭ (1969) made on single crystals showed one gradual transition, whereas those of Westrum and Grønvold (1969) on a synthetic specimen revealed two peaks in the heat capacity, a smaller one at 113·3 K and a larger one at 118·9 K, with a combined entropy change of $0 \cdot 68R$.) With ordered Fe^{2+} and Fe^{3+} ions, the magnetic field

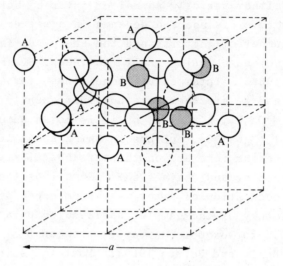

Fig.6.12. The normal spinel structure. The total cube is the unit cell. The open circles A are the cations in tetrahedral holes, the shaded circles are the B cations in the octahedral sites (Ward 1959).

would be expected to have different values for the two kinds of ion on the octahedral sites, and this is consistent with the observed Mössbauer spectrum (Bauminger, Cohen, Marinov, Ofer, and Segal 1961, Ito, Ôno, and Ishikawa 1963). The spectrum changes at the transition, however, in a way which indicates that in form I the field has an average value for all the octahedral sites. From this and other evidence, such as the considerable increase in electronic conductivity which accompanies the II→I transition, it appears that there is rapid electron interchange in form I between the two kinds of ion, which thereby effectively lose their identities, so that the condition can be regarded as one of dynamic disorder. However, in spite of the considerable amount of work already devoted to magnetite, much remains to be elucidated or resolved. More recent neutron diffraction evidence suggests that the charge ordering pattern in the rhombo-hedral low-temperature phase is not that originally pre-dicted for the Verwey model, though the details have yet to be settled (Iizumi and Shirane 1975). It appears that the charge ordering which takes place when the crystal is cooled to give the low-temperature form is induced by static displacements which result from the freezing or condensation of a lattice mode. Evans and Westrum (1972) pointed out that the Mössbauer spectra obtained by Romanov, Checherskii, and Eremenko (1969) show two changes which begin at nearly the same temperatures as those of the maxima in the heat capacity observed by Westrum and Gronvøld, and they consider that the combined information from these two sources supports the 'multiple ordering' theory of Cullen and Callen (1971), according to which three order parameters are needed to characterize the low-temperature phase.

If in the prototype spinel $MgAl_2O_4$ two Mg^{2+} ions are replaced by ($Li^+ + Al^{3+}$) we obtain the structure $LiAl_5O_8$. Up to 1570 K, this exists as a spinel in which the Li^+ and Al^{3+} are randomly distributed on the two sublattices. At 1570 K, it changes into a form with a non-spinel, primitive cubic structure in which Type 2 disorder of the cations still persists (Braun 1952, Datta and Roy 1963). Replacement of the A and B ions in a spinel by ions of different valencies can also be carried out to give a derivative which, while still stoichiometric and with the spinel structure, contains three or more kinds of cation, which of course enhances the *a priori* possibility of Type 2 disorder. Thus, the solids $LiNiVO_4$ and $LiCoVO_4$ have spinel structures in which the Li and Ni (or Co) ions are disordered on the octahedral sites (Corsmit and Blasse 1973). In the still more complex spinels $Li_2ZnGe_3O_8$ and $Li_2CoGe_3O_8$ the octahedral sites are occupied by ($4Li^+ + 12Ge^{4+}$), while [$4Zn^{2+}$ (or Co^{2+}) + $4Li^+$] are statistically distributed over the tetrahedral sites (Durif and Joubert 1962).

Spinels will be encountered again in Chapter 12, in section 12.12 in connection with cooperative Jahn-Teller effects, and in section 12.13.1 in respect of magnetic ordering.

Crystals of the compound $Bi_3(FeO_4)(MoO_4)_2$ as formed from solution are disordered. They have a structure like that of scheelite ($CaWO_4$), space group $I4_1/a$, with the Fe and Mo atoms randomly disposed on the tetrahedral cation

sites. They are metastable, and above 600°C change completely to a structure ($C2/c$) in which the Fe and Mo atoms are
ordered (Jeitschko, Sleight, McClellan, and Weiher 1976).

The possibility of Type 2 disorder increases even further with partial replacement of one ion by another of the
same charge and similar size. We shall not consider mixed
crystals in detail. They can, of course, be studied in many
types of solid, some of them much simpler than the spinels,
such as the alkali halides. A question presented by a mixed
crystal such as, say, KCl-KBr, is whether the chloride and
bromide ions are completely randomly disposed on the sites
available to them or whether there is some local order. On
the basis of his theory of such mixed crystals (which had
considerable success, for example in accounting for the observed enthalpies of formation), Wasastjerna (1949) concluded that in the example quoted there is a significant
degree of local ordering among the anions. Milnes and
Wallace (1961), however, obtained an experimental estimate
of the residual entropy of equimolar KCl-KBr mixed crystals
at 0 K of $5 \cdot 73 \pm 0 \cdot 17$ J K^{-1} mol^{-1}, equal within experimental error to the theoretical value of $R \ln 2$ for completely
random mixing.

REFERENCES

Alcock, N.W., Evans, D.A., and Jenkins, H.D.B. (1973). *Acta
crystallog.* B29, 360.

Asadov, Yu. G. and Yabrailova, G.A. (1972). *Phys.St.Solidi*
A12, K 13.

Baer, Y., Busch, G., Fröhlich, C., and Steigmeier, E. (1962).
Z.Naturforsch. 17a, 886.

Bauminger, R., Cohen, S.G., Marinov, A., Ofer, S., and Segal,
E. (1961). *Phys.Rev.* 122, 1447.

Becker, K.D., Herzog, G.W., Kanne, D., Richtering, H., and
Stadler, E. (1970). *Ber.Bunsenges.phys.Chem.* 74, 527.

Beevers, C.A. and Ross, M.A.S. (1937). *Z.Kristallog.
Kristallgeom.* 97, 59.

Bengtzelius, A., Kvist, A. and Trolle, U. (1968). *Z.
Naturforsch.* 23a, 2040.

Bentle, G.G. (1968). *J.appl.Phys*. 39, 4036.

Blasse,G. (1964). *Philips Res.Repts.Suppl*.

Bloch, R. and Möller, H. (1931). *Z.phys.Chem*. A152, 245.

Borchert, W. (1944). *Z.Kristallog.Kristallgeom*. 106, 5
    (volume covering 1945-1955).

Boucher, B., Buhl, R., and Perrin, M. (1969). *Acta crystallog.*
    B25, 2326.

Bradley, J.N. and Greene, P.D. (1966). *Trans.Faraday Soc*. 62,
    2069.

————————   ————————   (1967). (a) *Trans.Faraday Soc.*
    63, 424; (b) *Trans.Faraday Soc*. 63, 2516.

Braun, P.B. (1952). *Nature,Lond*. 170, 1123.

Bremer, F. and Nölting, J. (1973). *Ber.Bunsenges.phys.Chem.*.
    77, 398.

Brodersen,K. and Rüdorff,W.(1954). *Z.anorg.allgem.Chem*. 275, 141.

Browall, K.W., Kasper, J.S., and Wiedemeier, H. (1974).
    J.solid St.Chem. 10, 20.

Brown, I.D., Cutforth, B.D., Davies, C.G., Gillespie, R.J.,
    Ireland, P.R., and Vekris, J.E. (1974). *Can.J.Chem*. 52,
    791.

Buerger, M.J. and Buerger, N.W. (1944). *Am.Miner*. 29, 55.

Bührer, W. and Brüesch, P. (1975). *Solid St.Communs*. 16, 155.

Bundy, F.P., Kasper, J.S., and Moore, M.J. (1971). *High-Temp,*
    High Press. 3, 303.

Burley, G. (1963). *J.chem.Phys*. 38, 2807.

———————   (1964). *(J.)Phys.Chem.Solids*

———————   (1967). *Acta crystallog*.23, 1.

Burns, G., Dacol, F.H., and Shafer, M.W. (1976). *Solid*
    St.Communs. 19, 287,291.

Chivian, J.S., Claytor, R.N., Eden, D.D., and Hemphill, R.B.
    (1972). *Appl.Optics* 11, 2649.

Clark, J.B. and Rapoport, E. (1970). *(J.)Phys.Chem.Solids* 31
    247.

Coetzer, J., Kruger, G.J., and Thackeray, M.M. (1976).
    Acta crystallog. 32B, 1248.

Collongues, R. (1957). *Bull.Soc.chim.France* 261.

———————   and Chaudron, G. (1950). *C.r.hebd.Séanc.Acad.*
    Sci.,Paris 231, 143.

Corsmit, A.F. and Blasse, G. (1973). *Chem.Phys.Lett*. 20, 347.

Cullen, J.R. and Callen, E. (1971). *Solid St.Communs.* 9, 1041.

Datta, R.K. and Roy, R. (1963). *J.Am.Ceram.Soc.* 46, 388.

Davis, B.L. and Adams, L.H. (1964). *Science* 146, 519.

Delaney, M.J. and Ushioda, S. (1976). *Solid St.Communs.* 19, 297.

Djurle, S. (1958). *Acta chem.scand.* 12, 1427.

Durif, A. and Joubert, J.-C. (1962). *C.r.hebd.Séanc.Acad.Sci., Paris* 255, 2471.

Eckold, G. and Funke, K. (1973). *Z.Naturforsch.* 28a, 1042.

Evans, B.J. and Westrum, E.F. (1972). *Phys.Rev.* 5B, 3791.

Fischmeister, H. (1956). *Z.phys.Chem.N.F.* 7, 91.

Fletcher, N.H. (1971). *J.chem.Phys.* 55, 4681.

Førland, T. and Krogh-Moe, J. (1957). *Acta chem.scand.* 11, 565.

―――   ―――   (1958). *Acta crystallog.* 11, 224.

Forster, R.H. and Hall, E.O. (1965). *Acta crystallog.* 18, 857.

Frenzel, D. (1963). *Z.phys.Chem.N.F.* 36, 15.

Frueh, A.J. (1958). *Z.Kristallog.Kristallgeom.* 110, 136.

―――   (1961). *Am.Miner.* 46, 654.

Funke, K. and Hackenburg, R. (1972). *Ber.Bunsenges.phys.Chem.* 76, 885.

―――   and Jost, A. (1971). *Ber.Bunsenges.phys.Chem.* 75, 436.

Geller, S. (1967). *Science* 157, 310.

―――   (1972). *Science* 176, 1016.

―――   and Lind, M.D. (1970). *J.chem.Phys.* 52, 5854.

―――   and Owens, B.B. (1972). *(J.)Phys.Chem.Solids* 33, 1241.

Gmelin's Handbuch (1972). 61, T1.B2.

―――   (1973), 61, T1.B3.

Goodyear, J. and Steigmann, G.A. (1963). *Acta crystallog.* 16, 946.

Green, H.S. and Hurst, C.A. (1964). *Order-disorder phenomena* p.96. Interscience, London.

Greenwood, N.N. (1968). *Ionic crystals, lattice defects and nonstoichiometry.* Butterworths, London.

Guenther, B.D. and Hultsch, R.A. (1969). *J.mag.Res.* 1, 609.

Hahn, H. and Frank, G. (1952). *Z.anorg.allgem.Chem.* 269, 227.

Hahn, H., Frank, G. and Klingler, W. (1955). *Z.anorg. allgem.Chem.* <u>279</u>, 271.

——— ——— ——— Meyer, A.-D., and Störger, G. (1953). *Z.anorg.allgem.Chem.* <u>271</u>, 153.

——— and Klingler, W. (1949). *Z.anorg.allgem.Chem.* <u>259</u>, 135.

Hamilton, W.C. (1958). *Phys.Rev.* <u>110</u>, 1050.

Hara, M., Mori, T., and Ishiguro, M. (1973). *Jap.J.appl.Phys.* <u>12</u>, 343.

Hedvall, J.A., Lindler, R., and Hartler, N. (1950). *Acta chem. scand.* <u>4</u>, 1099.

Helmholtz, L. (1935). *J.chem.Phys.* <u>3</u>, 740.

Herrmann, K. and Ilge, W. (1931). *Z.Krystallog.Kristallgeom.* <u>80</u>, 402.

Herzog, G.W. and Richtering, H. (1967). *Z.phys.Chem.N.F.* <u>56</u>, 109.

Hibma, T., Beyeler, H.U., and Zeller, H.R. (1976). *J.Phys.* <u>C9</u>, 1691.

Hoshino, S. (1955). *J.phys.Soc.Japan* <u>10</u>, 197.

——— (1957). *J.phys.Soc.Japan* <u>12</u>, 315.

Iizumi, M. and Shirane, G. (1975). *Solid St.Commun.* <u>17</u>, 433.

Ingraham, T. and Marier, P. (1965). *Can.Met.Quart.* <u>4</u>, 169.

Ito, A. Ôno, K. and Ishikawa, Y. (1963). *J.phys.Soc.Japan* <u>18</u>, 1465.

Jacobs, R.B. (1938). *Phys.Rev.* <u>54</u>, 325.

Jeitschko, W., Sleight, A.W., McClennan, W.R., and Weiher, J.F. (1976). *Acta crystallog.* <u>32B</u>, 1163.

Johnston, W.V., Wiedersich, H., and Lindberg, G.W. (1969). *J.chem.Phys.* <u>51</u>, 3739.

Jost, W. (1971). *J.chem.Phys.* <u>55</u>, 4680.

——— and Kubaschewski, P. (1968). *Z.phys.Chem.N.F.* <u>60</u>, 69.

——— and Nölting, J. (1956). *Z.phys.Chem.N.F.* <u>7</u>, 383.

Kasper, J.S. and Browall, K.W. (1975). *J.Solid St.Chem.* <u>13</u>, 49.

Kelley, K.K. (1936). *U.S.Bur.Mines Bull.* No. 393.

Ketelaar, J.A.A. (1931). *Z.Kristallog.Kristallgeom.* <u>80</u>, 190.

——— (1934). (a) *Z.phys.Chem.* <u>B26</u>, 327; (b) *Z. Kristallog.Kristallgeom.* <u>87</u>, 436.

——— (1935). *Z.phys.Chem.* <u>B30</u>, 53.

Ketelaar, J.A.A. (1938) *Trans.Faraday Soc.* 34, 874.

Krogh-Moe, J. (1966). *Selected topics in high temperature chemistry* (ed. T. Førland, K. Grjotheim, K. Motzfeldt, and S. Urnes), *Universitetsforlaget Oslo*, p.79.

Krug, J. and Sieg, L. (1952). *Z.Naturforsch.*7a, 369.

Kubaschewski, P. and Nölting, J. (1973). *Ber.Bunsenges.phys. Chem.* 77, 70.

Kvist, A. (1966). *Z.Naturforsch.* 21a, 487.

———   (1967) *Z.Naturforsch.* 22a, 208.

———   and Josefson, A.-M. (1968). *Z.Naturforsch.* 23a, 625.

———   and Lundén, A. (1965). *Z.Naturforsch.* 20a, 235.

———   and Trolle, U. (1967). *Z.Naturforsch.* 22a, 213.

Lawn, B.R. (1964). *Acta crystallog.* 17, 1341.

Ledermann, F.L., Salamon, M.B. and Peisl, H. (1976). *Solid St. Communs.* 19, 147.

Lipscomb, W.N. (1953). *Anal.Chem.* 25, 737.

Llabres, G. and Messien, P. (1968). *Bull.Soc.R.Sci.Liege* 37, 329. (Chem.Abstr. 70, 32388u).

Milnes, M.V. and Wallace, W.E. (1961). *J.phys.Chem.* 65, 1456.

Miyake, S., Hoshino, S., and Takenaka, T. (1952). *J.phys. Soc.Japan* 7, 19.

Möbius, H.-H., Witzmann, H., and Hartung, R. (1964). *Z.phys. Chem.* 227, 40.

Moore, M.J. and Kasper, J.S. (1968). *J.chem.Phys.* 48, 2446.

Morosin, B. and Smith, D.L. (1967). *Acta crystallog.* 22, 906.

Nagao, M. and Kaneda, T. (1975). *Phys.Rev.* B11, 2711.

Natarajan, M. and Rao, C.N.R. (1970). *J.chem.Soc.* A3087.

Neubert, T.J. and Nichols, G.M. (1958). *J.Am.chem.Soc.* 80, 2619.

Nijssen, L. and Lipscomb, W.N. (1952). *Acta crystallog.* 5, 604.

Nolte, G. and Kordes, E. (1969). *Z.anorg.allgem.Chem.* 371, 149.

Nölting, J. (1963). *Ber.Bunsenges.phys.Chem.* 67, 172.

———   (1964). *Ber.Bunsenges.phys.Chem.* 68, 932.

———   and Rein, D. (1969). *Z.phys.Chem.N.F.* 66, 150.

———   ———   and Troe, J. (1969). *Nachr.Wiss. Göttingen.Math.-Phys.Kl.* 2, 4, 31.

Nord, A.G. (1973). *Chem.Comm.Univ.Stockholm* No.3. (*Chem. Abstr.* <u>79</u>, 24 447h).

Owens, B.B. and Argue, G.R. (1967). *Science* <u>157</u>, 308.

—————   —————   (1970). *J.electrochem.Soc.* <u>117</u>, 898.

Øye, H.A. (1963). *Thesis*, the Technical University of Norway, reported by Krogh-Moe (1966).

Pardee, W.J. and Mahan, G.D. (1974). *J.chem.Phys.* <u>61</u>, 2173.

Perrott, C.M. and Fletcher, N.H. (1968). (a) *J.chem.Phys.* <u>48</u>, 2143; (b) <u>48</u>, 2681.

—————   —————   (1969). (a) *J.chem.Phys.* <u>50</u>, 2344; (b) <u>50</u>, 2770.

Peters, C.R., Bettman, M., Moore, J.W., and Glick, M.D. (1971). *Acta crystallog.* <u>B27</u>, 1826.

Pfister, H. (1963). *Acta crystallog.* <u>16</u>, 153.

Polishchuk, A.F. and Shurzhal, T.M. (1973). *Elektrokhimiya* <u>9</u>, 838. (Soviet Electrochemistry <u>9</u>, 802)

Rahlfs, P. (1936). *Z.phys.Chem.* <u>B31</u>, 157.

Ramsdell, L.A. (1943). *Am.Miner.* <u>28</u>, 401.

Range, K.-J., Lindenberg, B., Keubler, M., Leeb, R. and Weiss, A. (1969). *Z.Naturforsch.* <u>24b</u>, 1651.

Reuter, B. and Hardel, K. (1960). *Angew.Chem.* <u>72</u>, 138.

—————   —————   (1965). *Z.anorg.allgem.Chem.*. <u>340</u>, 158, 168.

—————   —————   (1966). *Ber.Bunsenges.phys.Chem.* <u>70</u>, 82.

Rice, M.J. and Roth, N.L. (1972). *J.Solid St.Chem.* <u>4</u>, 294.

————— Strässler, S., and Toombs, G.A. (1974). *Phys.Rev. Lett.* <u>32</u>, 596.

Romanov, V.P., Checherskii, V.D., and Eremenko, V.V. (1969). *Phys.St.Solidi* <u>31</u>, K153.

Roth, W.L. (1972). *J.Solid St.Chem.* <u>4</u>, 60.

Schroeder, K. and Kvist, A. (1968). *Z.Naturforsch.* <u>23A</u>, 773.

Steigmann, G.A. (1967). *Acta crystallog.* <u>23</u>, 142.

Strock, L.W. (1934). *Z.phys.Chem.* <u>B25</u>, 441.

————— (1935). *Z.phys.Chem.* <u>B31</u>, 132.

Suchow, L. and Keck, P.H. (1953). *J.Am.chem.Soc.* <u>75</u>, 518.

————— and Pond, G.R. (1953). *J.Am.chem.Soc.* <u>75</u>, 5242.

Thompson, W.T. and Flengas, S.N. (1971). *Can.J.Chem.* <u>49</u>, 1550.

Tubandt, C. (1932). *Handbuch der Experimentalphysik*,
     Vol.XII, 1, p.383. Akad. Verlagsgesellschaft, Leipzig
     1932.

————   Eggert, S. and Schibbe, G. (1921). *Z.anorg.
allgem.Chem. 117, 1.

————   and Lorenz, E. (1914). *Z.phys.Chem.* 87, 513, 543.

——————— Reinhold, H. and Jost, W. (1929). *Z.anorg.
allgem.Chem. 177, 253.

————   Rindtorff, E. and Jost, W. (1927). *Z.anorg.
allgem.Chem. 165, 195.

Verwey, E.J., Haayman, P.W., and Romeijn, F.C. (1947). *J.
     chem.Phys.* 15, 181.

Voronel', A.V., Garber, S.R., and Mamnitskiĭ, V.M. (1969).
     Zh.eksp.teor.Fiz. 55, 2017 (Soviet Phys.JETP 1969, 28,
     1065).

Ward, R. (1959). *Progr.inorg.Chem.* 1, 465.

Wasastjerna, J.A. (1949). *Soc.Sci.Fenn.Comm.Phys.Math.XV*,
     3, 1.

Wehefritz, V. (1960). *Z.phys.Chem.* 26, 339.

Weidenborner, J.E., Stemple, N.R., and Okaya, Y. (1966).
     Acta crystallog. 20, 761.

Weil, R. and Lawson, A.W. (1964). *J.chem.Phys.* 41, 832.

Wells, A.F. (1975). *Structural inorganic chemistry*, 4th
     ed. Clarendon Press, Oxford.

Westrum, E.F. and Grønvold, F. (1969). *J.chem.Thermodynamics*
     1, 543.

Whittingham, M.S. and Huggins, R.A. (1971). (a) *J.chem.Phys.*
     54, 414; (b) *J.electrochem.Soc.* 118, 1.

Wiedersich, H. and Johnston, W.V. (1969). *(J.)Phys.Chem.
     Solids* 30, 475.

Wiegers, G.A. (1971). *Amer.Miner.* 56, 1882.

Worswick, R.D., Mayers, D.F., and Staveley, L.A.K. (1972).
     J.chem.Soc., Faraday Trans. II 68, 539.

7

ORIENTATIONAL DISORDER IN SALTS

7.1. INTRODUCTION

In this chapter we are concerned primarily with disorder in
ionic solids which arises because a diatomic or polyatomic
ion has available to it two or more distinguishable orientations in the lattice. This kind of disorder is a fairly
common occurrence, especially when the polyatomic ions are
sufficiently symmetrical. If these ions are associated with
monatomic ions of opposite charge, the situation **simplifies**
in that the diatomic or polyatomic ions are to some extent
protected from interference from ions of the same kind by
the intervening shell of monatomic ions. By contrast, for
a one-component *molecular* solid the interaction of the motion
of a particular molecule with that of its identical nearest
neighbours must make reorientation a matter of greater complexity, even when the molecules are very simple. It is
therefore not surprising to find that some salts of the kind
just mentioned, such as ammonium chloride **and sodium nitrate,**
provide cases of disorder which have been intensively studied
both experimentally and theoretically. Attention has already been drawn (page 102) to the encouraging correlation
which exists between the entropy changes at order-disorder
transitions in salts and $R \ln n$ for small integral values
of n.

Applications of almost all of the experimental methods
discussed in Chapter 4, as well as of other techniques which
are less generally useful, will be found in the following
sections of this chapter. Besides the essential structural
and thermodynamic investigation of a particular crystal,
and inquiry into such matters as whether the transition is
wholly or partly gradual, the extent to which some short-
range order still persists in the disordered phase, and so
on, it will be found that much of the more recent work has
been concerned with the dynamics of the ionic reorientation.
In this connection, it should be remembered that the estimation of the height of a barrier to rotation requires that

some assumption be made about the shape of the potential well, and that often the form assumed for this may be rather a gross oversimplification (Schlemper, Hamilton, and Rush 1966). For some of the more thoroughly studied systems information is now emerging not just on barrier heights for ionic rotation in general, but for this movement about particular axes, and on the degree to which the librational motion is anharmonic. Some progress has also been made in elucidating the way in which the actual change of orientation takes place. In salts in which one set of ions is monatomic, such as the alkali borohydrides MBH_4, the crystals may be isostructural for two or more different monatomic ions, and it can then be informative to examine the effect on the order-disorder transition, and on the parameters controlling the kinetics of ionic reorientation, of a change in size of the monatomic ion which thereby alters the interionic separations.

Salts in which both ions are polyatomic, such as ammonium nitrate, present such problems as which ion is to be held primarily responsible for an order-disorder transition, and whether the ions can in fact be regarded as behaving independently. We shall see that such questions may not yet have been satisfactorily resolved, even for a salt as common as ammonium sulphate.

7.2. DIATOMIC IONS

The salts in this category which have been most thoroughly studied are the cyanides and hydrogensulphides of the alkali metals. Some of the available information about the ordered and disordered forms of these compounds and about the transitions between them is summarized in Table 7.1.

The CN^- ions in the low-temperature form III of NaCN and KCN are considered to be orientationally ordered. Matsuo, Suga, and Seki (1968) predicted on electrostatic grounds that a polar arrangement of the CN^- ions would be preferred, but this seems unlikely since Gesi (1972) failed to observe any change in permittivity at the III-II transition in KCN, and the Raman spectrum favours an antipolar arrangement of the anions in KCN-III (Dultz 1974). From values of the

TABLE 7.1

Thermal and structural information on alkali cyanides and hydrogensulphides. T_t is the transition temperature, and ΔS_t the corresponding entropy increase. For the significance of F and λ and for a note on the references, see footnote on p.230.

Compound	III	T_t/K, $\Delta S_t/R$	II	T_t/K, $\Delta S_t/R$	I	References Cal.	Cryst.	NMR
NaCN	?Monoclinic	⟵ 171·9, 0·61 (λ) ⟶	Orthorhombic	⟵ 288·1, 1·41 (λ) ⟶	NaCl	1,2	3	4-6
KCN	?Monoclinic	⟵ 82·9, 0·665 (λ) ⟶	Orthorhombic	⟵ 168·3, 1·01 (λ) ⟶	NaCl	1,7	8,9	5,10
RbCN			?Monoclinic	⟵ 110·3, 0·695 (?F) ⟶	NaCl	11	12	-
CsCN			Rhombohedral	⟵ 193·1, 1·31 (λ) ⟶	CsCl	11	12	-
NaSH		⟵ 113 (?λ) a ⟶	Rhombohedral	⟵ 358 (?F) ⟶	NaCl	-	13-15	16
KSH			Rhombohedral	⟵ 453 (?F) ⟶	NaCl	-	13,14	-
RbSH		⟵ 123 (?λ) a ⟶	Rhombohedral	⟵ 403 (?F) ⟶	NaCl	-	13,14	-
CsSH		⟵ 113 (?λ) a ⟶	Tetragonal	⟵ 198·2 (?F) ⟶	NaCl	-	13,14,17	17

Footnotes to Table 7.1.

a.   From Raman spectra (Rush, Livingston, and Rosasco   1973).

References

1.   Messer and Ziegler (1941).

2.   Matsuo, Suga, and Seki (1968).

3.   Verweel and Bijvoet (1938); Siegel (1949) (X-ray).

4.   Coogan and Gutowsky (1964) (^{23}Na).

5.   O'Reilly, E.M. Peterson, Scheie, and Kadaba (1973)
      (^{14}N and ^{23}Na).

6.   O'Reilly (1973) (^{23}Na).

7.   Suga, Matsuo, and Seki (1965).

8.   Bijvoet and Lely (1940); Cimino, Parry, and Ubbelohde
      (1959); Parry (1962) (X-Ray).

9.   Elliott and Hastings (1961); Sequeira (1965); Atoji
      (1971); Price, Rowe, Rush, Prince, Hinks, and Susman
      (1972) (Neutron). Decker, Beyerlein, Roult, and Worlton
      (1974) (Neutron, high-pressure forms).

10.   Fukushima (1968) (^{13}C).

11.   Sugisaki, Matsuo, Suga, and Seki (1968).

12.   Lely (1942) (X-ray)

13.   West, C.D. (1934) (X-ray).

14.   Teichert and Klemm (1939) (X-ray).

15.   Schroeder, de Graaf, and Rush (1971) (Neutron).

16.   Coogan, Belford, and Gutowsky (1963) (H and ^{23}Na).
      Jeffrey (1974) (H).

17.   Albert, Grunzweig-Genossar, and Perel (1970) (X-ray)

torsional oscillational frequencies of the CN⁻ ions reached
by analysis of the heat capacity data, the barrier to the
rotation of these ions was estimated to be ~55 kJ mol^{-1}
in NaCN-III (Matsuo *et al*. 1968), and ~30 kJ mol^{-1} in
KCN-III (Suga, Matsuo, and Seki 1965). The entropy **gain of**
~R ln 2 at the III-II transition in NaCN and KCN strongly
suggests that in the orthorhombic forms II the CN⁻ ions are
randomly distributed between two orientations. The phases
which have been submitted to the closest scrutiny are the

high-temperature forms I. The entropy gains at the II-I
transition imply considerable further orientational disorder in the cubic lattices, and the question arises as to
whether free rotation of the CN⁻ ions or disorder among
a limited number of orientations is involved, and if the
latter whether the ions change their orientation by 'rotational diffusion', that is by progressing through a large
number of small steps, or by abrupt jumps from one orientation to another. A decision between the possibilities
for disorder cannot be made by an X-ray examination, since
they lead to almost identical calculated intensities. Neutron diffraction offers more hope of deciding between them,
but even here the earlier studies of this kind on KCN-I were
inconclusive (Elliott and Hastings 1961, Sequeira 1965).
However, reexamination of the neutron data by Atoji (1971)
eliminated free rotation in favour of the alternative, a
result supported by measurements of the depolarization
factor of the Raman line produced by the internal vibration of the CN⁻ ion (Mathieu 1954). A single crystal neutron diffraction study of KCN-I by Price, Rowe, Rush, Prince,
Hinks, and Susman (1972) confirmed that free rotation of the
anions does not take place, but whereas Atoji concluded that
these ions are oriented along the [111] directions, Price
and his colleagues doubted if a preferential direction could
be established with certainty. They made the interesting
observation that the root-mean-square amplitudes of the
vibration of the potassium ions and of the libration of
the anions are quite large even at 180 K, being ~0·025 nm
and ~24° respectively. This relatively considerable displacement of the cations may be a consequence of the local
stress induced in the lattice by the rapid switching of
the cyanide ions from one orientation to another. An inelastic neutron scattering study of the cubic forms of KCN
and NaCN gave a spectrum from which there was an absence
of well-defined peaks which could be assigned to phonons
of high frequency, and this too may be a result of the reorientational motion of the cyanide ions (Rowe, Rush, Vagelatos, Price, Hinks, and Susman 1975). It may well be a rather
general feature of disordered crystals of this kind that the

movement of one kind of ion is markedly influenced by the orientational disorder of the other (cf. section 3.6).

KCN and NaCN have been thoroughly studied by magnetic resonance techniques, as indicated by the references in Table 7.1. The results of these investigations favour the jump reorientation model. From measurements of the spin-lattice relaxation time T_1 for ^{13}C in KCN-I, Fukushima (1968) derived a value of 5 kJ mol^{-1} for E_R, the activation energy for reorientation of the CN$^-$ ions, while O'Reilly, Peterson, Scheie, and Kadaba (1973), from the temperature dependence of T_1 for the ^{14}N resonance in this phase, obtained $E_R = 2 \pm 1$ kJ mol^{-1}, and also a value of 5·9 kJ mol^{-1} for NaCN-I. For this last phase, ^{23}Na T_1 measurements gave $E_R = 6·2$ kJ mol^{-1}. Heat capacity analysis led to barrier heights of 8-12 kJ mol^{-1} for NaCN-I (Matsuo et al., 1968), and 5-6 kJ mol for KCN-I (Suga et al. 1965, D.Smith 1968, 1970). So the energy barriers to reorientation of the CN$^-$ ions in the cubic forms of the two salts are certainly quite small, and lower for KCN than for NaCN. Atoji has pointed out on the basis of calculations of the field in which the CN$^-$ ions move (Matsubara and Nagamiya 1949) that in KCN-I [111] reorientation of these ions should be easiest, followed by [110] and finally by [100] reorientation, for which the barrier height estimated from the potential field calculation is 5·2 kJ mol^{-1}. He considers, therefore, that as the cubic phase of KCN is heated, the tumbling of the cyanide ions from [111] to [111] begins via the [110] directions, but as the melting-point is approached makes use of the [100] directions also. It will be noted that while ΔS for the II-I transition in NaCN is close to $R \ln 4$, consistent with a change from two orientations in the orthorhombic phase to eight in the cubic phase, the corresponding quantity for KCN is somewhat less. Haussühl (1973), using an ultrasonic method to measure the elastic constants, found that the shear constant c_{44} tends to zero as the II→I transition is approached from below, suggesting the possible involvement of a soft shear mode.

In addition to the forms of KCN already discussed there is a metastable, low-temperature, monoclinic form, which is

probably ordered and which transforms into the cubic form
at 166·5 K (Suga *et al*. 1965, Cimino, Parry, and Ubbelohde
1959, Parry 1962). A rhombohedral form of NaCN can be
produced by quenching the cubic form from 300°C, and this
too is probably ordered (Siegel 1949). There are two high-
pressure forms of potassium cyanide. One of these (which
some authors have designated III) has a caesium chloride-
like structure with the cyanide ions randomly oriented along
the [111] directions, and once again the motion of the
cations has a relatively large amplitude attributable to the
rapid change in orientation of the anions (Decker, Beyerlein,
Roult, and Worlton, 1974). The other high-pressure form IV
has a distorted caesium chloride (monoclinic) structure,
and in this the cyanide ions are altogether more ordered.

Rubidium and caesium cyanides have been less thoroughly
investigated. RbCN has an NaCl-type lattice at ordinary
temperatures, and there is a low-temperature form which is
probably monoclinic and perhaps resembles the metastable
form of KCN. CsCN has a CsCl structure at room temperature
(as does thallium (I) cyanide) in which the CN⁻ ions must
be disordered, and a rhombohedral low-temperature form which
is a slightly distorted version of the CsCl structure. The
entropies of the II→I transition in RbCN and CsCN are approximately $R \ln 2$ and $R \ln 4$ respectively. Neither salt has a
lower transition, and since the disorder in the cubic phases
might be expected to be very similar to that in the corresponding phases of the sodium and potassium salts, Sugisaki,
Matsuo, Suga, and Seki (1968) concluded that in phase II of
RbCN and CsCN there is probably frozen-in disorder which
confers residual entropy on these salts at 0 K of $R \ln 4$ and
$R \ln 2$ respectively.

The most detailed structural study of a hydrogensulphide
is the neutron diffraction investigation of the rhombohedral
and cubic phases of NaSH by L.W. Schroeder, de Graaf, and
Rush (1971). Fig.7.1 illustrates the main conclusions
reached about the structure of both phases. In the high-
temperature form I it is probable that the SH⁻ ions are
randomly aligned along the trigonal axes. When this form
is cooled through the transition, the SH⁻ ions all take the

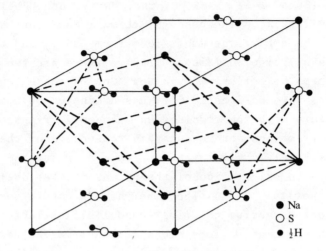

Fig.7.1. Composite drawing of phases I and II of NaSH. The SH⁻ ions are shown aligned along a single [111] direction of the high-temperature f.c.c. cell. The dashed lines outline the primitive trigonal cell of phase II (after L.W.Schroeder, de Graaf, and Rush 1971).

direction of one of the cube diagonals, which shortens as a result and so gives rise to the trigonal phase II. It is possible that in addition to the orientational disorder of the SH⁻ ions, both they and the sodium ions have increased freedom of translational movement in the cubic phase I. These findings are in agreement with the NMR H and ^{23}Na studies of Coogan, Belford, and Gutowsky (1963). The proton second moment at 90°C is consistent with rapid random reorientation of the SH⁻ ions among the eight [111] directions of the cubic phase, while diffusion of both cations and anions is indicated by the narrowing of the ^{23}Na and H resonances. For the trigonal phase, Coogan *et al*. concluded that the SH⁻ ions have six equivalent orientations, but the second moment and T_1 measurements of Jeffrey (1974) are better fitted by a model in which each anion switches between two orientations along the trigonal axis (Fig.7.1).

The neutron scattering investigations of Rush and his coworkers on the alkali hydrogensulphides provide an elegant demonstration of the insight which can be gained into the dynamics and mechanism of reorientational processes in crystal

lattices by using the evidence provided by both inelastic
and quasielastic studies. These investigations were carried
out on both forms of NaSH and on CsSH-I (Rush, de Graaf, and
Livingston 1973) and on RbSH-I and -II (Rowe, Livingston,
and Rush 1973a,b). We reproduce in Fig.7.2 the spectra
given by NaSH at temperatures above and below the transition

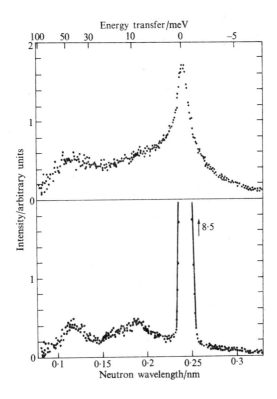

Fig.7.2. Inelastic neutron spectrum for NaSH in its cubic form I at 103°C
(upper figure), and in its trigonal phase II at 23°C (lower figure) ·
T_t = 85°C; scattering angle (65°) is the same for both phases (Rush,
de Graaf, and Livingston 1973).

at 85°C. The main conclusions that emerge from these comprehensive studies are the following: (a) As will be seen
from Fig.7.2, there are broad inelastic peaks in the spectra
given by phase II at ~50 and 10 meV.[†] These are attributed

[†]1 meV ≃ 96·50 J mol^{-1} ≃ 8·067 cm^{-1}.

to SH$^-$ librations and to translational lattice vibrations
respectively. Since the peak at ~50 meV is still perceptible
above the transition, free rotation of the SH$^-$ ions is
eliminated, and these ions must be regarded as continuing
to execute librational motion in the cubic phase with much
the same frequency (~400 cm^{-1}) as in the rhombohedral phase.
(b) The quasielastic peaks for NaSH, RbSH, and CsSH in the
cubic phase show a broadening dependent both on temperature
and on the momentum transfer, implying rapid reorientation
of the anions. Analysis of this broadening supports the jump
reorientation mechanism. (c) If an ion spends an average
time τ in one orientation before jumping to another, τ is
estimated to decrease from 0·4 to 0·15 ps in NaSH-I as the
temperature rises from 103°C to 212°C, and from 2·0 to 0·75
ps in CsSH-I between 23° and 140°C. Assuming an Arrhenius-
type equation is applicable, these τ values give 12 kJ mol^{-1}
and 8·7 kJ mol^{-1} for the reorientational activation energy
E_R in NaSH-I and CsSH-I respectively. (d) The quasielastic
peak of RbSH-I somewhat below the transition temperature
can be resolved into two components, an elastic component
and a broadened component (cf. the example of neopentane
cited on page 168). The momentum-transfer dependence of
the elastic peak was shown by Rowe *et al*. to be consistent
with the view that the SH$^-$ ions are switching between two equilibrium positions along the trigonal axis. Their estimate
of E_R for this reorientation was 17 kJ mol^{-1}, the value of
τ at 393 K being 4 ps, which is about an order of magnitude
larger than the values quoted for the cubic phases. Nevertheless, the mean-square amplitude of the vibrations of the
hydrogen atom appears to be *greater* in RbSH-II than in
RbSH-I.

If the SH$^-$ ions in the rhombohedral phases of NaSH,
KSH, and CsSH are disordered between two orientations, then
at sufficiently low temperatures these crystals should
transform to completely ordered phases. Rush, Livingston,
and Rosasco (1973) report having observed this transition,
which appears to be gradual, in the sodium, rubidium, and
caesium salts from changes in the Raman spectrum.

There are other salts with diatomic ions which are known

to exist in cubic forms in which the ions must be orientationally disordered, and in due course these will no doubt
be more thoroughly investigated. They include the hydro-
genselenides of Na, K, and Rb, which like the corresponding
hydrogensulphides are rhombohedral at ordinary temperatures,
and change at temperatures not very different from those for
their hydrogensulphide counterparts into NaCl-like high-
temperature forms (Teichert and Klemm 1939, Albert, Grunzweig-
Genossar, and Perel 1970). CsSeH shows dimorphism similar to
that of CsSH. The compounds BaNH, SrNH, and CaNH containing
the ion NH^{2-} have NaCl lattices at room temperature, while
the rhombic room-temperature form of sodium hydroxide transforms to an NaCl-like phase at 300°C, with KOH behaving
similarly. Another substance with an NaCl lattice is calcium
carbide, CaC_2, above 450°C (Vannerberg 1962, Atoji 1971).

   The nitrosyl salts contain the diatomic cation NO^+.
Examples of these salts have been listed by D.W.A. Sharp and
Thorley (1963). Some of them are isomorphous with the
corresponding ammonium and oxonium salts. Thus, the salts
$NOClO_4$, $NOBF_4$, and $(NO)_2SnCl_6$ are isomorphous with the
ammonium salts (Klinkenburg 1937). The NO^+ ions are therefore probably orientationally disordered, in which condition
they are effectively about as large as the H_3O^+ ion and
somewhat smaller than the ammonium ion. Transitions to
low-temperature ordered forms are to be expected, but do not
appear to have been reported. The NO^+ ion is isoelectronic
with the carbon monoxide molecule, and in solid carbon monoxide the molecules remain orientationally disordered down
to 0 K, but the NO^+ ion may be sufficiently polar for a
nitrosyl salt to achieve a completely ordered structure
at a suitably low temperature.

7.3. TRIATOMIC IONS

7.3.1. Linear ions

Potassium thiocyanate, KNCS, provides an example of a solid
containing linear triatomic ions which at sufficiently high
temperatures become orientationally disordered. At room
temperature the salt has an orthorhombic structure (Pbcm) in
which the NCS⁻ ions lie in planes parallel to the (001) face

(Klug 1933, Akers, S.W. Peterson, and Willett 1968).   It
will be seen from Fig.7.3 that the dipoles of the anions
have an ordered antiparallel arrangement, so that the structure can be regarded as an antiferroelectric.   As the crystal

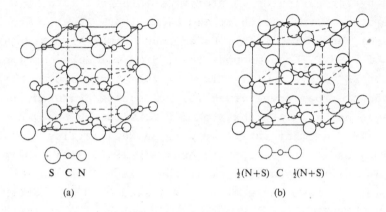

Fig.7.3. The arrangement of the thiocyanate ions in KNCS; (a) the low-
temperature, ordered orthorhombic form, (b) the high-temperature, disordered tetragonal form (Yamada and Watanabe 1963).

is heated it undergoes a λ-type transition culminating at
T_λ = 413 K, above which the compound is tetragonal ($I4/mcm$),
the transformation taking place without hysteresis and
without the crystal shattering (Yamada and Watanabe 1963).
In the high-temperature phase I the NCS$^-$ ions are still in
the same planes, but are now disordered between two orientations.   Evidence for this is provided by the entropy gain
at the II→I transition, which is $R\ln 2$ within experimental
error (Sakiyama, Suga, and Seki 1963), and by the changes
in the infrared and Raman spectra (Savoie and Pézolet 1967,
Iqbal, Sarma, and Möller 1972).   In phase I the Raman spectrum
associated with the external vibrational modes takes the form
of a broad band, consequent on the breakdown of the selection rules which operate in the orientationally ordered phase
II.   Short-range order does not appear to persist to any
marked extent above T_λ.
     Iqbal and coworkers have used their spectroscopic results
to examine whether the 'soft mode' interpretation of transi-

tions in certain ferroelectric crystals (section 3.9) is
applicable to the antiferroelectric - paraelectric transition in KNCS. If ω_{TO} is the transverse optic mode frequency
at $k \sim 0$, then its temperature dependence may be represented
by the relation

$$\omega_{TO}^2 = \omega_{LO}^2 \ (\varepsilon_\infty/C)(T-T_c) \ , \qquad (7.1)$$

where ω_{LO} is the longitudinal frequency corresponding to ω_{TO},
ε_∞ is the high-frequency permittivity, and C the Curie constant which appears in the equation for the temperature dependence of the static permittivity in the high-temperature
phase,

$$\varepsilon_0 = C/(T-T_c) \ .$$

According to equation (7.1), ω_{TO}^2 should decrease linearly
with temperature as the disordered phase is cooled, becoming
zero at T_c, so that the crystal is then unstable with respect to the mode in question (the 'soft mode'), and transforms to the ordered phase in which ω_{TO}^2 increases linearly
as the temperature continues to fall. Fig.7.4 shows the
plot of $\Pi(\omega_{TO})^2$ for the frequencies of the three Raman-active
external modes in KNCS, against temperature. The relation
is approximately linear, but $\Pi(\omega_{TO})^2$ is not zero at T_c.

Caesium thiocyanate transforms at 470 K from an ordered
orthorhombic form (space group $Pnma$) to a cubic CsCl-like
structure, the transition temperature being only 9 K below
the melting-point. The diffraction evidence on the cubic
form is consistent with 24-fold orientational disorder of
the NCS⁻ ions (Manolatos, Tillinger, and Post 1973). Ammonium thiocyanate has a first-order transition at 360·15 K
($\Delta S_t = 1 \cdot 205 R$), followed by a λ-type transition ($T_\lambda = 392 \cdot 2$ K,
$\Delta S_t = 0 \cdot 30 R$) (Seki, private communication).

The azide ion N_3^- is also linear, and while it cannot of
course show the end-for-end disorder of the thiocyanate ion,
order-disorder transitions occur in some of the azides of
monovalent metals. The caesium salt undergoes a first-order
transition at 423 K ($\Delta S_t \approx 0 \cdot 9 R$) from a tetragonal, distorted

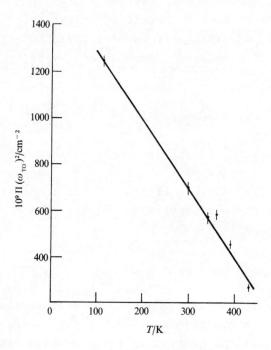

Fig.7.4. Plot of $\Pi(\omega_{TO})^2$ for the frequencies of the three Raman-active external modes in KNCS against temperature (Iqbal, Sarma, and Möller 1972).

CsCl structure (space group $I4/mcm$) to a cubic, CsCl-like lattice (Mueller and Joebstl 1965, Iqbal and Christoe 1975a). The azide ions in the latter are statistically oriented along the three axes of the unit cell, but as ΔS_t is somewhat less than $R \ln 3$, it would seem that interaction between neighbouring anions prevents any one of them from making full independent use of its three possible positions. The polymorphism of the rubidium salt is similar, but now the disordered phase I only exists over a range of 2 K, while the potassium salt is limited to the ordered tetragonal phase. The behaviour of the Cs, Rb, and Tl salts shows that the transition temperature rises with decreasing size of the cation, and in the potassium salt transformation to a high-temperature, cubic disordered form is forestalled by melting. Sodium azide has a rather more subtle transition, which was discovered by electron spin resonance experiments on crystals doped with 5 p.p.m. of Mn^{2+} as a probe, the spectra above

and below the transition being quite different (Fig.7.5;
B.S. Miller and King 1963). The high-temperature form I is
rhombohedral $R\bar{3}m$, (Hendricks and Pauling 1925). Pringle

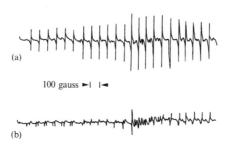

(a)

100 gauss ►| |◄

(b)

Fig.7.5. Part of the ESR spectrum of NaN_3 doped with 5 p.p.m. of Mn^{2+},
(a) at 22°C, (b) under the same conditions at 17°C, $T_t \approx 19°C$
(B.S.Miller and King 1963).

and Noakes (1968) found that the low-temperature phase II
is monoclinic, $C2/m$, and that the II→I transition takes
place over a long temperature range of ~100 K. Single
lines in the powder diffraction pattern of I are replaced
by split lines in II. The splittings gradually decrease
with rising temperature, and vanish at 286 K. Iqbal (1973)
observed very similar behaviour in a Raman study of the
librational mode, and suggested that the spectroscopic and
X-ray results implied an order-disorder transition, with the
disorder taking the form of random orientations of a terminal nitrogen atom of the azide ion to right or left of the
c axis of the crystal (see also Simonis and Hathaway 1974).
This proposal was essentially confirmed by a neutron diffraction study carried out by Choi and Prince (1976), who
concluded that the terminal nitrogen atom of the tilted azide
ion jumps between three sites which are occupied with equal
probability, the angle of tilt with respect to the c axis
being ~7°. However, the only visible anomaly in the heat
capacity - temperature curve is a very small transition at
293 K with $\Delta S_t = 0 \cdot 03$ J K^{-1} mol^{-1} (Fritzer and Torkar 1966,
Carling and Westrum 1976). Iqbal and Christoe (1975b) pre-

sented a theoretical treatment similar to that applied to
phosphorus pentachloride by Chihara and his coworkers
(p.405).

The thallium salt TlN_3 is interesting in that it undergoes the same II→I transition as the caesium and rubidium
salts but with a smaller entropy gain (~0·5R; Pistorius 1969b),
which may be a consequence of some covalency in the thallium
salt. In addition, on cooling the tetragonal phase II it
transforms at 248 K to an orthorhombic form III (Mauer,
Hubbard, and Hahn 1973). From the Raman spectrum, the gradual
III→II transition appears to involve the softening of a librational mode, and to be another case to which the Chihara
model applies reasonably well (Iqbal and Christoe 1974).

The salt caesium hydrogenfluoride with the linear
[F..H..F]$^-$ ion has a high-temperature form structurally like
that of the azide, with the HF_2^- ions orientationally disordered (Kruh, Fuwa, and McEver 1956). The high-temperature
phases of potassium and rubidium hydrogenfluorides, however,
have sodium-chloride-like lattices.

7.3.2. Non-linear ions
Since the discovery by Sawada, Nomura, Fujii, and Yoshida
(1958) that the form of sodium nitrite stable at room temperature is ferroelectric, a considerable amount of work
has been carried out on the ordered and disordered phases
of this salt, much of it by Japanese investigators. Interest has been stimulated partly because it has a relatively simple structure for a ferroelectric, and partly by
the discovery that between the ferroelectric phase III and
high-temperature, disordered paraelectric phase I there
exists an antiferroelectric phase II, the stability range
of which at atmospheric pressure is only ~1 K. Phase III
has an orthorhombic structure, space group *Im2m* (Ziegler
1931, Carpenter 1952). The triangular NO_2^- ions lie in the
bc planes, and the direction of spontaneous polarization is
parallel to the *b* axis (Fig.7.6). The transformation into
the paraelectric form I (space group *Immm*) involves the
gain of an *ac* mirror plane, the nitrite ions being disordered
between two orientations in the *bc* plane. Evidence to support

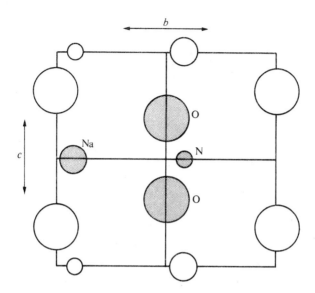

Fig.7.6. Projection along the a axis of the structure of the ordered form III of $NaNO_2$. The large, medium, and small circles represent O, Na, and N atoms respectively. Open circles are atoms at $a = 0$, shaded circles atoms at $a = \frac{1}{2}$ (Ziegler 1931).

this will be summarized shortly. It will be seen from Fig. 7.6 that relative to the oxygen atoms of the nitrite ions, the sodium ions in the ordered structure are displaced along the b axis, whereas they adopt central positions on this axis in the paraelectric phase.

The existence of phase II was first revealed in an X-ray study by the appearance at 436 K of satellite lines, which rapidly became diffuse with rising temperature and vanished at ~437 K (Yamada, Shibuya, and S.Hoshino 1963). The reality of this intermediate phase has since been abundantly confirmed by other investigations. The transition III→II starts gradually, the heat capacity and volume beginning to rise 'anomalously' at ~350 K, but it is completed isothermally at 436·5 K (T_c) (Sakiyama, Kimoto, and Seki 1965). Since phase II appears to be antiferroelectric, the temperature at which it gives place to I (~437·8 K) is designated T_N. Estimates of T_c and T_N differ slightly from one investigation to another. Fig.7.7 shows the heat capacity

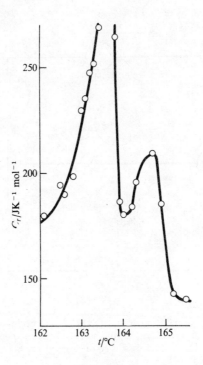

Fig.7.7. Heat capacity of NaNO$_2$ in the region of the two transitions (Sakiyama, Kimoto, and Seki 1965).

of NaNO$_2$ as a function of temperature between 435 K and 438 K, and Fig.7.8 the temperature dependence of the permittivity in the polar direction. These two figures display the two transitions very clearly. The molar volume shows an abrupt increase (of ~0·6 %) at 436·9 K, followed by a kink in the volume-temperature curve at 437·8 K, while the satellite lines in the ^{23}Na NMR spectrum are observed to be split into two components between T_c and T_N (Betsuyaku 1966). Under pressure, the range (T_N-T_c) increases, to become 8 K at ~10 kbar (Gesi, Ozawa, and Takagi 1965, Rapoport 1966).

That the transformation of III into II ends at T_c as a first-order transition has also been demonstrated by a careful study of the temperature dependence of the lattice parameters (Ismailzade, Anagiev, and Abdullaeva 1961), by the dilatometric experiments of Sakiyama *et al.*, by length

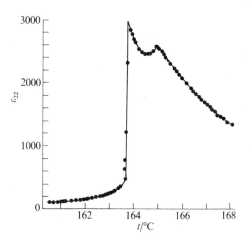

Fig.7.8. Permittivity ε_{22} of $NaNO_2$ in the polar direction in the region of the two transitions (Takagi and Gesi 1967).

measurements made using the sensitive capacitance technique (Ema, Hamano, and Hatta 1975), and by the appearance of hysteresis of ~0·5 K in the permittivity-temperature curves (Hamano 1964). On the other hand, there is no hysteresis associated with the II-I transition, which appears to be of higher order. Sakiyama and his coworkers made a careful analysis of the way in which additional entropy is gained in the passage through the two transitions. This increase amounts to $0·46R$ up to T_c (436·5 K), $0·13R$ from T_c to 438·1 K, and $0·05R$ above the last temperature, the total being $0·64R \pm 0·04R$. This is approximately $R \ln 2$, consistent with the belief that the essential disordering process is that two orientations become available to each NO_2^- ion. Support for this interpretation comes from the Raman studies of Chisler and Shur (1966) on the temperature dependence of the low-frequency lines arising from the torsional oscillations of the anions, which indicated that reorientation of these ions takes place about the a axis, and also from their work (1967) on the spectrum due to the fully symmetric vibration of the NO_2^- ion. [14]N NQR frequency and line-width measurements on the ferroelectric phase up to ~390 K also

favour a model in which the NO_2^- ions flip between two positions (Kadaba, O'Reilly, and Blinc 1970). From an infrared
study, Ivanova and Chisler (1974) concluded that the energy
barrier to reorientation of the nitrite ions in phase I at
438 K is fairly low ($6 \cdot 3$ kJ mol^{-1}). It appears probable
both from the heat capacity measurements and from diffraction
studies (Kay, Frazer, and Ueda 1962, Tanisaki 1963) that
short-range order persists along the b axis in the paraelectric phase to perhaps as high as 80 K above T_N. From
the small values of the second moment of the ^{23}Na resonance
at higher temperatures, Vinogradova and Lundin (1968) concluded that by 500 K the sodium ions have acquired considerable freedom to diffuse in the lattice.

Yamada *et al.* (1963) attributed the antiferroelectric
character of phase II to a sinusoidal modulation of the
electric moments along the a axis. This approach is similar
to Nagamiya's treatment of magnetic helices (section 12.9),
and like the latter requires that the ratio of the second
nearest-neighbour interaction to the first nearest-neighbour interaction exceeds a certain value. From a detailed
study of the alteration with temperature of the satellite
reflections in the X-ray diffraction of phase II, S.Hoshino
and Motegi (1967) deduced that the period of the sinusoidal
modulation along the a axis drops from $\sim 10a_0$ to $\sim 8a_0$ in
the narrow region of existence of this phase (Fig.7.9).
They presented evidence that the periodic variation of the
electric moments begins about $0 \cdot 2$ K below T_c.

It does not seem that the order-disorder change in
sodium nitrite crystals can be interpreted on the soft-mode
theory (section 3.9). Neither the information which can
be derived from dielectric relaxation observations (Andrade,
Prasad Rao, Katiyar, and Porto 1973) nor the Raman spectroscopic evidence (Hartwig, Wiener-Avnear, and Porto 1972)
favours the applicability of the theory in this instance.
Hartwig and his colleagues noted that in the paraelectric
phase the nitrite ions appear to be executing unusually
large torsional oscillations about the a axis, and they
considered that flipping of these ions from one position
to the other involves a temperature-dependent coupling of

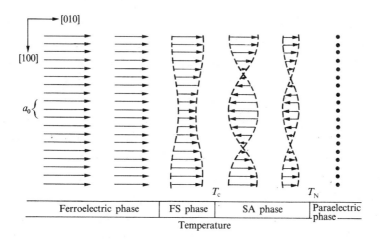

Fig.7.9. The changes in polarization in $NaNO_2$ in the passage from the ferroelectric to the paraelectric phase, as proposed by S.Hoshino and Motegi (1967). SA is the 'sinusoidal antiferroelectric' phase. Hoshino and Motegi suggest that the SA phase may be preceded by a region of ~0·2 K (the 'FS phase') in which a periodic variation of the electric moment sets in.

translational modes parallel to the c axis with librational modes about the a axis. I.R.Bonilla, Holz, and Rutt (1974) presented a molecular-field treatment of the order-disorder transition which recognizes the strong correlation between the orientation of the NO_2^- dipoles and the cation positions, so that when a nitrite ion changes its orientation the position of the adjacent sodium ions is altered.

At about 178 K, $NaNO_2$-III undergoes a transition to phase IV (Gesi 1969), which is probably identical with that into which III transforms at room temperature at a pressure of ~8 kbar (Rapoport 1966). There is also a high-pressure, high-temperature form V.

The double nitrite $AgNa(NO_2)_2$ is ferroelectric at ordinary temperatures, and changes, in a partly first-order transition at 311 K, to a paraelectric form without passing through an intermediate phase (Gesi 1970a). Both forms are orthorhombic, I and II having the space groups $Fddd$ and $Fd2d$ respectively. The nitrite ions in I are disordered between two orientations, but these are not equally occupied, the population ratio being about 7:3 at 323 K (Ishida and Mitsui 1974). This corresponds to a configurational entropy gain at the transition of ~1·2R. The observed ΔS_t is 1·45R (Gesi 1970b).

The polymorphism of potassium, rubidium, and caesium nitrites illustrates the preference of larger cations for CsCl-like structures. This can, of course, be discerned in other series of alkali metal salts, such as the nitrates. Increased pressure also favours the formation of the more compact CsCl-type lattice. There is at present some dis-agreement between the reports of various authors on the num-ber of phases which these three salts can form. It may be that some of the work on them was carried out on samples contaminated with nitrate ions, or with moisture, or both, and perhaps the phase behaviour is qualitatively changed by such impurities. Examples of this are provided by other salts discussed later in this chapter (e.g. ammonium nitrate, p. 343 , and tetramethylammonium chloride, p. 364). It is therefore possible that in the absence of impurities which act as a catalyst for phase changes a crystal may fail to un-dergo a transition and remain in a metastable state.

Potassium nitrite exists in at least three forms at ordinary pressure, the structures of which were examined by X-ray diffraction by Solbakk and K.O. Strømme (1969). I and II were also investigated by Tanisaki and Ishimatsu (1965), I by Parry, Schuyff, and Ubbelohde (1965), and III by K.O.Strømme (1974c). I has a sodium chloride-like lattice ($Fm3m$), II is rhombohedral ($R\bar{3}m$), while III is monoclinic ($P2_1/c$). The III→II and II→I transitions are both partly gradual and partly isothermal, reaching completion at 264·1 K and 314·7 K respectively. The lower transition is accom-panied by a volume increase of ~15 per cent, while the upper transition involves almost no volume change. The entropy changes are not known accurately, but there is certainly a configurational entropy gain in both cases, with the larger increase at the lower transition. There is little doubt that the nitrite ions are orientationally disordered in both I and II. From their structural work, Solbakk and Strømme con-cluded that each anion has six possible orientations in phase

II, and that in phase I there are two non-equivalent positions for each nitrite ion, associated with each of which there are 16 orientations. This gives 32 possibilities in all, though some mutual interference between neighbouring anions may prevent full independent use being made of them. An interesting point about KNO_2-II, itself suggestive of orientational disorder of the anions, is that to some extent it forms solid solutions with KNO_3-I.

The phase diagram of KNO_2 (Fig.7.10) is interesting in that there are three high-pressure phases, all of which were

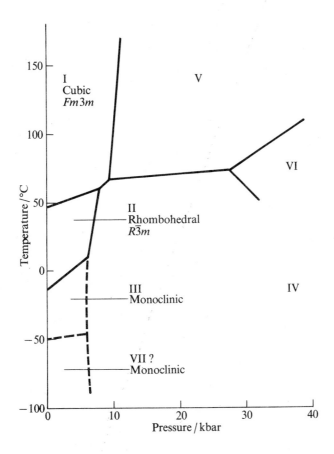

Fig.7.10. Phase diagram of KNO_2 (after Pistorius 1972).

considered by Pistorius (1972) to be disordered. The formation of CsCl-like structures by pressure is witnessed here, since V is cubic ($Pm3m$) like $CsNO_2$-I, while KNO_2-IV is rhombohedral ($R\bar{3}m$) and apparently isomorphous with $CsNO_2$-II. KNO_2-VI, which is tetragonal, has no counterpart in $RbNO_2$ or $CsNO_2$. Pistorius suggested that phases IV, VI, and V have configurational entropies of $R \ln 2$ to $R \ln 3$, $R \ln 4$, and $R \ln 12$ respectively, and if this is so then five out of the phases I to VI of this salt are disordered. Phase III may transform into a seventh, monoclinic ordered form on cooling (Pistorius and Richter 1972).

$CsNO_2$-II was shown to be rhombohedral by Richter and Pistorius (1972), while I is cubic like CsCl (Ferrari, Cavalca, and Tani 1957). The transition II→I is partly gradual and partly isothermal, reaching completion at 208·85 K. Mraw and Staveley (1976) obtained a value of 13·3 J K^{-1} mol^{-1} for ΔS_t, and found that at 408 K there is a minor thermal anomaly with an entropy gain of 0·05 J K^{-1} mol^{-1}. There was no sign of the transition variously reported as occurring at 393 K by Natarajan and C.N.R. Rao (1975), 353 K by Protsenko and Kolomin (1971), and 365 K by Natarajan and Hovi (1972). The anions in $CsNO_2$-I must be orientationally disordered, and Richter and Pistorius concluded that there is also partial disorder in $CsNO_2$-II. $RbNO_2$-I, the stable form of this salt at ordinary pressures and temperatures, has a face-centred cubic unit cell like KNO_2-I, and presumably therefore offers the nitrite ion 32 possible orientations. At a relatively low pressure (only 300 bar at the II→I transition) a denser form III is formed, which exists over a very extensive range of pressure and temperature (Fig.7.11). Richter and Pistorius suggested that III has the CsCl-like disordered structure of $CsNO_2$-I, and also that the other high-pressure form $RbNO_2$-IV may be isostructural with $CsNO_2$-II and KNO_2-IV. If, in fact, $RbNO_2$-IV is disordered, then the only ordered phase of this salt (II) occupies a remarkably small fraction of the phase diagram. Moreover, $RbNO_2$-IV and $CsNO_2$-II might well retain entropy at 0 K, as may also be the case with phases II of RbCN and CsCN (p.275).

7.4. TETRAATOMIC IONS
7.4.1. Planar ions
The salts falling in this category are nitrates, carbonates,

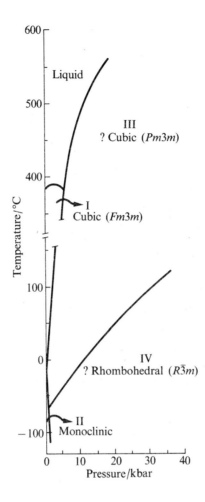

Fig.7.11. Phase diagram of $RbNO_2$ (after Richter and Pistorius 1972).

and borates containing the ion BO_3^{3-}. The temperature range
over which many nitrates and carbonates can be investigated
is limited by their thermal instability, and this section
will be largely devoted to the nitrates of the monovalent
ions sodium, potassium, rubidium, caesium, thallium, and
silver. (The special case of ammonium nitrate is dealt with
in section 7.5.2.) These six nitrates all have at least one
disordered phase, but no two of the six are completely identical in their phase behaviour, a reflection of its sensitivity to the cation size. Lithium nitrate may undergo minor
lattice changes (Rhodes and Ubbelohde 1959, Fermor and

Kjekshus 1969), but it lacks any significant order-disorder
transition. The physical properties of monovalent nitrates
have been generally reviewed by McClaren (1962), and Newns
and Staveley (1966) have more specifically considered the
significance of the entropies of transition.

Some of the structural information about the six salts
to be discussed is summarized in Table 7.2, which also gives
the temperatures and entropies of transitions. We have ad-
hered to our usual system of lettering phases (which is used
in most of the original papers on these salts), even though
this may obscure certain similarities - RbNO$_3$-III, for example, being the analogue of CsNO$_3$-I. Table 7.2 refers to the
most important stable phases encountered at atmospheric
pressure, and other phases exist. Potassium nitrate can be
obtained as a metastable phase III which we shall discuss in
due course, and silver nitrate probably forms a similar
phase. At 45 kbar, sodium nitrate transforms into a ferroelectric phase, the space group changing from $R\bar{3}c$ to $R3c$
(Barnett, Pack, and Hall 1969). Potassium nitrate has five
high-pressure forms, one being the form III just mentioned,
and four others, IV to VII.

In spite of the variety of behaviour which the six
nitrates display, they fall into two groups of three. Sodium,
potassium, and silver nitrates can be grouped together,
since their high-temperature phases are all rhombohedral. Of
the trio forming the other group, the disordered phase is
CsCl-like for CsNO$_3$ and TlNO$_3$, while rubidium nitrate (individually perhaps the most interesting of the six) presents
this phase as RbNO$_3$-III. Since the structures involved will
be discussed with particular reference to those of calcite
and aragonite, Fig.7.12 shows the calcite structure (which
is, for example, that of the room-temperature form of NaNO$_3$),
while Fig.7.13 shows the relation between the calcite and
aragonite structures. In the rhombohedral calcite lattice,
the cation has a coordination number of six, whereas in the
pseudo-hexagonal orthorhombic aragonite structure the coordination number is nine. The aragonite structure is therefore preferred by larger cations. In a calcite structure,
the X of the planar XO$_3$ ions is at the mid-point of a distorted

TABLE 7.2

Thermal and structural information on the nitrates of monovalent metals

Compound	IV ← $T_t/K, \Delta S_t/R$ → III	III ← $T_t/K, \Delta S_t/R$ → II	II ← $T_t/K, \Delta S_t/R$ → I	References Cal.	Cryst.
NaNO$_3$			548·6, 1·05 (λ) Rhombohedral $R\bar{3}c$ → Rhombohedral $R\bar{3}m$	1,2	3
KNO$_3$			401, 1·50 (F) Orthorhombic $Pnma$ → Rhombohedral $R\bar{3}m$	4	5
RbNO$_3$	437, 1·07 Orthorhombic → Cubic(CsCl)	493, 0·78 Cubic(CsCl) → Rhombohedral	564, 0·21 Rhombohedral → Cubic(NaCl)	6	7-10
CsNO$_3$			427, 1·09 Orthorhombic → Cubic(CsCl)	11	8-10,12
AgNO$_3$			432·6, 0·67 (F) Orthorhombic $Pbca$ → Rhombohedral $R\bar{3}m$	2,13	14
TlNO$_3$		348, 0·35 Orthorhombic $Pnma$ → Orthorhombic $P31m$	416, 1·10 Orthorhombic → Cubic(CsCl)	15	8,10,16

see footnotes on page 296

Footnotes to Table 7.2.

References

1.   Miekk-Oja (1941); Sokolov and Shmidt (1955); Mustajoki (1957a).

2.   Reinsborough and Whetmore (1967).

3.   Kracek, Posnjak, and Hendricks (1931), I; Bijvoet and Ketelaar
      (1932), I; Ketelaar and Strijk (1945), I; Tahvonen (1947), I;
      Siegel (1949), I; Shinnaka (1964), I; Cherin, Hamilton, and Post
      (1967), II; K.O. Strømme (1969a), I; K.V.K.Rao and Murthy (1970),
      I, II; Paul and Pryor (1971), I (neutron).

4.   Sokolov and Shmidt   (1956); Mustajoki (1962); Arell (1962a).

5.   Kracek, Barth, and Ksanda (1932), I, III; Finbak and Hassel (1937b),
      III; Barth (1939), III; Tahvonen (1947), I; Fischmeister (1956), I;
      Jamieson (1956), IV; Shinnaka (1962), I; K.O.Strømme (1969b), I,
      III; Nimmo and Lucas (1973), II (neutron); J.R.Holden and C.W.
      Dickinson (1975), II; Nimmo and Lucas (1976), I.

6.   Mustajoki (1958); Arell and Varteva (1961).

7.   Pauling and Sherman (1933), IV; Finbak, Hassel, and L.C.Strømme
      (1937), II; Korhonen (1951), III; R.N.Brown and McClaren (1962a),
      I, II, III, IV; Salhotra, Subbarao, and Venkateswarlu (1968), I, II,
      III, IV; Kennedy (1970), I; Courtenay and S.W.Kennedy (1974), II.

8.   Finbak and Hassel (1937a), III.

9.   Delacy and Kennard (1971), IV.

10.   K.O.Strømme, (1971), I.

11.   Mustajoki (1957b); Hovi, Arell, and Varteva (1959).

12.   Finbak and Hassel (1937c), II; Ferroni, Sabatini, and Orioli (1957),
      II; Shultin and Karpov (1968), II.

13.   Arell, (1962b).

14.   Pistorius (1961a), I, II; K.O. Strømme (1970), I; Levin (1969), I,
      II; Lindley and Woodward (1966), II.

15.   Bridgman (1916); Arell and Varteva (1962).

16.   Kennedy and Patterson (1961),III; Brown, R.N. and McClaren (1926b),
      III; Fraser, Kennedy, and Snow (1975), III.

octahedron.   In an aragonite structure, however, the X atom
is displaced along the c axis from the mid-point, so that
there are two possible positions for the XO_3 ion in the
unit cell, each associated with its own particular orientation of this ion.   It is worth noting that although there
is no question of orientational disorder in either the calcite or aragonite forms of calcium carbonate itself, Staveley and Linford (1969) found that the entropy of the former

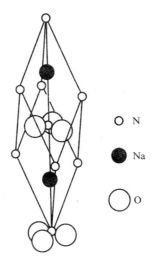

Fig.7.12. The calcite unit cell of NaNO₃-II. Only two groups of oxygen atoms are shown.

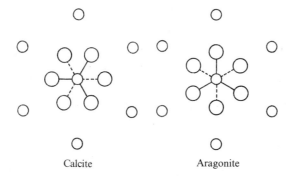

Calcite   Aragonite

Fig.7.13. Comparison of the calcite and aragonite structures, as seen in projection along the trigonal axis. Small circles, nitrogen atoms; large circles, oxygen atoms. The metal atoms are not shown. The dashed lines indicate the alternative positions of the nitrate ions in each case, achieved by 60° rotation.

polymorph exceeds that of the latter at room temperature by ~0.5R, and in fact this difference is effectively established at quite a low temperature (~80 K).

In what follows, it will be useful to bear in mind the

relation between a rhombohedral unit cell and the NaCl and
CsCl lattices. Fig.7.14 illustrates this relation using

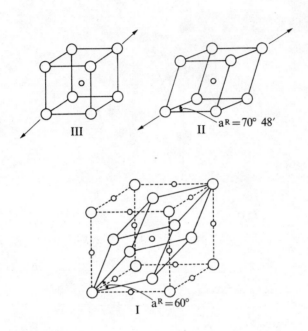

Fig.7.14. The structural relationship between phase III (CsCl-type),
phase II (rhombohedral), and phase I (NaCl-type) of RbNO$_3$. Large circles,
Rb atoms; small circles, N atoms. The oxygen atoms are not shown. The
arrows show the direction of elongation of the **rhombohedral** cell. α^R is
the rhombohedral angle (Salhotra, Subbarao, and Venkateswarlu 1969).

the structures of forms I, II, and III of rubidium nitrate.
The axial angles of the rhombohedral unit cells of the
nitrates under discussion are between 70° and 78°.   Rhombohedral angles of 60° and 90° correspond to NaCl and CsCl
lattices respectively, so that a rhombohedral structure
can be regarded as intermediate between the two cubic
lattices.

The low-temperature form II of sodium nitrate has a
rigid calcite lattice. The nitrate ions lie in planes
normal to the c axis, and have alternately the orientations
shown in Fig.7.12. The gradual transformation of II into
the disordered phase I was discovered by Kracek (1931), and
has come to be regarded as a typical example of a λ-type

transition. As shown by the heat capacity - temperature
plot in Fig.7.15, the transition extends over about 100 K.
The earlier X-ray experiments disclosed a gradual weakening

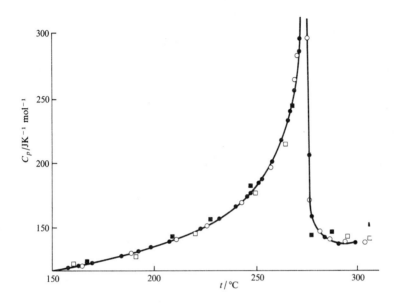

Fig.7.15. Heat capacity of $NaNO_3$ through the II-I transition, incorporating four sets of results (Reinsborough and Whetmore 1967).

of the reflection from the oxygen atoms, which was at first
interpreted as indicating the onset of rotation in the plane
of the ion. This interpretation appeared to be supported by
spectroscopic evidence. From a detailed infrared study of
various carbonates and nitrates, R.A.Schroeder, Weir, and
Lippincott (1962) reported a librational frequency for the
nitrate ion in $NaNO_3$ so low (20 cm^{-1}), and a consequential
barrier height so small (2·8 kJ mol^{-1}) that the barrier
could be overcome at quite low temperatures. Moreover, rotation of the nitrate ion would bring the oxygen atoms into
closer proximity than prevails in the staggered arrangement
of these ions in the calcite structure, and by virtue of
the greater repulsion between the oxygen atoms this would
account for the fact that as the II→I transition proceeds
the expansion is greatest along the c axis (K.V.K. Rao and

Murthy 1970, and earlier work cited by these authors). Nevertheless, free rotation can be eliminated on the grounds that
the entropy gain at the transition is too small, and that
there is little change in the vibration-libration spectrum
(Hexter 1958). Moreover, later X-ray and neutron work was
found to favour an orientationally disordered structure,
though Siegel (1949) considered I to be a disordered aragonite
phase, while Shinnaka (1964) concluded that it is a disordered calcite structure. In fact, both types of structure
may be involved. It is significant that the configurational
entropy gain at the II→I transition is larger than $R \ln 2$.
Taking changes in the lattice vibrational spectrum into consideration, Fermor and Kjekshus (1972) estimated this entropy
gain to be $0 \cdot 85R$, while K.O.Strømme (1969a) suggested a figure of $1 \cdot 05R$. Analysis of the relevant structural and thermal information led Strømme to conclude that in phase I
the nitrate ions are statistically disordered between both
aragonite-type and calcite-type environments, giving four
possibilities in all (Fig.7.13), the respective occupancies
of the two types of position being ~55 per cent and 45 per
cent at 563 K. From a calculation in which account was taken
not only of the two orientations possible to a nitrate ion
for each kind of environment and the relative weightings of
these environments, but also of the fact that some configurations would be rendered inaccessible because of the short
O-O distance between neighbouring ions, Strømme obtained a
value of $0 \cdot 95R$ for the configurational entropy gain accompanying the change from order to disorder. Studies of the
pressure and temperature dependence of the ^{23}Na nuclear quadrupole coupling constant (D'Alessio and Scott 1971) and of
the temperature dependence of the ^{14}N quadrupole coupling
constant (Gourdji, Guibé, and Peneau 1974) seem to support
Strømme's interpretation of the disorder in the high-temperature phase. Since a change from an ordered calcite lattice
to a disordered partially aragonite structure means that the
nitrate ions have to change both their orientation and their
relative position along the c axis, the disorder is brought
about not simply by reorientation of the anions in their
planes, but rather by a helicoidal motion.

Two further points about the disordered phase I may be noted. From a decrease in the ^{23}Na resonance line-width from 200°C to 280°C, it appears that diffusion of the cations in the lattice becomes increasingly facile (Andrew, Eades, Hennel, and Hughes 1962). And Chisler (1969) has suggested on the basis of Raman spectroscopic evidence that in phase I the anions are deformed. It may be added that the ferro-electric nature of the high-pressure phase discovered by Barnett *et al.* (1969) was attributed to the nitrogen atom of the anions being forced out of the plane of the oxygen atoms. A careful examination of the effect on the low-frequency Raman spectrum (~ 50 to 250 cm^{-1}) of sodium nitrate on proceeding from the ordered to the disordered crystal was made by Shen, Mitra, Prask, and Trevino (1975). They successfully interpreted the observed changes using values for an order parameter derived on a Bragg-Williams basis from heat capacity measurements.

Since sodium nitrate is a simple compound obtainable in a state of high purity which has an extended gradual transition, it has been regarded as a particularly suitable system on which to test some of the theories and relations proposed for higher order transitions. For example, Klement (1970a) has used the transition to test the Pippard relations (section 2.3). The temperature dependence of the volume V can be represented to within 5 K or so of the λ-point T_λ by the relation

$$|V - V_\lambda| = A (T - T_\lambda)^{2/3}$$

where V_λ is the volume at T_λ, and accordingly the coefficient of expansion α may be expressed as

$$\alpha = B |T - T_\lambda|^{-1/3}$$

Klement combined this with the Pippard relation (equation 2.7)

$$C_p = \alpha V T \left(\frac{\partial p}{\partial T} \right) + \text{const.}$$

to obtain

$$C_p/T \approx C + D|T-T_\lambda|^{-1/3}.$$

As will be seen from Fig.7.16, the experimental heat capacity results are reasonably consistent with the required

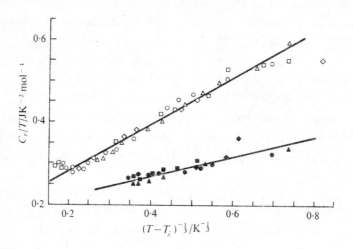

Fig.7.16. Test of the Pippard relation for the transition in NaNO$_3$. Open symbols, $T < T_\lambda$; filled symbols, $T > T_\lambda$ (Klement 1970a).

linear dependence of C_p/T on $|T-T_\lambda|^{-1/3}$. Moreover, the value $(\partial T_\lambda/\partial p)$ derived from the slope of the upper line in Fig. 7.16 is ~7·5 ± 0·5 K kbar^{-1}, in fair agreement with the directly determined value of 7·2 K kbar^{-1} (Klement 1970b).

Strømme (1970) concluded that in the high-temperature disordered form I of silver nitrate, as in NaNO$_3$-I, both calcite-like and aragonite-like environments of the nitrate ions are involved. However, while the structures of forms I of the two salts are certainly very similar the calorimetric work has shown that the II→I transition in AgNO$_3$ is at least partly isothermal, and the associated entropy increase is within a few per cent of $R\ln 2$. The temperature range of existence of I can be considerably extended by applying pressure (Rapoport and Pistorius 1966, Klement 1976). The ordered form of silver nitrate, AgNO$_3$-II, has a structure

unique among metallic nitrates (Lindley and Woodward 1966).
It is not unusual, of course, to find differences between
the crystal structures of silver salts and the corresponding alkali metal salts which reflect the greater propen-
sity of silver for forming covalent bonds.

The high-temperature disordered form I of potassium
nitrate is like that of the sodium salt, but the ordered
form KNO_3-II has an aragonite structure. The first-order
transformation of II into I involves a relatively small
volume increase of ~0·7%, and can be accomplished with a
single crystal without this breaking up (Davis and Oshier
1967). Kennedy and Odlyha (1974) investigated the mechanism
of this transformation by polarized light microscopy.
Strømme (1969b) calculated ΔS_t for the II→I transition in
KNO_3, again on the basis that in KNO_3-I both calcite-type and
aragonite-type environments are available to the nitrate
ions, obtaining a value of $1·03R$, which is somewhat less than
the experimental value. From their neutron diffraction
examination, Nimmo and Lucas (1973) concluded that the nitrate ions in phase II are non-planar, to an extent which
increases with rising temperature.

On cooling phase II in the absence of moisture, a
metastable phase III is obtained.[†] This usually appears
at about 123°C and transforms into II at about 115°C. Khanna,
Lingscheid, and Decius (1964), in a detailed study of the
infrared spectra of phases I, II, and III, found that if
phase III is produced in an evacuated vessel it can be cooled
to room temperature and kept there indefinitely. III achieves
stability at a minimum pressure of ~30 bar, and its stability
range widens considerably with increasing pressure, as will
be seen from the phase diagram reproduced in Fig.7.17.
KNO_3-III is hexagonal, space group $R3m$ (Barth 1939), and was
shown by Sawada, Nomura, and Fujii (1958) to be ferroelectric.
Mustajoki (1962) measured the enthalpy difference between
forms I and II, and between II and III, obtaining a value of
3·00 kJ mol^{-1} for ΔH(III→I) at 123°C, and 2·33 kJ mol^{-1} for

[†]Some authors refer to forms I, II and III of this salt as β, α, and γ
respectively.

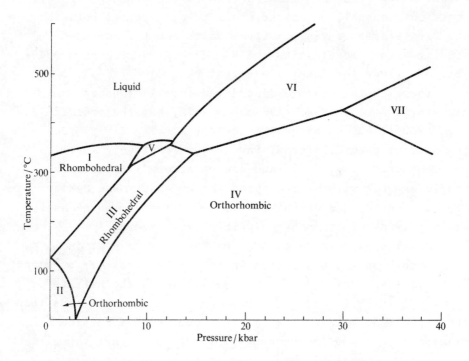

Fig.7.17. Phase diagram of KNO_3 (after Rapoport and G.C.Kennedy (1965), and also incorporating results of Bridgman (1916, 1937) and Babb, Chaney, and Owens (1964)).

$\Delta H(II{\rightarrow}III)$ at 113°C. Entropy differences can be estimated from the slope of the boundary lines on the phase diagram. This gives $\Delta S(III{\rightarrow}I) \approx 0{\cdot}91R$ and $\Delta S(II{\rightarrow}III) \approx 0{\cdot}45R$ at the triple-point of I, II, and III. The balance of evidence favours the view that III is an ordered structure, with the dipoles aligned along the c axis, which contracts by about 5 per cent when the paraelectric phase I transforms into the ferroelectric III. Chen and Chernow (1967) consider that this is not a transformation to which the soft-mode theory applies.

    Relatively little has been done on the other high-pressure forms of potassium nitrate. Form IV, which is not ferroelectric, is probably orthorhombic (Jamieson 1956), though the space group is not known with certainty. Possibilities are $Pmn2_1$ (Davis and Adams 1962), or $P2_1nb$ or Pmn (Weir, Piermarini, and Block 1969).

Turning to the nitrates of caesium, thallium, and rubidum, there is a clear correspondence between the II→I transition in the first two salts and the IV→III transition in rubidium nitrate. $CsNO_3$-I, $TlNO_3$-I and $RbNO_3$-III all have primitive cubic, CsCl-like structures, while $CsNO_3$-II, $TlNO_3$-II and $RbNO_3$-IV are orthorhombic. However, the latter structures depart so slightly from hexagonal symmetry that they can be referred to as being pseudohexagonal. Single crystals of the pseudohexagonal phases can be converted to the cubic forms without shattering. The structural relation between the two phases of each substance is illustrated for $RbNO_3$-IV and $RbNO_3$-III in Fig.7.18. The entropy changes of the II→I transition in the caesium and thallium

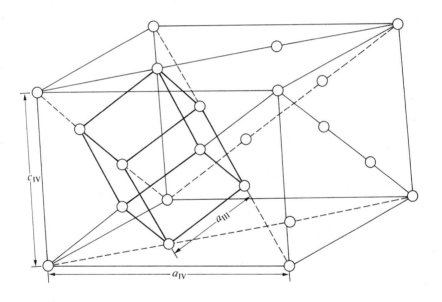

Fig.7.18. Structural relationship between phases III and IV of RbNO3 (Salhotra, Subbarao, and Venkateswarlu 1969).

salts and of the IV→III transition in the rubidium salt are all within two or three per cent of $R \ln 3$. At first this seems to be surprisingly small. Assuming that in the high-temperature form the threefold axis of the nitrate ion coincides with one of the four threefold axes of the cube,

in an isolated cube there will be eight equivalent aragonite-
type orientations, and eight calcite-type orientations. However, consideration of the restrictions imposed on the orientation of any one nitrate ion by neighbouring anions led Newns
and Staveley to propose an explanation of the entropy of
transition of $R \ln 3$ in terms of positional rather than orientational disorder. They suggested that in the high-temperature
cubic form the equilibrium positions of the nitrogen atoms do
not fall exactly on a threefold axis of a cube, but on one
of three unsymmetrical positions slightly off this axis.
More recently Strømme (1971), treating the problem once again
as one of orientational disorder of nitrate ions for which
both calcite-type and aragonite-type environments are possible and with detailed consideration of the limitations imposed on the orientation of a nitrate ion by its neighbours,
calculated $\Delta S = 1 \cdot 15R$ for the IV→III transition in $RbNO_3$, in
good agreement with the experimental value.

The low-temperature rhombic form (III) of $TlNO_3$ appears
to be the only one of its kind in the monovalent nitrates.
Since the structural evidence favours an ordered structure
for $TlNO_3$-II (Fraser, S.W. Kennedy, and Snow 1975), the
entropy change of $0 \cdot 35R$ at the III→II transition is another
indication of the magnitude of the entropy effect which can
be associated with alterations in the lattice vibrational
spectrum due to a crystal structure change.

There remain the two high-temperature forms of rubidium
nitrate. Of particular interest is $RbNO_3$-I, not only because it has a sodium chloride-type lattice, but because it
is sufficiently disordered to resemble the plastic molecular
crystals discussed in Chapters 9 and 10. Kennedy (1970)
has described crystals of this phase as 'soft and rather
plastic', and as having a structure 'close to that of the
melt'. On melting, there is actually a slight contraction
(Schinke and Sauerwald 1960). With regard to phase II,
Salhotra, Subbarao, and Venkateswarlu (1968) confirmed the
conclusion of Finbak, Hassel, and L.C.Strømme (1937) that
it is rhombohedral, resembling therefore KNO_3-I and $NaNO_3$-I,
and not tetragonal as R.N.Brown and McClaren had concluded
(1962a). As will be seen from Fig.7.19, at sufficiently

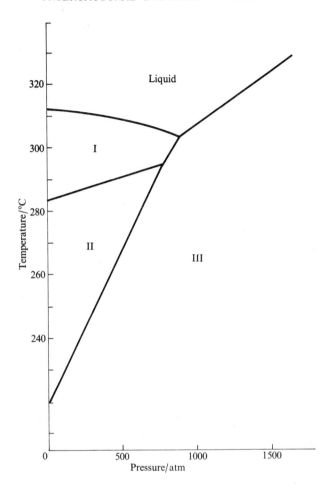

Fig.7.19. Phase diagram of RbNO₃ (after Cleaver and Williams 1968).

high pressures I and II disappear, leaving III as the high-
temperature phase. Likewise, phases I and II vanish from
solid solutions of caesium nitrate in rubidium nitrate when
the concentration of the caesium salt reaches ~25 mol %
(Fig.7.20). Iversen and Kennedy (1973) have called attention to the similarity between the change from NaCl-like to
CsCl-like structures in rubidium nitrate and the corresponding change in ammonium bromide.

Since the sum of the entropies of the IV→III
and III→II transition is approximately $R \ln 6$, Newns and
Staveley suggested that the disorder in II takes the form

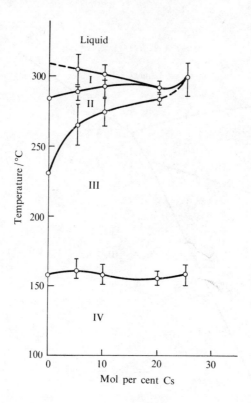

Fig. 7.20. Phase diagram of the system RbNO3-CsNO3, based on electrical conductivity measurements (Salhotra, Subbarao, and Venkateswarlu 1969).

of two orientational possibilities superimposed on the three-fold positional disorder they had supposed for phase II. The sum of the entropies of all three transitions is almost exactly $R \ln 8$, and consequently they ascribed this to two-fold orientational disorder of the nitrate ions in planes at right angles to each of the four threefold axes which pass through the nitrogen atom in the sodium chloride-type lattice. Strømme (1971), however, has given an alternative inter-pretation of the configurational entropies of phases II and I, involving consideration of unacceptable positions of the nitrate ions and of a statistical distribution between cal-cite-type and aragonite-type environments.

Investigations into orientational disorder in the al-kaline earth carbonates have been much less extensive, but disordered high-temperature forms of the calcium, strontium,

and barium salts certainly exist. At about 930°C - the
various values recorded for these high-temperature transitions differ somewhat - the orthorhombic (aragonite) form
of strontium carbonate changes into a rhombohedral (calcite)
form with an entropy increase of ~2·0R, and barium carbonate undergoes a corresponding transition at ~800°C with an
entropy gain of ~2·1R. The rhombohedral forms are regarded
as containing disordered carbonate ions (Lander 1949,
Rapoport and Pistorius 1967). Calcium carbonate appears to
have a similar transition at ~975°C, though Davis (1964) has
expressed doubts as to whether the high-temperature form is
disordered, and suggests that it may be isostructural with
KNO_3-III. At still higher temperatures (976°C for $BaCO_3$ and
1415°C for $SrCO_3$), the rhombohedral forms of the two salts
transform into sodium chloride-like structures, which must
of course be still more disordered and may well in this
respect closely resemble $RbNO_3$-I.

     With the still higher charges on the ions in borates
of the formula ABO_3, where A is a tervalent metal such as
a rare earth, it would be expected that any orientational or
order-disorder transitions would occur at even higher temperatures than those in the alkaline earth carbonates. The
principal forms in which these borates exist are aragonite,
calcite, and the metastable hexagonal form of calcium carbonate known as vaterite. Although transitions can occur
between these forms, usually above 1000°C, no evidence seems
to have been advanced to suggest that the high-temperature
forms are disordered (Levin, Roth, and Martin 1961).

7.4.2. Pyramidal ions
The pyramidal ion which we shall chiefly consider is the
oxonium (or hydronium) ion, H_3O^+, which occurs in the hydrates of certain acids, such as perchloric, nitric, and
sulphuric acids. The most thoroughly investigated crystal
containing it is the monohydrate of perchloric acid, $H_3O^+ClO_4^-$.
This melts at 322·7K, and at room temperature has an orthorhombic structure, space group *Pnma* (Volmer 1924, F.S.Lee
and Carpenter 1959). This structure is similar to that of
certain salts with monatomic cations such as barium sulphate,

and also to that of ammonium perchlorate, and it was therefore suggested that the oxonium ions are rotating, or at
least orientationally disordered. On cooling, the crystals
undergo a first-order phase change at 248·8 K to give an
ordered, monoclinic form, space group $P2_1/m$ (Nordman 1962).
Early NMR studies by Richards and Smith (1951) and Kakiuchi,
Shono, Komatsu, and Kigoshi (1951, 1952) confirmed the presence of the pyramidal H_3O^+ ion in this and other acid hydrates, and later more detailed second moment investigations
were carried out by Hennel and Pollak-Stachura (1969) and
by Cance and Potier (1971). As the temperature is raised from
100 K to room temperature, the second moment falls in two
stages. The first drop occurs between 140 K and 160 K, and
is believed to be due to the onset of reorientation about
the threefold axis of the H_3O^+ ions. The second fall takes
place at the phase change, and implies that more general
reorientation is possible in the high-temperature form.
This interpretation of the second moment changes was confirmed by an inelastic neutron scattering study carried out
by J.M. Janik, Pytasz, Rachwalska, J.A. Janik, Natkaniec, and
Nawrocik (1973). On the basis of his crystallographic results, Nordman proposed that the cations in phase I are disordered among at least four orientations. J.M. Janik,
Rachwalska, and J.A. Janik (1974) suggested that each H_3O^+
ion has eight configurations available to it, which can certainly be accommodated by their measured value for the
entropy of transition of $2·6R$ ($R\ln 8 = 2·08R$). From spin-
lattice relaxation time measurements, O'Reilly, E.M. Peterson, and
Williams (1971) obtained values of 20 and 17·5 Kj mol^{-1} for the
activation energy for reorientation of the H_3O^+ ions in phases
II and I respectively. The corresponding values obtained by
Janik *et al*. from their neutron scattering study are 19 and
16·5 kJ mol^{-1}. The barrier to rotation of the cations in
perchloric acid monohydrate is therefore appreciably higher
than that of ~4 kJ mol^{-1} for the more symmetrical ammonium
ion in ammonium perchlorate.
    The ion H_3O^+ also occurs in the interesting solid which
is precipitated when hydrogen chloride is passed into a
solution of caesium chloride. This has the formula

CsCl.1/3 $(H_2O.2HCl)$, and structurally is probably Cs^+Cl^-.
$1/3(H_3O^+).1/3(HCl_2^-)$.   In this salt (and in the analogous
bromide) the H_3O^+ ions form strings parallel to the c axis.
Within any one string these ions are ordered, but the z
co-ordinates of the oxygen atoms are not necessarily the
same from one string to another (L.W. Schroeder and Ibers
1968a,b). Disorder of exactly the same kind had previously been found in the monohydrate of hydrogen chloride,
which structurally is $H_3O^+Cl^-$ (Yoon and Carpenter 1959).
[Cf. the compound $Hg_{2.86}AsF_6$ (p. 256) and the urea-hydrocarbon adducts discussed in section 11.4.]

    The salt sodium chlorate is cubic (space group $P2_13$).
The frequency and temperature dependence of its permittivity
have been interpreted in terms of growing disorder due to
'apex reversal' within the pyramidal ClO_3^- ion, that is, as
arising from the chlorine atom jumping between two minima
in a double-well potential. It seems that with rising temperature the salt is, as it were, on its way to an order-
disorder transition when fusion supervenes (Mason 1946,
A.D.P. Rao, Andrade, and Porto 1974).

7.5. TETRAHEDRAL IONS

7.5.1. Ammonium halides

Structural and thermodynamic information relating to the
various phases of the ammonium halides is summarized in
Table 7.3. In the literature on these salts, both Roman
numerals and Greek letters are used to label the phases,
and both are given in the table. Some of the spectroscopic
and other work carried out on these salts has already been
mentioned in Chapter 4.

    We shall first discuss the III-II transition in am-
monium chloride, one of the most studied of all order-disorder
transformations in a crystal. Since its discovery by heat
capacity measurements by Simon in 1922, it has often been
cited as the prototype of a λ-type transition, though we
shall have to consider in more detail the question of its
order. Both II and III have CsCl-like structures, but whereas III is piezoelectric, II is not (Hettich 1934), so that
II has a centre of symmetry which III lacks. Evidence soon

TABLE 7.3

Thermal and structural information on ammonium halides

Compound	CsCl δ $P\bar{4}3m$	$T_t/K,\ \Delta S_t/R \rightarrow$ Tetragonal γ $P4/nmm$	$T_t/K,\ \Delta S_t/R \rightarrow$ CsCl β $Pm3m$	$T_t/K,\ \Delta S_t/R \rightarrow$ F.c.c. α $Fm3m$	Cal.	Cryst.	NMR
NH_4Cl	III	242·50 (λ), 0·60-0·76 →	II	457·6(F),1·18 → I	1-3	4,5	6-8
ND_4Cl	III	249·7 (λ) →	II	442(F),1·17 → I	2,9	5,10	11,12
NH_4Br	IV	III 235·1(λ),0·36 →	II	411·2(F),1·08 → I	3,13	14-16	7,8,17
ND_4Br	IV	III 215·05, 0·23 →	II	391(F), 1·09 → I	9,18	15,19, 20	11,12, 21
NH_4I		III 231·0(λ),0·55 →	II	257(F),1·58 → I	22	16,23, 24	8,25, 26
ND_4I		III 224(λ) →	II	~254 → I	—	20,24	12,26, 27

References

Footnotes on facing page

Footnotes to Table 7.3.

References

1.   Simon (1922)(C_p,20 - 290 K); Popov and Gal'chenko (1951)
      (ΔH_t, II→I); Arell (1966) (ΔH_t, III→I); Voronel' and Garber (1967)
      (C_p in transition region); Schwartz (1971) (C_p, 218-254 K); Amitin,
      Kovalevskaya, and Paukov (1972) (C_p under pressure).

2.   Stephenson, Blue, and Stout (1952) (C_p, 20 - 300 K, NH_4Cl, ND_4Cl).

3.   Arell (1960) (ΔH_t, II→I, NH_4Cl, NH_4Br).

4.   (X-ray) Dinichert (1942). (Electron diffraction) Stasova and
      Vainshtein (1956); Kuwabara (1959). (Neutron diffraction) Tokunaga
      and Koyano (1968).

5.   (X-ray) Boiko (1969) (NH_4Cl, ND_4Cl). (Neutron diffraction) Levy and
      Peterson (1952).

6.   Bersohn and Gutowsky (1954) (LW); Trappeniers (1966) (T_1 under
      pressure); Woessner and Snowden (1967a) (T_1); Ueda and Itoh (1967)
      (^{35}Cl under pressure); Kodama (1972) (T_1 and $T_{1\rho}$); Michel (1973);
      Speight and Jeffrey (1973) (^{14}N and ^{35}Cl, T_1); Mandema and Trap-
      peniers (1974 a,b) (T_1 under pressure).

7.   J.Itoh, Kusaka, and Saito (1962) (LW, NH_4Cl,NH_4Br); J.Itoh and
      Yamagata (1962) (^{35}Cl in NH_4Cl, ^{81}Br in NH_4Br).

8.   Gutowsky, Pake, and Bersohn (1954) (LW, NH_4Cl, NH_4Br, NH_4I).

9.   Arell, Roiha, and Aaltonen (1970) (ΔH_t, II→I, ND_4Br).

10.   (Neutron diffraction) Yelon and Cox (1972).

11.   Chiba (1962) (ND_4Cl, ND_4Br); Hovi and Pyykkö (1966) (ND_4Cl,ND_4Br).

12.   Hovi, Järvinen, and Pyykkö (1965) (LW, ND_4Cl, ND_4Br, ND_4I).

13.   Simon, von Simson, and Ruhemann (1927) (C_p, 210 - 290 K); Stephenson
      and Adams (1952); Sorai, Suga, and Seki (1965) (C_p, 13 - 305 K);
      Kostina and Mil'ner (1972).

14.   (X-ray) Hovi, Heiskanen, and Varteva (1964) (II, III); Pöyhönen,
      Mansikka, and Heiskanen (1964) (I, II); A. Bonilla, Garland, and
      Schumaker (1970) (5 - 150 K). (Electron diffraction) Kolomiichuk
      and Dvoryankin (1964); Kolomiichuk (1965) (III). (Neutron dif-
      fraction) Egert, Jahn, and Renz (1971).

15.   (X-ray) Ketelaar (1934); Hovi, Paavola, and Urvas (1968a) (NH_4Br,
      ND_4Br, III, IV); (1968b) (NH_4Br, I - IV).

16.   (Neutron diffraction) Seymour and Pryor (1970) (NH_4Br).

17.   Woessner and Snowden (1967b) (T_1); Shimomura, Kodama, and Negita
      (1969); Jeffrey, A.G.Brown, and Armstrong (1973) (^{81}Br).

18.   Stephenson and Karo (1968) (C_p, 17-300 K).

19.   (Neutron diffraction) Levy and Peterson (1951, 1953a) (I to IV).

20.   (Neutron diffraction) Levy and Peterson (1953b) (ND_4Br, ND_4I, I).

21.   Woessner and Snowden (1967c) (T_1).

22.   Stephenson, Landers, and Cole (1952) (C_p, 14 - 300 K); Arell and
      Alare (1964) (ΔH_t, II→I).

23.   (X-ray) Hovi and Varteva (1964) (I,II); Hovi and Lainio (1966)
       (II, III).

24.   (X-ray) Hovi, Paavola, and Nurmi (1969) (NH_4I, ND_4I, I, II, III).

25.   Hovi, Järvinen, and Pyykkö (1965) (LW); Pintar, A.R. Sharp, and
       Vrscaj (1968) (T_1); Niemelä and Ylinen (1969) (T_1); Shimomura,
       Kodama, and Negita (1969) (T_1); Tsang, Farrar, and Rush (1968) (T_1,SM).

26.   A.R.Sharp and Pintar (1970) (NH_4I, ND_4I, T_1).

27.   Niemelä and Ylinen (1969) (NH_4I, ND_4I, T_1).

accumulated to disprove the suggestion that the transition
marks the onset of free rotation of the ammonium ions. Their
torsional oscillational frequency, obtained spectroscopically,
was shown to be little changed by passage through the transition (section 4.5), and to indicate a considerable barrier
of ~22 kJ mol^{-1} to reorientation of the ions. The heat capacity of phase II at constant volume was demonstrated to be
consistent with three-dimensional torsional oscillation of
the cations, but not with their free rotation (Lawson 1940),
although, as we shall see, the analysis of the heat capacity
of this phase is not as simple as was at first supposed.
The entropy change at the III→II transition of ~0·7R is too
small for a change from libration to rotation in three degrees of freedom. It is now generally accepted that the
transition involves the gain of orientational disorder on
the part of the ammonium ions. Within any one cell, with
an NH_4^+ ion at its centre, the N-H bonds are directed towards
the neighbouring chloride ions. There are then two possible
orientations for each ion (Fig.7.21). In the ordered form
III at low temperatures, all ions have the same parallel
orientation - making the system an analogue of a ferromagnet - while in phase II the ions are disordered between
the two possible orientations available to each of them. A
block of cells in phase II therefore effectively has a centre
of symmetry. This interpretation of the transition is consistent with the entropy gain of ~R ln 2. Direct evidence
that the N-H bonds are directed towards the chloride ions was
provided by Levy and Peterson's classical neutron diffraction investigation (1952) and by Bersohn and Gutowsky's NMR
line-width and second-moment studies on single crystals
(1954). Basically, therefore, the nature of the transition

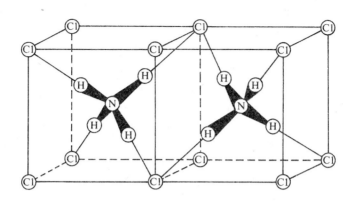

Fig.7.21. The two orientations available to an NH_4^+ ion at the centre of a cube of eight Cl^- ions.

is very simple, and it has accordingly been much used as a test case for order-disorder theories. Nevertheless, as we shall see, a number of rather subtle features prove to be involved, which are still being actively investigated both experimentally and theoretically.

Careful studies, particularly of properties which can be measured isothermally, have shown that while the transition begins gradually, at ordinary pressures it is undoubtedly completed isothermally, so that it is partly gradual and partly first-order. The properties investigated include the volume, measured in a dilatometer (Smits and MacGillavry 1933), the thermal expansion (Fredericks 1971), the refractive index (Adam and Searby 1973), the elastic constants (Garland and Renard 1966), the piezoelectricity (Mohler and Pitka 1974), and the effect known as second-harmonic generaton, to which we shall briefly refer later (Freund 1967, Bartis 1971). Such experiments have shown that the III-II transition is accompanied by hysteresis (Table 7.4). The partly first-order character of the transition is consistent with heat capacity measurements made with small temperature intervals (Voronel' and Garber 1967, Schwartz 1971).

However, with increasing pressure the character of the transition changes. It progressively loses its first-order discontinuity, and eventually becomes a wholly gradual

TABLE 7.4

Values of the volume change associated with the discontinuous part of the transitions in the ammonium halides, and of the width ΔT of the corresponding hysteresis loop. The volume change is expressed as $100\,\Delta V/V$, the percentage volume increase when the low-temperature form transforms into the high-temperature form

Salt	Transition	ΔT/K	$100\Delta V/V$
NH$_4$Cl	III–II	0·27[a], 0·35[b], 0·30[c], 0·21[d], 0·41[e,f]	0·43[b], 0·24[d], 0·42[g], 0·39[h]
	II–I	–	19·31[i], 19·43[j]
NH$_3$DCl	III–II	0·12[b]	0·32[b]
ND$_3$HCl	III–II	0·07[b]	0·20[b]
ND$_4$Cl	III–II	0·035[k], 0·035[l]	–
NH$_4$Br	IV–III	~30[m]	2·20[n]
	III–II	–	−0·43[n], −0·38[o], −0·17[p]
	II–I	–	18·3[n], 18·14[q], 18·23[r], 18·17[s]
ND$_4$Br	IV–III	8·5[t]	2·23[n], 2·81[u]
	III–II	0·19[u]	−0·73[n], −0·43[u]
	II–I	–	18·5[n], 18·19[s]
NH$_4$I	III–II	0·11[v]	~0·1[w], −0·28[x]
	II–I	–	16·73[w], 16·96[y]
ND$_4$I	III–II	–	~0·1[w]
	II–I	–	16·86[w]

Footnotes on facing page

Footnotes to Table 7.4.

a.   Smits and MacGillavry (1933).

b.   Thomas and Staveley (1951).

c.   Schwartz (1971).

d.   Fredericks (1971).

e.   Mandema and Trappeniers (1974b).

f.   This value, from proton T_1 measurements, is for a compact poly-
     crystalline sample. For a single crystal, ΔT was found to be some-
     what less.

g.   Dinichert (1942).

h.   Smits, Muller, and Kröger (1937).

i.   Pöyhönen (1960).

j.   Mansikka and Pöyhönen (1962).

k.   Yelon and Cox (1972).

l.   Garland, Bruins, and Greytak (1975).

m.   Stephenson and Adams (1952).

n.   Hovi, Paavola, and Urvas (1968a,b).

o.   Hovi, Heiskanen, and Varteva (1964).

p.   Smits, Ketelaar, and Muller (1936).

q.   Pöyhönen (1960).

r.   Pöyhönen, Mansikka, and Heiskanen (1964).

s.   Jaakkola, Pöyhönen, and Simola (1968).

t.   Stephenson and Karo (1968).

u.   Smits, Tollenaar, and Kröger (1938).

v.   Stephenson, C.C., private communication.

w.   Hovi, Paavola, and Nurmi (1969).

x.   Hovi and Lainio (1966).

y.   Hovi and Varteva (1964).

transition. Using a sensitive capacitance method to follow
the change in length of a single crystal, Weiner and Garland
(1972) found that the abrupt part of the change vanishes at
255·95 K and 1492 bar, and this result was essentially confirmed by measurements of the total Rayleigh scattering intensity carried out by Fritz and Cummins (1972). The disappearance of the discontinuity was also observed in determinations of the heat capacity of the salt under pressure

318   ORIENTATIONAL DISORDER IN SALTS

(Amitin, Kovalevskaya, and Paukov 1972), and in a study of
the effect of pressure on the spin-lattice relaxation time
T_1 (Fig.7.22; Trappeniers and Mandema 1966, Mandema and
Trappeniers 1974b). Mandema and Trappeniers, while admitting
the difficulty of determining precisely the critical temperature and pressure at which the discontinuity vanishes, obtained values of 251·3 K and ~950 bar respectively, somewhat
different from those of Weiner and Garland. The point at
which this transition in ammonium chloride just ceases to
have a first-order component has been classified as a tri-

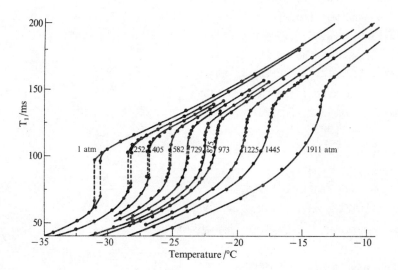

Fig.7.22. Proton spin-lattice relaxation time T_1 for NH_4Cl as a function
of temperature and pressure in the region of the III-II transition (after
Mandema and Trappeniers 1974b).

critical point, a term first introduced by Griffiths (1970)
with reference to the [3]He - [4]He system (section 2.6). The
significance of the prefix 'tri' is that this critical point
is where two second-order lines merge on a phase diagram
with one first-order line. We shall return to this aspect
of the transition later.

    Using differential thermal analysis, Trappeniers and

van der Molen (1966) studied the effect of pressure on the entropy change of the III→II transition, and found that this decreases considerably with increasing pressure, falling to only about one-quarter of $R \ln 2$ at 1 kbar.

Dinichert (1942) showed that within the hysteresis loop for NH_4Cl at atmospheric pressure two phases coexist, with recognizably different X-ray diffraction patterns. Most studies of the hysteresis associated with the III-II transition relate to the immediate neighbourhood of the discontinuity, but Nissilä and Pöyhönen (1970) concluded from a dilatometric study that the hysteresis persists down to ~200 K, and a later X-ray investigation by Hovi, Mutikainen, and Pirinen (1973) extended the hysteresis region to ~78 K.

Considerable effort has been devoted to estimating the height of the energy barrier opposing reorientation of the ammonium ion (Table 7.5). Passage between the two orientations shown in Fig.7.21 can be effected by rotation about a two-fold axis of the ion (or a fourfold S_4 axis of the cell), when it will reach the summit of a barrier of height V_0 after rotation through $\pi/4$. It should be noted that even if the III-II transition involved no change in lattice dimensions, V_0 would not be a constant quantity throughout the transition. The energy of a particular ammonium ion with respect to neighbouring cations depends on the degree of orientational order, so that the potential energy of the ion as it rotates must also be a function of the degree of order (Fig.7.23). This matter was considered by Sorai, Suga, and Seki (1965), and later by Mandema and Trappeniers (1974a), who accounted on this basis for the observed difference in activation energy for ammonium ion reorientation above and below the transition. The evaluation of V_0 requires an experimental value for the torsional oscillational frequency (and it is helpful if this is known in excited states of the torsional mode as well as in the ground state). This frequency can be derived from spectroscopic work, some of which has already been considered in section 4.5, from inelastic neutron scattering (section 4.6.1), or by analysis of heat capacity data. A potential function for the

TABLE 7.5

Estimates of V_0, the height of the barrier opposing rotation of the NH_4^+ or ND_4^+ ion, and of E, the activation energy for the reorientation of this ion deduced from NMR studies. For CsCl-like structures, values of V_0 refer to rotation about a two-fold axis of the ion, coincident with a fourfold axis of the unit cell. Most of the V_0 values have been derived from estimates of the torsional oscillational frequency, the source of which is shown by INS (inelastic neutron scattering), SPEC (infrared and Raman spectroscopy), or C_p (from analysis of heat capacity data). LW = from NMR line-width studies. Values of V_0 designated as 'CALC' have been calculated from an electrostatic model, assuming that each hydrogen atom carries a charge of e/4. The temperature range of validity of V_0 and E is given where stated by the authors. Unless otherwise indicated, the values of E have been obtained from spin-lattice relaxation time measurements (for H or D resonance, unless another nucleus is specified). The right-hand column gives the sum of the activation energy and the zero-point energy of the torsional oscillations of the ammonium ion ($3h\nu/2$).

Compound	V_0/kJ mol^{-1}	E/kJ mol^{-1}	$(E+3h\nu/2)$/kJ mol^{-1}
NH_4F	44(>253 K,INS)[a]	~42[b]	
NH_4Cl	22·0(SPEC)[c]	19·9(LW)[c]	26·4
	22·6(CALC)[c]	19·5(II)[d]	26
	26 (III,C_p)[e]	19(<195 K)[d]	25·5
	21 (LW)[f]	18·0(II,^{35}Cl)[h]	24·4
	21·2(100 K,INS)[i]	17·5(II)[i]	23·9
	18·3(300 K,INS)[i]	17·1(II)[k]	23·5
	19(>253 K,INS)[l]	21·8(III)[k]	28·7
	23(<123 K,INS)[l]	17·6(II)[m]	24·0
	22·2(III,SPEC)[n]	16·7(II,^{14}N)[o]	23·1
	18·6(II,SPEC)[p]	18·4(II,^{35}Cl)[o]	24·8
	24·3(III,SPEC)[p]	21·2(III)[q]	28·1
		17·7(II)[q]	24·1
ND_4Cl	21·2(100 K,INS)[i]	21(III,LW)[r]	-
	18·8(300 K,INS)[i]		
	22·2(III,SPEC)[n]		
	21 (LW)[g]		

continued......

Table 7.5 continued.....

NH$_4$Br	17·5(SPEC)[c]	14·0(LW)[c]	20·0
	15·6(CALC)[c]	17·8(III)[j]	23·8
	15·5(>253 K,INS)[l]	14·4(II)[j]	20·4
	18 (<123 K,INS)[l]	15·2(II)[s]	21·2
	16·7 (IV,C_p)[e]	16·7(III, <185 K)[s]	22·7
	18·2 (III,SPEC)[n]		
	15·35 (III,SPEC)[p]		
	19·9 (III,SPEC)[p]		-
ND$_4$Br	-	15·0(II)[t]	-
		15·0(IV)[t]	-
NH$_4$I	11·9(SPEC)[c]	10·7(LW)[c]	16·8
	12·2(CALC)[c]	13·0(II,239-268 K)[u]	19·1
	11·85 (II,SPEC)[p]	11·8(III,86-116 K)[u]	17·9
	12(>253 K,INS)[l]	13·4(III)[v]	19·5
	13(<123 K,INS)[l]		
ND$_4$I	-	3·5(I)[u]	
		12·5(II,225-266 K)[u]	18·6
		12·2(III,94-143 K)[u]	18·3

a.   Leung, Taylor, and Havens (1968).

b.   Drain (1955).

c.   Gutowsky, Pake, and Bersohn (1954).

d.   Woessner and Snowden (1967a).

e.   Sorai, Suga, and Seki (1965).

f.   Waugh and Fedin (1962).

g.   Hovi and Pyykkö (1966).

h.   Ueda and Itoh (1967).

i.   Venkataraman *et al*. (1966).

j.   Trappeniers and Mandema (1966).

k.   Kodama (1972).

l.   Leung, Taylor, and Havens (1968).

m.   Punkkinen (1973).

n.   Schumaker and Garland (1970).

o.   Speight and Jeffrey (1973).

p.   D.Smith (1974c).

q.   Mandema and Trappeniers (1974a).

r.   Rabideau and Waldstein (1965).

s.   Woessner and Snowden (1967b).

t.   Woessner and Snowden (1967c).

u.   Niemelä and Ylinen (1969).

v.   Tsang, Farrar, and Rush (1968).

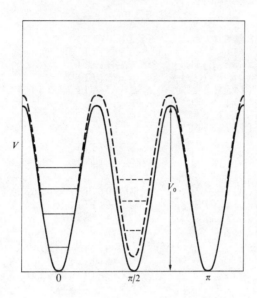

Fig.7.23. Potential energy V of an ammonium ion on rotation about one of its twofold axes. Full curve, orientationally disordered NH_4^+ ions; dotted curve, orientationally ordered ions (after Sorai, Suga, and Seki 1965).

rotation of the ion must then be assumed, which is used to solve for the energy levels by perturbation theory. The potential functions which have been employed, such as that of Gutowsky, Pake, and Bersohn (1954), derive from the pioneer work of Nagamiya (1942, 1943, 1952a), who based his function on electrostatic interaction combined with nearest-neighbour overlap repulsion. The experimental evidence shows that the librational motion of the NH_4^+ ion is anharmonic, and Garland and Weiner (1970) empirically modified the Gutowsky, Pake, and Bersohn potential to give a function which fits the overtones of NH_4Cl and ND_4Cl, and (with appropriate alterations) the fundamental and overtone frequencies of the torsional oscillations in the bromides. With an expression for the energy levels, the librational frequencies can then be related to V_0. Thus, for the frequency υ of the transition $E_{000}-E_{100}$, Gutowsky, Pake, and Bersohn found the relation

$$V_0 = \frac{1}{16} \frac{\{h\upsilon + (5h^2/8\pi^2 I)\}^2}{h^2/8\pi^2 I}$$

Strictly speaking, this equation applies to the disordered phase II, but D. Smith (1974c) has shown how it can be modified to deal with the ordered phase III.[†]

Quantitative information on the dynamics of ionic movement in ammonium halides has been obtained from NMR line-width and T_1 studies. The line-width transition in NH_4Cl takes place at 129 K, well below the λ-point, at which there is no further appreciable alteration. The earlier NMR studies failed to detect any change at the λ-point in T_1 either, but Kodama (1972) found that plots of both T_1 and $T_{1\rho}$ against $1/T$ show a kink at the λ-point, as did Woessner and Snowden (1967a) and Mandema and Trappeniers (1974a) for T_1. Woessner and Snowden pointed out that if values of T_1 in the region of the gradual part of the transition are used in the usual way to estimate an activation energy, the value of ~ 29 kJ mol^{-1} so obtained for NH_4Cl is unacceptably high. They suggest that this is because in this temperature region the pre-exponential factor in the Arrhenius equation is temperature-dependent, and that to arrive at meaningful values of the activation energy in the ordered phase T_1 data relating to lower temperatures should be used. For comparison with V_0, activation energies obtained from NMR must be corrected for zero-point energy, but even then they must not be expected necessarily to agree with V_0', since motion other than reorientation about the twofold axis of the ammonium ion may be involved in NMR effects, such as reorientation of the ion about one of its threefold axes. Motion about a C_3 axis, for which the potential energy barrier is $16V_0/9$, will not of course affect the population balance between the two orientations of Fig.7.21. Mandema and Trappeniers (1974a) investigated the dependence of T_1 for a single crystal on its orientation, and concluded from their results that an ammonium ion in ammonium chloride can in fact change its orientation directly from any one equilibrium position to any other, or in other words that it is not restricted to single-step reorientation about a

[†]In their paper, Gutowsky, Pake, and Bersohn use the symbol V_0 for two different quantities. In their equation (12), V_0 *is* the barrier height, whereas for the V_0 of their equation (8), the barrier height is $4V_0/9$.

symmetry axis. [On the other hand, Livingston, Rowe, and
Rush (1974) deduced from a quasielastic neutron scattering
study on single crystals of ammonium bromide that in this
salt the reorientation of the cation is dominated by jumps
of 90° about the C_2 axis, the average time between jumps
being 3·2 ps at 373 K.] It will be seen from Table 7.5 that
for all the ammonium halides the NMR activation energies,
corrected for zero-point energy, are in fact rather larger
than the V_0 values.

The relation between temperature and the degree of
order in phase III of ammonium chloride has been studied by
neutron diffraction experiments on single crystals (Tokunaga
and Koyano 1968), by infrared spectroscopy (see section
4.5), and by ^{35}Cl NMR studies (J. Itoh and Yamagata 1962).
With regard to these last experiments, owing to the dependence of the chlorine nuclear quadrupole interaction on the
orientations of the eight surrounding ammonium ions, T_1 is
a function of the degree of orientational order as well as
of temperature and activation energy. Of interest is the
extent to which both short-range and long-range order persist
in phase II above the λ-point. Short-range order is responsible for the high-temperature tail of the heat capacity, and
for the 'anomalous' thermal expansion coefficient for some
degrees above the transition (Nissilä and Pöyhönen 1970,
1972). Evidence for long-range order has been obtained
by an interesting optical technique, made possible by the
availability of lasers, which uses the effect of second-
harmonic generation.[†] This effect was predicted by Lajzerowicz
(1965), who pointed out that a condition for its production
is that the crystal, like NH_4Cl-III, should lack a centre of
symmetry. The experiment involves directing polarized laser
light of frequency ν onto an oriented slab of the crystal,
and measuring the intensity of the transmitted light of frequency 2ν. Fig.7.24 gives a plot showing the temperature
dependence of the intensity of the second harmonic (the
logarithmic scale is to be noted), from which it will be

[†] For a brief account of the origin of this effect, which is also referred
to as hyper Rayleigh scattering, see Long (1971).

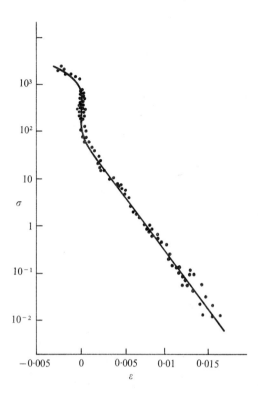

Fig.7.24. Relative second-harmonic intensity σ *vs.* ε for NH_4Cl;
$\varepsilon = (T-T_c)/T_c$ (Freund 1967).

seen that the second harmonic is still detectable above the
λ-point (Freund 1967; see also Luban, Wiser, and Greenfield
1970, Freund and Kopf 1970, Bartis 1971). Evidence for the
persistence of long-range order in form II of NH_4CL (for
up to 2·5 K above T_λ) was obtained by Bruins and Garland
(1975) from the piezoelectric behaviour of the crystal.

   Sakamoto (1954) and Marshall, Staveley, and Hart (1956)
pointed out that there appears to be an additional contribution
to the heat capacity of phase II of ammonium chloride, which
reaches a maximum of ~11 J K^{-1} mol^{-1} at 300 K. Chihara and

M. Nakamura (1972) have interpreted this as a manifestation
of the development of further phase II disorder in which
each ion makes use of orientations (subsidiary minima in the
three-dimensional potential energy function) over and above
the two principal orientations. Herrington and Staveley
(1964), however, on the basis of the observation that the
electrical conductivity of ammonium chloride is significantly
higher than that of comparable alkali halides, suggested
that the additional heat capacity in phase II might be associated with the formation by proton transference within the
lattice of an $(NH_3 + HCl)$ pair from the adjacent NH_4^+ and Cl^-
ions. The belief that such proton transference does take
place is supported by conductivity measurements on ND_4Cl
(Fuller and Patten 1970. See also Berteit, Kessler, and List
1976).

The III-II transition in ammonium chloride is one on
which both of the Pippard relations have been tested. These
relations (section 2.3) may be put in the forms (1) $C_p/T \propto V\alpha$,
where α is the thermal expansion coefficient, and
(2) $\kappa_s \propto T/VC_p$, where κ_s is the adiabatic compressibility.
In the first of an important series of papers on the ammonium
halides by Garland and coworkers, it was shown that the experimental data are in good accord with the relations below
T_λ, but above T_λ the agreement is less satisfactory. This
statement is illustrated for relation (1) in Fig.7.25 (Garland and Jones 1963).

The first important theoretical treatment of the transition was that presented by Nagamiya (1942, 1943), in which
the ordering influence was assumed to be the electrostatic
interaction between the cations, each regarded as a tetrahedron carrying positive charges at its apices. As in crystalline methane (section 9.7), the order therefore depends
on octupole-octupole interaction. The energy of this interaction, which favours parallelism of the ammonium ions, depends on a^{-7}, where a is the distance between neighbouring
NH_4^+ ions. On the Ising model the two spin states are, of
course, the two possible orientations of the ammonium ion,
and on this model the transition would be expected to be
gradual, whereas in fact it is partly first-order.   Garland

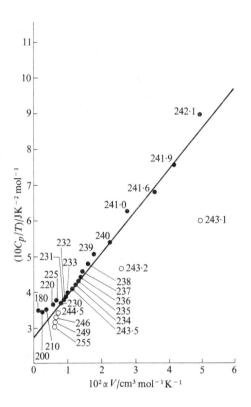

Fig.7.25. Test of the Pippard relation for NH_4Cl, α = expansivity. The temperature for each point is shown. Full circles, $T < T_\lambda$, open circles, $T > T_\lambda$; T_λ= 242·5 K (Garland and Jones 1963).

and his colleagues modified the model by recognizing that the lattice is compressible, i.e. that the interaction para- meter is volume-dependent. On this basis they were able to explain why the transition is partly isothermal, and accom- panied by hysteresis (Garland and Renard 1966, Renard and Garland 1966; see also Slichter, Seidel, Schwartz, and Fredericks 1971, and section 3.1.8). They were also able to account for the observed behaviour of the elastic and acoustic properties of the crystal in the neighbourhood of the λ-point (Garland and Yarnell 1966, Garland and Young 1968a). Never- theless, the Ising model must represent a simplification of the true state of affairs, and several authors have drawn

attention to the approximations involved in the treatments
just mentioned. An ordering energy proportional to a^{-7} would
require, for example, that T_λ also should be proportional
to a^{-7}, so that with a knowledge of the compressibility of
the crystal the dependence of T_λ on pressure could then be
calculated. Pistorius (1969a), noting that (dT_λ/dp) estimated
in this way is not in good agreement with the direct experimental value, pointed out that some of the factors which may
contribute to the discrepancy include the neglect of the interaction of higher multipoles, and the assumption that, with
increasing pressure and decreasing volume, the effective
charge on the hydrogen atoms and the N-H bond length both
remain constant. Perhaps still more important is the ability
of two adjacent ammonium ions to influence each other indirectly via their polarizing effect on the halide ions. This
indirect interaction appears to be responsible for the existence of the tetragonal phases of ammonium bromide and iodide
(*v.inf.*) (Yamada, Mori, and Noda 1972, Sokoloff 1972). Freund
and Kopf (1970) and Fredericks (1971) have drawn attention to
some of the features associated with the III-II transition
in ammonium chloride which do not appear to be consistent
with the Ising model (see also McKenzie and Seymour 1975).

We have already referred to a tricritical point at which
the first-order discontinuity in the III-II transition in
NH_4Cl disappears. For many years it was believed, on the
basis of careful dilatometric work carried out by Smits,
Müller, and Kröger (1937), that the corresponding transition
in ND_4Cl is continuous throughout and hysteresis-free (Fig.
4.3). In 1972, however, Yelon and Cox reported that it is
partly first-order, with a hysteresis ΔT of $0 \cdot 035$ K. In the
light of information obtained in the meanwhile on the effects
of partial deuteration (Table 7.4), this result seemed open
to doubt, as Yelon and Cox's sample had a deuterium content
of only 94 per cent. However, more recently Garland, Bruins,
and Greytak (1975), who made precise measurements of both
the piezoelectric constant and of the length of single crystals containing $99 \cdot 2$ per cent D, confirmed that there is a
small first-order component in the transition and a hysteresis loop $0 \cdot 035$ K wide. A critical point for the deuterated

salt at a comparatively low pressure is therefore possible,
and indeed Yelon, Cox, Kortman, and Daniels (1974), using
neutron diffraction (which promises to be a powerful tool
for the investigation of the critical region in non-magnetic
systems, as it has already proved to be for magnetic substances) had already established for a sample of composition
$N(D_{0.93}H_{0.07})_4Cl$ that the first-order discontinuity observable at atmospheric pressure vanishes at 128 bar and 250·2 K.
Although these critical points have been considered as tricritical points, this cannot as yet be regarded as established
beyond doubt, and it is theoretically possible that higher
(e.g. tetra) critical points are involved. In principle, a
decision could be made between the *a priori* possibilities on
the basis of the values of the critical exponents (section
3.3), and accordingly accurate measurement of these for the
ammonium halides has acquired a new importance. Writing
$\varepsilon = (T-T_c)/T_c$, an order parameter is taken as proportional
to $|\varepsilon|^\beta$, so the exponent β can be evaluated by measuring the
temperature dependence of a property such as a piezoelectric
constant, birefringence, or the intensity of a suitable reflection in an X-ray or neutron diffraction experiment. If
the 'excess' heat capacity c_p' (or 'excess' expansivity) is
measured, the critical exponent α' can be determined, where
$c_p'/T \propto |\varepsilon|^{-\alpha'}$. Before giving examples of the values obtained
for α' and β, it should be pointed out that the physical
properties which have to be studied may be extremely sensitive to the pretreatment or condition of the sample. This
was strikingly demonstrated by the experience of Garland
and his colleagues, who found a very noticeable difference
in the piezoelectric constant for two samples of ND_4Cl cut
from the same single crystal, the values of the temperature
T_c (which is usually regarded as a parameter to be obtained
by fitting the data in question) differing by 0·035 K. This
may have reflected dissimilarity in the domain structure of
the two samples, suggesting that the investigation of some
aspects of order-disorder transitions is reaching a stage
where it is desirable, or even essential, to use not just
single crystals but single-domain crystals - as was in fact
achieved by Mohler and Pitka in their measurements of the

piezoelectric constant of NH_4Cl.

With regard to the experimental values of the critical exponents associated with the III-II transition in ammonium chloride, Garland *et al.* found $\beta = 0\cdot125 \pm 0\cdot001$ for ND_4Cl from their piezoelectric measurements, somewhat less than the figure of $0\cdot16 \pm 0\cdot02$ obtained by Yelon and Cox from neutron diffraction estimates of the order parameter, while the length determinations gave $\alpha' = 0\cdot69$. These values do not seem to agree with those calculated for a tricritical point with any particular model so far proposed.

For NH_4Cl, Mohler and Pitka found $\beta = 0\cdot33$, close to the value of ~5/16 for a three-dimensional Ising model, but Bruins and Garland, likewise from measurements of the piezo-electric constant, obtained a much lower value of $0\cdot134$, close to that for ND_4Cl. For α', Schwartz (1971) obtained $0\cdot67$ from heat capacity measurements, and Fredericks (1971) $0\cdot75$ from measurements of the linear expansion. A useful discussion of the critical exponents in relation to the tri-critical region has been presented for ND_4Cl by Yelon *et al.* (1974). A tricritical point can arise when there are com-peting ordering influences. These exist in the ammonium halides, since besides the direct (octupole-octupole) interaction of neighbouring ammonium ions, which favours their parallel alignment, there is also, as we have observed, an indirect interaction, analogous to superexchange (sec-tion 12.11.2), in which the cations interact by virtue of a dipole induced in an intervening halide ion by an octupole, and this favours an antiparallel ordering of the tetrahed-ral cations. The effects observed on changing the pressure arise from the consequential alteration in the balance between these two opposing factors. In principle, a phase diagram can be constructed in which the two ordering fields are two of the variables, temperature being the third, and the tri-critical point is the point on the diagram at which two second-order lines and one first-order line coalesce (Fig. 2.7b).

We now turn to the bromides and iodides, postponing consideration of the disorder in the high-temperature form I of ammonium chloride, since this disorder has been more

thoroughly studied in the corresponding form of the bromide
and iodide. While both of these salts have phases II similar
to NH_4Cl-II, these transform on cooling into tetragonal
structures III. NH_4Br-III and ND_4Br-III revert at still
lower temperatures to CsCl-like forms IV, which correspond
to NH_4Cl-III, but the transformation III→IV is sluggish
particularly with NH_4Br, and for some time NH_4Br-IV eluded
discovery. The IV-III transition in this salt has an exceptionally wide thermal hysteresis loop (Table 7.4). The
structure of ND_4Br-III was determined by Levy and S.W.Peter-
son (1953a) by neutron diffraction, and is shown in Fig.7.26.

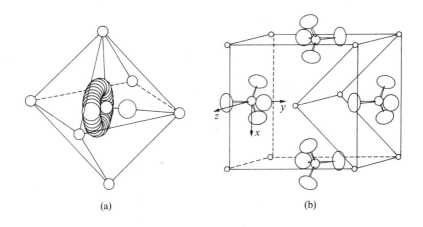

(a)   (b)

Fig.7.26. Structure of ammonium bromide in (a) phase I, (b) phase III
(Levy and Peterson 1953a, Couture-Mathieu and Mathieu 1952).

The ammonium ions are aligned in a parallel way along the
z axis, but have an antiparallel arrangement in the xy plane.
Adjacent chains of the halide ions are displaced antiparallel to each other along the z axis. Since the spontaneous polarization in any one chain of ions is cancelled
by the opposite polarization in a neighbouring chain, the
tetragonal phases of NH_4Br and NH_4I can be regarded as antiferroelectrics (Sonin 1961). The distortion from the cubic
structures which gives the tetragonal phases is very small.
In NH_4Br-III at 150 K, the longer side of the cell only

exceeds the two equal shorter sides by 0·4%, and in
NH_4I-III at 120 K by 0·7%.   As a result of studies of the
effect of pressure on the phase equilibria of the three
halides, Stevenson (1961) constructed a generalized phase
diagram, which later authors have developed, which correlates
the various forms of the three salts (Fig.7.27).   In an investigation of the effect of pressure on ultrasonic velocities

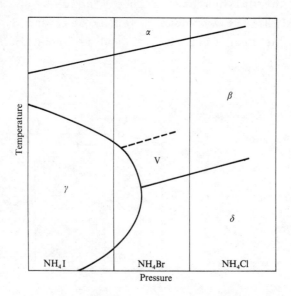

Fig.7.27. Generalized phase diagram for ammonium chloride, bromide,
and iodide (after Ebisuzaki 1973).

in ammonium bromide, Garland and Young (1968b) discovered
a third ordered form V of this salt, the existence of which
was confirmed by Ebisuzaki (1973) in a Raman study. This
new phase is separated from the disordered phase II by a
λ-transition, and from the ordered phase IV by a first-order
transition. The region of existence of V is approximately
indicated on the generalized phase diagram in Fig.7.27.
However, Hochheimer and Geisel (1976), who also used Raman
spectroscopy to monitor phase changes, failed to find phase
V, and suggested that whether or not this modification appears
may depend on how the sample has been prepared, or alternatively

that Garland and Young's phase V might in fact be phase IV.

Some interesting studies have been made of the change in order with temperature as the tetragonal phase III is heated. This form of the bromide or iodide is birefringent (but not piezoelectric) and Egert, Jahn, and Renz (1971) showed that from 100 K up to the III→II transition in ammonium bromide at 235 K there is close agreement between the birefringence and the square of the long-range order parameter as deduced from neutron diffraction data. Both of these lines of experimental evidence give $\beta = 0 \cdot 25 \pm 0 \cdot 02$ for the critical exponent. Heat capacity measurements on NH_4Br between 220 K and 232 K when fitted to the relation $C_p'/T \propto |\epsilon|^{-\alpha'}$ gave $\alpha' \approx 0 \cdot 5$ (Kostina and Mil'ner 1972). These values of α' and β are consistent with the mean field prediction for a tricritical point (section 3.3). However, a different value of β of $0 \cdot 34$ was obtained by Geisel and Keller (1975), who used the 56 cm^{-1} mode in the Raman spectrum (p. 158) to study the change in order with temperature on approaching the III-II transition.

To go from the orientationally ordered form III to the disordered form II requires that the ammonium ions should be able to flip through 90°. It is believed that this flipping movement is coupled to the displacements of the bromide ions, as shown in Fig.7.28. The crystal can accordingly be described as a pseudospin-phonon coupled system. Evidence supporting this view was provided by a neutron scattering study of ND_4Br (Yamada, Noda, Axe, and Shirane 1974), the coupled mode in question giving rise to a quasielastic central component in a triple peak in the spectrum along [110]. Furthermore, Jeffrey, A.G. Brown, and Armstrong (1973) investigated the temperature dependence of the nuclear quadrupole coupling constant of [81]Br in NH_4Br-III, which is proportional to the square of the displacement of the bromide ions. In Fig.7.29, the square of the long-range order parameter associated with the orientational ordering of the ammonium ions, as derived from the neutron work of Egert, Jahn, and Renz (1971), is compared with the reduced nuclear quadrupole coupling constant. The temperature dependences of the two quantities are almost identical, showing that the parameter

for the ordering of the NH_4^+ ions is directly proportional to
that associated with the bromide ion displacements, as predicted by Yamada, Mori, and Noda (1972).

It will be seen from Table 7.5 that the barrier heights
V_0 and the activation energies from NMR studies decrease in
the order chlorides > bromides > iodides. (This energy is
altogether larger for the fluoride, which has an ordered
wurtzite lattice.) Included in the table are V_0 values calculated on an electrostatic basis by Gutowsky, Pake, and
Bersohn, assuming the cation to be a tetrahedron with a charge
of $e/4$ at each apex. On this model $V_0 \propto a^{-5}$, where a is the
unit cell size. The agreement between the calculated V_0
values and those obtained from experimental libration frequencies is very fair, but there is no doubt that the electrostatic model is an over-simplification, especially for
the bromide and the iodide.

Finally, in the NaCl-like phases I, the disorder is
effectively still greater than in II. While the neutron diffraction work of Levy and S.W.Peterson (1953b) on ND_4Br-I
eliminated free rotation, they could not distinguish between
structures in which one, two, or three protons approach as
closely as possible to one, two, or three halide ions respectively. However, Couture-Mathieu and Mathieu (1952)
demonstrated convincingly by an elegant use of polarized
Raman spectra that the threefold axis of the ammonium ion
coincides with the fourfold axis of the crystal, or in
other words that the one approach model is correct, in which
an N-H bond of a cation points directly at one of the six
neighbouring halide ions (Fig.7.26). This leaves the problem
of whether or not there is free one-dimensional rotation about
this N-H bond. There is a drop of 16 J K^{-1} mol^{-1} in the heat
capacity of ammonium iodide at the II→I transition, which
Stephenson, Landers, and Cole (1952) interpreted as indicating
a change from libration to rotation. However, Sato (1965)
showed that the observed intensity distribution in the fundamental υ_4 band of the ammonium ion in the infrared spectrum of NH_4Br-I does not agree with that calculated for free
one-dimensional rotation, and concluded that the motion of
the ammonium ion is one of libration with comparatively large

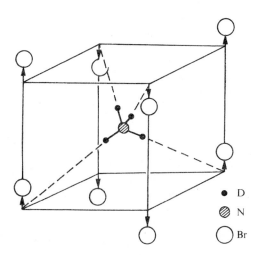

Fig.7.28. Mode in ND_4Br in which the Br^- displacements are coupled co-
herently to flipping through $90°$ of the NH_4^+ (Yamada et al. 1974).

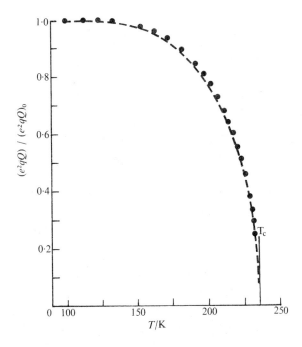

Fig.7.29. Comparison of the temperature dependence of the square of the
order parameter deduced from neutron scattering data (broken curve) and
the reduced quadrupole coupling constant (full circles) in NH_4Br-III
(Jeffrey, A.G.Brown, and Armstrong 1973).

amplitude about the N-H-Br axis. This axis is constantly
changing between any one of the six halide ions, and the
movement of the cation is therefore a complex one, involving
according to Sato no less than 72 potential minima. Sköld
and Dahlborg (1973) carried out inelastic neutron scattering studies on NH_4Cl-I and NH_4Cl-II, and while unable to
obtain a value for the reorientation rate of the cations
in phase I, concluded that this is considerably faster than
in phase II. An interesting inference made by Seymour and
Pryor (1970) from their neutron diffraction investigation is
that in NH_4l-I the ions appear to be somewhat displaced
(perhaps by $\sim 0\cdot 01$ nm) from the positions they might be expected to occupy.

Ammonium chloride and ammonium bromide form a complete
series of mixed crystals, and several investigations have
been made of the phase diagram of the binary system. The
results of these studies are summarized in Fig.7.30. It will
be seen that a comparatively small percentage of bromide ions
favours the formation of the tetragonal or γ-phase with the
antiparallel arrangement of the ammonium ions. The rapid fall
in the δ-γ (IV-III) transition temperature in ammonium
bromide with the introduction of chloride ions is also
noteworthy. Far infrared and Raman studies of the β, γ, and
δ phases of the mixed crystals have been made by Bauhofer,
Genzel, Perry, and Jahn (1974), and Bauhofer, Genzel, and
Jahn (1974). If Fig.7.30 is compared with the generalized
phase diagram (Fig.7.27) it will be noted that there is a
similarity in the relation between phases β, γ, and δ. An
increase in chloride content has the same sort of effect as
an increase in pressure, both changes of course causing the
lattice to contract, so that movement to the *right* in Fig.
7.27 should be compared with movement to the *left* in Fig.
7.30. Birefringence measurements on the mixed crystals revealed that the β-γ transition has a first-order discontinuity over the whole composition range, but that the system
could be near a tricritical point in the middle concentration region (Jahn, Brunskill, Bausch, and Dachs 1975).

Owing to the thermal instability of phosphonium halides,
they cannot be studied over such a wide temperature range

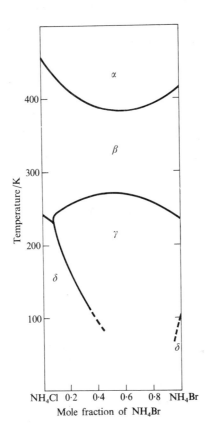

Fig.7.30. Phase diagram of the system NH_4Cl - NH_4Br, constructed from the results of Mandleberg and Staveley (1950), Costich, Maass, and N.O.Smith (1963), and Jahn and Neumann (1973). The lines are plotted from the transition temperatures observed on warming.

as the ammonium halides, at least at atmospheric pressure, and no transitions have been found in them. The structure of crystalline phosphonium iodide has been investigated by R.G.Dickinson (1922b), and by neutron diffraction by Sequeira and Hamilton (1967). It is the same as that of NH_4Br-III and NH_4I-III, namely a distorted CsCl structure. Estimates of the barrier hindering rotation of the phosphonium ion in this salt have been made from the librational frequencies

obtained from inelastic neutron scattering (Rush 1966) and
from far infrared and Raman spectra (Durig, Antion, and
Baglin 1968). The values so obtained are $29 \cdot 5$ kJ mol^{-1} and
27 kJ mol^{-1} respectively. As expected, the barrier to rotation is somewhat higher in the bromide ($32 \cdot 5$ kJ mol^{-1}) and
still higher in the chloride ($35 \cdot 5$ kJ mol^{-1}) (Durig, Antion,
and Pate 1969, 1970). The activation energy for the reorientation of the PH_4^+ ion in PH_4I as derived from proton
T_1 measurements was found to be $32 \cdot 3$ kJ mol^{-1} by Pyykkö
(1968) and $30 \cdot 7$ kJ mol^{-1} by Tsang, Farrar, and Rush (1968).

7.5.2. Other ammonium salts

When the anion in an ammonium salt is not monatomic, this
ion as well as the ammonium ion may be capable of orientational disorder, especially if it is planar, tetrahedral, or
octahedral. A transition may *a priori* involve the gain of
such disorder by either ion or both. The question as to
whether the movement of the anions and ammonium ions in such
salts can be considered to be more or less independent of
each other is one on which it does not seem possible to offer
any useful generalizations, and each case must really be
considered individually.

   In Table 7.6 we summarize some structural and thermal
information on some of the ammonium salts which undergo
transitions, though it must not be assumed that a transition
is necessarily to be attributed primarily to a change in the
behaviour of the ammonium ion. Table 7.7 presents estimates
of the barrier heights and activation energies for the
reorientation of the ammonium ion in the salts of Table 7.6,
as well as in other ammonium salts which may or may not display transitions.

   Two ammonium salts (apart from the halides) have attracted particular attention, namely the nitrate and the sulphate.
In view of the possibilities for orientational disorder
offered separately by ammonium ions and nitrate ions, it is
not surprising that the association of the two in ammonium
nitrate leads to a situation of some complexity. At ordinary pressures, there are at least five stable forms of this
salt (Table 7.8), of which I and II are certainly disordered

TABLE 7.6

Thermal and structural information on some ammonium salts (other than halides) with more than one phase

Salt	III	T_t/K, $\Delta S_t/R$	II	T_t/K, $\Delta S_t/R$	I	References Cal.	Cryst.	NMR
$(NH_4)_2SO_4$			Orthorhombic $Pnam$	←→ 223·1(λ), 2·1[a] ←→	Orthorhombic $Pna2$	1-3	3-5	6-9,16
$(ND_4)_2SO_4$				←→ 223·6(λ), 2·1[a] ←→	Orthorhombic	1,3	–	8,10-12
$(NH_4)_2BeF_4$			Orthorhombic $Pn2_1a$	←→ 176(λ), 0·95 ←→	Orthorhombic $Acan$	3	4	7,13,16
$(ND_4)_2BeF_4$				←→ 179(λ), 1·15 ←→		3	–	12
NH_4SO_4		←→ 154, 1·05 ←→	Orthorhombic	←→ 270(λ), 0·25 ←→	Monoclinic $P2_1/c$	14	15	16
$NaNH_4SO_4 \cdot 2H_2O$	$P2_1$ or $P1$	←→ 92 ←→	Orthorhombic $P2_12_12_1$	←→ 101 ←→	Orthorhombic $P2_12_12_1$	–	17	18
$NH_4ClO_4^{[b]}$			Orthorhombic $Pna2_1$ (?$Pnma$)	←→ 511·2, 2·26-2·43 ←→	Cubic	19	20,21	6,10,22,23

NH_4BF_4 [b]	Orthorhombic *Pnma*	$\xrightarrow{461.9,\ 2.3}$	Cubic	- 24,25 10,26-28
NH_4PF_6	$\xrightarrow{131.3(\lambda),1.24}$ Orthorhombic	$\xrightarrow{191.8(\lambda),\ 1.12}$	Cubic	29 30 23,31
$(NH_4)_2SiF_6$	$\xrightarrow{38.6(\lambda),\ 0.7}$ Trigonal $P\bar{3}m1$			32 33 34
$(NH_4)_2SnBr_6$	$\xrightarrow{144.8(\lambda),\ 2.25}$ Anti-fluorite			35 36 6,37

a. According to Hoshino *et al.*, these transitions culminate in twin heat capacity peaks, about 2 K apart. The temperatures quoted are those of the more pronounced peaks.

b. See Table 7.11 for further information on these two salts

Reference footnotes on facing page

REFERENCES   (to Table 7.6)

(The crystallographic references are to X-ray diffraction, unless otherwise stated.   In the NMR references, LW = line-width, SM = second moment).

1.   Nitta and Suenaga (1938) $(C_p$, 90-300 K).
2.   Shomate (1945) $(C_p$, 52-310 K).
3.   S.Hoshino, Vedam, Okaya, and Pepinsky (1958).
4.   Okaya, Vedam, and Pepinsky (1958).
5.   Schlemper and Hamilton (1966b) (neutron diffraction); Udalova and Pinsker (1963) (electron diffraction).
6.   Richards and Schaefer (1961) (LW).
7.   Blinc and Levstek (1960) (LW).
8.   O'Reilly and Tsang (1967a) $(T_1, T_{1\rho})$.
9.   Knispel, Petch, and Pintar (1975) (T_1).
10.   Chiba (1962) (D salts).
11.   Rabideau and Waldstein (1965).
12.   Kydon, Petch, and Pintar (1969) (T_1).
13.   O'Reilly, Peterson, and Tsang (1967) $(T_1, T_{1\rho}$, H and ^{19}F).
14.   Pepinsky, Vedam, Hoshino, and Okaya (1958).
15.   Nelmes (1971).
16.   S.R.Miller, Blinc, Brenman, and Waugh (1962) (T_1).
17.   Corazza, Sabelli, and Guiseppetti (1967).
18.   Todo and Tatsuzaki (1966) (T_1); Easwaran (1966); Makita, Tsuchiya, and M.Yamagita (1967) (SM); Genin and O'Reilly (1969) (H, D, and ^{23}Na, H and D forms).
19.   Westrum and Justice (1969) $(C_p$, 5-350 K).
20.   Venkatesan (1957); Peyronel and Pignedoli (1975); H.G.Smith and Levy (1962) (neutron); Choi, Prask, and Prince (1974) (neutron, 10-298 K).
21.   Stammler, Bruenner, Schmidt, and Orcutt (1966).
22.   Riehl, Wang, and Bernard (1973) (SM and T_1).
23.   Lalowicz, McDowell, and Raghunathan (1975).
24.   M.J.R.Clark and Lynton (1969).
25.   Finbak and Hassel (1936).
26.   Pendred and Richards (1955) (H and ^{19}F, SM).
27.   Caron, Huettner, Ragle, Sherk, and Stengle (1967) (H and ^{19}F, H and D salts).
28.   Huettner, Ragle, Sherk, Stengle, and Yeh (1968) $(^{19}$F, T_1 and LW, D salts).

29.   Staveley, Grey, and Layzell (1963) (C_p, 20-300 K).

30.   Bode and Clausen (1951).

31.   Albert and Gutowsky (1973) (H and ^{19}F, T_1 and SM); L.Niemelä
      and Tuohi (1970) (D and ^{19}F, T_1).

32.   Stephenson, Wulff, and Lundell (1964) (C_p, 25-300 K).

33.   Vainshtein and Stasova (1956) (electron diffraction, trigonal
      form); Schlemper and Hamilton (1966a) (neutron diffraction,
      trigonal form); Schlemper, Hamilton, and Rush (1966) (neutron
      diffraction, cubic form).

34.   Strange and Terenzi (1972) (T_1, $T_{1\rho}$); Blinc and Lahajnar (1967)
      [LW(H, D, ^{19}F) and T_1(H and ^{19}F), H and D salts, cubic form].

35.   Morfee, Staveley, Walters, and Wigley (1960) (C_p, 20-300 K).

36.   Ketelaar, Rietdijk, and van Staveren (1937).

37.   Norris, Strange, and Terenzi (1968) (T_1, $T_{1\rho}$).

to some degree. There is also a metastable phase V*, which
has a limited range of existence and which is only produced
when V is heated in the presence of a surface-active reagent
such as octadecylamine acetate. Amorós Portolés, Alonso,
and Canut (1958) reported that on heating IV rapidly to
328 K, a different version of phase II is produced, with the
same lattice constants as the stable phase II but probably
having the space group $P4$. Conflicting statements have been
made about the transition of V at low temperatures into yet
another form. From the careful heat capacity studies of
Nagatani, Seiyama, Sakiyama, Suga, and Seki (1967), it seems
that there is a minor thermal anomaly at 156 K. Under
pressure, phase III soon disappears, while II is replaced
at ~9 kbar by a form VI, which in turn vanishes at 19·5 kbar
to leave I and IV as the only crystalline phases (Fig.7.31;
Bridgman 1916, Rapoport and Pistorius 1966). On deuteration
the temperatures of the II→I and III→II transitions are
raised by 1·8 K and 3·6 K respectively, while those of the
IV→III and IV→II transitions are lowered by 2·5 K and 2·4 K.
(Pöyhönen, Nissilä, and Jaakkola 1968; Juopperi 1972).

A factor which has complicated the experimental investigations of this substance is that some of the transitions are sluggish, and their occurrence and characteristics

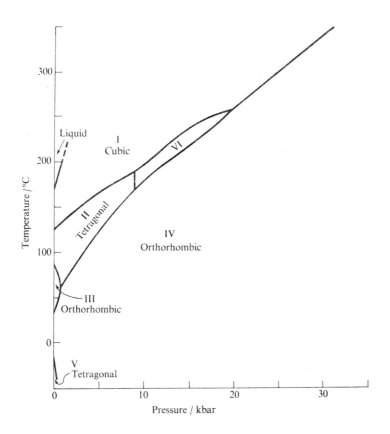

Fig.7.31. Phase diagram for NH_4NO_3 (after Bridgman 1916, and Rapoport and Pistorius 1966).

depend on how dry the sample is and on its thermal history. The IV↔III and III↔II transitions have been selected for investigation of the kinetics of phase transitions, (see e.g. Erofeev and Mitskevich 1952, 1953, Everett and Watson 1956, Wolf, Benecke, and Fuertig 1972).

The diffraction work has established that there is an affinity between the structures of phases V, IV, II, and I. That between IV and II, for example, is sufficiently close for a single crystal of IV to be preserved on conversion into II, while very little change in the positions of the centres of the ions is needed for the conversion of V into II. The phase which is out of line is III, and the transitions IV→III and III→II apparently take place only in the

presence of moisture. There is, of course, hydrogen bonding
between the cations and anions, but whereas in IV this gives
rise to infinite sheets of ions so bonded, in III the ions
are linked to give double chains. An interesting feature
of phase III is that its heat capacity is much less
($\sim$20 J K^{-1} mol^{-1}) than that of superheated IV or supercooled
II. (This is why the sum of the entropies of the IV$\rightarrow$III
and III$\rightarrow$II transitions given in Table 7.8 is considerably
greater than ΔS_t for the IV$\rightarrow$II transition.) Michaelis de
Saenz, Amonini, and Presa (1964) made a density study of the
IV$\rightarrow$III transition, taking special care to ensure that equilibrium between the phases had been established. Their
results for the temperature dependence of the density
through the transition are shown in Fig.7.32. This depen-

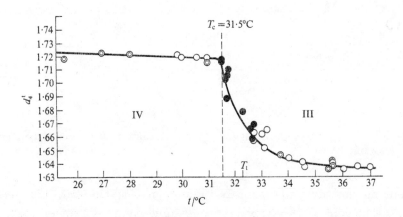

Fig.7.32. Relative density d_4^t vs. temperature for phases IV and III of
NH$_4$NO$_3$. Transition temperature (T_t) = 32$\cdot$2°C (after Michaelis de
Saenz, Amonini, and Presa 1964).

dence is unusual in being almost the reverse of that normally found in a gradual or partly gradual transition.

        There seems little doubt that in phases II and I the
nitrate ions are orientationally disordered, but the
position with regard to the ammonium ions is less clear.
The major drop in the proton resonance line-width occurs
between 20 K and 80 K, so that even in phase V the ammonium

TABLE 7.7

Experimental values of the barrier height V_0 *and of the activation energy* E *for reorientation of the ammonium ions in various salts. (See heading to Table 7.5 for explanation of abbreviations used.) Values of* V_0 *indicated by NSCS were obtained from neutron scattering cross-section measurements.*

Salt	V_0/kJ mol^{-1}	E/kJ mol^{-1}
$(NH_4)_2SO_4$	14·5(NSCS)[a]	16·5,11·5[b](II,<170 K), 9·5(I)[c]
$(ND_4)_2SO_4$	-	21·5,11·5[b](II), 10·5[d](I)[e]
$(NH_4)_2BeF_4$	-	14,9·5[b](II, < 110 K), 11·5f(I)g
$(ND_4)_2BeF_4$	-	18,10[b](II), 17, 10[b](I)[e]
$(NH_4)_2SeO_4$	~19(LW)[h]	19·5(I)[c]
$(NH_4)_2CrO_4$	17(NSCS)[j,k]	-
NH_4ClO_4	1·7(NSCS)[a], < 4(C_p)[l], <4(LW)[h]	2·7, 1·7[m]
NH_4SO_3F	3-4(NSCS)[k,n]	-
NH_4N_3	25(INS)[o]	-
NH_4CNS	17(NSCS)[j],15(SPEC)[p]	-
ND_4CNS	16·5(SPEC)[p]	-
$NaNH_4SO_4\cdot2H_2O$	-	8·5q(I), 18r(I), 13q(II, III)s
NH_4HSO_4	-	8·5(II), 12(III)[t]
NH_4PF_6	~1(NSCS)[n]	-
ND_4PF_6	-	3·4(III,< 70 K),3·0(I)[u]
$(NH_4)_2SiF_6$	13·4(C_p)[v],4-8(NSCS)[w]	9·2[x]
$(NH_4)_2GeF_6$	-	5·4y(> 60 K)
$(NH_4)_2SnCl_6$	6·15(C_p)[v]	5·2[x], 5·0[i]
$(NH_4)_2RuCl_6$	-	5·1[z]
$(NH_4)_2PdCl_6$	-	1·75[z]
$(NH_4)_2PtCl_6$	-	1·6[z]

Table 7.7 continued.......

$(NH_4)_2SnBr_6$	$<3(LW)^h$	$6 \cdot 0(II),\ 1 \cdot 1(I)^{aa}$
$(NH_4)_2Cr_2O_7$	$<3(LW)^h, \sim 6(NSCS)^w$	$8 \cdot 2^i$
$(NH_4)_2S_2O_8$	$<3(LW)^h, \sim 4(NSCS)^k,$ $3(NSCS)^n,\ 4\text{-}8(NSCS)^w$	7^i
$(NH_4)_2S_2O_3$	-	$7,12^i$
NH_4VO_3	-	$8^i,\ 21^r,\ 8^{q,bb}$
$NH_4H_2AsO_4$	-	16^{cc}
NH_4NO_3	-	$8 \cdot 7(V,\ <200\ K)^{dd},$ $12(IV,V)^{ee}$
ND_4NO_3	-	$10 \cdot 7(V,\ <200\ K)^{dd}$
NH_4ReO_4	-	$9 \cdot 2^{ff}$

a.   Leung, Taylor, and Havens (1968).

b.   These values refer to type I and type II NH_4^+ ions respectively (see text).

c.   O'Reilly and Tsang (1967a).

d.   For type II NH_4^+ ions.

e.   Kydon, Petch, and Pintar (1969).

f.   For type I NH_4^+ ions.

g.   O'Reilly, Peterson, and Tsang (1967).

h.   Richards and Schaefer (1961).

i.   Watton, Sharp, Petch, and Pintar (1972).

j.   Rush, Taylor, and Havens (1961).

k.   Rush, Safford, Taylor, and Havens (1962).

l.   Westrum and Justice (1969).

m.   Riehl, Wang, and Bernard (1973).

n.   Brajovic, Boutin, Safford, and Palevsky (1963).

o.   Boutin, Trevino, and Prask (1966).

p.   Durig and Pate (1972).

q.   For rotation about 3-fold axes.

r.   For rotation about 2-fold axes.

s.   Genin and O'Reilly (1969).

t.   S.R.Miller, Blinc, Brenman, and Waugh (1962).

Footnotes to Table 7.7 continued.....

u.   L.Niemelä, and Tuohi (1970).

v.   D. Smith (1974b).

w.   Leung, Rush, and Taylor (1972).

x.   Strange and Terenzi (1972).

y.   Ylinen, Tuohi, and L.Niemelä (1974).

z.   Bonori and Terenzi (1974).

aa. Norris, Strange, and Terenzi (1968).

bb. Peternelj, Valic, and Pintar (1971).

cc. Grosescu (1973).

dd. L.Niemelä and Lohikainen (1967).

ee. Anderson and Slichter (1966).

ff. Armstrong, Lourens, and Jeffrey (1976).

ions can have considerable orientational freedom. At 410 K
in form I the line-width is only ~0·06G, implying that the
cations have acquired not only still greater orientational
freedom but also the ability to diffuse with ease in the
lattice. In fact, this diffusion probably begins in phase
II, as the electrical conductivity rises by a factor of
about 25 at the III→II transition (R.N.Brown and McClaren
1962c), and simultaneously the permittivity increases
(Makosz and Gonsior 1971). The conductivity rises again
about thirtyfold at the II→I transition. From T_1 measurements, Hovi, Lohikainen, and Niemelä (1968) obtained a value
of 53 kJ mol^{-1} for the activation energy for diffusion of
the ammonium ions in I, in fair agreement with the figure
of 47 kJ mol^{-1} obtained by Suga, Sugisaki, and Seki (1966)
from a high-resolution NMR study. As for the nitrate ions,
it appears probable from the diffraction studies that in II
these are disordered between two orientations, which is consistent with the entropy change at the IV→II transition.
Shinnaka (1959a) suggested that in the cubic phase I each
nitrate ion may have four orientations in the planes parallel
to the cube faces, giving twelve possibilities in all, with
the qualification that there must be some correlation between
the orientations of neighbouring anions (Fig.7.33). These

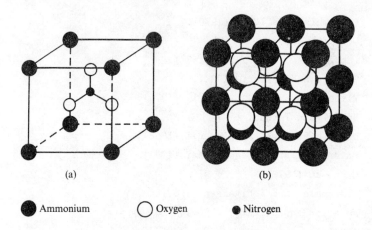

(a)   (b)

● Ammonium   ○ Oxygen   ● Nitrogen

Fig.7.33. (a) One of twelve equivalent orientations of a nitrate ion in
a possible structure for NH₄NO₃-I. (b) Illustrating how neighbouring
nitrate ions might pack on this model to give some local order (after
Yamamoto and Shinnaka 1974).

views on the nitrate ion disorder in I and II were upheld
by later X-ray work (Yamamoto and Shinnaka 1974), which also
suggested that the ammonium ions as well are orientationally
disordered in both phases. A mutually restrictive interaction
may also operate between the ammonium ions and the nitrate
ions. We may add that ammonium nitrate has a low entropy of
fusion of ~1·5R (cf. the plastic crystals discussed in Chapters 9 and 10). Only rubidium nitrate of the alkali metal
nitrates has an entropy of fusion smaller than this. Raman
studies on phases I, II, and IV showed that lattice modes
obtained with II and IV are absent from the spectrum of I,
which led Østerlund and Rosen (1974) to conclude that the
movement of the nitrate ion in the high-temperature phase I
approaches almost free rotation. Examination of phases III,
IV, and V by the same technique suggested that the anions may
be orientationally disordered to some extent even in phase
III (James, Carrick, and Leong 1974), which is not inconsistent with the entropy gain at the IV→III transition. These
authors also concluded that the partly gradual, partly first-
order, V→IV transition is associated with the development
of orientational disorder of the ammonium ions.

TABLE 7.8

Thermal and structural properties of ammonium nitrate

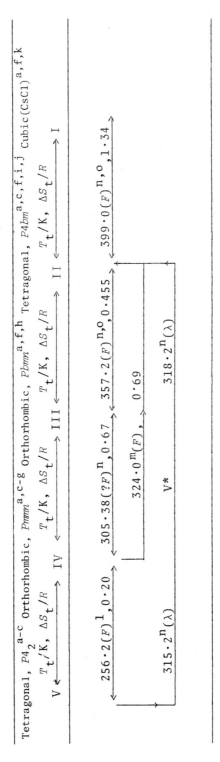

Footnotes on page 350

Footnotes to Table 7.8.

a.   Hendricks, Posnjak, and Kracek (1932).

b.   Amorós, Arrese, and Canut (1962).

c.   Amorós Portolés, Alonso, and Canut (1958).

d.   Choi, Mapes, and Prince (1972) (neutron diffraction).

e.   C.D.West (1932).

f.   R.N.Brown and McClaren (1962c).

g.   J.R.Holden and C.W.Dickinson (1975).

h.   Goodwin and Whetstone (1947).

i.   Shinnaka (1956, 1959b).

j.   Stasova (1959) (electron diffraction).

k.   Shinnaka (1959a); Yamamoto and Shinnaka (1974).

l.   Stephenson, Bentz, and Stevenson (1955).

m.   Everett and Watson (1956) (dilatometric, IV-III transition).

n.   Nagatani et $al.$ (1967) (C_p, 15-410 K).

o.   Hovi, Pöyhönen, and Paalassalo (1960).

     Ammonium sulphate transforms at 223 K from a high-
temperature paraelectric form I into a ferroelectric phase
II (Matthias and Remeika 1956). The discovery of ferroelectricity in such a simple salt led to a considerable amount
of experimental work being carried out on it, and it is therefore remarkable that there is still a lack of unanimity about
such matters as the cause of the ferroelectric character of
phase II, and whether or not the transition is of the order-
disorder type - and indeed about some of the physical properties of the two phases and about the condition and behaviour
of the ions therein. We will first summarize some of the
relevant information which is not in dispute. Although both
forms are orthorhombic, the space group of I is $Pnam$ while
that of form II is $Pna2_1$. On the usual convention for an
orthorhombic unit cell, that $b > a > c$, the c axis in II is
the direction of spontaneous polarization. The essential
structural difference between the two phases is that whereas
I has three reflection planes (ab, bc, and ac) and a centre
of inversion, phase II lacks the centre of inversion and
the ab plane of reflection. In both the paraelectric and

ferroelectric forms, the environment of the ammonium ions
in the lattice is of two kinds. The two types of ion are
designated by most authors as $NH_4(I)$ and $NH_4(II)$, so it is
important to avoid confusion between the Roman numerals as
used in this context and as applied to the phases. As shown,
for example, by the electron diffraction investigation of
Udalova and Pinsker (1963) and the neutron diffraction study
of Schlemper and Hamilton (1966b), an $NH_4(I)$ ion has five
nearest-neighbour sulphate ions while an $NH_4(II)$ ion has
six (in both phases). The existence of the two types of
ammonium ion is confirmed by NMR evidence. Thus, the proton
resonance line is narrow at room temperature, indicating that
reorientation of the cations is rapid on the NMR timescale,
but on cooling the line splits into two components at about
160 K. Down to about 90 K, one of the components is broad
while the other remains narrow, implying that in this temperature range the reorientation of one type of ammonium ion
is much more rapid than that of the other (Blinc and Levstek
1960). Also, plots of the spin-lattice relaxation time T_1
against temperature show two minima, which O'Reilly and Tsang
(1967a) interpreted as arising from the different frequencies
with which the two kinds of ion undergo reorientation, the
$NH_4(I)$ ions being the less mobile of the two. From T_1 measurements on mixed crystals of ammonium and potassium sulphates,
Kasahara, Sasakawa, and Tatsuzaki (1975) found that with increasing potassium ion content the transition temperature
falls and the activation energy for the $NH_4(I)$ ions decreases. Moreover, it is the latter type of ion which is
preferentially replaced, and in sufficiently potassium -
rich mixed crystals only $NH_4(II)$ ions remain. From relaxation time measurements on phase I of $(NH_4)_2SO_4$, it appears
that above 300 K the ammonium ions start to diffuse in the
lattice with an activation energy of 75 kJ mol^{-1} (Knispel,
Petch, and Pintar 1975).

The transition II→I is partly gradual, as was shown by
the heat capacity determinations. It is accompanied by a
gradual volume decrease, amounting to about 1·5 per cent
overall, the contraction being confined to the a axis
(S.Hoshino, Vedam, Okaya, and Pepinsky 1958). The gradual

onset of the transition was also apparent in the cold neutron
scattering experiments of Dahlborg, Larsson, and Pirkmajer
(1970). However, while it extends over a range of roughly
50 K, it is almost certainly completed isothermally. Thus,
there is a sudden change at the Curie point in the spontaneous
polarization (Hoshino *et al.*) and in the elastic compliance
coefficients (T.Ikeda, Fujibayashi, Nagai, and Kobayashi
1973). Nevertheless, there is no abrupt alteration in the
torsional oscillation frequencies, as determined by far infrared (Trefler 1971) and infrared and Raman spectra (Torrie,
Lin, Binbrek, and Anderson 1972). nor in the neutron scattering cross-section (Leung, Taylor, and Havens 1968). We
shall not discuss in detail the ferroelectric behaviour of
this salt, but it is worth noting that this is unusual in
some respects (see Ikeda *et al.*). In particular, the value
of the Curie-Weiss constant C is exceptionally low. This
constant, which appears in the Curie-Weiss equation for the
temperature dependence of the permittivity ε in the paraelectric phase

$$\varepsilon = \frac{C}{(T-T_0)} + \varepsilon_0$$

is of the order of 10^5 for a displacive ferroelectric such
as barium titanate, and about two orders of magnitude less
for a ferroelectric such as potassium dihydrogenphosphate
where the paraelectric and ferroelectric phases are separated
by an order-disorder transition. For ammonium sulphate,
however, C is only ~10 (E. Nakamura, Mitsui, and Furuichi
1963).

Since there is little change in the torsional oscillational frequency of the ammonium ions at the transition, or
in the neutron scattering cross-section for the hydrogen atoms,
the heights of the barrier opposing reorientation should be
much the same in the two phases. This was confirmed by the
values obtained by O'Reilly and Tsang (1967a) (Table 7.7),
who noted that once again the correlation times were anomalous in the region of the volume contraction below T_c (*cf.*
the comments made on the ammonium halides, p. 323).

A matter on which agreement does not appear to have been

reached is that of the distortion of the ammonium ions in
the lattice. This is clearly of importance in seeking a
reason for the existence of a ferroelectric phase, since such
distortion can make the ammonium ions polar. Blinc and
Levstek observed that the ν_4 band of the ammonium ion in the
infrared spectrum splits into three components below T_c, implying distortion of these ions in the ferroelectric phase.
(They reported that the sulphate ions appeared to be distorted as well.) Chiba (1962) measured the quadrupole coupling constant in $(ND_4)_2SO_4$, and attributed the coupling to
the effect of the distortion of the cations rather than to
crystal field effects. Udalova and Pinsker concluded from
their electron diffraction study that both the sulphate and
ammonium ions are strongly distorted. Various values, sometimes of 10° or more, have been advanced for the departure
of the H-N-H angle from the tetrahedral angle. Further evidence in support of ammonium ion distortion from deuteron
magnetic resonance experiments was provided by O'Reilly
and Tsang, but whereas they decided that the cations are
more distorted in the ferroelectric phase II than in the paraelectric phase I, Schlemper and Hamilton from their neutron
diffraction study reached the reverse conclusion. More
recently, Torrie *et al*., in a detailed study of the infrared
and Raman spectra of the H and D forms of the salt in the two
forms, failed to find any evidence that the ammonium ions are
distorted. Nor did their experiments give any indication
that the ferroelectric→paraelectric conversion is associated
with a soft mode. By contrast, Sawada, Takagi, and Ishibashi
(1973) have suggested that some of the properties of ammonium
sulphate (including its very small Curie-Weiss constant) can
be interpreted on the basis that a normal mode, having a
librational non-polar mode as its major component and a
translational polar mode as a minor component, becomes 'soft'
at the Curie point.

Two other properties of crystalline ammonium sulphate
about which there is still disagreement may be mentioned.
Whereas Hoshino *et al*. reported that in the ferroelectric
phase the spontaneous polarization is almost independent
of temperature, this was denied by Unruh (1970). And while

Kamiyoshi (1957) stated that the application of a d.c.
field in the [110] direction increased or decreased T_c, depending on the field direction, by ~1·2 K for a field of
1000 V cm^{-1}, Hoshino and his coworkers could not reproduce
this effect. Finally, there is the important matter of the
nature of the transition itself. Some authors regard this
as an order-disorder transition, the dipoles of the distorted NH_4^+ ions being disordered in the paraelectric phase with
respect to the ab plane. O'Reilly and Tsang advanced several
reasons in support of this view, one of the most cogent
being the considerable entropy increase at the transition of
~$2R$, which they suggested may be attributed to each ammonium
ion as well as each sulphate ion in the paraelectric phase
having two orientations. They also attached considerable
importance to the evidence provided by the NMR studies on
$(ND_4)_2SO_4$ on the relation between the deuteron electric
field gradient tensors just above and below T_c, on the basis
of which they proposed that the cations are symmetrically
tilted with respect to the ab plane below T_c, while
above this temperature they are tilted either above or
below this plane. O'Reilly and Tsang (1967b) applied a molecular-field treatment and showed that the partly first-order
character of the transition could result from a sufficiently
strong dependence of the interaction on the number of mis-
orientated ion pairs. Schlemper and Hamilton, however, concluded that the transition does not fall in the order-disorder category, but essentially involves a change in the
hydrogen bonding between the sulphate ions and ammonium ions,
the bonding in the ferroelectric phase being stronger than
that in the paraelectric phase (see also Hamilton 1969, and
Trefler 1971). Other authors have felt unable to support
either of these interpretations, and have placed the onus
on the sulphate ions rather than the ammonium ions. Thus,
Jain and his coworkers, from an infrared study of the υ_1 and
υ_2 modes of the SO_4^{2-} ions, inferred that while these ions are
tetrahedral in the paraelectric phase, they become distorted
in a narrow temperature range on entering the ferroelectric
phase (Jain, Bist, and Upreti 1973, Jain and Bist 1974).
They attributed the transition to this, and considered that

any change in the behaviour or characteristics of the ammonium ion should be regarded as a consequence of it, rather than its cause.

In considering the possible role of the cations in the transition in ammonium sulphate, two further points should be noted. The first is that, in marked contrast to some hydrogen-bonded ferroelectrics, replacing the hydrogen in ammonium sulphate by deuterium has virtually no effect on T_c. The second concerns the transition in ammonium hydrogen-sulphate, NH_4HSO_4, and in the corresponding rubidium salt $RbHSO_4$. Phase II of NH_4HSO_4 is ferroelectric, but its range of existence is now limited by a lower as well as an upper transition (Table 7.6). $RbHSO_4$ is similar in that it too has a ferroelectric phase II (Pepinsky and Vedam 1960). The inference from this comparison, namely that the ammonium ions are probably not responsible for the II→I ferro-electric→paraelectric transition in NH_4HSO_4, is supported by X-ray and neutron diffraction studies by Nelmes (1971), who showed that in phase I it is the anions which are dis-ordered between two orientations. The hydrogen bonds in the paraelectric phase of both $RbHSO_4$ and NH_4HSO_4 appear to be ordered (Ashmore and Petch 1975). The salt sodium ammonium sulphate, $NaNH_4SO_4 \cdot 2H_2O$ (lecontite), also has two transi-tions and both phases II and III are ferroelectric, but a comprehensive NMR study by Genin and O'Reilly (1969) using H, D, and ^{23}Na resonances showed that the ammonium ions are not distorted and that probably neither they nor the water molecules are primarily responsible for the ferroelectricity. The balance of the evidence favours the view that the transi-tion at 101 K in this salt is displacive in character, while that at 92 K involves minor lattice distortions.

While the salt ammonium fluoroberyllate, $(NH_4)_2BeF_4$, is similar to the sulphate in transforming below room tem-perature to a ferroelectric phase, there are interesting differences between the two. The space group of the fluoro-beryllate is $Acam$ in phase I (which may be antiferroelectric), and $Pn2_1a$ in the ferroelectric phase, in which the b and not the c axis is the polar axis. Blinc and Levstek (1960) con-cluded that the ammonium ions are distorted in the ferro-

electric phase, as the ν_4 band of the ion is split into
three components. Jain (1975), on the basis of infrared
evidence, ascribed the transition to distortion of the
anions in the low-temperature phase. $(NH_4)_2SO_4$ and
$(NH_4)_2BeF_4$ form a complete series of solid solutions. Each
depresses the transition temperature of the other, but between 20 and 70 mole per cent of the fluoroberyllate a new
phase is formed which has a different structure $(P2_12_12_1)$
from phase I of either salt and which does not change on
cooling, at least down to ~80 K (Hoshino, Vedam *et al*. 1958).

In ammonium salts containing a polyatomic anion, the
distribution of the charge on this ion over several atoms
must weaken the electrostatic attraction between any one of
these atoms and a hydrogen atom of an ammonium ion. It might
be expected that the barrier to reorientation of the ammonium
ion in such salts could accordingly be low enough to allow the
ammonium ion at higher temperatures to execute something approaching free rotation, especially if the anion only carries
a single charge. Salts for which the barrier height (or the
activation energy) are particularly small are NH_4ClO_4, NH_4SO_3F,
NH_4PF_6, and certain compounds of the type $(NH_4)_2MX_6$, where
X is a halogen atom (Table 7.7). In such cases, the question of how the rotational movement of the ammonium ions
should be regarded and how the nature of this movement will
change with temperature is best approached by first determining the torsional or rotational energy levels for the
ammonium ion in a field of symmetry appropriate to the particular crystal. A pioneer study of this kind was carried
out by King and Hornig (1966) on the energy levels of an
ammonium ion in an octahedral field, and D.Smith (1973) considered the case of a tetrahedral field. Strictly speaking,
these energy level calculations should be made with due
regard for the fact that for the ammonium ion, just as for
the methane molecule (section 9.7), there are three nuclear
spin states, *A*, *E*, and *T*. A possible scheme for the energy
levels for an ammonium ion in a tetrahedral field has been
given by Riehl, Wang, and Bernard (1973), and is reproduced
in Fig.7.34. For NH_4ClO_4, the barrier height V_0 is approximately 3 kJ mol^{-1}. With such low barriers, quantum-mechanical
tunnelling has to be considered as a mechanism by which the

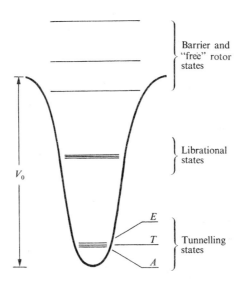

V_0

E

T

A

Barrier and "free" rotor states

Librational states

Tunnelling states

Fig.7.34. Schematic diagram of the energy levels for an ammonium ion in a tetrahedral field. The splitting of the tunnelling levels is actually much less than that of the librational levels (Riehl, Wang, and Bernard 1973).

ammonium ion can change its orientation. The possibility
of this is best examined by NMR studies at low temperatures,
when the ammonium ions are effectively all in the ground
state and a reorientation by a classical surmounting of the
barrier has become prohibitively difficult. We shall return
to this later. It will be seen from Fig.7.34 that there
is a librational level about half-way up the potential well,
and at temperatures at which this level is accessible reorientation could proceed by tunnelling from it. Higher
still there are levels which represent something approaching
free rotation, the attainment of which should be possible
within the range set by the thermal stability of ammonium
perchlorate and some other ammonium salts. If in addition
to these considerations there is added the possibility that
the barrier to rotation in the crystal may be markedly
anisotropic, the situation becomes one of some complexity
which is not capable of a simple verbal interpretation.
Moreover, it must be recognized that numerical estimates of

small barrier heights and activation energies, derived from
different kinds of evidence taken from different temperature
regions, cannot be given a precise quantitative significance.

The belief that the ammonium ions in NH_4ClO_4 at ordinary temperatures are approaching a condition of free rotation is supported by the neutron diffraction work and by
the infrared and Raman spectra of the salt (Waddington 1958,
Van Rensburg and Schutte 1972). The latter authors suggested
that at about 50 K weak hydrogen bonding may begin to restrict the rotational movement of the ion. A rather similar
conclusion was reached by Westrum and Justice (1969), who
pointed out that between 30 K and 40 K there is a shoulder
in the heat capacity-temperature curve and that the cause
of this may be that as the temperature falls the reorientation of the ammonium ion becomes confined to a single
axis. Westrum and Justice demonstrated that the orthorhombic
form II of ammonium perchlorate, though having no transition,
nevertheless approaches perfect order at 0 K. More recent
neutron diffraction work at 10 K, 78 K, and 298 K (Choi,
Prask, and Prince 1974) and an examination of the quasielastic neutron scattering (Prask, Trevino, and Rush 1975)
both confirmed that the motion of the ammonium ions
is a complex one right down to low temperatures. The picture
of the behaviour of the ammonium ion derived from these two
studies may be summarized as follows. At room temperature,
the NH_4^+ ions should not be regarded as undergoing free or
quasifree rotation. They still mostly librate about definite
equilibrium positions. These oscillations are however of
rather large amplitude, and the activation energy for reorientation is only $2 \cdot 3$ kJ mol^{-1}. This reorientation occurs
by random jumps of 120° about all four C_3 axes. The residence times for oscillation about a particular axis are
$9 \cdot 5$ps and $1 \cdot 8$ps at 78 K and 150 K respectively. Even at
10 K the amplitude of the librational movement of the ammonium ions about one of the three principal axes is quite
large, but the reorientation has still not become entirely
one-dimensional. It will be noted from Table 7.6 that ammonium perchlorate has a high-temperature cubic form. The
anions in this are orientationally disordered (p. 386).

In ammonium tetrafluoroborate, NH_4BF_4, the reorientation
of the ammonium ion is also very facile. It is still taking
place at 20 K, probably about a single twofold axis of the
ion (Pendred and Richards 1955).

Ammonium hexafluorophosphate, NH_4PF_6, is another salt
in which the restriction on rotation of the ammonium ion is relatively small. The detailed NMR studies of Albert and
Gutowsky (1973) and of Niemelä and Tuohi (1970) on this
compound are of interest not only for the information they
provide on the activation energies for reorientation of the
two ions, but also for the light they throw on the magnetic
interaction between the protons and the fluorine nuclei.
This salt has two transitions (Table 7.6), the upper of which
may be an order-disorder change primarily associated with
the PF_6^- ions, while the lower may be similarly linked with
the NH_4^+ ions, though even at 77 K in phase III the latter
are undergoing rapid, random reorientation, well below the
III→II transition at 131·3 K.

When ammonium fluorosilicate, $(NH_4)_2SiF_6$, is crystallized from solution above 5°C, it is obtained in a cubic
form, while below 5°C a trigonal form is produced. Spontaneous interconversion of the two forms is very sluggish.
The trigonal form undergoes a low-temperature order-disorder
transition (Table 7.6), whereas the cubic form has no transition. Both forms, however, become completely ordered at
0 K (Stephenson, Wulff, and Lundell 1964). The behaviour
of the ammonium ion in the cubic phase, as disclosed by a
combination of structural and spectroscopic studies, is
particularly interesting. In this form, each ammonium ion
is surrounded by twelve crystallographically equivalent
fluorine atoms. These form four groups (of three atoms each)
tetrahedrally disposed about the ammonium ion. Fig.7.35
shows the scattering density through the plane of a hydrogen
atom in cubic $(NH_4)_2SiF_6$ at room temperature, as evaluated
by Schlemper, Hamilton, and Rush (1966) from their neutron
diffraction investigation. Each peak in the figure is
equivalent to one-third of a hydrogen atom, and the positions
of the peaks correspond to the three fluorine atoms nearest
to the particular hydrogen atom. Schlemper *et al.* accordingly

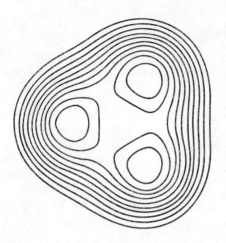

Fig.7.35. Observed hydrogen atom scattering density in the cubic form of $(NH_4)_2SiF_6$. Each peak corresponds to one-third of a hydrogen atom. The peaks are 0·075 nm apart (Schlemper, Hamilton, and Rush 1966).

prefer to regard the case as one of dynamic rather than static disorder, in that each hydrogen atom has a consider-able amount of thermal movement, covering an area of the order of 10^{-2} nm^2. Its motion must therefore be very an-harmonic. This picture is supported by the NMR study of Blinc and Lahajnar (1967), who also propose a mechanism for the reorientation of the ammonium ion, that is the movement in which any one hydrogen atom transfers its attention from one group of three fluorine atoms to another group. They suggest that the ammonium ion is excited from the ground torsional state to a level above the energy barrier, and after a short interval of almost free rotation lapses into one of the three possible equilibrium orientations of the ground state. Reorientation of the SiF_6^{2-} ions is altogether more restricted. The ^{19}F line-width transition occurs from ~30°C to 80°C, so reorientation of the anion only effective-ly begins above room temperature. Trigonal $(NH_4)_2SiF_6$ has a very different structure, in which there seems to be two-fold disorder of the ammonium ions accompanied by consider-able thermal motion. This disorder probably gives way to an ordered structure at the λ-transition at 38·6 K.

The transition in ammonium dihydrogenphosphate, $NH_4H_2PO_4$

(Table 7.14) is discussed on p. 420. Although it is not
one which can be ascribed to cooperative orientational ordering of the ammonium ions, we may remark here that proton T_1
and $T_{1\rho}$ measurements show that the NH_4^+ ions undergo reorientation about twofold axes, the activation energy
being 16 kJ mol^{-1} about all three axes in the paraelectric
phase I. In the antiferroelectric phase II, this activation
energy is larger for rotation about the c axis (17·5 kJ mol^{-1})
but smaller (12 kJ mol^{-1}) for reorientation about the a and
b axes. In phase II the ammonium ions suffer considerable
distortion (Kasturi and Moran 1975).

For some ammonium salts, it is found that at temperatures so low that virtually all the ammonium ions are in
the librational ground state and all classical motion can
be regarded as having ceased, the observed proton resonance
line-shapes are not those which would be expected for a
rigid lattice. This can be interpreted on the basis of
quantum-mechanical tunnelling, with its consequential
splitting of the torsional energy levels of the ammonium
ion. The magnitude of this splitting can be represented by
a quantity Δ, which can be estimated for a particular salt
by comparing the observed line-shapes at helium temperatures
with the shape calculated for various Δ values. The higher
the barrier opposing the rotation of the ammonium ion, the
smaller Δ, and as seen in Fig.7.36 for the few substances
for which data are available there appears to be a linear
relation between $\log \Delta$ and the barrier height (Dunn, Ikeda,
and McDowell 1972, Ikeda and McDowell 1973). For NH_4ClO_4
and NH_4PF_6, in which salts, as already noted, the barriers
to rotation of the ammonium ion are low, the proton resonance
line-shapes are narrower at liquid helium temperatures than
might be expected. The narrowing is temperature-dependent,
implying that it is influenced by a kinetic process involving a modulation of the tunnelling states (Lalowicz, McDowell,
and Raghunathan 1975).

7.5.3. Substituted ammonium salts
This class of compound is of interest for more than one
reason. In the first place, it links simple ionic solids

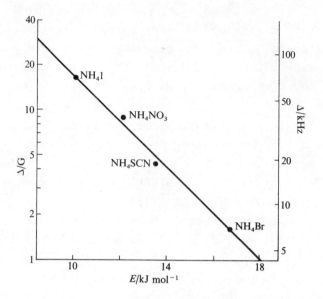

Fig.7.36. Tunnelling splitting constant Δ for the NH_4^+ ions $vs.$ E, the activation energy for reorientation (after Ikeda and McDowell 1973).

with the molecular crystals discussed in Chapters 9 and 10. For example, the tetramethylammonium ion, $N(CH_3)_4^+$, is iso-electronic with the neopentane molecule, $C(CH_3)_4$, and as with crystalline neopentane, so also with a tetramethyl-ammonium salt there are the a $priori$ possibilities of intra-molecular rotation of the methyl group, reorientation or rotation of the whole cation about one or more axes, and of diffusion in the lattice. Another similarity between the two types of solid can arise if an alkyl group of sufficient length is substituted into an ammonium ion, since the re-sulting solid can show order-disorder transitions related to the alkyl group in a way recalling the phenomena shown by solids composed of long-chain organic molecules (section 10.5). Furthermore, substitution in an ammonium ion can give rise to quite large cations which can be used in con-junction with suitable anions to produce magnetically dilute solids, in which the magnetic interaction is effectively limited to one or to two dimensions. A popular ion for this purpose is the tetramethylammonium ion, and a much-

studied salt, for example, is tetramethylammonium manganese
chloride, $(CH_3)_4NMnCl_3$, (TMMC), in which the anions are
infinite chains in which each manganese atom is coordinated
to six chlorine atoms (Fig.7.37). The parallel anion chains
are separated by the tetramethylammonium ions, and in consequence TMMC approaches very closely to a one-dimensional

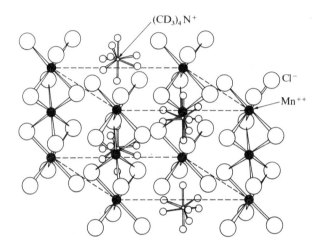

Fig.7.37. Structure of $(CD_3)_4NMnCl_3$ in the high-temperature disordered
phase I. The two possible orientations of the $(CD_3)_4N^+$ ion are shown.
The deuterium atoms have been omitted   (Hutchings *et al*. 1972).

magnetic system. Salts of the type $(RNH_3)_2MCl_4$, where R
is an alkyl group and M is a divalent metal atom, form layer
lattices, in which infinite anion sheets of metal and Cl
atoms are separated by the cations. Solids of this kind can
behave as two-dimensional magnetic systems, the type of
ordering within a layer depending on the nature of M (page
871). Such salts tend to have magnetic transitions at
lower temperatures and one or more transitions involving
the cation at higher temperatures.

Thermal and structural information on selected salts
with substituted ammonium ions is given in Table 7.9. Some
of the references accompanying this Table will be found to
contain data on similar salts. Some values for the activation energies (or barrier heights) opposing reorientation

(both intramolecular, and for the cation as a whole) are
listed in Table 7.10.

    Tetramethylammonium chloride exhibits a somewhat com-
plicated polymorphism, in that, as shown by Dufourcq, Haget-
Bouillaud, Chanh, and Lemanceau (1972), phase II when quite
dry readily supercools to room temperature, and does not
show the lower transitions recorded in Table 7.9. They
suggested that the II→III transition may belong to a hydrated
form of the salt, but it is perhaps more likely that its
occurrence is induced by the catalytic action of traces of
moisture in the crystals (cf. ammonium nitrate, p.343).
The high-temperature phase I is certainly disordered with
regard to the orientation of the cations, but whereas Pistorius and Gibson (1973) assigned a configurational entropy
of $R \ln 32$ to this phase, Dufourcq et al. attributed most of
the entropy gain at the II→I transition to the increase in
the restricted rotational entropy of the cation consequent
on the drop in the energy barrier opposing rotation, and
only allocated $\sim R \ln 2$ to the configurational entropy of
the high-temperature form. The cations do not diffuse with
any facility in this phase, since even above 550 K the proton
second moment is still of the order of 1 G^2. Opinions differ
as to whether the cations in phase II are orientationally
disordered or not. Pistorius and Gibson proposed a structure
for this phase which would give each cation two distinguishable orientations, while Dufourcq and his colleagues decided
that the cations are ordered. Phase II is piezoelectric,
so the unit cell lacks a centre of symmetry (Gibson and
Raab 1972). The several NMR studies agree in concluding
that, on the NMR time-scale, reorientation of the methyl
groups about their threefold axes begins at ~150 K, followed
by reorientation of the cation as a whole at about 230 K.
Plots of the spin-lattice relaxation time against temperature show two minima, which are attributed to the two motions.
The drop at the II→I transition in the barrier height opposing cation rotation is considerable, no doubt largely because of the volume increase of 12 per cent, and with a
barrier height of only ~ 4 kJ mol^{-1} in phase I, a not negligible fraction of the cations must be in a state of quasi-

TABLE 7.9

Thermal and structural properties of substituted ammonium salts

Compound	V	$T_t/K, \Delta S_t/R$ (→IV)	IV	$T_t/K, \Delta S_t/R$ (→III)	III	$T_t/K, \Delta S_t/R$ (→II)	II	$T_t/K, \Delta S_t/R$ (→I)	I	Cal.	Cryst.	NMR
$N(CH_3)_4Cl$		75·8(λ),0·19	Tetragonal	184·85(λ),0·07	Tetragonal $P4/nmm$	410, 0·46	Rhombohedral	537, 2·85	F.c.c.	1-3	2-4	5,6
$NH(CH_3)_3Cl$							Monoclinic, $P2_1/m$	308	Tetragonal	2	2,7	5
$NH_2(CH_3)_2Cl$						260	Orthothombic	313	?Hexagonal	2	2,8	5
$NH_3(CH_3)Cl$					(β)	220·4(F),0·97	(γ)	264·5(F),1·28	(α) Tetragonal $P4/nmm$	2,9	2,10	5,11
$(n\text{-}C_5H_{11}NH_3)Cl$ (quenched sample)						221·5(λ),0·64		246·5(λ),0·07		12	12	–
(annealed sample)						220·0(λ),0·49		246·5(λ),1·15				
$[(n\text{-}C_5H_{11})_4N]SCN$					315(F),8·5					13	–	–
$[(n\text{-}C_6H_{13})_4N]ClO_4$						355·91(λ),1·97		367·51(λ),0·87		14,15		
$(CH_3)_4N\ MnCl_3$			333·57(λ), 8·25				126·5(λ), 1·02^a Monoclinic $P2_1/a$		Hexagonal $P6_3/m$	16	17	18

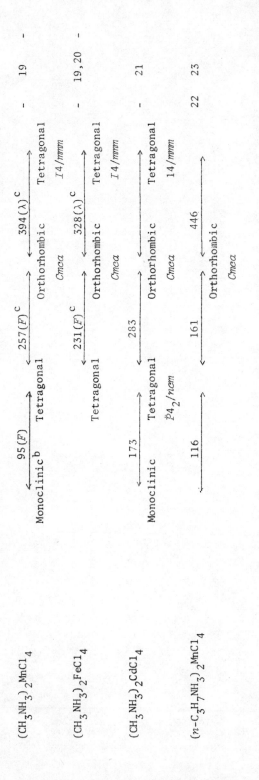

(CH₃NH₃)₂MnCl₄
Monoclinic[b] ⟶ 95(F) ⟶ Tetragonal ⟶ 257(F)[c] ⟶ Orthorhombic Cmca ⟶ 394(λ)[c] ⟶ Tetragonal I4/mmm — 19 —

(CH₃NH₃)₂FeCl₄
Tetragonal ⟶ 231(F)[c] ⟶ Orthorhombic Cmca ⟶ 328(λ)[c] ⟶ Tetragonal I4/mmm — 19,20 —

(CH₃NH₃)₂CdCl₄
Monoclinic ⟶ 173 ⟶ Tetragonal P4₂/ncm ⟶ 283 ⟶ Orthorhombic Cmca ⟶ 446 ⟶ Tetragonal I4/mmm — 21

(n-C₃H₇NH₃)₂MnCl₄
⟶ 116 ⟶ Orthorhombic Cmca ⟶ 161 ⟶ 446 ⟶ 22 23

a. Unpublished work by A.G. Dunn, M.Jewess, R.D. Worswick, and L.A.K. Staveley.

b. This form undergoes a magnetic transition at ~45 K.

c. Transition temperatures from optical birefringence studies, Ref. 19.

Further footnotes continued on facing page.

Footnotes to Table 7.9.

References

1.   Chang and Westrum (1962) (C_p, 5-300 K).

2.   Stammler (1967) (DTA).

3.   Pistorius and Gibson (1973) (DSC, X-ray I, II, III).

4.   Dufourcq, Haget-Bouillaud, Chanh, and Lemanceau (1972) (I, II, III);
      Vegard and Sollesnes (1927) (III); Wyckoff (1928) (III);
      Tench (1963) (IV).

5.   Andrew and Canepa (1972) (LW, SM).

6.   Dufourcq and Lemanceau (1970) (LW, SM); Albert, Gutowsky, and
      Ripmeester (1972) (T_1, $T_{1\rho}$); Gibson and Raab (1972) (LW, SM, T_1,
      $T_{1\rho}$, 77-567 K).

7.   Lindgren and Olovsson (1968a).

8.   Lindgren and Olovsson (1968b).

9.   Aston and Ziemer (1946) (C_p, 10-300 K).

10.   Hughes and Lipscomb (1946) (I).

11.   Albert and Ripmeester (1973) (T_1, $T_{1\rho}$, also CD_3NH_3Cl and CH_3ND_3Cl);
      Tsau and Gilson (1970) (LW, SM, also of bromide and iodide and
      of partially deuterated derivatives); Tegenfeldt and Ödberg (1972)
      (T_1, also CH_3ND_3Cl and CD_3NH_3Cl).

12.   Southard, Milner, and Hendricks (1933).

13.   Coker, Wunderlich, and Janz (1969) (DSC).

14.   Coker, Ambrose, and Janz (1970).

15.   Andrews and Gordon (1973).

16.   Takeda (1974); Dietz, Walker, Hsu, Haemmerle, Vis, Chau, and
      Weinstock (1974).

17.   Morosin and Graeber (1967); Peercy, Morosin, and Samara (1973);
      Hutchings, Shirane, Birgeneau, and Holt (1972).

18.   Mangum and Utton (1972); Hone, Scherer, and Borsa (1974) (T_1).

19.   Knorr, Jahn, and Heger (1974) (X-ray and neutron); Heger, Mullen,
      and Knorr (1975).

20.   Mostafa and Willett (1971).

21.   Chapuis, Arend, and Kind (1975).

22.   Arend, Hofmann, and Waldner (1973) (DTA).

23.   E.R.Peterson and Willett (1972).

free rotation above the barrier. The comparison of the
chloride with the bromide and iodide is interesting, in that
the last two salts, with tetragonal lattices isomorphous with

phase III of the chloride, show no transitions at all. (This
tetragonal structure is similar to that of phosphonium iodide,
being in effect a distorted caesium chloride lattice.) A
clue to the reason for the lack of polymorphism in the bromide and iodide may perhaps be found in the generalized phase
diagram for the simple ammonium halides (Fig.7.27), which
shows that increase in anion size extends the stability range
of the tetragonal structure (phase III of ammonium bromide).
It will be seen from Table 7.10 that with the progression
from chloride to bromide to iodide, the barrier height opposing reorientation of the cation falls, as is to be expected. Less predictably, perhaps, there is also a decrease
in the barrier to rotation of the methyl radicals. Values
of the parameters governing the rates of methyl group rotation and cation tumbling in the corresponding phosphonium
salts, i.e. $P(CH_3)_4X$ where $X = Cl, Br,$ or I, were obtained
from T_1 measurements by Ang and Dunell (1976).

The compound $(CH_3)_4NMnCl_3$, (TMMC), has already been mentioned. While interest has primarily centred on its magnetic properties and their interpretation, it appears to
provide another example of orientational disorder of the
tetramethylammonium ion. The salt has a partly gradual,
partly sharp transition with $T_\lambda = 126 \cdot 5$ K (or 128 K in the
deuterated form). It has been suggested on the basis of
the diffraction work that above this temperature the cations
are disordered between two orientations (Fig.7.37). A configurational entropy of $R \ln 2$ can certainly be accommodated
by the observed entropy of transition of $1 \cdot 02R$. It may be
that in the low-temperature phase the cations form ordered
chains along the c axis, but that these chains are disordered with respect to each other (Hutchings, Shirane,
Birgeneau, and Holt 1972). Proton resonance studies revealed
that the cations acquire the ability to change their orientation between 39 K and 50 K (Mangum and Utton 1972).

The ion $CH_3NH_3^+$ has a structure resembling that of the
ethane molecule, though it is of course less symmetrical
and carries a charge which is not uniformly distributed over
the hydrogen atoms. The salt monomethylammonium chloride,
$(CH_3NH_3)Cl$, has been subjected to a very thorough NMR study

TABLE 7.10

Activation energies (or barrier heights V_0) for reorientation in substituted ammonium salts, in kJ mol^{-1}. Unless otherwise stated, the values are for activation energies derived from relaxation time measurements. LW = line-width; the Roman numerals give the phase to which a value applies

Salt	Species involved	
	CH$_3$ radical (unless otherwise indicated)	Whole cation
N(CH$_3$)$_4$Cl	$27(V_0,$LW$)^a$; $28\cdot5($III$),28($II$)^b$; $\geq 18($I$),22\cdot9($II$),29($III$),$ $19\cdot5($IV$)^c$	$52(V_0,$LW$)^a$;$54\cdot5($III$),36($II$)^b$; $4($I$), 39($II$), 62($III$)^c$
N(CH$_3$)$_4$Br	$21\cdot5(V_0,$LW$)^a$; 27^b; 28^d; 22^i	$46(V_0,$LW$)^a$; 48^b; 49^d; $35($LW$)^i$
N(CH$_3$)$_4$I	$14\cdot5(V_0,$LW$)^a$; 23^b	$33\cdot5(V_0,$LW$)^a$; 46^b
N(CH$_3$)$_4$NO$_3$	$28\cdot5($LW$)^e$	$44\cdot5($LW$)^e$
[N(CH$_3$)$_4$]$_2$SO$_4$	$26\cdot5($LW$)^e$	$61\cdot5($LW$)^e$
[N(CH$_3$)$_4$]$_2$CO$_3$	$27($LW$)^e$	$60\cdot5($LW$)^e$
N(CH$_3$)$_4$ClO$_4$	$19($LW$)^e$	-
N(CH$_3$)$_4$ClO$_3$	$21($LW$)^e$	-
(CH$_3$NH$_3$)Cl	$18\cdot5($III$), 7\cdot6($II$),$ $24($III,NH$_3^+$$),$ $32($II,NH$_3^+$$)^f$	$4($I$)^f$
(CD$_3$NH$_3$)Cl	$26\cdot5($III,NH$_3^+$$),32(II,NH_3^+$$)^f$; $27($III,NH$_3^+$$),$ $32($II,NH$_3^+$$)^g$; $25\cdot5($III,NH$_3^+$,LW$)^h$	$4\cdot5($I$)^f$ $3\cdot9($I$)^g$
(CH$_3$ND$_3$)Cl	$18\cdot5($III$), 7\cdot6($II$)^f$; $21 ($III$), 10\cdot5($II$)^g$; $20($III,LW$)^h$	$4\cdot5($I$)^f$ $3\cdot4($I$)^g$

Footnotes on next page

Footnotes to Table 7.10.

a.   Dufourcq and Lemanceau (1970).

b.   Albert, Gutowsky, and Ripmeester (1972).

c.   Gibson and Raab (1972).

d.   Polak and Sheinblatt (1973).

e.   Mahajan and Nageswara Rao (1974).

f.   Albert and Ripmeester (1973).

g.   Tegenfeldt and Ödberg (1972).

h.   Tsau and Gilson (1970).

i.   Blears, Danyluk, and Bock (1968).

by Albert and Ripmeester (1973), who by using deuteration
were able to separate the movement of the CH_3 group about
the C-N axis from that of the NH_3^+ group. The activation
energy for the reorientation of the latter in phase II and
III is higher than that for the CH_3 group, presumably in
consequence of hydrogen bonding between the NH_3 group and
the halide ions. At the III→II (β→γ) transition the activation energy for the motion of the CH_3 radical decreases,
while that for the NH_3 group increases. Albert and Ripmeester suggest that this may be due to a change at the transition in the charge distribution within the cation. Deuteration of the methyl group has a surprisingly large effect on
the temperature of the β→γ transition, raising it by ~25 K.
In phase I (α), the cation revolves as a unit round the C-N
axis with relatively little hindrance. .Moreover, in this
form the C-N axis coincides with the fourfold axis of the
crystal. The entropy increase at the II→I transition is however considerably less than the $R \ln 4$ which would be associated with the gain of fourfold orientational disorder,
and Albert and Ripmeester prefer to attribute it to the
change in entropy of the NH_3 and CH_3 groups resulting from
the decrease in barrier height, treating these groups as
one-dimensional rotors. Phase II can be supercooled, but
its entropy approaches equality with that of phase III as
T→0 K, so probably neither phase retains any disorder at
very low temperatures.

In trimethylammonium chloride, the NMR evidence indicates that with rising temperature reorientation of the
methyl group is followed by reorientation of the whole
cation about its threefold axis.   Only the dimethylammonium
salt shows line-narrowing at 4 K due to tunnelling, so the
barrier to methyl group reorientation in this salt must be
less than in any of the other three methylammonium chlorides.

When alkyl chains are substituted for hydrogen atoms
in ammonium ions, the resulting salts may have remarkably
low melting-points.   Thus, that of the salt $[(n\text{-}C_5H_{11})_4N]$
SCN is 322·5 K, only 7·5 K above the transition temperature.
More often than not, such salts have transitions, which
are frequently associated with large entropy changes.   Thus,
in a study by differential scanning calorimetry (DSC) of
34 quaternary ammonium salts, Coker, Ambrose, and Janz (1970)
found that the salt $(n\text{-}C_7H_{15})(n\text{-}C_6H_{13})_3NBr$ has two transitions with entropy changes totalling $13R$, while the entropy
of fusion is only $2\cdot3R$, a state of affairs reminiscent of
the plastic crystals discussed in Chapters 9 and 10.   Other
features of this kind of salt are tendencies for solidifica-
tion of the melt to give incompletely crystalline solids
and for transitions to be delayed, or associated with long
equilibrium times.   As a result of this, information on
temperatures and heats of transition obtained by the DSC
technique, while useful as a guide, may be somewhat uncertain.   Thus, the salt $(n\text{-}C_6H_{13})_4NClO_4$ has been very carefully studied in an adiabatic calorimeter by Andrews and
Gordon (1973), whose results for the temperatures and
entropies of transitions are recorded in Table 7.9.   Their
values for these temperatures differ by up to 2 K from those
obtained by Coker and his colleagues by DSC, which is not
surprising in view of Andrews and Gordon's observation that
equilibrium is only very slowly established in the transition
region, this sometimes requiring times of the order of a
day.

Coker, Wunderlich, and Janz (1969) have made a thorough
study of the salt tetra-n-amylammonium thiocyanate, and have
proposed an explanation of the large entropy increase of
$8\cdot5R$ at the transition based on the 'kink-block' model which

Pechhold and his coworkers advanced to account for the
so-called rotational transitions in n-alkanes (section 10.5)
(Pechhold, Dollhopf, and Engel 1966, Blasenbrey and Pechhold
1967). This is based on the idea that the disorder gained
by an alkyl chain at such a transition derives from the
formation of conformational isomers. If the chain is straight,
the terminal carbon atoms in a C-C-C-C unit have a *trans*
relation to each other. But they can also adopt a *gauche*
configuration in one of two directions, designated + and -,
of higher energy than the *trans* configuration. A kink is
produced in a previously straight chain if a sequence of four
carbon atoms adopts either the arrangement *gauche*(+)-*trans*-
gauche(-) or *gauche*(-)-*trans*-*gauche*(+) (Fig.7.38). If the
chain length is such that there are three ways in which

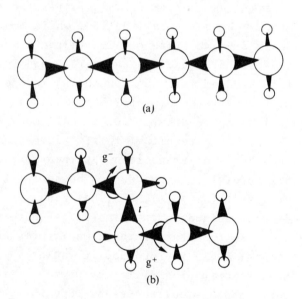

Fig.7.38. The kink-block model of Blasenbrey and Pechhold (1967) for
an aliphatic chain. The extended chain (a) is shortened in (b) by the
effective length of a CH_2 group by the introduction of a *gauche-trans-
gauche* kink (Coker, Wunderlich, and Janz 1969).

such a kink can be produced (which is possible for the amyl
group), then there are six conformations for each side-chain,
and 6^4 = 1296 for the tetra-n-amylammonium ion as a whole.
Coker *et al.* point out that by incorporating the nitrogen

atom the number of conformations Ω would be even higher than
this, and they suggest that in round numbers Ω may lie
between 10^3 and 10^4, corresponding to a conformational
entropy, $= R \ln \Omega$, between $6R$ and $9R$. With regard to the
three transitions in $(n\text{-}C_6H_{13})_4NClO_4$, Andrews and Gordon
suggest that that with the largest entropy gain, the IV→III
transition, is likewise to be interpreted on the basis of
kinking of the chains, but they give reasons for believing
that this kind of disorder is only fully developed on fusion.
They consider that the III→II and II→I transitions are associated with the gain of orientational disorder of the perchlorate ions (a common occurrence with this particular
anion), though it is probable that the anion and cation in
the salt cannot really be regarded as being independent of
each other. So phases I, II, and III are all disordered,
and even the possibility of some residual disorder in IV
(which may be resolved at a much lower temperature) cannot
be altogether ruled out.

Tsau and Gilson (1968) used DSC to investigate transitions in salts of the series $(n\text{-}C_nH_{2n+1}NH_3)X$, where
X = Cl or Br and n = 1 to 16. They also carried out NMR
studies on the chlorides with n = 3 to 10 (1973). With
$n < 10$, these salts tend to be tetragonal at room temperature, and with $n > 12$ monoclinic or orthorhombic. Most of
them have two transitions, and some have three. Several
when first heated undergo a transition with a large entropy
increase (~$11R$, for example, with X = Cl and n = 12) which
is not observed again, and the sum of the entropies of
transitions later found for the same specimen are less
than the entropy of transition experienced on the first
heating, suggesting that the disorder gained on this occasion is partially frozen into the lattice on cooling. The
temperatures of the lower transitions show an alternation
effect between odd and even members of the series (*cf.* section
10.5), which is not observed for the highest transitions
and the melting-points. The entropies of fusion are low,
being generally less than $5R/2$ (*cf.* the plastic crystals
discussed in Chapters 9 and 10). The line-width and second
moments of the chlorides fall in two stages with rising

temperature. The first change occurs somewhat below the lowest thermal transition, and is probably due to reorientation of the alkyl chain about its axis. The upper line-width transition coincides approximately with the thermal transition with the largest ΔS_t, which may mark transformation to a mesomorphic phase. Salts of this type would seem to offer scope for further investigation.

Compounds of the formula $(CH_3NH_3)_2MCl_4$ (and homologues with other alkyl groups), where M is the divalent ion of a metal of the first transition series (e.g. Mn) or of a B group (e.g. Cd) crystallize in perovskite-like layer structures (Fig.7.39) which have become model systems for the

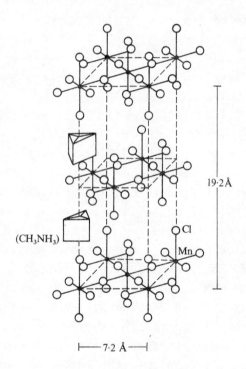

Fig.7.39. Simplified representation of the structure of $(CH_3NH_3)_2MnCl_4$ (Knorr, Jahn, and Heger 1974).

study of two-dimensional magnetic behaviour (section 12.13.2). The sequence of the four phases (Table 7.9) is crystallographically interesting, and its interpretation must be

sought in the changes in motion of the $CH_3NH_3^+$ ions. The
phases which concern us here are the orthorhombic II, which
is ordered, and the high-temperature tetragonal form I. This
is disordered with respect both to the $MnCl_6$ octahedra and
the $CH_3NH_3^+$ ions (Heger, Mullen, and Knorr 1975). The
$MnCl_6$ octahedra in I are tilted with respect to the fourfold axis and are statistically disordered among four orientations. The carbon atoms, but not the nitrogen atoms, lie
on the fourfold axis, and the C-N bonds are orientationally
disordered among eight positions, which form a cone around
the c axis. From their single crystal neutron diffraction
study, Heger et al. concluded that the hydrogen atoms of an
NH_3 group have 16 sites available to them, though these are
not all equivalent. In addition, the carbon atoms have considerable thermal movement in the ab plane. Knorr, Jahn,
and Heger (1974) made a careful study of the change with
temperature of the lattice constants and the birefringence
of salts with M = Mn and Fe over a wide range covering all
the transitions. If we assume that for the II→I transition
either the birefringence Δn or the lattice deformation
[which can be equated to $(a-b)/a$] is proportional to the
square of the order parameter (but see the case of the alloy
AuCu discussed in section 5.3), then we have

$$\Delta n \text{ or } (a-b)/a \propto (1 - T/T_c)^{2\beta}$$

As will be seen from the parallelism of the lines in Fig.
7.40, the birefringence and lattice parameter measurements
give the same result for β of 0·31 ± 0·01, the value for the
three-dimensional Ising model (section 3.3). In the series
$(C_nH_{2n+1}NH_3)_2MCl_4$, with increasing n the lattice remains
essentially a layer structure with the lengthening alkyl
chains forcing the ionic layers ever further apart. DSC
studies showed that these salts have order-disorder transitions, usually between 280 K and 380 K, for which ΔS_t increases as the chain lengthens, as is to be expected. Compounds so investigated include those with n from 9 to 17,
and M = Mn, Co, Fe, Hg, Cu, and Zn. (See Landi and
Vacatello 1975, who cite references to earlier work, and

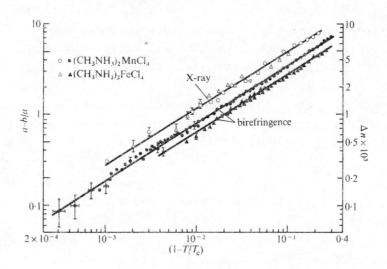

Fig.7.40. Comparison of the critical exponent β as evaluated from birefringence (Δn, = n_γ - n_β) and from the lattice constants $(a-b)/a$ for the
high-temperature phase transition in $(CH_3NH_3)_2MnCl_4$ and $(CH_3NH_3)_2FeCl_4$
(Knorr, Jahn, and Heger 1974).

also Bocanegra, Tello, Arriandiaga, and Arend 1975). With
n = 10, ΔS_t at the main order-disorder transition (there may
be other minor ones) can be ~110 J K^{-1} mol^{-1}, and for
n = 16 it may be as high as 215 J K^{-1} mol^{-1} (~R ln 10^{11}).
These compounds also merit further investigation.

7.5.4. Tetrahedral anions

The borohydride ion, BH_4^-, is isoelectronic with the methane
molecule and the ammonium ion, but owing to its negative
charge is larger than either of these. The relevant bond
lengths are B-H 0·1255 nm, C-H 0·1092 nm, and N-H 0·1035 nm.
All of the alkali borohydrides have transitions (Table 7.11).
The λ-transition in $NaBH_4$ has an entropy change approaching
R ln 2, which suggests the development of twofold orientational disorder of the BH_4^- ions, as for the NH_4^+ ions in
ammonium chloride. In fact, the structure of $NaBH_4$ is face-
centred cubic, like that of NH_4I, but in contrast to the
movement of the NH_4^+ ions in NH_4I there is no evidence of
facile reorientation of the BH_4^- ions in $NaBH_4$ about a threefold axis of the ion. Owing to the similarity of the

TABLE 7.11

Some structural and thermal information on salts with tetrahedral anions

Compound	III	T_t/K, $\Delta S_t/R$	II	T_t/K, $\Delta S_t/R$	I	Cal.	Cryst.	NMR
$LiBH_4$			Orthorhombic, *Pnma*	381·6, 2·0	Tetragonal, $I4_1$ or $I4_1/a$	1	1,2	3,4
$NaBH_4$			Tetragonal, $I\bar{4}m2$	189·9(λ), 0·61	Cubic, *Fm3m*	5	6–8	3,9
KBH_4			?Cubic, $F\bar{4}3m$[a]	77·16(λ), 0·35[b]	Cubic, *Fm3m*	10,11	6,8	3,9
$RbBH_4$				~44	Cubic, *Fm3m*	11	6	9
$CsBH_4$				~27	Cubic, *Fm3m*	11	6	–
$NaBF_4$			Orthorhombic, *Cmcm*	511·3, 1·3–1·55	Monoclinic, $P2_1/m$	12,13	13–16	16–19
KBF_4			Orthorhombic, *Pnma*	558·3, 2·95	Cubic, *Fm3m*	12,20	14,21,21	17,19,22,22
$RbBF_4$			Orthorhombic, *Pnma*	514·9, 2·75		12,23	22,23	17,19,22,24

Compound	Low-temperature phase	Transition (T, ratio)	Intermediate phase	Transition	High-temperature phase	References
CsBF₄ — $CsBF_4$	Orthorhombic, *Pnma*	←432·2, 2·1–2·2→	Cubic,	?723	?Cubic, ?*Fm3m*	12,25 22,25 17,19
NH₄BF₄ᶜ — $NH_4BF_4^{c}$	Orthorhombic, *Pnma*	←461·9, 2·3→	Cubic,	~733	?Cubic, ?*Fm3m*	21,48 14,21,17,19,22 24,26
TlBF₄ — $TlBF_4$	Orthorhombic, *Pnma*	←474·8, 2·27→	Cubic,	?7~5	?Cubic, ?*Fm3m*	27 27,28 –
AgBF₄ — $AgBF_4$	Orthorhombic, *Pnma*	←494·3→	Cubic, *Fm3m*			29 –
NaClO₄ — $NaClO_4$	Orthorhombic, *Pnma*	←581·4, 2·1–2·5→	Cubic, *Fm3m*			29 –
KClO₄ — $KClO_4$	Orthorhombic, *Cmcm*	←574·4, 2·84–3·2→	Cubic, *Fm3m*			30 31–33 –
RbClO₄ — $RbClO_4$	Orthorhombic, *Pnma*	←548·3, 2·25–2·5→	Cubic, *Fm3m*			33,34 31,33,35–37 –
CsClO₄ᶜ — $CsClO_4^{c}$	Orthorhombic, *Pnma*	←482·3→	Cubic, *Fm3m*	←758, 1·85→	?Cubic, ?*Fm3m*	23,33 31,33,35 –
NH₄ClO₄ᶜ — $NH_4ClO_4^{c}$	Orthorhombic, *Pna2₁*(?*Pnma*)	←511·2, 2·26–2·43→	Cubic, *Fm3m*			25,33 33,38,31,33,48 35,39 –

Table 7.11 continued........

Compound	Phase sequence (transition temperature, entropy)	References	
$TlClO_4$	Orthorhombic, $Pnma$ $\xrightarrow{540\cdot6,\ 2\cdot22-2\cdot33}$ Cubic $Fm3m$	27,33 31,35	–
$AgClO_4$	Orthorhombic, $Cmcm$ $\xrightarrow{428\cdot9,\ 0\cdot9-1\cdot1}$ Cubic, $Fm3m$ $\xrightarrow{?}$?Cubic, $?Fm3m$	29,33 29,31	–
Li_2SO_4	Monoclinic, $P2_1/c$ $\xrightarrow{843,\ 3\cdot63}$ Cubic, $F23$ or $F\bar{4}3m$	40,41 42	–
Na_2SO_4	(V) Monoclinic $\xrightarrow{458,\ 0\cdot082}$ (IV) $\xrightarrow{514,\ 2\cdot56}$ Hexagonal (I)	43 44,45	–
K_2SO_4	Orthorhombic, $Pmcn$ $\xrightarrow{855,\ 1\cdot26}$ Hexagonal, $P\bar{3}m1$	40 45	–
Li_2BeF_4	Trigonal, $R\bar{3}$ $\xrightarrow{449,\ 2\cdot25}$ $\xrightarrow{563,\ 0\cdot115}$ Trigonal	46 47	–

a. From infrared and Raman spectra (Harvey and McQuaker 1971).

b. Furukawa *et al*. (Ref.10) consider that there is a heat capacity anomaly extending from 200 to 450 K which is really a continuation of this transition, and which increases the transition entropy to $R\ln 2$, or even more.

c. See Table 7.6 for further information on these two salts.

Further footnotes continued on page 380

Footnotes for Table 7.11

REFERENCES

1.   Pistorius (1974); Hallett and Johnston (1953).
2.   P.M.Harris and Meibohm (1947); Semenenko, Chavgun, and Surov [1971).
3.   Tsang and Farrar (1969) (T_1, including ^{11}B and ^{23}Na measurements for NaBH$_4$).
4.   Niemelä and Auranen (1970).
5.   Johnston and Hallett (1953).
6.   Abrahams and Kalnajs (1954).
7.   Soldate (1947).
8.   Ford and Powell (1954).
9.   Ford and Richards (1955) (LW, SM).
10.   Furukawa, Reilly, and Piccirelli (1964).
11.   Stephenson, Rice, and Stockmayer (1955).
12.   Dworkin and Bredig (1970).
13.   Pistorius, Boeyens, and Clark (1969).
14.   Finbak and Hassel (1936).
15.   Brunton (1968).
16.   Weiss and Zohner (1967).
17.   Huettner, Ragle, Sherk, Stengle, and Yeh (1968) (^{19}F, T_1 and LW).
18.   Hurst, R.J.C. Brown, and Whittem (1968). (^{19}F, SM).
19.   Hurst (1970) (^{19}F, SM).
20.   Pistorius (1970a).
21.   Strømme (1974b).
22.   M.J.R. Clark and Lynton (1969).
23.   Pistorius and J.B.Clark (1969).
24.   Pendred and Richards (1955) (SM).
25.   Richter and Pistorius (1971a).
26.   Caron, Huettner, Ragle, Sherk, and Stengle (1967) (H, ^{19}F, LW and T_1; also ND$_4$BF$_4$).
27.   J.B. Clark and Pistorius (1973).
28.   Pistorius (1970b).
29.   J.B. Clark and Pistorius (1974).
30.   Results of Grønvold and Lyng-Nielsen, quoted by Strømme (1974a).
31.   Herrmann and Ilge (1931); Bräkken and Harang (1930).
32.   Zachariasen (1930).
33.   Strømme (1974a).

REFERENCES for Table 7.11 continued......

34.   Ozawa, Momota, and Isozaki (1967).

35.   Büssem and Herrmann (1928).

36.   Gottfried and Schusterius (1933).

37.   Mani (1957).

38.   Markowitz and Boryta (1962).

39.   Venkatesan (1957).

40.   Denielou, Fournier, Petitet, and Téqui (1970).

41.   Riccardi and Sinistri (1965); Ingraham and Marier (1965).

42.   Albright (1933); Førland and Krogh-Moe (1957).

43.   Kracek (1929); Coughlin (1955); Shmidt and Sokolov (1961); Brodale and Giauque (1972).

44.   Kracek and Ksanda (1930).

45.   Bredig (1941, 1942, 1943); Fischmeister (1962).

46.   Levina, Kalitin, and Kalinnikov (1961).

47.   Burns and Gordon (1966).

48.   Richter and Pistorius (1971b).

electronegativities of boron and hydrogen, the effective negative charge on the hydrogen atoms of the BH_4^- ion is presumably not as large numerically as the positive charge on the hydrogen atoms in the ammonium ion. With this in mind, Stockmayer and Stephenson (1953) suggested that the preferred orientations of the BH_4^- ions in $NaBH_4$ are determined by the minimization of the repulsive energy between hydrogen atoms of neighbouring ions rather than by electrostatic attraction. They concluded that the B-H bonds must lie on the cube diagonals. This gives each BH_4^- ion the two possible orientations necessary to account for the entropy of transition, but they pointed out that in the ordered state the H...H repulsions are reduced if in one layer of borohydride ions these ions all have one of these orientations, and the other orientation in the adjacent layers. This led them to predict that $NaBH_4$-II should be tetragonal, which Abrahams and Kalnajs (1954) and Ford and Powell (1954) later found to be the case. As will be seen from Table 7.11, there is a marked drop in the temperature of the transitions in the borohydrides from the sodium to the caesium salt.

Stephenson, Rice, and Stockmayer (1955) pointed out that
since the energy of repulsion of two atoms or ions at a distance r is approximately proportional to $\exp(-r/\rho)$, a roughly linear relation might be expected between $\log T_\lambda$ and r,
the distance between neighbouring borohydride ions, and this
proves to be so (Fig.7.41). The NMR results provide an

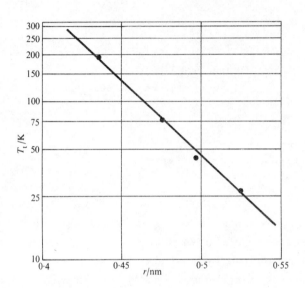

Fig.7.41. Transition temperature T_t for Na, K, Rb, and Cs borohydrides
(left to right) *vs*. distance r between neighbouring borohydride ions
(Stephenson, Rice, and Stockmayer 1955).

interesting contrast. Whereas with $NaBH_4$ the line-width
transition falls at 80 K to 100 K, which is well below the
λ-point, in KBH_4 it also occurs between 80 K and 100 K, and
between 75 K and 85 K for the rubidium salt, so that for
the last two salts the line-width transition is well above
T_λ. Moreover, the activation energies for reorientation do
not decrease, and may actually increase on passing from the
sodium salt to the potassium and then to the rubidium salt
(Table 7.12). Ford and Richards (1955) considered that
this supports the view of Stockmayer and Stephenson that
repulsion is the dominant factor in deciding the reorientational behaviour of the anion in these salts. At room

TABLE 7.12

Values of E, the activation energy for the reorientation of the anion in various salts, as derived from line-width (LW) or relaxation time (T_1) measurements. Values indicated as (V_0, C_p) are estimates of the barrier height to rotation from analysis of heat capacity data

Compound	E/kJ mol^{-1}
$NaBH_4$	$10\cdot1(LW)$[a]; $11\cdot2(T_1,I)$, $14\cdot8(T_1,II)$[b]; $12\cdot5(V_0,C_p)$[c]
$NaBD_4$[d]	$14\cdot5$-$16\cdot5(II,T_1,D)$, 14-$16\cdot5(II,T_1,{}^{11}B)$, $13(I,T_1,D)$, $12(I,T_1,{}^{11}B)$[e]
KBH_4	$15\cdot7(LW)$[a]; $14\cdot4(V_0,C_p)$[c]; $14\cdot8(T_1)$[b]
$RbBH_4$	$16\cdot3(LW)$[a]
$NaBF_4$	$49\cdot2$[f](T_1); $54\cdot5(LW)$[g]
KBF_4	$36\cdot7$[f](T_1); $35\cdot6(LW)$[g]
$RbBF_4$	$34\cdot0$[f](T_1); $31\cdot4(LW)$[g]
$CsBF_4$	$28\cdot5$[f](T_1); $22\cdot8(LW)$[g]
NH_4BF_4	$30\cdot7$[f](T_1)[g]; 27-$33(LW,II)$[h]
$NOBF_4$	$40\cdot7$[f](T_1)[g]
$(NH_4)_2BeF_4$	$30\cdot5(T_1,I)$[i]

a. Ford and Richards (1955).

b. Tsang and Farrar (1969).

c. D.Smith (1974a).

d. T_λ for this salt is 197 K (Huettner *et al.* 1968).

e. Niemelä and Ylinen (1970).

f. These are values for 'low temperature', i.e. for below the transition region. Except for $NOBF_4$, the 'high-temperature' values are somewhat higher.

g. Huettner *et al.* (1968).

h. Caron *et al.* (1967).

i. O'Reilly, Peterson, and Tsang (1967).

temperature the second moments are such that the BH_4^- ions appear to be undergoing reorientation about random axes.

The lithium salt has a different (orthorhombic) structure at ordinary temperatures, and shows no transition between 15 K and 300 K. Since form II is isomorphous with the room-temperature modification of most of the tetrafluoroborates and perchlorates, and since ΔS_t for the II→I transition in $LiBH_4$ is about the same as that for the transition experienced by the orthorhombic forms of these salts on heating, it is probable that the disorder in $LiBH_4$-I is similar to that in the cubic form of the tetrafluoroborates and perchlorates ($v.inf.$), even though $LiBH_4$-I itself is tetragonal. There is a high-pressure phase V of $LiBH_4$ which may also be disordered (Pistorius 1974). T_1 measurements on $LiBH_4$-II (Tsang and Farrar 1969) and on this salt and $LiBD_4$ (Niemelä and Auranen 1970) have led to the conclusion that there are two non-equivalent BH_4^- or BD_4^- ions in the orthorhombic modification, and moreover that these ions are somewhat distorted. In both respects, this recalls the case of the ammonium ions in ammonium sulphate. The activation energies for reorientation of the BH_4^- ions in $LiBH_4$-II are not much greater than those for the other alkali metal salts, being about 15 and 20 kJ mol^{-1} for the two kinds of ion.

The tetrafluoroborates and perchlorates of the alkali metals (except lithium) and of ammonium, silver and monovalent thallium all undergo transitions to forms in which the anions are orientationally disordered. There is a close affinity between the polymorphism of the two sets of salts (which extends to the phases formed under pressure), but the tetrafluorobates, owing to their greater thermal stability, can exist in high-temperature forms which may not be obtained with the perchlorates. This means that on our convention of numbering the phase stable at the highest temperature and at atmospheric pressure as I, comparable phases in the two types of salt may have to be assigned different Roman numerals. Important contributions to our factual knowledge of the polymorphism of perchlorates and tetrafluoroborates have been made by Pistorius and his coworkers. Relevant

thermal and structural information is summarized in Table
7.11. Since considerable use has been made by Pistorius
and by Strømme of the entropies of transition in considering
the disordered phases, it should be noted that the ΔS_t values
at present available are not as certain as one could wish.
Most of them depend on the use of DSC, and the results of
different authors may vary somewhat, as indicated by the
range of values given in Table 7.11. Moreover, although the
transitions we are about to discuss are no doubt all first-
order to some extent, there may be a gradual approach to the
isothermal part of the transition, and the entropy gained in
the earlier stages, which may not be inconsiderable, will
almost certainly not be included in the DSC estimate. An
extreme example of this is provided by sodium perchlorate,
as shown by the plot of heat capacity against temperature
in Fig.7.42 from which it can be seen that the transition

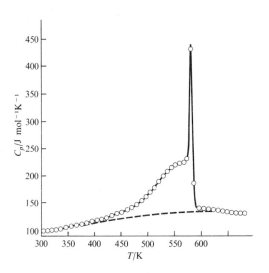

Fig.7.42. Heat capacity of sodium perchlorate $vs.T$ (results of Grønvold
and Lyng-Nielsen, presented by Strømme 1974a).

extends over at least 200 K, and furthermore (from the
shelf in the heat capacity just before the isothermal cul-
mination) that it appears to involve more than one stage.

All of the perchlorates and tetrafluoroborates in Table 7.11, with the exception of $NaClO_4$, $NaBF_4$, and $AgClO_4$, crystallize in the same orthorhombic lattice, namely that of barium sulphate. The other three salts at room temperature have the structure of calcium sulphate. All of these compounds transform on heating into a modification which, with the single exception of that produced by $NaBF_4$, has a sodium chloride-type lattice. These transitions show hysteresis (Connell and Gammel 1950, Syal and Yoganarasimhan 1973), and on this and other evidence are no doubt at least partly first-order. The entropies of transition are considerable, and comparable with the entropies of fusion where these are known. The transition temperatures for the K, Rb, and Cs salts fall with increasing size of the cation. It was at one time supposed that the anions rotate in the cubic phase (Finbak and Hassel 1936), but a combination of the structural, X-ray, and (for the fluoroborates) NMR evidence leaves little doubt that the anions are in fact disordered among a limited number of distinguishable orientations. Two main attempts to find an acceptable model for the cubic phase have been made, one by Pistorius and his colleagues, the other by Strømme (1974a,b). Pistorius, noting that the ΔS_t values for the transitions from the orthorhombic (*Pnma*) to the cubic (*Fm3m*) lattice are roughly $R \ln 8$, suggested that each anion has eight possible orientations, e.g. two for each of the four cube diagonals. Strømme's treatment is more sophisticated, and is similar to that which he had previously applied to nitrates (p. 308). The various *a priori* possibilities for the orientation of a perchlorate ion in the cubic unit cell consistent with the space group fall into six sets. Strømme (1974a) gave reasons for believing that two of the six sets, A and B (Fig.7.43) embody six and eight crystallographically equivalent orientations respectively. However, some of the possible configurations provided by these sets are unlikely to be realized, since they give rise to unacceptably small O--O distances ($< \sim 0\cdot 28$ nm) between neighbouring perchlorate ions. In principle, values of the occupancy factors x_A and x_B for the two sets of positions can be derived from the X-ray diffraction data. With due allowance for unaccept-

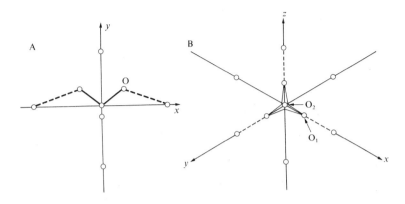

Fig.7.43. The two most probable orientations of the perchlorate ion in a face-centred cubic unit cell on the Strømme model (1974a).

able configurations (which must inevitably be made rather arbitrarily), the configurational entropy of the disordered lattice can be estimated. For ammonium perchlorate, for example, $x_A = 0·37$ and $x_B = 0·63$, and the calculated configurational entropy is $2·2R$ to $2·45R$, about the same as the experimental ΔS_t. For $KClO_4$, $x_A = 0·65$ and $x_B = 0·35$, and the calculated configurational entropy is $1·85R$ to $1·93R$, considerably less that ΔS_t. Conceivable reasons for a difference in this direction include the neglect of other sets of orientations, the possibility that movement of the metal ions may make some orientations more readily accessible, possible positional disorder in the high-temperature phase, and changes in the lattice vibrational spectrum at the transition. Strømme's treatment provides a plausible explanation of the relatively low ΔS_t for the III→II transition in $AgClO_4$, attributing it to the fact that the metal-oxygen distances in this salt are smaller than for the other perchlorates, so that a higher proportion of configurations derived from the A and B positions is rendered inaccessible.

The studies of Pistorius and his coworkers have led to the interesting discovery that forms of some of the fluoroborates and perchlorates exist which are probably still cubic ($Fm3m$), but substantially more disordered than the cubic phases we have already discussed. Some of these phases are capable of existing at atmospheric pressure, or apparently would do so were it not for thermal decomposition, and these phases we have designated as I. Some of the transition temperatures for the formation of these phases given in Table 7.11 were estimated by extrapolation of phase boundary lines on the p-T diagrams. $RbBF_4$ and KBF_4 have wholly high-pressure phases, labelled IV and III respectively, which are also probably examples of this further cubic modification. The entropy gain at the lower-cubic → higher-cubic transition may, on indirect evidence, be comparable with that at the transition producing the lower-cubic forms, so that the higher-cubic modifications may be considerably more disordered. Pistorius has suggested that they are comparable with the high-temperature phase I of NH_4Cl, with one Cl-O or B-F bond of each anion directed towards a metal ion and the anion then approaching rotation, or at least facile re-orientation, about this bond. Even these additional cubic phases may not represent the limit of disorder of which the fluoroborates are capable, since under pressure $RbBF_4$ has a modification V at still higher temperatures (Fig.7.44), and it is an interesting question how nearly the motion of the BF_4^- ion in this phase comes to free rotation. $CsBF_4$ probably has two high-temperature modifications V and VI which are still more disordered than I. We may add that Pistorius has pointed out that the phase diagrams for the perchlorates and tetrafluoroborates illustrate the empirical rule that in respect of their polymorphism, the effect of increased pressure is similar to that of increased cationic radius.

Unlike the borohydrides, the activation energies for anion reorientation in the potassium, rubidium, and caesium tetrafluoroborates run parallel to the transition temperatures in decreasing with increasing size of the cation (Table 7.12). An interesting point established by Huettner, Ragle, Sherk, Stengle, and Yeh (1968) is that the ^{19}F correlation time at the transition temperature is about the same for all the fluoroborates they studied, which included ND_4BF_4 and $NOBF_4$ as well as the salts listed in Table 7.11. The decreases in ^{19}F line-width and second moment take place

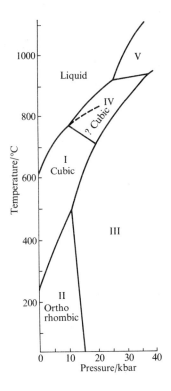

Fig.7.44. Phase diagram for $RbBF_4$ (Pistorius and Clark 1969).

a long way below the phase transitions, the second moment
for $NaBF_4$, for example, dropping between 230 K and 280 K.

An interesting perchlorate is Würster's blue perchlorate,
$[(CH_3)_2N-C_6H_4-N(CH_3)_2]^+ClO_4^-$, in which the cation is a
free radical. This has a partly gradual, partly isothermal
transition culminating at 190 K, for which Chihara, Nakamura,
and Seki (1965) found the entropy change to be $1 \cdot 1R$. There
is evidence that in the low-temperature form the cations
form dimers which have a singlet ground state and a triplet
excited state, and Chihara et al. suggested that the observed
entropy of transition may represent a combination of spin
disordering with orientational disordering of the perchlorate

ions. The structure of the salt $(C_6H_5)_3C^+ClO_4^-$, containing
carbonium cations, has been investigated at 85°C by Gomes
de Mesquita, MacGillavry, and Eriks (1965). It has a cubic
lattice ($F4_1 32$), in which there are two structurally different groups of perchlorate ions. Those of one group are
orientationally disordered, but not those of the other.

Anhydrous metal sulphates tend to be remarkably polymorphic. For example, including the phases formed under
pressure no less than eleven different forms of $ZnSO_4$ have
been reported (Pistorius 1961b), and eight of Na_2SO_4. A
valuable review of transitions in sulphates (and in other
salts with tetrahedral oxyanions) has been written by Prakash
and Rao (1975). While it is possible that some of the
high-temperature modifications of sulphates of divalent and
trivalent metals may involve orientational disorder of the
anion, at present relevant experimental information is somewhat fragmentary, partly no doubt because the necessary experiments must be performed at rather high temperatures.
We shall therefore confine ourselves to a brief discussion
of the anhydrous sulphates of univalent metals, perhaps the
most interesting of which is the lithium salt. This has a
high-temperature cubic phase which is undoubtedly highly disordered. Førland and Krogh-Moe (1957) consider that the
anions in this phase undergo 'strong rotational oscillations',
but in addition to this the lithium ions are positionally
disordered, as described in section 6.2. Sodium sulphate
has a surprisingly complex polymorphism, which has been
lucidly analysed by Brodale and Giauque (1972). It will be
noted that in Table 7.11 the transition which produces the
high-temperature form I is shown as proceeding from form IV.
This is because phase III is always metastable, as is the
phase II reported by Kracek and Ksanda (1930). The considerable entropy increase accompanying the formation of phase I
implies some disorder in this form. Potassium, rubidium,
caesium, and thallium (I) sulphates, as well as some of the
chromates of univalent metals, have an orthorhombic structure at room temperature, which changes to a hexagonal form
at higher temperatures. On passing along the series K_2SO_4 -
Rb_2SO_4 - Cs_2SO_4, the II→I transition temperature rises but

the entropy of transition appears to fall, though it may be
that entropy associated with the transition is gradually acquired over a range of temperature before the actual crystal
structure change occurs. Fischmeister (1962) surveyed the
relevant structural evidence on the sulphates of univalent
metals, and concluded that in the hexagonal phase I the sulphate ions are orientationally disordered. He noted that
while the volume available to the sulphate ion in this phase
is insufficient to permit its free rotation, the value of
this volume at the transition temperature is about the same
for all salts. He suggested that the orientational disorder
of the sulphate ions in the hexagonal phase takes the form
indicated in Fig.7.45. The orientation A and its mirror-

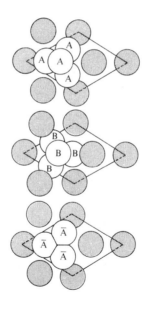

Fig.7.45. Possible orientations of the sulphate ion in the hexagonal
phase of sulphates such as Na_2SO_4-I. Open circles, oxygen atoms;
shaded circles, metal ions (Fischmeister 1962).

image $\bar{A}$ provide one pair of equal energy, and B and $\bar{B}$ a
second pair. The B positions require more space than the
A positions, so that the latter are energetically preferred,
but the possibility of two adjacent sulphate ions having

the orientations A and $\overline{A}$ can be ruled out on account of their
strong and unfavourable interaction when in this relationship. In other words, A and $\overline{A}$ positions can only be realized
if a B orientation intervenes. Accordingly, although there
are four orientational possibilities in all, the ions cannot
make full independent use of these, and moreover the relative number of ions in A orientations on the one hand and B
orientations on the other will depend on the temperature. It
is worth noting that sodium carbonate and sodium sulphate
in their high-temperature phases form an extensive series
of solid solutions, which can be supercooled to room temperature. On introducing Na_2CO_3 into Na_2SO_4-I, the carbonate ion presumably takes up a position with the carbon atom
on the three-fold axis and the plane of the ion normal to
this axis. Since the carbonate ion requires less room than
the sulphate ion, the c axis decreases considerably as the
carbonate content of the mixed crystals increases.

Attention has already been drawn to the fact that
fluoroberyllates and sulphates can have similar, though not
necessarily identical, structures (section 7.5.2). Li_2BeF_4,
which at room temperature is isotypic with Be_2SiO_4, has
been reported as undergoing two transitions (Table 7.11),
though the sum of the entropy changes of these is somewhat
less than the entropy gain at the II→I transition in
Li_2SO_4 (Levina, Kalitin, and Kalinnikov 1961). The thermal
properties of Li_2BeF_4 as reported by these authors seem
to be somewhat unusual, and deserve further investigation.
The potassium salt K_2BeF_4 exists in at least three modifications, and from the limited evidence available the
high-temperature form may be similar to K_2SO_4-I   (Levina
and Khromova 1963).

7.6. OCTAHEDRAL IONS
The salts with octahedral anions which are most likely to
display orientational disorder are those of the type $A^I M^V F_6$,
since the anion is relatively compact and carries only a
single charge which is dispersed over the six fluorine atoms,
so that the restriction on rotational movement attributable
to electrostatic interaction should be comparatively small.

Kemmitt, Russell, and D.W.A. Sharp (1963) have reviewed the structure of complex fluorides of this kind. Five varieties are encountered, two of which are rhombohedral, one tetragonal, and two cubic. One of the two cubic forms is based on a face-centred cubic unit cell, and is adopted by the hexafluorophosphates of potassium, thallium, rubidium, and caesium. The other derives from a primitive unit cell, and is the room-temperature structure of $NaPF_6$ as well as of the salts $NaMF_6$ where M = Re, Mo, W, Sb, Nb, and Ta. It may be that in $NaPF_6$ the six P-F bonds are directed towards the neighbouring sodium ions, whereas in the salts with larger cations these bonds are canted away from the cell edges. It will be seen from Table 7.13 that the activation energy for the reorientation of the anion in the alkali hexafluorophosphates decreases with increasing size of the cation. In the caesium salt the barrier to rotation is quite low, and the ^{19}F resonance line is still narrow at 77 K. These salts show interesting differences from one another and merit further investigation. The large entropy increase accompanying the II→I transition in KPF_6 suggests that the cubic phase I is highly disordered. The rubidium salt was found in both the calorimetric and NMR studies to show a dependence of its properties on thermal history which was unusually pronounced for such a comparatively simple substance.

More than one reference has been made in this chapter to the observation that the activation energy for reorientation as deduced from the change with temperature of the spin-lattice relaxation time T_1 can show an apparent increase as the substance is heated towards the peak of a gradual transition, and $RbPF_6$ provides another rather striking example of this. L. Niemelä, M. Niemelä, and Tuohi (1972) found that the apparent activation energy in kJ mol^{-1} was 1·6 from 63 K to 91 K, 2·1 from 92 K to 145 K, 4·0 from 146 K to 201 K, and no less than 12·6 in the last five degrees before T_λ (202 K to 207 K). At the upper transition in NH_4PF_6 and in ND_4PF_6 there is a discontinuity in the fluorine T_1, but little if any alteration in the proton or deuterium T_1, so that the transition is presumably associated with a change in the orientational behaviour of the PF_6^-

ions.

Comparison of $NaAsF_6$ with $NaPF_6$, and of $KAsF_6$ with KPF_6, shows that an increase in the size of the central atom in a molecule or ion, which therefore makes the latter less compact, leads to its reorientation in the lattice becoming less facile. The same effect can be seen, for example, in the comparison of ammonium and phosphonium salts (page 336) or in molecular crystals in the contrast between solid CCl_4 and solid $SiCl_4$ (page 514). Nevertheless, Andrew, Farnell, and Gledhill (1967) noted that the observed ^{19}F second moment of $1 \cdot 3$ G^2 for $KAsF_6$ at room temperature is considerably smaller than that calculated for the rigid lattice, being in reasonable agreement with the value of $1 \cdot 23$ G^2 estimated for rapid reorientation of the anions between the 24 equivalent orientations available to them. In salts containing doubly charged ions of the type MX_6^{2-} (X = halogen), the limited available evidence shows that, as expected, the reorientation of these ions is altogether more laborious, though there are indications from the NMR work that the anions in $(NH_4)_2SiF_6$, $(NH_4)_2SnCl_6$, and $(NH_4)_2SnBr_6$ are beginning to undergo reorientation, if rather slowly, above room temperature (Blinc and Lahajnar 1967, Strange and Terenzi 1972).

Potassium stannichloride [potassium hexachlorostannate (IV)], K_2SnCl_6, which has an antifluorite structure at room temperature, has a λ-type transition with an entropy change approximately equal to $R \ln 2$. This led Morfee, Staveley, Walters, and Wigley (1960) to suggest that it might be an order-disorder transition involving the orientation of the $SnCl_6^{2-}$ ions. Fig.7.46 shows the environment of this ion in an octant of the unit cell. For the simple antifluorite structure, $\theta = 0$. Attempts were made to estimate the change in potential energy as the anion is rotated about the axis AB. This estimate was bound to be uncertain, in view of the difficulty in assigning a value for the effective charge on the chlorine atoms and more particularly in evaluating the energy of repulsion between these atoms and the metal ions. However, the calculations indicated that according to the value of the parameters which determine the energies of

TABLE 7.13

Some thermal and structural properties of salts with octahedral anions. E is the activation energy (kJ mol^{-1}) for reorientation of the anion

Salt	Transitions: III ⟷ II ⟷ I (T_t/K, $\Delta S_t/R$)	E	Cal.	Cryst.	NMR
NaPF$_6$	II ⟷ 286^a(?F) ⟷ F.c.c. (I)	23(<170 K); 16·5(>287 K)	–	1,2	3,4
KPF$_6$	273·87(F),3·46 ⟷ F.c.c.	24(<213 K)	5	2,6,7	3,8
RbPF$_6$	II^b 207(λ), 1·22 ⟷ F.c.c.	6·7–8·8 (<145 K)	5	2	3,8
CsPF$_6$	89(?F) ⟷ F.c.c.	3·2(<56 K); 3·05(>90 K)	–	2,6,7	3,4
ND$_4$PF$_6$^{c}	III ⟷ 133^a ⟷ II; 194^a ⟷ I	23(<125 K); 17(142–194 K)	–	–	9
NaAsF$_6$	327·9^a ⟷ Rhombohedral, $R\bar{3}$,	35(<256 K); 20(316–500 K)	–	10	11
KAsF$_6$	391·7^a ⟷ Rhombohedral, $R\bar{3}m$ or $R\bar{3}$,		–	12	11,13
(ND$_4$)$_2$GeF$_6$		56(>300 K)	–	–	14
K$_2$SnCl$_6$	262·1(λ),0·57 ⟷ F.c.c.; Cubic ⟷ 103·4(λ),~0·61 ⟷ Cubic ⟷ 76·05(λ),~0·61 (III) Cubic, $Pn\bar{3}$?$Pn3m$		15	16	–
K$_2$ReCl$_6$	110·9(λ),~0·61 ⟷ Cubic, $Fm3m$, Cubic; (IV)^d 76·05(λ),~0·61 (III) Cubic		17	18	–

$(NH_4)_2SbBr_6$	$\xleftrightarrow{212(\lambda),0.34}$	$\xleftrightarrow{236(\lambda),0.35}$ Tetragonal,$I4_1amd$	19	20	-
Rb_2SbBr_6	$\xleftrightarrow{220(\lambda),\sim0.35}$	$\xleftrightarrow{230(\lambda),\sim0.35}$	21	-	-

a. Temperatures of discontinuities in spin-lattice relaxation time T_1.

b. According to Niemelä et al., there are anomalous changes in T_1 in phase II of this salt, with hysteresis, between 215 K and 255 K.

c. See Tables 7.6 and 7.7 for NH_4PF_6.

d. Form IV undergoes a further λ-type magnetic transition at 11·9 K to give a cubic, anti-ferromagnetic phase with an entropy loss of $\sim R\ln 4$.

Footnotes continued on facing page.

Footnotes to Table 7.13.

REFERENCES

1.   Bode and Teufer (1952).
2.   Cox (1956).
3.   Miller and Gutowsky (1963) (^{19}F, SM).
4.   L. Niemelä and Komu (1973) (^{19}F, T_1).
5.   Staveley, Grey, and Layzell (1963).
6.   Bode and Clausen (1951).
7.   Seifert (1931).
8.   L.Niemelä, M.Niemelä, and Tuohi (1972) (^{19}F, T_1).
9.   L.Niemelä and Tuohi (1970) (D and ^{19}F, T_1).
10.   Kemmitt, Russell, and D.W.A. Sharp (1963).
11.   L.Niemelä (1973) (^{19}F, T_1).
12.   Ibers (1956); Roof (1955).
13.   Andrew, Farnell, and Gledhill (1967) (^{19}F, SM).
14.   Tuohi, Ylinen, and L.Niemelä (1974) (D and ^{19}F, T_1).
15.   Morfee, Staveley, Walters, and Wigley, (1960).
16.   R.G.Dickinson (1922a); Engel (1935).
17.   Busey, Dearman, and Bevan (1962).
18.   Aminoff (1936); H.G. Smith and Bacon (1966).
19.   Lerbscher and Wulff (1970).
20.   Lawton and Jacobson (1966).
21.   S.H.Lee and Wulff (1974).

attraction and repulsion, the minimum potential energy of the
anion on rotation about the AB axis might either fall at $\theta = 0°$,
or alternatively there could be two minima. It was shown that
with parameters which appeared to be reasonable for K_2SnCl_6
the latter situation would obtain, with θ values for the
minima of $\pm 20°$, but that the single minimum at $\theta = 0°$ would
then be more likely for the salts K_2SnBr_6 and Rb_2SnCl_6, which
do in fact lack the transition shown by K_2SnCl_6. The compounds $(NH_4)_2SbBr_6$ and Rb_2SbBr_6 are particularly interesting,
since each contains equal numbers of the two anions $Sb^{III}Br_6^{3-}$
and $Sb^VBr_6^-$. The former ion is octahedral (O_h symmetry), while
the latter is distorted with D_{2h} symmetry. Each salt has two

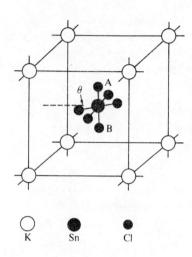

Fig.7.46. An octant of the unit cell of K_2SnCl_6, showing the environment of the $SnCl_6^{2-}$ ion (Morfee *et al.* 1960).

λ-transitions, the combined entropy change of which is approximately $R \ln 2$. This is divided roughly equally between the two transitions. Since the rubidium salt is very similar to the ammonium salt it is probable that the transitions in the latter are not directly related to the rotational state of the ammonium ions, but rather concern the anions. Wulff and his coworkers have interpreted the transitions in $(NH_4)_2SbBr_6$ and Rb_2SbBr_6 on the same basis as that suggested for K_2SnCl_6, namely that in the disordered room-temperature condition each anion makes use of two distinguishable orientations, and they suggest that this disorder is acquired in two stages, first for one type of anion and then at a slightly higher temperature for the other (Lerbscher and Wulff 1970, S.H. Lee and Wulff 1974).

The salt K_2ReCl_6 has no less than three cooperative transitions (in addition to a lower magnetic transition). Busey, Dearman, and Bevan (1962) estimated that the combined entropy change of the three transitions is $1 \cdot 83R$, and suggested that this could be averaged out at $\sim R \ln 2$ for each transition. The structure remains basically cubic down to helium temperatures. It may be noted that in some salts

of the type $A_2^I M^{IV} X_6$, where X = halogen, the structure is distorted from that of the prototype K_2PtCl_6 to allow a more
efficient packing of the large anions. Such structures may
then transform at higher temperatures to the cubic form
(I.D. Brown 1964).

Octahedral ions with a triple charge occur in such
salts as Na_3AlF_6, K_3AlF_6, $(NH_4)_3AlF_6$, and $(NH_4)_3FeF_6$. All
four compounds exist in more than one modification. The
sodium salt, monoclinic at room temperature, changes to a
cubic $Fm3m$ structure at ~820 K, while the potassium salt,
tetragonal at ordinary temperatures, becomes cubic at
~570 K. The ammonium salts are already cubic at room temperature, but on cooling transform to forms which are probably
tetragonal (Steward and Rooksby 1953). The salt Li_3AlF_6
exists in five different forms. On heating, it transforms at
~870 K into a cubic phase II which undergoes a further transition at 978 K into a form I. There are indications that
phase I, at least, is disordered (Holm 1966, Greene, Gross,
and Hayman 1968).

In the salt $(NH_4)_3ZrF_7$, it appears that both cations and
anions are involved in orientational disorder. The anion
is not, of course, octahedral, containing as it does a zir-
conium atom with the somewhat unusual coordination number of
seven. Hampson and Pauling (1938) considered that it is a
distorted octahedron with the seventh fluorine atom at the
centre of one of the faces, and that the threefold axis of
the anion is parallel to any one of the eight [111] directions, giving the ion 16 accessible orientations. Zachariasen
(1954), however, while agreeing that the anion ZrF_7^{3-} is orientationally disordered, proposed a pentagonal bipyramidal
structure for it similar to that of the ion UF_7^{3-}, which he
concluded was disordered among 24 possible orientations in
the salt K_3UF_7. Another anion involving 7-coordination which
appears to be disordered is that in the salt K_3NbOF_6
(Williams and Hoard 1942). The proton and ^{19}F second moments
for the salt $(NH_4)_3ZrF_7$ both fall between 100 K and 290 K to
values which indicate that cations as well as anions undergo
rapid reorientation at room temperature (Lahajnar, Pintar,
and Slivnik 1966).

In salts of the type $MSiF_6.6H_2O$ both cations and anions
are octahedral. At room temperature (or above ~25°C for the
magnesium compound), the salts have slightly distorted
caesium chloride structures in which there is some disorder.
(The copper salt is an exception, having an ordered lattice).
The SiF_6^{2-} ions prove to be regular octahedra, or very nearly
so, but there can be some distortion of the $M(H_2O)_6^{2+}$ ions.
Ray, Zalkin, and Templeton (1973) carried out single crystal
X-ray diffraction studies on the compounds with M = Co, Ni,
and Zn which led them to conclude that the space group is $R\bar{3}$
and that there are two possible orientations for the SiF_6^{2-}
ions, about 30° apart with respect to rotation about the
threefold axis. The two positions are not equally occupied,
and an unusual feature is that they are not related by any
symmetry element. Hamilton (1962) interpreted his neutron
diffraction results on a single crystal of $FeSiF_6.6H_2O$ as
showing that the space group is $R\bar{3}m$, and that both the
cations and anions are involved in disorder, each cation
having two orientations differing by rotation of 18° about
the threefold axis, and each SiF_6^{2-} ion having two positions
with a corresponding angle of 54°. Jehanno and Varret
(1975), however, in an X-ray examination of this salt and
also of those with M = Mg and Zn, reported finding reflections
inconsistent with the space group $R\bar{3}m$, and suggested that the
disorder in the high-temperature form might be dynamic. Some
of these salts on cooling show the expected transition to an
ordered phase, which appears to be monoclinic, space group
$P2_1/c$ (Syoyama and Osaki 1972). The transitions themselves
have not so far been investigated in detail. From H and ^{19}F
line-width studies on the compounds with M = Mn, Fe, Co, Ni,
Cu, and Zn, Skjaeveland and Svare (1974) demonstrated that
reorientation of the SiF_6^{2-} ion is generally easier than that
of the $M(H_2O)_6^{2+}$ ion, the only exception being the manganese
salt, for which the two ions seem to be on an equal footing
in this respect. For the cobalt compound, for example, the
proton line-width narrows at ~340 K and the estimate of the
barrier to rotation of the $Co(H_2O)_6^{2+}$ ion is 52 kJ mol^{-1}.
The corresponding quantities for the ^{19}F resonance and the
SiF_6^{2-} ion are ~200 K and 31 kJ mol^{-1} respectively. Values of

about the same magnitude for the activation energies for
reorientation of the cations and anions in the zinc and
magnesium salts were obtained by Jannek and Rager (1975)
from proton and ^{19}F T_1 measurements.

Octahedral cations are also to be found in the coordination compounds of transition metals. One salt which
has been particularly carefully studied is hexaamminenickel
iodide $Ni(NH_3)_6I_2$. This compound has a λ-transition culminating at 19·78 K, which is probably associated with the
mutual arrangement of the six ammonia molecules within a
cation. At a much lower temperature (~0·3 K) it shows the
expected magnetic transition to an antiferromagnetically
ordered state with an entropy change of $R \ln 3$. There is
also another large thermal anomaly, a Schottky effect with
its heat capacity maximum at about the same temperature as
the magnetic transition (Van Kempen, Duffy, Miedema, and Huiskamp 1964, Klaaijsen, Suga, and Dokoupil 1971). This
occurs because each ammonia molecule is librating in a potential well in the lowest possible energy level, and owing
to quantum-mechanical tunnelling the eightfold degeneracy
of the level is lifted, apparently to give two levels each
fourfold degenerate (Fig.7.47). At sufficiently low temperatures the upper level is vacated, so that each ammonia molecule loses entropy of $R \ln 2$. The loss of entropy per mole
of salt on this account is therefore $6R \ln 2$, which added
to the magnetic entropy loss of $R \ln 3$ gives a total decrease
of $5.26R$. The experimental figure is $5·3R$. On account of
the smaller tunnelling ability of the deuteron, the separation of the two fourfold degenerate levels is less in the
salt $Ni(ND_3)_6I_2$, so the Schottky anomaly must fall at a
lower temperature. In fact, only the magnetic transition is
observed for this salt, although the slight upturn of the
heat capacity at the very lowest temperatures may indicate
the high-temperature tail of the Schottky anomaly (Fig.7.48;
Van Kempen, Garofano, Miedema, and Huiskamp 1965).

Accordingly, above the λ-transition at ~20 K, hexaammine nickel iodide may be said to be disordered in three
different ways. Bates and Stevens (1969) carried out an
elaborate investigation based on a point-charge electrostatic

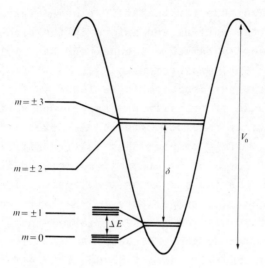

Fig.7.47 Schematic diagram of the energy levels of an NH_3 group in an $Ni(NH_3)_6^{2+}$ ion. δ is the energy difference between the two lowest librational states. The eightfold degenerate ground state is split by tunnelling into two quartets separated by ΔE. giving rise to the Schottky anomaly (after Van Kempen *et al*. 1965).

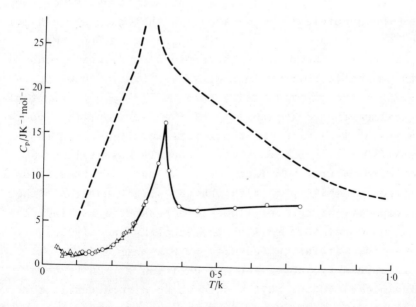

Fig.7.48. Heat capacity C_p of $Ni(ND_3)_6I_2$ (full curve) and of $Ni(NH_3)_6I_2$ (dashed curve) *vs*. temperature (Van Kempen *et al*. 1965).

model of the interaction between the ammonia molecules in
this salt, both within the same cation and between molecules
in nearest-neighbour cations, which must be one of the most
detailed of its kind yet undertaken. They suggested that
there may be 16 possible arrangements of the ammonia molecules within a cation which correspond to approximately equal
potential energy minima. If passage through the λ-transi-
tion at ~20 K on cooling means a change from a high-temperature disordered condition in which sixteen configurations
are fully utilized to a low-temperature ordered form of just
one configuration for each cation, the entropy loss should
be $R \ln 16$. In fact, Worswick, Cowell, and Staveley (1974)
found this entropy loss to be $9 \cdot 83$ J K^{-1} mol^{-1}, slightly
greater than $R \ln 3$. Moreover, they compared the apparent
calorimetric entropy $S(\text{cal})$ of $Ni(NH_3)_6I_2$ with the value
of $S(\text{eq})$ obtained from an equilibrium study. (This involved
studying the equilibrium between the hexaammine, ammonia,
and the diammine, and also that between the diammine, ammonia,
and NiI_2). Within experimental error, $S(\text{cal})$ and $S(\text{eq})$ were
equal, so that the hexaammine is approaching perfect order
at 0 K. (The same was found to be true of the diammine,
$Ni(NH_3)_2I_2$.) Klaaijsen, Suga, and Dokoupil (1971) have also
measured the heat capacities of the salts $M(NH_3)_6I_2$, where
M = Co, Mn, Zn, Cd, and Ca. All show λ-type transitions
(Fig.7.49), and as the series is traversed in the order
given, the transition temperature rises, the transition
broadens, and the accompanying entropy change ΔS_t increases,
reaching for the calcium compound the considerable value of
$29 \cdot 8$ J K^{-1} mol^{-1}, ($cf.$ $R \ln 32 = 28 \cdot 8$ J K^{-1} mol^{-1}). Nickel
hexaammine bromide and chloride also have λ-transitions, with
the heat capacity reaching its maximum at ~35 K and ~83 K
respectively (Matsuo, Suga, and Seki 1971; S.J.Smith, Bunting,
and Steeple 1974). The cobalt (II) complex $Co(NH_3)_6Cl_2$ has
a transition between 93 K and 99 K with $\Delta S_t \approx 35$ J K^{-1} mol^{-1},
$\approx R \ln 64$ (Matsuo, Tatsumi, Suga, and Seki 1973). Murray
and Waugh (1958) carried out proton and ^{19}F line-width and
second moment studies from 90 K to 400 K on the salts
$Co(NH_3)X_3$, with X = Cl, Br, I, NO_3, BF_4, and PF_6. The proton
second moments at 90 K are such that the ammonia molecules

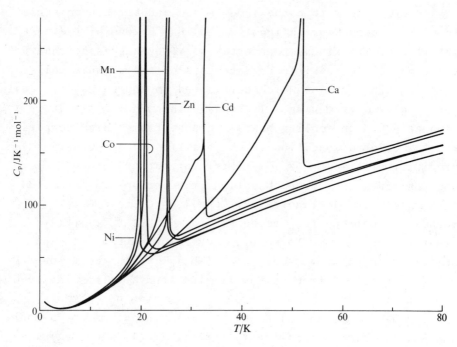

Fig.7.49. Heat capacity C_p of $X(NH_3)_6I_2$ vs. temperature for X = Ni, Co, Mn, Zn, Cd, and Ca (Klaaijsen, Suga, and Dokoupil 1971).

must be rapidly reorienting about the C-N axes. The first four salts then show a very broad line-width transition extending over about 200 K (that in the tetrafluoroborate is narrower) and at 300 K the octahedral cations are undergoing rapid tumbling - a condition already achieved by the BF_4^- and PF_6^- ions at 90 K. The results so far obtained on hexaammine salts should excite curiosity about the order-disorder phenomena which await discovery in the enormous number of coordination compounds and organometallic substances still to be investigated.

Electrically neutral octahedral entities are to be found in the solid compounds which can be crystallized from solutions of metals in liquid ammonia. Parker and Kaplan (1973) examined the Mössbauer spectrum of the europous compound $Eu(NH_3)_6$, and found a line-width decrease between 67 K and 77 K which might be the result of a phase change associated with hindered rotation of the ammonia molecules.

A salt containing both tetrahedral and octahedral ions
is phosphorus pentachloride, $[PCl_4^+][PCl_6^-]$. This substance
has a higher order transition with $\Delta S_t = 0 \cdot 20R$. The 'extra'
heat capacity reaches its maximum of $9 \cdot 1$ J K^{-1} mol^{-1} at 102 K,
and there is a high-temperature tail persisting to $\sim$ 110 K.
(Chihara, M. Nakamura, and Masukane 1973). Four ^{35}Cl
nuclear quadrupole resonance frequencies are observed in
phase I, and ten in phase II (Chihara and N.Nakamura 1973).
Chihara, M.Nakamura, and Masukane were able to account for
both the heat capacity and NQR results on a soft mode interpretation (Chihara, N.Nakamura, and Tachiki 1971), the transition being attributed to a change in the orientation of the
PCl_6^- ions in the lattice due to an anharmonic coupling between librational modes, which were represented by Einstein
functions. As the temperature rises, the tilt of the anions
changes, with an increase in potential energy, but simultaneously the librational frequencies of the Einstein modes
fall, and the entropy of the crystal accordingly rises.

7.7. SALTS WITH A FERROELECTRIC OR ANTIFERROELECTRIC PHASE

We shall end this chapter with a discussion of various salts
which show transitions to a disordered phase from an ordered
form which is either ferroelectric or antiferroelectric.
Examples of such salts have already been encountered earlier
in this chapter, and others will be found among the salt hydrates discussed in section 8.4. We shall not concern ourselves in any detail with the electrical, optical, elastic,
or related properties of ferroelectric and antiferroelectric
crystals. Good accounts of these will be found in such mono-
graphs as those of Jona and Shirane (1962) and Fatuzzo and
Merz (1967). Some relevant general information has, however,
already been presented in section 2.6. A valuable source
of factual material is the Landolt-Börnstein volume *Ferroelectric and Antiferroelectric Substances*, Group III (1969),
and a useful supplement to this is the article by Subbarao
(1973).

Thermal and structural information about the salts we
have selected for discussion is presented in the usual form
in Table 7.14. The letters P, F, and A stand for paraelectric,

ferroelectric and antiferroelectric respectively. Also shown
is the symbolism which is now in more or less common use for
many of these compounds. (We represent the deuterated form
of KDP, namely KD_2PO_4, by DKDP, although this is sometimes
indicated by KD*P or $KD^{\dagger}P$.) About half of the salts in
Table 7.14 are alkali dihydrogenphosphates and arsenates,
on which a great deal of experimental and theoretical work
has been carried out, especially on KDP itself - so much so
that our attempt to summarize this must necessarily omit much
of interest and importance. In Table 7.14 we have classified
the transitions in the phosphates and arsenates as being
first-order, since for all of them part of the transition is
discontinuous. This has been established, for example for
KDP, by careful measurements of heat capacity, of lattice
parameters (such as those of J. Kobayashi, Uesu, and Enomoto
1971), and by permittivity determinations, which show a discontinuous change in this property and also disclose hysteresis (e.g. Blinc, Burgar, and Levstik 1973). Further evidence
for a first-order stage in the KDP transition was supplied
by Vallade (1975) from an investigation of the SHG (second
harmonic generation, p. 324). and of the birefringence in the
neighbourhood of the transition. In fact, the transitions
in these salts in general qualify for the description we have
so often used of being partly gradual and partly isothermal,
and for some of them considerable trouble has been taken to
quantify this, for example to establish how much of the enthalpy gain at the transition is actually taken in as latent
heat. Thus, Reese (1969) concluded that whereas for KDP
only 10-12 % of the total entropy of transition is acquired
in the discontinuous stage, for DKDP the corresponding figure
is ~44 %, so for the deuterated salt the first-order component of the transition is much more prominent. When a
sufficiently large bias field (of the order of 10 kV cm^{-1})
is applied to the c faces of a KDP crystal the transition
becomes wholly gradual, as may be seen from Fig.4.7 (Kobayashi, Uesu, and Enomoto 1971; Eberhard and Horn 1975). This
is in agreement with the result found by Lieb for the two-
dimensional Slater KDP model (section 3.7).

    These phosphates and arsenates show some of the most

TABLE 7.14

Some structural and thermal information on salts with a ferroelectric or antiferroelectric ordered phase

Salt	Abbreviation	II $\xrightarrow{\;\;T_c/K,\; \Delta S_t/R\;\;}$ I	References Cal.	Cryst.	NMR
KH_2PO_4	KDP	F $\xrightarrow{121.71(F),\ 0.40}$ P Orthorhombic, $Fdd2$ — Tetragonal, $I\bar{4}2d$	1–3	4–7	8
KD_2PO_4	DKDP	F $\xrightarrow{219.62(F),\ 0.457}$ P	1,3	6,7,9	10,11
RbH_2PO_4	RDP	F $\xrightarrow{146.8(F),\ 0.36}$ P	12,13	–	–
RbD_2PO_4	DRDP	F $\xrightarrow{223^a(F),\ 0.39}$ P	13	–	–
CsH_2PO_4	CDP	F $\xrightarrow{159}$ P	–	7	–
$NH_4H_2PO_4$	ADP	A $\xrightarrow{147.9(F),\ 0.53}$ P Orthorhombic, $P2_12_12_1$ — Tetragonal, $I\bar{4}2d$	14,15	7,16,17	8,18
$ND_4D_2PO_4$	DADP	A $\xrightarrow{237.6(F),\ 0.37}$ P	15	17,65	18,19
KH_2AsO_4	KDA	F $\xrightarrow{96.15(F),\ 0.506}$ P Orthorhombic, $Fdd2$ — Tetragonal, $I\bar{4}2d$	1,20,21	5,7,22	8,62,63
KD_2AsO_4	DKDA	F $\xrightarrow{161.02(F),\ 0.500}$ P	21	5,7,22	–
RbH_2AsO_4	RDA	F $\xrightarrow{109.75(F),\ 0.50}$ P	23	7	63
CsH_2AsO_4	CDA	F $\xrightarrow{145.4(F),\ 0.45^b}$ P	24,25	7	–
CsD_2AsO_4	DCDA	F $\xrightarrow{190.2^c(F),\ 0.54}$ P	24	26	11

Compound	Abbrev.	Phase transition	Refs.
$NH_4H_2AsO_4$	ADA	Orthorhombic $P2_12_12_1$ $\xleftarrow{A}$ 216·1(F), 0·54 $\xrightarrow{P}$ Tetragonal, $I\bar{4}2d$	27 7,28 8,11, 29-31
$ND_4D_2AsO_4$	DADA	$\xleftarrow{A}$ 298·6 $\xrightarrow{P}$	– – 31
$Ag_2H_3IO_6$		$P\bar{1}$ $\xleftarrow{A}$ 227·25(λ), 0·81 $\xrightarrow{P}$ Hexagonal, $R\bar{3}$	32-34 34,35 36,37
$(NH_4)_2H_3IO_6$		Hexagonal, $R3$ $\xleftarrow{A}$ 246-255^d(F), 0·7 $\xrightarrow{P}$ Hexagonal, $R\bar{3}$	32,34 34,38 36
$NaH_3(SeO_3)_2$	STS	Triclinic, $P1$ $\xleftarrow{F}$ 194(F), 0·52 $\xrightarrow{P}$ Monoclinic, $P2$	39,59 40,41 42
$NaD_3(SeO_3)_2$	DSTS	Monoclinic, Pm $\xleftarrow{F}$ 270(F), 0·80 $\xrightarrow{P}$ Monoclinic, $P2_1/n$	39 – 43
$CsH_3(SeO_3)_2$		Triclinic, $P\bar{1}$ $\xleftarrow{A}$ 145(F), 0·41 $\xrightarrow{P}$ Triclinic, $P\bar{1}$	44 44,45 64
$(NH_2CH_2COOH)_3H_2SO_4$	TGS	Monoclinic, $P2_1$ $\xleftarrow{F}$ 332(λ), 0·55 $\xrightarrow{P}$ Monoclinic, $P2_1/m$	46,47 48,49 50,51
$(NH_2CH_2COOH)_3H_2BeF_4$		Monoclinic, $P2_1$ $\xleftarrow{F}$ 348(λ), 0·59 $\xrightarrow{P}$ Monoclinic, $P2_1/m$	46 49 51,52
$BaCa_2(CH_3CH_2COO)_6$		$\xleftarrow{F}$ 266·9(F), 3·25 $\xrightarrow{}$ Cubic, $F4_13$	53 54 –

Table 7.14 continued

$PbCa_2(CH_3CH_2COO)_6$

Tetragonal (II)F $\xleftarrow{\sim 333(\lambda)^e}$ P   55   56   –

III $\xrightarrow{191\cdot5\ (F),\ 2\cdot93}$ (II)

$SrCa_2(CH_3CH_2COO)_6$ DCSP

(II)F $\xrightarrow{282\cdot6(\lambda),\ 0.31}$ P   55   57   58

Tetragonal, 3 or $P4_1$ or   Tetragonal, $P4_12_12$ or $P4_32_12$

$P4_2$ or $P4_1$

III $\xleftarrow{104(F),\ 1\cdot6}$ (II)

$CH_3NH_3Al(SO_4)_2\cdot12H_2O$ ·MASD

F $\xleftrightarrow{177(?F),\ 0\cdot5}$ P   59   60   61

Monoclinic, $P2_1$ Cubic, $P2_13$

III

a. This transition temperature and entropy change refer to a salt of composition $Rb(D_{0\cdot8}H_{0\cdot2})_2PO_4$. The fully deuterated compound would probably form a non-ferroelectric, monoclinic modification.

b. Deutsch and Litov (1974) record a higher value of $\Delta S_t/R$ of 0.53.

c. A higher value of 212·4 K for this transition temperature was obtained by Stephenson, Corbella, and Russell (1953) from a cooling curve.

d. This is the range of 'anomalous' heat capacity, in which C_p has two peaks.

e. From permittivity measurements (Ferroni and Orioli 1959, Gesi and Ozawa 1975).

Footnotes to Table 7.14.

REFERENCES

1. Bantle (1942).

2. Stephenson and Hooley (1944); Danner and Pepinsky (1955); Garber and Smolenko (1973).

3. Reese (1969); Reese and May (1968) (DKDP); Strukov, Amin, and Koptsik (1968).

4. (X-ray) J.West (1930); de Quervain (1944); Frazer and Pepinsky (1953); J.Kobayashi, Uesu, Mizutani, and Enomoto (1970); J.Kobayashi, Uesu, and Enomoto (1971). (Neutron diffraction) Bacon and Pease (1953, 1955); Peterson, Levy, and Simonsen (1953); Levy, Peterson, and Simonsen (1954).

5. Ubbelohde and Woodward (1947).

6. Ubbelohde (1939).

7. Cook (1967).

8. Newman (1950) (LW, T_1).

9. Nakano, Shiozaki, and E.Nakamura (1974); Nelmes (1972); Thornley, Nelmes, and Rouse (1975) (neutron).

10. Bjorkstam and Uehling (1959) (T_1); Schmidt and Uehling (1962).

11. Blinc, Mali, Osredkar, Parker, Seliger, and Zumer (1973).

12. Amin and Strukov (1968).

13. Strukov, Baddur, Zinenko, Mishchenko, and Koptsik (1973).

14. Stephenson and Zettlemoyer (1944b).

15. Amin and Strukov (1970).

16. Keeling and Pepinsky (1955); Tenzer, Frazer, and Pepinsky (1958) (neutron).

17. Ubbelohde and Woodward (1942); Deshpande and Khan (1963).

18. Chiba (1965).

19. Chiba (1964); Blinc, Slak, and Zupančič (1974).

20. Stephenson and Zettlemoyer (1944a).

21. Fairall and Reese (1972); Knispel, Petch, and Pintar (1975).

22. Dickson and Ubbelohde (1950).

23. Fairall and Reese (1974).

24. Strukov, Baddur, Zinenko, Mikhailov, and Koptsik (1973).

25. Deutsch and Litov (1974).

26. Dietrich, Cowley, and Shapiro (1974) (neutron scattering).

27. Stephenson and Adams (1944a).

28. Delain (1958).

29. Grosescu (1973) (T_1, $T_{1\rho}$).

References to Table 7.14 continued.....

30. Bjorkstam (1970) (^{75}As).

31. Dalal, McDowell, and Srinivasan (1974) (T_1. Also ESR, ADA and DADA).

32. Baertschi (1945).

32. Stephenson and Adams (1944b).

34. Roos, Kind, and Petzelt (1976).

35. Gränicher, Meier, and Petter (1954).

36. Blinc (1959) (LW).

37. Roos and Kind (1974) (^{127}I).

38. Busch, Känzig, and Meier (1953); Aboav, Gränicher, and Petter (1955) (D salt); Gränicher, Kind, Meier, and Petter (1968).

39. Makita and Miki (1970).

40. Pepinsky, Vedam, Okaya, and Unterleitner (1959); Vijayan (1968); Miki (1973).

41. Shuvalov and Ivanov (1967).

42. Blinc and Pintar (1961); Blinc, Levstik, Stepisnik, Trontelj, and Zupančič (1968) (T_1, H, D, ^{23}Na); Adriaenssens (1974) (T_1, H); Stepisnik *et al.* (1973) (D, partially deuterated samples).

43. Soda and Chiba (1969).

44. Makita (1965).

45. Tellgren and Liminga (1974).

46. S.Hoshino, Mitsui, Jona, and Pepinsky (1957).

47. Tello and Gonzalo (1970); Strukov (1964); Reese and May (1972).

48. Wood and Holden (1957); S.Hoshino, Okaya, and Pepinsky (1959); K.Itoh and Mitsui (1973); Kay and Kleinberg (1973).

49. Pepinsky, Okaya, and Jona (1957).

50. R.Hoshino (1962) (SM); Blinc, Pintar, and Zupančič (1967) (D); Bjorkstam (1967) (D); Blinc, Mali, Osredkar, Prelesnik, Zupančič, and Ehrenberg (1971) (H, N double resonance).

51. Blinc, Lahajnar, Pintar, and Zupančič (1966) (T_1).

52. Blinc, and Zupančič (1963) (^{19}F, LW, SM).

53. Seki, Momotani, and Nakatsu (1951); Seki, Momotani, Nakatsu, and Oshima (1955).

54. Nitta and Watanabe (1935); Biefeld and Harris (1935).

55. N. Nakamura, Suga, Chihara, and Seki (1965).

56. Ferroni and Orioli (1959). Yamada, quoted in Ref. 55.

57. Orioli and Pieroni (1959); J.Kobayashi and Yamada (1962); Maruyama, Tomiie, Mizutani, Yamazaki, Uesu, Yamada, and J.Kobayashi (1967); Mizutani, Yamazaki, Uesu, Yamada, J.Kobayashi, Maruyama, and Tomiie (1967).

58. E.Nakamura, Hikichi, and Furuichi (1967) (SM).

59. Makita (1964).

60.   Jona, Mitsui , and Pepinsky, cited by Jona and Shirane (1962);
      Okaya, Ahmed, Pepinsky, and Vand (1957).

61.   R. Hoshino (1961).

62.   Adriaenssens (1975) (^{75}As).

63.   Blinc and Bjorkstam (1969) (^{75}As).

64.   Silvidi and Workman (1974) (LW, T_1).

65.   Wood, Merz, and Mathias (1952).

remarkable of all known isotope effects, the transition
temperature T_c rising in some cases by nearly 100 K on deuteration. Indeed, the substitution of hydrogen by deuterium
may even apparently produce changes in kind and not just in
degree. Thus, the data in Table 7.14 for DKDP relating to
phase I are for samples in which this phase is tetragonal
and isomorphous with KDP-I, but if the D/(D+H) ratio exceeds
0·98, the salt crystallizes at room temperature in a monoclinic ($P2_1$) and not a tetragonal form (Nelmes 1972, Nelmes
and Rouse 1974, Thornley, Nelmes, and Rouse 1975; see also
the footnote to Table 7.14 relating to DRDP). KDP itself
does in fact transform from its room-temperature tetragonal
modification into a monoclinic phase ($P2_1$ or $P2_1/m$) at
~460 K (K. Itoh, Matsubayashi, E. Nakamura, and Motegi (1975).
(We have nevertheless designated the tetragonal form as I,
for conformity with the considerable literature on this
salt.)

In the system $KH_{2(1-x)}D_{2x}PO_4$, T_c for the transition from
the ferroelectric to the paraelectric phase I does *not* rise
linearly with x. An interesting difference between KDP and
DKDP is that in the latter, and also in the deuterium-rich
mixed crystals, there is an 'excess' heat capacity above
the II→I transition which is not found for KDP itself (Strukov,
Baddur, Koptsik, and Velichko 1972). Evidence for the persistence of some order in the paraelectric phase of the
arsenate KDA just above the transition has been adduced by
Adriaenssens (1975), who ascribed additional lines in the
^{75}As NMR spectrum of the salt in this region to polarized
clusters with a life-time of ~10^{-3}s.

An important structural feature of the ordered phase of
KDP, highly relevant to its ferroelectric character, is that

when the paraelectric disordered form is cooled through the
transition, the potassium ions and phosphorus atoms are displaced relative to the oxygen framework by a few thousandths
nm in opposite directions along the z axis, which is the
polar axis in the ferroelectric phase.

In 1941, Slater published a paper on the transition in
KDP which has had an important influence on much of the later
theoretical work. He regarded the transition as presenting
an order-disorder problem in the disposition of the protons
in the hydrogen bonds which link the phosphate ions. The
essential features of his model have already been stated in
section 3.7. The belief that the protons are ordered in the
ferroelectric phase was later elegantly confirmed by the
neutron diffraction work of Bacon and Pease (1953) and of
Levy, S.W.Peterson, and Simonsen (1954). Several modifications and extensions of Slater's original theory have been
proposed, and we shall summarize a version put forward by
Silsbee, Uehling, and Schmidt (1964) which is a modified
mean-field treatment of the Slater model embodying most of
these developments. Fig.7.50 represents the structure of
KDP. There are chains of alternating potassium and phosphate
ions along the z axis, any one chain being displaced by $c/4$
with respect to the adjacent chain. Any one hydrogen bond
connects an O atom at the *top* of a given phosphate ion with
an O atom at the *bottom* of a neighbouring ion, or *vice versa*.
Within $0 \cdot 5°$, these hydrogen bonds lie in the xy plane. Slater
himself considered only those arrangements of the protons
which preserve the unit $H_2PO_4^-$. Since the proton in any one
hydrogen bond must occupy one of two off-centre positions,
this means that any phosphate ion can only have two 'near'
protons. This can be realized in six ways. Calling a bond
in which the hydrogen is near an oxygen atom at the top of
a particular PO_4 unit a + bond, and one in which it is near
an oxygen atom at the bottom of the PO_4 unit a - bond, the
six possibilities which give an $H_2PO_4^-$ ion are (1) two + bonds
(one possibility), (2) two - bonds (one possibility), and
(3) one + and one - (four possibilities). These are shown
in Fig.7.51. The ion $H_2PO_4^-$ is polar, and in configurations
(1) and (2) has a dipole moment in the z direction (but in

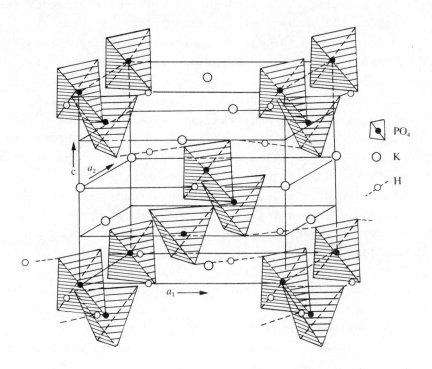

Fig.7.50. Structure of KH_2PO_4 (Slater 1941).

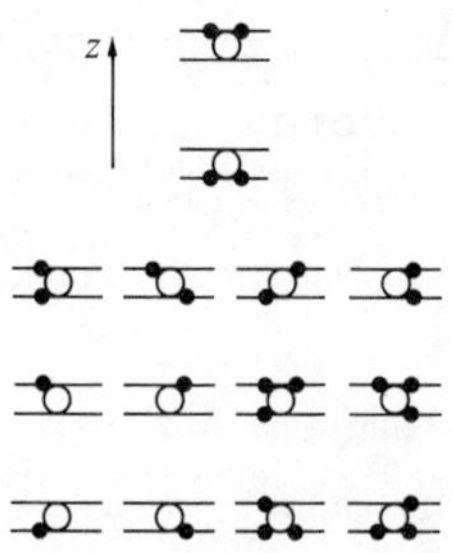

Configuration	Energy	Moment	Fractional population
	0	μ_0	x_2
	0	$-\mu_0$	x_{-2}
	ε_0	0	x_0 each
	ε_1	$\mu_0/2$	x_1 each
	ε_1	$-\mu_0/2$	x_{-1} each

Fig.7.51. Possible arrangements of a PO_4^{3-} ion (central open circles) and of a close proton (small filled circles) which produce the units $H_2PO_4^-$, HPO_4^{2-}, and H_3PO_4 (after Silsbee, Uehling, and Schmidt 1964).

opposite directions in the two cases), whereas the four
configurations (3) have no component of the dipole in this
direction. Silsbee *et al.* also allowed the possibility,
first considered by Takagi (1948), that the PO_4 unit might
have one or three near hydrogens, corresponding to the ion
HPO_4^{2-} and the molecule H_3PO_4. The arrangements which give
these species, with the associated contribution to the dipole moment in the z direction, are also given in Fig.7.51.
Grindlay and ter Haar (1959) went further and considered
the configurations $H_4PO_4^+$ and PO_4^{3-}, but as they represent a
condition of still higher energy than that needed to give
H_3PO_4 and HPO_4^{2-}, it is doubtful if they make a significant
contribution, and we shall ignore them. The participation
of the species H_3PO_4 and HPO_4^- (which can be regarded as a
form of lattice imperfection) can however have an important
influence on the finer details of the transition, such as
the balance between its first-order and second-order character. For each configuration there is a particular contribution to the energy, and the problem becomes one of finding the fractional populations of the various configurations
which minimize the Helmholtz function for a given value of
the order parameter p, which is defined by the equation

$$p = x_2 - x_{-2} + 2(x_1 - x_{-1}) \, ,$$

and can therefore be regarded as determining the resultant
dipole moment in the z direction. Silsbee *et al.* included
in the expression for the energy of the crystal a term
$-\beta p^2$, where β is an adjustable parameter, thereby recognizing the participation of long-range forces, as first
suggested by Senko (1961).

The expressions which then emerge for quantities such
as the heat capacity, the entropy of transition, and the
spontaneous polarization contain three adjustable parameters,
namely ε_0, ε_1 and β. This number can be reduced to two by
introducing the experimental value of the transition tem-
perature (i.e. the Curie temperature T_C), and an estimate
of ε_1 can be obtained from other properties - for DKDP, for
example, from deuterium relaxation time measurements (Schmidt

and Uehling 1962). Comparison of properties calculated with
various values of β can then be made with experiment. Broadly,
it may be said that the theory succeeds in reproducing rather
well some of the facts about the transitions in the hydro-
genphosphates and arsenates, though the parameters which give
the best fit for, say, the spontaneous polarization may not
necessarily do the same for another property such as the
elastic constants (see, e.g. Brody and Cummins 1974). However, the Slater theory, even in its modified forms, has two
more important failures. It fails to explain the dramatic
rise in T_c on replacing hydrogen by deuterium, and as incorporated for example in the Silsbee-Uehling-Schmidt
theory it tends to overestimate the transition entropy - especially for the hydrogen as compared with the deuterium
salts. Most of the theoretical work which has attempted to
deal with these shortcomings has involved consideration of
the quantum-mechanical tunnelling of the proton between the
two positions of minimum energy in a hydrogen bond. The
possible importance of such tunnelling was first recognized
by Blinc (1960), and its consequences have been explored by
Blinc and Svetina (1966) and others (see the review by Blinc
and Żekś 1972). The Hamiltonian in such treatments includes
a tunnelling integral

$$\Gamma_i, \text{ where } \Gamma_i = - \langle \psi_{i\uparrow} | H_t | \psi_{i\downarrow} \rangle ,$$

the arrows ↑ and ↓ denoting the two possible sites for the
proton in a hydrogen bond. The greatly reduced ability of
the deuteron for tunnelling of this kind can at once be
associated with the much higher T_c values for the deuterated
compounds. In the limit of no tunnelling ($\Gamma_i = 0$), which
appears to be virtually the case for the deuterated salts,
a classical treatment of the Slater type is applicable.
Thus, Fairall and Reese (1972) found that for KD_2AsO_4 the
Silsbee-Uehling-Schmidt theory predicts an entropy of transition of $0 \cdot 507R$, in agreement with the observed value of
$0 \cdot 500R$. For RbH_2AsO_4, however, the value predicted by this
theory is $0 \cdot 652R$ as compared with the experimental figure

of $0.50R$, and this discrepancy is regarded as arising from
the neglect of tunnelling. Imry, Pelah, Wiener, and Zafrir
(1967) made neutron scattering cross-section measurements
above and below T_c with the incident neutron beam parallel
and perpendicular to the z axis of a KDP crystal. They considered that the difference between the two sets of cross-
section results confirmed the proton tunnelling model in
this salt. Further evidence for the importance of tunnelling in KDP is provided by the temperature dependence of the
static permittivity above the II→I transition (Holakovský,
Březina, and Pacherová 1972).

When the hydrogen bond system in KDP and its isomorphs
becomes completely ordered, all the dipoles of the $H_2PO_4^-$ ion
point in one or other direction along the z axis of the
crystal. It was soon realized, however, that this in itself
was quite inadequate to account for the observed spontaneous
polarization of the ferroelectric phase, and that this must
be largely attributed to the displacement of the potassium
ions and phosphorus atoms. There must therefore be some
coupling between the proton movement and that of the potassium and phosphorus atoms. This was recognized by K.K.
Kobayashi (1968), who suggested that the proton tunnelling
mode couples with the optical vibrational mode for the K
and P atoms along the z axis, to give the ferroelectric mode
illustrated in Fig.7.52. This introduces the concept of
the soft mode (section 3.9), since as the crystal approaches
T_c from above, the frequency of the ferroelectric mode tends
to zero, the mode becomes frozen, and the large spontaneous
polarization along the z axis is generated. The ferroelectric soft mode in KDP was first observed by Kaminow and
Damen (1968) in the low-frequency Raman scattering. More
recent work on the Raman-active modes of hydrogenarsenates
has suggested that the coupling which produces the ferroelectric mode is more complicated than had originally been
supposed (Lowndes, Tornberg, and Leung 1974). An important
contribution was made by Peercy (1975), who studied the
temperature dependence of the soft-mode spectra of KDP at
high pressures and also the pressure dependence of these
spectra at various temperatures in both the paraelectric

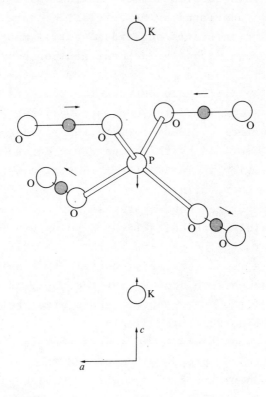

Fig.7.52. The coupling responsible for the ferroelectric mode in KH_2PO_4 (K.K.Kobayashi 1968).

and ferroelectric phases. Whereas the soft-mode response is overdamped at atmospheric pressure, it becomes under-damped under pressure, which makes it possible to obtain more exact information about the coupled-mode system. Peercy concluded that his results could not be adequately accounted for on a pure tunnelling basis, and that a better quantitative interpretation was afforded by a coupled-mode model incor-porating the tunnelling component of the proton motion.

The effect of pressure on the polymorphism of KDP is of considerable interest. With increasing pressure, the length of the hydrogen bonds decreases, and the energy barrier to proton movement and the separation of the two minima become less. Eventually the proton should oscillate about a single minimum in the centre of the bond, when the proton-lattice mode coupling should vanish and the transition disappear. This was found by Samara (1971) to be the case (Fig.7.53). As pressure is applied, T_c falls with increasing

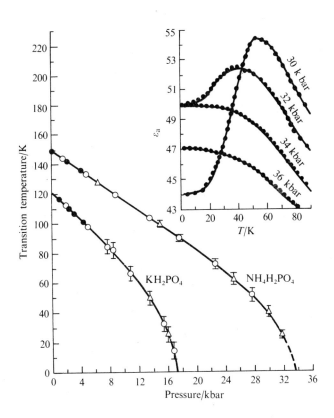

Fig.7.53. Effect of pressure on the transition temperatures of KH_2PO_4 and $NH_4H_2PO_4$. The inset shows the disappearance of the paraelectric→ antiferroelectric transition in $NH_4H_2PO_4$, as revealed by measurements of the permittivity along the a axis (Samara 1971).

rapidity and reaches 0 K at ~17 kbar. ADP behaves similarly, the transition vanishing at 33 kbar.

The above summary does not exhaust, even in outline, the treatments applied to transitions in hydrogen-bonded ferroelectrics. But it would appear that the transitions in KDP and allied salts, which are simultaneously both order-disorder and displacive in character, can in general only be dealt with successfully by combining more than one approach, and it seems inevitable that increasing refinement will mean increasing complexity.

The corresponding ammonium phosphates and arsenates are antiferroelectric in their ordered phases, a possibility first realized by Nagamiya (1952b). The ordered configurations here are the four shown in the third line of Fig.7.51, for which the dipole moment of the $H_2PO_4^-$ ion has no component along the z axis. The X-ray evidence requires that there should be two kinds of antiferroelectrically ordered domains, which are shown in Fig.7.54. The essential correctness of

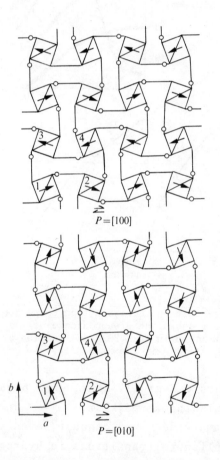

Fig.7.54. The two kinds of antiferroelectrically ordered domains in ADP and DADP (Blinc, Slak, and Zupančič 1974).

the Nagamiya theory has been demonstrated by NMR studies on DADP (Blinc, Slak, and Zupančič 1974) and on ADA and DADA

(Dalal, McDowell, and Srinivasan 1974, Blinc, Mali, Osredkar,
Parker, Seliger, and Zumer 1973). Dalal and his coworkers
concluded that above T_c the ammonium ions in ADA are undergoing rapid reorientation and effectively have spherical
symmetry, but that below T_c they make permanent hydrogen
bonds with the oxygens of the arsenate ions, which in consequence are somewhat distorted. It seems probable that the
original Nagamiya model for ADP and ADA needs some modification. Reference has already been made to the theoretical
treatments of antiferroelectrics proposed by Rys and by Wu
(section 3.7).

The two periodates $Ag_2H_3IO_6$ and $(NH_4)_2H_3IO_6$ are also
antiferroelectric in the ordered state. The transition
temperatures rise by about 40 K and 15 K respectively on
deuteration. The two salts have the same space group in
the paraelectric phase, but whereas in the antiferroelectric
modification of the silver salt the identity period doubles
in the a and c directions, in the ammonium salt this only
happens in the a direction. The transition in the silver
salt manifests itself in the heat capacity curve as an
unusually symmetrical anomaly. Stephenson and Adams (1944b),
treating the transition as a change from an ordered to a
random arrangement of the hydrogen atoms, showed that a
lower limit for ΔS_t on a Slater-type approach is $\frac{3}{4}R\ln 3$,
or $0\cdot815R$, which is in fact the experimental value. Roos,
Kind, and Petzelt (1976) reported that in both the silver
and ammonium salts the transition takes place in two stages.
They attributed the main stage to freezing-in of the proton
tunnelling mode. But the two transitions are by no means
alike, that in the silver salt being broad and gradual, while
that in the ammonium salt has a pronounced first-order component.

The alkali trihydrogenselenites form an interesting
group of salts. The sodium salt is ferroelectric in the
ordered state, as is the rubidium salt (Shuvalov, Ivanov,
Gordeeva, and Kirpichnikova 1969), whereas the caesium salt
is antiferroelectric. The lithium salt is ferroelectric up
to its melting-point of 383 K (Pepinsky and Vedam 1959).
The T_c values rise considerably on deuteration - by ~76 K

for the sodium salt, and by as much as 110-120 K for the
caesium salt.   Once again these order-disorder transitions
involve the position of the hydrogen atoms in the hydrogen
bonds, but here these hold the $H_3(SeO_3)_2^-$ ions together in
parallel layers, so the ordering is a two-dimensional matter
(Fig.7.55).   Several attempts have been made to interpret

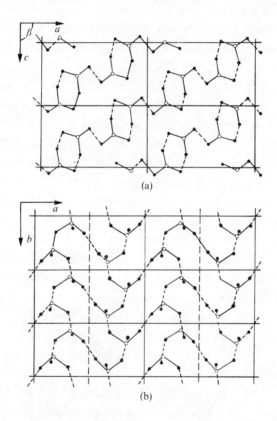

(a)

(b)

Fig.7.55. Layer structure of $NaH_3(SeO_3)_2$; (a) shows the layers of
$H_3(SeO_3)_2$ ions parallel to the (101) plane, and (b) shows one of these
layers projected onto the (001) plane.   Open circles, Se atoms; small
filled circles, O atoms; dotted lines, hydrogen bonds. The sodium ions
are not shown   (Makita and Miki, 1970).

the observed ΔS_t for the sodium salt.   Makita and Miki (1970)
adopted an approach which recalls the dimer problem, and in
fact a theoretical treatment of this problem using a model
based on the structure of $NaH_3(SeO_3)_2$ has already been summarized in section 3.8.   Any two SeO_3 units are linked by

a hydrogen bond, and Makita and Miki assumed (1) that a
hydrogen bond has one and only one hydrogen between the two
oxygens, (2) that any individual SeO_3 unit has one or two,
but not three, near protons, and (3) that the two SeO_3 units
of an $(SeO_3)_2$ pair have a total of three near protons.
Abraham and Lieb (1971) showed that the combinatorial problem
presented by this model could be exactly solved, and obtained
a value of $0 \cdot 95R$ for the configurational entropy in the disordered state. The experimental value of the sum of the
entropies of the two transitions ($v.inf.$) in $NaH_3(SeO_3)_2$ is
$0 \cdot 77R$. ΔS_t for the single transition in the deuterium salt,
as measured by Makita and Miki, is $0 \cdot 80R$. Nagle and Allen
(1971), however, questioned the applicability of assumption
(3), and considered that an Ising model is superior, while
Vaks and Zein (1974) noted the inability of the Makita-Miki
model to explain all the experimentally observed features
of the transition. Ishibashi and Takagi (1973), on theoretical grounds, gave upper and lower limits of $R \ln (5/4)$ and
$R \ln (9/2)$ for ΔS_t. Perhaps the most interesting fact about
the sodium trihydrogenselenites is the qualitative
difference between the deuterated form and the ordinary form.
The triclinic, ferroelectric phase II of the latter undergoes a first-order transition on cooling at ~100 K, with
$\Delta S_t \approx 0 \cdot 25R$, to give a monoclinic form III (space group Pm)
which is still ferroelectric. III can exist as a meta-
stable phase above the III→II transition, and can then be
converted directly at 194·5 K into form I. For $NaD_3(SeO_3)_2$,
however, the triclinic form II is absent, and on cooling
the high-temperature modification it changes at ~270 K
directly into a ferroelectric phase isomorphous with phase
III of $NaH_3(SeO_3)_2$ (Shuvalov, Ivanov, Kirpichnikova, and
Schagina 1968). This difference has prompted several investigations of the phase diagram of the system
$Na(D_xH_{1-x})_3(SeO_3)_2$, and the main features of this are
shown in Fig.7.56. Stepisnik, Slak, Blinc, Shuvalov, Ivanov,
and Schagina (1973) concluded from a deuteron NMR study of
the mixed crystals that it is only in phase I that the
deuterons are disordered. They also considered that their
relaxation time measurements demonstrated that the para-

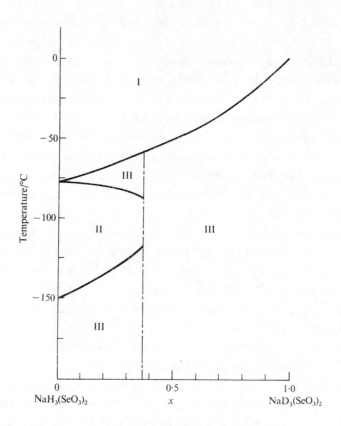

Fig.7.56. Phase diagram of the system $Na(H_{1-x}D_x)_3(SeO_3)_2$ (after Miki and Makita 1970; see also Kirikov, Shuvalov, and Zheludev 1974).

electric → ferroelectric transition is controlled by a ferroelectric soft mode. Torrie and Knispel (1973), however, on the basis of a Raman study, while in agreement on the disorder prevailing in phase I, concluded that the order in phase II might not be complete.

In triglycine sulphate (TGS) two of the glycine units are present as glycinium ions, $NH_3^+CH_2COOH$, while the third is a glycine molecule in the zwitterion form, $NH_3^+CH_2COO^-$. The salt is therefore really glycine diglycinium sulphate. From a detailed diffraction study, K.Itoh and Mitsui (1973) concluded that one of the glycinium ions (I) is permanently in this condition and is non-planar, while the other two glycine units (II and III) alternate between glycinium-

glycine and glycine-glycinium pairs (in which each glycine
unit is planar) by the movement of a proton along a hydrogen
bond. They agreed with the conclusion previously reached by
S.Hoshino, Okaya, and Pepinsky (1959) that above T_c
the glycine I units are statistically distributed between
two orientations, whereby the plane y = 1/4 becomes the
mirror-plane in the paraelectric phase. Blinc, Pintar,
and Zupančič (1967) pointed out that there is an analogy
between the transition in TGS and that in KDP, in that in
TGS order-disorder in the O(III) - H - O(II) bonds linking
glycines II and III is associated with a displacive-type
change affecting glycine I.

N.Nakamura, Suga, Chihara, and Seki (1965) considered
that the transitions in the three dicalcium propionates are
order-disorder transitions involving the position of the
methyl groups in the propionate anions. In the room-
temperature form of the strontium salt, two of the six
propionate ions have effectively twofold symmetry about
the bond joining the carbonyl carbon to the α-carbon atom,
implying that each methyl group (with the β-carbon atom)
has two equivalent positions available to it. In the ordered
modification, each methyl group has a definite position.
The configurational entropy gain on heating the crystal
through the transition should therefore be $2R \ln 2$. This is
considerably more than the entropy increase when the ferroelectric phase II passes into the paraelectric form I. When
pressure is applied to the strontium salt, and also to dicalcium lead propionate, the first-order component of the
III→II transition dwindles, and vanishes at a critical point
at a pressure of 3·35 kbar for the strontium compound and
1·73 kbar for the lead salt (cf. the case of ammonium chloride,
p. 317) (Gesi and Ozawa 1975).

The transition in methylammonium aluminium sulphate
(MASD) appears to be another order-disorder transition. In
the paraelectric phase, the $CH_3NH_3^+$ ions are inclined to the
cube body diagonals and statistically distributed among six
different configurations (Okaya, Ahmed, Pepinsky, and Vand,
1957). A small drop in the proton second moment ~16 K below
T_c indicates that the disappearance of ferroelectricity is

preceded by reorientation of these cations. In this compound, T_c is unchanged by deuteration.

REFERENCES

Aboav, D., Gränicher, H., and Petter, W. (1955). *Helv.phys. Acta.* 28, 299.

Abraham, D.B. and Lieb, E.H. (1971). *J.chem.Phys.* 54, 1446.

Abrahams, S.C. and Kalnajs, J. (1954). *J.chem.Phys.* 22, 434.

Adam, M. and Searby, G.M. (1973). *Phys.St.Solidi* 19(a), 185.

Adriaenssens, G.J. (1974). *Ferroelectrics* 7, 123. (1975). *Phys.Rev.* B12, 5116.

Akers, C., Peterson, S.W., and Willett, R.D. (1968). *Acta crystallogr.* B24, 1125.

Albert, S., Grunzweig-Genossar, J., and Perel, I. (1970). *J.chem.Phys.* 52, 5962.

──────   and Gutowsky, H.S. (1973). *J.chem.Phys.* 59, 3585.

──────   ──────   and Ripmeester, J.A. (1972). *J.chem.Phys.* 56, 3672.

──────   and Ripmeester, J.A. (1973). *J.chem.Phys.* 58, 541.

Albright, J.G. (1933). *Z.Kristallogr.Kristallgeom.* 84, 150.

Amin, M. and Strukov, B.A. (1968). *Fizika tverd.Tela* 10, 3158 (*Soviet Phys.Solid St.* 1969, 10, 2498).

──────   ──────   (1970). *Fizika tverd.Tela* 12, 2035 (*Soviet Phys. Solid St.* 1971, 12, 1616).

Aminoff, B. (1936). *Z.Kristallogr. Kristallgeom.* 94, 246.

Amitin, E.B., Kovalevskaya, Yu. A., and Paukov, I.E. (1972). *Fizika tverd. Tela* 14, 3438 (*Soviet Phys.Solid St.* 1973, 14, 2902).

Amorós Portolés, J.L., Alonso, P., and Canut, M.L. (1958). *Publs.Dept.Cryst.Mineral (Madrid)* 4, 30, 38 (*Chem.Abs.* 53, 17625c).

Amorós, J.L., Arrese, F., and Canut, M.L. (1962). *Z.Kristallogr.Kristallgeom.* 117, 92.

Anderson, J.E. and Slichter, W.P. (1966). *J.chem.Phys.* 44, 1797.

Andrade, P. da R., Prasad Rao, A.D., Katiyar, R.S., and Porto, S.P.S. (1973). *Solid St.Communs.* 12, 847.

Andrew, E.R. and Canepa, P.C. (1972). *J.mag.Res.* 7, 429.

——— Eades, R.G., Hennel, J.W., and Hughes, D.G. (1962). *Proc.phys.Soc.* 79, 954.

——— Farnell, L.F., and Gledhill, T.D. (1967). *Phys.Rev.Lett.* 19, 6.

Andrews, J.T.S. and Gordon, J.E. (1973). *J.chem.Soc., Faraday Trans.* I 69, 546.

Ang, T.T. and Dunell, B.A. (1976). *Can.J.chem.* 54, 1985.

Arell, A. (1960). *Annls.Acad.Sci.Fenn.,Ser.A* VI, no.57.

——— (1962a). *Annls.Acad.Sci.Fenn.,Ser.A* VI, No.101.

——— (1962b). *Annls.Acad.Sci.Fenn.,Ser.A* VI, No.100.

——— (1966). *Annls.Acad.Sci.Fenn.,Ser.A* VI, No.204.

——— and Alare, O. (1964). *Phys.kondens.Mater.* 2, 423.

——— Roiha, M., and Aaltonen, M. (1970). *Phys. kondens.Mater.* 12, 87.

——— and Varteva, M. (1961). *Annls.Acad.Sci.Fenn., Ser.A* VI, No.88.

——— ——— (1962). *Annls.Acad.Sci.Fenn.,Ser.A* VI, No.98.

Arend, H., Hofmann, R., and Waldner, F. (1973). *Solid St.Communs.* 13, 1629.

Armstrong, R.L., Lourens, J.A.J., and Jeffrey, K.R. (1976). *J.mag.Res.* 23, 115.

Ashmore, J.P. and Petch, H.E. (1975). *Can.J.phys.* 53, 2694.

Aston, J.G. and Ziemer, C.W. (1946). *J.Am.chem.Soc.* 68, 1405.

Atoji, M. (1971). *J.chem.Phys.* 54, 3514.

Babb, S.E., Chaney, P.E., and Owens, B.B. (1964). *J.chem. Phys.* 41, 2210.

Bacon, G.E. and Pease, R.S. (1953). *Proc.R.Soc.* A220, 397.

——— ——— (1955). *Proc.R.Soc.* A230, 359.

Baertschi, P. (1945). *Helv.phys.Acta* 18, 267.

Bantle, W. (1942). *Helv.phys.Acta* 15, 373.

Barnett, J.D., Pack, J., and Hall, H.T. (1969). *Trans.Am. cryst.Ass.* 5, 113.

Barth, T.F.W. (1939). *Z.phys.Chem.* B43, 448.

Bartis, F.J. (1971). *Phys.St.Solidi* B43, 665.

Bates, A.R. and Stevens, K.W.H. (1969). *J.Phys.* C2, 1573.

Bauhofer, W., Genzel, L., and Jahn, I.R. (1974). *Phys.St. Solidi* B63, 465.

———   ———   Perry, C.H., and Jahn, I.R. (1974). *Phys.St.Solidi* B63, 385.

Bersohn, R. and Gutowsky, H.S. (1954). *J.chem.Phys.* 22, 651.

Berteit, B., Kessler, A., and List, T. (1976). *Z.Phys.* B24, 15.

Biefeld, L.P. and Harris, P.M. (1935). *J.Am.chem.Soc.* 57, 396.

Betsuyaku, H. (1966). *J.phys.Soc.Japan* 21, 187.

Bijvoet, J.M. and Ketelaar, J.A.A. (1932). *J.Am.chem.Soc.* 54, 625.

———   and Lely, J.A. (1940). *Recl.Trav.chim.Pays-Bas* 59, 908.

Bjorkstam, J.L. (1967). *Phys.Rev.* 153, 599. (1970). *J.phys. Soc.Japan* 28, Suppl., 101.

———   and Uehling, E.A. (1959). *Phys.Rev.* 114, 961.

Blasenbrey, S. and Pechhold, W. (1967). *Rheol.Acta* 6, 174.

Blears, D.J., Danyluk, S.S., and Bock, E. (1968). *J.phys. Chem.* 72, 2269.

Blinc, R. (1959). *J.chem.Phys.* 31, 849.

———   (1960). *(J.)Phys.Chem.Solids* 13, 204.

———   and Bjorkstam, J.L. (1969). *Phys.Rev.Lett.* 23, 788.

———   Burgar, M., and Levstik, A. (1973). *Solid St. Communs.* 12, 573.

———   and Lahajnar, G. (1967). *J.chem.Phys.* 47, 4146.

———   ———   Pintar, M., and Zupančič, I. (1966). *J.chem.Phys.* 44, 1784.

———   and Levstek, I. (1960). *(J.)Phys.Chem.Solids* 12, 295.

———   Levstik, A., Stepisnik, J., Trontelj, Z., and Zupančič, I. (1968). *Phys.Lett.* 26A, 290.

———   Mali, M., Osredkar, R., Parker, R., Seliger, J., and Zumer, S. (1973). *J.chem.Phys.* 59, 2947.

———   ———   ———   Prelesnik, A., Zupančič, I., and Ehrenberg, L. (1971). *J.chem.Phys.* 55, 4843.

———   and Pintar, M. (1961). *J.chem.Phys.* 35, 1140.

———   ———   and Zupančič, I. (1967). *(J.) Phys. Chem.Solids* 28, 405.

Blinc, R., Slak, J., and Zupančič, I. (1974). *J.chem.Phys.*
61, 988.
——— and Svetina, S. (1966). *Phys.Rev.* 147, 423, 430.
——— and Žekš, B. (1972). *Adv.Phys.* 21, 693.
——— and Zupančič, I. (1963). *(J.)Phys.Chem.Solids* 24,
1379.
Bocanegra, E.H., Tello, M.J., Arriandiaga, M.A., and Arend, H.
(1975).*Solid St.Communs.* 17, 1221.
Bode, H. and Clausen, H. (1951). *Z.anorg.allg.Chem.* 265, 229.
——— and Teufer, G. (1952). *Z.anorg.allg.Chem.* 268, 20.
Boiko, A.A. (1969). *Kristallografiya* 14, 639 (*Soviet Phys.
Crystallogr.* 1970, 14, 539).
Bonilla, A., Garland, C.W., and Schumaker, N.E. (1970).
Acta crystallogr. A26, 156.
Bonilla, I.R., Holz, A., and Rutt, H.N. (1974). *Phys.St.
Solidi* B63, 297; B64, 709.
Bonori, M. and Terenzi, M. (1974). *Chem.Phys.Lett.* 27, 281.
Boutin, H., Trevino, S., and Prask, H. (1966). *J.chem.
Phys.* 45, 401.
Bräkken, H. and Harang, L. (1930). *Z.Kristallogr.Kristallgeom.*
75, 538.
Brajovic, V., Boutin, H., Safford, G.J., and Palevsky, H.
(1963).*(J.)Phys.Chem.Solids* 24, 617.
Bredig, M.A. (1941). *J.Am.chem.Soc.* 63, 2533.
——— (1942). *J.phys.Chem.* 46, 747.
——— (1943). *J.phys.Chem.* 47, 587.
Bridgman, P.W. (1916). *Proc.Am.Acad.Arts Sci.* 51, 582.
——— (1937). *Proc.Am.Acad.Arts Sci.* 72, 45.
Brodale, G.E. and Giauque, W.F. (1972). *J.phys.Chem.* 76, 737.
Brody, E.M. and Cummins, H.Z. (1974). *Phys.Rev.* B9, 179.
Brown, I.D. (1964). *Can.J.Chem.* 42, 2758.
Brown, R.N. and McClaren, A.C. (1962). (a) *Acta crystallogr.*
15, 974; (b) *Acta crystallogr.* 15, 977; (c) *Proc.R.Soc.*
A266, 329.
Bruins, D.E. and Garland, C.W. (1975). *J.chem.Phys.* 63, 4139.
Brunton, G. (1968). *Acta crystallogr.* B24, 1703.
Büssem, W. and Herrmann, K. (1928). *Z.Kristallogr.Kristallgeom.*
67, 405.

Burns, J.H. and Gordon, E.K. (1966). *Acta crystallogr.* <u>20</u>, 135.

Busch, G., Känzig, W., and Meier, W.M. (1953). *Helv.phys. Acta* <u>26</u>, 385.

Busey, R.H., Dearman, H.H., and Bevan, R.B. (1962). *J.phys. Chem.* <u>66</u>, 82.

Cance, M.-H. and Potier, A. (1971). *J.Chim.phys.* <u>68</u>, 941.

Carling, R.W. and Westrum, E.F. (1976). *J.chem.Thermodynamics* <u>8</u>, 565.

Caron, A.P., Huettner, D.J., Ragle, J.L., Sherk, L., and Stengle, T.R. (1967). *J.chem.Phys.* <u>47</u>, 2577.

Carpenter, G.B. (1952). *Acta crystallogr.* <u>5</u>, 132.

Chang, S.S. and Westrum, E.F. (1962). *J.chem.Phys.* <u>36</u>, 2420.

Chapuis, G., Arend, H., and Kind, R. (1975). *Phys.St.Solidi* <u>A31</u>, 449.

Chen, A. and Chernow, F. (1967). *Phys.Rev.* <u>154</u>, 493.

Cherin, P., Hamilton, W.C., and Post, B. (1967). *Acta crystallogr.* <u>23</u>, 455.

Chiba, T. (1962). *J.chem.Phys.* <u>36</u>, 1122.

——   (1964). *J.chem.Phys.* <u>41</u>, 1352.

——   (1965). *Bull.chem.Soc.Japan* <u>38</u>, 490.

Chihara, H. and Nakamura, M. (1972). *Bull.chem.Soc.Japan* <u>45</u>, 133.

——   ——   and Masukane, K. (1973). *Bull. chem.Soc.Japan* <u>46</u>, 97.

——   ——   and Seki, S. (1965). *Bull.chem. Soc.Japan* <u>38</u>, 1776.

——   and Nakamura, N. (1973). *Bull.chem.Soc.Japan.* <u>46</u>,94

——   ——   and Tachiki, M. (1971). *J.chem. Phys* . <u>54</u>, 3640.

Chisler, E.V. (1969). *Fizika tverd.Tela* <u>11</u>, 1272 (*Soviet Phys.Solid St.* 1969, <u>11</u>, 1032).

——   and Shur, M.S. (1966). *Phys.St.Solidi* <u>17</u>, 163, 173.

——   ——   (1967). *Soviet Phys.Solid St.* <u>9</u>, 796.

Choi, C.S., Mapes, J.E., and Prince, E. (1972). *Acta crystallogr.* <u>B28</u>, 1357.

Choi, C.S., Prask, H.J., and Prince, E. (1974). *J.chem.Phys.* 61, 3523.

———— and Prince, E. (1976). *J.chem.Phys.* 64, 4510.

Cimino, A., Parry, G.S., and Ubbelohde, A.R. (1959). *Proc. R.Soc.* A252, 445.

Clark, J.B. and Pistorius, C.W.F.T. (1973). *J.Solid St.Chem.* 7, 353.

———— ———— (1974). *Z.phys.Chem.N.F.* 88, 242.

Clark, M.J.R. and Lynton, H. (1969). *Can.J.Chem.* 47, 2579.

Cleaver, B. and Williams, J.F. (1968). *(J.) Phys.Chem.Solids,* 29, 877.

Coker, T.G., Ambrose, J., and Janz, G.J. (1970) *J.Am.chem. Soc.* 92, 5293.

———— Wunderlich, B., and Janz, G.J. (1969). *Trans. Faraday Soc.* 65, 3361.

Connell, L.F. and Gammel, J.H. (1950). *Acta crystallogr.* 3, 75.

Coogan, C.K., Belford, G.A., and Gutowsky, H.S. (1963). *J.chem.Phys.* 39, 3061.

———— and Gutowsky, H.S. (1964). *J.chem.Phys.* 40, 3419.

Cook, W.R. (1967). *J.appl.Phys.* 38, 1637.

Corazza, E., Sabelli, C., and Giuseppetti, G. (1967). *Acta crystallogr.* 22, 683.

Costich, P.S., Maass, G.J., and Smith, N.O. (1963). *J.chem. Eng.Data* 8, 26.

Coughlin, J.P. (1955). *J.Am.chem.Soc.* 77, 868.

Courtenay, E.W. and Kennedy, S.W. (1974). *Aust.J.Chem.* 27, 209.

Couture-Mathieu, L. and Mathieu, J.-P. (1952). *J.Chim.phys.* 49, 226.

Cox, B., (1956). *J.chem.Soc.* 876.

Dahlborg, U., Larsson, K.E., and Pirkmajer, E. (1970). *Physica* 49, 1.

Dalal, N.S., McDowell, C.A., and Srinivasan, R. (1974). *J.chem.Phys.* 60, 3787.

D'Alessio, G.J. and Scott, T.A. (1971). *J.mag.Res.* 5, 416.

Danner, D.R. and Pepinsky, R. (1955). *Phys.Rev.* 99, 1215.

Davis, B.L. (1964). *Science* 145, 489.

———   and Adams, L.H. (1962). *Z.Kristallogr.*
     Kristallgeom. 117, 399.

———   and Oshier, E.H. (1967). *Am.Min.* 52, 957.

Decker, D.L., Beyerlein, R.A., Roult, G., and Worlton, T.G.
     (1974). *Phys.Rev.* B10, 3584.

Delacy, T.P. and Kennard, C.H.L. (1971). *Aust.J.Chem.* 24,
     165.

Delain, C. (1958). *C.R.hebd.Séanc.Acad.Sci.,Paris* 247, 1451.

Denielou, L., Fournier, Y., Petitet, J.-P., and Téqui, C.
     (1970). *C.R.hebd.Séanc.Acad.Sci.,Paris* C270, 1854.

Deshpande, V.T. and Khan, A.A. (1963). *Acta crystallogr.*
     16, 936.

Deutsch, M. and Litov, E. (1974). *Ferroelectrics* 7, 209.

Dickinson, R.G. (1922). (a) *J.Am.chem.Soc.* 44, 276. (b) *J.
     Am.chem.Soc.* 44, 1489.

Dickson, D.H.W. and Ubbelohde, A.R. (1950). *Acta crystallogr.*
     3, 6.

Dietrich, O.W., Cowley, R.A., and Shapiro, S.M. (1974).
     J.Phys. C7, 1239.

Dietz, R.E., Walker, L.R., Hsu, F.S.L., Haemmerle, W.H.,
     Vis, B., Chau, C.K., and Weinstock, H. (1974). *Solid
     St. Communs.* 15, 462.

Dinichert, P. (1942). *Helv.phys.Acta* 15, 462.

Drain, L.E. (1955). *Disc.Faraday Soc.* 19, 200.

Dufourcq, J., Haget-Bouillaud, Y., Chanh, N.B., and
     Lemanceau, B. (1972). *Acta crystallog.* B28, 1305.

———   and Lemanceau, B. (1970). *J.Chim.phys.* 67, 9.

Dultz, W. (1974). *Solid St.Communs.* 15, 595.

Dunn, M.B., Ikeda, R., and McDowell, C.A. (1972). *Chem.Phys.
     Lett.* 16, 226.

Durig, J.R., Antion, D.J., and Baglin, F.G. (1968). *J.chem.
     Phys.* 49, 666.

———   ———   and Pate, C.B. (1969). *J.chem.
     Phys.* 51, 4449.

———   ———   ———   (1970). *J.chem.
     Phys.* 52, 5542.

Durig, J.R. and Pate, C.B. (1972). *Spectrochim.Acta* A28, 1031.

Dworkin, A.S. and Bredig, M.A. (1970). *J.chem.Eng.Data* 15, 505.

Easwaran, K.R.K. (1966). *J.chem.Phys.* 45, 403.

Eberhard, J.W. and Horn, P.M. (1975). *Solid St.Communs.* 16, 1343.

Ebisuzaki, Y. (1973). *Chem.Phys.Lett.* 19, 503.

Egert, G., Jahn, I.R., and Renz, D. (1971). *Solid St.Communs.* 9, 775.

Elliott, N. and Hastings, J. (1961). *Acta crystallogr.* 14, 1018.

Ema, K., Hamano, K., and Hatta, I. (1975). *J.phys.Soc.Japan*, 39, 726.

Engel, G. (1935). *Z.Kristallogr.Kristallgeom.* 90, 341.

Erofeev, B.V. and Mitskevich, N.I. (1952). *Zh.fiz.Khim.* 26, 1631.

———   ———   (1953). *Zh.fiz.Khim.* 27, 118.

Everett, D.H. and Watson, A.E.P. (1956). *Tercera reunion international sobre reactividad de los solidos, Madrid,* I, 301.

Fairall, C.W. and Reese, W. (1972). *Phys.Rev.* B6, 193.

———   ———   (1974). *Phys.Rev.* B10, 882.

Fatuzzo, E. and Merz, W.J. (1967). *Ferroelectricity*, North-Holland Publishing Co., Amsterdam.

Fermor, J.H. and Kjekshus, A. (1969). *Acta chem.scand.* 23, 1581.

———   ———   (1972). *Acta chem.scand.* 26, 2039.

Ferrari, A., Cavalca, L., and Tani, M.E. (1957). *Gazz.chim. ital.* 87, 310.

Ferroni, E. and Orioli, P. (1959). *Z.Kristallogr.Kristallgeom.* 111, 362.

———   Sabatini, A., and Orioli, P. (1957). *Gazz.chim. ital.* 87, 630.

Finbak, C. and Hassel, O. (1936). *Z.phys.Chem.* B32, 433.

Finbak, C. and Hassel, O. (1937). (a) *Z.phys.Chem.* B35, 25; (b) *Z.phys.Chem.* B37, 75; (c) *J.chem.Phys.* 5, 400.

―――   ―――   and Strømme, L.C. (1937). *Z.phys. Chem.* B37, 468.

Fischmeister, H.F. (1956). *J.inorg.nucl.Chem.* 3, 182.

―――   (1962). *Mh.Chem.* 93, 420.

Ford, P.T. and Powell, H.M. (1954). *Acta crystallogr.* 7, 604.

―――   and Richards, R.E. (1955). *Disc.Faraday Soc.* No.19, 230.

Førland, T. and Krogh-Moe, J. (1957). *Acta.chem.scand.* 11, 565.

Fraser, W.L., Kennedy, S.W., and Snow, M.R. (1975). *Acta. crystallogr.* B31, 365.

Frazer, B.C. and Pepinsky, R. (1953). *Acta crystallogr.* 6, 273.

Fredericks, G.E. (1971). *Phys.Rev.* B4, 911.

Freund, I. (1967). *Phys.Rev.Lett.* 19, 1288.

―――   and Kopf, L. (1970). *Phys.Rev.Lett.* 24, 1017.

Fritz, I.J. and Cummins, H.Z. (1972). *Phys.Rev.Lett.* 28, 96.

Fritzer, H.P. and Torkar, K. (1966). *Mh.Chem.* 97, 703.

Fukushima, E. (1968). *J.chem.Phys.* 49, 4721.

Fuller, R.G. and Patten, F.W. (1970). *(J.)Phys.Chem.Solids.* 31, 1539.

Furukawa, G.T., Reilly, M.L., and Piccirelli, J.H. (1964). *J.Res.natn.Bur.Stand.* 68A, 651.

Garber, S.R. and Smolenko, L.A. (1973). *Zh.eksp.teor.Fiz.* 64, 181. (*Sov.Phys.JETP* 1973, 37, 94.)

Garland, C.W., Bruins, D.E., and Greytak, T.J. (1975). *Phys.Rev.* B12, 2759.

―――   and Jones, J.S. (1963). *J.chem.Phys.* 39, 2874.

―――   and Renard, R. (1966). *J.chem.Phys.* 44, 1130.

―――   and Weiner, B.B. (1970). *J.chem.Phys.* 53, 1609.

―――   and Yarnell, C.F. (1966). *J.chem.Phys.* 44, 3678.

―――   and Young, R.A. (1968). (a) *J.chem.Phys.* 48, 146; (b) 49, 5282.

Geisel, T. and Keller, J. (1975). *J.chem.Phys.* 62, 3777.

Genin, D.J. and O'Reilly, D.E. (1969). *J.chem.Phys.* 50, 2842.

Gesi, K. (1969). *J.phys.Soc.Japan* 26, 953.

―――   (1970). (a) *J.phys.Soc.Japan* 28, 395; (b) 28, 1377.

Gesi, K. (1972). *J.phys.Soc.Japan* 33, 561.

────── and Ozawa, K. (1975). *J.phys.Soc.Japan* 39, 1026.

────── ────── and Takagi, Y. (1965). *J.phys.Soc.*
Japan 20, 1773.

Gibson, A.A.V. and Raab, R.E. (1972). *J.chem.Phys.* 57, 4688.

Gomes de Mesquita, A.H., MacGillavry, C.H., and Eriks, K.
(1965). *Acta crystallogr.* 18, 437.

Goodwin, T.H. and Whetstone, J. (1947). *J.chem.Soc.* 1455.

Gottfried, C. and Schusterius, C. (1933). *Z.Kristallogr.*
Kristallgeom. 84, 65.

Gourdji, M., Guibé, L., and Peneau, A. (1974). *J.Phys.* 35,
497.

Gränicher, H., Kind, R., Meier, W.M., and Petter, W. (1968).
Helv.phys.Acta 41, 843.

────── Meier, W.M., and Petter, W. (1954). *Helv.*
phys.Acta 27, 216.

Greene, P.D., Gross, P., and Hayman, C. (1968). *Trans.Faraday*
Soc. 64, 633.

Griffiths, R.B. (1970). *Phys.Rev.Lett.* 24, 715.

Grindlay, J. and ter Haar, D. (1959). *Proc.R.Soc.* A250, 266.

Grosescu, R. (1973). *Chem.Phys.Lett.* 21, 80.

Gutowsky, H.S., Pake, G.E., and Bersohn, R. (1954). *J.*
chem.Phys. 22, 643.

Hallett, N.C. and Johnston, H.L. (1953). *J.Am.chem.Soc.*
75, 1496.

Hamano, K. (1964). *J.phys.Soc.Japan* 19, 945.

Hamilton, W.C. (1962). *Acta crystallogr.* 15, 353.

────── (1969). *J.chem.Phys.* 50, 2275.

Hampson, G.C. and Pauling, L. (1938). *J.Am.chem.Soc.* 60, 2702.

Harris, P.M. and Meibohm, E.P. (1947). *J.Am.chem.Soc.* 69, 1231.

Hartwig, C.M., Wiener-Avnear, E., and Porto, S.P.S. (1972).
Phys.Rev. B5, 79.

Harvey, K.B. and McQuaker, N.R. (1971). *Can.J.Chem.* 49, 3272.

Haussühl, S. (1973). *Solid St.Communs.* 13, 147.

Heger, G., Mullen, D., and Knorr, K. (1975). *Phys.St.Solidi*
A31, 455.

Hendricks, S.B. and Pauling, L. (1925). *J.Am.chem.Soc.* 47, 2904.

────── Posnjak, E., and Kracek, F.C. (1932). *J.Am.*
chem.Soc. 54, 2766.

Hennel, J.W. and Pollak-Stachura, M. (1969). *Acta phys. polon.* <u>35</u>, 239.

Herrington, T.M. and Staveley, L.A.K. (1964). *(J.)Phys.Chem. Solids* <u>25</u>, 921.

Herrmann, K. and Ilge, W. (1931). *Z.Kristallogr.Kristallgeom.* <u>75</u>, 41.

Hettich, A. (1934). *Z.phys.Chem.* <u>A168</u>, 353.

Hexter, R.M. (1958). *Spectrochim. Acta* <u>10</u>, 291.

Hochheimer, H.D. and Geisel, T. (1976). *J.chem.Phys.* <u>64</u>, 1586.

Holakovský, J., Březina, B., and Pacherová, O. (1972). *Phys. St.Solidi* <u>B53</u>, K69.

Holden, J.R. and Dickinson, C.W. (1975). *J.phys.Chem.* <u>79</u>, 249.

Holm, J.L. (1966). *Acta chem.scand.* <u>20</u>, 1167.

Hone, D., Scherer, C., and Borsa, F. (1974). *Phys.Rev.* <u>B9</u>, 965.

Hoshino, R. (1961). *J.phys.Soc.Japan* <u>16</u>, 835.

——————   (1962). *J.phys.Soc.Japan* <u>17</u>, 119.

Hoshino, S., Mitsui, T., Jona, F., and Pepinsky, R. (1957). *Phys.Rev.* <u>107</u>, 1255.

——————   and Motegi, H. (1967). *Jap.J.appl.Phys.* <u>6</u>, 708.

——————   Okaya, Y., and Pepinsky, R. (1959). *Phys.Rev.* <u>115</u>, 323.

——————   Vedam, K., Okaya, Y., and Pepinsky, R. (1958). *Phys.Rev.* <u>112</u>, 405.

Hovi, V., Arell, A., and Varteva, M. (1959). *Annls.Acad.Sci. Fenn.,Ser.A* <u>VI</u>, No.39.

——————   Heiskanen, K.,and Varteva, M. (1964). *Annls.Acad. Sci.Fenn.,Ser.A.* <u>VI</u>, No.144.

——————   Järvinen, U., and Pyykkö, P. (1965). *Phys.kondens. Mater.* <u>4</u>, 103.

——————   and Lainio, J. (1966). *Annls.Acad.Sci.Fenn.,Ser.A* <u>VI</u>, No.215.

——————   Lohikainen, T., and Niemelä, L. (1968). *Annls.Univ. Turku.,Ser.* A1, 119.

——————   Mutikainen, P., and Pirinen, J. (1973). *Annls.Acad. Sci.Fenn.,Ser.A* <u>VI</u>, No.404.

——————   Paavola, K., and Nurmi, E. (1969). *Annls.Acad. Sci.Fenn.,Ser.A* <u>VI</u>, No.328.

Hovi, V., Paavola, K., and Urvas, O. (1968). (a) *Helv.phys.*
     Acta <u>41</u>, 938; (b) *Annls.Acad.Sci.Fenn.,Ser.A* <u>VI</u>, No. 291.

——— Pöyhönen, J., and Paalassalo, P. (1960). *Annls.*
     Acad.Sci.Fenn.,Ser.A <u>VI</u>, No.42.

——— and Pyykkö, P. (1966). *Phys.kondens.Mater.* <u>5</u>, 1.

——— and Varteva, M. (1964). *Phys.kondens.Mater.* <u>3</u>, 305.

Huettner, D.J., Ragle, J.L., Sherk, L., Stengle, T.R., and
     Yeh, H.J.C. (1968). *J.chem.Phys.* <u>48</u>, 1739.

Hughes, E.W. and Lipscomb, W.N. (1946). *J.Am.chem.Soc.* <u>68</u>,
     1970.

Hurst, H.J. (1970). *Chem.Phys.Lett.* <u>4</u>, 531.

——— Brown, R.J.C., and Whittem, R.N. (1968). *Chem.*
     Phys.Lett. <u>1</u>, 647.

Hutchings, M.T., Shirane, G., Birgeneau, R.J., and Holt,
     S.L. (1972). *Phys.Rev.* <u>B5</u>, 1999.

Ibers, J.A. (1956). *Acta crystallogr.* <u>9</u>, 967.

Ikeda, R. and McDowell, C.A. (1973). *Molec.Phys.* <u>25</u>, 1217.

Ikeda, T., Fujibayashi, K., Nagai, T., and Kobayashi, J.
     (1973). *Phys.St.Solidi* <u>A16</u>, 279.

Imry, Y., Pelah, I., Wiener, E., and Zafrir, H. (1967).
     Solid St.Communs. <u>5</u>, 41.

Ingraham, T.R. and Marier, P. (1965). *Can.Metall.Q.* <u>4</u>, 169.

Iqbal, Z. (1973). *J.chem.Phys.* <u>59</u>, 1769.

——— and Christoe, C.W. (1974). *Chem.Phys.Lett.* <u>29</u>, 623.

——— ——— (1975). (a) *J.chem.Phys.* <u>62</u>,
     3246; (b) *Solid St.Communs.* <u>17</u>, 71.

——— Sarma, L.H., and Möller, K.D. (1972). *J.chem.Phys.*
     <u>57</u>, 4728.

Ishibashi, Y. and Takagi, Y. (1973). *J.phys.Soc.Japan* <u>35</u>,814.

Ishida, K. and Mitsui, T. (1974). *Ferroelectrics* <u>8</u>, 475.

Ismailzade, I.G., Anagiev, M.Kh., and Abdullaeva, Kh.M.
     (1961). *Kristallografiya* <u>6</u>, 733. *(Soviet Phys.*
     Crystallogr. 1962, <u>6</u>, 585).

Itoh, J. Kusaka, R., and Saito, Y. (1962). *J.phys.Soc.Japan*
     <u>17</u>, 463.

——— and Yamagata, Y. (1962). *J.phys.Soc.Japan* <u>17</u>, 481.

Itoh, K., Matsubayashi, T., Nakamura, E., and Motegi, H.
     (1975). *J.phys.Soc.Japan* <u>39</u>, 843.

——— and Mitsui, T. (1973). *Ferroelectrics,* <u>5</u>, 235.

Ivanova, E.A. and Chisler, E.V. (1974). *Fizika tverd.* *Tela* 16, 3371. (*Soviet Phys.Solid St.* 1975, 16, 2185).

Iversen, A.J. and Kennedy, S.W. (1973). *Acta crystallogr.* B29, 1554.

Jaakkola, S., Pöyhönen, J., and Simola, K. (1968). *Annls.* *Acad.Sci.Fenn.,Ser.A* VI, No.295.

Jahn, I.R. Brunskill, I.H., Bausch, R., and Dachs, H. (1975). *J.Phys.* C8, 3280.

——— and Neumann, E. (1973). *Solid St.Communs.* 12, 721.

——— and Renz, D. (1971). *Solid St.Communs.* 9, 775.

Jain, Y.S. (1975). *Phys.St.Solidi* B71, K61.

——— and Bist, H.D. (1974). *Phys.St.Solidi* B62, 295.

——— ——— and Upreti, G.C. (1973). *Chem.* *Phys.Lett.* 22, 572.

James, D.W., Carrick, M.T., and Leong, W.H. (1974). *Chem.* *Phys.Lett.* 28, 117.

Jamieson, J.C. (1956). *Z.Kristallogr.Kristallgeom.* 107, 65.

Janik, J.M., Pytasz, G., Rachwalska, M., Janik, J.A., Natkaniec, I., and Nawrocik, W. (1973). *Acta phys.* *polon.* A43, 419.

——— Rachwalska, M., and Janik, J.A. (1974). *Physica* 72, 168.

Jannek, H.-D. and Rager, H. (1975). *Z.Naturf.* 30A, 1615.

Jeffrey, K.R. (1974). *Can.J.Phys.* 52, 2370.

——— Brown, A.G., and Armstrong, R.L. (1973). *Phys.Rev.* B8, 3071.

Jehanno, G. and Varret, F. (1975). *Acta crystallogr.* A31, 857.

Johnston, H.L. and Hallett, N.C. (1953). *J.Am.chem.Soc.* 75, 1467.

Jona, F. and Shirane, G. (1962). *Ferroelectric crystals.* Pergamon Press, Oxford.

Juopperi, O. (1972). *Annls.Acad.Sci.Fenn.,Ser.A* VI, No.383.

Kadaba, P.K., O'Reilly, D.E., and Blinc, R. (1970). *Phys.* *St.Solidi* 42, 855.

Kakiuchi, Y., Shono, H., Komatsu, H., and Kigoshi, K. (1951). *J.chem.Phys.* 19, 1069. (1952). *J.phys.Soc.* *Japan* 7, 102.

Kaminow, I.P. and Damen, T.C. (1968). *Phys.Rev.Lett.* 20, 1105.

Kamiyoshi, K. (1957). *J.chem.Phys.* **26**, 218.

Kasahara, M., Sasakawa, K., and Tatsuzaki, I. (1975). *J. phys.Soc.Japan* **39**, 1022.

Kasturi, S.R. and Moran, P.R. (1975). *Phys.Rev.* **B12**, 1874.

Kay, M.I., Frazer, B.C., and Ueda, R. (1962). *Acta crystallogr.* **15**, 506.

———— and Kleinberg, R. (1973). *Ferroelectrics* **5**, 45.

Keeling, R.O. and Pepinsky, R. (1955). *Z.Kristallogr. Kristallgeom.* **106**, 236.

Kemmitt, R.D.W., Russell, D.R., and Sharp, D.W.A. (1963). *J.chem.Soc.* 4408.

Kennedy, S.W. (1970). *Phys.St.Solidi* **A2**, 415.

———— and Odlyha, M. (1974). *Aust.J.Chem.* **27**, 1121.

———— and Patterson, J.H. (1961). *Z.Kristallogr. Kristallgeom.* **116**, 143.

Ketelaar, J.A.A. (1934). *Nature,Lond.* **134**, 250.

———— Rietdijk, A.A., and van Staveren, C.H. (1937). *Recl.Trav.chim.Pays-Bas* **56**, 907.

———— and Strijk, B. (1945). *Recl.Trav.chim.Pays-Bas* **64**, 174.

Khanna, R.K. Lingstheid, J., and Decius, J.C. (1964). *Spectrochim.Acta* **20**, 1109.

King, H.F. and Hornig, D.F. (1966). *J.chem.Phys.* **44**, 4520.

Kirikov, V.A., Shuvalov, L.A., and Zheludev, I.S. (1974). *Kristallografiya* **19**, 650. (*Soviet Phys.Crystallogr.* **19**, 402).

Klaaijsen, F.W., Suga, H., and Dokoupil, Z. (1971). *Physica* **51**, 630.

Klement, W. (1970). (a) *J.phys.Chem.* **74**, 2753; (b) **74**, 2751.

———— (1976). *J.chem.Soc.,Faraday Trans.I* **72**, 303.

Klinkenburg, L.J. (1937). *Recl.Trav.chim.Pays-Bas* **56**, 749.

Klug, H.P. (1933). *Z.Kristallogr.Kristallgeom.* **85**, 214.

Knispel, R.R., Petch, H.E., and Pintar, M.M. (1975). *J. chem.Phys.* **63**, 390.

Knorr, K., Jahn, I.R., and Heger, G. (1974). *Solid St. Communs.* **15**, 231.

Kobayashi, J. and Yamada, N. (1962). *Bull.Sci.Engng.Lab. Waseda Univ.* **18**, 63.

Kobayashi, J., Uesu, Y., and Enomoto, Y. (1971). *Phys.St. Solidi* B45, 293.

——   ——   Mizutani, I., and Enomoto, Y. (1970). *Phys.St.Solidi* A3, 63.

Kobayashi, K.K. (1968). *J.phys.Soc.Japan* 24, 497.

Kodama, T. (1972). *J.mag.Res.* 7, 137.

Kolomiichuk, V.N. (1965). *Kristallografiya* 10, 565. (*Soviet Phys.Crystallogr*. 1966, 10, 475).

——   and Dvoryankin, V.F. (1964). *Kristallografiya* 9, 50 (*Soviet Phys.Crystallogr*. 1964, 9, 35).

Korhonen, U. (1951). *Annls.Acad.Sci.Fenn*., Ser.AI, No.102.

Kostina, E.N. and Mil'ner, G.A. (1972). *Fizika tverd.Tela* 14, 3459. (*Soviet Phys.Solid St*. 1973, 14, 2923).

Kracek, F.C. (1929). *J.phys.Chem*. 33, 1281.

——   (1931). *J.Am.chem.Soc*. 53, 2609.

——   Barth, T.F.W., and Ksanda, C.J. (1932). *Phys. Rev*. 40, 1034.

——   and Ksanda, C.J. (1930). *J.phys.Chem*. 34, 1741.

——   Posnjak, E., and Hendricks, S.B. (1931). *J. Am.chem.Soc*. 53, 3339.

Kruh, R., Fuwa, K., and McEver, T.E. (1956). *J.Am.chem.Soc*. 78, 4256.

Kuwabara, S. (1959). *J.phys.Soc.Japan* 14, 1205.

Kydon, D.W., Petch, H.E., and Pintar, M. (1969). *J.chem. Phys*. 51, 487.

Lahajnar, G., Pintar, M., and Slivnik, J. (1966). *Croat.chem. Acta* 38, 63.

Lajzerowicz, J. (1965). *Solid St.Communs*. 3, 369.

Lalowicz, Z.T., McDowell, C.A., and Raghunathan, P. (1975). *Chem.Phys.Lett*. 35, 294.

Lander, J.J. (1949). *J.chem.Phys*. 17, 892.

Landi, E. and Vacatello M. (1975). *Thermochim.Acta* 13, 441.

Landolt-Börnstein (1969). *Ferroelectric and Antiferroelectric Substances, Group III*, Vol.3. Springer-Verlag, Berlin.

Lawson, A.W. (1940). *Phys.Rev*. 57, 417.

Lawton, S.L. and Jacobson, R.A. (1966). *Inorg.Chem*. 5, 743.

Lee, F.S. and Carpenter, G.B. (1959). *J.phys.Chem*. 63, 279.

Lee, S.H. and Wulff, C.A. (1974). *J.chem.Thermodynamics* 6, 85.

Lely, J.A. (1942). *Dissertation*, Utrecht, p.84.

Lerbscher, J.A. and Wulff, C.A. (1970). *J.chem.Thermodynamics* 2, 717.

Leung, P.S., Rush, J.J., and Taylor, T.I. (1972). *J.chem. Phys.* 57, 175.

———— , Taylor, T.I., and Havens, W.W. (1968). *J.chem. Phys.* 48, 4912.

Levin, E.M. (1969). *J.Am.Ceram.Soc.* 52, 53.

———— , Roth, R.S., and Martin, J.B. (1961). *Am.Miner.* 46, 1030.

Levina, M.E., Kalitin, V.I., and Kalinnikov, V.T. (1961). *Vest.Mosk.Univ.Khim.Ser.II* 16, No.4, 43 (*Chem.Abstr.* 56, 11010b).

———— and Khromova, N.V. (1963). *Izv.Vyssh.ucheb. Zaved.Khim.i Khim.Tekhnol.* 6, 717. (*Chem.Abstr.* 60, 7517e).

Levy, H.A. and Peterson, S.W. (1951). *Phys.Rev.* 83, 1270.

————   ———— (1952). *Phys.Rev.* 86, 766.

————   ———— (1953). (a) *J.Am.chem.Soc.* 75, 1536; (b) *J.chem.Phys.* 21, 366.

————   ———— and Simonsen, S.H. (1954). *Phys.Rev.* 93, 1120.

Lindgren, J. and Olovsson, I. (1968). (a) *Acta crystallogr.* B24, 554; (b) B24, 549.

Lindley, P.F. and Woodward, P. (1966). *J.chem.Soc.* A123.

Livingston, R.C., Rowe, J.M., and Rush, J.J. (1974). *J. chem.Phys.* 60, 4541.

Long, D.A. (1971) in *Essays in Structural Chemistry* (ed. Downs, A.J., Long, D.A., and Staveley, L.A.K.) Chap.2. Macmillan, London.

Lowndes, R.P., Tornberg, N.E., and Leung, R.C. (1974). *Phys. Rev.* B10, 911.

Luban, M., Wiser, N., and Greenfield, A.J. (1970). *J.Phys.* C3, 1.

Mahajan, M. and Nageswara Rao, B.D. (1974). *J.Phys.* C7, 995.

Makita, Y.(1964). *J.phys.Soc.Japan* 19, 576.

———— (1965). *J.phys.Soc.Japan* 20, 1567.

———— and Miki, H. (1970). *J.phys.Soc.Japan* 28, 1221.

———— Tsuchiya, T., and Yamagita, M. (1967). *J.phys.Soc. Japan*, 22, 938.

Makosz, J.J. and Gonsior, A. (1971). *Acta phys.pol.A* 39, 371.

Mandema, W. and Trappeniers, N.J. (1974). (a) *Physica* 76, 102; (b) 76, 123.

Mandleberg, C.J. and Staveley, L.A.K. (1950). *J.chem.Soc.* 2736.

Mangum, B.W. and Utton, D.B. (1972). *Phys.Rev.* B6, 2790.

Mani, N.V. (1957). *Proc.Indian Acad.Sci.* A46, 143.

Manolatos, S., Tillinger, M., and Post, B. (1973). *J.Solid St. Chem.* 7, 31.

Mansikka, K. and Pöyhönen, J. (1962). *Annls.Acad.Sci.Fenn.*, *Ser.A* VI, No.118.

Markowitz, M.M. and Boryta, D.A. (1962). *Am.Rocket Soc.J.* 32, 1941.

Marshall, J.G., Staveley, L.A.K., and Hart, K.R. (1956). *Trans.Faraday Soc.* 52, 19.

Maruyama, H., Tomiie, Y., Mizutani, I., Yamazaki, Y., Uesu, Y., Yamada, N., and Kobayashi, J. (1967). *J.phys.Soc.Japan* 23, 899.

Mason, W.P. (1946). *Phys.Rev.* 70, 529.

Mathieu, J.-P. (1954). *C.r.hebd.Séanc.Acad.Sci.*,*Paris* 238, 74.

Matthias, B.T. and Remeika, J.P. (1956). *Phys.Rev.* 103, 262.

Matsubara, T. and Nagamiya, T. (1949). *Scient.Pap.Fac.Sci. Osaka Univ.* No.14.

Matsuo, T., Suga, H., and Seki, S. (1968). *Bull.chem.Soc.Japan* 41, 583.

——— ——— ——— (1971). *Bull.chem.Soc.Japan* 44, 1171.

——— Tatsumi, M., Suga, H., and Seki, S. (1973). *Phys.Chem.Solids* 34, 136.

Mauer, F.A., Hubbard, C.R., and Hahn, T.A. (1973). *(J.) Phys.* 59, 3770.

Messer, C.E. and Ziegler, W.T. (1941). *J.Am.chem.Soc.* 63, 2703.

McClaren, A.C. (1962). *Rev.pure appl.Chem* 12, 54.

McKenzie, D.R. and Seymour, R.S. (1975). *J.Phys.* C8, 1071.

Michaelis de Saenz I., Amonini, N., and Presa, S. (1964). *Z.phys.Chem.N.F.* 43, 119.

Michel, K.H. (1973). *J.chem.Phys.* 58, 142.

Miekk-Oja, H. (1941). *Annls.Acad.Sci.Fenn.*,*Ser.A* I, No.7.

Miki, H. (1973). *J.phys.Soc.Japan* 34, 1314.

Miki, H. and Makita, Y. (1970). *J.phys.Soc.Japan* 29, 143.

Miller, B.S. and King, G.J. (1963). *J.chem.Phys.* 39, 2779.

Miller, G.R. and Gutowsky, H.S. (1963). *J.chem.Phys.* 39, 1983.

Miller, S.R., Blinc, R., Brenman, M., and Waugh, J.S. (1962). *Phys.Rev.* 126, 528.

Mizutani, I., Yamazaki, Y., Uesu, Y., Yamada, N., Kobayashi, J., Maruyama, H., and Tomiie, Y. (1967). *J.phys.Soc. Japan* 23, 900.

Mohler, E. and Pitka, R. (1974). *Solid St.Communs.* 14, 791.

Morfee, R.G.S., Staveley, L.A.K., Walters, S.T., and Wigley, D.L. (1960). *(J.)Phys.Chem.Solids* 13, 132.

Morosin, B. and Graeber, E.J. (1967). *Acta crystallogr.* 23, 766.

Mostafa, M.F. and Willett, R.D. (1971). *Phys.Rev.* B4, 2213.

Mraw, S.C. and Staveley, L.A.K. (1976). *J.chem.Thermodynamics* 8, 1001.

Mueller, H.J. and Joebstl, J.A. (1965). *Z.Kristallogr. Kristallgeom.* 121, 385.

Murray, G.R. and Waugh, J.S. (1958). *J.chem.Phys.* 29, 207.

Mustajoki, A. (1957). (a) *Annls.Acad.Sci.Fenn.,Physica, Ser.A.* VI, No.5; (b) No.7.

——————   (1958). *Annls.Acad.Sci.Fenn.,Physica,Ser.A* VI, No.9.

——————   (1962). *Annls.Acad.Sci.Fenn.,Physica,Ser.A* VI, No.99.

Nagamiya, T. (1942). *Proc. phys.-math.Soc.Japan* 24, 137.

——————   (1943). *Proc.phys.-math.Soc.Japan* 25, 540.

——————   (1952). (a) *Soc.Chim.phys.Changements de Phases*, 251; (b) *Progr.theoret.Phys.* 7, 275.

Nagatani, M., Seiyama, T., Sakiyama, M., Suga, H., and Seki, S. (1967). *Bull.chem.Soc.Japan* 40, 1833.

Nagle, J.F. and Allen, G.R. (1971). *J.chem.Phys.* 55, 2708.

Nakamura, E., Hikichi, K., and Furuichi, J. (1967). *J.phys. Soc.Japan*, 23, 471.

——————   Mitsui, T., and Furuichi, J. (1963). *J.phys. Soc.Japan*, 18, 1477.

Nakamura, N., Suga, H., Chihara, H., and Seki, S. (1965). *Bull.chem.Soc.Japan*, 38, 1779.

Nakano, J., Shiozaki, Y., and Nakamura, E. (1974).
  Ferroelectrics <u>8</u>, 483.
Natarajan, M. and Hovi, V. (1972). *Annls.Acad.Sci.Fenn.*,
  Ser.VI Phys., No.400.
───────   and Rao, C.N.R. (1975). Unpublished work,
  quoted by Rao, C.N.R., Prakash, B., and Natarajan, M.
  NBS-NSRDS Monograph - 53.
Nelmes, R.J. (1971). *Acta crystallogr.* <u>B27</u>, 272.
───────   (1972). *Phys.Stat.Solidi* <u>B52</u>, K89.
───────   and Rouse, K.D. (1974). *Ferroelectrics* <u>8</u>, 487.
Newman, R. (1950). *J.chem.Phys.* <u>18</u>, 669.
Newns, D.M. and Staveley, L.A.K. (1966). *Chem.Rev.* <u>66</u>, 267.
Niemelä, L. (1973). *Annls.Univ.Turku.,Ser.A*, No.162.
───────   and Auranen, J. (1970). *Annls.Univ.Turku.,Ser.A*
  <u>I</u>, No.132.
───────   and Komu, M. (1973). *Annls.Acad.Sci.Fenn.,Ser.A*
  <u>VI</u>, No.403.
───────   and Lohikainen, T. (1967). *Phys.kondens.Mater.*
  <u>6</u>, 376.
───────   Niemelä, M., and Tuohi, J. (1972). *Annls.Acad.*
  Sci.Fenn.,Ser.A <u>VI</u>, No.388.
───────   and Tuohi, J. (1970). *Annls.Univ.Turku.,Ser.A*
  <u>I</u>, No.137.
───────   and Ylinen, E. (1969). *Annls.Acad.Sci.Fenn.*,
  Ser.A <u>VI</u>, No.307.
───────   ───────   (1970). *Phys.Lett.* <u>31A</u>, 369.
Nimmo, J.K. and Lucas, B.W. (1973). *J.Phys.* <u>C6</u>, 201.
───────   ───────   (1976). *Acta crystallogr.*<u>B32</u>,
  1968.
Nissilä, P. and Pöyhönen, J. (1970). *Phys.Lett.* <u>33A</u>, 345.
───────   ───────   (1972). *Phys.Lett.* <u>39A</u>, 197.
Nitta, I. and Suenaga, K. (1938). *Bull.chem.Soc.Japan* <u>13</u>,
  36.
───────   and Watanabe, T. (1935). *Sci.Papers Inst.phys.*
  chem.Research (Tokyo) <u>26</u>, 164.
Nordman, C.E. (1962). *Acta crystallogr.* <u>15</u>, 18.
Norris, M.O., Strange, J.H., and Terenzi, M. (1968). *Rc.*
  Semin.Fac.Sci.Univ.Cagliari <u>38</u>, 309. (Chem.Abs.1971,
  <u>74</u>, 47859e).

Okaya, Y., Ahmed, M.S., Pepinsky, R., and Vand, V. (1957).
      Z.Kristallogr.Kristallgeom. <u>109</u>, 367.
────────   Vedam, K., and Pepinsky, R. (1958). *Acta
      crystallogr.* <u>11</u>, 307.
O'Reilly, D.E. (1973). *J.chem.Phys.* <u>58</u>, 3023.
────────   Peterson, E.M., Scheie, C.E., and Kadaba,
      P.K. (1973). *J.chem.Phys.* <u>58</u>, 3018.
────────   ────────   and Tsang, T. (1967). *Phys.
      Rev.* <u>160</u>, 333.
────────   ────────   and Williams, J.M. (1971).
      J.chem.Phys. <u>54</u>, 96.
────────   and Tsang, T. (1967). (a) *J.chem.Phys.* <u>46</u>,
      1291; (b) <u>46</u>, 130.
Orioli, P. and Pieroni, M. (1959). *Ricerca Scient.* <u>29</u>, 295.
Østerlund, K. and Rosen, H.J. (1974). *Solid St.Communs.*
      <u>15</u>, 1355.
Ozawa, T., Momota, M., and Isozaki, H. (1967). *Bull.chem.
      Soc.Japan* <u>40</u>, 1583.
Parker, F.T. and Kaplan, M. (1973). *Phys.Rev.* <u>B8</u>, 4318.
Parry, G.S. (1962). *Acta crystallogr.* <u>15</u>, 601.
────────   Schuyff, A., and Ubbelohde, A.R. (1965). *Proc.
      R.Soc.* <u>A285</u>, 360.
Paul, G.L. and Pryor, A.W. (1971). *Acta crystallogr.* <u>B27</u>,
      2700.
Pauling, L. and Sherman, J. (1933). *Z.Kristallogr.
      Kristallgeom.* <u>84</u>, 213.
Pechhold, W., Dollhopf, W., and Engel, A. (1966). *Acustica*
      <u>17</u>, 61.
Peercy, P.S. (1975). *Phys.Rev.* <u>B12</u>, 2725.
────────   Morosin, B., and Samara, G.A. (1973). *Phys.
      Rev.* <u>B8</u>, 3378.
Pendred, D. and Richards, R.E. (1955). *Trans.Faraday Soc.*
      <u>51</u>, 468.
Pepinsky, R., Okaya, Y., and Jona, F. (1957). *Bull.Am..
      phys.Soc.,Ser.II*, <u>2</u>, 220.
────────   Vedam, K., (1959). *Phys.Rev.* <u>114</u>, 1217.
────────   ────────   (1960). *Phys.Rev.* <u>117</u>, 1502.
────────   ────────   Hoshino, S., and Okaya, Y. (1958).
      Phys.Rev. <u>111</u>, 1508.

Pepinsky, R., Vedam, K., Okaya, Y., and Unterleitner, F.
    (1959). *Bull.Am.phys.Soc.* (2) <u>4</u>, 63.

Peternelj, J., Valic, M.I., and Pintar, M.M. (1971). *Physica*
    <u>54</u>, 604.

Peterson, E.R. and Willett, R.D. (1972). *J.chem.Phys.* <u>56</u>,
    1879.

Peterson, S.W., Levy, H.A., and Simonsen, S.H. (1953).
    J.chem.Phys. <u>21</u>, 2084.

Peyronel, G. and Pignedoli, A. (1975). *Acta crystallogr.* <u>B31</u>,
    2052.

Pintar, M.M., Sharp, A.R., and Vrscaj, S. (1968). *Phys.Lett.*
    <u>27A</u>, 169.

Pistorius, C.W.F.T. (1961). (a) *Z.Kristallogr.Kristallgeom.*
    <u>115</u>, 291; (b) <u>116</u>, 220.

——————   (1969). (a) *J.chem.Phys.* <u>50</u>, 1436; (b)
    <u>51</u>, 2604.

——————   (1970). (a) *(J.)Phys.Chem.Solids* <u>31</u>, 385.
    (b) *Z. anorg.allgem.Chem.* <u>376</u>, 308.

——————   (1972). *High Temp.-High Press.* <u>4</u>, 77.

——————   (1974). *Z.phys.Chem.N.F.* <u>88</u>, 253.

——————   Boeyens, J.C.A., and Clark, J.B. (1969).
    High Temp.-High Press. <u>1</u>, 41.

——————   and Clark, J.B. (1969). *High Temp.-*
    High Press. <u>1</u>, 561.

——————   and Gibson, A.A.V. (1973). *J.Solid St.*
    Chem. <u>8</u>, 126.

——————   and Richter, P.W. (1972). *Z.anorg.*
    allg.Chem. <u>389</u>, 315.

Polak, M. and Sheinblatt, M. (1973). *J.mag.Res.* <u>12</u>, 261.

Popov, M.M. and Gal'chenko, G.L. (1951).*Zh.obshch.Khim.*
    <u>21</u>, 2220.

Pöyhönen, J. (1960). *Annls.Acad.Sci.Fenn.,Ser A* <u>VI</u>, No.58.

——————   Mansikka, K., and Heiskanen, K. (1964). *Annls.*
    Acad.Sci.Fenn., Ser.A <u>VI</u>, No.168.

——————   Nissilä, P., and Jaakkola, S. (1968). *Annls.*
    Acad.Sci.Fenn.,Ser.A <u>VI</u>, 273.

Prakash, B. and Rao, C.N.R. (1975). *Crystal Structure Trans-*
    formations in Inorganic Sulfates, Phosphates, Per-

chlorates, and Chromates, NSRDS-NBS 56.

Prask, H.J., Trevino, S.F., and Rush, J.J. (1975). *J.chem. Phys.* 62, 4156.

Price, D.L., Rowe, J.M., Rush, J.J., Prince, E., Hinks, D.G., and Susman, S. (1972). *J.chem.Phys.* 56, 3697.

Pringle, G.E. and Noakes, D.E. (1968). *Acta crystallogr.* B24, 262.

Protsenko, P.I. and Kolomin, L.G. (1971). *Izv.Vyssh.Ucheb. Zaved.Fiz.* 14, 105 (Chem.Abstr. 1971, 75, 123665b).

Punkkinen, M. (1973). *Annls.Univ.Turku.* AI, No.162.

Pyykkö, P. (1968). *Chem.Phys.Lett.* 2, 559.

de Quervain, M. (1944). *Helv.phys.Acta* 17, 509.

Rabideau, S.W. and Waldstein, P. (1965). *J.chem.Phys.* 42, 3822.

Rao, A.D.P., Andrade, P. da R., and Porto, S.P.S. (1974). *Phys.Rev.* B9, 1077.

Rao, K.V.K. and Murthy, K.S. (1970). *(J.)Phys.Chem.Solids* 31, 887.

Rapoport, E. (1966). *J.chem.Phys.* 45, 2721.

────── and Kennedy, G.C. (1965). *(J.)Phys.Chem.Solids* 26, 1995.

────── and Pistorius, C.W F.T. (1966). *J.chem.Phys.* 44, 1514.

────── ────── (1967). *J.geophys.Res.* 72, 6353.

Ray, S., Zalkin, A., and Templeton, D.H. (1973). *Acta crystallogr.* B29, 2741, 2748.

Reese, W. (1969). *Phys.Rev.* 181, 905.

────── and May, L.F. (1968). *Phys.Rev.* 167, 504.

────── ────── (1972). *Ferroelectrics* 4, 65.

Reinsborough, V.C. and Whetmore, F.E.W. (1967). *Aust.J. Chem.* 20, 1.

Renard, R. and Garland, C.W. (1966). *J.chem.Phys.* 45, 763.

Rhodes, E. and Ubbelohde, A.R. (1959). *Proc.R.Soc.* A251, 156.

Riccardi, R. and Sinistri, C. (1965). *Ric.Sci.Rend.Sez.* A8, 1026.

Richards, R.E. and Schaefer, T. (1961). *Trans.Faraday Soc.* 57, 210.

────── and Smith, J.A.S. (1951). *Trans.Faraday Soc.* 47, 1261.

Richter, P.W. and Pistorius, C.W.F.T. (1971). (a) *J.Solid St.Chem.* 3, 197; (b) 3, 434.

———   ———   (1972). *J.Solid St. Chem.* 5, 276.

Riehl, J.W., Wang, R., and Bernard, H.W. (1973). *J.chem.Phys Phys.* 58, 508.

Roof, R.B. (1955). *Acta crystallogr.* 8, 739.

Roos, J. and Kind, R. (1974). *Ferroelectrics* 8, 553.

———   ———   and Petzelt, J. (1976). *Z.Phys.* B24, 99.

Rowe, J.M., Livingston, R.C., and Rush, J.J. (1973). (a) *J.chem.Phys.* 58, 5469; (b) 59, 6652.

———   Rush, J.J., Vagelatos, N., Price, D.L., Hinks, D.G. and Susman, S. (1975). *J.chem.Phys.* 62, 4551.

Rush, J.J. (1966). *J.chem.Phys.* 44, 1722.

———   de Graaf, L.A., and Livingston, R.C. (1973). *J. chem.Phys.* 58, 3439.

———   Livingston, R.C., and Rosasco, G.J. (1973). *Solid St.Communs.* 13, 159.

———   Safford, G.J., Taylor, T.I., and Havens, W.W. (1962). *Nucl.Sci.Eng.* 14, 339.

———   Taylor, T.I., and Havens, W.W. (1961). *J.chem. phys.* 35, 2265.

Sakamoto, Y. (1954). *J.Sci.Hiroshima Univ.* A18, 95.

Sakiyama, M., Kimoto, A., and Seki, S. (1965). *J.phys.Soc. Japan* 20, 2180.

———   Suga, H., and Seki, S. (1963). *Bull.chem. Soc.Japan* 36, 1025.

Salhotra, P.P., Subbarao, E.C., and Venkateswarlu, P. (1968). *Phys.St.Solidi* 29, 859.

———   ———   ———   (1969). *J.phys.Soc.Japan* 27, 621.

Samara, G.A. (1971). *Phys.Rev.Lett.* 27, 103.

Sato, Y. (1965). *J.phys.Soc.Japan* 20, 2304.

Savoie, R. and Pézolet, M. (1967). *Can.J.Chem.* 45, 1677.

Sawada, A., Takagi, Y., and Ishibashi, Y. (1973). *J. phys. Soc.Japan* 34, 748.

Sawada, S., Nomura, S., and Fujii, S. (1958). *J.phys.Soc. Japan* 13, 1549.

———   ———   Fujii, S., and Yoshida, I. (1958). *Phys.Rev.Lett.* 1, 320.

Schinke, H. and Sauerwald, F. (1960). *Z.anorg.angew.Chem.*
    304, 25.

Schlemper, E.O. and Hamilton, W.C. (1966). (a) *J.chem.Phys.*
    45, 408; (b) 44, 4498.

——   ——   and Rush, J.J. (1966).
    J.chem.Phys. 44, 2499.

Schmidt, V.H. and Uehling, E.A. (1962). *Phys.Rev.* 126, 447.

Schroeder, L.W., de Graaf, L.A., and Rush, J.J. (1971).
    J.chem.Phys. 55, 5363.

——   and Ibers, J.A. (1968). (a) *J.Am.chem.Soc.*
    88, 2601; (b) *Inorg.Chem.* 7, 594.

Schroeder, R.A., Weir, C.E., and Lippincott, E.R. (1962).
    J.Res.natn.Bur.Stand. 66A, 407.

Schumaker, N.E. and Garland C.W. (1970). *J.chem.Phys.* 53, 392.

Schwartz, P. (1971). *Phys.Rev.* B4, 920.

Seifert, H. (1931). *Z.Kristallogr.Kristallqeom.* 76, 455.

Seki, S., Momotani, M., and Nakatsu, K. (1951). *J.chem.*
    Phys. 19, 1061.

——   ——   ——   and Oshima, T. (1955).
    Bull.chem.Soc.Japan 28, 411.

Semenenko, K.N., Chavgun, A.P., and Surov, V.N. (1971).
    Russ.J.inorg.Chem. 16, 271.

Senko, M.E. (1961). *Phys.Rev.* 121, 1599.

Sequeira, A. (1965). *Acta crystallogr.* 18, 291.

——   and Hamilton, W.C. (1967). *J.chem.Phys.* 47, 1818.

Seymour, R.S. and Pryor, P.W. (1970). *Acta crystallogr.* B26, 1487.

Sharp, A.R. and Pintar, M.M. (1970). *J.chem.Phys.* 53, 2428.

Sharp, D.W.A. and Thorley, J. (1963). *J.chem.Soc.* 3557.

Shen, T.Y., Mitra, S.S., Prask, H., and Trevino, S.F. (1975).
    Phys.Rev. B12, 4530.

Shimomura, K., Kodama, T., and Negita, H. (1969). *J.phys.*
    Soc.Japan 27, 255.

Shinnaka, Y. (1956). *J.phys.Soc.Japan* 11, 393.

——   (1959). (a) *J.phys.Soc.Japan* 14, 1073; (b) 14,1707.

——   (1962). *J.phys.Soc.Japan* 17, 820.

——   (1964). *J.phys.Soc.Japan* 19, 1281.

Shmidt, N.E. and Sokolov, V.A. (1961). *Zh.neorg.Khim.* 6,
    2613 (*Russ.J.inorg.Chem.* 6, 1321.)

Shomate, C.H. (1945). *J.Am.chem.Soc.* 67, 1096.

Shultin, A.A. and Karpov, S.V. (1968). *Kristallografiya* 13, 705 (*Soviet Phys.Crystallogr.* 1969, 13, 601).

Shuvalov, L.A. and Ivanov, N.R. (1967). *Phys.St.Solidi* 22, 279.

——   ——   Gordeeva, N.V., and Kirpich-nikova, L.F. (1969). *Kristallografiya* 14, 658 (*Soviet Phys.Crystallogr.*, 1970, 14, 554).

——   ——   Kirpichnikova, L.F. and Schagina, N.M. (1968). *Sov.Phys.JETP Lett.* 8, 143.

Siegel, L.A. (1949). *J.chem.Phys.* 17, 1146.

Silsbee, H.B., Uehling, E.A., and Schmidt, V.H. (1964). *Phys.Rev.* 133, A165.

Silvidi, A.A. and Workman, D.T. (1974). *Ferroelectrics* 6, 183.

Simon, F. (1922). *Annln.Phys.* 68, 241.

——   von Simson, C., and Ruhemann, M. (1927). *Z.physik. Chem.* 129, 339.

Simonis, G.J. and Hathaway, C.E. (1974). *Phys.Rev.* B10, 4419.

Skjaeveland, S.M. and Svare, I. (1974). *Physica Scripta* 10, 273.

Sköld, K. and Dahlborg, U. (1973). *Solid St.Communs.* 13, 543.

Slater, J.C. (1941). *J.chem.Phys.* 9, 16.

Slichter, C.P., Seidel, H., Schwartz, P., and Fredericks, G. (1971). *Phys.Rev.* B4, 907.

Smith, D. (1968). *(J.)Phys.Chem.Solids.* 29, 525.

——   (1970). *J.phys.Chem.* 74, 2373.

——   (1973). *J.chem.Phys.* 58, 3833.

——   (1974). (a) *J.chem.Phys.* 60, 958; (b) *Chem.Phys. Lett.* 25, 348; (c) 25, 497.

Smith, H.G. and Bacon, G.E. (1966). *J.appl.Phys.* 37, 979.

——   and Levy, H.A. (1962). *Acta crystallogr.* 15, 1201.

Smith, S.J., Bunting, J.G., and Steeple, H. (1974) *(J.)Phys. Chem.Solids* 35, 893.

Smits, A., Ketelaar, J.A.A., and Muller, G.J. (1936). *Z. physik.Chem.* A175, 359.

——   and MacGillavry, C.H. (1933). *Z.physik.Chem.* A166, 97.

——   Muller, G.J., and Kröger, F.A. (1937). *Z.physik. Chem.* B38, 177.

Smits, A., Tollenaar, D., and Kröger, F.A. (1938). *Z.physik. Chem.* **B41**, 215.

Soda, G. and Chiba, T. (1969). *J.phys.Soc.Japan* **26**, 723.

Sokoloff, J.B. (1972). *(J.)Phys.Chem.Solids* **33**, 1899.

Sokolov, V.A. and Shmidt, N.E. (1955). *Izv.Sekt.fiz-khim., Analiza Inst.obshchei neorg.Khim.* **26**, 123.

———   ———   (1956). *Izv.Sekt.fiz-khim., Analiza Inst.Obshchei neorg.Khim.* **27**, 217.

Solbakk, J.K. and Strømme, K.O. (1969). *Acta chem.scand.* **23**, 300.

Soldate, A.M. (1947). *J.Am.chem.Soc.* **69**, 987.

Sonin, A.S. (1961). *Kristallografiya* **6**, 137 (*Soviet Phys. Crystallogr.* 1961, **6**, 112).

Sorai, M., Suga, H., and Seki, S. (1965). *Bull.chem.Soc. Japan* **38**, 1125.

Southard, J.C. Milner, R.T., and Hendricks, S.B. (1933). *J.chem.Phys.* **1**, 95.

Speight, P.A. and Jeffrey, K.R. (1973). *J.mag.Res.* **10**, 195.

Stammler, M. (1967). *J.inorg.nucl.Chem.* **29**, 2203.

———   Bruenner, R., Schmidt, W., and Orcutt, D. (1966). *Adv.X-Ray Analysis* **9**, 170.

Stasova, M.M. (1959). *Kristallografiya* **4**, 242 (*Soviet Phys. Crystallogr.* 1960, **4**, 219).

———   and Vainshtein, B.K. (1956). *Trudy Inst. Kristallog.* **12**, 18.

Staveley, L.A.K., Grey, N.R., and Layzell, M.J. (1963). *Z. Naturf.* **18a**, 148.

———   and Linford, R.G. (1969). *J.chem.Thermo-dynamics,* **1**, 1.

Stephenson, C.C. and Adams, H.E. (1944). (a) *J.Am.chem.Soc.* **66**, 1409; (b) **66**, 1412.

———   ———   (1952). *J.chem.Phys.* **20**, 1658.

———   Bentz, D.R., and Stevenson, D.A. (1955). *J.Am.chem.Soc.* **77**, 2161.

———   Blue, R.W., and Stout, J.W. (1952). *J. chem.Phys.* **20**, 1046.

———   Corbella, J.M., and Russell, L.A. (1953). *J.chem.Phys.* **21**, 1110.

Stephenson, C.C. and Hooley, J.G. (1944). *J.Am.chem.Soc.* <u>66</u>, 1397.

———— and Karo, A.M. (1968). *J.chem.Phys.* <u>48</u>, 104.

———— Landers, L.A., Cole, A.G. (1952). *J. chem.Phys.* <u>20</u>, 1044.

———— Rice, D.W., and Stockmayer, W.H. (1955). *J. chem.Phys.* <u>23</u>, 1960.

———— Wulff, C.A., and Lundell, O.R. (1964). *J. chem.Phys.* <u>40</u>, 967.

———— and Zettlemoyer, A.C. (1944). (a) *J.Am. chem.Soc.* <u>66</u>, 1402; (b) <u>66</u>, 1405.

Stepisnik, J., Slak, J., Blinc, R., Shuvalov, L.A., Ivanov, N.R., and Schagina, N.M. (1973). *Solid St.Communs.* <u>13</u>, 1053.

Stevenson, R. (1961). *J.chem.Phys.* <u>34</u>, 1757.

Steward, E.G. and Rooksby, H.P. (1953). *Acta crystallogr.* <u>6</u>, 49.

Stockmayer, W.H. and Stephenson, C.C. (1953). *J.chem.Phys.* <u>21</u>, 1311.

Strange, J.H. and Terenzi, M. (1972). *(J.)Phys.Chem.Solids* <u>33</u>, 923.

Strømme, K.O. (1969). (a) *Acta chem.scand.* <u>23</u>, 1616; (b) <u>23</u>, 1625.

———— (1970). *Acta chem.scand.* <u>24</u>, 1477.

———— (1971). *Acta chem.scand.* <u>25</u>, 211.

———— (1974). (a) *Acta chem.scand.* <u>A28</u>, 515; (b) <u>A28</u>, 546; (c) *Z.anorg.allg.Chem.* <u>403</u>, 176.

Strukov, B.A. (1964). *Fizika tverd.Tela*, <u>6</u>, 2862 (*Soviet Phys.Solid St.* 1965, <u>6</u>, 2278).

———— Amin, M., and Koptsik, V.A. (1968). *Phys.St. Solidi* <u>27</u>, 741.

———— Baddur, A., Koptsik, V.A., and Velichko, I.A. (1972). *Fizika tverd. Tela* <u>14</u>, 1034 (*Soviet Phys. Solid St.* 1972, 14, 885).

———— ———— Zinenko, V.I., Mikhailov, V.K., and Koptsik, V.A. (1973). *Fizika tverd.Tela* <u>15</u>, 2018 (*Soviet Phys.Solid St.* 1974, <u>15</u>, 1347).

———— ———— ———— Mishchenko, A.V., and Koptsik, V.A. (1973). *Fizika tverd.Tela* <u>15</u>, 1388 (*Soviet Phys.Solid St.* 1973, <u>15</u>, 939).

Subbarao, E.C. (1973). *Ferroelectrics* 5, 267.

Suga, H., Matsuo, T., and Seki, S. (1965). *Bull.chem.Soc.
Japan* 38, 1115.

———— Sugisaki, M., and Seki, S. (1966). *Molec.Cryst.* 1,
377.

Sugisaki, M., Matsuo, T., Suga, H., and Seki, S. (1968).
Bull.chem.Soc.Japan 41, 1747.

Syal, S.K. and Yoganarasimhan, S.R. (1973). *Inorg.nucl.Chem.
Lett.* 9, 1193.

Syoyama, S. and Osaki, K. (1972). *Acta crystallogr.* B28, 2626.

Tahvonen, P.E. (1947). *Ann.Acad.Sci.Fenn., Ser.AI*, Nos.43, 44.

Takagi, Y. (1948). *J.phys.Soc.Japan* 3, 271.

———— and Gesi, K. (1967). *J.phys.Soc.Japan* 22, 979.

Takeda, K. (1974). *Phys.Lett.* 47A, 335.

Tanisaki, S. (1963). *J.phys.Soc.Japan* 18, 1181.

———— and Ishimatsu, T. (1965). *J.phys.Soc.Japan* 20,
1277.

Tegenfeldt, J. and Ödberg, L. (1972). *(J.)Phys.Chem.Solids* 33,
215.

Teichert, T. and Klemm, W. (1939). *Z.anorg.allg.Chem.* 243,
86.

Tellgren, R. and Liminga, R. (1974). *Ferroelectrics* 8, 629.

Tello, M.J. and Gonzalo, J.A. (1970). *J.phys.Soc.Japan*, 28,
Suppl., 199.

Tench, A.J. (1963). *J.chem.Phys.* 38, 593.

Tenzer, L., Frazer, B.C., and Pepinsky, R. (1958). *Acta
crystallogr.* 11, 505.

Thomas, D.G. and Staveley, L.A.K. (1951). *J.chem.Soc.* 1420.

Thornley, F.R., Nelmes, R.J., and Rouse, K.D. (1975). *Chem.
Phys.Lett.* 34, 175.

Todo, I. and Tatsuzaki, I. (1966). *Phys.Lett.* 22, 22.

Tokunaga, M. and Koyano, N., (1968). *J.phys.Soc.Japan* 24,
1407.

Torrie, B.H. and Knispel, R.R. (1973). *Ferroelectrics* 5, 53.

———— Lin, C.C., Binbrek, O.S., and Anderson, A. (1972).
(J.)Phys.Chem.Solids 33, 697.

Trappeniers, N.J. (1966). *Ber.Bunsengesellschaft phys.Chem.*
70, 1080.

———— and Mandema, W. (1966). *Physica* 32, 1170.

Trappeniers, N.J. and van der Molen, T.J. (1966). *Physica* <u>32</u>, 1161.

Trefler, M. (1971). *Can.J.Phys.* <u>49</u>, 1694.

Tsang, T. and Farrar, T.C. (1969). *J.chem.Phys.* <u>50</u>, 3498.

———   ———   and Rush, J.J. (1968). *J.chem. Phys.* <u>49</u>, 4403.

Tsau, J. and Gilson, D.F.R. (1968). *J.phys.Chem.* <u>72</u>, 4082.

———   ———   (1970). *Can.J.Chem.* <u>48</u>, 717.

———   ———   (1973). *Can.J.Chem.* <u>51</u>, 1990.

Tuohi, J.E., Ylinen, E.E., and Niemelä, L.K.E. (1974). *Chem. Phys.Lett.* <u>28</u>, 35.

Ubbelohde, A.R. (1939). *Proc.R.Soc.* <u>A173</u>, 417.

———   and Woodward, I. (1942). *Proc.R.Soc.* <u>A179</u>, 399.

———   ———   (1947). *Proc.R.Soc.* <u>A188</u>, 358.

Udalova, V.V. and Pinsker, Z.G. (1963). *Kristallografiya* <u>8</u>, 538 (*Soviet Phys.Crystallogr.*1964, <u>8</u>, 433.)

Ueda, S. and Itoh, J. (1967). *J.phys.Soc.Japan* <u>22</u>, 927.

Unruh, H.-G. (1970). *Solid St.Communs.* <u>8</u>, 1951.

Vainshtein, B.K. and Stasova, M.M. (1976). *Kristallografiya* <u>1</u>, 311 (*Soviet Phys.Crystallogr.* 1956, <u>1</u>, 241).

Vaks, V.G. and Zein, N.E. (1974). *Ferroelectrics* <u>6</u>, 251.

Vallade, M. (1975). *Phys.Rev.* <u>B12</u>, 3755.

Van Kempen, H., Duffy, W.T., Miedema, A.R., and Huiskamp, W.J. (1964). *Physica* <u>30</u>, 1131.

———   Garofano, T., Miedema, A.R., and Huiskamp, W.J. (1965). *Physica* <u>31</u>, 1096.

Vannerberg, N.-G. (1962). *Acta chem.scand.* <u>16</u>, 1212.

Van Rensburg, D.J.J. and Schutte, C.J.H. (1972). *J.mol. Struct.* <u>11</u>, 229.

Vegard, L. and Sollesnes, K. (1927). *Phil.Mag.* <u>4</u>, 985.

Venkataraman, G., Usha Deniz, K., Iyengar, P.K., Roy, A.P., and Vijayaraghavan, P.R. (1966). *(J.)Phys.Chem.Solids.* <u>27</u>, 1103.

Venkatesan, K. (1957). *Proc.Ind.Acad.Sci.* <u>A46</u>, 134.

Verweel, H.J. and Bijvoet, J.M. (1938). *Z.Kristallogr. Kristallgeom.* <u>100</u>, 201.

Vijayan, M. (1968). *Acta crystallogr.* <u>B24</u>, 1237.

Vinogradova, I.S. and Lundin, A.G. (1968). *Fizika tverd.*
   Tela 10, 769 (*Soviet Phys.Solid St.* 1968, 10, 602).
Volmer, M. (1924). *Ann.Chem.* 440, 200.
Voronel' A.V. and Garber, S.R. (1967). *Zh.eksp.teor.Fiz.* 52,
   1464 (*Soviet Phys.*, *JETP*, 1967, 25, 970).
Waddington, T.C. (1958). *J.chem.Soc.* 4340.
Watton, A., Sharp, A.R., Petch, H.E., and Pintar, M.M.
   (1972). *Phys.Rev.* B5, 4281.
Waugh, J.S. and Fedin, E.I. (1962). *Fizika tverd.Tela* 4,
   2233 (*Soviet Phys.Solid St.*1963, 4, 1633).
Weiner, B.B. and Garland, C.W. (1972). *J.chem.Phys.* 56, 155.
Weir, C.E., Piermarini, G.J., and Block, S. (1969). *J.chem.*
   Phys. 50, 2089.
Weiss, A. and Zohner, K. (1967). *Phys.St.Solidi* 21, 257.
West, C.D. (1932). *J.Am.chem.Soc.* 54, 2256.
———   (1934). *Z.Kristallogr.Kristallgeom.* 88, 97.
West, J. (1930). *Z.Kristallogr.Kristallgeom.* 74, 306.
Westrum, E.F. and Justice, B.H. (1969). *J.chem.Phys.*
   50, 5083.
Williams, M.B. and Hoard, J.L. (1942). *J.Am.chem.Soc.* 64,
   1139.
Woessner, D.E. and Snowden, B.S. (1967). (a) *J.phys.Chem.* 71,
   952; (b) *J.chem.Phys.* 47, 378; (c) 47, 2361.
Wolf, F., Benecke, K., and Fuertig, H.(1972). *Z.phys.Chem.*
   (Leipzig) 249, 274.
Wood, E.A. and Holden, A.N. (1957). *Acta crystallogr.* 10,
   145.
———   Merz, W.J., and Matthias, B.T. (1952). *Phys.Rev.*
   87, 544.
Worswick, R.D., Cowell, J.C., and Staveley, L.A.K. (1974).
   *J.chem.Soc.,Faraday Trans.*I70, 1590.
Wyckoff, R.W.G. (1928). *Z.Kristallogr.Kristallgeom.* 67, 91.
Yamada, Y., Mori, M., and Noda, Y. (1972). *J.phys.Soc.Japan*
   32, 1565.
———   Noda, Y., Axe, J.D., and Shirane, G. (1974).
   Phys.Rev. B9, 4429.
———   Shibuya, I., and Hoshino, S. (1963). *J.phys.*
   Soc.Japan 18, 1594.
———   and Watanabe, T. (1963). *Bull.chem.Soc.Japan*
   36, 1032.

Yamamoto, S. and Shinnaka, Y. (1974). *J.phys.Soc.Japan*
    37, 724.
Yelon, W.B. and Cox, D.E. (1972). *Solid St.Communs.* 11, 1011.
————   ————   Kortman, P.J., and Daniels, W.B.
    (1974). *Phys.Rev.* B9, 4843.
Ylinen, E.E., Tuohi, J.E., and Niemelä, L.K.E. (1974).
    Chem.Phys.Lett. 24, 447.
Yoon, Y.K. and Carpenter, G.B. (1959). *Acta crystallogr.*
    12, 17.
Zachariasen, W.H. (1930). *Z.Kristallogr.Kristallgeom.* 73,
    141.
————   (1954). *Acta crystallogr.* 7, 792.
Ziegler, G.E. (1931). *Phys.Rev.* 38, 1040.

8

ICE AND HYDRATES

8.1. THE ORDINARY LOW-PRESSURE FORM OF ICE

Besides the ordinary low-pressure form of ice, which has an
hexagonal structure, there is an unstable cubic low-pressure
form and at least eight high-pressure forms. We shall refer
to the ordinary form as Ih. The existence of disorder in this
form was first established by a comparison of the value of
the molar entropy of water vapour derived from calorimetric
measurements with that calculated from the properties of the
water molecule obtained spectroscopically. Giauque and
Ashley's value (1933) of $188 \cdot 7$ J K^{-1} mol^{-1} for the spectroscopic entropy of a mole of water, considered as an ideal gas,
at 1 atm and 25°C, was ~ 4 J K^{-1} mol^{-1} greater than the estimate of the calorimetric entropy made on the information then
available. A later experimental study by Giauque and Stout
(1936) gave $(185 \cdot 25 \pm 0 \cdot 5)$J K^{-1} mol^{-1} for the calorimetric
entropy under the same conditions, implying that ice posses-
ses at 0 K residual entropy of $3 \cdot 45$ J K^{-1} mol^{-1}. For heavy
ice, Long and Kemp (1936) obtained a value of
$(192 \cdot 0 \pm 0 \cdot 5)$J K^{-1} mol^{-1} for the molar entropy of the ideal
vapour at 1 atm and 0°C, as compared with the spectroscopic
estimate of $195 \cdot 25$ J K^{-1} mol^{-1}. Since the difference of
$3 \cdot 25$ J K^{-1} mol^{-1} between these two figures is virtually
the same as the corresponding difference for ice formed
from ordinary water, the possibility that the disorder
is connected with *ortho* and *para* states can be ruled
out, since it would lead to values of the residual entropy which would be quite different for H$_2$O and D$_2$O, and
which in neither case would agree with the experimental
estimate. It is now generally accepted that the cause of
the disorder is that proposed by Pauling (1935). Bernal and
Fowler (1933) had previously postulated that in ice the
hydrogen atoms lie on the lines connecting the oxygen atoms,
that there is only one hydrogen atom between any pair of
oxygen atoms,[†] and that each oxygen atom has two hydrogen

[†] See page 458

atoms close to it, so that the unit of the water molecule
is preserved. These postulates are sometimes known as the
Bernal-Fowler rules, or simply as the ice rules. The water
molecule can be regarded as a tetrahedron with the oxygen
atom at its centre, which has two of the tetrahedral positions occupied by hydrogen atoms and the other two by lone
pairs of electrons. (The H-O-H angle in the molecule in
the gaseous state is actually 104°27'.) The structure of
ice-Ih is determined by the stereochemistry of the water
molecule and resembles that of wurtzite or tridymite (Fig.
8.1). It will be seen that the oxygen atoms lie in puckered

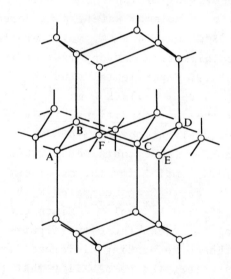

Fig.8.1. The structure of the hexagonal form of ice, ice-Ih, showing
the layers parallel to the hexagonal axis.

hexagonal layers. Adjacent layers are mirror images of each
other, and each oxygen atom is surrounded tetrahedrally by
four others. The frequency of the intramolecular vibration

[†]This postulate is occasionally violated by so-called Bjerrum faults.
These are of two kinds, D (doppelt = double) if there are two protons
between a pair of neighbouring oxygen atoms, and L (leer = empty) if
there are no protons between the oxygen atoms. It is estimated that
just below the melting-point of ice about one molecule in 10^6 is involved
in a Bjerrum fault. A simple account of these faults has been given by
Runnels (1966).

associated with the symmetrical stretching of the OH bonds
in the gaseous molecule is only ~12% larger than the value
for the molecule in ice just below 0°C. This relatively
small frequency change leaves no doubt that for the molecule
in the ice lattice the OH bond length is only slightly
greater - by ~0·002 nm - than its value for the gaseous
molecule. Consequently, the single proton lying between a
pair of nearest-neighbour oxygen atoms has two positions
available to it of minimum potential energy. Pauling has
shown that there is a very large number of ways of equal, or
almost equal, energy in which the hydrogen atoms can be disposed in ice to give a hydrogen-bonded structure which conforms to the Bernal-Fowler rules. One version of his famous
calculation of the residual entropy of ice runs as follows.
In a mole of ice containing N_A oxygen atoms and $2N_A$ hydrogen
atoms, any of the latter assigned to any one hydrogen bond
has two possible positions, and if there were no restrictions at all on the use which could be made of these, the
number of ways W of positioning the hydrogen atoms would be
2^{2N_A}. However, of the sixteen possible ways of siting the
hydrogen atoms round any one oxygen atom, only six are
acceptable in that only six give the molecular unit H_2O. Of
the ten unacceptable arrangements, one would represent the
species H_4O^{2+}, another the ion O^{2-}, four the ion H_3O^+, and
four the ion OH^-. And although there is evidence from the
electrical conductivity of ice that at any instant the
crystals do in fact contain a very small proportion of the
species H_3O^+ and OH^-, the amount of these is altogether too
small to have any significant effect on the overall disorder. [Eigen and De Maeyer (1958) have estimated that the
concentration of these ions in ice at -10°C is between
3×10^{-11} and $1·5 \times 10^{-10}$ mol dm^{-3}.] Consequently, as far
as any one oxygen atom is concerned, the total number of
possible ways of siting the protons is reduced by the factor
3/8. If the same restriction is exerted *independently* by
each of the N_A oxygen atoms, the total number of acceptable
configurations W becomes $W = 2^{2N_A} \times (3/8)^{N_A} = (3/2)^{N_A}$ and
the associated entropy is $S = k \ln (3/2)^{N_A} = 3·38$ J K^{-1} mol^{-1},
in close agreement with the observed values of the residual

entropy for both light and heavy ice.

Two assumptions made in this calculation demand closer
scrutiny, the first that each oxygen atom can be regarded
as independently determining the fraction of configurations
acceptable to itself, the second that all configurations
have effectively the same energy. Before discussing these,
however, it may be stated that the Pauling structure for
ice (sometimes referred to as the 'half-hydrogen' or
'statistical' structure) is now accepted as essentially
correct. Alternatives have been proposed, notably a polar
disordered structure advanced by Rundle (1953) in the belief
that ice crystals can be piezoelectric. As Lipscomb (1954)
pointed out, however, the Rundle model should lead to a residual entropy of ~4·0 J K^{-1} mol^{-1}, which is significantly
larger than the experimental value. Moreover, the balance
of the evidence seems to be that ice crystals do not show
piezoelectric or pyroelectric behaviour. On the basis of
experiments carried out on some unusually good ice crystals,
Mason and Owston (1952) stated that there were no indications of piezoelectric or pyroelectric properties, a conclusion confirmed by Steinemann (1953), Rossberg and Magun
(1957), and by Teichmann and Schmidt (1965). Deubner, Heise,
and Wenzel (1960),on the other hand, claimed that ice *is*
piezoelectric, but it seems probable that they were observing an effect due to inhomogeneous impurities (Gränicher
1969). In any case, the Pauling structure has been upheld
by a single crystal neutron diffraction study of heavy ice
at -50°C and -150°C (Peterson and Levy 1957), by a similar
investigation on ordinary ice at 77 K (Chamberlain, Moore,
and Fletcher 1973), and also by electron diffraction experiments on ordinary ice (Shimaoka 1960).

Returning to the estimate of W, the following argument,
due to Owston (1951) shows that the simple calculation outlined above cannot be exact. If we consider a sequence of
six oxygen atoms ABCDEF and assume that the protons round
A have a given acceptable distribution, there are three
possible ways of disposing the protons round B. For each
of these, there are three possible ways of siting the protons
round C, and so on, so the total number of possibilities for

the chain of six atoms is $3^5 = 243$. Since this is not a
multiple of six, the six possible acceptable configurations
of the protons round F cannot all be equally represented.
Therefore the configuration chosen for A has an influence,
even though slight, on the environment of F. Moreover, the
oxygen atoms form six-membered rings, and as shown in Fig.
8.1, F might in fact be a nearest neighbour of A, in virtue
of which the chosen configuration for A would require that
F should have one of three equally probable configurations -
a requirement clearly inconsistent with that reached by considering F as the end of the chain ABCDEF. Several authors
have attempted the altogether more sophisticated analyses
which recognition of the interdependence of the environments
of different oxygen atoms demands, treating both a two-
dimensional quadratic lattice (the so-called square ice
problem, section 3.7) as well as the actual three-dimensional
case. Their work shows that the number of complexions W,
and hence the entropy of disorder, is slightly greater than
the value given by Pauling's simple approach. Some of the
mathematics involved in these calculations is difficult, and
we may therefore mention that one of the first and simpler
attempts to improve on Pauling's estimate of W was that of
Meijering (1957), which, while superseded by later more
rigorous treatments, made it clear why Pauling's value for
W is an underestimate. Using matrix methods, DiMarzio and
Stillinger (1964) expressed the residual entropy as a
series expansion in which the first and by far the most important term is Pauling's $R \ln(3/2)$. Their approach was
developed by Nagle (1966), who obtained an even more accurate
result for W', where $W = (W')^N A$, (which was the same, in-
cidentally, for both hexagonal and cubic ice), namely
$W' = 1 \cdot 506085 \pm 0 \cdot 00015$, whence $S = k \ln (W')^N A = (3 \cdot 408 \pm 0 \cdot 001)$ J K^{-1} mol^{-1}. Shortly afterwards, Lieb (1967) succeeded in arriving at an exact solution of the square ice
problem, namely $W' = (4/3)^{3/2} = 1 \cdot 5396$, as compared with
Nagle's numerical estimate of $1 \cdot 540 \pm 0 \cdot 001$. These statistical methods have an importance outside the particular case
of ice, in that they point the way to the treatment of other
systems in which phase transitions involving hydrogen-bonding

can occur, such as ferroelectric and antiferroelectric solids.
     Turning now to the equality or otherwise of the energy
of different configurations of water molecules in ice, this
is of interest in its bearing on why the disorder apparently
persists to 0 K. We have to consider the relative positions
of the six oxygen atoms which form the neighbours of any two
linked oxygen atoms. In ice-Ih there are in fact two possible arrangements which are shown in Fig.8.2, and which are

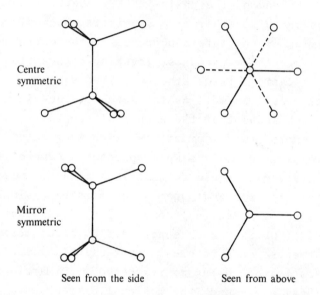

Fig.8.2. The two possible arrangements for the six oxygen atoms adjacent
to a pair of linked oxygen atoms in ice-Ih (Bjerrum 1952).

distinguished as being mirror-symmetric and centre-symmetric.
If viewed along the hexagonal (vertical) axis, these two
arrangements would appear to be eclipsed and staggered respectively. In ice-Ih, one quarter of the arrangements are
mirror-symmetric, and all other arrangements are centre-
symmetric, whereas in the unstable cubic form of ice, Ic,
which resembles diamond, *all* the arrangements are centre-
symmetric. Insertion of the protons in acceptable positions
causes the symmetry of both arrangements to become either
inverse or oblique, as may be seen from Fig.8.3, where +

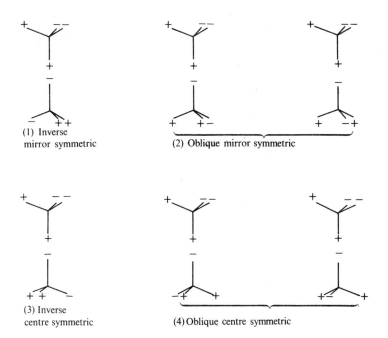

Fig.8.3. The six possible charge distributions for the mirror-symmetric and centre-symmetric arrangements in ice-Ih (Bjerrum 1952).

indicates a proton and - the effective negative charge due to a lone pair on an oxygen atom. Clearly these different arrangements will have different energies. From the charge distribution shown in Fig.8.3 one would intuitively expect that a mirror-symmetric disposition would have a lower energy than a centre-symmetric arrangement, that the inverse mirror arrangement (1) would have a lower energy than the oblique mirror arrangement (2), but that of the centre-symmetric arrangements the oblique (4) would have a lower energy than the inverse (3). Some experimental support for the expectation that a mirror-symmetric bond has a lower energy than a centre-symmetric bond is that in ice-Ih the former bonds appear to be slightly shorter than the others. If all the O--O bonds were equal in length, than the c/a ratio in ice-Ih should be $(8/3)^{\frac{1}{2}}$, $= 1·6330$. Megaw's report (1934) that the ratio is actually a little less than this was confirmed by LaPlaca and Post (1960) and later by Brill and Tippe

(1967), who found that between 0° and -180°C the c/a ratio
is virtually constant at 1·6280 ± 0·0002.   This is consistent with the mirror-symmetric bonds being ~0·001 nm shorter
than the centre-symmetric bonds.   Calculations of the energy
differences (2)-(1) and (3)-(4) were first made by
Bjerrum (1952), who assumed that the water molecule was a
regular tetrahedron with a centre to apex distance of 0·099
nm and with positive charges of 0·171e at two corners and
negative charges of the same magnitude at the other two -
a charge distribution which gives the correct dipole moment
for the water molecule.   Bjerrum's calculations appeared to
show that the energy differences (2)-(1) and (3)-(4)
were considerable, but Pitzer and Polissar (1956) pointed
out that he had only considered the interactions a and b of
Fig.8.4, neglecting the almost equally important interactions

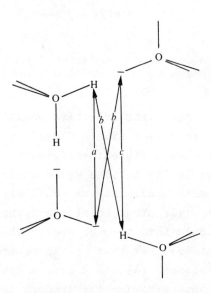

Fig.8.4. The interactions considered by Pitzer and Polissar (1956) in
evaluating the electrostatic energy of a group of water molecules in
ice.

c between water molecules separated by two other water molecules.   Pitzer and Polissar found that by taking the interactions c into account the differences in energy (2)-(1)
and (3)-(4) were much reduced.   The absolute magnitudes of

these differences depend on the value adopted for the relative permittivity appropriate to the interactions. With
a value of 3 for this - which, though low, is reasonable,
for since the dipoles are regarded as fixed, dipole orientation cannot be considered as contributing to the permittivity - the energy difference between the ordered and
disordered arrangements of the protons is such that, divided
by the entropy of disorder of $3\cdot45$ J K^{-1} mol^{-1}, the corresponding Curie temperature is ~60 K.

Doubts have been expressed as to whether even Pitzer
and Polissar's improved version of Bjerrum's calculation is
accurate enough to decide how the configurational energy of
a group of water molecules in ice depends on their mutual
arrangement, or whether, indeed, such a situation can be
adequately handled at all on the basis of a model in which
point charges are located within an individual molecule
to give the correct overall dipole moment (Hollins 1964,
Campbell, Gelernter, Heinen, and Moorti (1967). But at
least it appears that there are energy differences for different arrangements of the protons in ice which are relatively small - probably less than one per cent of the
lattice energy. The latter quantity is, of course, primarily determined by the interaction between nearest-
neighbour molecules, while the interactions which determine
the details of the hydrogen-bonding pattern are those
between more distant neighbours. The question therefore
arises as to whether these small energy differences for
different arrangements of the protons can give rise to sufficient ordering in the lattice to have observable consequences, or whether this would only happen at temperatures
so low that the atoms are no longer capable of the freedom
of movement necessary to achieve a more ordered condition.
There is in fact evidence that on cooling to temperatures
in the neighbourhood of 100 K some rearrangement of the
protons in ice-Ih does take place to produce a slight measure of order. The first indications of this were the observations of Giauque and Stout (1936) that there appears
to be a small anomaly in the heat capacity near 100 K and
that thermal equilibrium in ice is only slowly established

between 85 K and 100 K. In 1964, Dengel, Eckener, Plitz,
and Riehl reported that the permittivity of ice-Ih passes
through a maximum near 100 K, and they attributed this to a
transition to a ferroelectric state. Although a rather
different interpretation is now placed on their experimental
results, this work of Dengel and his colleagues stimulated
further useful research into the properties of ice at low
temperatures. The heat capacity was reinvestigated by van
den Beukel (1968), Pick, Wenzl, and Engelhardt (1971), and
Haida, Matsuo, Suga, and Seki (1972). All three studies
confirm that the heat capacity is anomalous near 100 K.
Haida *et al*. demonstrated that the magnitude of the thermal
anomaly can be increased by annealing the ice at 90 K (Fig.
8.5), though neither in their experiments nor in those of

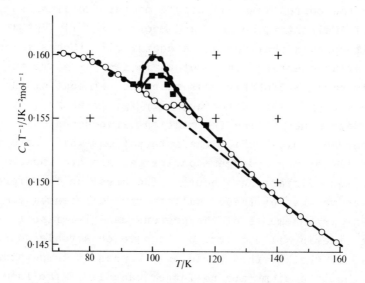

Fig.8.5. Temperature dependence of the molar heat capacity C_p of ice-Ih
(plotted as C_pT^{-1}) after different thermal treatments; o , quenched at
~1 K min^{-1}; ■ , annealed at 94·4 K for 71 h; ● annealed at 89·4 K for 624
h. The dotted line is the estimated 'normal' heat capacity (Haida
et al. 1972).

van den Beukel and Pick *et al*. did the entropy change associated with the heat capacity anomaly exceed two per cent of
the residual entropy of ice-Ih of 3·45 J K^{-1} mol^{-1}. The

Japanese investigators detected a measurable heat evolution
from samples of ice cooled into the region of slow thermal
equilibration, and from a quantitative study of this they
obtained an estimate of 22 kJ mol^{-1} for the activation energy
of the relaxation process involved. The experiments of van
den Beukel and of Pick and his coworkers showed that on
doping the ice with an acid impurity such as hydrogen fluoride the region of abnormal heat capacity becomes more prominent and tends to occur at lower temperatures, and may
appear as two humps on the heat capacity curve rather than
one. Such effects can be brought about by hydrogen fluoride
at a mole fraction of ~10^{-5}. The extra entropy gain on
warming such doped ice, however, is still less than five
per cent of the residual entropy. In a perfect ice crystal,
proton rearrangement can only be accomplished by infringing
the Bernal-Fowler rules, but as Pick *et al.* pointed out, a
real crystal will contain imperfections which facilitate such
rearrangement. An impurity such as hydrogen fluoride presumably acts as a catalyst by increasing the number of defects or imperfections and by lowering the activation energy
for proton movement.

An interesting technique which has been applied to ice-
Ih in the temperature region we are concerned with is that
of the measurement of the thermally stimulated depolarization
(TSD) current. A sample of ice is cooled in an electric
field, or maintained at a suitably low temperature under the
influence of such a field, and as a result becomes polarized.
The current which develops when the sample is heated is
measured. Fig.8.6 is an example of the results obtained for
ice-Ih, taken from the comprehensive study of Johari and
Jones (1975), who summarize the theory of the method. The
magnitude of the TSD current depends *inter alia* on the heating rate, the activation energy for the process responsible
for the decay of polarization, and on the difference between
the low- and high-frequency permittivities. Johari (1975)
pointed out that the TSD technique promises to be a valuable
source of information on permittivity changes in slow order-
disorder transitions for which the long relaxation times
render conventional methods of permittivity measurement

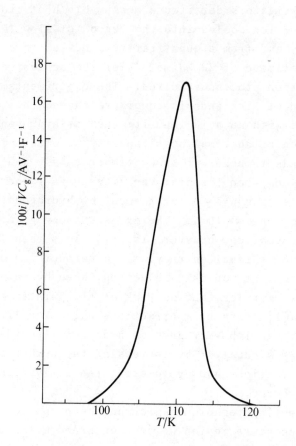

Fig.8.6. The thermally stimulated depolarization (TSD) current i measured in H_2O ice after being kept in an electric field at 99·2 K for 17 days. Heating rate $2·27 \times 10^{-3}$ K s^{-1}. In the quantity plotted as ordinate, V is the applied voltage and C_g the capacitance of the empty cell (Johari and Jones 1975).

impracticable, thus enabling a decision to be made in such cases as to whether the ordered phase is ferroelectric or antiferroelectric. On the basis of their own measurements and their reinterpretation of those of Dengel et al., Johari and Jones concluded that ice-Ih does not in fact become ferroelectric below 100 K.

There have been several theoretical examinations of the extent to which orientational order is to be expected in ice. These have aimed at calculating the Kirkwood orientational correlation factor g_K, a measure of the extent to

which neighbouring molecules tend to align their dipoles.
Treatments of this problem such as those of Rahman and
Stillinger (1972) and Stillinger and Cotter (1973) (who
briefly reviewed earlier work in this field) led to the conclusion that a not inconsiderable amount of local orientational order is to be expected in ice, sufficient to cause
the latter authors to express mild surprise that the simple
Pauling approximation is as good as it is.

To summarize, on cooling ice-Ih short-range proton order
begins to develop below 140 K, but as the temperature drops
further attempts to increase the order are defeated by the
exponential increase in the relaxation time for the ordering
process, and accordingly the disorder is very largely frozen-
in.

8.2. THE CUBIC FORM OF LOW-PRESSURE ICE
This form of ice, Ic, was first characterized by König
(1942, 1943) and by Blackman and Lisgarten (1957). In these
studies, and in all of the earlier work on Ic, it was prepared by allowing water vapour to condense slowly on a
surface cooled to below 193 K. Either a deposit of Ic is
produced directly, or else vitreous or partly vitreous ice
is formed which transforms on warming into Ic at about 150 K.
Whether vitreous ice or Ic is formed depends primarily on
the rate of deposition of the vapour and on the temperature
of the surface on which the deposit forms. When Ic is
heated, it changes irreversibly into Ih, the transition
becoming perceptible at temperatures which have been reported as being as far apart as 143 K and 200 K. It is now
known, however, that Ic can be made in quantity from the
high-pressure forms of ice. If any one of these is prepared by application of a suitable pressure and then cooled
under pressure to liquid nitrogen temperatures, it does
not revert to a low-pressure form when the pressure is
released. This has made it possible to carry out investigations at atmospheric pressure (and necessarily at low
temperatures) on the high-pressure forms of ice. All of
these, without exception, when warmed from liquid nitrogen
temperatures, change first into Ic. This happens at ~125 K

for ice-VII, at ~170 K for ice-II, and at intermediate temperatures for the other forms (Bertie, Calvert, and Whalley
1963, 1964).

Ic, like the stable form Ih, has a disordered structure.
This was clearly shown by an electron diffraction study
(Shimaoka 1960). Ic and Ih are in fact very similar, the
densities of the two forms and the O--O distances being virtually identical, as are the infrared spectra from 4000 cm^{-1}
to 50 cm^{-1}. The structural difference lies in the relation
between the planes of hexagonal rings in Fig.8.1, which in
Ic are joined to put the oxygen atoms in the same relation
as the atoms in diamond or β-cristobalite, thereby making
all the bonds centre-symmetric. The enthalpy of Ic only
exceeds that of Ih by about 160 J mol^{-1} (Sugisaki, Suga,
and Seki 1968). Pitzer and Polissar, on the basis of calculations discussed in the previous section, concluded that
the energies of the cubic and hexagonal forms are equal,
but pointed out that the slightest amount of proton ordering
about the mirror-symmetric bonds in the hexagonal structure
could account for the stability of this form over the cubic
modification.

8.3. THE HIGH-PRESSURE FORMS OF ICE
The pressure-temperature diagram, which is largely due to
experiments by Bridgman and by Whalley and his coworkers,
is reproduced in Fig.8.7. Of the high-pressure forms, IV
is a metastable phase which is not shown in Fig.8.7. Its
existence appeared probable from Bridgman's experiments
(1912) on ice formed from ordinary water, and was confirmed
in a later study of the modifications of heavy ice (Bridgman
1935). All the stable high-pressure forms have been examined by diffraction methods by Kamb and his coworkers, and
by a variety of techniques by Whalley and his collaborators.
The work of these groups has considerably extended our
knowledge of the polymorphism of ice. The diffraction
studies have not only included powder photographs taken
under pressure, but, as already mentioned, the high-pressure
forms can be examined at suitably low temperatures at atmospheric pressure, and use has been made of this to obtain

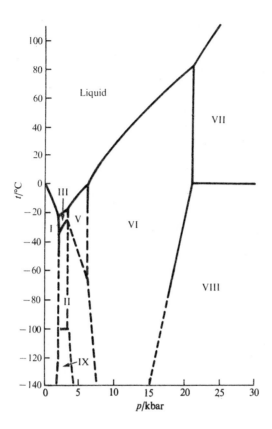

Fig.8.7. The ice phase diagram (Whalley, Heath, and Davidson 1968).

single crystals for both X-ray and neutron diffraction
work.

It seems that the protons are ordered virtually completely in forms II and VIII, and largely in IX, but disordered in all other forms, including IV, though the disorder is not necessarily complete. This conclusion about
II was reached by Kamb (1964) from a detailed analysis of X-
ray single-crystal rotation photographs taken at 123 K. The
puckered six-membered rings of Ih persist in II, but in the
latter they are more compactly linked (Fig.8.8). The structural evidence for long-range proton ordering in II from the
X-ray work is that there are two sorts of oxygen atom in the
crystal with different environments, whereas in a structure

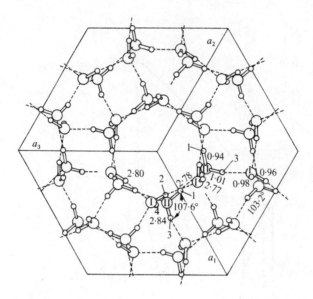

Fig.8.8. The structure of D_2O ice-II, shown as a projection along the hexagonal c axis. The two non-equivalent types of oxygen atom are labelled I and II. Each type of water molecule separately forms a hydrogen-bonded, puckered hexagonal ring. Hydrogen-bonded O--O distances and O-D bond lengths are given in Ångströms (from Hamilton, Kamb, LaPlaca, and Prakash 1969).

with disordered protons the average environment of all oxygen atoms should be the same, as in ice-I. As a result of the ordering, the symmetry of the rhombohedral lattice is degraded from $R\bar{3}c$ to $R\bar{3}$. The ordered structure was confirmed by neutron diffraction investigations on D_2O ice-II, on a powdered sample by Finch, Rabideau, Wenzel, and Nereson (1968), and on a single crystal by Kamb, Hamilton, La Placa, and Prakash (1971). The latter very detailed study left no doubt that the deuteron ordering is complete, especially in the light of the further analysis of the results by La Placa, Hamilton, Kamb, and Prakash (1973). We shall refer later to the information on interatomic distances and interbond angles obtained from this diffraction work.

     The conclusion that ice-II is an ordered form is supported by the values of the entropy differences ΔS_t for transitions involving this phase. These ΔS_t values (Table 8.1) have been obtained by applying the Clapeyron equation

TABLE 8.1

Values of the entropy of transition ΔS_t between various polymorphic forms of H_2O ice[a]. ΔS_t has been obtained from the measured slope of the appropriate phase boundary line[b].

Transition	$\Delta S_t / \text{J K}^{-1}\text{mol}^{-1}$	Reference
II → I	+3.3	1
III → II	-4·2, -4·2[b]	1,2
II → V	+4·2	1
I → III	+0·3	1
III → V	-0·25	1
V → VI	+0·2	1
IV → VI	+0·4	3
IV → VI	+0·04[a]	3
VI → VII	-1·45	4
VI → VII	-1·6[a]	4
VI → VIII	-4·2	5
III → IX	-1·35[b]	2

a. Values marked thus refer to D_2O ice.
b. Values marked thus derive from differential calorimetric measurements.

References
1. Kamb (1964), using Bridgman's results.
2. Nishibata and Whalley (1974).
3. Engelhardt and Whalley (1972).
4. Johari, Lavergne, and Whalley (1974).
5. Brown and Whalley (1966).

$dp/dT = \Delta S/\Delta V$ to the slopes of the phase-boundary lines in the phase diagram. In principle, there must be some contribution to each of these ΔS_t values from changes in the lattice vibrational entropy, but from the values for transitions involving phases other than II, VIII, and IX this contribution would seem to be small. The ΔS values for the three transitions from phase II are not far from 3.41 J K^{-1} mol^{-1}, the expected configurational entropy for disordered protons, and approximately the experimental value for the residual entropy of ice-I at 0 K. This strongly implies that in II the protons are ordered, and disordered in III and V. Further evidence for this comes from permittivity and infrared data. II, in contrast to I, III, V, and VI, has a low permittivity and shows no detectable dielectric relaxation (Wilson, Chan, Davidson, and Whalley, 1965). The static relative permittivity ε_0 of II is ~4, which is about the same as ε_∞ for I, III, V, and VI, for which ε_0 goes from ~99 (for I) to ~193 (for VI). As for the infrared evidence, Bertie and Whalley (1964) made a thorough study of the spectrum from 4000 to 340 cm^{-1} of ice in the forms Ih, Ic, II, III, and V, prepared from H_2O, D_2O, and dilute solutions of one isotopic species in the other (which give information on the vibration frequencies associated with the HDO molecule). The stretching bands of OH and OD in the HDO molecule proved to be rather broad in Ih, Ic, and V, the OD bond having, for example, a half-width of ~30 cm^{-1}. This was regarded as a consequence of the disordered proton arrangement in these forms, which would give rise to variability in the forces acting on the oxygen atoms and hence in the O--O equilibrium distances and the associated force constants. For II, the corresponding bands were much narrower (half-width ~5 cm^{-1} for the OD band). Likewise, the rotational-vibrational bands for the molecules in ice-II formed from pure H_2O or D_2O showed considerable fine structure, which was absent from the corresponding bands in phases I and V. It will be seen from Fig.4.16(b) that the O-D stretching vibration band obtained from a dilute solution of HOD in H_2O ice-II is resolved into four components. These correspond to the four non-equivalent sites for the H or D atoms which are occupied in the ordered structure.

What distinguishes ice-II from the other ordered forms, VIII and IX, is that II cannot be produced from a structurally similar proton-disordered phase, and this is presumably responsible for differences in the behaviour of ice-II as compared with the neighbouring phases I, III, and

V on the phase diagram (Bridgman 1912). With regard to
superheating and supercooling, for example, the relation
between II on the one hand and these three forms on the other
is analogous to that between the crystalline and liquid forms
of a pure substance. Thus, II can never be superheated into
the regions where III and V are stable, though these two
forms can easily be supercooled into the stability region
of II. II can only be produced under pressure from I at
temperatures much below the upper limits of the stability
region of II. Apparently conflicting statements have been
made, however, about the interconvertibility of II and III.
Bridgman reported that once II has been converted into III,
it is difficult to reform it, which would mean that there
was no sign of the 'memory effect' which can operate in
transitions between the other forms. But Nishibata and
Whalley (1974) found that after II had been converted by
warming into III, the latter phase always transformed into
II on cooling before finally giving phase IX.

We now turn to the forms III and IX. ΔS_t for the transformation of III into II is $-4 \cdot 2$ J K^{-1} mol^{-1} (Table 8.1),
implying that III is orientationally disordered. Whalley,
Heath, and Davidson (1968) discovered that when III is
cooled it undergoes a gradual transition to give a new form
IX. They measured the relative permittivity ε_0 (between
10^{-1} and 10^{-6} Hz) of form III on cooling to ~110 K and found
that between 208 K and $164 \cdot 5$ K ε_0 falls gradually to a limiting, very low value, equal to ε_∞ (Fig.8.9). Since the relaxation time in this temperature interval does not rise to
values sufficiently long to allow frozen-in disorder, being
~1s at 160 K, III must have changed into an orientationally
ordered form, IX. The similarity of the X-ray powder photographs of III at 203 K (under pressure) and of IX at 77 K
(at atmospheric pressure) shows that the positions of the
oxygen atoms in III and IX are essentially the same. The
unit cell in III and IX is tetragonal, space group $P4_1 2_1 2$
(Kamb and Prakash 1968). Evidence already existed in the
earlier infrared work of Bertie and Whalley (1964) to support
the view that IX is ordered. The spectroscopic features
observed in phase II with ice made from dilute solutions of

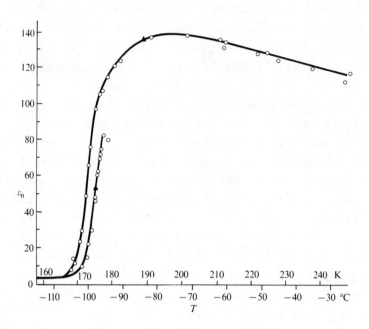

Fig.8.9. The limiting low-frequency relative permittivity of ice-III at 2·3 kbar on cooling and heating (Whalley, Heath, and Davidson 1968).

H_2O in D_2O, and *vice versa*, which have been cited above as evidence that the protons in II are ordered, were also observed in III on cooling to 173 K, namely after III had presumably almost completed the gradual transformation into IX. Subsequently, further confirmation that IX is ordered while III is disordered was provided by two neutron diffraction studies, one carried out on powdered samples of D_2O ice-III and -IX by Arnold, Wenzel, Rabideau, Nereson, and Bowman (1971), the other a single-crystal study of D_2O ice-IX (La Placa, Hamilton, Kamb, and Prakash 1973). In Fig.8.10 the neutron diffraction patterns of III and IX obtained by Arnold and his coworkers are compared. The peak broadening in form III is to be noted. A projection of the structure of D_2O ice-IX as determined by La Placa and his colleagues is shown in Fig.8.11. There are two types of water molecule, I and II. Type I has no point symmetry, while type II lies on a two-fold axis. The preferred positions for the deuterons are shown as small circles drawn with full lines. The

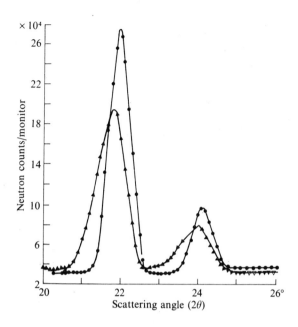

Fig.8.10. Superimposed neutron diffraction patterns of D_2O ice-III and
ice-IX at 2·8 kbar showing the peak broadening in III; •, ice-IX at 127 K,
▲, ice-III at 249 K (Arnold et al. 1971).

most interesting feature of this phase is that the order is
not complete, the very thorough analysis of La Placa et al.
indicating that a few per cent of the deuterons are to be
found in the sites shown in Fig.8.11 as the small circles
drawn in dashed lines. The same conclusion was reached independently by Nishibata and Whalley (1974) from a calorimetric determination of the entropy of the III→IX transition,
which they found to be -1·35 J K^{-1} mol^{-1}, numerically much
less than the configurational entropy change of -3·51 J K^{-1}
mol^{-1} to be expected for a transition from a fully disordered
III to a fully ordered IX. (Not only are the structures of
III and IX very similar, but the transition between the two
phases involves a volume change of less than one per cent,
so very probably the observed entropy change is essentially
that in the configurational entropy.) Nishibata and Whalley
showed that the thermodynamic data are consistent with the
degree of disorder in IX suggested by the diffraction experi-

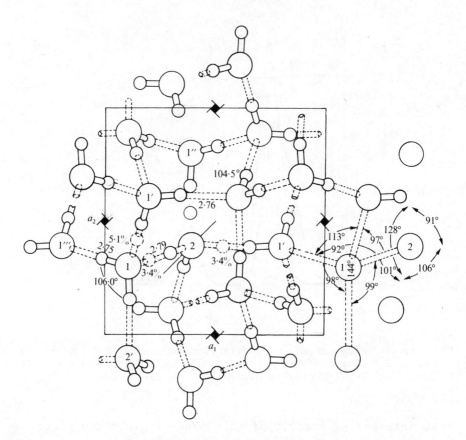

Fig.8.11. Structure of D_2O ice-IX, shown as a projection along the tetra-gonal c axis. Large circles represent oxygen atoms, the smaller circles deuterium atoms (see text). The percentages are the occupancy factors for the sites indicated, as found from the neutron diffraction study (Kamb 1973)

ments, and it is likely that the extent of disorder as re-vealed by the calorimetric experiments represents the true equilibrium situation prevailing in the ice-IX lattice at 168 K.

The metastable phase IV has been investigated by Engel-hardt and Whalley (1972), making use of the discovery by Evans (1967) that IV can be nucleated from the liquid by a variety of organic compounds. They estimated that the en-tropy changes for the IV→VI transformation in ice from H_2O and D_2O are 0·4 and 0·04 J K^{-1} mol^{-1} respectively. These increases are so small that since VI is orientationally disordered, the same must be true of IV. Engelhardt and

Whalley expressed the opinion that ice can probably form
other metastable phases, but of much shorter life-times than
that of IV.

From the entropy changes recorded in Table 8.1 for the
transitions II→V, III→V and V→VI it is clear that V and VI
are essentially disordered phases. In the case of V, this
inference is supported by dielectric evidence (Johari and
Whalley 1973), and by the infrared spectrum, as already
mentioned. X-ray and single-crystal neutron diffraction
studies have been carried out on ice-V and -VI at atmospheric
pressure on samples quenched to ~100 K. Since low-tempera-
tures favour ordering, it is not surprising that such experiments at ~100 K have revealed some degree of proton or
deuteron ordering in V and VI and indeed in all the high-
pressure forms of ice. The X-ray diffraction study of Kamb,
Prakash, and Knobler (1967) on H_2O ice-V at 110 K and the
neutron diffraction work of Hamilton, Kamb, LaPlaca, and
Prakash (1969) on single crystals of D_2O ice-V at the same
temperature established that the crystal is monoclinic with
the space group $A2/a$. This structure does not allow complete
ordering of the hydrogen atoms. Nevertheless, the neutron
results clearly indicated that there is some measure of
deuteron ordering in the quenched sample. Fig.8.12 shows

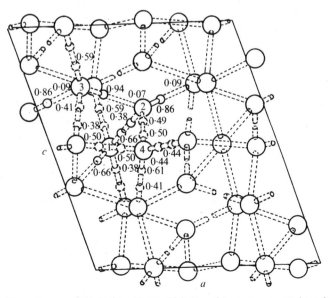

Fig.8.12. Structure of D_2O ice-V at 110 K, shown as a projection along
the c axis (see text) (Hamilton *et al.* 1969).

the structure of V, the oxygen atoms being represented by
the larger circles and the deuterium atoms by the smaller
circles.   The numbers adjacent to the latter give the population or occupancy factors of the sites.   These factors
were found to cover the range 0·08 to 0·94.   The deuteron
sites for which the population factor approaches unity are
shown as complete circles, while those for which this factor
is roughly 0·5 are shown as dashed circles.   For the fully
disordered ice-V all population factors would be 0·5.

      With ice-VI a new feature appears.   The crystal is made
up of two interpenetrating but independent frameworks (Kamb
1965).   Each of these consists of hydrogen-bonded chains of
water molecules cross-linked to give a rather open structure,
and each framework uses the vacant space available in the
other.   Kamb has described such a crystal as a 'self-clathrate'
The structures of phases VII and VIII (which together with
VI make up the three most dense forms of ice) are also self-
clathrates.   Kamb concluded that ice-VI has a tetragonal
lattice of space group $P4_2/nmc$, a structure only compatible
with complete disorder.   In the diffraction pattern which he
obtained at 100 K, however, there appeared some very weak
reflections which contravened the space group and suggested
the possibility that cooling produces ordering. That this
does in fact happen was confirmed by neutron diffraction.
The ordering is accompanied by a change to an orthorhombic
lattice of space group $Pmmn$.   This low-temperature form has
been designated ice-VI', and its structure is shown in Fig.
8.13.   The circles and decimals have the same significance
as in Fig.8.12.   In addition, the numbers within the circles
give the heights of the corresponding atoms above the base
of the unit cell as hundredths of the c axial length, and the
fractions in the upper left corner of the diagram are the
occupancy factors that would obtain for the sites in question
if the degree of long-range order were the maximum consistent with the space group $Pmmn$.   It will be noted that in
Fig.8.13 the central cluster of water molecules belongs to
one framework and that in the bottom left-hand corner to the
other, independent framework.   In ice-VI' each framework
is ferroelectrically ordered, the net polarization being

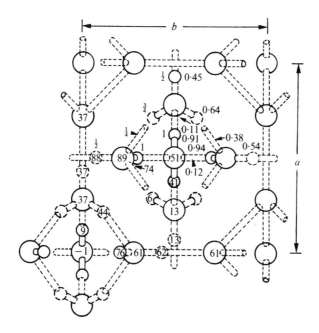

Fig.8.13. Structure of ice-VI' (Kamb 1973).

parallel to the c axis, but the polarization of one framework
is cancelled by that of the other to give an antiferroelectric
crystal.   A similar situation exists in ice-VIII.

Kamb (1973) has stressed that although the low-temperature form of VI has been provisionally designated as ice-VI',
the two forms are crystallographically distinct, and having
different space groups can justifiably be regarded as two
different phases. [Johari and Whalley (1976) measured the
low-frequency permittivity of ice-VI down to 128 K under a
pressure of 9 kbar. Their results confirmed that this phase
seems to be approaching a ferroelectrically ordered state
on cooling, but as the neutron diffraction study at atmospheric pressure and 100 K showed that ice-VI' is partly
ordered antiferroelectrically under these conditions, it
would seem that between 128 K at 9 kbar and 100 K at atmospheric pressure there is a hitherto undetected transition.]
Admittedly, owing to the limitations involved in carrying
out diffraction experiments under pressure, it still remains
to be proved that the high-temperature form VI has the space

group $P4_2/nmc$, but the balance of the available evidence
appears to favour this.   For the pair of ices III and IX,
however, in spite of the use of different Roman letters
to distinguish between them, the affinity between the two
forms is closer.   Among all the known forms of ice, III and
IX have a unique relation in that the structure allows for
a change from proton order to disorder without any alteration in the size or the symmetry of the unit cell.

Ice-VII is another 'self-clathrate', with a relatively
simple structure.   On the basis of X-ray powder photographs
at 25 kbar and 223 K, Kamb and Davis (1964) assigned to it
the structure shown in Fig.8.14, which consists of two

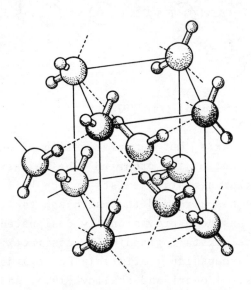

Fig.8.14. Structure of ice-VII (Kamb and Davis 1964).

identical hydrogen-bonded frameworks, each resembling the
lattice of ice-Ic, which interpenetrate but are not connected, making the whole structure like that of cuprite
(Cu_2O). Any one water molecule has eight neighbours.   It is
hydrogen-bonded to four of these, and in 'repulsive contact'
with the other four, in consequence of which the hydrogen
bond is rather longer (0·286 nm) than in I (0·276 nm).   The
transformation of VII into VIII, which occurs near 0°C at

a pressure of ~21 kbar, was discovered by Whalley, Davidson, and Heath (1966) by a permittivity study, under pressures established by an anvil technique. Whereas the dielectric properties of VII are much like those of I, III, V, and VI, when VII is cooled it transforms at about 0°C into a form VIII with a low permittivity. Accordingly, Kamb and Davis must have carried out their experiments on VIII and not on VII, but Weir, Block, and Piermarini (1965) studied a single crystal of VII at 25 kbar and 298 K and concluded that it has the body-centred cubic structure of Fig.8.14. It has since been stated that VIII may be slightly distorted into a tetragonal lattice [Kamb, quoted by Johari, Lavergne, and Whalley (1974), who suggest that the same may also be true of VII]. Be that as it may, the structures of VII and VIII are undoubtedly very similar, and moreover the two forms transform into each other with almost no volume change. From a further dielectric study of VII and VIII, Johari *et al.* established that the VII-VIII transition is first order, and that the two forms are in equilibrium at (0.82 ± 0.02)°C.

In ice-VIII the protons are ordered, as was first made apparent by the permittivity changes observed on cooling VII. The order is believed to take the form of a parallel arrangement of the molecular dipoles within each ice-I*c* sublattice, but with one sublattice polarized antiparallel with respect to the other. Ice-VIII, which has a tetragonal lattice, space group $I4_1/amd$ (Kamb, quoted by Wong and Whalley 1976), can in fact be considered to have the simplest structure of any form of ice. Johari and his colleagues found from their detailed dielectric investigation that disorder is by no means completely attained when VIII transforms to VII. The orientational correlation parameter[†] of ice-VII at room temperature proves to be only about one-half of that of, say, ice-I*h*. From measurements of dp/dT for the equilibria VI-VII and VI-VIII, Johari *et al.* estimated that ΔS_t for the conversion of VII into VIII

[†]This parameter is so defined that its value is reduced by ordering.

is $-2 \cdot 75$ J K^{-1} mol^{-1} for H_2O and $-2 \cdot 7$ J K^{-1} mol^{-1} for D_2O.
These values are numerically roughly one-quarter less than
the configurational entropy loss to be expected for a fully
disordered VII passing into a fully ordered VIII, which furnishes further proof that VII is not completely disordered.
It would seem likely that the order which persists in VII
resembles that which is fully achieved in VIII, that is that
it takes the form of a tendency to parallel ordering within
a sublattice, and also of antiparallel ordering between two
sublattices.

It is an interesting question whether at sufficiently
high pressures VII would transform into an 'ultimate', even
denser high-pressure form of ice, in which oxygen atoms
would form a close-packed array unfavourable to hydrogen
bonding, so forcing the protons into an ordered arrangement.
However, pressures of up to 200 kbar have been applied to
VII without producing any sign of such a transformation
(C.W.F.T. Pistorius, M.C.Pistorius, Blakey, and Admiraal,
1963). Holzapfel (1972) predicted on theoretical grounds
that a transition to a condition of symmetrical hydrogen
bonding in ice-VII might be expected to occur at a pressure
between 350 and 800 kbar. Kawai, Mishima, Togaya, and le
Neindre (1975), using an anvil technique, reported that on
applying a pressure which appears to have exceeded a megabar
a new form of ice is formed, accompanied by a dramatic fall
in electrical resistance by a factor of $\sim 10^6$.

Curiosity is naturally aroused as to why so many different forms of ice exist, and about the connexion between
these structures and the proton order or disorder. The problems involved here are very complex. The energy differences
between the various structures are small, of the order of one
per cent of the lattice energy, and sometimes less. Thus, in
spite of the structural difference between I and II, the
energy of II exceeds that of I by only ~ 40 J mol^{-1}. The
water molecule itself is only slightly distorted in the
crystal as compared with the configuration of a gaseous molecule. In an isolated D_2O molecule, the average O-D bond length
is $0 \cdot 0970$ nm, and the average D-O-D angle is $104 \cdot 5°$. In ice
IX, the average bond length is $0 \cdot 097$ nm and the D-O-D angles
for the two kinds of molecule are $104 \cdot 7°$ and $106 \cdot 0°$. In ice-

II, the corresponding distance is 0·097 nm, and the interbond angles are 103·2° and 107·6° (Fig.8.8). The quantity
which does vary considerably, both within the lattice of
one particular structure and from one form to another,
is the so-called donor angle O--O--O, where the three oxygen
atoms are part of the system O--H-O-H--O. In ice-Ih, this
angle differs by less than half a degree from the tetrahedral angle. In ice-II, by contrast, it covers the range
81° to 128°, and in IX one of these angles reaches the value
of 144° (Fig.8.11). No doubt an important factor in determining the structure and the ordering or disordering of the
protons or deuterons is how well the water molecules can
adapt themselves to O--O--O angles which differ considerably
from those best suited to hydrogen bonding. This matter has
been considered by Kamb *et al*. (1971), Kamb (1973) and
LaPlaca *et al*. The available structural information shows
that a water molecule need not take up a symmetrical disposition with regard to a particular O--O--O angle, and also
that it is not necessarily the O--O--O angles nearest the
tetrahedral angle which will be preferred. In the ordered
form ice-II, for example, donor angles of 88° and 99° are
used in preference to the pair 99° and 115°. One is forced
to the conclusion that other factors besides hydrogen bonding
must be considered, and that a decisive role may be played
by interactions between next-nearest neighbours, such as
dispersion forces and interproton repulsion. For instance,
as compared with I, each water molecule in II has a rather
close next-nearest neighbour 0·324 nm away, and the hydrogen-
bond energy lost in going from I to II, with its less favourable O--O--O angles, may be largely compensated by the dispersion energy gained from the closer packing.

We may add that for the phases of ice which display
dielectric relaxation, the activation energy for this process is much the same for all forms (~56 kJ mol^{-1}), suggesting a common mechanism. Whereas, however, ice-Ih and -Ic
have a single relaxation time, for III, V, and VI there is
a distribution of times, presumably as a result of the presence in their lattices of crystallographically non-equivalent bonds (Johari, Lavergne, and Whalley 1974).

8.4. HYDRATES

Since ice retains entropy, and hence disorder, at the absolute zero, it was inevitable that other crystals in which
hydrogen bonding is involved should be examined to see if
they are similar in this respect. A type of solid of this
kind which often lends itself to an accurate thermodynamic
search for residual disorder is the hydrate of an oxygen-
containing compound such as an oxy-salt, oxy-acid, or hydroxide. The principle of the thermodynamic approach is simple
(p.112). It involves the comparison of the calorimetric
entropy S(cal) at a reference temperature such as 298·15 K
with the value S(eq) obtained by measuring the standard entropy change $\Delta S^{\ominus}$ at this temperature for a suitable reaction
involving the compound concerned, it being assumed that for
the other substances which participate in the reaction
values of their entropies are available which within adequate
limits of precision are unambiguous. $\Delta S^{\ominus}$ is usually found
from measurements of the enthalpy change $\Delta H^{\ominus}$ and the Gibbs
energy change $\Delta G^{\ominus}$ for the reaction, using the relation
$\Delta S^{\ominus} = (\Delta H^{\ominus} - \Delta G^{\ominus})/T$. If the compound concerned is perfectly
ordered at 0 K, S(cal) and S(eq) will agree within experi-
mental error. If S(eq) exceeds S(cal) by an amount exceeding the experimental error, the substance retains disorder
at the absolute zero. It must be stressed that data of the
highest accuracy are needed, since a significant difference
between S(cal) and S(eq) may be only of the order of one per
cent of their absolute magnitudes.

Table 8.2 p.502 summarizes the results of investigations
of this kind, most of them the outcome of the impeccable work
of Giauque and his coworkers. The equilibrium studies needed
to give $\Delta S^{\ominus}$ were of three kinds.

(1) For a salt hydrate, the reaction chosen can be that
     between the hydrate, water vapour, and the anhydrous
     salt (or a lower hydrate). For example, S(eq) for
     crystalline $Na_2SO_4.10H_2O$ was obtained from a study at
     25°C of the equilibrium

$$Na_2SO_4(s) + 10H_2O(g) = Na_2SO_4.10H_2O(s)$$

If $p(H_2O)$ is the equilibrium pressure (strictly the
fugacity) of water vapour, $\Delta G^{\ominus} = RT \ln p(H_2O)^{10}$. $\Delta H^{\ominus}$
can be obtained from calorimetrically-determined values
of the heat of solution of the two salts and of the
heat of vaporization of water. Then

$$\Delta S^{\ominus} = S(\text{hydrate})^{\ominus} - S(Na_2SO_4)^{\ominus} - 10S[H_2O(g)]^{\ominus}.$$

The entropy of the anhydrous salt is obtained from heat
capacity measurements, assuming that it is perfectly
ordered at 0 K. This method of estimating S(eq) was
used for example for the hydrates of sodium, cadmium,
and cobalt sulphates, sodium carbonate, disodium hydrogenphosphate, and the monohydrates of lithium and
sodium hydroxides.

(2) The approach adopted for hydrates of sulphuric acid,
     nitric acid, and ammonia may be illustrated by the par-
     ticular example of sulphuric acid hemihexahydrate,
     $H_2SO_4 \cdot 6 \cdot 5H_2O$. The crystalline solid of this composi-
     tion melts at 220·28 K. (Strictly speaking, this phase
     is unstable at its melting-point, as there is a peri-
     tectic point in the phase diagram at 219·53 K at which
     the hemihexahydrate comes into equilibrium with the
     tetrahydrate and solution. Nevertheless, the unstable
     melting-point and the heat of fusion of the hemihexahy-
     drate could both be accurately determined.) The value
     of S(cal) at 298·15 K for this system given in Table
     8.2 therefore refers to a liquid sulphuric acid - water
     mixture of composition $H_2SO_4 \cdot 6 \cdot 5H_2O$, and is given by

$$S(\text{cal}) = \int_{0}^{220 \cdot 28} C_p \, \mathrm{d}\ln T \quad \text{for the crystal}$$

and

$$\Delta S(\text{fusion}) + \int_{220 \cdot 28}^{298 \cdot 15} C_p \, \mathrm{d}\ln T \quad \text{for the liquid.}$$

The 'reaction' chosen for the evaluation of S(eq) was

$$H_2SO_4(\ell) + 6 \cdot 5 \; H_2O(\ell) = H_2SO_4.6 \cdot 5 \; H_2O(\ell) \; .$$

$\Delta H^{\ominus}$ for this reaction can be determined by heat of mixing experiments, while $\Delta G^{\ominus}$, the Gibbs energy increase on forming the solution from the pure components, can be found by a suitable choice from the methods for measuring activities and activity coefficients. For the evaluation of $\Delta G^{\ominus}$ for the formation of solutions with a molar ratio of H_2O to H_2SO_4 of two or more, Giauque and his coworkers used measurements of the partial vapour pressure of water over the solutions. For the more concentrated solutions with a molar ratio of H_2O to H_2SO_4 of two or less, $\Delta G^{\ominus}$ was calculated from freezing-point measurements. Since such measurements give $\Delta G^{\ominus}$ well below 25°C, for the comparison of $S(\text{cal})$ and $S(\text{eq})$ to be made at 25°C values of $\Delta G^{\ominus}$ so obtained must be corrected on the basis of the equation

$$\left(\frac{\partial (\Delta G^{\ominus}/T)}{\partial T} \right)_p = - \frac{\Delta H^{\ominus}}{T^2} \; .$$

The correction requires a knowledge of $\Delta H^{\ominus}$ as a function of temperature, that is of the partial molal heat contents of the components at one temperature, of the partial molal heat capacities, and of the variation of the latter with temperature.

$\Delta G^{\ominus}$ for the 'reactions' in the systems involving nitric acid and ammonia was evaluated from vapour pressure measurements. The available data on the partial pressures of water and nitric acid over aqueous solutions at 25°C were found to be untrustworthy as they were inconsistent with the Gibbs-Duhem relation. As the vapour pressure data for higher temperatures appeared on this criterion to be more reliable, the comparison of $S(\text{cal})$ and $S(\text{eq})$ for the liquids of composition $HNO_3.H_2O$ and $HNO_3.3H_2O$ was made at 70°C and 50°C respectively. It will be seen from Table 8.2 that for $NH_3.H_2O(\ell)$ the agreement between $S(\text{cal})$ and $S(\text{eq})$ is virtually perfect at 298·15 K, whereas at 273·15 K there is a difference of 0·8 J K^{-1} mol^{-1}. This was attributed

by Hildenbrand and Giauque (1953) to errors in the published information on the vapour pressures of aqueous
ammonia, and illustrates the necessity for data of the
highest possible reliability.

(3)   In the third method for arriving at S(eq), $\Delta S^{\ominus}$ for the
reaction is determined by e.m.f. measurements on a suit-
able cell.   The only substance listed in Table 8.2 for
which this approach was adopted is $ZnSO_4.7H_2O$.   In this
case, the Clark cell was used, in which one electrode
is zinc, and the other mercury in contact with solid
mercury(I) sulphate, while the electrolyte is a solution
of zinc sulphate saturated with $ZnSO_4.7H_2O$.   The reaction taking place is essentially that between zinc and
solid mercury(I) sulphate to produce metallic mercury
and solid $ZnSO_4.7H_2O$, but the water needed for the latter
comes from the saturated solution of the heptahydrate,
and by virtue of the supersaturation which this removal
of water produces, more solid heptahydrate is produced
than corresponds to the quantity of electricity which
passes through the cell.   If there are A moles of water
per mole of $ZnSO_4$ in the saturated solution, the actual
reaction occurring in the cell is

$$Zn(s) + Hg_2SO_4(s) + \frac{7}{(A-7)} ZnSO_4.AH_2O \text{ (sat.soln)}$$

$$= \frac{A}{(A-7)} ZnSO_4.7H_2O(s) + 2Hg(\ell)$$

Since $\Delta G^{\ominus} = -2EF$, where E is the measured e.m.f. and
$\Delta S^{\ominus} = -[\partial(\Delta G^{\ominus})/\partial T]_p$, $\Delta S^{\ominus}$ for the above reaction can be
obtained from the measured temperature coefficient of
the e.m.f. $\Delta S^{\ominus}$ for the reaction

$$\frac{7}{(A-7)} ZnSO_4.7H_2O(s) + 7H_2O(\ell) = \frac{7}{(A-7)} ZnSO_4.AH_2O \text{ (sat.soln)}$$

can be derived from data on the heat of solution of
crystalline zinc sulphate and the vapour pressure of
water over the saturated solution.   Addition of $\Delta S^{\ominus}$
for the last two reactions gives $\Delta S^{\ominus}$ for the following

process:

$$Zn(s) + Hg_2SO_4(s) + 7H_2O(\ell) = ZnSO_4 \cdot 7H_2O(s) + 2Hg(\ell)$$

from which S (eq) for $ZnSO_4 \cdot 7H_2O(s)$ follows at once,
assuming values for the entropy of the other four substances involved in the reaction. This method of determining S (eq) requires that there should be no uncertainty about the precise reaction to which the measured
values of the e.m.f. relate, and it also demands an extremely accurate value for the temperature coefficient
of the e.m.f. An error of only one microvolt per degree
in dE/dT for the Clark cell would lead to an error of
$0 \cdot 2$ J K^{-1} mol^{-1} in S(eq). Owing to this sensitivity
of $\Delta S^{\ominus}$ to errors in dE/dT, Giauque, Barieau, and Kunzler
(1950) considered that when e.m.f. data are available
over a temperature range, it is better to use them on
a point-by-point basis rather than as a source of a
value of dE/dT at one temperature. If $ZnSO_4 \cdot 7H_2O$ is
completely ordered at 0 K, then its entropy at $298 \cdot 15$K
is correctly given by $\int_0^{298 \cdot 15} C_p \mathrm{d} \ln T$. Hence $\Delta G^{\ominus}$ at
T/K for the reaction above is given by the equation

$$\Delta G^{\ominus} = \Delta H^{\ominus}_{298 \cdot 15} + \int_{298 \cdot 15}^{T} \Delta C_p^{\ominus} \mathrm{d}T - T \left(\Delta S^{\ominus}_{298 \cdot 15} + \int_{298 \cdot 15}^{T} \Delta C_p^{\ominus} \mathrm{d} \ln T \right).$$

$\Delta G^{\ominus}$ can be calculated for each temperature T at which
the e.m.f. of the cell has been determined, and with
the available heat capacity data these lead to a set
of values of $\Delta H^{\ominus}_{298 \cdot 15}$. These values will be constant
if the right value for $\Delta S^{\ominus}_{298 \cdot 15}$ has been taken, that is
if the assumption that the heptahydrate is completely
ordered at 0 K is correct. If there were disorder in
the crystalline hydrate which conferred on it a residual
entropy of say $R \ln 2$, the values of $\Delta H^{\ominus}_{298 \cdot 15}$ derived
from e.m.f. measurements made over the range 0 - 25°C
would show a trend of $25R \ln 2$, or $\sim$145 J mol^{-1}. Since
the values of $\Delta H^{\ominus}_{298 \cdot 15}$ were constant to ± 8 J mol^{-1}, the
conclusion that $ZnSO_4 \cdot 7H_2O$ achieves a state of perfect
order at the absolute zero was confirmed.

It will be seen from Table 8.2 that out of the hydrates
listed, only four fail to achieve a perfectly ordered state
at 0 K, namely sodium sulphate decahydrate, sodium carbonate
decahydrate, disodium hydrogenphosphate dodecahydrate and
zinc fluoride tetrahydrate.   Since, however, the decahydrates
of sodium chromate, selenate, molybdate, and tungstate are
all isomorphous with that of sodium sulphate, it is probable
that these four salts would also prove to be disordered at
0 K. Barieau and Giauque (1950) studied zinc sulphate hexahydrate as well as the heptahydrate, and concluded that unlike the heptahydrate, it is disordered at 0 K, the residual
entropy being between 5·5 and 7·5 J K^{-1} mol^{-1}. The measurements on the hexahydrate were however complicated by the fact
that at low temperatures it is unstable with respect to the
heptahydrate and monohydrate, and tends to break down with
accompanying thermal effects to give these two hydrates in a
microcrystalline condition (Cox, Hornung, and Giauque 1955).
An X-ray study of cobalt sulphate hexahydrate and of the
isomorphous magnesium salt (Zalkin, Ruben, and Templeton
1962, 1964) gave no evidence for any disorder due to hydrogen
bonding, and it would therefore be rather surprising if zinc
sulphate hexahydrate were in fact still disordered at 0 K.

The question of the precise form taken by the disorder
in the four hydrates of Table 8.2 which still retain it at
0 K would be best pursued by neutron diffraction studies. So
far none of the four salts appears to have been investigated
in this way, but one of them, sodium sulphate decahydrate,
has been subjected to a detailed X-ray examination which
established the probable nature of the disorder (Ruben,
Templeton, Rosenstein, and Olovsson 1961). All of the water
molecules are involved in hydrogen bonding with other water
molecules and with the oxygen atoms of sulphate ions. For
some of the water molecules, there is no possibility of disorder of the protons in the hydrogen bonds in which they are
involved. The remaining water molecules, however, are bonded
in rings of four molecules. There is one such ring for each
formula unit Na_2SO_4, and two possible ways of arranging the
hydrogen atoms in any one ring, as shown in Fig.8.15.   Complete randomness between the two possible configurations for

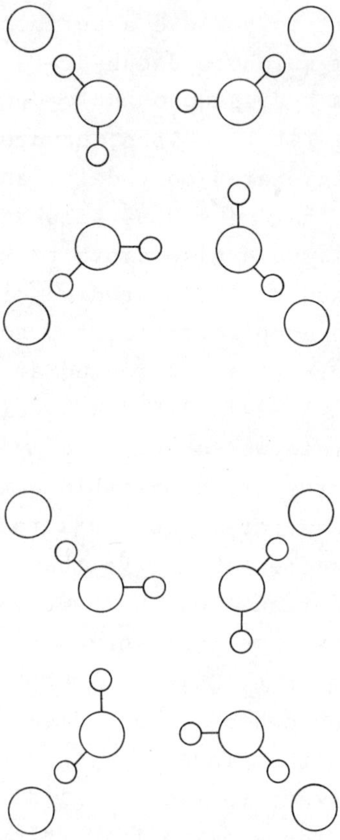

Fig.8.15. The two possibilities for hydrogen bonding in a ring of four water molecules in the lattice of $Na_2SO_4.10H_2O$. The large circles are oxygen atoms, the smaller circles hydrogen atoms.

each ring would lead therefore to an entropy of disorder of $R \ln 2$, in agreement with the experimental estimate of the residual entropy at 0 K. The two configurations are not in fact crystallographically equivalent, and the persistence of the entropy of disorder to very low temperatures must mean either that the energy differences associated with the two possibilities are very small, or that the coordinated movement of the protons which the change from one configuration of a ring to the other would require is prohibitively slow at low temperatures.

The disorder in sodium carbonate decahydrate may well have much the same origin. The hydrogen-bonding scheme in disodium hydrogenphosphate dodecahydrate is probably more complicated, since the anion can now contribute a hydrogen atom, but the larger residual entropy may partly derive from the higher ratio of water molecules to cations. The disorder in zinc fluoride tetrahydrate, however, may be rather different in character. The corresponding iron (II) compound, $FeF_2.4H_2O$, crystallizes in a rhombohedral form and an hexagonal form, both of which are disordered (Penfold and Taylor 1960). The unit in the crystal is an octahedron consisting of four water molecules and two fluorine atoms coordinated to a central iron atom, and the disorder arises because the crystal fails to distinguish between the fluorine and oxygen atoms - a phenomenon encountered in other solids with ions or molecules containing both fluorine and oxygen atoms. Each octahedron has two possible orientations, but adjacent octahedra are linked by hydrogen bonds of two kinds O-H---O and O-H---F, and the orientation of any one octahedron probably influences that of its neighbours, so reducing the overall disorder. The origin of the disorder in the zinc salt may be similar to that in the iron compound. It will be noted that $S(res)$ is rather less than $R \ln 2$.

Although from the evidence summarized in Table 8.2 it might be inferred that disorder in hydrates due to hydrogen bonding is rather uncommon, it may occur more often in salt hydrates with a high proportion of water. As an extreme example of such a solid might be cited the highest hydrate of aluminium sulphate, said to have the formula $Al_2(SO_4)_3.27H_2O$. While it would be interesting to study this hydrate and others like it, it will probably be necessary to characterize them more rigorously than has been done hitherto. Thus, the hydrate of aluminium sulphate which was for long regarded as $Al_2(SO_4)_3.18H_2O$ seems in fact to be the heptadecahydrate $Al_2(SO_4)_3.17H_2O$, in which moreover one molecule of water is zeolitic, the compounds $Al_2(SO_4)_3.16H_2O$ and $Al_2(SO_4)_3.17H_2O$ being mutually soluble (N.O. Smith 1942, N.O. Smith and Walsh 1954).

Disorder may also be found in salt hydrates with only a relatively small number of water molecules if the structure is such as to allow each molecule more than one orientation.

Examples of this are the β-forms of the monohydrates of
lithium iodide and lithium bromide, which simultaneously exhibit positional disorder of the lithium ions and orientational disorder of the water molecules. The crystals have a
perovskite-like structure (Fig.8.16), with the cations statistically distributed among the three times more numerous

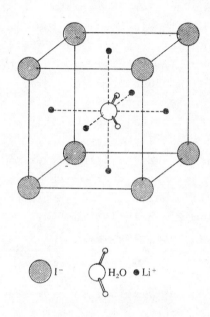

I^- H_2O • Li^+

Fig.8.16. Structure of $LiI.H_2O$ at room temperature. The lithium ions
occupy the face-centred sites with a statistical weight of 1/3.

face-centred sites. The water molecule at the unit cell
centre probably attempts to direct its hydrogen atoms towards a pair of the eight surrounding halide ions, which gives
it twelve possible orientations (Weiss 1965, Kessis 1965,
Weiss, Hensel, and Kühr 1969). Chihara, Kawakami, and
Soda (1969) carried out H, D, and [7]Li resonance studies on
$LiI.H_2O$ and $LiI.D_2O$. They concluded that at room temperature the water molecules are undergoing rapid reorientation
and that the lithium ions are migrating from site to site.
Both kinds of motion require about the same activation energy
of ~55 kJ mol^{-1}, and may therefore be coupled in some way.
Line-width changes for both the H and [7]Li resonances are

observed on cooling, but there is no major thermal anomaly, so presumably both kinds of disorder become frozen-in, at least to some extent. Another monohydrate with orientationally disordered water molecules is $UO_2Cl_2.H_2O$. A neutron diffraction study revealed that the water molecules are approximately equally distributed between two orientations, in one of which they are hydrogen-bonded to oxygen atoms, and in the other to chlorine atoms (Taylor and Wilson 1974). But needless to say, there are numerous lower hydrates in which there is no disorder, examples of which will be found in Table 8.2. For one of these, $Na_2CO_3.H_2O$, the conclusion reached on thermodynamic grounds that it has an ordered lattice was confirmed by neutron diffraction (Kang Kun Wu and Brown 1975).

Three salt hydrates have recently attracted particular attention. They are copper (II) formate tetrahydrate, $Cu(OOCH)_2.4H_2O$, tin (II) chloride dihydrate, $SnCl_2.2H_2O$, and the trihydrate of potassium ferrocyanide [potassium hexacyanoferrate (II)], $K_4Fe(CN)_6.3H_2O$. These three salts have a common structural feature, namely that the water molecules are hydrogen-bonded into layers. Copper formate tetrahydrate (Fig.8.17) is monoclinic (space group $P2_1/a$) in its room temperature form I (Kiriyama, R., Ibamoto, and Matsuo 1954). On cooling, this is converted into an antiferroelectric phase II (Kiriyama 1962, Okada 1965) with a doubling of the c axis (Tuberfield 1967). The II-I transition is partly gradual, but is completed isothermally at 235·78 K, the total entropy of transition ΔS_t being 3·55 J K^{-1} mol^{-1} (Matsuo, Kume, Suga, and Seki 1976). The corresponding temperature and ΔS_t for the deuterated salt are 245·64 K and 3·81 J K^{-1} mol^{-1}, so there is a not insignificant isotope effect (Okada 1967). [Kobayashi and Haseda (1963) found that at 17 K, the paramagnetic phase II transforms into a magnetically ordered form III which is antiferromagnetic but shows weak ferromagnetism (section 12.8).] The water molecules in phase I are two-dimensionally disordered (Okada, Kay, Cromer, and Almodovar 1966) whereas in II they are ordered to give a ferroelectric arrangement in any one ab plane, but in opposite directions in adjacent planes. The

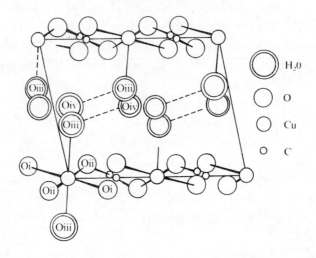

Fig.8.17. Structure of $Cu(HCOO)_2.4H_2O$ as shown by Kobayashi and Haseda (1963) as a projection on (010). Oi and Oii are oxygen atoms of formate ions, Oiii oxygen atoms of water molecules coordinated to Cu^{2+} ions, and Oiv oxygen atoms of water molecules not linked to Cu^{2+} ions.

statistical aspects of the order-disorder change in this salt have been considered by Okada (1967, 1974), Ishibashi, Ohya, and Takagi (1973), Allen (1974) and Allen and Nagle (1975). The approach of Ishibashi *et al*. is essentially an extension of the basic dimer model (section 3.8) by the addition of a mean-field treatment of intraplanar interactions between more distant neighbours, as well as of interplanar interactions. Their prediction that complete saturation of the polarization in any plane prevails throughout the whole range of the ordered phase was not upheld by the proton relaxation time studies of Žumer and Pirš (1974). Allen and Nagle solved the dimer part of the problem exactly, and showed that the interplanar interactions, while responsible for the antiferroelectric ordering, are about a thousand times less strong than the intraplanar interactions. Okada (1974) and Allen and Nagle predicted that there may exist a hitherto undiscovered partially ferroelectric phase of this hydrate.

In $SnCl_2.2H_2O$ the transition to the low-temperature ordered phase II manifests itself by a large peak in the permittivity measured along the b and c axes (but not the a

axis) (H.Kiriyama and R.Kiriyama 1970), and also by a remarkably symmetrical anomaly in the heat capacity - temperature
curve (Fig.8.18; Matsuo, Tatsumi, Suga, and Seki 1973). The
extra heat capacity is closely proportional to $(T-T_c)^{-\alpha}$ or
$(T_c-T)^{-\alpha'}$, where both α and α' are $0 \cdot 5$ within experimental
error (cf. Table 3.7), and where T_{c+} = $217 \cdot 9970$ K and
T_{c-} = $217 \cdot 9907$ K. There does appear to be a small first-
order component in the transition, though this only contributes about 3 per cent to the total entropy of transition of

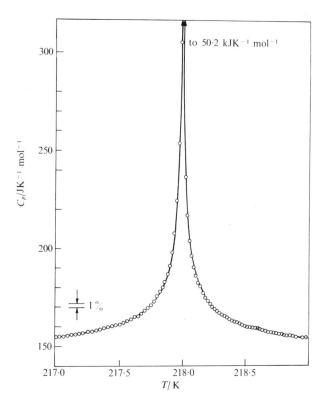

Fig.8.18. Heat capacity of a single crystal of $SnCl_2.2H_2O$ in the transition region (Matsuo *et al.* 1973).

$4 \cdot 6$ J K^{-1} mol^{-1}. Deuteration increases T_c by about 16 K,
a strong indication that proton or deuteron disordering is
involved (H.Kiriyama and R.Kiriyama 1970). X-ray diffraction
investigations of $SnCl_2.2H_2O$ were carried out by Kamenar and

Grdenic (1961) and by H.Kiriyama, Kitahama, Nakamura, and
R.Kiriyama (1973). This work was supplemented by a single-
crystal neutron diffraction study of $SnCl_2.2D_2O$ (R.Kiriyama,
H.Kiriyama, Kitahama, and Nakamura 1973). Fig.8.19 gives
an impression of the layered nature of the lattice. The

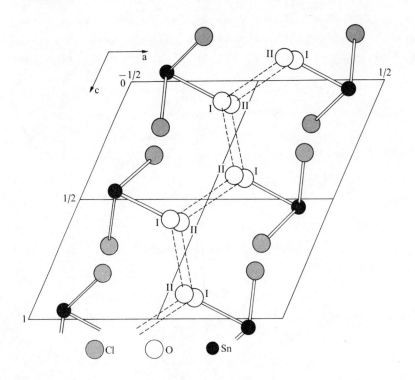

Fig.8.19. Structure of $SnCl_2.2H_2O$ seen along the monoclinic b axis
(H.Kiriyama, Kitahama, Nakamura, and R.Kiriyama 1973).

crystals are monoclinic ($P2_1/c$) above and below the transition, which leaves the positions of the Sn, Cl, and O atoms
unchanged. The lattice consists of layers parallel to the
(100) plane made up of the aquocomplex $SnCl_2.H_2O$, between
which there are layers composed of the remaining water molecules. In other words, the water molecules are of two kinds,
I and II, the O(I) atoms using one of their lone pairs to
coordinate with a tin atom. One of the H or D atoms of a
type II water molecule is not involved in hydrogen bonding
between oxygen atoms, but is directed towards a chlorine

atom. The remaining hydrogen bond-forming capacity of the
water molecules is used to link the two kinds of oxygen atom
to produce layers parallel to the (100) plane. The neutron
diffraction investigation of $SnCl_2.2D_2O$ showed that the deuterons are ordered in the layers in form II, and disordered
in I, and Kiriyama and his colleagues were able to obtain
quantitative information on the distribution of the deuterons
among the sites available to them in the disordered structure.
Matsuo, Oguni, Suga, and Seki (1972) have reported thermal
effects in the region of 155 K which indicate that complete
ordering of the protons in the low-temperature phase is only
rather slowly attained, the necessary rearrangement process
having an activation energy of ~50 kJ mol^{-1}.

The order-disorder problem presented by $SnCl_2.2H_2O$ has
a much more general interest than might at first be supposed,
and important advances in understanding it have followed
from the work of Matsuo, Oguni, Suga, Seki, and Nagle (1974)
and Salinas and Nagle (1974). It follows from what has been
said about the two types of oxygen atom that an O(II) atom
can only have one near proton in the plane of a layer of water
molecules, whereas the type I oxygens have two near protons
in this plane. It will be seen from Fig.8.20 that there are

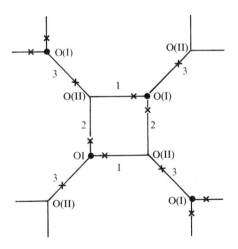

Fig.8.20. The hydrogen-bonded network in $SnCl_2.2H_2O$, with the two types
of oxygen atom O(I) and O(II). A cross indicates one of the two possible
positions for a proton in any one hydrogen bond. The three inequivalent
types of bond are numbered 1, 2, and 3 (Salinas and Nagle 1974).

three non-equivalent types of hydrogen bond, labelled 1, 2,
and 3, and also that the water molecule layers are made up
of four- and eight-sided rings. The theoretical treatments
of Matsuo *et al*. and of Salinas and Nagle are based on the
assumption that the ice rules (p. 458) are operative. The
crosses in Fig.8.20 indicate one possible disposition of the
protons in the bonds in the figure, which is in fact the low-
temperature ordered state as revealed by the neutron diffraction pattern at 88 K. What gives this case its more
general interest is that, as Salinas and Nagle showed, it
can be cast in the form of a dimer problem appropriate to
a two-dimensional 4-8 lattice, and this can be exactly solved.
A dimer must in effect replace an $O(I)$---$H-O(II)$ unit, so
that using the dimer approach the portion of the layer shown
in Fig.8.20 would appear as four dimers, all in the bonds
labelled 3. The calculations of Salinas and Nagle demonstrated that the model accounts rather well for the main
features of the transition between the two forms of $SnCl_2.2H_2O$,
and although there is not complete quantitative agreement
between theory and experiment it should be possible to reduce
the discrepancies by refining the model, for example, by re-
laxing the ice rules.

The third hydrate on which considerable effort has been
expended, $K_4Fe(CN)_6.3H_2O$, also has a layered structure and an
ordered low-temperature phase (Waku, Hirabayashi, Toyoda,
Iwasaki, and Kiriyama 1959). Both the paraelectric (I) and
ferroelectric (II) forms are monoclinic, space groups $A2/a$
and Aa respectively. The X-ray study of R.Kiriyama, H. Kiriyama, Wada, Niizeki, and Hirabayashi (1964) and the neutron
diffraction investigation of Taylor, Mueller, and Hitterman
(1970) showed that there is virtually no change in the heavy
atom positions in phases I and II, and that the order-disorder transition is once again concerned with the hydrogen-
bonding system. The lattice consists of double layers of
the octahedral anions surrounded by potassium ions, between
which layers of the water molecules are sandwiched. The
hydrogen-bond pattern is complex, both oxygen and nitrogen
atoms being used as acceptor atoms. There is more than one
kind of water molecule - two kinds in the disordered phase,

and probably four in phase II. The experimental work carried
out to provide detailed information about the hydrogen atom
positions and about the motion of the water molecules has
been summarized by Hamilton and Ibers (1968), and is a good
example of how contributions from a variety of techniques
can be combined in tackling problems of this kind. Even in
the ordered phase, the water molecules have considerable freedom of movement. The deuteron resonance study which Tsang
and O'Reilly (1965) carried out on $K_4Fe(CN)_6.3D_2O$ showed
that below the Curie point the water molecules can still
undergo fast reorientation through 180° about the bisectrix
of the D-O-D angle. In the paraelectric phase I the reorientation takes place about more than one axis, but the
motion of the water molecules is nevertheless strongly
coupled. The entropy of transition, which in the protonated
form of the salt was estimated to be 8·75 J K^{-1} mol^{-1} by
Malcolm, Staveley, and Worswick (1973) and 12·41 J K^{-1} mol^{-1}
by Oguni, Matsuo, Suga, and Seki (1975), is greater than the
$R \ln 2$ which would be expected if, as the structural evidence
suggests, the crystal has two different states per three
water molecules.

The nature of the II-I transition in this salt is
interesting. The heat capacity determinations of both
Malcolm *et al.* and of Oguni *et al.* showed that C_p remains
finite at the transition and that it falls rather abruptly
between 247 K and 248 K. Oguni and his colleagues also found
that there is a sudden change not in the molar volume but
in the coefficient of expansion α. This suggested that the
transition might fall in the Ehrenfest second-order category,
and that therefore the relation

$$(dp/dT)_{T_t} = \frac{\Delta C_p}{T_t V \Delta \alpha}$$

might apply (p. 13). The results of permittivity studies
carried out under pressure (Krasnikova and Polandov 1970)
gave $3·8 \times 10^7$ Pa K^{-1} for the left-hand side of the above
equation, while from their own work Oguni *et al.* found
$3·2 \times 10^7$ Pa K^{-1} for the right-hand side. The agreement is
probably within experimental error, so the II-I transition

in this salt may in fact be at least a close approximation
to a type of transition which is certainly rare in its ideal
form.

Disorder in hydrates which contain the ion H_3O^+ rather
than the water molecule as such is dealt with in Chapter
7.4.2.

TABLE 8.2

*Summary of thermodynamic studies of crystalline hydrates
for possible residual entropy at 0 K. S(cal) is the calorimetric entropy of the system given in the first column at
the temperature given in the second column. S(eq) is the
entropy of the same system at the same temperature derived
from a study of an equilibrium involving the system (see
text for details).*

$$S(res) = S(eq) - S(cal)$$

System	T/K	$S(cal)$	$S(eq)$	$S(res)$	Ref.
		($J\ K^{-1}\ mol^{-1}$)			
$H_2SO_4.H_2O$ (ℓ)	298·15	211·25	211·55		1
$H_2SO_4.2H_2O$ (ℓ)	298·15	276·3	276·4		1
$H_2SO_4.3H_2O$ (ℓ)	298·15	345·4	345·4		1
$H_2SO_4.4H_2O$ (ℓ)	298·15	414·5	414·6		1
$H_2SO_4.6·5H_2O$ (ℓ)	298·15	588·3	587·9	All zero	1
$HNO_3.H_2O$ (ℓ)	343·1	242·65	242·3	within	2
$HNO_3.3H_2O$ (ℓ)	323·1	373·35	373·3	experi-	2
$NH_3.2H_2O$ (ℓ)	292·15	232·9	233·5	mental	3
$NH_3.H_2O$ (ℓ)	273·15	152·35	151·55	error	4
$NH_3.H_2O$ (ℓ)	298·15	165·55	165·55		4
$2NH_3.H_2O$ (ℓ)	298·15	267·5	267·5		4
$CdSO_4.H_2O$ (s)	298·15	154·05	154·7		5

continued....

Table 8.2 continued.....

$CdSO_4.8/3H_2O$ (s)	298·15	229·65	229·75		5
$ZnSO_4.7H_2O$ (s)	298·15	388·7	389·1		6
$CoSO_4.7H_2O$ (s)	298·15	406·05	405·85		7
$LiOH.H_2O$ (s)	298·15	71·4	71·3		8
$NaOH.H_2O$ (s)	323·15	106·9	106·9		9
$NaOH.2H_2O$ (ℓ)	298·15	196·0	196·05	All zero	10
$NaOH.3·5H_2O$ (ℓ)	298·15	286·0	286·35	within	10
$NaOH.4H_2O$ (ℓ)	298·15	318·55[a](α)	318·7	experi-	11
$NaOH.4H_2O$ (ℓ)	298·15	318·7[a](β)	318·7	mental	11
$Na_2HPO_4.2H_2O$ (s)	298·15	221·35	221·4	error	12
$Na_2HPO_4.7H_2O$ (s)	298·15	434·6	436·15		12
$Na_2CO_3.H_2O$ (s)	298·15	168·15	168·05		13
$Na_4P_2O_7.10H_2O$ (s)	298·15	689·4	688·8		14
$K_4Fe(CN)_6.3H_2O$ (s)	298·15	593·8	593·7		15
$Na_2SO_4.10H_2O$ (s)	298·15	585·55	591·85	6·3	16
$Na_2HPO_4.12H_2O$ (s)	298·15	621·6	636·25	14·65	12
$Na_2CO_3.10H_2O$ (s)	298·15	558·25	564·55	6·3	13
$ZnF_2.4H_2O$ (s)	298·15	221·5	225·8[b]	4·3[b]	17

[a] The S(cal) values (α) and (β) are derived from heat capacity measurements made on the stable α form and unstable β form of the tetrahydrate respectively.

[b] The values of S(eq) and hence of S(res) have been revised by using the figure for the standard entropy of the zinc ion given by Berg and Vanderzee (1975).

Footnotes to Table 8.2   continued......

REFERENCES

1.   Giauque, Hornung, Kunzler, and Rubin (1960).
2.   Forsythe and Giauque (1942).
3.   Chan and Giauque (1964).
4.   Hildenbrand and Giauque (1953).
5.   Papadopoulos and Giauque (1955).
6.   Barieau and Giauque (1950); Giauque, Barieau, and Kunzler (1950).
7.   Rao and Giauque (1965).
8.   Bauer, Johnston, and Kerr (1950).
9.   Murch and Giauque (1962).
10.   Siemens and Giauque (1969).
11.   Mraw and Giauque (1974).
12.   Waterfield and Staveley (1967).
13.   Waterfield, Linford, Goalby, Bates, Elyard, and Staveley (1968).
14.   Reynolds, Worswick, and Staveley (1971).
15.   Malcolm, Staveley, and Worswick (1973).
16.   Pitzer and Coulter (1938); Brodale and Giauque (1958).
17.   Cook, Davies, and Staveley (1972).

REFERENCES

Allen, G.R. (1974). *J.chem.Phys.* $\underline{60}$, 3299.
Allen, G.R. and Nagle, J.F. (1975). *J.Phys.* $\underline{C8}$, 2788.
Arnold, G.F., Wenzel, R.G., Rabideau, S.W., Nereson, N.G.,
     and Bowman, A.L. (1971). *J.chem.Phys.* $\underline{55}$, 589.
Barieau, R.E. and Giauque, W.F. (1950). *J.Am.chem.Soc.* $\underline{72}$,
     5676.
Bauer, T.W., Johnston, H.L., and Kerr, E.C. (1950). *J.Am.
     chem.Soc.* $\underline{72}$, 5174.
Berg, R.L. and Vanderzee, C.E. (1975). *J.chem.Thermodynamics*,
     $\underline{7}$, 229.
Bernal, J.D. and Fowler, R.H. (1933). *J.chem.Phys.* $\underline{1}$, 515.
Bertie, J.E., Calvert, L.D., and Whalley, E. (1963). *J.
     chem.Phys.* $\underline{38}$, 840.
———   ———   ———   (1964). *Can.J.
     Chem.* $\underline{42}$, 1373.

Bertie, J.E. and Whalley, E. (1964). *J.chem.Phys.* <u>40</u>, 1637, 1646.

van den Beukel, A. (1968). *Phys.St.Solidi* <u>28</u>, 565.

Bjerrum, N. (1952). *Science* <u>115</u>, 385.

Blackman, M. and Lisgarten, N.D. (1957). *Proc.R.Soc.* <u>A239</u>, 93.

Bridgman, P.W. (1912).*Proc.Am.Acad.Arts Sci.* <u>47</u>, 441.

———   (1935). *J.chem.Phys.* <u>3</u>, 597.

Brill, R. and Tippe, A. (1967). *Acta crystallogr.* <u>23</u>, 343.

Brodale, G. and Giauque, W.F. (1958). *J.Am.chem.Soc.* <u>80</u>, 2042

Brown, A.J. and Whalley, E. (1966). *J.chem.Phys.* <u>45</u>, 4360.

Campbell, E.S., Gelernter, G., Heinen, H., and Moorti, V.R.G. (1967). *J.chem.Phys.* <u>46</u>, 2690.

Chamberlain, J.S., Moore, F.H., and Fletcher, N.H. (1973). *Symposium on the physical chemistry of Ice, Ottawa 1972.* (ed. E.Whalley, S.J.Jones, and L.W.Gold) p.283. Royal Society of Canada, Ottawa.

Chan, J.P. and Giauque, W.F. (1964). *J.phys.Chem.* <u>68</u>, 3053.

Chihara, H., Kawakami, T., and Soda, G. (1969). *J.mag.Res.* <u>1</u>, 75.

Cook, R.O., Davies, A., and Staveley, L.A.K. (1972). *J.chem. Soc.,Faraday Trans.* I, <u>68</u>, 1384.

Cox, W.P., Hornung, E.W., and Giauque, W.F. (1955). *J.Am. chem.Soc.* <u>77</u>, 3935.

Dengel, O., Eckener, U., Plitz, H., and Riehl, N. (1964). *Phys.Lett.* <u>9</u>, 291.

Deubner, A., Heise, R., and Wenzel, K.(1960). *Naturwiss.* <u>47</u>, 600.

DiMarzio, E.A. and Stillinger, F.H. (1964). *J.chem.Phys.* <u>40</u>, 1577.

Eigen, M. and Maeyer, L. De (1958). *Proc.R.Soc.* <u>A247</u>, 505.

Engelhardt, H. and Whalley, E. (1972). *J.chem.Phys.* <u>56</u>, 2678.

Evans, L.F. (1967). *J.appl.Phys.* <u>38</u>, 4930.

Finch, E.D., Rabideau, S.W., Wenzel, R.G., and Nereson, N.G. (1968). *J.chem.Phys.* <u>49</u>, 4361.

Forsythe, W.R. and Giauque, W.F. (1942). *J.Am.chem.Soc.* <u>64</u>, 48.

Giauque, W.F. and Ashley, M.F. (1933). *Phys.Rev.* <u>43</u>, 81.

———   Barieau, R.E., and Kunzler, J.E. (1950). *J.Am. chem.Soc.* <u>72</u>, 5685.

Giauque, W.F., Hornung, E.W., Kunzler, J.E., and Rubin, T.R. (1960). *J.Am.chem.Soc.* <u>82</u>, 62.

────────   and Stout, J.W. (1936). *J.Am.chem.Soc.* <u>58</u>, 1144.

Gränicher, H. (1969). *Proceedings International Symposium on the Physics of Ice, Munich, 1968* (ed. N.Riehl, B.Bullemer, and H.Engelhardt) p.1. Plenum Press, New York.

Haida, O., Matsuo, T., Suga, H., and Seki, S. (1972). *Proc. Japan Acad.* <u>48</u>, 489.

Hamilton, W.C. and Ibers, J.A. (1968). *Hydrogen bonding in solids*, W.A.Benjamin, Inc. New York.

────────   Kamb, B., LaPlaca, S.J., and Prakash, A. (1969). *Proceedings International Symposium on the Physics of Ice, Munich, 1968* (ed. N.Riehl, B.Bullemer, and H. Engelhardt), p.44. Plenum Press, New York.

Hildenbrand, D.L. and Giauque, W.F. (1953). *J.Am.chem.Soc.* <u>75</u>, 2811.

Hollins, G.T. (1964). *Proc.phys.Soc.* <u>84</u>, 1001.

Holzapfel, W.B. (1972). *J.chem.Phys.* <u>56</u>, 712.

Ishibashi, Y., Ohya, S., and Takagi, Y. (1973). *J.phys.Soc. Japan* <u>34</u>, 888.

Johari, G.P. (1975). *Phys.Lett.* <u>53A</u>, 144.

────────   and Jones, S.J. (1975). *J.chem.Phys.* <u>62</u>, 4213.

────────   Lavergne, A., and Whalley, E. (1974). *J.chem. Phys.* <u>61</u>, 4292.

────────   and Whalley, E. (1973). *Symposium on the physical chemistry of ice, Ottawa, 1972* (ed. E.Whalley, S.J.Jones, and L.W.Gold) p.278. Royal Society of Canada, Ottawa.

────────   ────────   (1976). *J.chem.Phys.* <u>64</u>, 4484.

Kamb, B. (1964). *Acta crystallogr.* <u>17</u>, 1437.

────────   (1965). *Science* <u>150</u>, 205.

────────   (1973). *Symposium on the physical chemistry of ice, Ottawa, 1972* (ed. E.Whalley, S.J.Jones, and L.W.Gold), p.28. Royal Society of Canada, Ottawa.

────────   and Davis, B.L. (1964). *Proc.Nat.Acad.Sci.(U.S.)* <u>52</u>, 1433.

────────   Hamilton, W.C., LaPlaca, S.J., and Prakash, A. (1971). *J.chem.Phys.* <u>55</u>, 1934.

────────   and Prakash, A. (1968). *Acta crystallogr.* <u>B24</u>, 1317.

Kamb, B., Prakash, A., and Knobler, C. (1967). *Acta crystallogr.* 22, 706.

Kamenar, B. and Grdenic, D. (1961). *J.chem.Soc.* 3954.

Kang Kun Wu and Brown, I.D. (1975). *Acta crystallogr.* B31, 890.

Kawai, N., Mishima, O., Togaya, M., and le Neindre, B. (1975). *Proc.Japan Acad.* 51, 627.

Kessis, J.-J. (1965). *Bull.Soc.chim.France* 32, 48.

Kiriyama, H. (1962). *Bull.chem.Soc.Japan* 35, 1199.

———— Kitahama, K., Nakamura, O., and Kiriyama, R. (1973). *Bull.chem.Soc.Japan* 46, 1389.

———— and Kiriyama, R. (1970). *J.phys.Soc.Japan Suppl.* 28, 114.

Kiriyama, R., Ibamoto, H., and Matsuo, K. (1954). *Acta crystallogr.* 7, 482.

———— Kiriyama, H., Kitahama, K., and Nakamura, O. (1973). *Chem.Lett.(Chem.Soc.Japan)* 1105.

———— ———— Wada, T., Niizeki, N., and Hirabayashi, H. (1964). *J.phys.Soc.Japan* 19, 540.

Kobayashi, H. and Haseda, T. (1963). *J.phys.Soc.Japan* 18, 541.

König, H. (1942). *Nachr.Akad.Wiss.Göttingen, Math.Phys.Kl.*, no.1, 1.

———— (1943). *Z.Kristallogr.Kristallgeom.* 105, 279.

Krasnikova, A.Ya. and Polandov, I.N. (1970). *Soviet Phys. Solid St.* 11, 1421.

LaPlaca, S.J., Hamilton, W.C., Kamb, B., and Prakash, A. (1973). *J.chem.Phys.* 58, 567.

———— and Post, B. (1960). *Acta crystallogr.* 13, 503.

Lieb, E.H. (1967). *Phys.Rev.* 162, 162.

Lipscomb, W.N. (1954). *J.chem.Phys.* 22, 344.

Long, E.A. and Kemp, J.D. (1936). *J.Am.chem.Soc.* 58, 1829.

Malcolm, I.R., Staveley, L.A.K., and Worswick, R.D. (1973). *J.chem.Soc.,Faraday Trans.I*, 69, 1532.

Mason, B.J. and Owston, P.G. (1952). *Phil.Mag.(7)* 43, 911.

Matsuo, T., Kume, Y., Suga, H., and Seki, S. (1976). *(J.)Phys. Chem.Solids* 37, 499.

———— Oguni, M., Suga, H., and Seki, S. (1972). *Proc. Japan Acad.* 48, 237.

Matsuo, T., Oguni, M., Suga, H., Seki, S., and Nagle, J.F. (1974). *Bull.chem.Soc.Japan* <u>47</u>, 57.

——— Tatsumi, M., Suga, H., and Seki, S. (1973). *Solid St.Communs.* <u>13</u>, 1829.

Megaw, H.D. (1934). *Nature,Lond.* <u>134</u>, 900.

Meijering, J.L. (1957). *Philips Res.Reports* <u>12</u>, 333.

Mraw, S.C. and Giauque, W.F. (1974). *J.phys.Chem.* <u>78</u>, 1701.

Murch, L.E. and Giauque, W.F. (1962). *J.phys.Chem.* <u>66</u>, 2052.

Nagle, J.F. (1966). *J.math.Phys.* <u>7</u>, 1484.

Nishibata, K. and Whalley, E. (1974). *J.chem.Phys.* <u>60</u>, 3189.

Oguni, M., Matsuo, T., Suga, H., and Seki, S. (1975). *Bull. chem.Soc.Japan* <u>48</u>, 379.

Okada, K. (1965). *Phys.Rev.Lett.* <u>15</u>, 252.

——— (1967). *Phys.Rev.* <u>164</u>, 683.

——— (1974). *J.phys.Soc.Japan* <u>37</u>, 1226.

——— Kay, M.I., Cromer, D.T., and Almodovar, I. (1966). *J.chem.Phys.* <u>44</u>, 1648.

Owston, P.G. (1951). *Quart.Rev.(Chem.Soc.,London)* 1951, V, 344.

Papadopoulos, M.N. and Giauque, W.F. (1955). *J.Am.chem.Soc.* <u>77</u>, 2740.

Pauling, L. (1935). *J.Am.chem.Soc.* <u>57</u>, 2680.

Penfold, B.R. and Taylor, M.R. (1960). *Acta crystallogr.* <u>13</u>, 953.

Peterson, S.W. and Levy, H.A. (1957). *Acta crystallogr.* <u>10</u>, 70.

Pick, M.A., Wenzl, H., and Engelhardt, H. (1971). *Z.Natur-forsch.* <u>26a</u>, 810.

Pistorius, C.W.F.T., Pistorius, M.C., Blakey, J.P., and Admiraal, L.J. (1963). *J.chem.Phys.* <u>38</u>, 600.

Pitzer, K.S. and Coulter, L.V. (1938). *J.Am.chem.Soc.* <u>60</u>, 1310.

——— and Polissar, J. (1956). *J.phys.Chem.* <u>60</u>, 1140.

Rahman, A. and Stillinger, F.H. (1972). *J.chem.Phys.* <u>57</u>, 4009.

Rao, R.V.G. and Giauque, W.F. (1965). *J.phys.Chem.* <u>69</u>, 1272.

Reynolds, R.E.D., Worswick, R.D., and Staveley, L.A.K. (1971). *Trans.Faraday Soc.* <u>67</u>, 618.

Rossberg, D. and Magun, S. (1957). *Naturwiss.* <u>44</u>, 59.

Ruben, H.W., Templeton, D.H., Rosenstein, R.D., and Olovsson, I. (1961). *J.Am.chem.Soc.* 83, 820.

Rundle, R.E. (1953). *J.chem.Phys.* 21, 1311.

Runnels, L.K. (1966). *Scient.Am.* 215, (Dec.), 118.

Salinas, S.R. and Nagle, J.F. (1974). *Phys.Rev.* B9, 4920.

Siemens, P.R. and Giauque, W.F. (1969). *J.phys.Chem.* 73, 149.

Shimaoka, K. (1960). *J.phys.Soc.Japan* 15, 106.

Smith, N.O. (1942). *J.Am.chem.Soc.* 64, 41.

───────   and Walsh, P.N. (1954). *J.Am.chem.Soc.* 76, 2054.

Steinemann, S. (1953). *Experientia* 9, 135.

Stillinger, F.H. and Cotter, M.A. (1973). *J.chem.Phys.* 58, 2532.

Sugisaki, M., Suga, H., and Seki, S. (1969). *Proceedings International Symposium on the Physics of Ice, Munich, 1968* (ed. N.Riehl, B.Bullemer, and H.Engelhardt) p.329. Plenum Press, New York.

Taylor, J.C., Mueller, M.H., and Hitterman, R.L. (1970). *Acta crystallogr.* A26, 559.

───────   and Wilson, P.W. (1974). *Acta crystallogr.* B30, 169.

Teichmann, I. and Schmidt, G. (1965). *Phys.St.Solidi* 8, K145.

Tsang, T. and O'Reilly, D.E. (1965). *J.chem.Phys.* 43, 4234.

Tuberfield, K.C. (1967). *Solid St.Communs.* 5, 887.

Waku, S., Hirabayashi, H., Toyoda, H., Iwasaki, H., and Kiriyama, R. (1959). *J.phys.Soc.Japan*, 14, 973.

Waterfield, C.G., Linford, R.G., Goalby, B.B., Bates, T.R., Elyard, C.A., and Staveley, L.A.K. (1968). *Trans.Faraday Soc.* 64, 868.

───────   and Staveley, L.A.K. (1967). *Trans.Faraday Soc.* 63, 2349.

Weir, C., Block, S., and Piermarini, G. (1965). *J.Res.natn. Bur.Stand.* 69C, 275.

Weiss, E. (1965). *Z.anorg.allg.Chem.* 341, 203.

───────   Hensel, H., and Kühr, H. (1969). *Chem.Ber.* 102, 632.

Whalley, E., Davidson, D.W., and Heath, J.B.R. (1966). *J. chem.Phys.* 45, 3976.

───────   Heath, J.B.R., and Davidson, D.W. (1968). *J. chem.Phys.* 48, 2362.

Wilson, G.J., Chan, R.K., Davidson, D.W., and Whalley, E.
     (1965). *J.chem.Phys.* <u>43</u>, 2384.

Wong, P.T.T. and Whalley, E. (1976). *J.chem.Phys.* <u>64</u>, 2359.

Zalkin, A., Ruben, H., and Templeton, D.H. (1962). *Acta
     crystallogr.* <u>15</u>, 1219.

──────   ──────   ──────   (1964). *Acta
     crystallogr.* <u>17</u>, 235.

Zŭmer, S. and Pirš, J. (1974). *Ferroelectrics* <u>7</u>, 119.

9

DISORDER IN MOLECULAR SOLIDS — I

9.1. INTRODUCTION

In this chapter and the next we shall discuss disorder in molecular crystals. Two particular kinds of disorder are commonly encountered, one due to the ability of molecules to switch from one orientation to another in the lattice, the other to their ability to migrate with comparative ease from site to site. As the crystal is heated up from low temperatures, it is generally orientational freedom which is acquired first. Increased freedom of the molecules to diffuse in the lattice is usually not observed until the crystal is in a condition in which the molecules have considerable orientational freedom, though cases are known in which the two kinds of disorder appear to develop simultaneously. We shall therefore first discuss reorientational movement, the limit of which is continuous rotation. The possibility of such rotation was suggested by Pauling (1930) and by Fowler (1935) and many references can be found in the literature to the 'rotation' of ions and molecules in crystal lattices. It is now known that this motion, in the literal sense, is rare. The molecules of *ortho*-hydrogen in the crystals near the melting-point are almost certainly rotating. Much higher up the scale of molecular complexity, it is likely that the molecules of the hydrocarbon adamantane ($C_{10}H_{16}$) in the high-temperature form near the melting-point are approaching a state of free rotation (section 10.3). But in general the situation in a crystal in which a molecule has orientational freedom is that first envisaged by Frenkel (1935), namely that the molecule has a number of orientations available to it and that it can flick from one of these orientations to another. In a lucid discussion of this model and its consequences, Darmon and Brot (1967) have shown that the contribution made to the thermodynamic properties of the crystal by the molecules actually in transit at any instant between one orientation and another is generally very small, even when the energy barrier separating the orientations is relatively low.

In many molecular crystals, the gain in orientational freedom is associated with a phase change or transition. The word 'associated' is here used rather loosely, since the molecules may begin to acquire this freedom well below the transition. But it is also possible for orientational freedom to develop without the appearance of a transition at all. The presence or absence of a transition depends on whether the possible orientations are distinguishable or not, that is on the relation between the symmetry of the molecule and the symmetry of its site in the lattice. Thus, there is no doubt that in crystalline benzene at higher temperatures the molecules can readily reorient themselves in the plane of the ring between six possible orientations. These six positions are indistinguishable from each other, and there is no thermodynamic transition associated with the reorientation. In solid hydrogen chloride, on the other hand, there is a phase change at which a substantial contribution to the entropy increase arises because whereas in the low-temperature form all the molecules have a unique orientation, in the high-temperature form each molecule has twelve nearest neighbours, and can direct its hydrogen atom towards any one of twelve chlorine atoms, so that any one molecule has twelve possible *distinguishable* orientations.

When a molecular crystal undergoes a transition, there is often a considerable increase of disorder in the lattice which is reflected in a relatively large entropy of transition and a correspondingly small entropy gain when the disordered crystal melts. Many of the examples of this are provided by organic substances. The existence of crystals with some remarkable properties in common, including a low entropy of fusion, was first recognized by Timmermanns (1938), who gave them the name of 'plastic crystals'. He realized that the molecules forming such crystals are usually 'globular' molecules, that is molecules of high symmetry, being for example often tetrahedral or approximately spherical in shape. It will be convenient to summarize briefly some of the properties of plastic crystals.

(1) Adopting the usual convention that the form stable at the highest temperatures is designated I, which on cooling

gives a form II, which on further cooling gives a form III,
and so on, the criterion originally used by Timmermanns was
that to qualify as a plastic crystal the entropy of fusion
of I should be less than 5 cal K^{-1} mol^{-1}, i.e. $< 5R/2$.
This criterion is useful, but must not be taken too literally.
Thus, hexachlorethane-I should probably be regarded as a
plastic crystal even though its entropy of fusion is $\sim 2 \cdot 75R$.
Usually, only phase I is plastic, and II and any other low-
temperature forms are 'normal', but examples can be cited
of substances, such as 2-propanethiol, where both phases I
and II are plastic, and cycloheptane actually has three plastic
phases.

(2) The transition from the ordered to the disordered plastic
phase (usually the II→I transition, therefore, but occasionally a lower transition) is sometimes isothermal, sometimes
non-isothermal, and sometimes begins gradually but is completed isothermally. The classification of these transitions
has been discussed by Jaffray (1948) and by McCullough (1961),
who recognized seven different types of transition, three of
which are at least partly isothermal, while the remaining
four are at no stage isothermal. Aston (1961) has pointed
out that when there is evidence that the passage to the disordered phase involves only an increase in orientational
freedom (and not in the ability of the molecules to diffuse),
then the transition is gradual and the heat capacity curve
above the transition is almost a continuation of that below,
whereas a transition such as the III→II transition in cyclopentane, at which it appears that molecular freedom of both
kinds is acquired, is a first-order transition at which there
is an increase in heat capacity similar to that which usually accompanies the fusion of a 'normal' molecular crystal.
Pople and Karasz's theoretical treatment (1961) of molecular
crystals which exhibit positional and orientational disorder
simultaneously has already been discussed (section 3.1.7).

(3) Phase I often has a cubic lattice, though this is not
always so. Examples of high-temperature phases of plastic
crystals which are not cubic will be found in the next chapter.

(4) The plastic, disordered phases give rather diffuse X-ray

diffraction patterns, having a relatively small number of
reflections with considerable background scattering. Much
of the work on these phases has been carried out on powder
photographs which yield only a very limited number of lines.
Thus, that used by Carter and Templeton (1953) in their study
of cyclobutane showed only two lines - the minimum necessary
to establish that phase I is body-centred cubic. A consequence of this is that the unit cell dimensions of plastic
crystals are often not known as precisely as one would like.
(5) The description of certain disordered molecular crystals
as 'plastic' derives from the observation by Michils (1948)
that they can be extruded by quite small pressures. As a
typical example, whereas a pressure of about 1 500 bar was
required to extrude carbon tetrabromide in its non-plastic
form II through a particular orifice, the corresponding
pressure for the plastic phase was only ~250 bar. Numerous
authors have described plastic crystals in their papers as
'soft' or 'waxy', and one or two extreme cases have been
noted. Thus, perfluorocyclohexane in its plastic phase
flows under gravity, like pitch, while Perdok and Terpstra
(1943) reported that tetrathiomethylmethane, even in phase
II, 'sinks under its own weight'. The ordered phases of such
substances are, by contrast, hard and brittle. We shall
briefly discuss in the next chapter the probable reason for
the plasticity of disordered crystals.
(6) Although plastic crystals are generally formed by substances with roughly spherical molecules, the converse is
not necessarily true. Thus, while CCl_4 and $C(CH_3)_4$ have
plastic phases, $SiCl_4$ and $Si(CH_3)_4$ do not. The hexafluorides
of the third series of transition metals such as tungsten
and platinum all undergo transitions to a body-centred cubic
phase I which has an entropy of fusion ΔS of ~1·6R, whereas
the hexafluorides of the actinide elements such as uranium
exist in only one form with $\Delta S \approx 6·5R$. The hydrocarbon adamantane forms a plastic crystal, whereas hexamethylenetetramine, with a non-polar molecule of very similar shape, does
not. It should be pointed out that it is possible for a
crystal to pass from a hard, brittle state into a plastic
condition without undergoing any transition. An example is

argon. Stewart (1955) found that at 77 K (about 7 K below
the triple-point), crystalline argon can be extruded through
a ~3mm diameter hole by only 260 bar, whereas at 63 K the
necessary pressure has increased to 580 bar. We must further
bear in mind that there is no question of a molecular crystal
being either completely ordered up to its melting-point, or
else giving a high-temperature phase which falls in the category of plastic crystals. Intermediate cases are known,
some of which will be considered in the next chapter, where
some limited disorder is acquired, such as reorientational
freedom in one plane only, the entropy of fusion remaining
relatively high.

The nature of the problems which arise in studies of
disorder in a molecular crystal should now be clear. The
form taken by the disorder has to be disclosed. The molecular dynamics associated with the disorder should be quantitatively investigated. In general, this will involve studies of rates of reorientation and diffusion, and as information on the parameters governing these rate processes accumulates it is natural to seek correlations between them and
other properties of the substances concerned. There is also
the question of the nature of the forces responsible for the
change at sufficiently low temperatures to an ordered condition. Possibilities here can include the anisotropy of dispersion forces and of short-range repulsive forces, interaction between dipoles, interaction between quadrupoles (as
in crystalline nitrogen or hydrogen), interaction between
octupoles (as in methane) and between even higher multipoles
(for example, hexadecapoles in sulphur hexafluoride), and hydrogen bonding. Finally, there is the matter of how successful any particular theoretical order-disorder treatment is
in correlating and accounting for the experimental observations. Understandably, most progress has been made with
solids consisting of simple molecules. For convenience, we
shall arbitrarily restrict ourselves in this chapter to solids
the molecules of which do not exceed in complexity the tetra-
hydrides of Group IV elements. In the following chapter we
shall first consider solids composed of somewhat larger molecules before finally reviewing certain general matters in the

light of the information which has been presented.

9.2. HYDROGEN AND DEUTERIUM

Crystalline hydrogen and deuterium are exceptional solids
from the standpoint of disorder, since they are examples,
rare if not unique, of crystals in which molecules can rotate
with almost unimpeded freedom. This is due to a combination
of factors. Because the intermolecular attraction is so weak,
the zero-point energy of the molecules is comparable with
the lattice energy, and the lattice is therefore very expanded.
A substantial part of the volume it occupies might be described as zero-point volume. As the moments of inertia of
the molecules are relatively very small, the rotational quanta
are correspondingly large, and though the intermolecular
forces are anisotropic (which has important consequences at
sufficiently low temperatures) the change in the potential
energy of a pair of molecules as their mutual orientation
alters is much smaller than the lowest values of the rotational energy. Analysis of molecular behaviour in the crystal
is facilitated by the comparison of hydrogen and deuterium,
and by the detailed information available on the intermolecular force field. One of the reasons why these crystals
have attracted so much attention is, in fact, the simplicity
of the hydrogen molecule. As we shall see, the force which
at sufficiently low temperatures induces the ordering of the
molecular axes is electric quadrupole-quadrupole interaction, and the quadrupole moment of the hydrogen and deuterium molecules can be reliably calculated by quantum mechanics. Another attractive feature is that there is a close
analogy between the ordering of the molecular axes in crystalline hydrogen and the ordering of spins in magnetic systems, the analogy extending to the dynamic aspects of the
ordering processes (Harris 1971). A molecule of hydrogen
in the lowest rotational level (J = 0) corresponds to a non-
magnetic particle, while a molecule with J = 1 resembles a
particle with a magnetic spin of S = 1.

Interest in crystalline hydrogen and deuterium is further enhanced by the fact that H_2 and D_2 molecules can exist
in *ortho* and *para* forms. The proton has two possible nuclear

spin wave functions, and there are therefore three possible
symmetric nuclear spin wave functions for the molecule H_2
and one antisymmetric wave function. Molecules with the
symmetric nuclear spin wave functions are *ortho* molecules,
and those with the antisymmetric function *para* molecules.
Since the complete wave function must be asymmetric in the
two protons, the *ortho* molecules have odd values of the rotational quantum number J, while for the *para* molecules J
must be even. Any *ortho* molecule therefore has a spin degeneracy of three, and at temperatures sufficiently high that
differences in the rotational energy levels available to
ortho and *para* molecules no longer matter, there are three
times as many *ortho* molecules as *para* molecules in the equilibrium mixture. At 25°C the percentage of *ortho* molecules
in the equilibrium mixtures is in fact 74·925, so that without introducing any serious error we can regard 'ordinary'
hydrogen $(n\text{-}H_2)$ as $\frac{3}{4}o\text{-}H_2$ and $\frac{1}{4}p\text{-}H_2$. At 0 K, however, $p\text{-}H_2$
is the stable form. The rotational energy of one *ortho* mole-
cule with $J = 1$ is 1·41 kJ mol^{-1} (= 118 cm^{-1}). Any rotational level is $(2J + 1)$-fold degenerate, so that in their
lowest possible rotational state the *ortho* molecules have
a *rotational* degeneracy of three.

The deuteron with a spin of one has three possible
nuclear spin wave functions, and therefore for D_2 the
possibilities for the molecular nuclear spin wave function
are six symmetric functions and three antisymmetric
functions. The *ortho* states must now be associated with
symmetric rotational wave functions for which J is even,
while the *para* molecules have odd values of J. The
equilibrium mixture at sufficiently high temperatures
$(n\text{-}D_2)$ therefore consists of *ortho* and *para* molecules in the
proportion of 2:1. If $n\text{-}D_2$ persists as such to very low
temperatures, it consists of two-thirds non-rotating $o\text{-}D_2$
molecules and one-third $p\text{-}D_2$ molecules with $J = 1$. The
stable form at very low temperatures is $o\text{-}D_2$.

Almost since the realization that hydrogen exists in
ortho and *para* forms it has been possible to prepare virtually pure $p\text{-}H_2$, and since the discovery of deuterium almost
pure $o\text{-}D_2$. More recently, by using a process of selective

adsorption on alumina at ~20 K devised by Cunningham, Chapin, and Johnston (1958) and developed by Depatie and Mills (1968), it has become possible to prepare almost pure o-H_2 and p-D_2. This has greatly assisted the elucidation of the order-disorder problems presented by the hydrogen isotopes, but it should be pointed out that even if virtually 100% o-H_2 and p-D_2 are initially obtained, the spontaneous conversion of o-H_2 into p-H_2 (and the corresponding, but slower, p-$D_2 \to o$-D_2 change) means in effect that the properties of pure o-H_2 and p-D_2 may still have to be obtained by extrapolation. These spontaneous conversions have, of course, an interest in their own right for some investigators, but are a nuisance to others.

Our primary concern is with the disorder which can prevail in solid H_2 and D_2, and with the change at lower temperatures to an ordered condition, and we shall begin with the state of affairs in the crystals near the melting-point. The first evidence for thinking that under these circumstances the o-H_2 molecules in a crystal of n-H_2 rotate almost freely was the following. When a mole of p-H_2 sublimes at its triple-point (13·81 K), absorbing 1·015 kJ, it gives a gas almost all the molecules of which are *not* rotating. When a mole of n-H_2 sublimes, the gas formed consists of $\frac{3}{4}o$-H_2, with molecules rotating with an energy of 1·41 kJ mol^{-1}, yet the molar heat of sublimation of n-H_2 (1·025 kJ) is almost the same as that of p-H_2. This is consistent with the retention of their rotational freedom by the o-H_2 molecules in the lattice of n-H_2. That such free rotation is possible in solid hydrogen was beautifully confirmed in a study by Allin, Feldman, and Welsh (1956) of the Raman spectrum, and later of the infrared spectrum (Allin, Gush, Hare, and Welsh 1958). The Raman spectrum of p-H_2 a few degrees below the melting-point reveals a rotational frequency of ~355 cm^{-1} for the $J = 0$ to $J = 2$ transition, which is almost identical with the value found for the gas, while n-H_2 shows both this line and that of ~589 cm^{-1} for the $J = 1$ to $J = 3$ transition for the *ortho* molecules. The same frequencies appear in association with the vibrational transition in the infrared spectrum of n-H_2 at 11 K. In solid HD, for any molecule of

which all J values are in principle possible, the fundamental i.r. band incorporates the $J = 0$ to $J = 1$ transition.
However, although such spectroscopic evidence confirms the
belief that the rotation of the molecules near the melting-
point is almost free, there must nevertheless be some effect
of the anisotropic intermolecular force field on the rotational energy levels, and this was discussed in detail by
Van Kranendonk and Karl (1968). Raman studies have provided
direct evidence of such interaction, as may be seen from
Fig.9.1 due to Bhatnagar, Allin, and Welsh (1962). This shows

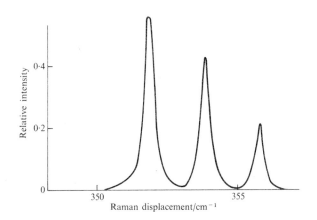

Fig.9.1. Raman spectrum of solid p-H$_2$, $S_0(0)$ transition (after Bhatnagar,
Allin, and Welsh 1962).

the spectrum due to the $S_0(0)$ rotational transition, for
which J changes from 0 to 2 while the vibrational quantum
number remains zero. Excited rotational states are broadened
by the anisotropic intermolecular forces into rotational
energy bands. For the $J = 2$ level, three levels of the band
combine with the $J = 0$ state, and the transition therefore
appears as a triplet.

Numerous NMR studies have been carried out on solid
hydrogen and deuterium. Particularly notable are the pioneer
investigation of Hatton and Rollin (1949), the later work of
Reif and Purcell (1953), and the papers of Meyer, Weinhaus,
and their collaborators. With hydrogen, the resonance line

derives only from the *ortho* molecules, with nuclear spin
quantum number $I = 1$, whereas with deuterium both the *ortho*
molecules with $I = 2$ and the *para* molecules ($I = 1$) give a
signal. These NMR studies have given particularly useful
information about molecular behaviour in the first two or
three degrees from 0 K, and we shall refer to this in due
course. Here we note that as the melting-point is approached
the resonance line becomes very narrow (being only ~0·1 G
wide for n-H_2 just below its melting-point), which is not
only consistent with almost free rotation of the *ortho* molecules, but also implies that the molecules can readily move
from site to site in the lattice. Since freedom of molecular movement in a lattice can be associated with exceptional softness of the crystal (as with the organic plastic
crystals discussed in Chapter 10), it is interesting that
solid hydrogen is viscoelastic ('non-rigid'), though it
hardens over a rather narrow pressure range at ~150 bar (Cook,
Dwyer, Berwaldt, and Nevins 1965). By measuring the relaxation time in the rotating frame below ~13 K, and the transverse relaxation time T_2 above this temperature, Weinhaus,
Meyer, Myers, and Harris (1973) obtained quantitative information on thermally activated diffusion in deuterium
from 9 to 17 K, in which range the characteristic time τ
between molecular jumps changes by ~10^7. The temperature
dependence of τ is shown in Fig. 9.2. The activation energy
for diffusion of 2·3 kJ mol^{-1} is essentially independent of
temperature and of the p-D_2 content of the crystals. The
corresponding activation energy for H_2 is 1·66 kJ mol^{-1}
(Weinhaus and Meyer 1973). There was no sign in these
studies that diffusion proceeds as predicted by Ebner and
Sung (1972), namely by quantum-mechanical tunnelling.

Manzhelii, Udovidchenko, and Esel'son (1973) reported
that when p-H_2 is heated under a pressure of ~30 bar, it
appears to undergo a first-order change when less than a
degree from the melting-point with a volume *decrease*. This
interesting observation merits further investigation.

When the statistical entropy of n-H_2 was compared with
the calorimetric entropy based on measurements carried down
to 10 K or so, it became clear that at this temperature

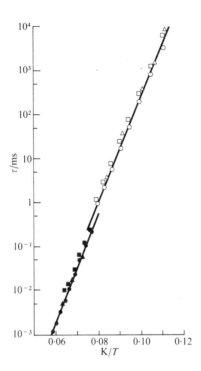

Fig.9.2. Temperature dependence of the characteristic time τ between jumps in classical diffusion region for D_2 for various mole fractions x of p-D_2. Solid symbols, high-field T_2 measurements; open symbols, rotating-frame measurements; circles, $x = 0 \cdot 05$; triangles, $x = 0 \cdot 54$; squares, $x = 0 \cdot 89$ (after Weinhaus, Meyer, Myers, and Harris 1973).

crystalline n-H_2 has an entropy larger by about 18 J K^{-1} mol^{-1} than the vibrational entropy of the lattice (Giauque and Johnston 1928, Giauque 1930). Regarding a mole of n-H_2 as a random mixture of $\frac{3}{4}$ mole o-H_2 and $\frac{1}{4}$ mole p-H_2, there will first be the entropy of mixing, $-R(\frac{3}{4} \ln \frac{3}{4} + \frac{1}{4} \ln \frac{1}{4})$, $= 4 \cdot 674$ J K^{-1} mol^{-1}. Since the *ortho* molecules are nine-fold degenerate (three-fold by virtue of the nuclear spin, and three-fold by virtue of their rotation), there will be a further entropy contribution of $\frac{3}{4} R \ln 9$, $= 13 \cdot 70$ J K^{-1} mol^{-1}. The sum of these two quantities, 18.37 J K^{-1} mol^{-1}, is in good agreement with the experimental value of 18$\cdot$0 J K^{-1} mol^{-1}. One would hardly expect that the nuclear spin dege-neracy of o-H_2 would be lifted until extremely low temperatures had been reached[†]. But with the *rotational* degeneracy of $o\text{-}H_2$ and $p\text{-}D_2$ the position is different. The first indication that the anisotropy of the intermolecular forces splits the $J = 1$ level of the *ortho* molecules in $n\text{-}H_2$ was obtained by Simon, Mendelssohn, and Ruhemann (1930). They found that the heat capacity of samples of hydrogen containing *ortho* molecules started to *rise* with decreasing temperature at about 5 K, pointing to a maximum in the heat capacity at a still lower temperature. The existence of this maximum was definitely established by Hill and Ricketson (1954). In brief, the position is that hydrogen with a sufficiently high proportion of *ortho* molecules undergoes a cooperative transition; for $n\text{-}H_2$, T_λ is ~1·6K. There is a corresponding transition in crystalline deuterium containing a sufficiently high proportion of $p\text{-}D_2$ molecules. We therefore have here systems in which the species capable of being in an ordered condition can be diluted by inert bodies, a situation discussed in section 3.4 under the title of the 'Percolation Problem'.

The following are the more important facts about the transition in hydrogen and deuterium.

(1) For hydrogen or deuterium containing more than about 50% of $o\text{-}H_2$ or $p\text{-}D_2$ respectively, there is a peak in the heat capacity curve. Although for brevity we shall refer to this as a λ-anomaly, the peak for hydrogen is in fact rather more symmetrical than a typical λ-point. In deuterium, on the other hand, the anomaly is very sharp, with a much less pronounced 'tail' above T_λ (Fig.9.3; Grenier and White, 1964). At lower concentrations of $o\text{-}H_2$ and $p\text{-}D_2$, there is a broad, hump-like anomaly in the heat capacity, which becomes less evident as the systems approach pure $p\text{-}H_2$ and $o\text{-}D_2$ respectively. (It may be mentioned here that Hill and Ricketson (1954), and later investigators, found that the calorimetric study at very low temperatures of solid hydrogen containing $o\text{-}H_2$ is complicated by the heat evolved

[†]In solid ^{3}He, in which the nuclear spin-spin exchange interaction is unusually large, a transition to an ordered nuclear spin state occurs at about 1·2 mK (see e.g. Halperin, Archie, Rasmussen, Buhrman, and Richardson 1974).

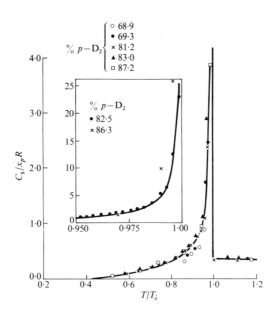

Fig.9.3. Heat capacity C_s of solid D_2 containing more than 68·9 per cent
p-D_2; x_p = mole fraction of p-D_2 (Grenier and White 1964).

in the *ortho→para* conversion caused by magnetic dipole-dipole
interaction. As the magnetic moment of the deuteron is smaller than that of the proton, the corresponding *para→ortho*
change for deuterium takes place more slowly, and so more
accurate measurements can be made on deuterium than on hydrogen.)

(2) Ahlers and Orttung (1964) made a particularly thorough
study of the heat capacity of solid hydrogen, not only as a
function of temperature and of c, the percentage of *ortho*
molecules, but also of volume. This revealed that the λ-
anomaly has structure, in that besides the main peak at a
temperature T_λ, there is one subsidiary maximum, and sometimes two (Fig.9.4). This work confirmed the observation
of Hill and Ricketson that T_λ rises linearly with increasing
c, a conclusion supported by NMR studies (*cf.* the relation
between T_t and composition for the methanol-quinol clathrate,
section 11.2.4).

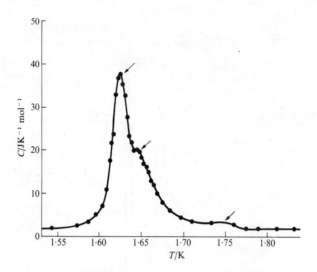

Fig.9.4. Heat capacity C of a sample of H_2 containing 74·1% o-H_2.   The arrows indicate distinguishable peaks (after Ahlers and Orttung 1964).

Extrapolation to c = 1 (for deuterium, c is the percentage of $para$ molecules) gives estimates of T_λ = 2·87 K for pure o-H_2 and T_λ = 4·06 K for pure p-D_2 (Orttung 1962).   These are useful figures, since the statistical theories which have been applied to the transitions in hydrogen and deuterium have primarily been developed for pure o-H_2 and pure p-D_2.

(3)   The weak intermolecular forces in hydrogen and deuterium coupled with the relatively high zero-point energies confer on their crystals exceptionally high compressibilities, so that by the application of moderate pressures the molar volume V can be considerably reduced.   In Ahlers and Orttung's experiments on hydrogen, V varied from 22·6 to 15·9 cm^3 mol^{-1}. As V falls, T_λ rises according to the equation

$$T_\lambda = (-226 + 6·93c) (V^{-5/3} + 1·20 \times 10^3 V^{-5}) .$$

The dominant term in the second bracket in this equation is $V^{-5/3}$, corresponding to a dependence of T_λ on R^{-5}, where R is the intermolecular separation.   This is striking evidence that quadrupole-quadrupole interaction is the chief factor tending to produce molecular order. The term with an even higher dependence on V, namely that in V^{-5}, presumably derives from short-range overlap repulsion. The theoretical treatments which we shall briefly review are all based on quadrupole interaction as the order-inducing influence.

(4)   The λ-anomaly is associated with hysteresis, T_{λ} differing by ~0·2 K on heating and cooling. This is confirmed by the NMR and infrared spectroscopic studies, and implies that the transition is partly isothermal.

(5)   The hump-like heat capacity anomalies in solid hydrogen and deuterium with <60 per cent o-H_2 and p-D_2 respectively have a pronounced high-temperature tail which is responsible for a considerable fraction of the entropy gained in the transition. At sufficiently high temperatures, the anomalous heat capacity C_{ex} is given approximately by the equation

$$C_{ex} \, T^2 = Ac + Bc^2 \, ,$$

where Bc^2 is the dominant term on the right-hand side. According to this equation, for a given c the excess heat capacity above the transition is proportional to T^{-2} (a dependence encountered both in magnetic transitions (section 3.1.4), and in Schottky anomalies), but a more detailed examination has shown that the relation between C_{ex} and T is less simple than this (Berlinsky and Harris 1970).

(6)   The hump-shaped anomalies at lower o-H_2 and p-D_2 concentrations cannot be fitted by Schottky curves for three energy levels, whether equally spaced or comprising a single ground level and a doubly degenerate upper level. The latter possibility is that to be expected for the removal of the triple degeneracy of the $J = 1$ rotational level in an axially symmetric field, the single level corresponding to the quantum number $M = 0$, and the upper doubly degenerate level to $M = \pm 1$. For either kind of splitting, cooling would lead to an entropy loss of $R \ln 3$ per mole of o-H_2 or p-D_2. The experiments of Hill and Ricketson on hydrogen and the

detailed study by Grenier and White of the more favourable
deuterium system showed that the expected entropy loss of
$(c/100)R\ln 3$ does in fact take place, being virtually complete when the temperature has fallen to ~$0\cdot6T_\lambda$ for $c > 80\%$,
but not until the temperature has fallen to within a few
tenths of a degree from 0 K for mixtures with $c < 60$.

(7)   A crystal structure change is associated with the λ-
anomaly in *ortho*-rich hydrogen and *para*-rich deuterium.
Keesom, De Smedt, and Mooy had shown in 1930 that p-H_2 at
helium temperatures has an hexagonal close-packed (h.c.p.)
lattice, which was confirmed by Kogan, Bulatov, and Yakimenko
(1964).   The h.c.p. lattice is also the stable form at higher
temperatures for n-H_2, n-D_2, and HD (Bostanjoglo and Kleinschmidt 1967). The first evidence of a crystal structure
change between $1\cdot3$ and $1\cdot9$ K was obtained by Clouter and
Gush (1965), who studied in this temperature region the
infrared absorption spectrum between 4 150 cm^{-1} and 5 100 cm^{-1}
of samples approximating to n-H_2. Features present in the
spectrum at $1\cdot9$ K, having their origin in quadrupole induc-
tion effects, had almost vanished at $1\cdot3$ K, from which it was
concluded that at $1\cdot3$ K the crystal had acquired a centre of
inversion which was lacking at $1\cdot9$ K. The change in the
spectrum took place over ~$0\cdot1$ K and showed thermal hysteresis.
The phase change was confirmed by an X-ray study by Mills
and Schuch (1965), who found that the h.c.p. lattice of
n-H_2 persists down to about $1\cdot3$ K, but then transforms to a
face-centred cubic (f.c.c.) lattice. The parameters of the
two structures as determined by Mills and Schuch are such
that the calculated molar volumes are the same within experimental error, but by confining a sample of hydrogen with
73% o-H_2 in a fixed volume and measuring the pressure change
as a function of temperature, Jarvis, Ramm, and Meyer (1967)
established that the volume of the h.c.p. phase exceeds that
of the f.c.c. phase by ~$0\cdot1\%$, which is about an order of
magnitude less than the volume difference between *para* and
ortho hydrogen. Mills and Schuch confirmed that the transition temperature falls with decreasing *ortho/para* ratio. A
neutron diffraction study (Mucker, Talhouk, Harris, White,

and Erickson 1965) of n-D_2 and o-D_2 at 13 K was interpreted
as favouring an h.c.p. lattice for both crystals, a result
confirmed by an electron diffraction study by Bostanjoglo
and Kleinschmidt (1967). Schuch and Mills (1966) carried
out an X-ray study on deuterium enriched up to 65% in p-D_2,
and found that with a p-D_2 content of 60% or more, the h.c.p.
structure transformed into an f.c.c. lattice below 1·4 K.
At lower p-D_2 concentrations, the structure remained h.c.p.
It is interesting that Mills and Schuch found that for n-H_2
in the h.c.p. form at 1·30 K, the c/a ratio is 1·623 ± 0·006,
a little less than the theoretical value for close packing of
$(8/3)^{\frac{1}{2}} = 1\cdot633$, whereas for the h.c.p. lattices of n-H_2, HD,
and n-D_2 at an unspecified, but higher temperature (perhaps
~4 K), the electron diffraction study of Bostanjoglo and
Kleinschmidt gave 1·634 ± 0·006 for the c/a ratio.

One outcome of an exceptionally thorough Raman study
of p-D_2 and o-H_2 carried out by Hardy, Silvera, and McTague
(1975), in which optically clear oriented single crystals
were used, was the confirmation that the ordered f.c.c.
forms have the space group $Pa3$, in agreement with the conclusion reached from neutron diffraction by Mills, Yarnell, and
Schuch (1974). This structure had been predicted theoretically as that to which electric quadrupole-quadrupole interaction would give rise ($v.inf$). It consists of four sublattices, in each of which the molecules are aligned along
a different diagonal of the unit cell (Fig.9.5).

It therefore appears that the prominent λ-type heat
capacity anomalies in hydrogen and deuterium of sufficiently
high o-H_2 and p-D_2 content respectively are associated with
phase changes between h.c.p. and f.c.c. lattices, whereas
samples showing the broader, hump-backed anomalies remain
in the h.c.p. form. In a sense, however, the crystal structure change between the f.c.c. and h.c.p. lattices is sub-
ordinate to the orientational order-disorder transition.
Bostanjoglo and Kleinschmidt noted that in the neighbourhood
of the helium boiling-point, thin layers of n-H_2 and n-D_2
can be deposited from the vapour as f.c.c. crystals, which
then change on warming into the stable h.c.p. form, and it
appears that sometimes such films can be formed as a mixture

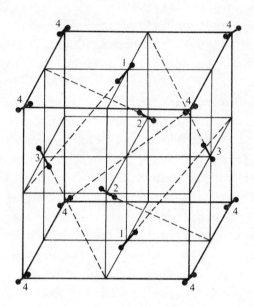

Fig.9.5. The four-sublattice structure of H_2 in the f.c.c. form (space group $Pa3$).

of the two structures. Subsequently, Schuch, Mills, and Depatie (1968) found that thermal cycling stabilizes the f.c.c. phase as compared with the h.c.p. phase, and the same observation was made by Meyer, Weinhaus, Maraviglia, and Mills (1972) in their NMR study of D_2. Clearly the f.c.c. and h.c.p. phases must have almost identical Gibbs energies. When, however, as a result of such thermal cycling, the crystal remains in the f.c.c. form throughout, the order-disorder (orientational) transition still persists. Moreover, Ramm, Meyer, and Mills (1970) had already shown that when the order-disorder transition *is* accompanied by the phase transformation, the observed changes in thermal properties result mainly from the transition and not from the crystal structure change. Accordingly, it has been possible in theoretical treatments of the order-disorder transition to disregard the phase change, and to consider the transition as taking place in an f.c.c. lattice throughout.

(8)   The first NMR investigation of solid hydrogen was carried
out by Hatton and Rollin (1949), and several later studies,
notably the particularly thorough examination of Reif and
Purcell (1953) confirmed and extended their observations and
conclusions.   The resonance line in n-H_2 broadens as the
temperature falls, becoming ~8 G wide at ~10 K.   From 10 K
down to about 1·5 K the width of the resonance line is almost constant, so presumably the rotational movement remains
relatively unaffected while diffusion is suppressed.   At
about 1·5 K the character of the line changes in a way which
suggests a rotational-librational transition.   Two widely
separated peaks begin to form, and at 1·15 K the NMR line
consists of a remnant of the central line with two peaks symmetrically disposed about it and separated from each other
by about 50 G.   These two peaks arise because molecular rotation is now hindered and no longer averages out the intramolecular magnetic dipole-dipole interaction of the two
protons.   The detailed structure of the two peaks, which
have humps on their outer sides, can however only be quantitatively interpreted by taking into consideration the
effect of the crystalline potential field in lifting the
rotational degeneracy of the $ortho$ molecules.   There is a
reasonable if not perfect correspondence between the temperature T_c at which the peaks appear and T_λ of the heat
capacity anomaly.   Moreover, T_c shows a dependence on the
percentage of $ortho$ molecules and on pressure similar to
that found for T_λ (Dickson and Meyer 1965), and the appearance and disappearance of the peaks displays hysteresis
(Sugawara, Masuda, T. Kanda, and E. Kanda 1955, G.W. Smith
and Housley 1960).

NMR measurements have been used to investigate quantitatively the change in orientational order with temperature.   A thorough study of this kind was carried out on D_2
by Meyer, Weinhaus, Maraviglia, and Mills (1972) which
covered the temperature range 0·4 - 4 K with mole fractions
of p-D_2 molecules ($J = 1$) from 0·55 to 0·96.   In the ordered
phase, there are two doublets symmetrically disposed about
the central Larmor frequency (Fig.9.6).   The outer one is
produced by the $J = 1$ molecules.   The doublet with the much

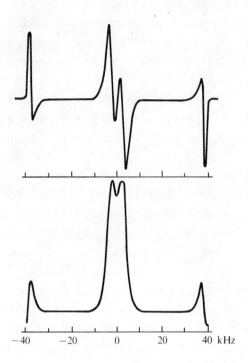

Fig.9.6. Observed derivative and integrated shape of a typical NMR line in orientationally ordered D_2. T = 1·26 K; mole fraction of p-D_2 = 0·81 (H. Meyer *et al*. 1972).

smaller splitting derives from the J = 0 molecules. The ordering parameters σ for the J = 1 and J = 0 molecules are proportional to the respective doublet splittings. (Although a molecule with J = 0 should behave as a spherically sym- metrical body, such molecules do in fact become orientationally ordered, as the perturbation from surrounding J = 1 mole- cules introduces a small degree of mixing of the J = 2 state.) The doublets disappear suddenly at T_λ, showing the first-order completion of the transition, to be replaced by the sharp central line, but it is interesting that the latter appears just below T_λ, indicating the presence of clusters of dis- ordered D_2 molecules. Fig.9.7 shows the change with tempera- ture of the order parameter σ, which can be regarded as a measure of the average degree of alignment of a molecular

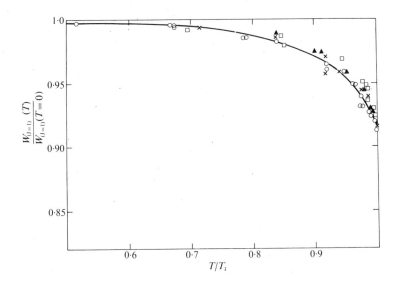

Fig.9.7. Temperature dependence of normalized line-width
$W_{(J=1)}(T)/W_{(J=1)}(T=0)$ for samples of D_2 of p-D_2 mole fraction ranging from
$0\cdot81$ to $0\cdot96$. The curve shows the normalized order parameter $\sigma(T)/\sigma(T=0)$
for pure p-D_2 (after H.Meyer et al. 1972).

axis with the direction characterizing a particular sublattice.

(9) Considerable interest has been taken in the motion of
the molecules in the ordered state which replaces the almost
free rotation in the disordered crystal. Below the transition,
the molecules undergo torsional oscillations (librations)
which combine to produce angular momentum waves or librons,
analogous to the spin waves in magnetically ordered solids.
Information on the libron state has been obtained from inelastic neutron scattering (Stein, Stiller, and Stockmeyer
1972), nuclear spin-lattice relaxation time measurements
(Ishimoto, Nagamine, Kimura, and Kumagai 1974), and Raman
spectra (Hardy, Silvera, and McTague 1975).

(10) As already stated, the dominant cause of orientational
ordering at low temperatures is electric quadrupole-quadrupole interaction. By comparison, the anisotropy of the dispersion and overlap forces has only a very minor influence.

The quadrupole coupling constant Γ_0 in a rigid lattice is given by the equation

$$\Gamma_0 = 6e^2 Q^2 / 25R^5 \ ,$$

where eQ is the molecular quadrupole moment and R is the nearest-neighbour separation. With the values of the quadrupole moment of H_2 and D_2 calculated quantum mechanically by Karl and Poll (1967), Γ_0 is $0 \cdot 698 \ cm^{-1}$ for H_2, and $0 \cdot 839 \ cm^{-1}$ for D_2. In the actual crystal, owing to the zero-point motion, the effective coupling constant Γ_{eff} is smaller than Γ_0 (see e.g. Stein *et al.* 1972). Writing $\Gamma_{eff} = \zeta \Gamma_0$, ζ can be found experimentally in more than one way, from appropriate measurements made on *ortho*-rich samples of H_2 or *para*-rich samples of D_2 extrapolated to give estimates for pure o-H_2 and p-D_2. Probably the most accurate method is neutron spectroscopy, by which Stein *et al.* found $\zeta = 0 \cdot 80 \pm 0 \cdot 01$ for H_2. This compares with $0 \cdot 82$ from measurements of $(\partial p / \partial T)_V$ (Jarvis, Meyer, and Ramm 1969) and $0 \cdot 83$ from Raman studies (Hardy *et al.* 1975). For p-D_2, ζ is ~$0 \cdot 89$.

Turning to the theoretical treatments of the order-disorder problems presented by H_2 and D_2, these systems can be regarded as generally falling between two extremes. At one extreme, we have pure o-H_2 and pure p-D_2, where cooperative interaction is inevitable. At the other, we may consider dilute solutions of o-H_2 in p-H_2, or of p-D_2 in o-D_2, where the problem is primarily the simpler one of the mutual influence of the molecules in the few nearest-neighbour pairs present at low concentration (though even here next-nearest-neighbour effects are not necessarily insignificant). Considering first the pure o-H_2 system, several authors have succeeded in showing that at 0 K, in agreement with experiment, the f.c.c. lattice is more stable than the h.c.p. lattice (Felsteiner 1965, Kitaigorodskii and Mirskaya 1965, Miyagi and Nakamura 1967). Their calculations are essentially based on the work of Nagai and Nakamura (1960), who extended Luttinger and Tisza's classic treatment of dipole-dipole interaction in crystals (1946) to quadrupole interactions.

The energy difference between the f.c.c. and h.c.p. lattices was estimated to be 5-10 J mol^{-1}.

With regard to statistical-mechanical treatments of the orientational order-disorder transition, these are now numerous. Our reference to them must necessarily be brief, and the original literature must be consulted for the details of the various models used and for the criticisms to which these models have been subjected. Some approaches have been limited to the f.c.c. phase, some have been applied to the h.c.p. phase, while yet others have attempted to account for the crystal structure change. An important advance was made by James and Raich (1967) who used a rigid lattice, molecular-field approach, and who criticized earlier theories such as those of Bell and Fairbairn (1964) and Danielian (1965) on the grounds that these had led to calculated orientational distributions which would not give rise to a molecular potential with a symmetry consistent with the calculated distributions. Accordingly James and Raich adopted an iterative approach, adaptable to high-speed computation, in which, for a given set of sublattices, a condition of the molecules was sought which gave a self-consistent description of the ordering. Moreover, both the f.c.c. lattice (James and Raich 1967) and the more difficult case of the h.c.p. lattice (James 1968) were examined. An interesting aspect of James' work is that it raised the possibility of the existence of structures other than the ordered f.c.c. and disordered h.c.p. phases, depending on the effective range of the coupling between the molecules in the lattice. This recalls Ahlers and Orttung's observation that the specific heat anomaly in *ortho*-rich hydrogen showed one or two subsidiary peaks besides the main peak. James concluded that the transition in o-H_2 (and *ortho*-rich mixtures) is made up of a main, first-order transition from an orientationally ordered f.c.c. structure to an orientationally ordered h.c.p. lattice, followed by one or two second-order transitions into an orientationally disordered form. He pointed out that among the several factors neglected in his treatment was the effect of lattice vibrations, which for H_2 have a considerable amplitude and are notably anharmonic. For deuterium, the amplitude of the vibration will be smaller and the anharmonicity relatively less, and James considered that this difference could lead in p-D_2 to a single transition from the ordered f.c.c. lattice to the orientationally disordered h.c.p. lattice, consistent with the apparent absence of any sign of maxima, other than the main peak, in the heat capacity anomaly in *para*-rich crystalline deuterium (Grenier and White 1964).

As an example of other theoretical treatments we may mention the cluster-variation approach of Lee and Raich (1971), which they applied to an assembly of pure ($J = 1$) H_2 or D_2 molecules on both h.c.p. and f.c.c. lattices. The principle of this method is that the interaction within a small cluster of spins (e.g. three) is treated exactly, while the interaction of the cluster with the rest of the crystal is approximated by an effective field. In the transition region, at least, this kind of theory is superior to a molecular-field treatment. Englman and Friedman (1973) have considered o-H_2 by superimposing correlations on the molecular-field approximation. Their theory leads to the correct ordered lattice and to a transition temperature of 2·56 K.

We turn finally to dilute solutions of o-H_2 in p-H_2 and of p-D_2 in o-D_2, which on the magnetic analogy are equivalent to magnetically dilute alloys. In a dilute solution of o-H_2 in p-H_2, the $J = 1$ level of a single (isolated) molecule is split into two levels, a lower level ($M = 0$), and a pair of upper levels ($M = \pm1$), where M is the component of J along the hexagonal axis. For two adjacent o-H_2 molecules, the triple degeneracy of each gives a nine-fold degeneracy for the pair. Owing to the electric quadrupole-quadrupole interaction the energy level system of the pair consists of a doublet at $-4\Gamma_0$, a fourfold degenerate level at zero, a doublet at $+\Gamma_0$ and a singlet at $+6\Gamma_0$, where Γ_0 is the coupling constant as previously defined (Nakamura 1955). The heat capacity of such a dilute solution therefore shows a Schottky anomaly which can still be detected even if the concentration of the o-H_2 molecules is only of the order of one per cent. The anomaly arises from the pairs of o-H_2 molecules, and to some extent from groups of three such

molecules. The energy level splitting for isolated molecules has a negligible effect in the temperature region in
question. The maximum of the anomaly occurs at ~1·3 K for
the H_2 system, and at about 1·4 K for p-D_2 in o-D_2 (Roberts
and Daunt 1970, 1972). On extending the heat capacity measurements on the latter (D_2) system down to 0·25 K, it was
found that as the temperature falls below 0·6 K, the heat
capacity rises again, so that there is a second, lower,
anomaly with a maximum below 0·3 K. To account for this it
was necessary to consider quadrupole-quadrupole interaction
between next-nearest, and even next-next-nearest neighbours
(Roberts and Daunt 1974, Roberts, Rojas, and Daunt 1976).

This heat capacity work provided confirmation of an interesting phenomenon which occurs in a dilute solution of
o-H_2 in p-H_2 (but *not* in the counterpart D_2 system). Meyer
and his coworkers had previously concluded from NMR studies
(Amstutz, Thompson, and Meyer 1968) and from measurements
of $(\partial p/\partial T)_V$ (Jarvis, Meyer, and Ramm 1969) that the o-H_2 molecules in the dilute solution tended to cluster together.
Roberts and Daunt showed that the crystals could ultimately
contain as many as ten times more o-H_2 pairs than would be
expected on a random distribution. This clustering has been
called 'rotation diffusion'. At such low temperatures it
could not possibly occur classically, by thermally activated
diffusion, and Oyarzun and Van Kranendonk (1971) suggested
that the mechanism is actually conversion of a $J = 1$ molecule to a $J = 0$ state with the simultaneous reverse change
of $J = 0$ to $J = 1$ for a neighbouring molecule, brought about
by magnetic dipole-dipole interaction. Rotation diffusion
is not observed in dilute solutions of p-D_2 in o-D_2, and as
little as 15 per cent of o-D_2 in solution in p-H_2 is sufficient to prevent clustering of the o-H_2 molecules.

9.3. NITROGEN, CARBON MONOXIDE, OXYGEN, FLUORINE, NITROGEN
OXIDE, AND ACETYLENE

These substances form a convenient group for discussion, since
there are some similarities in the order-disorder problems
they present. Nevertheless, no two of them are alike in all
respects. With carbon monoxide and nitrogen oxide orienta-

tional disorder persists until the absolute zero, while with
solid oxygen there is the question of the form taken by the
ultimate magnetic ordering.

It has become customary to distinguish the different
solid forms of the first four substances by Greek letters,
and we shall use these here to facilitate reference to the
original literature. The relation between this classification and that based on the Roman numerals I, II, etc. which
we have used generally in this book is shown in Table 9.1.
which summarizes relevant thermodynamic and crystallographic
information. Some of the latter derives from the elegant
X-ray diffraction investigations carried out by Lipscomb and
his coworkers, which have included single-crystal studies
of β-N_2 and β-F_2, and also of the low-temperature form of
nitrogen, α-N_2. Normally, single crystals of a high-temperature phase break up on cooling through a transition, but
in one case out of twenty a single crystal of β-N_2 gave
on cooling a single crystal of α-N_2.

The low-temperature, α-forms of nitrogen, fluorine,
and oxygen are ordered, as is shown by the agreement between
the entropy calculated from spectroscopic data, S(spec), and
the calorimetric entropy, S(cal). For example, for fluorine
S(spec) = 165·5 J K^{-1} mol^{-1} and S(cal) = 165·6 J K^{-1} mol^{-1}.
We shall discuss the case of carbon monoxide later. With
equal certainty, one can say that the high-temperature forms
of these three substances and of carbon monoxide are orientationally disordered. Indeed, on the basis of a comparison
of the melting behaviour of nitrogen and argon, Crawford,
Daniels, and Cheng (1975) concluded that there is probably
more local orientational order in *fluid* nitrogen than in
β-N_2 near the melting-point. (The same inference was made
about methane.) However, *free* molecular rotation in these
high-temperature solid phases can be ruled out on several
grounds. The heat capacities of β-N_2 and β-CO are consistent
with the molecules undergoing torsional oscillations, but
not free rotation (Staveley 1961, D. Smith 1971a, Krupskii,
Prokhvatilov, and Erenburg 1975). The same conclusion
follows from consideration of molecular volumes, which for
nitrogen, for example, are 44·5 × 10^{-24} cm^3 in the α-form,

TABLE 9.1

Thermal and structural information on nitrogen, carbon monoxide, oxygen, and fluorine. T_t is the transition temperature, and ΔS_t the corresponding entropy increase. For the significance of F and λ, see footnote on p.230.

Substance	III $\xleftarrow{T_t/K,\ \Delta S_t/R}$ II	II $\xrightarrow{T_t/K,\ \Delta S_t/R}$ I	I $\xrightarrow{T_m/K,\ \Delta S_m/R}$ Liq.	References Cal.	References Cryst.
N_2	α-N_2 35·61, 0·773(λ) $\xrightleftharpoons$ β-N_2 63·14, 1·373 $\xrightarrow{}$ Cubic, $P2_13$ or $Pa3$ H.c.p., $P6_3/mmc$			1, 2	3
CO	α-CO 61·55, 1·237(λ) $\xrightleftharpoons$ β-CO 68·09, 1·476 $\xrightarrow{}$ Cubic, $P2_13$ or $Pa3$ H.c.p.			2, 4	5
O_2	α-O_2 23·66, 0·477(F) $\xrightleftharpoons$ β-O_2 43·76, 2·042(F) $\xrightleftharpoons$ γ-O_2 54·39, 0·983 $\xrightarrow{}$ Monoclinic, $C2/m$ or $C2/c$ Rhombohedral, $R\bar{3}m$ Cubic, $Pm3n$			2, 6	7
F_2	α-F_2 45·55, 1·921(F) $\xrightleftharpoons$ β-F_2 53·54, 1·146 $\xrightarrow{}$ Monoclinic, $C2/m$ or $C2/c$ Cubic, $Pm3n$			8	9

Footnotes to table on page 538

Footnotes to Table 9.1.

REFERENCES

1.   Giauque and Clayton (1933).
2.   Burford and Graham (1969).
3.   Streib, Jordan, and Lipscomb (1962); Jordan, H.W.Smith, Streib,
      and Lipscomb (1964); LaPlaca and Hamilton (1972); Gannon and
      Morrison (1973); Lipscomb (1974); Venables and English (1974)
      (electron diffraction); Krupskii, Prokhvatilov, and Erenburg (1975).
4.   Clayton and Giauque (1932); Gill and Morrison (1966).
5.   Vegard (1930a, 1934); Krupskii, Prokhvatilov, Erenburg, and
      Yantsevich (1973); Lipscomb (1974).
6.   Giauque and Johnston (1929).
7.   Hörl (1962)(β, electron diffraction); Alikhanov (1963, 1964) (β,
      neutron diffraction);(1967)(α, neutron diffraction); Jordan,
      Streib, H.W.Smith, and Lipscomb (1964) (γ); Curzon and Pawlowicz
      (1965) (β, neutron diffraction); Collins (1966) (β, γ, neutron
      diffraction); Barrett, Meyer, and Wasserman (1967a) (α); Cox,
      Samuelsen, and Beckurts (1973) (γ, neutron diffraction).
8.   Hu, White, and Johnston (1953).
9.   Jordan, Streib, and Lipscomb (1964); L. Meyer, Barrett, and Greer,
      (1968).

$48 \cdot 1 \times 10^{-24}$ cm^3 in the β-form, and $57 \cdot 7 \times 10^{-24}$ cm^3 in the
liquid, whereas free rotation, as estimated from the observed
distance of closest approach in α-N_2 at 4 K, would require
a volume of $64 \cdot 7 \times 10^{-24}$ cm^3 (Bolz, Boyd, Mauer, and Peiser
1959). But while the broad infrared absorption band given
by β-CO was considered by Ewing (1962) to imply that molecular rotation was hindered, he expressed the view that a
few molecules in this phase might be undergoing free rotation (and in the *liquid* at 80 K, perhaps more than half of
them). This may be an oversimplification, but the barrier
to rotation in the β-phase is certainly much less than that
in α-CO, in which the 'rotational' motion of the molecules
is entirely librational with a frequency of ~70 - 85 cm^{-1}
(Ewing and Pimentel 1961, Gill and Morrison 1966). Smith (1971)

estimated that the barrier to rotation of the nitrogen
molecules in β-N_2 is only ~$0 \cdot 72$ kJ mol^{-1}.

More detailed information about the high-temperature
phase of nitrogen resulted from Streib, Jordan, and Lipscomb's
single-crystal study (1962) of the h.c.p. lattice of β-N_2,
carried out at 50 K. The arrangement of the molecular centres
in this structure is shown in Fig.9.8. The molecules are

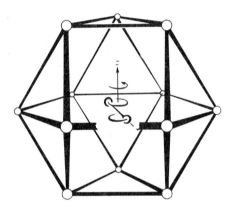

Fig.9.8. Structure of β-N_2 (= N_2-I) proposed by Streib, Jordan, and
Lipscomb (1962), showing a precessing molecule with its nearest neighbours
(small circles), each of which is also precessing.

disordered in the xy plane, and orientated at $56 \cdot 0° \pm 2 \cdot 5°$
with respect to the z axis. On the X-ray evidence, the molecules could either be statistically disordered among 24 positions, or precessing about the z axis. On spatial grounds
(based on the calculated electron density within the molecule), Schuch and Mills (1970) ruled out precession in
favour of the random orientation model. As pointed out elsewhere (section 4.7.1), for an angle of inclination of the
molecule to the z axis of 54°44' the electric field gradient
at the nitrogen nucleus averages to zero, and so β-N_2 fails
to give a pure quadrupole resonance spectrum (T.A. Scott 1962).
Accordingly, the picture which emerges of the high-temperature
disordered phase is one in which the molecules, tilted at
54°44' with respect to the z axis, switch between 24 possible

orientations at a rate rapid compared with the quadrupole frequency.

The information given by nuclear quadrupole resonance studies on the development of disorder as the $\alpha \to \beta$ transition in nitrogen is approached from below has been summarized in section 4.7.1. A mean-field treatment of orientational disorder in the β-phase has been presented by Dunmore (1976).

There has been considerable discussion as to whether the low-temperature ordered α-phases of N_2 and CO have the space group $Pa3$ (which would make them identical with the f.c.c. form of hydrogen) or $P2_13$. The latter is derived from the $Pa3$ structure by displacing the molecular centres along the cube diagonals (i.e. the [111] directions, which are those of the molecular axes). The observation that α-N_2 is piezoelectric (Brookeman and Scott 1972) supports the $P2_13$ structure, as does a comparison of the infrared and Raman spectra (Wachtel 1972). The X-ray evidence has been interpreted as favouring the space group $P2_13$ (Jordan, H.W.Smith, Streib, and Lipscomb 1964; LaPlaca and Hamilton 1972), and Lipscomb (1974) estimated that the displacement of the molecular centres is $\sim 0 \cdot 016$ nm. Venables and English (1974) and Krupskii, Prokhvatilov, and Erenburg (1975), however, concluded from their own diffraction work that these displacements from the centre-symmetric positions of the space group $Pa3$ could not exceed $0 \cdot 005$ nm. Whatever the outcome of this controversy, there is clearly a resemblance between the ordered and disordered forms of N_2 (and CO) on the one hand, and those of H_2 on the other. However, at the molecular level there are important differences. With N_2 and CO, in contrast to H_2, the energy barrier to rotation is large compared with the rotational quanta, and for N_2 and other diatomic molecules the anisotropy of the dispersion and overlap forces is relatively much more important than it is for H_2, where, as already explained, only quadrupole - quadrupole interaction really matters (English and Venables 1974, Goodings and Henkelman 1971, Slusarev, Freiman, Krupskii, and Burakhovich 1972). Nevertheless, it still remains true for N_2 and CO that the *principal* ordering influence in the α-phases is quadrupole-quadrupole interaction

(Jansen, Michels, and Lupton 1954, Kohin 1960, Melhuish and
R.L.Scott 1964). The quadrupole moment of $CO(-2 \cdot 5 \times 10^{-26}$
e.s.u. cm^2) is numerically greater than that of
$N_2(-1 \cdot 4 \times 10^{-26}$ e.s.u. cm^2) (D.E. Stogryn and A.P. Stogryn
1966; Billingsley and Krauss 1974). This difference is no
doubt responsible for the higher transition temperature in
CO. (The effect of the small dipole moment of CO (0·112 D)
is negligible.) However, the quadrupole-quadrupole coupling
constant is proportional to the square of the quadrupole
moment, and the ratio of the transition temperatures (CO
to N_2) of 1·73 is smaller than the ratio of the squares
of the quadrupole moments (3·2).

While nitrogen and carbon monoxide are very similar,
both molecularly and crystallographically, the β-phases are
nevertheless apparently not identical. Barrett and Meyer
studied the phase diagrams of the systems Ar-N_2 (1965a) and
Ar-CO (1965b), and these are *not* replicas of each other.
The chief difference is that with the former system, the
h.c.p. lattice of β-N_2 persists down to 0 K for solid solutions containing between 55 and 77 moles per cent of nitrogen,
whereas with the Ar-CO system the h.c.p. phase is never
stable below 53 K. And although the dimensions of the cubic
unit cells of β-CO and β-N_2 agree to within 10^{-4} nm, the
phase diagram of the CO-N_2 system is definitely asymmetric
(Angwin and Wasserman 1966).

The conclusions reached by Jordan, Streib, and Lipscomb
(1964) about the structure of β-F_2 are particularly interesting, since with regard to orientational disorder the
molecules fall into two groups. Those shown as circles in
the representation of the unit cell in Fig.9.9 are either
freely rotating or statistically disordered (almost isotropically) - the second possibility being much the more
likely. The remaining molecules are highly disordered in
one plane, so that they are cylindrically, and not spherically, disordered. Thus, the two molecules on the front
face of the cube in Fig.9.9, whose coordinates are $\frac{1}{2},0,\frac{1}{4}$
and $\frac{1}{2},0,\frac{3}{4}$, are disordered in the planes $z = \frac{1}{4}$, $z = \frac{3}{4}$. There
are therefore three cylindrically disordered molecules
for every one spherically disordered molecule.

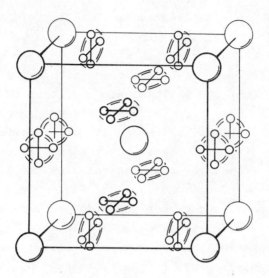

Fig.9.9. The structure of β-F_2 (=F_2-I). The spheres represent molecules orientationally disordered in three dimensions. The remaining molecules are orientationally disordered in two dimensions, as indicated (Jordan, Streib, and Lipscomb 1964).

Turning to oxygen, crystallographic and spectroscopic work has definitely disproved the conclusion reached in earlier studies that solid oxygen contains dimers. Jordan, Streib, H.W.Smith, and Lipscomb (1964) stated that 'any description of γ-O_2 based on O_2 dimers is untenable', adding that their work raised serious doubts about the existence of dimers in the other solid phases. Cairns and Pimentel (1965), who studied the infrared spectrum of α- and β-O_2, were equally emphatic: 'None of the spectral evidence presented suggests that dimeric O_4 molecules are present in α-O_2'. One piece of evidence for this statement was that the spectrum of an isotopic mixture of $^{16}O_2$ and $^{18}O_2$ is simply the separate spectrum of each species superimposed. Nothing was observed which could be attributed to the mixed dimers, $^{16}O_2$-$^{18}O_2$.

Although it has long been known that α-O_2 is ordered at 0 K, since S(spec) and S(cal) of oxygen gas at its boiling-point agree within 0.4 J K^{-1} mol^{-1}, it was some time before its structure was unambiguously determined, partly because

the temperatures at which earlier X-ray experiments were
carried out were such that the crystals studied were probably
a mixture of α- and β-forms. The unit cell, which is shown
in Fig.9.10, is in fact monoclinic (Alikhanov 1967, Barrett,

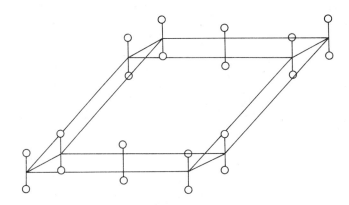

Fig.9.10. Monoclinic cell of α-O₂ (=O₂-III) (Barrett, Meyer, and Wasserman
1967a).

Meyer, and Wasserman 1967a). The transition between α and
β is rapid and reversible. The β-form has been investigated
by electron diffraction (Hörl 1962, Curzon and Pawlowicz
1965), and by neutron diffraction (Alikhanov 1963, 1964;
Collins 1966). All of these investigators agree in assigning a rhombohedral structure to β-O_2. The hexagonal unit
cell contains three molecules, whose axes are parallel to
the hexagonal axis and whose centres lie at (1/3,1/3,0),
(-1/3,0,1/3), and (0,-1/3,-2/3).

The high-temperature, cubic γ-form of oxygen is similar
to that of β-F_2 in containing two kinds of disordered molecule. The X-ray investigation of Jordan *et al*. revealed
that a quarter of the molecules have an effectively spherical
electron density distribution, while the rest have an oblate
spheroidal distribution. Further details were supplied by
Cox, Samuelsen, and Beckurts (1973) from a single-crystal
neutron diffraction study. The molecules at the corners
and centres of the cubic unit cell are randomly oriented
along the [111] axes, while the remainder, which occupy sites

on the faces at $(0, \frac{1}{4}, \frac{1}{2})$, lie along one of the [100] axes
perpendicular to the four-fold inversion axis at the site.
Moreover, both kinds of molecule undergo librational motion
with a considerable amplitude (~20°), a conclusion previously reached from Raman evidence (Cahill and Leroi 1969).
It is, of course, very probable that the reorientational
motion of the molecules in $\gamma\text{-}O_2$ is a cooperative matter (L.
Meyer 1969). There are grounds for thinking that the struc-
tures of $\beta\text{-}F_2$ and $\gamma\text{-}O_2$, while similar, are not identical
- for example, the diffraction results of Jordan *et al*. and
the comparison of the O_2-Ar phase diagram with that for F_2-Ar,
(Barrett, Meyer, and Wasserman 1967b). Whereas the formation of solid solutions of oxygen in argon (and also, inci-
dentally, of nitrogen and of carbon monoxide in argon)
changes the f.c.c. argon lattice into an h.c.p. form, fluorine
does not do this, and consequently the F_2-Ar and O_2-Ar diagrams
are quite different. The remarkably low entropy of fusion
of oxygen is worth noting. It is considerably less than that
of the rare gases, and less than that of any other diatomic
substance, including hydrogen. Kiefte and Clouter (1975)
determined the adiabatic elastic constants of $\gamma\text{-}O_2$ by
Brillouin spectroscopy, and on the basis of the elastic properties made an interesting comparison of $\gamma\text{-}O_2$ with the
plastic phase of the molecularly much more complex substance
succinonitrile (p.658).

With regard to the consequences of intermolecular magnetic effects in solid oxygen, the α-phase is antiferromagnetically ordered. It has a relatively low, almost temperature-independent susceptibility, and gives two low-angle
lines in its neutron diffraction pattern which are not observed in the X-ray pattern (Fig.9.11; Collins 1966). Barrett,
Meyer, and Wasserman (1967a) concluded that the magnetic
moments lie in the direction of the molecular axes, but it
seems more likely that they are perpendicular to these axes
(Alikhanov 1967). The susceptibility of $\gamma\text{-}O_2$, like that of
the gas and the liquid, follows a Curie law and is that to
be expected for two uncoupled electrons in a $^3\Sigma_1$ state (Kanda,
Haseda, and Otsubo 1954, Borovic-Romanov, Orlova, and Strelkov 1954). On cooling into the β-phase, the susceptibility

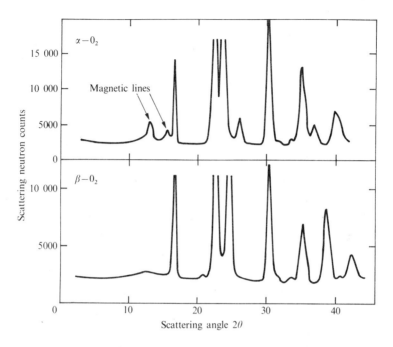

Fig.9.11. Neutron powder patterns from α-O_2 (=O_2-III) at 4·2 K, and from β-O_2 (=O_2-II) at 27 K (Collins 1966).

drops by a factor of ~2½, and then decreases further with falling temperature. The neutron diffraction pattern of the β-form has a *broad* peak at low angles (Fig.9.11) so it seems that while in this phase there is in fact some antiferromagnetic ordering, this is only short-range.

   The α-form of carbon monoxide provides a well-known example of frozen-in disorder. Clayton and Giauque (1932) found that the calculated entropy S(spec) for the ideal gas at 1 atm and 25°C exceeds the calorimetric entropy S(cal) by 4·64 J K^{-1} mol^{-1}. Since this difference is only a little short of $R \ln 2$, it was interpreted to mean that disorder persists to 0 K, with the molecules randomly distributed among two orientations (CO and OC). Since the dipole moment of the CO molecule is almost zero, and the two atoms must have effectively almost the same size, it was assumed that the energy difference between the two orientations CO and OC is very small, and hence that at temperatures low enough for this energy difference to matter the molecules would no longer be able to change their orientation. This view was confirmed by Melhuish and Scott (1964), who estimated that the energy difference for ordered and disordered orientations of the dipoles is only ~ 20 J mol^{-1}. However, Gill and Morrison (1966) made a later calorimetric study of carbon monoxide, and while they confirmed Clayton and Giauque's experimental results, by using more recent values of the molecular parameters to calculate S(spec), and by introducing an improved correction for the imperfection of the actual gas in estimating S(cal), they found that S(spec) - S(cal) is in fact only $3 \cdot 4 \pm 0 \cdot 8$ J K^{-1} mol^{-1}, which is definitely less than $R \ln 2$. In principle, the original explanation can hold, with the modification that there is partial ordering of the molecules. Permittivity measurements give no indication that there is any region of temperature in which the orientational movement of the molecules alters. On the other hand, Atake, Suga, and Chihara (1976) made very careful heat capacity measurements between 15 K and 20 K which disclosed a relaxation process in this region (*cf.* the behaviour of ice-I, (p. 466). They considered that down to ~ 20 K the carbon monoxide crystal is in an equilibrium condition, but that below ~ 19 K the remaining disorder becomes frozen in. It has been suggested that there may be a third, ordered phase of carbon monoxide at very low temperatures. Barrett and Meyer (1965b) indeed claimed to have found evidence of a new solid form in their study of the Ar-CO system, in that weak lines appeared repeatedly in the diffraction pattern of α-CO. On the other hand, there was no sign of a second transition in Gill and Morrison's heat capacity study, even though their measurements were carried down to $2 \cdot 5$ K. Swenson (1955) discovered that at low temperatures and high pressures, nitrogen exists in a third phase. Thus, at 0 K, for example, this is stable above $\sim 3 \cdot 50$ kbar (see also Thiéry, Fabre, Jean-Louis, and Vu 1973). A search by Stevenson (1957c) for a corresponding third solid form of carbon monoxide failed to find one, but his experiments were confined to applying pressures up to ~ 10 kbar at 60 K and 65 K. Subsequent calculations by Raich and Mills (1971) indicated that γ-CO would only become stable at ~48 kbar.

While the α-forms of nitrogen, oxygen, carbon monoxide, and fluorine are hard and brittle, the high-temperature forms deserve to be described as plastic crystals. Thus, Barrett, Meyer, and Wasserman (1967b) described β-F_2 as soft and transparent, and reported that its transformation on cooling into the α-form was often a rather spectacular process, accompanied by an audible click, frequently by an explosion, and sometimes by a flash of light. The same authors (1967c) made some interesting comments on the interconversion of the three forms of solid oxygen. They found that for the $\alpha \rightleftharpoons \beta$ conversion, at which the volume change is only small (~0·12 cm^3 mol^{-1}; Stevenson 1957c), the crystallites of the α- and β-forms are related in orientation in such a way that the (001) plane of the α-form transforms into the 00.1 of the β-form, and *vice versa*, suggesting a martensitic type of transformation. On the other hand, at the $\gamma \rightarrow \beta$ transition, where there is a much larger volume decrease of $1·18$ cm^3 mol^{-1}, the γ-crystals break up into near-randomly orientated, smaller β-crystallites.

Nitrogen oxide, NO, was shown by Johnston and Giauque (1929) to retain entropy at 0 K of $3·0 \pm 0.4$ $J K^{-1}$ per mole of NO, which is almost exactly $\frac{1}{2}R \ln 2$. The reason for this is that this compound is dimeric in the solid state, with the dimers randomly distributed between two orientations. The dimer in the solid has a planar, trapezium-like structure, with the nitrogen atoms of the two component NO units separated by $0·218$ nm, and the two oxygen atoms $0·262$ nm apart (Dulmage, Meyers, and Lipscomb 1953, Lipscomb, F.E. Wang, May, and Lippert 1961). It is possible that the structure of the dimer in the gaseous phase is somewhat different (Dinerman and Ewing 1971, Lipscomb 1971).

Assuming that it is permissible to regard acetylene as a quasi-diatomic molecule, we shall briefly deal here with its polymorphism. It exists in an orthorhombic low-temperature form, space group *Acam* (Koski and Sándor 1975), which transforms at 149 ± 1 K into a face-centred cubic modification, space group *Pa*3 (Sugawara and Kanda 1952). The latter is disordered, as is shown by its relatively low entropy of

fusion of $2 \cdot 3R$, by the broad, featureless absorption in the
far infrared (Schwartz, Ron, and Kimel 1969, 1971) and by
the NMR evidence. Measurements of proton T_1 and $T_{1\rho}$ values
for C_2H_2 (Albert and Ripmeester 1972) and a study of deuteron magnetic resonance in C_2D_2 (Scheie, E.M.Peterson, and
O'Reilly 1973) combined to show that in the high-temperature
plastic phase the molecules diffuse with an activation energy of 33 kJ mol^{-1}, and also undergo reorientation (either by
180° flips about a twofold axis or by general spherical
reorientation) with an activation energy of 22-23 kJ mol^{-1}.
Reorientation, probably by 180° flips, is also possible
in the low-temperature α-modification with almost the same
activation energy (24 kJ mol^{-1}). The influence of quadrupole-quadrupole interaction and of overlap repulsion in
determining the structure of solid acetylene has been considered by Masao Hashimoto, Michiko Hashimoto, and Isobe
(1971).

9.4. HYDROGEN AND DEUTERIUM HALIDES

The numerous solid forms of the hydrogen and deuterium halides
have been thoroughly studied, and almost all the techniques
described in Chapter 4 have been applied to them. But although much has been learnt, it cannot be said that a complete, self-consistent picture of the molecular behaviour
and intermolecular relations has yet emerged. It must rather
be accepted that in spite of the molecular simplicity of
these crystals, the movement of the molecules in them is
very intricate, especially in the disordered phases. A
feature which gives these compounds added interest is that
the low-temperature forms of HCl and HBr (i.e. HCl-II and
HBr-III) are ferroelectric (S.Hoshino, Shimaoka, and Niimura
1967), though HI-III is not (Cichanowski and Cole 1973).
Structurally, these two phases of HCl and HBr are presumably
the simplest known ferroelectrics, at least among molecular
solids.

Some facts about the various crystalline modifications
and transitions are summarized in Table 9.2. Hydrogen bromide

and deuterium bromide provide an example of a qualitative
difference between isotopic species, in that HBr exists in
one more phase than DBr. We have regarded this as an 'extra'
form of phase II, and Table 9.2 therefore shows HBr as having
phases IIa and IIb. [The 'extra' phase is IIa. Experiments
by Clusius (1946) on mixed crystals of HBr and DBr showed
that as the DBr content increases from zero, the temperature
interval over which IIa is stable decreases. Phase IIa
vanishes at a triple-point with I and IIb at 117 K and 47
moles per cent DBr.] The low-temperature form of HCl has been
designated as phase II, even though the agreement between the
calorimetric and spectroscopic entropies for this compound
leaves no doubt that II is orientationally ordered, and this
phase of HCl and DCl is really the analogue of phase III of
HBr and DBr.

    Although Table 9.2 records only two forms of HCl, there
is evidence that on cooling the cubic phase I it transforms
at about 120 K into an orthorhombic form. Shimaoka, Niimura,
Motegi, and Hoshino (1969) found that new lines attributable
to an orthorhombic lattice appeared at this temperature in
both neutron and X-ray diffraction experiments with single
crystals. Wang and Fleury (1970) reported the appearance of
satellite peaks in the Raman spectrum of crystalline HCl
below 120 K, implying a change to a structure of lower symmetry. Both pieces of evidence for a structural change
seem convincing, and it is surprising that Chihara and Inaba
(1976a,b), in a careful study of the heat capacity near 120 K,
could find no sign at all of any thermal anomaly or transition, as indeed Giauque and Wiebe (1928a) had failed to do
before them.

    It may be said at once that the possibility that the
molecules of any of the three halides rotate freely in phase
I, as originally suggested by Simon and von Simson (1924) and
by Pauling (1930), has been conclusively eliminated. An early
application of NMR to crystalline HCl, HBr, and HI by Alpert
(1949) failed to show at any transition a decrease in line-
width of the magnitude which would have accompanied the
change to a high-temperature form with free molecular rotation.
Later, Hiebert and Hornig (1957) investigated the infrared

TABLE 9.2

Thermal and structural information on hydrogen and deuterium halides

Compound	T_t/K III $\leftrightarrow$ II	T_t/K, $\Delta S_t/R$ II $\leftrightarrow$	T_m/K, $\Delta S_m/R$ I $\leftrightarrow$	References Liq·Cal·Cryst· NMR
HCl		98·67, 1·490(F) F.c.orthorhombic, $Pn2_1a$	159·05, 1·547 F.c.c.	1,2 3-5 6-9
DCl		104·63, 1·477(F) F.c.orthorhombic, $Pn2_1a$	158·41, 1·536 F.c.c.	2,10 4 7-9
HBr	89·53(λ)^a $\to$ IIb	113·60(λ) IIa 117·00(λ) Cubic	186·50, 1·559 F.c.c.	11,12 3,13 6,7, 14
DBr	93·67(λ) F.c.orthorhombic, $Bb2_1m$	119·96 (λ) F.c.orthorhombic, $Bbcm$	185·64, 1·557 F.c.c.	10,12 15 7,14
HI	70·1 (λ)	125·6 (λ) Orthorhombic Cubic	222·31, 1·554	16 17 6,7
DI	77·3 (λ)	128·28 (λ)	221·23, 1·557	10 - 7

Footnotes to Table 9.2

[a]ΔS_t values have not been quoted for this and the other λ transitions, since the enthalpy increases given in the literature are the total enthalpy increases over a temperature interval.

REFERENCES

1.   Giauque and Wiebe (1928a); Chihara and Inaba (1976a).

2.   Chihara and Inaba (1976b).

3.   Natta (1933).

4.   Sándor and Farrow (1967a,b).

5.   Niimura, Shimaoka, Motegi, and S.Hoshino (1972).

6.   Alpert (1949).

7.   Genin, O'Reilly, E.M.Peterson, and Tsang (1968).

8.   Okuma, N.Nakamura, and Chihara (1968).

9.   Norris, Strange, Powles, Rhodes, Marsden, and Krynicki (1968a).

10.   Clusius and Wolf (1947).

11.   Giauque and Wiebe (1928b).

12.   Chihara and Inaba (1976c).

13.   A.Simon (1971).

14.   Norris *et al.* (1968b).

15.   Sándor and Johnson (1968).

16.   Giauque and Wiebe (1929).

17.   A.Simon (1970).

spectrum of DC1 in dilute solution in HC1 (as a way of examining the crystal field acting on an individual molecule) and found no signs, either in phase I or phase II, of the structure which rotation would have imposed on the DC1 absorption peak at $\sim 2\ 000\ cm^{-1}$. Sándor and Farrow (1967b) made a thorough neutron diffraction study of DC1-I, which seemed to establish with certainty that the molecules are not freely rotating (or randomly oriented) (Fig.4.4). The chlorine atoms form a face-centred cubic lattice, and the disorder in the structure arises because the deuterium atom in a molecule can be directed towards any one of the twelve nearest-neighbour chlorine atoms.

The low-temperature phases II and III of the chlorides

and bromides have face-centred orthorhombic lattices in which
the molecules are arranged in zig-zag chains (resembling in
this latter respect the structure of solid HF, which exists
in only one form). The chains form layers parallel to the
(001) plane, and when the hydrogen in HCl-II is replaced by
deuterium there is a contraction which is confined to this
plane, the c parameter being virtually unaffected. The existence of the chains was first deduced from spectroscopic evidence, such as that furnished by the infrared study of Hornig
and Osberg (1955), and was later confirmed by the very thorough X-ray and neutron powder diffraction experiments of
Sándor and Farrow on HCl and DCl (1967a) and of Sándor and
Johnson (1968) on DBr. The structure of DCl-II as shown
in Fig.9.12. As far as the orientation of the molecules is

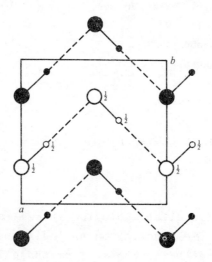

Fig.9.12. The structure of DCl-II. Large circles, chlorine atoms,
small circles, deuterium atoms; full circles, atoms in the plane of the
drawing ($z = 0$), open circles, atoms halfway up ($z = c/2$) (Sándor and
Farrow 1967b).

concerned it is a completely ordered arrangement. It is
probable that the chains are not quite planar, that is, that
the hydrogen atoms do not lie in the plane through the
halogen atoms. This was inferred by Savoie and Anderson
(1966) from investigations of the infrared and Raman spectra

of HCl, DCl, HBr, and DBr from 10 K to 77 K, and was confirmed for HCl by spectroscopic studies on a single crystal
by Brunel and Peyron (1967). The matter was taken a step
further by Ito, Suzuki, and Yokoyama (1969) who concluded
from an investigation of the Raman spectra of HCl, DCl, HBr,
and DBr that owing to the non-planarity of the chains the
space group in the orthorhombic form II of the chlorides and
III of the bromides is strictly $Pn2_1a$. They suggested that
the H or D atoms in a chain lie alternately above and below
the planes through the halogen atoms, with the angle between
the plane and the molecular axes probably not exceeding ~10°.
In other words, there is only a slight departure from the
space group $Bb2_1m$ proposed on the diffraction results, which
corresponds to linear chains.

The structure of DBr-II, shown in Fig.9.13, is intermediate between that of I and III in that each molecule has

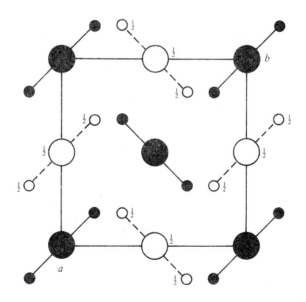

Fig.9.13. The structure of DBr-II, the disordered middle phase; symbols
as for Fig.9.12 (Sándor and Johnson 1968).

two possible orientations. The neutron diffraction study
of Sándor and Johnson threw an interesting light on the

gradual nature of the transition from DBr-III to phase II.
Values of the $F(101)$ structure factor, which is zero in phase
II, were observed to decrease gradually over a range of
several degrees as the λ-point was approached. This was interpreted to mean that small domains of II develop within
phase III, the coexistence of the two phases being made
possible by the relatively small volume difference between
them (~1·4 per cent). Small though this difference is, however, it could nevertheless set up mechanical strains in
the crystal, which might account for the blurred character
of the X-ray powder lines in the transition region. It
may be added that Arnold and Heastie (1967), who studied the
far infrared spectrum of DBr from 86 K to 125 K, reported
that the absorption intensities changed continuously with
temperature in the region of the λ-point.

   Information on molecular motion in crystalline hydrogen
halides has come from investigations of dielectric dispersion
and from NMR and nuclear quadrupole resonance (NQR) studies.
As phase I of the three hydrogen halides approaches the
melting-point there is a minimum in $T_{1\rho}$, the proton relaxation time in the rotating frame, which Genin, O'Reilly, E.M.
Peterson, and Tsang (1968) attributed to translational diffusion. The activation energies obtained for this mode of
motion, in kJ mol^{-1}, were 16·5 for HCl, 26 for HBr, and 25·5
for HI. Norris *et al.* (1968a) found 16·5 and 19 kJ mol^{-1}
for this quantity for the chloride (from line-width and T_1
measurements respectively), while the estimate of Okuma, N.
Nakamura, and Chihara (1968) was somewhat higher (23·5 kJ
mol^{-1}). There is a considerable body of quantitative kinetic
information on relaxation processes associated with molecular
reorientation, which is summarized in Table 9.3. In the dielectric dispersion investigations of Cole and his collaborators, special care was taken to eliminate as far as possible
voids in the crystalline sample. The presence of voids in the
specimens used by previous workers was no doubt primarily
responsible for discrepancies between the earlier and later
results. Smyth and Hitchcock (1933) had previously established that the permittivity of HCl, HBr, and HI in phase I

TABLE 9.3

Arrhenius parameters for relaxation times τ in the various phases of solid hydrogen halides

$$\log_{10}(\tau/s) = -\log_{10}A + E/(2 \cdot 3RT)$$

Halide	Phase	$\log_{10}A$	$E/\text{kJ mol}^{-1}$	Source
HCl	I	-	3	^{35}Cl, ^{37}Cl, NQR [a]
	II	13·0	11	Dielec.dispersion [b]
	II	13·6	9·5	^{35}Cl, NQR [c]
	II	-	6	Proton $T_{1\rho}$ [c]
	II	-	11·5	^{35}Cl, NQR [d]
DCl	I	14·5	3·5	Deuteron T_1 [e]
	I	-	3·5	Deuteron and ^{35}Cl T_1 [f]
	II	13·6	9·5	^{35}Cl, NQR [c]
	II	-	11·5	^{35}Cl, NQR [d]
HBr	II	18·3 [g]	17·5	Dielec. dispersion [h]
	III	11·2 [i]	11·5	Dielec. dispersion [b]
		12·1	6·5	
DBr	I	13·7	4·55	Deuteron T_1 [e]
	III	16·2 [i]	6·5	Dielec. dispersion [b]
		13·5	15	
	III	9·9	5	^{79}Br and ^{81}Br, NQR [j]
HI	II	15·1 [g]	12·5	Dielec. dispersion [h]
	II	17·2	15	Dielec. dispersion [b]
	III	13·6	9	Dielec. dispersion [b]
DI	I	13·5	4·05	Deuteron T_1 [e]
	II	15·6	13	Dielec. dispersion [b]
	II/III	13·3	9	Dielec. dispersion [b]

[a] Okuma, N.Nakamura, and Chihara (1968).

[b] Cole and Havriliak (1957).

[c] O'Reilly (1970).

[d] Marram and Ragle (1964).

[e] Genin, O'Reilly, E.M.Peterson, and Tsang (1968).

[f] Powles and Rhodes (1967).

continued on page 555

Footnotes to Table 9.3 continued.....

[g] For these two phases the relaxation rates only approximately conform to an Arrhenius equation.

[h] Groenewegen and Cole (1967).

[i] The bracketed values correspond to the two dispersion regions at lower and higher frequencies respectively.

[j] Kadaba and O'Reilly (1970).

is in every case high, and this evidence for facile molecular reorientation was confirmed by Swenson and Cole (1954) by measurements of the static permittivity ε_0 of HCl-I, and by their failure to detect any dielectric dispersion in this phase in the frequency range used (10 kHz to 1 MHz). The temperature dependence of ε_0 for the three halides is shown in Fig.9.14. That for HCl-I was shown by Swenson and Cole to be in remarkably good agreement with the dependence

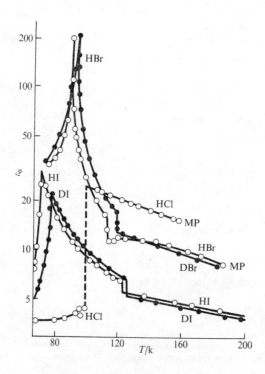

Fig.9.14. The static permittivity ε_0 vs. temperature for the hydrogen and deuterium halides (after Cichanowski and Cole 1973).

required by Onsager's equation for a polar *liquid* (section
4.8), as indeed Brown and Cole (1953) had already found to
be true of HBr-I. HBr-III shows two regions of dielectric
dispersion. That at lower frequencies with an activation
energy of $11·5$ kJ mol^{-1} is strongly dependent on the bias
field and on the thermal history of the sample, and was
ascribed by Cichanowski and Cole to dipole reorientation at
domain boundaries. The high frequency dispersion (activation energy $6·5$ kJ mol^{-1}) was attributed to dipole reorientation within domains. Only one dispersion region was found
in HBr-IIb, which appeared to be continuous with the higher
frequency process in phase III (Groenewegen and Cole 1967).
HI-II and -III each showed a single dispersion region in
the frequency range used (5-225 MHz), with little change
in the frequency of maximum loss on passing from III to II.
But an interesting difference is that whereas in III the
dispersion obeys a circular arc function, for HI-II (and
HBr-IIb) the dispersion fits a skewed arc function, an observation which is a novelty for a polar *solid*, though not
uncommon for a polar *liquid*. Since conformity with a circular arc function corresponds to persistence of dipole correlations to relatively long times, the loss of this with
passage into phase II is evidence that this latter phase
is more disordered in that the molecules reorient with less
mutual interference, as in the liquid.

Facile molecular reorientation in phase I of the halides
is apparent from the low activation energies for these phases
quoted in Table 9.3. Indeed, it is probable that the motion
of the molecules is much like that in the liquid. Powles and
Rhodes (1967) found that the spin-lattice relaxation time
T_1 for the deuteron in DCl showed no discontinuity or change
in its temperature dependence at the melting-point, and Wang
and Wright (1974) suggested on the basis of the Raman spectrum of HCl a mechanism for molecular reorientation which was
the same for phase I and the liquid.

Information on the lattice translational and librational
frequencies in some of the solid forms of the hydrogen and
deuterium halides has come from studies of their far infrared spectra. The absorption spectra of HCl- and DCl-II and

of HBr- and DBr-III which were obtained by Anderson,
Gebbie, and Walmsley (1964) between 20 and 400 cm^{-1} showed
considerable detail. Thus, for HBr, absorption peaks at
57 and 71 cm^{-1} were assigned to translational modes of
vibration. These frequencies bracket the Debye frequency
as calculated from heat capacity data, and the difference
between them and the corresponding frequencies for HCl is
close to that expected from the molecular weight difference.
(It is curious, however, that on deuteration the slight
change in these frequencies is to higher rather than to
lower values; thus for DBr they become 60 and 72 cm^{-1}. The
effect may be due, in part at least, to the slightly smaller
molar volumes of the deuterium compound.) Peaks at higher
frequencies, e.g. 200 and 269 cm^{-1} for HBr, can be assigned
to librations of the molecules. When the HBr passes into
phase IIb, the frequencies of the absorption peaks associated
with the translational modes persist almost unchanged, but
those at higher frequencies merge into a broad band, consistent with the view that the disorder in IIb is orientational
in nature. Similar results were obtained by Arnold and
Heastie (1967) in an investigation of HCl and DBr, which also
included an examination of phase I. The far infrared spectra
in this phase were still less like those of an ordered crystal,
showing only one very broad absorption band with a maximum
at about the frequency assigned to the librational modes
in the lower phases (Fig.4.17).

    Insight into the various modes of motion in condensed
HCl and HBr has also been obtained from the inelastic scattering of slow neutrons (Boutin and Safford 1964). While
some of the frequencies so obtained correspond reasonably
well with those assigned from the far infrared spectra, the
neutron time-of-flight spectra for HCl-I and HBr-I still
display several peaks which correspond with peaks in the
spectra of phases II and IIb, and even the spectra of the
liquids show some related structure (Fig.4.20). The zig-
zag chains of molecules must therefore be regarded as existing to some extent in phase I of HCl and HBr, and even in
the liquids. Raman spectroscopy appears to confirm this

conclusion (Ito 1970, Wang and Wright 1974), which must accordingly be taken into consideration in any attempt to form
a realistic picture of molecular behaviour in the solids
under discussion.

We may summarize what is known about molecular movement in these crystals as follows. In phase I, a molecule
switches rapidly between twelve orientations, but in between
the acts of reorientation it enters into part of a polymer
chain with its neighbours which exists for several periods
of vibration before being disrupted by reorientation (Sándor
and Farrow 1969). Wang and Wright considered that the reorientation itself takes place by rotational diffusion involving large angular steps. As phase I cools, it is possible that at about 120 K - where a transition has been
reported, as already mentioned - the chains lengthen considerably and the reorientation rate falls (Niimura, Shimaoka,
Motegi, and Hoshino 1972). Relaxation effects in the ordered
phases (III of HBr and HI, and II of HCl) have been interpreted by Genin *et al*. as implying a single-phase reorientation process, which may be a 90° flip in the plane of the
chains (O'Reilly 1970, Kadaba and O'Reilly 1970). Yi and
Gavrielides (1971) discussed molecular motion in these ferroelectric phases with special reference to its bearing on
the mechanism of polarization reversal. In the intermediate
phases II of HI and HBr, Genin *et al*. considered that both
two-plane and three-plane reorientation processes may be
involved. All in all, the molecular movement in the solid
phases of these substances must be one of considerable complexity, and a corollary of this is that no simple quantitative interpretation of the entropy changes at the transitions is to be expected.

It is worth briefly considering the nature of the
forces responsible for the ultimate ordering of the hydrogen
halide molecules. To regard this simply as dipole-dipole
interaction is undoubtedly an oversimplification. Thus,
the activation energies in Table 9.3 show no obvious connection with the dipole moments of the molecules involved
(or indeed with their polarizabilities or size). Moreover,
the chains of molecules in DCl-II and DBr-III, so far from

being linear as might be expected for a simple dipole array,
are such that the Cl-Cl-Cl and Br-Br-Br angles are 93°31'
and 91°48' respectively, suggesting that the intermolecular
attraction is primarily between a proton of one molecule and
a lone pair of electrons on an adjacent molecule. Some
authors therefore regard the interaction as a case of hydrogen bonding, and indeed all three halides show the considerable shifts of the fundamental stretching frequency
commonly associated with hydrogen-bond formation. For HCl,
this amounts to a change from 2 889 cm^{-1} for the gas to
2 707-2 758 cm^{-1} in phase II at 77 K. [Brunel and Peyron
(1967) found by using a single crystal that in this phase
of HCl the fundamental vibration band has three peaks, at
2 707, 2 718, and 2 758 cm^{-1}.] The corresponding shift for
HI from gas to phase III is proportionately much the same
(2 230 to 2 120 cm^{-1}). Moreover, the absorption coefficients
for HCl and HBr are much higher in the low-temperature phases
than in the gaseous phase, which again is characteristic of
hydrogen-bonded crystals (Friedrich and Person 1963). Tsang
and Shaw (1971) attempted to account for the dielectric and
other properties of the hydrogen halides on a molecular-field
basis. Their treatment, which achieved fair success, took
account of both hydrogen bonding and of dipole-dipole interaction. It should however be pointed out that a detailed
consideration of the intermolecular attraction within these
solids should not overlook the possibility that a significant
contribution may come from quadrupole-quadrupole interaction,
which, as stressed elsewhere, can be an important order-
promoting factor in solids composed of non-polar diatomic
molecules. The values of the quadrupole moments referred
to a centre of mass origin (in e.s.u. cm^2 × 10^{26}) of HCl,
HBr, and HI recommended by D.E.Stogryn and A.P.Stogryn (1966)
are +3·8, +4, and +6 respectively. These are large enough
to give significant quadrupole-quadrupole energies, and with
the dipole moments decreasing in the order HCl (1·08 D)
>HBr(0·82 D) >HI(0·42 D), for HBr and HI at least quadrupole
interaction may play an important order-inducing role.

9.5. TRIATOMIC MOLECULES

9.5.1. *Linear molecules - dinitrogen oxide, carbon dioxide, and carbon oxysulphide*

Dinitrogen oxide (nitrous oxide, N_2O) and carbon dioxide crystallize in f.c.c. lattices (space group $Pa3$) which are isomorphous with each other, and also with (or at least very similar to) the low-temperature forms of carbon monoxide and nitrogen. All four lattices are therefore a consequence of the interaction of the molecular quadrupoles. As with carbon monoxide, the dipole moment of N_2O is so small (0·166 D) that its orienting influence is negligible. But the quadrupole moments of N_2O and CO_2 (-3·0 × 10^{-26} and -4·3 × 10^{-26} e.s.u. cm^2 respectively) are larger than those of CO (-2·5 × 10^{-26} e.s.u. cm^2) and N_2 (-1·4 × 10^{-26} e.s.u. cm^2), and effectively prevent molecular reorientation in solid dinitrogen oxide and carbon dioxide, which unlike the two diatomic substances have no transition at ordinary pressures. N_2O, however, retains entropy at 0 K approximately equal to $R \ln 2$ (Clusius 1934, Blue and Giauque 1935). In the linear molecule of N_2O the atoms are approximately the same size and the two bonds are not very different in length (N-N = 0·1126 nm, N-O = 0·1186 nm), so the obvious interpretation of the residual entropy is that the molecules are in a state of frozen-in disorder involving the two possible orientations NNO and ONN. The first estimate of S(spec) - S(cal) of 4·77 ± 0·4 J K^{-1} mol^{-1} was slightly less than $R \ln 2$, implying some local order in the crystal, but Atake and Chihara (1974) extended the heat capacity measurements down to 2 K and obtained a revised estimate of 6·0 J K^{-1} mol^{-1}, i.e. $R \ln 2$ within experimental error. The scattering factors of the oxygen and nitrogen atoms for neutrons differ considerably, being 0·58 and 0·94 respectively, and Hamilton and Petrie (1961) obtained neutron diffraction results which were incompatible with an orientationally ordered structure. Kovalenko, Indan, Khudotyoplaya, and Krupskii (1973) found no signs of ordering in electron diffraction studies carried out from 2 K to 60 K on thin layers of the crystals. Anderson and Walmsley (1964) examined the far infrared spectrum of N_2O crystals at 77 K between 20 cm^{-1} and 400 cm^{-1}, and found only a single broad

band. This is consistent with a relaxation of the selection
rules in consequence of orientational disorder. For an ordered structure, four bands would be expected.

For the molecule of carbon oxysulphide, COS, the dipole
moment of $0 \cdot 72$ D is appreciably larger than that of N_2O, and
the terminal atoms differ considerably in size (C-O = $0 \cdot 116$ nm,
C-S = $0 \cdot 156$ nm). It is therefore not surprising that crystalline carbon oxysulphide has a different (rhombohedral) structure from f.c.c. dinitrogen oxide and carbon dioxide, and that
it is ordered at 0 K, since Kemp and Giauque (1937) showed
that S(spec) and S(cal) are equal within experimental error.
These authors reported, however, that in a temperature range
of about 75 K from the melting-point downwards, thermal equilibrium in COS was established unusually slowly, and it would
be interesting to apply other techniques to see if the crystals,
when first produced, show any evidence of orientational disorder which tends to disappear with time.

9.5.2. *Non-linear molecules - hydrogen and deuterium sulphide*
and selenide, sulphur dioxide
The four substances hydrogen and deuterium sulphide and
selenide all exist in three forms at ordinary pressures
(Table 9.4). In addition, there are two high-pressure phases
of hydrogen sulphide (Stevenson 1957a) but these do not seem
to have been investigated and we shall not refer to them
again. The compound which has been most thoroughly examined
is H_2S. The first X-ray studies led to the conclusion that
all three forms are face-centred cubic (Vegard 1930b, Natta
1931, Justi and Nitka 1936). While this is generally accepted
to be the case for I, it is not true of III, and II, though
cubic, is not face-centred. That III is not cubic was first
demonstrated by Kruis and Clusius (1937), who used a polarizing microscope to show that H_2S-III, unlike I and II, is optically anisotropic. Later, Reding and Hornig (1957) found
that the infrared spectrum of III, unlike that of I and II,
consists of extremely sharp lines, and concluded that III
must be an ordered crystal. The structure of this phase was
finally resolved by Sándor and Ogunade (1969) by combined X-
ray and neutron diffraction studies. X-ray photographs showed

TABLE 9.4

Thermal and structural information on hydrogen and deuterium sulphides and selenides

Compound	III ← T_t/K, $\Delta S_t/R$ → II	II ← T_t/K, $\Delta S_t/R$ → I	I ← T_m/K, $\Delta S_m/R$ → Liq.	References Cal.	Cryst.	NMR
H_2S	103·52(F),1·789 Tetragonal,$P4_2$	126·22(λ), 0·484 Cubic,$Pa3$	187·61, 1·524 F.c.c.	1,2	3-6	7-10
D_2S	107·82(F),1·88 Tetragonal,$P4_2$	132·85(λ), 0.47 Cubic,$Pa3$	187·14, 1·520 F.c.c.	2	4,6	–
H_2Se	82·3(?λ), 2·30 Cubic	172·54(λ), 0·78 Cubic	207·43, 1·46 Cubic	2	4,8	7,8,10
D_2Se	90·5(?λ), 2·59 Cubic	176·02(λ), 0·81 Cubic	206·24, 1·45 Cubic	2	4	–

1. Giauque and Blue (1936).
2. Kruis and Clusius (1937).
3. Vegard (1930b); Natta (1931); Justi and Nitka (1936).
4. Vegard and Oserød (1942); Vegard (1944).
5. Kitamura and Harada (1962); Harada and Kitamura (1964).
6. Sándor and Ogunade (1969).
7. Alpert (1949).
8. Loehlin, Mennitt, and Waugh (1966).
9. Look, Lowe, and Northby (1966).
10. El Saffar and Schultz (1972).

that the *sulphur* lattice is tetragonal, space group $P4_2/mnm$, with four atoms per unit cell. The positions of the deuterium atoms were derived from the neutron powder patterns, which were successfully interpreted on the basis of a unit cell containing sixteen molecules, space group $P4_2$. The D-S-D angle seems to be one to two degrees larger in the molecule in phase III than in the gas. The arrangement of the molecules in phase III projected onto the (001) plane is shown in Fig.9.15. There are zig-zag chains reminiscent of the hydrogen halides. Sándor and Ogunade describe the structure as

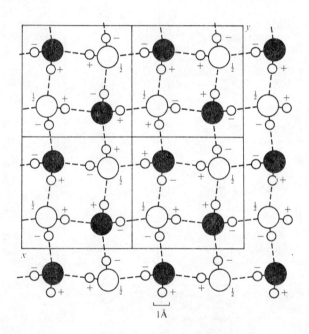

Fig.9.15. Arrangement of the molecules in D_2S-III, projected onto the (001) plane. The dashed lines indicate hydrogen bonds, which form zig-zag chains parallel to the [100] and [010] axes (Sándor and Ogunade 1969).

hydrogen-bonded, though the reduction in the intramolecular vibration frequencies on passing from gaseous hydrogen sulphide to the crystal does not exceed three per cent. Before Sándor and Ogunade's work, Kitamura and Harada (1962) had concluded that III consists of two tetragonal phases, IIIa which is stable, and IIIb which is transient. (These they

designated, rather regrettably, as I and II respectively.)
They considered that IIIa contains 16 and IIIb four molecules per unit cell, and that on warming the crystals from
low temperatures the sequence of transformations is
IIIa→IIIb→II. As for the middle phase II, Sándor and Ogunade
accounted for the neutron powder patterns for this modification at 112 K on the basis that the structure has the primitive cubic space group $Pa3$, with the molecules disordered
among six equally probable orientations.

The III→II transition is accompanied by hysteresis
which was studied by Clusius and Weigand (1938). They examined the effect of pressure on this transition, primarily
to determine the associated volume increase, obtaining values
of $0 \cdot 22$ cm^3 mol^{-1} (~$0 \cdot 8$ per cent) for H_2S, and $0 \cdot 18$ cm^3 mol^{-1}
(~$0 \cdot 65$ per cent) for D_2S. This study revealed that the hys-
teresis interval ($0 \cdot 42$ K for H_2S and $0 \cdot 23$ K for D_2S at zero
pressure) increases for both substances with rising pressure.
Less is known about the II→I transition, at which there is
a further volume increase of about 2 per cent for H_2S. The
III→II transition in hydrogen selenide is unusual in that the
NMR line-width transition and the thermal anomaly coincide.

Smyth and Hitchcock (1934) found that H_2S-III has a low
permittivity, whereas in II and I it is much higher (Fig.
4.28). Their results were essentially confirmed by Havriliak
Swenson, and Cole (1955). Clearly, therefore, there must be
considerable orientational freedom in phases II and I, for
which the temperature dependence of the permittivity is in
fact in fair agreement with the equation developed by Onsager
for polar liquids. In the measurements of Havriliak *et al*,
which extended over the frequency range 15 Hz to 500 kHz,
there was no evidence in any phase of dielectric dispersion.

Structural studies on hydrogen selenide are much less
extensive than those on hydrogen sulphide, but from a rather
cursory X-ray examination made by Loehlin, Mennitt, and Waugh
(1966) as an adjunct to a detailed NMR study, it seems that
H_2Se-II (and presumably H_2Se-I) is cubic, while H_2Se-III is
not, and may have a lattice of lower symmetry than tetragonal.
As with H_2S, the permittivity of H_2Se is high in phases I
and II (Smyth and McNeight 1936). It will be seen from

566   DISORDER IN MOLECULAR SOLIDS - I

Table 9.4 that the effect of replacing H by D is to raise
the temperature of every transition but to lower the melting-
points. The substitution of H by D causes the lattices of all
modifications of the sulphide and selenide to contract. For
H_2Se-II, the volume reduction is said to amount to as much as
4·5 per cent (Vegard and Oserød 1942, Vegard 1944).

Our knowledge of molecular motion in the three forms
of crystalline hydrogen sulphide and selenide derives very
largely from two NMR studies, one of H_2S by Look, Lowe, and
Northby (1966), the other of H_2S and H_2Se by Loehlin et al.
The former group measured the spin-lattice relaxation times
for both static and rotating magnetic fields (T_1 and $T_{1\rho}$),
while the latter measured T_1 and the transverse relaxation
time T_2. The two sets of results for T_1 are in good agreement. Fig.9.16 shows the dependence of the second moment

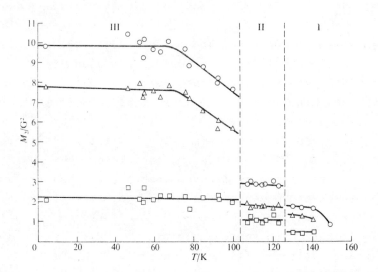

Fig.9.16. Second moment M_2 of the proton resonance line in H_2S as a function of temperature. Circles, total M_2; triangles, intramolecular M_2;
squares, intermolecular M_2 (Look, Lowe, and Northby 1966).

of H_2S on temperature, as determined by Look et al. In phase
III, its value starts to decrease at ~70 K. Both groups
of investigators consider that in this phase the lattice is
rigid and that the process taking place is one of rotational

flips about the C_2 axis. This is, of course, consistent
with the small permittivity, since the direction of the molecular dipoles is unaffected by such flips, the activation
energies for which are estimated from the temperature dependence of T_1 to be 16 kJ mol^{-1} for H_2S and 5·8 kJ mol^{-1} for
H_2Se. But whereas Loehlin and his colleagues regarded the
flips as taking place through 180°, Look et al. in an elaborate analysis gave reasons for believing that in one revolution a molecule of H_2S passes through absolute minima at 0°
and 180° and two relative minima at 90° and 270°, and that
the flips therefore involve a 90° rotation about the C_2 axis.
In phase II of both H_2S and H_2Se, the second moment is much
smaller (~2 G^2 for H_2Se), and since the permittivity is
much larger than in phase III it is considered that the
molecules (while still undergoing flips about their polar
axes, probably much more rapidly than in phase III) are now
undergoing reorientation in other directions as well. At
the II→I transition in both H_2S and H_2Se the second moment
falls again, and as the melting-points are approached it
decreases to unresolvably small values. This is attributed
to translational self-diffusion, with an activation energy
of 30·5 kJ mol^{-1} for H_2S and 25 kJ mol^{-1} for H_2Se.

Since in the ordered forms of the hydrogen sulphides
and selenides the molecules are linked in chains as in the
hydrogen halides, one would expect that the motion of the
molecules in the two types of compound is similar, and that
the acts of reorientation of a molecule in the disordered
phases are separated by brief periods of participation with
its neighbours in short chains. Again a simple quantitative
explanation of the entropies of transition should not be expected, but in view of Sándor and Ogunade's conclusion that
in the middle phase II of the sulphides each molecule has
six equivalent orientations available to it, it is interesting that ΔS_t for the III→II transition in H_2S is almost
exactly $R \ln 6$, and that in none of the other three similar
substances is it less than this.

Giauque and Stephenson (1938) obtained close agreement
between S(cal) and S(spec) for sulphur dioxide, so that the
crystal is perfectly ordered at 0 K. There are no transitions,

but it may be noted that these authors reported that from 130 K upwards thermal equilibrium was only established slowly (*cf*. carbon oxysulphide, section 9.5.1).

9.6. TETRAATOMIC MOLECULES

Crystalline phosphine is a system of some complexity, as may be seen from Fig.9.17, due to Stephenson and Giauque

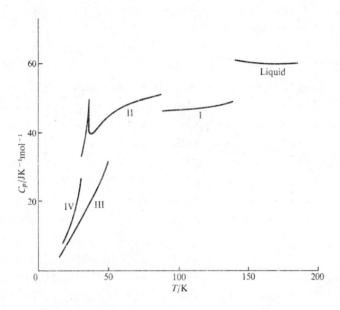

Fig.9.17. Molar heat capacity C_p of phosphine (after Stephenson and Giauque 1937).

(1937). The stable form at low temperatures is III, but the complete conversion of II to III requires several days. The unstable form at low temperatures is IV, which when heated undergoes a transition at 30·29 K which is free from superheating and supercooling and which has an entropy change of 2·7 J K^{-1} mol^{-1}. The form II so produced, unstable at this temperature, enters a region of abnormally high heat capacity between 30·29 K and 35·66 K, C_p falling at the latter temperature by about 15 per cent within a few hundredths of a degree. The final transition, II→I, occurs at 88·10 K,

and appears to be first order with an entropy change of
$5 \cdot 52$ J K^{-1} mol^{-1}. I melts at $139 \cdot 35$ K with an entropy gain
of only $8 \cdot 12$ J K^{-1} mol^{-1}. The largest entropy increase
($15 \cdot 73$ J K^{-1} mol^{-1}) is at the III→II transition at $49 \cdot 43$ K.
S(cal) for the ideal gas at $25°C$ is $210 \cdot 7$ J K^{-1} mol^{-1}, in
good agreement with S(spec) = $210 \cdot 2$ J K^{-1} mol^{-1}. Moreover,
the two values for the molar entropy of II at $49 \cdot 43$ K, as
derived from (a) the heat capacity of III and ΔS for the
III→II transition, (b) the heat capacity of IV and supercooled II and ΔS for the IV→II transition, are (a) $34 \cdot 06$,
(b) $34 \cdot 02$ J K^{-1} mol^{-1}.

The only structural study on phosphine seems to be an
early X-ray examination by Natta and Casazza (1930) of phase
I, which was found to be cubic. This fact and the low entropy of fusion together indicate that I is highly disordered.
An NMR study (Boden and Folland 1975) showed that whereas
with some plastic crystals there is no discontinuity in the
orientational correlation time or its temperature dependence
at the melting-point, this is not the case for PD_3. The
associated activation energy is actually less in phase I
($1 \cdot 3$ kJ mol^{-1}) than in the liquid ($2 \cdot 5$ kJ mol^{-1}). An infrared investigation by Francia and Nixon (1973) disclosed that
the spectrum of form II consists of broad, largely featureless bands, whereas that of IV shows much more structure.
This is illustrated in Fig.9.18, which shows part of the
spectrum in the region of the v_3 fundamental. Francia and
Nixon suggested that IV might be a complicated structure
with perhaps as many as six different types of molecular
site. On the spectroscopic evidence, therefore, II, like I,
is disordered, while IV is ordered, and although the spectrum of III was not obtained, on thermodynamic grounds this
too is an ordered phase.

Study of crystalline arsine seems to have been limited
so far to measurements of the permittivity ε by Smyth and
McNeight (1936). These show a transition at $32 \cdot 1$ K, at
which ε reaches a maximum, thereafter falling with rising
temperature like ε for a liquid. There is a further transition at $106 \cdot 6$ K, with a slight increase in ε.

Only one form of crystalline ammonia is known, even at

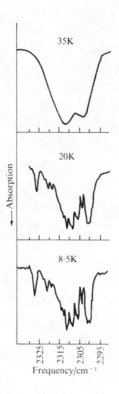

Fig.9.18. Infrared spectrum of crystalline PH_3 in the ν_3 region. The spectrum at 35 K is that of phase II. The spectra at 20 K and 8·5 K were recorded after depositing the film at 51 K and rapidly cooling to these temperatures, and are presumably the spectra of phase IV (Francia and Nixon 1973).

pressures up to $\sim 10^4$ bar, the structure being essentially determined by hydrogen bonding.

Turning to substances with tetraatomic but planar molecules, the only non-polar compound which appears to have been examined is boron trifluoride. Although the molecule of this compound is geometrically similar to the nitrate ion, which is often found in an orientationally disordered condition, solid boron trifluoride has no phase transitions (Kostryukov, Samorukov, and Strelkov 1958). Eucken and Schröder (1938) had reported a gradual transition with T_λ about 2·3 K below the melting-point and a small entropy effect of $\sim 0·55$ J K^{-1} mol^{-1}, but Kostryukov and his colleagues attributed this to impurities.

The conclusion reached by Giauque and Jones (1948), that crystalline phosgene ($COCl_2$) retains ~$6 \cdot 7$ J K^{-1} mol^{-1} of entropy at 0 K, was shown later to be untenable by Giauque and Ott (1960), who found that this substance has three solid forms, of which I has the highest melting-point, III is always unstable with respect to I and II, while II may be the stable form below ~40 K, although I showed no signs of instability during the calorimetric measurements. That I is ordered at 0 K was shown by the agreement between S(cal) and S(spec) (both equal to $280 \cdot 3$ J K^{-1} mol^{-1}) and confirmed by an X-ray study by Zaslow, Atoji, and Lipscomb (1952) who found a perfectly ordered structure at 113 K. On the other hand, the molar entropy of form II at the melting-point is $84 \cdot 68$ J K^{-1} mol^{-1}, while $\int_0^T c_p \mathrm{d} \ln T$ for this form is $83 \cdot 84$ J K^{-1} mol^{-1}. Giauque and Ott considered that the discrepancy is real, and attributed it to a small amount of frozen-in atomic exchange disorder. The difference of $0 \cdot 84$ J K^{-1} mol^{-1} corresponds to $1 \cdot 75$ per cent of molecules which are disordered with respect to the positions of the oxygen and chlorine atoms. Carbonyl fluoride has no transition, and is ordered at 0 K. [S(cal) = $238 \cdot 85$ J K^{-1} mol^{-1} for the gas at the boiling-point, S(spec) = $239 \cdot 45$ J K^{-1} mol^{-1}; Pace and Reno (1968).] On the other hand, for perchloryl fluoride, ClO_3F (Koehler and Giauque 1958), S(cal) for the ideal gas at the boiling-point is $251 \cdot 75$ J K^{-1}mol^{-1}, while S(spec) is $261 \cdot 9$ J K^{-1} mol^{-1}. The difference, S(res), of $10 \cdot 15$ J K^{-1} mol^{-1} is not far from $R \ln 4$ (= $11 \cdot 53$ J K^{-1} mol^{-1}), and clearly implies relatively little discrimination in the lattice between oxygen and fluorine atoms. [It is significant that the dipole moment of ClO_3F ($0 \cdot 013$ D) is very much less than that of COF_2 ($0 \cdot 951$ D) or that of $COCl_2$ ($1 \cdot 18$ D).] However, since S(res) falls short of $R \ln 4$ by $1 \cdot 38$ J K^{-1} mol^{-1}, it would appear that the orientational disorder of the ClO_3F molecules is not quite complete, and this conclusion finds support from the Raman spectrum (Sunder and McClung 1974).

9.7. METHANE AND DEUTERATED METHANES

These substances have attracted a good deal of attention.
All of them, except possibly CH_4, exist in three solid forms
at low pressures. In view of the highly symmetrical, compact nature of the molecules, and of the relatively non-polar
character of the carbon-hydrogen bond, it was clear at the
outset that something closely approaching free rotation, at
least near the melting-point, was an *a priori* possibility.
Moreover, by partial deuteration of CH_4, it is possible to
change the symmetry properties of the molecule without introducing any appreciable polarity. Finally, as we shall see,
phenomena are encountered which are a consequence of the
existence of different nuclear spin species (spin isomers).
As with hydrogen, different nuclear spin states are coupled
with different rotational states. For CH_4 and CD_4, three
such species exist, designated A, E, and T (or F) (sometimes
called *meta*, *para*, and *ortho* respectively). The proportions
of A, E, and T in the equilibrium high-temperature mixture
of gaseous CH_4 are 5:2:9. The lowest possible values of the
rotational quantum number J are 0 for A, 2 for E, and 1 for
T, so that A is the stable species at low temperatures. For
CD_4, the corresponding proportions of A, E, and T in the
equilibrium mixture are 5:4:18. As for the partially deuterated methanes, CH_3D and CD_3H each exist in two species,
A and E, in the proportions 1:1 for CH_3D and 11:16 for CHD_3,
while CH_2D_2 consists of the species A and B in the proportions of 5:7. The analogy drawn between crystalline hydrogen
and deuterium and magnetic alloys is therefore applicable
to the methanes as well, and the adjectives 'ferrorotational'
and 'antiferrorotational' have appeared in the literature
in descriptions of ordering in these crystals. Here too the
behaviour of the solid is complicated by spontaneous spin-
isomer conversion, especially for the proton-rich modifications. We shall return to this after presenting some of
the main facts about these compounds.

Table 9.5 summarizes some of the features of the transitions in crystalline methane and deuterated methanes, much
of the early calorimetric work on which was carried out by
Clusius and his coworkers. All of the transitions are partly

TABLE 9.5

Temperatures and entropies of transition and fusion for methane and deuterated methanes

Compound	III	T_t/K,ΔS_t/R	II	T_t/K,ΔS_t/R	I	T_m/K,ΔS_m/R	Liq.
CH_4		?8, 0·28[a]		20·6, 0·46[a]		90·67, 1·25[a]	
CH_3D		16·1, 0·26[b]		23·1, 0·54[b]		90·41, 1·26[c]	
CH_2D_2		19·1, 0·26[b]		24·9, 0·50[b]		90·17, 1·23[c]	
CHD_3		20·9, 0·28[b]		26·0, 0·59[b]		89·96, 1·23[c]	
CD_4		22·4, 0·40[a]		27·2, 0·62[a]		89·78, 1·22[a]	

[a] Colwell, Gill, and Morrison (1963).
[b] Sperandio (1961).
[c] Colwell, Gill, and Morrison (1965).

gradual and all show hysteresis, the most thorough study of which is that made by Colwell, Gill, and Morrison (1963). Different views have been expressed as to whether or not the transitions can properly be described as first order (see e.g. Bloom and Morrison 1973), and it may well be that the nature of the III-II transition in particular is affected by the extent to which spin-isomer conversion has occurred. The values in Table 9.5 of ΔS_t, the entropy of transition, are due to Sperandio (1961), and are estimates of the excess (or true) transition entropies. The failure of some of these to agree with $R \ln n$ for a simple value of n, and the difference between the ΔS_t values for CH_4 and CD_4, both discourage the hope of any facile interpretation of the ΔS_t figures.

For a long time it was believed that, at ordinary pressures, CH_4 (unlike the deuterated methanes) has only one order-disorder transition. In 1962, Colwell, Gill, and Morrison reported heat capacity evidence for a lower thermal anomaly in CH_4, which they were inclined to regard as a second transition. The new anomaly appeared to be much broader than all the other λ-type transitions, and thermal equilibrium was established only slowly. Bartholomé, Drikos, and Eucken (1938) had previously studied transitions in mixed crystals of CH_4 and CD_4 (Fig.9.19). It will be seen that the

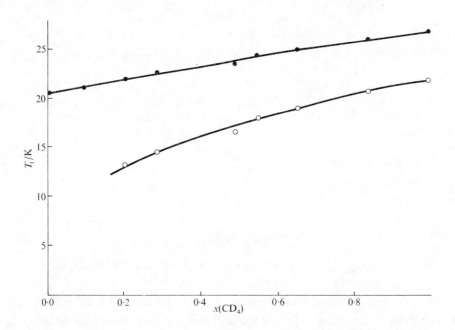

Fig.9.19. Temperatures of the upper and lower transitions in CH_4-CD_4 mixtures, plotted against x (CD_4), the mole fraction of CD_4, from the results of Bartholomé, Drikos, and Eucken (1938).

trend of the lower transition with decreasing deuterium content could certainly be regarded as consistent with a transition temperature of ~8 K in pure CH_4. However, doubts were cast on the correctness of regarding this new 'transition' in CH_4 as the analogue of the III-II transformation in the deuterated methanes. For example, it was observed that some properties of the crystal which changed

at the 20·6 K transition in CH_4 did not appear to alter in
the region of 8 K. These include the infrared spectrum
(Blanchard, Brunel, and Peyron 1971), the adiabatic compressibility (Wolf, Stahl, and Watrous 1973), and the neutron
scattering cross-section (Johnston and Collins 1972). It
now appears that the thermal effects observed in the region
of 8 K for CH_4 are connected with spin-isomer conversion,
and are dependent on time, thermal history, and the presence
of impurities, especially oxygen. We shall return to this
later.

Table 9.5 does not exhaust the thermal anomalies manifested by the solids concerned, since CH_3D, CH_2D_2, and CHD_3
also have Schottky anomalies at still lower temperatures,
all with maxima in the heat capacity below 1 K. Discussion
of these anomalies (and of the related question of the significance of apparent residual entropies) will be deferred
until the transitions between phases I, II, and III have
been considered.

The data in Table 9.5 refer to zero pressure. Several
studies have been made of the phase relations in CH_4 and CD_4
under pressure (Trapeznikowa and Miljutin 1939, Stevenson
1957b, Stewart 1959, Rosenshein and Whitney 1964). These
disclosed that under pressure a III-II transition *does*
appear in CH_4, but it cannot be detected until ~155 bar has
been attained (Fig.9.20). The III→II and II→I transition
temperatures both rise with increasing pressure, in such a
way that phase II is eventually squeezed out of existence,
the triple-point for I, II, and III for CH_4 having the coordinates 33 K and 2·7 kbar (Stewart 1959). Stevenson
claimed to have found a new, high-pressure form of CH_4,
which at 20 K, for example, was supposed to be stable above
~3 kbar, but Stewart, although taking the pressure to ~19
kbar, was unable to confirm this. He also reported that at
77 K solid methane is 'quite plastic'. As the temperature
falls, it becomes increasingly brittle.

X-ray work on CH_4 carried out between 4 K and 80 K has
shown that the carbon atoms are positioned on an f.c.c.
lattice throughout (Schallamach 1939, Greer and Meyer 1969,
Herczeg and Stoner 1971, Bol'shutkin, Gasan, and Prokhvatilov

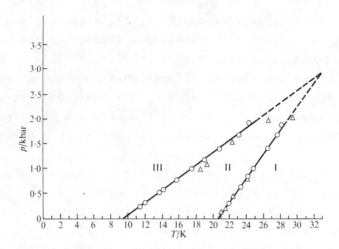

Fig.9.20. Phase diagram for CH_4, after Rosenshein and Whitney (1964), whose results are shown by circles. Triangles, results of Trapeznikowa and Miljutin (1939).

1971). A neutron diffraction study demonstrated that the carbon atoms in CD_4-I have the same arrangement (Gissler and Stiller 1965), and a subsequent single-crystal examination of CD_4-I at 77 K by Press, Dorner, and Will (1970), while confirming the f.c.c. structure (space group $Fm3m$), led to the important conclusion that the molecules are not freely rotating. Instead, they are distributed between twelve equivalent orientations, and they have large amplitudes of librational and translational movement. Further neutron diffraction work by Press (1972) on all three phases of CD_4 confirmed a remarkable prediction made about phase II by James and Keenan (1959), whose theory we shall consider in due course, namely that in phase II three molecules out of four are orientationally ordered, while the remainder are orientationally disordered (or freely rotating). The struc-ture of CD_4-III was shown by an X-ray study to be tetragonal (Bol'shutkin, Gasan, Prokhvatilov, and Yantsevich 1971), but the departure from a cubic lattice is only slight. At 10 K the c/a ratio is 1·013. (It decreases with rising tempera-ture, so that expansion in this phase is anisotropic.) The volume increase at the III→II transition is only ~0·1 per cent.

That CD_4-III is not cubic was also shown by Press's diffraction work, by the birefringence of CD_4-III (Ballik, Gannon, and
Morrison 1972), by the far infrared spectrum of this phase
(Savoie and Fournier 1970), and by the infrared spectra of dilute solid solutions of CH_4 and CHD_3 in CD_4 (Savitsky and
Hornig 1962, Chapados and Cabana 1970). Colwell, Gill, and
Morrison (1963) pointed out that c_p for CD_4-I is higher than
that of CH_4-I by amounts consistent with the differences in
molecular weight and moments of inertia of the two molecules,
that is with CD_4 having translational frequencies lower than
those of CH_4 by $(16/20)^{\frac{1}{2}}$, and librational frequencies lower
by $(\frac{1}{2})^{\frac{1}{2}}$. The molar volume of CH_4 is between 2·5 and 3·5%
larger than that of CD_4, according to the temperature.

Several investigations of the infrared and Raman spectra
of the methanes have been carried out. Savitsky and Hornig
(1962) examined the infrared spectra of CH_4 and CD_4 between
5 K and 40 K in the neighbourhood of the ν_3 and ν_4 fundamentals, and also of dilute solutions of CH_4 in CD_4, and of
CD_4 in CH_4 (see section 4.5). The spectra of these solutions
are particularly informative, since they are almost free
from the complications which can be caused by the interaction
between neighbouring identical molecules. The spectra in the
ν_4 region for the dilute solutions consists in all phases of
a single sharp peak, which could not possibly be the envelope
of a rotation-vibration band, but the band is wider in phase
I than in II or III, which is consistent with orientational
disorder in I. Ewing (1964) compared the infrared spectra
of CH_4 and CD_4 in the region of the ν_3 fundamental, extending
his observations into the liquid phase. The absorption band
shows no discontinuous change at the melting-point, and even
in the liquid its shape indicates some residual hindrance to
rotation. Ewing estimated that the barrier to rotation in
the crystal near the melting-point and in the liquid does
not exceed 0·75 kJ mol^{-1}. The essential similarity between
the molecular movement in the liquid and in I near the
melting-point was also apparent in a study of the Raman
spectra of CH_4 and CD_4 (Anderson and Savoie 1965). This investigation was extended down to 10 K, so that CD_4 was
examined in all three phases. There are marked changes in
the Raman spectrum on passing from I to II, but only small

differences between II and III. Chapados and Cabana (1972)
compared the infrared spectra of CH_4, CD_4, and mixed isotopic
crystals in phases I and II, and concluded that corresponding
phases of CH_4 and CD_4 have the same structures. Their results
also indicated that there is considerable molecular motion
in phase I, and that in II there are two types of sites for
the molecules, as predicted by James and Keenan. D.Smith
(1971b, 1974) analysed the heat capacity of CD_4 in phases I
and III and estimated that the barrier to rotation of the
molecules in III is $\sim 1 \cdot 5$ kJ mol^{-1}, but only $\sim 0 \cdot 63$ kJ mol^{-1}
in phase I. Manzhelii, Tarasenko, Bondarenko, and Gavrilko
(1975) measured the coefficient of expansion and the sound velo-
city for CH_4-I near the melting-point and used their results
to evaluate c_V, which they interpreted as showing that the
rotational contribution to c_V is near the value for free rotation, while that from the lattice vibrations reflects considerable anharmonicity in this motion.

Methane was one of the first solids having phase transitions to which NMR was applied, but unfortunately some of the
early work was vitiated by the presence of oxygen, which can
shorten the spin-lattice relaxation time by as much as 10^3.
More recent studies of the proton resonance in all four protonated methanes have given concordant results (Wolf and
Whitney 1964, Trappeniers, Gerritsma, and Oosting 1965,
de Wit and Bloom 1966). As found earlier by Thomas, Alpert,
and Torrey (1950), the line-width in CH_4-I starts to fall
rapidly with increasing temperature above ~ 60 K, reaching
very low values determined by the inhomogeneity of the magnetic field. This was attributed by Waugh (1957) to the onset of self-diffusion, an interpretation supported by the
fact that the activation energies given by the dependence of
both T_1 and T_2 (the spin-spin relaxation time) on temperature
between 60 K and the melting-point are almost the same (15
kJ mol^{-1}) for all four protonated methanes. In this region
of rapid molecular motion, the line-shape is Lorentzian
rather than Gaussian, which it becomes at sufficiently low
temperatures. There is no discontinuity in T_1 at the melting-
point. From ~ 60 K down to ~ 25 K the line-width and second
moment remain approximately constant, so presumably rapid

molecular reorientation continues while diffusion is suppressed. Below 25 K, the line-widths start to increase, but
do not change abruptly at either of the two transitions in
the partly deuterated methanes. On the other hand, in CH_3D
and CD_3H, T_1 drops sharply (by a factor of about two) at
each of the transitions I→II and II→III. (For CH_4 and CD_4,
similar pronounced changes only occur at the upper transition.) The reason for the difference is that the line-widths
are controlled by intermolecular interactions, while T_1 is
governed by intramolecular spin-lattice interactions. Even
at 1·8 K, the second moment is much smaller than would be
expected for a rigid lattice (de Wit and Bloom 1966).

Investigations of the scattering of slow neutrons by
crystalline and liquid methane once again bring out the similarity in molecular behaviour in phase I and in the liquid
near the melting-point, and confirm that there is some restriction on the freedom of rotation (Stiller and Hautecler
1962, Harker and Brugger 1965, Kosaly and Solt 1966). Harker
and Brugger (1967) studied both the inelastic and elastic
scattering for solid CH_4 from 22 K down to 5 K. The passage
from I to II is accompanied by a narrowing of the elastic
scattering peaks and by the development of some structure in
the inelastic scattering. These findings were analysed by
Sköld (1968), who suggested that in the region of the upper
transition the molecules undergo stepwise orientation. He
estimated that the average time between the jumps is 10^{-12} s
at 22 K, increasing to >5 × 10^{-12} s at 18 K.

We may therefore summarize our knowledge of molecular
movement in crystalline methane as follows. The motion in
the solid near the melting-point is very much like that in
the liquid. The molecules undergo very rapid reorientation,
without rotating absolutely freely, and have considerable
freedom of translational movement. As these soft crystals
are cooled, diffusion effectively ceases at ~65 K and the
crystals become harder, though reorientation remains facile
down to 25 K. To anticipate our discussion of theoretical
treatments, the barrier to rotation almost certainly derives
from intermolecular octupole-octupole interaction, the
energy of which depends on R^{-7}, and this sensitive dependence

on distance means that as the crystal cools and contracts
the barrier to rotation may increase from the rather low
value of ~0·63 kJ mol^{-1} which obtains near the melting-point.
The λ-type transitions which are then encountered on further
cooling are almost certainly intimately linked with changes
in the reorientational movement of the molecules, but quite
how is not yet clear. It is possible that phase III is a
structure of some complexity.

    We have already referred to the possibility of spon-
taneous conversion between nuclear spin species. There is
no doubt that this occurs in CH_4 and in CH_3D, and it compli-
cates the experimental study of these solids at low temperatures. The conversion is greatly accelerated by the presence
of oxygen, and detailed studies of this have been made, such
as those of Van Hecke, Grobet, and Van Gerven (1972) and Van
Hecke and Van Gerven (1973). The catalytic effect of oxygen
has been deliberately applied to try and establish equilibrium between the various spin isomers, for example, in the
heat capacity measurements made on CH_3D by Morrison and
Norton (1972) and on CH_4 by Vogt and Pitzer (1975), and in
the X-ray study of the temperature dependence of the lattice
parameters of CH_4 by Krupskii, Gasan, and Prokhvatilov (1974).
Code and Higinbotham (1976) measured the static proton magnetic susceptibility of oxygen-containing samples of CH_4
between 1·6 K and 80 K. They showed that their results could
be explained on the basis that within two hours spin conversion reaches equilibrium in phase II on the two disordered
sublattices on which the molecules are almost freely rotating
(*v.inf.*), but that no conversion takes place in this time on
the six ordered sublattices. Since it must be accepted that
spin-isomer conversion can and does take place in CH_4 at low
temperatures, it is accordingly not surprising to find reports
that the properties of this substance depend on the thermal
history of the sample. Thus, Ballik, Gannon, and Morrison
(1972) examined CH_4, CH_3D, CHD_3, and CD_4 for optical birefringence at low temperatures. Phase III of each of the
deuterated methanes proved to be birefringent, showing that
it has a symmetry lower than cubic. CH_4 behaved differently.
Below 20 K, solid CH_4 did indeed develop birefringence, but

this was temperature- and time-dependent. Another example
of the dependence of the behaviour of CH_4 on its thermal history was found by Blanchard, Brunel, and Peyron (1971) in a
comparison of the infrared spectrum at 7 K of quenched and
annealed specimens.

It is appropriate here to mention an unusual property
of CH_4 at low temperatures, namely that it has a negative
coefficient of expansion (Fig.9.21; Heberlein and Adams
1970). Yamamoto and Kataoka (1970) attributed this to the

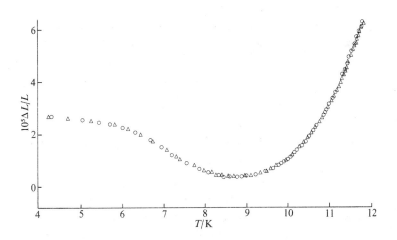

Fig.9.21. Relative length changes of solid CH_4 plotted against temperature, showing the negative coefficient of expansion below ~8·7 K. Circles
and triangles refer to warming and cooling runs respectively (Heberlein
and Adams 1970).

transformation of the species T and of the fewer molecules
of species E into species A, for which the lowest level has
$J = 0$. This change reduces the energy of the octupole-
octupole interaction and the volume of the crystal accordingly increases. This interpretation was confirmed by studying the expansion of samples containing small amounts of
oxygen to accelerate conversion (Aleksandrovskii, Kuchnev,
Manzhelii, and Tolkachev 1976). A curious consequence of
this spin conversion is that if on cooling CH_4-II, in which
three-quarters of the molecules are orientationally ordered,
conversion of the T and E species to the A species with

$J = 0$ takes place, then decreasing temperature brings about a reversion to an orientationally disordered condition (see also Alexander and Lerner-Naor 1972).

The order-disorder transitions in crystalline methanes were considered theoretically in an important paper by James and Keenan (1959). Their treatment is classical in that they disregarded the quantization of molecular rotation and the consequences of nuclear spin, and accordingly they applied their findings to CD_4 and not to CH_4. They assumed that the molecules are rigid and have a tetrahedral charge distribution, so that they are octupoles. If the charge distribution is represented by a charge q at each of the four vertices of a tetrahedron, all at a distance a from the central charge of $-4q$, then the octupole moment I_3 is given by $I_3 = 4(5/9)^{\frac{1}{2}}qa^3$[†]. The ordering force was assumed to be the nearest-neighbour octupole-octupole interaction, the energy of which is proportional to I_3^2/R^7. In the James and Keenan theory, I_3 is the only adjustable parameter. As in James's work on crystalline hydrogen, they used the mean-field approximation and ensured that any conclusion about the relative disposition of the molecules was consistent with the field assumed in its derivation. An elaborate analysis led them to conclude that there are in fact three possible stable phases. In I (assumed *ab initio* to be f.c.c.) the molecules are orientationally disordered. Their conclusion about phase III, that it has a tetragonal structure of space group $I\overline{4}2m$ with all molecular tetrahedra parallel, has not been upheld by later experimental work (Press 1972). On the other hand, as already mentioned, their prediction about phase II *has* been confirmed. This modification, sometimes referred to as the antiferrorotational phase, is an eight sublattice structure in which one molecule in four rotates quite freely, while its twelve nearest neighbours

[†]The following three definitions of octupole moment appear to be in current use:

$$I_3 = 15^{\frac{1}{2}} \sum_i e_i \, x_i \, y_i \, z_i$$
$$\omega = \sum_i e_i \, x_i \, y_i \, z_i$$
$$\Omega = (5/2) \sum_i e_i \, x_i \, y_i \, z_i$$

oscillate about preferred orientations. The methane molecules on any one of the eight sublattices all have the same
orientation, except for the two sublattices formed by the
rotating molecules. The structure of CD_4-II, as determined
by Press by neutron diffraction, is shown in Fig.9.22. The
value of the octupole moment I_3 assigned to CH_4 by James and

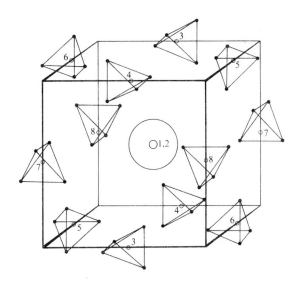

Fig.9.22. The arrangement of the eight sublattices in CD_4-II; the
disordered molecules are represented by circles (Press 1972).

Keenan to give the right value of T_c for the II→I transition
is ± $0·504 \times 10^{-24}$ electron cm^3, which is a reasonable figure
since it corresponds to a charge of ± $0·13e$ on each hydrogen
atom. (In principle, I_3 can be calculated by quantum mechanics, but depending on the choice of wave function the calculated value lies between $0·3$ and $1·8 \times 10^{-24}$ electron cm^3.
Experimental values fall between ~$0·8$ and $1·6 \times 10^{-24}$ electron cm^3.) With their value of I_3, James and Keenan's
estimate of T_c for the III→II transition was $24·4$ K, as compared with the experimental value of $22·4$ K, and the calculated height of the barrier to rotation in phase II was
~$0·83$ kJ mol^{-1}.

Further important advances have been made by Japanese

theoreticians, notably Yamamoto, Kataoka and their collaborators, references to whose work will be found in the paper
by Nishiyama and Yamamoto (1973). Their approach, while essentially based on the James-Keenan model, takes account of the
quantization of molecular rotation and of the existence of
the different nuclear spin species. This makes possible a
theoretical treatment of ordinary methane, CH_4. In one of
the first papers of the series, Yamamoto and Kataoka (1968),
instead of assuming that the crystal is an equilibrium mixture of the three species, A, E, and T, considered hypothetical solids composed only of either pure A or pure T. They
restricted themselves to values of the rotational quantum
number J of 4 or less, the possibilities for A being 0, 3,
and 4, and for T 1, 2, 3, and 4. (In later work, calculations have been extended to higher J values.) They assumed
that phases II and III have the sublattice structures predicted by James and Keenan. The strength of the coupling
between molecules was expressed as a parameter ξ, where
$\xi = I_3^2/R^7$, and depending on the magnitude of ξ, they found
that there are two other possibilities for a system of stable
phases, besides that predicted by the classical treatment.
These are (a) that the disordered phase I persists down to
0 K (essentially because the coupling is too weak to overcome the zero-point energy), (b) that phase II is formed,
but not phase III. In view of the dependence of the octupole-
octupole interaction on R^{-7}, it is qualitatively understandable why the temperature of transitions controlled by this
interaction should rise rapidly with increasing pressure.
Another interesting conclusion to emerge from the work of
this school is that the I-II transition should be first order
(Kataoka, Okada, and Yamamoto 1973).

Two further related theoretical contributions should be
mentioned. The first is that of Alexander and Lerner-Naor
(1972), who used the quantum-mechanical molecular-field
approach but also took proper account of the molecular and
site symmetries. Calculations were carried out for CH_4 and
CD_4 which considered all three spin species and covered rotational states up to $J = 6$. It was shown that whether a II-III
transition occurs in CH_4 or not should be very sensitive to

the spin-isomer composition. The second notable treatment
was that of Nakamura and Miyagi (1971), who, while recognizing the quantum nature of the phenomena under consideration, introduced the principle of corresponding states and
investigated the problem of the change of transition temperature T_c with isotopic composition. They predicted that
for the upper transition, the relation $T_c + \theta = $ constant
would obtain, where θ is a quantum-mechanical parameter (analogous to the Weiss parameter) calculable from the moment of
inertia of the molecules. This prediction agrees very well
with the facts (Fig.9.23). For the lower transition temperature they predicted the relation $T_c + 2\theta = $ constant, which

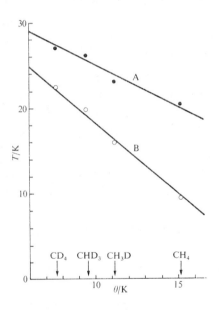

Fig.9.23. Plots of the transition temperatures in the methanes against
the parameter θ (see text). Lines A and B are drawn according to the
equations $T_c + \theta = 35 \cdot 0$ and $T_c + 5\theta/3 = 34 \cdot 9$ respectively (Nakamura and
Miyagi 1971).

is not very different from the empirical relation $T_c + 5\theta/3$
$= $ constant.

It remains to consider the question of apparent residual entropies and of the Schottky anomalies observed at

very low temperatures. In Table 9.6 are given the values of
S(cal) for the five methanes in the gaseous state at a specified temperature and pressure. These values are due to
Clusius and coworkers and to Colwell, Gill, and Morrison.
In evaluating S(cal) for CH_4, the anomaly centred round 8 K
which was reported by Colwell *et al*. has been disregarded,
as have the very low temperature Schottky anomalies for the
partially deuterated methanes. Also given in Table 9.6 are
the corresponding values of S(spec), the entropy calculated
from spectroscopic data taking no account of the consequences
of nuclear spin. S(spec) must be distinguished from S(stat),
which would embody the degeneracy due to nuclear spin and
the mixing entropy of the different nuclear spin species. If
x_i is the mole fraction of a nuclear spin species i, then
ΔS_m, the mixing entropy, is given by

$$\Delta S_m = -R \sum_i x_i \ln x_i$$

and if $g_0(i)$ is the effective degeneracy of the ground state
available to the species i, the resulting entropy contribution for all species is $R \sum_i x_i \ln g_0(i)$. For CD_4, for example, the equilibrium mixture is A:E:T in the proportions of
5:4:18, so that x_A = 5/27, x_E = 4/27, x_T = 18/27, while in a
field of tetrahedral symmetry $g_0(A)$ = 15, $g_0(E)$ = 12, and
$g_0(T)$ = 54. In this case, if the three species remain in
the proportions of the equilibrium mixture,

$$S(\text{stat}) - S(\text{spec}) = R \ln 81 = 4 \cdot 39 R.$$

It will be seen from Table 9.6 that, for CD_4 and CH_4,
S(spec) - S(cal) is zero within experimental error. If the
anomaly reported by Colwell *et al*. were to be brought into
the estimation of S(cal), S(spec) - S(cal) would be negative
($-2 \cdot 4$ J K^{-1} mol^{-1}), implying that a part of the nuclear spin
entropy is lost on cooling the crystals through the region
of the anomaly. However, $2 \cdot 4$ J K^{-1} mol^{-1} is so much less
than $R \ln 16$ (=$23 \cdot 0$ J K^{-1} mol^{-1}), the entropy which should be
lost for total conversion between spin isomers, that it is
clear that in the experiments of Colwell *et al*. the conver-

TABLE 9.6

Molar entropies of gaseous methane and deuterated methanes. The values refer to the temperature T and gaseous pressure p given in the table. S(cal) is the value calculated from calorimetric data, ignoring the possible thermal anomaly at ~8K for CH_4, and the low-temperature Schottky anomalies for the partially deuterated methanes. S(spec) is the calculated entropy disregarding the consequences of nuclear spin[a]

Compound	T/K	p/mmHg	S(spec) J K^{-1} mol^{-1}	S(cal) J K^{-1} mol^{-1}	S(spec)-S(cal) J K^{-1} mol^{-1}
CH_4	298·15	760	186·25	186·35	-0·1 ± 0·4
CH_3D	90·41	84·5	179·2	167·3	11·9 ± 0·4
CH_2D_2	90·17	82·0	185·6	170·9	14·7 ± 0·4
CHD_3	89·96	80·2	185·0	173·5	11·5 ± 0·4
CD_4	97·82	208·8	170·9	171·0	-0·1 ± 0·4

a. $R \ln 4 = 11·53$, $R \ln 6 = 14·90$ J K^{-1} mol^{-1}. References as for Table 9.5, and also Clusius, Popp, and Frank (1937), Clusius and Popp (1940).

sion was very far from complete.

For CH_3D and CD_3H, the values of $S(\text{spec}) - S(\text{cal})$ are
very close to $R \ln 4$, and the value for CH_2D_2 to $R \ln 6$.
Since the first two molecules can each have four distinguishable orientations for any one orientation of the tetrahedron,
while the CH_2D_2 molecule has six, the values of $S(\text{spec}) -$
$S(\text{cal})$ were taken to be residual entropies which at first
were naturally interpreted in terms of a random distribution among orientations rendered distinguishable by the
presence of the two isotopes. However, on making heat capacity measurements on the partially deuterated methanes down
to $2\cdot5$ K, Colwell, Gill, and Morrison (1965) found that C_p begins to increase below about 5 K, and extension of these measurements to $0\cdot3$ K by Colwell (1969) disclosed the essentially
Schottky-type anomalies shown in Fig.9.24. We may here re-

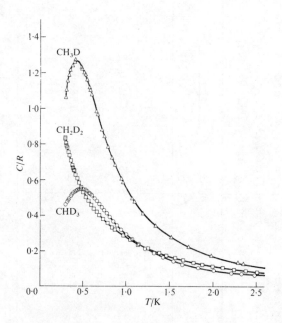

Fig.9.24. Heat capacities of CH_3D, CH_2D_2, and CHD_3 at low temperatures
(Colwell 1969).

call an important difference between hydrogen and deuterium,
as revealed by the rate of the spontaneous *ortho-para* inter-

conversion in H_2 as compared with the rate of the *para-ortho*
conversion in D_2, namely that the interaction between proton
spins is much stronger than that between deuteron spins. It
is therefore significant that between 0·3 K and 4 K, the
sample of CH_3D showed a pronounced thermal relaxation effect,
and that of CH_2D_2 a similar but smaller effect, while nothing
of the kind was observed with the sample of CHD_3 (Colwell
1969). (The effect manifested itself as an exponential decrease of temperature after the energy input of a heat capacity measurement, superimposed on the normal superheating of
the vessel containing the sample. The relaxation time was
of the order of one minute). For CH_3D, Colwell estimated
that the entropy lost on cooling from 4 K to 0·3 K, over and
above the small lattice contribution, is $1·624R$. This is
appreciably larger than $S(\text{spec})-S(\text{cal}) \approx R\ln 4$, $\approx 1·386R$, and
implies that for CH_3D there is some entropy loss due to
conversion between spin species. The thermal behaviour of
CH_3D below 10 K has been further examined particularly carefully by Morrison and Norton (1972), using a sample of exceptionally high isotopic purity (99·8 per cent), and with
less than 10 p.p.m. of other impurities. This study established that when solid CH_3D is cooled to helium temperatures,
there is a slow release of energy which is an intrinsic property, not to be attributed to the presence of impurities
or to the delayed release of energy from one of the λ-transi-
tions. This release of energy was ascribed to the spontaneous conversion of the nuclear spin species E into the
species A, which would be the only form present in the equilibrium crystal at 0 K. In a later experiment, in which the
sample was kept below 4 K for no less than three months, the
entropy lost in the Schottky anomaly was assessed at $1·80 R$
(Jones, Morrison,and Richards 1975). While this is somewhat
larger than the estimate resulting from Colwell's work it is
still about 14 per cent less than the value to be expected
for complete orientational ordering of the molecules· combined with total conversion of the spin isomers.

    Based on a theory due to Nagamiya (1951), attempts have
been made to construct energy-level schemes for the partially deuterated crystalline methanes which account for the

Schottky anomalies and for the entropy effects (Colwell, Gill, and Morrison 1965, Hopkins, Kasper, and Pitzer 1967, Colwell 1969). The energies of these levels and their degeneracies depend on the symmetry of the molecule and on that of the crystalline field. In spite of the restriction on rotation, molecular reorientation can still take place by tunnelling through the barrier, with consequential splitting of the energy levels to an extent which will be greater for proton tunnelling than for deuteron tunnelling and which will depend on the height of the potential barrier. The problem of finding a set of energy levels in any particular case which satisfactorily accounts for all the relevant facts is a difficult and challenging one, and it cannot yet be said to have been solved. Among the factors which contribute to its complexity are the uncertainty introduced by the possibility of nuclear spin conversion, ignorance of the symmetry of the crystalline field, the possibility that an anomaly may not be truly Schottky-like but (to a small extent at least) cooperative, and finally that in any case more than one set of levels can be made to fit a given particular anomaly. Special attention has been paid, both theoretically and experimentally, to CH_4-II, in which three-quarters of the molecules have site symmetry D_{2d} and one quarter site symmetry O_h. Two sets of energy levels must therefore be considered, schemes for which were proposed by Kataoka, Okada, and Yamamoto (1973). Experimental information on energy level separations has been obtained from NMR experiments, which give information on the tunnelling splittings (Glättli, Sentz, and Eisenkremer 1972), from neutron scattering (Kapulla and Gläser 1970, Press and Kollmar 1975), and from an analysis of low-temperature heat capacity data (Vogt and Pitzer 1975). From these investigations it appears that in the lowest group of A, T, and E levels for the molecules in sites of symmetry D_{2d}, the levels of the T and E molecules lie respectively 1·7 K - 1·9 K and 2·0 K - 2·9 K above the A level.

9.8. SILANES, GERMANES, AND STANNANES

These hydrides have been less thoroughly studied than the methanes, but on the evidence available they present some interesting features which it would be worth exploring further. It will be seen from Table 9.7 that whereas with SiH_4 and $SiHD_3$ each has only one transition, GeH_4 has two, quite close together. All four transitions in the three

TABLE 9.7

Thermal information on silanes, germanes, and stannanes

Compound IV	T_t/K → III	$T_t/K,\Delta S_t/R$ → II	$T_t/K,\Delta S_t/R$ → I	$T_m/K,\Delta S_m/R$ → Liq.
SiH_4	-	-	63·75(λ)	88·5,0·90[a,b]
$SiHD_3$	-	-	66·05(λ)	86·8, 0·85[b]
SiD_4	-	38(λ)[c]	67[d]	-
GeH_4	62·9(λ)	73·2(λ),0·35	76·5(λ),0·56	107·26,0·937[e]
GeD_4	67·7(λ)	75·5(?F)	77·8(?F)[f]	-
SnH_4	-	-	99·7(?F)[g]	-
SnD_4	-	-	102·6(?F)	122·5[h]

a. Clusius (1933)(calorimetric).
b. Klein, Morrison, and Weir (1969) (calorimetric).
c. Wilde and Srinivasan (1975) (infrared).
d. Lähteenmäki, Niemelä, and Pyykkö (1967) (NMR, deuteron T_1).
e. Clusius and Faber (1941, 1942) (calorimetric).
f. Hovi, Lähteenmäki, and Tuulensuu (1969) (NMR, deuteron T_1).
g. Niemelä, Hirvonen, and Lähteenmäki (1972) (NMR, proton T_1).
h. Niemelä and Mäkelä (1973) (NMR, deuteron T_1).

compounds are λ-type. In addition, GeH_4 shows a heat capacity anomaly in phase III with a peak at 62·9 K. There appear to be sufficiently significant changes in the infrared and Raman spectra of GeH_4 on cooling form III below this peak to regard the crystal so produced as a different modification IV (Nguyen Dinh The, Gagnon, Belzile, and Cabana 1974).

As for SiD_4, Wilde and Srinivasan (1975) concluded from an
infrared study of $SiHD_3$ in SiD_4 that fully deuterated silane
has a second λ-type transition with $T_\lambda \approx 38$ K. Since no corresponding transition has been reported for SiH_4, it would
be useful to investigate SiD_4 calorimetrically. As the entropies of melting of SiH_4-I and GeH_4-I are both quite low
they would appear to qualify for description as plastic crystals and to be disordered, and indeed studies of the infrared and Raman spectra were considered to confirm this expectation [Fournier, Savoie, Nguyen Dinh The, Belzile, and
Cabana (SiH_4) 1972, Nguyen Dinh The *et al*. 1974]. At the
same time, both SiH_4-I and GeH_4-I are birefringent and so cannot have the cubic structures of CD_4-I or CD_4-II. In fact,
from an X-ray powder examination, Sears and Morrison (1975)
concluded that both SiH_4-I and -II have body-centred tetragonal lattices, and moreover they considered that in I as
well as in II there is 'significant ordering of the molecular orientations'. Accordingly, there is an apparent
inconsistency with regard to disorder in SiH_4-I which needs
to be resolved. Since with the methanes structures with
two different kinds of site for the molecules are encountered,
it is worth noting that the spectroscopic study of germane
revealed that in all four forms the molecules occupy only one
set of equivalent sites.

Disregarding the consequences of nuclear spin, SiH_4 and
GeH_4 have no residual entropy while $SiHD_3$, like CHD_3, retains
$R \ln 4$. Relevant changes on passing from methane to silane are
a probable increase in octupole moment, an increase in nearest-
neighbour separation in the lattice, and a decrease in the
separation of the rotational energy levels due to an increase
in the moment of inertia. On balance we might expect any
Schottky anomalies in $SiHD_3$, leading to the removal of residual entropy, to take place at a lower temperature than in
the corresponding methane. As yet, heat capacity measurements
at sufficiently low temperatures have not been made.

From the temperatures recorded in Table 9.7, it will be
seen that the effect of replacing hydrogen by deuterium conforms to the usual pattern of a drop in melting-point combined with a rise in transition temperatures.

Activation energies for reorientation (E_R) and for diffusion (E_D) derived by Finnish investigators from their relaxation time measurements indicate considerable freedom of motion of these two kinds. Thus E_R in kJ mol^{-1} is 11 in SnD_4-II, 12 in SnH_4-II, and between 5 and 6 in GeH_4-II, -III and -IV. In phase I, E_R is as low as 2 kJ mol^{-1} in SnD_4 and 1·2 kJ mol^{-1} in GeH_4. E_D is 12·5 kJ mol^{-1} in SnH_4-I (see Table 9.7 for references).

REFERENCES

Ahlers, G. and Orttung, W.H. (1964). *Phys.Rev.* **133**,A 1642.

Albert, S. and Ripmeester, J.A. (1972). *J.chem.Phys.* **57**, 3953.

Aleksandrovskii, A.N., Kuchnev, V.I., Manzhelii, V.G., and Tolkachev, A.M. (1976). *Phys.St.Solidi* **B73**, K111.

Alexander, S. and Lerner-Naor, M. (1972). *Can.J.Phys.* **50**, 1568.

Alikhanov, R.A. (1963). *J.exptl.theoret.Phys. (U.S.S.R)* **45**, 812 (*Sov.Phys.JETP* 1964, **18**, 556).

———— (1964). *J.Phys.(Paris)* **25**, 449.

———— (1967). *JETP Lett.* **5**, 349.

Allin, E.J., Feldman, T., and Welsh, H.L. (1956). *J.chem. Phys.* **24**, 1116.

———— Gush, H.P., Hare, W.F.J., and Welsh, H.L. (1958). *Nuovo Cim.Suppl.* **9**, 77.

Alpert, N.L. (1949). *Phys.Rev.* **75**, 398.

Amstutz, L.I., Thompson, J.R., and Meyer, H. (1968). *Phys. Rev.Lett.* **21**, 1175.

Anderson, A., Gebbie, H.A., and Walmsley, S.H. (1964). *Molec. Phys.* **7**, 401.

———— and Savoie, R. (1965). *J.chem.Phys.* **43**, 3468.

———— and Walmsley, S.H. (1964). *Molec.Phys.* **7**, 583.

Angwin, M.J. and Wasserman, J. (1966). *J.chem.Phys.* **44**, 417.

Arnold, G.M. and Heastie, R. (1967). *Chem.Phys.Lett.* **1**, 51.

Aston, J.G. (1961). *Pure appl.Chem.* **2**, 231.

Atake, T. and Chihara, H. (1974). *Bull.chem.Soc.Japan* **47**, 2126.

———— Suga, H., and Chihara, H. (1976). *Chem.Lett.* 567.

Ballik, E.A., Gannon, D.J., and Morrison, J.A. (1972). *J. chem.Phys.* 57, 1793.

Barrett, C.S. and Meyer, L. (1965). (a) *J.chem.Phys.* 42, 107; (b) 43, 3502.

―――   ―――   and Wasserman, J. (1967). (a) *J. chem.Phys.* 47, 592; (b) 47, 740; (c) *Phys.Rev.* 163, 851.

Bartholomé, E., Drikos, G., and Eucken, A. (1938). *Z.phys. Chem.* B39, 371.

Bell, G.M. and Fairbairn, W.M. (1964). *Molec.Phys.* 8, 497.

Berlinsky, A.J. and Harris, A.B. (1970). *Phys.Rev.* A1, 878.

Bhatnagar, S.S., Allin, E.J., and Welsh, H.L. (1962). *Can. J.Phys.* 40, 9.

Billingsley, F.P. and Krauss, M. (1974). *J.chem.Phys.* 60, 2767.

Blanchard, J., Brunel, L.-C., and Peyron, M. (1971). *C.r. hebd.Séanc.Acad.Sci.,Paris* B273, 19.

Bloom, M. and Morrison, J.A. (1973).'Surface and defect properties of solids', *Specialist periodical Rept.chem.Soc.* 2, 140.

Blue, R.W. and Giauque, W.F. (1935). *J.Am.chem.Soc.* 57, 991.

Boden, N. and Folland, R. (1975). *Chem.Phys.Lett.* 32, 127.

Bol'shutkin, D.N., Gasan, V.M., and Prokhvatilov, A.I. (1971). *Zh.strukt.Khim.* 12, 734 (*J.struct.Chem.* 12, 670).

―――   ―――   ―――   and Yantsevich, L.D. (1971). *Zh.strukt.Khim.* 12, 1115 (*J.struct.Chem.* 12, 1036).

Bolz, L.H., Boyd, M.E., Mauer, F.A., and Peiser, H.S. (1959). *Acta crystallogr.* 12, 247.

Borovic-Romanov, A.S., Orlova, M.P., and Strelkov, P.G. (1954). *Dokl.Akad.Nauk SSSR* 99, 699.

Bostanjoglo, O. and Kleinschmidt, R. (1967). *J.chem.Phys.* 46, 2004.

Boutin, H. and Safford, G.J. (1964). *Proc.Symposium on Inelastic Scattering of Neutrons, Bombay,* II, 393.

Brookeman, J.R. and Scott, T.A. (1972). *Acta crystallogr.* B28, 983.

Brown, N.L. and Cole, R.H. (1953). *J.chem.Phys.* 21, 1920.

Brunel, L.-C. and Peyron, M. (1967). *C.R.hebd.Séanc.Acad.Sci., Paris,* C264, 821.

Burford, J.C. and Graham, G.M. (1969). *Can.J.Phys.* 47, 23.

Cahill, J.E. and Leroi, G.E. (1969). *J.chem.Phys.* 51, 97.

Cairns, B.R. and Pimentel, G.C. (1965). *J.chem.Phys.* <u>43</u>,
    3432.

Carter, G.F. and Templeton, D.H. (1953). *Acta crystallogr.* <u>6</u>,
    805.

Chapados, C. and Cabana, A. (1970). *Chem.Phys.Lett.* <u>7</u>, 191.
───────   ───────   (1972). *Can.J.Chem.* <u>50</u>, 3521.

Chihara, H. and Inaba, A. (1976). (a) *J.phys.Soc.Japan* <u>40</u>,
    597; (b) *J.chem.Thermodynamics* <u>8</u>, 915; (c) <u>8</u>, 935.

Cichanowski, S.W. and Cole, R.H. (1973). *J.chem.Phys.* <u>59</u>,
    2420.

Clayton, J.O. and Giauque, W.F. (1932). *J.Am.chem.Soc.* <u>54</u>,
    2610.

Clouter, M. and Gush, H.P. (1965). *Phys.Rev.Lett.* <u>15</u>, 200.

Clusius, K. (1933). *Z.phys.Chem.* <u>B23</u>, 213.
───────   (1934). *Z.Elektrochem.* <u>40</u>, 98.
───────   (1946). *Z.Naturforsch.* <u>1</u>, 142.
───────   and Faber, G. (1941). *Naturwiss.* <u>29</u>, 468.
───────   ───────   (1942). *Z.phys.Chem.* <u>B51</u>, 352.
───────   and Popp, L. (1940). *Z.phys.Chem.* <u>B46</u>, 63.
───────   ───────   and Frank, A. (1937). *Physica* <u>4</u>,
    1105.
───────   and Weigand, K. (1938). *Z.Elektrochem.* <u>44</u>, 674.
───────   and Wolf, G. (1947). *Z.Naturforsch.* <u>2a</u>, 495.

Code, R.F. and Higinbotham, J. (1976). *Can.J.Phys.* <u>54</u>, 1248.

Cole, R.H. and Havriliak, S. (1957). *Disc.Faraday Soc.* No.23,
    Molecular mechanism of rate processes in solids, p.31.

Collins, M.F. (1966). *Proc.phys.Soc.* <u>89</u>, 415.

Colwell, J.H. (1969). *J.chem.Phys.* <u>51</u>, 3820.
───────   Gill, E.K., and Morrison, J.A. (1962). *J.chem.
    Phys.* <u>36</u>, 2223.
                                              (1963). *J.chem.
───────   ───────   ───────
    Phys.* <u>39</u>, 635.
                                              (1965). *J.chem.
───────   ───────   ───────
    Phys.* <u>42</u>, 3144.

Cook, G.A., Dwyer, R.F., Berwaldt, O.E., and Nevins, H.E.
    (1965). *J.chem.Phys.* <u>43</u>, 1313.

Cox, D.E., Samuelsen, E.J., and Beckurts, K.H. (1973).
    Phys.Rev. <u>B7</u>, 3102.

Crawford, R.K., Daniels, W.B., and Cheng, V.M. (1975). *Phys.
    Rev.* <u>A12</u>, 1690.

Cunningham, C.M., Chapin, D.S., and Johnston, H.L. (1958).
      J.Am.chem.Soc. 80, 2382.

Curzon, A.E. and Pawlowicz, A.T. (1965). *Proc.phys.Soc.* 85,
      375.

Danielian, A. (1965). *Phys.Rev.* 138, A282.

Darmon, I. and Brot, C. (1967). *Mol.Crystallogr.* 2, 301.

Depatie, D.A. and Mills, R.L. (1968). *Rev.sci.Instr.* 39,
      105.

Dickson, S.A. and Meyer, H. (1965). *Phys.Rev.* 138, A1293.

Dinerman, C.E. and Ewing, G.E. (1971). *J.chem.Phys.* 54, 3660.

Dulmage, W.J., Meyers, E.A., and Lipscomb, W.N. (1953). *Acta
      crystallogr.* 6, 760.

Dunmore, P.V. (1976). *J.low Temp.Phys.* 24, 397.

Ebner, C. and Sung, C.C. (1972). *Phys.Rev.* A5, 2625.

English, C.A. and Venables, J.A. (1974). *Proc.R.Soc.* A340,
      57.

Englman, R. and Friedman, Z. (1973). *Phys.Rev.Lett.* 31, 816.

Eucken, A. and Schröder, E. (1938). *Z.phys.Chem.* B41, 307.

Ewing, G.E. (1962). *J.chem.Phys.* 37, 2250.

―――   (1964). *J.chem.Phys.* 40, 179.

―――   and Pimentel, G.C. (1961). *J.chem.Phys.* 35, 925.

Felsteiner, J. (1965). *Phys.Rev.Lett.* 15, 1025.

Fournier, R.P., Savoie, R., Nguyen Dinh The, Belzile, R., and
      Cabana, A. (1972). *Can.J.Chem.* 50, 35.

Fowler, R.H. (1935). *Proc.R.Soc.* A149, 1; A151, 1.

Francia, M.D. and Nixon, E.R. (1973). *J.chem.Phys.* 58, 1061.

Frenkel, J. (1935). *Acta physicochimica U.R.S.S.* 3, 23.

―――   (1946). Kinetic theory of liquids, Chap.II.
      Oxford University Press.

Friedrich, H.B. and Person, W.B. (1963). *J.chem.Phys.* 39, 811.

Gannon, D.J. and Morrison, J.A. (1973). *Can.J.Phys.* 51, 1590.

Genin, D.J., O'Reilly, D.E., Peterson, E.M., and Tsang, T.
      (1968). *J.chem.Phys.* 48, 4525.

Giauque, W.F. (1930). *J.Am.chem.Soc.* 52, 4816.

―――   and Blue, R.W. (1936). *J.Am.chem.Soc.* 58, 831.

―――   and Clayton, J.O. (1933). *J.Am.chem.Soc.* 55,
      4875.

―――   and Johnston, H.L. (1928). *J.Am.chem.Soc.* 50,
      3221.

―――   ―――   (1929). *J.Am.chem.Soc.* 51, 2300

Giauque, W.F. and Jones, W.M. (1948). *J.Am.chem.Soc.* 70, 120.

———   and Ott, J.B. (1960). *J.Am.chem.Soc.*, 82, 2689.

———   and Stephenson, C.C. (1938). *J.Am.chem.Soc.*
60, 1389.

———   and Wiebe, R. (1928). (a) *J.Am.chem.Soc.* 50,
101; (b) 50, 2193.

———   ———   (1929). *J.Am.chem.Soc.* 51, 1441.

Gill, E.K. and Morrison, J.A. (1966). *J.chem.Phys.* 45, 1585.

Gissler, W. and Stiller, H. (1965). *Naturwiss.* 52, 512.

Glättli, H., Sentz, A., and Eisenkremer, M. (1972). *Phys.
Rev.Lett.* 28, 871.

Goodings, D.A. and Henkelman, M. (1971). *Can.J.Phys.* 49,
2898.

Greer, S.C. and Meyer, L. (1969). *Z.angew.Phys.* 27, 198.

Grenier, G. and White, D. (1964). *J.chem.Phys.* 40, 3015.

Groenewegen, P.P.M. and Cole, R.H. (1967). *J.chem.Phys.*
46, 1069.

Halperin, W.P., Archie, C.N., Rasmussen, F.B., Buhrman, R.A.,
and Richardson, R.C. (1974). *Phys.Rev.Lett.* 32, 927.

Hamilton, W.C. and Petrie, M. (1961). *J.phys.Chem.* 65, 1453.

Harada, J. and Kitamura, N. (1964). *J.phys.Soc.Japan* 19,
328.

Hardy, W.N., Silvera, I.F., and McTague, J.P. (1975). *Phys.
Rev.* B12, 753.

Harker, Y.D. and Brugger, R.M. (1965). *J.chem.Phys.* 42, 275.

———   ———   (1967). *J.chem.Phys.* 46, 2201.

Harris, A.B. (1971). *J.appl.Phys.* 42, 1574.

Hashimoto, Masao, Hashimoto, Michiko, and Isobe, T. (1971).
Bull.chem.Soc.Japan, 44, 649.

Hatton, J. and Rollin, B.V. (1949). *Proc.R.Soc.* A199, 222.

Havriliak, S., Swenson, R.W., and Cole, R.H. (1955). *J.chem.
Phys.* 23, 134.

Heberlein, D.C. and Adams, E.D. (1970). *J.low Temp.Phys.* 3,
115.

Herczeg, J. and Stoner, R.E. (1971). *J.chem.Phys.* 54, 2284.

Hiebert, G.L. and Hornig, D.F. (1957). *J.chem.Phys.* 27, 1216.

Hill, R.W. and Ricketson, B.W.A. (1954). *Phil.Mag.* 45, 277.

Hopkins, H.P., Kasper, J.V.V., and Pitzer, K.S. (1967). *J.
chem.Phys.* 46, 218.

Hörl, E.M. (1962). *Acta crystallogr.* <u>15</u>, 845.

Hornig, D.F. and Osberg, W.E. (1955). *J.chem.Phys.* <u>23</u>, 662.

Hoshino, S., Shimaoka, K., and Niimura, N. (1967). *Phys.Rev. Lett.* <u>19</u>, 1286.

Hovi, V., Lähteenmäki, U., and Tuulensuu, R. (1969). *Phys. Lett.* <u>29A</u>, 520.

Hu, J.-H., White, D., and Johnston, H.L. (1953). *J.Am.chem. Soc.* <u>75</u>, 5642.

Ishimoto, H., Nagamine, K., Kimura, Y., and Kumagai, H. (1974). *J.phys.Soc.Japan* <u>37</u>, 956.

Ito, M. (1970). *Chem.Phys.Lett.* <u>7</u>, 439.

———   Suzuki, M., and Yokoyama, T. (1969). *J.chem.Phys.* <u>50</u>, 2949.

Jaffray, J. (1948). *Annls. Chim.Phys.* <u>3</u>, 5.

James, H.M. (1968). *Phys.Rev.* <u>167</u>, 862.

———   and Keenan, T.A. (1959). *J.chem.Phys.* <u>31</u>, 12.

———   and Raich, J.C. (1967).*Phys.Rev.* <u>162</u>, 649.

Jansen, L., Michels, A., and Lupton, J.M. (1954). *Physica* <u>20</u>, 1235.

Jarvis, J.F., Meyer, H., and Ramm, D. (1969). *Phys.Rev.* <u>178</u>, 1461.

———   Ramm, D. and Meyer, H. (1967). *Phys.Rev.Lett.* <u>18</u>, 119.

Johnston, H.L. and Giauque, W.F. (1929). *J.Am.chem.Soc.* <u>51</u>, 3194.

Johnston, N.T. and Collins, M.F. (1972). *J.chem.Phys.* <u>57</u>, 5007.

Jones, E.P., Morrison, J.A., and Richards, E.L. (1975). *Can. J.Phys.* <u>53</u>, 2546.

Jordan, T.H., Smith, H.W., Streib, W.E., and Lipscomb, W.N. (1964). *J.chem.Phys.* <u>41</u>, 756.

———   Streib, W.E., and Lipscomb, W.N. (1964). *J. chem.Phys.* <u>41</u>, 760.

———   ———   Smith, H.W., and Lipscomb, W.N. (1964). *Acta crystallogr.* <u>17</u>, 777.

Justi, E. and Nitka, H. (1936). *Physik.Z.* <u>37</u>, 435.

Kadaba, P.K. and O'Reilly, D.E. (1970). *J.chem.Phys.* <u>52</u>, 2403.

Kanda, E., Haseda, T., and Otsubo, A. (1954). *Physica* <u>20</u>, 131.

Kapulla, H. and Gläser, W. (1970). *Phys.Lett.* <u>31A</u>, 158.

Karl, G. and Poll, J.D. (1967). *J.chem.Phys.* 46, 2944.

Kataoka, Y., Okada, K., and Yamamoto, T. (1973). *Chem.Phys. Lett.* 19, 365.

Keesom, W.H., De Smedt, J., and Mooy, H.H. (1930). *Communs. K.Onnes Lab.Leiden* 19, 209d.

Kemp. J.D. and Giauque, W.F. (1937). *J.Am.chem.Soc.* 59, 79.

Kiefte, H. and Clouter, M.J. (1975). *J.chem.Phys.* 62, 4780.

Kitaigorodskii, A.I. and Mirskaya, K.V. (1965). *Kristallo-grafiya* 10, 162 (*Soviet Phys.Cryst.* 10, 121).

Kitamura, N. and Harada, J. (1962). *J.phys.Soc.Japan* 17, Suppl. B-II, 245.

Klein, M.L., Morrison, J.A., and Weir, R.D. (1969). *Disc. Faraday Soc.*, No.48, 93.

Koehler, J.K. and Giauque, W.F. (1958). *J.Am.chem.Soc.* 80, 2659.

Kogan, V.S., Bulatov, A.S., and Yakimenko, L.F. (1964). *Soviet Phys.JETP* 19, 107.

Kohin, B.C. (1960). *J.chem.Phys.* 33, 882.

Kosaly, G. and Solt, G. (1966). *Physica* 32, 1571.

Koski, H.K. and Sándor, E. (1975). *Acta crystallogr.* B31, 350; *Chem.Phys.Lett.* 30, 501.

Kostryukov, V.N., Samorukov, O.P., and Strelkov, P.G. (1958). *Zh.fiz.Khim.* 32, 1354.

Kovalenko, S.I., Indan, E.I., Khudotyoplaya, A.A., and Krupskii, I.N. (1973). *Phys.St.Solidi* A20, 629.

Kruis, A. and Clusius, K. (1937). *Z.phys.Chem.* B38, 156; *Physik.Z.* 38, 510.

Krupskii, I.N., Gasan, V.M., and Prokhvatilov, A.I. (1974). *Solid St.Communs.* 15, 803.

————   Prokhvatilov, A.I., and Erenburg, A.I. (1975). *Fiz.niz.Temp.* 1, 359.

————   ————   ————   and Yantsevich, L.D. (1973). *Phys.St.Solidi* A19, 519.

Lähteenmäki, U., Niemelä, L., and Pyykkö, P. (1967). *Phys. Lett.* 25A, 460.

LaPlaca, S.J. and Hamilton, W.C. (1972). *Acta crystallogr.* B28, 984.

Lee, R.J. and Raich, J.C. (1971). *Phys.Rev.Lett.* 27, 1137.

Lipscomb, W.N. (1971). *J.chem.Phys.* 54, 3659.

Lipscomb, W.N. (1974). *J.chem.Phys.* 60, 5138.

————   Wang, F.E., May, W.R., and Lippert, E.L. (1961).
    Acta crystallogr. 14, 1100.

Loehlin, J.H., Mennitt, P.G., and Waugh, J.S. (1966). *J.chem.
    Phys.* 44, 3912.

Look, D.C., Lowe, I.J., and Northby, J.A. (1966). *J.chem.
    Phys.* 44, 3441.

Luttinger, J.M. and Tisza, L. (1946). *Phys.Rev.* 70, 954.

Manzhelii, V.G., Tarasenko, L.M., Bondarenko, A.I., and
    Gavrilko, V.G. (1975). *Soviet Phys.Solid St.* 17, 1495.

————   Udovidchenko, B.G., and Esel'son, V.B. (1973).
    JETP Letters 18, 16 (Zh.ETF Pis.Red. 18, 30).

Marram, E.P. and Ragle, J.L. (1964). *J.chem.Phys.* 41, 3546.

McCullough, J.P. (1961). *Pure appl.Chem.* 2, 221.

Melhuish, M.W. and Scott, R.L. (1964). *J.phys.Chem.* 68, 2301.

Meyer, H., Weinhaus, F. Maraviglia, B., and Mills, R.L. (1972).
    Phys.Rev. B6, 1112.

Meyer, L. (1969). *Adv.chem.Phys.* 16, 343.

————   Barrett, C.S., and Greer, S.C. (1968). *J.chem.Phys
    .* 49, 1902.

Michils, A. (1948). *Bull.Soc.chim.Belg.* 57, 575.

Mills, R.L. and Schuch, A.F. (1965). *Phys.Rev.Lett.* 15, 722.

————   , Yarnell, J.L. and Schuch, A.F. (1974). *Low
    Temperature Physics* - LT 13, vol.2, 203. Ed. K.D.Timmer-
    haus, W.J.O'Sullivan and E.F.Hammel. Plenum Press, New
    York.

Miyagi, H. and Nakamura, T. (1967).*Progr.theoret.Phys.* 37,
    641.

Morrison, J.A. and Norton, P.R. (1972). *J.chem.Phys.* 56, 1457.

Mucker, K.F., Talhouk, S., Harris, P.M., White, D., and
    Erickson, R.A. (1965). *Phys.Rev.Lett.* 15, 586.

Nagai, O. and Nakamura, T. (1960).*Progr.theoret.Phys.* 24, 432.

Nagamiya, T. (1951). *Progr.theoret.Phys.* 6, 702.

Nakamura, T. (1955). *Progr.theoret.Phys.* 14, 135.

————   and Miyagi, H. (1971). *J.chem.Phys.* 54, 5276.

Natta, G. (1931).*Nature,Lond.* 127, 129.

————   (1933). *Gazz.chim.ital.* 63, 425.

————   and Casazza, E. (1930). *Gazz.chim.ital.* 60, 851.

Nguyen Dinh The, Gagnon, J.-M., Belzile, R., and Cabana, A.
    (1974). *Can.J.Chem.* 52, 327.

Niemelä, L., Hirvonen, M. and Lähteenmäki, U. (1972). *Phys. Lett.* 39A, 323.

————   and Mäkelä, J. (1973). *Phys.Lett.* 43A, 343.

Niimura, N., Shimaoka, K., Motegi, H., and Hoshino, S. (1972). *J.phys.Soc.Japan* 32, 1019.

Nishiyama, K. and Yamamoto, T. (1973). *J.chem.Phys.* 58, 1001.

Norris, M.O., Strange, J.H., Powles, J.G., Rhodes, M., Marsden, K., and Krynicki, K. (1968). (a) *J.Phys.* C1, 445; (b) C1, 422.

Okuma, H., Nakamura, N., and Chihara, H. (1968). *J.phys.Soc. Japan* 24, 452.

O'Reilly, D.E. (1970). *J.chem.Phys.* 52, 2396.

Orttung, W.H. (1962). *J.chem.Phys.* 36, 652.

Oyarzun, R. and Van Kranendonk, J. (1971). *Phys.Rev.Lett.* 26, 646.

Pace, E.L. and Reno, M.A. (1968). *J.chem.Phys.* 48, 1231.

Pauling, L. (1930). *Phys.Rev.* 36, 430.

Perdok, W.G. and Terpstra, P. (1943). *Recl.Trav.chim.Pays-Bas* 62, 687.

Pople, J.A. and Karasz, F.E. (1961). *(J.)Phys.Chem.Solids* 18, 28.

Powles, J.G. and Rhodes, M. (1967). *Phys.Lett.* 24A, 523.

Press, W. (1972). *J.chem.Phys.* 56, 2597.

Press, W., Dorner, B., and Will, G. (1970). *Phys.Lett.* 31A, 253.

Press, W. and Kollmar, A. (1975). *Solid St.Communs.* 17, 405.

Raich, J.C. and Mills, R.L. (1971). *J.chem.Phys.* 55, 1811.

Ramm, D., Meyer, H., and Mills, R.L. (1970). *Phys.Rev.* B1, 2763.

Reding, F.P. and Hornig, D.F. (1957). *J.chem.Phys.* 27, 1024.

Reif, R. and Purcell, E.M. (1953). *Phys.Rev.* 91, 631.

Roberts, R.J., and Daunt, J.G. (1970). *Phys.Lett.* 33A, 353.

————   ————   (1972). *J.low Temp.Phys.* 6, 97.

————   ————   (1974). *J.low Temp.Phys.* 16, 405.

————   , Rojas, E. and Daunt, J.G. (1976). *J.low Temp. Phys.* 24, 265.

Rosenshein, J.S. and Whitney, W.M. (1964). *Proc.9th Int. Conf.Low-Temp.Phys.* B, 1114.

El Saffar, Z.M. and Schultz, P. (1972). *J.chem.Phys.* 56, 2524.

Sándor, E. and Farrow, R.F.C. (1967). (a) *Nature,Lond.* 213, 171; (b) 215, 1265.

———   ———   (1969). *Disc.Faraday Soc.* No.48, *Motions in molecular Crystals*,p.78.

———   and Johnson, M.W. (1968). *Nature,Lond.* 217, 541.

———   and Ogunade, S.O. (1969). *Nature,Lond.* 224, 905.

Savitsky, G.B. and Hornig, D.F. (1962). *J.chem.Phys.* 36, 2634.

Savoie, R. and Anderson, A. (1966). *J.chem.Phys.* 44, 548.

———   and Fournier, R.P. (1970). *Chem.Phys.Lett.* 7, 1.

Schallamach, A. (1939). *Proc.R.Soc.* A171, 569.

Scheie, C.E., Peterson, E.M., and O'Reilly, D.E. (1973). *J. chem.Phys.* 59, 2758.

Schuch, A.F. and Mills, R.L. (1966). *Phys.Rev.Lett.* 16, 616.

———   ———   (1970). *J.chem.Phys.* 52, 6000.

———   ———   and Depatie, D.A. (1968). *Phys.Rev.* 165, 1032.

Schwartz, Y.A., Ron, A., and Kimel, S. (1969). *J.chem.Phys.* 51, 1666.

———   ———   ———   (1971). *J.chem.Phys.* 54, 99.

Scott, T.A. (1962). *J.chem.Phys.* 36, 1459.

Sears, W.M. and Morrison, J.A. (1975). *J.chem.Phys.* 62, 2736.

Shimaoka, K., Niimura, N., Motegi, H., and Hoshino, S. (1969). *J.phys.Soc.Japan* 27, 1078.

Simon, A. (1970). *Z.Naturforsch.* 25b, 1489.

———   (1971). *J.appl.Crystallogr.* 4, 138.

Simon, F., Mendelssohn, K., and Ruhemann, M. (1930). *Naturwiss.* 18, 34.

———   and von Simson, C. (1924). *Z.Phys.* 21, 168.

Sköld, K. (1968). *J.chem.Phys.* 49, 2443.

Slusarev, V.A., Freiman, Yu.A., Krupskii, I.N., and Bura-khovich, I.A. (1972). *Phys.St.Solidi* B54, 745.

Smith, D. (1971a). *Chem.Phys.Lett.* 11, 405.

———   (1971b). *Chem.Phys.Lett.* 10, 174.

———   (1974). *Chem.Phys.Lett.* 25, 268.

Smith, G.W. and Housley, R.M. (1960). *Phys.Rev.* 117, 732.

Smyth, C.P. and Hitchcock, C.S. (1933). *J.Am.chem.Soc.* 55,1830.

Smyth, C.P. and Hitchcock, C.S. (1934). *J.Am.chem.Soc.* <u>56</u>, 1084.

———————   and McNeight, S.A. (1936). *J.Am.chem.Soc.* <u>58</u>, 1723.

Sperandio, A. (1961). *Thesis*, University of Zürich, quoted by Colwell, Gill, and Morrison, (1963).

Staveley, L.A.K. (1961). *(J.)Phys.Chem.Solids* <u>18</u>, 46.

Stein,H., Stiller, H., and Stockmeyer, R. (1972). *J.chem. Phys.* <u>57</u>, 1726.

Stephenson, C.C. and Giauque, W.F. (1937). *J.chem.Phys.* <u>5</u>, 149.

Stevenson, R. (1957). (a) *J.chem.Phys.* <u>27</u>, 147; (b) <u>27</u>, 656; (c) <u>27</u>, 673.

Stewart, J.W. (1955). *Phys.Rev.* <u>97</u>, 578.

———————   (1959). *(J.)Phys.Chem.Solids* <u>12</u>, 122.

Stiller, H. and Hautecler, S. (1962). *Inelastic scattering of neutrons in solids and liquids, Proc. Symp. Chalk River, Canada* <u>2</u>, 281.

Stogryn, D.E. and Stogryn, A.P. (1966). *Molec.Phys.*<u>11</u>,371.

Streib, W.E., Jordan, T.H., and Lipscomb, W.N. (1962). *J. chem.Phys.* <u>37</u>, 2962.

Sugawara, T. and Kanda, E. (1952). *Sci.Rept.Res.Inst.Tohoku Univ.Ser.* <u>A4</u>, 607.

———————   , Masuda, Y., Kanda, T., and Kanda, E. (1955). *Sci.Rep.Res.Inst.Tohoku Univ.* <u>7</u>, 67.

Sunder, S. and McClung, R.E.D. (1974). *Can.J.Phys.* <u>52</u>, 2299.

Swenson, C.A. (1955). *J.chem.Phys.* <u>23</u>, 1963.

Swenson, R.W. and Cole, R.H. (1954). *J.chem.Phys.* <u>22</u>, 284.

Thiéry, M.M., Fabre, D., Jean-Louis, M., and Vu, H. (1973). *J.chem.Phys.* <u>59</u>, 4559.

Thomas, J.T., Alpert, N.L., and Torrey, H.C. (1950). *J.chem. Phys.* <u>18</u>, 1511.

Timmermanns, J. (1938). *J.Chim.phys.* <u>35</u>, 331.

Trapeznikowa, O.N. and Miljutin, G.A. (1939). *Nature,Lond.* <u>144</u>, 632.

Trappeniers, N.J., Gerritsma, C.J., and Oosting, P.H. (1965). *Physica* <u>31</u>, 202.

Tsang, T. and Shaw, E.L. (1971). *J.chem.Phys.* <u>55</u>, 2337.

Van Hecke, P. and Van Gerven, L. (1973). *Physica* <u>68</u>, 359.

Van Hecke, P., Grobet, P., and Van Gerven, L. (1972). *J.mag. Res.* <u>7</u>, 117.

Van Kranendonk, J. and Karl, G. (1968). *Rev.mod.Phys.* <u>40</u>, 531.

Vegard, L. (1930). (a) *Z.Phys.* <u>61</u>, 185; (b) *Nature,Lond.* <u>126</u>, 916.

———   (1934). *Z.Phys.* <u>88</u>, 235.

———   (1944). *Chem.Zent.* <u>44</u> (I), 342.

———   and Oserød, L.S. (1942). *Avh.Norske Vidensk.- Akad. Oslo. I.Mat.-Naturvidensk, Kl.* Nr. 7.

Venables, J.A. and English, C.A. (1974). *Acta crystallogr.* <u>B30</u>, 929.

Vogt, G.J. and Pitzer, K.S. (1975). *J.chem.Phys.* <u>63</u>, 3667.

Wachtel, E.J. (1972). *J.chem.Phys.* <u>57</u>, 5620.

Wang, C.H. and Fleury, P.A. (1970). *J.chem.Phys.* <u>53</u>, 2243.

———   and Wright, R.B. (1974). *Molec.Phys.* <u>27</u>, 345.

Waugh, J.S. (1957). *J.chem.Phys.* <u>26</u>, 966.

Weinhaus, F. and Meyer, H. (1973). *Phys.Rev.* <u>B7</u>, 2974.

———   ———   Myers, S.M., and Harris, A.B. (1973). *Phys.Rev.* <u>B7</u>, 2960.

Wilde, R.E. and Srinivasan, T.K.K. (1975). *(J.)Phys.Chem. Solids* <u>36</u>, 119.

de Wit, G.A. and Bloom, M. (1966). *Phys.Lett.* <u>21</u>, 39.

Wolf, R.P., Stahl, F.A., and Watrous, J.A. (1973). *J.chem. Phys.* <u>59</u>, 115.

———   and Whitney, W.M. (1964). *Proc.9th Int.Conf.Low- Temp.Phys.* <u>B</u>, 1118.

Yamamoto, T. and Kataoka, Y. (1968). *J.chem.Phys.* <u>48</u>, 3199.

———   ———   (1970).*Progr. theoret.Phys. Suppl.* No.46, 383.

Yi, P.-N. and Gavrielides, A.T. (1971). *J.chem.Phys.* <u>54</u>, 3777.

Zaslow, B., Atoji, M., and Lipscomb, W.N. (1952). *Acta crystallogr.* <u>5</u>, 833.

10

DISORDER IN MOLECULAR SOLIDS — II

10.1. TETRAHEDRAL MOLECULES

Structural and thermodynamic information on crystals whose
molecules fall in this category will be found in Table 10.1.
A cursory glance at this shows that the high-temperature
plastic phases of such compounds, while often cubic, are
not always so, and that polarity of the molecule does not
necessarily prevent the formation of a plastic phase. The
dipole moments of t-butyl chloride and t-nitrobutane, for
example, are considerable, being 2·1 D and 3·7 D respectively.

Values of $\Sigma \Delta S_t$, the sum of the transition entropies,
and of $(\Delta S_m + \Sigma \Delta S_t)$, where ΔS_m is the entropy of fusion,
are listed in Table 10.2 for some of the substances in Table
10.1. Data of this kind have an important part to play in
attempts to interpret and rationalize order-disorder transitions, as will appear from the summaries of such attempts
presented in the last section of this chapter. The reader
should perhaps be reminded that the experimental results from
which the figures in Table 10.2 are derived no doubt vary
considerably in their accuracy, and that in any case there
can be some uncertainty in evaluating ΔS_t, especially when
the transition is partly gradual and partly sharp.

That the high-temperature forms of the carbon tetra-
halides are disordered is evident from their low entropies
of fusion and from NMR studies. For CF_4, disorder in phase
I was confirmed by investigations of the infrared and Raman
spectra (Fournier, Savoie, Bessette, and Cabana 1968) and
of the far-infrared spectrum (Sataty, Ron, and Herbstein
1975). As with some of the substances discussed in the last
chapter, so also for many of the compounds considered in this,
experimental evidence of various kinds has been obtained
which shows how closely the motion of the molecules in the
plastic phases resembles that in the liquid state. For CCl_4,
for example, there is no discontinuity in the ^{35}Cl spin-spin
relaxation time T_2 when the plastic phase melts (O'Reilly,

TABLE 10.1

Thermodynamic and structural information on substances with tetrahedral molecules forming plastic crystals. E_R and E_D are estimates of the activation energies for reorientation and diffusion respectively, and unless otherwise stated are derived from NMR studies and refer to phase I

Name	Formula	II ← (structure)	T_t/K, $\Delta S_t/R$	→ I ← (structure)	T_m/K, $\Delta S_m/R$ → Liq.	E_R kJ mol⁻¹	E_D kJ mol⁻¹	Cal.	Cryst.	NMR
Carbon tetrafluoride	CF_4	Monoclinic C2/c	76·2, 2·71		89·6, 0·96	–	–	1 2	3	4
Carbon tetrachloride	CCl_4	Monoclinic	225·5(F), 2·45	Rhombohedral or f.c.c. (see text)	250·3, 1·21	–	–	5 6	7	8 9
Carbon tetrabromide	CBr_4	Monoclinic	320·0(F), 2·51		363·3, 1·31	–	–	10	11	–
Carbon tetramethyl (neopentane)	$C(CH_3)_4$	Hexagonal	140·0(λ), 2·21	F.c.c.	256·5, 1·53	4·2, 3·8	25, 34	12	13 14	15–17 50 51
t-butyl chloride	$C(CH_3)_3Cl$	Tetragonal P4/nmm	220, 3·2	F.c.c. Fm3m	248·1, 0·95	~6 ~12[a]	~21 33·5	18 19 20	14 15 16	9 21–23 26

(III ← 183, 1·2 → II) ?Monoclinic

Compound	Formula	Transition data (T/K, ΔS)					
t-butyl bromide	$C(CH_3)_3Br$	209, 3·3 ↔ 256·1, 0·9 ↔ II (III ↔ 231·5, 0·55 → II)	–		18	19	16, 22
2,2-Dichloropropane	$C(CH_3)_2Cl_2$	188, 3·82 (Orthorhombic) ↔ 239·4, 1·18 (Rhombohedral) ↔	~12	~25	24 (25)	14	15, 22, 23, 50
1,1,1-Trichloroethane (methylchloroform)	$C(CH_3)Cl_3$	224·8, 4·01 (Orthorhombic, *Pnma*) ↔ 243·1, 1·16 (Cubic) ↔	~19	–	27–29	14 (30)	9, 15, 16, 31, 51
2,2-Dinitropropane	$C(CH_3)_2(NO_2)_2$	~267 ↔ 326 (F.c.c.) ↔	–	–	27	32	16, 31
2-Chloro-2-nitropropane	$C(CH_3)_2ClNO_2$	213·8, 5·38 ↔ 251·6, 0·64 ↔	5·5^b	–	27	–	16
Pentaerythritol	$C(CH_2OH)_4$	457, 11·5 (Tetragonal $I\bar{4}$) ↔ 539, 1·59 (F.c.c.) ↔	105	102	33	34	35
Pentaerythritol fluoride	$C(CH_2F)_4$	249·9 (*F*), 6·37 ↔ 367·4, 1·69 ↔	–	–	36	–	–
2,2-Dicyanopropane (dimethylmalononitrile)	$C(CH_3)_2(CN)_2$	302·6 (*F*), 3·93 ↔ 307·5, 1·59 ↔	–	–	37	–	–

Trimethylacetic acid C(CH₃)₃COOH (pivalic acid)

$\xleftarrow{280\cdot1,\ 3\cdot05^c}$ F.c.c. $Fm3m$ $\xrightarrow{309\cdot7,\ 0\cdot78^c}$

25 50 38 39 40 –
16·7[d] 42

t-butylthiol C(CH₃)₃SH

$\xleftarrow{199\cdot4(F),\ 0\cdot58}$ B.c.c. (IV $\xleftarrow{151\cdot6(F),\ 3\cdot23}$ III $\xrightarrow{274\cdot4,\ 1\cdot09}$ F.c.c. $\xrightarrow{157\cdot0(F),\ 0\cdot50}$ II)
?H.c.p.

– 32 43 44 26
(in I) 45 46 –
– 35 – –
(in II)

Tetrathio-methylmethane C(SCH₃)₄

$\xleftarrow{318\cdot7,\ 2\cdot87}$ Tetragonal $I4/mmm$ $\xrightarrow{338\cdot7,\ 1\cdot47}$ Cubic $Im3m$ (III $\xrightarrow{296\cdot4,\ 2\cdot49}$ II) Tetragonal

– – 47 48 –

t-nitrobutane C(CH₃)₃NO₂

$\xleftarrow{260\cdot1(F),\ 2\cdot16}$ Triclinic $P42_1c$ $\xrightarrow{299\cdot2,\ 1\cdot04}$ Orthorhombic (III $\xleftarrow{215\cdot3(F),\ 2\cdot36}$ II)

49 49 –

Footnotes Table 10.1.

a.   For rotation about C-Cl axis in phases II and III.

b.   From a dielectric relaxation study (Clemett and Davies 1962).

c.   Quoted in Reference 40.

d.   For rotation of t-butyl group in phase II.

REFERENCES

1.   Eucken and Schröder (1938).

2.   J.H.Smith and Pace (1969).

3.   Greer and Meyer (1969); Bol'shutkin et al. (1972); Sataty, Ron, and Herbstein (1975).

4.   Aston, Stottlemyer, and Murray (1960) (^{19}F, LW, and SM); L.Niemelä and M.Niemelä (1970) (^{19}F, T_1, T_2).

5.   Hicks, Hooley, and Stephenson (1944).

6.   Arentsen and van Miltenburg (1972).

7.   Post (1959); Rudman and Post (1966).

8.   O'Reilly, E.M.Peterson, and Scheie (1974) (T_2, ^{35}Cl).

9.   Gutowsky and McCall (1960) (^{35}Cl, NQR).

10. Frederick and Hildebrand (1939); Marshall, Staveley, and Hart (1956).

11. Finbak and Hassel (1937); Finbak (1937).

12. Aston and Messerly (1936).

13. Mones and Post (1952).

14. Rudman and Post (1968b).

15. Stejskal et al. (1959) (proton, T_1).

16. Powles and Gutowsky (1953a) (LW, SM).

17. Allen, Liu, and Jonas (1975) (T_1 in I under pressure).

18. Kushner, Crowe, and Smyth (1950).

19. Schwartz, Post, and Fankuchen (1951).

20. Rudman (1967).

21. O'Reilly et al. (1973) (H, D, ^{35}Cl, T_1, and $T_{1\rho}$).

22. Anderson and Slichter (1966b) (H, under pressure).

23. Woessner and Gutowsky (1963) (^{35}Cl).

24. van de Vloed (1939).

25. van Miltenburg (1972).

26. Segel and Mansingh (1969) (LW).

Table 10.1 footnotes continued.....

27.   Crowe and Smyth (1950b).

28.   Rubin, Levedahl, and Yost (1944).

29.   Andon, Counsell, Lee and Martin (1973).

30.   Silver and Rudman (1972).

31.   Powles and Gutowsky (1955) (SM).

32.   Abrahams (1953).

33.   Nita, Seki, Momotani, Suzuki, and Nakagawa (1950); Nitta, Seki, and Momotani (1959).

34.   Llewellyn, Cox, and Goodwin (1937); Nitta and Watanabe (1937, 1938); Shiono, Cruickshank, and Cox (1958); Hvoslef (1958).

35.   Gupta and Agrawal (1967); G.W. Smith (1969a) (LW, SM, T_1).

36.   Trowbridge and Westrum (1964).

37.   Ribner and Westrum (1967).

38.   Murill and Breed (1970).

39.   Namba and Oda (1952); Kondo and Oda (1954).

40.   Suga, Sugisaki, and Seki (1966) (LW).

41.   Albert, Gutowsky, and Ripmeester (1976) (SM, T_1, $T_{1\rho}$, 77-310 K).

42.   Hood, Lockhart, and Sherwood (1972) (LW).

43.   McCullough, Scott, Finke, Hubbard, Cross, Katz, Pennington, Messerly, and Waddington (1953).

44.   Kondo (1957, 1965).

45.   Guthrie and McCullough (1961).

46.   G.W.Smith (1969b) (LW, SM).

47.   Backer and Perdok (1943).

48.   Perdok and Terpstra (1943, 1946).

49.   Urban, Tomkowicz, Mayer, and Waluga (1975).

50.   Roeder and Douglass (1970).

51.   Gutowsky and Pake (1950) (LW, SM).

E.M.Peterson, and Scheie 1974), nor in the reorientational correlation time as deduced from Raman line broadening, a source of information mentioned later in this section in connection with neopentane (Bartoli and Litovitz 1972). An interesting point about carbon tetrachloride is that on cooling the liquid it crystallizes in a face-centred cubic form (Ia) which a few degrees lower spontaneously transforms

TABLE 10.2

Values of $\Sigma \Delta S_t$, the sum of the entropies of transition, and of $\Sigma \Delta S_t$ plus the entropy of fusion, ΔS_m, for compounds with tetrahedral molecules

Compound	$\Sigma \Delta S_t / R$	$(\Delta S_m + \Sigma \Delta S_t)/R$
CF_4	2·71	3·67
CCl_4	2·45	3·66
CBr_4	2·51	3·82
$C(CH_3)_4$	2·21	3·74
$C(CH_3)_3Cl$	4·4	5·35
$C(CH_3)_3Br$	3·85	4·75
$C(CH_3)Cl_3$	4·01	5·17
$C(CH_3)_2Cl_2$	3·82	5·00
$C(CH_3)_2ClNO_2$	5·38	6·02
$C(CH_3)_2(CN)_2$	3·93	5·52
$C(CH_3)_3SH$	4·31	5·40
$C(CH_3)_3NO_2$	4·52	5·56
$C(SCH_3)_4$	5·36	6·83

into a rhombohedral phase (Ib) which is slightly denser and which has 21 molecules in the unit cell. On heating the low-temperature monoclinic form II, the rhombohedral form is always produced (Rudman and Post 1966). At first it was considered that Ia is always metastable and that Ib is the stable disordered phase. Arentsen and van Miltenburg (1972) measured the melting-point and enthalpy of fusion of the lower-melting of the two forms, obtaining values of 245·70 K and $0·905R$ for the temperature and entropy of fusion respectively, which they ascribed to the supposedly metastable face-centred cubic modification. On this interpretation the

melting parameters in Table 10.1 would refer to the rhombohedral form. However, on the basis of optical birefringence
studies Koga and Morrison (1975) concluded that Ia is probably stable at higher temperatures and Ib at lower temperatures, and if this is accepted the usually quoted melting-
point of 250·3 K is that of the face-centred form Ia. Koga
and Morrison considered that the temperature of the Ia-Ib
transition probably lies between 240 K and 249 K, but hysteresis prevents a more precise determination. As regards
the monoclinic form II, this (and CBr_4-II) appears to be a
structure of some complexity, with 32 molecules in the unit
cell, but nevertheless the relation between phases I and II
seems to be quite close.

Neopentane, $C(CH_3)_4$, has been the subject of several
cold neutron scattering studies. Pelah, Vulkan, and Zafrir
(1972) investigated the inelastic scattering in the acoustic
region ~1 K above and below the transition, and estimated
that the time between reorientational jumps is ~$0·7 \times 10^{-12}$ s.
The transition is accompanied by a relatively large volume
increase (~18 per cent), but in spite of this the inelastic
spectrum shows very little change, implying that there is not
much alteration in the effective intermolecular force field.
Moreover, Mössbauer measurements of the mean square displacement $\langle x^2 \rangle$ as a function of temperature showed that this
quantity is continuous throughout the transition. The work
carried out on the broadening of the elastic peak has already been summarized in section 4.6.2. This did not lead
to an unambiguous decision between large-angle jumps on the
one hand and rotational diffusion by small steps on the other
for the mechanism of reorientation, and indeed it was suggested that both processes operate simultaneously. A valuable
contribution was made by Livingston, Rothschild, and Rush
(1973) using a technique which will no doubt be increasingly
widely applied to the study of the dynamics of the rotational
movement of molecules and ions in crystals, namely analysis
of the infrared and Raman band shapes. It had already been
shown that the shapes of Raman lines given by liquids can
be made to yield quantitative information on molecular reorientation (Rakov 1959). The theory of the method of

analysis used by Livingston *et al.* was later developed by
Gordon (1965). A band is broadened by molecular reorientation - there can, of course, be other causes of broadening
which may have to be considered - and by Fourier analysis of
the line-shape it is possible to obtain an orientational correlation function from which quantitative information about
the reorientational motion can be derived. The method relates to motion which operates on a time-scale of ~0·1 to 3 ps
and which involves a single molecule rather than collective
movement. By choosing a suitable rotation-vibration band,
results can be obtained which refer to reorientation about
a particular molecular axis. In their investigation of neopentane, Livingston *et al.* selected the infrared and Raman
bands of the 924 cm^{-1} fundamental. The appearance of the
Raman spectrum at different temperatures is shown in Fig.10.1.

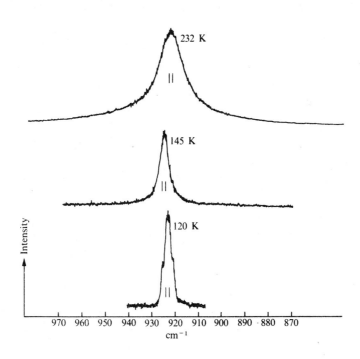

Fig.10.1. Raman spectra of the 924 cm^{-1} vibration-rotation band in crystalline neopentane (T_t = 140 K, T_m = 256·5 K) (Livingston, Rothschild, and
Rush 1973).

Their analysis demonstrated that the rotational behaviour of the molecules in the plastic phase is virtually unchanged when the crystal melts. The temperature dependence of the correlation time gave a value of $4 \cdot 1$ kJ mol^{-1} for the activation energy for reorientation, in good agreement with the estimates from NMR and inelastic neutron scattering. The *average* angle of 'rotation' in the plastic phase at 175 K was calculated to be 10° to 13°. The combined spectroscopic and neutron scattering evidence appears to eliminate small-step rotational diffusion as the reorientation mechanism.

By making T_1 measurements for proton resonance in phase I of neopentane under pressure, Allen, Liu, and Jonas (1975) found that whereas pressure has relatively little effect on reorientation, the self-diffusion of the molecules is strongly pressure-dependent. In fact, the volume of activation for the latter kind of movement is $\sim$110 cm^3 mol^{-1}, which is about the same as the molar volume of the crystal, and so supports the view that self-diffusion proceeds by a vacancy mechanism (see section 10.7). By contrast, the volume of activation for reorientation is only $\sim$5 cm^3 mol^{-1}. The activation energies for diffusion and reorientation were estimated to be 34 and $3 \cdot 8$ kJ mol^{-1} respectively.

Compounds of the group $C(CH_3)_n X_{4-n}$, where X = a halogen atom and n = 1, 2, or 3, show resemblances in their polymorphism to the substances already discussed in this section, but orientational disorder can now be acquired in stages. Thus, when n = 1 or 3, reorientation can begin about the threefold axis of the molecule, to be followed at higher temperatures by more general reorientation (isotropic tumbling). It will be seen from Table 10.1 that the compounds $C(CH_3)_3Cl$ and $C(CH_3)_3Br$ show two transitions. The first two heat capacity studies on methyl chloroform, $C(CH_3)Cl_3$, gave indications of a minor transition at 206 K, but there was no sign of this in a later calorimetric investigation (Andon, Counsell, Lee, and Martin 1973), and single crystal X-ray studies at 128 K and 213 K showed no significant structural difference (Silver and Rudman 1972).

Methyl chloroform and t-butyl chloride have been quite thoroughly examined. NMR studies of the former compound

revealed that the first fall in the second moment, associated
with the reorientation of the methyl group, occurs between
120 K and 150 K, and from a proton T_1 study Stejskal, Woessner, Farrar, and Gutowsky (1959) deduced a value of 19 kJ
mol^{-1} for the activation energy for this movement. This is
an apparent activation energy which is not the same as the
height of the barrier V_0 inhibiting rotation of the methyl
group with respect to the CCl_3 group, since it is probable
that methyl group reorientation involves tunnelling through
the barrier. The value given by Stejskal *et al.* for V_0 is
24 kJ mol^{-1}, which can be compared with two independent estimates. The frequency of the internal torsional mode was observed at ~ 290 cm^{-1} by Durig, Craven, Lau, and Bragin (1971)
in the far-infrared spectrum of methyl chloroform, while Rush
(1967) estimated ~ 300 cm^{-1} for this frequency from a cold
neutron scattering study. Assuming a cosine-type potential
and following the procedure of Fateley and Miller (1961), V_0
can then be calculated from the frequency. The values so
obtained are 23 kJ mol^{-1} from the far-infrared work and
24 kJ mol^{-1} from the neutron scattering investigation, in
good agreement with the NMR value, but appreciably higher
than estimates of V_0 for the molecule in the gaseous phase,
which range from 7 to 12·5 kJ mol^{-1}. Differences in the same
sense have been found for similar molecules. Since the frequency of the internal torsional mode in methylchloroform
is observed to be virtually unchanged on passage through
the solid phases into the liquid state, the difference in
the values given for V_0 cannot be attributed to the effect
of environment on what is essentially an intramolecular matter,
and it may be that the estimate of V_0 for the gaseous molecule
will have to be revised.

The abrupt increase in the permittivity of solid methylchloroform at the II→I transition and the simultaneous change
in the proton T_1 are evidence that on passage into phase I
the molecules gain orientational freedom. However, even in
phase II a considerable measure of freedom of molecular motion seems to be acquired, since the far-infrared spectrum
in the lattice mode region becomes much more diffuse over
the range 80 - 190 K.

There are thermal and structural grounds for believing
that methylchloroform and also 2,2-dichloropropane can both
form phases Ia and Ib similar to those given by carbon tetrachloride (Rudman 1970).

Turning to t-butyl chloride, there is an appreciable
entropy gain at each of the two transitions, and the inference that orientational freedom is acquired at both is
supported by other evidence. Rudman and Post (1968b) concluded from an X-ray diffraction study that in phase II
there is disorder of the methyl groups in the ab plane but
not in the direction of the c axis, implying that the molecules can reorient about the molecular axis passing through
the chlorine atom and the central carbon atom. A considerable amount of NMR work has been carried out on this substance, which was cited in section 4.4 as an example of a
solid for which three minima are observed in the spin-lattice
relaxation time T_1 (Fig.4.12). A very detailed investigation
was carried out by O'Reilly, E.M. Peterson, Scheie, and Seyfarth (1973), in which proton T_1 and $T_{1\rho}$ measurements were
made from 90 K to the melting-point, as well as studies of
deuteron resonance and of ^{35}Cl NQR. This work confirmed
that methyl group rotation commences in phase III, that motion of the molecule about the C-Cl bond also begins in phase
III and continues in II, and that in phase I the molecules
undergo isotropic tumbling and also diffuse quite rapidly.
Once again the similarity in molecular behaviour in the plastic phase and in the liquid was demonstrated, in this case
by the observation that the rotational correlation times
measured for D, H, and ^{35}Cl do not change when the liquid
freezes to give I, although they show a discontinuity at the
II-I transition (Fig.10.2). Quasielastic neutron scattering
results for phases III and II were interpreted on the basis
that reorientation of the molecule about its polar axis
occurs by jumps of 120° with an activation energy of 6 kJ
mol^{-1} (Goyal, Nawrocik, Urban, Domoslawski, and Natkaniec 1974).

The values given in Table 10.1 for E_R, the activation
energy for molecular reorientation, are those derived from
NMR investigations. They appear to decrease as chlorine
atoms are replaced by methyl groups, and an attempt has been

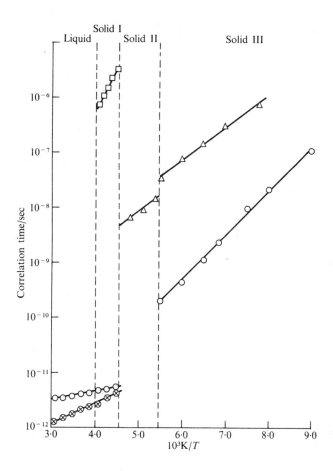

Fig.10.2. Correlation times for various types of motion in t-butyl chloride; O, methyl group rotation about triad axes, Δ, rotation about C-Cl bond, □, translational diffusion in solid I, ⊗ , molecular tumbling in liquid and solid I (O'Reilly, Peterson, Scheie, and Seyfarth 1973).

made to relate this decrease (and also the drop in temperature at which the lower or lowest phase changes to the one
above) to the fact that in the disordered phase I, at least,
the molecular volume increases with the introduction of the
methyl groups. As against this, the molecular volumes in
the *ordered* phases show no such systematic increase, and
moreover the few independent measurements of E_R are not in
good agreement with those in Table 10.1. Thus, for methyl
chloroform, Rush gave $E_R \leq 4$ kJ mol^{-1}, while Clemett and
Davies (1962a) from a dielectric relaxation study of 2,2-

dichloropropane found E_R = 6 kJ mol^{-1}. It may be, therefore, that E_R does not in fact vary much over the series $C(CH_3)_4$-CCl_4, and this may also be true of the rather higher values of E_D, the activation energy for self-diffusion.

For pentaerythritol, ΔS_t is as high as the molar entropy of vaporization of the average liquid at its boiling-point, and is approximately equal to $R \ln 10^5$! Attempts to interpret this quantity were made by Nitta and his colleagues, and improved and developed by Westrum in the light of his results for the somewhat simpler substance pentaerythrityl fluoride. In pentaerythritol, the hydrogen atom of any one hydroxyl group should have available to it three potential minima, and if in the disordered crystal each hydroxyl group uses these minima independently of the other three hydroxyl groups in the molecule, the contribution to the entropy will be $4R \ln 3$. The X-ray diffraction study of the high-temperature cubic form showed that the $-CH_2O-$ units are so disposed as to give rise to two possible arrangements for the molecule as a whole, which adds a term $R \ln 2$. The sum of $R \ln 2$ and $4R \ln 3$ is $5 \cdot 09R$, which is almost exactly the amount by which ΔS_t for pentaerythritol exceeds ΔS_t for the fluoride (Trowbridge and Westrum 1964).

Doshi, Furman, and Rudman (1973) examined several compounds of the formula $RC(CH_2OH)_3$ using the techniques of differential scanning calorimetry, the polarizing microscope, and X-ray powder photography. Face-centred cubic plastic crystalline phases were found for R = COOH, CH_3, and NO_2. The compound with R = NH_2 gave a plastic phase which yielded only one detectable diffraction line.

Certain features in the progression of crystalline 2-methyl-2-propanethiol from order to disorder deserve to be mentioned. As with t-butyl chloride, the development of orientational disorder appears to involve two stages. The line-width narrows at about 100 K (well below the IV→III transition), but the permittivity remains constant at a relatively low figure. This implies that molecular reorientation about the C-S axis (leaving the direction of the molecular dipole unaffected) begins in

phase IV. The permittivity in phase III is much higher, and
at the III→II transition there is virtually no change either
in the NMR characteristics or in the permittivity. Presumably
general molecular reorientation therefore occurs in both
phases III and II. At about 170 K the line-width starts to
decrease again, reaching very small values at the II→I transition, so that self-diffusion is now occurring. At the II→I
transition the line-width suddenly rises, subsequently to
decrease again to small values as the melting-point is
reached. In other words, at first the passage from phase II
into phase I makes self-diffusion more difficult, not less.
It is apparent that for this substance both phases I and II
can be regarded as plastic crystals, which together cover a
range of 117 K. By contrast, the plastic phase of dimethyl-
malononitrile exists over less than 5 K.

In spite of its polarity, t-nitrobutane exists in two
disordered phases. The larger entropy gain occurs at the
lower transition, which falls in the region of temperature
where the most marked change takes place in the far-infrared
spectrum (Haffmans and Larkin 1972).

Although pivalic acid (trimethylacetic acid) has been
included in Table 10.1 as a substance with a tetrahedral molecule, the unit in the crystal is really a hydrogen-bonded
dimer (Longueville and Fontaine 1976). From depolarized Rayleigh studies, Bird, Jackson, and Powles (1973) estimated
that the reorientational activation energy is 60 kJ mol^{-1},
and pointed out that this is about the same as the energy of
association of two molecules to form a dimer. This implies
that reorientation involves the breaking and reforming of
hydrogen bonds, and that there must be randomness in the di-
merization of any one molecule with its twelve nearest neighbours. In a comprehensive NMR investigation, Albert, Gutowsky, and Ripmeester (1976) noted that in the neighbourhood
of the transition there is a considerable difference in the
behaviour of $T_{1\rho}$ between the ordinary form of the acid and
the partially deuterated form $(CH_3)_3CCOOD$, which they regarded as an indication that quantum-mechanical tunnelling is
important in the making and breaking of hydrogen bonds which
occurs during the tumbling process. The kinetics of self-

diffusion in the plastic phase were particularly thoroughly studied by Sherwood and his coworkers. The activation energy for self-diffusion given by a tracer study using carbon-14 was $91 \cdot 2 \pm 0 \cdot 4$ kJ mol^{-1}. This agrees well with the value of $93 \cdot 4 \pm 2 \cdot 9$ kJ mol^{-1} for the activation energy for the creep (plastic flow) process, implying that this process is self-diffusion controlled (Hawthorne and Sherwood 1970a). There is a striking difference between these values of the activation energy for self-diffusion in phase I and those obtained from NMR experiments, which are roughly only half of the values quoted. Some preliminary remarks have been made on differences of this kind in section 4.4, and we shall discuss the matter further in the last section of this chapter. Hood, Lockhart, and Sherwood (1972), using tritium as a tracer, studied the self-diffusion of the acidic protons in the plastic phase, which proves to take place about 10^3 times more rapidly than that of the molecules, probably by an intermolecular exchange mechanism which involves molecular rotation.

Although bromoform, $CHBr_3$, does not form a plastic crystal, it presents an interesting example of disorder. The crystals are hexagonal, space group $P6_3$, with the c axis coincident with the threefold axis of the molecules, which are randomly oriented between the two possible positions which achieve this coincidence, i.e. upwards or downwards along the c axis (Kawaguchi, Takashina, Tanaka, and Watanabe 1972). This case was used by Coulson and Emerson (1974) in a theoretical treatment of the development of orientational order during crystal growth.

10.2. CYCLIC MOLECULES

Examples are given in Table 10.3 of organic substances with cyclic molecules which form plastic crystals, some of which (e.g. cyclopentane) have exceptionally low entropies of fusion. Where crystallographic and NMR results are available, they show that in the plastic phase there is considerable orientational disorder, which gives rise to some interesting structural similarities. Thus, the high-temperature cubic forms of cyclooctanone and cyclononanone, with

space group $Pm2n$, are identical not only with those of
cycloöctane and cycloheptatriene, but more surprisingly,
perhaps, with the high-temperature forms of fluorine and
oxygen (β-F_2 and γ-O_2).

We shall briefly discuss some of the more interesting
features shown by compounds in this group, beginning with
the polymorphism of cyclohexanol, a matter of some complexity. It has long been known (Kelley 1929) that the
plastic form I of cyclohexanol can be readily supercooled,
but whereas Kelley concluded that this form, like II, approaches zero entropy at 0 K, Adachi, Suga, and Seki (1968)
carried out a very thorough heat capacity study from which
they inferred that I retains entropy of $4 \cdot 72$ J K^{-1} mol^{-1}
at 0 K. At about 148 $K(T_g)$ there is a relatively sudden
increase in the heat capacity of supercooled I as the temperature rises (Fig.10.3). In other words, supercooled I
behaves very much like a supercooled liquid which eventually
gives a glass, and Seki and his colleagues have proposed
that it should be called a 'glassy crystal' (section
2.1). In addition to the forms I and II, there is a meta-

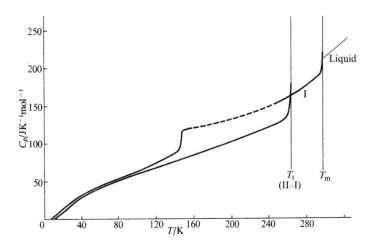

Fig.10.3. Molar heat capacity C_p of cyclohexanol as phase II (lower curve),
and as liquid, phase I, and supercooled I (upper curve). The dotted line
is an estimate (after Adachi, Suga, and Seki 1968).

stable form III, but this, like II, becomes perfectly ordered at 0 K. Adachi *et al.* used their calorimetric results
to compare the Gibbs energies of phases I, II, and III, which
are shown graphically as a function of temperature in Fig.
10.4. The disorder retained by supercooled I is believed

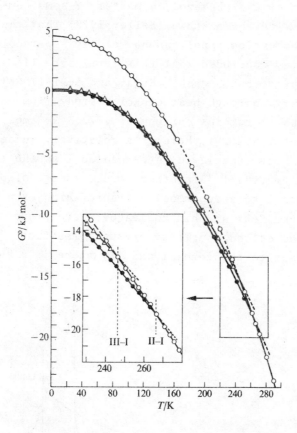

Fig.10.4. Gibbs energies of crystalline phases I, II, and III of cyclohexanol; open circles, I (both as stable crystal and as supercooled
crystal); full circles, II; triangles, III (Adachi, Suga, and Seki
1968).

to arise from the freezing-in of more than one orientation
and more than one molecular conformation. From the dielectric dispersion studies on I carried out by Meakins
(1962) and by Corfield and Davies (1964) it would certainly
seem plausible that orientational disorder is frozen-in
at low temperatures.

The polymorphism of cyclohexanol has been independently examined by Green and Griffith (1969). Their interpretation differs from that of Adachi *et al*. in that whereas the latter consider that III is always metastable with respect to II, Green and Griffith believe that there is a II→III transition at about 209 K, below which III is the stable phase[†]. An interesting feature of their work was the use of permittivity measurements to study the rate of transformation of one phase into another. These studies led them to conclude that, as previously suggested by Otsubo and Suguwara (1955), there must be at least one other form of cyclohexanol, which they designate pre-II. They regard this as being always metastable with respect to forms I and II, but they believe that it transforms into I at 229 K (at which temperature, of course, I itself is unstable with respect to both II and III). This interesting substance will undoubtedly receive further attention. Whatever the final verdict on its phase relations, the three (and quite possibly four) different forms which can exist cannot differ greatly in stability. Between 200 K and the melting-point, differences in Gibbs energy between any two forms do not exceed ~2 kJ mol^{-1}.

The ability shown by cyclohexanol to form a 'glassy crystal' is also possessed by *cis*-1,2-dimethylcyclohexane. Phase I of this substance can be supercooled, and at ~95 K the heat capacity shows the rather sudden drop characteristic of glass formation. Supercooled I retains residual entropy of 1·04R. Other examples, as revealed by DTA experiments, have been noted by Adachi, Suga, and Seki (1970). They include cyclohexene, for which (in addition to the glass given by the supercooled liquid) two kinds of glassy crystal were obtained, one derived from phase I, and the other from a metastable phase III (Haida, Suga, and Seki 1973).

[†]In their paper Green and Griffith (following Crowe and Smyth 1951) designate the metastable form as II, and the stable form as III. We have altered their labelling of the phases to conform to that of Adachi *et al*., which we have adopted here.

Cyclopentanol also presents some unusual features, especially with regard to its dielectric behaviour. This deserves attention since it has led to attempts to explain how an apparently high degree of orientational freedom in a solid composed of molecules containing hydroxyl groups can be reconciled with the simultaneous existence of intermolecular hydrogen bonds. In addition to the three phases of this substance noted in Table 10.3, there appears to be a phase IV formed by quenching III in liquid nitrogen, which on warming changes into III at about -80°C. Both I and II have high relative permittivities, whereas that of III and IV is about 2·5, so that in the latter pair of phases the molecules are effectively prevented from reorientation. The chief point of interest is the comparison between phases I and II with regard to the molecular interaction and molecular dynamics in these phases. From an X-ray study, Green and Wheeler (1969a) concluded that both phases I and II are disordered, I more so than II. Indeed, they state that in I 'the molecules are rotating with near spherical symmetry about their centre of mass', whereas in II the molecular disorder is probably restricted to movement about one axis. Corfield and Davies (1964) had previously carried out a dielectric relaxation study of cyclopentanol in phases I and II and in the liquid state, from which they derived values of κ, the (specific) d.c. conductivity. The temperature dependence of κ obeys the equation

$$\kappa = A e^{-E/RT}$$

and in phase I both A and E were found to be very much larger than in either the liquid state or in phase II. Attributing the conductivity to a proton-jump, Grotthus-type mechanism, Davies (1966) suggested that whereas in the liquid state and in phase II the molecules associate by hydrogen bonding into linear chains, in I they form rings of perhaps four molecules. Green, Dalich, and Griffith (1972) made the important observation that while as a dielectric phase I is isotropic, in phase II the permittivity is very large along the c axis. The high values (considerably greater

TABLE 10.3

Thermodynamic and structural information on substances with cyclic molecules

Name	Formula	III← T_t/K, $\Delta S_t/R$ →II	←T_t/K, $\Delta S_t/R$ →I	←T_m/K, $\Delta S_m/R$ →I Liq.	Cal.	Cryst.	NMR
						References	
Cyclobutane	C_4H_8	←145·7(λ),4·72→		←182·4, 0·72→ B.c.c.	1	2	3
Cyclopentane	C_5H_{10}	←122·4(F),4·80→	←138·1(F),0·30→	←179·7, 0·40→ Hexagonal	4	5	6
Cyclohexane	C_6H_{12}	←186·0(F),4·33→ Monoclinic $C2/c$		←279·8, 1·12→ F.c.c. $Fm3m$	7	8	9 / 11 / 12
Cycloheptane	C_7H_{14}	←198·2(F),0·176→ (IV←134·8(F),4·432→ III)	←212·4(F),0·255→	←265·12,0·854→	13	–	14
Cycloöctane	C_8H_{16}	←166·5(F),4·556→	←183·8(F),0·313→	←287·98,1·007→	13	15	–
Cyclopentene	C_5H_8	←87·07(λ),0·66[a]→		←138·13,2·93→	16	–	17
Cyclohexene	C_6H_{10}	←138·7(F),3·686→		←169·67,2·335→	16 / 18	–	19

Compound	Formula	Transition data	Refs.		
Cycloheptatriene	C_7H_8	$153\cdot98(\lambda),1\cdot833^a \rightarrow 197\cdot92,0\cdot706$ Cubic	13	20	–
1,2-*cis*-Dimethylcyclohexane	C_8H_{16}	$172\cdot5(F),5\cdot76 \rightarrow 223\cdot28,0\cdot886$	21	–	–
Cyclopentanol	C_5H_9OH	$\sim201 \qquad 202\cdot8(F),2\cdot19 \rightarrow 256\cdot9,0\cdot72$ Hexagonal	22	23	–
Cyclohexanol	$C_6H_{11}OH$	$(III \leftarrow 244\cdot8,4\cdot244 \rightarrow I)\ 265\cdot50(\lambda),4\cdot00 \rightarrow 299\cdot05,0\cdot717$	24	25	26
Cyclooctanone	$(CH_2)_7CO$	$183,2 \rightarrow 231,8\cdot6 \rightarrow 315,1\cdot0$ Monoclinic $\qquad$ Cubic $Pm3n$	27 28	27	27
Cyclononanone	$(CH_2)_8CO$	$301,0\cdot75$ Cubic $Pm3n$	27 28	27	27
Perfluorocyclohexane	C_6F_{12}	$168 \rightarrow 331$ F.c.c.	29	29	10
Thiacyclohexane	$C_5H_{10}S$	$201\cdot4(F),0\cdot65^a \rightarrow 240\cdot0(F),3\cdot89 \rightarrow 292\cdot25,1\cdot01$ F.c.c.	31	32	30
Furan	C_4H_4O	$150\cdot0(F),1\cdot642 \rightarrow 187\cdot55,2\cdot439$ Orthorhombic $Cmca$	33	34	35
Thiophene	C_4H_4S	$(III \leftarrow 138(\lambda)^b \rightarrow II)\ (IV \leftarrow 112(\lambda)^b \rightarrow III)\ 171\cdot6(F),0\cdot45 \rightarrow 234\cdot95,3\cdot40$ $P4_1 2_1 2$ or $P4_3 2_1 2$ Tetragonal $\qquad$ Orthorhombic	36	37	38

Compound	Formula	Transition data	References
Sulpholan	$C_4H_8SO_2$	$\xleftrightarrow{288\cdot59,\ 4} \xleftrightarrow{301\cdot61,\ 0\cdot55}$	39, –, 40
Hexamethylbenzene	$C_6(CH_3)_6$	$\xleftarrow{116\cdot48(\lambda),\ 1\cdot21} \xleftrightarrow{383} \xleftrightarrow{438}$ Hexagonal / Triclinic / Orthorhombic *P6mm*	41, 42, 11 43
Pentafluorochlorobenzene	C_6F_5Cl	$\xleftrightarrow{191,\ 2\cdot15} \xleftrightarrow{245,\ 0\cdot48} \xleftrightarrow{257\cdot49,\ 3\cdot90}$	44, –, –
Pentafluorophenol	C_6F_5OH	$\xleftrightarrow{287,\ 0\cdot47} \xleftrightarrow{310\cdot62,\ 6\cdot35}$	44, –, –
1,2,3-Trichloro-4,5,6-trimethylbenzene	$C_6(CH_3)_3Cl_3$	Monoclinic $\xleftrightarrow{140\text{-}270^c,\ 0\cdot46}$ Monoclinic $\xleftrightarrow{494}$ $P2_1/c$	45, 46, 47
1,3-Difluorobenzene	$C_6H_4F_2$	$\xleftrightarrow{186\cdot77,\ 0\cdot533} \xleftrightarrow{204\cdot03,\ 5\cdot06}$	48, –, –
1,2,3,4-Tetrafluorobenzene	$C_6H_2F_4$	$\xleftrightarrow{221,\ 2\cdot7} \xleftrightarrow{231\cdot25,\ 3\cdot21}$	49, –, –
1,2,3,5-Tetrafluorobenzene	$C_6H_2F_4$	$\xleftrightarrow{224\cdot2,\ 2\cdot3} \xleftrightarrow{226\cdot90,\ 3\cdot37}$	49, –, –

Footnotes to Table 10.3.

a. These transitions are preceded by an anomalous rise in the heat capacity which has not been taken into account in assessing the entropies of transition, which may therefore be too low.

b. These two transitions are stated to involve 'only small amounts of energy'.

c. Gradual transition, taking place in two stages (140-220 K, 220-270 K).

d. The data refer to a metastable phase. The stable phase has no transition, and melts at 233·26 K with $\Delta S = 5 \cdot 64 R$.

REFERENCES

1. Rathjens and Gwinn (1953).
2. Carter and Templeton (1953).
3. Hoch and Rushworth (1964) (LW, SM, T_1).
4. Douslin and Huffman (1946).
5. Post, Schwartz, and Fankuchen (1951).
6. Rushworth (1954) (LW, SM, T_1).
7. Ruehrwein and Huffman (1943); Aston, Szasz, and Fink (1943).
8. Hassel and Sommerfeldt (1938); Oda (1948); Krishna Murti (1958); Green and Wheeler (1969b); Renaud and Fourme (1966); Kahn *et al.* (1970), 1973).
9. Andrew and Eades (1953) (LW, SM, T_1); Roeder and Douglass (1970) $(T_{1\rho})$.
10. Roeder and Douglass (1970) $(T_{1\rho})$; Boden, Cohen, and Davis (1972) $(T_1, T_{1\rho}, T_2)$.
11. Van Steenwinkel (1969) (T in local dipolar field).
12. Tanner (1972) (spin-echo).
13. Finke, Scott, Gross, Messerly, and Waddington (1956).
14. Brookeman and Rushworth (1976) (LW, T_1, 50-265 K).
15. Sands and Day (1965).
16. Huffman, Eaton, and Oliver (1948).
17. Lawrenson and Rushworth (1958) (LW, SM).
18. Haida, Suga, and Seki (1973).
19. Eades, Finch, and El Saffar (1959); Andrew (1963) (SM).
20. Reed and Lipscomb (1953).
21. Huffman, Todd, and Oliver (1949).

Footnotes to Table 10.3 continued.....

22. Parks, Kennedy, Gates, Mosley, Moore, and Renquist (1956).

23. Green and Wheeler (1969a).

24. Kelley (1929); Adachi, Suga, and Seki (1968); Green and Griffith (1969).

25. Hassel and Sommerfeldt (1938); Oda (1949); Green and Wheeler (1969b).

26. Eguchi, Soda, and Chihara (1976) (LW, T_1, H and D).

27. Rudman and Post (1968a) (LW, SM).

28. Ziegler and Aurnhammer (1934).

29. Christoffers, Lingafelter, and Cady (1947).

30. Fratiello and Douglass (1964) (SM, T_1).

31. McCullough, Finke, Hubbard, Good, Pennington, Messerly, and Waddington (1954).

32. Kondo (1958).

33. Guthrie, Scott, Hubbard, Katz, McCullough, Gross, Williamson and Waddington (1952).

34. Fourme (1969).

35. Fried (1966) (LW, SM).

36. Waddington, Knowlton, Scott, Oliver, Todd, Hubbard, Smith and Huffman (1949).

37. Bruni and Natta (1929, 1930); Abrahams and Lipscomb (1952); Tranchant and Guérin (1972), Migliorini, Salvi, and Sbrana (1974).

38. Anderson (1970) (SM, T_1).

39. Monica, Jannelli, and Lamanna (1968).

40. Gilson and Saviotti (1974) (LW).

41. Frankonsky and Aston (1965).

42. Brockway and Robertson (1939); Watanabe, Saito, and Chihara (1949); Celotti, Bertinelli, and Stremmenos (1975).

43. Anderson and Slichter (1966a) (T_1 under pressure); Lemanceau, Chezeau, and Hache (1966) (LW, SM); Allen and Cowking (1967) (SM, T_1, 2-450 K); El Saffar (1962) (SM, 1-80 K).

44. Andon et al. (1968).

45. Lagarrigue (1972).

46. Fourme, Renaud, and André (1972); Fourme and Renaud (1972).

47. Brot, Darmon, and Dat-Xuong (1967) (SM).

48. Messerley and Finke (1970).

49. Andon and Martin (1973).

than those of phase I) which can be recorded when phase II
is formed by cooling I are therefore misleading, since the
crystals tend to have been formed with the c axis normal
to the plates of the condenser. When II is produced by
warming the low-temperature form III, it has an altogether
lower permittivity, a little less in fact than that of phase
I. By applying the Onsager equation, Green et al. concluded
that in both phases I and II about three molecules make up a
hydrogen-bonded unit. Any one such unit must, of course, be
regarded as a transitory entity, the molecules of which are
continually switching from one unit to another and changing
their orientation in so doing. Whereas in I the resulting
dipole moment of a unit may point in any direction, in II
the moment tends to be directed along the c axis. On this
basis, Green and his colleagues applied a Bragg-Williams
treatment to their results for phase II, in which the order
parameter is the fraction of the hydrogen-bonded chains
aligned along the c axis.

Turning to the cycloparaffins, cyclobutane and cyclopentane have not yet been investigated in detail. Cyclopentane has two highly disordered phases. The structure of
II (and of III) has still to be determined; that of I is
hexagonal and not cubic. From the phase diagram shown in
Fig.10.5 it will be seen that the application of pressure
considerably extends the temperature range of existence of
I and II, and gives rise to a new phase IV, which may also
be disordered. The volume changes at the III→II and II→I
transitions are only 0·85 and 0·07 per cent respectively.

Cyclohexane-I is one of the plastic crystals in which
self-diffusion has been examined both by the radiotracer
technique (Hood and Sherwood 1966a), and by studies of
plastic flow (creep) (Hawthorne and Sherwood 1970a). Within
the limits of experimental error, the values obtained by the
two methods for the activation energy for self-diffusion
agree, that given by the tracer technique being the more precise. The value of 68 kJ mol^{-1} so obtained, however, is
much larger than those derived from NMR experiments. The
estimates made from measurements of line-width, $T_{1\rho}$, and
the relaxation time in the local dipolar field all fall

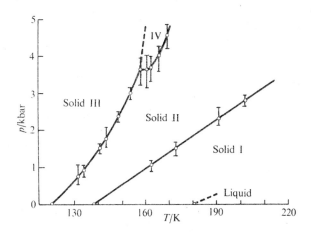

Fig.10.5. Phase diagram of cyclopentane (Webster and Hoch 1976).

between 35 and 45 kJ mol^{-1} (see section 10.7). Spectroscopic studies, such as that of the far-infrared spectrum by
Sataty and Ron (1974), confirm that a high degree of orientational disorder prevails in phase I. When this phase melts,
there is no discontinuity in the rotational correlation time
as deduced from Raman line-broadening (Bartoli and Litovitz
1972). As with cyclohexene, a metastable form III of cyclohexane can be obtained, in this case by quenching small
samples in liquid nitrogen (Kahn, Fourme, André, and Renaud
1970).

As the size of the ring increases in the cycloalkane
series, the molecule becomes increasingly flexible and the
number of possible conformations rises. For cycloheptane, the
ring is already very pliable, and there are four possible conformations (Fig.10.6), of which the 'twist-chair' is probably
the most stable. This substance, which has three disordered
phases, was subjected to a careful NMR study by Brookeman
and Rushworth (1976). Although the lack of structural information was a handicap in the interpretation of their results, some interesting conclusions nevertheless emerged.
Molecular movement influencing the second moment effectively
begins in phase IV at ~120 K, and it seems probable that in

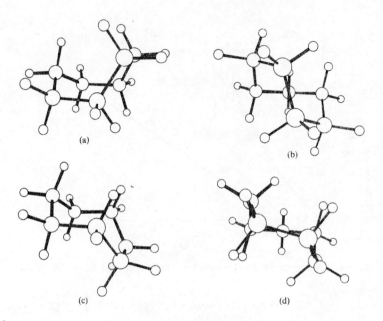

Fig.10.6. The four conformations of the cycloheptane molecule; (a) boat, (b) twist-boat, (c) chair, (d) twist-chair (Brookeman and Rushworth 1976).

III there is just one type of such motion, which is fully developed. Brookeman and Rushworth suggested that this might involve interconversion between the different conformations. One way (though not the only one) in which this could come about is by 'pseudo-rotation'. The possibility of this kind of motion was first raised by Kilpatrick, Pitzer, and Spitzer (1947) in connection with the puckered ring of cyclopentane. They coined the term pseudo-rotation to describe a process in which the angle of maximum puckering rotates round the ring. In cycloheptane it would take the form of concerted movement of the methylene groups, producing a sequence in the course of which each group takes up all possible ring positions. There is more than one way in which the CH_2 groups could move to achieve this, but a definite decision cannot be made between the several possibilities, and indeed more than one type of motion may be simultaneously involved. In phases II and I relatively free isotropic reorientation of

the molecule occurs, and diffusion begins as the melting-
point is approached.

From the observed entropy gain at the transition in
furan, which is within two per cent of $R \ln 5$, taken in con-
junction with the shape of the molecule, it might be inferred
that in I each molecule has access to five different orientations. In fact, Fourme (1969) demonstrated by a single-
crystal diffraction study that the molecules in the disordered phase are distributed among *four* equivalent positions (Fig.10.7). Fried and Lassier (1966) concluded from
a dielectric dispersion study of furan that the reorientation frequency at 171 K is remarkably high (6 000 MHz), the
activation energy being only $8 \cdot 5$ kJ mol^{-1} (not very different from the value for the liquid state). Darmon and

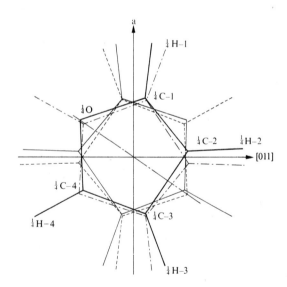

Fig.10.7. The four possible positions of a furan molecule in phase I
(Fourme 1969).

Brot (1967) showed that even with such facile reorientation
as this, the proportion of molecules which are actually in a
'state of jump' at any instant is only of the order of one
per cent. Thiophene, though structurally similar to furan,

shows interesting differences. Although it has three
transitions, no line-width changes are observed at any of
these, and the total entropy gained at them is not large.
Nevertheless, the relatively low value of the second moment
at 93 K ($2 \cdot 85$ G^2 as compared with the value of $6 \cdot 8$ G^2 for
fixed molecules) shows that some reorientational freedom
persists even at this low temperature. By comparing the
infrared spectra of the four forms, Paliani, Poletti, and
Cataliotti (1973) concluded that forms I, II, and III are
all disordered. The structures of these have still not
been definitely established. On spectroscopic evidence,
III may be orthorhombic and IV monoclinic, though tetragonal and orthorhombic structures have also been suggested
for this last phase (Migliorini, Salvi, and Sbrana 1974).
Abrahams and Lipscomb (1952) concluded from their X-ray
study of phase I that the orientational disorder takes the
form of the availability of a limited number of possible
orientations in the plane of the ring - either four or two.
The II→I transition is somewhat unusual, in that the heat
capacity remains abnormally high (by a factor of about two),
for ~4 K *above* the temperature at which energy is isothermally absorbed, before falling rapidly to normal values.

Sulpholan, the molecular structure of which is shown
in Fig.10.8, is another example of a compound which can
exist in a highly disordered phase even though the molecules
are strongly polar ($p = 4 \cdot 8$ D) and of low symmetry. The
NMR study of this compound revealed two line-width transitions, one at ~210 K which is probably associated with reorientation about the twofold axis, the other at 288 K
which is probably a consequence of more general reorientation and self-diffusion. The substance octaphenylsiloxane
(Fig.10.8) forms plastic crystals between a transition at
~461 K and the melting-point at 478 K. The ratio $\Delta S_t / \Delta S_m$
was estimated to have the very high value of ~22 (Keyes and
Daniels 1975).

Turning to benzene derivatives, an obvious possibility
at sufficiently high temperatures is limited orientational
disorder within the plane of the ring. For molecules with a
sixfold symmetry axis, such as benzene itself, hexamethyl-

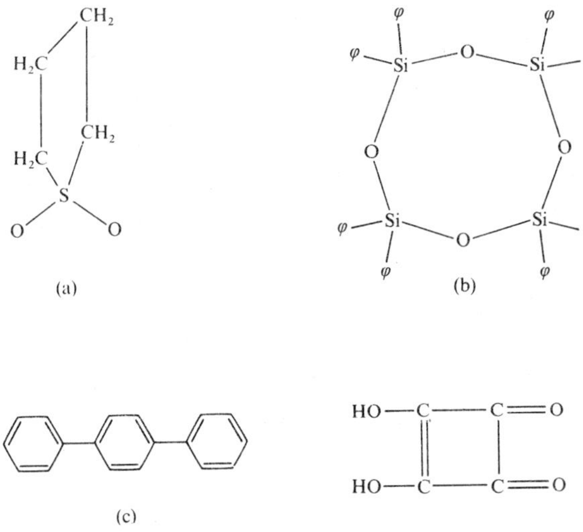

Fig.10.8. The structural formulae of (a) sulpholan, (b) octaphenylsiloxane, (c) terphenyl, (d) squaric acid.

benzene and hexafluorobenzene, the acquisition of freedom of orientational movement of this kind will not increase the configurational energy of the system, since the six possible orientations are indistinguishable, and there need not therefore be any concomitant thermal effects. Andrew's pioneering experiments on the effect of temperature on the NMR line-width in crystalline benzene made it clear that at higher temperatures the molecules switch rapidly from one orientation to another in the plane of the ring, but there is no transition or thermal anomaly. The situation is different, of course, for partially substituted benzene derivatives, and for some at least of the transitions in such compounds listed in Table 10.3 much of the entropy gain at the transition is the configurational contribution resulting from the distribution of the molecules among different distinguishable orientations within the molecular planes.

In benzene itself, measurements of the proton T_1 and $T_{1\rho}$ gave 19 kJ mol^{-1} for E_R, the activation energy for reorientation, and 94 kJ mol^{-1} for E_D (for diffusion) (Noack,

Weithase, and von Schütz 1975). This last value agrees reasonably well with those obtained from self-diffusion studies
carried out with tritium and ^{14}C (Fox and Sherwood 1971),
but the pre-exponential factor derived from the tracer work
exceeds the NMR value by $\sim 10^4$. In crystalline hexafluorobenzene there are two kinds of site. ^{19}F T_1 measurements gave
E_R = 31·2 kJ mol^{-1} for molecules at one kind of site, and
12·6 kJ mol^{-1} for those at the other (Boden, Davis, Stam, and
Wesselink 1973). For diffusion, E_D = 52 kJ mol^{-1} (Roeder
and Douglass 1970).

The most thoroughly studied benzene derivative is hexamethylbenzene. It was at one time thought that the lower
transition marked the onset of the rotation of the methyl
groups about the bonds joining them to the aromatic ring,
but this is not so, since an NMR study by El Saffar (1962)
showed that this movement is still quite facile even at temperatures as low as 1 K[†]. This is a consequence of quantum-
mechanical tunnelling by the protons, and is not because
the barrier to the rotation of the methyl groups is very
small. Rush and Taylor (1966) in a neutron scattering study
observed a band which they attributed to the torsional oscillations of the methyl groups which was peaked at 137 cm^{-1}
below the III→II λ-transition, but which shifted to 120 cm^{-1}
above the transition. Concordant estimates of the librational frequencies in phase II and III were obtained from the
Raman spectrum (Dumas and Michel 1971). Rush and Taylor estimated that the barrier to rotation of the methyl group
drops from 5·6 kJ mol^{-1} in phase III to 4·5 kJ mol^{-1} in phase
II (see also Section 4.6.1 and Fig.4.25). These values are
considerably less than that of 10-15 kJ mol^{-1} made by an
analysis of the entropy of the *vapour* by Overberger, Steele,
and Aston (1969), so this is another example - the case of
methylchloroform has already been cited - of a molecule in
which the barrier impeding the internal rotation of a methyl
group appears to be significantly different according to

[†]Another example of almost free methyl group rotation is provided by γ-
picoline (4-methyl-pyridine), for which the minimum in T_1 due to this
movement occurs at 2·3 K (Zweers, Brom, and Huiskamp 1974).

whether the molecule is isolated or in a crystal lattice.

The nature of the changes taking place at the III→II transition has not yet been unequivocally established. Two possibilities are that in II there is some distortion of the ring, or that the methyl groups tilt out of the plane of the ring. From observations of the Raman and infrared spectra, Prasad, Woodruff, and Kopelman (1973) concluded that the marked alterations which appear to take place in the phonon spectrum support the second alternative. This transition shows an isotope effect which is remarkably large for a non-hydrogen-bonded substance, T_λ rising by ~20 K on complete deuteration. Prasad et al. regarded this as also favouring tilting of the methyl groups rather than ring distortion. Little is known of the cause or consequences of the upper, II→I transition, where the neutron scattering spectrum scarcely alters. An interesting feature of phase I, noted by Chihara and Seki (1948), is that after the transition at 383 K the volume of phase I increases to a maximum at 403 K and then drops considerably (by about ten per cent) to a minimum. Hexamethylbenzene is one of the relatively few substances for which not only the temperature dependence but also the pressure dependence of the spin-lattice relaxation time T_1 has been measured. The activation energy of ~28 kJ mol^{-1} for what is presumably molecular reorientation is independent of pressure up to 680 bar, while the volume of activation is 13 per cent of the molar volume.

Partially substituted benzene derivatives have received some attention, especially from French investigators who have carried out thermal, NMR, and dielectric measurements. Some information on transitions in selected compounds of this type is given in Table 10.3. It will be noted that the entropies of transition are now less than the entropies of fusion. The disorder in the high-temperature phases is more limited than for most of the compounds already discussed in this section, and these crystals do not really fall in the plastic category.

A molecule of pentafluorochlorobenzene, C_6F_5Cl, will have six distinguishable orientations within the molecular plane, and if (as seems likely from the NMR work) the III→II

transition is associated with the gain of orientational freedom in this plane, the configurational entropy increase
would be $R \ln 6$, $= 14 \cdot 9$ J K^{-1} mol^{-1}. The observed transition
entropy of $17 \cdot 9$ J K^{-1} mol^{-1} is in fact rather larger than this.
An interesting feature of the development of disorder in 1,2,
3-trimethyl-4,5,6-trichlorobenzene $(C_6(CH_3)_3Cl_3)$ is that it
appears thermally as a very gradual anomaly which extends
from 140 K to 270 K and which involves two stages. Here,
the total entropy gain of $3 \cdot 8$ J K^{-1} mol^{-1} is much less than
$R \ln 6$. Further examples of benzene derivatives capable of
sixfold in-plane disorder are chloropentamethylbenzene
(Charbonneau and Trotter 1968), 1,2,4-trichloro-3,5,6-tri-
methylbenzene (Charbonneau and Trotter 1967, Eveno and
Meinnel 1966), 1,2-dichloro-3,4,5,6-tetramethylbenzene, and
pentachlorotoluene. These last two substances, together
with 1,2,3-trichloro-4,5,6-trimethylbenzene, were considered
by Brot and Darmon (1970) with special reference to their dielectric properties. They showed that the cooperative ordering which takes place on cooling produces an antiferroelectric arrangement of the polar molecules for which electrostatic interaction is responsible. In a quantitative treatment of this interaction, they demonstrated the superiority
of a localized charge model over a point-dipole model. The
compound dichlorodurene (1,2,4,5-tetramethyl-3,6-dichloro-
benzene) has a monoclinic lattice, space group $P2_1/a$, in
which there is statistical orientational disorder in the plane
of the ring. There is a gradual transition with its peak
at ~165 K, but even below this some disorder persists (Messager and Blot 1971, Messager and Sanquer 1974).

In-plane orientational disorder is also possible in
solids composed of molecules with fused ring systems. A
simple example is benzthiophene. This has a λ-transition with
$\Delta S_t = R \ln 4$ within one per cent. This suggests that whereas
all molecules have a unique orientation in the low-temperature
form, above the transition they make full use of the four
possibilities shown in Fig.10.9. The high-temperature form
can be supercooled, and then retains entropy at 0 K of approximately $R \ln 2$. Not surprisingly, therefore, changes
between one orientation and another of the set of four must

differ in the ease with which they can be accomplished.
The supercooled high-temperature form behaves like a glassy
crystal in that there is an 'extra' rise in the heat capacity between 110 K and 120 K.

   Monoclinic sulphur (space group $P2_1/c$) is a partially
disordered crystal, in that one-third of the cyclic S_8 molecules can have either of two orientations (Sands 1965).
This adds $(R/3)\ln2$ to the entropy of a mole (S_8) of monoclinic sulphur. Montgomery (1974) found that, within experimental error, all of this additional entropy is lost at a
λ-transition $(T_\lambda \approx 198$ K), so that this allotrope of sulphur,
like the rhombic form, is ordered at 0 K. An unusual kind
of disorder is shown by p-terphenyl (Fig.10.8). This compound has a transition at 178 K, above which the central
ring in the molecule has two possible inclinations with respect to the two outer rings (Baudour, Cailleau, Delugeard,
Desuche, Girard, Meinnel, and Yelon 1976).

   Finally, as something of a curiosity, we may mention
squaric acid (3,4-dihydroxy-3-cyclobut-3-ene-1,2-dione,
Fig.10.8). This undergoes a λ-type transition at 371 K which
shows an astonishingly large isotope effect, T_λ rising to
516 K on complete deuteration. The crystal, however, is essentially a two-dimensional hydrogen-bonded structure, and
so in the order-disorder context probably has more affinity

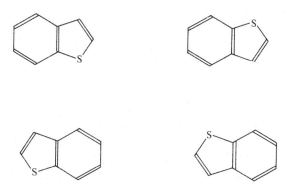

Fig.10.9. The four possible orientations of a benzthiophene molecule in
phase I.

with the ferroelectrics and antiferroelectrics discussed in
Chapter 7 and with the two-dimensional hydrates mentioned in
Chapter 8 than with the molecular solids dealt with in this
section (Semmingsen and Feder 1974, Samuelsen and Semmingsen
1975).

10.3. CAGE MOLECULES

The compounds in Table 10.4 are examples of substances with
cage-like (or bridged-ring) molecules, all of which have
a high-temperature disordered phase. Further compounds of
this kind will be found in the review by Timmermans (1961)
and in the paper of White and Bishop (1940). Some of the
solids listed in Table 10.4 have already been investigated
in some detail, and for these crystals we give in Table 10.5
experimental values for the parameters controlling the rates
of reorientation and diffusion.

A substance which has been particularly thoroughly
studied is the hydrocarbon adamantane, the structural formula
of which is shown in Fig.10.10. The differences between
phases I and II have been revealed by X-ray work. In the
low-temperature, ordered form II the molecules are distributed between two mutually perpendicular orientations such
that two adjacent molecules are normal to one another. In
the high-temperature form I, the molecules are randomly distributed between these two possible orientations. When I
transforms into II on cooling, one of the cubic axes contracts to become the tetragonal c axis. The reverse change,
II→I, begins gradually but is largely completed isothermally.
From an infrared spectroscopic study, Wu, Hsu, and Dows (1971)
concluded that in the region of the transition (which is accompanied by hysteresis) small regions of one crystal can
exist in a matrix of the other. Since there is a volume
difference of ~9% between the two phases, the small regions
of the new phase are presumably under considerable tension
or compression. The NMR studies of adamantane have been
carried out with exceptional thoroughness. McCall and
Douglass (1960) followed the line-width from 100 K to 340 K,
making the interesting observation that there is no line-
width change at the transition at 209 K in spite of the not

TABLE 10.4

Thermodynamic and structural information on substances with 'cage' molecules forming plastic crystals
(See Fig.10.10 for formulae 1–18)

		II ⟷ I: T_t/K, $\Delta S_t/R$	I	I ⟷ Liq.: T_m/K, $\Delta S_m/R$	References: Cal.	Cryst.	NMR
(1)	Bicyclo[2,2,2]octane	164·25(F), 3·35		447·5, 2·25	1	-	2
			F.c.c.				
(2)	Bicyclo[2,2,2]octa-2-ene	176·5(F), 3·86		389·75, 1·22	1	-	2
		(III ⟷ II) 110·5(λ), 0·39					
(3)	Bicyclo[2,2,1]heptane (norbornane)	306, 0·03		360, 1·53	3,4	5	6
		II: H.c.p. 6/mmm	F.c.c.				
		(III ⟷ II) 131, 3·79					
(4)	1-Azabicyclo[2,2,2]octane (quinuclidine)	196·0(F), 3·19		430·0, 1·61	7	8	2
			F.c.c.				
(5)	1,4-Diazabicyclo[2,2,2]octane (triethylenediamine)	351·1(F), 3·62		433·1, 2·06	9	10	6,11, 12
		II: Hexagonal $P6_3/m$	F.c.c.				
(6)	3-Azabicyclo[3,2,2]nonane	297·8(F), 5·85		467, 1·79	13	-	6
			F.c.c.				
(7)	3-Oxabicyclo[3,2,2]nonane	208·5(λ), 4·14		448·4, 1·82	7	-	-

No.	Compound	Transition data	Structure	Refs
(8)	Bicyclo[2,2,1]hepta-2-ene (norbornylene)	129, 4.52 → 320, 1.22 →	H.c.p. 6/mmm	4, 5, 6
(9)	Bicyclo[2,2,1]hepta-2,5-diene (norbornadiene)	202, 5.32 → 254, 0.80 →	H.c.p. 6/mmm	4, 5, 6
(10)	Nortricyclene	173, 4.5 → 330, 1.25 →		4, –, –
(11)	Exo-2-cyanobicyclo[2,2,1]heptane	238, 3.92 → 300, 1.18 →		27, –, –
(12)	Endo-2-cyanobicyclo[2,2,1]heptane	177, 1.42 → 332, 1.07 →		28, ·, –
(13)	Exo-2-methylbicyclo[2,2,1]heptane	152, 3.72 → 387, 0.70 →		28, –, –
(14)	Adamantane	208.6 (F), 1.95 → ~543 →	Tetragonal $P\bar{4}2_1c$ / F.c.c. $Fm3m$	14, 15, 16
(15)	Ortho-Carborane	273.6 (F), 1.70 → 569.5, 2.61 → (III ← 158.2 (F), 0.87 → II)	F.c.c.	17,18 / 17 / 17,19
(16)	Meta-Carborane	282.4 (F), 1.87 → 545.8, 2.70 → (III ← 162.5 (F), 1.51 → II)	F.c.c.	18 / 17 / 17

	Transitions	F.c.c. / structure	References
(17) *d*-Camphor	374, 0·076 ⟶ Hexagonal (III (?Tetragonal) ⟵ 244·5, 5·6 ⟶ II)	F.c.c. ⟶ 451, 1·82	20 21,22 21,23
dl-Camphor	350, 0·08 ⟶ (III ⟵ 203·8, 1·73 ⟶ II)	F.c.c. ⟶ 451, 1·82	20 21 21
(18) *dl*-Camphene	~153 ⟶	B.c.c. ⟶ ~324, 1·15	24 22,25 26

Footnotes overleaf

Footnotes to Table 10.4.

REFERENCES

1. Wong and Westrum (1970).

2. Darmon and Brot (1966) (SM).

3. Guthrie and McCullough (1961).

4. Westrum (1969).

5. Jackson and Strange (1972).

6. Folland, Jackson, Strange, and Chadwick (1973) (LW, SM, $T_{1\rho}$).

7. Westrum, Wong, and Morawetz (1970).

8. Nowacki (1946).

9. S.-S. Chang and Westrum (1960b); Trowbridge and Westrum (1963).

10. Wada, Kishida, Tomiie, Suga, Seki, and Nitta (1960); Weiss, Parkes, Nixon, and Hughes (1964); Reynolds (1974) (neutron); Nimmo and Lucas (1976) (neutron).

11. G.W.Smith (1965) (LW, SM, T_1); Suga, Sugisaki, and Seki (1966).

12. Bladon, Lockhart, and Sherwood (1971a) (LW).

13. Barber and Westrum (1963); Wulff and Westrum (1964).

14. S.-S. Chang and Westrum (1960a).

15. Nordman and Schmitkons (1965); Mirskaya (1963); Donohue and Goodman (1967).

16. McCall and Douglass (1960) (SM, T_1); G.W.Smith (1961) (SM); Resing (1965) (T_1), (1969) (T_1, T_1^*, T_2); Graham and Choi (1975) (LW, SM).

17. Baughman (1970) (LW, SM).

18. Westrum and Henriquez (1976).

19. Leffler, Alexander, Sagalyn, and Walker (1975) (LW and T_1, H, ^{10}B, ^{11}B).

20. Schäfer and Wagner (1958).

21. Anderson and Slichter (1964) (SM, T_1).

22. Finbak and Viervoll (1942).

23. Moskalev and Petrov (1963).

24. Roth (1936).

25. Green and Wheeler (1969a,b).

26. Blum and Sherwood (1970) (LW).

27. Kolesov, Seregin, and Skuratov, quoted by Westrum (1966).

28. Results of Russian investigators, quoted in Reference 4.

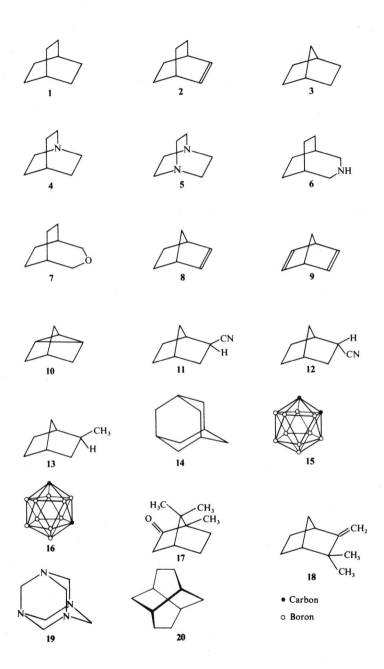

Fig.10.10. Structural formulae of the compounds numbered (1) to (18) in Table 10.4, and of hexamethylenetetramine (19) and 'twistane' (20).

inconsiderable volume change. Resing (1965, 1969) measured
not only the ordinary relaxation times T_1 and T_2 but also
T_1^*, the relaxation time in the local field, using the technique developed by Ailion and Slichter (section 4.4) to
measure very long diffusional jump times. The temperature
dependence of T_1, T_2, and T_1^* is shown in Fig.10.11. A detailed analysis demonstrated that the line-width reduction

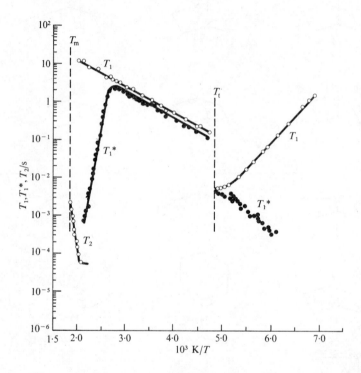

Fig.10.11. The temperature dependence of the relaxation times T_1, T_1^* and
T_2 for adamantane, after Resing (1969). T_2 and T_1^* on the left are determined by diffusion, whereas T_1 in both phases is dominated by molecular
reorientation.

at ~170 K is undoubtedly due to the onset of molecular reorientation, and the later narrowing of the line in phase I
from ~475 K upwards to diffusion. The latter movement is
also responsible for the course taken by T_2 and T_1^* at the
highest temperatures, while the trend in T_1 is dominated
by reorientation. In Fig.10.12 the logarithm of the jump
frequencies (reciprocal jump times) is plotted against

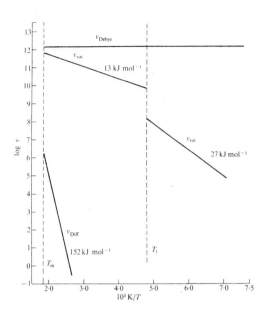

Fig.10.12. Jump frequencies for reorientation and diffusion in adamantane (after Resing 1969).

reciprocal temperature. It will be seen that altogether a range of jump rates of nearly 10^{12} is covered. The difference in the activation energy E_R for reorientation in phases I and II is noteworthy, as is the sudden increase in reorientational jump frequency at the II→I transition. At the melting-point, this frequency reaches a value of about one half of the Debye frequency, ν_D. Since the time spent by a molecule in the actual process of jumping is $\sim \nu_D^{-1}$, this means that this time is comparable with the interval between jumps. This is the basis for the statement in the general remarks about molecular rotation in crystals made in the previous chapter, that the molecules in crystalline adamantane near the melting-point are approaching a condition of free rotation.

Adamantane has frequently been compared with hexamethylenetetramine (HMT), the structural formula of which is shown in Fig.10.10. In spite of the molecular similarity, the differences in crystalline properties of the two compounds are considerable. HMT only exists in one phase, and although this is body-centred cubic and has about the same melting-point as adamantane, it is *not* a plastic crystal. The NMR estimates of the reorientational activation energy E_R in HMT are 65 kJ mol^{-1} (Alexander and Tzalmona 1965), 75 kJ mol^{-1} (G.W.Smith 1962) and 81 kJ mol^{-1} (Resing 1969), which are altogether higher than E_R for adamantane, while diffusion in HMT is too slow to be measured even by the ultra-slow-motion technique. Although the molecule of HMT is non-polar, pre-sumably there are strongly directional forces between the molecules in the crystal owing to the local polarity centred around the nitrogen atoms.

Mention should be made of two theoretical studies involving adamantane, one carried out by Reynolds (1975), the other by Fyfe and Harold-Smith (1976a,b). The object of Reynolds' work was to calculate the thermodynamic properties of the two phases and the changes in thermodynamic functions at the transition, as well as the volume and enthalpy of activation for molecular reorientation. An Ising model was used, and the intermolecular potential was constructed by summing over atom-atom interactions. The only experimentally determined property for which a value was assumed was the low-temperature thermal expansion. Using the mean-field Ising approximation, very fair agreement was obtained between the observed and calculated values of numerous crystal pro-perties in both modifications. This approach was less suc-cessful in accounting for the behaviour of the heat capacity in the transition region, but Reynolds showed that a con-siderable improvement in this respect could be brought about by replacing the mean-field approximation by a series expan-sion solution. This is tantamount to expanding the parti-tion function to take account of the effect of clusters (of increasing size) of disordered molecules in an ordered lattice, disorder with regard to the position of the mass centres of the molecules as well as with respect to their orientation being recognized. Fyfe and Harold-Smith also used a summed atom-atom potential to calculate first the energy barrier to reorientation of the adamantane molecules in both phases (1976a), and then to estimate the energy barriers opposing diffusion (1976b). They considered in

detail the influence on any one molecule of its orientational relation with its nearest neighbours, and showed what
a striking effect could be exerted on the energy required
by a molecule to move to a vacant nearest-neighbour site by
its neighbours adopting favourable orientations. They concluded that, as a result of this interdependence, the energetically favoured path for a molecule migrating from one
site to another is curved.

Adamantane has an isomer, 'twistane', (tricyclo[4,4,0,0]
decane; Fig.10.10), the molecule of which is formed exclusively from twist-boat cyclohexane rings. Little is known as yet
about this solid, but from NMR experiments it too appears
to form a plastic phase, permitting both self-diffusion and
facile molecular reorientation (Graham and Choi 1975).

The molecule of *ortho*-carborane has a lower symmetry
than that of adamantane, and it also has a large dipole
moment of $4 \cdot 5$ D. Nevertheless, at room temperature the
molecules in crystalline *ortho*-carborane have considerable
orientational freedom, since the second moment at 25°C of
$0 \cdot 71$ G^2 is very much less than the value of 34 G^2 calculated
for a rigid lattice. The only kind of reorientational motion
possible for this molecule which would not generate *distinguishable* reorientations is reorientation about the twofold
axis. If reorientation were limited to this, calculation
shows that the second moment would be at least $15 \cdot 5$ G^2.
There are thirty distinguishable ways in which the carbon
and boron atoms can be disposed at the twelve vertices of
the molecular icosahedron, so that if all molecules adopted
a unique orientation on cooling into phase II, the maximum
configurational entropy loss would be $R \ln 30$, $= 3 \cdot 4R$. In
fact, the sum of the entropy changes at the two transitions is
less than this, and disorder equivalent to a configurational
entropy of $\sim R \ln 2$ may be frozen-in in form III (Westrum and
Henriquez 1976). For the *meta* isomer, on the other hand,
the combined ΔS_t is almost exactly $R \ln 30$.

Some preliminary work has been carried out on substituted *ortho*-carboranes, several of which were found to form
plastic phases, though the temperature ranges over which
these exist are considerably smaller than for the parent

substance (Klingen and Kindsvater 1974). A plastic modification can still exist with substituents as large as a
propyl or a phenyl group. The most thoroughly studied derivative is 1-vinyl-*o*-carborane, which forms a face-centred,
disordered phase from 284 K to the melting-point at 352 K
which gives a very narrow NMR line (Klingen and Wright 1972).

     Molecular motion in crystalline triethylenediamine has
already been discussed in section 4.4. This solid was also
treated by Reynolds (1974) by combining Ising theory with
a summed atom-atom intermolecular potential. Using no adjustable parameters, good agreement was obtained between calculated and experimentally determined properties. An interesting deduction made by Reynolds, which is relevant to the
discussion of the significance of entropies of transition in
the last section (7.7) of this chapter, was that about 60%
of the entropy of the transition in triethylenediamine must
be ascribed to expansion, leaving only 40% for the configurational entropy gain.

     With regard to the bicyclic hydrocarbons listed in Table
10.4, until recently the information available on these was
limited to the results of careful calorimetric work, mostly
due to Westrum and his collaborators. These solids are now
attracting increasing attention, since they enable comparison to be made between crystals with highly symmetric and
rather similar molecules. Thus, an informative investigation of the proton magnetic resonance (line-width and T_1
measurements) was carried out by Folland, Jackson, Strange,
and Chadwick (1973) on norbornane, norbornylene, and nor-
bornadiene, as well as on triethylenediamine and 3-aza-
bicyclononane. Some of the results of this study are given
in Table 10.5, and their implications are considered in
Section 7.7. Quantitative information on the dynamics of
molecular reorientation in norbornylene has also resulted
from an analysis of Rayleigh and Raman line-broadening
(Folland, Jackson, and Rajagopal 1975), from which it was
inferred that the activation energy for reorientation increases from $6 \cdot 3$ kJ mol^{-1} at room temperature to $10 \cdot 5$ kJ
mol^{-1} at 129 K. Norbornane has two plastic phases, the
lower being hexagonal close-packed and the upper face-centred

TABLE 10.5

Experimental values of the parameters governing the rates of reorientation and diffusion in solids composed of cage molecules. E_R and E_D are the Arrhenius activation energies in $kJ\ mol^{-1}$ for reorientation and diffusion respectively. ν_∞ and D_0 refer to the equations $\nu = \nu_\infty exp(-E_R/RT)$ and $D = D_0 exp(-E_D/RT)$, where ν is the jump frequency (reciprocal mean molecular jump time) and D the self-diffusion coefficient; ν_∞ is in s^{-1} and D_0 in $cm^2 s^{-1}$

Substance	Reorientation				Diffusion			
	Phase	ν_∞	E_R	Ref.	Phase	ν_∞ or D_0	E_D	Ref.
Triethylene-diamine	II	10^{12}	30	1	I	$10^{12}(\nu_\infty)$	68	1
					I	$2\times10^{17}(\nu_\infty)$	91	2
					I	$1.3\times10^{18}(\nu_\infty)$	96.4	3
Adamantane	II	9×10^{14}	27.2	4	I	$5\times10^{5}(D_0)$	152	4
	I	10^{13}	12.9	4				
ortho-carborane	II	1.2×10^{14}	34.4	5	I	$3\times10^{11}(\nu_\infty)$	69.5	5
	II	-	~18	6				
	I	7×10^{11}	5.8	6				
d-Camphor	II	-	11.5	7				
	II	-.	7.5	8				
	II	1.5×10^{12}	11.5	9	I	-	61	9
	II,I		13.5	10	II,I	$3\times10^{12}(\nu_\infty)$	67	11
dl-Camphene	I	-	6.7	7	I	$3\times10^{8}(D_0)$	98	12
					I	-	50	13
	I	-	9.2	8	I	-	104	14
Norbornane					II	$2.2\times10^{14}(\nu_\infty)$	54.5	3
					I	$9\times10^{15}(\nu_\infty)$	64.8	3
Norbornylene	I	-	6.3 (300K)	15	I	$2.3\times10^{14}(\nu_\infty)$	48.6	3
		-	10.5 (129K)	15				
Norbornadiene					I	$1.6\times10^{14}(\nu_\infty)$	39.9	3
3-Azabicyclo-nonane					I	$6\times10^{15}(\nu_\infty)$	83.6	3

Footnotes to Table 10.5

REFERENCES

1.   G.W.Smith (1965) (NMR).

2.   Suga, Sugisaki, and Seki (1966) (NMR; ν_∞ calculated by Baughman 1970).

3.   Folland et al. (1973) (NMR).

4.   Resing (1969) (NMR).

5.   Baughman (1970) (NMR).

6.   Leffler et al. (1975) (NMR).

7.   Williams and Smyth (1962) (dielectric relaxation).

8.   Clemett and Davies (1962b) (dielectric relaxation).

9.   Anderson and Slichter (1964) (NMR).

10.   Powles (1952) (dielectric relaxation).

11.   Moskalev and Petrov (1963) (NMR).

12.   Sherwood (1969) (diffusion, by radiotracer).

13.   Blum and Sherwood (1970) (NMR).

14.   Hawthorne and Sherwood (1970b) (creep).

15.   Folland, Jackson, and Rajagopal (1975) (Raman and Rayleigh line-broadening).

cubic, with an entropy of transition of only $0 \cdot 03R$.

The case of camphor introduces a matter to which we have not referred before, namely the pronounced differences which can be found between an optically active form and the racemic form of a substance. With camphor, interest centres not so much on the minor high-temperature phase transition II→I (at which there is virtually no change in the disorder already existing in phase II, or in the molecular dynamics), but in the lower transition III→II and in the nature and properties of phase II. The relatively small amount of work so far carried out on l-camphor shows, as indeed is to be expected, that it is identical with d-camphor in the properties and behaviour of interest to us. But between d-camphor and dl-camphor there are striking differences, the chief of which are the following:-

(1) The III→II transition, while broad in both crystals, is

more diffuse in dl-camphor than in d-camphor.

(2) The same is true of the NMR line-width transition. As will be seen from Fig.10.13, this happens at a rather lower temperature for both solids than that at which the heat capacity reaches a maximum, but the line-width decrease is much less abrupt in dl-camphor than in d-camphor.

(3) The permittivity increase for dl-camphor at the III→II transition is only about half of that for d-camphor (Yager and Morgan 1935).

(4) The entropy loss on cooling II to give III is much larger for d-camphor than for dl-camphor.

(5) Whereas the powder photographs of d- and dl-camphor are identical at room temperature, they are quite different at 77 K, that for the racemic crystal having significantly fewer reflections. Again, the change from the low temperature to the room temperature structure is much less abrupt for dl- than for d-camphor.

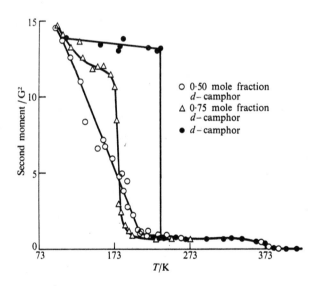

Fig.10.13. Temperature dependence of NMR second moment in d-camphor and in solid solutions of d- and l-camphor (Anderson and Slichter 1964).

These differences, especially (4) and (5), imply that

considerable disorder persists in phase III of the dl-crystal, but not of d-camphor, and this inference is supported by other evidence. Rossiter (1972) carried out a comprehensive dielectric relaxation study and showed that there is a difference in the Cole-Cole plots for d-camphor and dl-camphor which can be interpreted to mean that there is a much wider distribution of relaxation times in the dl-form. This would be associated with the retention of some disorder in the dl-lattice with a consequent variation in the local environment from molecule to molecule in the crystal (cf. Fig.4.13 and the comments on this on p.145). Camphor is one of the substances for which the pressure dependence of T_1 has been examined. Whereas pressures up to ~690 bar have no effect on T_1 for d-camphor in phase III, for dl-camphor T_1 is increased by applying pressure, indicating a decrease in molecular motion, and it may be that dl-camphor-III as first formed contains defects which are progressively reduced by the application of pressure.

The observed second moment is such that even at temperatures as low as 100 K the three methyl groups must be changing their orientations with a frequency of ~10^4 s^{-1}, the barrier to rotation being ~17 kJ mol^{-1}, and this motion must be regarded as responsible for the minimum in T_1 for d-camphor near 150 K. Molecular tumbling is, of course, the cause of the fall in the second moment shown in Fig.10.13. Rossiter considered that the dielectric evidence supports the view that there is a sudden increase in orientational freedom at the III→II transition, which White and Morgan (1935) had previously suggested might be associated with a change in the intramolecular vibrational condition - a change in the molecular rigidity, as it were. Be that as it may, the activation energy of ~11 kJ mol^{-1} for reorientation in phase II certainly seems small for molecules of such size.

Some work has been performed on crystals with a d-camphor content between 50 and 100 %. The concentration dependence of the transition temperatures as found by Schäfer and Wagner (1958) is shown in Fig.10.14, from which it will be seen that a minimum value of the temperature of the III→II transition is attained for a solid consisting of three d-

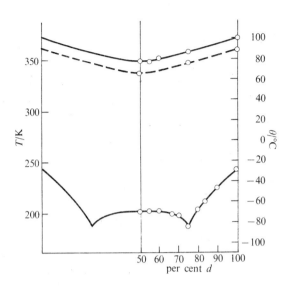

Fig.10.14. Transition temperatures in the d-camphor-l-camphor system. Lower curve, III-II transition; upper curve II-I transition (full line, heating; dotted line, cooling) (Schäfer and Wagner 1958).

molecules to one l-molecule. This solid, in phase III, has a different crystal structure from either d-camphor or dl-camphor, while the temperature dependence of the second moment (Fig.10.13) shows that while much of the molecular tumbling is arrested about 17 K below the thermodynamic transition temperature, some still persists down to 110 K.

For dl-camphene, Green and Wheeler's X-ray study (1969a) led them to conclude that the molecules do not achieve spherical symmetry by rotation, but are restricted to switching between a limited number of orientations, probably twelve. We shall refer to this substance again in discussing possible mechanisms of self-diffusion in plastic crystals (section 7.7).

10.4. OCTAHEDRAL AND OTHER MOLECULES
Table 10.6 (p.663) contains information on compounds which show order-disorder transitions and which are composed of molecules of a variety of shapes. The prevalence of body-centred cubic structures among the high-temperature disordered phases

will be noted, as well as some similarities between the structures of the ordered modifications, such as MoF_6-II and
C_2Br_6-II.

It is interesting that the hexafluorides of the actinide
elements uranium, neptunium, and plutonium do *not* give high-
temperature phases with low entropies of fusion. For UF_6,
NpF_6 and PuF_6, ΔS_m = 6·85R, 6·45R, and 6·9R respectively. In
the last three compounds the metal-fluorine bonds are 8-9%
longer than in their analogues WF_6, ReF_6, and OsF_6, so the
reason may simply be that this produces molecular inter-
locking in the actinide compounds to an extent which prevents
facile molecular reorientation - just as the compact molecule of carbon tetramethyl gives rise to a plastic crystal,
whereas the tetramethyls of silicon, germanium, tin, and
lead do not (*cf*. J.H. Levy, Taylor, and Wilson 1975b). The
structure of solid uranium hexafluoride (orthorhombic, space
group *Pnma*) is similar to that of the low-temperature forms
of the hexafluorides of metals of the second and third
transition series. It may be added that in addition to the
hexafluorides listed in Table 10.6, those of technetium,
ruthenium, and rhodium also undergo transitions to give high-
temperature phases which are almost certainly plastic crystals
(Chernick, Claassen, and Weinstock 1961).

The behaviour of xenon hexafluoride lives up to the re-
putation of this remarkable compound for producing the unexpected. Its comparatively low entropy of fusion qualifies
it for inclusion as a plastic crystal, though it should be
pointed out that the *liquid* produced on melting is highly
associated. Unlike the other hexafluorides listed in Table
10.6 with their single transition, xenon hexafluoride exists
in four solid forms. In addition to the three modifications
listed in Table 10.6, there is a form IV which is cubic
(space group *Fm3c*) and which is stable from its melting-point
of 301 K down to at least 93 K. Burbank and Jones (1974)
showed that XeF_6-IV is disordered in a very remarkable way.
Its structure is based on aggregates of XeF_5^+ and F^- units,
which associate in two ways: (1) by four ions of each kind
forming tetrameric rings, (2) by six pairs of ions giving
hexameric rings. The tetramers have two orientations avail-

able to them, and the hexamers have four. The unit cell contains no less than 144 XeF_6 entities, or 1 008 atoms in all, which are distributed among 1 600 positions. Phases I and II also contain tetrameric rings and they too are disordered.

Like the volatile metallic hexafluorides, the two heptafluorides ReF_7 and IF_7 exist in a high-temperature cubic form and a low-temperature, probably orthorhombic modification (Siegel and Northrop 1966, Burbank and Bensey 1957).

Quantitative information on molecular motion in hexafluorides has been obtained by ^{19}F NMR studies. These include an interesting investigation carried out by Virlet and Rigny (1975) on dilute solutions of UF_6 (~8 per cent) in MoF_6, and *vice versa*. Due to a difference in chemical shifts, the fluorine atoms in the two different molecules give separate signals in both the plastic and orthorhombic phases, so that the motion of each kind of molecule in the solid solution could be elucidated.

It has sometimes been pointed out that not infrequently plastic crystals have relatively high triple-point pressures, and this is certainly true of several of the substances in Table 10.6. For example, the triple-point pressure of sulphur hexafluoride is 2·3 bar, of platinum hexafluoride 0·77 bar, and of hexachloroethane 1·1 bar. But this property is not confined to plastic crystals, as witness the high triple-point pressures of uranium, neptunium, and plutonium hexafluorides, which are 1·5, 1·0, and 0·7 bar respectively, and of course other instances can be found in quite different substances such as carbon dioxide (5·1 bar).

The recent discovery that ethane has a transition only ~0·5 K below the triple-point means that this substance is almost certainly that giving the plastic crystalline phase with the shortest known range of existence at ordinary pressures. The stability range of this increases with rising pressure (Webster and Hoch 1971). There is a decrease in ΔS_t in the series $C_2F_6 \rightarrow C_2Cl_6 \rightarrow C_2Br_6$ which Koide, Tsujino, Sawada, and Oda (1974) attempted to rationalize. They proposed that in the disordered cubic phase of compounds of the type C_2X_6 the molecules are orientationally disordered in

that the C-C axis can be parallel to any one of the four
body-diagonals of the cube, which contributes $R \ln 4$, $= 1 \cdot 39R$,
to ΔS_t. They suggested that in addition disorder can be
acquired at the II→I transition by internal 'rotation' of
one CX_3 group with respect to the other and also by overall
'rotation' about the C-C axis. For C_2Br_6 these last two
modes of motion only make a minor contribution to ΔS_t, but
a considerable one for C_2F_6. Lewis and Pace (1973), who
determined the structure of C_2F_6-II, considered that in this
monoclinic phase some statistical disorder still persists.

Three of the most thoroughly studied substances of
Table 10.6 are hexamethylethane, hexamethyldisilane, and
succinonitrile. The NMR work on hexamethylethane showed
that, in contrast to some organic substances containing
methyl groups that we have already discussed, line-narrowing
due only to methyl group reorientation does not occur.
Instead, at ~90 K the second moment drops from ~30 G^2 (effectively the rigid lattice value) to $2 \cdot 2$ G^2 due to methyl group
reorientation and the simultaneous reorientation of the
$C(CH_3)_3$ groups about the C-C axis. At the transition at
152 K there is a further drop in second moment to $0 \cdot 9$ G^2
which reflects the onset of general molecular reorientation,
and above 270 K there is the usual approach of the second
moment to zero due to diffusion. The activation energy for
the reorientation which produces the 90 K line-narrowing was
estimated to be 13 kJ mol^{-1}, and that for diffusion to be
~63 kJ mol^{-1}. We would expect the barrier to the rotation
of the individual methyl groups in hexamethyldisilane to be
less than that in hexamethylethane, and in fact from their
NMR line-width and T_1 study Yukitoshi, Suga, Seki, and Itoh
(1957) concluded that even at 90 K these groups are rapidly
reorientating with an activation energy of 11 kJ mol^{-1}. At
~153 K reorientation about the Si-Si bond begins with an
activation energy of 24 kJ mol^{-1}. Above the transition,
there is general rapid reorientation, and self-diffusion
sets in with an activation energy of 42 kJ mol^{-1}.

The behaviour of succinonitrile is of interest for two
reasons, one that although it forms a plastic crystal the
molecule is far from 'globular', the other that a factor

which now enters into the disorder is the existence of the
molecule in two configurations, *gauche* and *trans* (Fig.10.15).
Spectroscopic studies (Fitzgerald and Janz 1957, Fontaine,

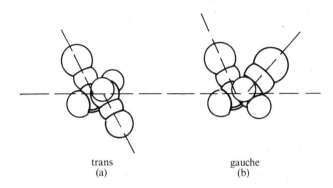

trans   gauche
(a)   (b)

Fig.10.15. The *trans* (a) and *gauche* (b) forms of the succinonitrile
molecule (Longueville, Fontaine, and Chapoton 1971).

Longueville, and Wallart 1972) showed that in phase II all
molecules are in the *gauche* form, whereas I is a mixture of
the two rotational isomers. (They are not present in equal
proportions, since the *gauche* form is more stable than the
trans by $1 \cdot 5$ kJ mol^{-1}.) Wulff and Westrum (1963) proposed
that the observed entropy of transition of $3 \cdot 20R$ is essentially the sum of three terms which arise as follows. (1)
It is assumed that any molecule in phase I (in which it has
eight nearest neighbours) has its principal axis along the
length of the molecule aligned with one of the four diagonals
of the cubic unit cell, so that orientational disorder among
these four diagonals will contribute an entropy term of
$R \ln 4$. (2) A molecule so aligned, whether *gauche* or *trans*,
will have two possible configurations (separated by rotation
through 180°), use of which contributes $R \ln 2$ to the entropy.
(3) The entropy of mixing of the *gauche* and *trans* forms, with
due consideration of their relative proportions, is estimated
to be $1 \cdot 05R$. The sum of these three entropy terms is $3 \cdot 13R$.
(For an alternative interpretation, see Descamps 1976).

The NMR studies of succinonitrile have been particularly thorough. The second moment drops sharply at 229 K owing to the onset of general molecular reorientation. (Although most of the heat of transition is absorbed isothermally, or near-ly so, at 234 K, the heat capacity starts to rise at 227 K.) The NMR estimate of the reorientation activation energy is 25 kJ mol^{-1}. Longueville, Fontaine, and Chapoton (1971), from dielectric relaxation experiments, obtained a lower value of 17·8 kJ mol^{-1} for this quantity, but it may be that the lack of agreement derives, at least in part, from the molecular flexibility, in that the transformation of the *gauche* form into a mixture of *gauche* and *trans* forms may affect the NMR and dielectric behaviour differently. Finally, in phase I self-diffusion occurs with an activation energy of 40·5 kJ mol^{-1}.

Clever, Westrum, and Cordes (1965) attempted to explain the large entropy of the transition in tetraphosphorus tri-sulphide, P_4S_3, of 3·95R (which is almost equal to $R \ln 48$, = 3·87R) on the lines laid down by Guthrie and McCullough (section 10.7). The structure of this C_{3v} molecule is shown in Fig.10.16. That of the plastic phase I is not known, but if it is assumed to be cubic it is reasonable to consider

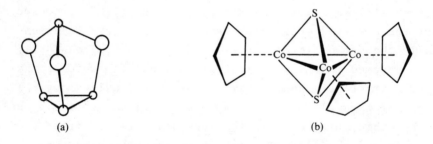

(a)   (b)

Fig.10.16. The structure of the molecules of (a) P_4S_3 (small circles = P, large circles = S); (b) $Co_3(C_5H_5)_3S_2$ (Sorai *et al.* 1971).

that the trigonal axis of the molecule is aligned, in either direction, with any one of the four diagonals of the cubic unit cell. For any one of these eight possibilities, the molecule can be rotated into six positions which cause the

three phosphorus atoms or the three sulphur atoms to coincide with other cube diagonals. The total number of possible
orientations per molecule would then be $2 \times 4 \times 6 = 48$.

From the thermodynamic properties of trimethylamino-
borane (Table 10.6) it is clear that phase I of this substance is disordered. Ang and Dunell (1972, 1974) carried
out detailed NMR investigations (which included measurements of T_1 and $T_{1\rho}$ as well as of the second moment) on the
chemically related compounds $(CH_3)_3N.X(CH_3)_3$, where X = B,
Al, or Ga. It seems likely from their results that each of
these substances has three solid phases. Reorientation of
the methyl groups about the C-X bonds (which are longer than
the C-N bonds) effectively begins first, being already quite
rapid at liquid nitrogen temperatures. The corresponding
motion about the C-N bonds commences at a higher temperature,
to be followed by reorientation of the whole molecule about
the N-X bond, and finally by isotropic tumbling and self-
diffusion. Calorimetric studies have been carried out on
ammonia-triborane, $NH_3B_3H_7$, the molecule of which contains
a triangle of boron atoms to one of which the nitrogen
atom is attached, and also on the related compound trimethyl-
amine-triborane, $(CH_3)_3N.B_3H_7$. Each of these two substances
has a transition with an entropy gain of $\sim 2R$ (Westrum and
Levitin 1959, Levitin, Westrum, and Carter 1959).

The transition in ferrocene effectively begins at about
125 K as far as the heat capacity C_p is concerned, with C_p
reaching a maximum at 163·9 K. At 169 K there is a second
subsidiary maximum in C_p (Fig.10.17). This, though small,
is reproducible and is independent of the main transition,
appearing in heat capacity determinations on a sample cooled
only to, say, 165 K. Edwards, Kington, and Mason (1960)
suggested in the light of the thermodynamic and structural
evidence that the low-temperature form has an ordered
lattice of staggered molecules and that above the λ-point the
crystal is partially disordered with respect to the ring
orientations. They proposed that each cyclopentadienyl ring
can have two orientations (related by rotation through 36°
in the plane of the ring), but that intermolecular hydrogen
-hydrogen repulsion prevents full use being made of all

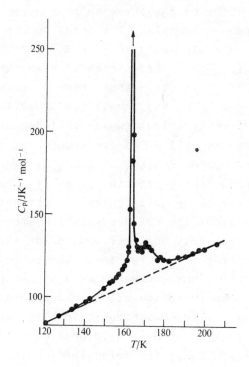

Fig.10.17. Heat capacity of ferrocene in the transition region (Edwards, Kington, and Mason 1960).

orientational possibilities. As a result, staggered molecules still predominate in the high-temperature phase. Support for the belief that some short-range order persists in
this phase comes from the infrared spectrum (Hyams and Ron
1973). Calvarin and Berar (1975) concluded from a careful
X-ray study that two processes are superimposed in the transition region. One is the development between ~130 K and
~220 K of orientational disorder in the plane of the rings,
which they regarded as responsible for the minor heat capacity peak at 169 K. The other effect is a sudden reorientation of the molecules in a stack, producing the crystal
structure change to which they attributed the major peak in
C_p at 164 K, since they observed a discontinuity in the
lattice parameters at this temperature.

In spite of the similarity of nickelocene to ferrocene,
the corresponding 'transition' in the nickel compound is

TABLE 10.6

Thermodynamic and structural information on various compounds with order-disorder transitions

Compound		II ← T_t/K, $\Delta S_t/R$ → I	I ← T_m/K, $\Delta S_m/R$ → Liq.	References Cal.	Cryst.	NMR
Sulphur hexafluoride	SF_6	94·3(F), 2·05	222·5, 2·7	1	–	2
Molybdenum hexafluoride	MoF_6	263·5(F), 3·73 Orthorhombic *Pnma*	290·8, 1·79 B.c.c.	3 / 4	4 / 5	6 / 7
Tungsten hexafluoride	WF_6	264·7, 3·93 Orthorhombic	275·2, 1·79 B.c.c.	8	5 / 9	6
Rhenium hexafluoride	ReF_6	269·8, 3·77 Orthorhombic	291·7, 1·79 B.c.c.	8	9	–
Osmium hexafluoride	OsF_6	274·5, 3·67 Orthorhombic	306·4, 1·83 B.c.c.	8	9	–
Iridium hexafluoride	IrF_6	272·0, 3·56 Orthorhombic	317·1, 1·90 B.c.c.	8	9	–
Platinum hexafluoride	PtF_6	276·5, 3·41 Orthorhombic	334·8, 1·91 B.c.c.	8	9	–

Compound	Formula	Transition data	Phases	Refs
Xenon hexafluoride	XeF_6	$291.8(\lambda), 0.505 \longrightarrow 322.63, 2.14$; $(III \longleftarrow -253.8(\lambda), 0.461 \longrightarrow II)$	Orthorhombic → Monoclinic; Monoclinic	10, 11, –
Ethane	C_2H_6	$89.813(F), 3.065 \longrightarrow 90.341, 0.78$		12, –, 13
Hexafluoroethane	C_2F_6	$104.0(F), 4.32 \longrightarrow 173.1, 1.86$	Monoclinic	14, 15, –
Hexachloroethane	C_2Cl_6	$344.6(F), 2.87 \longrightarrow 458, 2.77$; $(III \longleftarrow 318.1(F), 0.97 \longrightarrow II)$	Triclinic → Cubic; Orthorhombic	16, 17, –; 18
Hexabromoethane	C_2Br_6	$450, 1.45 \longrightarrow 487$	Orthorhombic; B.c.c.	19, 19, –; 20
Hexamethylethane	$C_2(CH_3)_6$	$152.5(F), 1.58 \longrightarrow 145.2, 2.4$	Orthorhombic Pnma; B.c.c.	21, 18, 22–24
2,2-Dimethylbutane	$(CH_3)_3C.CH_2.CH_3$	$140.8(F), 0.243 \longrightarrow 174.2, 0.40$; $(III \longleftarrow -126.8(F), 5.12 \longrightarrow II)$		25, –, –
Hexamethyldisilane	$Si_2(CH_3)_6$	$221.8(F), 5.28 \longrightarrow 287.6, 1.26$	B.c.c.	26, 27, 23; 28
Succinonitrile	$(CH_2CN)_2$	$233(F), 3.20 \longrightarrow 331.3, 1.35$	Monoclinic; B.c.c.	29, 30, 31

Compound		Transition data	Crystal system / Space group			
Trimethylamineborane	$(CH_3)_3N.BH_3$	$360 \cdot 4\,(F)$, $1 \cdot 982$ → $368 \cdot 7$, $1 \cdot 614$ (III ← $350 \cdot 1\,(F)$, $0 \cdot 871$ → II)		32	–	–
Tetraphosphorus trisulphide	P_4S_3	$313 \cdot 9\,(F)$, $3 \cdot 95$	Orthorhombic *Pnmb*	33	34	35
Ferrocene	$Fe(C_5H_5)_2$	$163 \cdot 9\,(\lambda)$, $0 \cdot 64$	Triclinic	Monoclinic $P2_1/a$	36 37	36 38	39
Nickelocene	$Ni(C_5H_5)_2$	$170\text{-}240$, $0 \cdot 6$	Monoclinic $P2_1/a$	Monoclinic $P2_1/a$	40	41	–

Footnotes overleaf

Footnotes to Table 10.6.

REFERENCES

1. Eucken and Schröder (1938).

2. Virlet and Rigny (1970b) (^{19}F,T_1,T_2,T_D).

3. Brady, Myers, and Clauss (1960).

4. Osborne, Schreiner, Malm, Selig, and Rochester (1966).

5. J.H. Levy, Taylor, and Wilson (1975a, MoF$_6$; 1975b, WF$_6$; neutron).

6. Rigny and Virlet (1969) (^{19}F, T_1, T_2).

7. Virlet and Rigny (1970a) (^{19}F,T_D).

8. Weinstock, Westrum, and Goodman (1963).

9. Siegel and Northrop (1966).

10. Schreiner, Osborne, Malm, and McDonald (1969).

11. Agron, Johnson, and H.A. Levy (1965) (I); Burbank and Jones (1970, IV; 1971, I, II, III; 1974, IV).

12. Atake and Chihara (1976). See also Eggers (1975) and Straty and Tsumara (1976).

13. Burnett and Muller (1976) (T_1).

14. Pace and Aston (1948).

15. Lewis and Pace (1973) (II).

16. Ivin and Dainton (1947); Seki and Momotani (1950).

17. Finbak (1937); Sasada and Atoji (1953); Atoji, Oda, and Watanabe (1953).

18. C.D. West (1934).

19. Koide *et al.* (1974) (I).

20. Snaauw and Wiebenga (1942) (II).

21. Calingaert, Soroos, Hnizda, and Shapiro (1944); Scott, Douslin, Gross, Oliver, and Huffman (1952).

22. Koide (1967) (LW, SM); G.W. Smith (1971) (LW, SM).

23. Albert, Gutowsky, and Ripmeester (1972) (T_1,$T_{1\rho}$).

24. Chezeau, Dufourcq, and Strange (1971) (SM, T_1, $T_{1\rho}$).

25. Kilpatrick and Pitzer (1946).

26. Suga and Seki (1959).

27. Chatani, Suga, and Taguchi, quoted in Reference 29.

28. Yukitoshi *et al.* (1957) (LW, SM, T_1).

29. Wulff and Westrum (1963).

30. Finbak (1938); Finbak and Viervoll (1942).

31. Petrakis and A. Rao (1963) (SM); Powles, Begum, and Norris (1969) (T_1, $T_{1\rho}$); Strange and Terenzi (1970) ($T_{1\rho}$); Bladon, Lockhart, and Sherwood (1971b) (LW).

Footnotes to Table 10.6. continued.......

32.   Finke, Todd, and Messerly (1970).

33.   Clever, Westrum, and Cordes (1965).

34.   Leung, Waser, van Houten, Vos, Wiegers, and Wiebenga (1957).

35.   Andrew, Hinshaw, Hutchins, and Jasinski (1974) (^{31}P).

36.   Edwards, Kington, and Mason (1960).

37.   Edwards and Kington (1962).

38.   Dunitz, Orgel, and Rich (1956); Calvarin and Berar (1975).

39.   Holm and Ibers (1959) (LW); Mulay and Attalla (1963) (LW, SM).

40.   Azokpota, Calvarin, and Pommier (1976).

41.   Calvarin and Weigel (1976).

very extended and appears to leave the structure unchanged.
Another compound which contains cyclopentadienyl rings and
undergoes an order-disorder transition is tris-(π-cyclo-
pentadienylcobalt) disulphide, $Co_3(C_5H_5)_3S_2$ (Fig.10.16).
This transition is certainly partly, and perhaps wholly,
gradual with T_λ = 192·5 K and an entropy gain ΔS_t of 28·9 J
K^{-1} mol^{-1}, which is almost exactly $R \ln 32$ (Sorai, Kosaki,
Suga, Seki, Yoshida, and Otsuka 1971). Sorai *et al.* suggested that there is cooperative coupling between the orientational movement of the rings and the electronic states of the
molecule, and that ΔS_t is made up of a magnetic contribution
of $R \ln 4$ and a configurational term of $R \ln 8$, the latter
being the result of each of the three cyclopentadienyl rings
in a molecule having two possible orientations in the high-
temperature disordered form.

10.5. LONG-CHAIN COMPOUNDS
Substances with long-chain molecules are very often polymorphic, with one or more of their phases disordered to
some degree. Their study is complicated by the sensitivity
of their phase behaviour to homologous impurities, as little
as one or two per cent of which can sometimes bring about
qualitative changes. Any experimentalist contemplating work
in this field should be aware of the extreme importance of
using samples of the highest possible purity, and regrettably

one must conclude that some of the earlier work was un-
reliable or misleading. With regard to certain aspects of
our subject it is still difficult to generalize with reasonable certainty about long-chain compounds, and recent work
suggests that it is unwise to take too much for granted
about the properties of compounds with chains longer than
say 30 carbon atoms on the basis of what has been established
for compounds with shorter chains. As for the types of disorder which can be encountered, it has been known for some
time, and indeed was only to be expected, that long-chain
compounds are prone to orientational disorder about the long
molecular axis. In general, this is once again a matter
of the molecules acquiring the ability to surmount potential
energy barriers between minima, the number of which for a
complete revolution may be relatively large, perhaps between
8 and 18. However, the amplitude of the torsional oscillations of the chains may be considerable, and in some cases
to speak of rotation, as has often been done, may not be so
wide of the mark. More recently, the possibility that two
other types of disorder may occur has been recognized, one
arising from longitudinal displacement of the chains by a
kind of screw motion, the other due to kinking of the chains,
which has already been mentioned in section 7.5.3 in connection with n-alkyl substituted ammonium salts. In many treatments of the orientational disorder the chains have been regarded as rigid, but this must always be to some extent an
oversimplification, and especially so if kinking takes place.
We shall defer further consideration of the last two types of
disorder, and deal first with orientational disorder after
summarizing some of the relevant physical properties of long-
chain compounds.

Crystals of compounds of the general formula $CH_3(CH_2)_nX$
usually fall into two categories, α-forms which are often
described as being translucent or waxy, and β-forms which
are white and opaque. Many such compounds give both types
of crystal, and a given substance may have more than one
α-form (butyl stearate, for example, having three) and more
than one β-form. In α-forms the molecules have considerable
orientational freedom about the chain axis, whereas in the

β-form such freedom is lacking, or at least less than in the α-modification. If an α-form is a possibility, it is produced when the melt solidifies. It may be metastable, and spontaneously change into a β-phase. We shall not attempt to translate the α,β classification of phases of such compounds into the I, II, III etc. symbolism used generally in this book, because in addition to making comparative reference to the literature rather laborious for the reader, the use of our general symbolism would be complicated by the frequent occurrence with long-chain compounds of metastable phases, and moreover retention of the α,β classification does have the virtue of bringing out similarities in the crystal forms of different compounds.

Homologous series which have been investigated include those for which X = -Br, -$COOC_2H_5$, and -CH_2OH, where the terminal group confers polarity on the molecule, and extensive studies have also been made of ketones, secondary alcohols, ethers, and esters (including esters of glycerol), where the polar group is more centrally placed. Our knowledge of disorder in long-chain polar compounds is largely based on permittivity and dielectric loss studies. For the paraffins (X = CH_3) permittivity measurements are not very informative, but NMR studies can throw light on the molecular movement.

A crystalline long-chain paraffin will have one of four possible crystal structures. These are an α-form which is hexagonal, and β-forms which may be orthorhombic, triclinic, or monoclinic. Some confusion has been introduced into the subject by the variety of notations used by different authors for the four crystalline forms, and a signal service was rendered by Broadhurst (1962) in correlating these notations as well as in analysing relevant experimental data. Following Broadhurst, we shall use the subscripts H, O, T, and M to indicate hexagonal, orthorhombic, triclinic, and monoclinic structures respectively. The results of structural studies on the n-paraffins have been summarized by Olf and Franconi (1973).

Andrew (1950) measured the NMR second moment for the two n-alkanes $C_{28}H_{58}$ and $C_{32}H_{66}$. There is a considerable drop

in this at the $\beta \to \alpha$ transition, but this is preceded by a
gradual fall in the second moment as the β-phase is heated.
The one-dimensional reorientation therefore begins in the
β-phase, but is much more pronounced in the α-form. Second
moment measurements were made on $n\text{-}C_{32}H_{66}$ by Olf and Peterlin (1970) and on $n\text{-}C_{19}H_{40}$ by Dehl (1974). From comparisons
of the observed second moments with calculated values it is
clear that in the rotator phases the movement of the molecules about their axes, if not unrestricted rotation, is at
least one of large-angle oscillation. Reference has already
been made (section 4.4) to experiments carried out by Anderson
and Slichter (1965) which showed that in $n\text{-}C_7H_{16}$ the terminal
methyl groups can readily change their orientation at 150 K,
while the methylene chains at this temperature are stationary.
They also made T_1 measurements on a series of alkanes, obtaining results typified by Fig.10.18, which shows the temperature dependence of T_1 for three n-paraffins. The minimum
in T_1 is attributed to the reorientation of the methyl groups,
the temperature of minimum T_1 being almost independent of
the chain length of the molecule from C_6H_{14} to $C_{40}H_{82}$. On

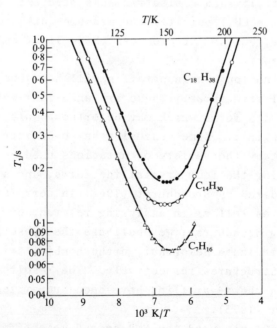

Fig.10.18. Temperature dependence of the spin-lattice relaxation time,
T_1, in $n\text{-}C_7H_{16}$, $n\text{-}C_{14}H_{30}$, and $n\text{-}C_{18}H_{38}$ (Anderson and Slichter 1965).

the other hand, the value of T_1 at the minimum increases
linearly with chain length. It is believed that the mechanism by which the spin energy of the methylene protons is
dissipated after irradiation by the r.f. field is by transmission by spin-spin coupling to the methyl group protons,
and from there to the lattice. Since the number of methyl
groups per molecule is the same throughout the series, it
is understandable on this basis that the shorter the chain
between the methyl groups, the less the relaxation time. A
few degrees below the melting-point - in other words, at
about the temperature of the $\beta \to \alpha_H$ transition - there is a
rather sudden fall in T_1, which presumably reflects the onset of one-dimensional reorientation of the whole chain.

Although in paraffins the molecules are orientationally
disordered about their long axis in the α_H form, but not (or
to a smaller extent) in the β_O form, these two structures
are similar in that the chains in both are perpendicular
to the end-group planes. In the other two structures, β_T
and β_M, the chains are tilted with respect to the end-group
planes, the angle of tilt being greater in β_M than in β_T.
In Figs. 10.19 and 10.20, which are based on Broadhurst's

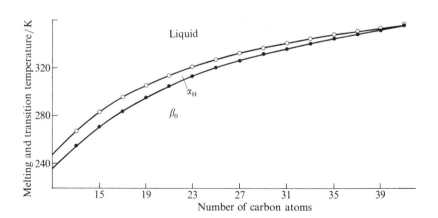

Fig.10.19. Melting-points (open circles) and transition temperatures
(full circles) of odd members of the n-alkane series.

critical assessment of available information, the melting-

points and transition temperatures are plotted for the odd
and even paraffins as a function of chain length. The disordered phase exists for the odd n-paraffins from the C-9
member up to (probably) the C-43 member, but for the even
paraffins only from C_{22} to C_{42}. The temperature range over
which α_H is stable is relatively small, and studies of the
effect of pressure (Richter and Pistorius 1972) have shown
that this phase disappears at comparatively low pressures
(~3 kbar or less). It will be seen from Figs. 10.19 and

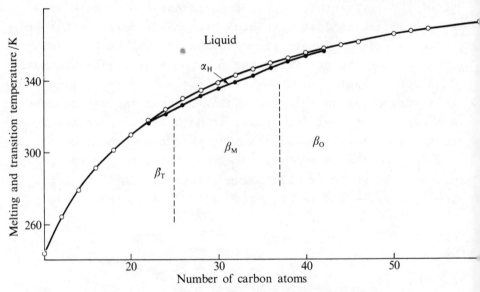

Fig.10.20. Melting-points (open circles) and transition temperatures
(full circles) of even members of the n-alkane series.

10.20 that the stable ordered phase for the odd paraffins is
always β_O, whereas it is β_T for the lower even members, then
β_M, the first member of the series to give this probably
being C_{26}. For the higher even members, perhaps from C_{38}
onwards, it is likely that β_O is the stable ordered modification. Information about the paraffins with $n > 40$ is still
rather meagre.

      The effect of homologous impurities on the crystalli-
zation of long-chain compounds from the melt is often to in-
duce the formation of an unstable or metastable phase. Thus,
impure n-$C_{18}H_{38}$ (which when pure has no *stable* α_H or β_O form)
freezes at 26·5°C to give one of these two forms (probably
β_O) which melts at the same temperature. When kept a little

below this temperature, transformation into the stable β_T form takes place. This melts at 27·0° C. If a partially transformed sample is melted, the melting-point appears to be somewhat unsharp, and this is now believed to be at least partly responsible for some of the 'premelting' effects reported in some of the earlier work on long-chain compounds (Ubbelohde 1938).

Reference is often made to the odd-even alternation effect in the melting-points of the n-paraffins. This arises when there is a β_M or β_T phase involved with tilted chains. Thus, the melting-points of the α_H forms for both odd and even members lie on a smooth curve. For the chains stacked perpendicularly to the end-group planes in the α_H and β_O phases, there is no difference in end-group packing for the odd and even members. When the chains are tilted, only the even paraffins can have equivalent packing for the two end-groups. For the odd members, if a favoured position of low energy is adopted by one end of a molecule, the other end is forced into a different position, presumably of higher energy (Broadhurst 1962).

In Fig. 10.21 the entropies of fusion of the n-paraffins and the entropies of transition of an ordered β-form into the disordered α_H phase are plotted against the number of carbon atoms in the chain. It would be interesting to know how the trends in these quantities continue with further increase in the length of the chains. For the members of the series with between 19 and 28 carbon atoms, the contraction on freezing is about 10 per cent (for both odd and even members), and the further contraction at the transition is about 6 per cent for the even members, and somewhat less (2·5 - 4·8%) for the odd (Schaerer, Busso, Smith, A.E., and Skinner 1955). In interpreting the entropy of transition, Hoffman and Decker (1953) ascribed a considerable part of this to the volume change, on the basis of the equation $\Delta S/\Delta V = \alpha/\kappa$, where α is the coefficient of expansion and κ the isothermal compressibility. They concluded that for the transitions in the paraffins with 22-30 carbon atoms, the configurational entropy gain is only about one-third of the total entropy of transition. [In this connection we may

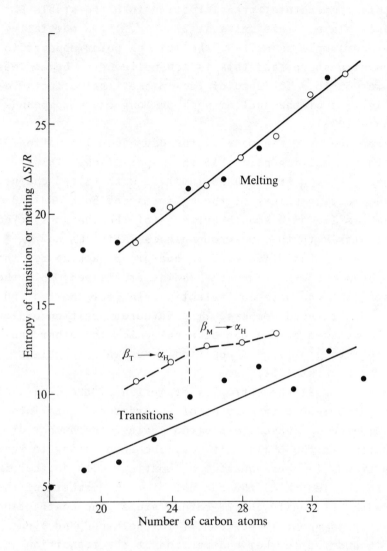

Fig.10.21. Entropies of transition and melting in the n-alkane series.
Open circles, even members; full circles, odd members.

note that McClure (1968) demonstrated that a substantial part
of the enthalpy change at a transition in an n-paraffin crystal can be attributed to the change in lattice energy.]
Hoffman (1952) had previously shown that the thermal and dielectric properties of long-chain compounds could be satisfactorily accounted for on the assumption that as a molecule
is rotated about its long axis through 2π it passes through

one deep energy minimum and Ω other minima with a potential
energy V_0 above that of the deep well (Fig.10.22). He
applied a Bragg-Williams treatment, with the fraction of molecules in the deep potential wells as the long-range order

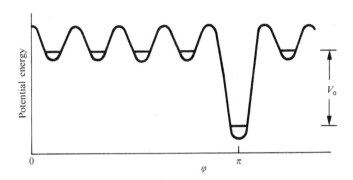

Fig.10.22. Illustrating the type of potential energy function suggested
by Hoffman for the rotation of a long-chain molecule.

parameter, and showed that a first-order transition would
be expected for values of Ω larger than ~8. If the configurational contribution to the entropy of transition, as
estimated by Hoffman and Decker, is equated with $R \ln \Omega$, a
value for Ω of ~14 is obtained. Since in the light of later
work it seems that the values of the total transition entropies they used were too small, they may have underestimated
the configurational contributions, and hence the values of Ω.
J.D. Barnes (1973) studied the inelastic scattering of neutrons from both the ordered and disordered phases of the n-
paraffin $C_{19}H_{40}$, obtaining results for the disordered phase
which were consistent with the molecules making rotational
jumps between 8 or more sites for each revolution of the
molecule about the chain axis.
     We now turn to the question of the participation of
other kinds of disorder in crystals of the n-paraffins. In
section 7.5.3 a brief description was given of the 'kink-
block' model developed by Pechhold and his collaborators (see
e.g. Blasenbrey and Pechhold 1967). We shall illustrate the

application of this to n-paraffins by reference to investigations carried out on n-tritriacontane ($C_{33}H_{68}$) by Piesczek and Strobl and their collaborators, since this will at the same time serve as an example both of the importance of working with pure specimens and of the revelation of unexpected features in the behaviour of a higher member of the n-alkane series. Piesczek, Strobl, and Malzahn (1974) found that their highly purified sample of n-$C_{33}H_{68}$ exhibited *three* transitions. In addition to the high-temperature α_H form (which they designated D) and the low-temperature orthorhombic form A (= β_0), there are two intermediate monoclinic modifications, B, space group Aa (which might be designated $\beta_M(II)$), and C, space group $A2$ [$\beta_M(I)$]. The transition and melting temperatures and entropy changes are as follows:

A, or β_0 — 327·6 K, 0·8R → B, or $\beta_M(II)$ —— 338·6 K, 1·6R→

C, or $\beta_M(I)$ —— 341·1 K, 10R → D, or α_H —— 344·9 K, 27·5 R→

   liquid

The results of small-angle X-ray scattering studies (Strobl, Ewen, Fischer, and Piesczek 1974) and infrared and NMR measurements (Ewen, Fischer, Piesczek, and Strobl 1974) were interpreted as showing that two other types of disorder are involved besides that associated with cooperative rotational jumps, and the following scheme was advanced for the changes taking place at the molecular level at the transitions. (1) The A → B transition is accompanied by a marked decrease in the NMR second moment, which was attributed to the molecules in B making cooperative rotational jumps of ~180°. (2) With the transition B → C, a screw motion begins which shifts the chains along their axis, so that longitudinal disorder is introduced. (3) On entering phase D, intramolecular defects (kinks) appear. These shorten the chains, and have the effect of introducing defects at the interface between molecular layers. These two kinds of disorder in (2) and (3) are represented in Fig.10.23. X-ray evidence for such kinking of chains had already been obtained for the hydrocarbon n-$C_{94}H_{190}$ by Sullivan and Weeks (1970), who

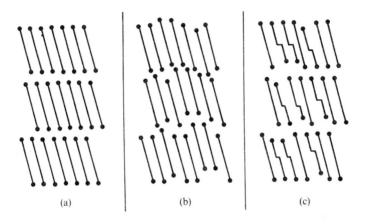

(a)   (b)   (c)

Fig.10.23. Illustrating the introduction into an ordered lattice of
paraffin molecules (a) of longitudinal disorder (b) and of intrachain
defects (c) (Strobl *et al*. 1974).

studied the intensity of the 001 reflections which depend on
the lamellar repeat distance. The kinks in modification D
should not be thought of as static, but as being capable of
diffusion along the chain. This kind of disorder affects,
and indeed facilitates, the rotational motion. It is interesting that in phase D the lateral packing of the chains approaches but does not attain the strict hexagonal symmetry which
the simple rotation model would require.

With the n-primary alcohols, at least three crystalline
forms are encountered. The transition temperatures show a
marked odd-even alternation. This is much less in evidence
for the melting-points, which when plotted against temperature give an almost smooth curve. In the monoclinic γ-phase
the chains are tilted with respect to the base of the unit
cell, whereas in the orthorhombic β-form they are more or
less normal to the base. The hexagonal α-modification is
disordered (see, e.g. Tasumi, Shimanouchi, Watanabe, and Goto
1964, and also Mosselman, Mourik, and Dekker 1974).

The members of the n-alkyl bromide series with 22, 26,
and 30 carbon atoms produce an orientationally disordered
α-phase on cooling. The changes in the permittivity ε for

n-docosyl bromide, $C_{22}H_{45}Br$, are consistent with one-dimensional orientational freedom in the α-phase, since on soli-
difying at 40°C the permittivity drops sharply, but only to
a value still well above ε_∞. On cooling this form, there is
an irreversible transition at 30°C at which the permittivity
falls again, this time to ε_∞, implying that the molecules
have now lost the one-dimensional freedom of movement about
the chain axis. (The transition at first produces an unstable β-form, which then changes into a stable β-form, which
melts at 44°C. The α-form will give the stable β-form directly if suitably nucleated at temperatures between 30°C and
40°C.) One-dimensional reorientation appears possible in the
ethers $(C_{16}H_{33})_2O$ and $(C_{18}H_{37})_2O$, but not in $(C_{12}H_{25})_2O$ and
$(C_{14}H_{29})_2O$.

The extensive studies of the dielectric properties of
long-chain polar substances have been reviewed by Smyth
(1955) and Meakins (1961). A considerable amount of this
work has been performed on dilute solid solutions of the
polar molecules in a hydrocarbon matrix, but we shall confine our attention to results obtained on the single substances. In a β-phase, a polar long-chain compound may or
may not show dielectric absorption at radiofrequencies, and
when it occurs it has been suggested that it is due to lattice
imperfections. Its magnitude, often small, can be considerably increased by cold working or by the addition of impurities, both of which would increase the number of imperfections in a particular sample. Some β-phase long-chain compounds show absorption at microwave frequencies as well.
Examples of such substances are the methyl esters
$C_nH_{2n+1}\cdot COOCH_3$, with n = 15, 17, and 21. Whereas for these
three substances the frequency of maximum absorption, f_{max},
in the radiofrequency region decreases with increasing chain
length, in the microwave region f_{max} is approximately independent of chain length. Also, the energy barrier and
frequency factor for microwave absorption are generally much
less than for the radiofrequency absorption. The microwave
absorption has therefore been attributed by Meakins to independent orientation of the dipoles, whereas the radiofrequency absorption is associated with movement of the whole
molecule.

Dielectric absorption is altogether more marked in an
α-phase, and appears as two or more absorption maxima at
audio, radio, or microwave frequencies. For the low-frequency
absorption, f_{max} is < 10^3 Hz at room temperature. The free
energy of activation for this absorption increases linearly
with chain length, showing that it is connected with reorientation of the whole molecule. The higher frequency absorptions have been less thoroughly studied, but it seems
that these too are associated with reorientation of the entire molecule, and that several potential minima are involved
in this reorientation. Hoffman showed that for n-docosyl
bromide, $C_{22}H_{45}Br$, the dielectric relaxation effects were
consistent with the estimate of 12 or so high-level minima
derived from the transition entropy. It may be, therefore,
that the low-frequency absorption is to be attributed to
jumps between a deep potential energy minimum and one of the
more numerous shallow high-level minima, whereas the high-
frequency absorption arises from the passage between two
shallow minima. Non-equivalent potential minima give rise
to a distribution of relaxation times. Cole-Cole arc plots
for hexadecyl and octadecyl ethers indicate a wide distribution of relaxation times, and a still broader distribution
is found for glycerides such as tripalmitin and tristearin.
It might be supposed that the potential barriers for long-
chain polar molecules are primarily due to dipole-dipole
interaction, but similarities between the β→α transitions
in paraffins and those in polar substances such as bromides
and alcohols suggest that the energy barriers may be essentially determined by dispersion forces.

The α-phases (some of which are unstable) of the higher
primary alcohols, besides showing dielectric absorption at
greater frequencies, also show absorption at a low frequency
accompanied by a high d.c. conductivity. In these crystals,
the hydroxyl groups are in double layers held together by
hydrogen bonds. It is believed that molecular reorientation
permits the transfer of a proton in a layer from one hydroxyl
group to another, and that this is responsible for the conductivity. The reality of proton migration in an electric
field in the orientationally disordered phase of n-hexadecanol

was demonstrated by Kakiuchi, Komatsu, and Kyoya (1951) who
showed that hydrogen was liberated on the passage of a current.

Long-chain molecules with a substituent at one end may
in principle give crystals with a different kind of disorder,
often referred to by the self-explanatory term of 'end-for-
end disorder'. The most certain examples of this are provided by some of the 1-alkenes, $CH_3(CH_2)_n.CH=CH_2$ (McCullough,
Finke, Gross, Messerly, and Waddington 1957). The calorimetric entropies at 25°C of the liquid alkenes from 1-hexene
($n = 3$) to 1-decene ($n = 7$) are less than those of the corresponding paraffins by the small and constant amount of $0 \cdot 1R$.
The value of the quantity $[S(\text{paraffin}) - S(\text{alkene}) - 0 \cdot 1R]$ is
$0 \cdot 70R$ (almost exactly $R \ln 2$) for 1-hexadecene, $0 \cdot 60R$ for 1-
dodecene, and $0 \cdot 10R$ for 1-undecene. This strongly suggests
that in crystalline 1-hexadecene there is complete end-for-
end disorder of the molecules, considerable disorder of the
same kind in 1-dodecene, and some slight disorder in 1-un-
decene. It was at one time supposed that disorder of this
type existed in crystals of the first member of the series,
propene ($CH_3CH=CH_2$), since Powell and Giauque (1939) concluded that the molar entropy of the gas calculated from
spectroscopic data exceeded the calorimetric entropy by
approximately $R \ln 2$. However, Guttman and Pitzer (1945)
showed that this result was due to the use of an erroneously
low value for the height of the energy barrier restricting
intramolecular rotation of the methyl group, and that crystalline propene does not in fact retain entropy at 0 K. Crowe
and Smyth (1950a) reported that λ-type transitions occurred
in metastable phases of $n\text{-}C_7H_{15}Br$, $n\text{-}C_9H_{19}Br$, and $n\text{-}C_{11}H_{23}Br$,
with entropy changes of $\sim R \ln 2$, and these have been attri-
buted to the development of end-for-end disorder. However,
it seems rather improbable that such molecules could reverse
the direction of their chains in the lattice, especially
at the relatively low temperatures (between 170 K and 185 K)
of the λ-transitions.

10.6. TWO-COMPONENT SYSTEMS
In this section we shall briefly review work carried out on

two-component solid systems in which one or both components have transitions from ordered to disordered phases. The thorough study of any one such system is a laborious matter, since several mixtures should be examined, the investigation of each of which may be expected to be just as time-consuming as that of a pure substance, and quite possibly more so, since equilibrium in a mixed crystal may be rather slowly established. Examples of some of the systems investigated are given in Table 10.7, which is meant to be illustrative rather than complete. It does not include the binary systems which have already been mentioned in this and the preceding chapter, for example argon-oxygen, argon-nitrogen, argon-carbon monoxide, argon-fluorine, methane-tetradeuteromethane, hydrogen bromide - deuterium bromide, and d- and l-camphor.

The krypton-methane system demonstrates the marked effect on the orientational freedom of molecules in a lattice of replacing some of these molecules (methane in this case) by others with a more symmetrical field of force (krypton). With the introduction of krypton, the temperature of the II→I transition falls, and the transition rapidly becomes less pronounced, vanishing altogether at a mole fraction of krypton of ~0·3. In the neighbourhood of the helium boiling-point, the v_3 band for CH_4 and CD_4 molecules in dilute solution in krypton shows considerable fine structure, implying that these molecules are rotating, so that the barrier to rotation, already quite small in pure methane, must be reduced to virtually zero in the mixed crystals. Contrary to what one might expect, the spectra suggest that at higher temperatures there is more interference with the rotation of the methane molecules in these dilute solutions rather than less, suggesting a greater degree of perturbation of the rotational energy levels the larger their quantum number. In recent years, the infrared spectra of various small molecules trapped in a rare-gas matrix have been shown to have rotational fine structure, but we shall not discuss studies of matrix-isolated species here. They have been reviewed by A.J. Barnes and Hallam (1969).

It will be noted that several of the systems in Table 10.7 involve carbon tetrachloride as one component, and of

TABLE 10.7

Two-component molecular crystals showing disorder

System	References and type of study
Krypton-methane	1. C_p measurements on six mixtures
	2. X-ray diffraction
	3. Infrared spectra
Carbon tetrachloride - carbon tetramethyl	4. C_p measurements on five mixtures
Carbon tetrachloride - t-butyl chloride	5. Thermal properties
	6. Permittivity measurements
	7. NMR
Carbon tetrachloride - t-butyl iodide	8. Permittivity and NMR
Carbon tetrachloride - carbon tetrabromide	9. Thermal study of phase diagram
Carbon tetrachloride - cyclohexanone	10. Phase diagram (liquidus-solidus curves only)
	11. Calorimetry (13 mixtures)
Cyclopentane - 2,2-dimethylbutane	12. Phase diagram by adiabatic calorimetry
	13. NMR
2,2-dimethylbutane - 2,3-dimethylbutane	12. Phase diagram by adiabatic calorimetry
	13. NMR
Benzene - thiophene	14. NMR
1,2-dichloroethane - 1,2-dibromoethane	15. C_p measurements on eight mixtures
Benzene - hexafluoro-benzene	16. Phase diagram
	17. DSC study of 1:1 complex
	18. NMR
n-$C_{20}H_{42}$ - $n\,C_{22}H_{46}$	19. Phase diagram. X-ray diffraction and calorimetry

Footnotes on facing page

Footnotes to Table 10.7.

REFERENCES

1.   Eucken and Veith (1936, 1937); Manzhelii, Chausov, and Freiman (1972).

2.   Greer (1973).

3.   Chamberland, Belzile, and Cabana (1970).

4.   E.T. Chang and Westrum (1965, 1970).

5.   Turkevich and Smyth (1940).

6.   Conner and Smyth (1941); Kotake, Nakamura, and Chihara (1970).

7.   Powles and Gutowsky (1953b).

8.   Chihara, Otsuru, and Seki (1966).

9.   Sackmann (1955).

10. Pariaud (1950).

11. van Miltenburg and Oonk (1974).

12. Fink, Cines, Frey, and Aston (1947).

13. Aston, Bolger, Trambarulo, and Segall (1954).

14. Anderson (1970).

15. Spice, Harrow, McGowan, and Smith, E.B. (1961).

16. Duncan and Swinton (1966).

17. Brennan, Brown, and Swinton (1974).

18. Gilson and McDowell (1966).

19. Lüth, Nyburg, Robinson, and Scott, H.G. (1974).

these one of the most thoroughly investigated is that with t-butyl chloride. The phase diagram, the result of a combination of thermal, permittivity and NMR measurements, is shown in Fig.10.24. The two solids are completely miscible in their plastic crystalline phases. This region is traversed by the line FG. On crossing this line from high to low temperatures there is a drop in permittivity, and the crystals (isotropic above FG) become somewhat anisotropic. Attendant thermal effects, however, seem to be very small. At low temperatures, the two solids are only mutually soluble between ~35 per cent and ~71 per cent of t-butyl chloride. For the solid solutions within this range, even at 78 K the second moment is much less than the value for pure t-butyl chloride at the same temperature, almost certainly because

intramolecular rotation of the methyl groups is less impeded
when the molecules are in solid solution with carbon tetrachloride molecules. On warming, crystals of all compositions,
whether within the one-phase or two-phase regions, show two

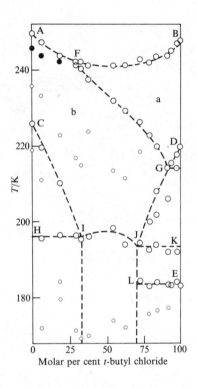

Fig.10.24. Phase diagram for the system CCl_4-$C(CH_3)_3Cl$. Large and small
circles represent phase changes or transitions as recorded on warming
or on cooling respectively. Full circles show the melting-points of the
metastable modification. (Kotake, Nakamura, and Chihara 1970, incorporating also the results of Conner and Smyth 1941, and Turkevich and Smyth
1940.)

line-width transitions. The first of these occurs between
~85 K and ~125 K and probably reflects the onset of reorientation of the $(CH_3)_3C$- units about the C-Cl bond. The
second line-width transition coincides with the line HIJK
of the phase diagram, and simultaneously there is an increase
in permittivity, so here overall reorientation of the molecules sets in, and presumably translational movement as well.
    The tentative phase diagram for the system carbon tetra-

chloride - carbon tetramethyl constructed by E.T. Chang and
Westrum (1970) from their heat capacity results, and reproduced in Fig.10.25 is very different from that for the system

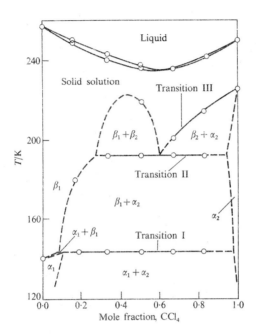

Fig.10.25. Tentative phase diagram for the system $C(CH_3)_4$-CCl4 (E.T.Chang
and Westrum 1970).

with t-butyl chloride, primarily because the transition temperatures in the pure components are now further apart. In
spite of the considerable amount of calorimetric work already
devoted to this system, it is clear that further information
is needed. E.T.Chang and Westrum (1965) have applied to the
solid solution of the plastic phases recent statistical-
mechanical theories developed to account for the excess thermodynamic functions of $liquid$ mixtures of non-electrolytes.

Whereas solid carbon tetrachloride and solid cyclohexane are immiscible at all temperatures, carbon tetrachloride and cyclohexanone are to some extent mutually soluble
in their plastic phases. However, the phase diagram for the
latter system (Fig.10.26) suggests that the plastic phases of

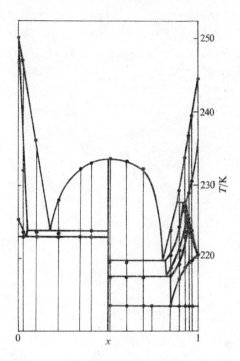

Fig.10.26. Phase diagram for the system CCl_4 - cyclohexanone; x = mole fraction of cyclohexanone (van Miltenburg and Oonk 1974).

the pure components do not have identical crystal structures. A 1:1 complex is formed which has no transition. By contrast, benzene and hexafluorobenzene, neither of which has a transition, give a 1:1 complex with a transition at 249·2 K (ΔS_t = 0·32R). This could involve partial disordering in the stacking sequence of the two kinds of molecule. There is a decrease in the NMR line-width for the C_6H_6-C_6F_6 complex between 90 K and 120 K for both H and ^{19}F resonances, which presumably reflects the development of reorientational movement of molecules of both types in the ring planes, but no thermal anomalies could be detected in this temperature region.

The detailed study of the cyclopentane - 2,2-dimethylbutane system showed that the plastic phases are completely miscible, and that a 2:1 complex is formed. But whereas each of the two pure components has two first-order transitions, in the complex there is only one transition, which is λ-type and occurs at a temperature below that of the lower transition in either pure substance. This complex clearly behaves as an independent solid, and it is probably no longer profitable to think in terms of the effect of one component on the orientational freedom of the other. One should rather consider the behaviour of a unit consisting of two molecules of cyclopentane and one of 2,2-dimethylbutane. The system 2,2-dimethylbutane - 2,3-dimethylbutane also forms a complex with the molecular ratio of 3:2 respectively, and this on cooling, forms a 'glassy crystal' (cf. p. 621).

The orthorhombic crystals of benzene and thiophene-I form a complete series of solid solutions with a melting-point which changes approximately linearly with composition. Anderson's measurements (1970) of the second moment and of T_1 for the solid solutions showed that, as with the pure solids, so also in the solutions the molecules undergo re-orientation in the plane of the rings. With increasing benzene concentration this motion of the benzene molecules becomes slower, while that of the thiophene molecules accelerates.

The phase diagram for the system $n\text{-}C_{20}H_{42}$ - $n\text{-}C_{22}H_{46}$ is remarkably complex, involving no less than six different solid phases. There is an orthorhombic β_0 form just below the solidus curve at all compositions, and at lower temperatures three new β-phases appear, and two γ-phases.

Two-component molecular complexes offering scope for further work are the charge transfer systems formed by donor and acceptor molecules. These have been comprehensively reviewed by Herbstein (1971). Some have been known for over a century, and the crystal structures of a considerable number have now been investigated. About 40% of those so examined show some degree of orientational disorder, but very little use has yet been made of other experimental techniques to study this in more detail. The donors in the complexes include benzene, naphthalene, pyrene, heterocyclic substances such as indole and 8-hydroxyquinoline (and its metal chelates), and organometallic compounds (e.g. ferrocene). Acceptors which are frequently used include polynitro- and polycyano-

compounds (e.g. 1,3,5-trinitrobenzene, tetracyanoethylene,
and 1,2,4,5-tetracyanobenzene), and acid anhydrides such as
pyromellitic dianhydride. Usually, though not always, the
donor-acceptor ratio is 1:1. The structural characteristic
of these complexes is that the molecules are arranged in
columns or stacks in which the donor and acceptor molecules
alternate. The stacks themselves are arranged in quasi-
hexagonal close packing. Interaction between adjacent molecules in a stack is stronger than that between molecules in
neighbouring stacks. When disorder is found, it takes the
form of orientational disorder of one or both of the two
components in the molecular plane. The disorder of the naphthalene molecules in the 1:1 naphthalene-tetracyanoethylene
complex is strikingly demonstrated by the electron density
contours in the plane of the rings (Fig.4.5).

Most of the crystallographic work on these donor-
acceptor complexes has been carried out at room temperature,
but some diffraction studies have been made well below this
and still revealed a disordered system. For example, the
tetracyanoethylene molecules in the 1:1 complex of this substance with pyrene are still disordered at 105 K between
two positions which are not energetically equivalent, one of
them being occupied only to the extent of 7 per cent (Larsen,
Little, and Coppens 1975). A calorimetric study of the
pyrene - 1,2,4,5-tetracyanobenzene adduct disclosed a gradual
transition between 220 K and 250 K, for which ΔS_t was estimated to be $1 \cdot 1R$. The heat capacity in the transition
region varied from run to run in an unusually capricious
manner (Clayton, Worswick, and Staveley 1976).

Alexandre and Rigny (1972) studied the temperature dependence of the spin-lattice relaxation times of the complexes
of 1,3,5-trinitrobenzene with azulene, naphthalene, indole,
and benzthiophene as donors. All four show dynamic disorder.
In the complexes with azulene and naphthalene the donor and
acceptor molecules make independent jumps in the plane of
the ring. For the indole complex, a combination of the NMR
and crystallographic evidence led to the conclusion that
besides the dynamic disorder there is static disorder as
well. The X-ray work of Hanson (1964, 1965) requires that

the indole molecule at a given site can have the positions
shown as (a) and (c) in Fig.10.27.   It will be seen that the
passage from one of these positions to the other could only

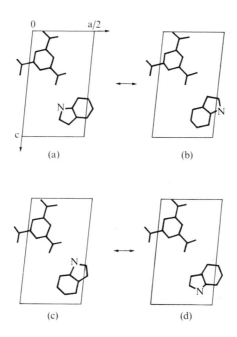

(a)   (b)

(c)   (d)

Fig.10.27. The four possible positions of the indole molecule in the
1,3,5-trinitrobenzene - indole complex (Alexandre and Rigny 1972).

be effected by rotation about an axis lying in the molecular
plane, an operation which would appear to be prohibitively
difficult.   Positions (a) and (c) therefore provide static
disorder.   On the other hand, dynamic disorder arises because
rotational jumps in the plane of the indole ring can take
molecules in position (a) to position (b), and those in orientation (c) to orientation (d).   Alexandre and Rigny pointed
out that the barrier height for the reorientation (a) → (b) need
not be the same as that for the change (c) → (d), and that the
barrier heights will depend on the orientation of neighbouring molecules, so that one must reckon with a range of activation energies for reorientation rather than with a single

value. The activation energies for reorientation in all
four of these complexes are in any case larger than the
corresponding quantities for molecules like benzene and hexamethylbenzene in their own lattices, which presumably reflects the enhancement of the intermolecular forces in the
complexes by the charge transfer contribution.

10.7. SOME GENERAL OBSERVATIONS ON DISORDER IN MOLECULAR
CRYSTALS

In this final section we shall briefly review some of the
attempts made to interpret, rationalize, or coordinate the
experimental facts about disorder in molecular crystals.
These facts fall into two categories, those relating on the
one hand to the equilibrium properties of the crystal and to
changes in these properties at transitions between ordered
and disordered phases, and on the other those concerned with
the dynamics of molecular movement. With regard to properties of the first kind, one of the main problems here is the
interpretation of entropies of transition in terms of orientational disorder. Also of interest is what determines the
temperature range over which a disordered phase is stable.
As for the dynamic aspects, there are of course two types
of motion to be considered, namely reorientation and diffusion, and we shall discuss possible mechanisms by which
these can take place.

An important contribution to the understanding of ΔS_t
values in terms of orientational disorder, which had a considerable influence on later work in this field, was made by
Guthrie and McCullough (1961). The essence of their approach
is to seek those orientations of a molecule in the lattice
of the disordered crystal for which there is some correspondence of the symmetry elements of the molecule with those
of the lattice. The symmetry elements common to the molecule
and the site will not, as a rule, represent the full symmetry
of the molecule. In general, there will be several possible
orientations of the molecule, and attempts to predict which
of these will be preferred must be based on steric and symmetry considerations. As an example, we take the case of a
regular tetrahedral molecule such as CCl_4 or $C(CH_3)_4$ in a

face-centred cubic lattice. Guthrie and McCullough suggested
that the preferred orientations would be those shown in Fig.
10.28; (a) in this figure gives two possible orientations, and
Guthrie and McCullough considered that (b) offers eight more,
with (a) and (b) having characteristics which they described
as follows:

(a) For these two orientations, the following symmetry
elements coincide (T_d symmetry): each threefold axis of the
molecule with a threefold axis of the cubic lattice, each
twofold axis of the molecule with a fourfold axis of the
lattice, and the six mirror planes of the molecule with the
diagonal mirror planes of the lattice.

(b) For the eight orientations, one threefold tetra-

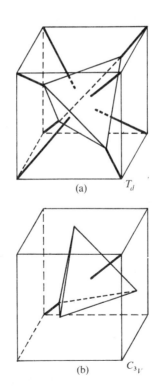

(a) T_d

(b) C_{3v}

Fig.10.28. The two most probable sets of orientations of a tetrahedral
molecule in a cubic cell, according to Guthrie and McCullough (1961).

hedral axis coincides with a threefold lattice axis (symmetry C_{3v}). These orientations are formed by rotating one
of the T_d orientations of (a) through 60° about a threefold
axis.

Guthrie and McCullough's approach has been criticized
with respect to the way they applied it in particular cases
by Clark, McKervey, Mackle, and Rooney (1974). However, before elaborating on this, we may mention that in the meanwhile a notable advance was made by Amzel and Becka (1969),
who combined the ideas of Guthrie and McCullough with the
theory of Pople and Karasz. This theory, which has been
summarized in section 3.1.7, examined the consequences of
both disorder of position and of orientation being simultaneously possible in a molecular crystal. In its original
form, the Pople-Karasz theory supposed that there were just
two orientations available to a molecule. Amzel and Becka
modified it to accommodate the larger number of orientations
suggested by the approach of Guthrie and McCullough. We
shall see that even if the latter sometimes overestimates
this number, it is certainly not infrequently greater than
two. For a transition from an ordered lattice in which
every molecule has a unique orientation to a disordered
lattice in which each molecule has N energetically equivalent but distinguishable orientations, ΔS_t as calculated
by Amzel and Becka is larger than $R \ln N$ by an amount depending on the parameter v. (This is the ratio $q'W'/qW$ of
section 3.1.7. It is a measure of the relative potential
energy increase when a change of orientation takes place to
the energy increase accompanying diffusion to an interstitial site.) However, the difference between the supposed
$R \ln N$ and ΔS_t as calculated by Amzel and Becka is not very
large. Thus, for bicyclo[2,2,2]octa-2-ene (Table 10.4 and
Fig. 10.10), they took $N = 20$. $R \ln 20$ is $3 \cdot 00R$, while the
calculated ΔS_t is $3.15R$ and the experimental value is $3 \cdot 35R$.

Clark et al. raised two objections to the original
version of the Guthrie-McCullough treatment. One was that
this overestimates the number of $distinguishable$ orientations. For example, for the case of a regular tetrahedral
molecule with full T_d symmetry in a cubic lattice which we

considered above, Clark *et al.* pointed out that the C_{3v} set
of eight orientations reduces to two, which are identical
with the two of the T_d set, so that the configurational entropy gain should be only $R \ln 2$ and not $R \ln 10$. A key role
in their argument is played by adamantane, the molecule of
which has T_d symmetry. Diffraction experiments showed that
in disordered adamantane-I each molecule has just two possible
orientations. The second criticism raised against the
Guthrie-McCullough approach is that they combined *non-
equivalent* sets of orientations to reach a total more or less
adequate to account for the whole of ΔS_t on a configurational
basis. Clark *et al.* defined an excess entropy of transition
ΔS_τ by the equation

$$\Delta S_t = \Delta S_\tau + R \ln(N_1/N_2) ,$$

where N_1 and N_2 are the number of possible molecular orientations in the high- and low-temperature phases respectively
For the hydrocarbon bicyclo[2,2,2]octa-2-ene cited above,
they considered that $N = N_1/N_2 = 8$ and not 20 as supposed by
Amzel and Becka, so that the configurational entropy gain
of $R \ln 8$ contributes only $2 \cdot 08R$ to ΔS_t, the balance of $1 \cdot 27R$
being ΔS_τ. It may be recalled that others had already attributed a non-configurational origin to a considerable part
of ΔS_t in certain order-disorder transitions, for example
Reynolds as a result of his calculations on triethylenediamine (p. 650), and Hoffman and Decker in their analysis
of ΔS_t for the $\beta \rightarrow \alpha$ transitions in n-paraffins (p. 673). The
question of the division of experimental ΔS_t values into configurational and non-configurational components is clearly
an important one which merits further attention. As Westrum
(1969) pointed out, if it is found possible to supercool the
high-temperature disordered form of a compound, thus freezing-
in the disorder, it will be helpful to determine the residual
entropy at 0 K of the disordered modification. Another relevant and difficult problem is the influence of molecular
correlation, that is the extent to which the adoption by a
molecule in a crystal of a possible orientation is affected
by the orientations its neighbours happen to have, a matter

to which we have already referred on more than one occasion.
A recent attempt to deal with this, using a method previously applied to the ice and dimer problems, has been
made by Descamps (1976), who chose as his examples succinonitrile, cyclohexane, and pivalic acid. In succinonitrile,
Descamps estimated that correlations reduce the configurational entropy gain at the transition to about 80 % of the
maximum possible value.

For solids composed of molecules with less than full
tetrahedral symmetry, a further contribution to ΔS_t can come
from the number of distinguishable ways in which the molecule can take up one allowed position. Thus, the maximum
contribution from this term will be $R \ln 4$ for $C(CH_3)_3Cl$,
$C(CH_3)Cl_3$, $C(CH_3)_3Br$ and $C(CH_3)_3SH$, $R \ln 6$ for $(CH_3)_2C(CN)_2$
and $R \ln 12$ for $C(CH_3)_2ClNO_2$. It may be that in the disordered
phase, and even in the liquid, some of these configurations
are energetically preferred over others, so that the full
contribution to the entropy from this source is not realized.
Finally, for molecules such as $C(CH_3)_3SH$ and $C(SCH_3)_4$, distinguishable configurations can be generated by rotation about
the C-S bond. For the former molecule, three such configurations can be expected. In fact, the amount by which $\Sigma \Delta S_t$ for
$C(CH_3)_3SH$ exceeds ΔS_t for $C(CH_3)_4$, namely $2 \cdot 10R$ (Table 10.2),
is less than $R \ln 12$ ($= 2 \cdot 48R$), but over a range of temperature preceding the IV→III transition in $C(CH_3)_3SH$ the heat
capacity is abnormally high, and allowance for this could
make up the deficit. In $C(SCH_3)_4$, each methyl group might
be expected in principle to have three possible positions,
but owing to the repulsion between these groups when they
approach too closely it is unlikely that each CH_3 can adopt
any one of these positions independently of the positions
occupied by the other methyl groups in the molecule, and it
is therefore not surprising that the amount by which $\Sigma \Delta S_t$ for
$C(SCH_3)_4$ exceeds ΔS_t for $C(CH_3)_4$ is only ~70% of $4R \ln 3$.

With regard to the temperature range of stability of
orientationally disordered phases, Amzel and Becka correlated
this with the ν parameter, and also with the volume changes
and entropy changes on melting. Clark *et al.* noted two interesting relationships, which, although based on results

for only five cage hydrocarbons, should be more widely
tested when the necessary information on suitable compounds
becomes available. One is that the quantity $\log_{10}$ $(\Delta S_\tau - 10 \cdot 3)$
is an approximately linear function of $(T_m - T_t)$ where ΔS_τ is
the excess entropy of transition as defined above in J K^{-1} mol^{-1}.
The larger ΔS_τ, the smaller is $(T_m - T_t)$, the range of stable
existence of the plastic phase. There is no connection between $(T_m - T_t)$ and N, the number of distinguishable orientations available to the molecules in the disordered phase.
The other relation connects $(T_m - T_t)$ with the molecular
dimensions. If D_1 and D_2 are the diameters of the molecule
perpendicular to the axes about which reorientation occurs,
then $(T_m - T_t)$ decreases linearly as $|D_2 - D_1|$ increases, or
in other words the range of the plastic phase contracts as
the molecule becomes less 'globular'.

Turning to the dynamics of molecular reorientation, there
have been a few attempts to establish and interpret empirical
relations between the activation energy E_R and a thermodynamic property of the system. Thus, for a number of molecules (mostly of the kind discussed in Chapter 9), Chihara
and Koga (1971) pointed out that there is a roughly linear
relation between E_R and the temperature of the order-disorder
transition, implying that the transition occurs when the
average thermal energy reaches an approximately constant
fraction of E_R. Bondi (1968) noted a linear dependence of
the ratio $E_R/\Delta H_S$, where ΔH_S is the enthalpy of sublimation
of the crystal, on the packing density, the ratio of the
actual volume of the molecules to the volume of the crystal.
The various models proposed for reorientation have been ad-
mirably reviewed by Brot and Lassier-Govers (1976). In
agreement with the impression which will have been given by
the individual cases we have discussed, they concluded that
the most probable mechanism for reorientation is one of
large-angle jumps between potential wells, the residence
time in a well being usually much longer than the duration
of the actual jump. Reorientation by rotational diffusion,
that is by a succession of relatively small stages, though
not impossible, is certainly much less common. The idea
of jumps between potential wells (as opposed to free rotation)

goes back to Frenkel, but whereas Frenkel envisaged a situation in which the wells were randomly disposed, in general
it is much more probable that their positions are fixed by
the symmetry of the lattice and of the molecule. With
regard to the difficult but fundamentally important question
of the correlation of the angular movements of neighbouring
molecules, Brot and Lassier-Govers pointed out that if a
particular molecule makes a reorientational jump, this may
in itself cause one or more of its neighbours to follow suit,
and that it will in any case affect the chances of their reorientation by changing the depths of their potential wells.
More may be learnt in the future about correlation effects
from a comparison of information which relates to individual
molecules (such as jump rates evaluated from NMR relaxation
times, quasielastic neutron scattering, and vibrational
line-shapes) with that derived from techniques such as dielectric relaxation and light-scattering experiments which
are concerned with the total orientational dynamics of a
larger region. We may add that several lines of evidence
show that in general molecular reorientation, unlike diffusion, does not require the presence of vacancies. For example, the reorientation jump rate is usually much higher than
the diffusion jump rate, and the volume of activation for
reorientation (as found from the pressure dependence of NMR
relaxation times) is much less than that for diffusion.

     There is a considerable literature on the subject of
diffusion in crystals, and we can only briefly summarize
the present state of our knowledge of the mechanism of this
type of movement and of the factors which determine its rate
in the kind of disordered solid discussed in this chapter
and the last. A useful review has been written by Sherwood
(1973). The methods yielding quantitative information on the
diffusion of molecules in solids are basically of two kinds,
those involving mass transport, and those depending on movement of the molecules on a very much smaller scale, namely
that of nearest-neighbour intermolecular separations. Methods
in the first category include the use of radiotracers (the
most accurate in this class), the study of plastic deformation (creep), and electron spin resonance. The experimental

techniques involved have been described in sections 4.7.2
and 4.9.   It will be appreciated that in a radiotracer investigation of diffusion, any one experiment may last for
perhaps 10^4 - 10^6 seconds and the movement of the labelled
molecules is monitored over macroscopic distances.   The
chief technique of the second kind is the measurement of the
NMR relaxation times T_1, T_2, T_1^* (or T_{1D}), and $T_{1\rho}$, the last
being especially valuable in view of the relatively low rate
with which diffusion often proceeds.   To compare results obtained from NMR measurements with those of an investigation
of the other type, a mean molecular jump time τ is first
derived from the measured relaxation time, usually on the
basis of Torrey's random walk model for uncorrelated isotropic diffusion (1953, 1954).   The self-diffusion coeffi-
cient D is then related to τ by the equation $D = \langle r^2 \rangle / 6\tau$,
where $\langle r^2 \rangle$ is the mean-square distance of the random jumps.
The Arrhenius activation energy for diffusion E_D follows
from the temperature dependence of D or τ, using the equations $D = D_0 \exp(-E_D/RT)$ or $\tau = \tau_0 \exp(E_D/RT)$.   As yet, the
number of plastic crystals on which both radiotracer and
relaxation time measurements have been made is not large,
but already it is clear that while for some of them the E_D
values from the two techniques agree well, for others (e.g.
cyclohexane, p. 630) this is not the case.   Before presenting the reasons advanced to explain this, we shall first
discuss the part which vacancies may play in the diffusion
process.

     The activation energy for diffusion E_D can be regarded
as the sum of two terms, one for the production of the defect which makes migration possible, the other for its movement.   The energy needed for the formation of a simple vacancy should be approximately equal to the lattice energy
of the crystal, and hence to the enthalpy of sublimation
ΔH_S.   On the other hand, calculations on the solid rare
gases suggest that the energy needed to put a molecule into
an interstitial site is appreciably larger (> $3\Delta H_S$).   The
experimental values of E_D from mass-transport experiments
fall between 1·6 and 2·4ΔH_S.   This therefore favours the
vacancy mechanism, and implies that the energy needed for

the migration of a vacancy is very roughly the same as that
required for its creation. Support for the vacancy mechanism
comes from estimates of $V^{\ddagger}$, the volume of activation, derived
from studies of the effect of pressure on relaxation times.
For example, Strange and Ross (1976) measured T_1 for hexamethylethane over a range of temperature and at pressures
up to 2·3 kbar, and obtained $V^{\ddagger} = 1·12V_m$, where V_m is the
molar volume.

Returning to the matter of the agreement or otherwise
between E_D values obtained from relaxation time measurements
and from mass-transport experiments, it was found that for
solids giving agreement E_D was about twice ΔH_S, whereas in
cases of disagreement the value of E_D from the NMR measurements was $<2\Delta H_S$. It was further noted that the solids giving
agreement were those with the higher entropies of melting ΔS_m,
while those yielding disagreement had relatively low values
of ΔS_m. For instance, for hexamethylethane the E_D values
from the two sources are virtually identical, with $E_D/\Delta H_S =$
2·0 and $\Delta S_m = 2·4R$. Folland, Jackson, Strange, and Chadwick
(1973) made a thorough NMR study of five compounds with cage
molecules, some of the results of which are shown in Table
10.8, from which it will be seen that as ΔS_m decreases, so
do both E_D and the ratio $E_D/\Delta H_S$.

It accordingly appeared that in some crystals diffusion
might have a more complex mechanism than that depending on
the formation and movement of a single vacancy, and for these
solids Hood and Sherwood (1966b) proposed a 'relaxed vacancy'
model. This had previously been advanced by Beaumont, Chihara, and Morrison (1961) to account for the trend in the
heat capacity and expansivity of argon on approaching the
melting-point. The idea is that on the formation of a vacancy
the nearest-neighbour molecules, and very possibly more distant molecules as well, relax into it, giving rise to a relatively large disordered region and making diffusion a
cooperative process. Since this will extend the disorder
within the crystal and increase its entropy, it is understandable that the presence of relaxed vacancies should be
associated with a decreased entropy of fusion. A further
consequence is that while the Torrey model may adequately

relate the relaxation time to the jump time τ when the simple
vacancy mechanism is valid, this may no longer be true when
relaxed vacancies are involved (Boden, Cohen, and Squires
1976). Moreover, the volume of activation $V^{\ddagger}$ might be expected to be less when the relaxed vacancy mechanism is
operative than for the simple vacancy mechanism. It is
therefore significant that $V^{\ddagger}$ appears to decrease with decreasing entropy of fusion. Thus, in contrast to hexa-
methylethane, for which $\Delta S_m = 2 \cdot 4R$ and $V^{\ddagger} = 1 \cdot 12 V_m$, for hexamethyldisilane $\Delta S_m = 1 \cdot 26R$ and $V^{\ddagger}$ ranges from $0 \cdot 55 V_m$ to as
little as $0 \cdot 17 V_m$ with increasing temperature and pressure

TABLE 10.8.

*Self-diffusion parameters for five plastic crystals composed
of cage molecules (see Table 10.4 and Fig.10.10 for formulae)*
ΔS_m = entropy of fusion, E_D = activation energy, ΔH_S = molar
enthalpy of sublimation, $\Delta S^{\ddagger}$ = entropy of diffusion,
τ (m.p.) = mean molecular jump time at melting-point (Folland
et al. 1973).

Substance	$\Delta S_m/R$	$E_D/$kJ mol^{-1}	τ(m.p.)/s	$E_D/\Delta H_S$	$\Delta S^{\ddagger}/R$
Triethylenediamine	2·06	96·4	$3 \cdot 4 \times 10^{-7}$	1·84	11·1
3-azabicyclo [3,2,2]nonane	1·79	83·6	$4 \cdot 0 \times 10^{-7}$	1·45	6·1
Norbornane	1·53	54·5[a]	$3 \cdot 0 \times 10^{-7}$	1·76[a]	2·8[a]
Norbornylene	1·22	48·6	$4 \cdot 2 \times 10^{-7}$	1·47	2·9
Norbornadiene	0·80	39·9	$1 \cdot 1 \times 10^{-6}$	1·31	2·5

a.   Data for h.c.p. form.

(Strange and Ross 1976). For cyclohexane (for which $V^{\ddagger}/V_m = 0 \cdot 70$; Folland and Strange 1972), there is evidence of another
kind that self-diffusion in the plastic phase proceeds by a
complicated mechanism involving many molecules. If it were
to occur by the simple vacancy mechanism, then the diffusion
coefficients for various isotopic forms of the cyclohexane

molecule should differ. In fact, Chadwick and Sherwood (1972) found the diffusion coefficients of the species $^{12}C_5{}^{14}C_1H_{12}$ and $C_6D_{11}T$ (T = tritium) to be the same as that of the ordinary C_6H_{12} molecule. Some idea of the possible size of the region affected by a relaxed vacancy was obtained from an investigation of Brillouin and Rayleigh scattering in succinonitrile and pivalic acid by Hyde, Kevorkian, and Sherwood (1969). They suggested that a small disordered region might contain about 20 molecules.

Attempts have been made to estimate the number of vacancies in plastic crystals by the well-known method of comparing the measured density of the crystal with that corresponding to the unit cell dimensions found by X-ray diffraction. The disordered nature of the crystal unfortunately has an adverse effect on the precision with which the cell dimensions can be estimated. For cyclohexane and cyclohexanol, a combination of the density measurements of Higgins, Ivor, Staveley, and Virden (1964) and of the X-ray work of Green and Wheeler (1969b) placed upper limits of 0·5 and 0·3 % respectively on the vacancy concentration. A similar approach applied to succinonitrile and cyclooctane by Baughman and Turnbull (1971) gave < 0·1 % and ~0·36 % respectively at the triple-points. For camphene, Green and Wheeler estimated that the vacancy concentration might reach the very high figure of 7·7 per cent at the melting-point, but Sherwood (1973) questioned the reliability of this conclusion.

For the few crystals on which investigations of plastic deformation (creep) as well as radiotracer studies have been carried out, the very fair agreement between the two activation energies resulting therefrom shows that plastic deformation is self-diffusion controlled. The plasticity of such solids is therefore a vacancy-dependent property, as suggested by Dunning (1961).

It will be seen from Table 10.8 that in spite of the considerable difference in E_D for the five substances (and also in the pre-exponential factor of the Arrhenius equation), the jump times for diffusion at the melting-points are remarkably constant, implying that the crystal melts when the jump time reaches a more or less constant critical value. The same point was made by Virlet and Rigny (1975), who pointed out that for sixteen substances of widely differing chemical types and with melting-points ranging from 90 K to 540 K, the τ values at the melting-point fell between $\sim 10^{-6}$ and $0 \cdot 8 \times 10^{-7}$ s.

REFERENCES

Abrahams, S.C. (1953). *J.chem.Phys.* 21, 1218.
———— and Lipscomb, W.N. (1952). *Acta crystallogr.* 5, 93.
Adachi, K., Suga, H., and Seki, S. (1968). *Bull.chem.Soc. Japan* 41, 1073.
————   ————   ———— (1970). *Bull.chem.Soc. Japan* 43, 1916.
Agron, P.A., Johnson, C.K., and Levy, H.A. (1965). *Inorg. nucl.Chem.Lett.* 1, 145.
Albert, S., Gutowsky, H.S., and Ripmeester, J.A. (1972). *J.chem.Phys.* 56, 1332.
————   ————   ———— (1976). *J. chem.Phys.* 64, 3277.
Alexander, S. and Tzalmona, A. (1965). *Phys.Rev.* 138, A845.
Alexandre, M. and Rigny, P. (1972). *Molecular Crystals and Liquid Crystals* 17, 19.
Allen, P.S. and Cowking, A. (1967). *J.chem.Phys.* 47, 4286.
Allen, W.C., Liu, N., and Jonas, J. (1975). *J.chem.Phys.* 63, 3317.
Amzel, L.M. and Becka, L.N. (1969). *(J.)Phys.Chem.Solids* 30, 521.
Anderson, J.E. (1970). *Molecular Crystals and Liquid Crystals* 11, 343.
———— and Slichter, W.P. (1964). *J.chem.Phys.* 41, 1922.
————   ———— (1965). *J.phys.Chem.* 69, 3099.
————   ———— (1966a). *J.chem.Phys.* 44, 1797.
————   ———— (1966b). *J.chem.Phys.* 44, 3647.
Andon, R.J.L., Counsell, J.F., Hales, J.L., Lees, E.B., and Martin, J.F. (1968). *J.chem.Soc.(A)* 2357.

———— ———— Lee, D.A., and Martin, J.F. (1973). *J.chem.Soc.,Faraday Trans.I* 69, 1721.

———— and Martin, J.F. (1973). *J.chem.Soc.,Faraday Trans.I* 69, 761.

Andrew, E.R. (1950). *J.chem.Phys.* 18, 607.

———— (1963). *Ber.Bunsenges.phys.Chem.* 67, 295.

———— and Eades, R.G. (1953). *Proc.R.Soc.* A216, 398.

———— Hinshaw, W.S., Hutchins, M.G., and Jasinski, A. (1974). *Chem.Phys.Lett.* 27, 96.

Ang, T.T. and Dunell, B.A. (1972). *J.chem.Soc.,Faraday Trans. II* 68, 1331.

———— ———— (1974). *J.chem.Soc.,Faraday Trans. II* 70, 17.

Arentsen, J.G. and van Miltenburg, J.C. (1972). *J.chem.Thermodynamics* 4, 789.

Aston, J.G., Bolger, B., Trambarulo, R., and Segall, H. (1954). *J.chem.Phys.* 22, 460.

———— and Messerly, G.H. (1936). *J.Am.chem.Soc.* 58, 2354.

———— Stottlemyer, Q.R., and Murray, G.R. (1960). *J.Am.chem.Soc.* 82, 1281.

———— Szasz, G.J., and Fink, H.L. (1943). *J.Am.chem. Soc.* 65, 1135.

Atake, T. and Chihara, H. (1976). *Chem.Lett.* 683.

Atoji, M., Oda, T., and Watanabe, T. (1953). *Acta crystallogr.* 6, 868.

Azokpota, C., Calvarin, G., and Pommier, C. (1976). *J.chem. Thermodynamics* 8, 283.

Backer, H.J. and Perdok, W.G. (1943). *Recl.trav.chim.Pays-Bas* 62, 533.

Barber, C.M. and Westrum, E.F. (1963). *J.phys.Chem.* 67, 2373.

Barnes, A.J. and Hallam, H.E. (1969). *Quart.Rev.chem.Soc.* 23, 392.

Barnes, J.D. (1973). *J.chem.Phys.* 58, 5193.

Bartoli, F.J. and Litovitz, T.A. (1972). *J.chem.Phys.* 56, 413.

Baudour, J.L., Cailleau, H., Delugeard, Y., Desuche, J., Girard, A., Meinnel, J., and Yelon, W.P. (1976). *Molecular Crystals and Liquid Crystals* 32, 5.

Baughman, R.H. (1970). *J.chem.Phys.* <u>53</u>, 3781.

———   and Turnbull, D. (1971). *(J.)Phys.Chem.Solids*
<u>32</u>, 1375.

Beaumont, R.H., Chihara, H., and Morrison, J.A. (1961).
Proc.phys.Soc. <u>78</u>, 1462.

Bird, M.J., Jackson, D.A., and Powles, J.G. (1973). *Molec.
Phys.* <u>25</u>, 1051.

Bladon, P., Lockhart, N.C., and Sherwood, J.N. (1971a).
Molec.Phys. <u>20</u>, 577

———   ———   ———   (1971b).
Molec.Phys. <u>22</u>, 365.

Blasenbrey, S. and Pechhold, W. (1967). *Rheol.Acta* <u>6</u>, 174.

Blum, H. and Sherwood, J.N. (1970). *Molecular Crystals and
Liquid Crystals* <u>10</u>, 381.

Boden, N., Cohen, J., and Davis, P.P. (1972). *Molec.Phys.*
<u>23</u>, 819.

———   ———   and Squires, R.T. (1976). *Molecular
Crystals and Liquid Crystals* <u>32</u>, 55.

———   Davis, P.P., Stam, C.H., and Wesselink, G.A.
(1973). *Molec.Phys.* <u>25</u>, 87.

Bol'shutkin, D.N., Gasan, V.M., Prokhvatilov, A.I., and
Erenburg, A.I. (1972). *Acta crystallogr.* <u>B28</u>, 3542.

Bondi, A. (1968). *Molecular Crystals* <u>3</u>, 479.

Brady, A.P., Myers, O.E., and Clauss, J.K. (1960). *J.phys.
Chem.* <u>64</u>, 588.

Brennan, J.S., Brown, N.M.D., and Swinton, F.L. (1974). *J.
chem.Soc.,Faraday Trans.I* <u>70</u>, 1965.

Broadhurst, M.G. (1962). *J.Res.natn.Bur.Stand.* <u>66A</u>, 241.

Brockway, L.O. and Robertson, J.M. (1939). *J.chem.Soc.* 1324.

Brookeman, J.H. and Rushworth, F.A. (1976). *J.Phys.* <u>C9</u>, 1043.

Brot, C. and Darmon, I. (1970). *J.chem.Phys.* <u>53</u>, 2271.

———   ———   and Dat-Xuong, N. (1967). *J.Chim.
phys.* <u>64</u>, 1061.

———   and Lassier-Govers, B. (1976). *Ber.Bunsenges.phys.
Chem.* <u>80</u>, 31.

Bruni, G. and Natta, G. (1929). *Recl.trav.chim.Pays-Bas*
<u>48</u>, 860.

———   ———   (1930). *Rend.Accad.Nazl.Lincei* <u>11</u>,
929.

Burbank, R.D. and Bensey, F.N. (1957). *J.chem.Phys.* <u>27</u>, 981.

———   and Jones, G.R. (1970). *Science* 168, 248.

———   ———   (1971). *Science* <u>171</u>, 485.

———   ———   (1974). *J.Am.chem.Soc.* <u>96</u>, 43.

Burnett, L.J. and Muller, B.H. (1976). *J.mag.Res.* <u>23</u>, 343.

Calingaert, G., Soroos, H., Hnizda, V., and Shapiro, H. (1944). *J.Am.chem.Soc.* <u>66</u>, 1389.

Calvarin, G. and Berar, J.F. (1975). *J.appl.Crystallogr.* <u>8</u>, 380.

———   and Weigel, D. (1976). *J.appl.Crystallogr.* <u>9</u>, 212.

Carter, G.F. and Templeton, D.H. (1953). *Acta crystallogr.* <u>6</u>, 805.

Celotti, G., Bertinelli, F., and Stremmenos, C. (1975). *Acta crystallogr.* <u>A31</u>, 582.

Chadwick, A.V. and Sherwood, J.N. (1972). *J.chem.Soc.,Faraday Trans.I* <u>68</u>, 47.

Chamberland, A., Belzile, R., and Cabana, A. (1970). *Can.J. Chem.* <u>48</u>, 1129.

Chang, E.T. and Westrum, E.F. (1965). *J.phys.Chem.* <u>69</u>, 2176.

———   ———   (1970). *J.phys.Chem.* <u>74</u>, 2528.

Chang, S.-S. and Westrum, E.F. (1960). (a) *J.phys.Chem.* <u>64</u>, 1547; (b) <u>64</u>, 1551.

Charbonneau, G.-P. and Trotter, J. (1967). *J.chem.Soc.(A)* 2032.

———   ———   (1968). *J.chem.Soc.(A)*1267.

Chernick, C.L., Claassen, H.H., and Weinstock, B. (1961). *J.Am.chem.Soc.* <u>83</u>, 3165.

Chezeau, J.M., Dufourcq, J., and Strange, J.H. (1971). *Molec. Phys.* <u>20</u>, 305.

Chihara, H. and Koga, Y. (1971). *Bull.chem.Soc.Japan* <u>44</u>, 2681.

———   Otsuru, M., and Seki, S. (1966). *Bull.chem.Soc. Japan* <u>39</u>, 2145.

———   and Seki, S. (1948). *Nature,Lond.* <u>162</u>, 773.

Christoffers, H.J., Lingafelter, E.C., and Cady, G.H. (1947). *J.Am.chem.Soc.* <u>69</u>, 2502.

Clark, T., McKervey, M.A., Mackle, H., and Rooney, J.J. (1974). *J.chem.Soc.,Faraday Trans.I* <u>70</u>, 1279.

Clayton, P.R., Worswick, R.D., and Staveley, L.A.K. (1976).
    Molecular Crystals and Liquid Crystals 36, 153.

Clemett, C. and Davies, M. (1962). (a) *Trans.Faraday Soc.* 58,
    1705; (b) 58, 1718.

Clever, H.L., Westrum, E.F., and Cordes, A.W. (1965). *J.phys.
    Chem.* 69, 1214.

Conner, W.P. and Smyth, C.P. (1941). *J.Am.chem.Soc.* 63, 3424.

Corfield, G. and Davies, M. (1964). *Trans.Faraday Soc.* 60,
    10.

Coulson, C.A. and Emerson, D. (1974). *Proc.R.Soc.* A337, 151.

Crowe, R.W. and Smyth, C.P. (1950). (a) *J.Am.chem.Soc.* 72,
    1098; (b) 72, 4009.

———   ———   (1951). *J.Am.chem.Soc.* 73, 5406.

Darmon, I. and Brot, C. (1966). *Molecular Crystals* 1, 417.

———   ———   (1967). *Molecular Crystals* 2, 301.

Davies, M. (1966). *J.Chim.phys.* 63, 67.

Dehl, R.E. (1974). *J.chem.Phys.* 60, 339.

Descamps, M. (1976). *Molecular Crystals and Liquid Crystals*
    32, 61.

Donohue, J. and Goodman, S.H. (1967). *Acta crystallogr.* 22,
    352.

Doshi, N., Furman, M., and Rudman, R. (1973). *Acta crys-
    tallogr.* B29, 143.

Douslin, D.R. and Huffman, H.M. (1946). *J.Am.chem.Soc.* 68,
    173.

Dumas, G.G. and Michel, J. (1971). *C.r.hebd.Séanc.Acad.Sci.,
    Paris* 272B, 836.

Duncan, W.A. and Swinton, F.L. (1966). *Trans.Faraday Soc.*
    62, 1082.

Dunitz, J.D., Orgel, L.E., and Rich, A. (1956). *Acta crys-
    tallogr.* 9, 373.

Dunning, W.J. (1961). *(J.)Phys.Chem.Solids* 18, 21.

Durig, J.R., Craven, S.M., Lau, K.K., and Bragin, J. (1971).
    J.chem.Phys. 54, 479.

Eades, R.G., Finch, N.D., and El Saffar, Z.M. (1959). *8è
    Colloque Ampère (London)*, p.109.

Edwards, J.W. and Kington, G.L. (1962). *Trans.Faraday Soc.*
    58, 1334.

———   ———   and Mason, R. (1960). *Trans.
    Faraday Soc.* 56, 660.

Eggers, D.F. (1975). *J.phys.Chem.* <u>79</u>, 2116.

Eguchi, T., Soda, G., and Chihara, H. (1976). *J.mag.Res.*
     <u>23</u>, 55.

El Saffar, Z.M. (1962). *J.chem.Phys.* <u>36</u>, 1093.

Eucken, A. and Schröder, E. (1938). *Z.phys.Chem.* <u>B41</u> 307.

────   and Veith, H. (1936). *Z.phys.Chem.* <u>B34</u>, 275.

────   ────   (1937). *Z.phys.Chem.* <u>B38</u>, 393.

Eveno, M. and Meinnel, J. (1966). *J.Chim.phys.* <u>63</u>, 108.

Ewen, B., Fischer, E.W., Piesczek, W., and Strobl, G. (1974).
     J.chem.Phys. 61, 5265.

Fateley, W.G and Miller, F.A. (1961). *Spectrochim.Acta* <u>17</u>,
     857.

Finbak, C. (1937). *Tids.Kjemi Bergvesen* <u>17</u>, No.9.

────   (1938). *Arch.Math.Naturvidenskab* <u>B42</u>, No.1.

────   and Hassel, O. (1937). *Z.phys.Chem.* <u>B36</u>, 301.

────   and Viervoll, H. (1942). *Tids.Kjemi Bergvesen* <u>2</u>,
     35.

Fink, H.L., Cines, M.R., Frey, F.E., and Aston, J.G. (1947).
     J.Am.chem.Soc. <u>69</u>, 1501.

Finke, H.L., Scott, D.W., Gross, M.E., Messerly, J.F., and
     Waddington, G. (1956). *J.Am.chem.Soc.* <u>78</u>, 5469.

────   Todd, S.S., and Messerly, J.F. (1970). *J.chem.*
     Thermodynamics <u>2</u>, 129.

Fitzgerald, W.E. and Janz, G.J. (1957). *J.molec.Spectrosc.* <u>1</u>, 49.

Folland, R., Jackson, D.A., and Rajagopal, S. (1975). *Molec.*
     Phys. <u>30</u>, 1063.

────   Jackson, R.L., Strange, J.H., and Chadwick,
     A.V. (1973). *(J.)Phys.Chem.Solids* <u>34</u>, 1713.

────   and Strange, J.H. (1972). *J.Phys.* <u>C5</u>, L50.

Fontaine, H., Longueville, W., and Wallart, F. (1972).
     C.r.hebd.Séanc.Acad.Sci.,Paris <u>274B</u>, 641.

Fourme, R. (1969). *C.r.hebd.Séanc.Acad.Sci.,Paris* <u>268C</u>, 931.

────   and Renaud, M. (1972). *Molecular Crystals and*
     Liquid Crystals <u>17</u>, 223.

────   ────   and André, D. (1972). *Molecular*
     Crystals and Liquid Crystals <u>17</u>, 209.

Fournier, R.P., Savoie, R., Bessette, F., and Cabana,A.
     (1968). *J.chem.Phys.* <u>49</u>, 1159.

Fox, R. and Sherwood, J.N. (1971). *Trans.Faraday Soc.* <u>67</u>, 3364.

Frankosky, M. and Aston, J.G. (1965). *J.phys.Chem.* 69, 3126.

Fratiello, A. and Douglass, D.C. (1964). *J.chem.Phys.* 41, 974.

Frederick, K.J. and Hildebrand, J.H. (1939). *J.Am.chem.Soc.* 61, 1555.

Fried, F. (1966). *C.r.hebd.Séanc.Acad.Sci.,Paris* 262C, 1497.

——— and Lassier, B.(1966). *J.Chim.phys.* 63, 75.

Fyfe, C.A. and Harold-Smith, D. (1976). (a) *Can.J.Chem.* 54, 769; (b) 54, 783.

Gilson, D.F.R. and McDowell, C.A. (1966). *Can.J.Chem.* 44,945.

——— and Saviotti, P.P. (1974). *J.chem.Soc., Faraday Trans.II* 70, 1.

Gordon, R.G. (1965). *J.chem.Phys.* 43, 1307.

Goyal, P.S., Nawrocik, W., Urban, S., Domoslawski, J., and Natkaniec, I. (1974). *Acta phys.pol.* 46A, 399.

Graham,J.D. and Choi, J.K. (1975). *J.chem.Phys.* 62, 2509.

Green, J.R., Dalich, S.J., and Griffith, W.T. (1972). *Molecular Crystals and Liquid Crystals* 17, 251.

——— and Griffith, W.T. (1969). *Molecular Crystals and Liquid Crystals* 6, 23.

——— and Wheeler, D.R. (1969). (a) *Molecular Crystals and Liquid Crystals* 6, 1; (b) 6, 13.

Greer, S.C. (1973). *Phys.Lett.* 43A, 73.

——— and Meyer, L. (1969). *J.chem.Phys.* 51, 4583.

Gupta, R.C. and Agrawal, V.C. (1967). *Ind.J.Phys.* 41, 559.

Guthrie, G.B. and McCullough, J.P. (1961). *(J.)Phys.Chem. Solids* 18, 53.

——— Scott, D.W., Hubbard, W.N., Katz, C., McCullough, J.P., Gross, M.E., Williamson, K.D., and Waddington, G. (1952). *J.Am.chem.Soc.* 74, 4662.

Gutowsky, H.S. and McCall, D.W. (1960). *J.chem.Phys.* 32, 548.

——— and Pake, G.E. (1950). *J.chem.Phys.* 18, 162.

Guttman, L. and Pitzer, K.S. (1945). *J.Am.chem.Soc.* 67, 324.

Haffmans, R. and Larkin, I.W. (1972). *J.chem.Soc.,Faraday Trans.* II 68, 1729.

Haida, O., Suga, H., and Seki, S. (1973). *Chem.Lett.* 79.

Hanson, A.W. (1964). *Acta crystallogr.* 17, 559.

——— (1965). *Acta crystallogr.* 19, 19.

Hassel, O. and Sommerfeldt, A.M. (1938). *Z.Phys.Chem.* B40, 391.

Hawthorne, H.M. and Sherwood, J.N. (1970a). *Trans.Faraday Soc.* <u>66</u>, 1783; (1970b). <u>66</u>, 1799.

Herbstein, F.H. (1971). *Perspectives in Structural Chemistry* Vol. IV, p.166. John Wiley and Sons, New York.

Hicks, J.F.G., Hooley, J.G., and Stephenson, C.C. (1944). *J.Am.chem.Soc.* <u>66</u>, 1064.

Higgins, P.F., Ivor, R.A.B., Staveley, L.A.K., and Virden, J.J. des C. (1964). *J.chem.Soc.* 5762.

Hoch, M.J.R. and Rushworth, F.A. (1964). *Proc.phys.Soc.* <u>83</u>, 949.

Hoffman, J.D. (1952). *J.chem.Phys.* <u>20</u>, 541.

———   and Decker, B. (1953). *J.phys.Chem.* <u>57</u>, 520.

Holm, C.H. and Ibers, J.A. (1959). *J.chem.Phys.* <u>30</u>, 885.

Hood, G.M., Lockhart, N.C., and Sherwood, J.N. (1972). *J. chem.Soc.,Faraday Trans.* I <u>68</u>, 736.

———   and Sherwood, J.N. (1966a). *Molecular Crystals.* <u>1</u>, 97.

———   ———   (1966b). *J.Chim.phys.* <u>63</u>, 121.

Huffman, H.M., Eaton, M., and Oliver, G.D. (1948). *J.Am. chem.Soc.* <u>70</u>, 2911.

———   Todd, S.S., and Oliver, G.D. (1949). *J.Am. chem.Soc.* <u>71</u>, 584.

Hvoslef, J. (1958). *Acta crystallogr.* <u>11</u>, 383.

Hyams, I.J. and Ron, A. (1973). *J.chem.Phys.* <u>59</u>, 3027.

Hyde, A.J., Kevorkian, J., and Sherwood, J.N. (1969). *Motions in molecular crystals, Disc.Faraday Soc.* No.48, p.19.

Ivin, K.J. and Dainton, F.S. (1947). *Trans.Faraday Soc.* <u>43</u>, 32.

Jackson, R.L. and Strange, J.H. (1972). *Acta crystallogr.* <u>B28</u>, 1645.

Kahn, R., Fourme, R., André, D., and Renaud, M. (1970). *C.r.hebd.Séanc.Acad.Sci.,Paris* <u>271B</u>, 1078.

———   ———   ———   ———   (1973). *Acta crystallogr.* <u>B29</u>, 131.

Kakiuchi, Y., Komatsu, H., and Kyoya, S. (1951). *J.phys.Soc. Japan* <u>6</u>, 321.

Kawaguchi, T., Takashina, K., Tanaka, T., and Watanabe, T. (1972). *Acta crystallogr.* <u>28B</u>, 967.

Kelley, K.K. (1929). *J.Am.chem.Soc.* 51, 1400.

Keyes, P.H. and Daniels, W.B. (1975). *J.chem.Phys.* 62, 2000.

Kilpatrick, J.E. and Pitzer, K.S. (1946). *J.Am.chem.Soc.* 68, 1066.

———   ———   and Spitzer, R. (1947). *J. Am.chem.Soc.* 69, 2483.

Klingen, T.J. and Kindsvater, J.H. (1974). *Molecular Crystals and Liquid Crystals*, 26, 365.

———   and Wright, J.R. (1972). *Molecular Crystals and Liquid Crystals*, 16, 283.

Koga, Y. and Morrison, J.A. (1975). *J.chem.Phys.* 62, 3359.

Koide, T. (1967). *Bull.chem.Soc.Japan* 40, 2026.

———   Tsujino, M., Sawada, K., and Oda, T. (1974). *Bull. chem.Soc.Japan* 47, 2998.

Kondo, S. (1957). *Mem.Fac.Osaka Gakugei University, Ser.B,* No.6, 25.

———   (1958). *Bull.chem.Soc.Japan* 29, 999.

———   (1965). *Bull.chem.Soc.Japan* 38, 527.

———   and Oda, T. (1954). *Bull.chem.Soc.Japan* 27, 567.

Kotake, K., Nakamura, N., and Chihara, H. (1970). *Bull. chem.Soc.Japan* 43, 2429.

Krishna Murti, G.S.R. (1958). *Ind.J.Phys.* 32, 460.

Kushner, L.M., Crowe, R.W., and Smyth, C.P. (1950). *J.Am. chem.Soc.* 72, 1091.

Lagarrigue, M. (1972). *Molecular Crystals and Liquid Crystals* 17, 237.

Larsen, F.K., Little, R.G., and Coppens, P. (1975). *Acta crystallogr.* B31, 430.

Lawrenson, I.J. and Rushworth, F.A. (1958). *Proc.phys.Soc.* 72, 791.

Leffler, A.J., Alexander, M.N., Sagalyn, P.L., and Walker, N. (1975). *J.chem.Phys.* 63, 3971.

Lemanceau, B., Chezeau, J.-M., and Hache, J.-Y. (1966). *J.Chim.phys.* 63, 94.

Leung, Y.C., Waser, J., van Houten, S., Vos, A., Wiegers, G.A., and Wiebenga, E.H. (1957). *Acta crystallogr.* 10, 574.

Levitin, N.E., Westrum, E.F., and Carter, J.C. (1959). *J. Am.chem.Soc.* 81, 3547.

Levy, J.H., Taylor, J.C., and Wilson, P.W. (1975). (a) *Acta crystallogr.* B31, 398; (b) *J.Solid St.Chem.* 15, 360.

Lewis, A. and Pace, E.L. (1973). *J.chem.Phys.* <u>58</u>, 3661.

Livingston, R.C., Rothschild, W.G., and Rush, J.J. (1973).
     J.chem.Phys. <u>59</u>, 2498.

Llewellyn, F.J., Cox, E.G., and Goodwin, T.H. (1937). *J.chem.
     Soc.* 883.

Longueville, W. and Fontaine, H. (1976). *Molecular Crystals
     and Liquid Crystals* <u>32</u>, 73.

――――   ――――   and Chapoton, A. (1971). *J.
     Chim.phys.* <u>68</u>, 436.

Lüth, H., Nyburg, S.C., Robinson, P.M., and Scott, H.G. (1974).
     Molecular Crystals and Liquid Crystals <u>27</u>, 337.

Manzhelii, V.G., Chausov, G.P., and Freiman, Yu. A. (1972).
     Soviet Phys.Solid St. <u>13</u>, 2902.

Marshall, J.G., Staveley, L.A.K., and Hart, K.R. (1956).
     Trans.Faraday Soc. <u>52</u>, 19.

McCall, D.W. and Douglass, D.C. (1960). *J.chem.Phys.* <u>33</u>, 777.

McClure, D.W. (1968). *J.chem.Phys.* <u>49</u>, 1830.

McCullough, J.P., Finke, H.L., Gross, M.E., Messerly, J.F.,
     and Waddington, G. (1957). *J.phys.Chem.* <u>61</u>, 289.

――――   ――――   Hubbard, W.N., Good, W.D.,
     Pennington, R.E., Messerly, J.F. and Waddington, G.
     (1954). *J.Am.chem.Soc.* <u>76</u>, 2661.

――――   Scott, D.W., Finke, H.L., Hubbard, W.N.,
     Gross, M.E., Katz, C., Pennington, R.E., Messerly, J.F.,
     and Waddington, G. (1953). *J.Am.chem.Soc.* <u>75</u>, 1818.

Meakins, R.J. (1961). *Progr.Dielectrics* <u>3</u>, 151.

――――   (1962). *Trans.Faraday Soc.* <u>58</u>, 1962.

Messager, J.-C. and Blot, J. (1971). *C.r.hebd.Séanc.Acad.Sci.,
     Paris* <u>272B</u>, 684.

――――   and Sanquer, M. (1974). *Molecular Crystals
     and Liquid Crystals*, <u>26</u>, 373.

Messerly, J.F. and Finke, H.L. (1970). *J.chem.Thermodynamics*
     <u>2</u>, 867.

Migliorini, M.G., Salvi, P.R., and Sbrana, G. (1974). *Chem.
     Phys.Lett.* <u>28</u>, 565.

Mirskaya, K.V. (1963). *Soviet Phys.Cryst.* <u>8</u>, 167.

Mones, A.H. and Post, B. (1952). *J.chem.Phys.* <u>20</u>, 755.

Monica, M.D., Jannelli, L. and Lamanna, U. (1968). *J.phys.
     Chem.* <u>72</u>, 1068.

Montgomery, R.L. (1974). *Science* 184, 562.

Moskalev, V.V. and Petrov, M.P. (1963). *Fiz.Tverd.Tela* 5, 1400 (*Soviet Phys.Solid St.* 5, 1018).

Mosselman, C., Mourik, J., and Dekker, H. (1974). *J.chem. Thermodynamics* 6, 477.

Mulay, L.N. and Attalla, A. (1963). *J.Am.chem.Soc.* 85, 702.

Murill, E. and Breed, L. (1970). *Thermochim.Acta* 1, 239.

Namba, Y. and Oda, T. (1952). *Bull.chem.Soc.Japan* 25, 225.

Niemelä, L. and Niemelä, M. (1970). *Ann.Acad.Sci.Fennicae*, *Ser.A* VI, No. 341.

Nimmo, J.K. and Lucas, B.W. (1976). *Acta crystallogr.* B32, 348.

Nitta, I., Seki, S., and Momotani, M. (1950). *Proc.Jap.Acad.* 26, (9), 25.

——— ——— ——— Suzuki, K., and Nakagawa, S. (1950). *Proc.Jap.Acad.* 26, (10), 11.

——— and Watanabe, T. (1937). *Nature,Lond.* 140, 365.

——— ——— (1938). *Sci.Papers Inst.phys. chem.Res.,Tokyo* 34, 1669; *Bull.chem.Soc.Japan* 13, 28.

Noack, F., Weithase, M., and von Schütz, J. (1975). *Z. Naturforsch.* 30a, 1707.

Nordman, C.E. and Schmitkons, D.L. (1965). *Acta crystallogr.* 18, 764.

Nowacki, W. (1946). *Helv.chim.Acta* 29, 1798.

Oda, T. (1948). *X-rays* 5, 26.

——— (1949). *X-rays* 5, 95.

Olf, H.G. and Franconi, B. (1973). *J.chem.Phys.* 59, 534.

——— and Peterlin, A. (1970). *J.Polymer Sci.* A-2 8, 791.

O'Reilly, D.E., Peterson, E.M., and Scheie, C.E. (1974). *J.chem.Phys.* 60, 1603.

——— ——— ——— and Seyfarth, E. (1973). *J.chem.Phys.* 59, 3576.

Osborne, D.W., Schreiner, F., Malm, J.G., Selig, H., and Rochester, L. (1966). *J.chem.Phys.* 44, 2802.

Otsubo, A. and Suguwara, T. (1955). *Sci.Rept.Res.Inst. Tohoku Univ.* A7, 583.

Overberger, J.E., Steele, W.A., and Aston, J.G. (1969). *J. chem.Thermodynamics* 1, 535.

Pace, E.L. and Aston, J.G. (1948). *J.Am.chem.Soc.* 70, 566.

712 DISORDER IN MOLECULAR SOLIDS - II

Paliani, G., Poletti, A., and Cataliotti, R. (1973). *Chem. Phys.Lett.* <u>18</u>, 525.

Pariaud, J.-C. (1950). *Bull.Soc.chim.Fr.* 1239.

Parks, G.S., Kennedy, W.D., Gates, R.R., Mosley, J.R., Moore, G.E., and Renquist, M.L. (1956). *J.Am.chem.Soc.* <u>78</u>, 56.

Pelah, I., Vulkan, U., and Zafrir, H. (1972). *J.chem.Phys.* <u>56</u>, 5186.

Perdok, W.G. and Terpstra, P. (1943). *Recl.trav.chim.Pays-Bas* <u>62</u>, 687.

———   ———   (1946). *Recl.trav.chim.Pays-Bas* <u>65</u>, 493.

Petrakis, L. and Rao, A. (1963). *J.chem.Phys.* <u>39</u>, 1633.

Piesczek, W., Strobl, G., and Malzahn, K. (1974). *Acta crystallogr.* <u>B30</u>, 1278.

Post, B. (1959). *Acta crystallogr.* <u>12</u>, 349.

———   Schwartz, R.S., and Fankuchen, I. (1951). *J.Am. chem.Soc.* <u>73</u>, 5113.

Powell, T.M. and Giauque, W.F. (1939). *J.Am.chem.Soc.* <u>61</u>, 2366.

Powles, J.G. (1952). *J.chem.Phys.* <u>20</u>, 1648.

———   Begum, A., and Norris, M.O. (1969). *Molec.Phys.* <u>17</u>, 489.

———   and Gutowsky, H.S. (1953a). *J.chem.Phys.* <u>21</u>, 1695.

———   ———   (1953b). *J.chem.Phys.* <u>21</u>, 1704.

———   (1955). *J.chem.Phys.* <u>23</u>, 1692.

Prasad, P.N., Woodruff, S.D., and Kopelman, R. (1973). *Chem. Phys.* <u>1</u>, 173.

Rakov, A.V. (1959). *Opt.Spectrosc.* <u>7</u>, 128.

Rathjens, G.W. and Gwinn, W.D. (1953). *J.Am.chem.Soc.* <u>75</u>, 5629.

Reed, T.B. and Lipscomb, W.N. (1953). *Acta crystallogr.* <u>6</u>, 108.

Renaud, M. and Fourme, R. (1966). *J.Chim.phys.* <u>63</u>, 27.

Resing, H.A. (1965). *J.chem.Phys.* <u>43</u>, 1828.

———   (1969). *Molecular Crystals and Liquid Crystals* <u>9</u>, 101.

Reynolds, P.A. (1974). *Molec.Phys.* <u>28</u>, 633.

——————   (1975). *Molec.Phys.* <u>30</u>, 1165.

Ribner, A. and Westrum, E.F. (1967). *J.phys.Chem.* <u>71</u>, 1208.

Richter, P.W. and Pistorius, C.W.F.T. (1972). *Molecular Crystals and Liquid Crystals* <u>16</u>, 153.

Rigny, P. and Virlet, J. (1969). *J.chem.Phys.* <u>51</u>, 3807.

Roeder, S.B.W. and Douglass, D.C. (1970). *J.chem.Phys.* <u>52</u>, 5525.

Rossiter, V. (1972). *J.Phys.* <u>C5</u>, 1969.

Roth, W.A. (1936). *Landolt-Börnstein Physikalisch-Chemische Tabellen Eg IIIC*, 2695.

Rubin, T.R., Levedahl, B.H., and Yost, D.M. (1944). *J.Am. chem.Soc.* <u>66</u>, 279.

Rudman, R. (1967). *J.chem.Educ.* <u>44</u>, 331.

——————   (1970). *Molecular Crystals and Liquid Crystals* <u>6</u>, 427.

——————   and Post, B. (1966). *Science* <u>154</u>, 1009.

——————   ——————   (1968a). *Molecular Crystals and Liquid Crystals* <u>3</u>, 325.

——————   ——————   (1968b). *Molecular Crystals and Liquid Crystals* <u>5</u>, 95.

Ruehrwein, R.A. and Huffman, H.M. (1943). *J.Am.chem.Soc.* <u>65</u>, 1620.

Rush, J.J. (1967). *J.chem.Phys.* <u>46</u>, 2285.

——————   and Taylor, T.I. (1966). *J.chem.Phys.* <u>44</u>, 2749.

Rushworth, F.A. (1954). *Proc.R.Soc.* <u>A222</u>, 526.

Sackmann, H. (1955). *Z.phys.Chem.* <u>204</u>, 299.

Samuelsen, E.J. and Semmingsen, D. (1975). *Solid St.Communs.* <u>17</u>, 217.

Sands, D.E. (1965). *J.Am.chem.Soc.* <u>87</u>, 1395.

——————   and Day, V.W. (1965). *Acta crystallogr.* <u>19</u>, 278.

Sasada, Y. and Atoji, M. (1953). *J.chem.Phys.* <u>21</u>, 145.

Sataty, Y.A. and Ron, A. (1974). *Chem.Phys.Lett.* <u>25</u>, 384.

——————   ——————   and Herbstein, F.H. (1975). *J.chem. Phys.* <u>62</u>, 1094.

Schaerer, A.A., Busso, C.J., Smith, A.E., and Skinner, L.B. (1955). *J.Am.chem.Soc.* <u>77</u>, 2017.

Schäfer, K.L. and Wagner, U. (1958). *Z.Elektrochem.* <u>62</u>, 328.

Schreiner, F., Osborne, D.W., Malm, J.G., and McDonald, G.N. (1969). *J.chem.Phys.* <u>51</u>, 4838.

Schwartz, R.S., Post, B., and Fankuchen, I. (1951). *J.Am. chem.Soc.* 73, 4490.

Scott, D.W., Douslin, D.R., Gross, M.E., Oliver, G.D., and Huffman, H.M. (1952). *J.Am.chem.Soc.* 74, 883.

Segel, S.L. and Mansingh, A. (1969). *J.chem.Phys.* 51, 4578.

Seki, S. and Momotani, M. (1950). *Bull.chem.Soc.Japan* 23, 30.

Semmingsen, D. and Feder, J. (1974). *Solid St.Communs.* 15, 1369.

Sherwood, J.N. (1969). *Molecular Crystals and Liquid Crystals* 9, 37.

——— (1973). *Chem.Soc.Specialist Periodical Reports, Surface and Defect Properties of Solids* 2, 250.

Shiono, R., Cruickshank, D.W.J., and Cox, E.G. (1958). *Acta crystallogr.* 11, 389.

Siegel, S. and Northrop, D.A. (1966). *Inorg.Chem.* 5, 2187.

Silver, L. and Rudman, R. (1972). *J.chem.Phys.* 57, 210.

Smith, G.W. (1961). *J.chem.Phys.* 35, 1134.

——— (1962). *J.chem.Phys.* 36, 3081.

——— (1965). *J.chem.Phys.* 43, 4325.

——— (1969). (a) *J.chem.Phys.* 50, 3595; (b) 51, 3569.

——— (1971). *J.chem.Phys.* 54, 174.

Smith, J.H. and Pace, E.L. (1969). *J.phys.Chem.* 73, 4232.

Smyth, C.P. (1955). *Dielectric behavior and structure.* McGraw-Hill, New York.

Snaauw, G.J. and Wiebenga, E.H. (1942). *Recl.trav.chim.Pays-Bas* 61, 253.

Sorai, M., Kosaki, A., Suga, H., Seki, S., Yoshida, T., and Otsuka, S. (1971). *Bull.chem.Soc.Japan* 44, 2364.

Spice, J.E., Harrow, G.A., McGowan, C.R., and Smith, E.B. (1961). *Pure and appl.Chem.* 2, 303.

Stejskal, E.O., Woessner, D.E., Farrar, T.C., and Gutowsky, H.S. (1959). *J.chem.Phys.* 31, 55.

Strange, J.H. and Ross,S.M. (1976). *Molecular Crystals and Liquid Crystals* 32, 67.

——— and Terenzi, M. (1970). *Molec.Phys.* 19, 275.

Straty, G.C. and Tsumara, R. (1976). *J.chem.Phys.* 64, 859.

Strobl, G., Ewen, B., Fischer, E.W., and Piesczek, W. (1974). *J.chem.Phys.* 61, 5257.

Suga, H. and Seki, S. (1959). *Bull.chem.Soc.Japan* 32, 1088.

———— Sugisaki, M., and Seki, S. (1966). *Molecular Crystals* 1, 377.

Sullivan, P.K. and Weeks, J.J. (1970). *J.Res.natn.Bur.Stand.* 74A, 203.

Tanner, J.E. (1972). *J.chem.Phys.* 56, 3850.

Tasumi, M., Shimanouchi, T., Watanabe, A., and Goto, R. (1964). *Spectrochim.Acta* 20, 629.

Timmermans, J. (1961). *(J.)Phys.Chem.Solids* 18, 1.

Torrey, H.C. (1953). *Phys.Rev.* 92, 962.

———— (1954). *Phys.Rev.* 96, 690.

Tranchant, F. and Guérin, R. (1972). *C.r.hebd.Séanc.Acad. Sci.,Paris* 274B, 795.

Trowbridge, J.C. and Westrum, E.F. (1963). *J.phys.Chem.* 67, 2381.

———— ———— (1964). *J.phys.Chem.* 68, 255.

Turkevich, A. and Smyth, C.P. (1940). *J.Am.chem.Soc.* 62, 2468.

Ubbelohde, A.R. (1938). *Trans.Faraday Soc.* 34, 282.

Urban, S., Tomkowicz, Z., Mayer, J., and Waluga, T. (1975). *Acta phys.pol.* A48, 61.

van Miltenburg, J.C. (1972). *J.chem.Thermodynamics* 4, 773.

———— and Oonk, H.A.J. (1974). *Molecular Crystals and Liquid Crystals* 28, 167.

Van Steenwinkel, R. (1969). *Z.Naturforsch.* 24a, 1526.

van de Vloed, A. (1939). *Bull.Soc.chim.Belg.* 48, 229.

Virlet, J. and Rigny, P. (1970a). *Chem.Phys.Lett.* 4, 501.

———— ———— (1970b). *Chem.Phys.Lett.* 6, 377.

———— ———— (1975). *J.mag.Res.* 19, 188.

Wada, T., Kishida, E., Tomiie, Y., Suga, H., Seki, S., and Nitta, T. (1960). *Bull.chem.Soc.Japan* 33, 1317.

Waddington, G., Knowlton, J.W., Scott, D.W., Oliver, G.D., Todd, S.S., Hubbard, W.N., Smith, J.C., and Huffman, H.M. (1949). *J.Am.chem.Soc.* 71, 797.

Watanabe, T., Saito, Y., and Chihara, H. (1949). *Sci.Papers Osaka Univ. Ser.C., Chem.* 11, No.2,9.

Webster, D.S. and Hoch, M.J.R. (1971). *(J.)Phys.Chem.Solids* 32, 2663.

Webster, D.S. and Hoch, M.J.R. (1976). *(J.)Phys.Chem.Solids* 37, 351.

Weinstock, B., Westrum, E.F., and Goodman, G.L. (1963). *Proceedings 8th International Conference on Low-temperature Physics* (ed. R.O. Davies), p.405. Butterworths, London.

Weiss, G.S., Parkes, A.S., Nixon, E.R., and Hughes, R.E. (1964). *J.chem.Phys.* 41, 3759.

West, C.D. (1934). *Z.Kristallogr.Kristallgeom.* 88, 195.

Westrum, E.F. (1966). *J.Chim.phys.* 63, 46.

——— (1969). *Molecular dynamics and structure of solids* (ed. R.S. Carter and J.J. Rush) p.459. NBS Special Publication No. 301.

——— and Henriquez, S. (1976). *Molecular Crystals and Liquid Crystals* 32, 31.

——— and Levitin, N.E. (1959). *J.Am.chem.Soc.* 81, 3544.

——— Wong, W.-K., and Morawetz, E. (1970). *J.phys. Chem.* 74, 2542.

White, A.H. and Bishop, W.S. (1940). *J.Am.chem.Soc.* 62, 8.

——— and Morgan, S.O. (1935). *J.Am.chem.Soc.* 57, 2078.

Williams, D.E. and Smyth, C.P. (1962). *J.Am.chem.Soc.* 84, 1808.

Woessner, D.E. and Gutowsky, H.S. (1963). *J.chem.Phys.* 39, 440.

Wong, W.-K. and Westrum, E.F. (1970). *J.phys.Chem.* 74, 1303.

Wu, P.-J., Hsu, L., and Dows, D.A. (1971). *J.chem.Phys.* 54, 2714.

Wulff, C.A. and Westrum, E.F. (1963). *J.phys.Chem.* 67, 2376.

——— ——— (1964). *J.phys.Chem.* 68, 430.

Yager, W.A. and Morgan, S.O. (1935). *J.Am.chem.Soc.* 57, 2071.

Yukitoshi, T., Suga, H., Seki, S., and Itoh, J. (1957). *J. phys.Soc.Japan* 12, 506.

Ziegler, K. and Aurnhammer, R. (1934). *Justus Liebigs Annln. Chem.* 513, 43.

Zweers, A.E., Brom, H.B., and Huiskamp, W.J. (1974). *Phys. Lett.* 47A, 347.

11

CLATHRATES AND CHANNEL COMPOUNDS

11.1. CLATHRATES - INTRODUCTION

A very interesting class of two-component systems exhibiting various types of disorder is that of the clathrates (Gk. *clathros* = cage). These substances consist essentially of a 'host' substance, e.g. quinol or water, which forms a fairly rigid lattice, and a 'guest' substance which can fill certain interstitial positions in this lattice. It is usually unnecessary for all of the available interstitial positions to be occupied by 'guest' molecules, though if there are too many vacancies of this type the substance may be unstable. The first type of disorder which may be expected is in the distribution of these vacancies. If the 'host' lattice is sufficiently inert and the distance between neighbouring 'guest' positions is sufficiently large we may expect there to be no correlation in the occupancies of these positions and the vacancies therefore to be distributed at random. Once the crystal has been formed there is, in general, no possibility of redistributing the vacancies, even though thermodynamics may demand that this should be done. Thus we would expect on thermodynamic grounds that on cooling to a sufficiently low temperature the 'guest' molecules would move to mutually adjacent sites, leaving the remaining parts of the crystal empty. In most cases, however, it would require the breakdown of the 'host' lattice before such movements of the 'guest' molecules would be possible. We might also expect orientational disorder of the 'guest' molecules if the 'host' lattice sufficiently reduces the angular-dependent part of the interaction between the 'guest' molecules and does not, itself, exert too strong an orientating influence. We leave further discussion of the possible types of disorder until they arise in dealing with the individual clathrates.

11.2. β-QUINOL CLATHRATES

Although compounds of this type were prepared as long ago as 1849 by Wöhler, their nature was not understood

until Palin and Powell (1947) made a detailed X-ray structure determination of the SO_2 compound. It was found that
the quinol molecules were hydrogen-bonded together so as to
form two interpenetrating three-dimensional arrays, the β-
structure (Fig.11.1a and b). This arrangement leaves almost

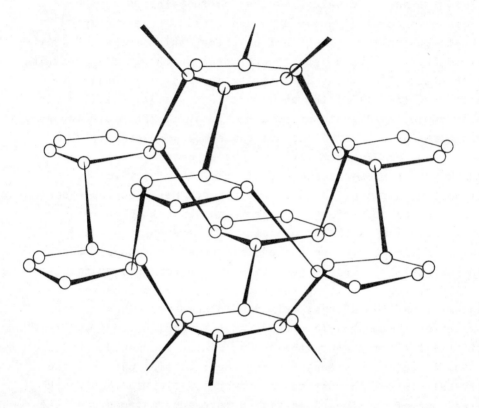

Fig.11.1(a). The bonding in β-quinol. Circles represent oxygen atoms.
The hexagons of O atoms are held together by hydrogen bonds. Aromatic
rings (not shown) are situated on all other bonds shown (from Palin and
Powell 1947).

spherical cavities in the lattice bounded on top and bottom
by the hexagons of oxygen atoms. Usually not all of these
cavities are occupied and, since no superlattice is found,
it is generally assumed that the vacancies are distributed
randomly. The crystal lattice parameters were found to be
independent of the nature of the 'guest' provided that its
molecules were not too large. However, long molecules, such

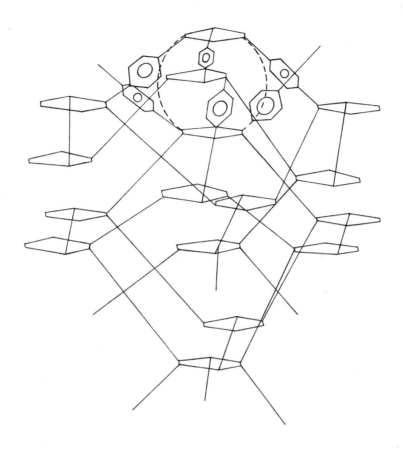

Fig.11.1(b). A cavity in the β-quinol structure is indicated by a broken line. ⟨ O ⟩ : aromatic ring; ⊂⟩ : hexagons of oxygen atoms held together by hydrogen bonds (from Palin and Powell 1947).

as CH_3CN, caused trellis-like distortion of the 'host' lattice (Palin and Powell 1947). Larger molecules still are not capable of acting as 'guests'.

It is important to realize that the 'host' lattice described above is not the stable form for pure quinol. The latter adopts the so-called α-structure ($\rho = 1 \cdot 33 \times 10^3$ kg m^{-3}), which is of higher density than the empty β-structure ($\rho = 1 \cdot 26 \times 10^3$ kg m^{-3}). Powell (1948) found that under pressure CO_2 preferred to be encaged in a structure which was very similar to the α-form, even though this structure is less open than the β-alternative. The α-structure is, perhaps,

favoured here because it can provide elongated cavities
which are a better fit for the CO_2 molecules. It is difficult to understand, however, why this pseudo α-structure,
providing a smaller number of correctly shaped cavities, is
not favoured at low pressures, at which only a relatively
small amount of 'guest' is introduced; at higher pressures,
adoption of the β-structure would then be expected so as to
accommodate a larger number of 'guest' molecules. Thus the
observed behaviour is the reverse of what would be expected.

When the thermodynamics of formation of, say, the argon
clathrate from gaseous argon and pure α-quinol is considered
it is clear that the entropy of inclusion into the β-quinol
will be negative since much of the considerable freedom of
the argon molecules in the gas phase is lost on clathration.
We must also take into account that there will be an increase in the contribution of the quinol to the free energy
on going from the α- to the less stable β-form. To compensate for both of these effects the enthalpy of inclusion
must be negative and sufficiently large. With this in mind,
it is not surprising that helium and neon, which would have
very weak interactions with the quinol walls, do not form
stable compounds. This, of course, does not completely rule
out the possibility of including a small amount of one of
these gases in, say, a krypton clathrate. Since the β-lattice
is then already stabilized by the presence of the krypton
'guest' molecules it is only the loss of entropy on inclusion
of the helium or neon into the krypton β-quinol clathrate
which opposes the clathration of these small molecules.

In this section we shall first consider the present
knowledge about the clathrates of the simplest substances,
the *noble* gases, before proceeding to those of diatomic
molecules and then to polyatomic molecules. A final sub-
section is devoted to inter-'guest' interactions.

11.2.1. β-*Quinol clathrates of the noble gases*

The enthalpy of formation of the argon clathrate was determined calorimetrically by Evans and Richards (1954). They
found that ΔH varied linearly with y, the fraction of the
total number of cavities which were occupied. Consequently,

by extrapolation to $y = 0$ and $y = 1$ they were able to evaluate ΔH for the reaction α-quinol$\rightarrow\beta$-quinol $(y=0)$ $(+0\cdot67$ kJ mol$^{-1})$ and also the molar enthalpy of intercalation of the 'guest' into the β-lattice (Table 11.1). A value for the krypton clathrate was obtained by the same technique by Grey,

TABLE 11.1.

Enthalpy of clathration in β-quinol

'Guest' molecule	$-\Delta H/[\text{kJ}(\text{mol.'guest'})^{-1}]$	Reference
Ar	25·1	1
Kr	26·4	2
	25·5	3
Xe	40·6	3
CH_4	30·2	4
	25·5	3
N_2	24·3	1
O_2	23·0	1
HCl	38·5	1
HBr	42·7	1
CH_3OH	46	1
HCOOH	51·0	1

References

1. Evans and Richards (1954).
2. Grey, Parsonage, and Staveley (1961).
3. Allison and Barrer (1968).
4. Parsonage and Staveley (1960).

Parsonage, and Staveley (1961) and for the krypton and xenon clathrates from isotherm data by Allison and Barrer (1968). There are two features of importance in this work. Firstly, the included molecules appear to behave independently of each other. Secondly, the enthalpy values are such that they could be explained purely in terms of dispersion inter-

actions. Thus Evans and Richards, who also studied the
clathrates of several other substances, observed from their
data that the enthalpy of intercalation was, to a good
approximation, proportional to the polarizability of the
'guest' molecules, as would be expected if the important
interactions were dispersion forces between the 'guest'
molecules and the quinol walls. However, this proportion-
ality would also hold if the interactions arose from dipoles
in the quinol structure and induced dipoles in the 'guest'
molecules. Subsequently J.H. van der Waals (1956) demonstrated that the magnitude of these enthalpies was consistent with the forces between the 'guest' and 'host' molecules being entirely of dispersion type.

A theoretical treatment based on the statistical mechanics of the cell model of liquids was at this time proposed by van der Waals (1956). It was assumed that each
'guest' molecule was only influenced by the quinol molecules
which made up the walls of the cage in which it was situated.
In the spirit of the cell model the centres of force in the
walls were considered to be smeared out uniformly over the
surface of a sphere of radius a. Since it is assumed that
the encaged molecule interacts with each element of the wall
according to the Lennard-Jones 6-12 potential, the expression
derived by Lennard-Jones and Devonshire (1937, 1938) gives
the potential of a 'guest' molecule when a distance r from
the centre of the cell. When the equilibrium condition is
applied, namely that the chemical potential of the 'guest'
substance in the clathrate and in the gas phase (assumed to
be perfect) are equal, then an equation for y as a function
of T and p is obtained. It is

$$p = kT\{Z_g(T)/Z_{c1}(T)\}\{y/(1-y)\} \qquad (11.1)$$

where Z_g and Z_{c1} are the configurational parts of the
canonical partition function for a 'guest' molecule when
in the gaseous and enclathrated situations, respectively.
The Langmuir form of equation (11.1) has been confirmed by
experimental measurements by Platteeuw (1958). For the
system to be also in equilibrium with α-quinol, equality

of the chemical potentials of quinol in the α- and β-
phases is required. It is then found that the system is
univariant: for each temperature there is only one value of
y (and p) which can satisfy these conditions, these being
connected by the additional relationship

$$\ln(1-y) = -3\Delta\mu(T,p)/kT \tag{11.2}$$

where $\Delta\mu$ is the difference in chemical potential of the pure
β- and α-phases. Since $\Delta\mu$ is extremely insensitive to p,
it follows that at any given T the value of y for this three-
phase equilibrium should be very nearly independent of the
nature of the 'guest'. This is supported by experiments on
the argon and krypton systems at 25°C; it is found that
$y = 0\cdot34$ for both.

Van der Waals' treatment contained two adjustable parameters, one of which was chosen by consideration of the distance of closest approach of aromatic molecules in crystals,
the other being then chosen to give a fit with the enthalpy
of formation data for the argon clathrate. With these values,
there was striking agreement for the equilibrium (T,p,y)
values for the clathrate+gas equilibrium. Thus for the
pressure of gas in equilibrium with clathrate of composition
$y = 0\cdot34$ at 25°C the calculated and observed values, respectively, were (in atm). Ar,$3\cdot4,3\cdot4$; Kr,$0\cdot4,0\cdot4$; Xe,$0\cdot06$,
$0\cdot058$; $N_2,5\cdot2,5\cdot8$; HCl,$0\cdot02,0\cdot01$ (van der Waals and Platteeuw,
1959, Helle, Kok, Platteeuw, and van der Waals 1962).

Measurements of C_p on the argon and krypton clathrates
over a wide temperature range (12 - 300 K) also showed a
simple pattern (Parsonage and Staveley 1959, Grey, Parsonage,
and Staveley 1961). C_p at any given temperature was again
a linear function of y over almost the entire temperature
range, and it was therefore a simple matter to separate out
the molar contributions associated with an empty β-quinol
lattice and with the 'guest' molecules. The agreement with
van der Waals' theory was very good for that part of the temperature range over which the 'guest' molecules appeared to
be behaving classically. Fig. 11.2(a) and (b) shows plots
of the molar 'guest' contribution (C_{vib}) in the argon and

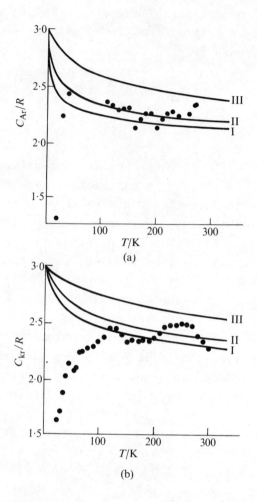

Fig.11.2. Comparison of experimental values and values calculated from classical theory for the heat capacity contributions of (a) argon and (b) krypton in their quinol clathrates; ● : experimental values. Calculated values: I for $\overline{\sigma}$ = 0·29 nm; II for $\overline{\sigma}$ = 0·30 nm; III for $\overline{\sigma}$ = 0·33 nm (from Grey, Parsonage, and Staveley 1961).

krypton clathrates as a function of temperature together with the values predicted from van der Waals' theory. The predicted values are sensitive to the value chosen for one of the parameters $(\overline{\sigma})$, and it is found that for the best fit $\overline{\sigma}$ must be lowered from 0·33 nm, the value used by van der Waals, to 0·29 nm. In the low-temperature region ($T < 40$ K for Ar, $T < 110$ K for Kr) it is clearly necessary to treat the 'guest' contribution quantum-mechanically. The first

attempt to deal with this problem was by Parsonage (1959),
who expanded the Lennard-Jones and Devonshire potential
in ascending powers of r^2. Retaining only the term in r^2
gives the harmonic oscillator approximation, whilst if both
the r^2 and r^4 terms are kept an anharmonic oscillator expression results. In view of the simplification made, the
agreement with experiment is good for argon and fair for
krypton (Fig.11.3a and b). The frequencies of the harmonic

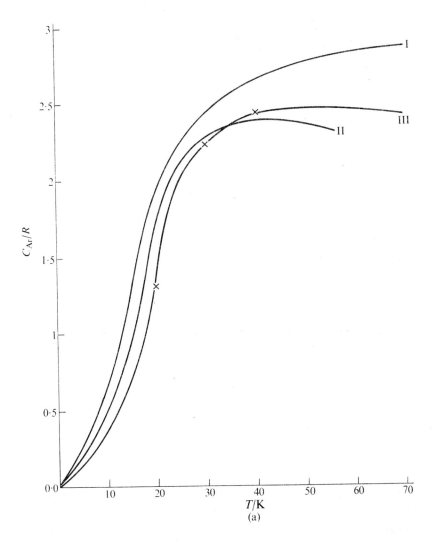

Fig.11.3. (a) Comparison of experimental values and values calculated
from quantum-mechanical theories for the heat capacity contributions of
argon in the quinol clathrates. I: harmonic oscillator approximation;
II: anharmonic oscillator approximation; III: experimental values.

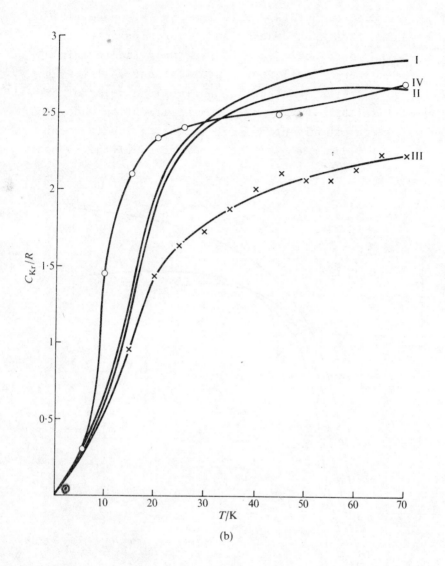

(b)

Fig.11.3.(b) Corresponding curves for Krypton. IV is for the quantum-mechanical cell model (Grey and Staveley 1963).

oscillators in these treatments were found to be 33·1 and 33·5 cm^{-1} for the argon and krypton clathrates, respectively, in surprisingly good agreement with the spectroscopic values obtained subsequently by Burgiel, Meyer, and Richards (1965) (Table 11.2). A quantum-mechanical treatment using the full

TABLE 11.2

Far infrared frequencies attributed to the 'guest' molecules in β-quinol clathrates at 1·2 K (Burgiel, Meyer, and Richards 1965).

'Guest' molecule	$\bar{\nu}/cm^{-1}$
Ar	35·5
Kr	36·0
Xe	43·5
CO	55·2
	81·5
N_2	53·5
NO	46·5
	33·0
O_2	40·0
CH_4	31
	~82

Lennard-Jones and Devonshire potential was carried out by Grey and Staveley (1963) who solved the Schrödinger equation for the lowest 200 energy levels of the krypton clathrate and then inserted these energy values into the partition function. Unfortunately, there was little improvement over the harmonic and anharmonic oscillator approximations (Fig.11.3b), and in particular the agreement for the krypton system remained only fair. The first suggestion for the relative failure of the fit to the low-temperature data for the krypton clathrate was that it arose from an error in the potential energy function. It is well known that there is a considerable discrepancy in the parameters put forward by different workers (Hirschfelder, Curtiss, and Byrd 1954). The alternative, and more likely, proposal is that of Hazony and Ruby (1968), who pointed out that the krypton atom is similar in mass to the quinol with which it is associated

(if $y = 1$, 83·8 g Kr is associated with 330·3 g quinol).
Because of this, they argue, it is not reasonable to assume
that the phonon distribution of the 'host' lattice is unaffected by the presence of the 'guest' molecules, as has
been done in all the treatments mentioned previously. Now
we have seen above that the 'rattling' frequency of krypton
is found from the harmonic oscillator model to be 33·5 cm^{-1},
and spectroscopy yields a similar value. We would expect
strong mechanical coupling of these vibrations only with
comparable frequencies of the β-quinol lattice. Oscillations with such frequencies would, in any case, be making
their full classical contribution to C_p at all temperatures
above ~110 K. Thus although the temperature at which the
classical behaviour could be said to have been reached would
be affected by modification of the frequencies, the value
of the contribution to C_p thereafter would be only slightly
altered. Hazony and Ruby's explanation of the failure of
the cell model at low temperatures is, therefore, also consistent with the fact that the model is very satisfactory
at higher temperatures.

At first sight one would not expect the 'rattling' mode
of the *noble* gas clathrates to be observable at all by infrared spectroscopy. However, apparently because of the effect
of the 'guest'-'host' forces on the polar molecules of the
cage, bands due to these modes are found in the far infrared
(Burgiel, Meyer, and Richards 1965). This would seem to be
the effect discussed by Hazony and Ruby, the oscillations of
the 'guest' and the 'host' being coupled so that the 'rattling' mode acquires some dipolar character from the contribution of the lattice. The frequencies of the centres of
the absorptions, which are an order of magnitude less in-
tense than ordinary electric dipole transitions, are given
in Table 11.2. One other result of this work stands in
opposition to Hazony's model: the frequencies assigned to
the β-quinol lattice do not change with occupancy. One
cannot rule out the possibility, of course, that some of the
unobserved modes are associated with frequencies which do
vary with the degree of filling of the cavities.

The Mössbauer spectrum of the krypton clathrate also

gives indirect evidence on the 'rattling' frequency. The
recoil-free fraction, f, falls smoothly from ~0·85 at 4·2 K
to ~0·05 at 300 K (Fig.11.4a). Since f is related to the mean‾

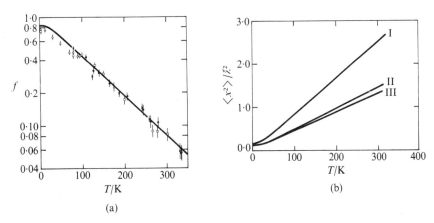

(a)   (b)

Fig.11.4. Krypton in the krypton quinol clathrate. (a) The recoil-free
fraction (f) against temperature. The different symbols indicate different runs, using two different techniques and done at different times.
Each run is normalized to give the same f value at 80 K. The curve is
that of a harmonic oscillator having $\bar{\nu} = 27 \cdot 1$ cm^{-1}. (b) Mean-square
displacement $\langle x^2 \rangle$ against temperature. I : Harmonic oscillator with
$\bar{\nu} = 27 \cdot 1$ cm^{-1}; II : harmonic oscillator with $\bar{\nu} = 36 \cdot 0$ cm^{-1}; III : Pöschl-
Teller oscillator with parameter chosen to fit the infrared data (see
Burgiel, Meyer, and Richards 1965) (after Hazony and Ruby 1968).

square displacement of the krypton atoms by the equation
$\ln f = -\langle x^2 \rangle / \chi^2$ where $\chi^2 [= (\lambda / 2\pi)^2]$ was $4 \cdot 5 \times 10^{-18}$ m^2 for the γ-
radiation involved in this experiment, it is possible to
obtain $\langle x^2 \rangle$ as a function of temperature (Fig.11.4b). The
data may be fitted by an Einstein oscillator of frequency
$27 \cdot 1$ cm^{-1}, but this conflicts with the directly determined
far infrared value of $36 \cdot 0$ cm^{-1}. The authors suggest that
this probably arises because the Mössbauer experiment is
affected by long wavelength modes in which the krypton atoms
participate, whilst the infrared experiment sees only the relative motion of krypton atom and wall (Hazony and Ruby 1968).

11.2.2. β-Quinol clathrates of diatomic molecules
Interest has centred here on the question of the extent to
which the diatomic molecules in the clathrate can be

considered as free rotors. Evidence that N_2 is not behaving
as a free rotor even at room temperature comes from the observation that the dissociation pressure of the $y = 0\cdot34$
clathrate at $298\cdot15$ K is $5\cdot8$ atm rather than $5\cdot2$ atm, the
value expected from van der Waals' theory, which assumes
that the molecules are rotating freely (van der Waals and
Platteeuw 1959). The higher value for the real system
suggests that the rotation is hindered. Too much should not
be made of the corresponding values for HCl (p.   ) as the
experimental data for that substance are much less reliable.

The heat capacities of the CO clathrates have been
studied in two laboratories. Both sets of workers calculated the contribution from the 'rattling' mode using van der
Waals' theory. However, whereas Grey and Staveley (1963)
took the values for the two parameters in this theory to be
those deduced from previous work on the argon and krypton
clathrates, Stepakoff and Coulter (1963) chose these parameters, along with that representing the height of the potential barrier (see below), so as to optimize the fit at the
higher temperatures. After making an allowance for the very
small contribution from the internal vibrations of the molecules, both groups discussed the residual heat capacity
(C_{rot}) in terms of statistical-mechanical treatments of
hindered rotation. Grey and Staveley concluded that the rotational contribution from about 100 to 300 K could be represented by two one-dimensional restricted rotors, each
having a barrier slightly larger than $4\cdot6$ kJ mol^{-1} (Fig.11.5a),
the values for these restricted rotors being taken from the
tables of Pitzer and Gwinn (1942). Stepakoff and Coulter
found values for the total molar contribution of the CO and
also for C_{rot} at 300 K which were higher than those of Grey
and Staveley by about 5 and $2\cdot5$ J K^{-1} mol^{-1}, respectively.
Their treatment of the rotational motion also differed in
that they approximated to the partition function for this
mode by the equation $Q^{hr} = Q_c^{hr} (q_{qmo}/q_c)^2$, where Q_c^{hr} is obtained by treating the two-dimensional motion as classical
and integrating over all orientations, and q_{qmo} and q_c are
the quantum-mechanical and classical partition functions of
a one-dimensional simple harmonic oscillator with a frequency

given by the curvature of the bottom of the potential well.
This analysis is in the spirit of Pitzer and Gwinn's treatment of a one-dimensional restricted rotor, but at the higher
temperatures gives values for C_{rot} which are appreciably
lower than would be estimated for two one-dimensional rotors
of the same barrier height. These two differences, in the
raw data and in the treatment, both contribute to making
the estimated barrier height of Stepakoff and Coulter
higher than that of Grey and Staveley, and it is found to be
$12 \cdot 0$ kJ mol^{-1}. For the range 15 - 40 K, where they used a
three-dimensional simple harmonic oscillator model for C_{vib},
Stepakoff and Coulter found a barrier hindering rotation of
$3 \cdot 12$ kJ mol^{-1}, in closer agreement with the value found by
Grey and Staveley.

A study of the infrared absorption due to the CO stretching mode in the clathrate showed pronounced 'wings' ~42
cm^{-1} on either side of the central peak (Q-branch) which was
attributed to combination with rotational transitions (Ball
and McKean 1962). Since this increment is larger than would
be expected for a free rotor they were led to suggest hindered rotation with a barrier height of ~240 cm^{-1} ($2 \cdot 87$ kJ
mol^{-1}), in good agreement with the low-temperature value of
Stepakoff and Coulter and in tolerable agreement with that
of Grey and Staveley. However, it is possible that the combination involved is that with the 'rattling' mode rather
than with the hindered rotation (McKean 1973). Indeed,
the assignment of the $81 \cdot 5$ cm^{-1} band of the far infrared
spectrum by Burgiel et $al.$ (1965) to torsional oscillation
corresponds to a value of 860 cm^{-1} ($10 \cdot 29$ kJ mol^{-1}) for the
barrier height, in fair agreement with the high-temperature
value of Stepakoff and Coulter. The problems involved in
the making of assignments for the spectra of these substances,
which generally invoke the dependence of the spectrum on
isotopic composition and on temperature, are clearly discussed in McKean's review article (1973). Confusion has
arisen not only between translational and rotational bands of
the 'guest' molecules but also, less pardonably, between
these and bands of the 'host' lattice.

Heat capacity studies have been made on the N_2 clathrates

by the two groups of workers mentioned above in connection
with the CO clathrates. So far, Coulter, Stepakoff, and
Roper (1963) have only discussed their results in terms of
a torsional oscillator model, for which they gave the frequency as $37 \cdot 9 \ cm^{-1}$. Grey and Staveley, on the other hand,
used a restricted rotor model and found the barrier to be
$4 \cdot 60 \ kJ \ mol^{-1}$. This result is in fair accord with the value
of $3 \cdot 93 \ kJ \ mol^{-1}$ suggested by nuclear quadrupole resonance
experiments (section 4.6).

Grey and Staveley (1963) also studied the O_2 clathrates,
for which they found the much lower barrier of $0 \cdot 84 \ kJ \ mol^{-1}$
(Fig.11.5b). This falls between the values of $0 \cdot 54$ and $1 \cdot 05$

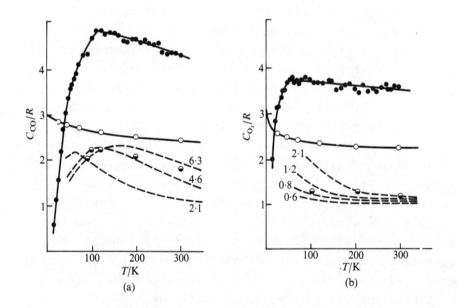

Fig.11.5. Analysis of the heat capacity contribution *versus* temperature
curves for (a) carbon monoxide and (b) oxygen in their quinol clathrates.
● : experimental values; o : calculated values of C_{vib}/R; ◐ : derived
values of $C_{rot}/R = (C_{CO}-C_{vib,CO})/R$ or $(C_{O_2}-C_{vib,O_2})/R$. Broken curves,
calculated values of C_{rot}/R for hindering barriers with values (in kJ
mol^{-1}) shown (from Grey and Staveley 1963).

$kJ \ mol^{-1}$ found from magnetic susceptibility and ESR experiments, respectively (see below). The lower barrier for O_2

as compared with CO and N_2, in spite of the greater length
of the interatomic bond, is consistent with the smaller
diameter found for the molecule by second virial coefficient
and viscosity methods (Hirschfelder *et al*., 1954). Magnetic
susceptibility measurements by Cooke, Meyer, Wolf, Evans,
and Richards (1954) and Meyer, O'Brien, and van Vleck (1957)
cover the range 0·25 - 20 K. Above 10 K the data are well
described by Curie's Law (χT = const.) (Fig.11.6a), which

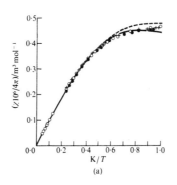

(a)

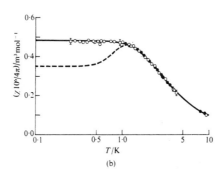

(b)

Fig.11.6. The molar magnetic susceptibility (χ) against temperature for
the oxygen clathrate of β-quinol. (a) The range 1-20 K; o,●: normal
oxygen, different runs; + : oxygen enriched to 11% in $^{16}O^{18}O$. Full and
broken lines are values calculated for the freely rotating model of normal
and enriched oxygen, respectively (from Cooke, Meyer, Wolf, Evans, and
Richards (1954). (b) The range 0·25 - 10K; ● : Cooke *et al*. (1954);
o : Meyer *et al*. (1957).

results from considering the O_2 molecules as classical free
rotors; from 2 to 10 K a quantum-mechanical free rotor model
fits the data well. At still lower temperatures the results
gave a very good fit to a hindered rotor model with a barrier

of $0 \cdot 54$ kJ mol^{-1} (Fig.11.6b).

The nitric oxide clathrates, which are somewhat unstable, particularly in the presence of air, have been studied only by the magnetic susceptibility and far infrared spectroscopic techniques. Two sets of susceptibility measurements were made which between them covered the range 1 - 300 K (Cooke and Duffus 1954, Meyer 1961), but unfortunately there is some disagreement between the two sets of results. Theoretical discussion of the results is also more difficult than for the O_2 clathrates (van Vleck 1961). This is partly because NO has orbital as well as spin angular momentum, but of greater importance is the fact that the spin multiplet separation in NO is comparable in magnitude to the potential barrier hindering rotation. Since it is the points below 20 K which essentially determine the potential barrier and as it is precisely in that range that the two sets of measurements disagree importantly, it has not been possible to fit a potential barrier for the system. In estimating the magnitudes of various terms in the theoretical expressions for χ, van Vleck chose the torsional oscillation frequency such that $h\nu/k = 45°$ or $\bar{\nu} = 32 \cdot 5$ cm^{-1}. Burgiel *et al.* (1965) did, indeed, find a band at $33 \cdot 0$ cm^{-1} in the far infrared spectrum and assigned it to torsional oscillation or hindered rotation. They found one other band attributable to the 'guest' at $46 \cdot 5$ cm^{-1}, and this they assigned to the 'rattling' mode.

The HCl clathrate has a far infrared band near 55 cm^{-1} which is accepted as being due to the 'rattling' mode; there is more controversy about the band near 20 cm^{-1} which arises from rotational motion of some type. The latter band, which is sensitive to both temperature and the composition of the sample, is explained in terms of free rotation by Allen (1966) and Barthel, Gerbaux, and Hadni (1970), but as hindered rotation by M. Davies (see McKean 1973).

The Raman spectra of the HCl and HBr clathrates at room temperature also indicate by the breadth of the internal vibrational bands that the 'guest' molecules are rotating: the half-width of the HCl band is more than halved on cooling to 78 K, and a similar reduction in width occurs for the HBr clathrate. The much greater sharpness of the bands for

the N_2 and O_2 clathrates may be due merely to the smaller
rotational constants (higher moments of inertia) of these
'guest' molecules, rather than to an absence of rotation
(J.E.D. Davies 1972).

11.2.3. β-*Quinol clathrates of polyatomic molecules*
The CH_4 clathrates were first studied by Parsonage and
Staveley (1960), who found that C_p was a linear function of
y over the entire range studied, 12 - 300 K. As for the
diatomic 'guest' molecules described in section 11.2.2, the
contribution of the 'rattling' mode was calculated by means
of van der Waals' theory. It was then found that, at least
above 150 K, the contribution from the rotational motion
(C_{rot}) was just $1 \cdot 5R$, that to be expected for a three-dimensional free rotor in the classical region (Fig.11.7a). Below
80 K the harmonic oscillator approximation for C_{vib} (with
$\bar{\nu} = 96 \cdot 2$ cm^{-1}) enabled C_{rot} to be calculated (Fig.11.7b).
Also shown is the rotational contribution for free gaseous
CH_4 in which equilibrium between the *ortho*, *meta*, and *para*
forms is maintained. The difference between these two
curves becomes very large near 20 K.

Against the above evidence for almost free rotation is
the fact that in the far infrared spectrum the bands due
to the β-quinol lattice are somewhat displaced (Burgiel
et al. 1965). This suggests that the lattice is distorted
by the inclusion of the CH_4 molecules, which, if true,
would mean that free rotation would be unlikely. A band
at ~82 cm^{-1} was indeed attributed to torsional oscillations
of the 'guest' molecules. A wide-line NMR study (W.G.
Schneider, unpublished work) showed that the signal from the
protons of the CH_4 molecules was very broad, which suggests
that the CH_4 molecules are not rotating even on the NMR
time-scale. However, incomplete narrowing of the resonance
line may occur even if the 'guest' molecules are rotating
because the fields arising from the protons of the quinol do
not average to zero even then.

The preferred orientations of molecules containing
fluorine have been established by observing the anisotropy
of the ^{19}F chemical shift. This is possible because the

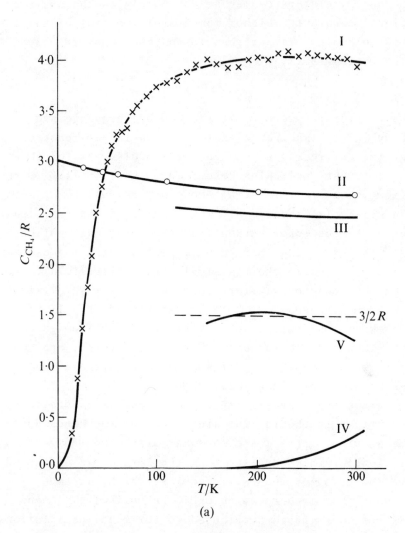

(a)

Fig.11.7. Analysis of the contribution of methane to the heat capacity
of the quinol clathrate (C_{CH_4}); (a) 12-300 K; (b) 12-70 K. I : C_{CH_4}
(expt.); II : C_{vib} from (a) classical theory of van der Waals or (b)
quantum-mechanical theory of the harmonic oscillator; III : corrected
value of $C_{vib}(C'_{vib})$; IV: the contribution of the internal vibrational
modes of methane (C_{int}); V : value deduced for the rotational contribution
(C_{rot}); VI : calculated values of the rotational contribution for an
equilibrium mixture of the three nuclear spin isomers of free methane
molecules (from Parsonage and Staveley 1960).

    Fig.11.7(b) overleaf

[19]F shift, unlike the ^{1}H shift, is big enough to be dis-

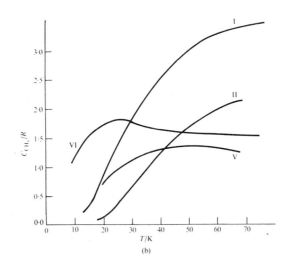

Fig.11.7(b).

tinguished even in solids. Thus for the CH_3F clathrate it
was found that the 'guest' molecules were aligned with their
CF bonds along the crystal c axis, as would be expected
(Hunt and Meyer 1964). Similar examination of the clathrates of the fairly similar compounds NF_3 and CHF_3 showed
that the molecular three fold axis was in each case directed
at $80 \pm 10°$ to the c axis of the crystal (Harris, Hunt, and
Meyer 1965). The general principle is clearly for the
molecules to align themselves so that their greatest
diameter is approximately along the c axis.

CH_3CN clathrates have been studied by many workers.
Palin and Powell (1947) found that the lattice was considerably distorted, the c parameter being increased and the a
dimension reduced so that their ratio was increased by
~17%. Dryden (1953) interpreted his permittivity data by a
single relaxation process having an activation energy of 75·3
kJ mol^{-1}. This very high value is consistent with the X-ray
evidence that the molecule is a very tight fit in the cavity
and indeed requires distortion of the lattice. The far
infrared study of P.R.Davies (1969) showed that the spectrum
is very different from those of α- and β-quinol, which again

is consistent with distortion of the lattice by the 'guest'
molecules. Fukushima (1973a) found infrared bands at 98
and 93 cm^{-1} for the clathrates of CH_3CN and CD_3CN, respectively, which he assigned either to 'rattling' or to torsional
oscillational movement, with a slight preference for the
latter. At an unspecified low temperature achieved by the
use of liquid nitrogen he observed bands at 115 and 106 cm^{-1}
respectively, which he then assigned to the 'rattling' mode.
Raman spectroscopy (Fukushima 1973b) also shows a band at
96 cm^{-1} for the CH_3CN clathrate which was attributed to the
'guest' molecules, but appears to include a superimposed
band of the 'host' lattice (see below). Second-moment values
of the proton magnetic resonance of this clathrate are consistent with the CH_3CN molecules displaying rotation of the
methyl group about the C-C bond but being otherwise fixed in
the lattice (Gregoire, Gallier, and Meinnel 1973, Gallier
1975).

Other clathrates whose permittivity data have given
evidence of hindered rotation are those of CH_3OH (Dryden
1953), HCN, HCOOH, and SO_2 (M.Davies and Williams 1968), the
respective enthalpies of activation of the single relaxation
process being 9·6, 5·3, 14·0 and <4·2 kJ mol^{-1}. These values
are similar to those associated with relaxation in liquids.
At ~225 K there appeared to be a break in the data for the
HCN clathrate. This point will be discussed in section 11.2.4.

Anthonsen (1975), using Raman spectroscopy, assigned
the following frequencies to the 'rattling' mode: HCl (51
cm^{-1}), HCN (55 cm^{-1}), H_2S (45 cm^{-1}), C_2H_4 (57, 43 cm^{-1}),
CH_3OH (49 cm^{-1}), CH_2O (55,29 cm^{-1}), CH_3CHO (43,27 cm^{-1}),
and bands at 69,80, and 99 cm^{-1}, which were present in the
spectrum of the empty β-quinol as well as those of the
clathrates, were assigned to the 'host' lattice. Fukushima
(1973a) found no bands in the infrared spectrum down to 30
cm^{-1} for the CH_3OH clathrate which he could attribute to
the 'rattling' mode.

An unusual, positive shift of the frequency of the C-Cl
and C-Br vibrations on going from the gaseous to the enclathrated state has been found for the methyl halide clathrates at room temperature by Raman spectroscopy (Cleaver,
J.E.D. Davies, and Wood 1975). This shift is said to arise

from compression of the C-X bonds by the lattice, which is
itself distorted. As the fraction of the cavities filled is
increased the shift is reduced.

11.2.4. Cooperative behaviour and transitions in β-quinol
clathrates
So far all the results discussed have supported the contention that correlations between molecules in neighbouring cages
can be ignored. Clear indications that this may not always
be so come from the ESR work on O_2 clathrates at 1·5 to 4·2 K
by Foner, Meyer, and Kleiner (1961). Hyperfine splittings
were found which were explained satisfactorily on the basis
that the different lines correspond to different occupancies
of the adjacent cavities. Thus a clathrate containing a
small concentration of O_2 and a large concentration of N_2
gave a spectrum at 1·6 K having a resolved fine structure of
three lines. This splitting was attributed to interaction
with N_2 molecules in the two neighbouring cages lying along
the c axis. There are three possible occupancies of these
two cages and calculation of the relevant dispersion interactions shows that they are of the right order of magnitude
to account for the splitting observed. Furthermore, the
relative intensities of the three lines were consistent with
the known N_2 concentration.

Likewise, a study of the ^{14}N nuclear quadrupole resonances of N_2 clathrates with $y = 0·2-0·8$ at 1·5-4·2 K by Meyer
and Scott (1959) showed a splitting into seven lines. The
relative intensities, though not the frequencies of these
lines, varied with y. They concluded that the **splitting arose**
from the different occupancies of neighbouring cages, which
caused small distortions of the lattice, these distortions
in turn leading to changes in the electric field gradient
at the resonant nucleus. These distortions must be sufficiently small to be unobservable by X-ray diffraction, yet
they must produce variations in electric field gradient of up
to 0·3%, the splitting between the first and seventh lines
as a percentage of the resonant frequency. The figure of
0·3% may not seem large, but it must be remembered that most
of the field gradient comes from within the N_2 molecule.

Support for the above explanation is provided by the observation that annealing of a specimen (with a small loss of N_2) caused a change in the relative intensities, though not of the frequencies, of the lines. It is difficult to see, however, why there should be seven hyperfine lines. It seems certain that one must go beyond the two nearest-neighbour cells (0·56 nm distant), the adjacent cells along the c axis, and take account of the next-nearest neighbours. However the number of neighbours to be considered then jumps rapidly: there are six cells at 0·95 nm and a further six at 1·01 nm. The original purpose of this experiment was to determine the librational frequency of the N_2 molecule, and this it also served to do (section 4.6).

The most striking evidence of interaction between 'guest' molecules is provided by the observations of thermodynamic transitions in several clathrates at low temperatures. Generally, the 'guest' substances involved are strongly dipolar and it is believed that it is the direct dipole-dipole interactions which lead to the ordering transition. As compared with ordinary order-disorder transitions we have in these systems an extra parameter, y. In this respect, the clathrates are analogous to ferromagnetic alloys on which a large amount of work, both theoretical and experimental has been concentrated in recent years (sections 3.1.7 and 3.4). Pursuing this analogy, the vacant sites in the clathrate become the atoms of non-ferromagnetic diluent in the alloy system. We would expect that at low values of y the available dipole-dipole network would not be sufficiently well-connected to sustain long-range order. A lower limit to y would be set by the value in the corresponding Atom Percolation Problem below which infinite clusters do not exist, e.g. $y = 0·307$ for a simple cubic lattice.

A heat capacity study from 10 to 300 K of the HCN clathrate with $y \approx 1$ shows a sharp peak at 178·1 K (Fig. 11.8) (Matsuo, Suga, and Seki 1968). The evaluation of the entropy of transition depends upon the estimation of the position of the background curve. With two extreme choices for this background, values of $0·687R$ and $0·730R$ were found.

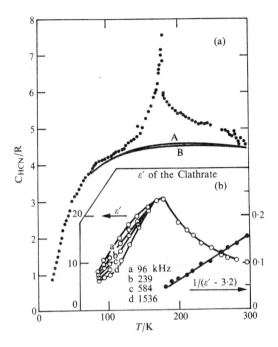

Fig.11.8. A quinol+HCN clathrate: (a) the heat capacity contribution of the HCN(C_{HCN}); (b) the permittivity. Lines A and B of graph (a) are the two estimates used for the background heat capacity (from Matsuo *et al.*, 1968).

These bracket $R \ln 2 = 0 \cdot 693R$, which suggests that the process is a simple order-disorder one with each dipole being able to take either of the two possible orientations along the c axis. When the dielectric properties were measured in the same laboratory it was found that above 180 K there was an orientational contribution to ε', but below 170 K, ε' fell as T fell. This behaviour is consistent with the deduction from the heat capacity data. By contrast, M. Davies and Williams (1968), studying a clathrate with $y \approx 0 \cdot 8$, reported a break in the plot of ε' against $1/T$ at ~225 K which they attributed to a transition. This result is very surprising, since with the lower value of y one would expect any transition temperature to be lower, and probably much lower, than $178 \cdot 1$ K, the value of T_t for $y = 1$. The experiments of Davies and Williams did not extend below 113 K, and it may well be that a transition corresponding to that at $178 \cdot 1$ K

in the y = 1 clathrate would have been found at lower temperatures.

Belliveau (1970) has made heat capacity measurements
from 15 to 300 K on four clathrates of CH_3OH with compositions of y = 0·552, 0·644, 0·750, and 0·989. No anomaly
was observed for y = 0·552, but T_t varied linearly with y
from 35 K for y = 0·644 to 71 K for y = 0·989 (compare
the transition in solid H_2, section 9.2). Matsuo et $al.$
(1967) found T_t = 66 K for y = 0·974 using DTA and calcula-
ted ΔH_t = 0·23 kJ mol^{-1} and ΔS_t = 0·42R = R ln 1·52 from
their data. They also found an abrupt increase of dielectric
loss at 66 K, a result which was confirmed by Jaffrain,
Siemons, and Lebreton (1969) for a clathrate of which the
composition was not reported.

Nobody has reported definite evidence of transitions in
the HCl and HBr clathrates, although the dipole moments of
1·08 D and 0·79 D, respectively, should be adequate to support an ordered structure up to readily accessible temperatures. Following Matsuo et $al.$ (1968), who noted that for
the HCN and CH_3OH clathrates T_t was proportional to p^2, where
p is the dipole moment of the 'guest' molecules, we would
estimate that for the y = 1 clathrates of HCl and HBr T_t
would be ~24 and ~13 K, respectively. M. Davies and
Williams (1968) did, indeed, find that for the HCl clathrate
with y = 0·5 the permittivity at 88 K was higher than would
have been expected from the values at higher temperatures,
which gave a linear plot for ε' against $1/T$. However, it
seems unlikely that such a dilute HCl clathrate would show
a transition at such a high temperature. Roper (1966), who
measured the heat capacity of one HCl clathrate over the
range 15-300 K made no mention of a transition. Stepakoff
(1963), on the other hand, found two maxima in the curve of
C_{rot} against T for an HBr clathrate having y = 0·811. Because of the uncertainties surrounding the hydrogen halide
clathrates it is difficult to assess the far infrared
spectroscopic results of Allen (1966), who studied HCl
clathrates having y = 0·07, 0·40, 0·62, and 0·77 at 1·2 K.
Some, at least, of these would be in the ordered form at this
temperature. Apart from bands assigned to the 'host'

lattice and the 'rattling' motion, Allen found an absorption near 20 cm^{-1}, which he ascribed to rotational oscillation. These rotational frequencies were dependent upon the y value. It would seem likely that the absorptions near 20 cm^{-1} arise from excitations of the coupled dipole system.

Belliveau (1970) has found a thermal anomaly at 110·3 K in a CH_3F clathrate with $y = 0·868$. His heat capacity measurements covered the range 15-300 K. Since the dipole moment of CH_3F is ~1·8 D (J.W. Smith 1955), this transition occurs at a higher temperature than would be expected from the results of Matsuo *et al*. on the HCN clathrate.

McTague (1969) studied the wide-line NMR spectrum of an H_2S clathrate for which, although no composition was reported, it may be assumed from the conditions of the preparation that $y > 0·8$. The quinol lattice gave a very broad background which did not interfere with the analysis of the spectrum. However, between -50° and -40°C there was a dramatic change and a well-resolved line appeared. He suggested that this change marked either the occurrence of a cooperative process or the onset of rotation of the H_2S molecules. Because of the fairly small dipole moment of H_2S the transition temperature would be expected to be very much lower than -50°C. It therefore appears more likely that the H_2S molecules are undergoing hindered rotation and that the temperature range -50° to -40°C corresponds to the achievement by the molecules of the degree of rotational excitation necessary to narrow the line.

11.3. CLATHRATE HYDRATES

There are two important groups of hydrates which are of the clathrate type (Muller and von Stackelberg 1951, 1952). In these there are no specific or chemical interactions of the 'guest' with the water molecules. The crystal structure of the water 'host' lattice is the same within each group but differs between the groups, and both of the possible 'host' lattice structures are different from all of the known ice structures.

The type I structure is depicted in Fig.11.9. There are two dodecahedral and six tetradecahedral cavities per

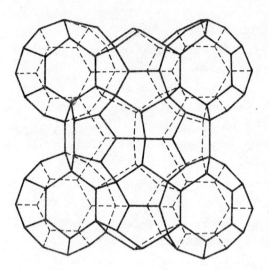

Fig.11.9. The stacking of dodecahedra and tetradecahedra in the hydrates of type I (from Wells 1975).

unit cell, each of which contains 46 water molecules. If every cavity were occupied by one 'guest' molecule the composition would be $M.5\frac{3}{4}H_2O$, whereas if only the larger cavities were occupied it would be $M.7\frac{2}{3} H_2O$. The largest molecules which can be accommodated appear to be those having van der Waals' diameters of 0·59 and 0·52 nm for the larger and the smaller cavities, respectively. Some molecules are able to occupy both the large and the small cages. These include Ar, CH_4, H_2S, CO_2, C_2H_2, PH_3, N_2O, and H_2Se. Larger molecules tend to occupy only the large cages. Among these are C_2H_6, C_2H_4, CH_3Cl, SO_2, Cl_2, and CHF_3.

The Type II structure is shown in Fig.11.10. Here there are also two types of cavity, both nearly spherical but of different size, being able to include molecules of van der Waals' diameter up to 0·69 and 0·48 nm. There are eight large hexadecahedral cavities and sixteen smaller, dodecahedral cavities per unit cell, which itself comprises 136 water molecules. If every cage were singly occupied the overall formula would be $M.5\frac{2}{3} H_2O$; if only the larger cavities were so occupied it would be $M.17H_2O$. Since structure II is only adopted if the 'guest' molecules are

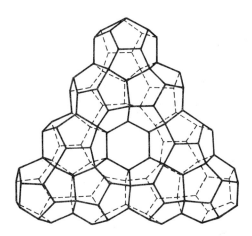

Fig.11.10. The stacking of dodecahedra and hexadecahedra in the hydrates
of type II (from Wells 1975).

too large for the cavities of structure I it follows that
the 'guest' molecules must necessarily be too large for
the smaller cages of structure II.   These smaller
cavities will therefore be unoccupied if only a single
'guest' substance is available.   However, if two 'guest'
substances are simultaneously present, one having molecules of suitable size to fill the large cages, the other
having molecules suitable for the small cavities, it is possible to fill both types of cavity and thereby achieve greater
stability than would be obtained in the absence of the 'guest'
having the smaller molecules.   Von Stackelberg gave the name
'hilfgas' to the substance having the smaller molecules in
such a system.   Waller (1960) examined the effect of the
choice of 'hilfgas' on the temperature at which the hydrate
decomposed under 1 atmosphere pressure.   He found, for example, that with argon, krypton, and xenon as 'hilfgas' the
$CHCl_3$ hydrate decomposed at $-4 \cdot 8$, $+9 \cdot 0$, and $+10 \cdot 9°C$, respectively.   The 'hilfgas' normally occupies only a fraction
of the available small cavities, but this fraction increases
in going from argon to xenon.   Examples of hydrates of Type
II which have been prepared are those of $CHCl_3$, CH_3I, CH_2Cl_2,
$CBrClF_2$, and CH_3CHCl_2.   Cyclopropane is one of a small number

of substances capable of forming both types of hydrate.

Theories similar to that of van der Waals for the quinol clathrates have been put forward by Barrer and Stuart (1957) and Platteeuw and van der Waals (1958) for the clathrate hydrates. The statistical mechanics is somewhat more complicated than for the quinol clathrates because of the presence in each of the hydrate structures of two kinds of cavity. However, the assumptions made and the development of the theory are similar in most respects. Corresponding to equations (11.1) and (11.2) we now have, provided that there is only a single 'guest' substance involved,

$$p = kT\{Z_g(T)/Z_{c1,1}(T)\}\{y_1/(1-y_1-y_2)\} =$$

$$kT\{Z_g(T)/Z_{c1,2}(T)\} \{y_2/(1-y_1-y_2)\}. \qquad (11.3)$$

for the hydrate+gas equilibrium, and

$$\nu_1 \ln(1-y_1) + \nu_2 \ln(1-y_2) = -\Delta\mu(T,p)/kT \qquad (11.4)$$

for the hydrate+gas+ice equilibrium,
where y_1 and y_2 are the occupancies of the first and second kinds of site, respectively; ν_1 and ν_2 are stoichiometric constants characteristic of the 'host' lattice (their values are $\nu_1 = 1/23$, $\nu_2 = 3/23$ for structure I, and $\nu_1 = 2/17$, $\nu_2 = 1/17$ for structure II); $Z_{c1,1}(T)$ and $Z_{c1,2}(T)$ are the configurational parts of the partition functions for a 'guest' molecule when in cavities of types 1 and 2, respectively; $Z_g(T)$ is the configurational part of the partition function for a 'guest' molecule in the gas phase; and $\Delta\mu(T,p)$ is the difference in chemical potential of the empty hydrate and ice-Ih. For the 'mixed' hydrates, which contain more than one 'guest' substance, the equations are again somewhat more complicated.

An important feature of these equations is that the presence of two kinds of cavity in the lattice confers extra flexibility on the system. Thus, for the quinol clathrates+α-quinol equation (11.2) ensured that, whatever the 'guest' substance, y would be for all intents and

purposes the same function of T. For hydrate+ice-Ih, equation (11.4) shows that a continuous range of combinations
of values of y_1 and y_2 would be satisfactory for any given
T. To find out what values of y_1 and y_2 are actually adopted
we must revert to equation (11.3), eliminating p between the
two parts. From this it is seen that y_1 and y_2 are related
by an equation which involves $z_{cl,1}$ and $z_{cl,2}$, and that they
will therefore be sensitive to the nature of the 'guest' substance. In those cases, however, where the molecules are unable to occupy one type of cavity (say type 2) the y_2 is
necessarily zero and the situation becomes the same as for
the quinol clathrates, y_1 being no longer sensitive to the
properties of the 'guest' molecules.

Table 11.3 shows the results of calculations of y_1, y_2
and p using equations (11.3) and (11.4) and evaluating the
partition functions for molecules in the two kinds of cavity
by the Lennard-Jones and Devonshire method. The results,
therefore, refer to the three-phase equilibrium: hydrate I
+ice+gas.

TABLE 11.3

*Cage occupancies (calculated) and dissociation pressures (cal-
culated and observed) for some structure I hydrates at 273 K*

'Guest'	ε^*/k	σ/nm	Occupancies		Dissociation pressure/atm	
			y_1	y_2	Obs.	Calc.
Ar	119·5°	0·3408	0·825	0·841	95·5	95·5
Kr	166·7°	0·3679	0·832	0·830	14·5	15·4
Xe	225·3°	0·4069	0·813	0·835	1·15	1·0
CH_4	142·7°	0·3810	0·818	0·836	26	19·0
CF_4	152·5°	0·470	0·282	0·894	~1	1·6
C_2H_6	243°	0·3954	0·837	0·827	5·2	1·1
C_2H_4	199·2°	0·4523	0·523	0·879	5·44	0·5
O_2	117·5°	0·358	0·821	0·839	120	63
N_2	95·05°	0·3698	0·810	0·845	160	90

(after van der Waals and Platteeuw 1959).

The second and third columns give the values used for the
Lennard-Jones parameters of the 'guest' substance. There is
generally good agreement between theory and experiment for
the first five substances, all of which have spherical or
near spherical molecules, and to a lesser extent for N_2 and
O_2. The poorer agreement for C_2H_6 and C_2H_4 is attributed primarily to some loss of freedom of rotation in the hydrate,
which is not allowed for in the theory. As ΔH for the process ice-I$h \rightarrow$ empty 'host' lattice is not known for either
hydrate structure it is not possible to make a direct comparison of ΔH calculated for formation of the hydrate from
the empty 'host' lattice with the measured value for formation from ice. However, it has been remarked by Platteeuw
and van der Waals (1958) that if ΔH for ice-I$h \rightarrow$ empty 'host'
lattice is assumed to be zero, good agreement is obtained
for the hydrates of Kr, Xe, CH_4, and C_2H_6 (Table 11.4).

TABLE 11.4

*Calculated and observed values of the enthalpy of formation
of several type I clathrate hydrates. The values refer to
the reaction:*

$$mH_2O(1) + M(g) = M.mH_2O(hydrate)$$

and are for $-\Delta H/(kJ\ mol^{-1})$ *(from Platteeuw and van der Waals
1958)*

	Ar	Kr	Xe	CH_4	C_2H_6	CF_4	O_2	N_2
Calc.	13·16	14·39	16·28	14·38	16·13	17·88	13·49	13·34
Obs.	–	14·0	16·7	14·5	16·3	–	–	–

In support of this assumption are the observations that ΔH
for transitions between the different forms of high-pressure
ice are usually found to be remarkably small (section 8.3).
     So far there does not appear to be any method available
for the experimental determination of y_1 and y_2 separately:
only the overall composition can be obtained.

11.3.1. Molecular motion in the hydrates

Most attention has been directed towards the motion of the
'guest' molecules, but there has also been a limited amount
of work concerned with the much slower motions which the
water molecules undergo. Table 11.5 summarizes the results
of the water relaxation observations for a number of hydrates.

TABLE 11.5

The motion of 'host' molecules in the clathrate hydrates.
The dielectric relaxation time (τ) and the activation energy
(E_a).

'Guest'	$\tau/\mu s$	$E_a/(kJ\ mol^{-1})$	Reference
Structure I hydrates at 0°C			
Ar (at 2 000 bar)	16	23·9	1
N_2 (at 1 200 bar)	15	33·1	1
Ethylene oxide	0·027	28·0	1
Trimethylene oxide	0·005	24·3	1
Structure II hydrates at -40°C			
SF_6	780	51·5	2
1,3-Dioxolane	5·4	36·4	2
2,5-Dihydrofuran	1·5	31·4	2
Tetrahydrofuran	1·0	31·0	2
Trimethylene oxide	0·48	29·3	2
Propylene oxide	2·0	33·5	2
c-Butanone	0·49	27·2	2
Acetone	0·57	27·2	2
Isoxazole	-	29·8	3

REFERENCES

1. Gough, Whalley, and Davidson (1968).

2. Morris and Davidson (1971).

3. Gough, Garg, and Davidson (1974).

For comparison, the corresponding activation enthalpy for
ice-Ih is 55·4 kJ mol^{-1}. Morris and Davidson (1971) suggest
that the relatively fast relaxation of the hydrates of the
ethers and ketones may be due to transient hydrogen-bond
formation, which in turn injects Bjerrum defects into the
lattice (see footnote, section 8.1). However, the argon and
nitrogen hydrates (structure I), for which this mechanism
is certainly not possible, also show low activation enthalpies for water relaxation (23·9 and 33·1 kJ mol^{-1}, respectively), although it is also true that the relaxation time
at 0°C (16 µs) is similar to that for ice-Ih (21·5 µs)
(Majid, Garg, and Davidson 1969).

A NMR and dielectric study of the type I hydrate of
trimethylene oxide, $(CH_2)_3O$, showed that the lattice does
not behave as if it is rigid until below 5 K : a residual,
very broad dielectric absorption of activation energy 8·8
kJ mol^{-1} persists down to these temperatures. The motion
responsible is thought to be a hindered rotation about the
polar axis, these axes themselves being fairly well aligned
along four directions at T < 105 K.

The much more rapid rotation of the 'guest' molecules
has been widely studied by dielectric methods and by NMR line-
width experiments. The results are briefly summarized in
Table 11.6. In the dielectric study of the tetrahydrofuran
hydrate (Davidson, Davies, and Williams 1964) two dispersion
regions were found, one at low frequencies due to water
relaxation and one at much higher frequencies. The latter
process gave a relaxation time of only 10^{-11} s at 88 K and
the low activation energy of 2·7 kJ mol^{-1}, and is confiden-
tly attributed to motion of the tetrahydrofuran molecules.
Morris and Davidson (1971) carried the study of the c-
butanone hydrate (structure II) down to 4·2 K. They found
dielectric loss curves for which the temperature of the maximum varied from 25·8 K for 10 Hz to 38·5 K for 50 kHZ. From
these data they obtained an activation energy of 6·02 kJ
mol^{-1}. The loss curves are too broad for a simple, single
relaxation process, and the authors believe this to be due
to the variation of electric field from cell to cell which,
in turn, arises from the disordered arrangement of the

TABLE 11.6

The motion of 'guest' molecules in the clathrate hydrates.
The relaxation time (τ) and activation energy (E_a)

Ref.	'Guest'	Structure	τ/s	T/K	$E_a/(kJ\ mol^{-1})$	Remarks
Dielectric studies						
1	Tetrahydro-furan (THF)	II	10^{-11}	88	~1	-
2	c-Butanone	II	$\begin{cases}1 \cdot 5 \times 10^{-2}\\ 3 \times 10^{-6}\end{cases}$	$\begin{matrix}25 \cdot 8\\ 38 \cdot 5\end{matrix}$	$6 \cdot 0$	broad due to H-bond disorder
1	Ethylene oxide	I	$\begin{cases}2 \times 10^{-10}\\ 2 \times 10^{-12}\\ 2 \cdot 6 \times 10^{-12}\\ 4 \cdot 2 \times 10^{-12}\end{cases}$	$\left.\begin{matrix}77\\ 243\\ 197\\ 155\end{matrix}\right\}$	$2 \cdot 1$	-
3	Trimethylene oxide	I	-	<105	$8 \cdot 8$	-
4	Isoxazole	II	-	17-30	$5 \cdot 2$	-
NMR studies						
5	c-propane	I&II	10^{-5}	240	-	-
5	Acetone	II	-	77	-	Rapid rotation of methyl group only
			-	172	$16 \cdot 5$	Diffusion of molecules over barrier
6	Sulphur hexafluoride	II	10^{-5}	150	-	Rotation about C_4 axis
				150-245	-	Rotation, isotropic or about random axes
6	Carbon tetra-fluoride	I	10^{-5}	240	-	Isotropic rotation+diffusion
				77	-	Second moment: rigid lattice value
7	Ethylene oxide	I	-	200-273	-	V.narrow line: almost free isotropic rotation
8	H_2S+iso-butane	II	-	100-273	-	Isobutane reorients isotropically; H_2S free to reorient and diffuse

continued overleaf

continuation of Table 11.6

8	H_2S+CCl_4	II				H_2S reorientates fairly freely and also diffuses. THF and thiophene reorient isotropically. CCl_4-reorientation was not studied.
8	H_2S+THF	II		110-270		
8	H_2S+thiophene	II				
9	n-propane	II	10^{-5}	~85	7·1	Reorients about C_2 axis
10	Methyl bromide	I	10^{-5}	~155	39·0	Some 'guest' alignment. Reorients about C_3-axis
7	THF	II	10^{-9}	223-273 212-261	~0	From T_1. No min. found from second moments. Rapid rotation
7	Trimethylamine	II		200-273		From sec. moments. Rapid rotation

REFERENCES

1.   Davidson *et al*. (1964).

2.   Morris and Davidson (1971).

3.   Gough, Garg, and Davidson (1974).

4.   Gough, Garg, Ripmeester, and Davidson (1974).

5.   Khanzada and McDowell (1971).

6.   McDowell and Raghunathan (1967).

7.   Brownstein, Davidson, and Fiat (1967).

8.   Chassonneau, Dufourcq, and Lemanceau (1971).

9.   McDowell and Raghunathan (1970).

10.   McDowell and Raghunathan (1968).

hydrogen bonds. The structure I hydrate of ethylene oxide (Davidson *et al*. 1964) shows very similar behaviour to that of the tetrahydrofuran hydrate. Apart from the low

frequency relaxation of the 'host' lattice there is a fast
process which causes an absorption peak near 6 GHz at ~77 K.
The relaxation times reported were $2 \cdot 0 \times 10^{-12}$, $2 \cdot 6 \times 10^{-12}$
and 4.2×10^{-12} s at 243, 197, and 155 K, respectively,
leading to the value of $3 \cdot 8$ kJ mol^{-1} for the activation
energy. For both the tetrahydrofuran and ethylene oxide
hydrates the amplitude of the high-frequency absorptions
were shown to be in excellent accord with the values expected for rotation of molecules having the known dipole
moments of the 'guest' molecules. Furthermore, the contribution to the static permittivity made by the orienta-
tional polarization (evaluated as $\varepsilon_0' - \varepsilon_\infty'$, where ε_0' and
ε_∞' are the real parts of the permittivity at zero and infinite frequency, respectively) is proportional to p^2, where
p is the dipole moment of the 'guest' molecule, for a range
of structure II hydrates (Fig.11.11). The corresponding

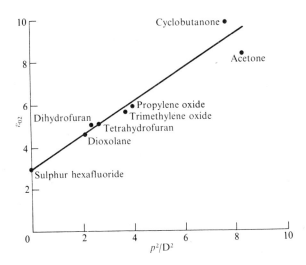

Fig.11.11. ε_{02}, the static permittivity less the contribution from the
reorientation of host molecules, for structure II hydrates at 168 K,
plotted against the square of the dipole moment (p) (from Morris and
Davidson 1971).

contribution to the permittivity in the structure I hydrate
of CH_3Cl also agrees with the value expected for isotropic
rotation or reorientation between equally favourable sites.

McDowell and coworkers have studied the narrowing of
the nuclear resonance line for a number of hydrates. To
avoid confusion between the protons of 'guest' and 'host'
molecules two devices were employed. Either the 'host'
molecules were deuterated, which greatly reduces the dipole
field which they exert; or, in the case of fluorine-con-
taining 'guest' molecules, the ^{19}F resonance was observed.
Cyclopropane (Khanzada and McDowell 1971), which can form
both structure I and structure II hydrates, gave second
moments which corresponded to the rotation being highly restricted up to ~240 K in both types of clathrate. At higher
temperatures there appeared to be almost free rotation about
the C_3 axis of the molecule. It is surprising that the
greater space available in the cells of structure II does
not lead to the line remaining narrow down to lower temperatures than for the structure I hydrate, and perhaps down to
liquid nitrogen temperatures. This is particularly so when
one bears in mind that reorientation at $>10^5$ Hz should be
indistinguishable from free rotation in the NMR line-width
experiments. Furthermore, the dielectric experiments on the
hydrate of tetrahydrofuran, a larger molecule, showed its
relaxation rate to be ~10^{11} Hz even at 88 K, as discussed
above. A similar NMR study of the acetone hydrate (structure II) pointed to there being rotation of the methyl
groups only at 77 K, but diffusion of acetone molecules over
a barrier at 172 K (Khanzada and McDowell 1971). The SF_6
hydrate (structure II) (McDowell and Raghunathan 1967) showed
dramatic changes in the second moment of the fluorine resonance at 150 and 245 K whether the 'host' lattice was deuterated or not (Fig.11.12). From 77 K (the lowest temperature studied) to 150 K the second moment corresponds
to the value calculated for rotation about a C_4 axis; between
150 and 245 K the value could be interpreted as arising either
from isotropic rotation or from reorientation about random
axes. The data for the CF_4 hydrate (McDowell and Raghunathan
1967) (structure I) is more difficult to interpret. The
sudden drop in second moment at 240 K is attributed by the
authors to a change from reorientation about random axes
to a state in which there is both isotropic rotation

and diffusion. Isotropic rotation alone is not sufficient
to explain the narrowness of the resonance line. It is
significant that even at 77 K the second moment is less than
the value calculated for the rigid lattice.

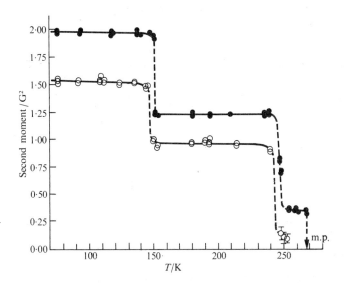

Fig.11.12. The temperature variation of the second moments of the ^{19}F
resonance of the light and heavy hydrate of SF_6; ● : $SF_6 + H_2O$; o :
$SF_6 + D_2O$ (from McDowell and Raghunathan 1967).

Brownstein, Davidson, and Fiat (1967) found very narrow
resonance lines at temperatures near 273 K for all the hydrates and deuterates they investigated [structure I : SO_2,
C_2H_4O, Cl_2; structure II : tetrahydrofuran, dihydrofuran,
propylene oxide; other structures : Br_2, $(CH_3)_3N$]. Indeed
the second moments were less than would be expected if the
'guest' molecules and the water molecules were all rotating
isotropically. It was therefore deduced that the further
narrowing must arise from diffusion of the water molecules.
T_1 measurements were also made on the tetrahydrofuran hydrate
from 223 to 272 K at two frequencies (56·4 and 8·13 MHz) so
as to show up the rapid motions of the 'guest' molecules.
Since T_1 was found to be independent of temperature over
this range a single correlation time ($=10^{-9}$ s) was assigned,
the activation energy of the process being very nearly zero.

The disordered nature of the 'host' lattice in the type I hydrate of cyclopropane has been indicated by the far infrared spectrum (Bertie, Bates, and Hendricksen 1975): the disorder causes some lattice modes to be allowed in the infrared which would otherwise be forbidden. Bands at 103, 88, and 130 cm^{-1} have been found by Raman spectroscopy of the hydrates of Cl_2, BrCl, and Br_2, respectively (Anthonsen 1975b). In assigning these frequencies to lattice modes, the author rejects the 'rattling' mode of the 'guest' on the grounds that the frequency should then decrease with increasing mass. This argument seems to be unsafe as the change in the potential energy well in going from Cl_2 to Br_2 may compensate for the increase in mass, as is found in the quinol clathrates (Table 11.2). While the assignment of Anthonsen may be correct, further evidence is required.

11.4. CHANNEL COMPOUNDS OF UREA

The stable form of pure urea under ordinary conditions is tetragonal. However, it also forms loose compounds, or adducts, with many organic substances in which the urea molecules lie in a hexagonal lattice with space group $P6_12$ (Fig.11.13). In these adducts the urea molecules are joined by hydrogen bonds so as to form interpenetrating helices, resulting in a lattice which has hexagonal channels of infinite length, the organic molecules lying along these cavities. The helices, three of which form the boundary to each channel, may have screw axes of either sense, though in any one crystal they must all be similarly directed. Whether a crystal contains left- or right-handed helices is determined at the time it is nucleated: by seeding with adduct crystals having, say, the right-handed configuration a product consisting of crystals of that configuration can be obtained. This fact has been used to resolve racemic mixtures, since a given configuration of the 'host' lattice will generally favour the inclusion of one or the other of the two enantiomers. A detailed summary of about twenty years of work on this topic carried out in his laboratory has been given by Schlenk (1973).

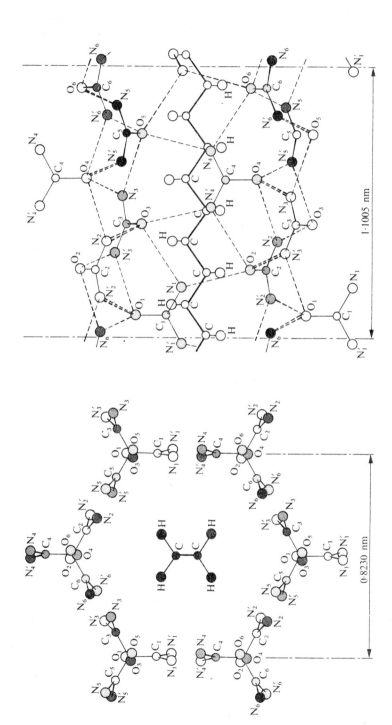

Fig.11.13. The crystal structure of a urea adduct: (a) view along the *c* axis; (b) view perpendicular to the *c* axis. The subscript attached to an atom indicates the *ab* plane in which the oxygen atom of that molecule lies (from Parsonage and Pemberton 1967).

Suitable 'guest' substances are straight-chain aliphatic compounds, of which the simplest are the *n*-alkanes.
The stability of the adducts increases with the chain length
(section 11.4.1). Replacement of a $>CH_2$ group by $>O$ or
$>SiH_2$ (Mueller and Meier 1964) in the *n*-alkanes leads to compounds which also form adducts. However, complete fluori-
nation to the perfluoroalkanes causes the molecules to have
cross-sections which are too large to be accommodated in the
channel. At the terminal positions of the chain there is
much greater tolerance with regard to the choice of substituents. Thus, compounds having the following end-groups all
form stable adducts: $-CH_2COOH$, $-CH_2Br$, $-CH_2I$ (Radell, Brodman, and Bergmann 1964), $-CH_2SH$, $-CH-CH_2$ (Radell *et al*. 1963).
However, compounds having substituents of similar size in
non-terminal positions are much less good as adduct formers.
A methyl group in the 2-position does not prevent adduct
formation, but an ethyl group would. A $>C=O$ group in
the chain is also tolerated. Apart from the saturated compounds cited above, the corresponding chain compounds with
double and treble bonds also form adducts (Radell, Connolly,
and Yuhas 1960), although these have been much less studied.
Thermodynamic evidence is that they are somewhat less stable
than the corresponding saturated compounds (Fetterly 1964).
Apart from the epoxy compounds mentioned above, ring compounds are generally too wide to fit into the channels and
do not form adducts. However, where a potential 'guest'
molecule has a long paraffin chain to confer stability it
may be possible to tolerate the distortion caused by introduction of a ring elsewhere in the molecule. Examples of
such adduct formers are 1-phenyl-octadecane and 1-cyclo-
hexyleicosane (Fetterly 1964). From the point of view
of the physicochemical study of the urea adducts it is un-
fortunate that the empty 'host' lattice cannot be prepared.
Attempts to achieve this by pumping out the 'guest' molecules cause reversion to the stable, tetragonal form of
urea. Indeed, it is not even possible to make the partly
filled adducts: these immediately disproportionate giving
tetragonal urea and the normal adduct with the cavities

filled.

It has been shown by Laves, Nicolaides, and Peng (1965) that the distance between the terminal carbon atoms of successive alkane molecules in the same channel is $0 \cdot 374$ nm. This is much less than the normal van der Waals' distance for $-CH_3$ groups, which is usually taken to be that for CH_4 molecules, namely $0 \cdot 41$ nm. Such a shortening of this distance was also found by Parsonage and Pemberton (1967) to be necessary in order to explain the thermodynamic anomalies which they had observed (section 11.4.2). The explanation of the effect lies in the fact that a gap between alkane molecules involves a 'waste' of the strong, attractive interactions between the 'host' lattice and its 'guest' molecules. The equilibrium $CH_3 - - - CH_3$ distance will then be reached when the lowering of the 'host'-'guest' potential energy brought about by decreasing the gap is balanced by the corresponding increase in the 'guest'-'guest' potential energy. Parsonage and Pemberton showed that using reasonable values for the parameters of the $CH_3 - - - CH_3$ interaction the potential energy was minimized when the $CH_3 - - - CH_3$ distance was $0 \cdot 375$ nm, in remarkable agreement with the X-ray observations of Laves et al. (1965).

Fig.11.13(a) shows a view of the structure along the c axis; Fig.11.13(b) is a view perpendicular to the c axis. Proceeding along the c axis there are six levels at which urea molecules can be situated (1 to 6 in Fig.11.13) before the cycle is repeated. At any one level three of the six vertices of the hexagonal channel are occupied by urea molecules. In only one of these three does the oxygen atom of the carbonyl group project into the channel; in the other two the planes of the urea skeletons are tangential to the wall of the cavity. A.E.Smith (1952) observed that alkane molecules in the adducts were in the fully extended conformation with the carbon skeleton as a planar zig-zag. Since, in general, the repeat distance along the c axis for the 'guest' molecules is not a simple multiple or fraction of the c parameter of the 'host' lattice, successive 'guest' molecules are in different environments. Alternatively, it can be said that the 'guest' molecules are not in register with the 'host' lattice.

It is generally assumed that molecules in different channels are staggered with respect to each other at room temperature. Of course, the 'guest' molecules may well come into register with each other at low temperatures. Such a process has not yet been observed, however.

The n-$C_{16}H_{34}$ adduct has attracted some special attention because the length of the fully extended alkane molecule is slightly greater than twice the c dimension of the 'host' lattice: the discrepancy is ~4% or ~0·9 nm. Smith (1952) found that the chain was able to contract, presumably by some slight rotation about the internal C-C bonds, so that the molecules were exactly twice the c parameter. This is supported by an examination of the compositions of the adducts as a function of chain length (Fig.11.14). It is seen that the composition of the n-$C_{16}H_{34}$ adduct deviates from the line through the other points by approximately the amount expected on the basis of Smith's observations. Lenné (1954, 1963) and Laves et $al.$ (1965), on the other hand, concluded from their X-ray data that the n-$C_{16}H_{34}$ molecules were fully extended.

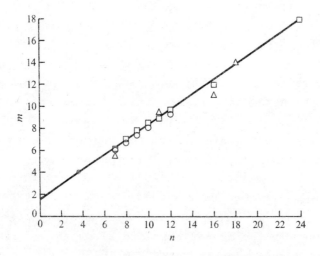

Fig.11.14. The variation of the mole ratio (m) of urea+n-alkane adducts with the number of carbon atoms in the alkane(n). □ : Schlenk (1949); △ : Zimmerschied et $al.$ (1950); o : Redlich et $al.$ (1950a) (from Smith 1952).

11.4.1. Thermodynamic properties

The most comprehensive series of measurements on the thermodynamic properties of the adducts is that of Redlich, Gable,
Dunlop, and Millar (1950). For low molecular weight 'guest'
substances measurement of the decomposition pressure gave
directly the standard Gibbs free energy of formation from
the 'guest' substance in the vapour state ($\Delta G^{\ominus}_{fg}$); for the
adducts of higher molecular weight substances, where the
decomposition pressure is too low to be accurately measure-
able, studies of equilibria in which the urea and the 'guest'
substance were dissolved in an appropriate solvent were
used. $\Delta G^{\ominus}_{fg}$ was found to increase in magnitude approximately
linearly with chain length for any one homologous series
of adducts at a given temperature. Thus at 298·15 K the
data for three classes of 'guest' substance were well represented by the straight lines:

$$\Delta G^{\ominus}_{fg}/\{kJ \ (mol.'guest')^{-1}\} = -9\cdot11+1\cdot59n \quad \text{for } n\text{-alkanes}, \quad (11.5)$$

$$\Delta G^{\ominus}_{fg}/\{kJ \ (mol.'guest')^{-1}\} = -8\cdot39+1\cdot62n \quad \text{for } n\text{-acids}, \quad (11.6)$$

$$\Delta G^{\ominus}_{fg}/\{kJ \ (mol.'guest')^{-1}\} = -10\cdot47+1\cdot62n \quad \text{for } n\text{-alcohols}, (11.7)$$

where n is the number of carbon atoms in the 'guest' molecule.

The corresponding enthalpy of formation of the n-alkane
adducts was determined from the temperature derivative of
$\Delta G^{\ominus}_{fg}$ and for the n = 7 - 16 members was found to be a fairly
good fit to the straight line:

$$\Delta H^{\ominus}_{fg}/\{kJ \ (mol.'guest')^{-1}\} = -10\cdot23+11\cdot74n \ . \quad (11.8)$$

Fetterly (1964) attributed a large part of the stability
of the adducts to the shortening of some hydrogen bonds in
the hexagonal urea structure as compared with the tetragonal
structure. He argued that, although this contribution was
partly offset by lengthening of other hydrogen bonds, the
balance was in favour of the hexagonal form. However, if this
is so, why is the hexagonal form not the stable form of urea?

An alternative explanation comes from the potential energy
calculations of Parsonage and Pemberton (1967) which showed
that the Lennard-Jones type interactions of the 'guest' molecules with the 'host' lattice were sufficient on their own to
account for the observed $\Delta H^{\ominus}_{fg}$ values. Using two alternative
sets of intermolecular potential energy parameters, values
of 14·23 and 10·88 kJ (mol.CH_2 units)$^{-1}$ for the energy of
interaction were found. Table 11.7 shows the experimental
values of $\Delta H^{\ominus}_{fg}$ and the mean increment per CH_2 unit. Although

TABLE 11.7

*The enthalpy of formation ($\Delta H^{\ominus}_{fg}$) from tetragonal urea and
gaseous hydrocarbon and the mean increment (δ) per CH_2 unit
for several n-alkanes (from Parsonage and Pemberton 1967).*

Alkane	$-\Delta H^{\ominus}_{fg}$/{kJ(mol.'guest')$^{-1}$}	δ/{kJ(mol.'guest')$^{-1}$}
C_7H_{16}	66·9	
		15·1
C_8H_{18}	82·0	
		13·8
C_9H_{20}	95·8	
		10·5
$C_{10}H_{22}$	106·3	
		11·1
$C_{12}H_{26}$	128·4	
		10·2
$C_{16}H_{34}$	169·0	

changes in the hydrogen-bond energy may occur on forming
the adducts, the effect is probably not large (*cf.* α- and
β-quinol for which the enthalpy difference is only 0·54 kJ
mol^{-1}), and is, in any case, not necessary in order to explain
the stability.

11.4.2. *Thermal anomalies*
Heat capacity measurements from 12 to 300 K have been made on
the adducts of a number of alkanes by Parsonage and coworkers
(Pemberton and Parsonage 1965, 1966, Cope and Parsonage 1969,
Gannon and Parsonage 1972). Apart from the adducts of dec-1-
ene (the shortest alk-1-ene studied) and 2-methylpentadecane

(the only branched-chain compound studied), all the samples showed a region of anomalously high heat absorption (Fig. 11.15). First inspection suggests that the process involved

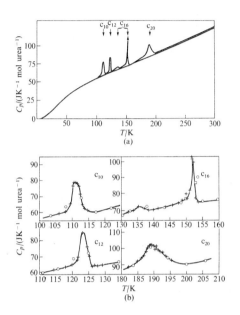

Fig.11.15. Heat capacity against temperature for four urea+n-alkane adducts. The quantity of adduct referred to is that which contains 1 mole of urea. (a) Overall plot for the four adducts; (b) detailed plots in the transition region for each adduct (from Pemberton and Parsonage 1965).

occurs over 20 to 30 K, but closer analysis shows that an appreciable part of the entropy is gained in the 'wings', the more remote temperature regions. Information about the transitions is collected in Table 11.8. The transition temperature (T_t) is defined as the temperature at which the maximum occurs in the graph of C_p against T. The enthalpy (ΔH_t) and entropy (ΔS_t) of transition depend upon the estimation of where the C_p-T curve would have run in the absence of the transition. For the adducts of the four even n-alkanes the T_t, ΔH_t, and ΔS_t values all vary smoothly and monotonically with chain length (n) (Fig.11.16): the two odd n-alkane adducts have values which suggest curves some-

TABLE 11.8

Transition temperatures and enthalpies and entropies of transition of the urea adducts. (The quantities of adduct referred to are those which contain one mole of hydrocarbon.)

'Guest'	T_t/K	$\Delta H_t/(kJ\ mol^{-1})$	$\Delta S_t/(J\ K^{-1}mol^{-1})$	Reference
$n\text{-}C_{10}H_{22}$	110·9	0·85	8·1	1
$n\text{-}C_{12}H_{26}$	123·2	1·11	9·5	1
$n\text{-}C_{16}H_{34}$	135·3 151·8	1·77	12·2	1
$n\text{-}C_{20}H_{42}$	189·3	2·79	15·1	1
$n\text{-}C_{11}H_{24}$	122·4	1·39	10·8	2
$n\text{-}C_{15}H_{32}$	158·4	1·44	9·5	3
$1\text{-}C_{10}H_{20}$	-	-	- (6·3)[a]	2
$1\text{-}C_{12}H_{24}$	82·0	1·21	10·8 (7·9)[a]	4
$1\text{-}C_{14}H_{28}$	256·6	3·63	12·0	4
$1\text{-}C_{16}H_{32}$	141·7	1·63	11·7(11·7)[a]	2
$1\text{-}C_{18}H_{36}$	155·9	1·93	12·7	4
$1\text{-}C_{20}H_{40}$	153·9	1·42	9·3(13·5)[a]	2

a. Values for ΔS_t in brackets are the values corrected after analysis of the data as described by Cope and Parsonage (1969).

REFERENCES

1. Pemberton and Parsonage (1965).
2. Cope and Parsonage (1969).
3. Pemberton and Parsonage (1966).
4. Gannon and Parsonage (1972).

what displaced from those for the even members. Odd-even alternations in the physical properties of members of aliphatic homologous series are, of course, commonplace.

A possible explanation of the transitions is not difficult to find. The pure n-alkanes (even, n = 22 and above;

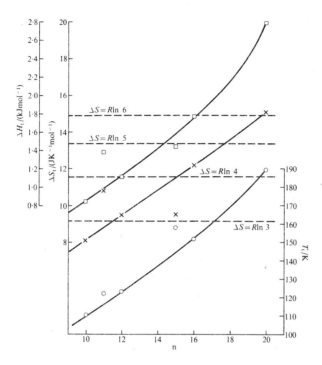

Fig.11.16. The enthalpies (□) and entropies (×) of transition per mole of hydrocarbon and the transition temperatures (○) of the urea+n-alkane adducts; n = the number of carbon atoms in the n-alkane molecule. Also shown are the ordinates corresponding to $\Delta S = R \ln 3$, $R \ln 4$, $R \ln 5$, and $R \ln 6$ (after Pemberton and Parsonage 1965).

odd, n = 9 and above) all exhibit gradual transitions a few degrees below their melting-points which are due to the onset of rotational or reorientational motion of the molecules about their long axes (section 10.5) (Fig.11.17). Similar motion in the corresponding adducts would, therefore, not be surprising. The fact that the 2-methylpentadecane adduct does not show a transition is strong evidence for this suggestion. What is surprising, however, is that the process appears to be quite strongly cooperative and that it occurs at such a high temperature.

In discussing these adducts it is almost invariably assumed that the 'guest' molecules in one channel are oblivious of those in all other channels. It also seems reasonable to assume that each 'guest' molecule will interact only

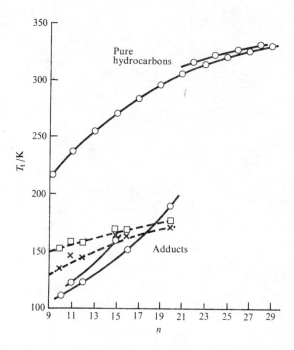

Fig.11.17. The transition temperature against n, the number of carbon atoms in the n-alkane, for the pure hydrocarbons and their urea adducts; o : experimental values; □ and × : calculated values for the adducts using two different sets of interaction parameters (after Parsonage and Pemberton 1967).

with the two 'guest' molecules which are immediately adjacent to it in its channel. If both of these assumptions are accepted then it would appear likely from van Hove's Theorem (section 3.14; the theorem is actually concerned with the possibility of non-analytic behaviour and is not strictly related to the gradual transitions discussed here) that there would be no order-disorder transition and indeed no long-range order above 0 K. One mental reservation which must be made here is brought out by the work of Casey and Runnels (1969) on a system of hard 'squares' with their centres equally spaced on a line. The 'squares' are able to rotate but their centres cannot move. The potential energy of the system is infinite if any of the 'squares' overlap, but zero otherwise. For such a system a phase transition

occurs as the distance apart of the centres of the 'squares'
decreases. This result is not an exception to van Hove's
Theorem because for each 'square' there are two coordinates,
one defining the position of its centre, the other its
orientation. Are, then, the adduct transitions of the Runnels
type? If they are we would expect the transition to be independent of chain length for a classical system since the
potential energy of the interaction of adjacent molecules in
the same channel is itself independent of chain length.
Since this is contrary to the observations, the Runnels
model may be omitted from further consideration. Although
van Hove's Theorem does not actually forbid gradual transitions for systems which satisfy its criteria, nevertheless
it would appear advisable to abandon the assumption that
there is no interaction between 'guest' molecules in neighbouring channels. On computing the interactions between
such neighbouring molecules two facts emerge (Parsonage
and Pemberton 1967). Firstly, the barriers to relative
rotation arising from direct interactions of the Lennard-
Jones form lie in the range 31 - 53 J (mol.hydrocarbon)$^{-1}$
for the n = 10 to n = 20 n-alkane adducts. Secondly, the
barriers for the odd members do not fall in line with those
for the even members. The latter fact is almost certainly
the cause of the odd-even alternation in T_t. In the same
study, the potential energies of the urea-alkane interactions and the interactions between adjacent molecules in
the same channel were also computed.

Parsonage and Pemberton (1967) used the above-mentioned
computed results of the potential energy contributions in a
statistical-mechanical treatment of the adducts. In their
model they represented the orientation of the molecules and
the angular-dependent part of their interactions by an Ising
model in which each 'spin' could be in either of two states.
This is equivalent to allowing each molecule to adopt either
of two orientations, rather than giving each the choice of
six as in the real system. Previous work on Ising systems by
Domb and coworkers (Domb and Miedema 1964) has, however,
shown that T_t is not very sensitive to the number of permitted states: indeed, in going from 2 to ∞, T_t is only

reduced by a factor of ~2 (Table 3.3). The orienting influence of the urea lattice is represented by the difference
in potential energy ($2V$) between the greatest and the least
of the six minima. However, as the position of the molecule
in its channel (the z value) is changed, the direction in
which this orienting influence is exerted (towards the deep-
est minimum) will change. That is, the relative potentials
of the six minima vary periodically with the z value. Since
only one pair of wells is considered in the model, the component of the orienting influence tending to favour one of
the two states is set equal to $2V \cos \phi$, where ϕ is a phase
angle which is directly proportional to the z value. The
interactions between nearest neighbour 'guest' molecules are
written as $-J\mu_1\mu_2$, where J is a constant which depends upon
the nature of the 'guest' substance and also on whether they
are longitudinal or lateral neighbours, and μ_1 and μ_2, which
are equivalent to s_1^z/s and s_2^z/s respectively of equation (3.1),
may be either +1 or -1 according to the orientation of the
molecule represented by the subscript. The model may be described as a three-dimensional Ising system with equal interactions in two directions (the lateral) but stronger interactions in the third (the longitudinal), and with the influence of the urea lattice being to impose a field of which
the relevant component varies periodically along the longitudinal direction. Since exact solutions have not been found,
so far, for either of the simpler Ising systems, the three-
dimensional lattice in zero field or the two-dimensional
lattice in a uniform field (section 3.1.1), it is necessary
to make an approximation: the lateral interaction term for
the ith molecule in a channel is replaced by $-J\langle \mu_i \rangle\mu_i$, where
$\langle \mu_i \rangle$ is the average value of μ_i taken over all molecules
having the same z value. This is equivalent to adopting a
Weiss or Bragg-Williams model for the lateral interactions
whilst retaining the exact Ising model for the much stronger,
longitudinal interactions. The potential energy for any configuration is then

$$-J \sum_{\substack{\text{long} \\ nn}} \mu_i\mu_j \quad -V \sum_i \mu_i \cos \phi \quad -6J' \sum_i \langle \mu_i \rangle\mu_i \qquad (11.9)$$

The partition function for this system can then be evaluated
by the transfer matrix method without further approximation.
Using values of J, J', and V derived from the previously mentioned potential energy calculations, and with no adjustable parameters, order-disorder transitions are found at temperatures which are in fair agreement with those observed
experimentally (Fig.11.17). The predicted transition temperature increases with n and is higher for odd than even
alkanes, thereby agreeing in both respects with the experimental results. The shapes of the theoretical heat capacity
curves are, however, quite different from the experimental
curves. This is no doubt due to the use of the Bragg-
Williams approximation in treating the lateral interactions,
for the shape of the theoretical curve is very similar to
the saw-tooth plot obtained from simple Bragg-Williams
theory; the experimental curves, on the other hand, are
much more similar to the curves found for exact Ising calculations, differing from them primarily in being rounded
off instead of showing a divergence. Had it been possible
to avoid the use of the Bragg-Williams approximation for
the lateral interactions then it is probable that the
shapes as well as the temperatures of the transitions
would have been in good agreement with experiment.

In the real system, the regular increase in ΔS_t with
n suggests that internal rotations within the alkane chains
occur simultaneously with the reorientations of the whole
molecule. This is similar to a suggestion made by Temperley (1956) concerning the transitions in the pure hydrocarbons.

The importance of the theory described above is that
it demonstrates how even weak interactions in the lateral
directions, provided they are supported by strong interactions in the other direction, can lead to order-disorder
transitions at readily accessible temperatures. Of course,
the transition would disappear altogether, being replaced
by a non-cooperative gain in energy of the Schottky type,
if the lateral interactions were zero. Nevertheless, it is
not true to say that the only factor of importance in
determining the transition temperature is the strength of

the weakest interactions.

The n-alkane adducts have also been studied by wide-line NMR. Although Gilson and McDowell (1961) examined the line-widths and second moments of the n-$C_{13}H_{28}$ and n-$C_{16}H_{34}$ adducts from 77 to 300 K they did not find any sudden changes on passing through the transition temperatures. Indeed, the only sudden changes they reported were at ~250 K, which they attributed to small structural changes of the 'host' lattice. In the previously discussed C_p measurements very small extra heat intakes were found at about this temperature, but since the enthalpies involved varied erratically from adduct to adduct the effect was thought to be due to the presence of very small amounts of occluded impurity. Takahashi (1967) found from wide-line NMR spectra of the n-alkane adducts with n = 12,14,16 and 18 that even at 95 K, the lowest temperature employed, there were methyl group rotations as well as rotations about the long axis. 95 K is much lower than T_t for all these adducts, but it must be remembered that reorientations at 10^4-10^5 s^{-1} are sufficient to cause narrowing of the NMR lines, although the same rate of reorientation would have virtually no effect on the thermodynamic properties.

Bell and Richards (1969) determined the spin-lattice relaxation time (T_1) for the n-alkane adducts with n = 10, 12,16 and 20, the same set of even adducts as were studied by Pemberton and Parsonage (1965). For any given process having a correlation time τ_c, T_1 is assumed to be given by the equation

$$1/T_1 = C[\tau_c/(1+\omega^2\tau_c^2) + 4\tau_c/(1+4\omega^2\tau_c^2)] \qquad (11.10)$$

where ω is the Larmor frequency and C is a constant. From this equation it can easily be shown that a graph of T_1 against T^{-1} should show a minimum when $\omega\tau_c \approx 0 \cdot 62$ at which $1/T_1(\text{min}) = 1 \cdot 42C/\omega$ (Fig.11.18). By locating the minimum in T_1 the values of C and the τ_c at the temperature at which the minimum occurs can be evaluated. The values found for C were $9 \cdot 6 \times 10^8$, $6 \cdot 4 \times 10^8$, $1 \cdot 3 \times 10^9$, and $4 \cdot 9 \times 10^8$ s^{-2} for the adducts with n = 10,12,16 and 20,

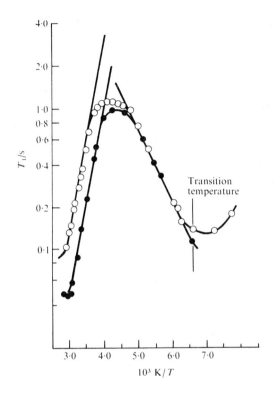

Fig.11.18. The proton spin-lattice relaxation time (T_1) for the urea+n-hexadecane adduct; o : measurements at 35 MHz; • : measurements at 20 MHz (from Bell and Richards 1969).

respectively. Since the corresponding adducts made with d_4-urea gave very similar results it is thought probable that the relaxation proceeds by intramolecular magnetic dipole coupling. Various models were then considered and the predicted values of C compared with experiment. The models and the conclusions with regard to them were as follows. (1) A model in which the molecules rotate freely about their long axes, and dipolar coupling is present between protons of the same CH_2 group but not between those of different CH_2 or CH_3 groups. The value predicted for C is $5 \cdot 2 \times 10^9$ s^{-2}, which is much higher than is observed for any of these compounds. (2) A model in which 'spin diffusion' to the methyl groups is the rate-controlling step, with relaxation of the methyl protons then occurring relatively rapidly. This model, which corresponds to that found to hold for the

pure n-alkanes, leads to the prediction that the T_1 minimum
should occur at the same temperature for all the adducts,
that the value of T_1 at the minimum should be directly proportional to the chain length, and that the activation
energy should be the same for all the adducts. None of these
predictions are fulfilled. (3) A model in which the alkane
molecules make torsional oscillations of large amplitude.
This would lead to values of C which were less than for
free rotation, but it would be expected that it would give
way to rotation as the temperature is raised. (4) A model
in which molecular reorientation between potential minima
of unequal depth occurs. The tendency of the molecule to
remain in the deeper well causes T_1 to rise and C to fall.
If there are only two wells it can be shown that the apparent
activation energy obtained by plotting $\ln T_1$ against T^{-1}
for temperatures above that at which the minimum occurs is
equal to $E_a - \Delta E$, where E_a is the activation energy from the
lower potential minimum and E is the difference in energy
of the bottoms of the wells; at temperatures below that
of the T_1 minimum, the apparent activation energy is equal
to $E_a + \Delta E$. The results obtained by an application of model
(4) are summarized in Table 11.9. The values for E_a(exp.)
are similar to one of the two sets of values calculated by
Parsonage and Pemberton (their set II). If one adds to the
computed potential barrier values of the latter workers
$3 \cdot 00$ kJ mol^{-1} for the barrier to rotation arising from
the interactions with the longitudinal neighbours, then
the values obtained are in agreement with those of Bell
and Richards for all the adducts except that of n-$C_{16}H_{34}$.
It thus appears that model (4) gives the best representation of the NMR relaxation data and is also in reasonable
accord with the theory which was proposed to explain the
thermal anomalies. Bell and Richards did not find any
sudden change at T_t, but they did find abrupt changes in
dT_1/dT at 250 K, in agreement with the wide-line experiments
(Gilson and McDowell 1961). They were unable to decide,
however, whether this arose from the onset of rotation of
the urea molecules, which in turn relaxes the protons of
the hydrocarbon, or from the beginning of segmental motion

of the alkane chain. In view of what has been said about
the entropy changes associated with the thermal anomalies,
however, it seems probable that segmental motion of the
hydrocarbon chain starts at lower temperatures.

TABLE 11.9

*Proton relaxation of the 'guest' molecules in urea adducts.
The temperature at which the minimum in T_1 occurs (T_{min}), the
difference in energy of the bottoms of the potential wells (ΔE),
and the experimental and theoretical values of the activation
energy (E_a) for adducts with ordinary and fully deuterated urea.*

Adduct	T_{min}/K	ΔE/(kJ mol^{-1})	E_a/(kJ mol^{-1})	
			Expt.	Theory (including longitudinal barriers)
h_4-urea+				
$C_{10}H_{22}$	130	3·05	6·90	7·11
$C_{12}H_{26}$	135	3·64	9·00	8·16
$C_{16}H_{34}$	142	3·10	12·89	8·74
$C_{20}H_{42}$	156	4·60	11·30	10·75
$\omega,\omega'-C_{10}H_{20}Br_2$	175	5·44	16·53	-
$\omega,\omega'-C_{10}H_{20}(CN)_2$	245	7·78	16·32	-
d_4-urea+				
$C_{12}H_{26}$	133	3·89	12·51	-
$C_{16}H_{34}$	142	3·05	11·63	-
$\omega,\omega'-C_{10}H_{20}Br_2$	170	4·23	16·53	-

(after Bell and Richards 1969).

11.4.3. Disorder in alk-1-ene adducts
The system becomes more complicated if the two ends of each
'guest' molecule are dissimilar, as in the alk-1-enes. Three
kinds of juxtaposition of end-groups of neighbouring mole-

cules in the same channel are then possible: ane-ane, ane-
ene and ene-ene, where ane and ene refer to the end-groups
$-CH_2-CH_3$ and $-CH=CH_2$, respectively. There are, therefore,
two possible types of disorder in these substances: orientational disorder, as found in the n-alkane adducts, and
'head-tail' or 'end-for-end' disorder (cf. section 10.5).
The latter kind of disorder would, of course, be 'frozen-in'
when the crystal is formed: it is not possible for the molecules to undergo subsequent 'head-tail' reversal. There
is a similarity here with the situation in ferromagnetic
alloys (section 3.1.7), in which the positional configuration is frozen-in but the magnetic configuration can change.

      The C_p-T curves of the n = 12,14,16,18, and 20 alk-1-
ene adducts each showed one transition region, but the curve
for the n = 10 adduct was free from this (Cope and Parsonage
1969, Gannon and Parsonage 1972). A careful analysis of
the data, however, showed that in the latter case there was,
in fact, an entropy gain spread over about 120 K, and that
for the n = 10,12,16, and 20 adducts ΔS_t was in each case
similar to the value for the corresponding n-alkane adduct.
Because of lack of auxiliary data, similar analyses for the
n = 14 and n = 18 adducts were not possible. The general
impression for this set of alk-1-ene adducts is, however,
of a lack of regularity in the results. A particularly
striking example of this is that T_t for the tetradec-1-ene
adduct is 256·6 K, about twice the temperature that would
be expected from interpolation between the values for the
remainder of the series. Again, for the eicos-1-ene adduct
the transition is much more diffuse than one would expect:
only about one-half of ΔS_t is gained within ±20° of T_t.

      From the theoretical point of view, it would be inter-
esting to examine the effect on the predicted C_p-T curve of
changes in the 'head-tail' order. Three simple situations
can be envisaged: random orientations, and the two types
of order shown in Fig.11.19. In terms of the model of
Parsonage and Pemberton (1967) the choice of 'head-tail'
arrangement affects J strongly, but has little or no effect
on J' and V. Unfortunately it is not possible to adapt
their treatment to the 'head-tail' disordered system.

(a)

(b)

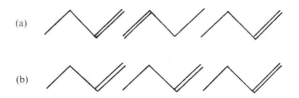

Fig.11.19. Possible ordered arrangements of the alk-1-ene molecules in an adduct channel. (a) Head-head ordered; (b) head-tail ordered.

Indeed, no analytic treatment, at the moment, can deal with such a situation. It is necessary, therefore, to resort to computer simulations. Monte Carlo evaluations have been attempted by Parsonage (1969) in which an Ising model simi-lar to that of Parsonage and Pemberton is initially adopted and in which the 'head-tail' ordering of the system is determined randomly before the start of the Monte Carlo run. Such studies are, however, bedevilled by the slowness with which the equilibrium values are reached in Monte Carlo calculations in the neighbourhood of transitions. This diffi-culty makes comments on the shapes of the heat capacity curves very uncertain, but it is clear that T_t is shifted appreciably on altering the 'head-tail' ordering.

11.4.4. Dielectric phenomena
The reorientation of polar adducted molecules has been studied by dielectric relaxation. Using microwave fre-quencies in the range 1×10^8 to 3×10^{10} Hz, Meakins (1955) observed absorption maxima at room temperature in the adducts of $CH_3(CH_2)_7CO(CH_2)_7CH_3$, $CH_3(CH_2)_{14}CO(CH_2)_{14}CH_3$, $CH_3(CH_2)_{16}CO(CH_2)_{16}CH_3$, $CH_3(CH_2)_{14}COOCH_3$, $CH_3COO(CH_2)_{15}CH_3$, $CH_3(CH_2)_{11}O(CH_2)_{11}CH_3$, $CH_3(CH_2)_{10}CHBr(CH_2)_{10}CH_3$, $CH_3(CH_2)_{14}CHBr(CH_2)_{14}CH_3$, $CH_3(CH_2)_{17}Br$, and $Br(CH_2)_{10}Br$. The adduct of the non-polar $CH_3(CH_2)_{20}CH_3$ showed no dielectric absorp-tion, indicating that the effects observed in the other compounds are, indeed, due to the 'guest' molecules rather than to the 'host' lattice. Another feature of interest

is that the $Br(CH_2)_{10}Br$ adduct shows absorption. If this
molecule remained rigidly in the fully extended form throughout, with the bromine atoms always occupying the *trans* positions, then the molecules would always make no contribution
to the polarization and so no dielectric absorption would
occur. The experimental observations, therefore, indicate
that some rotation or reorientation about the internal C-C
bonds can occur, even if only about the terminal C-C bond.

Meakins reported results for two of the adducts, those
of $CH_3(CH_2)_{14}CO(CH_2)_{14}CH_3$ and $CH_3(CH_2)_{11}O(CH_2)_{11}CH_3$, over
a considerable temperature range (197-293 K) and in greater
detail. The results for the former were subsequently
treated by Lauritzen (1958), who assumed that for this adduct
the variation of potential energy with orientation arose
entirely from the interactions of the CO group with the urea
framework. This assumption is supported by Meakins' observation that the adducts of the three ketones had absorption peaks at almost the same frequency. The calculations of Parsonage and Pemberton also showed that, although
the magnitude of the urea-*n*-alkane interaction was
~12·5 kJ (mol CH_2 units)$^{-1}$, its angular variation was indeed
small, as Lauritzen had argued. With this simplification
Lauritzen found the potential energy curve to have six unequal minima (Fig.11.20) and that the very shallow minimum
at 180° had negligible influence on the predicted results
and could be ignored. Assuming that the molecule could only
jump between adjacent wells the kinetic dielectric system
became one having four rate constants, each being written in
the Arrhenius form $k_i = A \exp(-W_i/kT)$, where W_i is the potential barrier for the process concerned. Using a procedure
developed by Hoffman which is applicable to a system with
several relaxation times ($\tau_1, \tau_2, \ldots$) and rate constants,
Lauritzen was able to express the four relaxation times in
terms of the four rate constants. The static permittivity
could also be expressed in terms of the τ_i and k_i. Fig.11.21
(a) shows a comparison of the experimental results of Meakins
for the static permittivity and the curve calculated by
Lauritzen. In obtaining such a good fit Lauritzen had permitted some variation of the potential barriers with tempera-

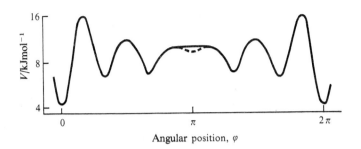

Fig.11.20. Potential energy (V) against orientation (ϕ) for a carbonyl group in the $z=0$ plane (from Lauritzen 1958).

ture, the justification for this being that the 'host' lattice would expand with rise in temperature. Fig.11.21 (b) and (c) shows the striking agreement achieved at all temperatures for the dielectric loss. Similar calculations were also made for the adduct of $CH_3(CH_2)_{10}CHBr(CH_2)_{10}CH_3$. Because of the greater size of the Br substituent the variations of potential energy with angle are greater. There is also an added complexity arising from the lower symmetry of the 'guest' molecule, and this caused Lauritzen to assume a displacement of the molecule by 0.07 nm from the c axis of the crystal in his calculations. Since the experimental results for this substance were confined to a single temperature it was not possible to make such a thorough test of the theory as was done for the ketone adduct.

Dielectric studies from 293 K down to 77 K using lower frequencies (10^2-10^6 Hz) have subsequently been made by Jaffrain et al. on the adducts of $CH_3(CH_2)_{10}CHBr(CH_2)_{10}CH_3$ (Jaffrain et al. 1969), $CH_3(CH_2)_{15}OH$, and $HO(CH_2)_{15}OH$ (Jaffrain and Schuster 1968). The results for the real part of the permittivity (ε') suggest that order-disorder transitions occur near 115 K for the last two. DTA examination confirmed the presence of thermal transitions for the alcohol adduct but not for the diol adduct.

11.4.5. Other NMR studies
Kiriyama, Kondo, and Asaki (1965) used the wide-line tech-

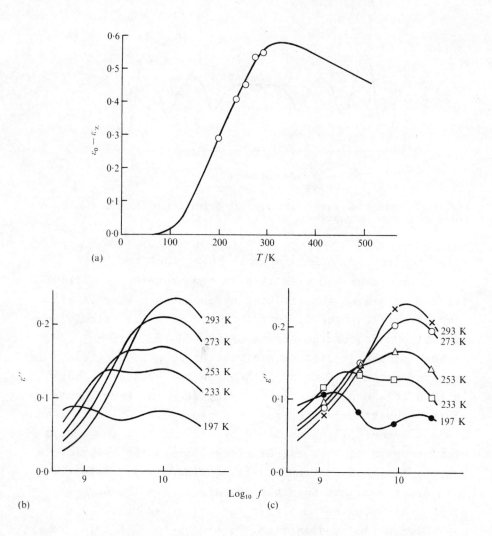

Fig.11.21. (a) Comparison of theory and experiment for the urea adduct of $CH_3(CH_2)_{14}CO(CH_2)_{14}CH_3$ for the variation with temperature of the contribution of the orientation of the ketone to the static permittivity $(\varepsilon_0-\varepsilon_\infty)$; o : experimental values, curve: theory. (b) Theoretical dielectric loss curves for the same adduct; (c) corresponding experimental curves (from Lauritzen 1958).

nique to study the adducts of $CH_3(CH_2)_8COOCH_3$ and $CH_3(CH_2)_{16}COOCH_3$. The former adduct showed motional narrowing over the range 173 - 223 K; the latter showed a similar, though more gradual effect. Their conclusion about the motion of the 'guest' molecules is similar to that put forward by Gilson and McDowell (1961) for the n-alkane adducts, namely

that at room temperature the molecules undergo twisting
about the C-C bonds as well as overall rotation.

11.5. CHANNEL COMPOUNDS OF THIOUREA

Thiourea forms a large number of inclusion compounds which
are similar in many ways to those formed by urea. Again
it is not the form stable at room temperature, the orthorhombic, which constitutes the 'host' lattice of the inclusion compounds. Rather, a rhombohedral structure, which
has never been found in the absence of 'guest' molecules, is
adopted by the thiourea when forming these compounds.

Fig.11.22(a) shows the 'host' lattice structure as

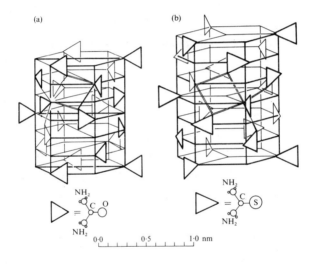

Fig.11.22. Host lattice structures of (a) urea and (b) thiourea (from
Lenné 1954).

determined by Lenné (1954) for the thiourea+cyclohexane
adduct. The space group is $R32/c$ with lattice constants
a = 1·58 nm and c = 1·25 nm. The similarities and differences between the urea and thiourea 'host' structures are
evident from Fig.11.22(a) and (b). As with the urea system,
the thiourea molecules are hydrogen-bonded together to form
interpenetrating helices. The decision as to whether a particular crystal should have right- or left-handed helices

is made when the crystal is grown, and in the absence of
directing factors, is made randomly. It will be noticed
that at levels 1 and 4 the thiourea molecules are oriented
so that the three sulphur atoms are projected into the
channel; at the other levels the sulphur atoms project into
adjacent channels. The constrictions in the channel at
levels 1 and 4 caused by the sulphur atoms appear to be
favoured sites for many 'guest' molecules. Lenné found that
the cyclohexane 'guest' molecules were centred at these
positions and thereby led to X-ray reflections from the
lattice of 'guest' molecules. If all these favoured sites,
and only these, are occupied by adducted molecules then
all thiourea adducts would have the stoichiometric formula
$3SC(NH_2)_2.X$, where X represents one molecule of the 'guest'
substance. It is indeed found that many, though by no
means all, thiourea channel adducts have this formula (Table
11.10). This is in contrast to the behaviour in the urea
adducts, where there appears to be virtually no tendency
for the adducts to form with simple molar ratios between
the 'guest' and 'host'.

The types of substance which form stable adducts with
thiourea are in some ways complementary to those forming
stable urea adducts. In both series of adducts the 'guest'
molecules should be able to fill the cavities without
leaving too much free space. However, since the channels
are broader in the thiourea than in the urea 'host' lattice,
the 'guest' molecules also should be broader. Thus, straight-
chain alkanes, which so readily form urea compounds, do not
adduct with thiourea unless the chain is long enough (sixteen or more carbon atoms) for the alkane to be able by
coiling to occupy most of the available space (McLaughlin
and McClenahan 1952). On the other hand, branched-chain
alkanes, which are of larger cross-section than the n-
alkanes, frequently form stable thiourea adducts. Ring compounds such as cyclohexane are also of about the correct
cross-section and form stable adducts. For reasons which
are not clear, benzene and its simple derivatives are not
suitable 'guest' substances, although they would appear to
be of about the optimum size. Some more complicated molecules

containing aromatic rings do, however, form adducts, e.g. 3-benzylcyclohexane. A short list of known thiourea adducts is given in Table 11.10.

TABLE 11.10

Thiourea adducts. The composition and enthalpy of formation from the 'guest' as liquid (ΔH_{fl}) and as gas (ΔH_{fg}).

	Molar ratio thiourea/guest	$-\Delta H_{fl}$ kJ(mol.'guest')$^{-1}$	$-\Delta H_{fg}$ kJ(mol.'guest')$^{-1}$	Ref.
$(CH_3)_3C.C_2H_5$	2·6, 2·9	18·4	46·1	1, 2
$(CH_3)_2CH.CH(CH_3)_2$	2·4	-	-	2
$(CH_3)_3C.CH(CH_3)_2$	2·9	15·5	47·5	2
$(CH_3)_3C.CH_2CH(CH_3)_2$	3·3	14·2	49·3	2
$(CH_3)_3C.CH_2.C(CH_3)_3$	4·0	14·2	50·4	2
$c\text{-}C_5H_{10}$	2·4	9·2	38·4	2
$c\text{-}C_5H_9.CH_3$	2·9	-	-	2
$c\text{-}C_6H_{12}$	3·0, 3·1	15·1	48·1	1, 2
$c\text{-}C_6H_{11}.CH_3$	2·9	-	-	3
$c\text{-}C_6H_{11}.CH(CH_3)_2$	4·1	6·3	46·5	2
$c\text{-}C_6H_8(1,4)$	2·9	-	-	3
$c\text{-}C_7H_{14}$	3·0	-	-	1
$c\text{-}C_8H_{16}$	3·1, 3·0	-	-	1
Decalin	4·0	-	-	3

REFERENCES

1.   Cope, Gannon, and Parsonage (1972a).
2.   Redlich, Gable, Beason, and Millar (1950).
3.   Fetterly (1964).

An interesting series of adducts are those formed by the dicyclohexyl compounds of general formula

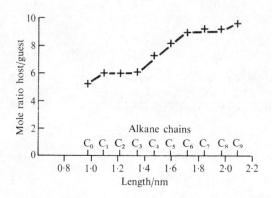

where n = 0 to 9. Schlenk (1951) and Lenné (1954) found that the mole ratio jumped almost discontinuously at certain points as n was increased (Fig.11.23). This behaviour is believed to arise from the tendency of the rings to take up positions in the planes of the sulphur atoms. Thus as n

Fig.11.23. Composition against length of the extended guest molecule for adducts of thiourea+ω,ω'-dicyclohexylalkanes (after Lenné 1954).

increases the rings of any one molecule remain in their positions in the planes of the sulphur atoms until the chain has been lengthened sufficiently to enable one of the rings to jump to the next available favoured site, 0·625 nm away.

11.5.1. *Thermodynamic properties*

Redlich, Gable, Beason, and Millar (1950) have made similar studies on the thiourea adducts to those which they carried out on the urea compounds. Some of these results are shown in Table 11.10. Generally speaking, the enthalpies and free energies of formation from the 'guest' substance in its liquid state are of smaller magnitude than for the urea adducts.

11.5.2. *Thermal anomalies*

Clément, Gourdji, and Guibé (1971) found a fairly sharp endo-
thermic peak near 131 K in the DTA trace of the cyclohexane
adduct, and found supporting evidence for the existence of
a transition near this temperature from nuclear quadrupole
resonance studies. In the latter they found that the number
of NQR lines dropped from five below 133 K to one above
158 K, there being a 'fuzzy' region between these temperatures in which consistent results could not be obtained.
Above 241 K no resonance at all was observed, this being
attributed to the hindered rotation of the thiourea molecules about the C=S bond.

When four adducts, those of cyclohexane, cycloheptane,
cycloöctane, and 2,2-dimethylbutane, were examined over a
wide range of temperature (12 - 300 K) by adiabatic calorimetry (Parsonage 1969, Cope, Gannon, and Parsonage 1972a)
it was found that the situation was more complex than was
the case with the urea adducts, all showing more than one
region of anomalously high heat absorption (Table 11.11,
Fig.11.24). DTA measurements on the same compounds up to

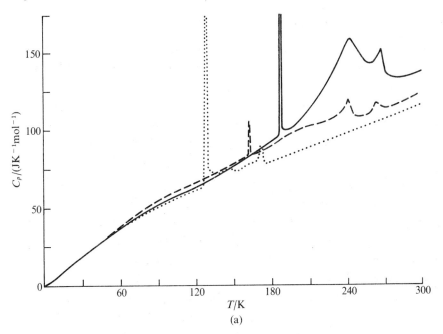

Fig.11.24. Heat capacity against temperature for thiourea adducts. (a) Dotted
line: c-C_6H_{12}; dashed line: c-C_7H_{14}; full line: c-C_8H_{16}.

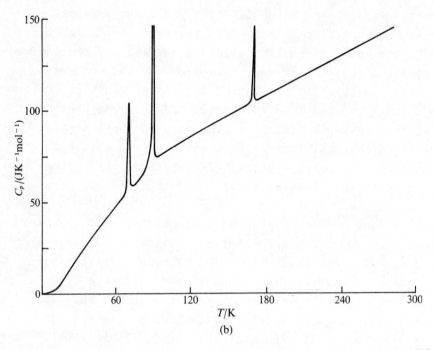

Fig.11.24. (b) $(CH_3)_3C.C_2H_5$ (after Cope, Gannon, and Parsonage 1972).

the points at which they melt and decompose showed that there
were no further anomalies of sufficient size to be observed
by that method. None of the transitions appears to be common
to all four substances, which suggests that none of the
transitional processes are concerned with the 'host' lattice
alone. This may be considered surprising since the stable,
tetragonal form of pure thiourea shows a complicated system
of thermodynamic transitions (Westrum and McCullough 1963).
The above conclusion does not, of course, rule out the possibility that in some of the adduct transitions both the 'host'
and the 'guest' molecules are intimately involved. All of
the transitions are very small [$\Delta S_t < 1$ J K^{-1} (mol.'guest')$^{-1}$]
and are therefore suggestive of the displacive transitions
which are exhibited by many ferroelectric substances (section
3.9). In particular, they are too small for it to be at all
likely that their origin lies in order-disorder processes.
     The most striking feature of the set of heat capacity
curves is the extremely large hump with its maximum at

TABLE 11.11

Transition temperatures and enthalpies and entropies of transition of thiourea adducts. (The quantities referred to are those which contain one mole of hydrocarbon.) (After Cope, Gannon, and Parsonage 1972a).

'Guest'	$\Delta T_t / K$	$\Delta H_t / (\text{kJ mol}^{-1})$	$\Delta S_t / (\text{J K}^{-1} \text{ mol}^{-1})$
$c\text{-}C_6H_{12}$	128·8	1·142	8·87
	130-150	0·331	2·34
	153-161	0·036	0·25
	170·8	0·142	0·84
	210-240	0·084	0·38
$c\text{-}C_7H_{14}$	162·4	0·123	0·75
	241	0·190	0·79
	262	0·031	0·12
	Shallow hump	1·606	11·54
$c\text{-}C_8H_{16}$	187·2	0·708	3·78
	240	7·186	31·68
	265	0·236	0·89
$(CH_3)_3C.C_2H_5$	69·9	0·310	4·35
	89·5	1·160	12·93
	169·6	0·240	1·42

~240 K in the graph for the cyclooctane adduct. The magnitude of this anomaly is best appreciated by equating the entropy change per mole of hydrocarbon with $R \ln n$, when n is found to be 45·1. Such a large value makes it very unlikely that the process is simply one of order-disorder involving rigid molecules. It is much more probable that in this temperature region the cyclooctane molecules are undergoing conformational changes in a fairly non-cooperative manner. The relative energies of the various conformers may, of course, be appreciably affected by the 'straight-jacket' imposed by the thiourea 'host' lattice. Nevertheless,

calculations of the conformational energies of free cycloöctane molecules (Bixon and Lifson 1967, Hendrickson 1967)
show that between the most stable form, on the one hand, and
the next five forms, on the other, there are gaps of 5·9 to
11·7 kJ mol^{-1}. The size of these energy increments are comparable with the ΔH_t value found from the heat capacity curve
of the adduct, and the large value of ΔS_t may well be due
to the large number of high energy forms and their greater
flexibility. A more shallow hump in the curve for the cycloheptane adduct has been assigned with much less certainty
to corresponding conformational changes of that 'guest' substance. Since the chair form of cyclohexane is much more
stable (by 22·2 kJ mol^{-1}) than the twist-boat it is not
surprising that none of the transitions of its adduct appear
to be conformational. Of relevance to this discussion is
the observation of conformational changes in three solid,
pure cycloalkanes (cyclobutane, cycloheptane, and cycloöctane) by means of wide-line NMR (Andrew 1971, Brookeman
and Rushworth, 1976; section 10.2 and Fig.10.6).

The adducts of cyclopentane, cyclohexane, and their
monomethyl derivatives, as well as cyclohexene, were examined
by Gilson and McDowell (1961) at 298 K using the wide-line
technique. They found that with the cyclopentane adduct
the line was only of modulation width at 298 K. The other
four adducts all showed fairly narrow lines of width 0·7-
1·6 G. At 77 K, the cyclohexane adduct had a line-width
of 4·6 G and a second moment of 2·7 G^2. Since the latter
value is less than would be expected for reorientation about
the triad axis (3·6 G^2) it is inferred that isotropic reorientation must be occurring even at this low temperature.
The results for the cyclohexane adduct have been confirmed
by Nakajima (1965), who found that the narrowing of the line
occurred between 120 and 170 K.

In the above discussion of conformational changes of
the 'guest' molecules it has been remarked that the relative
energies of the conformers may well be different for the
enclathrated molecule and the free molecule. Direct observation of this has been reported by Nishikawa (1963), who
compared the polarized infrared spectra of free chloro- and

bromocyclohexane in the liquid state with the corresponding
spectra for the thiourea inclusion compounds. He found that
certain bands are much stronger in the inclusion compound
than in the liquid. These bands are absent from the spectra
of the pure solids, which are known to be in the equatorial
form, from which he concluded that inclusion tended to favour
the axial as against the equatorial form.

There have been several suggestions that planar or near-
planar ring molecules do not always lie with their planes
perpendicular to the channel axis. Lenné (1954) noted that
the projection of the cyclohexane molecules onto a plane
perpendicular to the channel axis was such as to suggest that
the cyclohexane 'plane' was inclined at ~35° to the plane of
the sulphur atoms. If this is so, it raises the possibility
of disorder in the adducts, in that the axis about which the
cyclohexane molecule is tilted could vary from molecule to
molecule. On reasonable suppositions it might be expected
that there would be three or six possible axes of tilt.
Cope, Gannon, and Parsonage (1972b) treated such a model by
statistical mechanics to see whether it could explain the
existence of the transition at 128·8 K, for which ΔS_t is very
close to $R \ln 3$. It was found that the direct interactions
between 'guest' molecules in the same and in adjacent channels
were much too weak to sustain the ordered structure up to
the experimentally observed transition temperature. The
disordering process in the model system was found to occur
at too low a temperature and to be almost non-cooperative.
This leaves open the possibility of there being strong indirect interactions, employing the thiourea molecules as in-
termediates, and that the transition is indeed of the order-
disorder type discussed above. Clément, Jegoudez, and Mazieres
(1974) have observed changes in the X-ray diffraction patterns
of the adducts of cyclohexane (at 148 K), cycloheptane (at
238 K), and cyclooctane (at 268 K) which arise in each case
from a change of crystal symmetry from rhombohedral to monoclinic. Apart from the associated change in size of the unit
cell (the monoclinic unit cell = 2 x the rhombohedral unit
cell) the changes in the crystals at these temperatures are
small. On further cooling, gradual distortion of the mono-

clinic structure occurs, reaching its ultimate extent at
~126 K, ~173 K, and ~213 K, respectively, for the three
adducts. Below 186 K extra spots appear in the pattern for
the cycloöctane adduct and the b parameter is doubled.
Clément *et al.* suggest that on cooling into the last mentioned state the cycloöctane molecules, which would by then
all be in the conformational state of lowest energy, form
an ordered arrangement.

Further information on the tilting of planar 'guest'
molecules has come from studies of the cyclopentanone adduct
by circular dichroism (Nishikawa 1963). The results were
interpreted as showing that the CO group was at an angle of
~30° to the channel axis. Since the CO group must lie almost,
if not exactly, in the plane of the molecule this must be
approximately the angle by which the plane of the 'guest'
molecule deviates from the plane of the sulphur atoms.

11.6. GRAPHITE INTERCALATES

A variety of substances are able to form loose compounds with
graphite in which the former are incorporated between the
layers of the graphite, the spacing between the layers being
greatly increased in order to accommodate the 'guest' molecules. The interaction between the components of the compounds are, to a large extent, of the charge-transfer type
with the graphite host acting as either donor or acceptor
according to the nature of the 'guest' substance. Thus in the
alkali metal+graphite intercalates the graphite acts as the
acceptor, whereas in the graphite nitrates it is the donor.
The general pattern is for each interlamellar space to be
either empty or full of the 'guest', rather than partly filled.

Starting from pure graphite it is usually possible to
discern several distinct stages in the addition. For example,
compounds with the heavier alkali metals K, Rb, and Cs with
the formulae C_8M and $(C_{12})_nM$, where $n \geq 2$, can be distinguished. These compounds, which are discussed in greater
detail below, correspond to there being 1,2,3...n layers of
carbon atoms between successive layers of the intercalated
substance. As the composition of the compound is changed some
interlayer positions previously occupied become empty, and

vice versa (Fig.11.25). As will be seen, even though the
total amount of M is being increased on going from $C_{36}M$ to
$C_{24}M$ there are some interlayer positions which become empty.
The fact that these successive stages each have regular,
rather than random, sandwich arrangements of this type is an

C_{24} M C_{36} M

Fig.11.25. The layer structure of two stages of the alkali metal+graphite
intercalate system. Full lines: carbon layers; broken lines: alkali
metal layers.

indication that there are fairly strong interactions between
successive layers of guest particles and also that the process of intercalation is readily reversible. To explain
the regular sequence of intercalate layers, Nixon, Parry,
and Ubbelohde (1966) adopted an idea somewhat similiar to
that used in the theory of alloys to account for long-period
ordering (sections 5.4.3 and 5.5). According to their discussion, a change in the *c* periodicity of the lattice
changes the Brillouin zone system, and this may or may not
be advantageous to the system according to the number of
electrons which are to be accommodated.

     So far, the discussion has centred on the ordering per-
pendicular to the basal planes of the graphite. Of equal
or greater interest is the way in which the arrangement
within any layer is related to that in adjacent layers, the
'stacking'. We first distinguish between three possible
situations for the graphite planes, these differing by a
simple shift of the layer in its own plane. The stacking
sequence in pure graphite is then ABAB..., and in the first,
second, third, and fourth stages of both the graphite

nitrates and the potassium graphites it is |A|A|A|...,
|AB|BC|CA|A..., |ABA|ACA|ABA|..., and |ABAB|BCBC|CACA|A...,
respectively, where the symbols | represent the intercalate
layers, which it may be noted are each sandwiched between
two graphite layers of the same kind, e.g. two A layers.
Ordering of the intercalate layers is more uncertain, and is
discussed below for the only two systems for which there is
good evidence.

From X-ray diffraction studies Parry and Nixon (1967,
1968) have shown that the K atoms in the potassium graphites
are located above the centres of the hexagonal rings of the
immediately adjacent graphite layers. In the first stage
compound (C_8K) the arrangement of the K atoms is as shown
in Fig.11.26. There are four equivalent arrays of K atoms

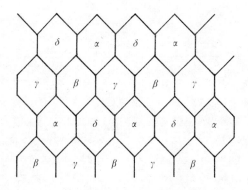

Fig.11.26. Arrangement of the atoms in a single alkali-metal plane of
C_8K. The potassium atoms occupy all the sites of one kind (α,β,γ, or δ).

($\alpha,\beta,\gamma,\delta$), and the stacking sequence for graphite and intercalate layers can be represented as $A\alpha A\beta A\gamma A\delta A$... At room
temperature the intercalate layers of higher stage ($n>1$) compounds are disordered within the layer. However, on lowering the temperature the K atoms in $C_{24}K$ were found to take up
three-dimensional order at ~98 K, the arrangement of the
graphite layers remaining unchanged. The stacking sequence
proposed by Parry and Nixon is $A\alpha_1 AB\beta_1 BC\gamma_1 CA\alpha_2 AB\beta_2 BC\gamma_2 CA\alpha_1 A$..,
where the members of the set $[\alpha_1,\beta_1,\gamma_1]$ are believed to be

related to the corresponding members of the set $[\alpha_2, \beta_2, \gamma_2]$
by a small displacement parallel to the graphite planes.
As before, A, B, and C refer to the host and α, β, and γ to
the guest arrangements. A compound of formula $C_{10}K$ has been
reported by Aronson, Salzano, and Bellafiore (1968) as being
stable above 588-598 K (at lower temperatures a mixture of
C_8K and $C_{24}K$ is obtained). There seems, however, to be no
structural evidence for this compound yet. In the case of
the caesium compound, Parry, Hatibarua, Lester, and Scruby
(1975) have briefly reported that there is X-ray evidence
that within a caesium layer there is ordering of the atoms
so as to give a $3a \times 7a$ layer superlattice, this being a com-
promise between the tendency to split the electronic band
system so as to minimize the energy of the conduction electrons and the tendency to maintain registry with the graphite
lattice. The lighter alkali metals form a somewhat different
range of compounds, e.g. C_6Li, $C_{12}Li$, $C_{18}Li$, and $C_{64}Na$
(Salzano and Aronson 1967).

The graphite nitrates, which have been extensively
studied by Ubbelohde and coworkers (Bottomley, Parry, Ubbelohde, and Young 1963, Bottomley, Parry, and Ubbelohde 1964,
Nixon, Parry, and Ubbelohde 1966) show behaviour which is
very similar to that of the potassium graphites. Unfortunately, the composition of the nitrates is rather uncertain as
a consequence of the compounds being fairly unstable. Both
NO_3^- ions and HNO_3 molecules are present, and for the second
stage compound the approximate formula $C_{48}NO_3 \cdot 3HNO_3$ (or
$C_{12} \cdot 0 \cdot 25NO_3 \cdot 0 \cdot 75HNO_3$) has been found (Bottomley, Parry, and
Ubbelohde, 1964). The stacking sequences of the graphite
layers are identical with those for the corresponding
potassium graphites. Turning to the intercalate layers,
we find an immediate difference in that the first stage
compound is similar to the subsequent stages in the nitrates,
the formula $C_{6n}H_xNO_3$ being applicable to all, but this is not
the case for the potassium compounds. The room-temperature
forms of at least the first four stages of the nitrates
are disordered both within the intercalate layers and from
one such layer to another. Each has, however, a transition
at ~253 K (designated as a λ-point on the basis of measure-

ments of c parameter *versus* temperature) to a form which is certainly ordered within the layers and is at least partly ordered in the c direction. The ordering between the layers at such a high temperature is surprising in view of the large distances separating successive layers (~1·78 nm for the stage four compound). Also, two transitions (rather than one) might have been expected for this ordering of the inter-calated molecules, the three-dimensional long-range order disappearing at the lower transition temperature and the two-dimensional order at the upper one. The absence of two separate transitions is, nevertheless, in line with the be-haviour of the pseudo two-dimensional magnetic compounds (section 12.13.2). Of particular relevance here are the series of complexes of general formula $(C_nH_{2n+1}NH_3)_2CuX_4$: only a single ordering temperature is observed and this is fairly insensitive to n for $n > 2$.

Karimov (1974-5) has made careful measurements of the magnetization (M) (parallel to the layers) and C_p for inter-calates of $NiCl_2$ and $CoCl_2$ in which successive 'guest' layers are separated by two carbon layers. The magnetic measure-ments showed two transitions for each substance ($NiCl_2$: 20·3, 18·1 K; $CoCl_2$: 9·05, 8·1 K). The phases stable at the highest and lowest temperatures, are, respectively, para- and ferromagnetic. The intermediate phase has zero long-range order, but was found to have a divergent susceptibility, and in this respect it recalls the phenomena predicted by Stanley and Kaplan (section 12.13.2). For each substance the effect of the lower transition is barely discernible in the C_p results, indicating that the corresponding energy change must be at least two orders of magnitude smaller than that associated with the upper transition.

REFERENCES

Allen, S.J., jnr. (1966). *J.chem.Phys*. **44**, 394.

Allison, S.A. and Barrer, R.M. (1968). *Trans.Faraday Soc*. **64**, 549.

Andrew, E.R. (1971). *Phys.Lett*. **34A**, 30.

Anthonsen, J.W. (1975). (a) *Acta chem.scand*. **A29**, 179; (b) A29, 175.

Aronson, S., Salzano, F.J., and Bellafiore, D. (1968). *J.chem.Phys.* <u>49</u>, 434.

Ball, D.F. and McKean, D.C. (1962). *Spectrochim.Acta* <u>18</u>, 933.

Barrer, R.M. (1964). *In Non-stoichiometric compounds* (ed. L.Mandelcorn) p.310. Academic Press, New York and London.
——————— and Stuart, W.I. (1957). *Proc.R.Soc.* <u>A243</u>, 172.

Barthel, C., Gerbaux, X., and Hadni, A. (1970). *Spectrochim. Acta* <u>A26</u>, 1183.

Bell, J.D. and Richards, R.E. (1969). *Trans.Faraday Soc.* <u>65</u>, 2529.

Belliveau, J.F. (1970). *Diss.Abstr.* <u>B31</u>, 2591.

Bertie, J.E., Bates, F.E., and Hendricksen, D.K. (1975). *Can.J.Chem.* <u>53,</u> 71.

Bixon, M. and Lifson, S. (1967). *Tetrahedron* <u>23</u>, 769.

Bottomley, M.J., Parry, G.S., and Ubbelohde, A.R. (1964). *Proc.R.Soc.* <u>A279</u>, 291.
——————— ——————— ——————— and Young, D.A. (1963). *J.chem.Soc.* 5674.

Brookeman, J.H. and Rushworth, F.A. (1976). *J.Phys.* <u>C9</u>, 1043.

Brownstein, S., Davidson, D.W., and Fiat, D. (1967). *J. chem.Phys.* <u>46</u>, 1454.

Burgiel, J.C., Meyer, H., and Richards, P.L. (1965). *J. chem.Phys.* <u>43</u>, 4291.

Casey, L.M. and Runnels, L.K. (1969). *J.chem.Phys.* <u>51</u>, 5070.

Chassonneau, M.A., Dufourcq, J., and Lemanceau, B. (1971). *C.r.hebd.Séanc.Acad.Sci.,Paris* <u>C273</u>, 793.

Cleaver, K.D., Davies, J.E.D., and Wood, W.J. (1975). *J. mol.Struct.* <u>25</u>, 222.

Clément, R., Gourdji, M., and Guibé, L. (1971). *Molec.Phys.* <u>21</u>, 247.
——————— Jegoudez, J., and Mazieres, C. (1974). *J.Solid St.Chem.* <u>10</u>, 46.

Cooke, A.H. and Duffus, H.J. (1954). *Proc.phys.Soc.(London)* <u>A67</u>, 525.
——————— Meyer, H., Wolf, W.P., Evans, D.F., and Richards, R.E. (1954). *Proc.R.Soc.* <u>A225</u>, 112.

Cope, A.F.G., Gannon, D.J., and Parsonage, N.G.(1972). (a) *J.chem.Thermodynamics* <u>4</u>, 829; (b) <u>4</u>, 843.

Cope, A.F.G. and Parsonage, N.G. (1969). *J.chem.Thermo-dynamics*, 1, 99.

Coulter, L.V., Stepakoff, G.L., and Roper, G.C. (1963). *(J.)Phys.Chem.Solids* 24, 171.

Davidson, D.W., Davies, M.M., and Williams, K. (1964). *J.chem.Phys.* 40, 3449.

Davies, J.E.D. (1972). *J.chem.Soc.,Dalton Trans.* 1182.

Davies, M. and Williams, K. (1968). *Trans.Faraday Soc.* 64, 529.

Davies, P.R. (1969). *Disc.Faraday Soc.* No. 48, 181.

Domb, C. and Miedema, A.R. (1964). *Prog.low temp.Phys.* 4, 296.

Dryden, J.S. (1953). *Trans.Faraday Soc.* 49, 1333.

Evans, D.F. and Richards, R.E. (1954). *Proc.R.Soc.* A223, 238.

Fetterly, L.C. (1964). In *Non-stoichiometric compounds* (ed. L.Mandelcorn) p.501. Academic Press, New York and London.

Foner, S., Meyer, H., and Kleiner, W.H. (1961). *(J.)Phys.Chem.Solids* 18, 273.

Fukushima, K. (1973). (a) *J.mol.Struct.* 18, 277; (b) *Chem.Lett.* 617.

Gallier, J. (1975). *Chem.Phys.Lett.* 30, 306.

Gannon, D.J. and Parsonage, N.G. (1972). *J.chem.Thermodynamics* 4, 745.

Gilson, D.F.R. and McDowell, C.A. (1961). *Molec.Phys.* 4, 125.

Gough, S.R., Garg, S.K., and Davidson, D.W. (1974). *Chem.Phys.* 3, 239.

——— ——— Ripmeester, J.A., and Davidson, D.W. (1974). *Can.J.Chem.* 52, 3193.

——— Whalley, E., and Davidson, D.W. (1968). *Can.J.Chem.* 46, 1673.

Gregoire, P., Gallier, J., and Meinnel, J. (1973). *J.Chim.phys.* 70, 1247.

Grey, N.R., Parsonage, N.G., and Staveley, L.A.K. (1961). *Molec.Phys.* 4, 153.

——— and Staveley, L.A.K. (1963). *Molec.Phys.* 7, 83.

Harris, A.B., Hunt, E., and Meyer, H. (1965). *J.chem.Phys.* 42, 2851.

Hazony, Y. and Ruby, S.L. (1968). *J.chem.Phys.* 49, 1478.

Helle, J.N., Kok, D., Platteeuw, J.C., and van der Waals,
     J.H. (1962). *Recl.trav.chim.Pays-Bas* <u>81</u>, 1068.
Hendrickson, J.B. (1967). *J.Am.chem.Soc.* <u>89</u>, 7036.
Hirschfelder, J.O., Curtiss, C.F., and Byrd, R.B. (1954).
     Molecular theory of gases and liquids, p.1110. Wiley,
     New York.
Hunt, E. and Meyer, H. (1964). *J.chem.Phys.* <u>41</u>, 353.
Jaffrain, M., Dansas, P., and Sixou, P. (1969). *J.Chim.
     phys.* <u>66</u>, 841.
————   and Schuster, P. (1968). *C.r.hebd.Séanc.Acad.
     Sci.,Paris* <u>B267</u>, 1011.
————   Siemons, J-L., and Lebreton, A. (1969). *C.r.
     hebd.Séanc.Acad.Sci.,Paris*, <u>C268</u>, 2240.
Karimov, Yu.S. (1974-5). *Sov.Phys. JETP*, <u>38</u>, 129; <u>39</u>, 547;
     <u>41</u>, 772.
Khanzada, A.W.K. and McDowell, C.A. (1971). *J.mol.Struct.* <u>7</u>,
     241.
Kiriyama, H., Kondo, T., and Asaki, Y. (1965). *Kogyo Kagaku
     Zasshi* <u>66</u>, 1491.
Lauritzen, J.I. (1958). *J.chem.Phys.* <u>28</u>, 118.
Laves, F., Nicolaides, N., and Peng, K.C. (1965). *Z.
     Kristallogr.Kristallgeom.* <u>121</u>, 258.
Lennard-Jones, J.E. and Devonshire, A.F. (1937). *Proc.R.Soc.*
     <u>A163</u>, 53.
————   ————   (1938). *Proc.R.Soc.*
     <u>A165</u>, 1.
Lenné, H-U. (1954). *Acta crystallogr.* <u>7</u>, 1.
————   (1963). *Z.Kristallogr.Kristallgeom.* <u>118</u>, 439.
McDowell, C.A. and Raghunathan, P. (1967). *Molec.Phys.* <u>13</u>, 331.
————   ————   (1968). *J.mol.Struct.* <u>2</u>,
     359.
————   ————   (1970). *J.mol.Struct.* <u>5</u>,
     433.
McKean, D.C. (1973). *Vibrational spectroscopy of trapped
     molecules* (ed. H.E. Hallam). Wiley, London, New York,
     Sydney, and Toronto.
McLaughlin, R.L. and McClenahan, W.S. (1952). *J.Am.chem.
     Soc.* <u>74</u>, 5804.
McTague, J.P. (1969). *J.chem.Phys.* <u>50</u>, 47.

Majid, Y.A., Garg, S.K., and Davidson, D.W. (1969). *Can.J. Chem.* <u>47</u>, 4697.

Matsuo, T., Suga, H., and Seki, S. (1967). *J.phys.Soc.Japan* <u>22</u>, 677.

———   ———   ——— (1968). *J.phys.Soc.Japan* <u>25</u>, 641.

Meakins, R.J. (1955). *Trans.Faraday Soc.* <u>51</u>, 953.

Meyer, H. (1961). *(J.) Phys.Chem.Solids* <u>20</u>, 238.

———   O'Brien, M.C.M., and van Vleck, J.H. (1957). *Proc. R.Soc.* <u>A243</u>, 414.

———   and Scott, T.A. (1959). *(J.)Phys.Chem.Solids* <u>11</u>, 215.

Morris, B. and Davidson, D.W. (1971). *Can.J.Chem.* <u>49</u>, 1243.

Mueller, R. and Meier, G. (1964). *Z.anorg.allg.Chem.* <u>332</u> 81.

Muller, H.R. and von Stackelberg, M. (1951). *Naturwiss.* <u>38</u>, 456; *J.chem.Phys.* <u>19</u>, 1319.

———   ——— (1952). *Naturwiss.* <u>39</u>, 20.

Nakajima, H. (1965). *J.phys.Soc.Japan* <u>20</u>, 555.

Nishikawa, M. (1963). *Chem.Ind.* 256.

Nixon, D.E., Parry, G.S., and Ubbelohde, A.R. (1966). *Proc. R.Soc.* <u>A291</u>, 324.

Palin, D.E. and Powell, H.M. (1947). *J.chem.Soc.* 208.

Parry, G.S., Hatibarua, J.A., Lester, K.M., and Scruby, C.B. (1975). *Acta crystallogr.*<u>A31</u>, Pt.S3, S60.

———   and Nixon, D.E. (1967). *Nature,Lond.* <u>216</u>, 909.

———   ——— (1968). *Brit.J.appl.Phys.* (J. Phys.D) <u>1</u>, 291.

Parsonage, N.G. (1959). *D.Phil.Thesis*, Oxford.

———   (1969). *Disc.Faraday Soc.* No.48, 215.

———   and Pemberton, R.C. (1967). *Trans.Faraday Soc.* <u>63</u>, 311.

———   and Staveley, L.A.K. (1959). *Molec.Phys.* <u>2</u>, 212.

———   ——— (1960). *Molec.Phys.* <u>3</u>, 59.

Pemberton, R.C. and Parsonage, N.G. (1965). *Trans.Faraday Soc.* <u>61</u>, 2112.

———   ——— (1966). *Trans.Faraday Soc.* <u>62</u>, 553.

Pitzer, K.S. and Gwinn, W.D. (1942). *J.chem.Phys.* 10, 428.

Platteeuw, J.C. (1958). *Recl.trav.chim.Pays-Bas* 77,
    403.

————————   and van der Waals, J.H. (1958). *Molec.Phys.* 1
    91.

Powell, H.M. (1948). *J.chem.Soc.* 61.

Radell, J., Brodman, B.W., and Bergmann, E.D. (1963).
    Tetrahedron 19, 873.

————————   ————————   ————————   (1964). *Can.J.*
    Chem. 42, 1069.

————————   Connolly, J.W., and Yuhaş, L.D. (1960). *U.S.Dept.*
    Commerce, Office Tech.Services, P.B.Rept. 161, 686.
    J.Org.Chem. (1960), 26, 2022.

Redlich, O., Gable, C.M., Dunlop, A.K., and Millar, R.W.
    (1950a). *J.Am.chem.Soc.* 72, 4153.

————————   ————————   Beason, L.R., and Millar, R.W.
    (1950b). *J.Am.chem.Soc.* 72, 4161.

Roper, G.C. (1966). *Diss.Abstr.* B27, 1444.

Salzano, F.J. and Aronson, S. (1967). *J.chem.Phys.* 47, 2978.

Schlenk, W., jnr. (1949). *Annln.Chem.* 565, 204.

————————   (1951). *Annln.Chem.* 573, 142.

————————   (1973). *Annln.Chem.* 1145, 1156, 1179, 1195.

Smith, A.E. (1952). *Acta crystallogr.* 5, 224.

Smith, J.W. (1955). *Electric dipole moments*, p.84. Butter-
    worths, London.

Staveley, L.A.K. (1964). In *Non-stoichiometric compounds*
    (ed. L. Mandelcorn), p.606. Academic Press, New York
    and London.

Stepakoff, G.L. (1963). *Diss.Abstr.* 24, 1424.

————————   and Coulter, L.V. (1963). *(J.)Phys.Chem.Solids*
    24, 1435.

Takahashi, K. (1967). *Diss.Abstr.* B28, 639.

Temperley, H.N.V. (1956). *J.Res.natn.Bur.Stand.* 56, 55.

Van der Waals, J.H. (1956). *Trans.Faraday Soc.* 52, 184.

————————   and Platteeuw, J.C. (1959). *Adv.chem.*
    Phys. 2, 1.

Van Vleck, J.H. (1961). *(J.)Phys.Chem.Solids,* 20, 241.

Waller, J.G. (1960). *Nature,Lond.* 186, 429.

Wells, A.F. (1975). *Structural inorganic chemistry*, 4th edition.
    Clarendon Press. Oxford.

Westrum, E.F., jnr. and McCullough, J.P. (1963). In *Physics and chemistry of the organic solid state* (eds. Fox, D., Labes, M.M., and Weissberger, A.), vol.1, Chap.1. Interscience, New York.

Wöhler, F. (1849). *Annln.Chem.* <u>69</u>, 297.

Zimmerschied, W.J., Dinerstein, R.A., Weitkamp, A.W., and Marschner, R.F. (1950). *Ind.eng.Chem.* <u>42</u>, 1300.

12

MAGNETIC SYSTEMS

12.1. INTRODUCTION

The number of substances now known to exhibit magnetic order
is so great that in this book it has been necessary to make
some decisions on which classes of substances to include and
which to omit. We have decided, in the main, to restrict
consideration to insulators, omitting thereby the itinerant
ferromagnetism and antiferromagnetism as displayed by metals
and alloys. Non-stoichiometric systems and nuclear magnetism
will also be omitted. Furthermore, we shall concentrate,
though not exclusively, on properties in the limit of zero
field.

12.2. DEMAGNETIZATION AND DOMAIN EFFECTS

We shall frequently be concerned with the field inside a
specimen when it is placed in an applied magnetic field, for
it is the field inside the sample which is of relevance when
we are considering the effect of the field on magnetic dipoles within the sample. If the specimen has a magnetization
M, then the internal field ($\mathcal{H}_{int}$) will differ from the applied
field ($\mathcal{H}_a$) by an amount proportional to M:

$$\mathcal{H}_{int} = \mathcal{H}_a - DM \qquad (12.1)$$

where the constant D is known as the demagnetization factor.
(The second term is important if M is large, as with a ferromagnet; for paramagnetic substances this term is usually much
smaller.) D is determined by the shape of the specimen, and
its value has been calculated for various common shapes.
From these calculations it emerges that for $\mathcal{H}_{int}$ to be uniform inside the sample the latter must have a quadratic surface. Since the only solid figure of this type is an ellipsoid, that is the shape of crystal which should be used for
studies on ferromagnets wherever possible. Clearly, a powder specimen is very unsatisfactory in this respect, since
the particles are of varied and ill-defined shapes. Though

most of the early work on ferromagnetic systems was done on
powders, an increasing amount of work is being done on samples which are ellipsoids, and usually ellipsoids of revolution. The source of the demagnetization term is easy to
appreciate; it is the field arising at an internal point from
uncompensated magnetic dipoles at the surfaces of the sample. It may be calculated by the methods of classical magnetic theory.

The demagnetization term has one other important effect:
it tends to lead to the formation of domains. This has already been discussed in Chapter 2 with respect to the occurrence of hysteresis. In antiferromagnets, on the other hand,
since the demagnetization term is absent, we would not expect to find this tendency. Domains in antiferromagnets
have, however, been observed. Under polarized light, a crystal of NiO in the form of a thin section (< 100 μm thick)
was observed to have a domain structure (Roth 1960). NiO
undergoes a contraction in the [111] direction on becoming
antiferromagnetic and this would be expected to cause stresses
in the crystal. It appears that the crystal can relieve
this stress by breaking up into domains in which each displays its contraction along one of the [111] axes. It is
also possible that in some instances the domains are formed
for kinetic reasons during the crystal formation and are
thereafter stabilized by pinning of the domain walls at defects.

In all that follows it will be assumed that $\mathcal{H}$ is $\mathcal{H}_{int}$
and that single-domain crystals are being studied.

12.3. BASIC MAGNETIC MODELS

Most of the features of the substances we shall be concerned
with can be explained qualitatively by mean-field theories
(section 3.1.2). These have, however, the deficiency that
they do not take proper account of short-range order. Since
the energy of the system, and hence also the heat capacity,
is strongly dependent upon the interactions between near
neighbours it is not surprising that the predicted values
of the magnetic contribution to the heat capacity in zero

magnetic field $(c_{\mathcal{H}=0}^m)^{\dagger}$ can be quite seriously in error.
For example, mean-field theories predict a finite discon-
tinuity in the c^m against T curve at the critical point,
instead of the infinite divergence which is often observed.
To apply mean-field theories to antiferromagnets it is
necessary to break the lattice down into sublattices, such
that in the ordered state all the spins on the same sublattice are similarly orientated. This is normally done
after observation of the actual ordered state, and so the
theory is in this sense empirical. The mean-field principle is then applied to each sublattice in that, in calculating the field at a point, the s_i for all spins on a sublattice are replaced by the mean value for that sublattice.
Calculations of this type can be carried through to completion even for substances requiring many sublattices, and
it is for these complicated systems that the mean-field
method is retained.

For simple systems of one or two sublattices the more
realistic Ising and Heisenberg models (and hybrids of these)
are used. The Ising model may be considered as the case of
extreme anisotropy in which only the spin component along
one direction is of importance; the Heisenberg model represents the other extreme, that of complete isotropy. In
zero field and for suitable ordering lattices the two sublattice antiferromagnet is entirely equivalent to the
ferromagnet for the Ising model, both yielding a divergence
in the heat capacity in two or three dimensions, though not
in one. By contrast, in the Heisenberg model the ferro- and
antiferromagnets in zero field are only equivalent in the
limit of $s \to \infty$. The Heisenberg ferromagnet with $s = 1/2$
shows a critical point below which there is long-range order
in three dimensions, though not in one or two. This raises
a general point when using the Heisenberg model to explain
the behaviour of some real layer systems, which may be
classed as pseudo-two-dimensional. If a critical point is
found for such a substance it may be attributed either to

$\dagger$Unless otherwise indicated we shall use the symbol c^m to denote the
magnetic contribution to C_p with the magnetic field held at zero.

the deviation from two-dimensional character, that is, to
the non-zero nature of the interactions in the third dimension, or alternatively to some anisotropy in the system
causing it to be partly Ising-like, the Ising model having
a transition in two dimensions.

12.4. SPIN WAVES

This approximate treatment of the Heisenberg model has not
been covered in Chapter 3 because it does not have the
general interest for order-disorder phenomena of the other
material dealt with there.

    Consider first a Heisenberg ferromagnet in its ground
state at 0 K, that is with all the spins aligned. Now proceed to an excited state by overturning a spin. Instead of
the excitation being localized at a particular spin it is
spread out over the whole array (Fig.12.1). This is

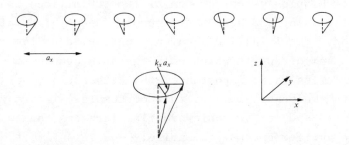

Fig.12.1. Equivalent semiclassical picture of a spin wave. Spins precess about the z direction.

represented by the eigenfunction, which is $\sum_j \exp(i\underline{k}.\underline{R}_j).\psi_j$,
where ψ_j is the eigenfunction for the state with the
overturned spin localized at the jth position, $\underline{R}_j$ is the
vector from the origin to the position of the jth spin,
and $\underline{k}$ is the wave-vector, which, because of boundary conditions, can only have components which satisfy relations of
the type:

$$k_x a_x N_x / 2\pi = 0, \pm 1, \pm 2, \ldots \ldots \quad \pm N_x / 2 \qquad (12.2)$$

where a_x is the spin spacing in the x direction and N_x is
the total number of spins in the x direction. From an
examination of the eigenfunction it is clear that the phase
changes regularly as one proceeds along a line in the spin
lattice. It is this which confers the wave nature upon the
excitation. For a system of cubic symmetry the energy of
the excited state is found to be $E_0 + 2J[q - \sum_{nn} \exp(i\underline{k}.\underline{r})]$,
where E_0 is the energy of the ground state, q is the number
of nearest neighbours (nn) which each spin has, and $\underline{r}$ is
the vector from a spin to a particular nn, and the summation
is over all nn of the particular spin. For small values of
k, the energy may be approximated by $E_0 + J \sum_{nn} (\underline{k}.\underline{r})^2$, from
which the quadratic dispersion relation $\nu = const.k$ is im-
mediately obtained. At a non-zero temperature the spin-wave
modes represented by the different allowed values of $\underline{k}$ will
be excited to various extents. In the simplest type of spin-
wave treatment, as put forward by Bloch (1930), it is assumed
that there are no interactions between the spin waves. This
assumption is most nearly valid at low temperatures, when
the density of excitations is very low. The error arising in
the predicted value of the magnetization from this assumption
is < 5% for s = 1/2 spins (and less still if s > 1/2) at
temperatures as high as $0 \cdot 5T_c$ (Dyson (1956). The above
dispersion relation leads to $c^m \propto T^{3/2}$. For a metallic
ferromagnet at low temperatures the electronic contribution
to C_p, which is $\propto T$, will become dominant. However, for insulators this problem does not arise and C_p measurements at
very low temperatures on substances such as yttrium iron
garnet and magnetite have been used to test spin-wave predictions. The quadratic dependence of ν on k has been independently confirmed by neutron scattering experiments on
cobalt (Sinclair and Brockhouse 1960) and subsequently on
other substances.

Dyson (1956) extended the temperature range of the
theory. He obtained for the heat capacity contribution:

$$c^m/R = b_0(kT/J)^{3/2} + b_1(kT/J)^{5/2} + b_2(kT/J)^{7/2} + b_3(kT/J)^4 + \cdots$$

$$(12.3)$$

where the second and third terms arise from the discreteness

of the lattice and the fourth term takes account of the interactions of the spin waves. A similar expression is obtained
for the spontaneous magnetization:

$$M_0(T)/M_0(0) = 1 - a_0(kT/J)^{3/2} - a_1(kT/J)^{5/2} - a_2(kT/J)^{7/2} - a_3(kT/J)^4.$$

$$(12.4)$$

The coefficients a_i and b_i are known numerical constants
dependent upon the lattice. For a two-dimensional system
the corresponding equations would each have a principal term
in T^1 instead of those in $T^{3/2}$ given in (12.3) and (12.4).

The spin-wave model for antiferromagnets shows a striking difference in behaviour in that the dispersion relation
for small k is $\nu = \text{const.}k$ (rather than k^2). This causes
the first-order contribution to C^m to be proportional to T^3.
Additional terms for C^m have also been obtained. Thus

$$C^m/R = b_0'(kT/J)^3 + b_1'(kT/J)^5 + b_2'(kT/J)^7 + b_3'(kT/J)^7 \quad ..(12.5)$$

(Oguchi 1960), where, again, the last term arises from the
spin-wave interactions, and the second and third terms are
corrections for deviation from the linear dispersion relation.

Even at 0 K there is a small amount of spin disorder,
which may be compared with the zero-point vibrational motion
in solids. Because of this the saturation value of the
sublattice magnetization in an antiferromagnet is less than
would be expected classically, when the completely ordered
spin system is permissible. The amount by which the saturation magnetization falls short of that to be expected for
complete alignment is known as the zero-point spin reduction ($\Delta s = s - s_z$). For the pseudo-two-dimensional antiferromagnet Rb_2MnF_4 it is ~7% of s, whereas for the rather
similar three-dimensional structure of $RbMnF_3$ it is only
~3% (Schrama 1973). These results illustrate a general observation, that the spin deviation is considerably greater
for two-dimensional than for three-dimensional systems. For
this reason recent attempts to check the applicability of
spin-wave theory by comparison of experimental and theoretical

values of Δs have concentrated on two-dimensional systems. Although Δs depends upon the anisotropy, it is not very sensitive to it (de Jongh and Miedema 1974). The expression for the sublattice magnetization to the same degree of approximation as (12.5) is then:

$$M_0(T)/M_0(0) = 1 - a_0'(kT/|J|)^2 - a_1'(kT/|J|)^4 - a_2'(kT/|J|)^6 - a_3'(kT/|J|)^6 ..$$

$$(12.6)$$

where $M_0(0)$ takes account of the spin reduction, and the correspondence with the terms in (12.5) is indicated by the subscripts on a' and b', e.g. terms involving a_2' and b_2' correspond.

Accepting the applicability of the spin-wave model, it is then possible by fitting equations (12.3) and (12.4) or (12.5) and (12.6) to data obtained well below the critical point to obtain a value of J, e.g. for $FeCl_2$ by Birgeneau, Yelon, Cohen, and Makovsky (1972). De Jongh and Miedema (1974) have, however, noted that values of J obtained by the application of spin-wave theory to c^m data are lower than those from high-temperature susceptibility data, the discrepancy being greater the lower the dimensionality and the spin number. Thus, for linear chains of $s = 1/2$ spins the spin-wave results are too large by a factor of about three. For a similar system of $s = 1$ spins this factor is found to be reduced to $1\cdot4$. $\chi_\perp{}^\dagger$ for antiferromagnetic Heisenberg chains, which is fairly well known from treatments such as that of Bonner and Fisher (1964), is wrongly predicted by spin-wave theory to diverge to infinity as $T \to 0$. For two-dimensional systems, spin-wave theory appears to give a fair account if $s > 1/2$, but the agreement for $s = 1/2$ is more doubtful.

$\dagger$ Prior to this section it has been assumed that χ is isotropic. In general this is not so, χ being a second-rank tensor linking the vectors $\underline{M}$ and $\underline{\mathcal{H}}$, i.e. $\underline{M} = \chi.\mathcal{H}$ It is found that the magnetization tends to lie along certain crystallographic axes, these being known as the 'easy' directions. The diagonal components of the tensor for the 'easiest' direction and for directions perpendicular to this are $\chi_\parallel$ and $\chi_\perp$, respectively.

A comprehensive account of spin-wave theory has been presented by Keffer (1966).

12.5. FERROMAGNETISM

When ferromagnetic materials in zero field go over to their paramagnetic form at the critical or Curie temperature (T_c) there is a complete loss of long-range magnetic order, although some short-range order will remain and will be lost more gradually as the temperature is raised further. Thermodynamically the Curie point can be recognized by the occurrence of singularities in both the heat capacity and the magnetic susceptibility. Above T_c, the heat capacity shows a considerable 'tail' corresponding to the slow loss of the residual short-range order. The susceptibility above T_c approximates to the Curie-Weiss Law, $\chi = C/(T+\Delta)$ or lost. $1/\chi = T/C + \Delta/C$. The spontaneous magnetization (M_0) falls to zero at T_c in a critical or second-order manner. However, in the presence of an applied field this transition is lost

Until about 1960 all ferromagnetic substances known were electronic conductors. Among the conducting ferromagnets are the transition elements Fe, Co, and Ni and the rare-earth metals Gd and Dy, although at low temperatures further rare-earth elements (Tb, Er, Ho, and Tm) also display ferromagnetism. Alloys containing these elements are ferromagnetic, as, indeed, are some substances containing, instead of the above, the elements Mn and Cr, which are adjacent to Fe in the Periodic Table. Thus, Mn with N, P, As, Sb, or Bi, and Cr with S, Te, and Pt, all yield conducting ferromagnets (Morrish 1965). There are also a large number of ferromagnetic substances to be found among the elements and compounds of the second and third transition series. Other ferromagnets not containing any of these elements include $ZrZn_2$ and Sc_3In (Rhodes and Wohlfarth 1963). Ferromagnetic insulators, several of which will be discussed in detail below, include $GdCl_3$, $CrBr_3$, $K_2CuCl_4 \cdot 2H_2O$ and several divalent europium compounds (EuO, EuS, EuI_2, and Eu_2SiO_4) (McGuire and Shafer 1964).

12.6. ANTIFERROMAGNETISM

Among insulators antiferromagnets are far more widespread
than ferromagnets, but they are also somewhat more difficult to recognize by magnetic measurements. In zero field
the heat capacity *versus* temperature curve is similar to that
for ferromagnets, the singularity occurring at the Néel
temperature (T_N). χ, however, does not show a singularity,
but only a maximum at a temperature (T_χ) which is higher
than T_N by an amount which depends upon the crystal structure,
and particularly on the dimensionality (Fig.12.2). According

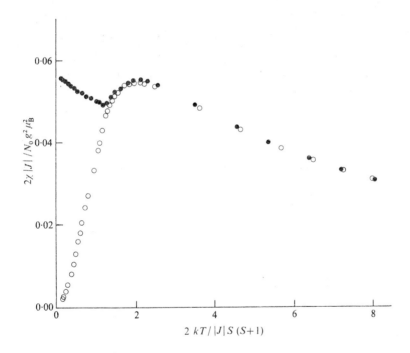

Fig.12.2. Parallel (o) and perpendicular (•) susceptibilities of K_2MnF_4
against temperature. Axes are in reduced units. J = coupling parameter
within layers; $s = 5/2$ (after de Jongh and Miedema 1974).

to the Ising model $T_\chi/T_N \approx 1 \cdot 08$ and $\approx 1 \cdot 5$ for three- and two-
dimensional systems, respectively, and this is in fair
agreement with the experimental observations, e.g. MnF_2(3D),
$1 \cdot 05$ and $KFeF_4$(2D), $1 \cdot 61$ (Heger, Geller, and Babel 1971).

Below T_N the χ *versus* T curve splits into two, $\chi_\perp$ remaining
very roughly constant at a value determined by the coupling
constant between the two sublattices, and $\chi_\parallel$ falling rapidly
towards zero.   Fisher (1962) (see also Skalyo, Cohen, Friedberg, and Griffiths 1967) has argued in favour of a relation
of the form $C^m = A(\partial \chi_\parallel T / \partial T)$, where A is a slowly varying
function of T near T_N.   This suggests that T_N should be
marked by a maximum in $(\partial \chi_\parallel / \partial T)$.   For the Ising model it is,
indeed, known that the latter quantity is infinite at T_N.
In discussing antiferromagnets a useful quantity to define
is the staggered susceptibility (χ'), which corresponds to
the ordinary susceptibility for a ferromagnet.   It is defined
as $(\partial M' / \partial \mathcal{H}')_T$ where M' is the magnetization of one sublattice
when the substance is subjected to a field of magnitude $\mathcal{H}'$
which alternates in sign from site to site. χ' may be determined from the observed magnetic fluctuations in the sublattice magnetization as obtained by neutron scattering. In
a large magnetic field parallel to the 'easy' axis antiferromagnets often go over to a 'spin-flop' phase in which
the spins lie in the plane perpendicular to the applied field
(Fig.12.3).   The existence of such a transition is dependent

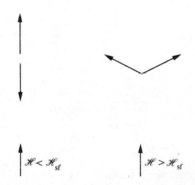

Fig.12.3. Spin orientations in the antiferromagnetic ($\mathcal{H} < \mathcal{H}_{sf}$) and spin-
flop ($\mathcal{H} > \mathcal{H}_{sf}$) phases.

upon there being a crystalline anisotropy which is not too
large, and indeed it furnishes a method of determining this
anisotropy.   The crystalline anisotropy energy (K) is defined

as the work required to make the moments lie along a particular direction rather than along the 'easiest' direction.
If a small field is applied parallel to the 'easy' axis the
spins will remain parallel to that axis (and antiparallel
to each other). On increasing the field beyond a critical
value ($\mathcal{H}_{sf}$) the moments will suddenly switch in a first-
order transition to the plane perpendicular to the field
because $\chi_\perp > \chi_\parallel$ (Fig.12.4). At this critical condition:

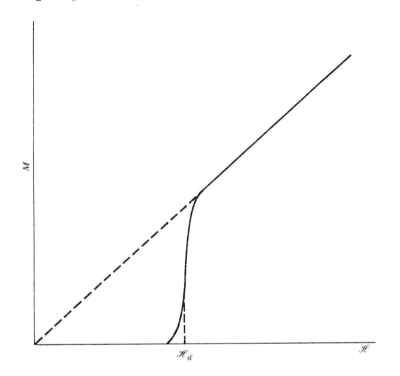

Fig.12.4. M-$\mathcal{H}$ isotherm showing the spin-flop transition.

$$-\tfrac{1}{2}\,\chi_\parallel \mathcal{H}_{sf}^2 = K - \tfrac{1}{2}\,\chi_\perp \mathcal{H}_{sf}^2 \qquad (12.7)$$

or
$$\mathcal{H}_{sf} = [2K/(\chi_\perp - \chi_\parallel)]^{1/2} \qquad (12.8)$$

Fig.12.4 is a plot of M against internal field ($\mathcal{H}_{int}$); if,
however, the applied field $\mathcal{H}_a$ is used as the abscissa then, instead of the discontinuity in M, there is a region in which

M rises steeply and linearly with $\mathcal{H}_a$. Examples of substances
in which 'spin-flopping' has been observed are $CuCl_2.2H_2O$
($T = 1 \cdot 51$ K, $\mathcal{H}_{sf} \approx 6 \cdot 5$ kOe ; $T_N = 4 \cdot 3$ K) (C.J.Gorter 1953),
MnF_2(4K, 93 kOe; $T_N = 67 \cdot 34$ K) (Jacobs 1961) and $MnCl_2.4H_2O$
($1 \cdot 25$ K, $7 \cdot 5$ kOe; $T_N = 1 \cdot 62$ K) (Rives and Benedict 1975)[†].
Fig.12.5 shows part of the $\mathcal{H}\text{-}T$ phase diagram for MnF_2

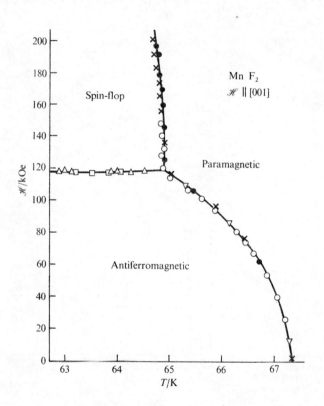

Fig.12.5. $\mathcal{H}\text{-}T$ phase diagram for MnF_2 (from Shapira and Foner 1970).

(Shapira and Foner 1970). The point at which the three
phases coexist has been called the bicritical point and the
theory of such points has been discussed by Fisher and
Nelson (1974), who have also drawn an analogy between 'spin-

[†] Throughout this chapter magnetic field strengths are given in oersteds,
the c.g.s. unit. This unit is related to the corresponding S.I. unit
(Am^{-1}) by the equation: 1 Oe = $10^3/4\pi$ Am^{-1}.

flop' and superfluid phases. At still higher fields the
'spin flop' phase gives way to the paramagnetic phase in
what is believed to be a second-order transition.

12.6.1. Metamagnetism

There exist a number of layer compounds, such as $FeCl_2$ and
$CoBr_2$, which have strong ferromagnetic interactions within
the layers and much weaker antiferromagnetic interactions
between them. In zero applied field the stable state will
be the antiferromagnetic one provided that the temperature
is less than the critical value. However, fairly small
applied fields are able to overturn the moments of some
of the layers giving a state with a large overall magnetization which is said to be metamagnetic. This behaviour is
well illustrated by the M-T and $\mathcal{H}$-T diagrams of Fig.12.6.
For $T^* > T > T_N$, where T^* is the tricritical temperature
(section 2.6), an internal field of value given by the
line tT_N (Fig.12.6b) is associated with a gradual transition,
the (net) magnetization being given by the corresponding
point on the line tT_N of Fig.12.6(a). For $T < T^*$ there is
a first-order transition when the field lies on the line Dt
of Fig.12.6(b), the (net) magnetization of the two coexisting
phases being given by the extremities of the tie-line drawn
through the two-phase region of Fig.12.6(a). These magnetization values correspond to the quantities M_{dis} and M_{ord}
which are discussed in the mean-field approximation in
equation (2.25). It is not surprising that the first-order
region is subject to hysteresis, as has been shown for
$FeCl_2$ by Jacobs and Lawrence (1967).

A fairly successful simulation of magnetic tricritical
behaviour has been achieved by Landau (1972). Two arrays
were examined, one being 50×50 simple quadratic and the
other $12 \times 12 \times 12$ simple cubic. In each system the interactions were supposed to be weak and antiferromagnetic in one
direction and strong and ferromagnetic in the remaining
directions. Phase diagrams of approximately the correct
form (as Fig.12.6a) were found and the tricritical exponent
(β_u) describing the disappearance of the two-phase region

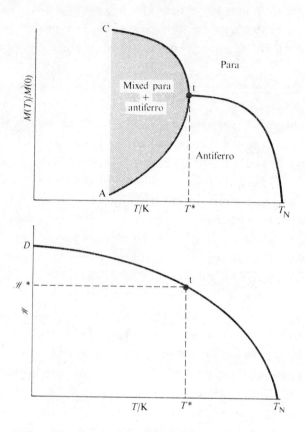

Fig.12.6. Metamagnetism. (a) Magnetization $[M(T)/M(0)]$ against tempera-
ture (T); (b) internal field $(\mathcal{H})$ against T. $(T*,\mathcal{H}*)$ is the tricritical
point.

at the tricritical point $[\Delta(M/M_s) \sim R(1-T/T*)^{\beta}u$, where
M_s = saturation magnetization and R is a constant] was found
to take the values $0\cdot58$ and $0\cdot78$ for the simple quadratic and
the simple cubic lattices, respectively. For $T > T*$ and a
path of constant $M = M*$, the susceptibility was found to
diverge like $\chi(M = M*) \sim (T/T*-1)^{-\gamma}u$ with $\gamma_u = 0\cdot53$ and $0\cdot29$
for, again, the quadratic and the simple cubic arrays.

12.7. FERRIMAGNETISM

The simplest case of an antiferromagnet is one with two
sublattices having equal but opposite magnetizations. If
the magnetizations are opposite in direction but not equal

in magnitude then we have the simplest kind of ferrimagnet.
The first substances found with this property were some
of the spinels (section 12.13). Ferrimagnets with three
or more sublattices are also known, e.g. some garnets
(section 12.13.1).

Because the magnetizations of the individual sublattices
may fall with increase of temperature at different rates the
resultant magnetization can show a variety of different types
of temperature variation (Fig.12.7). It will be noted that

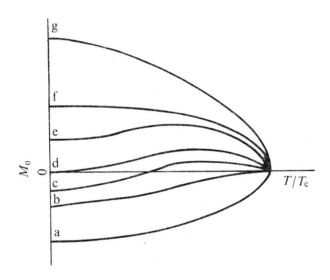

Fig.12.7. Possible patterns for resultant spontaneous magnetization (M_0)
against temperature for a simple two sublattice ferrimagnet
$[Fe_{x_A}M_{1-x_A}]_A[Fe_{x_B}M_{1-x_B}]_B$. The ratio (x_A/x_B) of magnetic ions on A and B
sites is varied monotonically (curves a to g) whilst keeping the interaction parameters constant (after E.W.Gorter 1955).

under some conditions there is a temperature, the compensation temperature (T_{comp}), at which the opposing sublattice
magnetizations are equal in magnitude, leading to zero resultant magnetization. Fig.12.8 shows the variation in sublattice magnetization with temperature for gadolinium iron
garnet, considered as a three sublattice system.

Whereas for an antiferromagnet, cooling through the
transition temperature is marked by the appearance in the
neutron diffraction pattern of 'extra' magnetic spots,

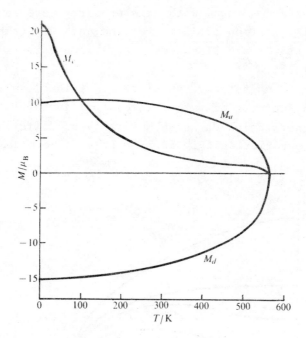

Fig.12.8. Temperature variation of the spontaneous magnetization of the sublattices of gadolinium iron garnet considered as a three sublattice (a,c,d) mean-field system. Magnetization is expressed in Bohr magnetons per single $Gd_3Fe_5O_{12}$ unit (after Morrish 1965).

the same is not true for ferrimagnets. In the latter the different types of site are inequivalent even in the disordered form, so that it is necessary to utilize the changes in the intensities of the various reflections.

Several mean-field treatments have been carried out which predict qualitatively, and to some extent quantitatively, the behaviour of a ferrimagnet in a magnetic field, the first of these being by Néel (1948). When the sublattice magnetizations are permitted to be non-collinear with each other and with the applied field then interesting $\mathcal{H}$-T phase diagrams are predicted. In the absence of crystalline anisotropy Clark and Callen (1968) obtained for the two sublattice system representing a rare-earth iron garnet (section 12.13.1) the phase diagrams shown in Fig.12.9(a) or (b) according to whether at 0 K the sublattice magnetization of the rare earth (M_R) was greater or less than that of the

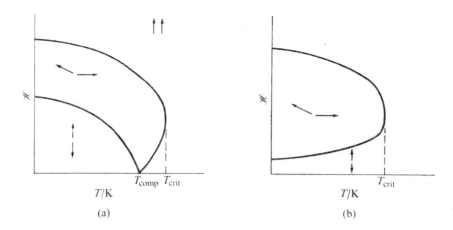

Fig.12.9. Theoretical $\mathcal{H}$-T phase diagrams for rare-earth iron garnets considered as two sublattice ferrimagnets. (a) $M_R(0 \text{ K}) > M_{Fe}(0 \text{ K})$; (b) $M_R(0 \text{ K}) < M_{Fe}(0 \text{ K})$.

iron (M_{Fe}). Fig.12.9(b) may be regarded as being derived from Fig.12.9(a) by truncating the latter at a value of $T > T_{comp}$. Yablonskii (1973) has derived similar phase diagrams by a somewhat different approach. He has observed that no second-order transition would be expected on crossing the $M = 0$ line because no symmetry change is involved. The existence of a field-induced phase with non-collinear spins is reminiscent of the spin-flop phase of antiferromagnets (section 12.6). In order to reach many parts of the calculated phase diagram very large fields indeed would be required. For this reason it is usually only the region near the compensation temperature, where the fields required to cause a transition are arbitrarily small, which is examined experimentally. Further discussion of this topic is presented in the section on garnets (section 12.13.1).

12.8. 'WEAK FERROMAGNETISM'

This is a modification of simple antiferromagnetism which can arise if the magnetizations of the two sublattices are equal in magnitude and nearly, but not quite, opposite in direction. A canted arrangement of the spins (Fig.12.10a)

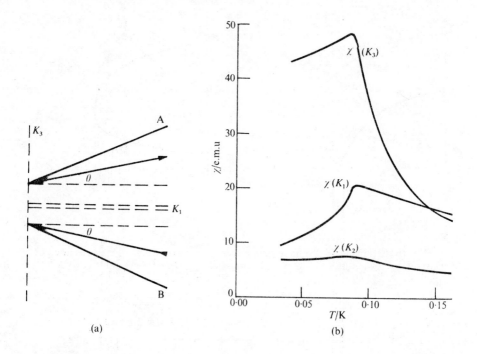

Fig.12.10. (a) Spin-canting due to crystalline anisotropy. K_1 = magnetically 'easy' direction. A and B are the directions preferred by
the crystalline anisotropy for spins on the two sublattices, and the
arrows are the corresponding resultant spin orientations. The direction of the 'weak ferromagnetism' is along K_3, perpendicular to K_1
(after Domb and Miedema 1964). (b) Temperature variation of the susceptibility of $(NH_4)_2Co(SO_4)_2.6H_2O$ along the three crystal axes
(after Garrett 1951).

results in a cancellation of the large horizontal components,
leaving a small magnetization (a ferromagnetism) in the vertical direction. Crystals containing such arrangements of
spins appear to be antiferro- or ferromagnetic according to
their orientation in susceptibility experiments. Fig.12.10(b)
shows the **results** of χ versus T measurements taken
along three different directions in cobalt ammonium Tutton
salt, $(NH_4)_2Co(SO_4)_2.6H_2O$, K_1 being the 'easiest' direction
(Garrett 1951). The results for K_1 and K_2 are typical of
antiferromagnets, whilst the very steep rise found for the
K_3 direction is indicative of ferromagnetic behaviour. In
this salt the spin-spin forces are tending to align the

spins with antiparallel orientations, but this is opposed
by the anisotropy which tends to align spins which are on
different sublattices in different directions (A and B).
The outcome of these conflicting tendencies is that there
is a non-zero canting angle (θ), which for this particular
salt has the large value of 23°. In similar fashion,
$Fe_3(PO_4)_2.4H_2O$ (ludlamite) (Meijer, Adair, and van den
Handel 1968) shows a large 'weak ferromagnetism' below
15·3 K, the value of the saturation magnetization at 0 K
pointing to a canting angle of ~11° out of the ac plane.

Other substances displaying 'weak ferromagnetism' include NiF_2, $MnCO_3$, $CoCO_3$, $KMnF_3$, α-Fe_2O_3, and
$Mn(CH_3COO)_2.4H_2O$. The magnetization is here much weaker
than in the case of the Tutton salts, being only about
10^{-2}-10^{-5} times the value which would be obtained for full
ferromagnetic alignment. Moriya (1960, 1963) has discussed
these systems and has suggested that anisotropic superexchange, rather than crystalline anisotropy, is responsible
for the canting in many of these substances ($MnCO_3$, $CoCO_3$,
α-Fe_2O_3, CrF_3).

12.9. HELICAL SPIN ARRANGEMENTS
These are again classed as modifications of antiferromagnetism
because there is a cancellation of magnetization. Examples
are the rare-earth elements Tb, Dy, and Ho, which in their
intermediate temperature forms have the close-packed hexagonal structure with the magnetic moments lying within the
layers and ordered ferromagnetically within them. On proceeding along the c axis the direction of the moments is
rotated (Fig.12.11). Spinels (section 12.13.1) with interactions between spins on B sites often have ground states
with helical spin arrangements. Other examples include the
electronic conductors MnP, Mn_3Sn, and CrAs, and the insulators $MnSO_4$, $FeCl_3$, and MnI_2.

Nagamiya (1967) has shown that it is necessary for
there to be non-zero interactions between other than nn
spins for a helical arrangement to be stable. For the
ground state of a substance having a layer lattice with
interlayer spacing c, he considers the possibility of a

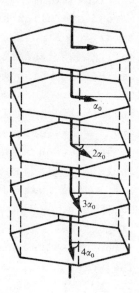

Fig.12.11. Orientation of the spins in successive layers of a helical arrangement (from Enz 1961).

helical arrangement with the axis perpendicular to the layers and with wave vector $\underline{q}$ (Fig.12.12). J_0 is the sum

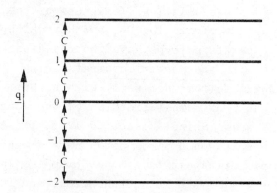

Fig.12.12. Spacing and numbering of layers in Nagamiya's theory; $\underline{q}$ is the propagation vector.

of the J_0 values for all interactions between a chosen spin and all other spins in its own layer; likewise J_1 and J_2

are sums referring to interactions with all spins in a neighbouring and a next-neighbouring layer, respectively. The
total interaction for the spin is then
$J_{tot} = J_0 + 2J_1\cos(cq) + 2J_2\cos(2cq)$. The maximum interaction energy is then given by the equation:

$$0 = dJ_{tot}/dq = -2c\{J_1 + 4J_2\cos(cq)\}\sin(cq) . \qquad (12.9)$$

Apart from solutions arising from $\sin(cq) = 0$, namely $q = 0$
(ferromagnetic) and $q = \pi/c$ (antiferromagnetic), there is
the helical solution, $\cos(cq) = -J_1/4J_2$. This is the stable
form provided $J_2 < 0$ and $|J_1| < |4J_2|$.

12.10. TRIANGULAR SPIN ARRANGEMENTS
A possible variant of ferrimagnetism in which the spins are
non-collinear is shown in Fig.12.13 (Yafet and Kittel 1952).

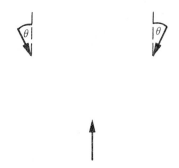

Fig.12.13. Triangular spin arrangement.

If $\theta = \pi/3$ the resultant moment is zero and the substance
is an antiferromagnet; for other angles there is a non-zero
resultant moment. In terms of a mean-field model it is
easily shown that the most stable configuration is given by:

$$\cos\theta = -N_{AB}/2N_{BB} \qquad \text{if } N_{AB} < 2N_{BB}$$

$$\qquad\qquad\qquad\qquad\qquad\qquad\qquad\qquad (12.10)$$

$$\text{or} \qquad\qquad \theta = 0 \qquad\qquad \text{if } N_{AB} < 2N_{BB}$$

where N_{AB} and N_{BB} are the values of the molecular-field
constants at the B sites due to the A and B spins, respectively.

Kaplan, Dwight, Lyons, and Menyuk (1961, 1962) have
concluded that any spinel system with a non-collinear magnetic ground state must pass through two stages of disordering. In the first of these it would transform into a
collinear state and in the second it would become paramagnetic.

$KFe_3(OH)_6(SO_4)_2$ is believed to be an example of a substance showing the triangular spin arrangement (section
12.13.5).

12.11. ORIENTATIONAL FORCES BETWEEN SPINS

12.11.1. Isotropic exchange

Heisenberg (1928) showed that strong ferromagnetic interactions could arise from quantum-mechanical exchange provided that the magnetic ions are fairly close together,
as they are in all real ferromagnets. If, however, the
atoms are too close together spin pairing, giving an antiferromagnetic interaction, occurs. The strength and,
indeed, the existence of a ferromagnetic interaction is
very sensitive to this interatomic distance. Heisenberg
concluded that the possible energies of a simple two-
electron exchange system are the eigenvalues of the operator
$(K - J_{12} - 4J_{12}\underline{s}_1 \cdot \underline{s}_2)$. Usually only the spin-dependent part of
this operator is considered, and it is written as
$-4J_{12}\,\underline{s}_1 \cdot \underline{s}_2$. In practice, a Hamiltonian of the latter type
is employed with J_{12} being treated as an adjustable para-
meter.

12.11.2. Superexchange

The weaker, superexchange interactions, which are the main
cause of the large number of antiferromagnetic substances
found in nature, were first explained by Kramers (1934)
(see also Anderson 1950) as being due to the participation
of excited states in which there is a transfer of charge
involving an intermediate diamagnetic ion. In the case
of the three-ion system $(Mn^{2+})_1 - - - O^{2-} - - - (Mn^{2+})_2$, Anderson

has set this out as follows. Consider four electrons, one from each of the Mn^{2+} ions and two from the O^{2-} ion. The ground orbital states with spin singlet or triplet are then as in the following scheme:

electron no.	1	2	3	4
on ion	$(Mn^{2+})_1$	O^{2-}	O^{2-}	$(Mn^{2+})_2$
in orbital	d_1	p	p	d_2
singlet	↑	↓	↑	↓
triplet	↑	↓	↑	↑

In the excited state at least one of the electrons from the oxygen atom is transferred to an s or d orbital on one of the Mn^{2+} ions. The Mn orbital into which the electron jumps must be fairly strongly coupled with the d orbital already occupied for there to be a superexchange interaction. We then have for the excited state:

electron no.	1	2	3	4
on ion	$(Mn^{2+})_1$	$(Mn^{2+})_1$	O^{2-}	$(Mn^{2+})_2$
in orbital	d_1	s_1	p	d_2
singlet	↑	↓	↑	↓
triplet	↑	↓	↑	↑

That part of the Hamiltonian causing transitions between the ground and excited orbital states will not mix the singlet and triplet states. Therefore, if the singlet and triplet wave functions are each written as $\psi^{s/t} = a\psi^{s/t}_{ground} + b\psi^{s/t}_{excited}$, $\psi^{s/t}$ being normalized, then the singlet-triplet splitting will be given as:

$$\Delta E_{s-t} = b^2 \, \Delta E^{excited}_{s-t} \tag{12.11}$$

That is, ΔE_{s-t} will be of the order of a normal exchange coupling $(\Delta E^{excited}_{s-t})$ but reduced by the factor b^2. This is in accord with the observation that Néel temperatures tend to be lower than Curie temperatures. There are, neverthe-less, a number of substances having high Néel temperatures, such as α-Fe_2O_3(953 K), NiO(523 K), and $Ca_2Fe_2O_5$(725 K).

A very important feature which comes out of this treatment of superexchange is the importance of the angle sub-
tended at the central ion by the two magnetic ions. The
above discussion refers to the 180° arrangement. Had the
angle been 90° the situation would have been quite different.
The two electrons on the oxygen atom would then have been in
different p orbitals in order to obtain overlap with the
respective magnetic ions, and it would then not have been
necessary for their spins to be antiparallel. Superexchange
in which the angle is 90° will therefore be much weaker than
that with an angle of 180°. This is important in MnO, for
which the strong interactions are found to be between the
nnn Mn^{2+} ions, which form a 180° arrangement with an O^{2-}
ion, rather than with the nn Mn^{2+} ions, which interact via
a 90° arrangement.

12.11.3. *Double exchange (Zener 1951)*
A related type of interaction can occur if the two magnetic
ions are in different valency states. Tbus if the ions
involved are Mn^{3+}---O^{2-}---Mn^{4+}, and each is assumed to be
in the spin state of maximum multiplicity, then only if the
moments are parallel will exchange to the corresponding
state, Mn^{4+}---O^{2-}---Mn^{3+}, be possible. This interaction
favouring ferromagnetic alignment is known as double exchange. It should be emphasized that this mechanism involves only the ground states of the ions; superexchange, in
contrast, utilizes excited states.

12.11.4. *Anisotropic exchange*
The exchange interactions which have been discussed may be
dependent upon the direction of the interspin vector with
respect to the quantization direction. The interaction
energy term can then have the same angular form as the
classical dipole-dipole term, although it is a true exchange
term, and it is then often called a pseudo-dipolar term.
Van Vleck (1937) showed that this term arose from the directional interaction of the atomic orbitals, which were themselves coupled to their respective magnetic spins. For a
pair of interacting atoms the leading term is found from

second-order perturbation theory to be proportional to the
square of the spin-orbit coupling constant. (Van Vleck was
concerned with cubic crystals, for which the leading term in
the *resultant* of these interactions for the whole system was
one encountered only in the fourth-order perturbation theory.)
Because of its exchange origin it is a short-range interaction and in this respect differs from the true dipole-dipole
term.

12.11.5. *Dipole-dipole forces*

These are the classical interactions which would be expected
for pairs of magnetic dipoles. The dipoles concerned are the
total dipoles, both orbital and spin contributions being
taken into account. The angular dependence of the interaction is as in section 12.11.4, but the fall-off with distance is much slower ($\propto r_{ij}^{-3}$) than for the exchange interaction described there. Since these interactions are relatively weak their effects are usually evident only at very
low temperatures. However, where they are important, as
in some rare-earth compounds, e.g. $GdCl_3, Dy(C_2H_5SO_4)_2 \cdot 9H_2O$,
their long-range character may influence the nature of any
magnetic ordering transition.

A detailed discussion of spin interaction energies,
dealing both with the cases where the orbital angular momentum is and is not quenched has been given by Baker (1971).
However, it is worth noting here that quenching leads to
the exchange interaction being isotropic (as in Mn^{2+}); where
the orbital angular momentum is incompletely quenched the
exchange interaction is anisotropic (as in Co^{2+}). Thus,
among the examples discussed later, it will be found that
Mn^{2+} and Co^{2+} compounds of the same kind show Heisenberg-
and Ising-type behaviour, respectively.

12.12. COOPERATIVE JAHN-TELLER EFFECTS

These have been included here, although they are not magnetic transitions, because they occur in the compounds
of the transition and rare-earth metals which are also
of interest magnetically. It is convenient, therefore,
to include them in this chapter.

According to the Jahn-Teller theorem, when the ground electronic state of an ion has degeneracy other than the Kramers degeneracy then a distortion of the environment of the ion will occur so as to remove that degeneracy. In the case of an ion in a crystal, the extent of the distortion is determined by the balance between the elastic forces of the crystal opposing the change and the lowering in electronic energy resulting from the splitting of the previously degenerate levels. For an octahedral environment the Jahn-Teller splitting of the two e_g states, which lie above the t_{2g} states as a result of the octahedral crystal field, is greater than the corresponding splitting of the three t_{2g} states (Fig.12.14a). This being so, the greatest electronic advantage arises if the 'distorting' ion has either one or three e_g electrons and adopts the high-spin form. Ions satisfying these requirements include Cr^{2+}, Mn^{3+}, and Cu^{2+}.

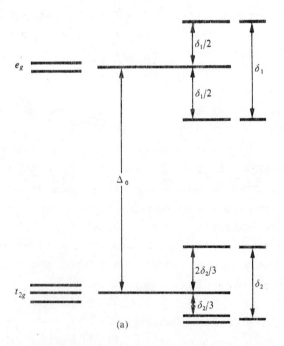

(a)

Fig.12.14(a). The splitting of the d orbitals by an octahedral crystal field (Δ_0) and the further splitting (δ_1 and δ_2) by a Jahn-Teller distortion. The diagram is not to scale: relative to Δ_0, δ_1 and δ_2 are smaller than shown (from Cotton and Wilkinson 1972).

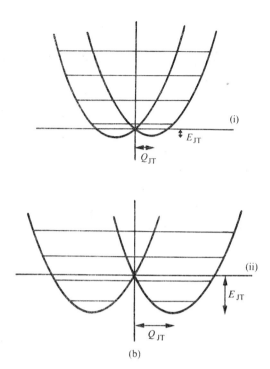

Fig.12.14(b). Energy levels in a system undergoing Jahn-Teller distortion. E_{JT} = Jahn-Teller energy; Q_{JT} = the distortion. (i) Weak coupling case: $E_{JT} < h\nu/2$; (ii) strong coupling case: $E_{JT} > h\nu/2$ (from Elliott, Gehring, Malozemoff, Smith, Staude, and Tyte 1971).

At low temperatures it may be expected that the distortions of the individual cells would be aligned, but that with rise of temperature the correlation between the directions of the distortions would tend to disappear. Because of the cooperative nature of the process the disappearance of the long-range order of the distortions occurs in a manner similar to that of magnetic transitions. Where the 'distorting' ion is that of a transition element, the interaction of the unpaired spins of the ion with the lattice is large and the Jahn-Teller energy, the lowering in energy produced by the distortion, is correspondingly large (Fig.12.14b). The zero-point energy of the ion is small compared with this Jahn-Teller energy, and a permanent distortion (often called the static Jahn-Teller effect) is observed. The corresponding disordering temperatures (T_D) are often of the order of 1 000 K.

Substances containing rare-earth 'distorting' ions
present quite a different picture. Since the relevant
electrons interact only weakly with the lattice the Jahn-
Teller energy is small. Indeed it will normally be less
than the zero-point energy, and it was for some time thought
that no Jahn-Teller effect would therefore be found. This
has been shown to be wrong by studies on rare-earth compounds having the zircon structure (section 12.13.1), many
of which show Jahn-Teller transitions at temperatures of
the order of 10 K.

The first successful theoretical treatment of cooperative Jahn-Teller effects was by Wojtowicz (1959) for the
transitions of spinels such as Mn_3O_4 (T_D = 1445 K, c/a = 1·16
at room temperature) and $CuFe_2O_4$ (T_D = 633 K, c/a = 1·06 at
room temperature). These spinels have the 'distorting'
cations (Mn^{3+} and Cu^{2+}, respectively) only in the octahedral (B) sites, the copper ferrite being an inverse spinel
(section 12.13.1). Each B site has six nn B sites, with
each of which it shares two O^{2-} ions, or alternatively, it
could be said that each octahedron shares one edge with
each neighbouring octahedron (Fig.12.15). The axis which

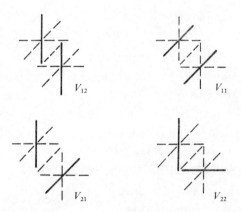

Fig.12.15. Possible juxtapositions of adjacent distorted octahedra. Full
line indicates the elongated axis of each octahedron. Adjacent octahedra share a common edge (from Wojtowicz 1959).

increases in length is indicated by a full line, and it can
be seen that there are four situations with each of which a
characteristic energy could be expected to be associated.
Wojtowicz assumed that the order of increasing energies was
$V_{12} < V_{11} \lessapprox V_{22} < V_{21}$, and was thereby able to obtain qualitative agreement with experiment. Other workers have, how-
ever, disputed the correctness of the order of energies used
(Novak 1969, Englman and Halperin 1970).

Wojtowicz's treatment took no account of the motion
of the ion in its cell. Subsequent workers have corrected
for this by including the kinetic energy of the ion and
treating its motion quantum-mechanically. Englman and Halperin (1970, 1971) have carried out such treatments for
spinels and perovskites, the latter having transition temperatures of the order of 300 K. This procedure yielded
transition temperatures lower by a factor of about one-half
than those from Wojtowicz's model, but did not alter the
predictions qualitatively. An account of the experimental
and theoretical work on the rare-earth zircons is given in
section 12.13.1. A comprehensive review of this topic
has been presented by G.A.Gehring and K.A.Gehring (1975).

12.13. SPECIFIC SYSTEMS
12.13.1. *Three-dimensional systems*
MnO. This compound is antiferromagnetic below T_N = 122 K.
The chemical structure is the same as that of NaCl; the magnetic structure of the ordered form, which has been determined by neutron diffraction, is more complicated (Fig.12.16).
The dimensions of the magnetic unit cell are twice those
of the chemical unit cell in each of the three directions. The moments are ordered ferromagnetically within
the (111) plane and it appears that the spin directions lie
within the same plane. Each (111) plane is antiferromagnetically ordered with respect to the adjacent (111) planes.
The magnetic transition has a large first-order component,
the order parameter dropping from 60% of its 0 K value to
zero at T_N. However, application of a 5 kbar stress in the
[111] direction causes the transition to become continuous,
this effect recalling the effect of pressure on NH_4Cl

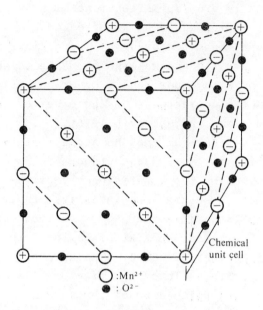

Fig.12.16. Magnetic unit cell of ordered MnO; (111) planes of Mn^{2+} ions
are indicated by broken lines; +, - indicate the two possible directions
of the spins, which are believed to lie in the (111) planes (from
Morrish 1965).

(section 7.5.1) (D. Bloch, Hermann-Ronzaud, Vettier, Yelon,
and Alben 1975).

    NiO, CoO, FeO, MnS, and MnSe have the same magnetic
structure, with the exception that it is probable that in
NiO, and perhaps also in FeO, the moments lie in the
[111] direction, that is, perpendicular to the ferromagnetic
(111) sheets. FeO is also somewhat rhombohedrally distorted
(Roth 1958, Lines and Jones 1965, Michel, Poix, and Bernier
1970).

MnF_2. This has the rutile, body-centred tetragonal structure
(Fig.12.17) and is antiferromagnetic below T_N = 67·34 K
(Heller 1966). The spins are directed along the c axis.
Each Mn^{2+} ion has two nn Mn^{2+} ions at ~0·32 nm and eight nnn
at ~0·36 nm. The latter interact more strongly with the
central spins and are found to be antiparallel to it in the
ordered state; the more weakly interacting nn spins are

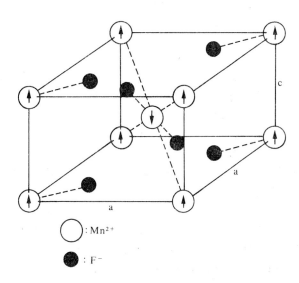

Fig.12.17. Unit cell of ordered MnF_2; o : Mn^{2+}; $\bullet$: F^- (from Erickson 1953).

parallel to the central ion.   This has already been discussed in section 12.11.2.

MnF$_2$ behaves as a good Heisenberg antiferromagnet,
yielding index values of $\beta = 0\cdot335$, $\gamma = 1\cdot27$, $\gamma' = 1\cdot32$,
$\nu = 0\cdot634$, and $\nu' = 0\cdot56$ (Schulhof, Nathans, Heller, and
Linz 1971).   Nevertheless, the anisotropy, which mostly
comes from the dipolar interactions, is much greater than
for RbMnF$_3$, another favoured Heisenberg antiferromagnet
(de Jongh and Miedema 1974).

FeF$_2$ (T_N = 78$\cdot$3 K), CoF$_2$ (T_N = 37$\cdot$7 K), and NiF$_2$
(T_N = 73$\cdot$5 K) have similar chemical and magnetic structures
to MnF$_2$, although in NiF$_2$ the spins lie in the basal plane
and are slightly canted (Richards 1963, 1964).   From C_p
measurements on FeF$_2$, the indices α and α' were both found
to be 0$\cdot$16, in fair agreement with predictions for the
three-dimensional Ising model and also with experimental
values from gas-liquid critical data (Ahlers, Kornblit, and
Salamon 1974).   However, for the same substance Hutchings,
Schulhof, and Guggenheim (1972) have obtained the indices

$\gamma = 1\cdot38$ and $\nu = 0\cdot67$, the former of which is more suggestive
of a three-dimensional Heisenberg system.

Europium chalcogenides (EuO, EuS, EuSe, EuTe). These all
have the NaCl structure. The interactions between nn Eu^{2+}
ions ($\varepsilon = 7/2$) (along face diagonals) and nnn ions (along
a cube side) are, in general, comparable in size. An analysis of C_p and M data for EuO suggested that these interactions
are opposite in sign, the former being ferro- and the latter
antiferromagnetic. However, neutron scattering experiments
on EuO (Passell, Dietrich, and Als-Nielsen, unpublished work
reported in de Jongh and Miedema 1974) and further analysis
of the bulk data for that substance lead to the conclusion
that both interactions are ferromagnetic (Dietrich, Henderson,
and Meyer 1975). There is a gradual change in properties
on increasing the mass of the chalcogen: EuO and EuS are
ferromagnetic at low temperatures, EuSe shows a complicated
behaviour to be described below, and EuTe is antiferromagnetic. The magnetic structure of the latter is of the same
type as MnO: each Eu^{2+} ion is surrounded by six parallel and
six antiparallel nn spins and six antiparallel nnn spins.

The complexity of the behaviour of EuSe is well illus-
trated by its $\mathcal{H}\text{-}T$ phase diagram (Fig.12.18). Immediately
below $T_N = 4\cdot6$ K the stable state in zero field has ferromagnetic (111) layers which are stacked so that the moment
is reversed after every second layer, i.e. NNSSNN.. (Fischer,
Hälg, von Wartburg, Schwob, and Vogt 1969). As is common
with antiferromagnetic systems having ferromagnetic layers,
metamagnetism can be induced by the application of a small
field. A very similar phase, having NNSNNS.. stacking, and
which is therefore ferrimagnetic, is stable over a large
part of the $\mathcal{H}\text{-}T$ field. Below $1\cdot8$ K and in zero and low fields
the MnO structure [antiferro (II) in Fig.12.18] is adopted.

EuO and EuS have been well studied because they are
often considered to be good representations of three-dimensional Heisenberg ferromagnets. Evidence which apparently
contradicted this was reported by Kornblit, Ahlers, and
Buehler (1973), who found that within the range
$|1-T/T_c| < 2 \times 10^{-2}$ of $T_c = 77$ K, the critical indices α and

α' are both -0·04. However, an alternative treatment of the
same data has led to the values α = α' = -0·10 (Kornblit
and Ahlers 1975), which are more typical of Heisenberg
ferromagnets. The value γ = 1·396 obtained for EuO by Als-
Nielsen, Dietrich, Kunnmann, and Passell (1971) is also in
excellent agreement with the best theoretical value for the
Heisenberg system. For EuS, c^m is also found not to diverge
as $T \to T_c$ (= 16·426 K) from below, although there appears
to be a logarithmic divergence on approaching from above.
This deviation from the predictions of the Heisenberg model
has been attributed to the presence of a (non-isotropic)
dipolar contribution in addition to the usual isotropic exchange interactions (van der Hoeven, Teaney, and Moruzzi
1968).

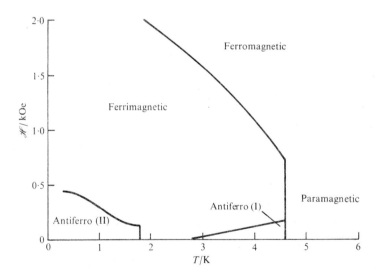

Fig.12.18. $\mathcal{H}$-T phase diagram of EuSe (after Griessen et al. 1971).

$M_2CuX_4 \cdot 2H_2O$, where M=K, Rb, Cs, or NH_4, and X = Br or Cl.
These compounds have been frequently studied because they
are considered to be good examples of Heisenberg ferromagnets. The crystal structure (Fig.12.19) is nearly body-
centred cubic, there being a tetragonal distortion such
that c/a = 1·05. Data for the transitions are collected

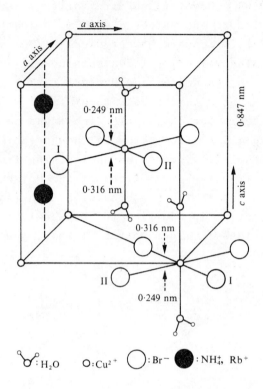

Fig.12.19. Crystal structure of $M_2CuBr_4.2H_2O$ (after Klaassen *et al.* 1972).

in Table 12.1. All of these compounds have transitions near
1 K.

Whilst a fall in J and hence in T_c as the crystal dimensions are enlarged is to be expected, this is not borne out
by these results. Thus the Rb-Cl salt has a higher Curie
point than the corresponding K-Cl salt although the former
has crystal dimensions which are about 5% larger. Again, the
ammonium salts have their T_c values in the inverse order to
that which would be expected.

Fig.12.20 shows c^m *versus* T/T_c for four of these salts.
The points fall on a common curve, supporting the suggestion
of the general simplicity of these systems (Miedema, Wielinga,
and Huiskamp 1965). Evidence for the Heisenberg nature of
the interactions comes from the fact that the c^m data for
temperatures up to $\sim 0\cdot 5T_c$ can be fitted to Dyson's formula
for spin waves with scattering (12.3) with only J as a

TABLE 12.1.

Transition temperatures and critical indices of the salts
$$M_2CuX_4 \cdot 2H_2O$$

M	X = Cl			X = Br			
	β	γ	T_c/K	β	γ	δ	T_c/K
K	-	$1\cdot36^a$	$0\cdot88^a$	-	-	-	-
Rb	$0\cdot35^b$	-	$1\cdot02^b$	-	-	-	$1\cdot876^d$ $1\cdot874^e$
Cs	$0\cdot35^b$	$1\cdot33^c$	$0\cdot75^b$, $0\cdot76^c$	-	-	-	-
NH$_4$	-	$1\cdot36^a$	$0\cdot70^a$	$0\cdot37^e$, $0\cdot38^f$, $0\cdot38^g$, $0\cdot34^j$	$1\cdot25^f$, $1\cdot31^h$, $1\cdot30^j$, $1\cdot33^k$	$3\cdot9^f$, $4\cdot3^g$	$1\cdot831^d$, $1\cdot836^e$, $1\cdot74^f$, $1\cdot828^g$, $1\cdot773^h$

a.   Miedema, van Kempen, and Huiskamp (1963).

b.   Klaassen, Gevers, Looyestijn, and Poulis (1973).

c.   Wielinga (1970).

d.   Velu, Renard, and Dupas (1972).

e.   Klaassen, Gevers, and Poulis (1972).

f.   Wielinga and Huiskamp (1969).

g.   Velu, Cadoul, Lécuyer, and Renard (1971).

h.   De Jongh, Miedema, and Wielinga (1970).

j.   Suzuki and Watanabe (1971).

k.   Cerdonio and Paroli (1970).

disposable parameter. Similar agreement with spin-wave
theory up to $\sim 0\cdot5\,T_c$ has been found for the NH$_4$-Br and
Rb-Br salts (Velu, Renard, and Dupas 1972). A comparison
of the effectiveness of the Heisenberg and Ising models
in representing the transition behaviour has been made by
Miedema, van Kempen, and Huiskamp (1963). They plotted

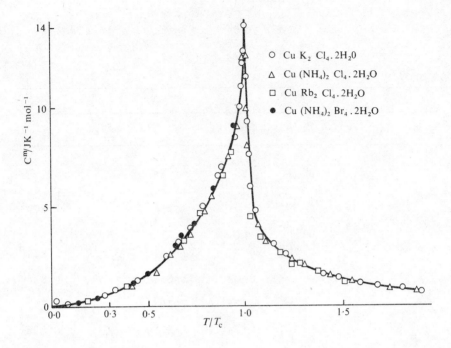

Fig.12.20. C^m against T/T_c for four salts of general formula $M_2CuX_4.2H_2O$ (from Miedema *et al.* 1965).

their results for the K-Cl and NH_4-Cl compounds on the same reduced curve (as Fig.12.20), and from this they took the experimental data used in Table 12.1. It is apparent that the system is closer to being a Heisenberg than an Ising system, at least as far as these criteria are concerned. A further improvement in agreement between theory and experiment for the critical data is obtained if it is supposed that nnn interactions with strength about one-quarter of that of the nn interactions are present (Wood and Dalton 1966). Van Amstel, de Jongh, and Matsuura (1974) have concluded from determinations of J for a number of these compounds that the interactions with non-nn spins are even more important than was supposed by Wood and Dalton. They have explained this by an examination of the various super-exchange paths available.

The related compounds $Rb_2MnBr_4.2H_2O$ and $Cs_2MnBr_4.2H_2O$

show λ-transitions to the antiferromagnetic state at 3·33 and 2·82 K, respectively (Forstat, McElearney, and Bailey 1968). This contrasts with the behaviour of the copper compounds discussed above, all of which ordered to ferro-magnetic states. The entropy changes associated with the transitions in the manganese salts are 15·02 and 15·06 J K^{-1} mol^{-1}, respectively, which are very close to $R \ln (2s+1)$ ($= 14·90$ J K^{-1} mol^{-1}). Only ~25% of this entropy is gained above T_N, which indicates the **three-dimensional** nature of the transition.

$GdCl_3$. This substance has the hexagonal UCl_3-type lattice (Fig.12.21), each Gd^{3+} ion being surrounded by nine Cl^- ions. Three of these Cl^- ions lie in each of three planes perpendicular to the c axis, there being one plane above and one below the Gd^{3+} ion with the remaining one passing through the cation. Considering only the Gd^{3+} ions, each

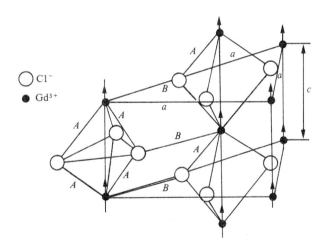

Fig.12.21. The structure of GdCl₃. Distances shown are: a = 0·7363 nm, c = 0·4105 nm, A = 0·286 nm, B = 0·305 nm (from Wolf, Leask et al., 1962).

ion, e.g. the central ion in Fig.12.21, has two nearest neighbours on the c axis at 0·4105 nm and six nnn at 0·4721 nm (the ions at the corner of the triangular prism in

Fig.12.21). In spite of the nn ions being coupled antiferromagnetically to the central ion, when the substance orders
at 2·20 K it does so ferromagnetically (Wolf, Leask, Mangum,
and Wyatt 1962). This was originally thought to be a simple
system on account of the Gd^{3+} ion being in an orbital s state
with $s = 7/2$, but it turns out to be fairly complicated because of the comparable importance of dipole-dipole and the
nn and nnn exchange forces. For the two kinds of exchange
interaction the ratio $J_{nnn}/J_{nn} = -1·2$ has been found (Clover
and Wolf 1968).

GdBr$_3$ has quite a different structure. It is monoclinic, and has a layer structure which is very similar to
that of CrCl$_3$. In this lattice, successive 'honeycomb'
layers of Gd^{3+} ions are separated by two hexagonal layers
of Br$^-$ ions. At ~2 K the substance becomes antiferromagnetically ordered with somewhat canted spins (Varsanyi,
Andres, and Marezio 1969).

Spinels. These solids have the general formula AB_2X_4, where
A and B are cations and X is a divalent chalcogenide anion.
Their structure (Fig.6.12), and the possible positional
disorder of the cations, has been discussed in section 6.3.
For most of the spinels the magnetically 'easy' directions
are along the body diagonals. However, some of these substances show distortions of the unit cell and associated
departures from this 'rule'. Thus, Mn$_3$O$_4$ below T_N = 42 K
has a tetragonal structure with the spins lying in the basal
plane but canted, as indicated by the value of M_0 when
extrapolated to 0 K. Fe$_3$O$_4$, which also shows departures
from cubic symmetry, is examined in detail in section 6.3.

An interesting example of the effect of partial inversion of cation positions (section 6.3) on magnetic be--
haviour has been provided by C_p measurements on ZnFe$_2$O$_4$.
When annealed this is a normal spinel, with all the Fe^{3+}
ions being in octahedral sites, and shows a λ-transition
near 9·5 K at which antiferromagnetic ordering of the Fe^{3+}
spins occurs. In contrast, a sample quenched from 1 100°C
showed only a small heat capacity anomaly in this region.
This is attributable to frozen-in positional disorder of

the cations, many Fe^{3+} ions being left in A sites when the sample is quenched (Grimes and Westrum 1958).

$MgCr_2O_4$, which is a normal spinel, appears to show transitions at ~16 K and ~13·5 K (Shaked, Hastings, and Corliss 1970, Plumier and Sougi 1969). At the upper of these it orders to a non-collinear antiferromagnet, and then goes to a mixture of two non-collinear phases at the lower temperature (Fig.12.22) (Plumier 1968b). $CuCr_2O_4$ (Prince 1957) has likewise been reported as adopting a non-collinear, possibly triangular, spin arrangement, but this is still in dispute (Jacobs 1959, Dwight and Menyuk 1960). The helical spin arrays originally proposed for $CoCr_2O_4$ and $MnCr_2O_4$ (Hastings and Corliss 1962, Menyuk, Dwight, and Wold 1964) have also been challenged as a result of further neutron diffraction work (Plumier 1968a). According to Plumier the set of B sites (containing the Cr^{3+} ions) splits into two sublattices, within one of which the transverse components of the spins

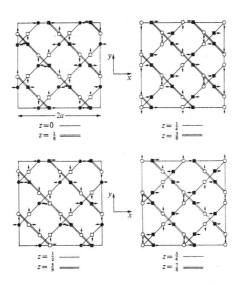

Fig.12.22. Projection of the magnetic structure of $MgCr_2O_4$ along the c axis. Only the magnetic ions (in the B sites) are shown. The projections shown refer to a cube of side $2a$ (Fig.6.12); z coordinates of the spins are indicated by the type of line through them (from Plumier 1968b).

are antiparallel (B_1), whilst the A spins and those in B_2
have transverse components which change their orientation
helically according to a propagation vector in the [110]
direction (Fig.12.23).

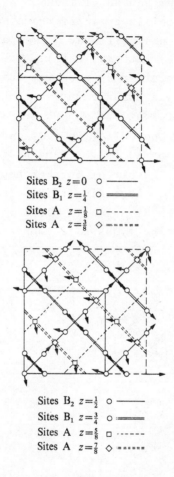

Sites B_2 $z=0$ ○ ——————
Sites B_1 $z=\frac{1}{4}$ ○ ══════
Sites A $z=\frac{1}{8}$ □ - - - - -
Sites A $z=\frac{3}{8}$ ◇ ══ ══ ══

Sites B_2 $z=\frac{1}{2}$ ○ ——————
Sites B_1 $z=\frac{3}{4}$ ○ ══════
Sites A $z=\frac{5}{8}$ □ - - - - -
Sites A $z=\frac{7}{8}$ ◇ ══ ══ ══

Fig.12.23. Projection of the magnetic structure of $CoCr_2O_4$ along the c
axis. The square indicated by full lines is of side a (Fig.6.12). The
nature (Co^{2+} or Cr^{3+}) and z coordinate of each spin is indicated by the
symbol (square or circle) and the type of line through it (from
Plumier 1968a).

Among many other oxides having the spinel structure
and showing at least one magnetic transition are $GeFe_2O_4$,
$FeCr_2O_4$, and FeV_2O_4 (Hartmann-Bouton and Imbert 1968).
The properties of a large number of spinel-type oxides have

been recorded by Schieber (1967).

Compounds of the general formula MCr_2X_4, where X = S, Se, or Te, may also have the spinel structure. They are of interest because some, but not all, are ferromagnetic. Thus, considering the set of group IIB spinels with X = S, Se (Table 12.2), all of which are normal spinels, it is found that the Zn compounds are antiferromagnets whereas the remainder are ferromagnets (Baltzer, Lehmann, and Robbins 1965).

TABLE 12.2

Transition temperatures and effective magnetic moments of spinels containing S and Se

(after Baltzer, Lehmann, and Robbins 1965 and Baltzer, private communication)

	$CdCr_2S_4$	$CdCr_2Se_4$	$HgCr_2S_4$	$HgCr_2Se_4$	$ZnCr_2S_4$	$ZnCr_2Se_4$
μ_{eff}/μ_B	5·2	· 5·4	5·3	5·4	-	-
T_c/K	84·5	129·5	36	106	$T_N = 18$	$T_N = 20$
a/nm	1·0244	1·0755	1·0237	1·0753	0·9988	1·0500

That factors other than the separation between adjacent Cr^{3+} ions must be important is shown by the fairly large differences in T_c between the Cd and Hg compounds, there being only very small differences in their cell dimensions. The Cd and Hg compounds are semiconductors in both para- and ferromagnetic states. $HgCr_2S_4$ is somewhat more complicated than is indicated in the Table in that at $T < 25$ K it is metamagnetic. The spin arrangement in the antiferromagnetic form (Hastings and Corliss 1968) is identical with that of $ZnCr_2S_4$ (Plumier 1966), being a simple helical arrangement with ferromagnetically ordered sheets, which are turned by ~42° between successive layers of spins, and with a propagation vector parallel to the axis of the helix and directed along a particular cube edge. The pitch of the helix in $HgCr_2S_4$ was found to decrease steadily from ~9·0 nm at 30 K to ~4·2 nm at lower temperatures; in $ZnCr_2Se_4$ the pitch did not vary with temperature.

Many of these substances, e.g. $FeCr_2S_4$, $CoCr_2S_4$, $MnCr_2S_4$, and $CdCr_2Se_4$, undergo a transformation to a monoclinic structure related to that of NiAs under elevated pressures and at high temperatures. This form can be quenched to room temperature and will then remain metastable at 1 atmosphere indefinitely. It can be looked upon as having close-packed anions with Cr^{3+} ions between alternate layers and the remaining interlayer sites being occupied by an ordered array of vacancies and Cd^{2+} ions (or other divalent ions). The monoclinic form orders antiferromagnetically at low temperatures. Thus $CdCr_2Se_4$ has T_N = 55 K; by contrast the same substance in its spinel form is a ferromagnet at low temperatures (Banus and Lavine 1969).

$CuCr_2Se_4$ and $CuCr_2Te_4$, which are also normal spinels, are interesting because the copper ion carries no moment (Colominas 1967). This indicates that the would-be Cu^{2+} ion has gained an electron from the conduction band to become Cu^+, a suggestion which is supported by the observed p-type conductivity.

Perovskites. The structure of a typical magnetic perovskite, $RbMnF_3$, is shown in Fig.12.24. It is cubic, with the Rb^+ ions at the corners, the Mn^{2+} at the centre, and the F^- ions at the six face-centres. This substance is one of the best examples of an isotropic, Heisenberg system. It becomes antiferromagnetic at T_N = 83·08 K. Like $KNiF_3$, another good isotropic antiferromagnet, the Néel point is too high for the lattice contribution to C_p to be easily separable from the magnetic. However, it seems certain that C^m remains finite at the transition and the indices $\alpha = \alpha' = -0·14$ have been assigned (Kornblit, Ahlers, and Buehler 1973). A neutron-scattering determination of the sublattice magnetization by Corliss, Delapalme, Hastings, Lau, and Nathans

(1969) yielded β = 0·316, somewhat low for a Heisenberg
system; however, γ = 1·397, obtained by Lau, Corliss, Delapalme, Hastings, Nathans, and Tucciarone (1970), is in good
accord with the theoretical value for such a system.

Bearing in mind the properties of the many titanates

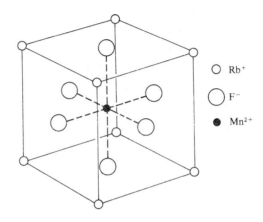

○ Rb$^+$

○ F$^-$

● Mn^{2+}

Fig.12.24. Perovskite structure of RbMnF$_3$ (from Kittel 1956).

and niobates which also have the perovskite structure,
it is not surprising to find that KMnF$_3$, which has the
perovskite structure at room temperature, shows a non-
magnetic transition of ferroelectric-type at 186 K. The
nature and mechanism of the transition, which is mainly
gradual but has a small first-order component, is similar
to that in SrTiO$_3$, which is entirely gradual. Below this
transition temperature KMnF$_3$ is tetragonal (Borsa 1973).
At lower temperatures still KMnF$_3$ undergoes rather a
strange magnetic transformation (Heeger, Beckman, and
Portis 1961). On cooling in zero field it goes over to
a uniaxial antiferromagnet at 88·3 K and to a canted structure at 81·5 K. Between these temperatures, the structure
becomes partly canted in fields greater than a critical
value. Above 88·3 K and below 81·5 K the magnetic structure is unaffected by the applied field. It was suggested,
on the basis of observations of hysteresis and discontinuities in the magnetization, that the transition at 81·5 K

is first order. Further, it was proposed that it is of the cooperative Jahn-Teller type (section 12.12; see also zircons, section 12.13.1), since this would explain its sensitivity applied magnetic fields.

The rare-earth ferrites, of general formula $RFeO_3$, show a number of interesting properties. They have high Néel points $[T_N(Fe) \approx 650 \text{ K}]$, at which the Fe spins become ordered antiferromagnetically although with a slight canting of the spins ($0 \cdot 57°$ in $GdFeO_3$). If the rare-earth ions have non-zero spins these interact with the weak ferromagnetism which is a consequence of the canting and tend to become oriented as the temperature is lowered. Reciprocally, a torque may be exerted on the Fe^{3+} spins tending to change their orientation from that adopted at $T_N(Fe)$, this being opposed by the uniaxial anisotropy of the crystal. This may result in a spin-reorientation transition, which involves typically a 90° change of orientation of the Fe spins occurring over a range of temperature and centred at a temperature (T_r) which is usually less than 100 K. Rare-earth ions which do not have spins (La^{3+}, Lu^{3+}, Eu^{3+}, and also Y^{3+}) do not display this kind of transition, because in them no orientating force is being exerted on the Fe^{3+} spins by other spins in the substance. Theories of the reorientation transitions have been proposed by Horner and Varma (1968), Wood, Remeika, Holmes, and Gyorgy (1969) and Yamaguchi (1974). A neutron scattering study has shown that the transitions in $TmFeO_3$ and $ErFeO_3$ (partly) are driven by a soft-mode mechanism (Shapiro, Axe, and Remeika 1974) (section 3.9). Reorientation transitions are sensitive to an applied magnetic field, which generally causes T_r to be lowered or even leads to disappearance of the transition. Thus for the transition in $HoFeO_3$ (between the a and c axes), application of a strong field along the b axis to a sample at $T < T_r$ tends to cause the Fe^{3+} spins to revert to their high-temperature orientation (Walling and White 1974).

At still lower temperatures (< 6 K) the spins of the rare-earth ions become ordered, in some cases in a fairly sharp cooperative transition (Gd, Tb, Dy, Er) but in others in a very gradual Schottky-like manner (Ho,Yb).

Results for the rare-earth ferrites are summarized in Table 12.3. The uniformity of the Néel points contrasts

TABLE 12.3

Transition temperatures of rare-earth ferrite perovskites
($RFeO_3$). T_r is the temperature of the spin-reorientation
transition

R	$T_N(R)/K$	T_r/K	$T_N(Fe)/K$
La	None	None	738^a
Nd	None above 1·3K	-	693^a
Sm	-	$\sim448^b$	673^a
Eu	None	None	663^a
Gd	$1·47^c$, $2·2^d$	$78^{\cdot} < T_r^{\cdot} < 295^e$	650^a
Tb	$3·2^d$, $3·1^f$, $3·2^g$	$\sim6·5^d$	653^a
Dy	$3·7^d$ $4·5^h$ $3·2^g$	$\sim35^i$	645^a
Ho	$6·5^j$ (Schottky)	$45-60^k$	643^a
Er	$3·9^d$, $4·3^j$	$\sim95^l$ $87·3 - 95·8^m$	641^a
Tm	-	$101·5^n$ $\sim100^p$, $\sim86^b$, $82·5 - 92·8^m$	631^a
Yb	$4·6^q$ (Schottky)	$6·5 - 7·8^q$ $6·31 - 7·59^r$	632^a 630^s
Lu	None	None	622^a
Y	None	None	648^a

Footnotes to Table 12.3.

a.   Schieber (1967).

b.   Gyorgy, Remeika, and Hagedorn (1968).

c.   Cashion, Cooke, Martin, and Wells (1970).

d.   Peyrard and Sivardière (1969).

e.   Gilleo (1956).

f.   Mareschal, Sivardière, de Vries, and Bertaut (1968).

g.   De Combarieu, Mareschal, Michel, and Sivardière (1968).

h.   Schuchert, Hüfner, and Faulhaber (1968).

i.   Levinson and Shtrikman (1970).

j.   Koehler, Wollan, and Wilkinson (1960).

k.   Walling and White (1974).

l.   Pinto, Shachar, Shaked, and Shtrikman (1971).

m.   Shapiro, Axe, and Remeika (1974).

n.   D.L. Wood *et al.* (1969).

p.   Kuroda, Miyadai, Naemura, Nuzeki, and Takata (1961).

q.   Moldover, Sjölander, and Weyhmann (1971).

r.   Schaffer, Bene, and Walser (1974).

s.   Treves (1965).

with the rather erratic behaviour of the reorientation transitions. Some of the evidence for the low value of T_r for $YbFeO_3$, the C_p measurements of Moldover, Sjölander, and Weyhmann (1971), is shown in Fig.12.25: a Schottky anomaly followed by a sharper transition may be clearly seen. This interpretation of the C_p data is supported by a Mössbauer study of the environment of the Yb nucleus (Davidson, Dunlap, Eibschütz, and van Uitert 1975). This work also shows that in the reorientation transition region near 7 K the net Fe^{3+} spin and the net Yb^{3+} spins are being orientated in opposite directions.

Similar effects are found in the corresponding ortho-chromites of general formula $RCrO_3$. The Néel points for ordering of the Cr^{3+} spins are lower than for the ferrites, ranging from 282 K for $LaCrO_3$ to 113 K for $LuCrO_3$. Canting

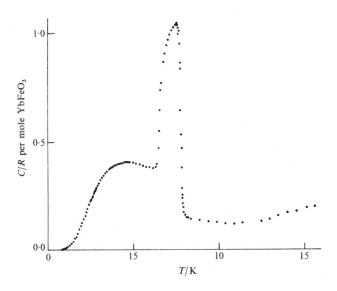

Fig.12.25. C_p against T for YbFeO$_3$ (from Moldover *et al*. 1971).

of the Cr^{3+} again leads to interaction with the rare-earth
spins and the possibility of reorientation transitions.   Thus
ErCrO$_3$ has an upper Néel point at 133 K (Bertaut and Mareschal 1967).   In the same study a lower Néel point at 16·8 K
was reported at which the Er^{3+} spins become ordered and the
Cr^{3+} spins suffered reorientation simultaneously.   Meltzer
and Moos (1970) were unable to find any change in the optical spectrum at 16·8 K, however.   Subsequently, C_p measurements (Eibschütz, Holmes, Maita, and van Uitert 1970) showed
that the temperature of the lower transition was 9·82 K and
there was, in addition, a Schottky anomaly with its maximum
near 5 K due to a splitting of the Er^{3+} electronic levels.
Magnetic and magneto-optical experiments have confirmed that
the transition at ~10 K involves the spin reorientation of
the Cr^{3+} spins (Hasson, Hornreich, Komet, Wanklyn, and
Yaeger 1975). T_r was found to decrease when the sample was
subjected to applied magnetic fields, as is found for the
orthoferrites.   In DyCrO$_3$, also, the reorientation transition which occurs as the temperature drops below 5 K, and
the ordering of Dy^{3+} spins (at 2·2 K) are very close together
(Tsushima, Aoyagi, and Sugano 1970, van Laar and Elemans

1971). NdCrO$_3$ has T_r = 35 K, the transition being first order. A Schottky anomaly centred at ~27 K appears to mark the non-cooperative ordering of the Nd^{3+} spins (Hornreich, Komet, Nolan, Wanklyn, and Yaeger 1975). The theoretical discussion of Yamaguchi (1974) classifies and treats the transitions in the chromites as well as the ferrites.

The aluminates, RAlO$_3$, with the same structure are simpler because the Al^{3+} ion has no spin. GdAlO$_3$ becomes ordered antiferromagnetically at 3·87 K (Cashion, Cooke, Thorp, and Wells 1970) and DyAlO$_3$ at T_N = 3·5 K (Schuchert, Hüfner, and Faulhaber 1968, Cashion, Cooke, Thorp, and Wells 1968). Bidaux and Meriel (1968) have observed that DyAlO$_3$ behaves as a good Ising system with effectively s = 1/2, and this is attributed to a distortion of the perovskite lattice which causes there to be a low-lying doublet in the Dy^{3+} energy-level system.

PrAlO$_3$ is noted for the richness of its structural transitions. The cubic perovskite lattice undergoes a trigonal distortion at ~1 640 K at which staggered rotations of the AlO$_6^{3-}$ octahedra about the [111] direction set in. On further cooling a first-order transition occurs at 205 K, the axis of the AlO$_6^{3-}$ rotations shifting discontinuously to [10$\bar{1}$]. With further cooling a gradual transition occurs at 151 K, below which the rotation axis moves continuously towards the [001] direction. The last two transitions are of the cooperative Jahn-Teller type with coupling of the lowest lying levels of the Pr^{3+} ion to the rotational movement of the AlO$_6^{3-}$ ions. Throughout these transitions the amplitude of the rotational oscillations of the AlO$_6^{3-}$ ions remains fairly constant at ~9·4° (Lyons, Birgeneau, Blount, and van Uitert 1975). The nature of the transition at ~151 K has also been studied by observing, by means of ESR, the change in direction of the principal axes of the field experienced by substitutional Gd^{3+} impurities. The results obtained pointed to a Landau value of β = 0·5. This behaviour, which suggests that the orientating forces are long-range, is reasonable when it is borne in mind that the interaction of the Pr^{3+} ions is mediated by the lattice strain (Sturge, Cohen, van Uitert, and van Stapele 1975). The pseudo-

tetragonal axis of this phase can be rotated by means of an
applied field of ~20 kOe, the axis orientating itself parallel to the field. In this behaviour it is similar to some
of the rare-earth zircons (see below), though in those the
fields required are much smaller (Riseberg, Cohen, Nordland,
and van Uitert, 1969). A further gradual transition, at
~118 K, has also been found. This is associated with a
partial softening of a mode, but there does not seem to be
any appreciable effect on the electronic levels (Fleury,
Lazay, and van Uitert 1974). Other rare-earth aluminates
show some of the variations displayed by $PrAlO_3$. The La,
Ce, and Nd compounds do not show the Jahn-Teller transitions and retain the trigonal structure down to the lowest
temperatures examined. $SmAlO_3$ has the trigonal and orthorhombic phases, and the Y, Gd, and Eu compounds can also adopt
the latter structure (Harley, Hayes, Perry, and Smith 1973).

Most of the ferrites, chromites and aluminates show
orthorhombic and rhombohedral distortions of the cubic
unit cell. These distortions are largest for the ferrites
and least for the aluminates, this being determined by the
size of the cations: Fe^{3+} (0·0645 nm) is larger than
Cr^{3+} (0·0615 nm), which in turn is larger than Al^{3+} (0·0530
nm), where the values given are the ionic radii for coordination number 6 (Prewitt, Shannon, Rogers, and Sleight 1969).

Garnets. As found in nature these have the general formula
$P_3Q_2R_3O_{12}$, where P, Q, and R are di-, tri- and tetra-valent
ions, respectively. Fig.12.26 shows the unit cell. As with
the spinels, it is easier to visualize the lattice as being
formed by placing cations in interstices between the O^{2-}
ions. The octahedral (a) and tetrahedral (d) sites are occupied by the Q and R ions, respectively, the divalent P
ions being surrounded by eight O^{2-} ions at the corners of a
triangular dodecahedron (c site) (Fig.12.27). The tetra-
valent R ion may be Si^{4+}, as in natural garnets, or Ge^{4+}.
The most interesting garnets are, however, obtained when a
PR pair of ions is replaced by two trivalent ions, as with
$(Y_3)_c(Fe_2)_a(Fe_3)_dO_{12}$ or YIG. The Y^{3+} ions are diamagnetic,
but the presence of Fe^{3+} ions in two different environments

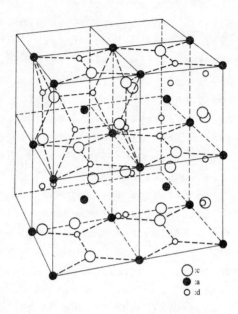

Fig.12.26. Garnet unit cell, showing the types of cation site. Oxygen ions are not shown (from Geller, Williams, Espinosa, and Sherwood 1964).

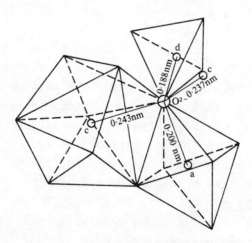

Fig.12.27. Environments of the three types of site in garnets. Oxygen ions are at the vertices of each of the three solid figures (from Gilleo and Geller 1958).

leads to ferrimagnetism, with an ordering temperature of
~550 K. Magnetic interactions within either of the sublattices occupied by the Fe^{3+} ions are weak (see the work on
$Ca_2Fe_2Ge_3O_{12}$ and related compounds, below), but there are
strong antiferromagnetic superexchange interactions between
the sublattices. If the Y^{3+} ions of YIG are replaced by trivalent rare-earth ions then the rare-earth iron garnets (RIG)
are obtained. The rare-earth ions chosen must not be larger
than Sm^{3+} so as to fit into the available cavity: the ions
of the lightest rare earths, La, Ce, Pr, and Nd, are too
large and complete substitution cannot be achieved. Because of the extra magnetic component these systems are magnetically more complex than YIG. The ferrimagnetic Néel
points are all found to lie close to that of YIG, being in
the range 548 K (for Lu) to 578 K (for Sm) (Néel, Pauthenet,
and Dreyfus 1964), showing that the c sites, containing the
rare-earth ions, are only weakly coupled to the a and d
sites. Another consequence of the weak coupling of the c sublattice to the other sublattices is that the spontaneous
magnetization associated with it falls off rapidly with
increase of temperature. Since the magnetization at 0 K
due to this sublattice is larger than and of opposite sign
to that from the a and d sublattices a compensation temperature (T_{comp}) exists at which $M_0 = 0$. Above this temperature M_0 adopts the sign associated with the iron sublattices
(Fig. 12.28).

The easy axis for Fe^{3+} spins in both a and d sublattices
is [111], the sense of the magnetization being, however,
opposite for the two Fe^{3+} sublattices. In DyIG, ErIG, YbIG,
and HoIG the rare-earth spins have been shown by neutron
diffraction to tilt away from the [111] axis (Herpin, Koehler,
and Meriel 1960, Pickart, Alperin, and Clark 1970). The magnetic moments of the Ho^{3+} ions in HoIG are found to adopt
a double conical arrangement about the [111] axis. This was
first proposed by Herpin et al. (1960) on the basis of their
powder neutron diffraction studies, and has been subsequently
confirmed by measurements of the spontaneous magnetization
as a function of crystal orientation at 4·2 K (Allain,
Bichara, and Herpin 1966). The vertex of the double cone

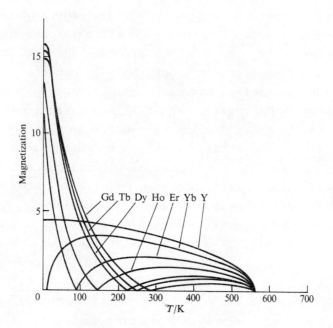

Fig.12.28. Magnetization against temperature for several rare-earth iron garnets, expressed in Bohr magnetons per single $R_3Fe_5O_{12}$ unit. On passing through the compensation temperature the sign of the magnetization is reversed (after Pauthenet 1958).

was found in the latter work to be 39° or 54°, according to the value assumed for the moment of the Ho^{3+} ion. The main influence on the orientation of the rare-earth spins in a RIG is the local crystal field, the effect of the R-Fe exchange interaction being about an order of magnitude less (Wolf 1964). For GdIG (Gd^{3+}, $L=0$), Néel *et al.* (1964) give the field at a Gd^{3+} ion due to other Gd^{3+} ions and to Fe^{3+} ions as being ~50 kOe and ~350 kOe, respectively, and the field at a Fe^{3+} ion due to other Fe^{3+} spins as being ~5 000 kOe.

YIG, which contains the non-magnetic rare-earth-like Y^{3+} ion, has been studied a great deal. For the investigation of the disordering of the Fe^{3+} spins at $T_N = 550 \cdot 41$ K, Berkner and Litster (1972) have measured the Faraday rotation, which is assumed to be proportional to the magnetization of each sublattice in the critical region, in fields up to 8 kOe. Their results ($\beta = 0 \cdot 370$, $\gamma = 1 \cdot 35$, $\delta = 4 \cdot 65$) correspond more closely with those expected for a three-dimensional Heisenberg system than for the Ising system.

The generation of canted or oblique spin phases under
the influence of applied magnetic fields has been briefly
discussed in section 12.7. Several mean-field treatments
similar to that of Clark and Callen (1968) have been proposed which are more specifically directed towards the situation obtaining in RIGs. For example, an isotropic model
having three sublattices (one for the rare-earth ions and
one each for the Fe^{3+} ions on the a and d sites) has been
developed by Féron, Fillion, and Hug (1973) and applied to
GdIG. Using the molecular-field parameters of Pauthenet
(1958) they obtained the $\mathcal{H}\text{-}T$ phase diagram of Fig.12.29. For

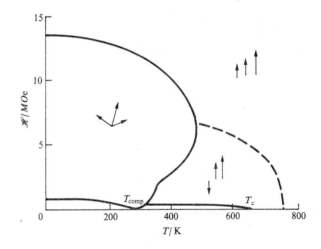

Fig.12.29. $\mathcal{H}\text{-}T$ phase diagram for gadolinium iron garnet calculated from
the mean-field coefficients of Pauthenet (from Féron *et al.* 1973).

temperatures less than or only slightly greater than T_{comp}
the diagram agrees with that of Clark and Callen for their
two sublattice system. Levitin, Ponomarev, and Popov (1971)
have measured the magnetization in fields up to 240 kOe for
the iron garnets of Gd, Tb, Dy, and Ho near T_{comp} and have
confirmed the nature of the phase diagram in that region.

A detailed calculation for YbIG, taking account of
anisotropy and allowing for the existence of six rare-earth
sublattices, as first suggested by Herpin *et al.* (1960), has
been made by Alben (1970). Because of the anisotropy, the

behaviour depends strongly upon the direction of the magnetic field with respect to the crystal axes. Alben also
presented an anisotropic two-sublattice model to simulate
the same system. Fig.12.30 shows the phase diagrams obtained.

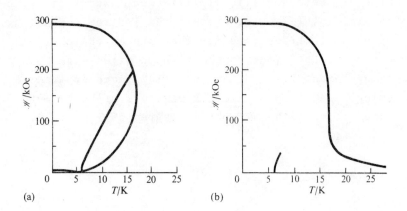

(a)   (b)

Fig.12.30. $\mathcal{H}$-T phase diagrams calculated for an anisotropic two sublattice model for fields directed along (a) the [111] and (b) the [100]
axes (from Alben 1970).

Two canted phases are predicted. When $\mathcal{H}$ is parallel to
[111] the transition between these is second order, whereas
for $\mathcal{H} \parallel [100]$ it is predicted to be first order, with the
transition line ending in a critical point. The magnetiza-
tion measurements on YbiG over the range 2-30 K with
fields up to 23 kOe by Levinson, Alben, and Jacobs (1971)
provide some support for Alben's model as against that of
Clark and Callen, although the existence of two separate
canted phases is not established.

   Partly in order to help to understand the magnetic contributions in the RIGs and partly because of their own intrinsic interest and industrial importance, there have been
extensive studies of the garnets corresponding to the RIGs,
but in which the Fe^{3+} ions are replaced by Al^{3+} or Ga^{3+} ions.
Thus only the c sublattice positions are occupied by magnetic ions. Because of the weakness of the cc interactions,
ordering of the rare-earth spins occurs at low temperatures.
From χ measurements, Cooke, Thorp, and Wells (1967) found

Néel points at 1·35 K, 0·85 K, and ~0·8 K for TbAlG, HoAlG,
and ErAlG, respectively. For GdGaG and TbGaG they did not
observe any behaviour which suggested a Néel point within
the temperature range of their experiments (0·6 - 4·0 K).
They remarked, however, that because the gallium garnets
have volumes ~7% larger than those of the aluminium garnets
it would be expected that the cc interactions in the former
would be correspondingly weaker and their ordering temperatures lower. Heat capacity measurements have been employed
by Onn, Meyer, and Remeika (1967), who found Néel points of
0·516 K, 0·967 K, and 0·789 K for the gallium garnets of Nd,
Sm, and Er, respectively. The behaviour of all three garnets
corresponded well with that expected of s = 1/2 Heisenberg
f.c.c. systems (there being no theoretical data for the
garnet structure) with regard to the amount of the entropy
increase above and below T_N; also, C^m goes to a finite maximum, although because of rounding near T_N it was not possible
to assign values of α and α'. GdGaG showed a Schottky anomaly, rather than the cooperative ordering of the Nd, Sm, and
Er compounds, and from this the splitting due to the crystalline field was obtained. DyGaG displayed a maximum in
C_p at ~0·36 K, but they were unable to fit the data adequately with any choice of J_{cc}. Hammann (1969) obtained T_N = 1·35 K
and ~0·95 K for TbAlG and HoAlG, respectively, in fair agreement with the results of Cooke et al. (1967), by observation
of the disappearance as the temperature is raised of the intensity of neutron diffraction reflections from the magnetic
superstructure. Indications of the relatively large crystal
fields (though not large compared with the spin-orbit coupling) and anisotropy in many garnets have come from a variety
of sources. Such evidence was reported by Wolf, Ball,
Hutchings, Leask, and Wyatt (1962), who measured χ over the
range 1·5 - 20 K for the eight garnets of aluminium and
gallium with Gd, Tb, Ho, and Tm. From the same results they
also deduced that the rare-earth spins lay in non-collinear
fashion on six sublattices (Hutchings and Wolf 1964). For
TbAlG, the spins on the six rare-earth sublattices have been
found by neutron diffraction studies to lie along the ±x,
±y and ±z axes (Hammann 1969, Gavignet-Tillard, Hammann, and

de Seze 1973a). Because of the large crystal fields at the Tb^{3+} sites, which results in two singlets lying well below the remaining levels, the magnetic and thermal properties can be well fitted by a model which takes account only of the two low-lying singlets (Gavignet-Tillard, Hammann, and de Seze 1973b). Thus, above T_N, here found to be 1·31 K, the heat capacity curve fits the high-temperature tail of a Schottky anomaly (Fig.12.31). With a magnetic field applied

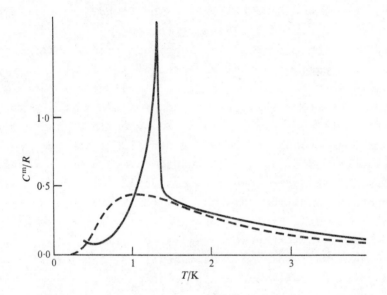

Fig.12.31. C^m against T for terbium aluminium garnet. The quantity of garnet referred to is that which contains 1 mole of Tb^{3+} ions. The broken curve is that for a simple two-level Schottky anomaly with $\Delta = 2\cdot5$ K. The rise in C^m with fall in T below 0·5 K is thought to be due to a nuclear spin contribution (from Gavignet-Tillard et al. 1973b).

along the [111] axis, the six rare-earth sublattices of TbAlG split into two groups of three, the members of each group being related by rotations of $2\pi/3$ about the [111] axis. The substance then behaves as a two sublattice metamagnet, with a tricritical point at 0·71 K.

Of all the gallium and aluminium garnets DyAlG has been the object of the most searching experimental and theoretical study. Because of its large anisotropy it behaves as a very good Ising antiferromagnet ($s = 1/2$) (Landau, Keen, Schneider,

and Wolf 1971, Wolf, Schneider, Landau, and Keen 1972).
Like TbAlG, it is metamagnetic for fields parallel to the
[111] axis, the tricritical point being 1·66 K, 3·25 kOe and
the tricritical indices (section 12.6.1: $\rho = \beta_u$, $\varepsilon = \gamma_u$)
$\beta_u = 0·65$ and $\gamma_u = 1·3$. These values are to be compared
with $\beta_u = \gamma_u = 1$, the values predicted for a classical Ising
model ($-\infty \leq s^z \leq \infty$) by a renormalization group method
(Riedel and Wegner 1972, Tuthill, Harbus, and Stanley 1973);
for a classical (Landau) system the indices would also be
$\beta_u = \gamma_u = 1$ (as follows from the equations in section 2.5).
The sublattice magnetization as a function of T and $\mathcal{H}$ has
been calculated from the measured intensities of neutron
diffraction peaks [intensity $\propto (M')^2$] (Blume, Corliss, Hastings,
and Schiller 1974). This shows that for $T_t < T < T_N$ M' does
not fall to zero at the antiferromagnet-paramagnet phase boundary but instead shows a point of inflexion. For $T < T_t$ and
fields greater than the upper critical field the long-range
antiferromagnetic order persists.

Some experiments have also been done on garnets in which
only the a sites contain magnetic ions. Examples of such
substances are $Ca_3Fe_2Ge_3O_{12}$ ($T_N = 11·5$ K, $J_{aa}/k = 4·7$ K),
$Ca_3Mn_2Ge_3O_{12}$ ($T_N = 13·0$ K, $J_{aa}/k = 5·3$ K), $NaCa_2Co_2V_3O_{12}$
($T_N = 8·1$ K, $J_{aa}/k = 3·3$ K), and $NaCa_2Ni_2V_3O_{12}$ ($T_N = 8·9$ K,
$J_{aa}/k = 3·7$K) (Belov, Mill', Ronninger, Sokolov, and Hien
1970). The values of J_{aa} were calculated by utilizing the
theoretical results of Rushbrooke and Wood (1963). A
Mössbauer study of $Ca_3Fe_2Ge_3O_{12}$, leading to $T_N = 12·6$ K, has
also been carried out (Dodokin, Lyubutin, Mill', and Peshkov
1973). In this work, T_N was determined as the temperature
at which the magnetic hyperfine splitting of the Mössbauer
spectrum was reduced to zero.

Zircons. A number of rare-earth phosphates, vanadates, and
arsenates having this structure (Fig.12.32) hage been extensively studied since it was found that $DyVO_4$ had a cooperative Jahn-Teller transition which could be controlled
by quite small magnetic fields (Cooke, Ellis, Gehring, Leask,
Martin, Wanklyn, Wells, and White 1970). They have the advantage that good, transparent crystals can be grown, enabling a variety of techniques to be employed in studying

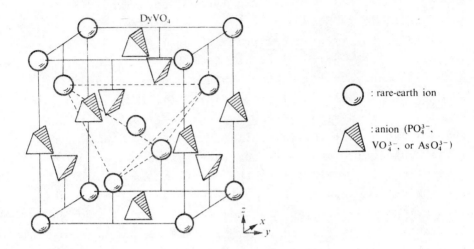

Fig.12.32. The zircon structure (after Göbel and Will 1972).

them. The arrangement of the magnetic ions can be considered
as a distorted diamond lattice, each rare-earth ion having
four similar nearest-neighbour ions (for the central ion in
Fig.12.32 these are the ions at the vertices of the tetrahedron indicated by broken lines).

On cooling through the Jahn-Teller transition the substances go from tetragonal to orthorhombic symmetry, although the distortion is small: in $DyAsO_4$ below the transition temperature (T_D) the axes are $a = 0 \cdot 7078$ nm, $b = 0 \cdot 7048$
nm, $c = 0 \cdot 6306$ nm, giving a fractional distortion $(1 - b/a)$
of $4 \cdot 29 \times 10^{-3}$. The fractional distortion for $DyVO_4$ is
$4 \cdot 76 \times 10^{-3}$ and for $TbVO_4$ is $21 \cdot 7 \times 10^{-3}$ (Will, Göbel,
Sampson, and Forsyth 1972). For the Dy compounds the ortho-
rhombic axes are parallel to the original tetragonal axes;
in the Tb and Tm compounds, on the other hand, the orthorhombic axes are parallel to the [110] and [1$\bar{1}$0] axes of
the undistorted form. Similar differences occur in the
nature of the heat capacity curve in the vicinity of T_D.
The Dy compounds have λ-shaped anomalies, as is usually
found in ordering transitions in which the interactions are
short-range; the vanadates and arsenates of Tb and Tm all
show typical Bragg-Williams curves, suggesting that long-range

interactions are important (Fig.2.3b). The transitions involve almost no change in volume and are of second or higher
order. When the transition occurs, the elastic mode corresponding to the distortion is found to go 'soft', i.e. the
elastic constant goes to zero. Thus, Sandercock, Palmer,
Elliott, Hayes, Smith, and Young (1972), using Brillouin
scattering and ultrasonic methods, have shown that $(c_{11}-c_{12})$
goes to zero for $DyVO_4$, but that in $TbVO_4$ it is c_{66} which
becomes 'soft'. Because of the very short time-scale associated with the Brillouin scattering experiments the c values
obtained from them were, in some instances, rather too high.
Again, in $TmVO_4$ it is c_{66} which becomes zero at T_D, although
$(c_{11}-c_{12})$ also falls by a considerable amount (18·6%) on
approaching T_D from above (Melcher, Pytte, and Scott 1973).
Although the next highest doublet in $TmVO_4$ is 138 cm^{-1} above
the ground doublet, it was found that it made a significant
contribution to the elastic constants: the reason for this
is that this doublet, although sparsely populated, is much
more strongly coupled to the phonon modes.

Many of these substances also have a Néel point at a
lower temperature. In the case of $DyVO_4$ (Cooke *et al.* 1970,
Cooke, Martin, and Wells 1971) the magnetic and the Jahn-
Teller transitions were each found to be associated with an
entropy change very close to $R \ln 2$ (= $0·693R$), the values
being $0·677R$ and $\sim 0·68R$, respectively. The heat capacity
curve was found to be logarithmic on the low-temperature
side of the Néel point but to correspond to the numerically
large value of $\alpha = -0·30$ on the high-temperature side. For
the magnetic transition in $DyAsO_4$ (Kahle, Klein, Müller-Vogt,
and Schopper 1971) the entropy change is $0·69R$, which is
also very close to $R \ln 2$. Furthermore, the entropy and energy
gained below the Néel point are found to be $0·43R$ and $0·35RT_N$,
respectively, as compared with $0·511R$ and $0·418RT_N$, calculated
by Essam and Sykes (1963) for an Ising model on a diamond
lattice. Although corresponding values for a Heisenberg
system on a diamond lattice are not available, a comparison
of Heisenberg and Ising values for simple cubic, body-centred
cubic and face-centred cubic lattices shows that the former
are uniformly smaller by $\sim 0·13R$ and $\sim 0·15RT_N$, indicating that

the $DyAsO_4$ behaviour is intermediate between those of the
Ising and Heisenberg systems. For the same substance the
Jahn-Teller anomaly was found to have $\Delta S = 0 \cdot 50R$ and
$\Delta E = 0 \cdot 48RT_D$, and these values have been interpreted in
terms of the splitting of the two lowest, near-degenerate,
orbital levels leaving them as Kramers doublets (as for
$DyVO_4$ in Fig.12.33). $DyPO_4$, which has only the magnetic

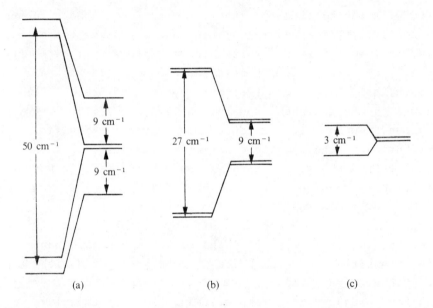

Fig.12.33. The lowest electronic energy levels of (a) $TbVO_4$, (b) $DyVO_4$,
and (c) $TmVO_4$ below T_D (to the left) and above T_D (to the right) (from
G.A.Gehring and K.A.Gehring 1975).

transition, conforms particularly well to the $s = 1/2$ Ising
model for that transition, the entropy and energy gained
below the Néel point being $0 \cdot 505R$ and $0 \cdot 408RT_N$, respectively.
This has been attributed to cancellation of the exchange
and dipolar contributions from the more remote neighbours
(de Jongh and Miedema 1974). The divergence of c^m at T_N
is also in approximate agreement with the predictions of
the Ising model, being logarithmic when approached from below
and sharper than logarithmic from above. In $TbAsO_4$, the magnetic anomaly has $\Delta S = 0 \cdot 6997R$, which again is very close
to $R \ln 2$ (Berkhahn, Kahle, Klein, and Schopper 1973). The

transition is logarithmic below T_N but has a critical exponent $\alpha = 0.47$, a very high value which may be due to the
considerable distance from T_N at which the measurements were
made $(3.3 \times 10^{-2} \leq (T/T_N)-1 \leq 0.2)$.

The directions of the rare-earth magnetic spins vary
within the group of compounds. In $DyPO_4$ the spins are
aligned along the c axis (Scharenberg and Will 1971). In
$TbPO_4$, on the other hand, the spins are canted, lying $40\pm1°$
off the c axis in the (100) planes (Zeeman splitting of the
optical spectrum, Lee, Moos, and Mangum 1971, neutron diffraction, Spooner, Lee, and Moos 1971). $DyVO_4$ has spins
pointing along the a (or b) axis, but in the thermodynamically very similar $DyAsO_4$ the spins are non-collinear and
lie in the ab plane making angles of $\pm22°$ with the b axis
(Schäfer and Will 1971). The spin arrangements for the
three Dy compounds are shown in Fig.12.34.

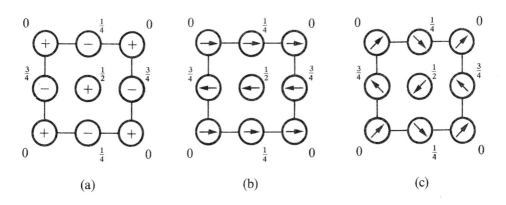

(a)   (b)   (c)

Fig.12.34. The magnetic structure of (a) $DyPO_4$, (b) $DyVO_4$, and (c)
$DyAsO_4$. Projections of the orientations of the magnetic spins onto the
ab plane; $+$, $-$ indicate the two possible directions perpendicular to the
ab plane. The z coordinate of each spin, expressed as a fraction of the
c cell constant, is shown (after Will, Schäfer, Scharenberg, and Göbel
1971).

The sensitivity of these compounds to applied magnetic
fields is manifested in several ways. Metamagnetic behaviour is shown by $TbPO_4$ at 0.4 K when a field of 6.1 kOe
is applied parallel to the c axis or ~9.5 kOe perpendicular

to the c axis (Lee, Moos, and Mangum 1971). Likewise, the
antiferromagnetic form of $DyVO_4$ (below T_N = 3·0 K) when subjected to a field of 2·1 ± 0·1 kOe in the a direction undergoes a metamagnetic spin-flip (Cooke et al. 1971). $DyPO_4$ at
0·5 K shows a metamagnetic transition when a field of
5·7 ± 0·1 kOe is applied along the c axis (Ellis, Leask,
Martin, and Wells 1971), the tricritical temperature being
1·95 K (Battison, Kasten, Leask, and Lowry 1975). The Jahn-
Teller transition of $TmAsO_4$ is lost when a field of 20 kOe
or more is applied along the c axis at 2·5 K (Harley, Hayes,
and Smith 1972). The critical field required for elimination of the Jahn-Teller distortion falls off as T_D is approached in a manner reminiscent of the relationship between
T_N and applied field for an ordinary antiferromagnet (Mangum,
Lee, and Moos 1971). In contrast, Hudson and Mangum (1971)
found that fields applied along the a axis raised T_D of
$DyAsO_4$ and $DyVO_4$ by ~2° for an applied field of 5 kOe, as
judged from measurements of the susceptibility. The direction of the Jahn-Teller distortion can also be rotated by
application of quite small fields in the basal plane. Thus,
at 4·2 K a field of 1 kOe along the b axis is adequate to
interchange the a and b axes of the orthorhombic structure
of $DyVO_4$ (Cooke et al. 1970). For $TbVO_4$ below T_D a field of
'a few kilooersteds' is sufficient; in $TbAsO_4$ at 2·4 K a
field of only 0·7 kOe along the [110] direction will turn
all the domains into the direction of the field (Wüchner,
Böhm, Kahle, Kasten, and Laugsch 1972).

        Theoretical work on the rare-earth zircons has taken
advantage of the fact that in most instances only a small
number of the electronic states of the Jahn-Teller ion, as
split by the crystal field, are effective contributors to
the thermodynamic and other properties: the remaining
states of the ion are so much higher in energy that they
are sparsely populated at the temperatures of interest. In
the simplest case, where only two states need be considered,
then a so-called pseudo-spin operator having the eigenvalues
$\pm\frac{1}{2}$ can be employed, the two eigenstates corresponding to
the two electronic states of the Jahn-Teller ion. This
formalism can be used for $DyVO_4$, where each eigenstate

represents a Kramers doublet, as well as for the simpler
TmVO$_4$ (Fig.12.33). For TbVO$_4$, in which four states must be

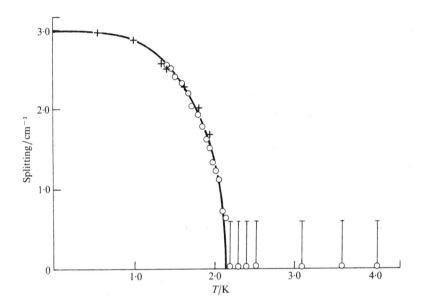

Fig.12.35. Splitting of the ground electronic state in TmVO$_4$ due to Jahn-
Teller distortion as a function of temperature; o : spectroscopic data,
+ : magnetization data. The line is calculated from mean-field theory.
This curve is equivalent to the M-T curve for a ferromagnet (from Becker,
Leask, and Tyte 1972).

included, a somewhat more complicated operator system has
been used successfully (Elliott, Harley, Hayes, and Smith
1972); a system involving a single s = 3/2 pseudo-spin
operator has also been tried (Sivardière and Blume 1972), but
it does not give an adequate description of this substance.
The arsenates, though not the phosphates, have energy-level
schemes which are similar to those of the vanadates (Wright
and Moos 1971). This accounts for the rather different
behaviour with regard to transitions displayed by the phosphates [so far the only phosphate found to have a Jahn-
Teller transition is that of terbium (Lewis and Prinz 1974)].
The energy levels for all these systems have been determined by direct spectroscopic methods (high-resolution optical, electronic Raman and far infrared), rather than by

fitting to thermodynamic data.

Elliott *et al.* (1972) have used as a mean-field Hamiltonian for the two-state system the expression:

$$\hat{\mathcal{H}} = -(\varepsilon + \lambda'\langle \sigma^x \rangle)\sigma^x - \lambda\langle \sigma^z \rangle\sigma^z \qquad (12.12)$$

where 2ε is the crystal field splitting of the levels in the undistorted phase (above T_D), σ^x and σ^z are Pauli operators which, respectively, cause interchanges between the electronic states and 'count' the difference in the number of spins in the two electronic states, and λ and λ' are mean-field coupling coefficients which are proportional to the interaction between the z and x components, respectively, of the operator at different sites. However, it is known that λ' is very small compared to λ. Ignoring the term containing λ', the ordering properties of the system can be expressed in the form:

$$\langle \sigma^z \rangle = (\lambda/W)\langle \sigma^z \rangle \tanh(W/kT) \qquad (12.13)$$

where $W = (\lambda^2\langle \sigma^z \rangle^2 + \varepsilon^2)^{1/2}$; as $\varepsilon \to 0$, $kT_D \to \lambda$. This treatment was originally applied to the results for $DyVO_4$ and $DyAsO_4$, for which, as we have seen, the experimental evidence does not suggest mean-field type behaviour. The thulium compounds, which were studied after those of Dy and Tb, and do show pronounced mean-field characteristics, are more suited to this simple treatment (Figs. 2.3b and 12.35), though in $TmAsO_4$ the presence of the first excited state (a singlet) at only ~ 14 cm^{-1} above the ground doublet requires that it be taken into account in some work, e.g. the heat capacity measurements of Colwell and Mangum (1972) lead to $\Delta S = 0\cdot835R$ for the Jahn-Teller transition.

For $TbVO_4$ a second operator (τ), such that τ^z gives different eigenvalues for the two states of a doublet and τ^x and τ^y cause interchange between these states, is introduced in addition to the operator σ. The mean-field Hamiltonian is then:

$$\hat{\mathcal{H}} = \{\varepsilon + \lambda'\langle (1+\tau^z)\sigma^x/2 \rangle\}(1+\tau^z)\sigma^x/2 + \lambda\langle \sigma^z \rangle\sigma^z . \qquad (12.14)$$

If the term in λ' is again neglected, the energy levels are found to be $\pm W_1$ and $\pm W_2$, with $W_1 = (\varepsilon^2 + \lambda^2 \langle \sigma^z \rangle^2)^{1/2}$ and $W_2 = \lambda \langle \sigma^z \rangle$. The solutions for $\langle \sigma^z \rangle$ and $\langle \sigma^x \rangle$ are:

$$\langle \sigma^z \rangle = \left\{ \frac{\lambda \langle \sigma^z \rangle}{W_1} \sinh(W_1/kT) + \sinh(W_2/kT) \right\} \Big/ \{\cosh(W_1/kT) + \cosh(W_2/kT)\}$$

$$(12.15)$$

$$\langle \sigma^x \rangle = \langle \tau^z \sigma^x \rangle = \frac{\varepsilon}{W_1} \sinh(W_1/kT) \Big/ \{\cosh(W_1/kT) + \cosh(W_2/kT)\} \quad \text{for}$$

$$T \leq T_D \qquad (12.16)$$

and

$$\langle \sigma^z \rangle = 0$$

$$\langle \sigma^x \rangle = \langle \tau^z \sigma^x \rangle = \sinh(\varepsilon/kT)/\{1 + \cosh(\varepsilon/kT)\} = \tanh(\varepsilon/2kT) \quad \text{for}$$

$$T > T_D \qquad (12.17)$$

No Jahn-Teller distortion occurs if $\varepsilon > 1 \cdot 2\lambda$. For $\varepsilon < \lambda$, which is true for $TbVO_4$, there is a single transition with $kT_D \approx \lambda$. Both $TbVO_4$ and $TbAsO_4$ conform well to mean-field predictions.

12.13.2. Pseudo two-dimensional systems
K_2NiF_4. The structure is as shown in Fig.12.36. Successive NiF_2 layers are separated by two KF planes. In the anti-ferromagnetically ordered state neighbouring Ni^{2+} spins within a layer are antiparallel. A Ni^{2+} spin in one plane has four equidistant neighbouring spins in each of the two adjacent layers. Since of these four spins two point in each of the two possible directions, their net effect on the central spin is zero. It is, therefore, only second and higher order interactions which cause spins in one plane to influence those in another. In fact, it is found that the adjacent spins of nnn planes are parallel. De Jongh and Miedema (1974) have estimated the ratio of the inter- and intra-layer parameters $|J'/J|$ to be $\sim 10^{-6}$.

K_2NiF_4 is frequently used in tests of theories of layer

TABLE 12.4

Temperatures of the Jahn-Teller (T_D) and magnetic (T_N) transitions in rare-earth zircons

Compound	T_D/K	T_N/K
$GdVO_4$	-	$2 \cdot 495$[a]
$TbPO_4$	$3 \cdot 5$[b]	$2 \cdot 2$[b], $2 \cdot 25$[c], $2 \cdot 17$[d]
$TbAsO_4$	$25 \cdot 5$[e], $27 \cdot 7$[f]	$1 \cdot 50$[f], $1 \cdot 48$[g]
$TbVO_4$	$33 \cdot 0$[h,i]	$0 \cdot 61$[j]
$DyPO_4$	-	$3 \cdot 391$[k]
$DyAsO_4$	$11 \cdot 17$[l], $11 \cdot 2$[m]	$2 \cdot 44$[m]
$DyVO_4$	$13 \cdot 8$[n]	$3 \cdot 04$[p], $3 \cdot 4$[q], $3 \cdot 0$[r]
$ErPO_4$	-	$0 \cdot 100$[s]
$ErVO_4$	-	$0 \cdot 4 \pm 0 \cdot 1$[t]
$TmAsO_4$	$6 \cdot 0$[u], $6 \cdot 1$[v]	-
$TmVO_4$	$2 \cdot 10$[w]	-

a. Metcalfe and Rosenberg (1972a).

b. Lewis and Prinz (1974).

c. Lee and Moos (1972).

d. Lee, Moos, and Mangum (1971).

e. Klein, Wüchner, Kahle, and Schopper (1971).

f. Berkhahn, Kahle, Klein, and Schopper (1973).

g. Wüchner *et al*. (1972).

h. K.A.Gehring *et al*. (1971).

i. Wells and Worswick (1972).

j. Kahle, Simon, and Wüchner (1974).

k. Colwell, Mangum, Thornton, Wright, and Moos (1969).

l. Brüesch and Kalbfleisch (1971a).

m. Kahle *et al*. (1971).

n. Brüesch and Kalbfleisch (1971b).

p.   D'Ambrogio, Brüesch, and Kalbfleisch (1972).

q.   Wright, Moos, Colwell, Mangum, and Thornton (1971).

r.   Will and Schäfer (1971).

s.   Mangum and Utton (1974).

t.   Metcalfe and Rosenberg (1972b).

u.   Mangum, Lee, and Moos (1971).

v.   Colwell and Mangum (1972).

w.   Cooke, Swithenby, and Wells (1972).

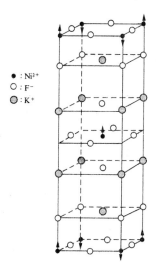

● : Ni²⁺
○ : F⁻
◎ : K⁺

Fig.12.36. Crystal structure of K_2NiF_4.

antiferromagnets. In these tests it is usually considered
to be a Heisenberg antiferromagnet with a small amount of
anisotropy. [However, see the C_p measurements of Salamon
and Hatta (1971) (below), according to which it behaves
like an Ising system.] In particular, the question of the
existence of the Stanley-Kaplan transition has been examined
by means of measurements on this compound (Salamon and
Hatta 1971, Salamon and Ikeda 1973). According to Stanley
and Kaplan (1966) it is possible for a two-dimensional

Heisenberg system with ferromagnetic (or antiferromagnetic) interactions to show a divergence in χ (or χ') at a finite temperature, even though it cannot have long-range order except at 0 K (Mermin and Wagner 1966). It has been proposed that the temperature concerned, the so-called Stanley-Kaplan temperature (T_{SK}), is given by the expression:

$$T_{SK} = 2J(q-1)\{2s(s+1)-1\}/5k \quad \text{for } s \geq 1; \tag{12.17}$$

for $s = \frac{1}{2}$ the value of T_{SK} has not been obtained with certainty. Although for Heisenberg systems there is no symmetry between ferro- and antiferromagnetic systems, it is thought that application of (12.13) to antiferromagnets should not introduce any serious error. A good discussion of the experimental evidence for the existence of this effect, drawing particularly on the results for K_2NiF_4, has been given by de Jongh and Miedema (1974), in which they conclude that it is probably genuine. A corresponding singularity in c^m was not predicted by Stanley and Kaplan, and indeed would be forbidden (Mermin and Wagner 1966). The actual C_p results for K_2NiF_4, after deduction of an amount taken to be the non-magnetic contribution, show a change in slope at ~98 K together with a small hump at about the same temperature. The hump is thought to reflect the small amount of anisotropy and the change in slope to correspond qualitatively, though not too well quantitatively, with the theories of Stanley and Kaplan and also Lines (1971).

The two-dimensional nature of the lattice is also indicated by the fact that the sublattice magnetization approaches zero as $T \rightarrow T_N = 97 \cdot 23$ K with the critical index $\beta = 0 \cdot 138$ (Birgeneau, Guggenheim, and Shirane 1970). This is much closer to the Ising value for two-dimensional systems ($\beta = 0 \cdot 125$) than to that for three ($\beta = 0 \cdot 31$). No comparison can be made for Heisenberg systems because the two-dimensional system then does not show a critical point. χ *versus* T curves show a smooth maximum at a temperature much higher than T_N, this being another characteristic of two-dimensional systems (Srivastava 1963, Maarschall, Botterman, Vega, and Miedema 1969).

K_2CoF_4 and Rb_2CoF_4 (Breed, Gilijamse, and Miedema 1969) have the same structure as K_2NiF_4, but their magnetic properties are in very good agreement with the $s = \frac{1}{2}$ two-dimensional Ising model up to T_χ; above T_χ there is an increasing discrepancy between theory and experiment which is attributable to population of the next higher electronic level (de Jongh and Miedema 1974). The K and Rb compounds order at 101 K and 107 K, respectively. Over the range $5 \times 10^{-4} < 1-T/T_N < 1 \times 10^{-1}$, β for Rb_2CoF_4 was found to be $0 \cdot 119$, in good accord with the two-dimensional Ising value.

Rb_2MnF_4 and K_2MnF_4. The chemical and magnetic structures are similar to those of K_2NiF_4, except that domains with the Ca_2MnO_4 magnetic structure have also been reported. [The latter differs from K_2NiF_4 only in that nnn planes have their spins antiparallel (Birgeneau *et al.* 1970).] There is a hump in the curve of c^m against T at the estimated Stanley-Kaplan temperature which is somewhat broader than that found for K_2NiF_4 and is likewise attributed to anisotropy. The main source of the anisotropy in K_2MnF_4 is believed to be dipole-dipole interaction, as against single ion anisotropy for K_2NiF_4 (Bucci and Guidi 1974). The critical index values of $\beta = 0 \cdot 18$ for Rb_2MnF_4 (Birgeneau *et al.* 1970) and $0 \cdot 188$ at $1-T/T_N \geq 4 \times 10^{-3}$ for K_2MnF_4 (Ikeda and Hirakawa 1972, 1973) support the view that these substances can be considered as two-dimensional. As T approaches T_N more closely, β for K_2MnF_4 was found to increase towards a value more typical of a three-dimensional array. In K_2MnF_4, the domains with the Ca_2MnO_4 structure were reported as having a much higher Néel point (58$\cdot$0 K) than those with the normal structure ($T_N = 42 \cdot 1$ K) (Ikeda and Hirakawa 1972). However, Birgeneau, Guggenheim, and Shirane (1973) were unable to find any evidence for the presence of a Ca_2MnO_4 form in their sample of K_2MnF_4, and de Jongh and Miedema (1974) have suggested that the second phase is, in fact, an impurity.

Rb_2FeF_4. This has the same chemical structure as K_2NiF_4, but the magnetic structure is slightly different in that the

spins lie in the *ab* plane along one of the base diagonals
(Birgeneau *et al.* 1970). For $0 \cdot 3 \geq 1 - T/T_N \geq 0 \cdot 02$, β was
found to be ~$0 \cdot 2$, indicating a fair amount of two-dimensional
character; however, closer to T_N the value of β jumped to
one more typical of a three-dimensional system.

KFeF$_4$. This has a layer structure with the layers composed
of FeF_6 octahedra, each sharing four F^- ions with four different octahedra in the same layer (Fig.12.37). The planes

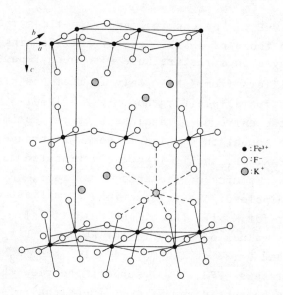

Fig.12.37. Crystal structure of $KFeF_4$ (from Heger *et al.* 1971).

are quite strongly puckered, the 'vertical' FeF bonds being
at $11 \cdot 65°$ to the *c* axis. Nevertheless, if one considers
only the magnetic ions it is found that these form unpuckered
planes perpendicular to the *c* axis. Antiferromagnetic
ordering sets in below T_N = $137 \cdot 2$ K with a value of β of
$0 \cdot 185$ (Eibschütz, Guggenheim, Holmes, and Bernstein 1972).
A broad maximum in the graph of χ against *T* occurs at ~222 K,
this being ~$1 \cdot 61 T_N$ and a good indication of the essentially
two-dimensional nature of the magnetic structure. Within
each layer of Fe^{3+} spins there is simple antiferromagnetic
ordering. The spins in any layer do not lie immediately

above those of the preceding layer (Fig.12.37) and as a
consequence each layer should exert no orientating influence
on the spins in the immediately adjacent layers (as is also
the case with K_2NiF_4). The ordering between spins in second-
neighbour layers has not been determined.

Similar results have been obtained for $RbFeF_4$ and
$CsFeF_4$, in which however the Fe atoms of one layer lie immediately above or below those of the next layer. The critical index β is found to vary from system to system, being
0·185, 0·245, and 0·278 for the K, Rb, and Cs salts, respectively. The lower value for $KFeF_4$ is consistent with
the greater two-dimensional character which arises from
the cancellations of the orientating influences associated
with its staggered structure. $CsFeF_4$ also shows somewhat
more three-dimensional character in that the ratio T_χ/T_N
has the lower value of 1·47 (Eibschütz, Davidson, and Guggenheim 1974). Estimates of the ratio of the coupling para-
meters $|J'/J|$ are ·10^{-4} for $KFeF_4$ and 10^{-2}-10^{-3} for $RbFeF_4$
and $CsFeF_4$.

$FeCl_2$, $FeBr_2$, and FeI_2. Planes of Fe^{2+} ions are separated
from each other by two planes of halide ions. The six
halide ions forming the immediate environment of a Fe^{2+}
ion are at the corners of a distorted octahedron. There is
a slight difference between these substances in that $FeCl_2$
has the $CdCl_2$ structure, whilst $FeBr_2$ and FeI_2 adopt the
very similar CdI_2 structure. The difference between these
is that, although the layers are the same, they are stacked
in different ways: the halide ions are cubic close-packed
in $CdCl_2$, but hexagonal close-packed in CdI_2. Above 5·9
kbar $FeCl_2$ goes over to the CdI_2 structure (Vettier and
Yelon 1975).

In the ordered structure the spins within a plane
are parallel, but adjacent planes are oppositely aligned.
It is not surprising, therefore, that $FeCl_2$ and $FeBr_2$ are
metamagnetic (section 12.6.1). The values obtained for T_N
are collected in Table 12.5.

De Jongh and Miedema (1974) have estimated the ratio
of the coupling constants $|J'/J|$ for $FeCl_2$ to be ~0·074.

TABLE 12.5

T_N and T_χ for the iron (II) halides

Compound	T_N/K	T_χ/K
$FeCl_2$	$23 \cdot 8^a$, $23 \cdot 5^b$, $24 \cdot 71^c$	-
$FeBr_2$	$14 \cdot 2^a$, $11 \cdot 4^d$	11^e
FeI_2	$8 \cdot 9^d$	10^e

a.   Lanusse, Carrara, Fert, Mischler, and Redoules (1972).
b.   Bizette, Terrier, and Tsai (1956).
c.   Chisholm and Stout (1962).
d.   Brade and Yates (1971).
e.   Bizette, Terrier, and Tsai (1957).

This value is much higher than those accorded to most of the other pseudo-two-dimensional systems in this section, and is consistent with the almost three-dimensional value for β of 0·29 (Yelon and Birgeneau 1972). De Jongh and Miedema have also suggested that the fact that even better agreement with the accepted three-dimensional values is not found is merely because the experiments included only a single point closer to T_N than is given by $1 - T/T_N = 10^{-3}$.

The T-$\mathcal{H}$ phase diagram of $FeCl_2$ has been mapped by means of optical studies (Griffin, Schnatterly, Farge, Regis, and Fontana 1974). This work depended upon the lifting of the restriction on a spin-forbidden transition by the internal magnetic fields created when the magnetic spins become disordered. The tricritical point was found to be at 21·5 K and ~9 kOe. Magnetic circular dichroism, which is very nearly proportional to the magnetization, has also been used to follow the changes in ordering (Griffin and Schnatterly 1974). This work led to values for the tricritical parameters of 20·79 K and $M^*/M_0(0) = 0·38$. Representing the magnetization

on lines Ct and At (Fig.12.6a) by M_{dis} and M_{ord}, respective-
ly, and setting $M_{dis} - M_{ord} = A(1-T/T*)^{\beta u}$, $(M_{dis} - M*)/M* = A_+(1-T/T*)^{\beta +}$ and $(M* - M_{ord})/M* = A_-(1-M/M*)^{\beta -}$, the indices
were found to be $\beta_u = 1\cdot 11 \pm 0\cdot 11$, $\beta_+ = 1\cdot 03 \pm 0\cdot 05$ and
$\beta_- = 1\cdot 13 \pm 0\cdot 14$. These results correspond fairly well
with the classical, Landau value of $\beta = 1\cdot 0$ [as deduced from
section 2.5, equation (2.25)], but do not agree with Birgeneau, Shirane, Blume, and Koehler (1974), who found, from
neutron diffraction studies of the sublattice magnetization,
that $2\beta_u = 0\cdot 38$.

Complexes of formula $(C_nH_{2n+1}NH_3)_2CuX_4$. The structure is
shown in Fig.12.38. It may be considered as being made up

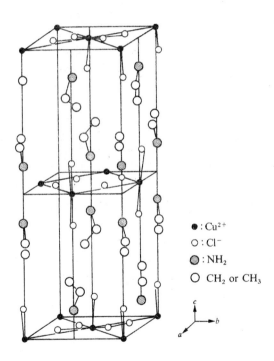

$\bullet$: Cu^{2+}

$\circ$: Cl^-

$\circledcirc$: NH_2

$\bigcirc$ CH_2 or CH_3

Fig.12.38. Crystal structure of $(C_2H_5NH_3)_2CuCl_4$ (from de Jongh *et al.*
1972).

of CuX_4^{2-} layers, each being separated by two layers of
amine cations from the next layer; the separation of the
layers increases as the length of the aliphatic chain

increases, being $0 \cdot 997$ nm for $n = 1$ and $2 \cdot 58$ nm for $n = 10$ (de Jongh and Miedema 1974). Within the layers each Cu^{2+} ion is surrounded by six X^- ions at the corners of a distorted octahedron, four of these anions being shared with adjacent octahedra. As there are strong ferromagnetic interactions between spins within the layers these compounds behave in some respects as two-dimensional ferromagnets. Theoretical estimates of $|J'/J|$ (de Jongh and Miedema 1974) show it to vary from 10^{-3} to 10^{-6} as n goes from 1 to 10. At sufficiently low temperatures three-dimensional ordering sets in, but it is difficult to predict whether this ordering will be ferromagnetic or antiferromagnetic. In fact, only the $n = 1$ system yields a ferromagnetically ordered phase. Indeed, because of the very small values of J' in these compounds it is difficult to determine experimentally whether the interlayer interaction is ferro- or antiferromagnetic. Data for several of these substances is given in Table 12.6. De Jongh and Miedema (1974) have concluded that it is the ratio $|J'/J|$ that is of prime importance in determining T_C, at least for small values of n.

At very low temperatures $c^m \propto T^1$, in agreement with the spin-wave theory for a two-dimensional Heisenberg ferromagnet. Indeed, Bloembergen has analysed the C_p results up to ~70 K, and compared the resultant c^m values with the spin-wave and high-temperature series predictions (Fig.12.39). The very small amounts of entropy and enthalpy associated with the three-dimensional ordering 'spikes' is at once evident.

Phenomena at much higher temperatures in these and related compounds have been treated in section 7.5.3. None of the matters dealt with there are magnetic in origin.

$CrBr_3$ and $CrCl_3$. These substances have often been studied as examples of approximately two-dimensional systems, though they are less satisfactory in this respect than K_2NiF_4 or the various compounds represented by the formula $(C_nH_{2n+1}NH_3)_2CuCl_4$.

$CrBr_3$ has the BiI_3 structure (Fig.12.40a). The layers of Cr^{3+} ions have the honeycomb configuration, and between successive Cr^{3+} layers there are two layers of Br^- ions. The

TABLE 12.6.

Ordering characteristics of the compounds $(C_nH_{2n+1}NH_3)_2CuCl_4$
for various values of n

n	T_t/K	Ferro(F) or antiferro (A) ordering	$|J'/J| \times 10^4$(Expt.)
0[a]	11·2	A	32
1[b]	8·9	F	5·5
2[c]	10·20	A	8·5
3[b]	7·61	A	0·5
4[b]	7·27	A	1
5[b]	7·26	A	0·1 - 1
6[b]	7·65	A	0·1 - 1
10[c]	7·92	A	0·1

a. Lécuyer, Renard, and Herpe (1972).
b. De Jongh, Botterman, de Boer, and Miedema (1969).
c. De Jongh, van Amstel, and Miedema (1972).

stacking of the halide ions is almost close-packed hexagonal.
It is found that within each layer of Cr^{3+} ions the interactions between the spins are ferromagnetic and, being mediated by only a single halide ion, are strong. The interactions between spins from adjacent layers are much weaker, because two halide ions intervene, and are of several kinds, some interspin vectors being parallel to the c axis and some not. A simplified model in which only one interlayer interaction parameter is employed is shown in Fig.12.40(b) (Gossard, Jaccarino, and Remeika 1961). By fitting their model to data for M_0 versus T obtained from ^{53}Cr magnetic resonance they found $J'/k = 0·44$ K and $J/k = 2·72$ K. A relatively smaller

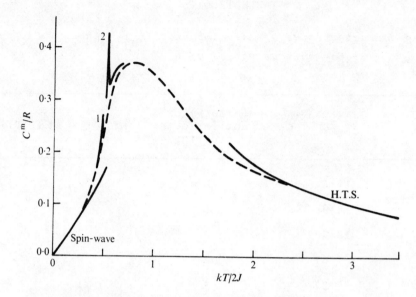

Fig.12.39. C^m against T (in reduced units) for $(C_nH_{2n+1}NH_3)_2CuX_4$. The broken curve is fitted to the experimental points for various n, ignoring critical regions. The 'spikes' for $n=1$ and 2 are shown. Also shown are theoretical curves based on spin-wave and high-temperature susceptibility expansion methods (de Jongh and Miedema 1974).

value for the interlayer parameter has been found by Davis and Narath (1964) using the same model but a different treatment.

CrCl$_3$ has a structure which is similar to that of CrBr$_3$, differing only in the stacking of the halide ions. In CrCl$_3$ these have an approximately f.c.c. packing, as against the approximately h.c.p. packing in CrBr$_3$. Whereas the interlayer interactions in CrBr$_3$ are ferromagnetic, leading to three-dimensional ferromagnetic ordering at 32·5 K, in CrCl$_3$ these interactions are antiferromagnetic and give a Néel point of 16·8 K (Hansen and Griffel 1959, Narath 1963). The different sign of the effective interlayer parameter in the two substances is not surprising when it is borne in mind that this J value arises from a delicate balance between a number of interactions of opposite sign (Samuelsen, Silberglitt, Shirane, and Remeika 1971).

De Jongh and Miedema (1974) have estimated $|J'/J|$ for CrBr$_3$ and CrCl$_3$ as 0·06 and 0·0034, respectively. Relative

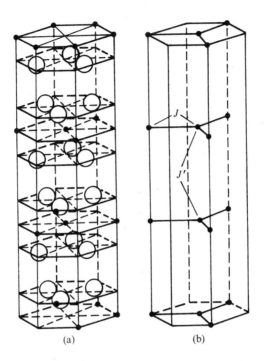

Fig.12.40. (a) Crystal structure of CrBr$_3$; • : Cr^{3+}; o : Br$^-$. (b) Simplified magnetic model (from Gossard *et al.* 1961).

to most other pseudo-two-dimensional substances discussed in this section the ratios of the inter- to intra-layer parameters are high, and in consequence the transitions are found to approximate closely to normal three-dimensional behaviour.

$Mn(HCOO)_2 \cdot 2H_2O$. Fig.12.41(a), in which only the Mn^{2+} ions are shown, reveals the magnetic structure of this compound. It can be considered as being composed of layers of Mn^{2+} ions parallel to the *bc* plane. There are two non-equivalent types (A and B) of Mn^{2+} site in the lattice, and the layers, each of which contains only one kind, are composed alternately of A and B sites. The important difference between the A and B sites lies in their coupling to other sites. Each A site is coupled to its four nn in its own layer by an antiferromagnetic interaction, this occurring by way of a

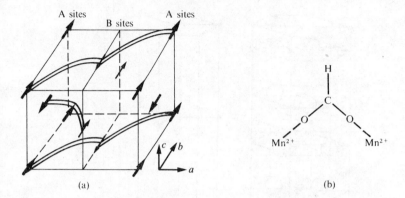

Fig.12.41. (a) Magnetic crystal structure of the fully ordered form of
Mn(HCOO)$_2$.2H$_2$O (from Skalyo *et al.* 1969).

carboxyl group which acts as a bridge between the spins (Fig.
12.41b). There are no such interactions between the B sites.
Each B site does, however, have an antiferromagnetic interaction with two A sites, one from each of the adjacent layers
(Fig.12.41a), carboxyl groups again being the superexchange
mediators.

Neutron diffraction measurements (Skalyo, Shirane, and
Friedberg 1969) showed that the magnetization of the B sublattice was less by a factor of 10 than that of the A sublattice over most of the range examined, although the two
sublattices contain equal numbers of Mn^{2+} ions (Fig.12.42).
This behaviour is readily explicable in terms of the weakness
of the magnetic interactions of the B ions. c_p measurements
also show up the different behaviour of the A and B sites
(Pierce and Friedberg 1968). Apart from the main peak at
T_N = 3·62 K, there is a much smaller spike at 1·7 K which
is associated with a spin-reorientation transition at which
the weak ferromagnetism appearing at T_N changes its direction from the b axis to (below 1·7 K) a direction in the
ac plane (Fig.12.43). Perhaps of greater interest is that
the total magnetic entropy removed by cooling to 1·4 K was
found to correspond to $\frac{1}{2}R \ln 6$, the value expected if only
half of the Mn^{2+} ions (s = 5/2) were being ordered. χ shows
corresponding maxima at 3·68 and 1·72 K (Abe, Morigaki,

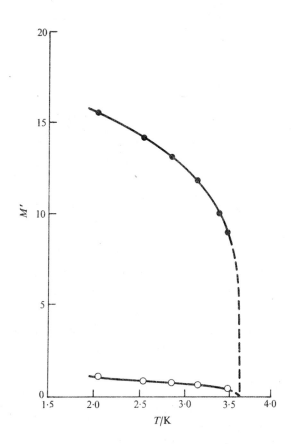

Fig.12.42. Mn(HCOO)$_2$.2H$_2$O. Relative sublattice magnetizations (in arbitrary units); o : A sites, ● : B sites (from Skalyo *et al*. 1969).

Matsuura, Torii, and Yamagata 1964). On further cooling a
Schottky anomaly with its maximum near 0·2 K is observed
which is believed to mark the ordering of the B spins in the
field of the A spins (see section 12.13.1, the perovskites)
(Matsuura, Blote, and Huiskamp 1970).

The decline of the magnetization of the A sublattice
near T_N proceeds with the critical index β = 0·23 for the
range 5·5 × 10^{-2} < 1-T/T_c < 0·55 (Skalyo *et al*. 1969). This
value, which is supported by an NMR experiment yielding
β = 0·22 (Ajiro, Terata, Matsuura, and Haseda 1970), lies
almost equidistant between the theoretical values for the
Ising model in two dimensions (β = 0·125) and in three

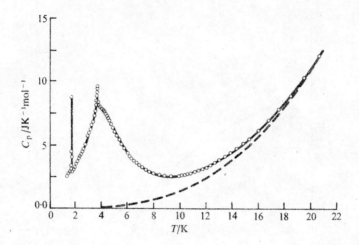

Fig.12.43. C_p against T for Mn(HCOO)$_2$.2H$_2$O. Broken line shows the estimated lattice contribution (after Pierce and Friedberg 1968).

dimensions (β = 0·31). The Heisenberg model in three dimensions has β = 0·345 (Stanley 1971).

12.13.3. Pseudo one-dimensional systems
A detailed review of the properties of a number of systems of this class has been given by Steiner, Villain, and Windsor (1976). The substances considered there are (CH$_3$)$_4$N.MnCl$_3$, CsNiF$_3$, CoCl$_2$.2NC$_5$H$_5$, CuCl$_2$.2NC$_5$H$_5$, and CoCl$_2$.2D$_2$O.

CsMnCl$_3$.2H$_2$O. This is frequently taken as a good example of a one-dimensional Heisenberg system. A projection on the (001) plane of half of the unit cell is shown in Fig.12.44. Each Mn^{2+} ion is surrounded in a distorted octahedral manner by four Cl$^-$ ions and two H$_2$O molecules. Two of these Cl$^-$ ions form superexchange links with adjacent Mn^{2+} ions in the a direction. The distance between adjacent Mn^{2+} ions within the chain is 0·456 nm, whereas the separation between ions belonging to neighbouring chains is 0·729 nm. (The Cl$^-$ — Mn^{2+} — Cl$^-$ chains are slightly kinked, but this small deviation can be ignored for most purposes when discussing possible magnetic effects.) The Heisenberg parameter for

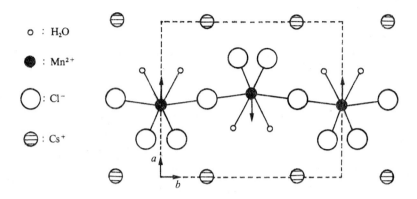

o : H₂O

● : Mn²⁺

◯ : Cl⁻

⊖ : Cs⁺

Fig.12.44. Structure of $CsMnCl_3 \cdot 2H_2O$: projection on the (001) plane. A one-dimensional magnetic chain is indicated (after Smith and Friedberg 1968).

interchain interactions (J') is correspondingly much smaller than the intrachain parameter (J):

$$J' \approx 0 \cdot 0035J \approx -0 \cdot 0125k \qquad (12.18)$$

(Skalyo, Shirane, Friedberg, and Kobayashi 1970). (The difference between the interchain parameters for neighbours in the b and c directions may be safely neglected.) Ferrieu (1974) has proposed a much greater equality of the coupling parameters, $J' \approx 0 \cdot 03J$, as a result of his measurements of the spin-lattice relaxation time (T_1). Three-dimensional ordering does not set in until T_N = 4·89 K (Spence, Casey, and Nagarajan 1968). Neutron scattering has indicated that correlations along the a axis persist up to ~$10T_N$; correlations perpendicular to a only appear as the temperature falls below ~$2T_N$. Consistent with the almost one-dimensional character of this magnetic system are the c^m measurements, which show that ~80% of the entropy associated with the magnetic ordering is gained above T_N (Forstat, McElearney, and Love, in Skalyo, Shirane, Friedberg, and Kobayashi 1970). χ measurements along all three axes from 0·35 K to 77 K show that sufficiently far above T_N (from ~9 K) the system behaves as a classical Heisenberg antiferromagnetic chain.

That is, the spin number (s = 5/2) is sufficiently large
that it is possible to replace the spin operators in the
energy expression by vectors (Smith and Friedberg 1968,
Kobayashi, Tsujikawa, and Friedberg 1973). The critical
index β has been found from neutron diffraction experiments
to be 0·30 for the range $5 \times 10^{-4} < 1-T/T_N < 7 \times 10^{-2}$, which
is close to the value for three-dimensional systems (Skalyo
et al. 1970). The three-dimensional antiferromagnetic
phase is subject to spin-flopping, the bicritical point
being 4·36 K, 20·55 kOe (Butterworth and Woollam 1969), with
a further point on the antiferromagnet spin-flop line at
1·07 K, 17·3 kOe (Botterman, de Jonge, and de Leeuw 1969).
The easy direction for the spins is the b axis, but the anisotropy is small ($\mathcal{H}^c$ = 450 Oe, $\mathcal{H}^a$ = 1 440 Oe, Nagata and
Tazuke 1970; $\mathcal{H}^c$ = 480 Oe, Botterman *et al.* 1969, also Nagata,
Tazuke, and Tsushima 1972).

$CsCoCl_3.2H_2O$. The chemical structure is the same as that of
$CsMnCl_3.2H_2O$. However, because of the anisotropy which is
frequently associated with the Co^{2+} ion, this substance behaves to a fairly good approximation as a one-dimensional
Ising system. At T_N = 3·38 K three-dimensional magnetic
ordering occurs to a structure in which the direction of the
spins is somewhat uncertain. Herweijer, De Jonge, Botterman,
Bongaarts, and Cowen (1972) were unable to decide whether
the moments lay in the b direction (as for $CsMnCl_3.2H_2O$) or
in the ac plane. The latter choice, with moments canted from
the c direction by ϕ_m = 17 ± 6° (Fig.12.45), was favoured by
the neutron diffraction results for the sublattice magnetization as a function of temperature (Bongaarts and van Laar 1972).
  C_p results for this compound (Herweijer *et al.* 1972)
were difficult to analyse because of the problem of allowing
for the lattice contribution; no suitable isomorphous non-
magnetic salt could be found, and a plot of $C_p T^2$ against T^5
(based on contributions proportional to T^{-2} and T^3 from the
magnetic and lattice systems, respectively) was found to
be non-linear. A crude allowance for the lattice contribution led to the observation that only 16% of the total magnetic entropy ($R \ln 2$) was gained below T_N, a result which
can be attributed to the essentially one-dimensional magnetic

nature of the substance. At temperatures well above T_N the
broad maximum in χ which would be expected for one-dimensional antiferromagnetically coupled chains of Ising spins
is modified by the residual 'weak ferromagnetism' of the
individual chains. This complication does not arise for
$CsMnCl_3.2H_2O$, where the spins are not canted. As can be seen
from Fig.12.45, the 'weak ferromagnetism' of each ac plane

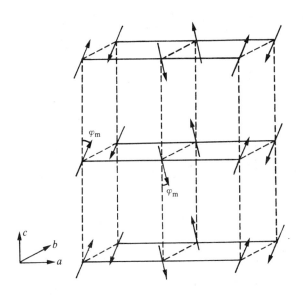

Fig.12.45. Magnetic structure of $CsCoCl_3.2H_2O$. Only the positions and
orientations of the magnetic spins, all of which lie in the ac-plane,
are shown (from Herweijer *et al.* 1972).

is oppositely directed to that of the adjacent planes. This
arrangement, not surprisingly, leads to metamagnetism: at
1·1 K a field of only 2·85 kOe is sufficient to render the
residual moments of all the ac planes parallel (de Jonge,
Rama Rao, Swüste, and Botterman 1971, Bongaarts 1974).

$Cu(NH_3)_4SO_4.H_2O$ and related compounds. In $Cu(NH_3)_4SO_4.H_2O$
each copper atom has as its nearest neighbours four NH_3
molecules disposed in a planar manner and two H_2O molecules
which complete an octahedral arrangement around the metal
atom (Mazzi 1955). For our purposes the structure can be

considered as being made up of $-Cu^{2+}-H_2O-Cu^{2+}-H_2O-$ chains
along the c axis with some superexchange cross-linking between the Cu^{2+} ions by means of $-NH_3-SO_4^{2-}-NH_3-$ bridges (Fig.
12.46). De Jongh and Miedema (1974) give for the ratio of

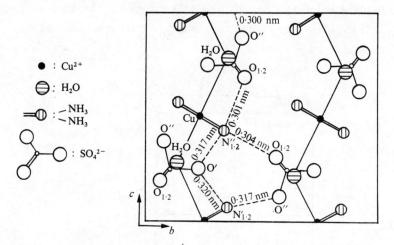

Fig.12.46. Structure of $Cu(NH_3)_4SO_4.H_2O$: projection onto the bc plane.
Each H_2O molecule is linked by hydrogen-bonds to O atoms of two different
SO_4^{2-} ions to form chains in the a direction. Layers in the ac planes are
held together by $NH_3...SO_4^{2-}$ bonds (after Mazzi 1955).

the coupling parameters along and perpendicular to the chains
$|J'|/|J| \approx 6 \times 10^{-3}$. Watanabe and Haseda (1958) found
from χ measurements on a single crystal over the range
1·04 - 20·4 K that the results were similar for fields
parallel to all three axes. χ_a, χ_b, and χ_c each show a
smooth maximum at ~3·4 K, and below ~3·2 K all three decrease
towards zero as the temperature falls. Fritz and Pinch
(1957) had previously found from their C_p measurements over
the range 1·3 - 24 K a Schottky-like anomaly with its maximum at ~3·0 K. Although this result was discussed by these
authors in terms of a simple Schottky anomaly, the same
type of curve is also produced by a linear chain of spins,
as was first realized for a one-dimensional Ising model.
In fact, above the three-dimensional ordering temperature
(T_N = 0·37 K; Haseda and Miedema 1961) the substance behaves as a one-dimensional Heisenberg system. Griffiths
(1964) has shown that the χ and C^m data above T_N accord
well with the calculations of Bonner and Fisher (1964) for

finite chains of antiferromagnetically coupled Heisenberg
spins and their extrapolations for infinite chains provided
$J = -1 \cdot 58k$. In particular c^m has a smooth maximum of value
$0 \cdot 360R$ at ~$10T_N$, as compared with $0 \cdot 35R$ deduced by Bonner
and Fisher for infinite chains. By contrast, a similar
Ising chain would have a maximum in c^m of $0 \cdot 439R$. The calculations also showed that χ for an infinite chain would
be bracketed by the values for finite chains with odd and even
numbers of spins n. Fig.12.47 for χT $versus$ T shows that the

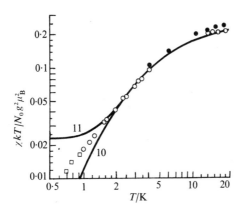

Fig.12.47. χT against T for $Cu(NH_3)_4SO_4.H_2O$. The susceptibility is
normalized by division by $N_0g^2\mu_B^2/k$. o : Watanabe and Haseda (1958),
□: Haseda and Miedema (1961), ● : Fritz and Pinch (1957). Solid lines
are calculated values of Bonner and Fisher for chains with 10 and 11
spins (from Griffiths 1964).

theoretical values for $n = 10$ and $n = 11$ do indeed bracket
the experimental results at low temperatures, the experimental and the two sets of theoretical results being virtually coincident at higher temperatures. Haseda and Kobayashi (1964) measured the magnetization at temperatures of
$1 \cdot 1$, $2 \cdot 0$, and $4 \cdot 2$ K and at fields up to 90 kOe. Again, comparison of the data obtained with that predicted for the
linear Heisenberg chain model by Inawashiro and Katsura
(1965) using a linked-cluster expansion method showed very
good agreement, with the Ising model being a much poorer
representation of the real system. The c^m data of Fritz and

Pinch, and also that of Haseda and Miedema (1961) at
~0·3 - 0·85 K, are also well reproduced by the one-dimensional Heisenberg model.

The corresponding selenate, $Cu(NH_3)_4SeO_4.H_2O$, has
been studied by Lowndes, Finegold, Rogers, and Morosin (1969),
who, from an analysis of the C_p data over the range 2-20 K
on a mixed sample containing much anhydrous salt, were
nevertheless able to show that experiment was in good agreement with the Bonner-Fisher treatment if $J = -1·18k$ was taken
(as against -1·58k for the sulphate).

The related, isostructural compound $Cu(NH_3)_4SO_4.NH_3$
has similar C^m properties (Rogers, Finegold, and Morosin
1972). It has a numerically lower value of $J(-1·48k)$ than
$Cu(NH_3)_4SO_4.H_2O$ ($J = -1·58k$), and since the compounds have
almost identical crystallographic parameters, the difference
is likely to be due to the different effectiveness of NH_3
and H_2O as media for superexchange.

$CuSO_4.5H_2O$ and $CuSeO_4.5H_2O$ have somewhat similar structures to the previous compounds, half of the Cu^{2+} ions
(designated I) being in a similar environment to those in
$Cu(NH_3)_4SO_4.H_2O$. They show broad maxima in their curves of
C^m against T at ~1·35 and 0·8 K, respectively (Geballe and
Giauque 1952, Miedema, van Kempen, Haseda, and Huiskamp 1962).
These maxima correspond to the maximum found for
$Cu(NH_3)_4SO_4.H_2O$ and arise from the one-dimensional chains
of type I copper atoms. Below these temperatures, C^m falls
to a minimum at ~0·2 K in both cases and then rises again
in a somewhat sharper transition at ~0·035 K for $CuSO_4.5H_2O$
and ~0·045 K for $CuSeO_4.5H_2O$ (Miedema et al. 1962, Giauque.
Fisher, Hornung, and Brodale 1968, 1970). The magnetic
entropy lost on cooling to the minimum (~0·2 K) is found
to be ~$\frac{1}{2}R \ln 2$ for both substances, thus corresponding to
complete magnetic ordering of the copper spins of type I;
the region below 0·2 K, and in particular the fairly sharp
transition, correspond to the ordering of the remaining Cu^{2+}
spins (type II).

Wittekoek and Poulis (1966) have used the observation
of the line-width of the ^{1}H resonance in $CuSO_4.5H_2O$ to make
inferences about the reorientation of the Cu^{2+} spins of

types I and II. Exchange coupling of the Cu^{2+} spins leads to their reorientation, and if this is sufficiently rapid the ions concerned make no contribution to the width of the ^{1}H resonance line. The type II spins are so weakly coupled that they make a constant contribution to the line-width over the whole range studied (0·31 - 20 K) as well as causing a line shift. This displacement is, however, different for each of the ten protons in the unit cell, thus giving ten widely spaced ^{1}H resonance lines. Type I spins, on the other hand, make no contribution above ~3 K, but below that the correlations between the type I Cu^{2+} spins leads to broadening of the resonance line. Application of a magnetic field tends to break up the antiferromagnetic correlations within the chains and so to eliminate that source of line broadening. By assuming the validity of the Curie-Weiss Law for the paramagnetic ions and employing fairly large applied fields (up to ~11 kOe), Wittekoek, Klaassen, and Poulis (1968) have been able to separate out the contributions to the line *shift* (rather than the *width*) arising from the paramagnetic and the chain spins. They found that the susceptibility contribution from the chain spins showed a maximum at ~1·7 K for $CuSO_4.5H_2O$ and at ~0·9 K for $CuSeO_4.5H_2O$. The results were in excellent agreement with predictions for an antiferromagnetic Heisenberg chain with coupling parameters of J = -0·73k and -0·40k for the sulphate and selenate, respectively. From resonance shifts of protons adjacent to paramagnetic Cu^{2+} ions it was found that the susceptibility contribution of the paramagnetic spins corresponded to $J_{12} \approx$ 0·04k. Bagguley and Griffiths (1950), from an interpretation of the splitting of the ESR spectrum, had concluded that $|J_{12}| \approx$ 0·05k. The weak coupling between the chains of type I spins has been studied by van Tol and Poulis (1973). They attempted to eliminate the effect of the type II spins in their proton resonance experiments by saturating that sublattice by the application of sufficiently large fields. They found that below 0·098 K the resonance frequencies were split, presumably as a result of the three-dimensional ordering of the type I spins. This effect occurred at the same temperature for the resonance

lines due to all the different types of proton in the crystal.
For the interchain interaction parameter they deduced
$qJ' = -0.035k$, where q is the number of neighbouring chains
in the crystal. $\mathcal{H}-T$ phase diagrams of the sulphate and
selenate were found to be superimposable, provided that it
was assumed that $J'(SO_4)/J'(SeO_4) = 0.83$ (Fig.12.48).

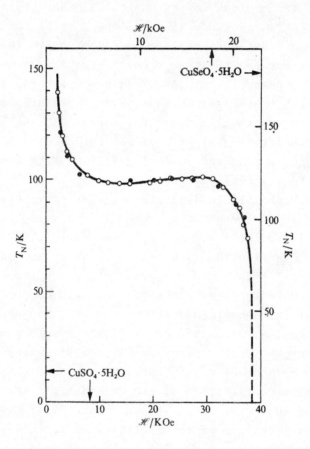

Fig.12.48. T_N against $\mathcal{H}$ ($\perp$ to c axis) for $CuSO_4.5H_2O$ (o) and $CuSeO_4.5H_2O$
(•) (from van Tol and Poulis 1973).

Reconciliation with the results of Geballe and Giauque (1952)
may be achieved if it is supposed that the heat capacity
'spike' arising from the three-dimensional ordering is in-
sufficiently large to be detected and becomes merged into
the smooth hump arising from the chains. The anomaly at

~0·035 K would then be attributed to the ordering of the
type II spins in the field of the type I spins.

$LiCuCl_3.2H_2O$. The structure, which is monoclinic with
$\beta = 108°50'$, is shown in Fig.12.49. Planar $Cu_2Cl_6^{2-}$ units,

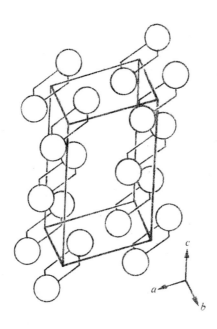

Fig.12.49. Magnetic structure of $LiCuCl_3.2H_2O$. Only the positions of
the Cu^{2+} ions are shown. Bridged dimers are indicated (after Abrahams
and Williams 1963).

having symmetric Cu-Cl-Cu bridges, are joined by longer,
weaker, links to other such units to form approximately one-
dimensional magnetic chains lying in the a direction. (X-
ray diffraction, Vossos, Jennings, and Rundle 1960; neutron
diffraction and magnetic susceptibility, Abrahams and
Williams 1963.) Within the dimers the Cu-Cu distance is
only 0·347 nm, whereas the other Cu-Cu distances in the
chain are 0·384 nm. Abrahams and Williams found that the
spins lay in the ac plane and were probably directed along
the Cu-Cu axis of each $Cu_2Cl_6^{2-}$ unit (35°30' from c).
Zimmerman, Bastmeijer, and van den Handel (1972), on the

other hand, have concluded that the spin direction makes
an angle of 16° with the c axis.

Three-dimensional antiferromagnetic ordering takes
place at T_N ($4\cdot40 \pm 0\cdot02$ K, Forstat and McNeely 1961;
$4\cdot45 \pm 0\cdot01$ K, Clay and Staveley 1966; $4\cdot440$ K, Zimmerman
et al. 1972). It is probable that below T_N the spin arrange-
ment within a chain is $\alpha\alpha\beta\beta\alpha\alpha\beta\beta...$, with the pair of Cu^{2+}
ions belonging to each $Cu_2Cl_6^{2-}$ unit having parallel spins
and pairs of weakly linked Cu^{2+} ions having antiparallel
spins. That the tightly bound spins within a unit form a
triplet spin state was first suggested from the observa-
tion that χ above T_χ (= $5\cdot9$ K) fits a Curie-Weiss Law for
the triplet state (Vossos et al. 1960). It was also in
accord with the general observation that chains in other
substances in which the bonds are of the weak, asymmetric
type, e.g. $CuCl_2.2H_2O$, have antiferromagnetic interactions
between nearest neighbours in the chain, whereas those
with strong, symmetric bonds usually showed ferromagnetic
tendencies, e.g. the iron group (II) halides. The C_p
measurements of Clay and Staveley (1966) supported this
contention, since they found the magnetic entropy of the
transition to be $4\cdot47$ J K^{-1} mol^{-1}, as compared with $4\cdot55$ J
K^{-1} mol^{-1} (= $\frac{1}{2}R \ln 3$) for the above model and $5\cdot76$ J K^{-1}
mol^{-1} (= $R \ln 2$) for a model in which all spins become ran-
domized independently at the transition. In contrast
earlier C_p measurements (Forstat and McNeely 1961) on a
much smaller sample had led to a value of $5\cdot64$ J K^{-1} mol^{-1},
very close to $R \ln 2$, and the neutron diffraction study of
Abrahams and Williams (1963) had also suggested that coupling within the units was antiferromagnetic.

Spin-flopping can occur when fields greater than 9 kOe
are applied along the easy axis to the sample cooled below
~$4\cdot2$ (Forstat, Bailey, and Ricks 1971).

12.13.4. Substances with helical spin arrangements
$FeCl_3$. This has the BiI_3 layer-lattice structure. The
Cl^- ions form a hexagonal close-packed (ABABAB..) lattice,
the Fe^{3+} ions being present in 'honeycomb' sheets in alternate interlayer spaces, where they occupy two-thirds of

the octahedral interstices (Wooster 1932, Blairs and Shelton
1966). Below the Néel temperature there is helical order
of the Fe^{3+} spins with a propagation vector along the [140]
direction and with a rotation of $2\pi/15$ between successive
layers. The individual moments lie in a plane perpendicular
to the propagation vector. Domains having their propagation
vectors along the various possible [140] directions are formed
(Cable, Wilkinson, Wollan, and Koehler 1962b). The value
of T_N = 15 ± 2 K found by Cable *et al*. seems to be much too
high, most subsequent work indicating $T_N \approx$ 8-10 K. Thus, a
more recent neutron diffraction study found T_N = 7·98 K
(Endoh, Skalyo, Oosterhuis, and Stampfel 1972), although
their results are otherwise consistent with those of Cable
et al. with regard to the spiral structure. The transition
was found to be partly first-order, and displayed hysteresis, but over the range 4·6 - 7·945 K the results could be
fitted with the critical index β = 0·158 ± 0·005 if T_N were
taken as 8·06 K. Jones, Morton, Cathey, Auel, and Amma
(1969) found the maximum in χ to occur at ~9·75 K, suggesting
a Néel point about 5% lower than that. The same authors
drew attention to the changes in properties which can arise
if the $FeCl_3$ is permitted to pick up moisture to form some
$FeCl_3.6H_2O$ as impurity. Possibly the presence of this
impurity accounts for the variability of some of the reported properties of $FeCl_3$.

There are indications from Mössbauer experiments that,
in the presence of fields greater than 15 kOe along the *c*
axis, the helical structure gives way to a simple two-
sublattice antiferromagnetic structure, which on further
increasing the field to 39-49 kOe, depending upon the temperature, shows spin-flopping (Stampfel, Oosterhuis, Window,
and Barros 1973).

MnI$_2$. This has the CdI_2 layer structure: I^- ions form a
hexagonal close-packed array, with the Mn^{2+} ions forming
hexagonal two-dimensional arrangements in every other interlayer space. Ordering occurs at T_N = 3·40 K, and at 1·3 K
the magnetic structure was found to be helical with the
propagation vector along the [307] direction and a rotation

of $2\pi/16$ per layer. Domains are formed with their vectors
along the three possible [307] axes. The helical axis has
a direction which bears no simple relationship to the positions of the neighbouring atoms (Cable, Wilkinson, Wollan,
and Koehler 1962a).

$MnSO_4$. The positions of the Mn^{2+} ions in this orthorhombic
structure are shown in Fig.12.50. It was found to be impossible to obtain agreement with the neutron diffraction

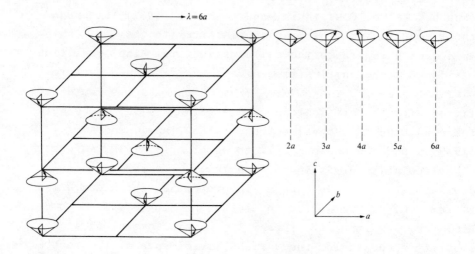

Fig.12.50. Magnetic structure of $MnSO_4$, showing the helix propagating in
in the [100] direction with wavelength $6a$ (from Will *et al*. 1965).

results on an ordered sample at 4·2 K (T_N = 11·5 K) with any
magnetic structure involving only collinear spins (Will,
Frazer, Shirane, Cox, and Brown 1965). The structure proposed has ferromagnetic (001) sheets coupled antiparallel
with the adjacent sheets. The spins all lie along the
conical surfaces (Fig.12.50), with the component in the
ab plane being subject to a periodicity of about $6a$ along
the a direction.

    The system appears to be of considerable complexity as
C_p measurements (Lecomte, de Gunzbourg, Teyrol, Miedan-Gros,
and Allain 1972) show three other peaks between 5 K and T_N.

It is suggested that the spin structure transforms from the
cone spiral form at the lowest temperatures, via a form
having periodically varying components along the a (or b)
direction, to a Néel-type collinear arrangement and finally
to the paramagnetic form.

12.13.5. $KFe_3(OH)_6(SO_4)_2$.
This compound, which is antiferromagnetic below ~60 K, is of
interest because its magnetic structure can be considered
as being made up of layers, each of which is a Kagomé lattice.
A considerable amount of theoretical work has been devoted
to study of this two-dimensional lattice, although it is uncommon in nature. In the more detailed chemical structure,
each Fe^{3+} ion is surrounded octahedrally by two O^{2-} ions
and four OH^- ions. Neighbouring octahedra are linked by
the sharing of an OH corner (Fig.12.51a). Strong magnetic

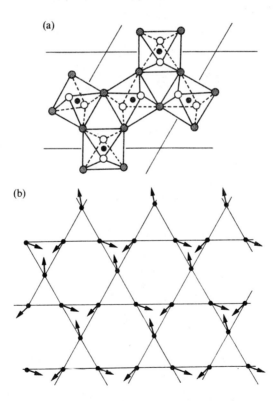

Fig.12.51. The structure of $KFe_3(OH)_6(SO_4)_2$. (a) Linking of FeO_6 octahedra to form the Kagomé array of Fe ions; ● : Fe^{3+}, ○ : O^{2-}, ◉ : OH.
(b) The non-collinear spin arrangement (from Takano *et al.* 1971).

coupling exists between each Fe^{3+} ion and the four nn Fe^{3+}
ions in the same sheet, O acting as the mediator. This interaction is believed to be antiferromagnetic, since otherwise
each individual layer would be ferromagnetic and the substance would then probably be metamagnetic, which it is not.
Herein lies the interest: it is not possible to achieve zero
magnetization with equal numbers of oppositely orientated
spins on the Kagomé lattice if nn pairs are always oppositely orientated. The spin system which has been suggested is
that shown in Fig.12.51(b), the deviation of each spin from
its nearest lattice line being uniform (Takano, Shinjo, and
Takada 1971).

Takano, Shinjo, Kiyama, and Takada (1968), who measured
χ from $1 \cdot 2$ to 400 K, found a broad maximum at ~60 K. For
the corresponding Na and NH_4 compounds maxima were found at
~53 K and ~55 K, respectively. Powers, Rossman, Schugar, and
Gray (1975) found T_χ for the K compound to be 45 K, but their
measurements were at intervals of ~15 K. The corresponding
chromate shows a magnetic transition, indicated by a sharp
change in χ (by a factor of ~$4 \cdot 7$ over 2 K) at 73 K, and it
has been suggested that this transition marks a switch from
a triangular to a collinear spin arrangement. There is
evidence for 'weak ferromagnetism' below the transition in
that saturation phenomena are observed, but with the saturation magnetization indicating a magnetic moment of only $0 \cdot 05$
μ_B, as compared with $5 \cdot 9$ μ_B for a spin-free Fe^{3+} ion.

REFERENCES

Abe, H., Morigaki, H., Matsuura, M., Torii, K., and Yamagata,
     K. (1964). *J.phys.Soc.Japan* 19, 775.
Abrahams, S.C. and Williams, H.J. (1963). *J.chem.Phys.* 39, 2923.
Ahlers G., Kornblit, A., and Salamon, M.B. (1974). *Phys.Rev.* B9,
     3932
Ajiro, Y., Terata, N., Matsuura, M., and Haseda, T. (1970).
     J.phys.Soc.Japan, 28, 1587.
Alben, R. (1970). *Phys.Rev.* B2, 2767.
Allain, Y., Bichara, M., and Herpin, A. (1966). *J.appl.Phys.*
     37, 1316.

Als-Nielsen, J., Dietrich, O.W., Kunnmann, W., and Passell, L.
    (1971). *Phys.Rev.Lett.* 27, 741.

Anderson, P.W. (1950). *Phys.Rev.* 79, 350.

Bagguley, D.M.S. and Griffiths, J.H.E. (1950). *Proc.R.Soc.*
    A201, 366.

Baker, J.M. (1971). *Rep.Prog.Phys.* 34, 109.

Baltzer, P.K., Lehmann, H.W., and Robbins, M. (1965). *Phys.
    Rev.Lett.* 15, 493.

Banus, M.D. and Lavine, M.C. (1969). *J.Solid.St.Chem.* 1, 109.

Battison, J.E., Kasten, A., Leask, M.J.M., and Lowry, J.B.
    (1975). *Solid St.Communs.* 17, 1363.

Becker, P.J., Leask, M.J.M., and Tyte, R.N. (1972). *J.Phys.*
    C5, 2027.

Belov, K.P., Mill', B.V., Ronninger, G., Sokolov, V.I., and
    Hien, T.D. (1970). *Soviet Phys. Solid St.* 12, 393.

Berkhahn, W., Kahle, H.G., Klein, L., and Schopper, H.C.
    (1973). *Phys.St.Solidi* B55, 265.

Berkner, D.P. and Litster, J.D (1972). *AIP Conf.Proc.* No.10.
    Pt.2., 894.

Bertaut, E.F. and Mareschal, J. (1967). *Solid St.Communs.*
    5, 93.

————   ————   (1968). *J.Phys.(Paris)* 29,
    67.

Bidaux, R. and Meriel, P. (1968). *J.Phys.(Paris)* 29, 220.

Birgeneau, R.J., Guggenheim, H.J., and Shirane, G. (1970).
    Phys.Rev. B1, 2211.

————   ————   ————   (1973).
    Phys.Rev. B8, 304.

————   Shirane, G., Blume, M., and Koehler, W.C.
    (1974). *Phys.Rev.Lett.* 33, 1098.

————   Yelon, W.B., Cohen, E., and Makovsky, J.
    (1972). *Phys.Rev.* B5, 2607.

Bizette, H., Terrier, C., and Tsai, B. (1956). *C.r.hebd.
    Séanc.Acad.Sci.,Paris* 243, 895.

————   ————   ————   (1957). *C.r.hebd.
    Séanc.Acad.Sci.,Paris* 245, 507.

Blairs, S. and Shelton, R.A.J. (1966). *J.inorg.nucl.Chem.*
    28, 1855.

Bloch, D., Hermann-Ronzaud, D., Vettier, C., Yelon, W.B.,
    and Alben, R. (1975). *Phys.Rev.Lett.* 35, 963.

Bloch, F. (1930). *Z.Physik* $\underline{61}$, 206.

Bloembergen, P. (———). In de Jongh and Miedema (1974).

Blume, M., Corliss, L.M., Hastings, J.M., and Schiller, E. (1974). *Phys.Rev.Lett.* $\underline{32}$, 544.

Bongaarts, A.L.M.(1974). *Phys.Lett.* $\underline{49A}$, 211.

——— and van Laar, B. (1972). *Phys.Rev.* $\underline{B6}$, 2669.

Bonner, J.C. and Fisher, M.E. (1964). *Phys.Rev.* $\underline{135}$, A640.

Borsa, F. (1973). *Phys.Rev.* $\underline{B7}$, 913.

Botterman, A.C., de Jonge, W.J.M., and de Leeuw, P. (1969). *Phys.Lett.* $\underline{30A}$, 150.

Brade, R.M. and Yates, B. (1971). *J.Phys.* $\underline{C4}$, 876.

Breed, D.J., Gilijamse, K., and Miedema, A.R. (1969). *Physica* $\underline{45}$, 205.

Brüesch, P. and Kalbfleisch, H. (1971a). *Phys.St.Solidi* $\underline{B45}$, K103.

——— ——— (1971b). *Phys.St.Solidi* $\underline{B44}$, K97.

Bucci, C. and Guidi, G. (1974). *Phys.Rev.* $\underline{B9}$, 3053.

Butterworth, G.J. and Woollam, J.A. (1969). *Phys.Lett.* $\underline{29A}$, 259.

Cable, J.W., Wilkinson, M.K., Wollan, E.O., and Koehler, W.C. (1962a). *Phys.Rev.* $\underline{125}$, 1860;

——— ——— ——— ——— (1962b). *Phys.Rev.* $\underline{127}$, 714.

Cashion, J.D., Cooke, A.H., Martin, D.M., and Wells, M.R. (1970). *J.appl.Phys.* $\underline{41}$, 1193.

——— ——— Thorp, T.L., and Wells, M.R. (1968). *J.Phys.* $\underline{C1}$, 539.

——— ——— ——— (1970). *Proc.R.Soc.* $\underline{A318}$, 473.

Cerdonio, M. and Paroli, P. (1970). *Phys.Lett.* $\underline{33A}$, 217.

Choh, S.H. and Stager, C.V. (1971). *Can.J.Phys.* $\underline{49}$, 144.

Chisholm, R.C. and Stout, J.W. (1962). *J.chem.Phys.* $\underline{36}$, 972.

Clark, A.E. and Callen, E. (1968). *J.appl.Phys.* $\underline{39}$, 5972.

Clay, R.M. and Staveley, L.A.K. (1966). *Ann.Acad.Sci.Fenn.*, Ser. AVI, No.210, 194.

Clover, R.B. and Wolf, W.P. (1968). *Solid St.Communs.* $\underline{6}$, 331.

Colominas, C. (1967). *Phys.Rev.* $\underline{153}$, 558.

Colwell, J.H. and Mangum, B.W. (1972). *Solid St.Communs*. $\underline{11}$, 83.

Colwell, J.H., Mangum, B.W., Thornton, D.D., Wright, J.C., and Moos, H.W. (1969). *Phys.Rev.Lett.* <u>23</u>, 1245.

Cooke, A.H., Ellis, C.J., Gehring, K.A., Leask, M.J.M., Martin, D.M., Wanklyn, B.M., Wells, M.R., and White, R.L. (1970). *Solid St.Communs.* <u>8</u>, 689.

────────── Martin, D.M., and Wells, M.R. (1971). *Solid St.Communs.* <u>9</u>, 519.

────────── Swithenby, S.J., and Wells, M.R. (1972). *Solid St.Communs.* <u>10</u>, 265.

────────── Thorp, T.L., and Wells, M.R. (1967). *Proc.phys. Soc.* <u>92</u>, 400.

Corliss, L.M., Delapalme, A., Hastings, J.M., Lau, H.Y., and Nathans, R. (1969). *J.appl.Phys.* <u>40</u>, 1278.

Cotton, F.A. and Wilkinson, G. (1972). *Advanced inorganic chemistry*, *3rd ed.* p.591. Interscience, New York, London, Sydney, and Toronto.

D'Ambrogio, F., Brüesch, P., and Kalbfleisch, H. (1972). *Phys.St.Solidi* <u>B49</u>, 117.

Davidson, G.R., Dunlap, B.D., Eibschütz, M.E., and van Uitert, L.G. (1975). *Phys.Rev.* <u>B12</u>, 1681.

Davis, H.L. and Narath, A. (1964). *Phys.Rev.* <u>134</u>, A433.

De Combarieu, A., Mareschal, J., Michel, J.C., and Sivardière, J. (1968). *Solid St.Communs.* <u>6</u>, 257.

De Jonge, W.J.M., Rama Rao, K.V.S., Swüste, C.H.W., and Botterman, A.C. (1971). *Physica* <u>51</u>, 620.

De Jongh, L.J., Botterman, A.C., de Boer, F.R., and Miedema, A.R. (1969). *J.appl.Phys.* <u>40</u>, 1363.

────────── and Miedema, A.R. (1974). *Adv.Phys.* <u>23</u>, 1.

────────── ────────── and Wielinga, R.F. (1970). *Physica* <u>46</u>, 44.

────────── van Amstel, W.D., and Miedema, A.R. (1972). *Physica* <u>58</u>, 277.

Dietrich, O.W., Henderson, A.J., and Meyer, H. (1975). *Phys. Rev.* <u>B12</u>, 2844.

Dodokin, A.P., Lyubutin, I.S., Mill', B.V., and Peshkov, V.P. (1973). *Soviet Phys.JETP* <u>36</u>, 526.

Domb, C. and Miedema, A.R. (1964). *Prog.low Temp.Phys.* <u>4</u>, 296.

Dwight, K. and Menyuk, N. (1960). *Phys.Rev.* <u>119</u>, 1470.

Dyson, F.J. (1956). *Phys.Rev.* <u>102</u>, 1217, 1230.

Eibschütz, M., Davidson, G.R., and Guggenheim, H.J. (1974). *Phys.Rev.* B9, 3885.

———— Guggenheim, H.J., Holmes, L., and Bernstein, J.L. (1972). *Solid St.Communs.* 11, 457.

———— Holmes, L., Maita, J.P., and van Uitert, L.G. (1970). *Solid St.Communs.* 8, 1815.

Elliott, R.J., Gehring, G.A., Malozemoff, A.P., Smith, S.R.P., Staude, W.S., and Tyte, R.N. (1971). *J.Phys.* C4, L179.

———— Harley, R.T., Hayes, W., and Smith, S.R.P. (1972). *Proc.R.Soc.* A328, 217.

Ellis, C.J., Leask, M.J.M., Martin, D.M., and Wells, M.R. (1971). *J.Phys.* C4, 2937.

Endoh, Y., Skalyo, J., Oosterhuis, W.T., and Stampfel, J.P. (1972). *AIP Conf.Proc.* No.10, Pt.1, 98.

Englman, R. and Halperin, B. (1970). *Phys.Rev.* B2, 75.

———— ———— (1971). *Phys.Rev.* B3, 1698.

Enz, U. (1961). *J.appl.Phys.* 32, 22S.

Erickson, R.A. (1953). *Phys.Rev.* 90, 779.

Essam, J.W. and Sykes, M.F. (1963). *Physica* 29, 378.

Féron, J.L., Fillion, G., and Hug, G. (1973). *J.Phys.* *(Paris)* 34, 247.

Ferrieu, F. (1974). *Phys.Lett.* 49A, 253.

Fischer, P., Hälg, W., von Wartburg, W., Schwob, P., and Vogt, O. (1969). *Phys.kondens.Mater.* 9, 249.

Fisher, M.E. (1962). *Phil.Mag.* 7, 1731.

———— and Nelson, D.R. (1974). *Phys.Rev.Lett.* 32, 1350.

Fleury, P.A., Lazay, P.D., and van Uitert, L.G. (1974). *Phys.Rev.Lett.* 33, 492.

Forstat, H., Bailey, P.T., and Ricks, J.R. (1971). *J.appl. Phys.* 42, 1559.

———— McElearney, J.N., and Bailey, P.T. (1968). *Proc.11th Int.Conf.Low Temp.Phys.* St. Andrews, 1968, 1349, 1365.

———— ———— and Love, N.D. (1970). In Skalyo *et al.* (1970).

———— and McNeely, D.R. (1961). *J.chem.Phys.* 35, 1594.

Fritz, J.J. and Pinch, H.L. (1957). *J.Am.chem.Soc.* 79. 3644.

Fujii, Y., Hoshino, S., Yamada, Y., and Shirane, G. (1974). *Phys.Rev.* B9, 4549.

Garrett, C.G.B. (1951). *Proc.R.Soc.* A206, 242.

Gavignet-Tillard, A., Hammann, J., and de Seze, L. (1973a). *(J.) Phys.Chem.Solids* 34, 241.

────────   ────────   ──────   (1973b). *J.Phys.(Paris)* 34, 27.

Geballe, T.H. and Giauque, W.F. (1952). *J.Am.chem.Soc.* 74, 3513.

Gehring, G.A. and Gehring, K.A. (1975). *Rep.Prog.Phys.* 38, 1.

Gehring, K.A., Malozemoff, A.P., Staude, W., and Tyte, R.N. (1971). *Solid St.Communs.* 9, 511.

Geller, S., Williams, H.J., Espinosa, G.P., and Sherwood, R.C. (1964). *Bell Systems Tech.J.* 43, 565.

Giauque, W.F., Fisher, R.A., Hornung, E.W., and Brodale, G.E. (1968). *J.chem.Phys.* 48, 3728.

────────   ────────   ──────   ──────

(1970). *J.chem.Phys.* 53, 3733.

Gilleo, M.A.(1956). *J.chem.Phys.* 24, 1239.

────────   and Geller, S. (1958). *Phys.Rev.* 110, 73.

Göbel, H. and Will, G. (1972). *Phys.St.Solidi* B50, 147.

Gorter, C.J. (1953). *Rev.mod.Phys.* 25, 332.

Gorter, E.W. (1954). *Phillips Res. Reports* 9, 295.

────────   (1955). *Proc.Inst.Radio Eng.* 43, 1945.

Gossard, A.C., Jaccarino, V., and Remeika, J.P. (1961). *Phys.Rev.Lett.* 7, 122.

Griessen, R., Landolt, M., and Ott, H.R. (1971). *Solid St. Communs.* 9, 2219.

Griffin, J.A. and Schnatterly, S.E. (1974). *Phys.Rev.Lett.* 33, 1576.

────────   ────────   Farge, Y., Regis, M., and Fontana, M.P. (1974). *Phys.Rev.* B10, 1960.

Griffiths, R.B. (1964). *Phys.Rev.* 135, A659.

Grimes, D.M. and Westrum, E.F. jr. (1958). *J.appl.Phys.* 29, 384.

Gyorgy, E.M., Levinstein, H.J., Dillon, J.F. jr., and Guggenheim, H.J. (1969). *J.appl.Phys.* 40, 1599.

────────   Remeika, J.P., and Hagedorn, F.B. (1968). *J.appl.Phys.* 39, 1369.

Hammann, J. (1969). *Acta crystallogr.* B25, 1853.

Hansen, W.N. and Griffel, M. (1959). *J.chem.Phys.* 30, 913.

Harley, R.T., Hayes, W., Perry, A.M., and Smith, S.R.P. (1973). *J.Phys.* C6, 2382.

────   ────   and Smith, S.R.P. (1972). *J.Phys.* C5, 1501.

Hartmann-Bouton, F. and Imbert, P. (1968). *J.appl.Phys.* 39, 775.

Haseda, T. and Kobayashi, H. (1964). *J.phys.Soc.Japan* 19, 1260.

────   and Miedema, A.R. (1961). *Physica* 27, 1102.

Hasson, A., Hornreich, R.M., Komet, Y., Wanklyn, B.M., and Yaeger, I. (1975). *Phys.Rev.* B12, 5051.

Hastings, J.M. and Corliss, L.M. (1962). *Phys.Rev.* 126, 556.

────   ────   (1968). *(J.)Phys.Chem.Solids* 29, 9.

Heeger, A.J., Beckman, O., and Portis, A.M. (1961). *Phys. Rev.* 123, 1652.

Heger, G., Geller, R., and Babel, D. (1971). *Solid St. Communs.* 9, 335.

Heisenberg, W. (1928). *Z.Physik* 49, 619.

Heller, P. (1966). *Phys.Rev.* 146, 403.

Herpin, A., Koehler, W.C., and Meriel, P. (1960). *C.r.hebd. Séanc.Acad.Sci.,Paris* 251, 1359.

Herweijer, A., de Jonge, W.J.M., Botterman, A.C., Bongaarts, A.L.M., and Cowen, J.A. (1972). *Phys.Rev.* B5, 4618.

Horner, H. and Varma, C.M. (1968). *Phys.Rev.Lett.* 20, 845.

Hornreich, R.M., Komet, Y., Nolan, R., Wanklyn, B.M., and Yaeger, I. (1975). *Phys.Rev.* B12, 5094.

Hudson, R.P. and Mangum, B.W. (1971). *Phys.Lett.* 36A, 157.

Hutchings, M.T., Schulhof, M.P., and Guggenheim, H.J. (1972). *Phys.Rev.* B5, 154.

────   and Wolf, W.P. (1964). *J.chem.Phys.* 41, 617.

Ikeda, H. and Hirakawa, K. (1972). *J.phys.Soc.Japan* 33, 393.

────   ────   (1973). *J.phys.Soc.Japan* 35, 617.

Inawashiro, S. and Katsura, S. (1965). *Phys.Rev.* 140, 892A.

Jacobs, I.S. (1959). *(J.) Phys.Chem.Solids* 11, 1.

────   (1961). *J.appl.Phys.* 32, 61S.

Jacobs, I.S. and Lawrence, P.E. (1967). *Phys.Rev.* 164, 866.

Jones, E.R., Morton, O.B., Cathey, L., Auel, T., and Amma,
    E.L. (1969). *J.chem.Phys.* 50, 4755.

Kahle, H.G., Klein, L., Müller-Vogt, G., and Schopper, H.C.
    (1971). *Phys.St.Solidi* B44, 619.

———   Simon, A., and Wüchner, W. (1974). *Phys.St.*
    Solidi B61, K53.

Kaplan, T.A., Dwight, K., Lyons, D., and Menyuk, N. (1961).
    J.appl.Phys. 32, 13S; (1962). *Phys.Rev.* 126, 540; 127,
    1983.

Keffer, F. (1966). *Handbuch der Physik*, 18/2. Springer-Verlag,
    Berlin, Heidelberg, and New York.

Kittel, C. (1956). *Introduction to solid state physics* (2nd
    ed.) Wiley, New York.

Klaassen, T.O., Gevers, A., Looyestijn, W.J., and Poulis,
    N.J. (1973). *Physica* 64, 149.

———   ———   and Poulis, N.J. (1972). *Physica*
    61, 95.

Klein, L., Wüchner, W., Kahle, H.G., and Schopper, H.C.
    (1971). *Phys.St.Solidi* B48, K139.

Kobayashi, H., Tsujikawa, I., and Friedberg, S.A. (1973). *J.*
    low Temp.Phys. 10, 621.

Koehler, W.C., Wollan, E.O., and Wilkinson, M.K. (1960).
    Phys.Rev. 118, 58.

Kornblit, A. and Ahlers, G. (1975). *Phys.Rev.* B11, 2678.

———   ———   and Buehler, E. (1973). *Phys.*
    Lett. 43A, 531.

Kramers, H.A. (1934). *Physica* 1, 182.

Kuroda, C., Miyadai, T., Naemura, A., Nuzeki, N., and Takata,
    H. (1961). *Phys.Rev.* 122, 446.

Landau, D.P. (1972). *Phys.Rev.Lett.* 28, 449.

———   Keen, B.E., Schneider, B., and Wolf, W.P. (1971).
    Phys.Rev. B3, 2310.

Lanusse, M.C., Carrara, P., Fert, A.R., Mischler, G., and
    Redoules, J.P. (1972). *J.Phys.(Paris)* 33, 429.

Lau, H.Y., Corliss, L.M., Delapalme, A., Hastings, J.M.,
    Nathans, R., and Tucciarone, A. (1970). *J.appl.Phys.* 41,
    1384.

Lecomte, M., de Gunzbourg, J., Teyrol, M., Miedan-Gros, A.,
    and Allain, Y. (1972). *Solid St.Communs.* 10, 235.

Lécuyer, B., Renard, J-P., and Herpe, A. (1972). *C.r.hebd. Séanc.Acad.Sci.,Paris* B275, 73.

Lee, J.N. and Moos, H.W. (1972). *Phys.Rev.* B5, 3645.

———   ———   and Mangum, B.W. (1971). *Solid St. Communs.* 9, 1139.

Levinson, L.M., Alben, R. and Jacobs, I.S. (1971). *AIP Conf. Proc.* No.5, 1, 685.

———   and Shtrikman, S. (1970). *Solid St.Communs.* 8, 209.

Levitin, R.Z., Ponomarev, B.K., and Popov, Yu.F. (1971). *Sov.Phys.JETP* 32, 1056.

Lewis, J.F.L. and Prinz, G.A. (1974). *Phys.Rev.* B10, 2892.

Lines, M.E. (1971). *Phys.Rev.* B3, 1749.

———   and Jones, E.D. (1965). *Phys.Rev.* 139, A1313.

Lowndes, D.H., Finegold, L., Rogers, R.N., and Morosin, B. (1969). *Phys.Rev.* 186, 515.

Lyons, K.B., Birgeneau, R.J., Blount, E.I., and van Uitert, L.G. (1975). *Phys.Rev.* B11, 891.

Maarschall, E.P., Botterman, A.C., Vega, S., and Miedema, A.R. (1969). *Physica* 41, 473.

McGuire, T.R. and Shafer, M.W. (1964). *J.appl.Phys.* 35, 984.

Mangum, B.W., Lee, J.N., and Moos, H.W. (1971). *Phys.Rev. Lett.* 27, 1517.

———   and Utton, D.B. (1974). *AIP Conf.Proc.* No.24,65.

Mareschal, J., Sivardière, J., de Vries, G.F., and Bertaut, E.F. (1968). *J.appl.Phys.* 39, 1364.

Matsuura, M., Blote, H.W.J., and Huiskamp, W.J. (1970). *Physica* 50, 444.

Mazzi, F. (1955). *Acta crystallogr.* 8, 137.

Meijer, H.C., Adair, T.W. III, and van den Handel, J. (1968). *Physica* 38, 233.

Melcher, R.L., Pytte, E., and Scott, B.A. (1973). *Phys.Rev. Lett.* 31, 307.

Meltzer, R.S. and Moos, H.W. (1970). *J.appl.Phys.* 41, 1240.

Menyuk, N., Dwight, K., and Wold, A. (1964). *J.Phys.(Paris)* 25,528

Mermin, N.D. and Wagner, H. (1966). *Phys.Rev.Lett.* 17, 1133.

Metcalfe, M.J. and Rosenberg, H.M. (1972a). *J.Phys.* C5, 459.

———   ———   (1972b). *J.Phys.* C5, 474.

Michel, A., Poix, P., and Bernier, J-C. (1970). *Annls.Chim.* 5,261.

Miedema, A.R., van Kempen, H., and Huiskamp, W.J. (1963). *Physica* 29, 1266.

Miedema, A.R., van Kempen, H., Haseda, T., and Huiskamp, W.J.
    (1962). *Physica* 28, 119.
─────   Wielinga, R.F., and Huiskamp, W.J. (1965).
    Physica 31, 1585.
Minkiewicz, V.J. and Shirane, G. (1969). *J.phys.Soc.Japan*
    26, 674.
Moldover, M.R., Sjölander, G., and Weyhmann, W. (1971).
    Phys.Rev.Lett. 26, 1257.
Moriya, T. (1960). *Phys.Rev.* 120, 91.
─────   (1963). In *Magnetism* (ed. Rado, G.T. and Suhl, H.)
    Vol.1. Academic Press, New York and London.
Morrish, A.H. (1965). *The physical principles of magnetism*
    p.309. Wiley, New York, London, and Sydney.
Nagamiya, T. (1967). *Solid St.Phys.* 20, 305.
Nagata, K. and Tazuke, Y. (1970). *Phys.Lett.* 31A, 293.
─────   ─────   and Tsushima, K. (1972). *J.phys.*
    Soc.Japan 32, 1486.
Narath, A. (1963). *Phys.Rev.* 131, 1929.
Néel, L. (1948). *Annls.Phys.* 3, 137.
─────   Pauthenet, R., and Dreyfus, B. (1964). *Prog.low Temp.*
    Phys. 4, 344.
Novak, P. (1969). *(J.)Phys.Chem.Solids* 30, 2357.
Oguchi, T. (1960). *Phys.Rev.* 117, 117.
Onn, D.G., Meyer, H., and Remeika, J.P. (1967). *Phys.Rev.*
    156, 663.
Passell, L., Dietrich, O.W., and Als-Nielsen, J. (-).
    Unpublished work cited in de Jongh and Miedema (1974).
Pauthenet, R. (1958). *Annls.Phys.Chim.* 3, 424.
Peyrard, J. and Sivardière, J. (1969). *Solid St.Communs.* 7,
    605.
Pickart, S.J., Alperin, H.A., and Clark, A.E. (1970). *J.*
    appl.Phys. 41, 1192.
Pierce, R.D. and Friedberg, S.A. (1968). *Phys.Rev.* 165, 680.
Pinto, H., Shachar, G., Shaked, H., and Shtrikman, S. (1971).
    Phys.Rev. B3, 3861.
Plumier, R. (1966). *J.Phys.(Paris)* 27, 213.
─────   (1968a). *J.appl.Phys.* 39, 635.
─────   (1968b). *C.r.hebd.Séanc.Acad.Sci.,Paris* B267, 98.
─────   and Sougi, M. (1969). *C.r.hebd.Séanc.Acad.Sci.,*
    Paris B268, 365.

Powers, D.A., Rossman, G.R., Schugar, H.J., and Gray, H.B. (1975). *J.Solid St.Chem.* 13, 1.

Prewitt, C.T., Shannon, R.D., Rogers, D.B., and Sleight, A.W. (1969). *Inorg.Chem.* 8, 1985.

Prince, E. (1957). *Acta crystallogr.* 10, 554.

Rhodes, P. and Wohlfarth, E.P. (1963). *Proc.R.Soc.* A273, 247.

Richards, P.L. (1963). *J.appl.Phys.* 34, 1237.

———   (1964). *J.appl.Phys.* 35, 850.

Riedel, E.K. and Wegner, F.J. (1972). *Phys.Rev.Lett.* 29, 349.

Riseberg, L.A., Cohen, E., Nordland, W.A., and van Uitert, L.G. (1969). *Phys.Lett.* 30A, 4.

Rives, J.E. and Benedict, V. (1975). *Phys.Rev.* B12, 1908.

Rogers, R.N., Finegold, L., and Morosin, B. (1972). *Phys. Rev.* B6, 1058.

Roth, W.L. (1958). *Phys.Rev.* 111, 772.

———   (1960). *J.appl.Phys.* 31, 2000.

Rushbrooke, G.S. and Wood, P.J. (1963). *Molec.Phys.* 6, 409.

Salamon, M.B. and Hatta, I. (1971). *Phys.Lett.* 36A, 85.

———   and Ikeda, H. (1973). *Phys.Rev.* B7, 2017.

Samuelsen, E.J., Silberglitt, R., Shirane, G., and Remeika, J.P. (1971). *Phys.Rev.* B3, 157.

Sandercock, J.R., Palmer, S.B., Elliott, R.J., Hayes, W., Smith, S.R.P., and Young, A.P. (1972). *J.Phys.* C5, 3126.

Schäfer, W. and Will, G. (1971). *J.Phys.* C4, 3224.

Schaffer, W.J., Bene, R.W., and Walser, R.M. (1974). *Phys. Rev.* B10, 255.

Scharenberg, W. and Will, G. (1971). *Int.J.Mag.* 1, 277.

Schieber, M.M. (1967). *Experimental magnetochemistry*, North-Holland, Amsterdam.

Schuchert, H., Hüfner, S., and Faulhaber, R. (1968). *J.appl. Phys.* 39, 1137.

Schulhof, M.P., Nathans, R., Heller, P., and Linz, A. (1971). *Phys.Rev.* B4, 2254.

Schrama, A.H.M. (1973). *Physica* 66, 131; 68, 279.

Shaked, H., Hastings, J.M., and Corliss, L.M. (1970). *Phys. Rev.* B1, 3116.

Shapira, Y. and Foner, S. (1970). *Phys.Rev.* B1, 3083.

Shapiro, S.M., Axe, J.D., and Remeika, J.P. (1974). *Phys.Rev.* B10, 2014.

Sinclair, P.N. and Brockhouse, B.N. (1960). *Phys.Rev.* <u>120</u>, 1638.

Sivardière, J. and Blume, M. (1972). *Phys.Rev.* <u>B5</u>, 1126.

Skalyo, J. jr., Cohen, A.F., Friedberg, S.A., and Griffiths, R.B. (1967). *Phys.Rev.* <u>164</u>, 705.

────────   Shirane, G., and Friedberg, S.A. (1969). *Phys.Rev.* <u>188</u>, 1037.

────────   ────────   ────────   and Kobayashi, H. (1970). *Phys.Rev.* <u>B2</u>, 1310, 4632.

Smith, T. and Friedberg, S.A. (1968). *Phys.Rev.* <u>176</u>, 660.

Spence, R.D., Casey, J.A., and Nagarajan, V. (1968). *J.appl. Phys.* <u>39</u>, 1011.

Spooner, S., Lee, J.N., and Moos, H.W. (1971). *Solid St. Communs.* <u>9</u>, 1143.

Srivastava, K.G. (1963). *Phys.Lett.* <u>4</u>, 55.

Stampfel, J.P., Oosterhuis, W.T., Window, B., and Barros, F. de S. (1973). *Phys.Rev.* <u>B8</u>, 4371.

Stanley, H.E. (1971). *Introduction to phase transitions and critical phenomena.* Clarendon Press, Oxford.

────────   and Kaplan, T.A. (1966). *Phys.Rev.Lett.* <u>17</u>, 913.

Steiner, M., Villain, J., and Windsor, C.G.,(1976). *Adv. Phys.* <u>25</u>, 87.

Sturge, M.D., Cohen, E., van Uitert, L.G., and van Stapele, R.P. (1975). *Phys.Rev.* <u>B11</u>, 4768.

Suzuki, H. and Watanabe, T. (1971). *J.phys.Soc.Japan* <u>30</u>, 367.

Takano, M., Shinjo, T., Kiyama, M., and Takada, T. (1968). *J.phys.Soc.Japan* <u>25</u>, 902.

────────   ────────   and Takada, T. (1971). *J.phys.Soc. Japan* <u>30</u>, 1049.

Testardi, L.R., Levinstein, H.J., and Guggenheim, H.J. (1967). *Phys.Rev.Lett.* <u>19</u>, 503.

Treves, D. (1965). *J.appl.Phys.* <u>36</u>, 1033.

Tsushima, K., Aoyagi, K., and Sugano, S. (1970). *J.appl.Phys.* <u>41</u>, 1238.

Tuthill, G.F., Harbus, F., and Stanley, H.E. (1973). *Phys. Rev.Lett.* <u>31</u>, 527.

Van Amstel, W.D., de Jongh, L.J., and Matsuura, M. (1974). *Solid St.Communs.* <u>14</u>, 491.

Van der Hoeven, B.J.C., Teaney, D.T., and Moruzzi, V.L. (1968). *Phys.Rev.Lett.* <u>20</u>, 719.

Van Laar, B. and Elemans, J.B.A.A. (1971). *J.Phys.(Paris)* 32, 301.

Van Tol, M.W. and Poulis, N.J. (1973). *Physica* 69, 341.

Varsanyi, F., Andres, K., and Marezio, M. (1969). *J.chem. Phys.* 50, 5027.

Van Vleck, J.H. (1937). *Phys.Rev.* 52, 1178.

Velu, E., Cadoul, D., Lécuyer, B., and Renard, J-P. (1971). *Phys.Lett.* 36A, 443.

——— Renard, J-P., and Dupas, C. (1972). *Solid St. Communs.* 11, 1.

Vettier, C. and Yelon, W.B. (1975). *Phys.Rev.* B11, 4700.

Vossos, P.H., Jennings, L.D., and Rundle, R.E. (1960). *J. chem.Phys.* 32, 1590.

Walling, J.C. and White, R.L. (1974). *Phys.Rev.* B10, 4737, 4748.

Wang, F.F.Y., Cox, D.E., and Kestigian, M. (1971). *Phys.Rev.* B3, 3946.

Watanabe, T. and Haseda, T. (1958). *J.chem.Phys.* 29, 1429,

Wells, M.R. and Worswick, R.D. (1972). *Phys.Lett.* 42A, 269.

White, R.L. (1969). *J.appl.Phys.* 40, 1061.

Wielinga, R.F. (1970). *Prog.low Temp.Phys.* Vol.6, Ch.8.

——— and Huiskamp, W.J. (1969). *Physica* 40, 602.

Will, G., Frazer, B.C., Shirane, G., Cox, D.E., and Brown, P.J. (1965). *Phys.Rev.* 140, A2139.

——— , Göbel, H., Sampson, C.F., and Forsyth, J.B. (1972). *Phys.Lett.* 38A, 207.

——— and Schäfer, W. (1971). *J.Phys.* C4, 811.

——— ——— Scharenberg, W., and Göbel, H. (1971) *Z.angew.Phys.* 32, 122.

Wittekoek, S., Klaassen, T.O., and Poulis, N.J. (1968). *Physica* 39, 693.

——— and Poulis, N.J. (1966). *Physica* 32, 693.

Wojtowicz, P.J. (1959). *Phys.Rev.* 116, 32.

Wolf, W.P. (1964). *Proc.Int.Conf.Magnetism, Nottingham, Inst. of Phys and Phys.Soc., London,* p. 555.

——— Ball, M., Hutchings, M.T., Leask, M.J.M., and Wyatt, A.F.G. (1962). *J.phys.Soc.Japan,* 17, Suppl.BI,443.

——— Leask, M.J.M., Mangum, B.W., and Wyatt, A.F.G. (1962). *J.phys.Soc.Japan.* 17, Suppl.BI, 487.

Wolf, W.P., Schneider, B., Landau, D.P., and Keen, B.E. (1972). *Phys.Rev.* B5, 4472.

Wood, D.L., Remeika, J.P., Holmes, L.M., and Gyorgy, E.M. (1969). *J.appl.Phys.* 40, 1245.

Wood, D.W. and Dalton, N.W. (1966). *Proc.phys.Soc.* 87, 755.

Wooster, N. (1932). *Z.Kristallogr.Kristallgeom.* 83, 85.

Wright, J.C. and Moos, H.W. (1971). *Phys.Rev.* B4, 163.

———   ———   Colwell, J.H., Mangum, B.W., and Thornton, D.D. (1971). *Phys.Rev.* B3, 843.

Wüchner, W., Böhm, W., Kahle, H.G., Kasten, A., and Laugsch, J. (1972). *Phys.St.Solidi* B54, 273.

Yablonskii, D.A. (1973). *Soviet Phys.Solid St.* 14, 2468.

Yafet, Y. and Kittel, C. (1952). *Phys.Rev.* 87, 290.

Yamaguchi, T. (1974). *(J.) Phys.Chem.Solids* 35, 479.

Yelon, W.B. and Birgeneau, R.J. (1972). *Phys.Rev.* B5, 2615.

Zener, C. (1951). *Phys.Rev.* 82, 403.

Zimmerman, N.J., Bastmeijer, J.D., and van den Handel, J. (1972). *Phys.Lett.* 40A, 259.

SUBSTANCE INDEX

Salts in which disorder can be attributed to one ion only are listed under that ion. Thus, metallic nitrates are given under N, dihydrogenphosphates under P, and hydrogensulphides under S. Ammonium salts appear under N. Salts in which both anion and cation may be involved in disorder are listed twice, under the letters appropriate to each ion. For example, NH_4BF_4 is given under B and under N.

Carbon compounds are listed in order of increasing number of carbon atoms, using structural formulae where possible. Names have been added for structurally more complex compounds.

Two-component systems are entered under that component which stands first alphabetically, e.g. Ar + CO under Ar, and NH_4Br + NH_4Cl under NH_4Br.

SUBJECT INDEX